Route planner

FERRY INFORMATION

Hebrides and west coast Scotland
calmac.co.uk	0800 066 5000
skyeferry.co.uk	01599 522 756
western-ferries.co.uk	01369 704 452

Orkney and Shetland
northlinkferries.co.uk	0845 6000 449
pentlandferries.com	01856 831 226
orkneyferries.co.uk	01856 872 044
shetland.gov.uk/ferries	01595 693 535

Isle of Man
steam-packet.com	08722 992 992

Ireland
irishferries.com	08717 300 400
poferries.com	08716 642 020
stenaline.co.uk	08447 70 70 70

North Sea (Scandinavia and Benelux)
dfdsseaways.co.uk	08715 229 955
poferries.com	08716 642 020
stenaline.co.uk	08447 70 70 70

Isle of Wight
wightlink.co.uk	0871 376 1000
redfunnel.co.uk	0844 844 9988

Channel Islands
condorferries.co.uk	0845 609 1024

Channel hopping (France and Belgium)
brittany-ferries.co.uk	0871 244 0744
condorferries.co.uk	0845 609 1024
eurotunnel.com	08443 35 35 35
ldlines.co.uk	0844 576 8836
dfdsseaways.co.uk	08715 229 955
poferries.com	08716 642 020
transeuropaferries.com	01843 595 522
transmancheferries.com	0844 576 8836

Northern Spain
brittany-ferries.co.uk	0871 244 0744
poferries.com	08716 642 020

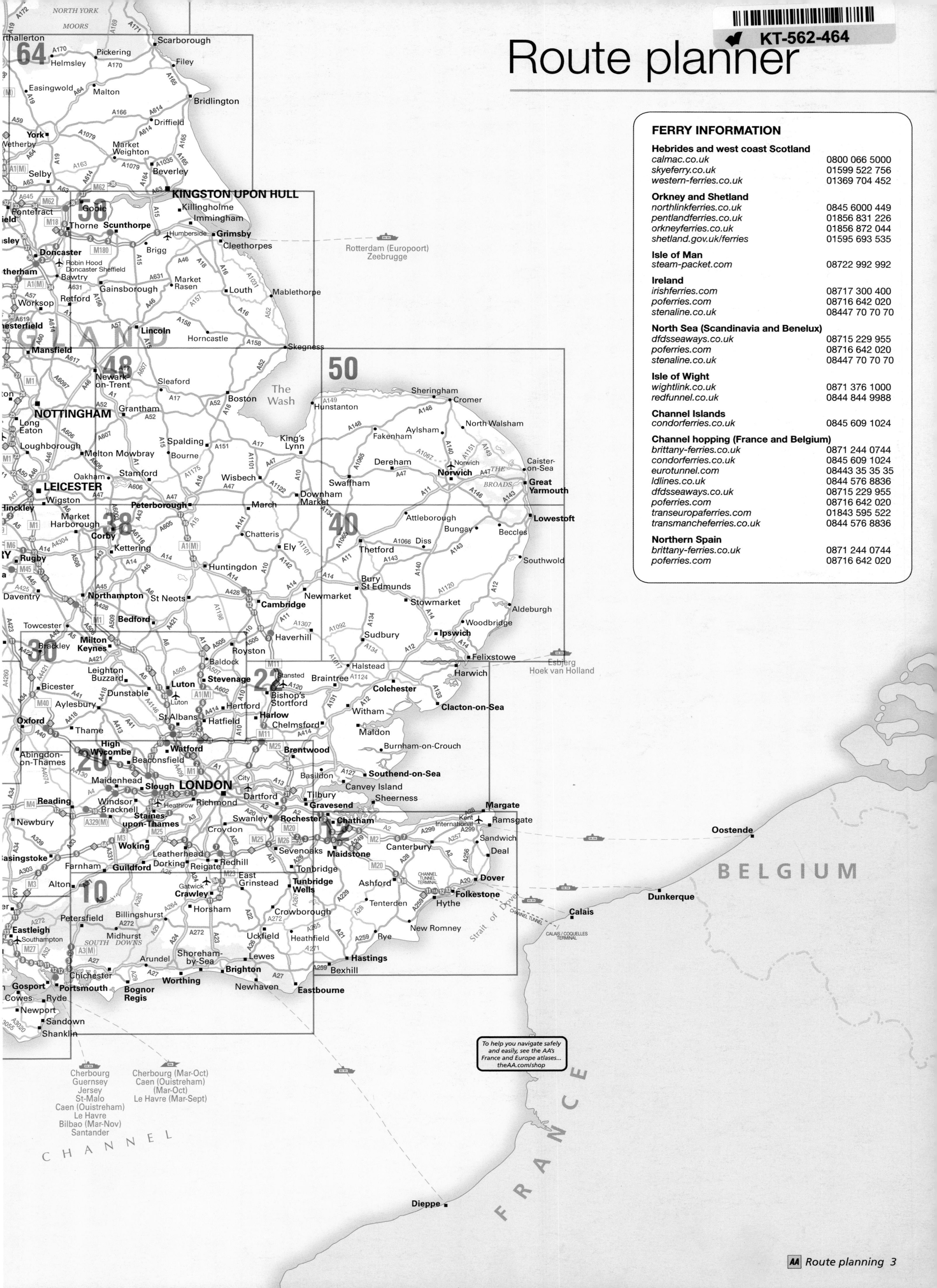

To help you navigate safely and easily, see the AA's France and Europe atlases... theAA.com/shop

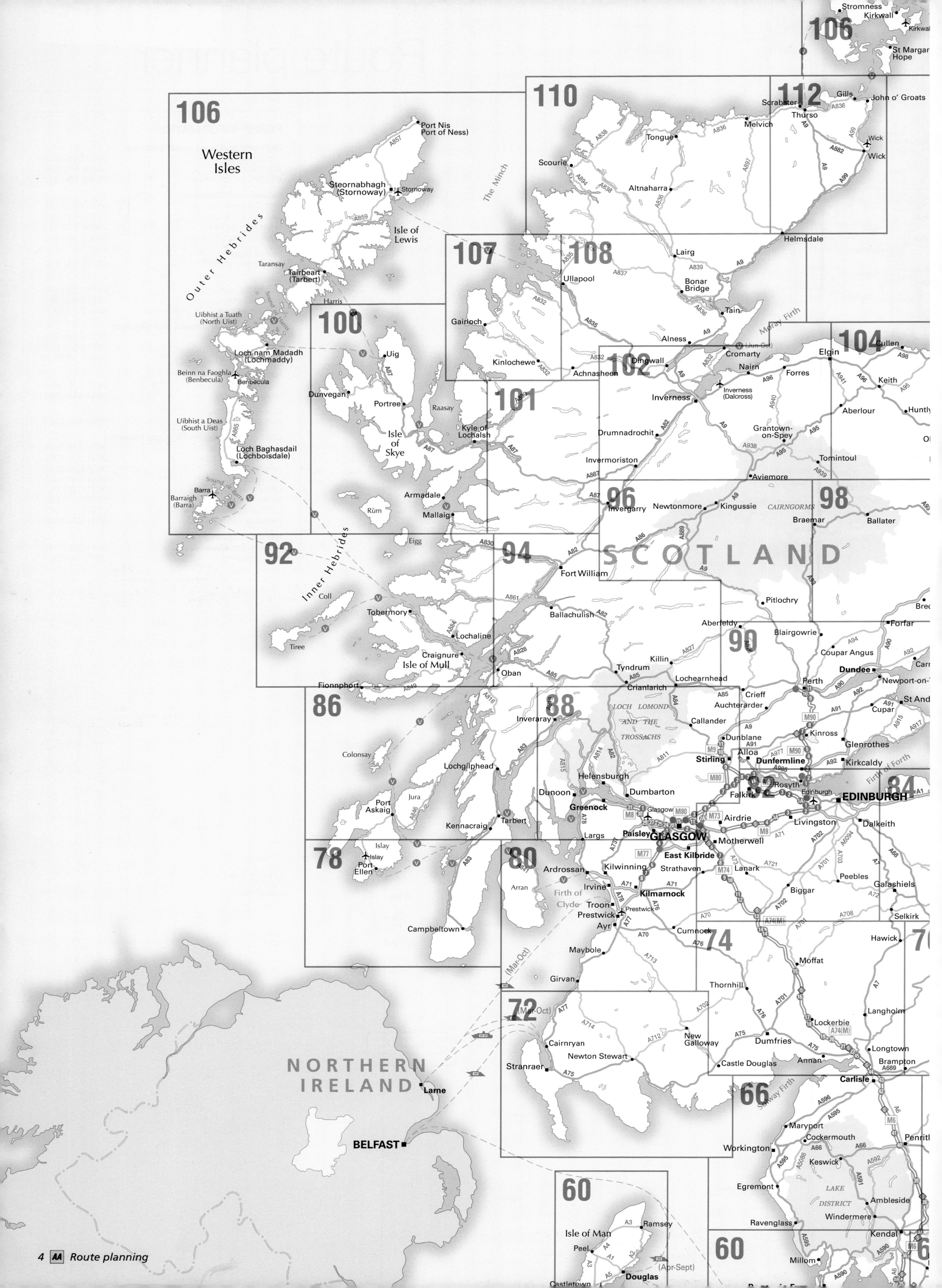
106
Western Isles
Outer Hebrides
Port Nis
Port of Ness)
Steornabhagh
(Stornoway)
Stornoway
Isle of Lewis
The Minch
Taransay
Tairbeart
(Tarbert)
Harris
Sound of Harris
Uibhist a Tuath
(North Uist)
Loch nam Madadh
(Lochmaddy)
Beinn na Faoghla
(Benbecula)
Benbecula
Uibhist a Deas
(South Uist)
Loch Baghasdail
(Lochboisdale)
Sound of Barra
Barra
Barraigh
(Barra)
100
Uig
Dunvegan
Portree
Raasay
Isle of Skye
Kyle of Lochalsh
Armadale
Mallaig
Rùm
Eigg
110
Scourie
Tongue
Melvich
Altnaharra
112
Scrabster
Thurso
Gills
John o' Groats
Wick
Helmsdale
107
108
Ullapool
Lairg
Bonar Bridge
Tain
Gairloch
Kinlochewe
Achnasheen
Alness
Moray Firth
Cromarty
102
Dingwall
Nairn
Forres
Elgin
104
Cullen
Keith
Huntly
Aberlour
Inverness
Inverness (Dalcross)
101
Drumnadrochit
Grantown-on-Spey
Invermoriston
Tomintoul
Aviemore
96
Invergarry
Newtonmore
Kingussie
CAIRNGORMS
98
Braemar
Ballater
92
Inner Hebrides
Coll
Tiree
94
Fort William
SCOTLAND
Pitlochry
Tobermory
Lochaline
Ballachulish
Craignure
Isle of Mull
Oban
Fionnphort
Tyndrum
Killin
Crianlarich
Lochearnhead
Aberfeldy
90
Blairgowrie
Coupar Angus
Forfar
Dundee
Perth
Newport-on-Tay
Crieff
Auchterarder
86
88
Inveraray
LOCH LOMOND AND THE TROSSACHS
Callander
Dunblane
Kinross
Glenrothes
Cupar
Stirling
Alloa
Dunfermline
Kirkcaldy
Firth of Forth
Colonsay
Lochgilphead
Helensburgh
Dumbarton
Dunoon
Greenock
Falkirk
82
Rosyth
Edinburgh
EDINBURGH
84
Glasgow
Airdrie
Livingston
Dalkeith
Jura
Port Askaig
Kennacraig
Tarbert
Largs
Paisley
GLASGOW
Motherwell
East Kilbride
Islay
78
Port Ellen
80
Ardrossan
Kilwinning
Strathaven
Lanark
Peebles
Galashiels
Arran
Irvine
Kilmarnock
Firth of Clyde
Troon
Prestwick
Biggar
Selkirk
Ayr
Cumnock
Campbeltown
74
Hawick
Maybole
Moffat
Girvan
Thornhill
(Mar-Oct)
72
Langholm
Lockerbie
New Galloway
Cairnryan
Newton Stewart
Dumfries
Longtown
Brampton
Stranraer
Castle Douglas
Annan
Carlisle
NORTHERN IRELAND
Larne
66
Solway Firth
BELFAST
Maryport
Cockermouth
Penrith
Workington
Keswick
LAKE DISTRICT
Egremont
Ambleside
Windermere
Ravenglass
Kendal
60
Isle of Man
Ramsey
Peel
Douglas
Castletown
(Apr-Sept)
Millom
106
Stromness
Kirkwall
St Margaret's Hope

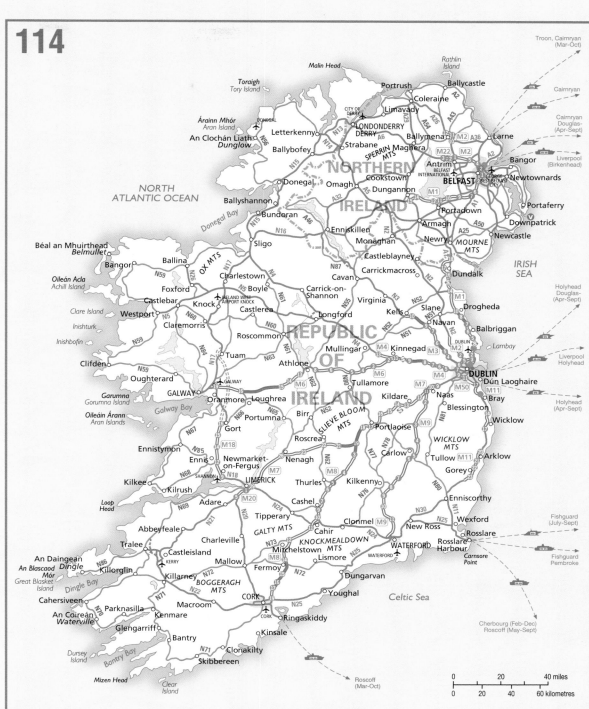
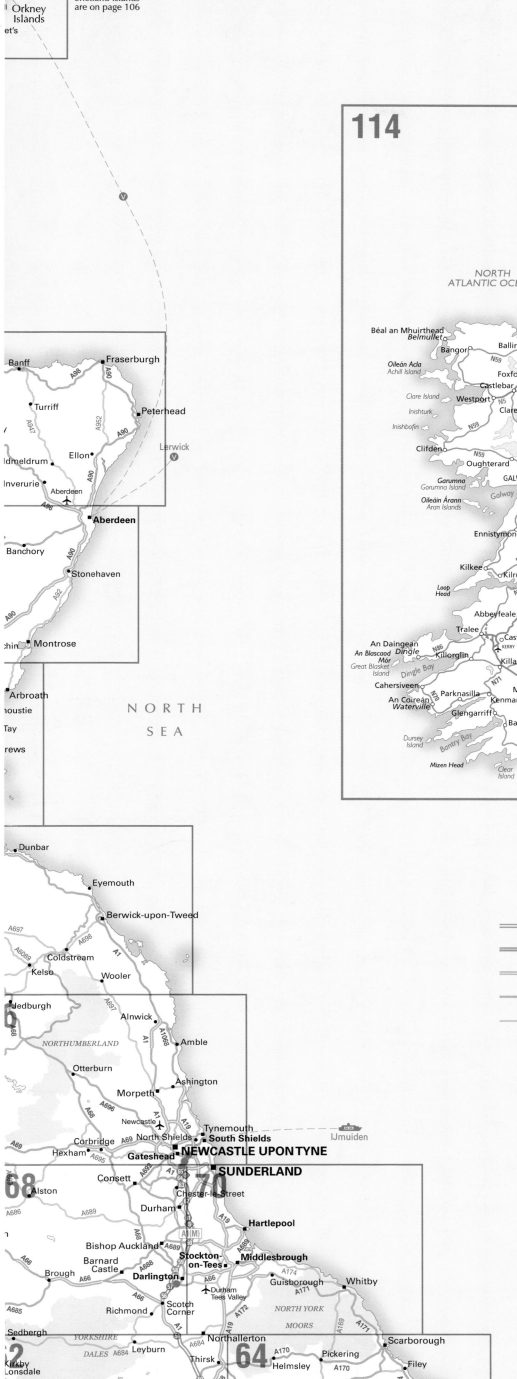
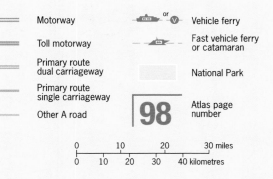

114

	Motorway			Vehicle ferry
Toll motorway			Fast vehicle ferry or catamaran
Primary route dual carriageway			National Park
Primary route single carriageway			
Other A road		**98**	Atlas page number

EMERGENCY DIVERSION ROUTES

In an emergency it may be necessary to close a section of motorway or other main road to traffic, so a temporary sign may advise drivers to follow a diversion route. To help drivers navigate the route, black symbols on yellow patches may be permanently displayed on existing direction signs, including motorway signs. Symbols may also be used on separate signs with yellow backgrounds.

For further information see www.highways.gov.uk

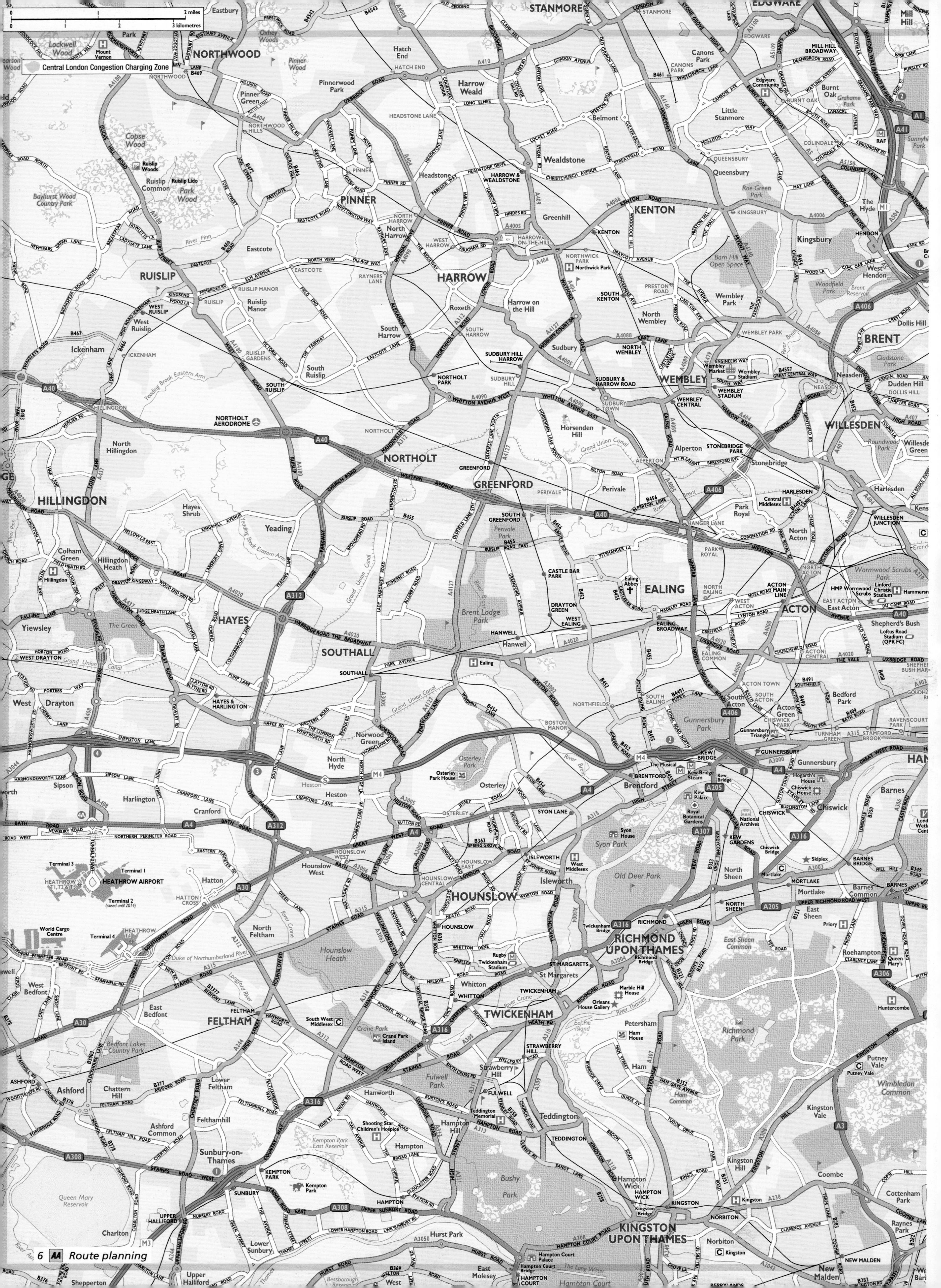

0 1 2 miles
0 1 2 3 kilometres
Central London Congestion Charging Zone
STANMORE
EDGWARE
NORTHWOOD
Hatch End
Harrow Weald
Pinner Green
Canons Park
Mill Hill
Belmont
Little Stanmore
Wealdstone
Queensbury
Colindale
PINNER
Headstone
KENTON
Greenhill
Kingsbury
The Hyde
HENDON
Eastcote
RUISLIP
HARROW
West Hendon
Ruislip Manor
Harrow on the Hill
Wembley Park
South Kenton
North Wembley
Dollis Hill
West Ruislip
Roxeth
BRENT
Ickenham
South Harrow
Sudbury
South Ruislip
WEMBLEY
Neasden
WILLESDEN
NORTHOLT AERODROME
Horsenden Hill
Alperton
North Hillingdon
NORTHOLT
Stonebridge
GREENFORD
Perivale
Harlesden
HILLINGDON
Hayes Shrub
Park Royal
Yeading
North Acton
Colham Green
Hillingdon Heath
EALING
Wormwood Scrubs Park
ACTON
HAYES
East Acton
Yiewsley
Brent Lodge Park
Hanwell
Shepherd's Bush
SOUTHALL
West Drayton
Drayton
Bedford Park
Norwood Green
Gunnersbury Park
North Hyde
Sipson
Harlington
Heston
Osterley
Brentford
Gunnersbury
Cranford
Chiswick
Barnes
HEATHROW AIRPORT
Hatton
Hounslow West
Isleworth
Syon Park
Old Deer Park
Mortlake
HOUNSLOW
North Sheen
East Sheen
North Feltham
Hounslow Heath
RICHMOND UPON THAMES
Roehampton
West Bedfont
East Bedfont
Whitton
St Margarets
FELTHAM
TWICKENHAM
Petersham
Richmond Park
Bedfont Lakes Country Park
Crane Park
Ham
Putney Vale
Lower Feltham
Strawberry Hill
Fulwell Park
Wimbledon Common
Ashford
Chattern Hill
Hanworth
Kingston Vale
Felthamhill
Teddington
Ashford Common
Hampton Hill
Hampton
Sunbury-on-Thames
Kingston Hill
Coombe
Bushy Park
Hampton Wick
Queen Mary Reservoir
Cottenham Park
Hurst Park
KINGSTON UPON THAMES
Raynes Park
Charlton
Upper Halliford
Lower Sunbury
Norbiton
East Molesey
New Malden
Upper Halliford
Shepperton
West

FINCHLEY
HENDON
HARINGEY
TOTTENHAM
WALTHAM FOREST
WALTHAMSTOW
HAMPSTEAD
CAMDEN
HACKNEY
ISLINGTON
TOWER HAMLETS
CITY
KENSINGTON
WESTMINSTER
LAMBETH
CHELSEA
HAMMERSMITH
FULHAM
SOUTHWARK
GREENWICH
LEWISHAM
PUTNEY
WANDSWORTH
CLAPHAM
CATFORD
STREATHAM
WIMBLEDON
BECKENHAM
MERTON
MITCHAM

Road safety cameras

First, the advice you would expect from the AA – we advise drivers to always follow the signed speed limits - breaking the speed limit is illegal and can cost lives.

Both the AA and the Government believe that safety cameras ('speed cameras') should be operated within a transparent system. By providing information relating to road safety and speed hotspots, the AA believes that the driver is better placed to be aware of speed limits and can ensure adherence to them, thus making the roads safer for all users.

Most fixed cameras are installed at accident 'black spots' where four or more fatal or serious road collisions have occurred over the previous three years. It is the policy of both the police and the Department for Transport to make the location of cameras as well known as possible. By showing speed camera locations in this atlas the AA is identifying the places where extra care should be taken while driving. Speeding is illegal and dangerous and you MUST keep within the speed limit at all times.
There are currently more than 4,000 fixed cameras in Britain and the road mapping in this atlas identifies their on-the-road locations.

 This symbol is used on the mapping to identify **individual** camera locations - with speed limits (mph)

 This symbol is used on the mapping to identify **multiple** cameras on the same stretch of road - with speed limits (mph)

 This symbol is used on the mapping to highlight SPECS™ camera systems which calculate your **average speed** along a stretch of road between two or more sets of cameras - with speed limits (mph)

    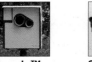

Gatso™   **Truvelo™**   **SPECS™**   **Traffipax™**

Mobile cameras are also deployed at other sites where speed is perceived to be a problem and mobile enforcement often takes place at the fixed camera sites shown on the maps in this atlas. Additionally, regular police enforcement can take place on any road.

Camera locations – read this before you use the atlas

1 The camera locations were correct at the time of finalising the information to go to press.

2 Camera locations are approximate due to limitations in the scale of road mapping used in this atlas.

3 In towns and urban areas camera locations are shown only on roads that appear on the road maps in this atlas.

4 Where two or more cameras occur close together, a special symbol is used to indicate multiple cameras on the same stretch of road.

5 Our symbols do not indicate the direction in which cameras point.

6 On the mapping we symbolise more than 4,000 fixed camera locations. Mobile laser device locations, roadwork cameras and 'fixed red light' cameras cannot be shown.

Speed Limits

Types of vehicle	Built up areas* MPH (km/h)	Single carriageways MPH (km/h)	Dual carriageways MPH (km/h)	Motorways MPH (km/h)
Cars & motorcycles (including car derived vans up to 2 tonnes maximum laden weight)	30 (48)	60 (96)	70 (112)	70 (112)
Cars towing caravans or trailers (including car derived vans and motorcycles)	30 (48)	50 (80)	60 (96)	60 (96)
Buses, coaches and minibuses (not exceeding 12 metres (39 feet) in overall length)	30 (48)	50 (80)	60 (96)	70 (112)
Goods vehicles (not exceeding 7.5 tonnes maximum laden weight)	30 (48)	50 (80)	60 (96)	70† (112)
Goods vehicles (exceeding 7.5 tonnes maximum laden weight)	30 (48)	40 (64)	50 (80)	60 (96)

* The 30mph (48km/h) limit usually applies to all traffic on all roads with street lighting unless signs show otherwise.
† 60mph (96km/h) if articulated or towing a trailer.

The fixed camera symbols on the mapping show the maximum speed in mph that applies to that particular stretch of road and above which the camera is set to activate. The actual road speed limit however will vary for different vehicle types and you must ensure that you drive within the speed limit for your particular class of vehicle at all times.
The chart above details the speed limits applying to the different classes. Don't forget that mobile enforcement can take account of vehicle class at any designated site.

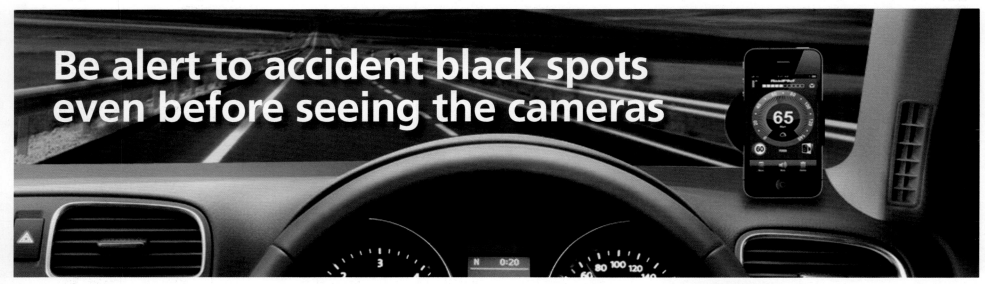

Be alert to accident black spots even before seeing the cameras

The AA brings you a Smart Phone app that provides 'real-time' updates of safety camera locations

The AA Safety Camera app brings the latest safety camera location system to your Smart Phone. It improves road safety by alerting you to the location of fixed and mobile camera sites and accident black spots.

The AA Safety Camera app ensures that you will always have the very latest data of fixed and mobile sites on your Smart Phone without having to connect it to your computer. Updates are made available automatically.

Powered by  **RoadPilot**®    Available on the **App Store**   Available in **Android Market**

Visual Countdown
To camera location

Your Speed
The speed you are travelling when approaching a camera. Dial turns red as an additional visual alert

Camera Types Located
Includes fixed cameras (Gatso, Specs etc.) and mobile cameras

Speed Limit at Camera

Smart Phone Apps

Tourist sites with satnav friendly postcodes

ENGLAND

- Acorn Bank Garden CA10 1SP Cumb 68 D7
- Aldborough Roman Site YO51 9ES N York 63 U6
- Alfriston Clergy House BN26 5TL E Susx 11 S10
- Alton Towers ST10 4DB Staffs 46 E5
- Anglesey Abbey CB25 9EJ Cambs 39 R8
- Anne Hathaway's Cottage CV37 9HH Warwks 36 G10
- Antony House PL11 2QA Cnwll 5 L9
- Appuldurcombe House PO38 3EW IoW 9 Q12
- Apsley House W1J 7NT Gt Lon 21 N7
- Arlington Court EX31 4LP Devon 15 P4
- Ascott LU7 0PS Bucks 30 J8
- Ashby-de-la-Zouch Castle LE65 1BR Leics 47 L10
- Athelhampton House & Gardens DT2 7LG Dorset 7 U6
- Attingham Park SY4 4TP Shrops 45 M11
- Audley End House & Gardens CB11 4JF Essex 39 R13
- Avebury Manor & Garden SN8 1RF Wilts 18 G6
- Baconsthorpe Castle NR25 6LN Norfk 50 K6
- Baddesley Clinton Hall B93 0DQ Warwks 36 H6
- Bamburgh Castle NE69 7DF Nthumb 85 T11
- Barnard Castle DL12 8PR Dur 69 M9
- Barrington Court TA19 0NQ Somset 17 L13
- Basildon Park RG8 9NR W Berk 19 T5
- Bateman's TN19 7DS E Susx 12 C11
- Battle of Britain Memorial Flight LN4 4SY Lincs 48 K2
- Beamish Open Air Museum DH9 0RG Dur 69 R2
- Beatrix Potter Gallery LA22 0NS Cumb 67 N13
- Beaulieu House SO42 7ZN Hants 9 M8
- Belton House NG32 2LS Lincs 48 D6
- Belvoir Castle NG32 1PD Leics 48 B7
- Bembridge Windmill PO35 5SQ IoW 9 S11
- Beningbrough Hall & Gardens YO30 1DD N York 64 C8
- Benthall Hall TF12 5RX Shrops 45 Q13
- Berkeley Castle GL13 9BQ Gloucs 28 C8
- Berrington Hall HR6 0DW Herefs 35 M8
- Berry Pomeroy Castle TQ9 6NJ Devon 5 U8
- Beth Chatto Gardens CO7 7DB Essex 23 Q3
- Biddulph Grange Garden ST8 7SD Staffs 45 U2
- Bishop's Waltham Palace SO32 1DH Hants 9 R5
- Blackpool Zoo FY3 8PP Bpool 61 Q12
- Blenheim Palace OX20 1PX Oxon 29 T4
- Blickling Hall NR11 6NF Norfk 51 L8
- Blue John Cavern & Mine S33 8WP Derbys 56 H10
- Bodiam Castle TN32 5UA E Susx 12 E10
- Bolsover Castle S44 6PR Derbys 57 Q12
- Boscobel House ST19 9AR Staffs 45 T12
- Bovington Tank Museum BH20 6JG Dorset 8 A11
- Bowes Castle DL12 9LD Dur 69 L10
- Bradford Industrial Museum BD2 3HP W Yorks 63 P13
- Bradley Manor TQ12 6BN Devon 5 U6
- Bramber Castle BN44 3WW W Susx 10 K8
- Brinkburn Priory NE65 8AP Nthumb 77 N6
- Bristol Zoo BS8 3HA Bristl 27 V13
- British Library NW1 2DB Gt Lon 21 N6
- British Museum WC1B 3DG Gt Lon 21 N6
- Brockhampton Estate WR6 5TB Herefs 35 Q10
- Brough Castle CA17 4EJ Cumb 68 G10
- Buckfast Abbey TQ11 0EE Devon 5 S7
- Buckingham Palace SW1A 1AA Gt Lon 21 N7
- Buckland Abbey PL20 6EY Devon 5 M7
- Buscot Park SN7 8BU Oxon 29 P8
- Byland Abbey YO61 4BD N York 64 C4
- Caldicot Castle & Country Park NP26 4HU Mons 27 T10
- Calke Abbey DE73 7LE Derbys 47 L9
- Canons Ashby House NN11 3SD Nhants 37 Q10
- Canterbury Cathedral CT1 2EH Kent 13 N4
- Carisbrooke Castle PO30 1XY IoW 9 P11
- Carlyle's House SW3 5HL Gt Lon 21 N7
- Castle Drogo EX6 6PB Devon 5 S2
- Castle Howard YO60 7DA N York 64 G5
- Castle Rising Castle PE31 6AH Norfk 49 U9
- Charlecote Park CV35 9ER Warwks 36 J9
- Chartwell TN16 1PS Kent 21 S12
- Chastleton House GL56 0SU Oxon 29 P2
- Chatsworth DE45 1PP Derbys 57 L12
- Chedworth Roman Villa GL54 3LJ Gloucs 29 L5
- Chessington World of Adventures KT9 2NE Gt Lon 21 L10
- Chester Cathedral CH1 2HU Ches 54 K13
- Chester Zoo CH2 1LH Ches 54 K12
- Chesters Roman Fort NE46 4EP Nthumb 76 J11
- Chiswick House W4 2RP Gt Lon 21 M7
- Chysauster Ancient Village TR20 8XA Cnwll 2 D10
- Clandon Park GU4 7RQ Surrey 20 H12
- Claremont Landscape Garden KT10 9JG Surrey 20 K10
- Claydon House MK18 2EY Bucks 30 F7
- Cleeve Abbey TA23 0PS Somset 16 D8
- Clevedon Court BS21 6QU N Som 17 M2
- Cliveden SL6 0JA Bucks 20 F5
- Clouds Hill BH20 7NQ Dorset 7 V6
- Clumber Park S80 3AZ Notts 57 T12
- Colchester Zoo CO3 0SL Essex 23 N3
- Coleridge Cottage TA5 1NQ Somset 16 G9
- Coleton Fishacre TQ6 0EQ Devon 6 B14
- Compton Castle TQ3 1TA Devon 5 V8
- Conisbrough Castle DN12 3HH Donc 57 R7
- Corbridge Roman Site NE45 5NT Nthumb 76 K13
- Corfe Castle BH20 5EZ Dorset 8 D12
- Corsham Court SN13 0BZ Wilts 18 C6
- Cotehele PL12 6TA Cnwll 5 L7
- Coughton Court B49 5JA Warwks 36 E8
- Courts Garden BA14 6RR Wilts 18 C8
- Cragside NE65 7PX Nthumb 77 M5
- Crealy Adventure Park EX5 1DR Devon 6 D6
- Crich Tramway Village DE4 5DP Derbys 46 K2
- Croft Castle HR6 9PW Herefs 34 K7
- Croome Park WR8 9DW Worcs 35 U12
- Deddington Castle OX15 0TE Oxon 29 U1
- Didcot Railway Centre OX11 7NJ Oxon 19 R2
- Dover Castle CT16 1HU Kent 13 R7
- Drayton Manor Theme Park B78 3TW Staffs 46 G13
- Dudmaston WV15 6QN Shrops 35 R3
- Dunham Massey WA14 4SJ Traffd 55 R9
- Dunstanburgh Castle NE66 3TT Nthumb 77 R1
- Dunster Castle TA24 6SL Somset 16 C8
- Durham Cathedral DH1 3EH Dur 69 S4
- Dyrham Park SN14 8ER S Glos 28 D12
- East Riddlesden Hall BD20 5EL Brad 63 M11
- Eden Project PL24 2SG Cnwll 3 R6
- Eltham Palace SE9 5QE Gt Lon 21 R8
- Emmetts Garden TN14 6AY Kent 21 S12
- Exmoor Zoological Park EX31 4SG Devon 15 Q4
- Farleigh Hungerford Castle BA2 7RS Somset 18 B9
- Farnborough Hall OX17 1DU Warwks 37 M11
- Felbrigg Hall NR11 8PR Norfk 51 L6
- Fenton House NW3 6RT Gt Lon 21 N5
- Finch Foundry EX20 2NW Devon 5 Q2
- Finchale Priory DH1 5SH Dur 69 S3
- Fishbourne Roman Palace PO19 3QR W Susx 10 C9
- Flag Fen Bronze Age Centre & Archaeology Park PE6 7QJ Cambs 48 K14
- Flamingo Land YO17 6UX N York 64 H4
- Forde Abbey TA20 4LU Somset 7 L3
- Fountains Abbey & Studley Royal HG4 3DY N York 63 R6
- Gawthorpe Hall BB12 8UA Lancs 62 G13
- Gisborough Priory TS14 6HG R & Cl 70 K9
- Glendurgan Garden TR11 5JZ Cnwll 2 K11
- Goodrich Castle HR9 6HY Herefs 28 A4
- Great Chalfield Manor SN12 8NH Wilts 18 C8
- Great Coxwell Barn SN7 7LZ Oxon 29 Q9
- Greenway TQ5 0ES Devon 5 V9
- Haddon Hall DE45 1LA Derbys 56 K13
- Hailes Abbey GL54 5PB Gloucs 28 L1
- Ham House TW10 7RS Gt Lon 21 L8
- Hampton Court Palace KT8 9AU Gt Lon 21 L9
- Hanbury Hall WR9 7EA Worcs 36 B8
- Hardwick Hall S44 5QJ Derbys 57 Q14
- Hardy's Cottage DT2 8QJ Dorset 7 T6
- Hare Hill SK10 4QB Ches 56 C11
- Hatchlands Park GU4 7RT Surrey 20 J12
- Heale Gardens SP4 6NT Wilts 18 H13
- Helmsley Castle YO62 5AB N York 64 E3
- Hereford Cathedral HR1 2NG Herefs 35 M13
- Hergest Croft Gardens HR5 3EG Herefs 34 G9
- Hever Castle & Gardens TN8 7NG Kent 21 S13
- Hidcote Manor Garden GL55 6LR Gloucs 36 G12
- Hill Top LA22 0LF Cumb 67 N13
- Hinton Ampner SO24 0LA Hants 9 R3
- Holkham Hall NR23 1AB Norfk 50 E5
- Housesteads Roman Fort NE47 6NN Nthumb 76 F12
- Howletts Wild Animal Park CT4 5EL Kent 13 N4
- Hughenden Manor HP14 4LA Bucks 20 E3
- Hurst Castle SO41 0TR Hants 9 L11
- Ickworth House & Gardens IP29 5QE Suffk 40 D8
- Ightham Mote TN15 0NT Kent 21 U12
- Ironbridge Gorge Museums TF8 7DQ Wrekin 45 Q13
- Kedleston Hall DE22 5JH Derbys 46 K5
- Kenilworth Castle CV8 1NE Warwks 36 J6
- Kenwood House NW3 7JR Gt Lon 21 N5
- Kew Gardens TW9 3AB Gt Lon 21 L7
- Killerton House & Garden EX5 3LE Devon 6 C4
- King John's Hunting Lodge BS26 2AP Somset 17 M6
- Kingston Lacy BH21 4EA Dorset 8 D8
- Kirby Hall NN17 3EN Nhants 38 D2
- Knightshayes Court EX16 7RQ Devon 16 C13
- Knole House TN15 0RP Kent 21 T12
- Knowsley Safari Park L34 4AN Knows 55 L8
- Lacock Abbey SN15 2LG Wilts 18 D7
- Lamb House TN31 7ES E Susx 12 H11
- Lanhydrock House PL30 5AD Cnwll 3 R4
- Launceston Castle PL15 7DR Cnwll 4 J4
- Leeds Castle ME17 1PL Kent 12 F5
- Lindisfarne Castle TD15 2SH Nthumb 85 S10
- Lindisfarne Priory TD15 2RX Nthumb 85 S10
- Little Moreton Hall CW12 4SD Ches 45 T2
- Liverpool Cathedral L1 7AZ Lpool 54 J9
- Longleat BA12 7NW Wilts 18 B12
- Losely Park GU3 1HS Surrey 20 G13
- Lost Gardens of Heligan PL26 6EN Cnwll 3 P7
- Ludgershall Castle SP11 9QR Wilts 19 L10
- Lydford Castle EX20 4BH Devon 5 N4
- Lyme Park SK12 2NX Ches 56 E10
- Lytes Cary Manor TA11 7HU Somset 17 P11
- Lyveden New Bield PE8 5AT Nhants 38 E3
- Maiden Castle DT2 9PP Dorset 7 S7
- Mapledurham House RG4 7TR Oxon 19 U5
- Marble Hill House TW1 2NL Gt Lon 21 L8
- Marwell Zoological Park SO21 1JH Hants 9 Q4
- Melford Hall CO10 9AA Suffk 40 E11
- Merseyside Maritime Museum L3 4AQ Lpool 54 H9
- Minster Lovell Hall OX29 0RR Oxon 29 R5
- Mompesson House SP1 2EL Wilts 8 G3
- Monk Bretton Priory S71 5QD Barns 57 N5
- Montacute House TA15 6XP Somset 17 N13
- Morwellham Quay PL19 8JL Devon 5 L7
- Moseley Old Hall WV10 7HY Staffs 46 B13
- Mottisfont Abbey & Garden SO51 0LP Hants 9 L3
- Mottistone Manor Garden PO30 4ED IoW 9 N12
- Mount Grace Priory DL6 3JG N York 70 F13
- National Gallery WC2N 5DN Gt Lon 21 N6
- National Maritime Museum SE10 9NF Gt Lon 21 Q7
- National Motorcycle Museum B92 0EJ Solhll 36 H4
- National Portrait Gallery WC2H 0HE Gt Lon 21 N6
- National Railway Museum YO26 4XJ York 64 D9
- National Space Centre LE4 5NS C Leic 47 Q12
- Natural History Museum SW7 5BD Gt Lon 21 N7
- Needles Old Battery PO39 0JH IoW 9 K12
- Nene Valley Railway PE8 6LR Cambs 38 H1
- Netley Abbey SO31 5FB Hants 9 P7
- Newark Air Museum NG24 2NY Notts 47 V2
- Newtown Old Town Hall PO30 4PA IoW 9 N10
- North Leigh Roman Villa OX29 6QB Oxon 29 S4
- Norwich Cathedral NR1 4DH Norfk 51 M12
- Nostell Priory WF4 1QE Wakefd 57 P3
- Nunnington Hall YO62 5UY N York 64 F4
- Nymans RH17 6EB W Susx 11 M5
- Old Royal Naval College SE10 9LW Gt Lon 21 Q7
- Old Sarum SP1 3SD Wilts 8 G2
- Old Wardour Castle SP3 6RR Wilts 8 C3
- Oliver Cromwell's House CB7 4HF Cambs 39 R4
- Orford Castle IP12 2ND Suffk 41 R10
- Ormesby Hall TS7 9AS R & Cl 70 H9
- Osborne House PO32 6JY IoW 9 Q9
- Osterley Park & House TW7 4RB Gt Lon 20 K7
- Overbeck's TQ8 8LW Devon 5 S13
- Oxburgh Hall PE33 9PS Norfk 50 B13
- Packwood House B94 6AT Warwks 36 G6
- Paignton Zoo TQ4 7EU Torbay 6 A13
- Paycocke's CO6 1NS Essex 22 K3
- Peckover House & Garden PE13 1JR Cambs 49 Q12
- Pendennis Castle TR11 4LP Cnwll 3 L10
- Petworth House & Park GU28 0AE W Susx 10 F6
- Pevensey Castle BN24 5LE E Susx 11 U10
- Peveril Castle S33 8WQ Derbys 56 J10
- Polesden Lacey RH5 6BD Surrey 20 K12
- Portland Castle DT5 1AZ Dorset 7 S10
- Portsmouth Historic Dockyard PO1 3LJ C Port 9 S8
- Powderham Castle EX6 8JQ Devon 6 C8
- Prior Park Landscape Garden BA2 5AH BaNES 17 U4
- Prudhoe Castle NE42 6NA Nthumb 77 M13
- Quarry Bank Mill SK9 4LA Ches 55 T10
- Quebec House TN16 1TD Kent 21 R12
- Ramsey Abbey Gatehouse PE17 1DH Cambs 39 L3
- Reculver Towers CT6 6SU Kent 13 P2
- Red House DA6 8JF Gt Lon 21 S7
- Restormel Castle PL22 0EE Cnwll 4 E8
- Richborough Roman Fort CT13 9JW Kent 13 R3
- Richmond Castle DL10 4QW N York 69 Q12
- Roche Abbey S66 8NW Rothm 57 R9
- Rochester Castle ME1 1SX Medway 12 D2
- Rockbourne Roman Villa SP6 3PG Hants 8 G5
- Roman Baths & Pump Room BA1 1LZ BaNES 17 U4
- Royal Observatory Greenwich SE10 8XJ Gt Lon 21 Q7
- Rufford Old Hall L40 1SG Lancs 55 L3
- Runnymede SL4 2JJ W & M 20 G8
- Rushton Triangular Lodge NN14 1RP Nhants 38 B4
- Rycote Chapel OX9 2PA Oxon 30 E12
- Salisbury Cathedral SP1 2EJ Wilts 8 G3
- Saltram PL7 1UH C Plym 5 N9
- Sandham Memorial Chapel RG20 9JT Hants 19 Q8
- Sandringham House & Grounds PE35 6EN Norfk 49 U8
- Saxtead Green Post Mill IP13 9QQ Suffk 41 N8
- Scarborough Castle YO11 1HY N York 65 P2
- Science Museum SW7 2DD Gt Lon 21 N7
- Scotney Castle TN3 8JN Kent 12 C8
- Shaw's Corner AL6 9BX Herts 31 Q9
- Sheffield Park Garden TN22 3QX E Susx 11 Q6
- Sherborne Old Castle DT9 3SA Dorset 17 R13
- Sissinghurst Castle Garden TN17 2AB Kent 12 F8
- Sizergh Castle & Garden LA8 8AE Cumb 61 T2
- Smallhythe Place TN30 7NG Kent 12 G10
- Snowshill Manor WR12 7JU Gloucs 36 E14
- Souter Lighthouse SR6 7NH S Tyne 77 U13
- Speke Hall L24 1XD Lpool 54 K10
- Spinnaker Tower PO1 3TT C Port 9 S9
- St Leonard's Tower ME19 6PE Kent 12 C4
- St Michael's Mount TR17 0HT Cnwll 2 E11
- St Paul's Cathedral EC4M 8AD Gt Lon 21 P6
- Stokesay Castle SY7 9AH Shrops 34 K4
- Stonehenge SP4 7DE Wilts 18 H12
- Stourhead BA12 6QD Wilts 17 U10
- Stowe Landscape Gardens MK18 5EH Bucks 30 E5
- Sudbury Hall DE6 5HT Derbys 46 G7
- Sulgrave Manor OX17 2SD Nhants 37 Q11
- Sunnycroft TF1 2DR Wrekin 45 Q11
- Sutton Hoo IP12 3DJ Suffk 41 N11
- Sutton House E9 6JQ Gt Lon 21 Q5
- Tate Britain SW1P 4RG Gt Lon 21 N7
- Tate Liverpool L3 4BB Lpool 54 H9
- Tate Modern SE1 9TG Gt Lon 21 P6
- Tattershall Castle LN4 4LR Lincs 48 K2
- Tatton Park WA16 6QN Ches 55 R10
- The Lowry M50 3AZ Salfd 55 T7
- The Vyne RG24 9HL Hants 19 T9
- The Weir HR4 7QF Herefs 34 K12
- Thornton Abbey DN39 6TU N Linc 58 K3
- Thorpe Park KT16 8PN Surrey 20 H9
- Tilbury Fort RM18 7NR Thurr 22 G12
- Tintagel Castle PL34 0HE Cnwll 4 C3
- Tintinhull Garden BA22 8PZ Somset 17 P13
- Totnes Castle TQ9 5NU Devon 5 U8
- Tower of London EC3N 4AB Gt Lon 21 P6
- Townend LA23 1LB Cumb 67 P12
- Treasurer's House YO1 7JL York 64 E9
- Trelissick Garden TR3 6QL Cnwll 3 L9
- Trengwainton Garden TR20 8RZ Cnwll 2 C10
- Trerice TR8 4PG Cnwll 3 L5
- Twycross Zoo CV9 3PX Leics 46 K12
- Upnor Castle ME2 4XG Medway 22 J13
- Uppark House & Garden GU31 5QR W Susx 10 B7
- Upton House & Garden OX15 6HT Warwks 37 L11
- Victoria & Albert Museum SW7 2RL Gt Lon 21 N7
- Waddesdon Manor HP18 0JH Bucks 30 F9
- Wakehurst Place RH17 6TN W Susx 11 N4
- Wall Roman Site WS14 0AW Staffs 46 E12
- Wallington House NE61 4AR Nthumb 77 L9
- Walmer Castle & Gardens CT14 7LJ Kent 13 S6
- Warkworth Castle NE65 0UJ Nthumb 77 Q4
- Warwick Castle CV34 4QU Warwks 36 J8
- Washington Old Hall NE38 7LE Sundld 70 D1
- Waterperry Gardens OX33 1JZ Oxon 30 D11
- Weeting Castle IP27 0RQ Norfk 40 C3
- Wenlock Priory TF13 6HS Shrops 45 P13
- West Midland Safari Park DY12 1LF Worcs 35 T5
- West Wycombe Park HP14 3AJ Bucks 20 D4
- Westbury Court Garden GL14 1PD Gloucs 28 D5
- Westminster Abbey SW1P 3PA Gt Lon 21 N7
- Westonbirt Arboretum GL8 8QS Gloucs 28 G9
- Westwood Manor BA15 2AF Wilts 18 B9
- Whitby Abbey YO22 4JT N York 71 R10
- Wightwick Manor WV6 8EE Wolves 45 U14
- Wimpole Hall & Home Farm SG8 0BW Cambs 39 M10
- Winchester Cathedral SO23 9LS Hants 9 P3
- Winchester City Mill SO23 0EJ Hants 9 P3
- Windsor Castle SL4 1NJ W & M 20 G7
- Winkworth Arboretum GU8 4AD Surrey 10 F2
- Wisley RHS Garden GU23 6QB Surrey 20 J11
- Woburn Safari Park MK17 9QN Beds 31 L6
- Wookey Hole Caves BA5 1BB Somset 17 P7
- Woolsthorpe Manor NG33 5NR Lincs 48 D9
- Wordsworth House CA13 9RX Cumb 66 H6
- Wrest Park MK45 4HS Beds 31 N5
- Wroxeter Roman City SY5 6PR Shrops 45 N12
- WWT Arundel Wetland Centre BN18 9PB W Susx 10 G9
- Yarmouth Castle PO41 0PB IoW 9 M11
- York Minster YO1 7JF York 64 E9
- ZSL London Zoo NW1 4RY Gt Lon 21 N6
- ZSL Whipsnade Zoo LU6 2LF Beds 31 M9

SCOTLAND

- Aberdour Castle KY3 0SL Fife 83 N1
- Alloa Tower FK10 1PP Clacks 90 C13
- Angus Folk Museum DD8 1RT Angus 91 N2
- Arbroath Abbey DD11 1EG Angus 91 T3
- Arduaine Garden PA34 4XQ Ag & B 87 P3
- Bachelors' Club KA5 5RB S Ayrs 81 N7
- Balmoral Castle Grounds AB35 5TB Abers 98 D5
- Balvenie Castle AB55 4DH Moray 104 C7
- Bannockburn Heritage Centre FK7 0LJ Stirlg 89 S7
- Blackness Castle EH49 7NH Falk 83 L2
- Blair Castle PH18 5TL P & K 97 P10
- Bothwell Castle G71 8BL S Lans 82 C7
- Branklyn Garden PH2 7BB P & K 90 H7
- Brodick Castle KA27 8HY N Ayrs 80 E5
- Brodie Castle IV36 2TE Moray 103 Q4
- Broughton House & Garden DG6 4JX D & G 73 R9
- Burleigh Castle KY13 9GG P & K 90 H11
- Burrell Collection G43 1AT C Glas 89 N13
- Caerlaverock Castle DG1 4RU D & G 74 K12
- Cardoness Castle DG7 2EH D & G 73 P8
- Carnasserie Castle PA31 8RQ Ag & B 87 Q5
- Castle Campbell FK14 7PP Clacks 90 E12
- Castle Fraser AB51 7LD Abers 105 L13
- Castle Kennedy & Gardens DG9 8BX D & G 72 E7
- Castle Menzies PH15 2JD P & K 90 B2
- Corgarff Castle AB36 8YL Abers 98 D2
- Craigievar Castle AB33 8JF Abers 98 K2
- Craigmillar Castle EH16 4SY C Edin 83 Q4
- Crarae Garden PA32 8YA Ag & B 87 T6
- Crathes Castle & Garden AB31 5QJ Abers 99 N4
- Crichton Castle EH37 5QH Mdloth 83 S6
- Crossraguel Abbey KA19 5HQ S Ayrs 80 K12
- Culloden Battlefield IV2 5EU Highld 102 K6
- Culross Palace KY12 8JH Fife 82 J1
- Culzean Castle & Country Park KA19 8LE S Ayrs 80 J10
- Dallas Dhu Distillery IV36 2RR Moray 103 R4
- David Livingstone Centre G72 9BT S Lans 82 C7
- Dirleton Castle EH39 5ER E Loth 84 E2
- Doune Castle FK16 6EA Stirlg 89 R5
- Drum Castle AB31 5EY Abers 99 P3
- Dryburgh Abbey TD6 0RQ Border 84 F12
- Duff House AB45 3SX Abers 104 K3
- Dumbarton Castle G82 1JJ W Duns 88 J11
- Dundrennan Abbey DG6 4QH D & G 73 S10
- Dunnottar Castle AB39 2TL Abers 99 R7
- Dunstaffnage Castle PA37 1PZ Ag & B 94 B12
- Edinburgh Castle EH1 2NG C Edin 83 Q4
- Edinburgh Zoo EH12 6TS C Edin 83 P4
- Edzell Castle DD9 7UE Angus 98 K10
- Elgin Cathedral IV30 1HU Moray 103 V3
- Falkland Palace & Garden KY15 7BU Fife 91 L10
- Fort George IV2 7TE Highld 103 L4
- Fyvie Castle AB53 8JS Abers 105 M8
- Georgian House EH2 4DR C Edin 83 P4
- Gladstone's Land EH1 2NT C Edin 83 Q4
- Glamis Castle DD8 1RJ Angus 91 N2
- Glasgow Botanic Gardens G12 0UE C Glas 89 N12
- Glasgow Cathedral G4 0QZ C Glas 89 P12
- Glasgow Science Centre G51 1EA C Glas 89 N12
- Glen Grant Distillery AB38 7BS Moray 104 B6
- Glenluce Abbey DG8 0AF D & G 72 F8
- Greenbank Garden G76 8RB E Rens 81 R1
- Haddo House AB41 7EQ Abers 105 P9
- Harmony Garden TD6 9LJ Border 84 E12
- Hermitage Castle TD9 0LU Border 75 U6
- Highland Wildlife Park PH21 1NL Highld 97 N3
- Hill House G84 9AJ Ag & B 88 G9
- Hill of Tarvit Mansionhouse & Garden KY15 5PB Fife 91 N9
- Holmwood G44 3YG C Glas 89 N14
- House of Dun DD10 9LQ Angus 99 M12
- House of the Binns EH49 7NA W Loth 83 L3
- Hunterian Museum G12 8QQ C Glas 89 N12
- Huntingtower Castle PH1 3JL P & K 90 G6
- Huntly Castle AB54 4SH Abers 104 G7
- Hutchesons' Hall G1 1EJ C Glas 89 N12
- Inchmahome Priory FK8 3RA Stirlg 89 N5
- Inveresk Lodge Garden EH21 7TE E Loth 83 R4
- Inverewe Garden IV22 2LG Highld 107 Q8
- Inverlochy Castle PH33 6SN Highld 94 G3
- Kellie Castle & Garden KY10 2RF Fife 91 R10
- Kildrummy Castle AB33 8RA Abers 104 F12
- Killiecrankie Visitor Centre PH16 5LG P & K 97 Q11
- Leith Hall Garden AB54 4NQ Abers 104 G10
- Linlithgow Palace EH49 7AL W Loth 82 K3
- Lochleven Castle KY13 8AS P & K 90 H11
- Logan Botanic Garden DG9 9ND D & G 72 D11
- Malleny Garden EH14 7AF C Edin 83 N5
- Melrose Abbey TD6 9LG Border 84 E12
- National Museum of Scotland EH1 1JF C Edin 83 Q4
- Newark Castle PA14 5NH Inver 88 H11
- Palace of Holyroodhouse EH8 8DX C Edin 83 Q4
- Pitmedden Garden AB41 7PD Abers 105 P10
- Preston Mill EH40 3DS E Loth 84 F3
- Priorwood Garden TD6 9PX Border 84 E12
- Robert Smail's Printing Works EH44 6HA Border 83 R11
- Rothesay Castle PA20 0DA Ag & B 88 C13
- Royal Botanic Garden Edinburgh EH3 5LR C Edin 83 P3
- Royal Yacht Britannia EH6 6JJ C Edin 83 Q3
- Scone Palace PH2 6BD P & K 90 H6
- Smailholm Tower TD5 7PG Border 84 G12
- Souter Johnnie's Cottage KA19 8HY S Ayrs 80 J11
- St Andrews Aquarium KY16 9AS Fife 91 R8
- Stirling Castle FK8 1EJ Stirlg 89 S7
- Sweetheart Abbey DG2 8BU D & G 74 J12
- Tantallon Castle EH39 5PN E Loth 84 F1
- Tenement House G3 6QN C Glas 89 N12
- The Lighthouse G1 3NU C Glas 89 N12
- Threave Castle DG7 1TJ D & G 74 D13
- Threave Garden DG7 1RX D & G 74 E13
- Tolquhon Castle AB41 7LP Abers 105 P10
- Traquair House EH44 6PW Border 83 R11
- Urquhart Castle IV63 6XJ Highld 102 F10
- Weaver's Cottage PA10 2JG Rens 88 K13
- Whithorn Priory DG8 8PY D & G 73 L11

WALES

- Aberconwy House LL32 8AY Conwy 53 N7
- Aberdulais Falls SA10 8EU Neath 26 D8
- Beaumaris Castle LL58 8AP IoA 52 K7
- Big Pit: National Coal Museum NP4 9XP Torfn 27 N6
- Bodnant Garden LL28 5RE Conwy 53 P8
- Caerleon Roman Amphitheatre NP18 1AE Newpt 27 Q9
- Caernarfon Castle LL55 2AY Gwynd 52 G10
- Cardiff Castle CF10 3RB Cardif 27 M12
- Castell Coch CF15 7JS Cardif 27 L11
- Chirk Castle LL14 5AF Wrexhm 44 G6
- Colby Woodland Garden SA67 8PP Pembks 25 L9
- Conwy Castle LL32 8AY Conwy 53 N7
- Criccieth Castle LL52 0DP Gwynd 42 K6
- Dan-yr-Ogof Showcaves SA9 1GJ Powys 26 E4
- Dinefwr Park SA19 6RT Carmth 25 V6
- Dolaucothi Gold Mines SA19 8US Carmth 33 N12
- Erddig LL13 0YT Wrexhm 44 H4
- Ffestiniog Railway LL49 9NF Gwynd 43 L6
- Harlech Castle LL46 2YH Gwynd 43 L7
- Llanerchaeron SA48 8DG Cerdgn 32 J8
- Penrhyn Castle LL57 4HN Gwynd 52 K8
- Plas Newydd LL61 6DQ IoA 52 H9
- Plas yn Rhiw LL53 8AB Gwynd 42 D8
- Portmeirion LL48 6ET Gwynd 43 L6
- Powis Castle & Garden SY21 8RF Powys 44 F12
- Raglan Castle NP15 2BT Mons 27 S6
- Sygun Copper Mine LL55 4NE Gwynd 43 M4
- Tintern Abbey NP16 6SE Mons 27 U7
- Tudor Merchant's House SA70 7BX Pembks 24 K10
- Tŷ Mawr Wybrnant LL25 0HJ Conwy 43 Q3
- Valle Crucis Abbey LL20 8DD Denbgs 44 F5

Caravan and camping sites in Britain

These pages list the top 300 AA-inspected Caravan and Camping (C & C) sites in the Pennant rating scheme. Five Pennant Premier sites are shown in **green**, Four Pennant sites are shown in **blue**.

Listings include addresses, telephone numbers and websites together with page and grid references to locate the sites in the atlas. The total number of touring pitches is also included for each site, together with the type of pitch available. The following abbreviations are used: C = Caravan CV = Campervan T = Tent

To find out more about the AA's Pennant rating scheme and other rated caravan and camping sites not included on these pages please visit ***theAA.com***

ENGLAND

Abbey Farm Caravan Park
Dark Lane, Ormskirk
L40 5TX
Tel: 01695 572686 **54 K5**
abbeyfarmcaravanpark.co.uk
Total Pitches: 56 (C, CV & T)

Alders Caravan Park
Home Farm, Alne, York
YO61 1RY
Tel: 01347 838722 **64 C6**
alderscaravanpark.co.uk
Total Pitches: 87 (C, CV & T)

Alpine Grove Touring Park
Forton, Chard
TA20 4HD
Tel: 01460 63479 **6 K3**
alpinegrovetouringpark.com
Total Pitches: 40 (C, CV & T)

Andrewshayes Caravan Park
Dalwood, Axminster
EX13 7DY
Tel: 01404 831225 **6 H5**
andrewshayes.co.uk
Total Pitches: 150 (C, CV & T)

Appuldurcombe Gardens Holiday Park
Appuldurcombe Road, Wroxall, Isle of Wight
PO38 3EP
Tel: 01983 852597 **9 Q12**
appuldurcombegardens.co.uk
Total Pitches: 100 (C, CV & T)

Ayr Holiday Park
St Ives, Cornwall
TR26 1EJ
Tel: 01736 795855 **2 E8**
ayrholidaypark.co.uk
Total Pitches: 40 (C, CV & T)

Back of Beyond Touring Park
234 Ringwood Rd, St Leonards, Dorset
BH24 2SB
Tel: 01202 876968 **8 F8**
backofbeyondtouringpark.co.uk
Total Pitches: 80 (C, CV & T)

Bagwell Farm Touring Park
Knights in the Bottom,
Chickerell, Weymouth
DT3 4EA
Tel: 01305 782575 **7 R8**
bagwellfarm.co.uk
Total Pitches: 320 (C, CV & T)

Bardsea Leisure Park
Priory Road, Ulverston
LA12 9QE
Tel: 01229 584712 **61 P4**
bardsealeisure.co.uk
Total Pitches: 83 (C & CV)

Barn Farm Campsite
Barn Farm, Birchover, Matlock
DE4 2BL
Tel: 01629 650245 **46 H1**
barnfarmcamping.com
Total Pitches: 25 (C, CV & T)

Barnstones C & C Site
Great Bourton, Banbury
OX17 1QU
Tel: 01295 750289 **37 N12**
Total Pitches: 49 (C, CV & T)

Beaconsfield Farm Caravan Park
Battlefield, Shrewsbury
SY4 4AA
Tel: 01939 210370 **45 M10**
beaconsfield-farm.co.uk
Total Pitches: 60 (C & CV)

Bellingham C & C Club Site
Brown Rigg, Bellingham
NE48 2JY
Tel: 01434 220175 **76 G9**
campingandcaravanningclub.co.uk/bellingham
Total Pitches: 64 (C, CV & T)

Bingham Grange Touring & Camping Park
Melplash, Bridport
DT6 3TT
Tel: 01308 488234 **7 N5**
binghamgrange.co.uk
Total Pitches: 150 (C, CV & T)

Bo Peep Farm Caravan Park
Bo Peep Farm, Aynho Road,
Adderbury, Banbury
OX17 3NP
Tel: 01295 810605 **37 N14**
bo-peep.co.uk
Total Pitches: 104 (C, CV & T)

Briarfields Motel & Touring Park
Gloucester Road, Cheltenham
GL51 0SX
Tel: 01242 235324 **28 H3**
briarfields.net
Total Pitches: 72 (C, CV & T)

Broadhembury C & C Park
Steeds Lane, Kingsnorth, Ashford
TN26 1NQ
Tel: 01233 620859 **12 K8**
broadhembury.co.uk
Total Pitches: 110 (C, CV & T)

Brokerswood Country Park
Brokerswood, Westbury
BA13 4EH
Tel: 01373 822238 **18 B10**
brokerswoodcountrypark.co.uk
Total Pitches: 69 (C, CV & T)

Budemeadows Touring Park
Widemouth Bay, Bude
EX23 0NA
Tel: 01288 361646 **14 F12**
budemeadows.com
Total Pitches: 145 (C, CV & T)

Burrowhayes Farm C & C Site
West Luccombe, Porlock, Minehead
TA24 8HT
Tel: 01643 862463 **16 B7**
burrowhayes.co.uk
Total Pitches: 120 (C, CV & T)

Burton Constable Holiday Park & Arboretum
Old Lodges, Sproatley, Hull
HU11 4LN
Tel: 01964 562508 **65 R12**
burtonconstable.co.uk
Total Pitches: 140 (C, CV & T)

Calloose C & C Park
Leedstown, Hayle
TR27 5ET
Tel: 01736 850431 **2 F10**
calloose.co.uk
Total Pitches: 109 (C, CV & T)

Camping Caradon Touring Park
Trelawne, Looe
PL13 2NA
Tel: 01503 272388 **4 G10**
campingcaradon.co.uk
Total Pitches: 85 (C, CV & T)

Carlton Meres Country Park
Rendham Road, Carlton, Saxmundham
IP17 2QP
Tel: 01728 603344 **41 Q7**
carlton-meres.co.uk
Total Pitches: 96 (C & CV)

Carlyon Bay C & C Park
Bethesda, Cypress Avenue, Carlyon Bay
PL25 3RE
Tel: 01726 812735 **3 R6**
carlyonbay.net
Total Pitches: 180 (C, CV & T)

Carnevas Holiday Park & Farm Cottages
Carnevas Farm, St Merryn
PL28 8PN
Tel: 01841 520230 **3 M2**
carnevasholidaypark.co.uk
Total Pitches: 195 (C, CV & T)

Carnon Downs C & C Park
Carnon Downs, Truro
TR3 6JJ
Tel: 01872 862283 **3 L8**
carnon-downs-caravanpark.co.uk
Total Pitches: 150 (C, CV & T)

Carvynick Country Club
Summercourt, Newquay
TR8 5AF
Tel: 01872 510716 **3 M5**
carvynick.co.uk
Total Pitches: 47 (CV)

Castlerigg Hall C & C Park
Castlerigg Hall, Keswick
CA12 4TE
Tel: 017687 74499 **67 L8**
castlerigg.co.uk
Total Pitches: 48 (C, CV & T)

Cheddar Bridge Touring Park
Draycott Rd, Cheddar
BS27 3RJ
Tel: 01934 743048 **17 N6**
cheddarbridge.co.uk
Total Pitches: 45 (C, CV & T)

Cheddar C & C Club Site
Townsend, Priddy, Wells
BA5 3BP
Tel: 01749 870241 **17 P6**
campingandcaravanningclub.co.uk/cheddar
Total Pitches: 90 (C, CV & T)

Chiverton Park
East Hill, Blackwater
TR4 8HS
Tel: 01872 560667 **2 J7**
chivertonpark.co.uk
Total Pitches: 12 (C, CV & T)

Church Farm C & C Park
The Bungalow, Church Farm, High Street,
Sixpenny Handley, Salisbury
SP5 5ND
Tel: 01725 552563 **8 D5**
churchfarmcandcpark.co.uk
Total Pitches: 35 (C, CV & T)

Claylands Caravan Park
Cabus, Garstang
PR3 1AJ
Tel: 01524 791242 **61 T10**
claylands.com
Total Pitches: 30 (C, CV & T)

Clippesby Hall
Hall Lane, Clippesby, Great Yarmouth
NR29 3BL
Tel: 01493 367800 **51 R11**
clippesby.com
Total Pitches: 120 (C, CV & T)

Cofton Country Holidays
Starcross, Dawlish
EX6 8RP
Tel: 01626 890111 **6 C8**
coftonholidays.co.uk
Total Pitches: 450 (C, CV & T)

Colchester Holiday Park
Cymbeline Way, Lexden,
Colchester
CO3 4AG
Tel: 01206 545551 **23 N2**
colchestercamping.co.uk
Total Pitches: 168 (C, CV & T)

Constable Burton Hall Caravan Park
Constable Burton, Leyburn
DL8 5LJ
Tel: 01677 450428 **63 P1**
cbcaravanpark.co.uk
Total Pitches: 120 (C & CV)

Coombe Touring Park
Race Plain, Netherhampton,
Salisbury
SP2 8PN
Tel: 01722 328451 **8 F3**
coombecaravanpark.co.uk
Total Pitches: 50 (C, CV & T)

Corfe Castle C & C Club Site
Bucknowle, Wareham
BH20 5PQ
Tel: 01929 480280 **8 C12**
campingandcaravanningclub.co.uk/corfecastle
Total Pitches: 80 (C, CV & T)

Cornish Farm Touring Park
Shoreditch, Taunton
TA3 7BS
Tel: 01823 327746 **16 H12**
cornishfarm.com
Total Pitches: 50 (C, CV & T)

Cosawes Park
Perranarworthal, Truro
TR3 7QS
Tel: 01872 863724 **2 K9**
cosawestouringandcamping.co.uk
Total Pitches: 40 (C, CV & T)

Cote Ghyll C & C Park
Osmotherley, Northallerton
DL6 3AH
Tel: 01609 883425 **70 G13**
coteghyll.com
Total Pitches: 77 (C, CV & T)

Cotswold View Touring Park
Enstone Road, Charlbury
OX7 3JH
Tel: 01608 810314 **29 S3**
cotswoldview.co.uk
Total Pitches: 125 (C, CV & T)

Dell Touring Park
Beyton Road, Thurston,
Bury St Edmunds
IP31 3RB
Tel: 01359 270121 **40 F8**
thedellcaravanpark.co.uk
Total Pitches: 60 (C, CV & T)

Diamond Farm C & C Park
Islip Road, Bletchingdon
OX5 3DR
Tel: 01869 350909 **30 B9**
diamondpark.co.uk
Total Pitches: 37 (C, CV & T)

Dibles Park
Dibles Road, Warsash,
Southampton
SO31 9SA
Tel: 01489 575232 **9 Q7**
diblespark.co.uk
Total Pitches: 14 (C, CV & T)

Dolbeare Park C & C
St Ive Road, Landrake, Saltash
PL12 5AF
Tel: 01752 851332 **4 K8**
dolbeare.co.uk
Total Pitches: 60 (C, CV & T)

Dornafield
Dornafield Farm, Two Mile Oak,
Newton Abbot
TQ12 6DD
Tel: 01803 812732 **5 U7**
dornafield.com
Total Pitches: 135 (C, CV & T)

East Fleet Farm Touring Park
Chickerell, Weymouth
DT3 4DW
Tel: 01305 785768 **7 R9**
eastfleet.co.uk
Total Pitches: 400 (C, CV & T)

Eden Valley Holiday Park
Lanlivery, Nr Lostwithiel
PL30 5BU
Tel: 01208 872277 **3 R5**
edenvalleyholidaypark.co.uk
Total Pitches: 56 (C, CV & T)

Eskdale C & C Club Site
Boot, Holmrook
CA19 1TH
Tel: 019467 23253 **66 J12**
campingandcaravanningclub.co.uk/eskdale
Total Pitches: 80 (CV & T)

Exe Valley Caravan Site
Mill House, Bridgetown, Dulverton
TA22 9JR
Tel: 01643 851432 **16 B10**
exevalleycamping.co.uk
Total Pitches: 50 (C, CV & T)

Fallbarrow Park
Rayrigg Road, Windermere
LA23 3DL
Tel: 015394 44422 **67 P13**
slholidays.co.uk
Total Pitches: 32 (C & CV)

Fernwood Caravan Park
Lyneal, Ellesmere
SY12 0QF
Tel: 01948 710221 **45 L7**
fernwoodpark.co.uk
Total Pitches: 60 (C & CV)

Fields End Water Caravan Park & Fishery
Benwick Road, Doddington, March
PE15 0TY
Tel: 01354 740199 **39 N2**
fieldsendcaravans.co.uk
Total Pitches: 52 (C, CV & T)

Fishpool Farm Caravan Park
Fishpool Road, Delamere, Northwich
CW8 2HP
Tel: 01606 883970 **55 N13**
fishpoolfarmcaravanpark.co.uk
Total Pitches: 50 (C, CV & T)

Flusco Wood
Flusco, Penrith
CA11 0JB
Tel: 017684 80020 **67 Q7**
fluscowood.co.uk
Total Pitches: 53 (C & CV)

Forest Glade Holiday Park
Kentisbeare, Cullompton
EX15 2DT
Tel: 01404 841381 **6 F3**
forest-glade.co.uk
Total Pitches: 80 (C, CV & T)

Globe Vale Holiday Park
Radnor, Redruth
TR16 4BH
Tel: 01209 891183 **2 J8**
globevale.co.uk
Total Pitches: 138 (C, CV & T)

Golden Cap Holiday Park
Seatown, Chideock, Bridport
DT6 6JX
Tel: 01308 422139 **7 M6**
wdlh.co.uk
Total Pitches: 108 (C, CV & T)

Golden Square Touring Caravan Park
Oswaldkirk, Helmsley
YO62 5YQ
Tel: 01439 788269 **64 E4**
goldensquarecaravanpark.com
Total Pitches: 129 (C, CV & T)

Golden Valley C & C Park
Coach Road, Ripley
DE55 4ES
Tel: 01773 513881 **47 M3**
goldenvalleycaravanpark.co.uk
Total Pitches: 45 (C, CV & T)

Goosewood Caravan Park
Sutton-on-the-Forest, York
YO61 1ET
Tel: 01347 810829 **64 D7**
flowerofmay.com
Total Pitches: 100 (C & CV)

Greenacres Touring Park
Haywards Lane, Chelston, Wellington
TA21 9PH
Tel: 01823 652844 **16 G12**
greenacres-wellington.co.uk
Total Pitches: 40 (C & CV)

Greenhill Leisure Park
Greenhill Farm, Station Road,
Bletchingdon, Oxford
OX5 3BQ
Tel: 01869 351600 **29 U4**
greenhill-leisure-park.co.uk
Total Pitches: 92 (C, CV & T)

Grouse Hill Caravan Park
Flask Bungalow Farm, Fylingdales,
Robin Hood's Bay
YO22 4QH
Tel: 01947 880543 **71 R12**
grousehill.co.uk
Total Pitches: 175 (C, CV & T)

Gunvenna Caravan Park
St Minver, Wadebridge
PL27 6QN
Tel: 01208 862405 **4 B5**
gunvenna.co.uk
Total Pitches: 75 (C, CV & T)

Gwithian Farm Campsite
Gwithian Farm, Gwithian, Hayle
TR27 5BX
Tel: 01736 753127 **2 F8**
gwithianfarm.co.uk
Total Pitches: 87 (C, CV & T)

Harbury Fields
Harbury Fields Farm, Harbury,
Nr Leamington Spa
CV33 9JN
Tel: 01926 612457 **37 L8**
harburyfields.co.uk
Total Pitches: 32 (C & CV)

Hawthorn Farm Caravan Park
Station Road, Martin Mill, Dover
CT15 5LA
Tel: 01304 852658 **13 R6**
keatfarm.co.uk
Total Pitches: 147 (C, CV & T)

Heathfield Farm Camping
Heathfield Road, Freshwater,
Isle of Wight
PO40 9SH
Tel: 01983 407822 **9 L11**
heathfieldcamping.co.uk
Total Pitches: 60 (C, CV & T)

Heathland Beach Caravan Park
London Road, Kessingland
NR33 7PJ
Tel: 01502 740337 **41 T3**
heathlandbeach.co.uk
Total Pitches: 63 (C, CV & T)

Hele Valley Holiday Park
Hele Bay, Ilfracombe, North Devon
EX34 9RD
Tel: 01271 862460 **15 M3**
helevalley.co.uk
Total Pitches: 50 (C, CV & T)

Heron's Mead Fishing Lake & Touring Park
Marsh Lane, Orby, Skegness
PE24 5JA
Tel: 01754 811340 **59 T13**
heronsmeadtouringpark.co.uk
Total Pitches: 21 (C, CV & T)

Hidden Valley Park
West Down, Braunton, Ilfracombe
EX34 8NU
Tel: 01271 813837 **15 M4**
hiddenvalleypark.com
Total Pitches: 115 (C, CV & T)

Highfield Farm Touring Park
Long Road, Comberton, Cambridge
CB23 7DG
Tel: 01223 262308 **39 N9**
highfieldfarmtouringpark.co.uk
Total Pitches: 120 (C, CV & T)

Highlands End Holiday Park
Eype, Bridport, Dorset
DT6 6AR
Tel: 01308 422139 **7 N6**
wdlh.co.uk
Total Pitches: 195 (C, CV & T)

Hill Cottage Farm C & C Park
Sandleheath Road, Alderholt,
Fordingbridge
SP6 3EG
Tel: 01425 650513 **8 G6**
hillcottagefarmcampingandcaravanpark.co.uk
Total Pitches: 35 (C, CV & T)

Hill Farm Caravan Park
Branches Lane, Sherfield English,
Romsey
SO51 6FH
Tel: 01794 340402 **8 K4**
hillfarmpark.com
Total Pitches: 70 (C, CV & T)

Hill of Oaks & Blakeholme
Windermere
LA12 8NR
Tel: 015395 31578 **61 R2**
hillofoaks.co.uk
Total Pitches: 43 (C & CV)

Hillside Caravan Park
Canvas Farm, Moor Road, Thirsk
YO7 4BR
Tel: 01845 537349 **63 U2**
hillsidecaravanpark.co.uk
Total Pitches: 35 (C & CV)

Hollins Farm C & C
Far Arnside, Carnforth
LA5 0SL
Tel: 01524 701508 **61 S4**
holgates.co.uk
Total Pitches: 12 (C, CV & T)

Homing Park
Church Lane, Seasalter, Whitstable
CT5 4BU
Tel: 01227 771777 **13 L3**
homingpark.co.uk
Total Pitches: 43 (C, CV & T)

Honeybridge Park
Honeybridge Lane, Dial Post, Horsham
RH13 8NX
Tel: 01403 710923 **10 K7**
honeybridgepark.co.uk
Total Pitches: 130 (C, CV & T)

Hurley Riverside Park
Park Office, Hurley, Nr Maidenhead
SL6 5NE
Tel: 01628 824493 **20 D6**
hurleyriversidepark.co.uk
Total Pitches: 200 (C, CV & T)

Hutton-le-Hole Caravan Park
Westfield Lodge, Hutton-le-Hole
YO62 6UG
Tel: 01751 417261 **64 G2**
westfieldlodge.co.uk
Total Pitches: 42 (C, CV & T)

Hylton Caravan Park
Eden Street, Silloth
CA7 4AY
Tel: 016973 31707 **66 H2**
stanwix.com
Total Pitches: 90 (C, CV & T)

Isle of Avalon Touring Caravan Park
Godney Road, Glastonbury
BA6 9AF
Tel: 01458 833618 **17 N9**
Total Pitches: 120 (C, CV & T)

Jacobs Mount Caravan Park
Jacobs Mount, Stepney Road,
Scarborough
YO12 5NL
Tel: 01723 361178 **65 N2**
jacobsmount.com
Total Pitches: 156 (C, CV & T)

Jasmine Caravan Park
Cross Lane, Snainton, Scarborough
YO13 9BE
Tel: 01723 859240 **65 L3**
jasminepark.co.uk
Total Pitches: 94 (C, CV & T)

Juliot's Well Holiday Park
Camelford, North Cornwall
PL32 9RF
Tel: 01840 213302 **4 D4**
juliotswell.com
Total Pitches: 39 (C, CV & T)

Kenneggy Cove Holiday Park
Higher Kenneggy, Rosudgeon,
Penzance
TR20 9AU
Tel: 01736 763453 **2 F11**
kenneggycove.co.uk
Total Pitches: 45 (C, CV & T)

Kennford International Caravan Park
Kennford, Exeter
EX6 7YN
Tel: 01392 833046 **6 B7**
kennfordinternational.co.uk
Total Pitches: 96 (C, CV & T)

King's Lynn Caravan & Camping Park
New Road, North Runcton,
King's Lynn
PE33 0RA
Tel: 01553 840004 **49 T10**
kl-cc.co.uk
Total Pitches: 150 (C, CV & T)

Kloofs Caravan Park
Sandhurst Lane, Bexhill
TN39 4RG
Tel: 01424 842839 **12 D14**
kloofs.com
Total Pitches: 50 (C, CV & T)

Kneps Farm Holiday Park
River Road, Stanah, Thornton-Cleveleys,
Blackpool
FY5 5LR
Tel: 01253 823632 **61 R11**
knepsfarm.co.uk
Total Pitches: 60 (C & CV)

Knight Stainforth Hall Caravan & Campsite
Stainforth, Settle
BD24 0DP
Tel: 01729 822200 **62 G6**
knightstainforth.co.uk
Total Pitches: 100 (C, CV & T)

Ladycross Plantation Caravan Park
Egton, Whitby
YO21 1UA
Tel: 01947 895502 **71 P11**
ladycrossplantation.co.uk
Total Pitches: 130 (C, CV & T)

Lamb Cottage Caravan Park
Dalefords Lane, Whitegate, Northwich
CW8 2BN
Tel: 01606 882302 **55 P13**
lambcottage.co.uk
Total Pitches: 45 (C & CV)

Langstone Manor C & C Park
Moortown, Tavistock
PL19 9JZ
Tel: 01822 613371 **5 N6**
langstone-manor.co.uk
Total Pitches: 40 (C, CV & T)

Larches Caravan Park
Mealsgate, Wigton
CA7 1LQ
Tel: 016973 71379 **66 K4**
Total Pitches: 73 (C, CV & T)

Lebberston Touring Park
Filey Road, Lebberston,
Scarborough
YO11 3PE
Tel: 01723 585723 **65 P3**
lebberstontouring.co.uk
Total Pitches: 125 (C & CV)

Lee Valley Campsite
Sewardstone Road,
Chingford, London
E4 7RA
Tel: 020 8529 5689 **21 Q3**
Total Pitches: 100 (C, CV & T)

Lemonford Caravan Park
Bickington (near Ashburton),
Newton Abbot
TQ12 6JR
Tel: 01626 821242 **5 T6**
lemonford.co.uk
Total Pitches: 82 (C, CV & T)

Lickpenny Caravan Site
Lickpenny Lane, Tansley,
Matlock
DE4 5GF
Tel: 01629 583040 **46 K2**
lickpennycaravanpark.co.uk
Total Pitches: 80 (C & CV)

Lime Tree Park
Dukes Drive, Buxton
SK17 9RP
Tel: 01298 22988 **56 G12**
limetreeparkbuxton.co.uk
Total Pitches: 106 (C, CV & T)

Lincoln Farm Park Oxfordshire
High Street, Standlake
OX29 7RH
Tel: 01865 300239 **29 S7**
lincolnfarmpark.co.uk
Total Pitches: 90 (C, CV & T)

Little Cotton Caravan Park
Little Cotton, Dartmouth
TQ6 0LB
Tel: 01803 832558 **5 V10**
littlecotton.co.uk
Total Pitches: 95 (C, CV & T)

Little Lakeland Caravan Park
Wortwell, Harleston
IP20 0EL
Tel: 01986 788646 **41 N3**
littlelakeland.co.uk
Total Pitches: 38 (C, CV & T)

Little Trevarrack Holiday Park
Laity Lane, Carbis Bay, St Ives
TR26 3HW
Tel: 01736 797580 **2 E9**
littletrevarrack.co.uk
Total Pitches: 200 (C, CV & T)

Long Acre Caravan Park
Station Road, Old Leake, Boston
PE22 9RF
Tel: 01205 871555 **49 N3**
longacres-caravanpark.co.uk
Total Pitches: 40 (C, CV & T)

Lowther Holiday Park
Eamont Bridge, Penrith
CA10 2JB
Tel: 01768 863631 **67 R7**
lowther-holidaypark.co.uk
Total Pitches: 180 (C, CV & T)

Lytton Lawn Touring Park
Lymore Lane, Milford on Sea
SO41 0TX
Tel: 01590 648331 **8 K10**
shorefield.co.uk
Total Pitches: 136 (C, CV & T)

Manor Wood Country Caravan Park
Manor Wood, Coddington, Chester
CH3 9EN
Tel: 01829 782990 **45 L2**
cheshire-caravan-sites.co.uk
Total Pitches: 45 (C, CV & T)

Maustin Caravan Park
Kearby with Netherby, Netherby
LS22 4DA
Tel: 0113 288 6234 **63 S10**
maustin.co.uk
Total Pitches: 25 (C, CV & T)

Mayfield Touring Park
Cheltenham Road, Cirencester
GL7 7BH
Tel: 01285 831301 **28 K6**
mayfieldpark.co.uk
Total Pitches: 72 (C, CV & T)

Meadowbank Holidays
Stour Way, Christchurch
BH23 2PQ
Tel: 01202 483597 **8 G10**
meadowbank-holidays.co.uk
Total Pitches: 41 (C & CV)

Merley Court
Merley, Wimborne Minster
BH21 3AA
Tel: 01590 648331 **8 E9**
shorefield.co.uk
Total Pitches: 160 (C, CV & T)

Middlewood Farm Holiday Park
Middlewood Lane, Fylingthorpe,
Robin Hood's Bay, Whitby
YO22 4UF
Tel: 01947 880414 **71 R12**
middlewoodfarm.com
Total Pitches: 100 (C, CV & T)

Minnows Touring Park
Holbrook Lane, Sampford Peverell
EX16 7EN
Tel: 01884 821770 **16 D13**
ukparks.co.uk/minnows
Total Pitches: 59 (C, CV & T)

Moon & Sixpence
Newbourn Road, Waldringfield,
Woodbridge
IP12 4PP
Tel: 01473 736650 **41 N11**
moonandsixpence.eu
Total Pitches: 65 (C, CV & T)

Moss Wood Caravan Park
Crimbles Lane, Cockerham
LA2 0ES
Tel: 01524 791041 **61 T10**
mosswood.co.uk
Total Pitches: 25 (C, CV & T)

Naburn Lock Caravan Park
Naburn
YO19 4RU
Tel: 01904 728697 **64 E10**
naburnlock.co.uk
Total Pitches: 100 (C, CV & T)

Newberry Valley Park
Woodlands, Combe Martin
EX34 0AT
Tel: 01271 882334 **15 N3**
newberryvalleypark.co.uk
Total Pitches: 120 (C, CV & T)

New House Caravan Park
Kirkby Lonsdale
LA6 2HR
Tel: 015242 71590 **62 C4**
Total Pitches: 50 (C & CV)

Newlands C & C Park
Charmouth, Bridport
DT6 6RB
Tel: 01297 560259 **7 L6**
newlandsholidays.co.uk
Total Pitches: 240 (C, CV & T)

Newperran Holiday Park
Rejerrah, Newquay
TR8 5QJ
Tel: 01872 572407 **2 K6**
newperran.co.uk
Total Pitches: 357 (C, CV & T)

Newton Mill Holiday Park
Newton Road, Bath
BA2 9JF
Tel: 0844 272 9503 **17 T4**
newtonmillpark.co.uk
Total Pitches: 106 (C, CV & T)

Northam Farm Caravan & Touring Park
Brean, Burnham-on-Sea
TA8 2SE
Tel: 01278 751244 **16 K5**
northamfarm.co.uk
Total Pitches: 350 (C, CV & T)

North Morte Farm C & C Park
North Morte Road, Mortehoe,
Woolacombe, N Devon
EX34 7EG
Tel: 01271 870381 **15 L3**
northmortefarm.co.uk
Total Pitches: 180 (C, CV & T)

Oakdown Country Holiday Park
Gatedown Lane, Sidmouth
EX10 0PT
Tel: 01297 680387 **6 G6**
oakdown.co.uk
Total Pitches: 150 (C, CV & T)

Oathill Farm Touring & Camping Site
Oathill, Crewkerne
TA18 8PZ
Tel: 01460 30234 **7 M3**
oathillfarmleisure.co.uk
Total Pitches: 13 (C, CV & T)

Old Barn Touring Park
Cheverton Farm,
Newport Road, Sandown
PO36 9PJ
Tel: 01983 866414 **9 R12**
oldbarntouring.co.uk
Total Pitches: 60 (C, CV & T)

Old Hall Caravan Park
Capernwray, Carnforth
LA6 1AD
Tel: 01524 733276 **61 U5**
oldhallcaravanpark.co.uk
Total Pitches: 38 (C & CV)

Orchard Farm Holiday Village
Stonegate, Hunmanby
YO14 0PU
Tel: 01723 891582 **65 Q4**
orchardfarmholidayvillage.co.uk
Total Pitches: 91 (C, CV & T)

Orchard Park
Frampton Lane,
Hubbert's Bridge, Boston
PE20 3QU
Tel: 01205 290328 **49 L5**
orchardpark.co.uk
Total Pitches: 87 (C, CV & T)

Ord House Country Park
East Ord, Berwick-upon-Tweed
TD15 2NS
Tel: 01289 305288 **85 P8**
ordhouse.co.uk
Total Pitches: 79 (C, CV & T)

Otterington Park
Station Farm, South Otterington,
Northallerton
DL7 9JB
Tel: 01609 780656 **63 T2**
otteringtonpark.com
Total Pitches: 62 (C & CV)

Oxon Hall Touring Park
Welshpool Road, Shrewsbury
SY3 5FB
Tel: 01743 340868 **45 L11**
morris-leisure.co.uk
Total Pitches: 105 (C, CV & T)

Padstow Touring Park
Padstow
PL28 8LE
Tel: 01841 532061 **3 N2**
padstowtouringpark.co.uk
Total Pitches: 150 (C, CV & T)

Park Cliffe Camping & Caravan Estate
Birks Road, Tower Wood, Windermere
LA23 3PG
Tel: 01539 531344 **61 R1**
parkcliffe.co.uk
Total Pitches: 60 (C, CV & T)

Parkers Farm Holiday Park
Higher Mead Farm, Ashburton, Devon
TQ13 7LJ
Tel: 01364 654869 **5 T6**
parkersfarmholidays.co.uk
Total Pitches: 100 (C, CV & T)

Pear Tree Holiday Park
Organford Road, Holton Heath,
Organford, Poole
BH16 6LA
Tel: 0844 272 9504 **8 C10**
peartreepark.co.uk
Total Pitches: 154 (C, CV & T)

Penrose Holiday Park
Goonhavern, Truro
TR4 9QF
Tel: 01872 573185 2 K6
penroseholidaypark.com
Total Pitches: 110 (C, CV & T)

Polmanter Touring Park
Halsetown, St Ives
TR26 3LX
Tel: 01736 795640 2 E9
polmanter.com
Total Pitches: 270 (C, CV & T)

Porlock Caravan Park
Porlock, Minehead
TA24 8ND
Tel: 01643 862269 15 U3
porlockcaravanpark.co.uk
Total Pitches: 40 (C, CV & T)

Portesham Dairy Farm Campsite
Portesham, Weymouth
DT3 4HG
Tel: 01305 871297 7 R7
poreshamdairyfarm.co.uk
Total Pitches: 90 (C, CV & T)

Porth Beach Tourist Park
Porth, Newquay
TR7 3NH
Tel: 01637 876531 3 L4
porthbeach.co.uk
Total Pitches: 200 (C, CV & T)

Porthtowan Tourist Park
Mile Hill, Porthtowan, Truro
TR4 8TY
Tel: 01209 890256 2 H7
porthtowantouristpark.co.uk
Total Pitches: 80 (C, CV & T)

Quantock Orchard Caravan Park
Flaxpool, Crowcombe, Taunton
TA4 4AW
Tel: 01984 618618 16 F9
quantock-orchard.co.uk
Total Pitches: 69 (C, CV & T)

Ranch Caravan Park
Station Road, Honeybourne, Evesham
WR11 7PR
Tel: 01386 830744 36 F12
ranch.co.uk
Total Pitches: 120 (C & CV)

Ripley Caravan Park
Knaresborough Road, Ripley, Harrogate
HG3 3AU
Tel: 01423 770050 63 R7
ripleycaravanpark.com
Total Pitches: 100 (C, CV & T)

River Dart Country Park
Holne Park, Ashburton
TQ13 7NP
Tel: 01364 652511 5 S7
riverdart.co.uk
Total Pitches: 170 (C, CV & T)

Riverside C & C Park
Marsh Lane, North Molton Road,
South Molton
EX36 3HQ
Tel: 01769 579269 15 R7
exmoorriverside.co.uk
Total Pitches: 42 (C, CV & T)

Riverside Caravan Park
High Bentham, Lancaster
LA2 7FJ
Tel: 015242 61272 62 D6
riversidecaravanpark.co.uk
Total Pitches: 61 (C & CV)

Riverside Caravan Park
Leigham Manor Drive, Marsh Mills,
Plymouth
PL6 8LL
Tel: 01752 344122 5 N9
riversidecaravanpark.com
Total Pitches: 259 (C, CV & T)

Riverside Holidays
21 Compass Point, Ensign Way, Hamble
SO31 4RA
Tel: 023 8045 3220 9 P7
riversideholidays.co.uk
Total Pitches: 77 (C, CV & T)

Riverside Meadows Country Caravan Park
Ure Bank Top, Ripon
HG4 1JD
Tel: 01765 602964 63 S5
flowerofmay.com
Total Pitches: 80 (C, CV & T)

River Valley Holiday Park
London Apprentice, St Austell
PL26 7AP
Tel: 01726 73533 3 Q6
rivervalleyholidaypark.co.uk
Total Pitches: 45 (C, CV & T)

Rosedale C & C Park
Rosedale Abbey, Pickering
YO18 8SA
Tel: 01751 417272 71 M13
flowerofmay.com
Total Pitches: 100 (C, CV & T)

Rose Farm Touring & Camping Park
Stepshort, Belton, Nr Great Yarmouth
NR31 9JS
Tel: 01493 780896 51 S13
rosefarmtouringpark.co.uk
Total Pitches: 145 (C, CV & T)

Ross Park
Park Hill Farm, Ipplepen, Newton Abbot
TQ12 5TT
Tel: 01803 812983 5 U7
rossparkcaravanpark.co.uk
Total Pitches: 110 (C, CV & T)

Rudding Holiday Park
Follifoot, Harrogate
HG3 1JH
Tel: 01423 871350 63 S9
ruddingpark.co.uk/caravans-camping
Total Pitches: 109 (C, CV & T)

Rutland C & C
Park Lane, Greetham, Oakham
LE15 7FN
Tel: 01572 813520 48 D11
rutlandcaravanandcamping.co.uk
Total Pitches: 130 (C, CV & T)

Seaview International Holiday Park
Boswinger, Mevagissey
PL26 6LL
Tel: 01726 843425 3 P8
seaviewinternational.com
Total Pitches: 201 (C, CV & T)

Severn Gorge Park
Bridgnorth Road, Tweedale, Telford
TF7 4JB
Tel: 01952 684789 45 R12
severngorgepark.co.uk
Total Pitches: 10 (C & CV)

Shamba Holidays
230 Ringwood Road, St Leonards,
Ringwood
BH24 2SB
Tel: 01202 873302 8 G8
shambaholidays.co.uk
Total Pitches: 150 (C, CV & T)

Shrubbery Touring Park
Rousdon, Lyme Regis
DT7 3XW
Tel: 01297 442227 6 J6
shrubberypark.co.uk
Total Pitches: 120 (C, CV & T)

Silverbow Park
Perranwell, Goonhavern
TR4 9NX
Tel: 01872 572347 2 K6
chycor.co.uk/parks/silverbow
Total Pitches: 100 (C, CV & T)

Silverdale Caravan Park
Middlebarrow Plain, Cove Road,
Silverdale, Nr Carnforth
LA5 0SH
Tel: 01524 701508 61 T4
holgates.co.uk
Total Pitches: 80 (C, CV & T)

Skelwith Fold Caravan Park
Ambleside, Cumbria
LA22 0HX
Tel: 015394 32277 67 N12
skelwith.com
Total Pitches: 150 (C & CV)

Somers Wood Caravan Park
Somers Road, Meriden
CV7 7PL
Tel: 01676 522978 36 H4
somerswood.co.uk
Total Pitches: 48 (C & CV)

Southfork Caravan Park
Parrett Works, Martock
TA12 6AE
Tel: 01935 825661 17 M13
southforkcaravans.co.uk
Total Pitches: 27 (C, CV & T)

South Lytchett Manor C & C Park
Dorchester Road,
Lytchett Minster, Poole
BH16 6JB
Tel: 01202 622577 8 D10
southlytchettmanor.co.uk
Total Pitches: 150 (C, CV & T)

Springfield Holiday Park
Tedburn St Mary, Exeter
EX6 6EW
Tel: 01647 24242 5 U2
springfieldholidaypark.co.uk
Total Pitches: 48 (C, CV & T)

Stanmore Hall Touring Park
Stourbridge Road, Bridgnorth
WV15 6DT
Tel: 01746 761761 35 R2
morris-leisure.co.uk
Total Pitches: 131 (C, CV & T)

St Helens Caravan Park
Wykeham, Scarborough
YO13 9QD
Tel: 01723 862771 65 M3
sthelenscaravanpark.co.uk
Total Pitches: 250 (C, CV & T)

Stowford Farm Meadows
Berry Down, Combe Martin
EX34 0PW
Tel: 01271 882476 15 N4
stowford.co.uk
Total Pitches: 700 (C, CV & T)

Stroud Hill Park
Fen Road, Pidley
PE28 3DE
Tel: 01487 741333 39 M5
stroudhillpark.co.uk
Total Pitches: 60 (C, CV & T)

Sumners Ponds Fishery & Campsite
Chapel Road, Barns Green, Horsham
RH13 0PR
Tel: 01403 732539 10 J5
sumnersponds.co.uk
Total Pitches: 85 (C, CV & T)

Sun Haven Valley Holiday Park
Mawgan Porth, Newquay
TR8 4BQ
Tel: 01637 860373 3 M3
sunhavenvalley.com
Total Pitches: 109 (C, CV & T)

Sun Valley Holiday Park
Pentewan Road, St Austell
PL26 6DJ
Tel: 01726 843266 3 Q7
sunvalleyholidays.co.uk
Total Pitches: 29 (C, CV & T)

Swiss Farm Touring & Camping
Marlow Road, Henley-on-Thames
RG9 2HY
Tel: 01491 573419 20 C6
swissfarmcamping.co.uk
Total Pitches: 140 (C, CV & T)

Tanner Farm Touring Caravan & Camping Park
Tanner Farm, Goudhurst Road, Marden
TN12 9ND
Tel: 01622 832399 12 D7
tannerfarmpark.co.uk
Total Pitches: 100 (C, CV & T)

Tattershall Lakes Country Park
Sleaford Road, Tattershall
LN4 4RL
Tel: 01526 348800 48 K2
tattershall-lakes.com
Total Pitches: 186 (C, CV & T)

Teversal C & C Club Site
Silverhill Lane, Teversal
NG17 3JJ
Tel: 01623 551838 47 N1
campingandcaravanningclub.co.uk/teversal
Total Pitches: 126 (C, CV & T)

The Inside Park
Down House Estate, Blandford Forum
DT11 9AD
Tel: 01258 453719 8 B8
theinsidepark.co.uk
Total Pitches: 125 (C, CV & T)

The Old Brick Kilns
Little Barney Lane, Barney, Fakenham
NR21 0NL
Tel: 01328 878305 50 H7
old-brick-kilns.co.uk
Total Pitches: 65 (C, CV & T)

The Old Oaks Touring Park
Wick Farm, Wick, Glastonbury
BA6 8JS
Tel: 01458 831437 17 P9
theoldoaks.co.uk
Total Pitches: 100 (C, CV & T)

The Orchards Holiday Caravan Park
Main Road, Newbridge, Yarmouth,
Isle of Wight
PO41 0TS
Tel: 01983 531331 9 N11
orchards-holiday-park.co.uk
Total Pitches: 171 (C, CV & T)

The Quiet Site
Ullswater, Watermillock
CA11 0LS
Tel: 07768 727016 67 P8
thequietsite.co.uk
Total Pitches: 100 (C, CV & T)

Tollgate Farm C & C Park
Budnick Hill, Perranporth
TR6 0AD
Tel: 01872 572130 2 K6
tollgatefarm.co.uk
Total Pitches: 102 (C, CV & T)

Townsend Touring Park
Townsend Farm, Pembridge, Leominster
HR6 9HB
Tel: 01544 388527 34 J9
townsendfarm.co.uk
Total Pitches: 60 (C, CV & T)

Treloy Touring Park
Newquay
TR8 4JN
Tel: 01637 872063 3 M4
treloy.co.uk
Total Pitches: 223 (C, CV & T)

Trencreek Holiday Park
Hillcrest, Higher Trencreek, Newquay
TR8 4NS
Tel: 01637 874210 3 L4
trencreekholidaypark.co.uk
Total Pitches: 194 (C, CV & T)

Trethem Mill Touring Park
St Just-in-Roseland,
Nr St Mawes, Truro
TR2 5JF
Tel: 01872 580504 3 M9
trethem.com
Total Pitches: 84 (C, CV & T)

Trevalgan Touring Park
Trevalgan, St Ives
TR26 3BJ
Tel: 01736 792048 2 D8
trevalgantouringpark.co.uk
Total Pitches: 120 (C, CV & T)

Trevarth Holiday Park
Blackwater, Truro
TR4 8HR
Tel: 01872 560266 2 J7
trevarth.co.uk
Total Pitches: 30 (C, CV & T)

Trevella Tourist Park
Crantock, Newquay
TR8 5EW
Tel: 01637 830308 3 L5
trevella.co.uk
Total Pitches: 313 (C, CV & T)

Troutbeck C & C Club Site
Hutton Moor End, Troutbeck,
Penrith
CA11 0SX
Tel: 017687 79149 67 N7
campingandcaravanningclub.co.uk/troutbeck
Total Pitches: 54 (C, CV & T)

Truro C & C Park
Truro
TR4 8QN
Tel: 01872 560274 2 K7
trurocaravanandcampingpark.co.uk
Total Pitches: 51 (C, CV & T)

Tudor C & C
Shepherds Patch, Slimbridge,
Gloucester
GL2 7BP
Tel: 01453 890483 28 D7
tudorcaravanpark.com
Total Pitches: 75 (C, CV & T)

Two Mills Touring Park
Yarmouth Road, North Walsham
NR28 9NA
Tel: 01692 405829 51 N8
twomills.co.uk
Total Pitches: 81 (C, CV & T)

Ulwell Cottage Caravan Park
Ulwell Cottage, Ulwell, Swanage
BH19 3DG
Tel: 01929 422823 8 E12
ulwellcottagepark.co.uk
Total Pitches: 77 (C, CV & T)

Vale of Pickering Caravan Park
Carr House Farm, Allerston, Pickering
YO18 7PQ
Tel: 01723 859280 64 K3
valeofpickering.co.uk
Total Pitches: 120 (C, CV & T)

Warcombe Farm C & C Park
Station Road, Mortehoe
EX34 7EJ
Tel: 01271 870690 15 L3
warcombefarm.co.uk
Total Pitches: 250 (C, CV & T)

Wareham Forest Tourist Park
North Trigon, Wareham
BH20 7NZ
Tel: 01929 551393 8 B10
warehamforest.co.uk
Total Pitches: 200 (C, CV & T)

Waren Caravan Park
Waren Mill, Bamburgh
NE70 7EE
Tel: 01668 214366 85 S12
meadowhead.co.uk
Total Pitches: 150 (C, CV & T)

Watergate Bay Touring Park
Watergate Bay, Tregurrian
TR8 4AD
Tel: 01637 860387 3 L4
watergatebaytouringpark.co.uk
Total Pitches: 171 (C, CV & T)

Waterrow Touring Park
Wiveliscombe, Taunton
TA4 2AZ
Tel: 01984 623464 16 E11
waterrowpark.co.uk
Total Pitches: 45 (C, CV & T)

Wayfarers C & C Park
Relubbus Lane, St Hilary,
Penzance
TR20 9EF
Tel: 01736 763326 2 F10
wayfarerspark.co.uk
Total Pitches: 39 (C, CV & T)

Wells Holiday Park
Haybridge, Wells
BA5 1AJ
Tel: 01749 676869 17 P7
wellsholidaypark.co.uk
Total Pitches: 72 (C, CV & T)

Westwood Caravan Park
Old Felixstowe Road, Bucklesham,
Ipswich
IP10 0BN
Tel: 01473 659637 41 N12
westwoodcaravanpark.co.uk
Total Pitches: 100 (C, CV & T)

Whitefield Forest Touring Park
Brading Road, Ryde, Isle of Wight
PO33 1QL
Tel: 01983 617069 9 S11
whitefieldforest.co.uk
Total Pitches: 80 (C, CV & T)

Whitemead Caravan Park
East Burton Road, Wool
BH20 6HG
Tel: 01929 462241 8 A11
whitemeadcaravanpark.co.uk
Total Pitches: 95 (C, CV & T)

Whitsand Bay Lodge & Touring Park
Millbrook, Torpoint
PL10 1JZ
Tel: 01752 822597 5 L10
whitsandbayholidays.co.uk
Total Pitches: 49 (C, CV & T)

Widdicombe Farm Touring Park
Marldon, Paignton
TQ3 1ST
Tel: 01803 558325 5 V8
widdicombefarm.co.uk
Total Pitches: 180 (C, CV & T)

Widemouth Fields C & C Park
Park Farm, Poundstock, Bude
EX23 0NA
Tel: 01288 361351 14 F12
widemouthbaytouring.co.uk
Total Pitches: 156 (C, CV & T)

Widend Touring Park
Berry Pomeroy Road, Marldon, Paignton
TQ3 1RT
Tel: 01803 550116 5 V8
widend.co.uk
Total Pitches: 207 (C, CV & T)

Wild Rose Park
Ormside, Appleby-in-Westmorland
CA16 6EJ
Tel: 017683 51077 68 E9
wildrose.co.uk
Total Pitches: 226 (C, CV & T)

Wilksworth Farm Caravan Park
Cranborne Road, Wimborne Minster
BH21 4HW
Tel: 01202 885467 8 E8
wilksworthfarmcaravanpark.co.uk
Total Pitches: 85 (C, CV & T)

Wolds Way Caravan & Camping
West Farm, West Knapton, Malton
YO17 8JE
Tel: 01944 728463 64 K5
rydalesbest.co.uk
Total Pitches: 70 (C, CV & T)

Wooda Farm Holiday Park
Poughill, Bude
EX23 9HJ
Tel: 01288 352069 14 F11
wooda.co.uk
Total Pitches: 200 (C, CV & T)

Woodclose Caravan Park
High Casterton, Kirkby Lonsdale
LA6 2SE
Tel: 01524 271597 62 C4
woodclosepark.com
Total Pitches: 29 (C, CV & T)

Wood Farm C & C Park
Axminster Road, Charmouth
DT6 6BT
Tel: 01297 560697 7 L6
woodfarm.co.uk
Total Pitches: 216 (C, CV & T)

Woodhall Country Park
Stixwold Road, Woodhall Spa
LN10 6UJ
Tel: 01526 353710 59 L14
woodhallcountrypark.co.uk
Total Pitches: 80 (C, CV & T)

Woodlands Grove C & C Park
Blackawton, Dartmouth
TQ9 7DQ
Tel: 01803 712598 5 U10
woodlands-caravanpark.com
Total Pitches: 350 (C, CV & T)

Woodland Springs Adult Touring Park
Venton, Drewsteignton
EX6 6PG
Tel: 01647 231695 5 R2
woodlandsprings.co.uk
Total Pitches: 81 (C, CV & T)

Woodovis Park
Gulworthy, Tavistock
PL19 8NY
Tel: 01822 832968 5 L6
woodovis.com
Total Pitches: 50 (C, CV & T)

Woolsbridge Manor Farm Caravan Park
Three Legged Cross, Wimborne
BH21 6RA
Tel: 01202 826369 8 G8
woolsbridgemanorcaravanpark.co.uk
Total Pitches: 60 (C, CV & T)

Yeatheridge Farm Caravan Park
East Worlington, Crediton
EX17 4TN
Tel: 01884 860330 15 S10
yeatheridge.co.uk
Total Pitches: 85 (C, CV & T)

Zeacombe House Caravan Park
Blackerton Cross, East Anstey, Tiverton
EX16 9JU
Tel: 01398 341279 15 U8
zeacombeadultretreat.co.uk
Total Pitches: 50 (C, CV & T)

SCOTLAND

Aird Donald Caravan Park
London Road, Stranraer
DG9 8RN
Tel: 01776 702025 72 D7
aird-donald.co.uk
Total Pitches: 100 (C, CV & T)

Anwoth Caravan Site
Gatehouse of Fleet, Castle Douglas
DG7 2JU
Tel: 01557 814333 73 P8
auchenlarie.co.uk
Total Pitches: 28 (C, CV & T)

Beecraigs C & C Site
Beecraigs Country Park, The Park Centre,
Linlithgow
EH49 6PL
Tel: 01506 844516 82 K4
beecraigs.com
Total Pitches: 36 (C, CV & T)

Blair Castle Caravan Park
Blair Atholl, Pitlochry
PH18 5SR
Tel: 01796 481263 97 P10
blaircastlecaravanpark.co.uk
Total Pitches: 241 (C, CV & T)

Brighouse Bay Holiday Park
Brighouse Bay, Borgue
DG6 4TS
Tel: 01557 870267 73 Q10
gillespie-leisure.co.uk
Total Pitches: 190 (C, CV & T)

Cairnsmill Holiday Park
Largo Road, St Andrews
KY16 8NN
Tel: 01334 473604 91 Q9
cairnsmill.co.uk
Total Pitches: 62 (C, CV & T)

Castle Cary Holiday Park
Creetown, Newton Stewart
DG8 7DQ
Tel: 01671 820264 73 M8
castlecary-caravans.com
Total Pitches: 50 (C, CV & T)

Craigtoun Meadows Holiday Park
Mount Melville, St Andrews
KY16 8PQ
Tel: 01334 475959 91 Q8
craigtounmeadows.co.uk
Total Pitches: 57 (C, CV & T)

Crossburn Caravan Park
Edinburgh Road, Peebles
EH45 8ED
Tel: 01721 720501 83 P10
crossburncaravans.co.uk
Total Pitches: 45 (C, CV & T)

Drum Mohr Caravan Park
Levenhall, Musselburgh
EH21 8JS
Tel: 0131 665 6867 83 S4
drummohr.org
Total Pitches: 120 (C, CV & T)

East Bowstrips Caravan Park
St Cyrus, Nr Montrose
DD10 0DE
Tel: 01674 850328 99 N10
caravancampingsites.co.uk/aberdeenshire/eastbowstrips.htm
Total Pitches: 32 (C, CV & T)

Gart Caravan Park
The Gart, Callander
FK17 8LE
Tel: 01877 330002 89 P4
theholidaypark.co.uk
Total Pitches: 128 (C & CV)

Glenearly Caravan Park
Dalbeattie
DG5 4NE
Tel: 01556 611393 74 F13
glenearlycaravanpark.co.uk
Total Pitches: 39 (C, CV & T)

Glen Nevis C & C Park
Glen Nevis, Fort William
PH33 6SX
Tel: 01397 702191 94 G4
glen-nevis.co.uk
Total Pitches: 380 (C, CV & T)

Hoddom Castle Caravan Park
Hoddom, Lockerbie
DG11 1AS
Tel: 01576 300251 75 N11
hoddomcastle.co.uk
Total Pitches: 200 (C, CV & T)

Huntly Castle Caravan Park
The Meadow, Huntly
AB54 4UJ
Tel: 01466 794999 104 G7
huntlycastle.co.uk
Total Pitches: 90 (C, CV & T)

Invercoe C & C Park
Glencoe, Ballachulish
PH49 4HP
Tel: 01855 811210 94 F7
invercoe.co.uk
Total Pitches: 60 (C, CV & T)

Linnhe Lochside Holidays
Corpach, Fort William
PH33 7NL
Tel: 01397 772376 94 F3
linnhe-lochside-holidays.co.uk
Total Pitches: 85 (C, CV & T)

Lomond Woods Holiday Park
Old Luss Road, Balloch, Loch Lomond
G83 8QP
Tel: 01389 755000 88 J9
holiday-parks.co.uk
Total Pitches: 100 (C & CV)

Machrihanish Caravan Park
East Trodigal, Machrihanish,
Mull of Kintyre
PA28 6PT
Tel: 01586 810366 79 L11
campkintyre.co.uk
Total Pitches: 90 (C, CV & T)

Milton of Fonab Caravan Site
Bridge Road, Pitlochry
PH16 5NA
Tel: 01796 472882 97 Q12
fonab.co.uk
Total Pitches: 154 (C, CV & T)

River Tilt Caravan Park
Blair Atholl, Pitlochry
PH18 5TE
Tel: 01796 481467 97 P10
rivertilt.co.uk
Total Pitches: 30 (C, CV & T)

Riverview Caravan Park
Marine Drive, Monifieth
DD5 4NN
Tel: 01382 535471 91 R5
riverview.co.uk
Total Pitches: 49 (C & CV)

Sands of Luce Holiday Park
Sands of Luce, Sandhead, Stranraer
DG9 9JN
Tel: 01776 830456 72 E9
sandsofluceholidaypark.co.uk
Total Pitches: 120 (C, CV & T)

Seaward Caravan Park
Dhoon Bay, Kirkudbright
DG6 4TJ
Tel: 01557 870267 73 R10
gillespie-leisure.co.uk
Total Pitches: 26 (C, CV & T)

Shieling Holidays
Craignure, Isle of Mull
PA65 6AY
Tel: 01680 812496 93 S11
shielingholidays.co.uk
Total Pitches: 90 (C, CV & T)

Silver Sands Leisure Park
Covesea, West Beach, Lossiemouth
IV31 6SP
Tel: 01343 813262 103 V1
silver-sands.co.uk
Total Pitches: 140 (C, CV & T)

Skye C & C Club Site
Loch Greshornish, Borve, Arnisort,
Edinbane, Isle of Skye
IV51 9PS
Tel: 01470 582230 100 c4
campingandcaravanningclub.co.uk/skye
Total Pitches: 105 (C, CV & T)

Springwood Caravan Park
Kelso
TD5 8LS
Tel: 01573 224596 84 J12
springwood.biz
Total Pitches: 20 (C & CV)

Thurston Manor Leisure Park
Innerwick, Dunbar
EH42 1SA
Tel: 01368 840643 84 J4
thurstonmanor.co.uk
Total Pitches: 120 (C, CV & T)

Trossachs Holiday Park
Aberfoyle
FK8 3SA
Tel: 01877 382614 89 M6
trossachsholidays.co.uk
Total Pitches: 66 (C, CV & T)

Witches Craig C & C Park
Blairlogie, Stirling
FK9 5PX
Tel: 01786 474947 89 T6
witchescraig.co.uk
Total Pitches: 60 (C, CV & T)

WALES

Anchorage Caravan Park
Bronllys, Brecon
LD3 0LD
Tel: 01874 711246 34 D13
anchoragecp.co.uk
Total Pitches: 110 (C, CV & T)

Barcdy Touring C & C Park
Talsarnau
LL47 6YG
Tel: 01766 770736 43 M6
barcdy.co.uk
Total Pitches: 80 (C, CV & T)

Beach View Caravan Park
Bwlchtocyn, Abersoch
LL53 7BT
Tel: 01758 712956 42 F8
Total Pitches: 47 (C, CV & T)

Bodnant Caravan Park
Nebo Road, Llanrwst, Conwy Valley
LL26 0SD
Tel: 01492 640248 53 P10
bodnant-caravan-park.co.uk
Total Pitches: 54 (C, CV & T)

Bron Derw Touring Caravan Park
Llanrwst
LL26 0YT
Tel: 01492 640494 53 N10
bronderw-wales.co.uk
Total Pitches: 43 (C & CV)

Bron-Y-Wendon Caravan Park
Wern Road, Llanddulas, Colwyn Bay
LL22 8HG
Tel: 01492 512903 53 R7
northwales-holidays.co.uk
Total Pitches: 130 (C & CV)

Bryn Gloch C & C Park
Betws Garmon, Caernarfon
LL54 7YY
Tel: 01286 650216 52 H11
campwales.co.uk
Total Pitches: 160 (C, CV & T)

Caerfai Bay Caravan & Tent Park
Caerfai Bay, St David's, Haverfordwest
SA62 6QT
Tel: 01437 720274 24 C6
caerfaibay.co.uk
Total Pitches: 106 (C, CV & T)

Cenarth Falls Holiday Park
Cenarth, Newcastle Emlyn
SA38 9JS
Tel: 01239 710345 32 E12
cenarth-holipark.co.uk
Total Pitches: 30 (C, CV & T)

Deucoch Touring & Camping Park
Sarn Bach, Abersoch
LL53 7LD
Tel: 01758 713293 42 F8
deucoch.com
Total Pitches: 70 (C, CV & T)

Dinlle Caravan Park
Dinas Dinlle, Caernarfon
LL54 5TW
Tel: 01286 830324 52 F11
thornleyleisure.co.uk
Total Pitches: 175 (C, CV & T)

Eisteddfa
Eisteddfa Lodge, Pentrefelin, Criccieth
LL52 0PT
Tel: 01766 522696 42 K6
eisteddfapark.co.uk
Total Pitches: 100 (C, CV & T)

Erwlon C & C Park
Brecon Road, Llandovery
SA20 0RD
Tel: 01550 721021 33 Q14
erwlon.co.uk
Total Pitches: 75 (C, CV & T)

Hendre Mynach Touring C & C Park
Llanaber Road, Barmouth
LL42 1YR
Tel: 01341 280262 43 M10
hendremynach.co.uk
Total Pitches: 240 (C, CV & T)

Home Farm Caravan Park
Marian-Glas, Isle of Anglesey
LL73 8PH
Tel: 01248 410614 52 G6
homefarm-anglesey.co.uk
Total Pitches: 98 (C, CV & T)

Hunters Hamlet Caravan Park
Sirior Goch Farm, Betws-yn-Rhos,
Abergele
LL22 8PL
Tel: 01745 832237 53 R8
huntershamlet.co.uk
Total Pitches: 23 (C & CV)

Islawrffordd Caravan Park
Tal-y-bont, Barmouth
LL43 2AQ
Tel: 01341 247269 43 L9
islawrffordd.co.uk
Total Pitches: 105 (C, CV & T)

Llys Derwen C & C Site
Ffordd Bryngwyn, Llanrug, Caernarfon
LL55 4RD
Tel: 01286 673322 52 H10
llysderwen.co.uk
Total Pitches: 20 (C, CV & T)

Pencelli Castle C & C Park
Pencelli, Brecon
LD3 7LX
Tel: 01874 665451 26 K3
pencelli-castle.com
Total Pitches: 80 (C, CV & T)

Penisar Mynydd Caravan Park
Caerwys Road, Rhuallt, St Asaph
LL17 0TY
Tel: 01745 582227 54 C11
penisarmynydd.co.uk
Total Pitches: 75 (C, CV & T)

Pen-y-Bont Touring Park
Llangynog Road, Bala
LL23 7PH
Tel: 01678 520549 43 T7
penybont-bala.co.uk
Total Pitches: 95 (C, CV & T)

Plas Farm Caravan Park
Betws-yn-Rhos, Abergele
LL22 8AU
Tel: 01492 680254 53 Q8
plasfarmcaravanpark.co.uk
Total Pitches: 40 (C, CV & T)

Pont Kemys C & C Park
Chainbridge, Abergavenny
NP7 9DS
Tel: 01873 880688 27 Q6
pontkemys.com
Total Pitches: 65 (C, CV & T)

Riverside Camping
Seiont Nurseries, Pont Rug, Caernarfon
LL55 2BB
Tel: 01286 678781 52 H10
riversidecamping.co.uk
Total Pitches: 60 (C, CV & T)

River View Touring Park
The Dingle, Llanedi, Pontarddulais
SA4 0FH
Tel: 01269 844876 25 U9
riverviewtouringpark.com
Total Pitches: 60 (C, CV & T)

The Plassey Leisure Park
The Plassey, Eyton, Wrexham
LL13 0SP
Tel: 01978 780277 44 J4
plassey.com
Total Pitches: 90 (C, CV & T)

Trawsdir Touring C & C Park
Llanaber, Barmouth
LL42 1RR
Tel: 01341 280999 43 L10
barmouthholidays.co.uk
Total Pitches: 70 (C, CV & T)

Trefalun Park
Devonshire Drive, St Florence, Tenby
SA70 8RD
Tel: 01646 651514 24 J10
trefalunpark.co.uk
Total Pitches: 90 (C, CV & T)

Tyddyn Isaf Caravan Park
Lligwy Bay, Dulas, Isle of Anglesey
LL70 9PQ
Tel: 01248 410203 52 G5
tyddynisaf.co.uk
Total Pitches: 30 (C, CV & T)

Tyn Cornel C & C Park
Frongoch, Bala
LL23 7NU
Tel: 01678 520759 43 S5
tyncornel.co.uk
Total Pitches: 67 (C, CV & T)

Well Park C & C Site
Tenby
SA70 8TL
Tel: 01834 842179 24 K10
wellparkcaravans.co.uk
Total Pitches: 100 (C, CV & T)

Ynysymaengwyn Caravan Park
Tywyn
LL36 9RY
Tel: 01654 710684 43 M13
ynysy.co.uk
Total Pitches: 80 (C, CV & T)

CHANNEL ISLANDS

Beuvelande Camp Site
Beuvelande, St Martin, Jersey
JE3 6EZ
Tel: 01534 853575 7 e2
campingjersey.com
Total Pitches: 150 (T)

Fauxquets Valley Campsite
Castel, Guernsey
GY5 7QL
Tel: 01481 236951 6 d3
fauxquets.co.uk
Total Pitches: 120 (T)

Rozel Camping Park
Summerville Farm, St Martin, Jersey
JE3 6AX
Tel: 01534 855200 7 f2
rozelcamping.co.uk
Total Pitches: 100 (C, CV & T)

Traffic signs and road markings

Traffic signs

Signs giving orders

Signs with red circles are mostly prohibitive.
Plates below signs qualify their message.

Entry to 20mph zone	End of 20mph zone	Maximum speed	National speed limit applies	School crossing patrol
Stop and give way	Give way to traffic on major road	Manually operated temporary STOP and GO signs	GO	No entry for vehicular traffic

Signs with blue circles but no red border mostly give positive instruction.

Warning signs

Mostly triangular

STOP 100 yds — Distance to 'STOP' line ahead	Dual carriageway ends	Road narrows on right (left if symbol reversed)	Road narrows on both sides	GIVE WAY 50 yds — Distance to 'Give Way' line ahead
Crossroads	Junction on bend ahead	T-junction with priority over vehicles from the right	Staggered junction	Traffic merging from left ahead

The priority through route is indicated by the broader line.

Double bend first to left (symbol may be reversed) · Bend to right (or left if symbol reversed) · Roundabout · Uneven road · Plate below some signs (REDUCE SPEED NOW)

Two-way traffic crosses one-way road · Two-way traffic straight ahead · Opening or swing bridge ahead · Low-flying aircraft or sudden aircraft noise · Falling or fallen rocks

Traffic signals not in use · Traffic signals · Slippery road · Steep hill downwards · Steep hill upwards

Gradients may be shown as a ratio i.e. 20% = 1:5

Tunnel ahead · Trams crossing ahead · Level crossing with barrier or gate ahead · Level crossing without barrier or gate ahead · Level crossing without barrier

School crossing patrol ahead (some signs have amber lights which flash when crossings are in use) · Frail (or blind or disabled if shown) pedestrians likely to cross road ahead · Pedestrians in road ahead · Zebra crossing · Overhead electric cable; plate indicates maximum height of vehicles which can pass safely (Safe height 16'·6")

Available width of headroom indicated

Sharp deviation of route to left (or right if chevrons reversed) · Light signals ahead at level crossing, airfield or bridge · Miniature warning lights at level crossings

Cattle · Wild animals · Wild horses or ponies · Accompanied horses or ponies · Cycle route ahead

Risk of ice · Traffic queues likely ahead · Distance over which road humps extend · Other danger; plate indicates nature of danger · Soft verges

Side winds · Hump bridge · Worded warning sign · Quayside or river bank · Risk of grounding

Direction signs

Mostly rectangular

Signs on motorways – blue backgrounds

At a junction leading directly into a motorway (junction number may be shown on a black background) · On approaches to junctions (junction number on black background) · Route confirmatory sign after junction

Downward pointing arrows mean 'Get in lane'
The left-hand lane leads to a different destination from the other lanes.

The panel with the inclined arrow indicates the destinations which can be reached by leaving the motorway at the next junction

Signs on primary routes - green backgrounds

On approaches to junctions · At the junction · On approaches to junctions · Route confirmatory sign after junction · On approach to a junction in Wales (bilingual)

Blue panels indicate that the motorway starts at the junction ahead.
Motorways shown in brackets can also be reached along the route indicated.
White panels indicate local or non-primary routes leading from the junction ahead.
Brown panels show the route to tourist attractions.
The name of the junction may be shown at the top of the sign.
The aircraft symbol indicates the route to an airport.
A symbol may be included to warn of a hazard or restriction along that route.

Primary route forming part of a ring road · R

Signs on non-primary and local routes - black borders

On approaches to junctions · At the junction · Direction to toilets with access for the disabled

Green panels indicate that the primary route starts at the junction ahead.
Route numbers on a blue background show the direction to a motorway.
Route numbers on a green background show the direction to a primary route.

Other direction signs

 Picnic site ·  Wrest Park — Ancient monument in the care of English Heritage · 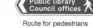 Saturday only — Direction to a car park

 Zoo — Tourist attraction · Direction to camping and caravan site · Advisory route for lorries

Route for pedal cycles forming part of a network · Marton 3 — Recommended route for pedal cycles to place shown ·  Public library Council offices — Route for pedestrians

Emergency diversion routes

 Northtown — Diversion route

Symbols showing emergency diversion route for motorway and other main road traffic

In an emergency it may be necessary to close a section of motorway or other main road to traffic, so a temporary sign may advise drivers to follow a diversion route. To help drivers navigate the route, black symbols on yellow patches may be permanently displayed on existing direction signs, including motorway signs. Symbols may also be used on separate signs with yellow backgrounds.

For further information see www.highways.gov.uk

Note: Although this road atlas shows many of the signs commonly in use, a comprehensive explanation of the signing system is given in the AA's handbook *Know Your Road Signs*, which is on sale at theaa.com/shop and booksellers. The booklet also illustrates and explains the vast majority of signs the road user is likely to encounter. The signs illustrated in this road atlas are not all drawn to the same scale. In Wales, bilingual versions of some signs are used including Welsh and English versions of place names. Some older designs of signs may still be seen on the roads.

Road markings

Information signs

All rectangular

Controlled ZONE Mon-Fri 8.30am-6.30pm Saturday 8.30am-1.30pm
Entrance to controlled parking zone

Entrance to congestion charging zone

Greater London Low Emission Zone (LEZ)

Advance warning of restriction or prohibition ahead

Parking place for solo motorcycles

With-flow bus lane ahead which pedal cycles and taxis may also use

Lane designated for use by high occupancy vehicles (HOV) – see rule 142

Vehicles permitted to use an HOV lane ahead

End of motorway

Start of motorway and point from which motorway regulations apply

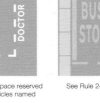

Appropriate traffic lanes at junction ahead

Traffic on the main carriageway coming from right has priority over joining traffic

Additional traffic joining from left ahead. Traffic on main carriageway has priority over joining traffic from right hand lane of slip road

Traffic in right hand lane of slip road joining the main carriageway has priority over left hand lane

'Countdown' markers at exit from motorway (each bar represents 100 yards to the exit). Green-backed markers may be used on primary routes and white-backed markers with black bars on other routes. At approaches to concealed level crossings white-backed markers with red bars may be used. Although these will be erected at equal distances the bars do not represent 100 yard intervals.

Traffic has priority over oncoming vehicles

Hospital ahead with Accident and Emergency facilities

Tourist information point

No through road for vehicles

Recommended route for pedal cycles

Home Zone Entry

Area in which cameras are used to enforce traffic regulations

Bus lane on road at junction ahead

Home Zone Entry – You are entering an area where people could be using the whole street for a range of activities. You should drive slowly and carefully and be prepared to stop to allow people time to move out of the way.

Roadworks signs

Road works

Loose chippings

SLOW WET TAR Temporary hazard at roadworks

800 yards Temporary lane closure (the number and position of arrows and red bars may be varied according to lanes open and closed)

Slow-moving or stationary works vehicle blocking a traffic lane. Pass in the direction shown by the arrow.

50 ¾ mile ahead — Mandatory speed limit ahead

Delays possible until Sept — Roadworks 1 mile ahead

Sorry for any delay End — End of roadworks and any temporary restrictions including speed limits

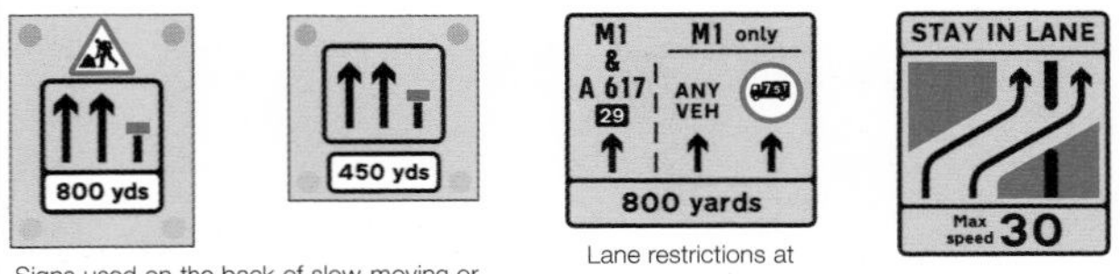

800 yds Signs used on the back of slow-moving or stationary vehicles warning of a lane closed ahead by a works vehicle. There are no cones on the road.

450 yds

M1 & A617 29 / M1 only ANY VEH / 800 yards Lane restrictions at roadworks ahead

STAY IN LANE Max speed 30 One lane crossover at contraflow roadworks

Across the carriageway

Stop line at signals or police control

Stop line at 'Stop' sign

Stop line for pedestrians at a level crossing

Give way to traffic on major road (can also be used at mini roundabouts)

Give way to traffic from the right at a roundabout

Give way to traffic from the right at a mini-roundabout

Along the carriageway

Edge line

Centre line See Rule 127

Hazard warning line See Rule 127

Double white lines See Rules 128 and 129

See Rule 130

Lane line See Rule 131

Along the edge of the carriageway

Waiting restrictions

Waiting restrictions indicated by yellow lines apply to the carriageway, pavement and verge. You may stop to load or unload (unless there are also loading restrictions as described below) or while passengers board or alight. Double yellow lines mean no waiting at any time, unless there are signs that specifically indicate seasonal restrictions. The times at which the restrictions apply for other road markings are shown on nearby plates or on entry signs to controlled parking zones. If no days are shown on the signs, the restrictions are in force every day including Sundays and Bank Holidays. White bay markings and upright signs (see below) indicate where parking is allowed.

No waiting at any time

8 am - 6 pm → No waiting during times shown on sign

P Mon-Sat 8 am-7pm 20 mins No return within 40 mins Waiting is limited to the duration specified during the days and times shown

Red Route stopping controls

Red lines are used on some roads instead of yellow lines. In London the double and single red lines used on Red Routes indicate that stopping to park, load/unload or to board and alight from a vehicle (except for a licensed taxi or if you hold a Blue Badge) is prohibited. The red lines apply to the carriageway, pavement and verge. The times at which the red line prohibitions apply are shown on nearby signs, but the double red line ALWAYS means no stopping at any time. On Red Routes you may stop to park, load/unload in specially marked boxes and adjacent signs specify the times and purposes and duration allowed. A box MARKED IN RED indicates that it may only be available for the purpose specified for part of the day (e.g. between busy peak periods). A box MARKED IN WHITE means that it is available throughout the day.

RED AND SINGLE YELLOW LINES CAN ONLY GIVE A GUIDE TO THE RESTRICTIONS AND CONTROLS IN FORCE AND SIGNS, NEARBY OR AT A ZONE ENTRY, MUST BE CONSULTED.

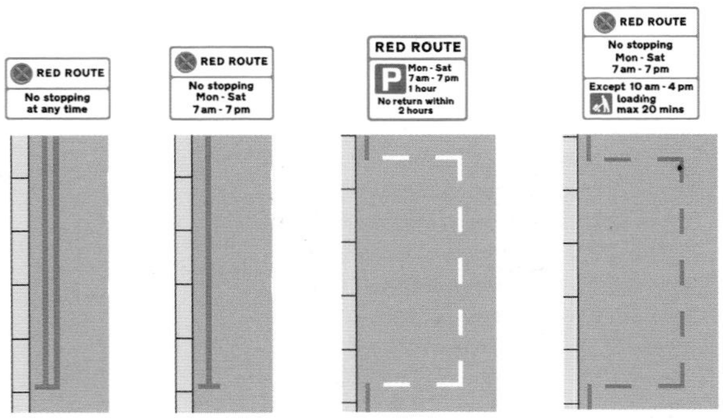

RED ROUTE No stopping at any time — No stopping at any time

RED ROUTE No stopping Mon-Sat 7am-7pm — No stopping during times shown on sign

RED ROUTE P 1 hour No return within 2 hours — Parking is limited to the duration specified during the days and times shown

RED ROUTE No stopping Mon-Sat 7am-7pm Except 10 am-4 pm loading max 20 mins — Only loading may take place at the times shown for up to a maximum duration of 20 mins

On the kerb or at the edge of the carriageway

Loading restrictions on roads other than Red Routes

Yellow marks on the kerb or at the edge of the carriageway indicate that loading or unloading is prohibited at the times shown on the nearby black and white plates. You may stop while passengers board or alight. If no days are indicated on the signs the restrictions are in force every day including Sundays and Bank Holidays.

ALWAYS CHECK THE TIMES SHOWN ON THE PLATES.

Lengths of road reserved for vehicles loading and unloading are indicated by a white 'bay' marking with the words 'Loading Only' and a sign with the white on blue 'trolley' symbol. This sign also shows whether loading and unloading is restricted to goods vehicles and the times at which the bay can be used. If no times or days are shown it may be used at any time. Vehicles may not park here if they are not loading or unloading.

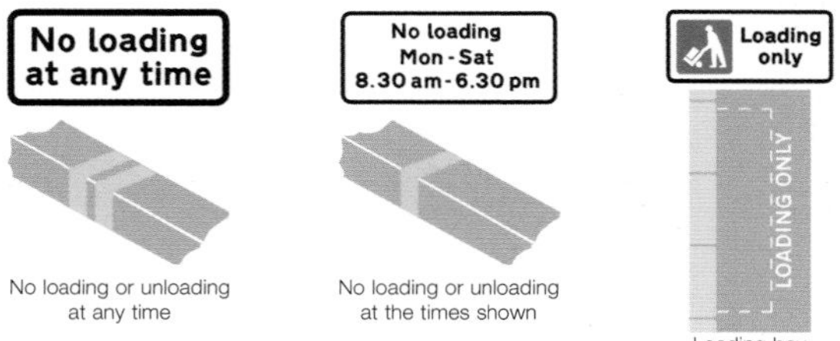

No loading at any time — No loading or unloading at any time

No loading Mon-Sat 8.30 am-6.30 pm — No loading or unloading at the times shown

Loading only — Loading bay

Other road markings

SCHOOL — KEEP — CLEAR
Keep entrance clear of stationary vehicles, even if picking up or setting down children

Warning of 'Give Way' just ahead

DOCTOR — Parking space reserved for vehicles named

BUS STOP — See Rule 243

BUS LANE — See Rule 141

Box junction - See Rule 174

KEEP CLEAR — Do not block that part of the carriageway indicated

CITY A3 YORK ST — Indication of traffic lanes

Light signals controlling traffic

Traffic Light Signals

RED means 'Stop'. Wait behind the stop line on the carriageway

RED AND AMBER also means 'Stop'. Do not pass through or start until GREEN shows

GREEN means you may go on if the way is clear. Take special care if you intend to turn left or right and give way to pedestrians who are crossing

AMBER means 'Stop' at the stop line. You may go on only if the AMBER appears after you have crossed the stop line or are so close to it that to pull up might cause an accident

A GREEN ARROW may be provided in addition to the full green signal if movement in a certain direction is allowed before or after the full green phase. If the way is clear you may go but only in the direction shown by the arrow. You may do this whatever other lights may be showing. White light signals may be provided for trams

Flashing red lights

Alternately flashing red lights mean YOU MUST STOP

At level crossings, lifting bridges, airfields, fire stations, etc.

Motorway signals

You MUST NOT proceed further in this lane

Change lane

Reduced visibility ahead

Lane ahead closed

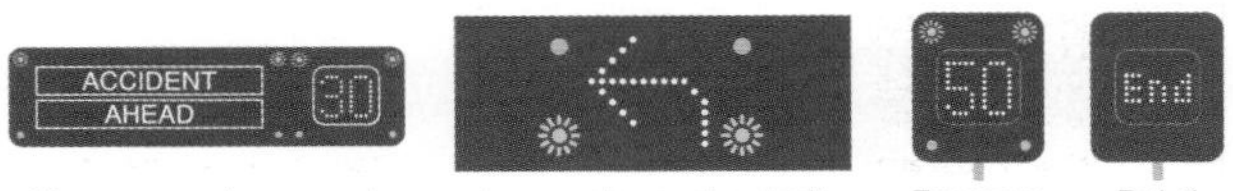

ACCIDENT AHEAD 30 Temporary maximum speed advised and information message

Leave motorway at next exit

Temporary maximum speed advised

End of restriction

Lane control signals

Green arrow - lane available to traffic facing the sign
Red crosses - lane closed to traffic facing the sign
White diagonal arrow - change lanes in direction shown

Channel hopping

For business or pleasure, hopping on a ferry across to France, Belgium or the Channel Islands has never been easier.

The vehicle ferry routes shown on this map give you all the options, together with detailed port plans to help you navigate to and from the ferry terminals. Simply choose your preferred route, not forgetting the fast sailings; then check the colour-coded table for ferry operators, crossing times and contact details.

Bon voyage!

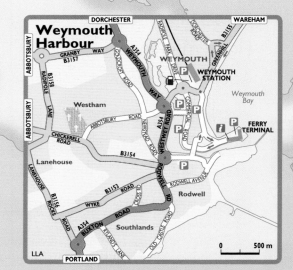

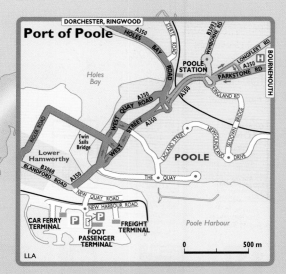

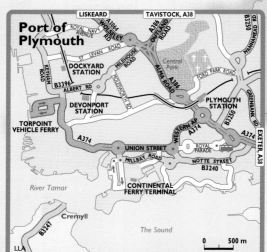

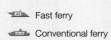 Fast ferry

Conventional ferry

ENGLISH

Plymouth

Weymouth

Poole

Isle of Wight

Alderney

St Peter Port
Herm
Guernsey
Sark

Channel Islands

Jersey

St Helier

Cherbourg

Roscoff

St-Malo

ENGLISH CHANNEL FERRY CROSSINGS AND OPERATORS					
To	**From**	**Journey Time**	**Operator**	**Telephone**	**Website**
Caen (Ouistreham)	Portsmouth	6 - 7 hrs	Brittany Ferries	0871 244 0744	brittany-ferries.co.uk
Caen (Ouistreham)	Portsmouth	3 hrs 45 mins (Mar-Oct)	Brittany Ferries	0871 244 0744	brittany-ferries.co.uk
Calais	Dover	1 hr 30 mins	P&O Ferries	0871 664 2020	poferries.com
Calais (Coquelles)	Folkestone	35 mins	Eurotunnel	08443 35 35 35	eurotunnel.com
Cherbourg	Poole	2 hrs 30 mins (April-Oct)	Brittany Ferries	0871 244 0744	brittany-ferries.co.uk
Cherbourg	Portsmouth	3 hrs (Mar-Oct)	Brittany Ferries	0871 244 0744	brittany-ferries.co.uk
Cherbourg	Portsmouth	4 hrs 30 mins(day) 8 hrs(o/night)	Brittany Ferries	0871 244 0744	brittany-ferries.co.uk
Cherbourg	Portsmouth	5 hrs 30 mins (May-Sept)	Condor	0845 609 1024	condorferries.co.uk
Dieppe	Newhaven	4 hrs	Transmanche Ferries	0844 576 8836	transmancheferries.co.uk
Dunkerque	Dover	2 hrs	DFDS Seaways	0871 522 9955	dfdsseaways.co.uk
Guernsey	Poole	2 hrs 30 mins (April-Oct)	Condor	0845 609 1024	condorferries.co.uk
Guernsey	Portsmouth	7 hrs	Condor	0845 609 1024	condorferries.co.uk
Guernsey	Weymouth	2 hrs 10 mins	Condor	0845 609 1024	condorferries.co.uk
Jersey	Poole	3 hrs (April-Oct)	Condor	0845 609 1024	condorferries.co.uk
Jersey	Portsmouth	10 hrs 30 mins	Condor	0845 609 1024	condorferries.co.uk
Jersey	Weymouth	3 hrs 25 mins	Condor	0845 609 1024	condorferries.co.uk
Le Havre	Portsmouth	5 hrs 30 mins - 8 hrs	LD Lines	0844 576 8836	ldlines.co.uk
Le Havre	Portsmouth	3 hrs 15 mins (Mar-Sept)	LD Lines	0844 576 8836	ldlines.co.uk
Oostende	Ramsgate	4 hrs - 4hrs 30 mins	Transeuropa	01843 595 522	transeuropaferries.com
Roscoff	Plymouth	6 - 8 hrs	Brittany Ferries	0871 244 0744	brittany-ferries.co.uk
St-Malo	Poole	4 hrs 35 mins (May-Sept)	Condor	0845 609 1024	condorferries.co.uk
St-Malo	Portsmouth	9 - 10 hrs 45 mins	Brittany Ferries	0871 244 0744	brittany-ferries.co.uk
St-Malo	Weymouth	5 hrs 15 mins	Condor	0845 609 1024	condorferries.co.uk

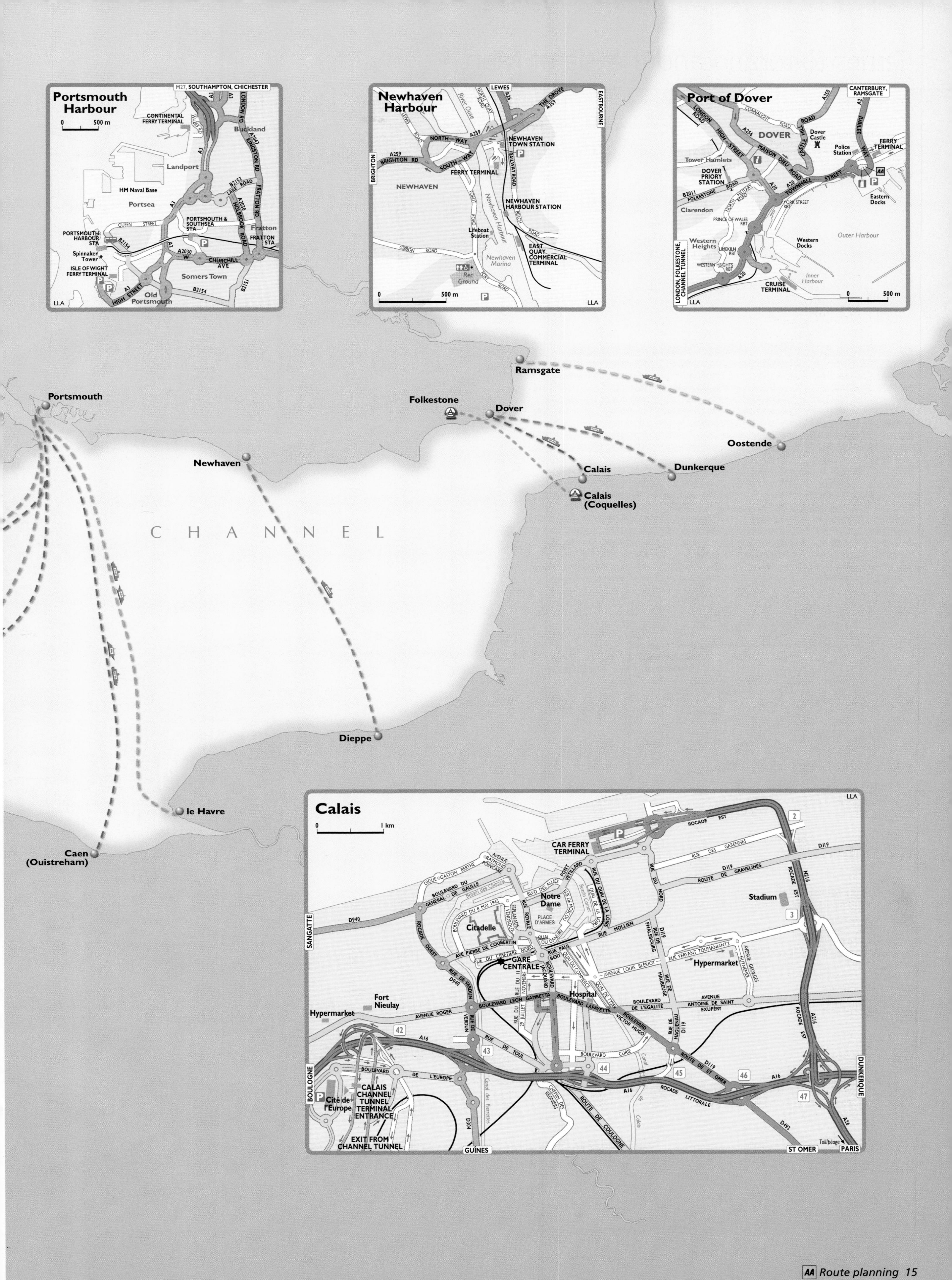

Portsmouth Harbour

SOUTHAMPTON, CHICHESTER · M27

CONTINENTAL FERRY TERMINAL

Buckland

Landport

HM Naval Base

Portsea

PORTSMOUTH HARBOUR STA

PORTSMOUTH & SOUTHSEA STA

FRATTON STA

Spinnaker Tower

ISLE OF WIGHT FERRY TERMINAL

Somers Town

Old Portsmouth

QUEEN STREET

HIGH STREET

CHURCHILL AVE

A2030

B2154

B2151

LLA

0   500 m

Newhaven Harbour

LEWES

THE DROVE · A259

EASTBOURNE

NORTH—WAY

SOUTH—WAY

NEWHAVEN TOWN STATION

FERRY TERMINAL

RAILWAY ROAD

NEWHAVEN HARBOUR STATION

BRIGHTON

A259 · BRIGHTON RD

NEWHAVEN

Lifeboat Station

Newhaven Marina

EAST QUAY COMMERCIAL TERMINAL

GIBBON ROAD

Rec Ground

0   500 m

LLA

Port of Dover

CANTERBURY, RAMSGATE

CONNAUGHT ROAD

JUBILEE WAY

DOVER

Dover Castle

Police Station

FERRY TERMINAL

Tower Hamlets

Dover Priory Station

HIGH STREET

MAISON DIEU ROAD

CASTLE HILL ROAD

A20

TOWNWALL STREET

AA

Eastern Docks

Clarendon

FOLKESTONE

B2011

PRINCE OF WALES RBT

YORK STREET RBT

Western Heights

Western Docks

Outer Harbour

WESTERN HEIGHTS RBT

LIMEKILN RBT

LONDON, FOLKESTONE, CHANNEL TUNNEL

CRUISE TERMINAL

Inner Harbour

0   500 m

LLA

Ramsgate

Folkestone

Dover

Oostende

Portsmouth

Calais

Dunkerque

Newhaven

Calais (Coquelles)

C H A N N E L

Dieppe

le Havre

Caen (Ouistreham)

Calais

0   1 km

ROCADE EST

CAR FERRY TERMINAL

Notre Dame

Stadium

BOULEVARD DU GÉNÉRAL DE GAULLE

Citadelle

GARE CENTRALE

Hypermarket

Hospital

SANGATTE

D940

Fort Nieulay

Hypermarket

AVENUE ROGER

BOULEVARD LÉON GAMBETTA

BOULEVARD DE L'EGALITE

A16

CALAIS CHANNEL TUNNEL TERMINAL ENTRANCE

EXIT FROM CHANNEL TUNNEL

Cité de l'Europe

BOULEVARD DE L'EUROPE

GUINES

ROUTE DE COULOGNE

ST OMER

DUNKERQUE

Toll/péage · PARIS

ROCADE LITTORALE

A16

N116

LLA

Ferries to Ireland and the Isle of Man

With so many sea crossings to Ireland and the Isle of Man this map will help you make the right choice.

The vehicle ferry routes shown on this map give you all the options, together with detailed port plans to help you navigate to and from the ferry terminals. Simply choose your preferred route, not forgetting the fast sailings; then check the colour-coded table for ferry operators, crossing times and contact details.

🚢 Fast ferry 🚢 Conventional ferry

IRISH SEA FERRY CROSSINGS AND OPERATORS

To	From	Journey Time	Operator	Telephone	Website
Belfast	Birkenhead	8 hrs	Stena Line	08447 70 70 70	stenaline.co.uk
Belfast	Douglas	2 hrs 55 mins (April–Sept)	Steam Packet Co	08722 992 992	steam-packet.com
Belfast	Cairnryan	2 hrs 15mins	Stena Line	08447 70 70 70	stenaline.co.uk
Douglas	Birkenhead	4 hrs 15 mins (Nov–Mar)	Steam Packet Co	08722 992 992	steam-packet.com
Douglas	Heysham	3 hrs 30 mins	Steam Packet Co	08722 992 992	steam-packet.com
Douglas	Liverpool	2 hrs 40 mins (Mar–Oct)	Steam Packet Co	08722 992 992	steam-packet.com
Dublin	Douglas	2 hrs 55 mins (April–Sept)	Steam Packet Co	08722 992 992	steam-packet.com
Dublin	Holyhead	1 hr 50 mins	Irish Ferries	08717 300 400	irishferries.com
Dublin	Holyhead	3 hrs 15 mins	Irish Ferries	08717 300 400	irishferries.com
Dublin	Holyhead	3 hrs 15 mins	Stena Line	08447 70 70 70	stenaline.co.uk
Dublin	Liverpool	8 hrs	P&O Ferries	08716 642 020	poferries.com
Dún Laoghaire	Holyhead	2 hrs (April–Sept)	Stena Line	08447 70 70 70	stenaline.co.uk
Larne	Cairnryan	2 hrs	P&O Ferries	08716 642 020	poferries.com
Larne	Cairnryan	1 hr (Mar–Oct)	P&O Ferries	08716 642 020	poferries.com
Larne	Troon	2 hrs (Mar–Oct)	P&O Ferries	08716 642 020	poferries.com
Rosslare	Fishguard	2 hrs (July–Sept)	Stena Line	08447 70 70 70	stenaline.co.uk
Rosslare	Fishguard	3 hrs 30 mins	Stena Line	08447 70 70 70	stenaline.co.uk
Rosslare	Pembroke Dock	3 hrs 45 mins	Irish Ferries	08717 300 400	irishferries.com

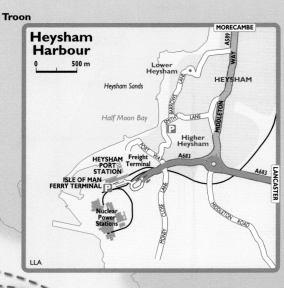

Heysham Harbour

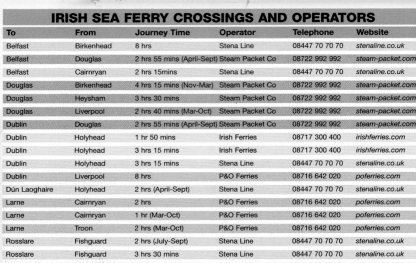

Holyhead Harbour

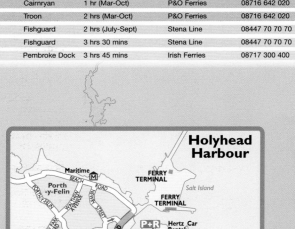

Liverpool Docks

Fishguard Harbour

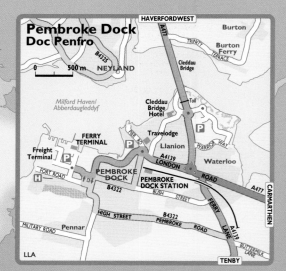

Pembroke Dock Doc Penfro

IRISH SEA

Troon
Cairnryan
Larne
BELFAST
Isle of Man
Douglas
Heysham
DUBLIN
Dún Laoghaire
Holyhead
Anglesey
Liverpool
Birkenhead
Rosslare Harbour
Fishguard
Pembroke Dock

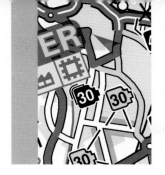

Atlas symbols

Motoring information

M4	Motorway with number	3	Restricted primary route junctions
Toll T4	Toll motorway with toll station	S	Primary route service area
11	Motorway junction with and without number	BATH	Primary route destination
3	Restricted motorway junctions	A1123	Other A road single/dual carriageway
S Fleet	Motorway service area	B2070	B road single/dual carriageway
	Motorway and junction under construction		Minor road more than 4 metres wide, less than 4 metres wide
A3	Primary route single/dual carriageway		Roundabout
11	Primary route junction with and without number		Interchange/junction

	Narrow primary/other A/B road with passing places (Scotland)		Railway line, in tunnel
	Road under construction/ approved	X	Railway station and level crossing
=======	Road tunnel	+++++++	Tourist railway
Toll	Road toll, steep gradient (arrows point downhill)	Y	City, town, village or other built-up area
5	Distance in miles between symbols	✈ H	Airport, heliport
or V	Vehicle ferry	H H	24-hour Accident & Emergency hospital, other hospital
	Fast vehicle ferry or catamaran	C	Crematorium
F	International freight terminal		Sandy beach

30	Speed camera site (fixed location) with speed limit in mph		
50	Section of road with two or more fixed speed cameras, with speed limit in mph		
40 40	Average speed (SPECS™) camera system with speed limit in mph		
V	Fixed speed camera with variable speed limit		
P·R	Park and Ride (at least 6 days per week)		
628 ▲ 637 Lecht Summit	Height in metres, mountain pass		
	National boundary		
	County, administrative boundary		

Touring information   To avoid disappointment, check opening times before visiting

	Scenic Route	M	Museum or art gallery	Aquarium	Steam railway centre
i	Tourist Information Centre		Industrial interest	RSPB site	Cave
i	Tourist Information Centre (seasonal)		Aqueduct or viaduct	National Nature Reserve (England, Scotland, Wales)	Windmill, monument
V	Visitor or heritage centre	✿	Garden	Wildlife Trust reserve	Golf course
	Picnic site		Arboretum	Local nature reserve	County cricket ground
	Caravan site (AA inspected)		Vineyard	Forest drive	Rugby Union national stadium
▲	Camping site (AA inspected)		Country park	National trail	International athletics stadium
	Caravan & camping site (AA inspected)		Agricultural showground	Viewpoint	Horse racing, show jumping
	Abbey, cathedral or priory		Theme park	Hill-fort	Motor-racing circuit
	Ruined abbey, cathedral or priory		Farm or animal centre	Roman antiquity	Air show venue
✗	Castle		Zoological or wildlife collection	Prehistoric monument	Ski slope (natural, artificial)
	Historic house or building		Bird collection	Battle site with year /1066	National Trust property

	National Trust for Scotland property
	English Heritage site
	Historic Scotland site
	Cadw (Welsh heritage) site
★	Other place of interest
	Boxed symbols indicate attractions within urban areas
⊙	World Heritage Site (UNESCO)
	National Park
	National Scenic Area (Scotland)
	Forest Park
	Heritage coast
	Major shopping centre

Town plans (pages 116–122)

2	Motorway and junction		Railway station	Toilet, with facilities for the less able	Tourist Information Centre
	Primary road single/ dual carriageway		Tramway	Building of interest	Visitor or heritage centre
	A road single/ dual carriageway		London Underground station	Ruined building	Post Office
	B road single/ dual carriageway		London Overground station	City wall	Public library
	Local road single/ dual carriageway		Rail interchange	Cliff lift	Shopping centre
	Other road single/ dual carriageway, minor road		Docklands Light Railway (DLR) station	Cliff escarpment	Shopmobility
	One-way, gated/ closed road	o	Light rapid transit system station	River/canal, lake	Theatre or performing arts centre
	Restricted access		Airport, heliport	Lock, weir	Cinema
	Pedestrian area	R	Railair terminal	Park/sports ground/ open space	Museum
-----	Footpath	P+	Park and Ride (at least 6 days per week)	Cemetery	Castle
	Road under construction	P	Car park	Woodland	Castle mound
|:::::|	Road tunnel		Bus/coach station	Built-up area	Monument, statue
	Level crossing	H H	24-hour Accident & Emergency hospital, other hosptial	Beach	Viewpoint

+	Abbey, chapel, church
✡	Synagogue
☾	Mosque
	Golf Course
	Racecourse
	Nature reserve
	Aquarium
⊙	World Heritage Site (UNESCO)
	English Heritage site
	Historic Scotland site
	Cadw (Welsh heritage) site
	National Trust site
	National Trust Scotland site

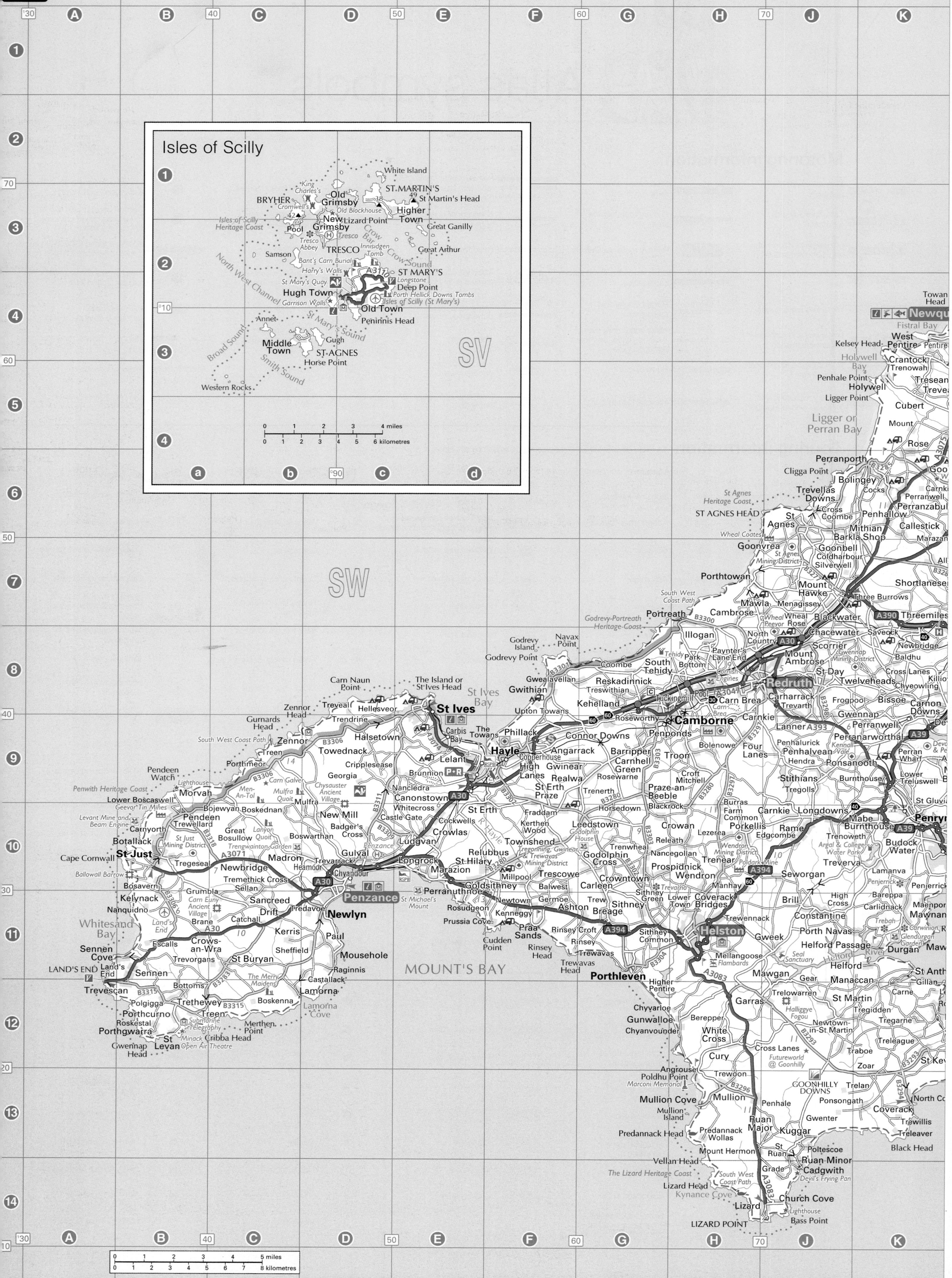
Isles of Scilly
White Island
ST MARTIN'S
St Martin's Head
BRYHER
Old Grimsby
Old Blockhouse
Higher Town
New Grimsby
Lizard Point
Isles of Scilly Heritage Coast
Pool
Great Ganilly
Tresco Abbey
TRESCO
Great Arthur
Samson
Bant's Carn Burial
Harry's Walls
ST MARY'S
Longstone
St Mary's Quay
Hugh Town
Deep Point
Porth Hellick Down Tombs
Garrison Walls
Isles of Scilly (St Mary's)
Old Town
North West Channel
Annet
Peninnis Head
St Mary's Sound
Middle Town
Gugh
ST AGNES
Horse Point
Broad Sound
Smith Sound
Western Rocks
SV
4 miles
6 kilometres
SW
Newquay
Fistral Bay
Kelsey Head
West Pentire
Holywell Bay
Crantock
Trenowah
Penhale Point
Holywell
Tresean
Ligger Point
Cubert
Ligger or Perran Bay
Mount
Rose
Perranporth
Cligga Point
Bolingey
St Agnes Heritage Coast
Trevellas
Downs
Cocks
Perranzabuloe
ST AGNES HEAD
St Agnes
Cross Coombe
Penhallow
Mithian
Callestick
Barkla Shop
Wheal Coates
Goonvrea
Goonbell
Coldharbour
Silverwell
St Agnes Mining District
Porthtowan
Mount Hawke
Shortlanesend
South West Coast Path
Mawla
Menagissey
Three Burrows
Portreath
Cambrose
Blackwater
Threemilestone
Godrevy-Portreath Heritage Coast
Wheal Rose
Illogan
Chacewater
Saveock
North Country
Scorrier
Newbridge
Godrevy Island
Navax Point
Paynter's Lane End
Mount Ambrose
Baldhu
Godrevy Point
Coombe
South Tehidy
Park Bottom
St Day
Cross Lanes
Gwealavellan
Reskadinnick
Redruth
Twelveheads
Chyeowling
Carn Naun Point
The Island or St Ives Head
Gwithian
Treswithian
Tuckingmill
Pool
Carn Brea
Carharrack
Trevarth
Frogpool
Bissoe
Carnon Downs
St Ives Bay
Kehelland
Zennor Head
Treveal
Hellesveor
St Ives
Upton Towans
Roseworthy
Camborne
Carnkie
Gwennap
Trendrine
Lanner
Perranwell
Gurnards Head
Halsetown
Carbis Bay
The Towans
Phillack
Connor Downs
Penponds
Four Lanes
Perranarworthal
South West Coast Path
Zennor
Towednack
Hayle
Angarrack
Barripper
Troon
Bolenowe
Penhalurick
Penhalvean
Perran Wharf
Treen
Lelant
Copperhouse
Carnhell Green
Hendra
Ponsanooth
Pendeen Watch
Porthmeor
Cripplesease
High Lanes
Gwinear
Rosewarne
Croft Mitchell
Stithians
Burnthouse
Lower Treluswell
Penwith Heritage Coast
Lighthouse
Carn Galver
Georgia
Brunnion
Realwa
St Erth Praze
Trenerth
Praze-an-Beeble
Tregolls
Lower Boscaswell
Morvah
Men-An-Tol
Mulfra Quoit
Chysauster Ancient Village
Nancledra
Canonstown
Horsedown
Blackrock
Burras
Farm Common
Carnkie
Longdowns
Geevor Tin Mines
Bojewyan
Boskednan
Mulfra
Whitecross
St Erth
Fraddam
Levant Mine and Beam Engine
Pendeen
Trewellard
New Mill
Castle Gate
Cockwells
Leedstown
Crowan
Lezerea
Porkellis
Rame
Mabe Burnthouse
Penryn
Carnyorth
Great Bosullow
Lanyon Quoit
Badger's Cross
Crowlas
Kerthen Wood
Godolphin House
Releath
Edgcombe
Trenowth
Budock Water
Botallack
St Just Mining District
Trengwainton Garden
Boswarthan
Ludgvan
Townshend
Trenwheal
Nancegollan
Wendron Mining District
Argal & College Water Park
Cape Cornwall
St Just
Madron
Gulval
Relubbus
Tregonning, Gwinear & Trewavas Mining District
Godolphin Cross
Trenear
Poldark Mine
Treverva
Ballowall Barrow
Tregeseal
Newbridge
Heamoor
Trevarrack
Longrock
St Hilary
Prospidnick
Wendron
Lamanva
Tremethick Cross
Chyandour
Marazion
Millpool
Trescowe
Crowntown
Seworgan
Bosavern
Sellan
Penzance
Perranuthnoe
Goldsithney
Carleen
Manhay
Penjerrick
Kelynack
Grumbla
Carn Euny Ancient Village
Sancreed
St Michael's Mount
Newtown
Germoe
Balwest
Trew
Sithney Green
Lower Town
Coverack Bridges
High Cross
Nanquidno
Drift
Tredavoe
Newlyn
Rosudgeon
Kenneggy
Ashton
Breage
Sithney
Brill
Barerpa
Carlidnack
Land's End
Brane
Catchall
Prussia Cove
Trewennack
Constantine
Mawnan
Whitesand Bay
Kerris
Paul
Praa Sands
Rinsey Croft
Helston
Trebah
Sennen Cove
Escalls
Crows-an-Wra
Sheffield
Cudden Point
Rinsey
Sithney Common
Gweek
Porth Navas
Glendurgan Garden
LAND'S END
Sennen
Trevorgans
St Buryan
Mousehole
Rinsey Head
Trewavas
Mellangoose
Flambards
Helford Passage
Durgan
Raginnis
MOUNT'S BAY
Trewavas Head
Seal Sanctuary
Helford River
Trevescan
Bottoms
The Merry Maidens
Castallack
Porthleven
Mawgan
Helford
St Anthony
Lamorna
Higher Pentire
Gear
Manaccan
Gillan
Polgigga
Trethewey
Boskenna
Lamorna Cove
Garras
Trelowarren
St Martin
Carne
Porthcurno
Treen
Chyvarloe
Halligye Fogou
Tregidden
Roskestal
Submarine Telegraphy
Merthen Point
Gunwalloe
Berepper
Newtown-in-St Martin
Tregarne
Porthgwarra
Minack Open Air Theatre
Cribba Head
Chyanvounder
White Cross
Treleague
Gwennap Head
St Levan
Cross Lanes
Traboe
Cury
Futureworld @ Goonhilly
Zoar
St Keverne
Angrouse
Poldhu Point
Marconi Memorial
Trewoon
GOONHILLY DOWNS
Trelan
Ponsongath
Mullion Cove
Mullion
Penhale
Coverack
North Corner
Mullion Island
Ruan Major
Gwenter
Trewillis
Predannack Head
Predannack Wollas
Kuggar
Treleaver
Black Head
Mount Hermon
St Ruan
Poltescoe
Ruan Minor
Vellan Head
Grade
Cadgwith
The Lizard Heritage Coast
South West Coast Path
Devil's Frying Pan
Lizard Head
Kynance Cove
Church Cove
Lizard
Lighthouse
Bass Point
LIZARD POINT
5 miles
8 kilometres

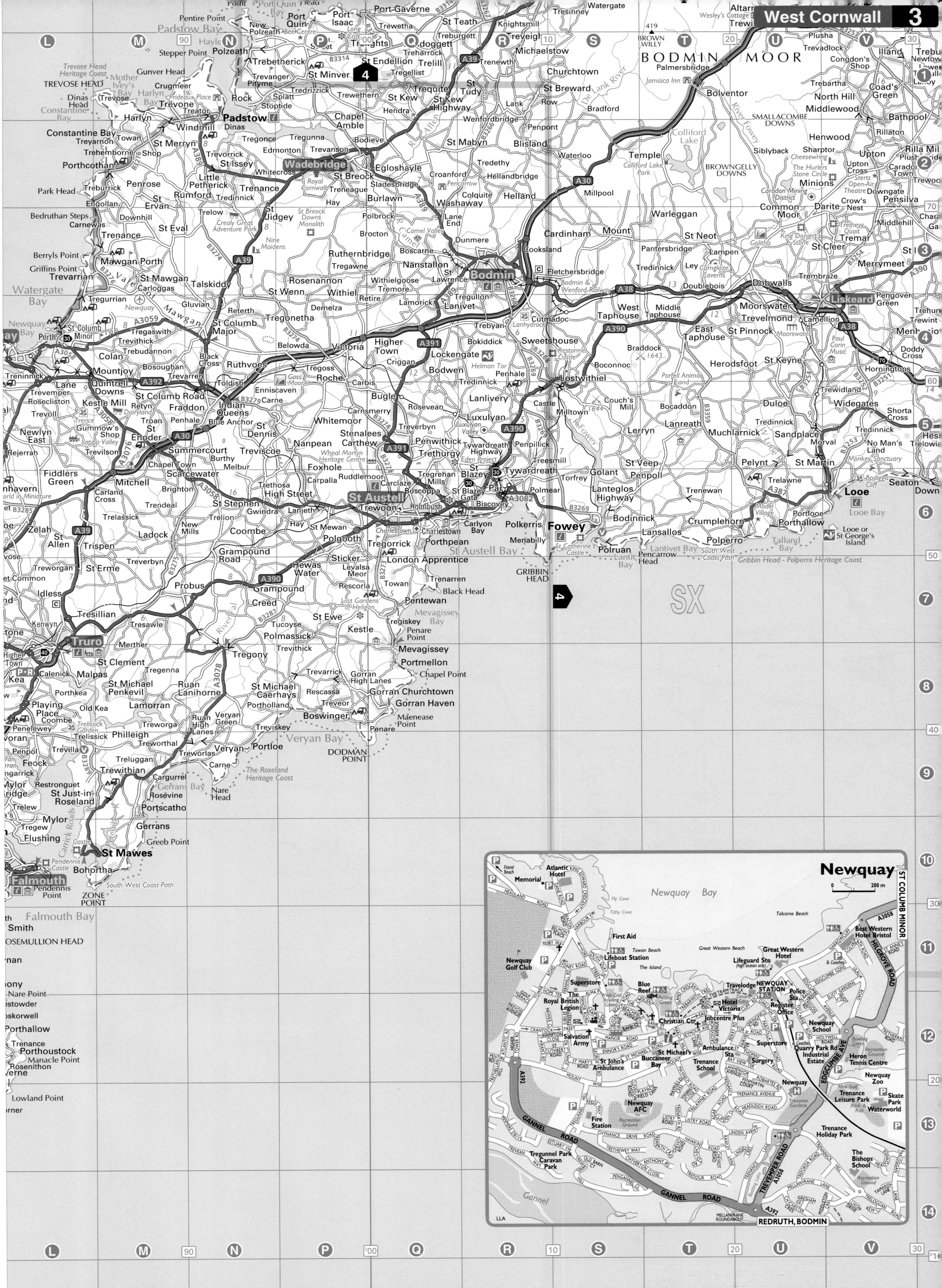
BODMIN MOOR
Padstow Bay
Padstow
Wadebridge
Bodmin
St Austell
Truro
Falmouth
Fowey
Looe
Liskeard
Lostwithiel
Newquay
St Mawes
St Columb Major
Indian Queens
St Austell Bay
Veryan Bay
Mevagissey Bay
Gerrans Bay
Falmouth Bay
Watergate Bay
Looe Bay
Lantivet Bay
GRIBBIN HEAD
DODMAN POINT
ZONE POINT
TREVOSE HEAD
Trevose Head Heritage Coast
The Roseland Heritage Coast
Gribbin Head - Polperro Heritage Coast
South West Coast Path
Mevagissey
Gorran Haven
Polperro
Polruan
Charlestown
Par
Lanivet
Roche
Probus
Tregony
Grampound
Camelford
Polzeath
Rock
St Minver
St Endellion
St Kew
St Tudy
St Breward
St Mabyn
Blisland
Helland
Cardinham
St Neot
Dobwalls
Menheniot
St Cleer
Minions
Upton Cross
Herodsfoot
Duloe
St Keyne
Widegates
Morval
St Martin
Seaton
Pelynt
Lerryn
Lanreath
Golant
Tywardreath
St Blazey
Luxulyan
Lanlivery
Bugle
Stenalees
Nanpean
St Dennis
Summercourt
Mitchell
St Stephen
Sticker
St Ewe
Polgooth
Pentewan
Portmellon
Gorran Churchtown
Boswinger
Portloe
Veryan
Ruan Lanihorne
Philleigh
St Just-in-Roseland
Portscatho
Gerrans
St Clement
Malpas
Kea
Feock
Mylor Bridge
Flushing
Pendennis Point
Constantine Bay
Harlyn
St Merryn
Trevone
Porthcothan
Mawgan Porth
St Mawgan
St Eval
St Issey
Little Petherick
Egloshayle
Washaway
Nanstallon
Lanhydrock
A30
A38
A39
A389
A390
A391
A392
A3058
A3059
A3075
A3076
A3078
A3082
A387
B3266
B3268
B3269
B3274
B3275
B3276
B3287
B3314
SX
4
Newquay
Newquay Bay
0
200 m
Fistral Beach
Towan Beach
Tolcarne Beach
Great Western Beach
Atlantic Hotel
Newquay Golf Club
First Aid
Lifeboat Station
Superstore
Blue Reef
Royal British Legion
Salvation Army
St John's Ambulance
Buccaneer Bay
St Michael's
Christian Ctr
Jobcentre Plus
Hotel Victoria
Travelodge
NEWQUAY STATION
Police Sta
Register Office
Ambulance Sta
Trenance School
Surgery
Newquay School
Quarry Park Rd Industrial Estate
Heron Tennis Centre
Newquay Zoo
Trenance Leisure Park
Skate Park
Waterworld
Trenance Holiday Park
The Bishops School
Newquay AFC
Fire Station
Tregunnel Park Caravan Park
Great Western Hotel
Best Western Hotel Bristol
Lifeguard Stn
Gannel
GANNEL ROAD
TREVEMPER ROAD
EDGCUMBE AVE
HILGROVE ROAD
ST COLUMB MINOR
REDRUTH, BODMIN
A392
A3058
LLA

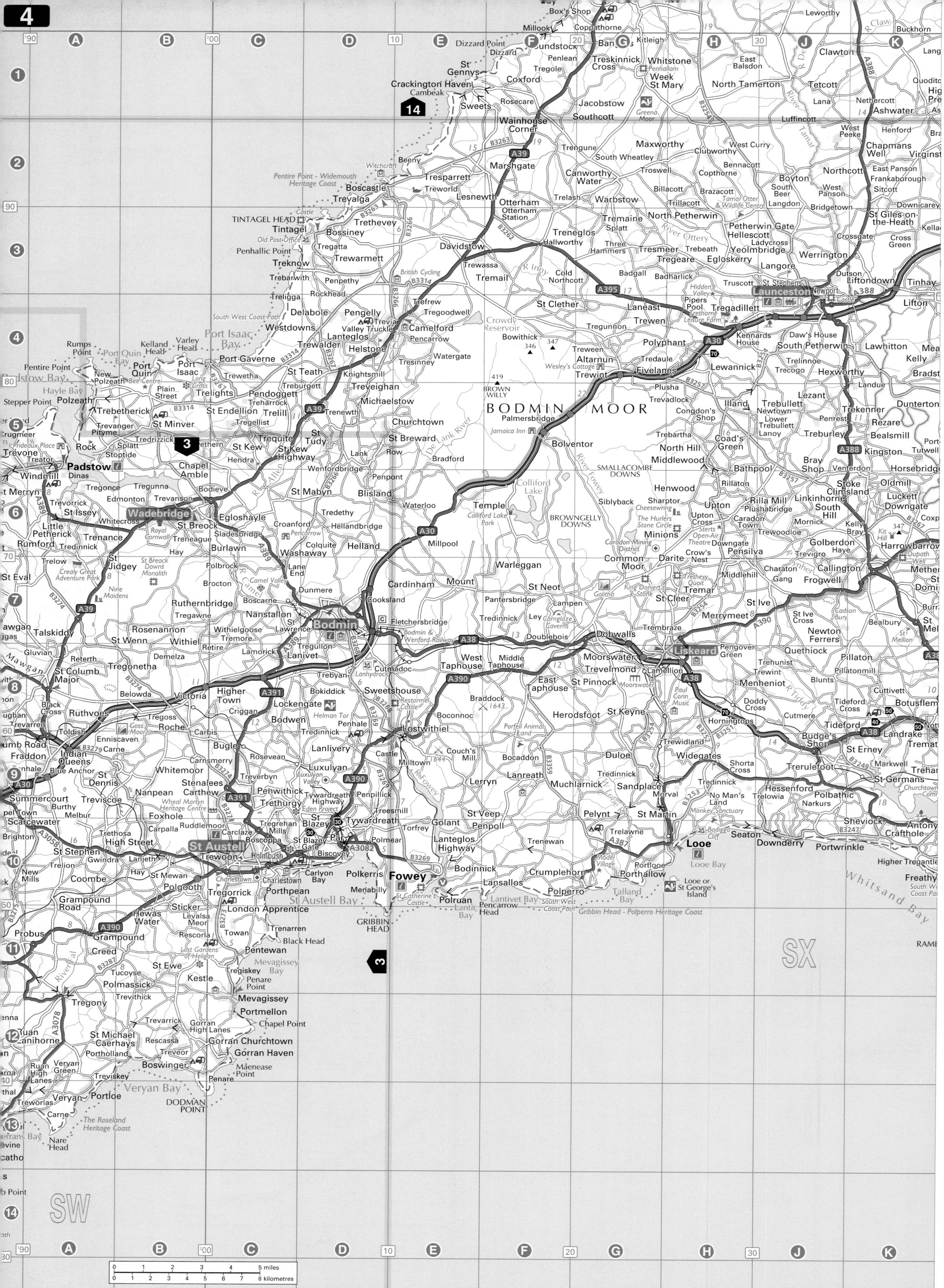
Crackington Haven
Cambeak
St Gennys
Dizzard Point
Millook
Box's Shop
Coppathorne
Bangors
Kitleigh
Lewforthy
Buckhorn
Penlean
Treskinnick Cross
Whitstone
Week St Mary
Tregole
Coxford
Rosecare
Sweets
Wainhouse Corner
Jacobstow
Southcott
North Tamerton
Tetcott
Clawton
East Balsdon
Lana
Nethercott
Ashwater
Luffincott
Henford
West Peeke
Chapmans Well
Virginstow
Beeny
Witchcroft
Pentire Point - Widemouth Heritage Coast
Boscastle
Trevalga
Tresparrett
Treworld
Marshgate
Lesnewth
Trengune
South Wheatley
Canworthy Water
Maxworthy
Clubworthy
West Curry
Bennacott
Copthorne
Troswell
Boyton
South Beer
Langdon
Northcott
East Panson
Frankaborough
Sitcott
West Panson
Bridgetown
Downicarey
St Giles-on-the-Heath
TINTAGEL HEAD
Tintagel
Old Post Office
Trethevey
Bossiney
Penhallic Point
Tregatta
Trewarmett
Treknow
Trebarwith
Treligga
Otterham
Otterham Station
Davidstow
Trelash
Warbstow
Treneglos
Hallworthy
Tremaine
Splatt
Three Hammers
North Petherwin
Petherwin Gate
Hellescott
Ladycross
Yeolmbridge
Crossgate
Cross Green
Werrington
River Ottery
Tresmeer
Trebeath
Tregeare
Egloskerry
Langore
Dutson
Liftondown
Tinhay
Lifton
Penpethy
Rockhead
British Cycling
Trewassa
Tremail
Cold Northcott
Badgall
Badharlick
Truscott
St Stephens
Launceston
Newport
Delabole
Pengelly
Trevia
Valley Truckle
Trefrew
Trewoodwell
Camelford
Pencarrow
Crowdy Reservoir
Bowithick
St Clether
Laneast
Trewen
Tregunnon
Hidden Valley
Pipers Pool
Tregadillett
Kennards House
Daw's House
South Petherwin
Lawhitton
South West Coast Path
Westdowns
Lanteglos
Helstone
Trewalder
Watergate
Tresinney
Treween
Altarnun
Wesley's Cottage
Polyphant
Tredaule
Fivelanes
Trewint
Lewannick
Trelinnoe
Trecogo
Hexworthy
Kelly
Bradstone
Rumps Point
Port Quin Bay
Kelland Head
Varley Head
Port Isaac Bay
Port Quin
Port Isaac
Port Gaverne
Pentire Point
New Polzeath
Trewetha
St Teath
Treburgett
Knightsmill
Treveighan
Padstow Bay
Hayle Bay
Polzeath
Plain Street
Trelights
Pendoggett
Treharrock
Trelill
Michaelstow
Stepper Point
Trebetherick
Trevanger
Pityme
St Minver
St Endellion
Tregellist
Trequite
St Tudy
Trenewth
Churchtown
BROWN WILLY
BODMIN MOOR
Palmersbridge
Jamaica Inn
Plusha
Trevadlock
Congdon's Shop
Illand
Trebullett
Newtown
Lower Trebullett
Lanoy
Lezant
Landue
Trekenner
Rezare
Treburley
Bealsmill
Dunterton
Rock
Prideaux Place
Splatt
Tredrizzick
Stoptide
St Kew
St Kew Highway
Hendra
Chapel Amble
St Breward
Lank
Row
De Lank River
Bradford
Bolventor
Trebartha
North Hill
Middlewood
Coad's Green
Bathpool
Bray Shop
Venterdon
Kingston
Horsebridge
Trevone
Treator
Padstow
Windmill
Dinas
St Merryn
Tregonce
Tregunna
Trevanson
Edmonton
Bodieve
Wenfordbridge
Penpont
St Mabyn
Blisland
Colliford Lake
SMALLACOMBE DOWNS
Henwood
Rillaton
Stoke Climsland
Oldmill
Luckett
Downgate
Trevorrick
St Issey
Little Petherick
Wadebridge
Royal Cornwall
Whitecross
St Breock
Egloshayle
Tredethy
Croanford
Hellandbridge
Waterloo
Temple
Colliford Lake Park
Siblyback
Sharptor
Cheesewring
The Hurlers Stone Circle
Minions
Upton
Upton Cross
Rilla Mill
Plushabridge
Caradon Town
Linkinhorne
South Hill
Mornick
Kelly Bray
Trewoodloe
Rumford
Tredinnick
Trenance
Treneague
Sladesbridge
Burlawn
Pencarrow
Colquite
Washaway
Helland
A30
Millpool
BROWNGELLY DOWNS
Caradon Mining District
Sterts Open-Air Theatre
Downgate
Golberdon
Harrowbarrow
Trelow
St Jidgey
St Breock Downs Monolith
Hay
Polbrock
Crealy Great Adventure Park
Nine Maidens
Camel Valley
Lane End
Dunmere
Warleggan
Common Moor
Darite
Crow's Nest
Pensilva
Trevigro
Charaton
Callington
St Eval
Brocton
Cardinham
Mount
St Neot
Golitha
Trethevy Quoit
Tremar
Frogwell
Rutherbridge
Boscarne
Cooksland
Pantersbridge
Lampen
King Doniert's Stone
St Cleer
St Ive
Merrymeet
Tregawne
Nanstallon
Bodmin
Fletchersbridge
Bodmin & Wenford Railway
Tredinnick
Ley
Carnglaze Caverns
Doublebois
Dobwalls
Trembraze
St Ive Cross
Newton Ferrers
Bealbury
Talskiddy
Rosenannon
Withielgoose
Tremore
St Wenn
Withiel
St Lawrence
Retire
Lamorick
Tregullon
Lanivet
West Taphouse
Middle Taphouse
Moorswater
Trevelmond
Liskeard
Lamellion
Pengover Green
Quethiock
Pillaton
Trehunist
Trewint
Pillatonmill
Gluvian
Reterth
Demelza
Tregonetha
St Columb Major
Belowda
Victoria
Higher Town
Trebyan
Lanhydrock
Cutmadoc
Sweetshouse
Braddock
East Taphouse
St Pinnock
Menheniot
Blunts
Cuttivett
Black Cross
Ruthvoes
Tregoss
Goss Moor
Roche
Criggan
Bokiddick
Lockengate
Helman Tor
Restormel Castle
Boconnoc
Porfell Animal Land
Herodsfoot
St Keyne
Paul Corin Music
Doddy Cross
Tideford Cross
Botusfleming
Toldish
Indian Queens
Enniscaven
Carne
Carbis
Bodwen
Penhale
Lostwithiel
Trewidland
Horningtops
Cutmere
Tideford
Landrake
Fraddon
St Dennis
Bugle
Tredinnick
Lanlivery
Castle
Couch's Mill
Bocaddon
Duloe
Widegates
Budge's Shop
St Erney
Trematon
Blue Anchor
Whitemoor
Carnsmerry
Rosevean
Luxulyan
Luxulyan Valley
Eden Project
Milltown
Lerryn
Lanreath
Muchlarnick
Tredinnick
Sandplace
Tredinnick
Shorta Cross
Trerulefoot
Markwell
Trehan
St Germans
Churchtown
Summercourt
Burthy
Treviscoe
Nanpean
Stenalees
Carthew
Wheal Martyn Heritage Centre
Treverbyn
Penwithick
Trethurgy
Tywardreath Highway
Penpillick
Morval
No Man's Land
Monkey Sanctuary
Hessenford
Trelowia
Polbathic
Narkurs
Melbur
Foxhole
Ruddlemoor
Tregrehan Mills
St Blazey
Par
Tywardreath
Treesmill
Golant
St Veep
Penpoll
Pelynt
St Martin
Sheviock
Antony
Crafthole
Scarcewater
Trethosa
Carpalla
Carclaze
Boscoppa
St Blazey Gate
Biscovey
Polmear
Torfrey
Lanteglos Highway
Trenewan
Trelawne
Model Village
Bodigga Cliff
Seaton
Downderry
Portwrinkle
High Street
St Stephen
Gwindra
Lanjeth
St Austell
Trewoon
Holmbush
Carlyon Bay
Polkerris
Fowey
Bodinnick
Crumplehorn
Portlooe
Looe
Looe Bay
Higher Tregantle
Trelion
New Mills
Coombe
Hay
St Mewan
Polgooth
Charlestown
Menabilly
Lansallos
Polperro
Porthallow
Looe or St George's Island
Freathy
Whitsand Bay
Grampound Road
Tregorrick
Porthpean
St Austell Bay
St Catherine's Castle
Polruan
Lantivet Bay
Pencarrow Head
Lantic Bay
South West Coast Path
Talland Bay
Gribbin Head - Polperro Heritage Coast
Sticker
Hewas Water
Levalsa Meor
London Apprentice
GRIBBIN HEAD
Probus
Grampound
Rescorla
Towan
Trenarren
Black Head
SX
RAME
Creed
Lost Gardens of Heligan
Pentewan
St Ewe
Mevagissey Bay
Tucoyse
Kestle
Tregiskey
Penare Point
Polmassick
Trevithick
Mevagissey
Tregony
Portmellon
Chapel Point
Trevarrick
Gorran High Lanes
Ruan Lanihorne
St Michael Caerhays
Rescassa
Gorran Churchtown
Portholland
Treveor
Gorran Haven
Veryan Green
Boswinger
Maenease Point
Ruan High Lanes
Treviskey
Penare
Veryan Bay
Veryan
Portloe
DODMAN POINT
Treworlas
Carne
The Roseland Heritage Coast
Nare Head
SW
A
B
C
D
E
F
G
H
J
K
0 1 2 3 4 5 miles
0 1 2 3 4 5 6 7 8 kilometres

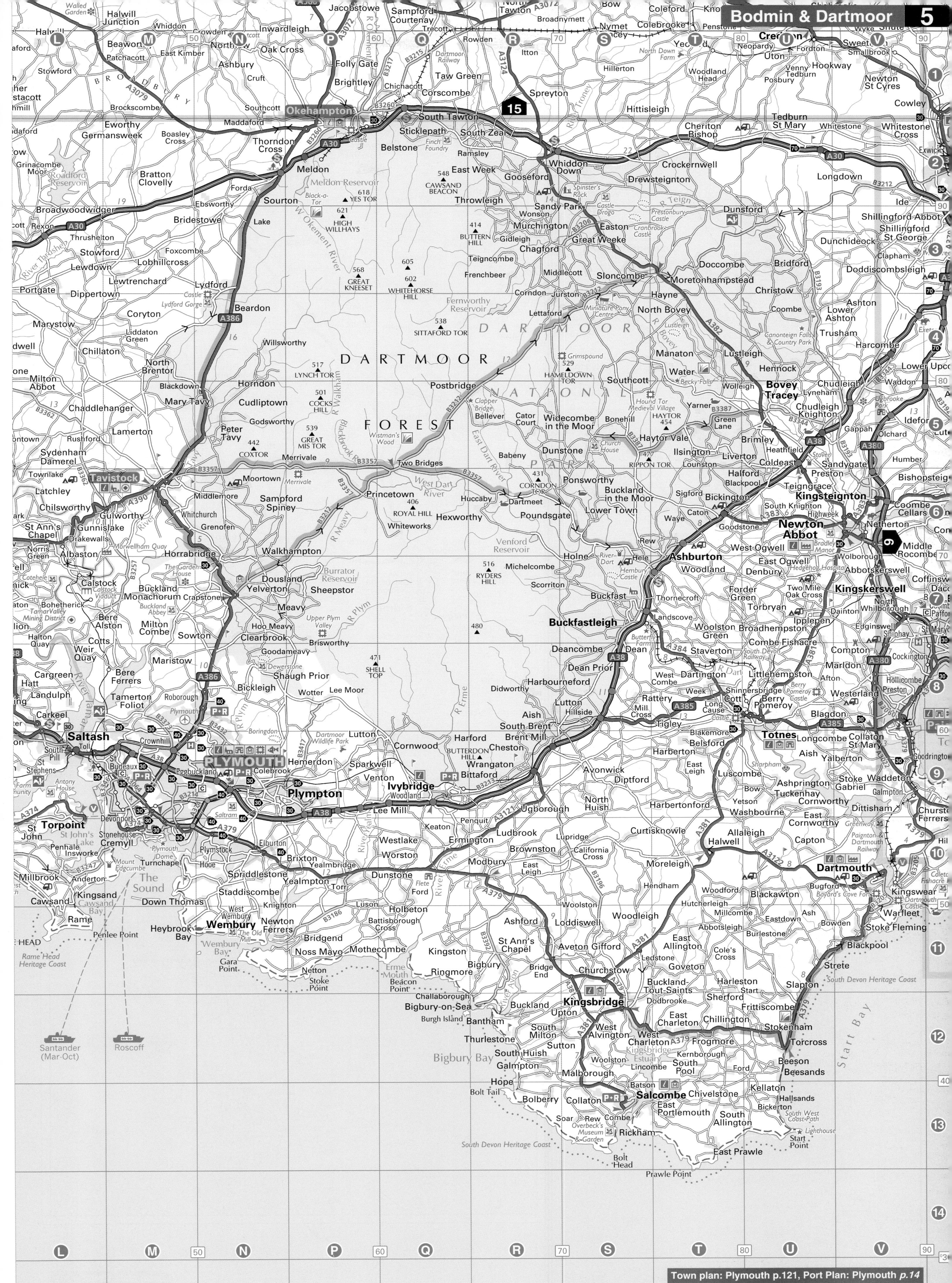
Walled Garden
Halwill Junction
Jacobstowe
Sampford Courtenay
Tawton
Broadnymett
Bow
Coleford
Colebrooke
Penstone
Nymet Tracey
Crediton
Whiddon
Crowden
Inwardleigh
Trecott
Rowden
Itton
Yeoford
Neopardy
Uton
Fordton
Sweetham
Shute
Smallbrook
Halwill
Beaworthy
Northlew
Oak Cross
North Down Farm
Hillerton
Woodland Head
Venny Tedburn
Posbury
Hookway
Newton St Cyres
Patchacott
East Kimber
Ashbury
Folly Gate
Dartmoor Railway
Taw Green
Stowford
Cruft
Brightley
Chichacott
Corscombe
Spreyton
B R O A D B U R Y
Southcott
Okehampton
Hittisleigh
Cowley
Brockscombe
Maddaford
South Tawton
Sticklepath
South Zeal
Finch Foundry
Cheriton Bishop
Tedburn St Mary
Whitestone
Whitestone Cross
Exwick
Eworthy
Germansweek
Boasley Cross
Thorndon Cross
Castle
Belstone
Ramsley
Whiddon Down
Crockernwell
Longdown
Grinacombe Moor
Roadford Reservoir
Bratton Clovelly
Meldon
Meldon Reservoir
548 CAWSAND BEACON
East Week
Gooseford
Drewsteignton
Spinster's Rock
Forda
Black-a-Tor
618 YES TOR
Throwleigh
Sandy Park
Castle Drogo
Prestonbury Castle
Dunsford
Ide
Broadwoodwidger
Sourton
Ebsworthy
621 HIGH WILLHAYS
Wonson
Murchington
Easton
Cranbrook Castle
Shillingford Abbot
Shillingford St George
Rexon
Bridestowe
Lake
W Okement River
414 BUTTERN HILL
Gidleigh
Great Weeke
Chagford
Dunchideock
Thrushelton
Stowford
Foxcombe
Teigncombe
Clapham
Lewdown
Lobhillcross
605
568 GREAT KNEESET
602 WHITEHORSE HILL
Frenchbeer
Middlecott
Sloncombe
Doccombe
Bridford
Doddiscombsleigh
Portgate
Lewtrenchard
Lydford
Moretonhampstead
Dippertown
Lydford Gorge
Fernworthy Reservoir
Corndon
Jurston
Christow
Hayne
Beardon
Miniature Pony Centre
North Bovey
Lettaford
Coombe
Ashton
Lower Ashton
Coryton
538 SITTAFORD TOR
D A R T M O O R
Lustleigh
Canonteign Falls & Country Park
Trusham
Marystow
Liddaton Green
Willsworthy
Manaton
Chillaton
Harcombe
Lustleigh
Grimspound
529 HAMELDOWN TOR
Hennock
D A R T M O O R
Water
Becky Falls
North Brentor
Blackdown
517 LYNCH TOR
Horndon
Postbridge
Southcott
Bovey Tracey
Chudleigh
Waddon
Lower Upcott
Milton Abbot
Mary Tavy
Cudliptown
501 COCKS HILL
N A T I O N A L
Clapper Bridge
Hound Tor Medieval Village
Wolleigh
Yarner
Lyneham
Ugbrooke Park
Chudleigh Knighton
Chaddlehanger
Godsworthy
539 GREAT MIS TOR
F O R E S T
Bellever
Cator Court
Widecombe in the Moor
Bonehill
HAYTOR 454
Haytor Vale
Green Lane
Gappah
Ideford
Olchard
Lamerton
Peter Tavy
Wistman's Wood
Church House
Brimley
Heathfield
Rushford
442 COXTOR
Merrivale
Two Bridges
Babeny
Dunstone
Ilsington
Liverton
Stover
Sandygate
Sydenham Damerel
477 RIPPON TOR
Lounston
Coldeast
Humber
Townlake
Tavistock
Moortown
P A R K
431 CORNDON TOR
Ponsworthy
Halford
Preston
Bishopsteignton
Latchley
Middlemoor
Merrivale
West Dart River
Buckland in the Moor
Blackpool
Teigngrace
Kingsteignton
Sampford Spiney
Princetown
Huccaby
Dartmeet
Sigford
Bickington
Chilsworthy
Gulworthy
Whitchurch
406 ROYAL HILL
Hexworthy
Lower Town
Poundsgate
Caton
South Knighton
Highweek
Coombe Cellars
Newton Abbot
Netherton
Gunnislake
St Ann's Chapel
Grenofen
Whiteworks
Waye
Goodstone
Drakewalls
Morwellham Quay
R Meavy
Venford Reservoir
Rew
Bradley Manor
Middle Rocombe
Norris Green
Albaston
Horrabridge
Walkhampton
West Ogwell
Holne
River Dart
Hele
Ashburton
East Ogwell
Wolborough
The Garden House
Burrator Reservoir
516 RYDERS HILL
Michelcombe
Hembury Castle
Woodland
Denbury
Hedgehog Hospital
Abbotskerswell
Coffinswell
Cotehele
Calstock
Dousland
Yelverton
Sheepstor
Scorriton
Buckfast
Forder Green
Two Mile Oak Cross
Kingskerswell
Calstock Viaduct
Buckland Monachorum
Crapstone
Thornecroft
Torbryan
Dainton
North Whilborough
Bohetherick
Tamar Valley Mining District
Buckland Abbey
Meavy
Upper Plym Valley
Landscove
Ipplepen
Bere Alston
Milton Combe
Hoo Meavy
480
Buckfastleigh
Woolston Green
Broadhempston
Edginswell
Halton Quay
Cotts
Sowton
Clearbrook
Briswworthy
Butterfly Farm
Combe Fishacre
Shiphay
Weir Quay
Goodameavy
Deancombe
Dean
Staverton
South Devon Railway
Compton
Cockington
Maristow
Dewerstone
471 SHELL TOP
Dean Prior
Dartington
Marldon
Cargreen
Bere Ferrers
Shaugh Prior
Littlehempston
Afton
Hollicombe
Hatt
Harbourneford
West Combe
Landulph
Tamerton Foliot
Roborough
Bickleigh
Wotter
Lee Moor
Didworthy
Week
Shinnersbridge
Berry Pomeroy Castle
Preston
Westerland
R Erme
Rattery
Cott
Berry Pomeroy
Carkeel
Lutton
Hillside
Mill Cross
Long Cause
Aish
Blagdon
Saltash
Boringdon
Dartmoor Wildlife Park
Lutton
Tigley
Castle
Crownhill
South Brent
Brent Mill
Blakemore
Totnes
Longcombe
Collaton St Mary
South Pill
Harford
Belsford
Goodrington
St Stephens
St Budeaux
PLYMOUTH
Hemerdon
Cornwood
Butterdon Hill
Cheston
Harberton
Aish
Yalberton
Antony House
Eggbuckland
Colebrook
Sparkwell
Wrangaton
Avonwick
East Leigh
Sharpham
Bittaford
Luscombe
Ashprington
Stoke Gabriel
Waddeton
Venton
Ivybridge
Diptford
Plympton
Woodland
Bow
Tuckenhay
Galmpton
Torpoint
Devonport
Lee Mill
North Huish
Harbertonford
Yetson
Cornworthy
Dittisham
Churston Ferrers
Saltram
Penquit
Ugborough
Washbourne
East Cornworthy
Greenway
St John
St John's Lake
Stonehouse
Cremyll
Keaton
Ermington
Ludbrook
Lupridge
Curtisknowle
Allaleigh
Paignton & Dartmouth Railway
Capton
Penhale
Insworke
Plymouth Dome
Plymstock
Elburton
Westlake
Brownston
California Cross
Halwell
Mount Edgcumbe
Turnchapel
Hooe
Brixton
Worston
Modbury
Moreleigh
Dartmouth
Millbrook
Anderton
Spriddlestone
Yealmbridge
East Leigh
Hendham
Woodford
Bugford
Kingswear
The Sound
Yealmpton
Dunstone
Flete
Torr
Ford
Blackawton
Bayard's Cove Fort
Dartmouth Castle
Cawsand
Kingsand
Cawsand Bay
Down Thomas
Staddiscombe
Woolston
Hutcherleigh
Millcombe
Eastdown
Ash
Warfleet
Knighton
Luson
Holbeton
Woodleigh
Bowden
Rame
West Wembury
Battisborough Cross
Ashford
Loddiswell
Abbotsleigh
Burlestone
Stoke Fleming
Penlee Point
Heybrook Bay
Wembury
The Old Mill
Newton Ferrers
Bridgend
HEAD
Rame Head Heritage Coast
Wembury Bay
Noss Mayo
Mothecombe
Kingston
St Ann's Chapel
Aveton Gifford
East Allington
Cole's Cross
Blackpool
Gara Point
Netton
Stoke Point
Erme Mouth
Beacon Point
Ringmore
Bigbury
Bridge End
Churchstow
Ledstone
Goveton
Strete
South Devon Heritage Coast
Challaborough
Bigbury-on-Sea
Burgh Island
Bantham
Buckland
Kingsbridge
Upton
Buckland-Tout-Saints
Dodbrooke
Harleston
Sherford
Start
Slapton
Frittiscombe
Start Bay
Thurlestone
South Milton
West Alvington
East Charleton
Chillington
Stokenham
West Charleton
Frogmore
Torcross
Santander (Mar-Oct)
Roscoff
Bigbury Bay
South Huish
Sutton
Woolston
Kingsbridge Estuary
Kernborough
Beeson
Galmpton
Malborough
Lincombe
South Pool
Ford
Beesands
Hope
Bolt Tail
Batson
Salcombe
Chivelstone
Kellaton
Hallsands
Bolberry
Collaton
East Portlemouth
Bickerton
South Allington
South West Coast Path
Lighthouse
Soar
Rew
Combe
Overbeck's Museum & Garden
Rickham
Start Point
South Devon Heritage Coast
East Prawle
Bolt Head
Prawle Point
L
M
N
P
Q
R
S
T
U
V
50
60
70
80
90
1
2
3
4
5
6
7
8
9
10
11
12
13
14
15
9

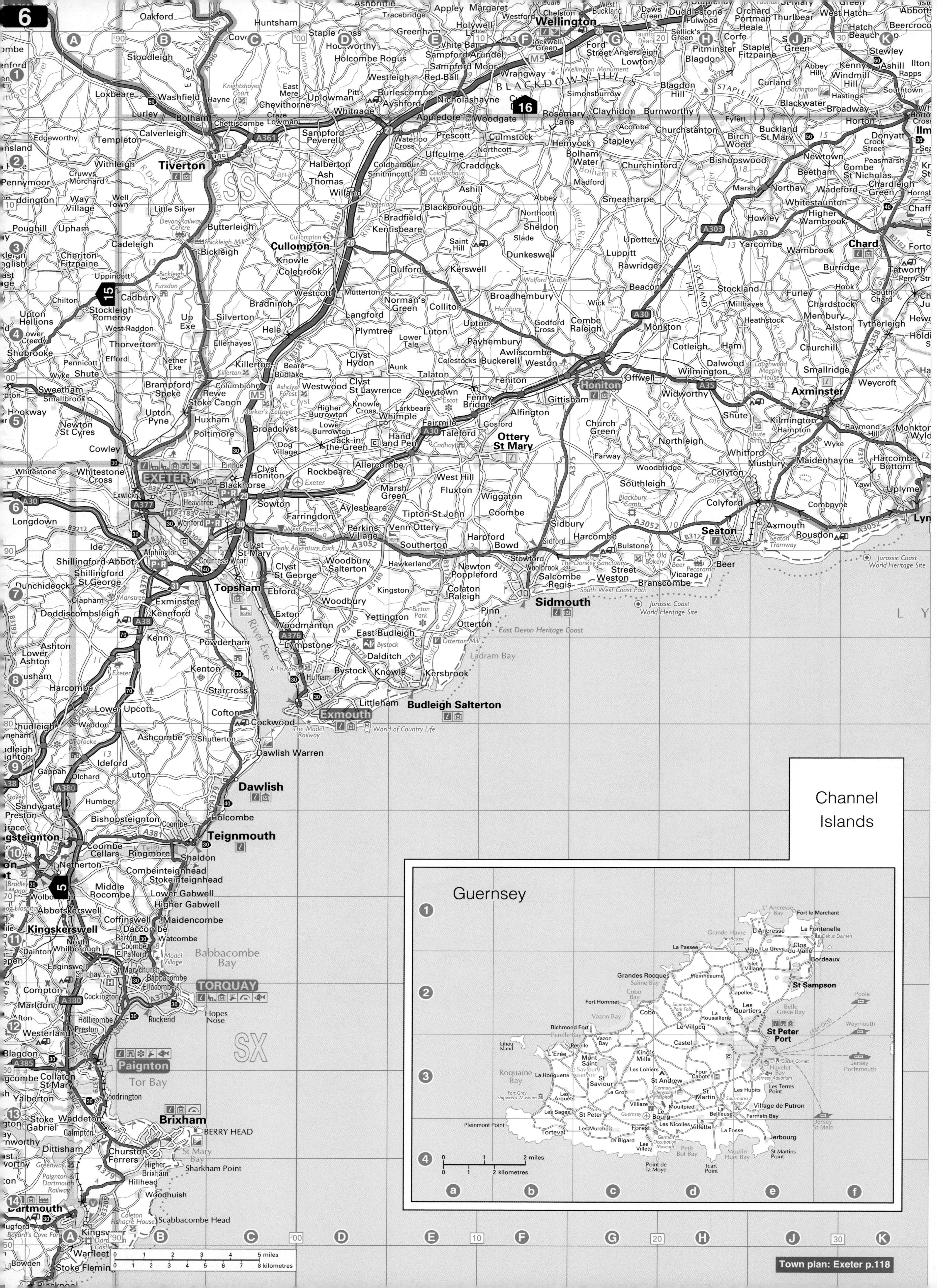
Oakford
Huntsham
Staple Cross
Hockworthy
Holcombe Rogus
Greenham
White Ball
Sampford Arundel
Sampford Moor
Red Ball
Appley
Holywell Lake
Wellington
Westford
Rockwell Green
Ford Street
Angersleigh
Lowton
West Buckland
Chelston
Daws Green
Duddlestone
Fulwood
Sellick's Green
Pitminster
Blagdon
Orchard Portman
Thurlbear
Heale
Corfe
Staple Fitzpaine
Stoodleigh
Loxbeare
Washfield
Hayne
Knightshayes Court
East Mere
Chevithorne
Uplowman
Pitt
Burlescombe
Ayshford
Westleigh
Whitnage
Lurley
Bolham
Chettiscombe
Craze Lowman
Sampford Peverell
Nicholashayne
Appledore
Woodgate
Wrangway
Wellington Monument
BLACKDOWN HILLS
Simonsburrow
Rosemary Lane
Clayhidon
Burnworthy
Blagdon Hill
Barrington Court
Hastings
Blackwater
Broadway
Southtown
Ashill
Ilton
Rapps
Stewley
Abbey Hill
Kenny
Windmill Hill
Curland
Beercrocombe
Abbotts
Hatch Beauchamp
West Hatch
Edgeworthy
Templeton
Calverleigh
Tiverton
Withleigh
Cruwys Morchard
Pennymoor
Way Village
Well Town
Little Silver
Devon Railway Centre
Butterleigh
Bickleigh Mill
Bickleigh
Cadeleigh
Poughill
Upham
Cheriton Fitzpaine
Uppincott
Fursdon
Cadbury
Chilton
Upton Hellions
Stockleigh Pomeroy
West Raddon
Thorverton
Shobrooke
Lower Creedy
Pennicott
Efford
Wyke
Shute
Nether Exe
Sweetham
Smallbrook
Hookway
Newton St Cyres
Brampford Speke
Upton Pyne
Rewe
Stoke Canon
Columbjohn
Killerton
Huxham
Poltimore
Cowley
Ellerhayes
Up Exe
Silverton
Hele
Bradninch
Westcott
Cullompton
Knowle
Colebrook
Halberton
Ash Thomas
Willand
Waterloo Cross
Prescott
Culmstock
Uffculme
Northcott
Coldharbour
Smithincott
Craddock
Ashill
Blackborough
Bradfield
Kentisbeare
Diggerland
Saint Hill
Hemyock
Bolham Water
Stapley
Acombe
Churchstanton
Churchinford
Madford
Abbey
Northcott
Sheldon
Slade
Dunkeswell
Smeatharpe
Upottery
Luppitt
Rawridge
Beacon
Birch Wood
Bishopswood
Buckland St Mary
Fyfett
Horton
Donyatt
Crock Street
Peasmarsh
Newtown
Beetham
Combe St Nicholas
Chardleigh Green
Marsh
Northay
Wadeford
Whitestaunton
Higher Wambrook
Howley
Yarcombe
Wambrook
Chard
Forton
Burridge
Tatworth
Perry Street
Hook
South Chard
Stockland
Furley
Chardstock
Millhayes
Heathstock
Membury
Alston
Tytherleigh
Holditch
Hewood
Churchill
Smallridge
Weycroft
Axminster
Kilmington
Hampton
Raymond's Hill
Monkton Wyld
Wyke
Maidenhayne
Harcombe Bottom
Yawl
Uplyme
Musbury
Whitford
Colyton
Colyford
Combpyne
Axmouth
Rousdon
Seaton
Seaton Tramway
Beer
Jurassic Coast World Heritage Site
Mutterton
Norman's Green
Colliton
Langford
Plymtree
Lower Tale
Luton
Upton
Payhembury
Broadhembury
Wolford Chapel
Hembury
Godford Cross
Combe Raleigh
Wick
Monkton
Cotleigh
Ham
Dalwood
Loughwood Meeting House
Wilmington
Offwell
Widworthy
Shute
Shute Barton
Northleigh
Honiton
Gittisham
Awliscombe
Weston
Buckerell
Colestocks
Feniton
Fenny Bridges
Alfington
Escot
Talaton
Aunk
Clyst Hydon
Clyst St Lawrence
Westwood
Ashclyst Forest
Beare
Budlake
Marker's Cottage
Higher Burrowton
Lower Burrowton
Knowle Cross
Larkbeare
Whimple
Newtown
Fairmile
Taleford
Gosford
Cadhay
Ottery St Mary
Hand and Pen
Jack-in-the-Green
Dog Village
Broadclyst
Allercombe
Rockbeare
Exeter
Clyst Honiton
West Hill
Fluxton
Marsh Green
Aylesbeare
Tipton St John
Wiggaton
Coombe
Church Green
Farway
Woodbridge
Southleigh
Blackbury Camp
Sidbury
Sidford
Harcombe
Bulstone
The Old Bakery
Pecorama
Branscombe
Vicarage
Street
Weston
Salcombe Regis
The Donkey Sanctuary
South West Coast Path
Sidmouth
Jurassic Coast World Heritage Site
Stowford
Woolbrook
Harpford
Bowd
Southerton
Newton Poppleford
Colaton Raleigh
Hawkerland
Venn Ottery
Perkins Village
Farringdon
West Point
Whitestone
Whitestone Cross
EXETER
Whipton
Blackhorse
Sowton
Heavitree
Exwick
Wonford
Longdown
Ide
Alphington
Countess Wear
Clyst St Mary
Crealy Adventure Park
Clyst St George
Woodbury Salterton
Shillingford Abbot
Shillingford St George
Dunchideock
Clapham
Exminster
Kennford
Topsham
Ebford
Woodbury
Kingston
Bicton Park
Exton
Woodmanton
Yettington
Otterton
Pinn
East Devon Heritage Coast
East Budleigh
Bystock
Dalditch
Otterton Mill
Ladram Bay
Lympstone
Knowle
Bystock
Kersbrook
Hulham
A La Ronde
Littleham
Budleigh Salterton
Exmouth
World of Country Life
The Model Railway
Doddiscombsleigh
Kenn
Powderham
River Exe
Kenton
Starcross
Cofton
Cockwood
Dawlish Warren
Ashton
Lower Ashton
Trusham
Harcombe
Lower Upcott
Waddon
Chudleigh
Ugbrooke Park
Ashcombe
Shutterton
Ideford
Luton
Gappah
Olchard
Dawlish
Holcombe
Humber
Sandygate
Preston
Bishopsteignton
Coombe
Teignmouth
Coombe Cellars
Ringmore
Shaldon
Netherton
Combeinteignhead
Stokeinteignhead
Middle Rocombe
Lower Gabwell
Higher Gabwell
Maidencombe
Abbotskerswell
Coffinswell
Daccombe
Kingskerswell
Barton
Watcombe
North Whilborough
Dainton
Coombe
Pafford
Model Village
Babbacombe Bay
Edginswell
Shiphay
St Marychurch
Babbacombe
Ellacombe
TORQUAY
Compton
Cockington
Marldon
Hollicombe
Preston
Rockend
Hopes Nose
Westerland
Blagdon
Paignton
Collaton St Mary
Tor Bay
Goodrington
Yalberton
Stoke Gabriel
Waddeton
Galmpton
Brixham
BERRY HEAD
Dittisham
Churston Ferrers
St Mary Bay
Sharkham Point
Higher Brixham
Hillhead
Greenway
Paignton & Dartmouth Railway
Woodhuish
Dartmouth
Coleton Fishacre House
Scabbacombe Head
Kingswear
Dart Castle
Warfleet
Bowden
Stoke Fleming
Bayard's Cove Fort
Newton Abbot
SS
SX
LY
Channel Islands
Guernsey
L' Ancresse Bay
Fort le Marchant
L'Ancresse
La Fontenelle
Dehus Dolmen
Grande Havre
Rousse Tower
La Passee
Vale
La Greve
Clos du Valle
Bordeaux
Islet Village
Grandes Rocques
Saline Bay
Pleinheaume
St Sampson
Cobo Bay
Capelles
Fort Hommet
Les Quartiers
Saumarez Park Folk
La Rousaillerie
Belle Greve Bay
Cobo
Vazon Bay
Le Villocq
Richmond Fort
Perelle Bay
Vazon Bay
St Peter Port
Castel
Lihou Island
Perelle
L'Erée
Mont Saint
St Saviour Reservoir
King's Mills
Castle Cornet
Havelet Bay
Guernsey Aquarium
Roquaine Bay
La Houguette
Les Lohiers
St Andrew
Four Cabots
St Saviour
German Underground Hospital
Le Gron
Les Hubits
Les Terres Point
Fort Grey Shipwreck Museum
Les Arquêts
St Martin
Saumarez Manor
Village de Putron
Les Sages
St Peter's
Villiaze
Le Bourg
Mouilpied
La Bellieuse
Fermain Bay
Pleinmont Point
Torteval
Les Murchez
Forest
Les Nicolles
La Villette
La Fosse
Jerbourg
Le Bigard
Les Villets
German Occupation Museum
Petit Bot Bay
Moulin Huet Bay
St Martins Point
Point de la Moye
Icart Point
Poole
Weymouth
Jersey Portsmouth
Jersey St Malo
(Apr-Oct)
2 miles
2 kilometres
5 miles
8 kilometres

Town plan: Exeter p.118

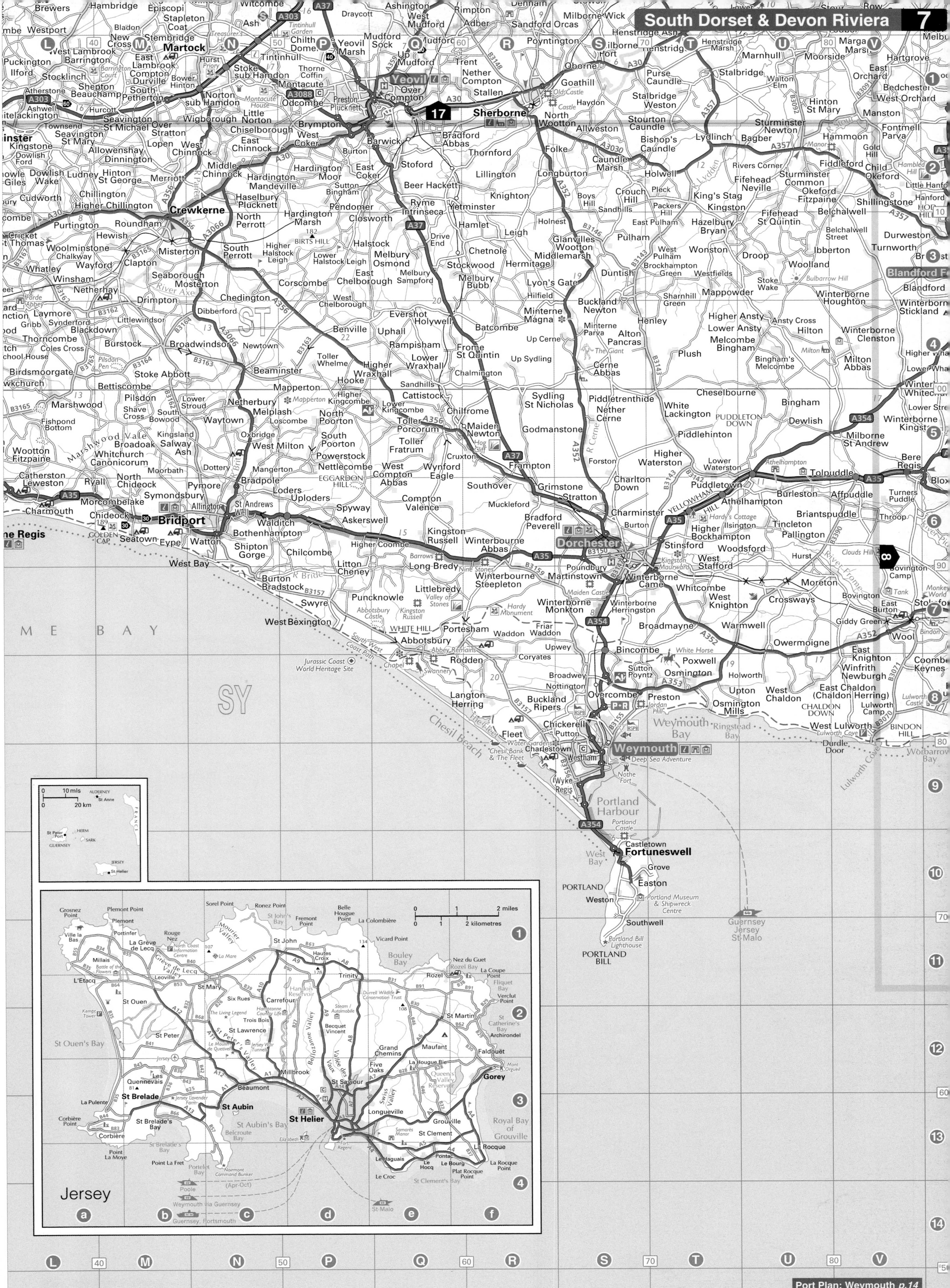
Yeovil
Martock
Crewkerne
Sherborne
Bridport
Dorchester
Weymouth
Fortuneswell
Portland Harbour
Portland Bill
Chesil Beach
Lyme Bay
Abbotsbury
Beaminster
West Bay
Charmouth
Portesham
Chickerell
Wyke Regis
Weymouth Bay
Durdle Door
Bere Regis
Puddletown
Cerne Abbas
Maiden Newton
Broadwindsor
Jurassic Coast World Heritage Site
Guernsey
Jersey
St Malo
Jersey
St Helier
St Aubin
St Brelade
Gorey
St Ouen's Bay
St Aubin's Bay
Royal Bay of Grouville
Bouley Bay
Poole
Weymouth via Guernsey
Guernsey, Portsmouth

Port Plan: Weymouth p.14

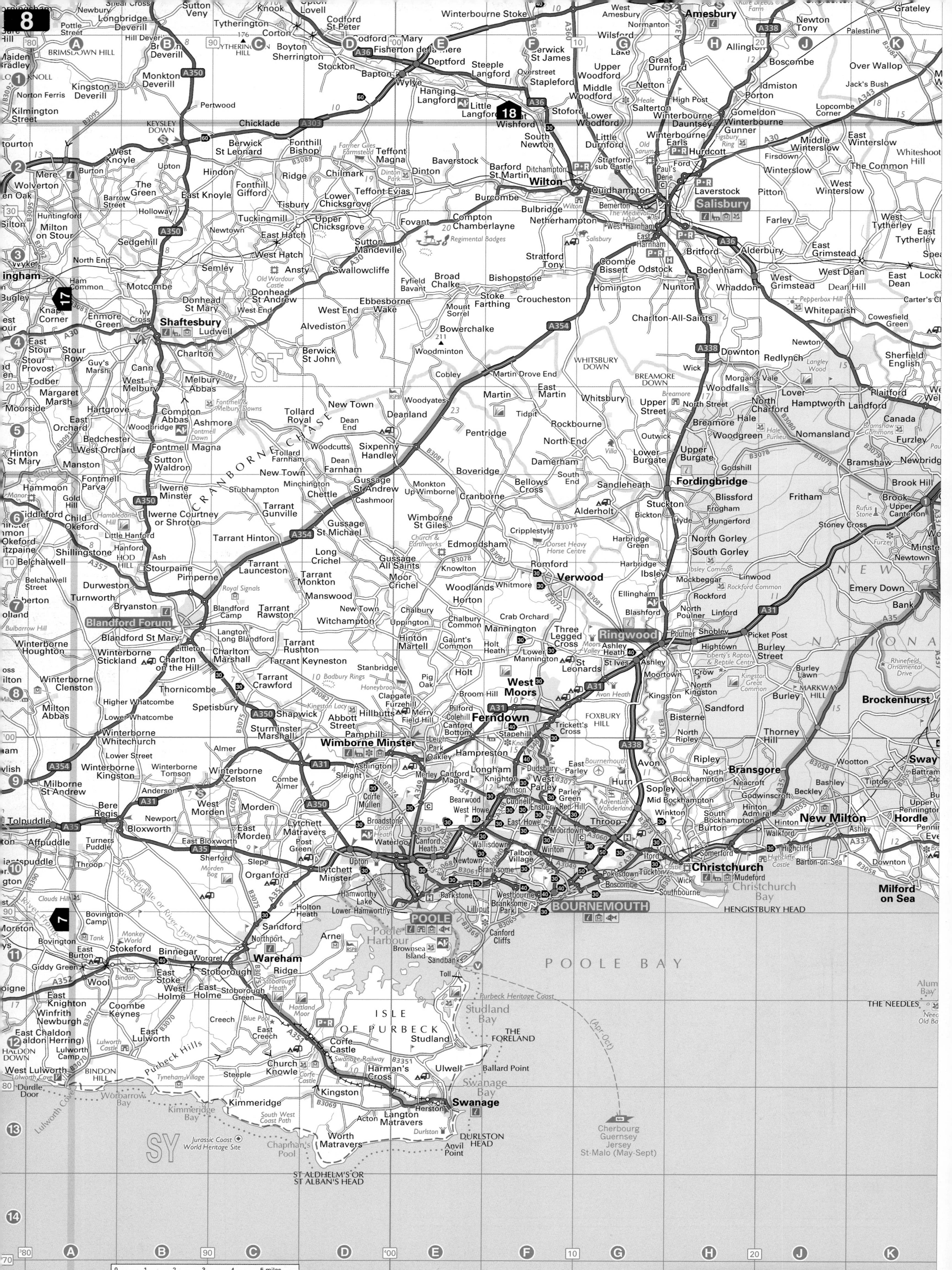
Amesbury
Salisbury
Wilton
Shaftesbury
Blandford Forum
Wimborne Minster
Ferndown
Verwood
Ringwood
Fordingbridge
West Moors
Poole
BOURNEMOUTH
Christchurch
New Milton
Wareham
Swanage
Brockenhurst
Sway
Hordle
Milford on Sea
Barton-on-Sea
Highcliffe
Sherfield English
Downton
Whiteparish
Alderbury
Laverstock
Stratford sub Castle
Old Sarum
Wishford
Stapleford
Wylye
Deptford
Fisherton de la Mere
Codford St Mary
Codford St Peter
Sutton Veny
Longbridge Deverill
Monkton Deverill
Kingston Deverill
Mere
West Knoyle
East Knoyle
Hindon
Tisbury
Fonthill Bishop
Chilmark
Teffont Magna
Dinton
Barford St Martin
Baverstock
Fovant
Compton Chamberlayne
Broad Chalke
Bishopstone
Coombe Bissett
Odstock
Britford
Bodenham
Nunton
Charlton-All-Saints
Donhead St Andrew
Donhead St Mary
Ludwell
Semley
Motcombe
Gillingham
East Stour
West Stour
Stour Provost
Todber
Margaret Marsh
Cann
Melbury Abbas
Compton Abbas
Ashmore
Fontmell Magna
Sutton Waldron
Iwerne Minster
Iwerne Courtney or Shroton
Child Okeford
Shillingstone
Stourpaine
Pimperne
Bryanston
Blandford St Mary
Durweston
Turnworth
Winterborne Houghton
Winterborne Stickland
Winterborne Clenston
Winterborne Whitechurch
Winterborne Kingston
Winterborne Zelston
Milton Abbas
Milborne St Andrew
Bere Regis
Bloxworth
Tolpuddle
Affpuddle
Charlton Marshall
Spetisbury
Sturminster Marshall
Tarrant Hinton
Tarrant Gunville
Tarrant Launceston
Tarrant Monkton
Tarrant Rawston
Tarrant Rushton
Tarrant Keyneston
Tarrant Crawford
Cranborne Chase
Tollard Royal
Sixpenny Handley
Farnham
Gussage St Andrew
Gussage St Michael
Gussage All Saints
Chettle
Long Crichel
Moor Crichel
Witchampton
Wimborne St Giles
Cranborne
Edmondsham
Alderholt
Damerham
Rockbourne
Martin
Whitsbury
Breamore
Woodgreen
Hale
Godshill
Bramshaw
Stuckton
Ibsley
Harbridge
Linwood
Ellingham
Burley
Bransgore
Sopley
Hurn
Avon
St Leonards
St Ives
Ashley Heath
Three Legged Cross
Holt
Colehill
Hampreston
Longham
West Parley
Corfe Mullen
Broadstone
Lytchett Matravers
Lytchett Minster
Upton
Hamworthy
Parkstone
Branksome
Canford Cliffs
Sandbanks
Poole Harbour
Brownsea Island
Poole Bay
Christchurch Bay
HENGISTBURY HEAD
Studland
Studland Bay
THE FORELAND
Ballard Point
Swanage Bay
DURLSTON HEAD
Anvil Point
Worth Matravers
Langton Matravers
Kingston
Corfe Castle
Harman's Cross
Kimmeridge
Kimmeridge Bay
Worbarrow Bay
Lulworth Cove
West Lulworth
East Lulworth
Wool
Bovington Camp
Stoborough
Sandford
Organford
Isle of Purbeck
Purbeck Hills
ST ALDHELM'S OR ST ALBAN'S HEAD
Chapman's Pool
Jurassic Coast World Heritage Site
South West Coast Path
Purbeck Heritage Coast
Cherbourg Guernsey Jersey St-Malo (May-Sept)
(Apr-Oct)
New Forest National Park
THE NEEDLES
A36
A30
A303
A338
A350
A354
A31
A35
A351
A352
A348
A3049
SY
ST
0 1 2 3 4 5 miles
0 1 2 3 4 5 6 7 8 kilometres

Town plan: Salisbury p.121, Port Plan: Poole p.14

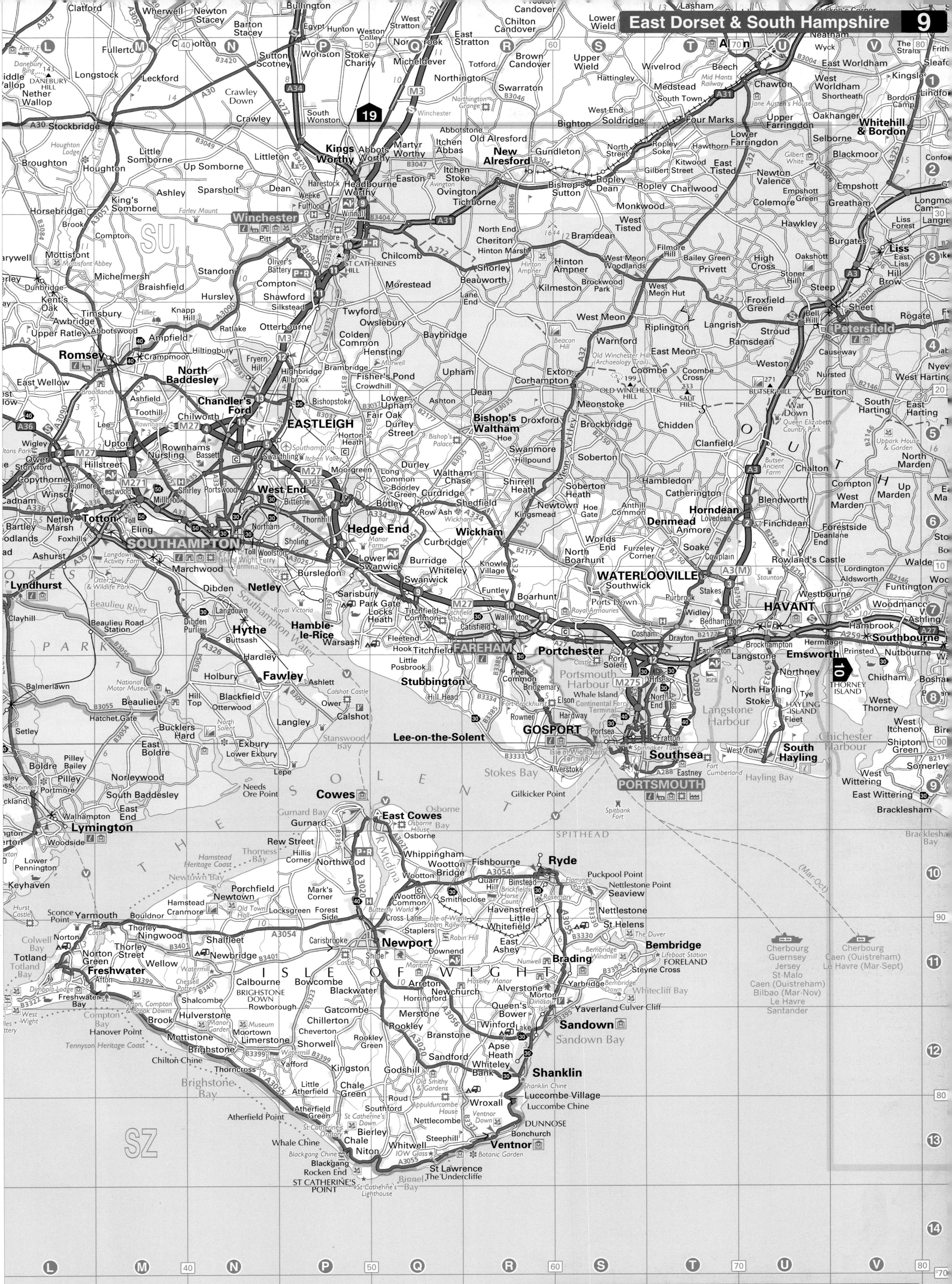
Stockbridge
Romsey
Totton
SOUTHAMPTON
Winchester
Kings Worthy
New Alresford
Alton
Petersfield
EASTLEIGH
Chandler's Ford
North Baddesley
West End
Hedge End
Bishop's Waltham
Wickham
WATERLOOVILLE
HAVANT
Emsworth
Southbourne
Fareham
Portchester
GOSPORT
Southsea
PORTSMOUTH
Lee-on-the-Solent
Stubbington
Fawley
Hythe
Netley
Hamble-le-Rice
Lyndhurst
Lymington
Cowes
East Cowes
Ryde
Newport
Yarmouth
Freshwater
Brading
Bembridge
Sandown
Shanklin
Ventnor
ISLE OF WIGHT
THE SOLENT
SPITHEAD
Southampton Water
Portsmouth Harbour
Langstone Harbour
Chichester Harbour
Hayling Island
Whitehill & Bordon
Liss
South Harting
Horndean
Denmead
Cherbourg
Guernsey
Jersey
St-Malo
Caen (Ouistreham)
Bilbao (Mar-Nov)
Le Havre
Santander
Cherbourg
Caen (Ouistreham)
Le Havre (Mar-Sept)
SU
SZ
19
10

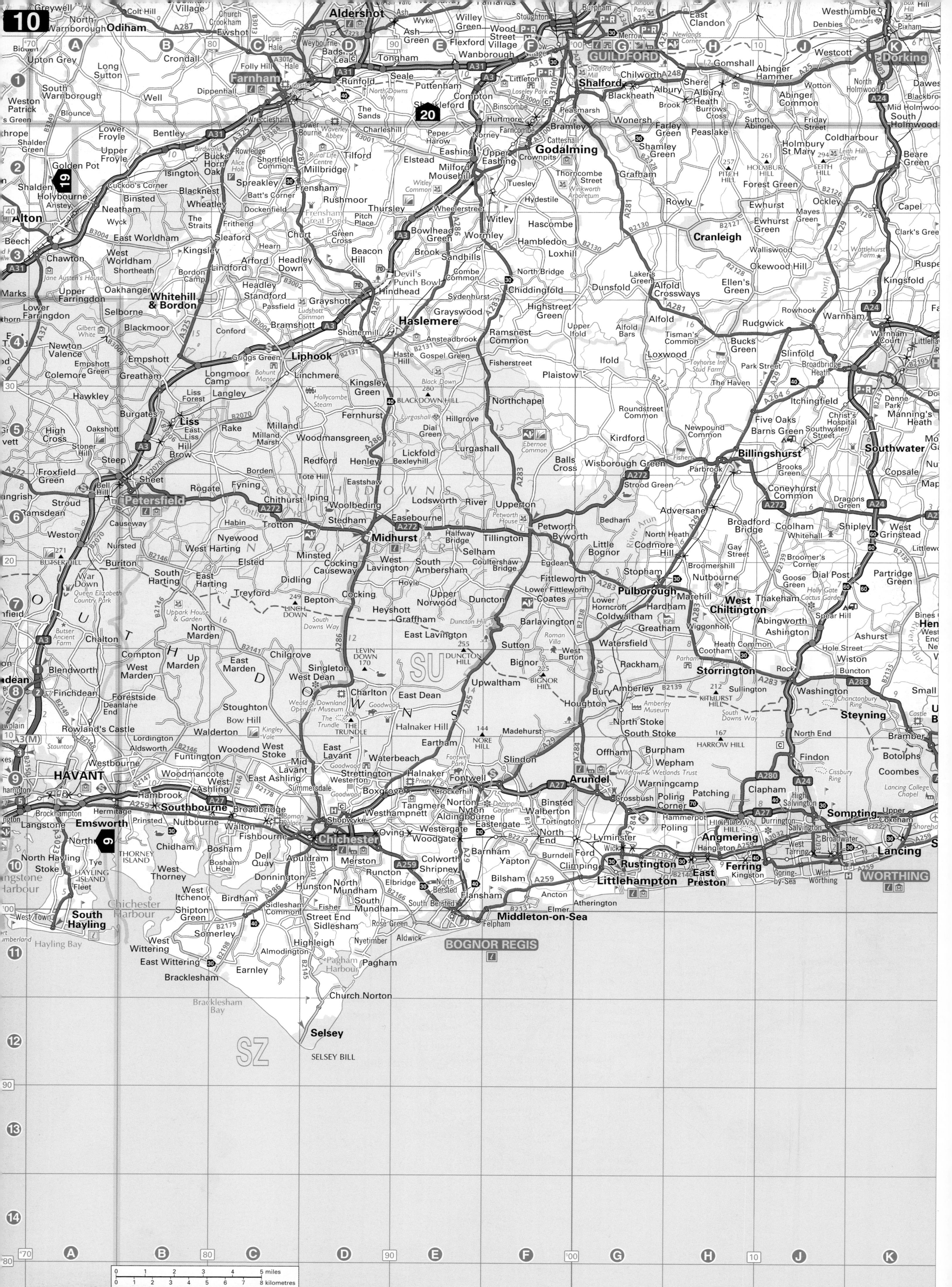
Odiham
Aldershot
Guildford
Dorking
Farnham
Shalford
Godalming
Bramley
Cranleigh
Haslemere
Hindhead
Grayshott
Liphook
Whitehill & Bordon
Alton
Liss
Petersfield
Midhurst
Petworth
Pulborough
Billingshurst
Southwater
West Chiltington
Storrington
Steyning
Arundel
Chichester
Havant
Emsworth
Southbourne
South Hayling
Bognor Regis
Middleton-on-Sea
Littlehampton
Rustington
Angmering
East Preston
Ferring
Worthing
Lancing
Sompting
Selsey
Selsey Bill
Chichester Harbour
Hayling Bay
Bracklesham Bay
South Downs National Park
Cocking
Singleton
Charlton
Goodwood
Tangmere
Fontwell
Slindon
Amberley
Findon
Washington
Wisborough Green
Kirdford
Rudgwick
Slinfold
Alfold
Dunsfold
Chiddingfold
Milford
Elstead
Tilford
Frensham
Churt
Bentley
Selborne
Chawton
Buriton
Rowland's Castle
Westbourne
Bosham
West Wittering
East Wittering
Bracklesham
Pagham
Felpham
Yapton
Barnham
Clapham
Patching
Wiston
Ashington
Thakeham
Coolham
Shipley
West Grinstead
Partridge Green
Dial Post
SU
SZ
0 1 2 3 4 5 miles
0 1 2 3 4 5 6 7 8 kilometres

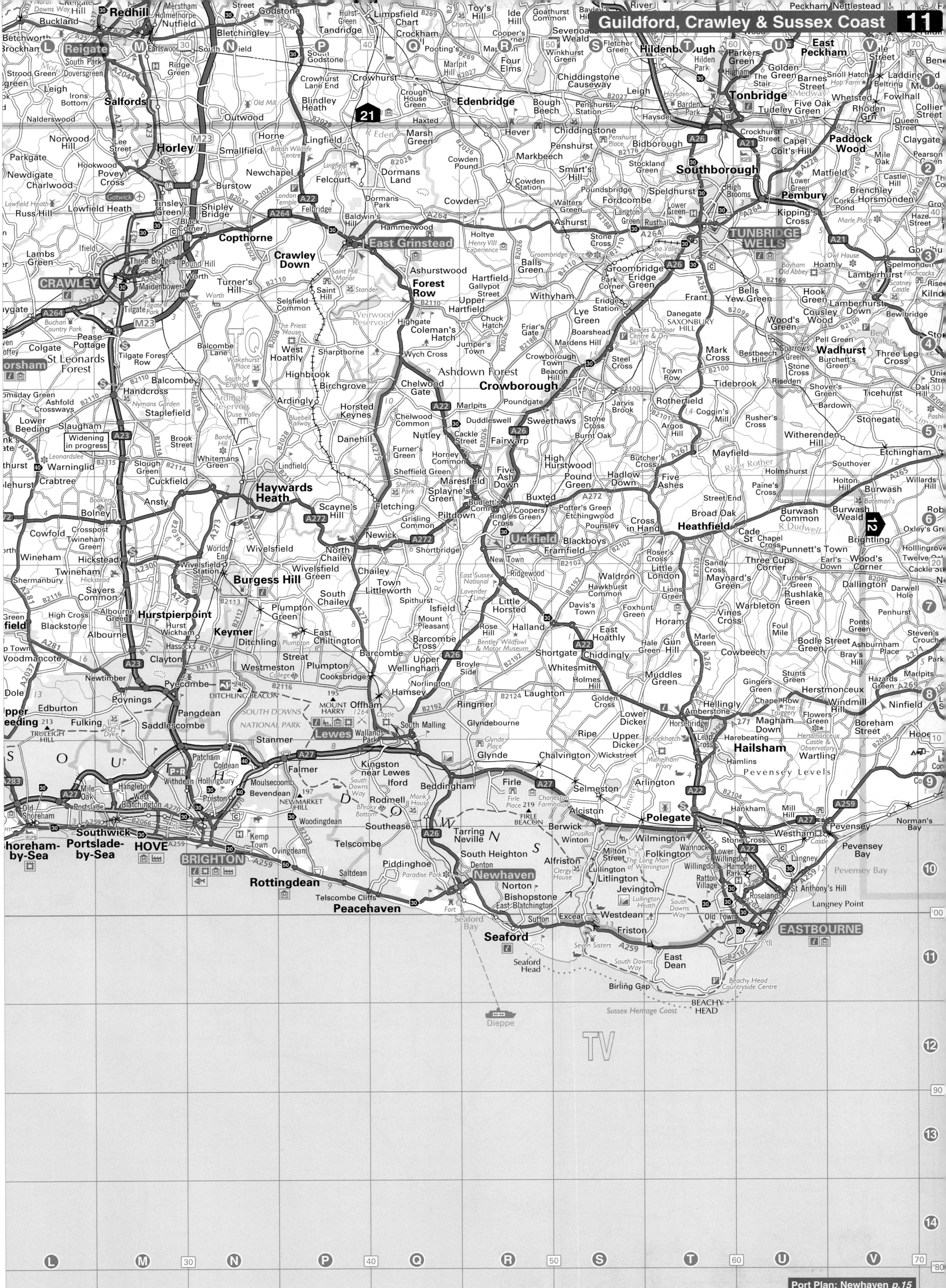
Redhill
Reigate
Horley
Salfords
Gatwick
Copthorne
CRAWLEY
Crawley Down
East Grinstead
Forest Row
Edenbridge
Lingfield
Tonbridge
Southborough
TUNBRIDGE WELLS
Pembury
Paddock Wood
Wadhurst
Crowborough
Ashdown Forest
Haywards Heath
Burgess Hill
Hurstpierpoint
Keymer
Uckfield
Heathfield
Hailsham
Polegate
Lewes
BRIGHTON
HOVE
Shoreham-by-Sea
Southwick
Portslade-by-Sea
Rottingdean
Peacehaven
Newhaven
Seaford
EASTBOURNE
Pevensey
Pevensey Bay
Westham
Beachy Head
BEACHY HEAD
Birling Gap
Seven Sisters
Sussex Heritage Coast
Dieppe
TQ
TV
SOUTH DOWNS NATIONAL PARK
DITCHLING BEACON
FIRLE BEACON
Widening in progress

Port Plan: Newhaven p.15

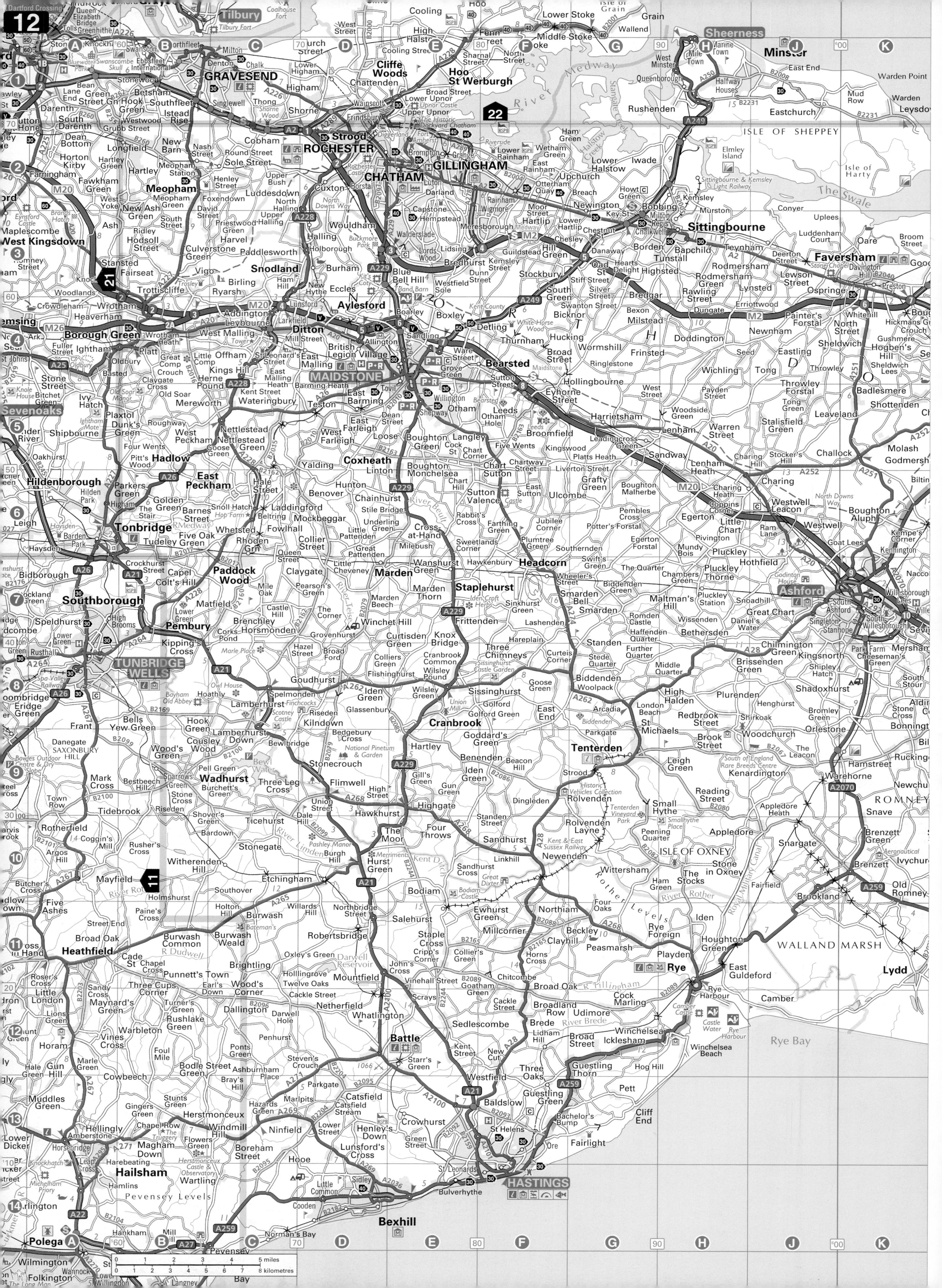
Dartford Crossing
Tilbury
Tilbury Fort
Coalhouse Fort
Cooling
Lower Stoke
Isle of Grain
Grain
Wallend
Sheerness
Minster
Warden Point
Eastchurch
Leysdown
ISLE OF SHEPPEY
Elmley Island
Isle of Harty
The Swale
Queen Elizabeth II Bridge
Greenhithe
Swanscombe
Northfleet
GRAVESEND
Chalk
Higham
Cliffe Woods
Hoo St Werburgh
Strood
ROCHESTER
CHATHAM
GILLINGHAM
River Medway
Lower Halstow
Iwade
Upchurch
Rainham
Newington
Sittingbourne
Teynham
Faversham
Kemsley
Milton Regis
Bapchild
Conyer
Darenth
South Darenth
Longfield
Hartley
Meopham
New Barn
Cobham
Shorne
Sole Street
Luddesdown
Cuxton
Borstal
Wouldham
Walderslade
Lordswood
Bredhurst
Hempstead
Wigmore
Hartlip
Borden
Tunstall
Rodmersham
Lynsted
Ospringe
West Kingsdown
Stansted
Vigo
Snodland
Burham
Eccles
Birling
Ryarsh
Trottiscliffe
Addington
Leybourne
Aylesford
Ditton
Larkfield
Blue Bell Hill
Boxley
Detling
Thurnham
Bicknor
Hucking
Wormshill
Milstead
Frinsted
Bredgar
Doddington
Newnham
Eastling
Throwley
Sheldwich
Badlesmere
Molash
Challock
Wrotham
Borough Green
Ightham
Platt
Offham
West Malling
Kings Hill
East Malling
MAIDSTONE
Bearsted
Sutton Street
Hollingbourne
Harrietsham
Lenham
Charing
Sevenoaks
Plaxtol
Shipbourne
Mereworth
Wateringbury
Teston
Barming
Leeds
Langley
Otham
Broomfield
Kingswood
Hadlow
East Peckham
West Peckham
Nettlestead
Yalding
Coxheath
Linton
Loose
Boughton Monchelsea
Chart Sutton
Sutton Valence
Ulcombe
Grafty Green
Egerton
Pluckley
Little Chart
Westwell
Boughton Aluph
Hildenborough
Tonbridge
Leigh
Golden Green
Laddingford
Beltring
Collier Street
Marden
Staplehurst
Headcorn
Smarden
Bethersden
Ashford
Kennington
Willesborough
Sevington
Great Chart
Kingsnorth
Southborough
Paddock Wood
Matfield
Brenchley
Horsmonden
Pembury
Speldhurst
Rusthall
TUNBRIDGE WELLS
Lamberhurst
Goudhurst
Kilndown
Frittenden
Sissinghurst
Biddenden
High Halden
Woodchurch
Orlestone
Hamstreet
Frant
Wadhurst
Bewl Water
Flimwell
Hawkhurst
Cranbrook
Benenden
Rolvenden
Tenterden
Newenden
Wittersham
Appledore
Snargate
Brenzett
Ivychurch
ROMNEY
Old Romney
Brookland
Fairfield
WALLAND MARSH
Lydd
Isle of Oxney
Stone in Oxney
Kent & East Sussex Railway
Royal Military Canal
Mayfield
Rotherfield
Heathfield
Burwash
Etchingham
Hurst Green
Bodiam
Salehurst
Robertsbridge
Northiam
Beckley
Peasmarsh
Rye
Rye Harbour
Camber
Winchelsea
Winchelsea Beach
Rye Bay
Icklesham
Pett
Fairlight
Brede
Udimore
Sedlescombe
Westfield
Battle
Dallington
Netherfield
Catsfield
Crowhurst
Ninfield
Herstmonceux
Hailsham
Hellingly
Horam
Pevensey Levels
Bexhill
HASTINGS
St Leonards
Bulverhythe
St Helens
Ore
Pevensey
Polegate
Wilmington
Folkington
Norman's Bay
Cooden
Sidley
Little Common
Hooe
Boreham Street
Windmill Hill
0 1 2 3 4 5 miles
0 1 2 3 4 5 6 7 8 kilometres
M20
M2
M26
A2
A20
A21
A26
A28
A229
A249
A259
A268
A271
A22
A27

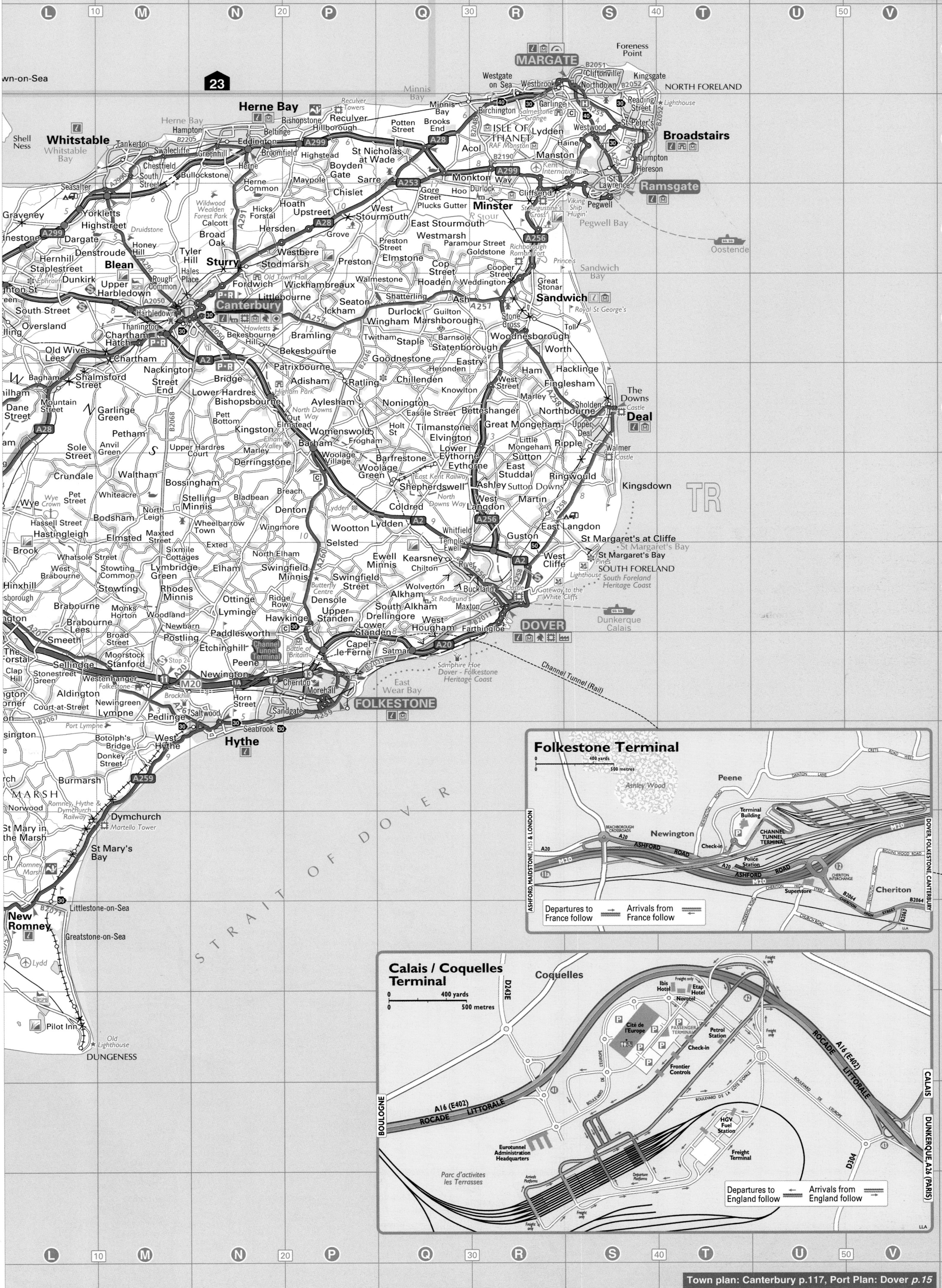

MARGATE
Foreness Point
Westgate on Sea
Westbrook
Cliftonville
Kingsgate
NORTH FORELAND
Birchington
Garlinge
Reading Street
ISLE OF THANET
RAF Manston
Lydden
Westwood
St Peter's
Broadstairs
Haine
Manston
Dumpton
Hereson
Kent International
St Lawrence
Ramsgate
Pegwell
Pegwell Bay
Oostende
Minnis Bay
Herne Bay
Reculver
Bishopstone
Hillborough
Beltinge
Hampton
Eddington
Broomfield
Greenhill
Swalecliffe
Tankerton
Whitstable
Whitstable Bay
Shell Ness
Chestfield
South Street
Bullockstone
Herne
Herne Common
Highstead
St Nicholas at Wade
Boyden Gate
Sarre
Maypole
Chislet
Potten Street
Brooks End
Acol
Monkton
Gore Street
Hoo
Plucks Gutter
Minster
Cliffsend
Seasalter
Graveney
Yorkletts
Highstreet
Dargate
Hernhill
Denstroude
Staplestreet
Dunkirk
Blean
Upper Harbledown
Rough Common
Tyler Hill
Broad Oak
Hales Place
Sturry
Fordwich
Stodmarsh
Westbere
Hoath
Upstreet
Hersden
Grove
West Stourmouth
East Stourmouth
Preston
Westmarsh
Paramour Street
Goldstone
Richborough Roman Fort
Sandwich Bay
Great Stonar
Sandwich
Royal St George's
Cop Street
Cooper Street
Hoaden
Weddington
Ash
Wickhambreaux
Littlebourne
Seaton
Ickham
Durlock
Guilton
Wingham
Marshborough
Stone Cross
Woodnesborough
Canterbury
Harbledown
Thanington
South Street
Oversland
Chartham Hatch
Chartham
Old Wives Lees
Shalmsford Street
Bekesbourne
Bramling
Twitham
Staple
Barnsole
Statenborough
Worth
Goodnestone
Eastry
Heronden
Nackington
Patrixbourne
Bridge
Adisham
Ratling
Chillenden
Knowlton
Ham
Hackling
Finglesham
West Street
Marley
Sholden
The Downs
Deal
Northbourne
Upper Deal
Walmer
Kingsdown
Ringwould
Ripple
Great Mongeham
Betteshanger
Little Mongeham
Sutton
East Studdal
Sutton Downs
Martin
West Langdon
East Langdon
St Margaret's at Cliffe
St Margaret's Bay
SOUTH FORELAND
South Foreland Heritage Coast
Guston
West Cliffe
Whitfield
Temple Ewell
River
Buckland
DOVER
Dunkerque
Calais
Maxton
West Hougham
Farthingloe
Capel-le-Ferne
Satmar
Samphire Hoe
Dover - Folkestone Heritage Coast
East Wear Bay
Channel Tunnel (Rail)
FOLKESTONE
Cheriton
Morehall
Sandgate
Seabrook
Hythe
West Hythe
Saltwood
Pedlinge
Lympne
Newington
Peene
Etchinghill
Postling
Aldington
Sellindge
Stanford
Brabourne
Smeeth
Wye
Dymchurch
St Mary's Bay
St Mary in the Marsh
Burmarsh
Littlestone-on-Sea
New Romney
Greatstone-on-Sea
Lydd
Pilot Inn
DUNGENESS
STRAIT OF DOVER
TR
Folkestone Terminal
400 yards
500 metres
Ashley Wood
Peene
Terminal Building
CHANNEL TUNNEL TERMINAL
Newington
Check-in
ASHFORD ROAD
Police Station
Cheriton
Superstore
ASHFORD, MAIDSTONE, M25 & LONDON
DOVER, FOLKESTONE, CANTERBURY
Departures to France follow
Arrivals from France follow
Calais / Coquelles Terminal
400 yards
500 metres
Coquelles
Ibis Hotel
Etap Hotel
Novotel
Cité de l'Europe
PASSENGER TERMINAL
Petrol Station
Check-in
Frontier Controls
ROCADE LITTORALE
A16 (E402)
BOULOGNE
CALAIS
DUNKERQUE, A26 (PARIS)
HGV Fuel Station
Freight Terminal
Eurotunnel Administration Headquarters
Parc d'activites les Terrasses
Departures to England follow
Arrivals from England follow

Town plan: Canterbury p.117, Port Plan: Dover p.15

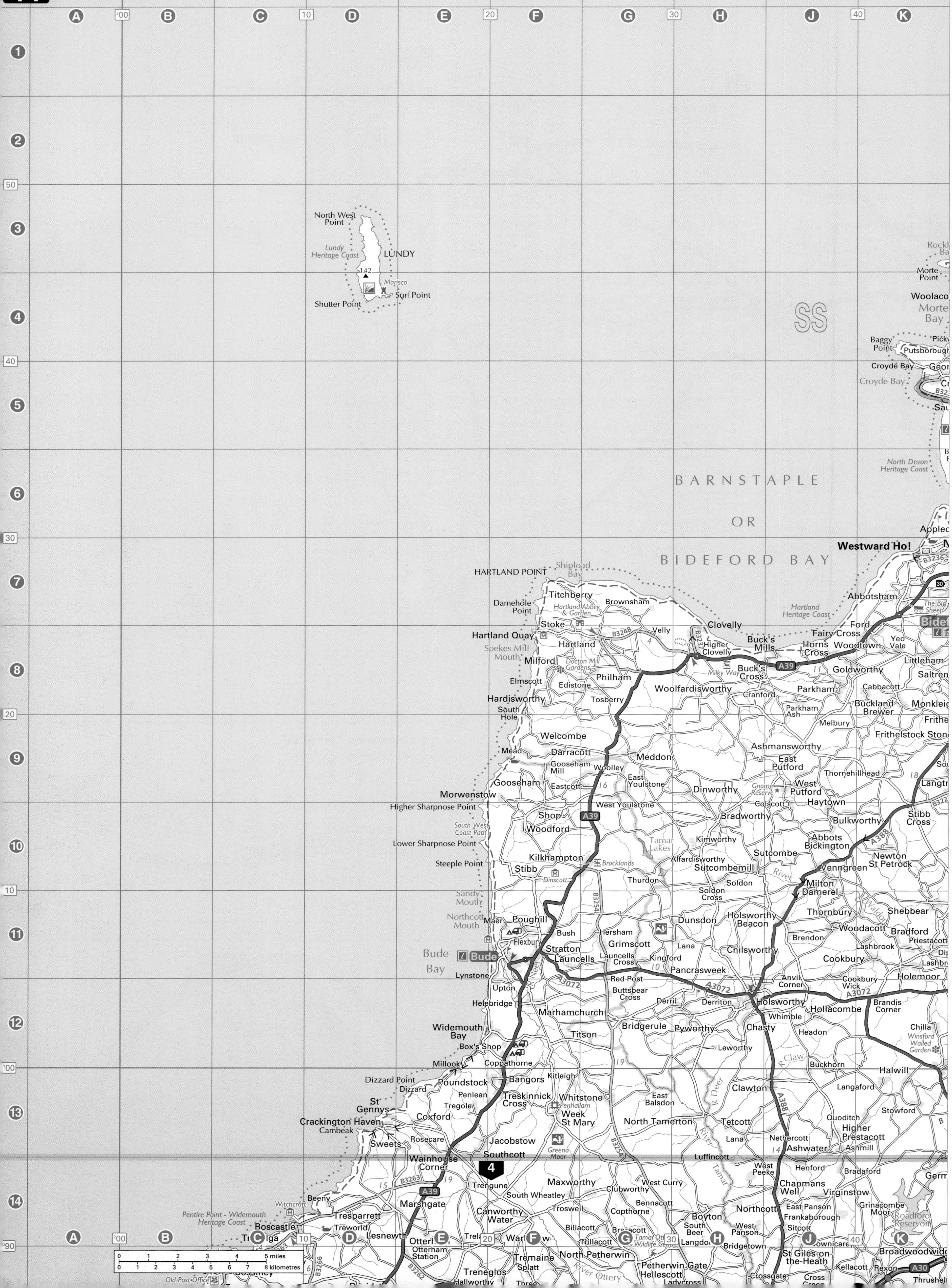
North West Point
Lundy Heritage Coast
LUNDY
142
Marisco
Surf Point
Shutter Point
SS
Rockham Bay
Morte Point
Woolacombe
Morte Bay
Baggy Point
Putsborough
Croyde Bay
North Devon Heritage Coast
BARNSTAPLE
OR
BIDEFORD BAY
Westward Ho!
Appledore
HARTLAND POINT
Shipload Bay
Titchberry
Brownsham
Damehole Point
Hartland Abbey & Garden
Stoke
Hartland Quay
Hartland
Velly
Clovelly
Higher Clovelly
Buck's Mills
Buck's Cross
Hartland Heritage Coast
Abbotsham
The Big Sheep
Fairy Cross
Ford
Horns Cross
Woodtown
Yeo Vale
Spekes Mill Mouth
Milford
Docton Mill Gardens
Philham
Milky Way
Goldworthy
Littleham
Elmscott
Edistone
Woolfardisworthy
Cranford
Parkham
Cabbacott
Saltren
Hardisworthy
Tosberry
Parkham Ash
Buckland Brewer
Monkleigh
South Hole
Melbury
Frithelstock
Frithelstock Stone
Welcombe
Ashmansworthy
Mead
Darracott
Meddon
East Putford
Gooseham Mill
Woolley
Thornehillhead
Gooseham
East Youlstone
Eastcott
Dinworthy
Gnome Reserve
West Putford
Langtree
Morwenstow
Colscott
Haytown
Higher Sharpnose Point
Shop
West Youlstone
Bradworthy
Stibb Cross
South West Coast Path
Woodford
Tamar Lakes
Bulkworthy
Lower Sharpnose Point
Kimworthy
Abbots Bickington
Steeple Point
Kilkhampton
Brocklands
Alfardisworthy
Sutcombe
Newton St Petrock
Stibb
Dinscott
Sutcombemill
Venngreen
Thurdon
Soldon
Milton Damerel
Sandy Mouth
Soldon Cross
Northcott Mouth
Maer
Poughill
Holsworthy Beacon
Thornbury
Shebbear
Dunsdon
Bush
Hersham
Woodacott
Bradford
Flexbury
Grimscott
Brendon
Priestacott
Bude Bay
Bude
Stratton
Launcells
Launcells Cross
Kingford
Lana
Chilsworthy
Lashbrook
Cookbury
Lynstone
Red Post
Pancrasweek
Anvil Corner
Cookbury Wick
Holemoor
Upton
Buttsbear Cross
Derril
Derriton
Holsworthy
Hollacombe
Brandis Corner
Helebridge
Marhamchurch
Whimble
Widemouth Bay
Titson
Bridgerule
Pyworthy
Chasty
Headon
Chilla
Winsford Walled Garden
Box's Shop
Lewworthy
Coppathorne
Millook
Buckhorn
Halwill
Dizzard Point
Bangors
Kitleigh
Dizzard
Poundstock
Penlean
Clawton
Langaford
St Gennys
Treskinnick Cross
Whitstone
Penhallam
East Balsdon
Tregole
Stowford
Crackington Haven
Coxford
Week St Mary
North Tamerton
Tetcott
Quoditch
Higher Prestacott
Cambeak
Sweets
Rosecare
Jacobstow
Greena Moor
Lana
Nethercott
Ashwater
Ashmill
Wainhouse Corner
Southcott
Luffincott
4
Trengune
Maxworthy
West Peeke
Henford
Bradaford
Beeny
Witchcraft
South Wheatley
Clubworthy
West Curry
Chapmans Well
Virginstow
Marshgate
Bennacott
Grinacombe Moor
Pentire Point - Widemouth Heritage Coast
Tresparrett
Canworthy Water
Troswell
Copthorne
Northcott
East Panson
Roadford Reservoir
Boscastle
Treworld
Boyton
Frankaborough
Lesnewth
South Beer
West Panson
Sitcott
Otterham Station
Billacott
Trillacott
Tamar Otter Wildlife Centre
Bridgetown
Broadwoodwidger
Tremaine
North Petherwin
St Giles-on-the-Heath
Splatt
Petherwin Gate
Kellacott
Rexon
Treneglos
Hellescott
Thrushelton
Old Post Office
Hallworthy
River Ottery
Ladycross
Crossgate
River Tamar
R Deer
R Claw
River Waldon
A39
A388
A3072
B3248
B3237
B3254
B3263
B3266
B3262
B3236
A30
0 1 2 3 4 5 miles
0 1 2 3 4 5 6 7 8 kilometres

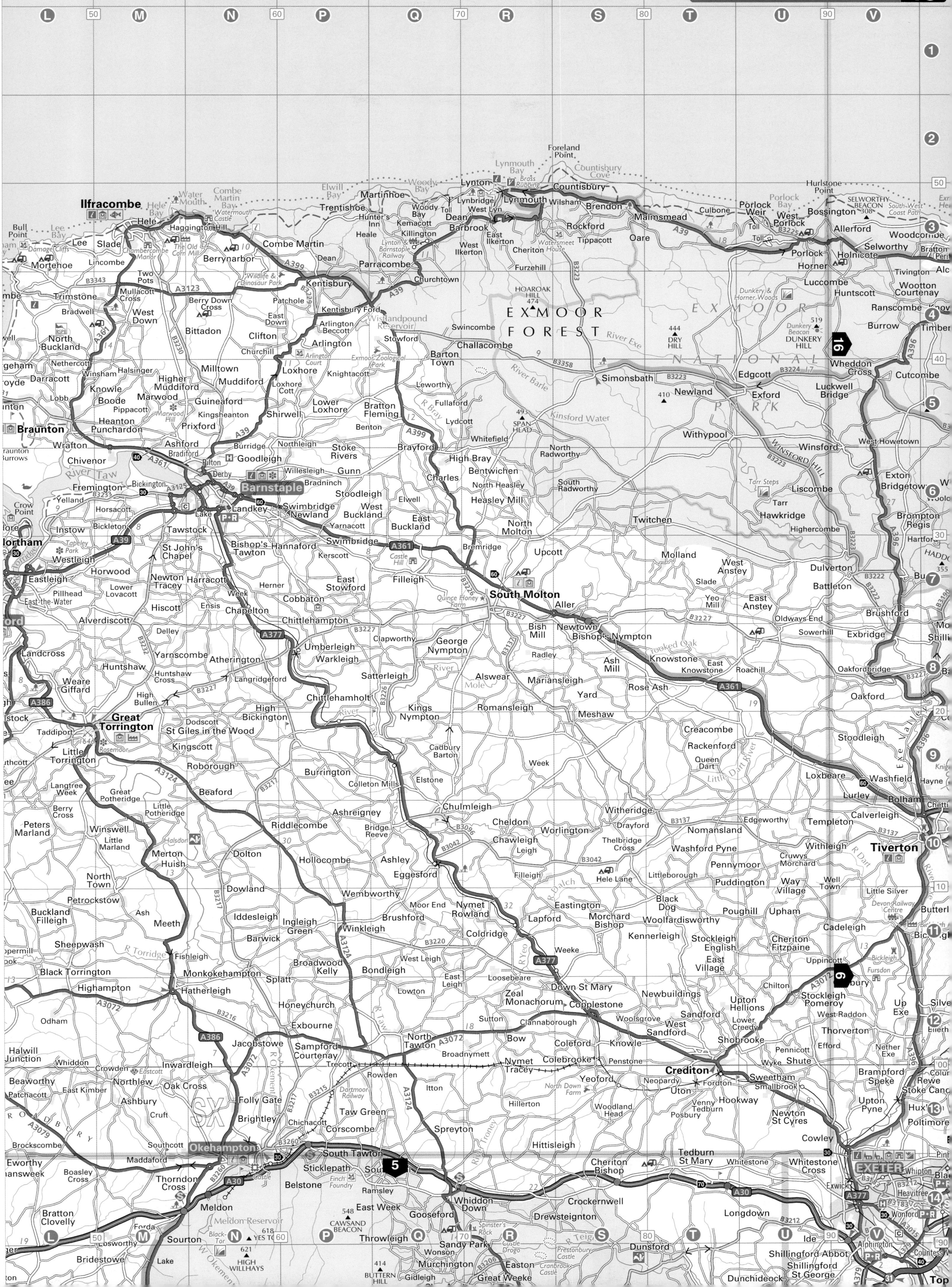
Ilfracombe
Combe Martin
Lynton
Lynmouth
Countisbury
Foreland Point
Porlock
Porlock Weir
Bossington
Allerford
Selworthy
Minehead
EXMOOR FOREST
EXMOOR NATIONAL PARK
Simonsbath
Exford
Withypool
Winsford
Dulverton
Braunton
Barnstaple
South Molton
Great Torrington
Tiverton
Crediton
Okehampton
EXETER
Mortehoe
Woolacombe
Lee
Berrynarbor
Kentisbury
Parracombe
Martinhoe
Trentishoe
Barbrook
Brendon
Malmsmead
Oare
Rockford
Challacombe
Bratton Fleming
Shirwell
Landkey
Swimbridge
Chittlehampton
Umberleigh
Atherington
Kings Nympton
Chulmleigh
Burrington
Eggesford
Winkleigh
Hatherleigh
Sampford Courtenay
North Tawton
Bow
Copplestone
Witheridge
Bishop's Nympton
Molland
Knowstone
Oakford
Bampton
Cadeleigh
Thorverton
Shobrooke
Sandford
Yeoford
Cheriton Bishop
Tedburn St Mary
Whiddon Down
Sticklepath
South Zeal
Belstone
Chagford
Moretonhampstead
Dunsford
Sourton
Meldon Reservoir
Bridestowe
Lydford
Black Torrington
Highampton
Merton
Dolton
Beaford
Roborough
Bideford
Northam
Appledore
Instow
Fremington
Westleigh
Horwood
Alverdiscott
Yarnscombe
Huntshaw
Weare Giffard
Peters Marland
A39
A361
A377
A386
A3072
A3124
A30
A396
B3227
B3223
B3224
B3358

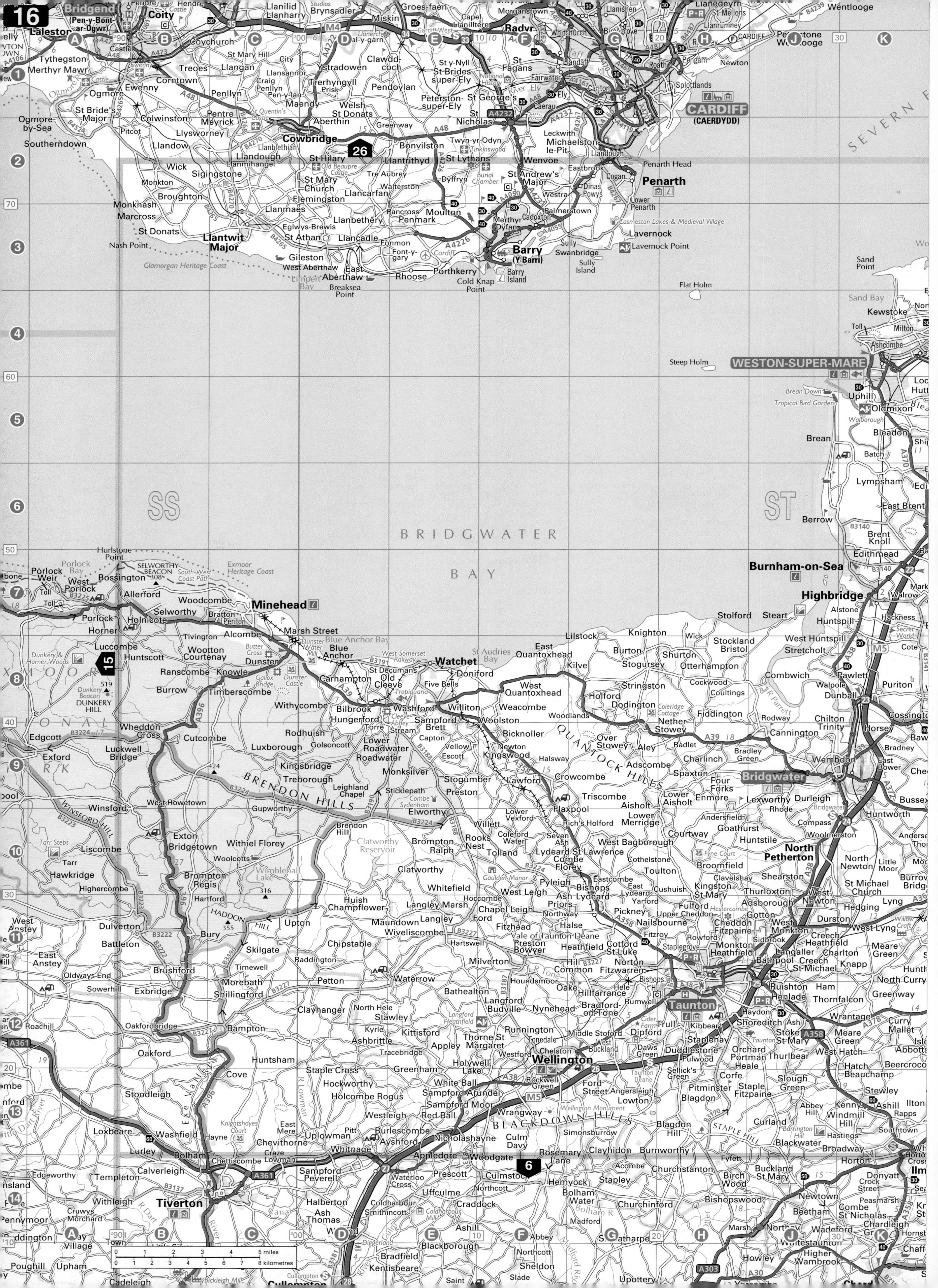
Bridgend (Pen-y-Bont-ar-Ogwr)
Coity
Laleston
Tythegston
Merthyr Mawr
Ogmore
Ewenny
Corntown
Treoes
Llangan
St Mary Hill
Penllyn
Ogmore-by-Sea
St Bride's Major
Colwinston
Southerndown
Pentre Meyrick
Llysworney
Cowbridge
Aberthin
Llanblethian
Llandow
Wick
Sigingstone
Monkton
Broughton
Monknash
Marcross
St Donats
Nash Point
Llantwit Major
Glamorgan Heritage Coast
Gileston
West Aberthaw
East Aberthaw
Limpert Bay
Breaksea Point
Rhoose
Porthkerry
Cold Knap Point
Barry (Y Barri)
Barry Island
Sully
Sully Island
Swanbridge
Lavernock
Lavernock Point
Penarth
Penarth Head
Lower Penarth
Cosmeston Lakes & Medieval Village
CARDIFF (CAERDYDD)
Llandaff
Canton
Roath
Splottlands
Llanrumney
St Mellons
Llanedeyrn
Wentlooge
Peterstone Wentlooge
Whitchurch
Radyr
Morganstown
St Fagans
Fairwater
Ely
Caerau
Culverhouse Cross
Michaelston-le-Pit
Llandough
Dinas Powys
Wenvoe
St Andrew's Major
Dyffryn
St Lythans
Twyn-yr-Odyn
St Nicholas
Bonvilston
Llantrithyd
St Hilary
St Mary Church
Flemingston
Llancarfan
Llanbethery
Penmark
Moulton
Font-y-gary
Fonmon
Llancadle
St Athan
Eglwys-Brewis
Llanmaes
Pendoylan
Peterston-super-Ely
St Brides super-Ely
St y-Nyll
St George's
Welsh St Donats
Ystradowen
Clawdd-coch
Trerhyngyll
Maendy
Miskin
Brynsadler
Llanharry
Groes-faen
Flat Holm
Steep Holm
Sand Point
Sand Bay
Kewstoke
WESTON-SUPER-MARE
Uphill
Oldmixon
Bleadon
Brean Down
Tropical Bird Garden
Brean
Lympsham
Berrow
East Brent
Brent Knoll
Edithmead
Burnham-on-Sea
Highbridge
Huntspill
Stolford
Steart
Pawlett
Puriton
Dunball
Bridgwater
Wembdon
Chilton Trinity
Cannington
Combwich
North Petherton
SS
ST
BRIDGWATER BAY
SEVERN
Hurlstone Point
Porlock Bay
Porlock Weir
Porlock
West Porlock
Bossington
Selworthy Beacon 308
Exmoor Heritage Coast
South West Coast Path
Allerford
Selworthy
Holnicote
Horner
Luccombe
Huntscott
Minehead
Alcombe
Woodcombe
Bratton
Periton
Marsh Street
Dunster
Blue Anchor Bay
Blue Anchor
Carhampton
West Somerset Railway
Watchet
St Audries Bay
Doniford
Williton
Washford
Old Cleeve
Five Bells
East Quantoxhead
West Quantoxhead
Kilve
Lilstock
Stogursey
Knighton
Burton
Shurton
Wick
Stockland Bristol
Otterhampton
Stringston
Holford
Dodington
Nether Stowey
Over Stowey
QUANTOCK HILLS
Crowcombe
Bicknoller
Stogumber
Monksilver
BRENDON HILLS
Dunkery Beacon 519
DUNKERY HILL
EXMOOR
Wheddon Cross
Cutcombe
Timberscombe
Exford
Winsford
Exton
Withiel Florey
Clatworthy Reservoir
Wimbleball Lake
Brompton Regis
Dulverton
Bury
Skilgate
Upton
Wiveliscombe
Milverton
Taunton
Bishops Lydeard
Staplegrove
Norton Fitzwarren
Bathpool
Creech St Michael
Ruishton
Henlade
Durston
North Newton
West Monkton
Wellington
Blackdown Hills
Wellington Monument
Tiverton
Bampton
Oakford
Washfield
Halberton
Sampford Peverell
Uffculme
Culmstock
Hemyock
Bolham
Chevithorne
Cullompton
Kentisbeare
Bradfield
Sheldon
Upottery
Churchinford
Chard
Ilminster
Wambrook
Higher Wambrook
Staple Fitzpaine
Blagdon Hill
Pitminster
Corfe
Orchard Portman
Thurlbear
Stoke St Mary
Hatch Beauchamp
Curry Mallet
Bishopswood
Buckland St Mary
Broadway
Donyatt
Combe St Nicholas
Whitestaunton
Howley
M4
M5
A48
A38
A39
A361
A396
A358
A303
A30
0 1 2 3 4 5 miles
0 1 2 3 4 5 6 7 8 kilometres

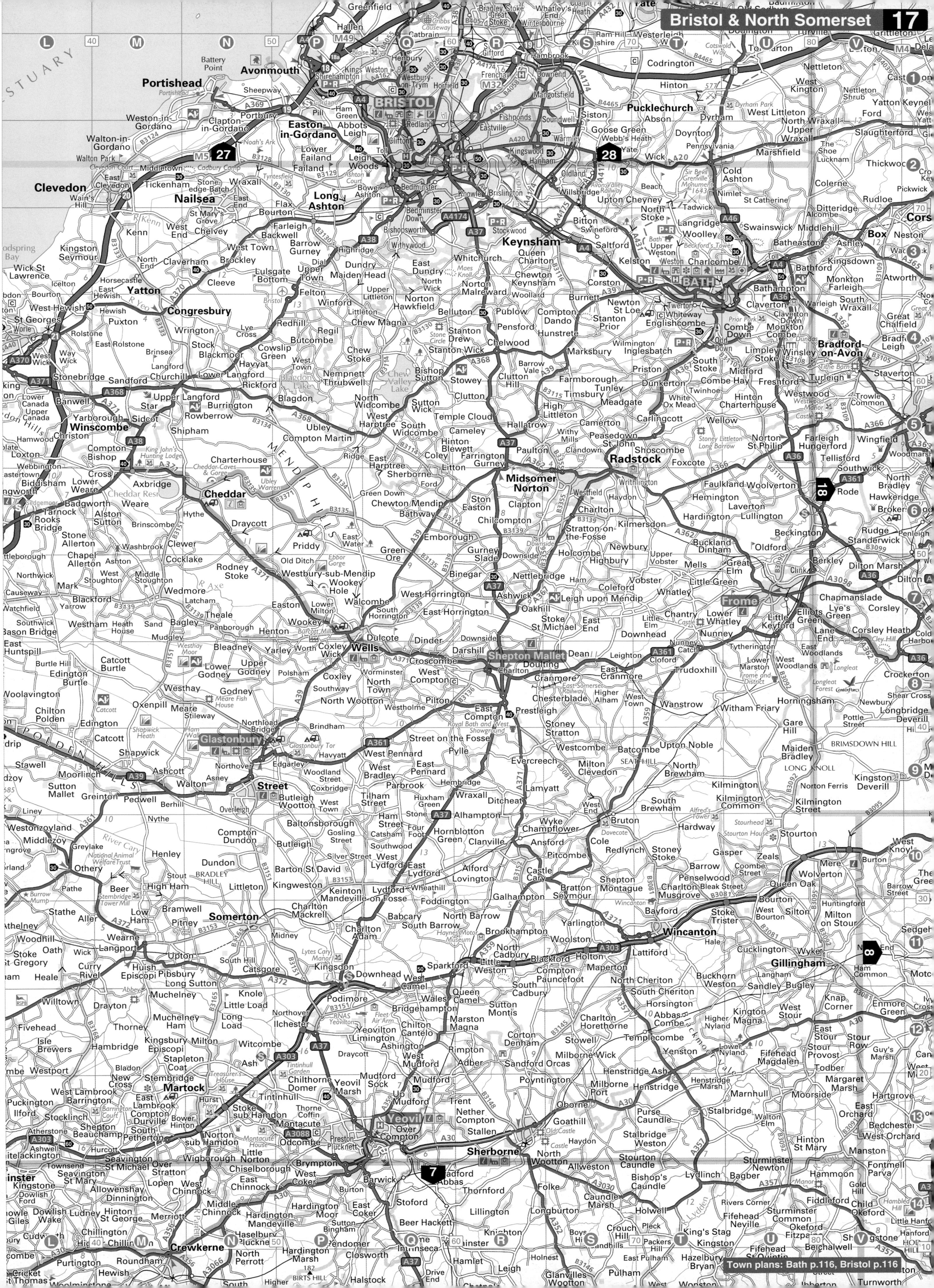
Portishead
Avonmouth
Clevedon
Nailsea
Long Ashton
BRISTOL
Keynsham
BATH
Pucklechurch
Yatton
Congresbury
Winscombe
Cheddar
MENDIP HILLS
Radstock
Midsomer Norton
Bradford-on-Avon
Frome
Wells
Shepton Mallet
Glastonbury
Street
POLDEN HILLS
Somerton
Wincanton
Gillingham
Martock
Yeovil
Sherborne
Crewkerne
Ilchester
Castle Cary
Bruton
Langport
M5
M4
M32
M49
A4
A37
A38
A39
A303
A361
A371
27
28
18
7
8

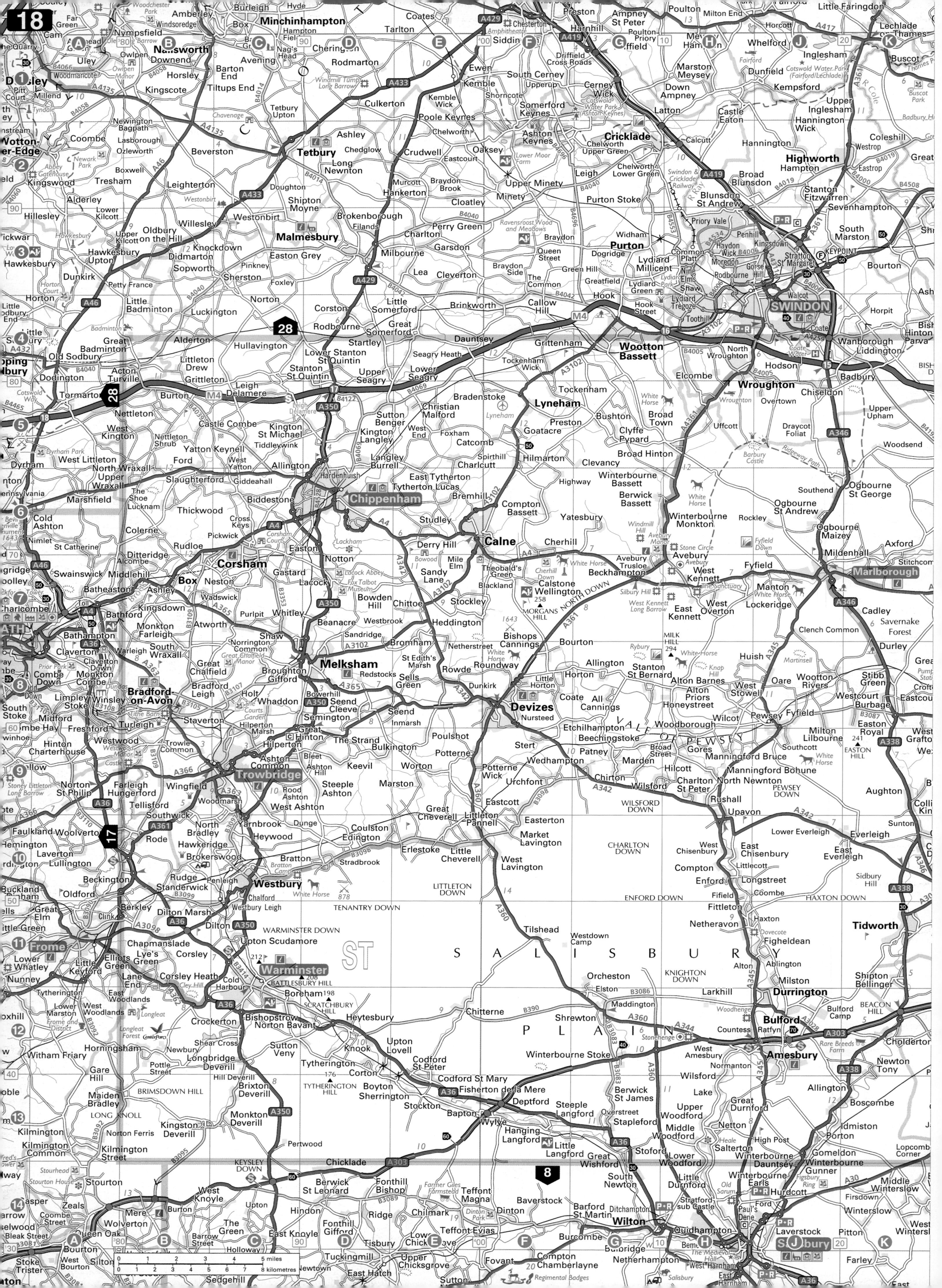
Amberley
Burleigh
Minchinhampton
Coates
Chesterton
Preston
Ampney St Peter
Poulton
Little Faringdon
Lechlade on-Thames
Nympsfield
Nailsworth
Avening
Cherington
Rodmarton
Tarlton
Siddington
Harnhill
Driffield
Fairford
Whelford
Inglesham
Buscot
Uley
Owlpen
Horsley
Barton End
Tiltups End
Kingscote
Kemble
Ewen
South Cerney
Cerney Wick
Marston Meysey
Down Ampney
Dunfield
Kempsford
Dursley
Culkerton
Kemble Wick
Poole Keynes
Somerford Keynes
Latton
Castle Eaton
Upper Inglesham
Hannington Wick
Wotton-under-Edge
Coombe
Beverston
Tetbury
Ashley
Crudwell
Oaksey
Ashton Keynes
Cricklade
Hannington
Coleshill
Highworth
Kingswood
Tresham
Leighterton
Long Newnton
Hankerton
Eastcourt
Upper Minety
Minety
Leigh
Purton Stoke
Blunsdon St Andrew
Broad Blunsdon
Stanton Fitzwarren
Sevenhampton
Alderley
Hillesley
Westonbirt
Shipton Moyne
Brokenborough
Cloatley
Charlton
Braydon
Purton
Widham
Hawkesbury Upton
Malmesbury
Perry Green
Garsdon
Milbourne
Lea
Cleverton
Lydiard Millicent
Haydon Wick
Penhill
Stratton St Margaret
South Marston
Bourton
Didmarton
Sopworth
Sherston
Easton Grey
Knockdown
Dunkirk
Horton
Little Badminton
Luckington
Norton
Corston
Rodbourne
Little Somerford
Great Somerford
Brinkworth
Callow Hill
Hook
Lydiard Tregoze
Toothill
SWINDON
Walcot
Horpit
Bishopstone
Badminton
Great Badminton
Old Sodbury
Chipping Sodbury
Alderton
Hullavington
Startley
Dauntsey
Grittenham
Wootton Bassett
Wroughton
Wanborough
Liddington
Dodington
Acton Turville
Littleton Drew
Grittleton
Stanton St Quintin
Lower Stanton St Quintin
Upper Seagry
Lower Seagry
Tockenham
Lyneham
Elcombe
Chiseldon
Badbury
Tormarton
Burton
Leigh Delamere
Sutton Benger
Christian Malford
Bradenstoke
Preston
Bushton
Broad Town
Nettleton
West Kingston
Castle Combe
Kington St Michael
Kington Langley
Foxham
Goatacre
Clyffe Pypard
Uffcott
Upper Upham
Dyrham
West Littleton
Yatton Keynell
Ford
Langley Burrell
Charlcutt
Hilmarton
Clevancy
Broad Hinton
Woodsend
Marshfield
Slaughterford
Allington
Chippenham
Tytherton Lucas
East Tytherton
Bremhill
Highway
Winterbourne Bassett
Berwick Bassett
Ogbourne St George
Ogbourne St Andrew
Cold Ashton
Biddestone
Thickwood
Studley
Compton Bassett
Yatesbury
Winterbourne Monkton
Rockley
Ogbourne Maizey
Colerne
Rudloe
Corsham
Derry Hill
Calne
Cherhill
Avebury
Mildenhall
Axford
Marlborough
Fyfield
Batheaston
Box
Neston
Gastard
Lacock
Sandy Lane
Calstone Wellington
Beckhampton
West Kennett
East Kennett
West Overton
Lockeridge
Manton
Bath
Bathford
Bathampton
Kingsdown
Atworth
Bowden Hill
Chittoe
Stockley
Heddington
Cadley
Savernake Forest
Monkton Farleigh
South Wraxall
Shaw
Whitley
Beanacre
Bromham
Bishops Cannings
Bourton
Clench Common
Durley
Claverton
Combe Down
Monkton Combe
Great Chalfield
Melksham
Rowde
Roundway
Allington
Stanton St Bernard
Alton Barnes
Huish
Oare
Wootton Rivers
Bradford-on-Avon
Winsley
Bradford Leigh
Holt
Whaddon
Seend
Sells Green
Devizes
Horton
Coate
All Cannings
Alton Priors
Honeystreet
Pewsey
Stibb Green
Burbage
Westcourt
Midford
Freshford
Turleigh
Staverton
Hilperton
Semington
Inmarsh
Nursteed
Etchilhampton
Woodborough
Wilcot
Easton Royal
Hinton Charterhouse
Westwood
Trowle Common
Great Hinton
The Strand
Bulkington
Poulshot
Potterne
Beechingstoke
Stert
Patney
Marden
Gores
Manningford Bruce
Milton Lilbourne
Norton St Philip
Farleigh Hungerford
Wingfield
Trowbridge
Keevil
Worton
Potterne Wick
Wedhampton
Chirton
Manningford Bohune
Hilcott
North Newnton
Charlton St Peter
Tellisford
Southwick
Steeple Ashton
Marston
Urchfont
Wilsford
Rushall
Upavon
Aughton
Faulkland
Woolverton
Rode
North Bradley
Yarnbrook
Heywood
Dunge
Coulston
Edington
Great Cheverell
Littleton Pannell
Eastcott
Easterton
Market Lavington
Lower Everleigh
Everleigh
East Everleigh
East Chisenbury
West Chisenbury
Laverton
Lullington
Beckington
Hawkeridge
Brokerswood
Standerwick
Westbury
Bratton
Erlestoke
Little Cheverell
West Lavington
Compton
Enford
Longstreet
Coombe
Oldford
Berkley
Dilton Marsh
Westbury Leigh
Chalford
Fittleton
Haxton
Netheravon
Tidworth
Frome
Chapmanslade
Corsley
Dilton
Upton Scudamore
Warminster
Tilshead
Westdown Camp
Figheldean
Lower Whatley
Nunney
Keyford
Lye's Green
Corsley Heath
Cold Harbour
Boreham
SALISBURY PLAIN
Orcheston
Elston
Ablington
Milston
Durrington
Shipton Bellinger
Tytherington
West Woodlands
Crockerton
Bishopstrow
Norton Bavant
Heytesbury
Chitterne
Shrewton
Maddington
Larkhill
Bulford
Bulford Camp
Witham Friary
Horningsham
Longbridge Deverill
Sutton Veny
Knook
Upton Lovell
Tytherington
Codford St Peter
Codford St Mary
Winterbourne Stoke
Stonehenge
Amesbury
Countess
West Amesbury
Cholderton
Newton Tony
Gare Hill
Maiden Bradley
Brixton Deverill
Boyton
Sherrington
Fisherton de la Mere
Stockton
Bapton
Deptford
Wylye
Steeple Langford
Berwick St James
Wilsford
Lake
Great Durnford
Allington
Boscombe
Kilmington
Kingston Deverill
Monkton Deverill
Pertwood
Hanging Langford
Little Langford
Great Wishford
Stapleford
Middle Woodford
Netton
High Post
Idmiston
Porton
Gomeldon
Stourton
Zeals
Mere
West Knoyle
Chicklade
Berwick St Leonard
Fonthill Bishop
Teffont Magna
Dinton
Baverstock
South Newton
Stoford
Lower Woodford
Little Durnford
Salterton
Winterbourne Dauntsey
Winterbourne Gunner
Winterbourne Earls
Hurdcott
Middle Winterslow
Winterslow
Wolverton
Queen Oak
Bourton
Burton
Hindon
Ridge
Chilmark
Teffont Evias
Barford St Martin
Wilton
Ditchampton
Quidhampton
Stratford sub Castle
Laverstock
Pitton
Silton
Stoke Trister
Sedgehill
East Knoyle
Fonthill Gifford
Tisbury
Tuckingmill
Upper Chicksgrove
East Hatch
Fovant
Compton Chamberlayne
Burcombe
Bulbridge
Netherhampton
West Harnham
Salisbury
Farley
Sutton
Longleat
Center Parcs
Savernake Forest
Vale of Pewsey
0 1 2 3 4 5 miles
0 1 2 3 4 5 6 7 8 kilometres

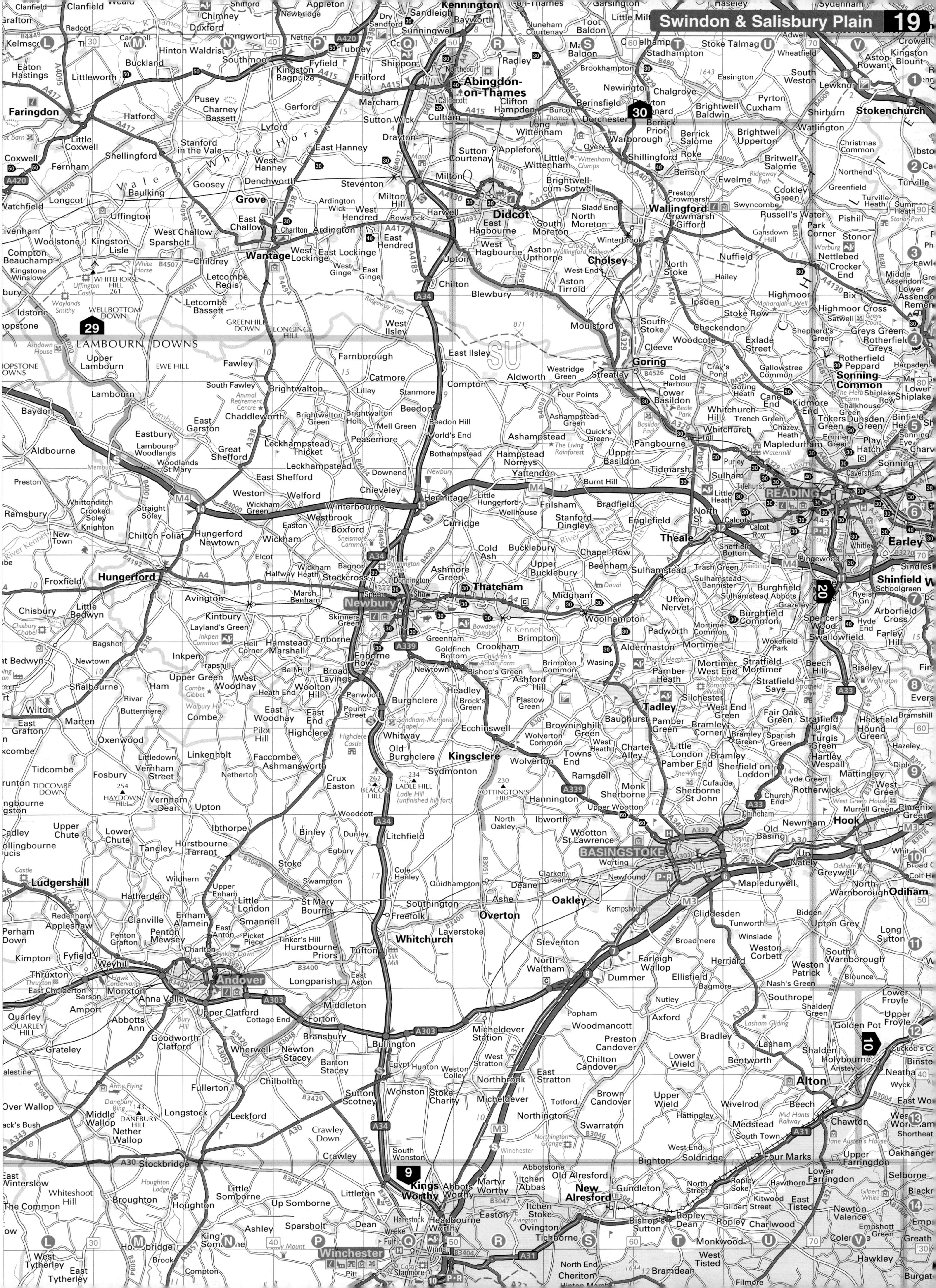
Faringdon
Abingdon-on-Thames
Wantage
Grove
Didcot
Wallingford
Cholsey
Goring
Streatley
Sonning Common
Reading
Earley
Theale
Hungerford
Newbury
Thatcham
Kingsclere
Tadley
Basingstoke
Oakley
Overton
Whitchurch
Ludgershall
Andover
Stockbridge
Kings Worthy
Winchester
New Alresford
Alton
Odiham
Hook
Lambourn Downs
Lambourn
Vale of White Horse
Ridgeway Path
Woodcote
Shinfield
Wokingham
Burghclere
Highclere
Hurstbourne Tarrant
Sutton Scotney
Micheldever
Bullington
Chilton Foliat
Ramsbury
Aldbourne
Baydon
Mapledurwell
Chawton
Four Marks

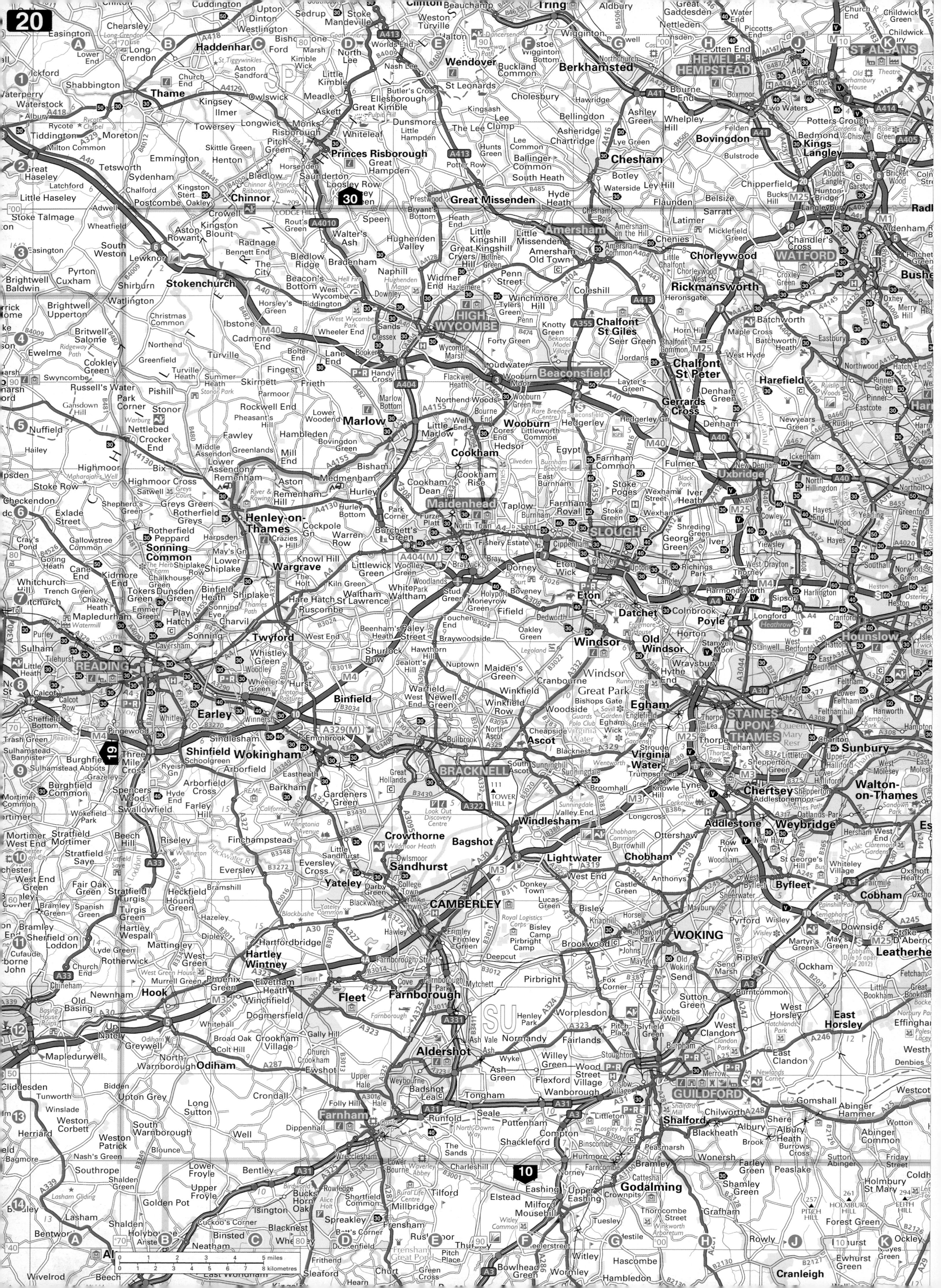
Haddenham
Thame
Wendover
Berkhamsted
Tring
HEMEL HEMPSTEAD
ST ALBANS
Princes Risborough
Chinnor
Great Missenden
Chesham
Kings Langley
Amersham
WATFORD
Chorleywood
Rickmansworth
Stokenchurch
HIGH WYCOMBE
Chalfont St Giles
Chalfont St Peter
Beaconsfield
Gerrards Cross
Harefield
Marlow
Wooburn
Cookham
Uxbridge
Henley-on-Thames
Maidenhead
SLOUGH
Wargrave
Eton
Datchet
Windsor
Old Windsor
Hounslow
Twyford
READING
Earley
Binfield
Egham
STAINES-UPON-THAMES
Sunbury
Shinfield
Wokingham
Ascot
Virginia Water
BRACKNELL
Chertsey
Walton-on-Thames
Windlesham
Addlestone
Weybridge
Crowthorne
Bagshot
Sandhurst
Lightwater
Chobham
Yateley
CAMBERLEY
Byfleet
Cobham
WOKING
Hartley Wintney
Hook
Fleet
Farnborough
Aldershot
Odiham
East Horsley
GUILDFORD
Farnham
Shalford
Godalming
Cranleigh
5 miles
8 kilometres

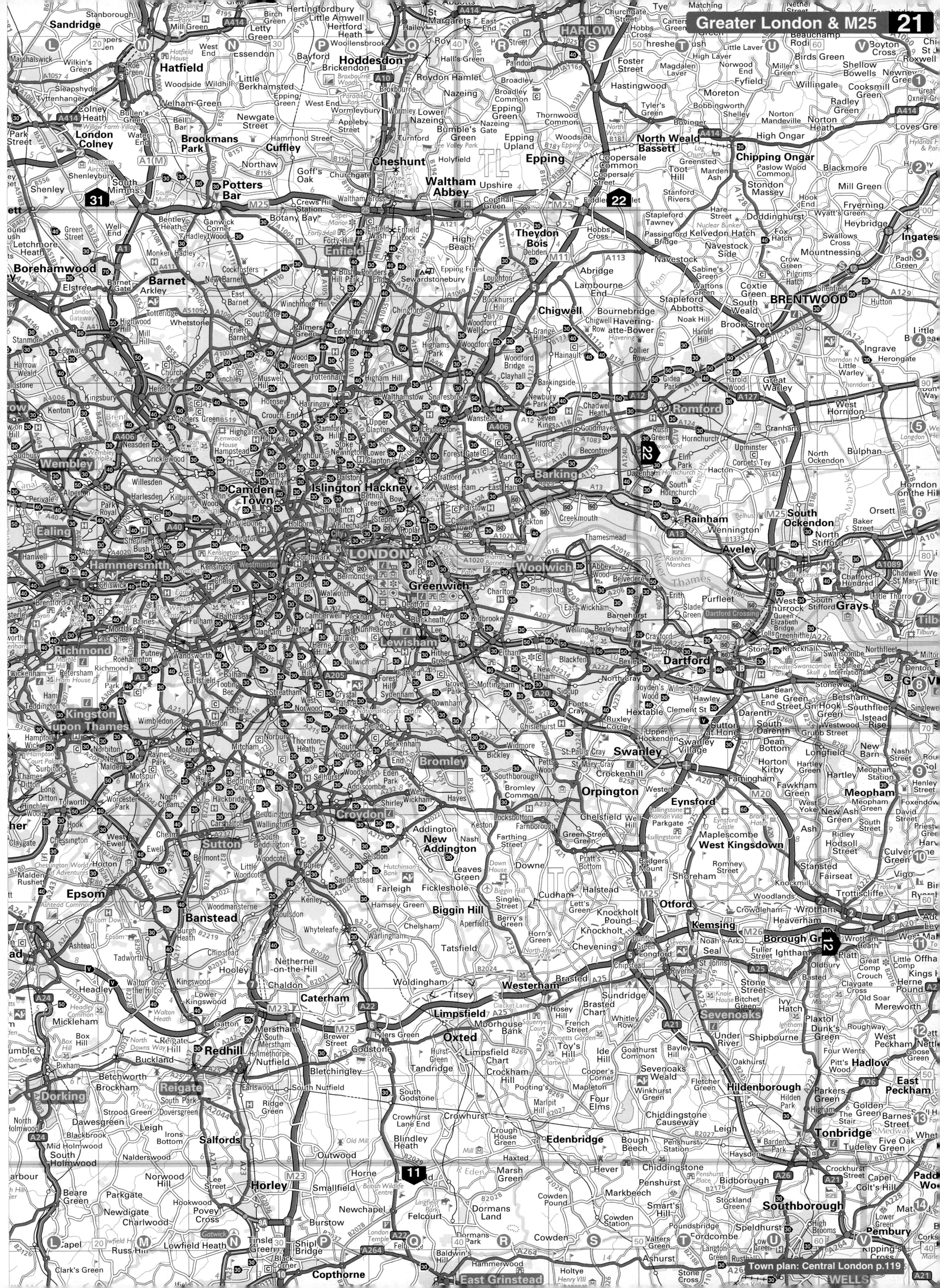
Sandridge
Hatfield
London Colney
Brookmans Park
Cuffley
Potters Bar
Hoddesdon
Cheshunt
Waltham Abbey
HARLOW
Epping
North Weald Bassett
Chipping Ongar
Borehamwood
Barnet
Enfield
Theydon Bois
Chigwell
BRENTWOOD
Romford
Wembley
Camden Town
Islington
Hackney
Barking
Rainham
South Ockendon
Ealing
Hammersmith
LONDON
Greenwich
Woolwich
Aveley
Grays
Richmond
Lewisham
Dartford
Kingston upon Thames
Bromley
Swanley
Epsom
Croydon
Sutton
Orpington
Eynsford
West Kingsdown
Meopham
Banstead
Biggin Hill
Otford
Kemsing
Borough Green
Caterham
Westerham
Redhill
Oxted
Sevenoaks
Hadlow
East Peckham
Dorking
Reigate
Hildenborough
Tonbridge
Salfords
Edenbridge
Horley
Southborough
Copthorne
East Grinstead
M25
M11
M26
M23
M20

Town plan: Central London p.119

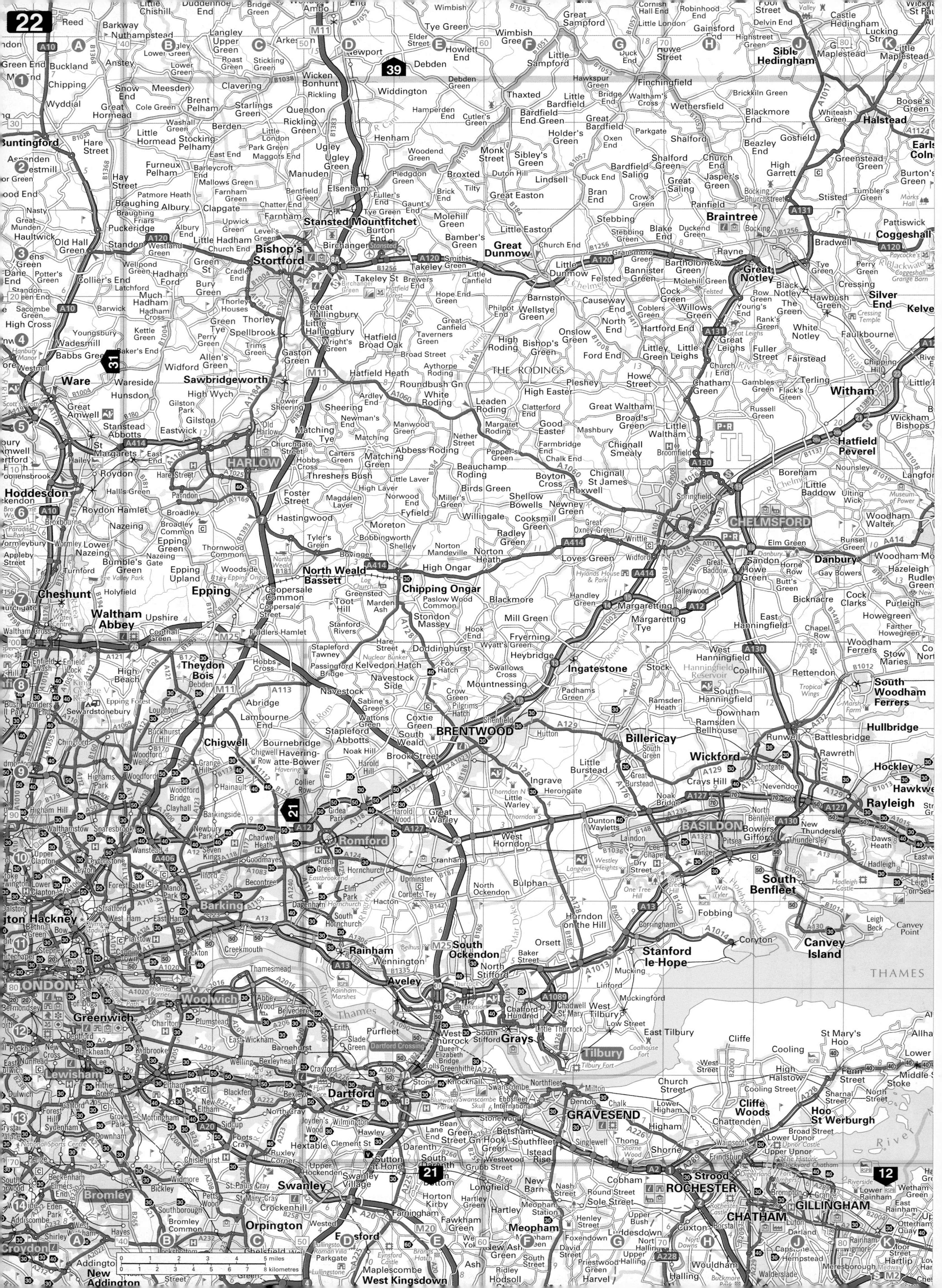
Reed
Barkway
Buntingford
Ware
Hoddesdon
Cheshunt
Waltham Abbey
Epping
Harlow
Sawbridgeworth
Bishop's Stortford
Stansted Mountfitchet
Newport
Thaxted
Great Dunmow
Finchingfield
Great Sampford
Sible Hedingham
Halstead
Braintree
Coggeshall
Witham
Great Notley
Hatfield Peverel
Chelmsford
Chipping Ongar
North Weald Bassett
Theydon Bois
Chigwell
Loughton
Brentwood
Ingatestone
Billericay
Wickford
Basildon
Rayleigh
Hockley
South Woodham Ferrers
Danbury
South Benfleet
Canvey Island
Stanford le Hope
Grays
Tilbury
Romford
Barking
Woolwich
Greenwich
Lewisham
Hackney
LONDON
Bromley
Croydon
Orpington
Swanley
Dartford
Gravesend
Rochester
Strood
Chatham
Gillingham
Hoo St Werburgh
Cliffe Woods
South Ockendon
Aveley
Rainham
THE RODINGS
THAMES
Thames
Dartford Crossing
TL
M11
M25
M20
M2
A12
A13
A120
A127
A130
A414
5 miles
8 kilometres
39
31
21
12

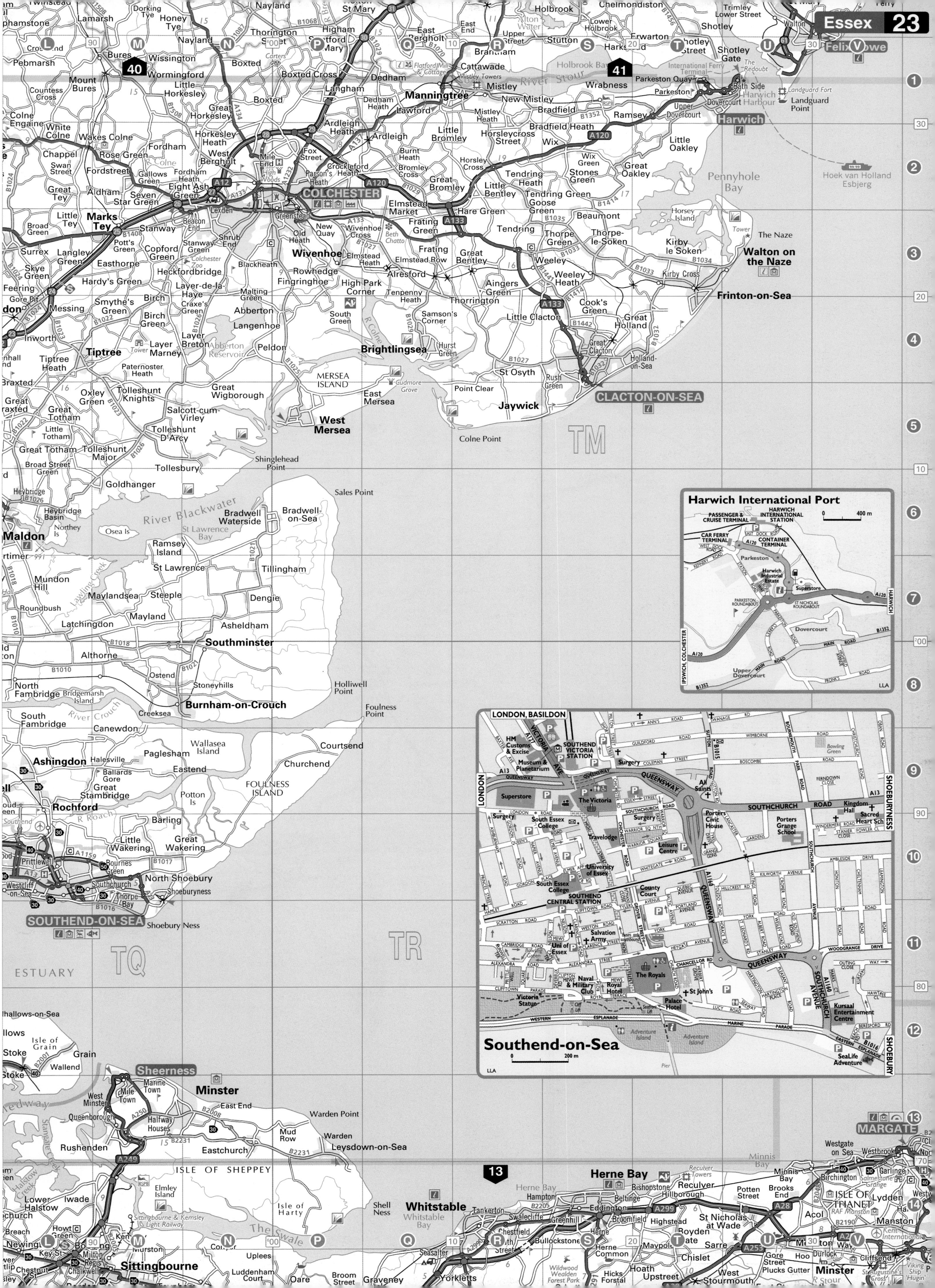
Nayland
Higham
Stratford St Mary
East Bergholt
Holbrook
Chelmondiston
Trimley Lower Street
Shotley
Shotley Gate
Felixstowe
Lamarsh
Dorking Tye
Honey Tye
Bures
Wissington
Wormingford
Boxted
Boxted Cross
Dedham
Langham
Brantham
Cattawade
Mistley
Manningtree
Lawford
Holbrook Bay
River Stour
Wrabness
Parkeston Quay
Parkeston
Harwich
Dovercourt
Upper Dovercourt
Landguard Point
Landguard Fort
Bath Side
The Redoubt
International Ferry Terminal
Pebmarsh
Mount Bures
Countess Cross
Colne Engaine
White Colne
Wakes Colne
Chappel
Swan Street
Fordstreet
Great Tey
Aldham
Little Horkesley
Great Horkesley
West Bergholt
Fordham
Fordham Heath
Eight Ash Green
Mile End
Ardleigh
Ardleigh Heath
Fox Street
Crockleford Heath
Parson's Heath
Dedham Heath
Little Bromley
Great Bromley
Horsleycross Street
Horsley Cross
Bradfield
Bradfield Heath
Wix
New Mistley
Mistley Heath
Ramsey
Little Oakley
Great Oakley
Wix Green
Stones Green
Tendring Heath
Little Bentley
Tendring Green
Goose Green
Hare Green
Tendring
Beaumont
Horsey Island
Pennyhole Bay
Hoek van Holland
Esbjerg
The Naze
Walton on the Naze
Kirby le Soken
Kirby Cross
Thorpe-le-Soken
Thorpe Green
Frinton-on-Sea
Marks Tey
Little Tey
Broad Green
Copford
Copford Green
Stanway
Stanway Green
Lexden
COLCHESTER
Greenstead
Old Heath
Wivenhoe
Wivenhoe Cross
New Quay
Elmstead Market
Frating Green
Frating
Elmstead Heath
Elmstead Row
Great Bentley
Alresford
Aingers Green
Weeley
Weeley Heath
Thorrington
Little Clacton
Cook's Green
Great Holland
Great Clacton
Holland-on-Sea
CLACTON-ON-SEA
Jaywick
Point Clear
St Osyth
Rush Green
Colne Point
Brightlingsea
Hurst Green
Samson's Corner
Tenpenny Heath
High Park Corner
Rowhedge
Fingringhoe
South Green
Langenhoe
Abberton
Abberton Reservoir
Peldon
Layer Breton
Layer Marney
Layer-de-la-Haye
Malting Green
Blackheath
Heckfordbridge
Birch
Birch Green
Easthorpe
Hardy's Green
Smythe's Green
Messing
Tiptree
Tiptree Heath
Inworth
Paternoster Heath
Tolleshunt Knights
Oxley Green
Great Wigborough
MERSEA ISLAND
East Mersea
West Mersea
Salcott-cum-Virley
Tolleshunt D'Arcy
Tolleshunt Major
Great Totham
Little Totham
Broad Street Green
Tollesbury
Goldhanger
Heybridge
Heybridge Basin
Maldon
Northey Is
Osea Is
River Blackwater
Shinglehead Point
Sales Point
Bradwell Waterside
Bradwell-on-Sea
St Lawrence Bay
Ramsey Island
St Lawrence
Tillingham
Mundon Hill
Maylandsea
Steeple
Dengie
Mayland
Latchingdon
Asheldham
Roundbush
Southminster
Althorne
Ostend
Stoneyhills
North Fambridge
Bridgemarsh Island
Burnham-on-Crouch
Creeksea
Holliwell Point
Foulness Point
River Crouch
South Fambridge
Canewdon
Wallasea Island
Courtsend
Churchend
Ashingdon
Paglesham
Eastwood
FOULNESS ISLAND
Rochford
Great Stambridge
Ballards Gore
Potton Is
Barling
Little Wakering
Great Wakering
North Shoebury
Shoeburyness
Shoebury Ness
SOUTHEND-ON-SEA
Westcliff-on-Sea
Prittlewell
Southchurch
Thorpe Bay
ESTUARY
TQ
TR
TM
Isle of Grain
Grain
Stoke
Wallend
Sheerness
Minster
Marine Town
Mile Town
West Minster
Queenborough
Halfway Houses
East End
Eastchurch
Rushenden
Warden Point
Warden
Mud Row
Leysdown-on-Sea
ISLE OF SHEPPEY
Elmley Island
Isle of Harty
The Swale
Shell Ness
Lower Halstow
Iwade
Sittingbourne
Milton Regis
Murston
Uplees
Luddenham Court
Oare
Broom Street
Graveney
Whitstable
Whitstable Bay
Seasalter
Yorkletts
Tankerton
Swalecliffe
Chestfield
Greenhill
Eddington
Herne Bay
Herne
Hampton
Beltinge
Bishopstone
Reculver
Reculver Towers
Hillborough
Broomfield
Herne Common
Bullockstone
Hicks Forstal
Hoath
Upstreet
Maypole
Highstead
Boyden Gate
Chislet
St Nicholas at Wade
Sarre
West Stourmouth
Potten Street
Brooks End
Minnis Bay
Birchington
ISLE OF THANET
Acol
Monkton
Minster
Manston
Westgate on Sea
Westbrook
Garlinge
Margate
MARGATE
Lydden
Cliffsend
Gore Street
Plucks Gutter
Hoo
Durlock
Minnis Bay
Harwich International Port
PASSENGER & CRUISE TERMINAL
HARWICH INTERNATIONAL STATION
CAR FERRY TERMINAL
CONTAINER TERMINAL
Parkeston
Harwich Industrial Estate
Superstore
PARKESTON ROUNDABOUT
ST NICHOLAS ROUNDABOUT
Dovercourt
Upper Dovercourt
MAIN ROAD
IPSWICH, COLCHESTER
HARWICH
0
400 m
LLA
Southend-on-Sea
LONDON, BASILDON
HM Customs & Excise
Museum & Planetarium
SOUTHEND VICTORIA STATION
VICTORIA AVE
QUEENSWAY
Superstore
The Victoria
Surgery
South Essex College
Travelodge
Leisure Centre
University of Essex
SOUTHEND CENTRAL STATION
County Court
Salvation Army
Uni of Essex
The Royals
Naval & Military Club
Royal Hotel
Palace Hotel
St John's
Victoria Statue
WESTERN ESPLANADE
MARINE PARADE
Adventure Island
Pier
All Saints
Porters Civic House
Porters Grange School
SOUTHCHURCH ROAD
Kingdom Hall
Sacred Heart Sch
Bowling Green
Kursaal Entertainment Centre
SeaLife Adventure
SOUTHCHURCH AVENUE
SHOEBURYNESS
SHOEBURY
LONDON
0
200 m
LLA

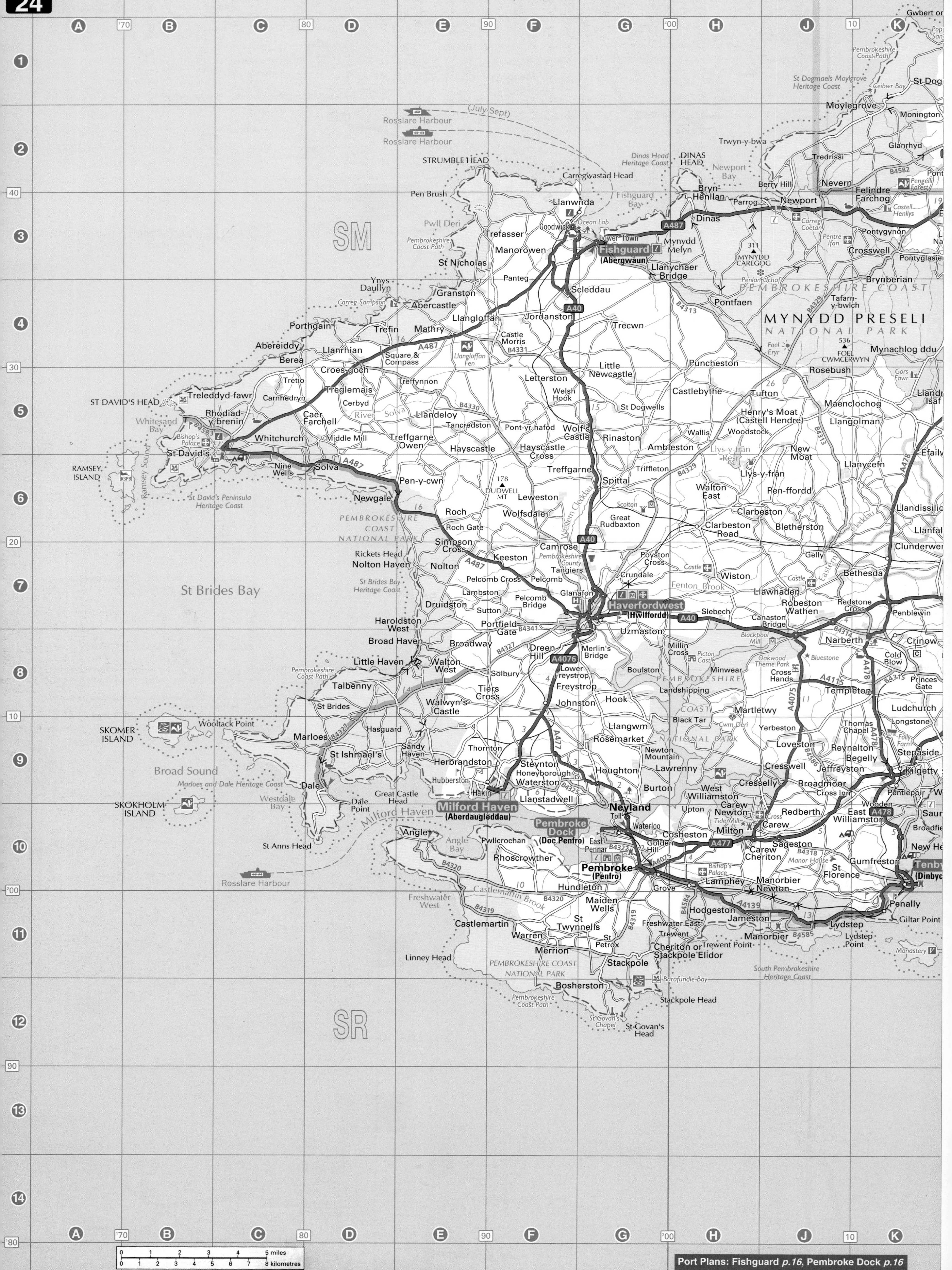
SM
SR
St Brides Bay
Broad Sound
Milford Haven
RAMSEY ISLAND
SKOMER ISLAND
SKOKHOLM ISLAND
Rosslare Harbour
(July Sept)
STRUMBLE HEAD
Pen Brush
Pwll Deri
Carregwastad Head
Llanwnda
Goodwick
Fishguard Bay
Fishguard
(Abergwaun)
Lower Town
Dinas Head Heritage Coast
DINAS HEAD
Newport Bay
Bryn-Henllan
Dinas
Newport
Berry Hill
Nevern
Felindre Farchog
Trwyn-y-bwa
Tredrissi
Glanrhyd
Moylegrove
Monington
St Dogmaels Moylgrove Heritage Coast
Pembrokeshire Coast Path
Ceibwr Bay
Gwbert on Sea
Mynydd Melyn
Llanychaer Bridge
MYNYDD CAREGOG
Pontfaen
Crosswell
Pontygynon
Brynberian
Tafarn-y-bwlch
PEMBROKESHIRE COAST
MYNYDD PRESELI
NATIONAL PARK
FOEL CWMCERWYN
Mynachlog ddu
Rosebush
Trefasser
Manorowen
St Nicholas
Panteg
Scleddau
Ynys Daullyn
Granston
Abercastle
Carreg Sampson
Llangloffan
Jordanston
Trecwn
Porthgain
Trefin
Mathry
Castle Morris
Abereiddy
Berea
Llanrhian
Square & Compass
Croes-goch
Treffynnon
Letterston
Little Newcastle
Puncheston
ST DAVID'S HEAD
Treleddyd-fawr
Tretio
Carnhedryn
Treglemais
Cerbyd
Welsh Hook
Castlebythe
Tufton
Maenclochog
Whitesand Bay
Rhodiad-y-brenin
Caer Farchell
Llandeloy
Tancredston
St Dogwells
Henry's Moat (Castell Hendre)
Llangolman
Bishop's Palace
Whitchurch
Middle Mill
Treffgarne Owen
Hayscastle
Pont-yr-hafod
Wolf's Castle
Rinaston
Woodstock
Wallis
Ambleston
Llys-y-frân
New Moat
St David's
Ramsey Sound
Nine Wells
Solva
Pen-y-cwn
Hayscastle Cross
Treffgarne
Spittal
Triffleton
Llanycefn
St David's Peninsula Heritage Coast
Newgale
DUDWELL MT
Leweston
Walton East
Pen-ffordd
Roch
Wolfsdale
Clarbeston
Roch Gate
Great Rudbaxton
Clarbeston Road
Bletherston
Simpson Cross
Camrose
Poyston Cross
Gelly
Rickets Head
Nolton Haven
Nolton
Keeston
Tangiers
Crundale
Wiston
Bethesda
St Brides Bay Heritage Coast
Pelcomb Cross
Pelcomb
Fenton Brook
Llawhaden
Robeston Wathen
Lambston
Glanafon
Haverfordwest
(Hwlffordd)
Druidston
Pelcomb Bridge
Sutton
Slebech
Canaston Bridge
Redstone Cross
Penblewin
Haroldston West
Portfield Gate
Uzmaston
Narberth
Crinow
Broad Haven
Broadway
Dreen Hill
Merlin's Bridge
Millin Cross
Blackpool Mill
Little Haven
Walton West
Lower Freystrop
Boulston
Picton Castle
Minwear
Oakwood Theme Park
Bluestone
Cold Blow
Solbury
Freystrop
Cross Hands
Princes Gate
Talbenny
Tiers Cross
Landshipping
Templeton
St Brides
Walwyn's Castle
Johnston
Hook
Martletwy
Ludchurch
Wooltack Point
Black Tar
Cwm Deri
Yerbeston
Thomas Chapel
Longstone
Marloes
Hasguard
Llangwm
Rosemarket
Loveston
St Ishmael's
Sandy Haven
Thornton
Newton Mountain
Reynalton
Stepaside
Begelly
Herbrandston
Steynton
Honeyborough
Houghton
Lawrenny
Cresswell
Jeffreyston
Kilgetty
Marloes and Dale Heritage Coast
Hubberston
Waterston
Cresselly
Broadmoor
Dale
Westdale Bay
Great Castle Head
Hakin
Llanstadwell
Burton
West Williamston
Cross Inn
Pentlepoir
Dale Point
Milford Haven
(Aberdaugleddau)
Neyland
Upton
Carew Newton
Redberth
East Williamston
Wooden
Saundersfoot
Toll
Tide Mill
Carew
Broadfield
Angle
Pembroke Dock
(Doc Penfro)
Waterloo
Cosheston
Milton
St Anns Head
Angle Bay
Pwllcrochan
East Pennar
Golden Hill
Carew Cheriton
Sageston
New Hedges
Rhoscrowther
Manor House
Gumfreston
Tenby
(Dinbych-y-pysgod)
Pembroke
(Penfro)
Bishop's Palace
Lamphey
Manorbier Newton
St Florence
Freshwater West
Castlemartin Brook
Hundleton
Grove
Penally
Maiden Wells
Hodgeston
Castlemartin
St Twynnells
Freshwater East
Jameston
Lydstep
Giltar Point
Trewent
Manorbier
Warren
St Petrox
Trewent Point
Lydstep Point
Merrion
Cheriton or Stackpole Elidor
Linney Head
PEMBROKESHIRE COAST NATIONAL PARK
Stackpole
South Pembrokeshire Heritage Coast
Monastery
Barafundle Bay
Bosherston
Stackpole Head
St Govan's Chapel
St Govan's Head
A40
A487
A4076
A477
A4075
A478
A4139
A4115
B4583
B4330
B4331
B4313
B4329
B4582
B4327
B4341
B4325
B4320
B4319
B4322
B4584
B4585
B4318
B4586
B4314
B4315
0 1 2 3 4 5 miles
0 1 2 3 4 5 6 7 8 kilometres

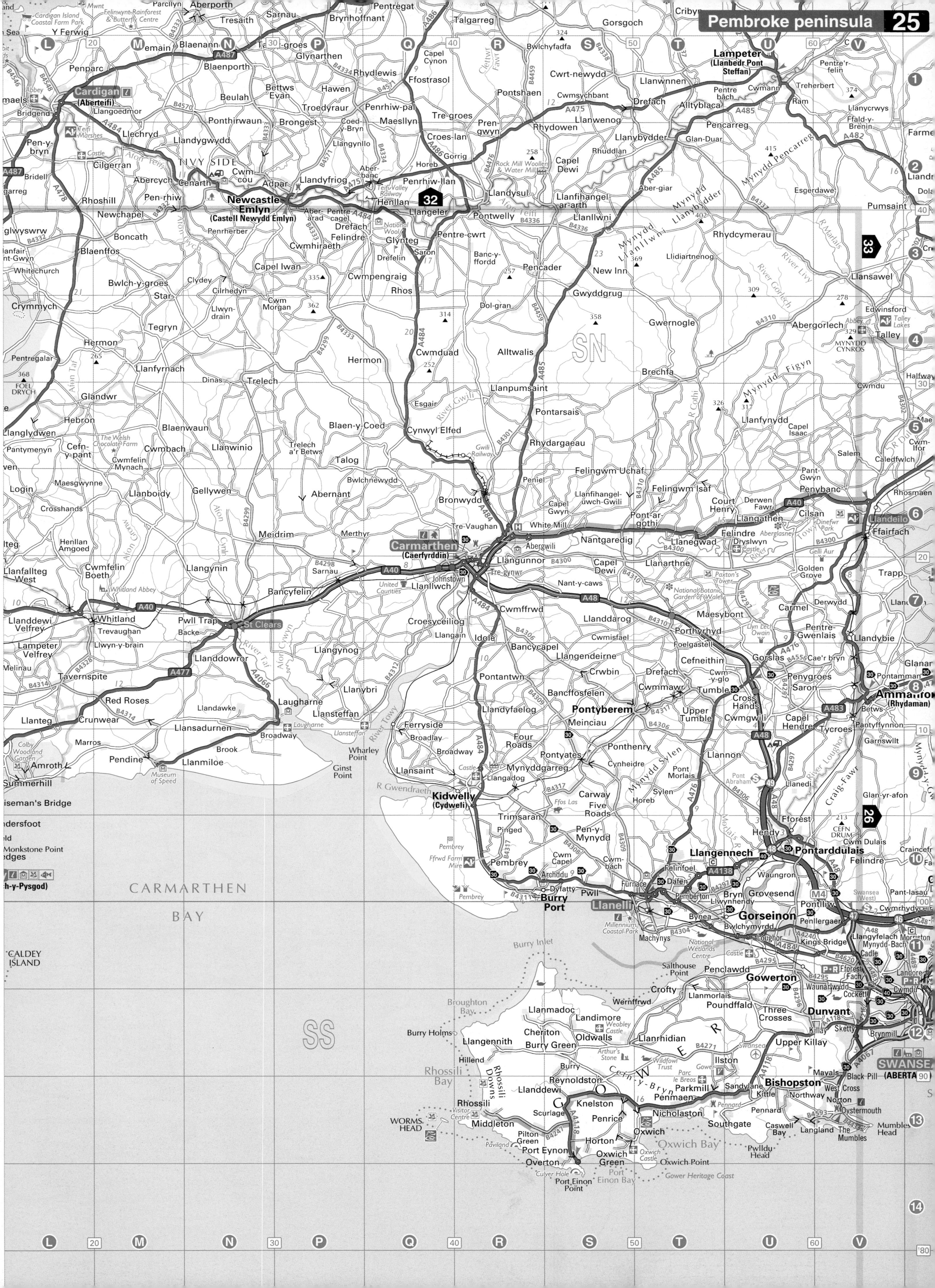
Aberporth
Tresaith
Sarnau
Brynhoffnant
Pentregat
Talgarreg
Gorsgoch
Cribyn
Cardigan Island Coastal Farm Park
Felinwynt Rainforest & Butterfly Centre
Mwnt
Y Ferwig
Blaenannerch
Glynarthen
Bwlchyfadfa
Lampeter (Llanbedr Pont Steffan)
Capel Cynon
Rhydlewis
Ffostrasol
Cwrt-newydd
Llanwnnen
Pentre'r-felin
Treherbert
Penparc
Blaenporth
Hawen
Bettws Evan
Pontshaen
Cwmsychbant
Drefach
Alltyblaca
Pentre bach
Cwmann
Ram
Llanycrwys
Ffald-y-Brenin
Cardigan (Aberteifi)
Llangoedmor
Beulah
Troedyraur
Penrhiw-pal
Llanwenog
Pencarreg
Glan-Duar
Farmers
Bridgend
Ponthirwaun
Brongest
Coed-y-Bryn
Maesllyn
Tre-groes
Pren-gwyn
Rhydowen
Llanybydder
Teifi Marshes
Llechryd
Llandygwydd
Croes-lan
Llangynllo
Gorrig
Rhuddlan
Capel Dewi
Mynydd Pencarreg
Pen-y-bryn
Cilgerran
Castle
TIVY SIDE
Cwm-cou
Horeb
Rock Mill Woollen & Water Mill
Llandre
Bridell
Abercych
Cenarth
Adpar
Llandyfriog
Aber-banc
Teifi Valley Railway
Penrhiw-llan
Aber-giar
Esgerdawe
Rhoshill
Pen-rhiw
Newcastle Emlyn (Castell Newydd Emlyn)
Henllan
Llandysul
Llanfihangel-ar-arth
Mynydd Llanybydder
Pumsaint
Newchapel
Aber-arad
Pentre-cagel
Llangeler
Pontwelly
Llanllwni
Penrherber
Drefach
National Wool Museum
Felindre
Pentre-cwrt
Mynydd Llanllwni
Rhydcymerau
Boncath
Cwmhiraeth
Glynteg
Saron
Banc-y-ffordd
Blaenffos
Drefelin
Llidiartnenog
Whitechurch
Capel Iwan
Pencader
New Inn
Lansawel
Bwlch-y-groes
Clydey
Cilrhedyn
Cwmpengraig
Rhos
River Gorlech
River Livy
Crymmych
Star
Cwm Morgan
Llwyn-drain
Dol-gran
Gwyddgrug
Edwinsford
Talley Lakes
Abbey
Tegryn
Gwernogle
Abergorlech
Talley
Mynydd Cynros
Hermon
Cwmduad
Alltwalis
SN
Pentregalar
Foel Drych
Llanfyrnach
Dinas
Trelech
Brechfa
Mynydd Figyn
Glandwr
Llanpumsaint
Esgair
River Gwili
Hebron
Pontarsais
Llanfynydd
Blaen-y-Coed
Capel Isaac
Llanglydwen
Blaenwaun
Cynwyl Elfed
The Welsh Chocolate Farm
Pantymenyn
Cefn-y-pant
Cwmbach
Llanwinio
Trelech a'r Betws
Rhydargaeau
Gwili Railway
Salem
Caledfwlch
Cwmfelin Mynach
Talog
Pant-Gwyn
Login
Maesgwynne
Gellywen
Bwlchnewydd
Felingwm Uchaf
Peniel
Felingwm Isaf
Penybanc
Rhosmaen
Llanboidy
Abernant
Bronwydd
Llanfihangel-uwch-Gwili
Court Henry
Derwen Fawr
Crosshands
Capel Gwyn
Pont-ar-gothi
Cilsan
Dryslwyn
Llangathen
Llandeilo
Ffairfach
Dinefwr Park
White Mill
Tre-Vaughan
Henllan Amgoed
Meidrim
Merthyr
Carmarthen (Caerfyrddin)
Abergwili
Nantgaredig
Llanegwad
Felindre
Aberglasney
Castle
Gelli Aur
Llanfallteg West
Cwmfelin Boeth
Llangynin
Sarnau
Llangunnor
Capel Dewi
Llanarthne
Golden Grove
Trapp
Whitland Abbey
Johnstown
Tre-gynwr
Nant-y-caws
Paxton's Tower
United Counties
Llanllwch
National Botanic Garden of Wales
Bancyfelin
Llandyfan
Llanddewi Velfrey
Whitland
Trevaughan
Pwll Trap
Backe
St Clears
Cwmffrwd
Llanddarog
Maesybont
Carmel
Derwydd
Croesyceiliog
Llangain
Idole
Cwmisfael
Porthyrhyd
Llyn Llech Owain
Pentre-Gwenlais
Llandybie
Lampeter Velfrey
Llwyn-y-brain
River Taf
Llangynog
Bancycapel
Foelgastell
Melinau
Llanddowror
Llangendeirne
Cefneithin
Gorslas
Cae'r bryn
Glanaman
Pontamman
Tavernspite
Pontantwn
Crwbin
Drefach
Cwm-y-glo
Penygroes
Saron
Ammanford (Rhydaman)
Red Roses
Llanybri
Bancffosfelen
Cwmmawr
Tumble
Cross Hands
Laugharne
Llandawke
Llansteffan
Llandyfaelog
Pontyberem
Upper Tumble
Capel Hendre
Betws
Llanteg
Crunwear
Llansadurnen
Laugharne Castle
Ferryside
Meinciau
Cwmgwili
Tycroes
Pantyffynnon
Colby Woodland Garden
Marros
Broadway
Brook
Llansteffan Castle
Broadway
Four Roads
Ponthenry
Garnswllt
Amroth
Pendine
Llanmiloe
Wharley Point
River Towy
Broadway
Pontyates
Cynheidre
Llannon
Summerhill
Museum of Speed
Ginst Point
Llansaint
Castle
Mynyddgarreg
Llangadog
Mynydd Sylen
Pont Morlais
Pont Abraham
Llanedi
Craig-Fawr
Glan-yr-afon
Wiseman's Bridge
R Gwendraeth
Kidwelly (Cydweli)
Carway
Five Roads
Sylen
Horeb
Saundersfoot
Monkstone Point
Ffos Las
Trimsaran
Fforest
Cefn Drum
Cwm Dulais
Pinged
Pen-y-Mynydd
Hendy
Pontarddulais
Felindre
Craigcefn
Pembrey
Ffrwd Farm Mire
Cwm Capel
Cwm-bach
Llangennech
Pembrey
Archddu
Felinfoel
Dafen
Waungron
CARMARTHEN BAY
Caldey Island
Furnace
Pemberton
Bryn
Llwynhendy
Grovesend
Pant-lasau
Swansea (West)
Pembrey
Dyfatty
Pwll
Burry Port
Llanelli
Pontlliw
Penllergaer
Cwmrhydyceirw
Bynea
Gorseinon
Millennium Coastal Park
Machynys
Bwlchymyrdd
Loughor
Kingsbridge
Langyfelach
Mynydd-Bach
Cadle
Morriston
Burry Inlet
National Wetlands Centre
Castle
Penclawdd
Fforestfach
Landore
Salthouse Point
Gowerton
Waunarlwydd
Cockett
Crofty
Llanmorlais
Cwmdu
Wernffrwd
Poundffald
Three Crosses
Dunvant
Broughton Bay
Llanmadoc
Landimore
Weobley Castle
Cheriton
Burry Holms
Oldwalls
Killay
Sketty
Brynmill
SS
Llangennith
Burry Green
Llanrhidian
Upper Killay
Arthur's Stone
Hillend
Wildfowl Trust
Ilston
Swansea
SWANSEA (ABERTAWE)
Rhossili Bay
Rhossili Downs
Burry
Reynoldston
Cefn-y-Bryn
Parc le Breos
Parkmill
Gower
Bishopston
Mayals
Black Pill
West Cross
Llanddewi
Sandylane
Kittle
Northway
Rhossili
Visitor Centre
Knelston
Penmaen
Pennard
Oystermouth
Worms Head
Scurlage
Nicholaston
Mumbles Head
Middleton
Penrice
Oxwich
Southgate
Caswell Bay
Langland
The Mumbles
Pilton Green
Paviland
Horton
Oxwich Bay
Pwlldu Head
Port Eynon
Oxwich Castle
Overton
Oxwich Green
Oxwich Point
Culver Hole
Port Einon Point
Port Einon Bay
Gower Heritage Coast
32
33
26

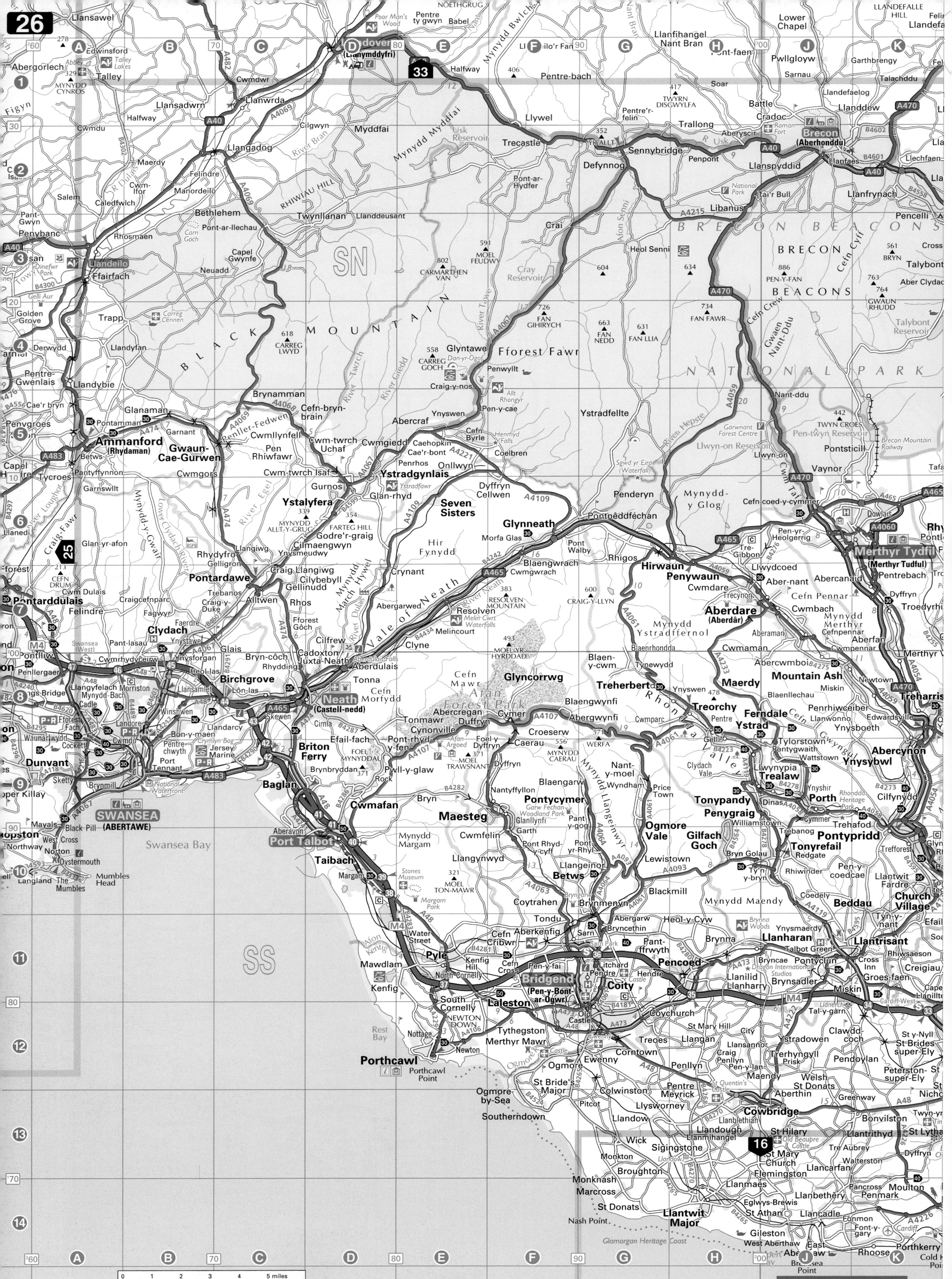
Llansawel
Llandovery (Llanymddyfri)
Abergorlech
Talley
Edwinsford
Cwmdwr
Halfway
Llanwrda
Llansadwrn
Llangadog
Myddfai
Mynydd Myddfai
Usk Reservoir
Trecastle
Llywel
Sennybridge
Defynnog
Trallong
Brecon (Aberhonddu)
Llanfaes
Llanspyddid
Libanus
Tai'r Bull
Llanfrynach
Penpont
Aberyscir
Battle
Cradoc
Llanddew
Pentre-bach
Pwllgloyw
Garthbrengy
Lower Chapel
Llanfihangel Nant Bran
Soar
Sarnau
Llandefaelog
Talachddu
TWYRN DISGWYLFA
Crai
Heol Senni
Pont-ar-Hydfer
Llanddeusant
Twynllanan
Bethlehem
Pont-ar-llechau
Capel Gwynfe
Rhosmaen
Llandeilo
Ffairfach
Neuadd
Salem
Caledfwlch
Manordeilo
Felindre
Maerdy
Cwmdu
Trapp
Carreg Cennen
Golden Grove
Derwydd
Llandyfan
Pentre-Gwenlais
Llandybie
Cae'r bryn
Penygroes
Glanaman
Pontamman
Garnant
Ammanford (Rhydaman)
Betws
Gwaun-Cae-Gurwen
Brynamman
Cefn-bryn-brain
Cwmllynfell
Pen Rhiwfawr
Cwmgors
Cwm-twrch Uchaf
Cwm-twrch Isaf
Gurnos
Ystradgynlais
Glan-rhyd
Ystalyfera
Godre'r-graig
Cilmaengwyn
Ynysmeudwy
Pantyffynnon
Tycroes
Capel Hendre
Garnswllt
Glan-yr-afon
Mynydd-y-Gwair
Rhydyfro
Gelligron
Pontardawe
Trebanos
Craig-y-Duke
Alltwen
Pontarddulais
Felindre
Craigcefnparc
Fagwyr
Clydach
Ynystawe
Glais
Pant-lasau
Pontlliw
Penllergaer
Cwmrhydyceirw
Ynysforgan
Bryn-côch
Heol-las
Birchgrove
Lôn-las
Llansamlet
Morriston
Llangyfelach
Mynydd-Bach
Cadle
Fforest Fach
Landore
Cwmdu
Waunarlwydd
Cockett
Winshwen
Bon-y-maen
Llandarcy
Pentre-chwyth
Jersey Marine
Port Tennant
Dunvant
Killay
Sketty
Brynmill
SWANSEA (ABERTAWE)
Black Pill
Mayals
West Cross
Norton
Oystermouth
Mumbles Head
Langland
The Mumbles
Swansea Bay
BLACK MOUNTAIN
CARREG LWYD
CARMARTHEN VAN
MOEL FEUDWY
Cray Reservoir
Glyntawe
CARREG GOCH
Dan-yr-Ogof
Craig-y-nos
Penwyllt
Fforest Fawr
FAN GIHIRYCH
FAN NEDD
FAN LLIA
FAN FAWR
Pen-y-cae
Ynyswen
Abercraf
Cefn Byrle
Coelbren
Caehopkin
Cae'r-bont
Penrhos
Onllwyn
Dyffryn Cellwen
Seven Sisters
Ystradfellte
Penderyn
Sgwd yr Eira (Waterfall)
BRECON BEACONS
NATIONAL PARK
PEN-Y-FAN
BRYN
Talybont
Aber Clydach
GWAUN RHUDD
Talybont Reservoir
Pencelli
Cefn Crew
Gwaen Nant-Ddu
Nant-ddu
TWYN CROES
Pen-twyn Reservoir
Pontsticill
Brecon Mountain Railway
Vaynor
Llwyn-on Reservoir
Llwyn-on
Garwnant Forest Centre
Mynydd-y Glog
Cefn-coed-y-cymmer
Dowlais
Merthyr Tydfil (Merthyr Tudful)
Pentrebach
Pen-yr-Heolgerrig
Pontnêddfechan
Glynneath
Morfa Glas
Pont Walby
Rhigos
Hirwaun
Penywaun
Tre-Gibbon
Llwydcoed
Aber-nant
Abercanaid
Cwmdare
Trecynon
Aberdare (Aberdâr)
Cefn Pennar
Cwmbach
Dyffryn
Troedyrhiw
Mynydd Merthyr
Aberfan
Merthyr Vale
Hir Fynydd
Blaengwrach
Cwmgwrach
Crynant
Mynydd March Hywel
Cilybebyll
Gellinudd
Craig Llangiwg
Rhos
Fforest Gôch
Cilfrew
Vale of Neath
Aberdulais
Resolven
RESOLVEN MOUNTAIN
CRAIG-Y-LLYN
Melincourt
Clyne
Cadoxton-Juxta-Neath
Rhyddings
Tonna
Neath (Castell-nedd)
Cefn Morfydd
Skewen
Cimla
Efail-fach
Briton Ferry
Baglan
FOEL MYNYDDAU
Pont-rhyd-y-fen
Pwll-y-glaw
Cwmafan
Brynbryddan
Port Talbot
Aberavon
Taibach
Margam
Stones Museum
Margam Park
MOEL TON-MAWR
Mynydd Margam
Cefn Mawr
Afan Forest Park
Glyncorrwg
Tonmawr
Abercregan
Duffryn
Cynonville
Cymer
Croeserw
Caerau
MYNYDD CAERAU
Foel-y-Dyffryn
MOEL TRAWSNANT
Dyffryn
Nantyffyllon
Maesteg
Bryn
Cwmfelin
Llangynwyd
Garth
Pontycymer
Blaengarw
Garw Fechan Woodland Park
Pant-y-gog
Pont Rhyd-y-cyff
Pont-yr-Rhyl
Llangeinor
Betws
Nant-y-moel
Wyndham
Price Town
Ogmore Vale
Lewistown
Gilfach Goch
Blaen-y-cwm
Treherbert
Blaenrhondda
Tynewydd
Ynyswen
Treorchy
Cwmparc
Blaengwynfi
Abergwynfi
WERFA
Pentre
Gelli
Ystrad
Ferndale
Maerdy
Cwmaman
Abercwmboi
Mountain Ash
Miskin
Penrhiwceiber
Llanwonno
Rhondda Valley
Tylorstown
Pontygwaith
Wattstown
Clydach Vale
Llwynypia
Trealaw
Tonypandy
Penygraig
Williamstown
Dinas
Porth
Ynyshir
Rhondda Heritage Park
Trehafod
Cymmer
Trebanog
Tonyrefail
Pontypridd
Edwardsville
Ynysboeth
Abercynon
Ynysybwl
Cilfynydd
Treharris
Bryn Golau
Ty'n-y-bryn
Blackmill
Mynydd Maendy
Redgate
Rhiwinder
Pen-y-coedcae
Llantwit Fardre
Church Village
Beddau
Coedely
Tyn-y-nant
Llantrisant
Llanharan
Ynysmaerdy
Talbot Green
Pontyclun
Brynna
Heol-y-Cyw
Abergarw
Bryncethin
Brynmenyn
Coytrahen
Tondu
Aberkenfig
Sarn
Pant-ffrwyth
Pencoed
Cefn Cribwr
Kenfig Hill
Cefn Cross
Pyle
Water Street
Mawdlam
Kenfig
North Cornelly
South Cornelly
Bridgend (Pen-y-Bont-ar-Ogwr)
Litchard
Pendre
Coity
Hendre
Laleston
Old Castle
Coychurch
Llanilid
Llanharry
Brynsadler
Bryncae
Crosss Inn
Groes-faen
Creigiau
Miskin
Tal-y-garn
Rest Bay
Nottage
NEWTON DOWN
Newton
Tythegston
Merthyr Mawr
Porthcawl
Porthcawl Point
Ogmore
Ewenny
Corntown
Treoes
St Mary Hill
Llangan
Llansannor
Craig Penllyn
Pen-y-lan
Penllyn
City
Ystradowen
Trerhyngyll
Prisk
Maendy
Clawdd-coch
Pendoylan
St y-Nyll
St Brides super-Ely
Peterston-super-Ely
Welsh St Donats
Aberthin
Cowbridge
Greenway
Bonvilston
Llantrithyd
St Hilary
Old Beaupre Castle
Ogmore-by-Sea
St Bride's Major
Colwinston
Pitcot
Southerndown
Pentre Meyrick
Llysworney
Llandow
Llanblethian
Llandough
Llanmihangel
Wick
Sigingstone
Monkton
Broughton
Monknash
Marcross
St Donats
Nash Point
Llantwit Major
Llanmaes
St Mary Church
Flemingston
Llancarfan
Tre Aubrey
Walterston
Dyffryn
Moulton
Pancross
Penmark
Llanbethery
Eglwys-Brewis
St Athan
Llancadle
Fonmon
Font-y-gary
Gileston
West Aberthaw
East Aberthaw
Breaksea Point
Rhoose
Porthkerry
Glamorgan Heritage Coast
SN
SS
0 1 2 3 4 5 miles
0 1 2 3 4 5 6 7 8 kilometres

Town plan: Swansea p.122

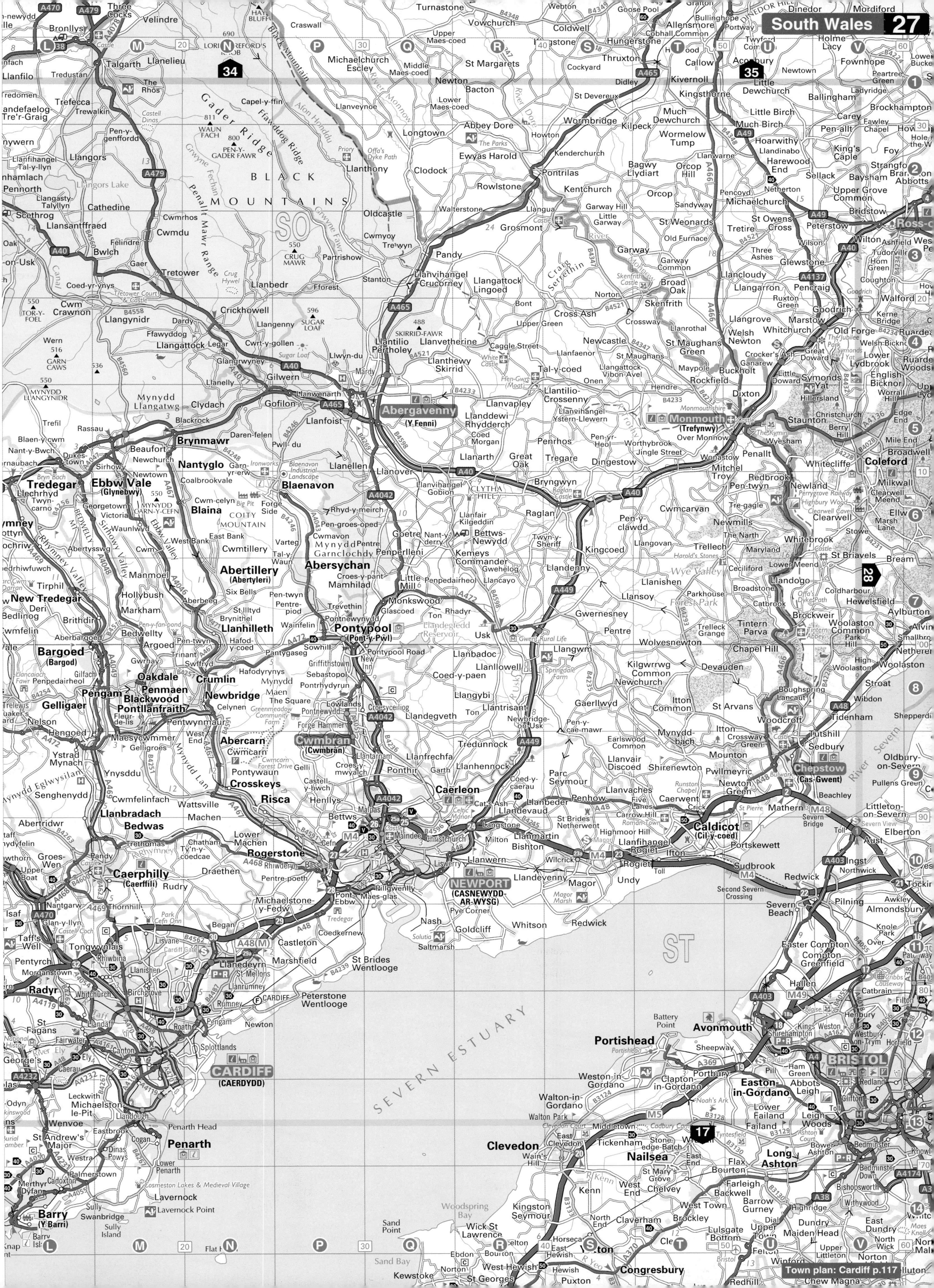
BLACK MOUNTAINS
Abergavenny
(Y Fenni)
Monmouth
(Trefynwy)
Chepstow
(Cas-Gwent)
NEWPORT
(CASNEWYDD-AR-WYSG)
CARDIFF
(CAERDYDD)
BRISTOL
Cwmbran
(Cwmbrân)
Pontypool
(Pont-y-Pŵl)
Caerphilly
(Caerffili)
Barry
(Y Barri)
Penarth
Portishead
Clevedon
Nailsea
Caldicot
(Cil-y-coed)
Coleford
Tredegar
Ebbw Vale
(Glynebwy)
Abertillery
(Abertyleri)
Blaenavon
Brynmawr
Bargoed
Blackwood
Risca
Usk
Caerleon
Crickhowell
Talgarth
Raglan
Avonmouth
SEVERN ESTUARY
Second Severn Crossing
Severn Bridge
Wye Valley
Ross-on-Wye
Lydney
Congresbury
Long Ashton
Easton-in-Gordano

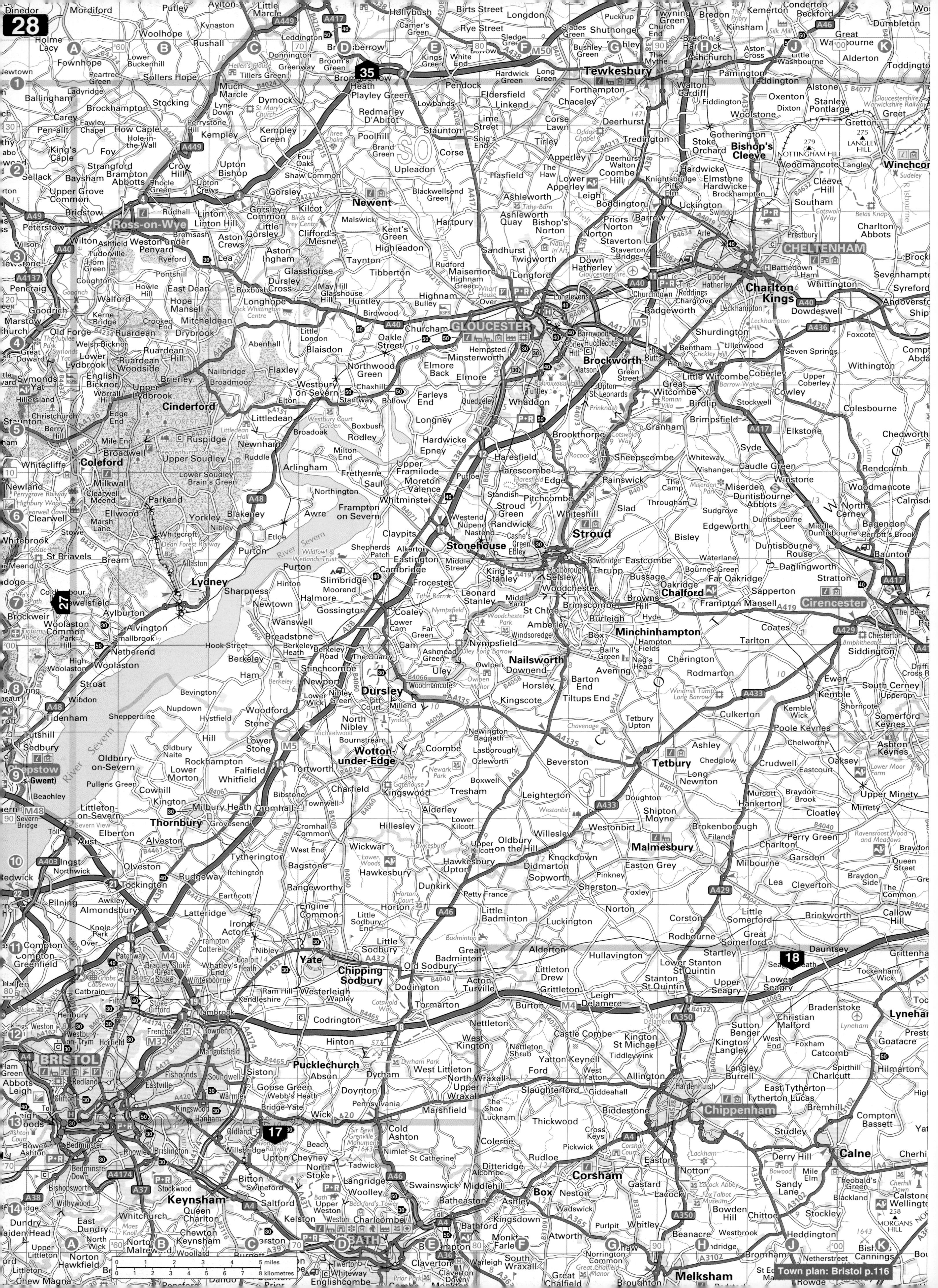

Ross-on-Wye
Newent
Tewkesbury
Bishop's Cleeve
Winchcombe
CHELTENHAM
Charlton Kings
GLOUCESTER
Brockworth
Cinderford
Coleford
Lydney
Stonehouse
Stroud
Chalford
Cirencester
Nailsworth
Minchinhampton
Dursley
Wotton-under-Edge
Tetbury
Malmesbury
Thornbury
Chepstow (Cas-Gwent)
Yate
Chipping Sodbury
BRISTOL
Keynsham
BATH
Corsham
Chippenham
Calne
Melksham
Lyneham
River Severn
Severn Bridge
Dean Forest Railway
Gloucestershire Warwickshire Railway
Cotswold Way
Wildfowl & Wetlands Trust
SO
ST
35
27
17
18
0 1 2 3 4 5 miles
0 1 2 3 4 5 6 7 8 kilometres
Town plan: Bristol p.116

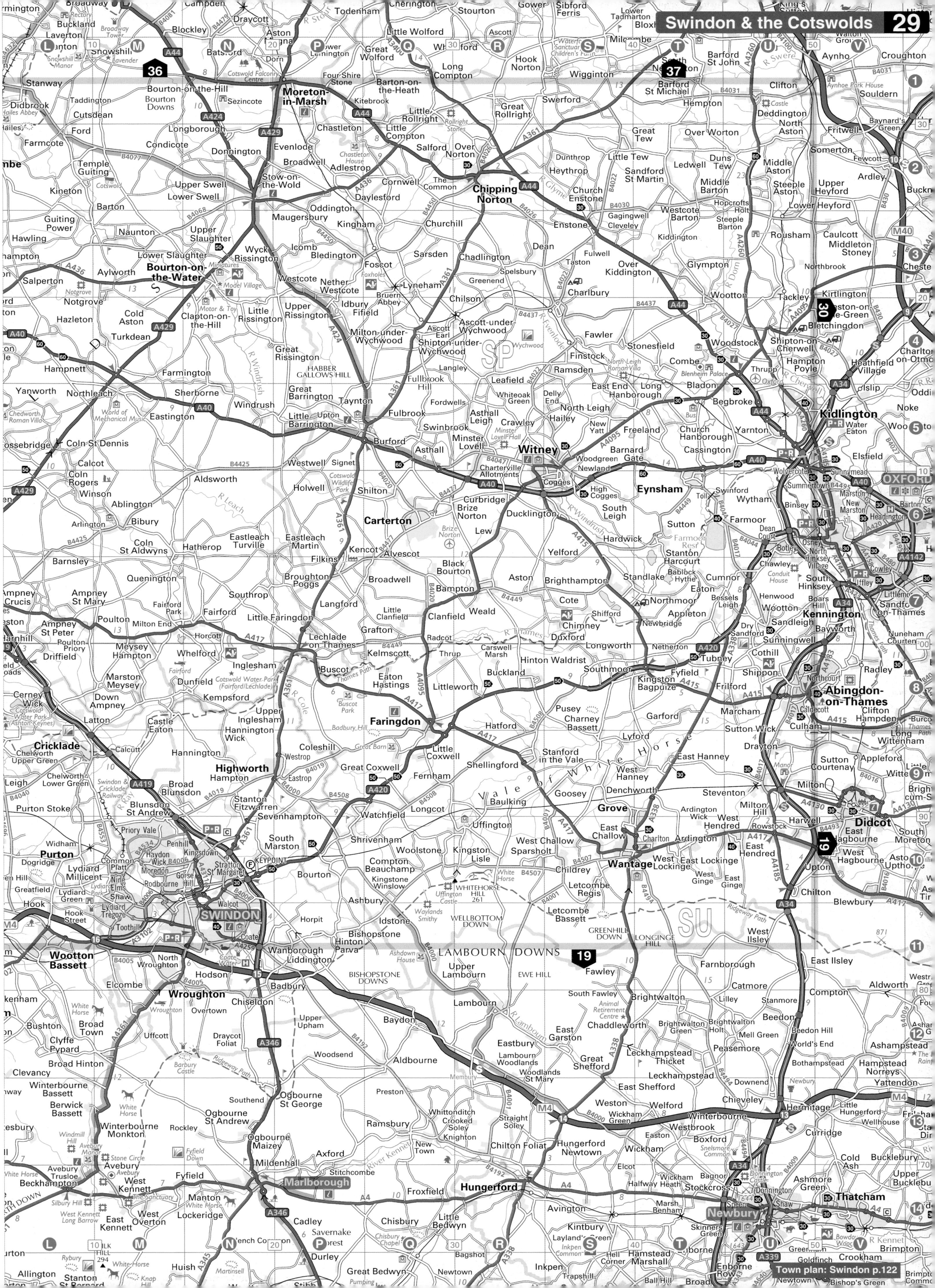

Buckland
Laverton
Snowshill
Blockley
Batsford
Draycott
Aston Magna
Todenham
Little Wolford
Great Wolford
Long Compton
Stourton
Hook Norton
Sibford Ferris
Milcombe
Wigginton
South Newington
Barford St John
Barford St Michael
Aynho
Croughton
Souldern
Stanway
Bourton-on-the-Hill
Sezincote
Moreton-in-Marsh
Barton-on-the-Heath
Four Shire Stone
Kitebrook
Little Rollright
Great Rollright
Swerford
Hempton
Deddington
North Aston
Didbrook
Taddington
Cutsdean
Ford
Farmcote
Longborough
Condicote
Donnington
Evenlode
Chastleton
Little Compton
Salford
Over Norton
Great Tew
Over Worton
Little Tew
Dunthrop
Heythrop
Sandford St Martin
Ledwell
Duns Tew
Middle Aston
Steeple Aston
Somerton
Fritwell
Ardley
Temple Guiting
Kineton
Upper Swell
Lower Swell
Stow-on-the-Wold
Broadwell
Adlestrop
Cornwell
Daylesford
Chipping Norton
Church Enstone
Enstone
Westcote Barton
Middle Barton
Upper Heyford
Lower Heyford
Barton
Guiting Power
Naunton
Hawling
Upper Slaughter
Lower Slaughter
Wyck Rissington
Oddington
Maugersbury
Kingham
Churchill
Icomb
Bledington
Sarsden
Chadlington
Spelsbury
Dean
Fulwell
Taston
Over Kiddington
Glympton
Rousham
Caulcott
Middleton Stoney
Northbrook
Aylworth
Bourton-on-the-Water
Salperton
Notgrove
Westcote
Foscot
Nether Westcote
Lyneham
Chilson
Charlbury
Wootton
Tackley
Kirtlington
Hazleton
Cold Aston
Clapton-on-the-Hill
Little Rissington
Upper Rissington
Idbury
Fifield
Bruern Abbey
Ascott-under-Wychwood
Ascott Earl
Bletchingdon
Turkdean
Milton-under-Wychwood
Shipton-under-Wychwood
Fawler
Stonesfield
Woodstock
Shipton-on-Cherwell
Hampnett
Great Rissington
Farmington
Finstock
Combe
Hampton Poyle
Heathfield Village
Charlton-on-Otmoor
Yanworth
Northleach
Sherborne
Great Barrington
Little Barrington
Taynton
Fullbrook Hill
Leafield
Ramsden
East End
Hanborough
Long Hanborough
Bladon
Begbroke
Islip
Kidlington
Eastington
Windrush
Fulbrook
Asthall Leigh
Crawley
North Leigh
Hailey
New Yatt
Freeland
Church Hanborough
Yarnton
Water Eaton
Coln St Dennis
Burford
Swinbrook
Minster Lovell
Witney
Barnard Gate
Cassington
Elsfield
Calcot
Coln Rogers
Westwell
Signet
Asthall
Charterville Allotments
Woodgreen
Newland
Wolvercote
Summertown
OXFORD
Aldsworth
Winson
Holwell
Shilton
Curbridge
Cogges
High Cogges
Eynsham
Swinford
Wytham
Marston
Binsey
Headington
Ablington
Bibury
Arlington
Carterton
Brize Norton
Ducklington
South Leigh
Sutton
Farmoor
Coln St Aldwyns
Hatherop
Eastleach Turville
Eastleach Martin
Filkins
Kencot
Alvescot
Lew
Hardwick
Stanton Harcourt
Yelford
Botley
North Hinksey Village
Cowley
Barnsley
Quenington
Southrop
Broughton Poggs
Broadwell
Black Bourton
Bampton
Aston
Brighthampton
Standlake
Cumnor
Eaton
South Hinksey
Ampney Crucis
Ampney St Mary
Fairford
Langford
Little Clanfield
Clanfield
Weald
Cote
Shifford
Chimney
Northmoor
Appleton
Kennington
Sandford-on-Thames
Ampney St Peter
Poulton
Little Faringdon
Lechlade on Thames
Grafton
Radcot
Duxford
Newbridge
Longworth
Dry Sandford
Sunningwell
Bayworth
Meysey Hampton
Driffield
Whelford
Inglesham
Kelmscott
Buscot
Eaton Hastings
Thrup
Carswell Marsh
Buckland
Hinton Waldrist
Southmoor
Kingston Bagpuize
Fyfield
Tubney
Cothill
Shippon
Radley
Marston Meysey
Dunfield
Kempsford
Down Ampney
Littleworth
Frilford
Abingdon-on-Thames
Cerney Wick
Latton
Castle Eaton
Upper Inglesham
Hannington Wick
Faringdon
Hatford
Pusey
Charney Bassett
Garford
Marcham
Culham
Clifton Hampden
Sutton Wick
Long Wittenham
Cricklade
Calcutt
Hannington
Highworth
Coleshill
Great Coxwell
Little Coxwell
Fernham
Shellingford
Stanton in the Vale
Lyford
West Hanney
East Hanney
Drayton
Sutton Courtenay
Appleford
Broad Blunsdon
Stanton Fitzwarren
Sevenhampton
Watchfield
Longcot
Baulking
Goosey
Denchworth
Grove
Steventon
Milton
Didcot
Purton Stoke
Blunsdon St Andrew
Priory Vale
Shrivenham
Uffington
Woolstone
Kingston Lisle
West Challow
Sparsholt
East Challow
Wantage
Ardington
West Hendred
East Hendred
Harwell
East Hagbourne
West Hagbourne
South Moreton
Purton
Lydiard Millicent
Haydon Wick
Stratton St Margaret
South Marston
Bourton
Compton Beauchamp
Childrey
West Lockinge
East Lockinge
Upton
Chilton
Blewbury
Shaw
Nine Elms
Lydiard Green
Hook
Lydiard Tregoze
Walcot
SWINDON
Coate
Ashbury
Idstone
Bishopstone
Hinton Parva
Letcombe Regis
Letcombe Bassett
West Ilsley
East Ilsley
Wootton Bassett
Wanborough
Liddington
North Wroughton
Hodson
Elcombe
Wroughton
Chiseldon
Badbury
Upper Lambourn
Fawley
Lambourn Downs
Farnborough
Catmore
Aldworth
Compton
Broad Town
Bushton
Clyffe Pypard
Broad Hinton
Uffcott
Overtown
Draycot Foliat
Upper Upham
Baydon
Lambourn
South Fawley
Brightwalton
Chaddleworth
East Garston
Beedon
Clevancy
Winterbourne Bassett
Berwick Bassett
Woodsend
Aldbourne
Eastbury
Lambourn Woodlands
Great Shefford
Leckhampstead Thicket
Leckhampstead
Peasemore
Ashampstead
Hampstead Norreys
Yattendon
Southend
Ogbourne St George
Preston
Woodlands St Mary
East Shefford
Ogbourne St Andrew
Winterbourne Monkton
Rockley
Ramsbury
Whittonditch
Crooked Soley
Knighton
Straight Soley
Weston
Welford
Wickham Green
Winterbourne
Chieveley
Hermitage
Curridge
Westbrook
Boxford
Avebury
Avebury Trusloe
Beckhampton
Ogbourne Maizey
Mildenhall
Axford
New Town
Chilton Foliat
Hungerford Newtown
Wickham
Cold Ash
Bucklebury
Fyfield
West Kennett
East Kennett
West Overton
Manton
Lockeridge
Marlborough
Froxfield
Hungerford
Avington
Halfway
Wickham Heath
Stockcross
Bagnor
Donnington
Newbury
Thatcham
Upper Bucklebury
Ashmore Green
Cadley
Savernake Forest
Chisbury
Little Bedwyn
Kintbury
Skinners Green
Greenham
Crookham
Brimpton
Durley
Bagshot
Inkpen
Hamstead Marshall
Enborne Row
Allington
Stanton St Bernard
Huish
Great Bedwyn
Newtown
Trapshill
Ball Hill
Bishop's Green

Town plan: Swindon p.122

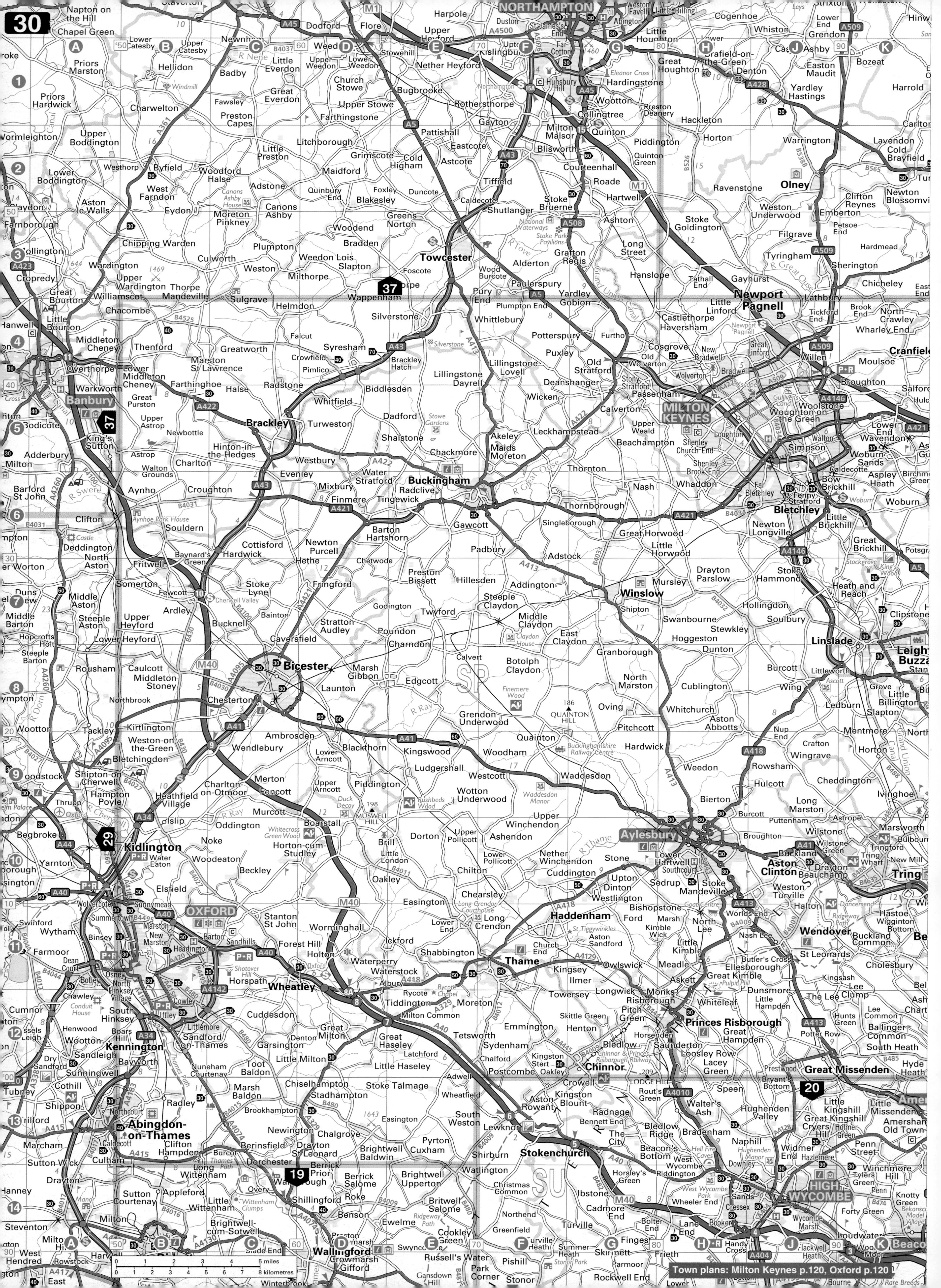
Napton on the Hill
Chapel Green
Dodford
Flore
Harpole
NORTHAMPTON
Cogenhoe
Whiston
Lower End
Grendon
Priors Marston
Lower Catesby
Upper Catesby
Newnham
Weedon
Upper Heyford
Kislingbury
Little Houghton
Grafield-on-the-Green
Ashby
Bozeat
Hellidon
Badby
Little Everdon
Upper Weedon
Lower Weedon
Stowehill
Nether Heyford
Hunsbury Hill
Eleanor Cross
Great Houghton
Hardingstone
Denton
Easton Maudit
Harrold
Priors Hardwick
Charwelton
Fawsley
Church Stowe
Great Everdon
Upper Stowe
Bugbrooke
Rothersthorpe
Wootton
Collingtree
Preston Deanery
Yardley Hastings
Preston Capes
Farthingstone
Gayton
Milton Malsor
Quinton
Hackleton
Horton
Carlton
Wormleighton
Upper Boddington
Little Preston
Litchborough
Pattishall
Eastcote
Blisworth
Piddington
Warrington
Lavendon
Cold Brayfield
Grimscote
Cold Higham
Astcote
Courteenhall
Quinton Green
Lower Boddington
Westhorp
Byfield
Woodford Halse
Maidford
Tiffield
Roade
Ravenstone
Olney
West Farndon
Canons Ashby House
Adstone
Quinbury End
Foxley
Duncote
Caldecote
Hartwell
Weston Underwood
Clifton Reynes
Newton Blossomville
Claydon
Aston le Walls
Eydon
Moreton Pinkney
Canons Ashby
Blakesley
Greens Norton
Shutlanger
Stoke Bruerne
Ashton
Emberton
Petsoe End
Farnborough
Chipping Warden
Woodend
National Waterways
Stoke Park Pavilions
Stoke Goldington
Filgrave
Mollington
Culworth
Plumpton
Bradden
Towcester
Grafton Regis
Long Street
Hardmead
Tyringham
Sherington
Wardington
Upper Wardington
Weston
Weedon Lois
Slapton
Foscote
Wood Burcote
Alderton
Hanslope
Cropredy
Thorpe Mandeville
Milthorpe
Wappenham
Pury End
Paulerspury
Tathall End
Gayhurst
Chicheley
Great Bourton
Williamscot
Sulgrave
Helmdon
Plumpton End
Yardley Gobion
Little Linford
Newport Pagnell
Lathbury
Little Bourton
Chacombe
Silverstone
Whittlebury
Castlethorpe
Haversham
Tickford End
Brook End
North Crawley
Wharley End
Hanwell
Middleton Cheney
Thenford
Greatworth
Falcut
Syresham
Crowfield
Pimlico
Brackley Hatch
Potterspury
Furtho
Cosgrove
New Bradwell
Great Linford
Willen
Cranfield
Marston St Lawrence
Lillingstone Lovell
Puxley
Old Stratford
Old Wolverton
Wolverton
Bradwell
Moulsoe
Overthorpe
Lower Middleton Cheney
Farthinghoe
Halse
Radstone
Lillingstone Dayrell
Deanshanger
Stony Stratford
Passenham
Broughton
Salford
Warkworth
Banbury
Great Purston
Biddlesden
Whitfield
Wicken
Calverton
MILTON KEYNES
Woolstone
Woughton on the Green
Hulcote
Bodicote
Upper Astrop
Brackley
Turweston
Dadford
Stowe Gardens
Akeley
Leckhampstead
Upper Weald
Beachampton
Shenley Church End
Loughton
Walton
Lower End
Wavendon
King's Sutton
Newbottle
Hinton-in-the-Hedges
Shalstone
Maids Moreton
Simpson
Woburn Sands
Adderbury
Astrop
Charlton
Westbury
Chackmore
Shenley Brook End
Caldecotte
Aspley Heath
Milton
Walton Grounds
Evenley
Water Stratford
Buckingham
Thornton
Bow Brickhill
Barford St John
Aynho
Croughton
Mixbury
Radclive
Nash
Whaddon
Far Bletchley
Fenny Stratford
Woburn
Finmere
Tingewick
Thornborough
Bletchley
Clifton
Aynhoe Park House
Souldern
Barton Hartshorn
Gawcott
Singleborough
Great Horwood
Little Brickhill
Newton Longville
Deddington
Cottisford
Newton Purcell
Padbury
Little Horwood
Great Brickhill
North Aston
Baynard's Green
Hardwick
Hethe
Chetwode
Adstock
Drayton Parslow
Potsgrove
Fritwell
Preston Bissett
Hillesden
Stoke Hammond
Somerton
Stoke Lyne
Fringford
Addington
Mursley
Winslow
Heath and Reach
Duns Tew
Middle Aston
Fewcott
Cherwell Valley
Steeple Claydon
Middle Claydon
Shipton
Hollingdon
Middle Barton
Steeple Aston
Ardley
Bainton
Godington
Stratton Audley
Twyford
Swanbourne
Soulbury
Clipstone
Upper Heyford
Bucknell
Poundon
Claydon House
East Claydon
Stewkley
Linslade
Hopcrofts Holt
Lower Heyford
Caversfield
Charndon
Hoggeston
Dunton
Leighton Buzzard
Steeple Barton
Rousham
Caulcott
Middleton Stoney
Bicester
Marsh Gibbon
Calvert
Botolph Claydon
Granborough
North Marston
Burcott
Littleworth
Launton
Edgcott
Cublington
Wing
Ascott
Grove
Little Billington
Northbrook
Chesterton
Finemere Wood
Quainton Hill
Oving
Whitchurch
Aston Abbotts
Ledburn
Slapton
Wootton
Tackley
Kirtlington
Grendon Underwood
Pitchcott
Mentmore
Ambrosden
Nup End
Weston-on-the-Green
Wendlebury
Blackthorn
Kingswood
Quainton
Buckinghamshire Railway Centre
Hardwick
Crafton
Woodstock
Bletchingdon
Lower Arncott
Woodham
Rowsham
Wingrave
Horton
Shipton-on-Cherwell
Charlton-on-Otmoor
Merton
Ludgershall
Westcott
Waddesdon
Weedon
Cheddington
Hampton Poyle
Heathfield Village
Fencott
Upper Arncott
Piddington
Wotton Underwood
Waddesdon Manor
Hulcott
Ivinghoe
Blenheim Palace
Thrupp
Murcott
Duck Decoy
Muswell Hill
Rushbeds Wood
Upper Winchendon
Bierton
Long Marston
Islip
Oddington
Whitecross Green Wood
Boarstall
Dorton
Upper Pollicott
Ashendon
Aylesbury
Burcott
Puttenham
Astrope
Marsworth
Begbroke
Kidlington
Noke
Brill
Lower Pollicott
Nether Winchendon
Broughton
Wilstone
Bulbourne
Yarnton
Water Eaton
Woodeaton
Horton-cum-Studley
Little London
Stone
Lower Hartwell
Buckland
Wilstone Green
Tring Wharf
New Mill
Beckley
Oakley
Chilton
Cuddington
Southcourt
Aston Clinton
Tring
Elsfield
Upton
Dinton
Sedrup
Stoke Mandeville
Weston Turville
Wolvercote
Sunnymead
Summertown
Westlington
Easington
Chearsley
Long Crendon Courthouse
Bishopstone
Halton
OXFORD
Stanton St John
Haddenham
Ford
Marsh
World's End
Swinford
Wytham
Worminghall
Lower End
Long Crendon
St Tiggywinkles
Kimble Wick
North Lee
Hastoe
Wigginton Bottom
Binsey
Marston
New Marston
Barton
Headington
Sandhills
Forest Hill
Ickford
Aston Sandford
Little Kimble
Nash Lee
Wendover
Buckland Common
Farmoor
Dean Court
Holton
Oxford
Shotover Hill
Shabbington
Church End
Thame
Owlswick
Butler's Cross
St Leonards
Cholesbury
Botley
Osney
North Hinksey Village
Horspath
Wheatley
Waterperry
Waterstock
Kingsey
Ilmer
Meadle
Ellesborough
Great Kimble
Pulpit Hill
Kingsash
Chawley
Cowley
Albury
Rycote
Rycote Chapel
Tiddington
Moreton
Towersey
Longwick
Askett
Monks Risborough
Dunsmore
Lee
Clump
The Lee
Cumnor
Conduit House
South Hinksey
Iffley
Cuddesdon
Milton Common
Skittle Green
Pitch Green
Whiteleaf
Little Hampden
Ashley Green
Chartridge
Henwood
Boars Hill
Littlemore
Sandford-on-Thames
Great Milton
Great Haseley
Tetsworth
Emmington
Henton
Horsenden
Princes Risborough
Great Hampden
Hunts Green
Lee Common
Ballinger Common
Wootton
Kennington
Garsington
Denton
Latchford
Sydenham
Bledlow
Saunderton
South Heath
Sandleigh
Bayworth
Little Milton
Little Haseley
Chalford
Kingston Stert
Chinnor & Princes Risborough Railway
Loosley Row
Lacey Green
Prestwood
Great Missenden
Hyde Heath
Sunningwell
Nuneham Courtenay
Toot Baldon
Postcombe
Oakley
Chinnor
Lodge Hill
Bryant's Bottom
Cothill
Marsh Baldon
Chiselhampton
Stoke Talmage
Adwell
Crowell
Kingston Blount
Speen
Tubney
Radley
Stadhampton
Wheatfield
Aston Rowant
Radnage
Walter's Ash
Hughenden Valley
Little Kingshill
Great Kingshill
Little Missenden
Amersham Old Town
Shippon
Brookhampton
Northcourt
Abingdon-on-Thames
Easington
South Weston
Lewknor
Bennett End
Bledlow Ridge
Bradenham
Cryers Hill
Holmer Green
Frilford
Newington
Chalgrove
Pyrton
The City
Naphill
Marcham
Caldecott
Clifton Hampden
Berinsfield
Drayton St Leonard
Brightwell Baldwin
Cuxham
Beacon's Bottom
Hell Fire Caves
Widmer End
Penn Street
Sutton Wick
Culham
Burcot
Dorchester
Berrick Prior
Shirburn
Stokenchurch
West Wycombe
Downley
Hughenden Manor
Hazlemere
Drayton
Long Wittenham
Wallingford
Berrick Salome
Brightwell Upperton
Watlington
Horsley's Green
Piddington
Tylers Hill
Winchmore Hill
Hanney
Sutton Courtenay
Appleford
Overy
Shillingford
Christmas Common
Ibstone
West Wycombe Park
Sands
HIGH WYCOMBE
Penn
Little Wittenham
Wittenham Clumps
Roke
Britwell Salome
Cadmore End
Wheeler End
Cressex
Knotty Green
Beaconsfield Model Village
Steventon
Milton
Brightwell-cum-Sotwell
Benson
Ewelme
Ridgeway Path
Northend
Cookley Green
Turville
Bolter End
Lane End
Booker
Wycombe Marsh
Forty Green
Milton Hill
Harwell
Slade End
Preston Crowmarsh
Swyncombe
Greenfield
Turville Heath
Fingest
Frieth
Handy Cross
Loudwater
West Hendred
Rowstock
Crowmarsh Gifford
Russell's Water
Pishill
Summer Heath
Skirmett
Parmoor
Flackwell Heath
Wooburn Moor
East Hendred
Winterbrook
Park Corner
Stonor
Stonor Park
Rockwell End
Gangsdown Hill
Lower
Bourne End
Rare Breeds
0 1 2 3 4 5 miles
0 1 2 3 4 5 6 7 8 kilometres
Town plans: Milton Keynes p.120, Oxford p.120

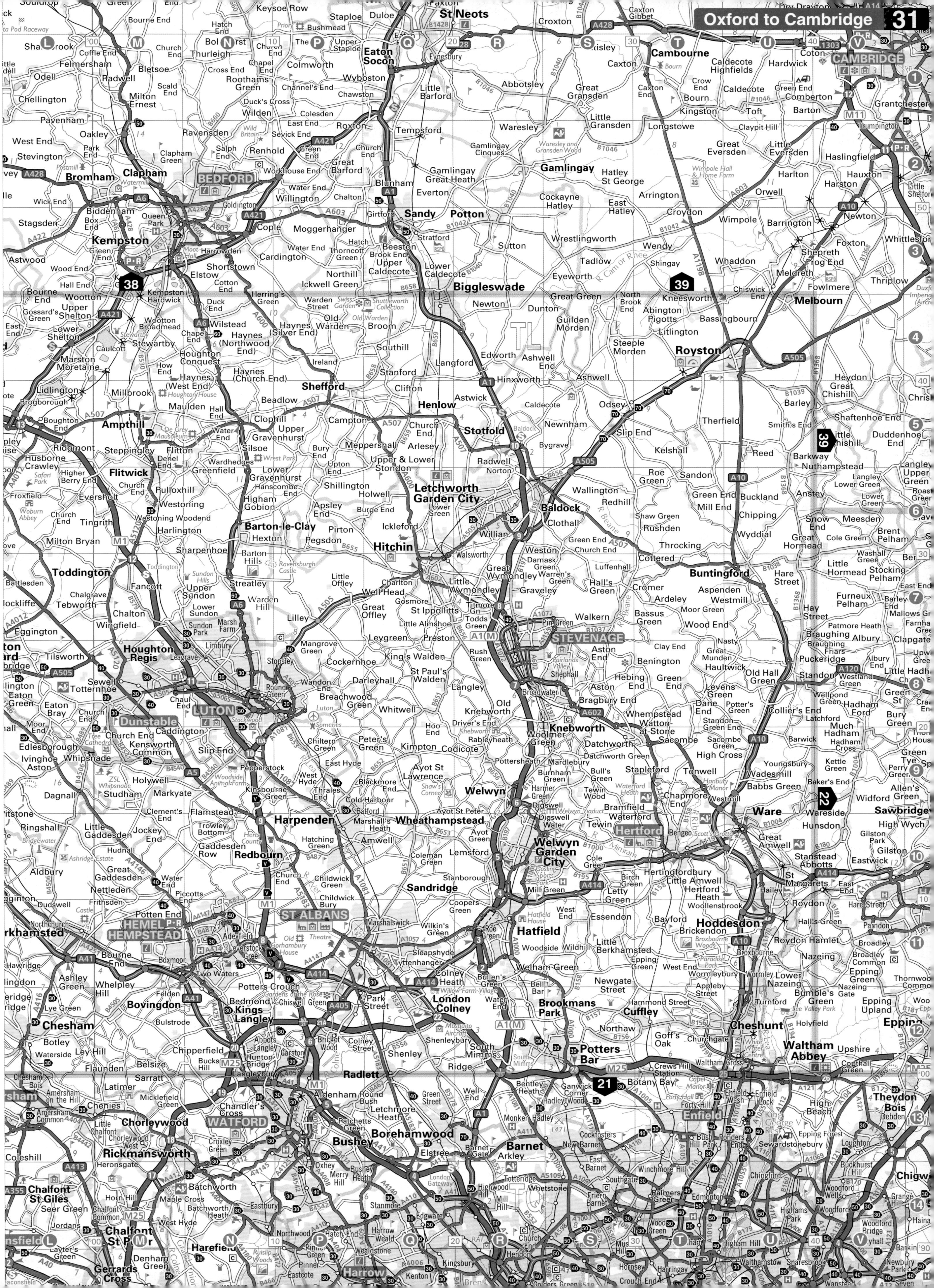
St Neots
Eaton Socon
Cambourne
CAMBRIDGE
BEDFORD
Kempston
Sandy
Potton
Biggleswade
Gamlingay
Royston
Melbourn
Shefford
Henlow
Stotfold
Letchworth Garden City
Baldock
Hitchin
Ampthill
Flitwick
Buntingford
STEVENAGE
Toddington
Houghton Regis
Dunstable
LUTON
Harpenden
Welwyn
Welwyn Garden City
Hertford
Ware
Hoddesdon
Hatfield
ST ALBANS
HEMEL HEMPSTEAD
Berkhamsted
Kings Langley
Chesham
Radlett
London Colney
Potters Bar
Cheshunt
Waltham Abbey
Enfield
Barnet
Borehamwood
Bushey
WATFORD
Chorleywood
Rickmansworth
Chalfont St Giles
Chalfont St Peter
Gerrards Cross
Harefield
Harrow
Theydon Bois
Sawbridgeworth
Epping

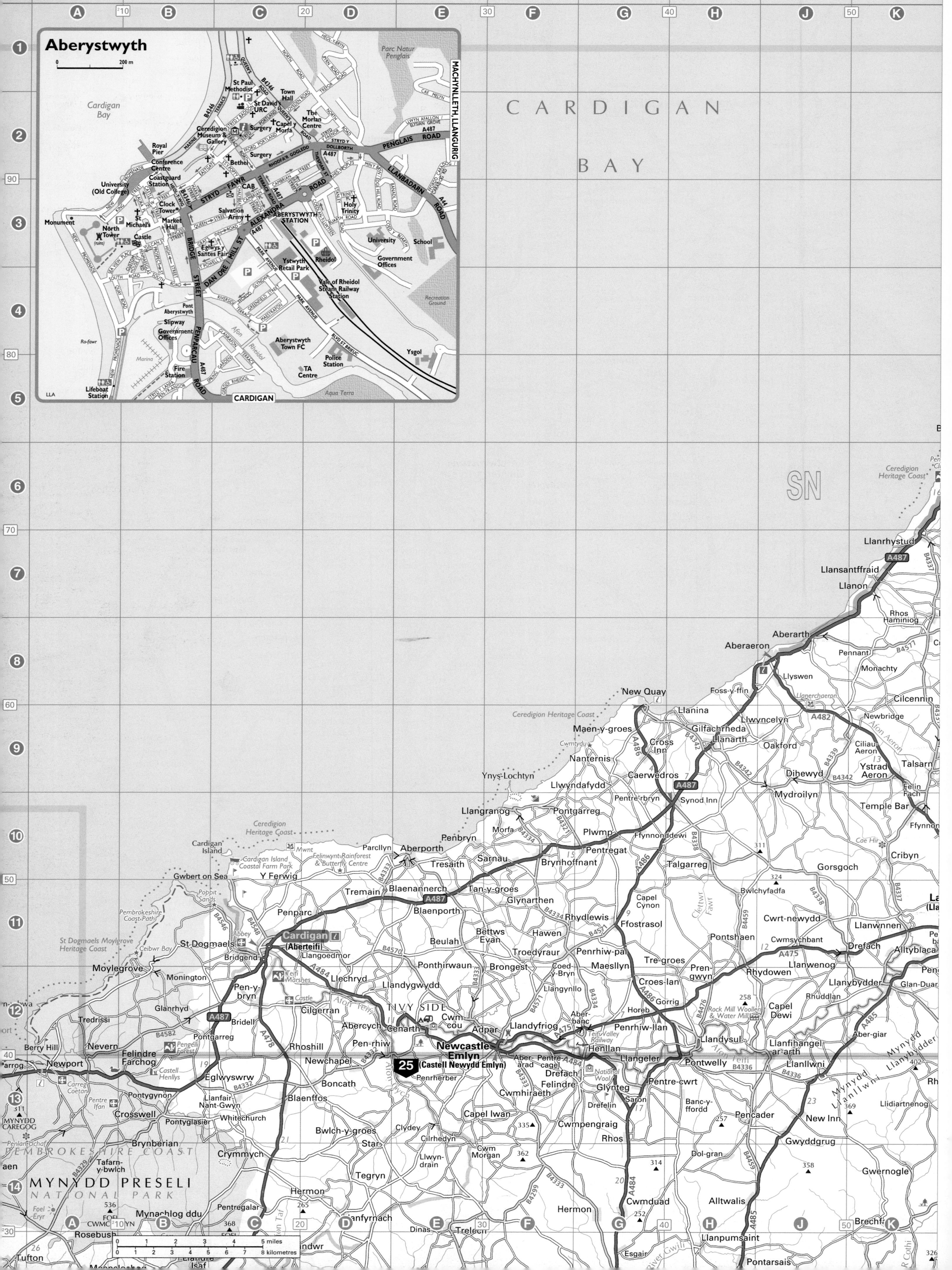
Aberystwyth
0
200 m
Cardigan Bay
Parc Natur Penglais
MACHYNLLETH, LLANGURIG
St Paul Methodist
Town Hall
St David's URC
Capel y Morfa
The Morlan Centre
Ceredigion Museum & Gallery
Surgery
Royal Pier
Conference Centre
Bethel
Coastguard Station
University (Old College)
PENGLAIS ROAD
STRYD FAWR
CAB
Clock Tower
Market Hall
Salvation Army
Monument
North Tower
St Michael's
Castle
Eglwys y Santes Fair
ABERYSTWYTH STATION
Holy Trinity
University
School
Government Offices
Rheidol
Ystwyth Retail Park
Vale of Rheidol Steam Railway Station
Recreation Ground
Pont Aberystwyth
Slipway
Government Offices
Ro-fawr
Marina
Aberystwyth Town FC
Police Station
Ysgol
Fire Station
TA Centre
Lifeboat Station
Aqua Terra
CARDIGAN
LLA
ALEXANDRA ROAD
LLANBADARN ROAD
BRIDGE STREET
PENPARCAU ROAD
DAN DRE / MILL ST
PARK AVENUE
A487
A44
B4346
CARDIGAN
BAY
SN
Ceredigion Heritage Coast
Llanrhystud
Llansantffraid
Llanon
Rhos Haminiog
Aberarth
Aberaeron
Pennant
Monachty
Llyswen
Foss-y-ffin
New Quay
Llanina
Llanerchaeron
Cilcennin
Newbridge
Llwyncelyn
Gilfachrheda
Llanarth
Oakford
Maen-y-groes
Cwmtydu
Cross Inn
Nanternis
Ciliau Aeron
Ystrad Aeron
Talsarn
Dihewyd
Caerwedros
Ynys-Lochtyn
Llwyndafydd
Pentre'rbryn
Synod Inn
Mydroilyn
Felin Fach
Temple Bar
Llangranog
Pontgarreg
Ffynnon
Morfa
Plwmp
Ffynnonddewi
Cae Hir
Cribyn
Penbryn
Cardigan Island
Parcllyn
Aberporth
Mwnt
Pentregat
Talgarreg
Gorsgoch
Cardigan Island Coastal Farm Park
Felinwynt Rainforest & Butterfly Centre
Tresaith
Sarnau
Brynhoffnant
Gwbert on Sea
Y Ferwig
Bwlchyfadfa
Poppit Sands
Tremain
Blaenannerch
Tan-y-groes
Glynarthen
Capel Cynon
Cletwr Fawr
Pembrokeshire Coast Path
Penparc
Blaenporth
Rhydlewis
Ffostrasol
Cwrt-newydd
Llanwnnen
Cardigan (Aberteifi)
Abbey
St Dogmaels Moylgrove Heritage Coast
Ceibwr Bay
St Dogmaels
Beulah
Bettws Evan
Hawen
Pontshaen
Cwmsychbant
Drefach
Alltyblaca
Bridgend
Llangoedmor
Troedyraur
Penrhiw-pal
Moylegrove
Monington
Teifi Marshes
Llechryd
Ponthirwaun
Brongest
Coed-y-Bryn
Maesllyn
Tre-groes
Pren-gwyn
Rhydowen
Llanwenog
Llanybydder
Glan-Duar
Pen-y-bryn
Castle
Llandygwydd
Llangynllo
Croes-lan
Gorrig
Rhuddlan
Capel Dewi
Glanrhyd
Tredrissi
Cilgerran
TIVY SIDE
Cwm-cou
Horeb
Rock Mill Woollen & Water Mill
Aber-banc
Abercych
Cenarth
Adpar
Llandyfriog
Penrhiw-llan
Teifi Valley Railway
Llandysul
Llanfihangel-ar-arth
Aber-giar
Bridell
Pontgarreg
Berry Hill
Nevern
Felindre Farchog
Pengelli Forest
Pen-rhiw
Newcastle Emlyn
25 (Castell Newydd Emlyn)
Rhoshill
Henllan
Llangeler
Pontwelly
Llanllwni
Mynydd Llanybydder
Newport
Newchapel
Aber-arad
Pentre-cagel
Drefach
National Wool Museum
Castell Henllys
Eglwyswrw
Penrherber
Carreg Coetan
Pentre Ifan
Pontygynon
Boncath
Felindre
Cwmhiraeth
Glynteg
Pentre-cwrt
Mynydd Llanllwni
MYNYDD CAREGOG
Llanfair-Nant-Gwyn
Blaenffos
Saron
Drefelin
Banc-y-ffordd
Crosswell
Pontyglasier
Whitechurch
Capel Iwan
Pencader
New Inn
Llidiartnenog
Penlan Uchaf
Bwlch-y-groes
Clydey
Cwmpengraig
PEMBROKESHIRE COAST
Brynberian
Star
Cilrhedyn
Rhos
Gwyddgrug
Crymmych
Tafarn-y-bwlch
Llwyn-drain
Cwm Morgan
Dol-gran
Gwernogle
MYNYDD PRESELI
NATIONAL PARK
Tegryn
Hermon
Foel Eryr
Mynachlog ddu
Pentregalar
Hermon
Cwmduad
Alltwalis
Rosebush
Llanfyrnach
Dinas
Trelech
Llanpumsaint
Brechfa
Tufton
Esgair
Pontarsais
River Gwili
Afon Teifi
Afon Aeron
A487
A486
A484
A478
A475
A485
A4329
B4333
B4334
B4338
B4342
B4459
B4336
B4570
B4548
B4546
B4582
B4332
B4299
B4571
B4337
B4339
B4476
B4321
0
1
2
3
4
5 miles
6
7
8 kilometres

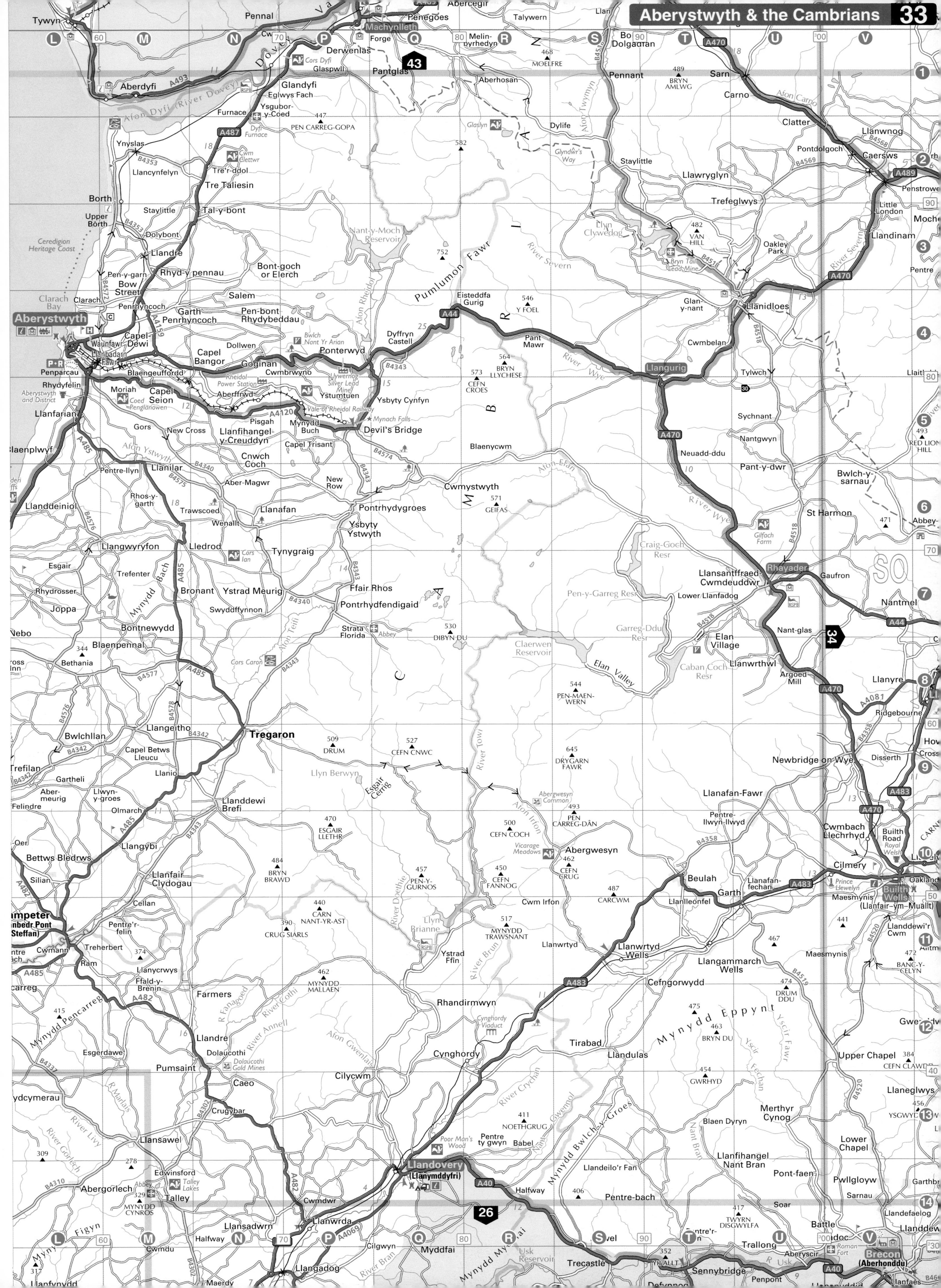

Tywyn
Pennal
Machynlleth
Abercegir
Penegoes
Talywern
Llan
Derwenlas
Forge
Melin-byrhedyn
Bont Dolgadfan
Pantglas
43
Aberdyfi
Afon Dyfi (River Dovey)
Glandyfi
Eglwys Fach
Glaspwll
Cors Dyfi
Furnace
Ysgubor-y-Coed
Dyfi Furnace
447 PEN CARREG-GOPA
468 MOELFRE
Aberhosan
Glaslyn
Dylife
Afon Twymyn
Glyndŵr's Way
Pennant
489 BRYN AMLWG
Sarn
Carno
Afon Carno
Clatter
Llanwnog
Pontdolgoch
Caersws
Staylittle
Llawryglyn
Trefeglwys
Penstrowed
Little London
Llandinam
Oakley Park
River Severn
Pentre
Llyn Clywedog
482 VAN HILL
Bryn Tail Lead Mine
Ynyslas
Llancynfelyn
Tre'r-ddôl
Cwm Clettwr
Tre Taliesin
582
Borth
Upper Borth
Staylittle
Tal-y-bont
Dolybont
Ceredigion Heritage Coast
Llandre
Rhyd-y-pennau
Bont-goch or Elerch
Nant-y-Moch Reservoir
752
Pumlumon Fawr
River Severn
Pen-y-garn
Bow Street
Clarach Bay
Clarach
Salem
Aberystwyth
Penrhyncoch
Garth
Penrhyncoch
Pen-bont Rhydybeddau
Afon Rheidol
Eisteddfa Gurig
546 Y FOEL
Glan-y-nant
Llanidloes
Capel Dewi
Waunfawr
Llanbadarn Fawr
Bwlch Nant Yr Arian
Dyffryn Castell
Pant Mawr
Cwmbelan
Penparcau
Capel Bangor
Dollwen
Goginan
Ponterwyd
564 BRYN LLYCHESE
573 CEFN CROES
River Wye
Llangurig
Tylwch
Rhydyfelin
Blaengeuffordd
Cwmbrwyno
Llywernog Silver Lead Mine
Rheidol Power Station
Moriah
Capel Seion
Aberffrwd
Ystumtuen
Ysbyty Cynfyn
Aberystwyth and District
Coed Penglanowen
Vale of Rheidol Railway
Mynach Falls
Llanfarian
Gors
New Cross
Pisgah
Llanfihangel-y-Creuddyn
Mynydd Bach
Devil's Bridge
Sychnant
Blaenplwyf
Capel Trisant
Blaenycwm
Nantgwyn
493 RED LION HILL
Afon Ystwyth
Cnwch Coch
Neuadd-ddu
Pentre-llyn
Llanilar
Afon Elan
Pant-y-dwr
Aber-Magwr
New Row
Cwmystwyth
Bwlch-y-sarnau
Rhos-y-garth
571 GEIFAS
Llanddeiniol
Trawscoed
Llanafan
Pontrhydygroes
River Wye
St Harmon
Wenallt
Ysbyty Ystwyth
471
Abbey-cwm-hir
Llangwyryfon
Lledrod
Cors Ian
Tynygraig
Gilfach Farm
Craig-Goch Resr
Esgair
Trefenter
Rhayader
Gaufron
Bronant
Ystrad Meurig
Ffair Rhos
Llansantffraed-Cwmdeuddwr
Rhydrosser
Mynydd Bach
Pontrhydfendigaid
Pen-y-Garreg Resr
Lower Llanfadog
Nantmel
Joppa
Swyddffynnon
Bontnewydd
Strata Florida
Abbey
530 DIBYN DU
Garreg-Ddu Resr
Elan Village
Nant-glas
34
Nebo
344
Blaenpennal
Afon Teifi
Claerwen Reservoir
Elan Valley
Caban Coch Resr
Llanwrthwl
Bethania
Cors Caron
Argoed Mill
Llanyre
544 PEN-MAEN-WERN
Ridgebourne
Bwlchllan
Llangeitho
Tregaron
509 DRUM
527 CEFN CNWC
645 DRYGARN FAWR
Capel Betws Lleucu
River Tywi
Newbridge on Wye
Disserth
Trefilan
Llanio
Llyn Berwyn
Esgair Cerrig
Gartheli
Aber-meurig
Llwyn-y-groes
Llanafan-Fawr
Felindre
Olmarch
Llanddewi Brefi
Abergwesyn Common
Afon Irfon
493 PEN CARREG-DÂN
Pentre-llwyn-llwyd
470 ESGAIR LLETHR
500 CEFN COCH
Cwmbach Llechrhyd
Builth Road
Royal Welsh
Llangybi
Vicarage Meadows
Abergwesyn
462 CEFN CRUG
Bettws Bledrws
484 BRYN BRAWD
457 PEN-Y-GURNOS
450 CEFN FANNOG
Beulah
Cilmery
Llanfair Clydogau
River Doethie
487 CARCWM
Garth
Llanafan-fechan
Prince Llywelyn
Silian
Cellan
Cwm Irfon
Llanlleonfel
Builth Wells (Llanfair-ym-Muallt)
Maesmynis
Lampeter
Llanbedr Pont Steffan
440 CARN NANT-YR-AST
390 CRUG SIARLS
Llyn Brianne
517 MYNYDD TRAWSNANT
441
Llanddewi'r Cwm
Pentre'r-felin
467
Cwmann
Treherbert
374
Llanwrtyd
Llanwrtyd Wells
Llangammarch Wells
Maesmynis
472 BANC-Y-CELYN
Ram
Llanycrwys
Ystrad Ffin
462 MYNYDD MALLAEN
Cefngorwydd
Ffald-y-Brenin
River Brân
474 DRUM DDU
Farmers
R Fanagoed
River Cothi
Rhandirmwyn
Cynghordy Viaduct
475
Mynydd Eppynt
Mynydd Pencarreg
415
River Annell
463 BRYN DU
Ysgir Fawr
Llandre
Afon Gwenlais
Tirabad
Esgerdawe
Dolaucothi
Cynghordy
Llandulas
Upper Chapel
384 CEFN CLAWDD
Pumsaint
Dolaucothi Gold Mines
Caeo
Cilycwm
454 GWRHYD
Ysgir Fechan
Llanybydder
R Marlais
River Crychan
Crugybar
411 NOETHGRUG
Merthyr Cynog
Llaneglwys
River Gorlech
Llansawel
Poor Man's Wood
Pentre ty gwyn
Babel
Mynydd Bwlch-y-Groes
Nant Brân
Blaen Dyryn
456 YSGWYDD
309
278
Edwinsford
Talley Lakes
Llandovery (Llanymddyfri)
Llandeilo'r Fan
Llanfihangel Nant Bran
Lower Chapel
Pont-faen
Abergorlech
Abbey
329 MYNYDD CYNROS
Talley
Halfway
406
Pentre-bach
Pwllgloyw
Sarnau
26
417 TWYRN DISGWYLFA
Soar
Llandefaelog
Llansadwrn
Llanwrda
Cwmdwr
Figyn
Halfway
Cwmdu
Cilgwyn
Myddfai
Mynydd Myddfai
Usk Reservoir
Trecastle
352
Pentre'r-felin
Trallong
Battle
Aberyscir
Roman Fort
Brecon (Aberhonddu)
Llangadog
River Brân
Sennybridge
Penpont
Maerdy
Llanfynydd
A470
A489
A44
A4120
A485
A487
A482
A483
A40
A4069
A4081
A493
B4353
B4572
B4340
B4343
B4574
B4575
B4576
B4577
B4578
B4342
B4337
B4310
B4302
B4518
B4358
B4519
B4520
B4568
B4569

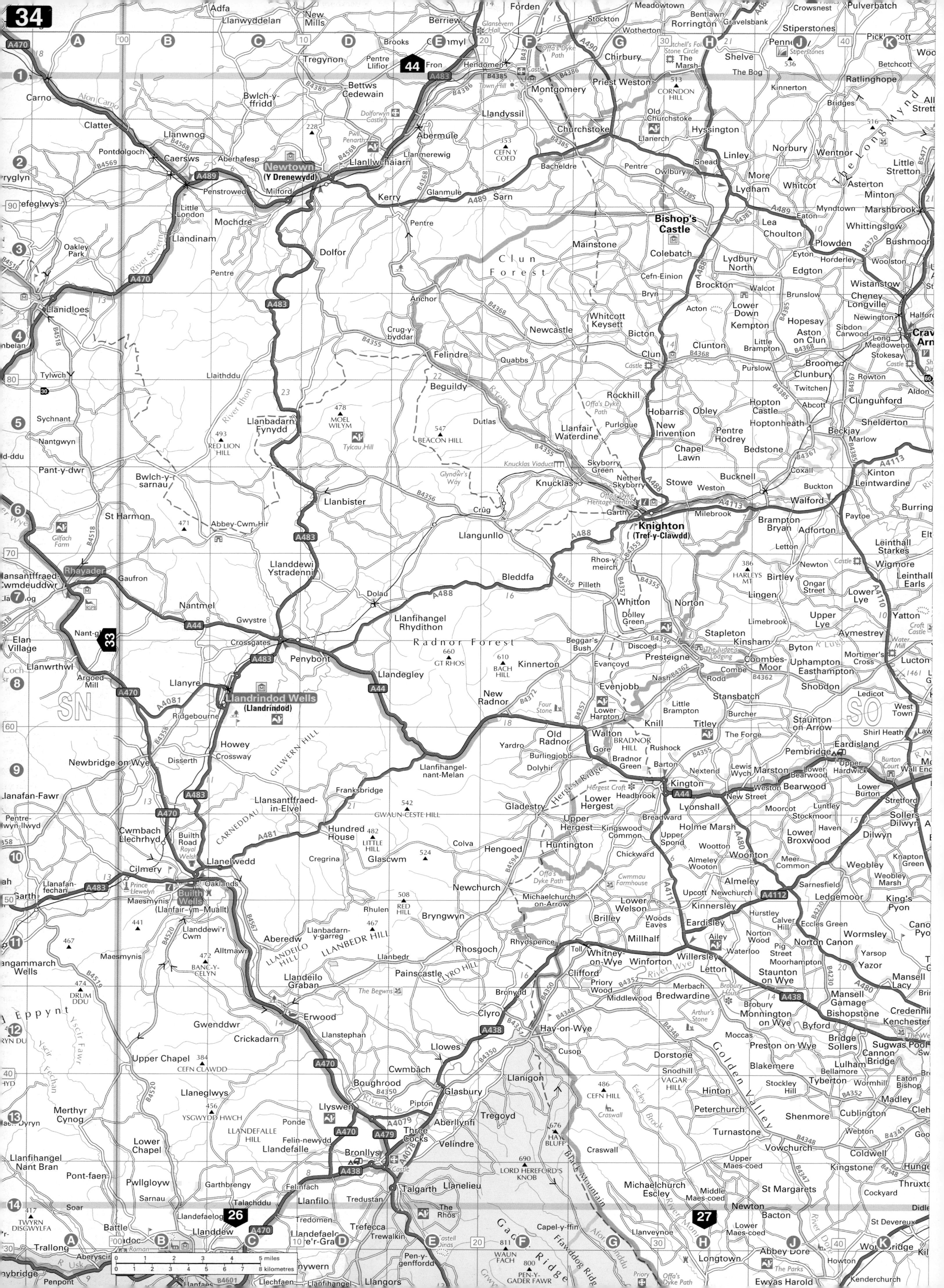
Adfa
Llanwyddelan
New Mills
Berriew
Forden
Meadowtown
Stockton
Bentlawn
Rorrington
Gravelsbank
Crowsnest
Pulverbatch
Stiperstones
Tregynon
Pentre Llifior
Brooks
Fron
Hendomen
Wotherton
Chirbury
Shelve
Pennerley
Stiperstones
Carno
Afon Carno
Bwlch-y-ffridd
Bettws Cedewain
Dolforwyn Castle
Montgomery
Priest Weston
Corndon Hill
The Bog
Kinnerton
Ratlinghope
Clatter
Llanwnog
Caersws
Pontdolgoch
Aberhafesp
Pwll Penarth
Abermule
Llandyssil
Churchstoke
Old Churchstoke
Hyssington
Llanerch
Cefn y Coed
Llanmerewig
Llanllwchaiarn
Newtown
(Y Drenewydd)
Bacheldre
Pentre
Owlbury
Snead
Linley
Norbury
Wentnor
The Long Mynd
Little Stretton
More
Lydham
Whitcot
Asterton
Minton
Penstrowed
Milford
Kerry
Glanmule
Sarn
Little London
Mochdre
Pentre
Bishop's Castle
Lea
Choulton
Myndtown
Marshbrook
Whittingslow
Eaton
Plowden
Bushmoor
Llandinam
Oakley Park
River Severn
Dolfor
Clun Forest
Mainstone
Colebatch
Lydbury North
Eyton
Horderley
Woolston
Edgton
Cefn-Einion
Brockton
Walcot
Wistanstow
Brunslow
Cheney Longville
Llanidloes
Pentre
Anchor
Bryn
Acton
Lower Down
Kempton
Hopesay
Aston on Clun
Sibdon Carwood
Newington
Craven Arms
Crug-y-byddar
Newcastle
Whitcott Keysett
Bicton
Clun
Clunton
Little Brampton
Long Meadowend
Stokesay
Felindre
Quabbs
Purslow
Broome
Clunbury
Rowton
Tylwch
Llaithddu
Beguildy
River Teme
Rockhill
Twitchen
Aldon
Hopton Castle
Clungunford
Sychnant
Llanbadarn Fynydd
Moel Wilym
Tylcau Hill
Dutlas
Hobarris
Obley
Abcott
Nantgwyn
Red Lion Hill
Beacon Hill
Llanfair Waterdine
Offa's Dyke Path
Purlogue
New Invention
Pentre Hodrey
Hoptonheath
Beckjay
Shelderton
Marlow
Bedstone
Chapel Lawn
Pant-y-dwr
Knucklas Viaduct
Skyborry Green
Coxall
Kinton
Leintwardine
Bwlch-y-sarnau
Glyndŵr's Way
Knucklas
Nether Skyborry
Stowe
Bucknell
Weston
Buckton
Llanbister
Offa's Dyke Heritage Centre
Walford
St Harmon
Crûg
Garth
Milebrook
Burrington
Abbey-Cwm-Hir
Knighton
(Tref-y-Clawdd)
Brampton Bryan
Adforton
Paytoe
Gilfach Farm
Llangunllo
Leinthall Starkes
Letton
Llanddewi Ystradenni
Rhos-y-meirch
Harleys Mt
Birtley
Newton
Wigmore
Rhayader
Gaufron
Bleddfa
Pilleth
Ongar Street
Leinthall Earls
Llansantffraed-Cwmdeuddwr
Whitton
Lingen
Lower Lye
Nantmel
Dolau
Norton
Llanfihangel Rhydithon
Dolley Green
Limebrook
Upper Lye
Yatton
Elan Village
Nant-glas
Gwystre
Crossgates
Radnor Forest
Beggar's Bush
Stapleton
Aymestrey
Discoed
Kinsham
Byton
Mortimer's Cross
Croft Castle
Lucton
Llanwrthwl
Penybont
Gt Rhos
Bach Hill
Kinnerton
Evancoyd
Presteigne
The Judge's Lodging
Coombes-Moor
Upphampton
Eastthampton
Argoed Mill
Llanyre
Llandegley
Nash
Rodd
Combe
Shobdon
Llandrindod Wells
(Llandrindod)
Evenjobb
Stansbatch
Ledicot
SN
Ridgebourne
New Radnor
Four Stones
Little Brampton
Lower Harpton
Bircher
Staunton on Arrow
SO
West Town
Walton
Knill
Titley
The Forge
Shirl Heath
Howey
Crossway
Gilwern Hill
Yardro
Old Radnor
Bradnor Hill
Rushock
Eardisland
Pembridge
Gore
Burlingjobb
Dolyhir
Bradnor Green
Barton
Newbridge on Wye
Disserth
Llanfihangel-nant-Melan
Nextend
Lewis Wych
Marston
Lower Bearwood
Burton Court
Upper Hardwick
Kington
Hergest Croft
Headbrook
Weston
Bearwood
New Street
Lower Burton
Llanafan-Fawr
Franksbridge
Llansantffraed-in-Elvel
Gwaun-Ceste Hill
Gladestry
Hergest Ridge
Lower Hergest
Lyonshall
Moorcot
Luntley
Stretford
Sollers Dilwyn
Pentre-llwyn-llwyd
Carneddau
Hundred House
Little Hill
Upper Hergest
Kingswood Common
Breadward
Holme Marsh
Stockmoor
Haven
Dilwyn
Cwmbach Llechrhyd
Builth Road
Royal Welsh
Llanelwedd
Colva
Hengoed
Huntington
Upper Spond
Wootton
Lower Broxwood
Cregrina
Glascwm
Chickward
Almeley Wootton
Woonton
Meer Common
Weobley
Knapton Green
Cilmery
Prince Llewelyn
Builth Wells
(Llanfair-ym-Muallt)
Oaklands
Llanafan-fechan
Garth
Maesmynis
Offa's Dyke Path
Cwmmau Farmhouse
Newchurch
Almeley
Weobley Marsh
Sarnesfield
Red Hill
Rhulen
Michaelchurch-on-Arrow
Upcott
Newchurch
Lower Welson
Kinnersley
Ledgemoor
King's Pyon
Llanddewi'r Cwm
Bryngwyn
Brilley
Woods Eaves
Hurstley
Calver Hill
Eccles Green
Canon Pyon
Llangammarch Wells
Maesmynis
Alltmawr
Banc-y-Celyn
Aberedw
Llanbadarn-y-garreg
Llanbedr Hill
Llandeilo Hill
Rhosgoch
Rhydspence
Millhalf
Eardisley
Ailey
Norton Wood
Norton Canon
Wormsley
Pipe Street
Waterloo
Toll
Whitney-on-Wye
Winforton
Willersley
Letton
Moorhampton
Yarsop
Llanbedr
Painscastle
Clyro Hill
Clifford
River Wye
Staunton on Wye
Yazor
Drum Ddu
Llandeilo Graban
Priory Wood
Merbach
Brobury House
Mansell Lacy
Mynydd Eppynt
The Begwns
Bronydd
Middlewood
Bredwardine
Mansell Gamage
Erwood
Clyro
Brobury
Monnington on Wye
Bishopstone
Credenhill
Gwenddwr
Crickadarn
Llanstephan
Hay-on-Wye
Arthur's Stone
Byford
Kenchester
Moccas
Bridge Sollers
Preston on Wye
Sugwas Pool
Llowes
Cusop
Dorstone
Cannon Bridge
Upper Chapel
Cefn Clawdd
Cwmbach
Snodhill
Vagar Hill
Golden Valley
Blakemere
Lulham
Bellamore
Tyberton
Eaton Bishop
Boughrood
Glasbury
Llanigon
Cefn Hill
Hinton
Stockley Hill
Wormhill
Madley
Llaneglwys
Merthyr Cynog
Ysgwydd Hwch
Llyswen
Pipton
Tregoyd
Craswall
Eskley Brook
Peterchurch
Shenmore
Cublington
Ponde
Aberllynfi
Three Cocks
Velindre
Hay Bluff
Turnastone
Webton
Llandefalle Hill
Felin-newydd
Llandefalle
Craswall
Vowchurch
Lower Chapel
Bronllys
Castle
Lord Hereford's Knob
Black Mountain
Upper Maes-coed
Coldwell
Kingstone
Llanfihangel Nant Bran
Pont-faen
Pwllgloyw
Garthbrengy
Felinfach
Talgarth
Llanelieu
Michaelchurch Escley
Middle Maes-coed
St Margarets
Cockyard
Sarnau
Talachddu
Llanfilo
Tredustan
The Rhos
River Monnow
Newton
Bacton
Soar
Twyn Disgwylfa
Llandefaelog
Llanddew
Tredomen
Trefecca
Trewalkin
Capel-y-ffin
Llanveynoe
Lower Maes-coed
St Devereux
Battle
Aberyscir
Llandefaelog-fach
Castell Dinas
Gader Ridge
Waun Fach
Pen-y-Gader Fawr
Fawddog Ridge
Longtown
Abbey Dore
Howton
Trallong
River Usk
Brecon
Pen-y-genffordd
Llangors
Llechfaen
Priory
Offa's Dyke Path
The Parks
Ewyas Harold
Kenderchurch
Penpont
44
33
26
27
0 1 2 3 4 5 miles
0 1 2 3 4 5 6 7 8 kilometres

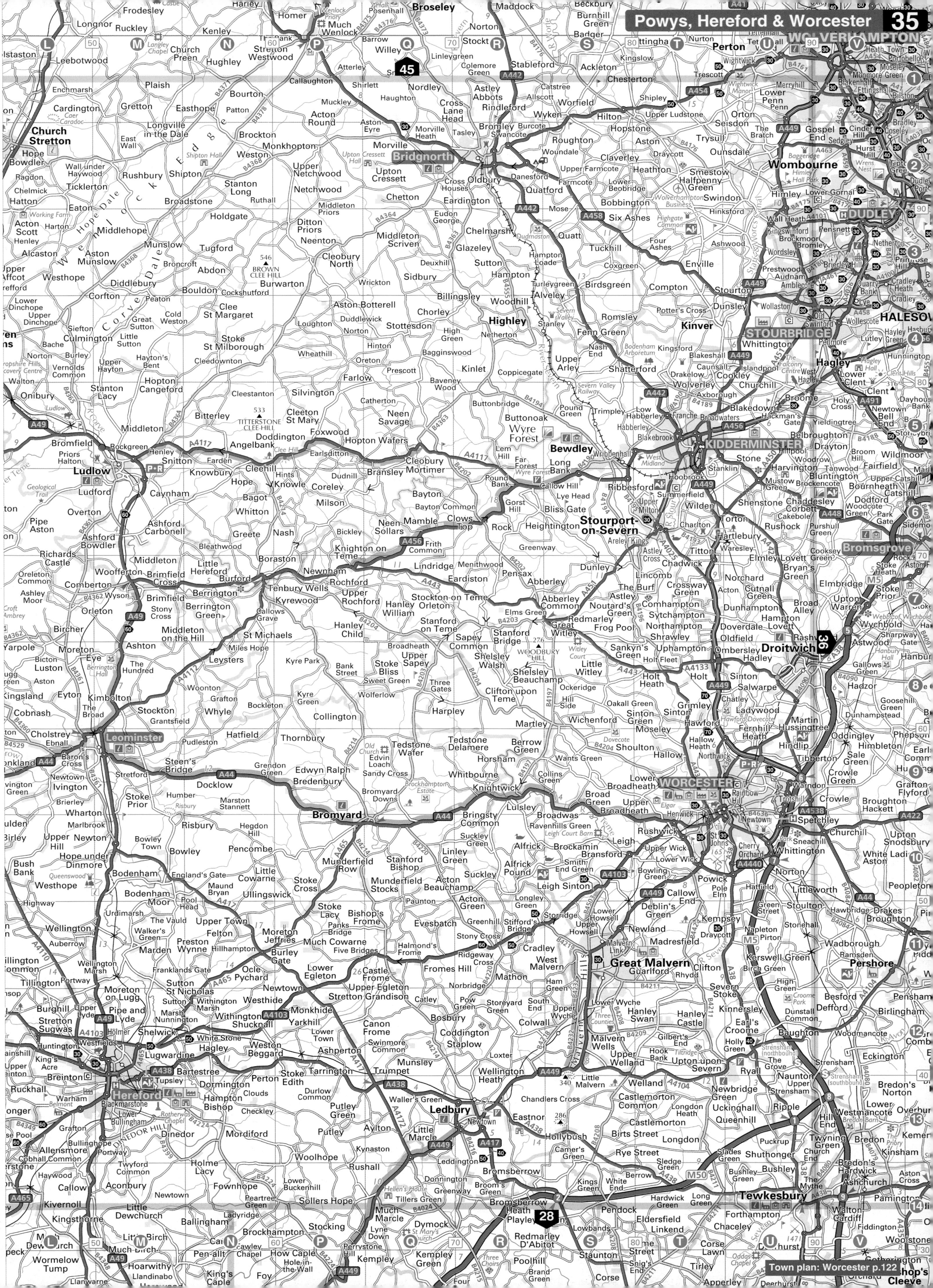
Church Stretton
Ludlow
Leominster
Hereford
Bridgnorth
Kidderminster
Bewdley
Stourport-on-Severn
Droitwich
Bromsgrove
Worcester
Great Malvern
Malvern Wells
Ledbury
Bromyard
Tenbury Wells
Tewkesbury
Pershore
Wombourne
Dudley
Stourbridge
Halesowen
Hagley
Kinver
Highley
Wyre Forest
Much Wenlock
Broseley
Wolverhampton
Cleobury Mortimer
Brown Clee Hill
Titterstone Clee Hill
Woodbury Hill
Wenlock Edge
Corve Dale
Severn Valley Railway
West Midland Safari Park
Upton upon Severn
Much Marcle
Great Witley
Kington
Ashton
Shobdon
A44
A49
A438
A449
A456
A442
A4117
A4103
A417
M5
M50
45
28
36

Town plan: Worcester p.122

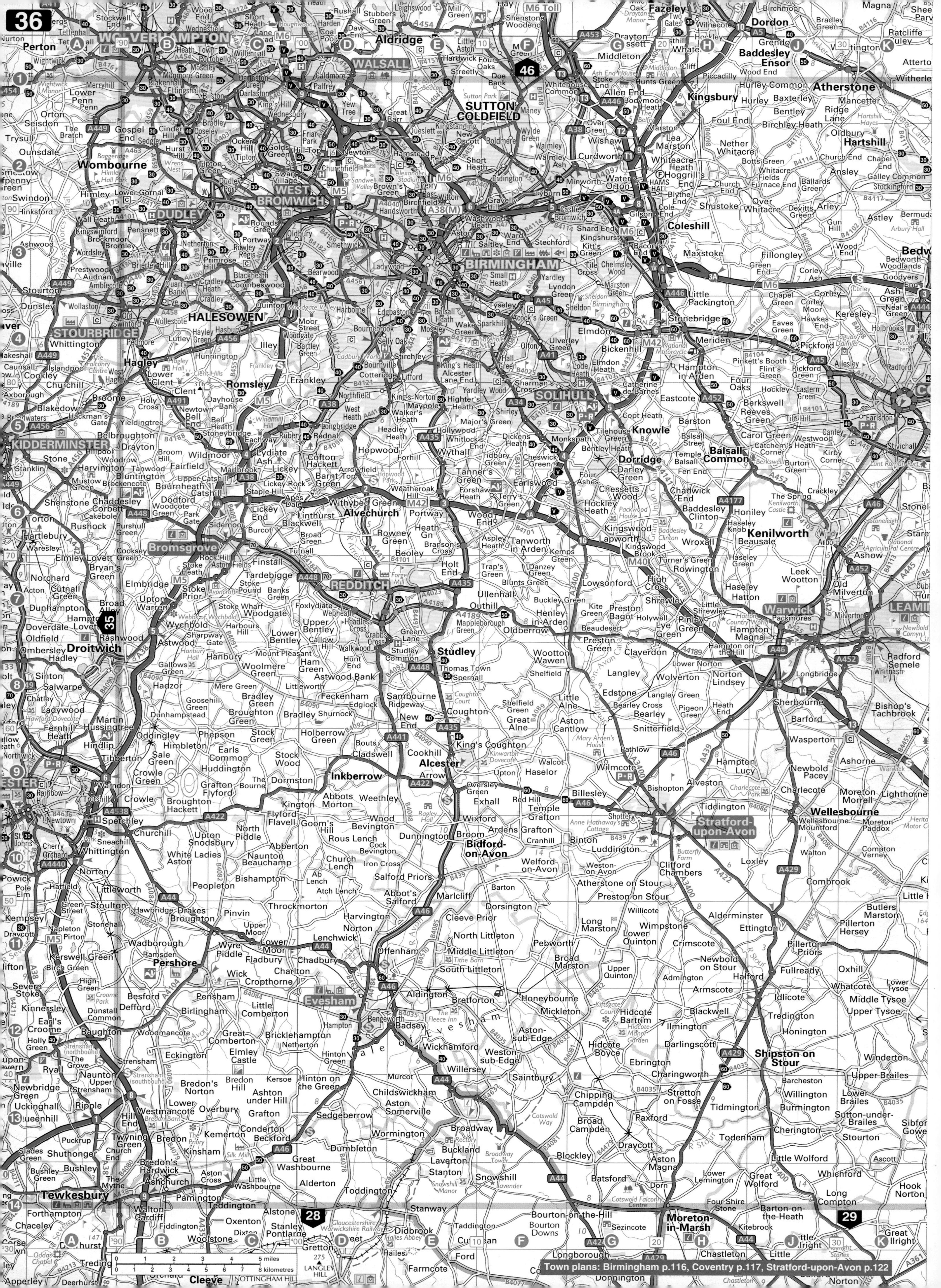
WOLVERHAMPTON
WALSALL
Aldridge
SUTTON COLDFIELD
WEST BROMWICH
DUDLEY
BIRMINGHAM
HALESOWEN
STOURBRIDGE
SOLIHULL
KIDDERMINSTER
Bromsgrove
REDDITCH
Droitwich
Warwick
Kenilworth
Stratford-upon-Avon
Evesham
Pershore
Tewkesbury
Atherstone
Coleshill
Knowle
Dorridge
Alvechurch
Studley
Alcester
Inkberrow
Bidford-on-Avon
Wellesbourne
Shipston on Stour
Chipping Campden
Broadway
Moreton-in-Marsh
Wombourne
Hagley
Romsley
Kingsbury
Hartshill
Balsall Common
Meriden
M6 Toll
M6
M5
M42
M40
M50
Town plans: Birmingham p.116, Coventry p.117, Stratford-upon-Avon p.122

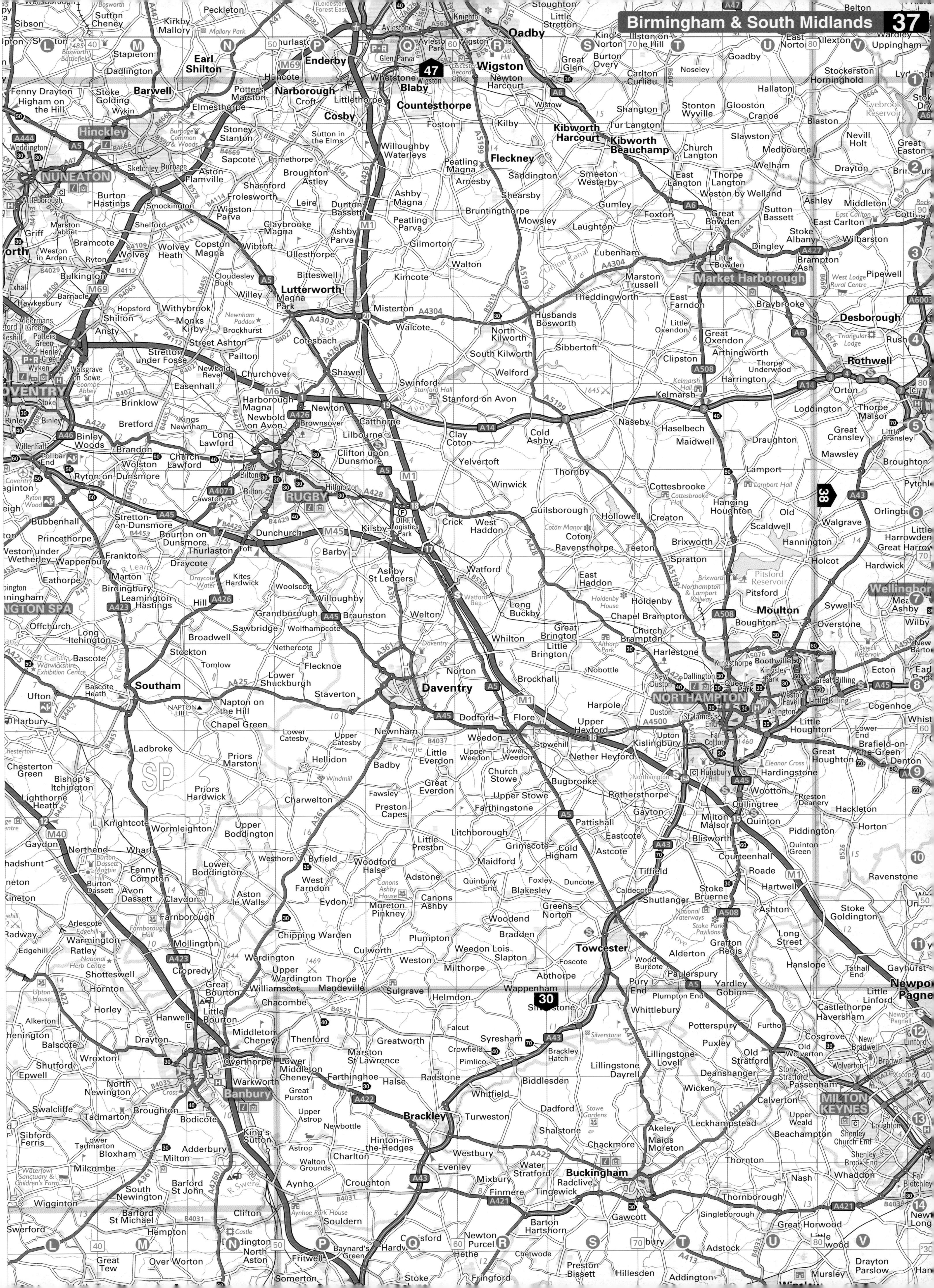

Hinckley
NUNEATON
COVENTRY
Earl Shilton
Enderby
Wigston
Oadby
Blaby
Countesthorpe
Narborough
Cosby
Barwell
Lutterworth
Kibworth Harcourt
Kibworth Beauchamp
Fleckney
Market Harborough
Desborough
Rothwell
RUGBY
Daventry
Southam
NORTHAMPTON
Moulton
Towcester
Brackley
Banbury
Buckingham
MILTON KEYNES
Newport Pagnell
Stony Stratford
Husbands Bosworth
Welford
Crick
Long Buckby
Dunchurch
Braunston
Weedon
Silverstone
Ashby St Ledgers
Guilsborough
Brixworth
Wellingborough
Leamington Spa
Dunsmore
Pitsford Reservoir
Stanford on Avon
Kelmarsh
Naseby
Harbury
Ladbroke
Fenny Compton
Cropredy
Adderbury
Bloxham
Deddington
Aynho
Croughton
Evenley
Deanshanger
Hanslope
Roade
Blisworth

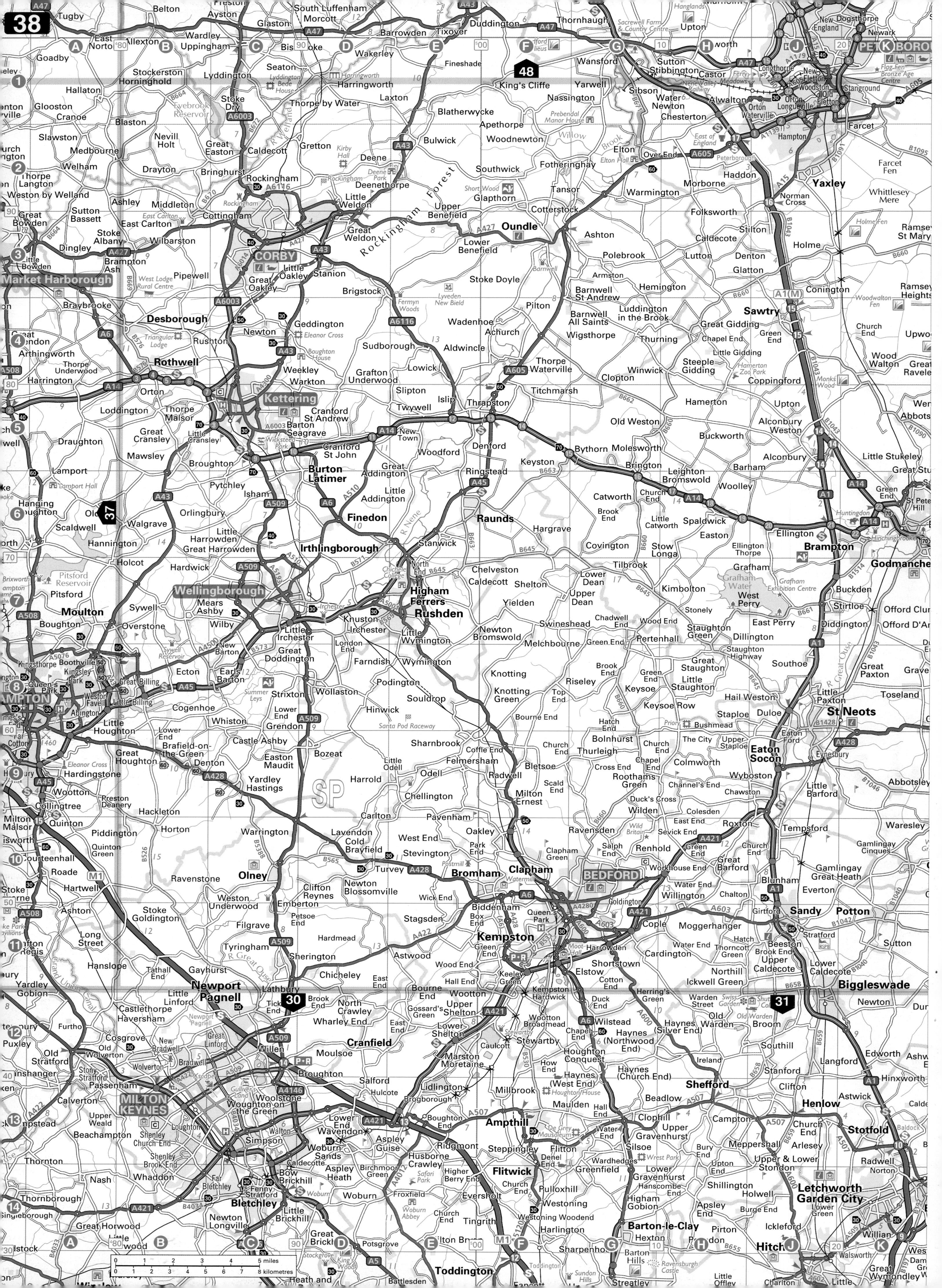
Tugby
Belton
Ayston
South Luffenham
Morcott
Glaston
Wardley
Uppingham
East Norton
Allexton
Bisbrooke
Barrowden
Tixover
Duddington
Thornhaugh
Sacrewell Farm & Country Centre
Upton
Wakerley
Fineshade
Wansford
Sutton
Stibbington
Castor
Longthorpe
New England
Dogsthorpe
Newark
PETERBOROUGH
Goadby
Stockerston
Horninghold
Lyddington
Seaton
Lyddington Bede House
Harringworth
King's Cliffe
Yarwell
Sibson
Water Newton
Alwalton
Orton Longueville
Orton Waterville
Woodston
Old Fletton
Stanground
Flag Fen Bronze Age Centre
Ferry Meadows
Nene Valley Railway
Hallaton
Glooston
Cranoe
Blaston
Eyebrook Reservoir
Stoke Dry
Thorpe by Water
Laxton
Blatherwycke
Apethorpe
Nassington
Prebendal Manor House
Chesterton
Hampton
Farcet
Slawston
Medbourne
Nevill Holt
Great Easton
Caldecott
Gretton
Kirby Hall
Bulwick
Woodnewton
Elton
Elton Hall
Over End
Peterborough
Fotheringhay
Welham
Drayton
Bringhurst
Rockingham
Deene
Deene Park
Deenethorpe
Southwick
Haddon
Farcet Fen
Thorpe Langton
Weston by Welland
Ashley
Middleton
Cottingham
Rockingham Forest
Little Weldon
Short Wood
Glapthorn
Tansor
Warmington
Morborne
Yaxley
Norman Cross
Whittlesey Mere
Great Bowden
Sutton Bassett
East Carlton
Stoke Albany
Wilbarston
Upper Benefield
Cotterstock
Oundle
Folksworth
Great Weldon
Lower Benefield
Ashton
Stilton
Holme Fen
Ramsey St Mary's
Dingley
Brampton Ash
Little Bowden
CORBY
Little Oakley
Stanion
Polebrook
Caldecote
Lutton
Denton
Holme
Market Harborough
West Lodge Rural Centre
Pipewell
Great Oakley
Stoke Doyle
Barnwell
Armston
Glatton
Brigstock
Fermyn Woods
Lyveden New Bield
Barnwell St Andrew
Hemington
Conington
Ramsey Heights
Braybrooke
Desborough
Geddington
Eleanor Cross
Pilton
Barnwell All Saints
Luddington in the Brook
Sawtry
Woodwalton Fen
Great Oxendon
Triangular Lodge
Rushton
Newton
Wadenhoe
Achurch
Wigsthorpe
Great Gidding
Chapel End
Green End
Church End
Upwood
Arthingworth
Thorpe Underwood
Boughton House
Sudborough
Aldwincle
Thurning
Little Gidding
Hamerton Zoo Park
Wood Walton
Great Raveley
Rothwell
Harrington
Weekley
Warkton
Grafton Underwood
Lowick
Thorpe Waterville
Winwick
Steeple Gidding
Coppingford
Monks Wood
Orton
Kettering
Slipton
Islip
Thrapston
Titchmarsh
Clopton
Loddington
Thorpe Malsor
Cranford St Andrew
Barton Seagrave
Twywell
Hamerton
Upton
Great Cransley
Little Cransley
Wicksteed Park
Cranford St John
New Town
Denford
Old Weston
Alconbury Weston
Abbots Ripton
Draughton
Mawsley
Broughton
Woodford
Bythorn
Molesworth
Buckworth
Alconbury
Little Stukeley
Great Stukeley
Lamport
Lamport Hall
Burton Latimer
Great Addington
Ringstead
Keyston
Brington
Leighton Bromswold
Barham
Pytchley
Isham
Little Addington
Catworth
Church End
Woolley
Green End
Hanging Houghton
Old
Scaldwell
Walgrave
Orlingbury
Finedon
Raunds
Brook End
Little Catworth
Spaldwick
Easton
Ellington
Huntingdon
St Peter's Hill
Hannington
Little Harrowden
Great Harrowden
Irthlingborough
Stanwick
Hargrave
Covington
Stow Longa
Ellington Thorpe
Brampton
Hinchingbrooke
Brixworth
Pitsford Reservoir
Holcot
Hardwick
North End
Chelveston
Caldecott
Tilbrook
Grafham
Grafham Water
Grafham Exhibition Centre
Godmanchester
Pitsford
Wellingborough
Chichele College
Higham Ferrers
Shelton
Lower Dean
Upper Dean
Kimbolton
West Perry
Buckden
Moulton
Sywell
Mears Ashby
Irchester
Rushden
Yielden
Stonely
Stirtloe
Offord Cluny
Offord D'Arcy
Boughton
Overstone
Wilby
Knuston
Little Irchester
Little Wymington
Newton Bromswold
Swineshead
Chadwell End
Wood End
Pertenhall
Staughton Green
East Perry
Dillington
Diddington
Sywell Reservoir
New Barton
Great Doddington
London End
Farndish
Wymington
Melchbourne
Green End
Staughton Highway
Southoe
Great Paxton
Graveley
Kingsthorpe
Boothville
Kingsley Park
Great Billing
Ecton
Earls Barton
Podington
Knotting
Brook End
Riseley
Keysoe
Little Staughton
Great Staughton
NORTHAMPTON
Queen's Park
Weston Favell
Little Billing
Abington
Summer Leys
Strixton
Wollaston
Souldrop
Knotting Green
Top End
Keysoe Row
Hail Weston
Little Paxton
Toseland
Cogenhoe
Whiston
Lower End
Grendon
Hinwick
Santa Pod Raceway
Bourne End
Hatch End
Bushmead
Staploe
Duloe
St Neots
Little Houghton
Lower End
Brafield-on-the-Green
Castle Ashby
Sharnbrook
Coffle End
Church End
Bolnhurst
Church End
The City
Upper Staploe
Eaton Ford
Eaton Socon
Eynesbury
Cotton End
Great Houghton
Denton
Easton Maudit
Bozeat
Little Odell
Felmersham
Thurleigh
Chapel End
Colmworth
Hardingstone
Eleanor Cross
Yardley Hastings
Harrold
Odell
Radwell
Bletsoe
Cross End
Roothams Green
Wyboston
Abbotsley
Hunsbury Hill
Wootton
Preston Deanery
Chellington
Scald End
Channel's End
Chawston
Little Barford
Collingtree
Hackleton
Milton Ernest
Duck's Cross
Wilden
Quinton
Horton
Carlton
Pavenham
Colesden
Roxton
Tempsford
Waresley
Milton Malsor
Piddington
Warrington
Lavendon
Cold Brayfield
Oakley
Ravensden
East End
Sevick End
Gamlingay Cinques
Blisworth
Quinton Green
West End
Stevington
Park End
Wild Britain
Salph End
Renhold
Church End
Green End
Courteenhall
Ravenstone
Olney
Turvey
Bromham
Clapham Green
Clapham
Great Barford
Gamlingay Great Heath
Roade
Clifton Reynes
Newton Blossomville
Postmill
BEDFORD
Workhouse End
Blunham
Everton
Hartwell
Weston Underwood
Emberton
Wick End
Water End
Willington
Chalton
Stoke Bruerne
Ashton
Stoke Goldington
Petsoe End
Biddenham
Box End
Queen's Park
Goldington
Cople
Moggerhanger
Girtford
Sandy
Potton
Stagsden
Stratford
RSPB
Long Street
Filgrave
Hardmead
Kempston
Castle Mill
Hatch
Beeston
Thorncote Green
Sutton
Grafton Regis
Tyringham
Sherington
Astwood
Green End
Harrowden
Cardington
Brook End
Upper Caldecote
Lower Caldecote
Hanslope
Tathall End
Gayhurst
Chicheley
East End
Wood End
Kempston Hardwick
Shortstown
Water End
Northill
Yardley Gobion
Little Linford
Newport Pagnell
Lathbury
Tickford End
Brook End
Hall End
Keeley Green
Elstow
Cotton End
Ickwell Green
Biggleswade
Castlethorpe
Haversham
North Crawley
Bourne End
Wootton
Herring's Green
Warden Street
Swiss Garden
Shuttleworth Collection
Old Warden
Newton
Cosgrove
Furtho
Great Linford
Willen
Wharley End
Upper Shelton
Lower Shelton
Wootton Broadmead
Duck End
Wilstead
Haynes (Silver End)
Haynes Warden
Broom
Puxley
Old Stratford
Old Wolverton
Wolverton
New Bradwell
Bradwell
Cranfield
Moulsoe
Caulcott
Stewartby
Chapel End
Haynes (Northwood End)
Southill
Edworth
Ashwell
Deanshanger
Stony Stratford
Passenham
Broughton
Marston Moretaine
Houghton Conquest
How End
Haynes (Church End)
Ireland
Langford
Hinxworth
Salford
Hulcote
Lidlington
Millbrook
Haynes (West End)
Houghton House
Stanford
Shefford
Clifton
Calverton
MILTON KEYNES
Gulliver's Land
Woolstone
Woughton on the Green
Brogborough
Maulden
Beadlow
Henlow
Astwick
Caldecote
Upper Weald
Beachampton
Shenley Church End
Loughton
Walton
Lower End
Wavendon
Aspley Guise
Boughton End
Ampthill
Clophill
Campton
Church End
Stotfold
Simpson
Woburn Sands
Ridgmont
De Grey Mausoleum
Water End
Gravenhurst
Upper Gravenhurst
Meppershall
Arlesey
Thornton
Shenley Brook End
Husborne Crawley
Steppingley
Flitton
Silsoe
Bury End
Upper & Lower Stondon
Radwell
Caldecotte
Bow Brickhill
Aspley Heath
Birchmoor Green
Safari Park
Higher Berry End
Flitwick
Denel End
Wardhedges
Wrest Park
Upton End
Norton
Nash
Whaddon
Far Bletchley
Fenny Stratford
Woburn
Woburn Abbey
Froxfield
Eversholt
Church End
Greenfield
Pulloxhill
Lower Gravenhurst
Hanscombe End
Shillington
Holwell
Letchworth Garden City
Thornborough
Bletchley
Little Brickhill
Church End
Westoning
Higham Gobion
Apsley End
Burge End
Lower Green
Singleborough
Great Horwood
Newton Longville
Tingrith
Westoning Woodend
Barton-le-Clay
Pirton
Ickleford
William
Little Horwood
Great Brickhill
Potsgrove
Milton Bryan
Harlington
Hexton
Hitchin
Walsworth
Weston
Mursley
Stockgrove
Sharpenhoe
Barton Hills
Ravensburgh Castle
Great Wymondley
Toddington
Sunden Hills
Little Offley
Streatley
Heath and Reach
Battlesden
Charlton
Little Wymondley
SP
miles
kilometres
0 1 2 3 4 5 miles
0 1 2 3 4 5 6 7 8 kilometres
A B C D E F G H J K
1 2 3 4 5 6 7 8 9 10 11 12 13 14
A47 A6003 A43 A605 A1(M) A15 A6116 A427 A14 A6 A509 A45 A4500 A428 A421 A428 A422 A5 A6 A600 A603 A507 A1 A4146 A5120 A4012 A508 M1
37
48
30
31

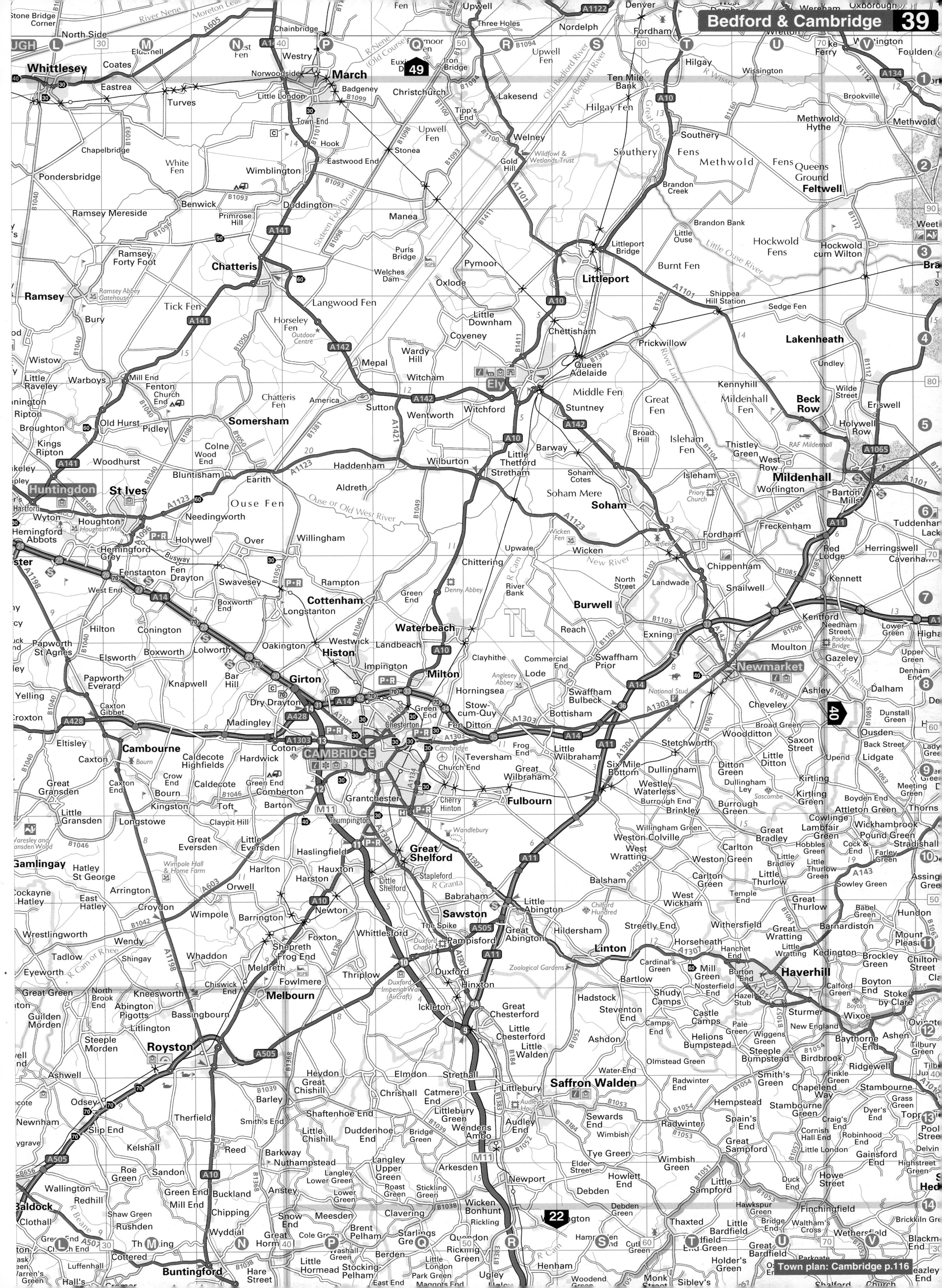
Whittlesey
March
Chatteris
Ramsey
Huntingdon
St Ives
Somersham
Littleport
Ely
Soham
Mildenhall
Lakenheath
Feltwell
Newmarket
Cambridge
Royston
Saffron Walden
Haverhill
Baldock
Buntingford
Linton
Sawston
Great Shelford
Histon
Girton
Milton
Waterbeach
Cottenham
Burwell
Fulbourn
Melbourn
Cambourne
Gamlingay
Upwell
Welney
Manea
Chatteris
Stonea
Mepal
Sutton
Witchford
Haddenham
Wilburton
Stretham
Fordham
Kennett
Kentford
Exning
Bottisham
Teversham
Grantchester
Trumpington
Comberton
Barton
Duxford
Pampisford
Great Abington
Little Abington
Balsham
Ickleton
Great Chesterford
Littlebury
Newport
Wimbish
Thaxted
Clavering
Barkway
Barley
Reed
Therfield
Kelshall
Ashwell
Bassingbourn
Litlington
Steeple Morden
Guilden Morden
Abington Pigotts
Shingay
Whaddon
Meldreth
Shepreth
Foxton
Fowlmere
Thriplow
Whittlesford
Harston
Hauxton
Haslingfield
Harlton
Orwell
Barrington
Wimpole
Croydon
Arrington
Longstowe
Kingston
Toft
Bourn
Caxton
Eltisley
Madingley
Dry Drayton
Oakington
Longstanton
Swavesey
Over
Willingham
Rampton
Earith
Bluntisham
Needingworth
Holywell
Fenstanton
Hilton
Conington
Elsworth
Boxworth
Knapwell
Lolworth
Bar Hill
Papworth Everard
Papworth St Agnes
Yelling
Houghton
Wyton
Hemingford Abbots
Hemingford Grey
Warboys
Wistow
Pidley
Bury
Benwick
Doddington
Wimblington
Christchurch
Littleport Bridge
Hilgay
Denver
Southery
Methwold
Hockwold cum Wilton
Brandon Creek
Burnt Fen
Shippea Hill Station
Prickwillow
Queen Adelaide
Stuntney
Isleham
Worlington
Barton Mills
Freckenham
Chippenham
Snailwell
Landwade
Reach
Swaffham Prior
Swaffham Bulbeck
Lode
Horningsea
Fen Ditton
Stow-cum-Quy
Great Wilbraham
Little Wilbraham
Six Mile Bottom
Dullingham
Stetchworth
Woodditton
Cheveley
Ashley
Moulton
Gazeley
Dalham
Kirtling
Burrough Green
Brinkley
Westley Waterless
Weston Colville
West Wratting
Weston Green
Carlton
Great Bradley
Little Thurlow
Great Thurlow
Withersfield
West Wickham
Horseheath
Hildersham
Bartlow
Castle Camps
Shudy Camps
Ashdon
Hadstock
Helions Bumpstead
Steeple Bumpstead
Sturmer
Kedington
Radwinter
Hempstead
Sewards End
Debden
Wendens Ambo
Arkesden
Elmdon
Chrishall
Heydon
Great Chishill
Little Chishill
Langley
Wicken
Upware
Chittering
Landbeach
Impington
Westwick
Coton
Hardwick
Caldecote
Great Eversden
Little Eversden
Great Gransden
Little Gransden
Hatley St George
East Hatley
Tadlow
Wrestlingworth
Eyeworth
Sandon
Rushden
Wallington
Clothall
Wyddial
Anstey
Meesden
Brent Pelham
Berden
Stocking Pelham
Hormead
Henham
Ugley
Rickling
Quendon
Wicken Bonhunt
Widdington
Radwinter
Great Sampford
Little Sampford
Finchingfield
Great Bardfield
Birdbrook
Ridgewell
Stambourne
A14
A10
A11
A505
A1198
A142
A141
A1101
A1123
A1307
A1303
A1304
A428
A603
A1301
M11
A1065
A134
A1122
A605
A507
B1040
B1050
B1049
B1102
B1085
B1063
B1052
B1053
B1054
B1383
B1368
B1039
B1038
49
40
22
TL

Town plan: Cambridge p.116

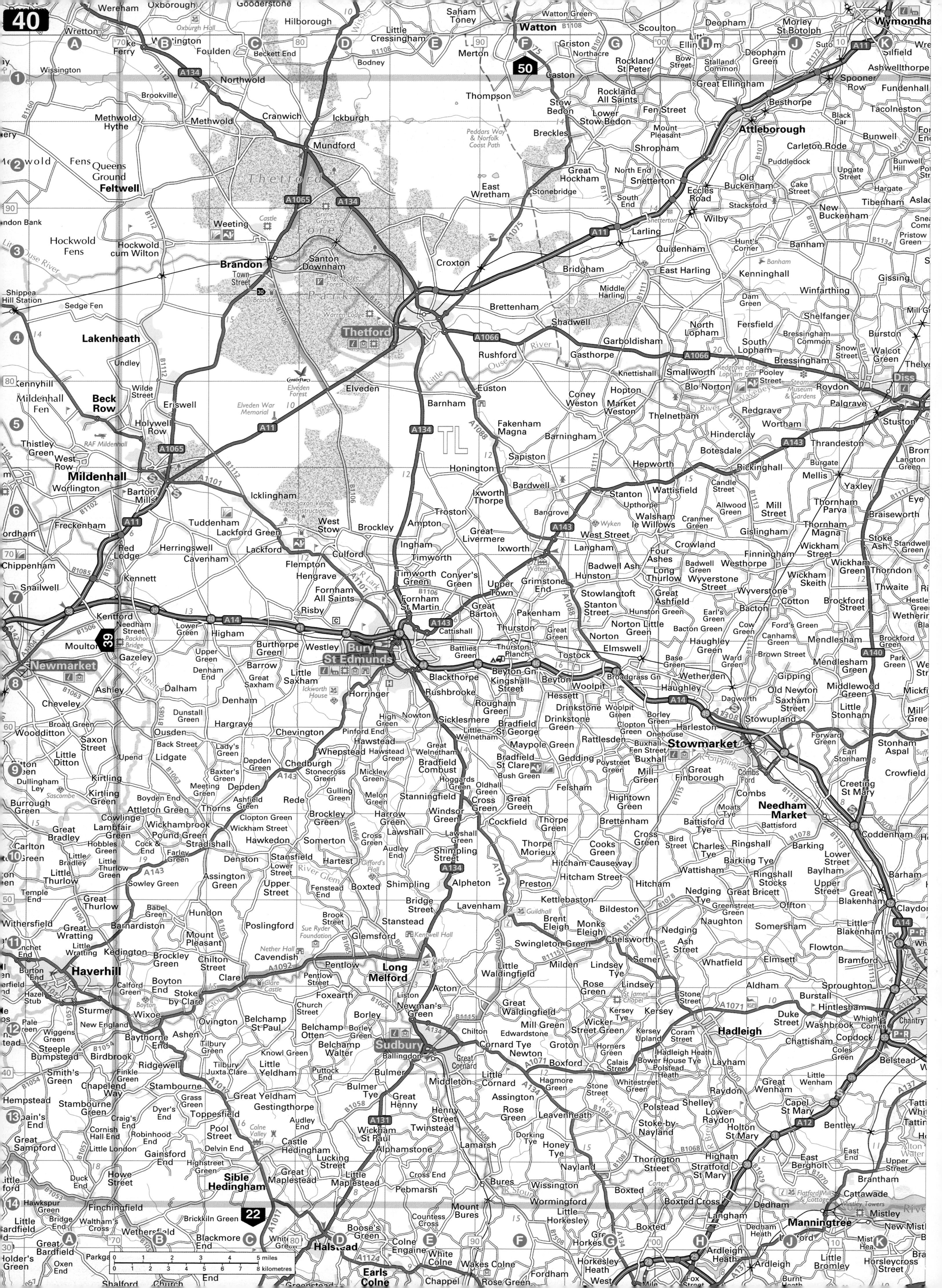
Wereham
Oxborough
Gooderstone
Hilborough
Saham Toney
Watton
Watton Green
Scoulton
Deopham
Morley St Botolph
Wymondham
Wretton
Wretton
Oxburgh Hall
Foulden
Beckett End
Little Cressingham
Bodney
Merton
Griston
Northacre
Rockland St Peter
Bow Street
Stalland Common
Deopham Green
Suton
Silfield
Ashwellthorpe
Wissington
Northwold
Caston
Thompson
Rockland All Saints
Great Ellingham
Spooner Row
Fundenhall
Brookville
Cranwich
Ickburgh
Stow Bedon
Lower Stow Bedon
Fen Street
Besthorpe
Tacolneston
Methwold Hythe
Methwold
Mundford
Peddars Way & Norfolk Coast Path
Breckles
Mount Pleasant
Attleborough
Black Car
Bunwell
Fens
Queens Ground
Feltwell
Thetford Forest
Shropham
Carleton Rode
Puddledock
Great Hockham
North End
Snetterton
Old Buckenham
Upgate Street
Bunwell Hill
East Wretham
Stonebridge
Eccles Road
Cake Street
Hargate
Tibenham
South End
Stacksford
New Buckenham
Weeting
Castle
Grime's Graves
Wilby
Larling
Snetterton
Hockwold Fens
Hockwold cum Wilton
Quidenham
Hunt's Corner
Banham
Pristow Green
Brandon
Town Street
Santon Downham
Croxton
Bridgham
East Harling
Kenninghall
Gissing
Banham
High Lodge Forest Centre
Shippea Hill Station
Sedge Fen
Park
Middle Harling
Dam Green
Winfarthing
Brettenham
Warren Lodge
Shelfanger
Lakenheath
Thetford
Shadwell
North Lopham
Fersfield
Burston
Bressingham Common
Garboldisham
South Lopham
Snow Street
Walcot Green
Undley
Rushford
Gasthorpe
Bressingham
Thelveton
Little Ouse River
Kennyhill
Mildenhall Fen
Beck Row
Wilde Street
Center Parcs Elveden Forest
Elveden
Euston
Knettishall
Smallworth
Redgrave and Lopham Fen
Pooley Street
Diss
Eriswell
Elveden War Memorial
Barnham
Coney Weston
Hopton
Blo' Norton
Steam Museum & Gardens
Roydon
Holywell Row
Market Weston
Thelnetham
Redgrave
Palgrave
Thistley Green
RAF Mildenhall
Fakenham Magna
Barningham
Hinderclay
Wortham
Stuston
West Row
Sapiston
Botesdale
Thrandeston
Mildenhall
Honington
Hepworth
Rickinghall
Burgate
Mellis
Langton Green
Worlington
Barton Mills
Icklingham
Bardwell
Stanton
Candle Street
Wattisfield
Yaxley
Anglo-Saxon Village Reconstruction
Ixworth Thorpe
Upthorpe
Allwood Green
Mill Street
Thornham Parva
Eye
Freckenham
Troston
Bangrove
Walsham le Willows
Cranmer Green
Braiseworth
Tuddenham
West Stow
Ampton
Great Livermere
Wyken
Thornham Magna
Lackford Green
Brockley
West Street
Gislingham
Stoke Ash
Standwell Green
Herringswell
Red Lodge
Lackford
Culford
Ingham
Ixworth
Langham
Crowland
Wickham Street
Chippenham
Cavenham
Flempton
Timworth
Four Ashes
Finningham
Westhorpe
Wickham Green
Thorndon
Kennett
Hengrave
Timworth Green
Conyer's Green
Grimstone End
Badwell Ash
Long Thurlow
Badwell Green
Wyverstone Street
Wickham Skeith
Snailwell
Fornham All Saints
Upper Town
Hunston
Stowlangtoft
Great Ashfield
Wyverstone
Thwaite
Fornham St Martin
Great Barton
Stanton Street
Hunston Green
Earl's Green
Bacton
Cotton
Brockford Street
Hestley Green
Kentford
Risby
Pakenham
Norton Little Green
Ford's Green
Wetheringsett
Needham Street
Lower Green
Higham
Cattishall
Thurston
Great Green
Cow Green
Bacton Green
Canhams Green
Moulton
Packhorse Bridge
Upper Green
Burthorpe Green
Westley
Bury St Edmunds
Battlies Green
Thurston Planch
Norton
Haughley Green
Mendlesham
Brockford Green
Newmarket
Gazeley
Denham End
Barrow
Little Saxham
Tostock
Elmswell
Brown Street
Mendlesham Green
Park Green
Great Saxham
Blackthorpe
Beyton Green
Beyton
Broadgrass Green
Base Green
Ward Green
Wetherden
Gipping
Ashley
Dalham
Kingshall Street
Woolpit
Haughley
Old Newton
Middlewood Green
Mickfield
Cheveley
Ickworth House
Horringer
Rushbrooke
Hessett
Dagworth
Saxham Street
Little Stonham
Mill Green
Denham
Dunstall Green
Nowton
Rougham Green
Drinkstone
Woolpit Green
Borley Green
High Green
Sicklesmere
Bradfield St George
Drinkstone Green
Clopton Green
Onehouse
Harleston
Stowupland
Broad Green
Hargrave
Chevington
Pinford End
Little Welnetham
Forward Green
Wood Ditton
Saxon Street
Ousden
Hawstead
Great Welnetham
Maypole Green
Rattlesden
Buxhall Fen Street
Stowmarket
Stonham Aspal
Back Street
Lady's Green
Whepstead
Hawstead Green
Bradfield Combust
Bradfield St Clare
Gedding
Poystreet Green
Buxhall
Earl Stonham
Little Ditton
Upend
Lidgate
Depden Green
Chedburgh
Mickley Green
Bush Green
Great Finborough
Combs Ford
Crowfield
Ditton Green
Baxter's Green
Stonecross Green
Mill Green
Combs
Dullingham Ley
Kirtling
Meeting Green
Depden
Gulling Green
Hoggards Green
Oldhall Green
Felsham
Creeting St Mary
Saxon Street
Kirtling Green
Boyden End
Ashfield Green
Rede
Melon Green
Stanningfield
Great Green
Hightown Green
Needham Market
Burrough Green
Attleton Green
Thorns
Brockley Green
Windsor Green
Cross Green
Moats Tye
Battisford
Cowlinge
Clopton Green
Harrow Green
Cockfield
Thorpe Green
Brettenham
Battisford Tye
Great Bradley
Lambfair Green
Wickhambrook
Wickham Street
Lawshall
Lawshall Green
Cross Green
Bird Street
Charles Tye
Ringshall
Barking
Coddenham
Carlton
Hobbles Green
Cock & End
Pound Green
Stradishall
Hawkedon
Somerton
Cross Green
Shimpling Street
Thorpe Morieux
Cooks Green
Barking Tye
Lower Street
Baylham
Carlton Green
Little Bradley
Farley Green
Denston
Stansfield
Hartest
Audley End
Gifford's Hall
Hitcham Causeway
Wattisham
Ringshall Stocks
Little Thurlow Green
Little Thurlow
Lower Street
Hitcham Street
Barham
Sowley Green
Assington Green
River Glem
Fenstead End
Boxted
Shimpling
Alpheton
Preston
Hitcham
Nedging Tye
Great Bricett
Upper Street
Temple End
Great Thurlow
Upper Street
Bridge Street
Lavenham
Kettlebaston
Great Blakenham
Claydon
Babel Green
Hundon
Brook Street
Guildhall
Bildeston
Greenstreet Green
Offton
Withersfield
Great Wratting
Barnardiston
Poslingford
Sue Ryder Foundation
Stanstead
Brent Eleigh
Monks Eleigh
Naughton
Somersham
Little Blakenham
Mount Pleasant
Nedging
Little Wratting
Kedington
Nether Hall
Cavendish
Glemsford
Kentwell Hall
Swingleton Green
Chelsworth
Ash Street
Flowton
Brockley Green
Chilton Street
Pentlow
Long Melford
Melford Hall
Little Waldingfield
Milden
Lindsey Tye
Semer
Whatfield
Elmsett
Bramford
Haverhill
Calford Green
Boyton End
Clare
Clare Castle
Pentlow Street
Acton
Rose Green
Lindsey
St James' Chapel
Stone Street
Aldham
Sproughton
Hazel Stub
Boyton Hall
Stoke by Clare
Foxearth
Liston
Newman's Green
Great Waldingfield
Kersey Tye
Kersey
Burstall
Hintlesham
Sturmer
Wixoe
Ovington
Church Street
Borley
Mill Green
Wicker Street Green
Hadleigh
Duke Street
Whight's Corner
Chantry
New England
Baythorne End
Ashen
Belchamp St Paul
Belchamp Otten
Borley Green
Chilton
Edwardstone
Kersey Upland
Coram Street
Washbrook
Copdock
Steeple Bumpstead
Tilbury Green
Belchamp Walter
Sudbury
Ballingdon
Cornard Tye
Newton
Groton
Horners Green
Hadleigh Heath
Chattisham
Birdbrook
Knowl Green
Great Cornard
Boxford
Calais Street
Bower House Tye
Polstead Heath
Layham
Coles Green
Belstead
Smith's Green
Ridgewell
Tilbury Juxta Clare
Little Yeldham
Puttock End
Bulmer
Little Cornard
Hagmore Green
Whitestreet Green
Little Wenham
Hempstead
Chapelend Way
Finkle Green
Stambourne
Grass Green
Great Yeldham
Bulmer Tye
Middleton
Assington
Stone Street
Raydon
Great Wenham
Capel St Mary
Stambourne Green
Dyer's End
Toppesfield
Gestingthorpe
Great Henny
Henny Street
Rose Green
Leavenheath
Polstead
Shelley
Lower Raydon
Bentley
Bain's End
Craig's End
Pool Street
Colne Valley
Audley End
Wickham St Paul
Twinstead
Stoke-by-Nayland
Holton St Mary
Great Sampford
Cornish Hall End
Robinhood End
Castle Hedingham
Alphamstone
Lamarsh
Dorking Tye
Honey Tye
Tattingstone
Delvin End
Little London
Gainsford End
Highstreet Green
Lucking Street
Nayland
Thorington Street
Higham
East Bergholt
East End
Upper Street
Duck End
Howe Street
Sible Hedingham
Great Maplestead
Little Maplestead
Cross End
Bures
Wissington
Boxted
Stratford St Mary
Brantham
Cattawade
Flatford Mill & Cottage
Hawkspur Green
Finchingfield
Mount Bures
Wormingford
Boxted Cross
Dedham
Mistley Towers
Mistley
Little Sampford
Bridge End
Waltham's Cross
Brickkiln Green
Countess Cross
Little Horkesley
Langham
Manningtree
New Mistley
Great Bardfield
Wethersfield
Blackmore End
Boose's Green
Halstead
Colne Engaine
Great Horkesley
Dedham Heath
Ford
Mistley Heath
Holder's Green
Oxen End
Parkgate
White Colne
Wakes Colne
Horkesley Heath
Ardleigh Heath
Ardleigh
Little Bromley
Horsleycross Street
Shalford
Church End
Earls Colne
Chappel
Rose Green
Fordham
West
Fox Street
Burnt
Greenstead
TL
50
39
22
0 1 2 3 4 5 miles
0 1 2 3 4 5 6 7 8 kilometres

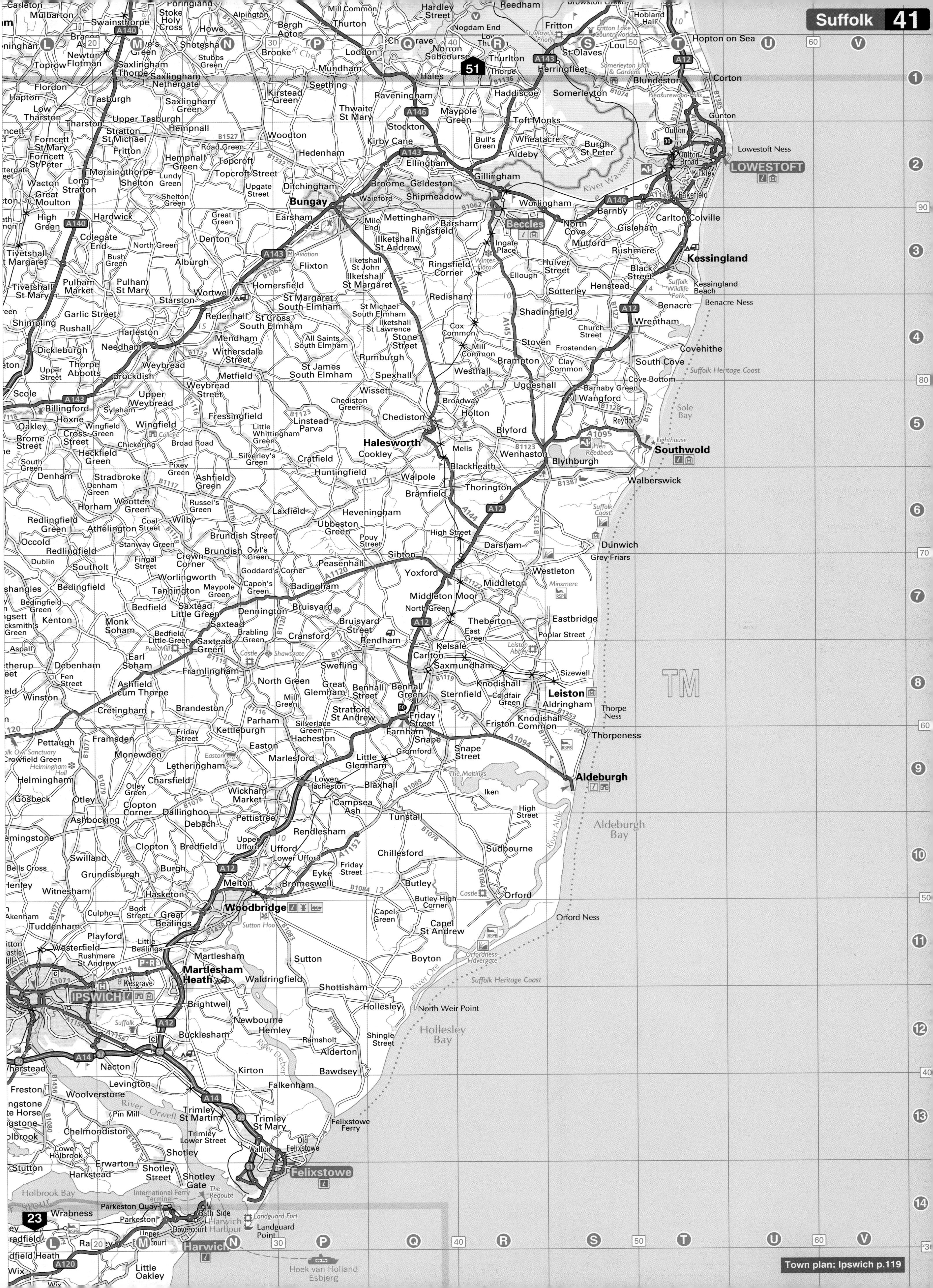
LOWESTOFT
Lowestoft Ness
Hopton on Sea
Corton
Gunton
Oulton Broad
Kirkley
Pakefield
Carlton Colville
Kessingland
Kessingland Beach
Benacre Ness
Benacre
Wrentham
Covehithe
South Cove
Suffolk Heritage Coast
Sole Bay
Southwold
Walberswick
Dunwich
Grey Friars
Westleton
Minsmere
Eastbridge
Sizewell
Leiston
Aldringham
Thorpe Ness
Thorpeness
Aldeburgh
Aldeburgh Bay
Orford
Orford Ness
Hollesley Bay
North Weir Point
Felixstowe Ferry
Felixstowe
Landguard Point
Harwich
Harwich Harbour
Holbrook Bay
Hoek van Holland
Esbjerg
TM
Beccles
Bungay
Halesworth
Saxmundham
Framlingham
Woodbridge
Martlesham Heath
IPSWICH
Haddiscoe
Herringfleet
St Olaves
Fritton
Somerleyton
Blundeston
Gillingham
Worlingham
Barnby
Wangford
Blythburgh
Wenhaston
Yoxford
Middleton
Theberton
Kelsale
Knodishall
Friston
Snape
Iken
Tunstall
Rendlesham
Sudbourne
Butley
Sutton
Shottisham
Hollesley
Alderton
Bawdsey
Ramsholt
Kirton
Falkenham
Trimley St Martin
Trimley St Mary
Walton
Nacton
Levington
Bucklesham
Brightwell
Newbourne
Hemley
Waldringfield
Melton
Ufford
Wickham Market
Campsea Ash
Otley
Grundisburgh
Debenham
Eye
Hoxne
Scole
Diss
Harleston
Stradbroke
Fressingfield
Laxfield
Peasenhall
Sibton
Badingham
Dennington
Earl Soham
Wrabness
Shotley Gate
Chelmondiston
Woolverstone
Freston
Stutton
River Orwell
River Deben
River Alde
River Ore
River Waveney
A12
A14
A140
A143
A144
A145
A146
A1094
A1095
A1120
A1152
A1214
Suffolk Wildlife Park
Hen Reedbeds
Somerleyton Hall & Gardens
Fritton Lake Countryworld
Sutton Hoo
The Maltings
Shawsgate
Landguard Fort
Suffolk Owl Sanctuary
Helmingham Hall
Leiston Abbey
Orfordness-Havergate
International Ferry Terminal
The Redoubt
Lighthouse

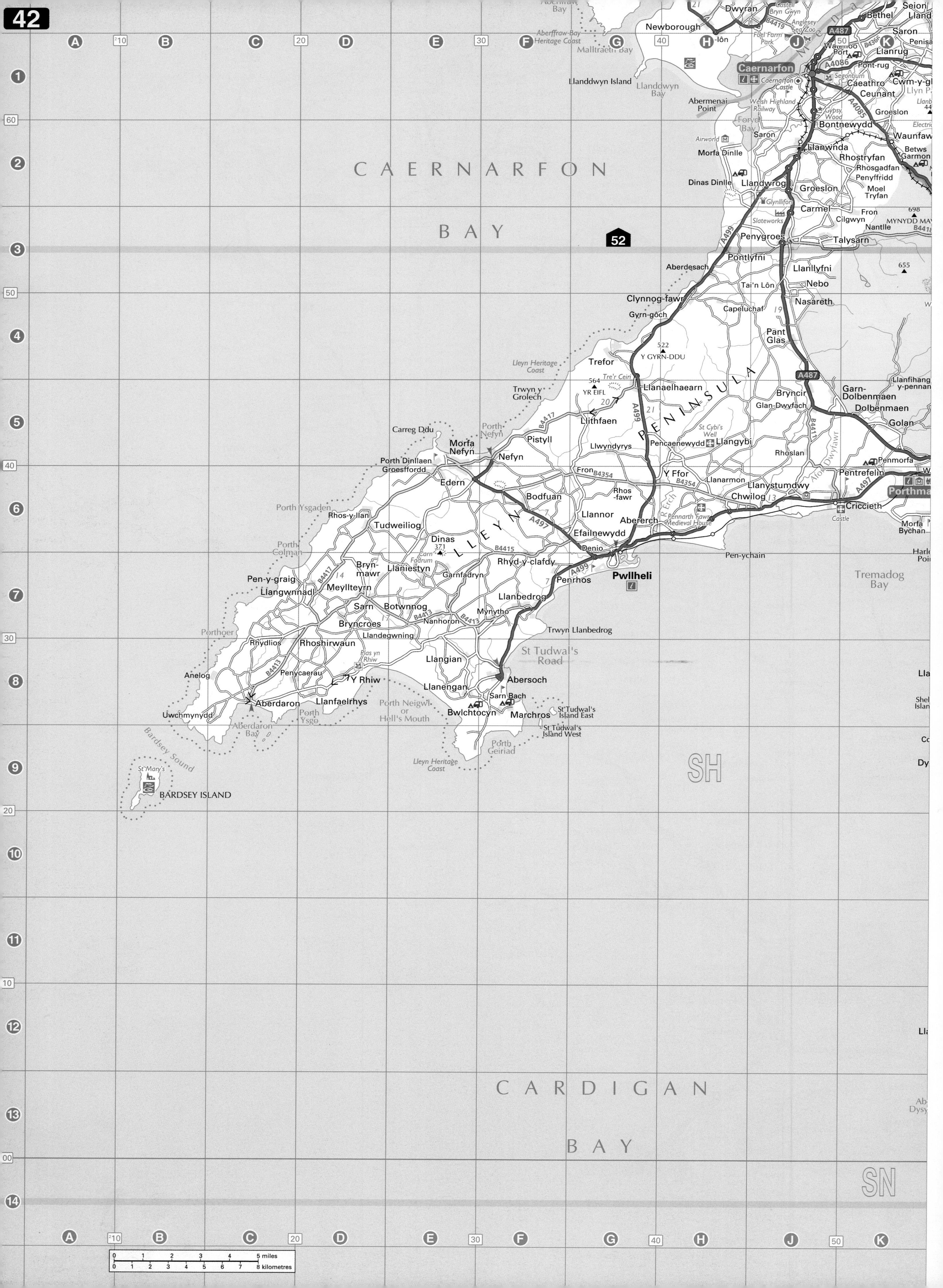
CAERNARFON BAY
CARDIGAN BAY
LLEYN PENINSULA
52
Newborough
Dwyran
Malltraeth Bay
Aberffraw Bay Heritage Coast
Llanddwyn Island
Llanddwyn Bay
Abermenai Point
Caernarfon
Caernarfon Castle
Segontium
Welsh Highland Railway
Foryd Bay
Saron
Airworld
Morfa Dinlle
Dinas Dinlle
Llandwrog
Glynllifon
Slateworks
Bethel
Llanrug
Pont-rug
Caeathro
Cwm-y-glo
Ceunant
Bontnewydd
Groeslon
Waunfawr
Llanwnda
Rhostryfan
Rhosgadfan
Betws Garmon
Penyffridd
Moel Tryfan
Carmel
Fron
Cilgwyn
Nantlle
MYNYDD MAWR
698
Penygroes
Talysarn
Pontllyfni
Aberdesach
Llanllyfni
655
Nebo
Tai'n Lôn
Clynnog-fawr
Nasareth
Gyrn-goch
Capeluchaf
Pant Glas
522
Y GYRN-DDU
Lleyn Heritage Coast
Trefor
Tre'r Ceiri
564
YR EIFL
Llanaelhaearn
A487
Bryncir
Garn-Dolbenmaen
Dolbenmaen
Glan-Dwyfach
Llanfihangel-y-pennant
Golan
Trwyn y Grolech
Llithfaen
Porth Nefyn
Carreg Ddu
Morfa Nefyn
Pistyll
Nefyn
Llwyndyrys
Pencaenewydd
Llangybi
St Cybi's Well
Rhoslan
Penmorfa
Afon Dwyfawr
Porth Dinllaen
Groesffordd
Edern
Fron
Rhos-fawr
Y Ffor
Llanarmon
Llanystumdwy
Pentrefelin
Porthmadog
Chwilog
Criccieth
Castle
Porth Ysgaden
Bodfuan
Rhos-y-llan
Tudweiliog
Llannor
Abererch
Pennarth Fawr Medieval House
Efailnewydd
Morfa Bychan
Porth Colman
Dinas
371
Carn Fadrum
Denio
Pen-y-chain
Pen-y-graig
Bryn-mawr
Llaniestyn
Rhyd-y-clafdy
Llangwnnadl
Meyllteyrn
Garnfadryn
Penrhos
Pwllheli
Tremadog Bay
Sarn
Botwnnog
Llanbedrog
Mynytho
Bryncroes
Nanhoron
Porthoer
Llandegwning
Trwyn Llanbedrog
Rhydlios
Rhoshirwaun
Plas yn Rhiw
St Tudwal's Road
Llangian
Anelog
Penycaerau
Y Rhiw
Abersoch
Llanengan
Aberdaron
Llanfaelrhys
Sarn Bach
Uwchmynydd
Porth Neigwl or Hell's Mouth
Bwlchtocyn
Marchros
St Tudwal's Island East
St Tudwal's Island West
Aberdaron Bay
Porth Ysgo
Porth Ceiriad
Lleyn Heritage Coast
Bardsey Sound
St Mary's
BARDSEY ISLAND
SH
SN
A B C D E F G H J K
1 2 3 4 5 6 7 8 9 10 11 12 13 14
A499
A497
A4085
A4086
B4417
B4354
B4415
B4413
B4411
0 1 2 3 4 5 miles
0 1 2 3 4 5 6 7 8 kilometres

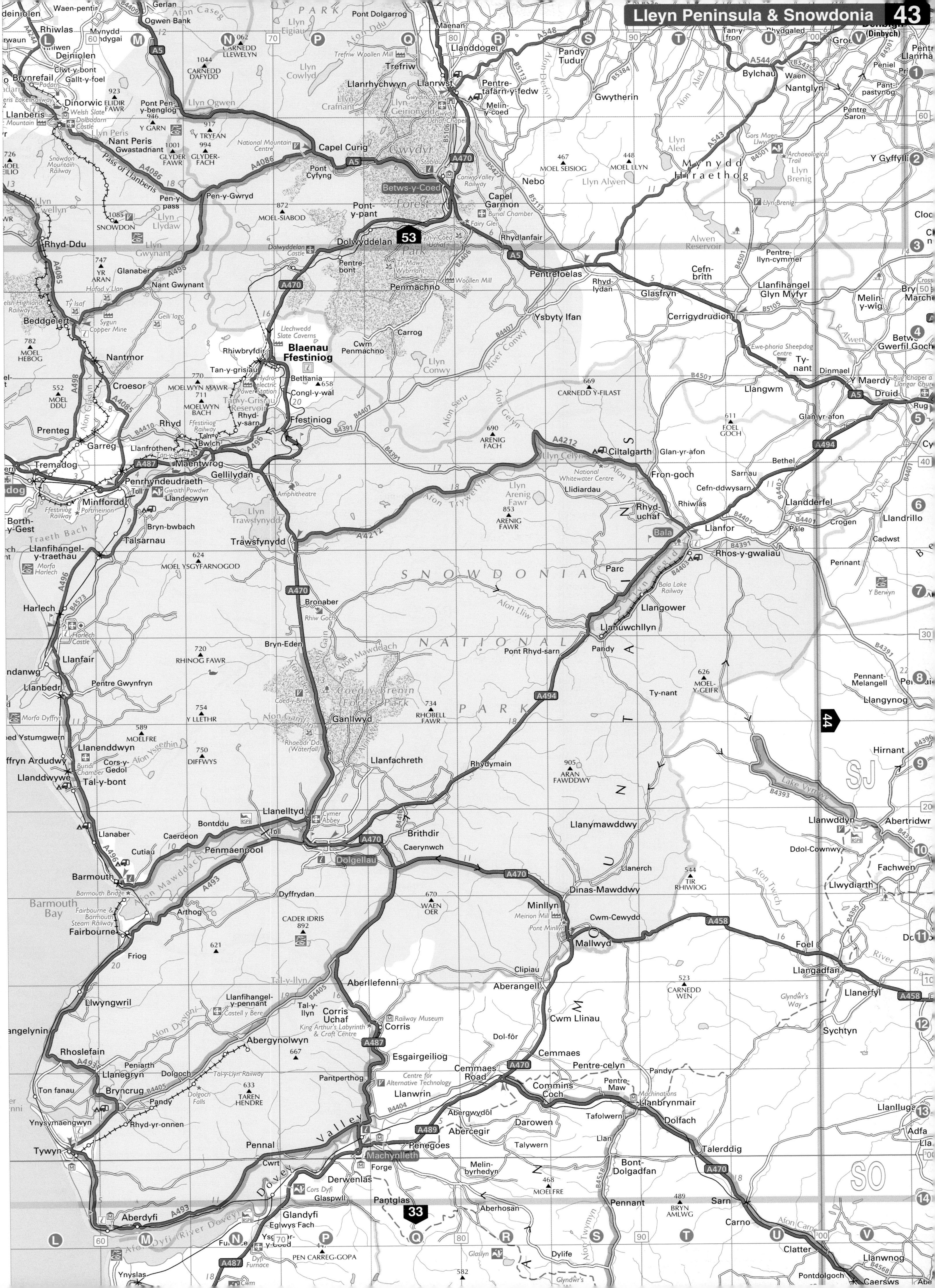
Llanberis
Dinorwic
Nant Peris
Capel Curig
Betws-y-Coed
Dolwyddelan
Blaenau Ffestiniog
Ffestiniog
Penmachno
Pentrefoelas
Cerrigydrudion
Trefriw
Llanrwst
Nebo
Bylchau
Nantglyn
Llyn Brenig
Alwen Reservoir
Mynydd Hiraethog
Beddgelert
Nantmor
Croesor
Prenteg
Garreg
Tremadog
Penrhyndeudraeth
Minffordd
Maentwrog
Gellilydan
Talsarnau
Trawsfynydd
Harlech
Llanfair
Llanbedr
Llanenddwyn
Tal-y-bont
Llanaber
Barmouth
Barmouth Bay
Fairbourne
Arthog
Penmaenpool
Dolgellau
Llanelltyd
Ganllwyd
Bronaber
Llanfachreth
Rhydymain
Brithdir
Bala
Llanfor
Rhos-y-gwaliau
Llangower
Llanuwchllyn
Parc
Ciltalgarth
Frongoch
Dinas-Mawddwy
Minllyn
Mallwyd
Llanymawddwy
Lake Vyrnwy
Llanwddyn
Abertridwr
Llangadfan
Llanerfyl
Foel
Corris
Corris Uchaf
Tal-y-llyn
Abergynolwyn
Llwyngwril
Rhoslefain
Llanegryn
Bryncrug
Tywyn
Aberdyfi
Pennal
Machynlleth
Derwenlas
Glandyfi
Cemmaes Road
Cemmaes
Commins Coch
Llanbrynmair
Talerddig
Carno
Caersws
Dovey Valley
SNOWDONIA NATIONAL PARK
SNOWDON 1085
CADER IDRIS 892
ARAN FAWDDWY 905
ARENIG FAWR 853
RHINOG FAWR 720
A5
A470
A487
A493
A494
A496
A4212
A458
A489
SJ
SO
53
44
33

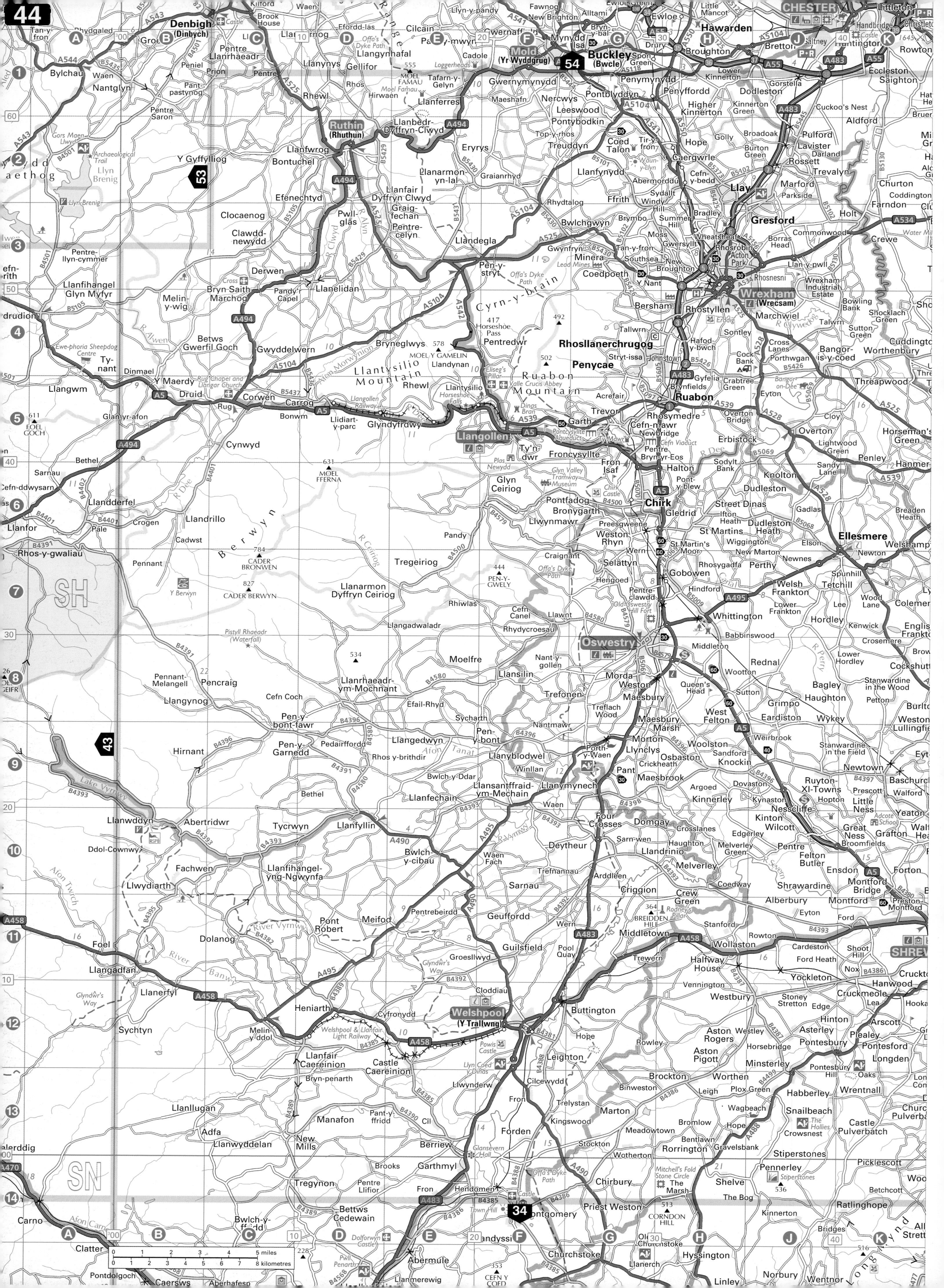
CHESTER
Denbigh (Dinbych)
Mold (Yr Wyddgrug)
Buckley (Bwcle)
Hawarden
Ruthin (Rhuthun)
Wrexham (Wrecsam)
Llangollen
Oswestry
Welshpool (Y Trallwng)
Chirk
Ruabon
Ellesmere
Gresford
Llay
Corwen
Rhosllanerchrugog
Penycae
Llanfyllin
Montgomery
Churchstoke
Bishop's Castle
Berwyn
Cyrn-y-brain
Llantysilio Mountain
Ruabon Mountain
Lake Vyrnwy
Llyn Brenig
Y Gyffylliog
Clocaenog
Llanfair Caereinion
Castle Caereinion
Meifod
Guilsfield
Llanymynech
Four Crosses
Llansantffraid-ym-Mechain
Llanrhaeadr-ym-Mochnant
Llanarmon Dyffryn Ceiriog
Glyn Ceiriog
Pontfadog
Bronygarth
Gobowen
St Martins
Whittington
Ruyton-XI-Towns
Nesscliffe
Montford Bridge
Westbury
Pontesbury
Minsterley
Chirbury
Forden
Berriew
Manafon
New Mills
Tregynon
Bettws Cedewain
Abermule
Carno
Caersws
Llangadfan
Llanerfyl
Foel
Dolanog
Llanwddyn
Abertridwr
Pen-y-bont-fawr
Llangynog
Pennant-Melangell
Llandrillo
Llandderfel
Cynwyd
Glyndyfrdwy
Carrog
Druid
Betws Gwerfil Goch
Gwyddelwern
Bryneglwys
Llandegla
Pen-y-stryt
Minera
Coedpoeth
Caergwrle
Hope
Penyffordd
Broughton
Saltney
Eccleston
Aldford
Farndon
Holt
Bangor-is-y-coed
Overton
Penley
Hanmer
Welsh Frankton
Tetchill
Knockin
Kinnerley
Maesbrook
Melverley
Alberbury
Criggion
Middletown
Buttington
Leighton
Marton
Priest Weston
Shelve
Stiperstones
Snailbeach
Habberley
Longden
Pontesford
Hanwood
Cruckmeole
Yockleton
Wollaston
Halfway House
Hinton
Ratlinghope
Bridges
Wentnor
Norbury
Linley
Hyssington
Llanerch
Corndon Hill
Cefn y Coed
Heniarth
Cyfronydd
Sylfaen
Pool Quay
Trewern
Moelfre
Llansilio
Trefonen
Morda
Maesbury
Llynclys
Pant
Porth-y-Waen
Llanyblodwel
Pen-y-bont
Llangedwyn
Pen-y-Garnedd
Hirnant
Llanwddyn
Bwlch-y-cibau
Llanfihangel-yng-Ngwynfa
Fachwen
Pont Robert
Llwydiarth
Sychtyn
Adfa
Llanllugan
Llanwyddelan
Clatter
Pontdolgoch
Offa's Dyke Path
Glyndŵr's Way
SH
SN
5 miles
8 kilometres

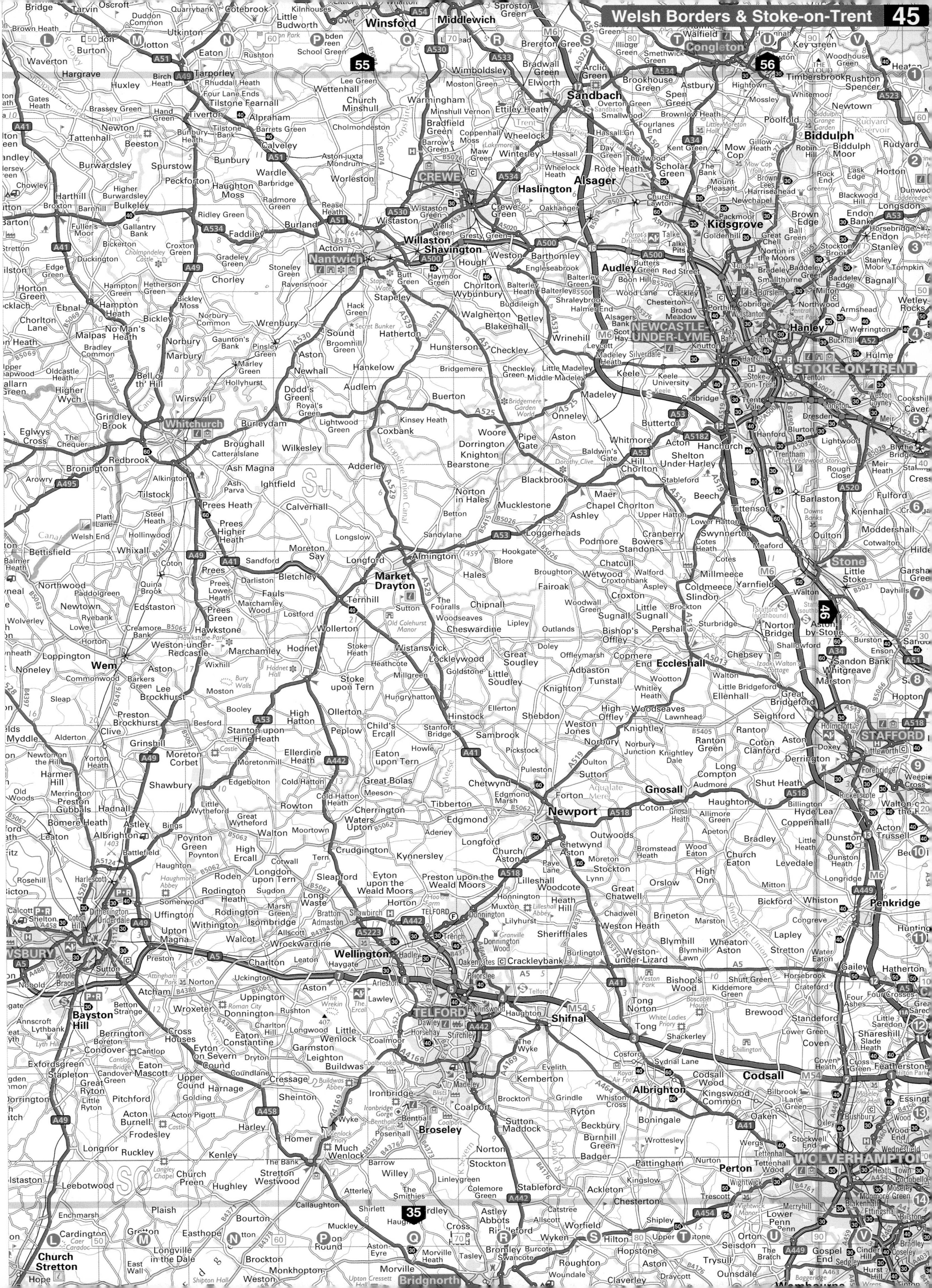
Winsford
Middlewich
Congleton
Sandbach
Biddulph
Crewe
Alsager
Kidsgrove
Haslington
Nantwich
Willaston
Shavington
Audley
Newcastle-under-Lyme
Hanley
Stoke-on-Trent
Whitchurch
Market Drayton
Stone
Eccleshall
Stafford
Wem
Newport
Gnosall
Penkridge
Wellington
Telford
Shifnal
Codsall
Albrighton
Shrewsbury
Bayston Hill
Broseley
Much Wenlock
Wolverhampton
Church Stretton
Bridgnorth
SJ
SO
M6
M54
A5
A41
A49
A51
A53
A500
A442
A518
A34
A529
55
56
46
35

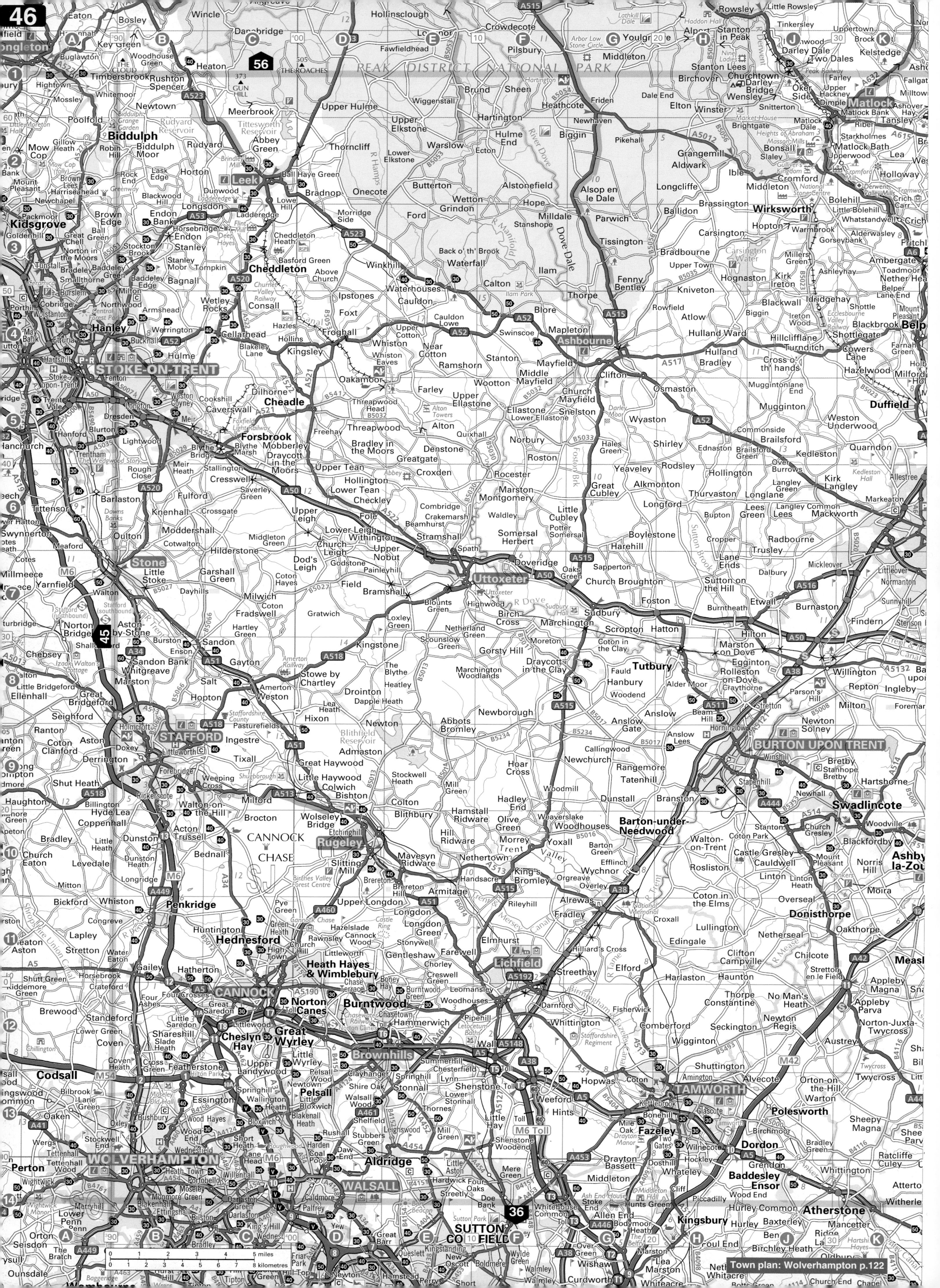
56
45
36
PEAK DISTRICT NATIONAL PARK
CANNOCK CHASE
Congleton
Biddulph
Kidsgrove
Leek
Cheddleton
Hanley
STOKE-ON-TRENT
Cheadle
Stone
STAFFORD
Uttoxeter
Ashbourne
Matlock
Wirksworth
Belper
Duffield
Tutbury
BURTON UPON TRENT
Swadlincote
Rugeley
Hednesford
CANNOCK
Heath Hayes & Wimblebury
Burntwood
Lichfield
Brownhills
Great Wyrley
Cheslyn Hay
Penkridge
Codsall
WOLVERHAMPTON
WALSALL
Aldridge
SUTTON COLDFIELD
TAMWORTH
Fazeley
Dordon
Polesworth
Atherstone
Barton-under-Needwood
Donisthorpe
Measham
5 miles
8 kilometres
Town plan: Wolverhampton p.122

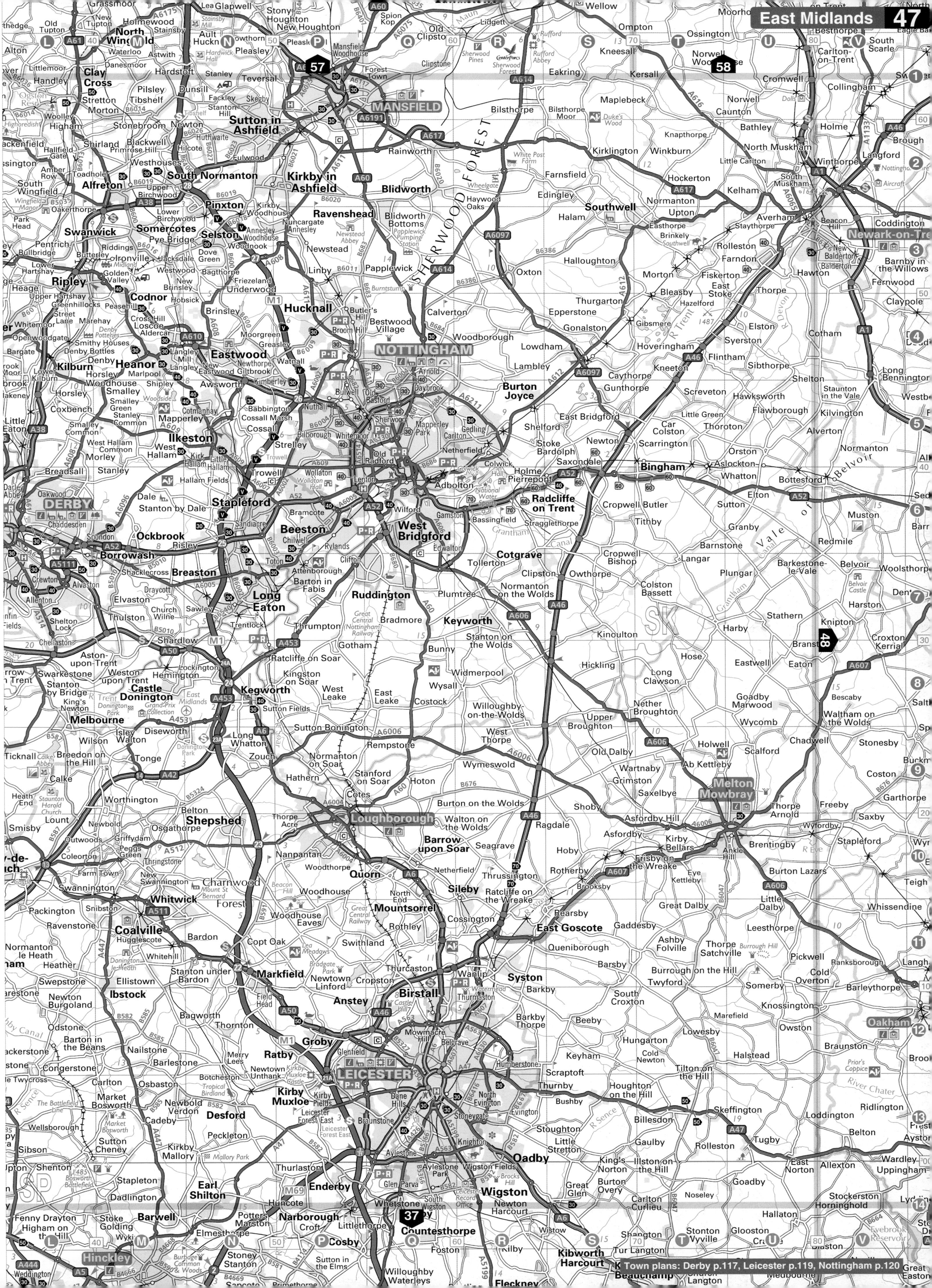

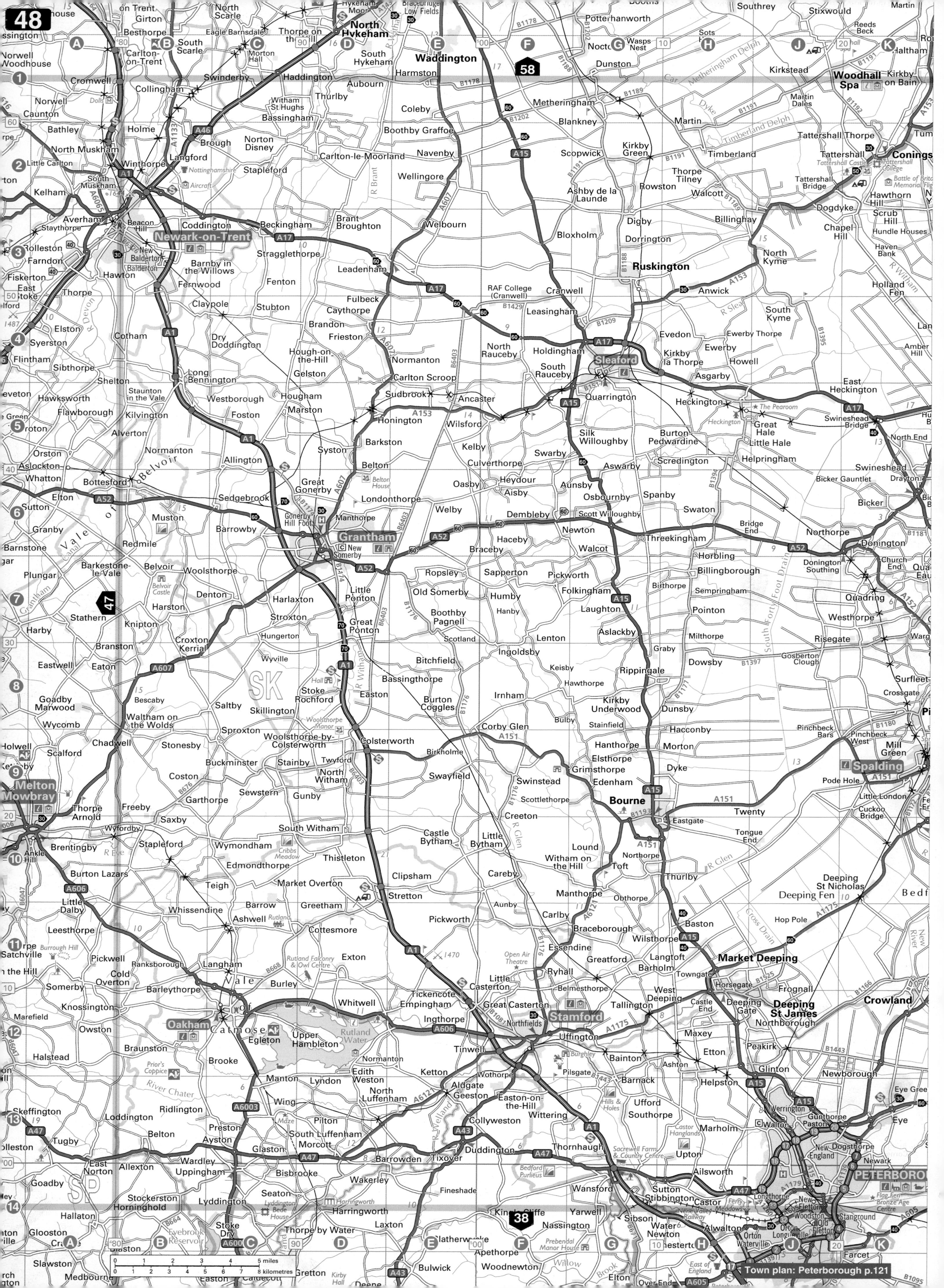
Girton
Besthorpe
South Scarle
Eagle Barnsdale
North Scarle
Thorpe on the Hill
North Hykeham
South Hykeham
Waddington
Potterhanworth
Nocton
Wasps Nest
Sots Hole
Southrey
Stixwould
Reeds Beck
Martin
Haltham
Carlton-on-Trent
Morton Hall
Norwell Woodhouse
Cromwell
Swinderby
Haddington
Harmston
Aubourn
Dunston
Metheringham Delph
Kirkstead
Woodhall Spa
Kirkby on Bain
Norwell
Caunton
Collingham
Witham St Hughs
Thurlby
Bassingham
Coleby
Metheringham
Blankney
Martin
Martin Dales
Timberland Delph
Bathley
Holme
North Muskham
Brough
Norton Disney
Boothby Graffoe
Carlton-le-Moorland
Navenby
Scopwick
Kirkby Green
Timberland
Tattershall Thorpe
Tattershall
Tattershall Castle
Coningsby
Little Carlton
Winthorpe
Langford
Stapleford
Wellingore
Thorpe Tilney
Rowston
Walcott
Ashby de la Launde
Tattershall Bridge
Kelham
South Muskham
Nottinghamshire
Aircraft
Hawthorn Hill
Dogdyke
Scrub Hill
Averham
Staythorpe
Beacon Hill
Newark-on-Trent
Coddington
Beckingham
Brant Broughton
Welbourn
Digby
Bloxholm
Dorrington
Billinghay
Chapel Hill
Hundle Houses
Rolleston
Farndon
Fiskerton
East Stoke
New Balderton
Balderton
Hawton
Barnby in the Willows
Stragglethorpe
Fernwood
Leadenham
Ruskington
North Kyme
Haven Bank
Holland Fen
Thorpe
Claypole
Fenton
Stubton
Fulbeck
Caythorpe
RAF College (Cranwell)
Cranwell
Leasingham
Anwick
South Kyme
Elston
Syerston
Cotham
Dry Doddington
Brandon
Frieston
Hough-on-the-Hill
North Rauceby
Holdingham
Evedon
Ewerby Thorpe
Ewerby
Kirkby la Thorpe
Howell
Amber Hill
Flintham
Sibthorpe
Long Bennington
Normanton
Gelston
Carlton Scroop
South Rauceby
Sleaford
Asgarby
Shelton
Staunton in the Vale
Westborough
Hougham
Sudbrook
Ancaster
Quarrington
Heckington
The Pearoom
East Heckington
Hawksworth
Flawborough
Kilvington
Foston
Marston
Honington
Wilsford
Great Hale
Little Hale
Swineshead Bridge
Orston
Alverton
Barkston
Syston
Kelby
Swarby
Silk Willoughby
Burton Pedwardine
Helpringham
North End
Aslockton
Whatton
Normanton
Allington
Belton
Belton House
Culverthorpe
Aswarby
Scredington
Swineshead
Bottesford
Belvoir
Great Gonerby
Heydour
Aisby
Oasby
Aunsby
Osbournby
Spanby
Bicker Gauntlet
Elton
Sedgebrook
Londonthorpe
Welby
Swaton
Bicker
Sutton
Muston
Gonerby Hill Foot
Manthorpe
Dembleby
Scott Willoughby
Newton
Bridge End
Northorpe
Granby
Barrowby
Grantham
New Somerby
Haceby
Braceby
Walcot
Threekingham
Horbling
Donington
Barnstone
Redmile
Vale of Belvoir
Plungar
Barkestone-le-Vale
Belvoir
Woolsthorpe
Ropsley
Sapperton
Pickworth
Billingborough
Donington Southing
Church End
Belvoir Castle
Denton
Harlaxton
Little Ponton
Old Somerby
Humby
Folkingham
Birthorpe
Sempringham
Quadring
Stathern
Harston
Stroxton
Great Ponton
Boothby Pagnell
Hanby
Laughton
Pointon
Westhorpe
Harby
Knipton
Croxton Kerrial
Hungerton
Scotland
Lenton
Aslackby
Milthorpe
Risegate
Branston
Wyville
Ingoldsby
Graby
Gosberton Clough
Eastwell
Eaton
Bitchfield
Keisby
Rippingale
Dowsby
South Forty Foot Drain
Goadby Marwood
Bescaby
Saltby
Skillington
Holt
Stoke Rochford
Bassingthorpe
Easton
Burton Coggles
Irnham
Hawthorpe
Kirkby Underwood
Dunsby
Surfleet
Crosgate
Waltham on the Wolds
Wycomb
Sproxton
Woolsthorpe Manor
Woolsthorpe-by-Colsterworth
Colsterworth
Corby Glen
Bulby
Stainfield
Hacconby
Pinchbeck Bars
Pinchbeck West
Holwell
Scalford
Chadwell
Stonesby
Buckminster
Stainby
Twyford
North Witham
Birkholme
Swayfield
Hanthorpe
Elsthorpe
Grimsthorpe
Morton
Dyke
Mill Green
Spalding
Melton Mowbray
Coston
Garthorpe
Sewstern
Gunby
Swinstead
Scottlethorpe
Edenham
Bourne
Pode Hole
Little London
Thorpe Arnold
Freeby
Saxby
South Witham
Castle Bytham
Little Bytham
Creeton
Eastgate
Twenty
Cuckoo Bridge
Wyfordby
Brentingby
Stapleford
Wymondham
Cribbs Meadow
Thistleton
Lound
Witham on the Hill
Northorpe
Toft
Tongue End
Ankle Hill
Burton Lazars
Edmondthorpe
Teigh
Market Overton
Clipsham
Careby
Manthorpe
Obthorpe
Thurlby
Deeping St Nicholas
Deeping Fen
Little Dalby
Whissendine
Barrow
Greetham
Stretton
Aunby
Carlby
Baston
Hop Pole
Cross Drain
Leesthorpe
Ashwell
Cottesmore
Pickworth
Braceborough
Wilsthorpe
Burrough Hill
Pickwell
Ranksborough
Exton
Essendine
Greatford
Langtoft
Market Deeping
Satchville
Cold Overton
Langham
Rutland Falconry & Owl Centre
Open Air Theatre
Ryhall
Barholm
Towngate
Somerby
Barleythorpe
Burley
Little Casterton
Belmesthorpe
West Deeping
Horsegate
Frognall
Crowland
Knossington
Whitwell
Tickencote
Empingham
Great Casterton
Tallington
Castle End
Deeping Gate
Deeping St James
Northborough
Marefield
Owston
Oakham
Vale of Catmose
Egleton
Upper Hambleton
Rutland Water
Ingthorpe
Northfields
Stamford
Uffington
Maxey
Peakirk
Braunston
Normanton
Tinwell
Burghley
Bainton
Etton
Halstead
Prior's Coppice
Brooke
Edith Weston
Ketton
Wothorpe
Pilsgate
Barnack
Ashton
Helpston
Glinton
Newborough
River Chater
Manton
Lyndon
North Luffenham
Aldgate
Geeston
Easton-on-the-Hill
Wittering
Hills & Holes
Ufford
Southorpe
Eye Green
Skeffington
Loddington
Ridlington
Wing
Maze
Pilton
Collyweston
Castor Hanglands
Marholm
Werrington
Gunthorpe
Paston
Walton
Eye
Tugby
Belton
Preston
Ayston
South Luffenham
Morcott
Duddington
Thornhaugh
Sacrewell Farm & Country Centre
Upton
Dogsthorpe
New England
Newark
Allexton
East Norton
Wardley
Uppingham
Glaston
Barrowden
Tixover
Bedford Purlieus
Ailsworth
Goadby
Bisbrooke
Seaton
Wakerley
Fineshade
Wansford
Sutton
Stibbington
Castor
Ferry Meadows
Longthorpe
New Fletton
Woodston
Flag Fen Bronze Age Centre
Peterborough
Stockerston
Horninghold
Lyddington
Lyddington Bede House
Harringworth
King's Cliffe
Yarwell
Sibson
Nene Valley Railway
Water Newton
Alwalton
Orton Waterville
Orton Longueville
Old Fletton
Stanground
Hallaton
Eyebrook Reservoir
Stoke Dry
Thorpe by Water
Laxton
Nassington
Prebendal Manor House
Chesterton
Glooston
Blaston
Apethorpe
Woodnewton
Farcet
Slawston
Medbourne
Easton
Gretton
Kirby Hall
Deene
Bulwick
Elton
Overend
East of England
Town plan: Peterborough p.121
5 miles
8 kilometres

58
47
38

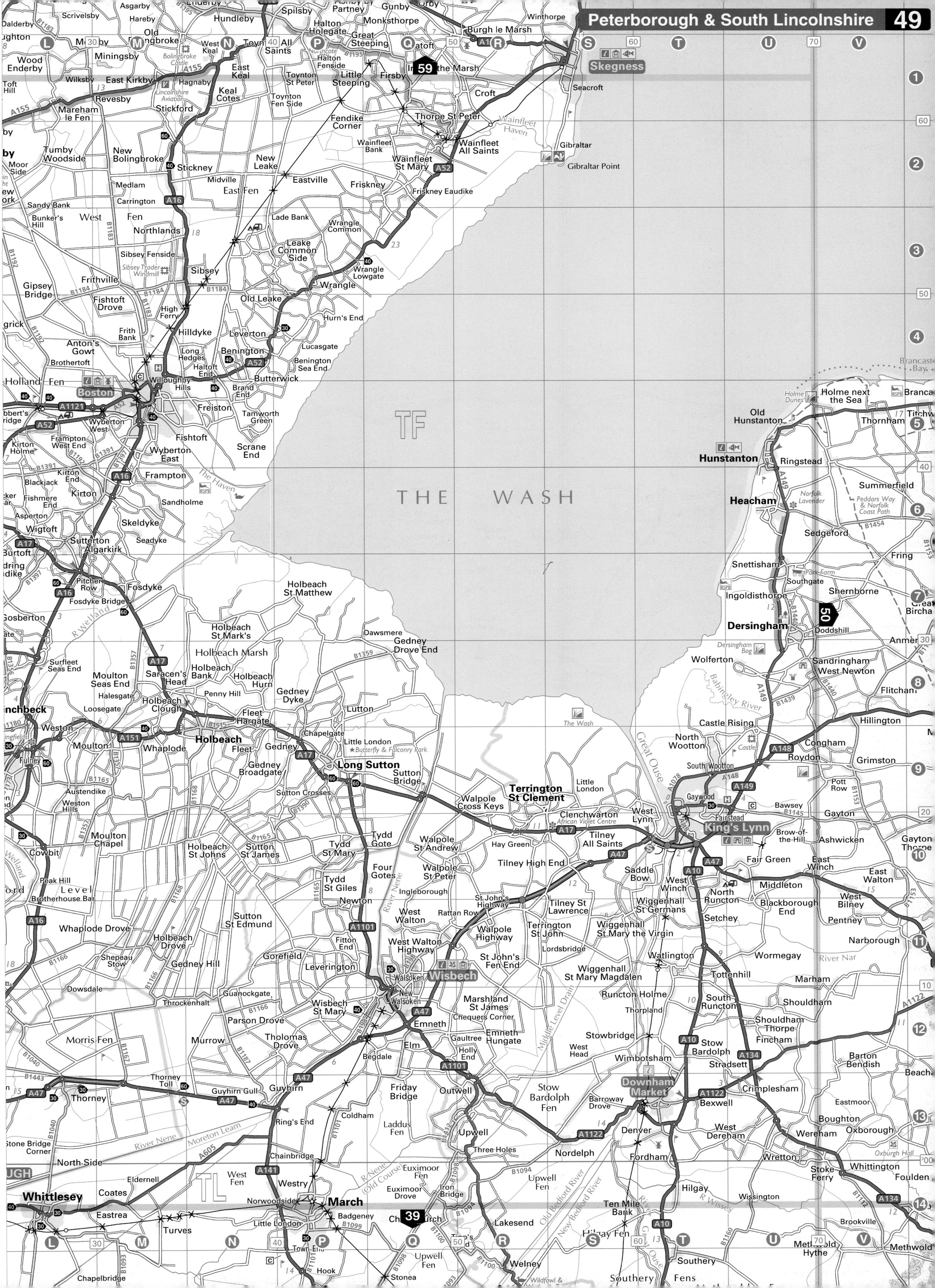
Skegness
Burgh le Marsh
Winthorpe
Seacroft
Croft
Gibraltar
Gibraltar Point
Wainfleet Haven
Wainfleet All Saints
Wainfleet St Mary
Wainfleet Bank
Thorpe St Peter
Firsby
Little Steeping
Great Steeping
Halton Holegate
Spilsby
Partney
Gunby
Monksthorpe
Hundleby
Enderby
Asgarby
Scrivelsby
Hareby
Old Bolingbroke
West Keal
East Keal
Keal Cotes
Toynton All Saints
Toynton St Peter
Toynton Fen Side
Fendike Corner
Miningsby
Wood Enderby
Wilksby
East Kirkby
Hagnaby
Revesby
Stickford
Mareham le Fen
Tumby Woodside
New Bolingbroke
Stickney
Moor Side
Medlam
Carrington
Midville
East Fen
Eastville
New Leake
Friskney
Friskney Eaudike
Sandy Bank
Bunker's Hill
West Fen
Northlands
Lade Bank
Wrangle Common
Leake Common Side
Sibsey Fenside
Sibsey Trader Windmill
Sibsey
Wrangle Lowgate
Wrangle
Frithville
Gipsey Bridge
Fishtoft Drove
High Ferry
Old Leake
Hurn's End
Frith Bank
Hilldyke
Leverton
Anton's Gowt
Long Hedges
Benington
Lucasgate
Benington Sea End
Brothertoft
Haltoft End
Butterwick
Holland Fen
Boston
Willoughby Hills
Brand End
Freiston
Tamworth Green
Wyberton West
Frampton West End
Kirton Holme
Fishtoft
Wyberton East
Scrane End
Kirton End
Blackjack
Frampton
The Haven
Fishmere End
Kirton
Sandholme
Asperton
Skeldyke
Wigtoft
Seadyke
Sutterton
Algarkirk
Burtoft
Pitcher Row
Fosdyke
Fosdyke Bridge
Gosberton
R Welland
Holbeach St Matthew
Holbeach St Mark's
Dawsmere
Gedney Drove End
Holbeach Marsh
Surfleet Seas End
Moulton Seas End
Saracen's Head
Holbeach Bank
Holbeach Hurn
Halesgate
Penny Hill
Gedney Dyke
Loosegate
Holbeach Clough
Fleet Hargate
Lutton
Spalding
Weston
Moulton
Whaplode
Holbeach
Fleet
Gedney
Chapelgate
Little London
Butterfly & Falconry Park
Long Sutton
Sutton Bridge
Gedney Broadgate
Fulney
Austendike
Sutton Crosses
Weston Hills
Moulton Chapel
Holbeach St Johns
Sutton St James
Tydd St Mary
Tydd Gote
Cowbit
Peak Hill
Tydd St Giles
Four Gotes
Deeping Fen
Brotherhouse Bar
Newton
Sutton St Edmund
Whaplode Drove
Holbeach Drove
Shepeau Stow
Gedney Hill
Gorefield
Fitton End
Leverington
Dowsdale
Throckenhalt
Guanockgate
Parson Drove
Wisbech St Mary
Murrow
Tholomas Drove
Morris Fen
Thorney Toll
Guyhirn Gull
Guyhirn
Thorney
Begdale
Ring's End
Coldham
Stone Bridge Corner
North Side
River Nene
Moreton Leam
Chainbridge
Eldernell
Coates
West Fen
Westry
Whittlesey
Eastrea
Turves
Norwoodside
March
Little London
Badgeney
Town End
Hook
Stonea
Chapelbridge
THE WASH
Walpole Cross Keys
Terrington St Clement
Little London
Clenchwarton
African Violet Centre
West Lynn
Walpole St Andrew
Hay Green
Tilney All Saints
Walpole St Peter
Tilney High End
Saddle Bow
Ingleborough
St John's Highway
West Walton
Rattan Row
Tilney St Lawrence
Terrington St John
Walpole Highway
West Walton Highway
St John's Fen End
Lordsbridge
Wiggenhall St Germans
Wiggenhall St Mary the Virgin
Wiggenhall St Mary Magdalen
Wisbech
Walsoken
New Walsoken
Emneth
Marshland St James
Chequers Corner
Elm
Emneth Hungate
Gaultree
Holly End
Outwell
Friday Bridge
Upwell
Laddus Fen
Three Holes
Euximoor Fen
Euximoor Drove
Iron Bridge
Upwell Fen
Lakesend
Welney
Stow Bardolph Fen
Barroway Drove
Nordelph
Middle Level Drain
West Head
Stowbridge
Wimbotsham
Downham Market
Denver
Fordham
Old Bedford River
New Bedford River
Ten Mile Bank
Hilgay Fen
Hilgay
Southery
Southery Fens
Runcton Holme
Thorpland
Watlington
Tottenhill
South Runcton
Stow Bardolph
Stradsett
Bexwell
Crimplesham
West Dereham
Wretton
Stoke Ferry
Wissington
Methwold Hythe
Methwold
Brookville
Whittington
Foulden
Oxburgh Hall
Oxborough
Boughton
Wereham
Eastmoor
Barton Bendish
Beachamwell
Fincham
Shouldham Thorpe
Shouldham
Marham
Wormegay
River Nar
Narborough
Pentney
West Bilney
East Walton
Blackborough End
Setchey
North Runcton
Middleton
West Winch
East Winch
Fair Green
Ashwicken
Gayton Thorpe
Brow-of-the-Hill
King's Lynn
Fairstead
Gaywood
Bawsey
Gayton
Pott Row
South Wootton
North Wootton
Castle Rising
Roydon
Congham
Grimston
Hillington
Flitcham
Babingley River
Wolferton
Sandringham
West Newton
Anmer
Dersingham
Dersingham Bog
Doddshill
Ingoldisthorpe
Shernborne
Snettisham
Park Farm
Southgate
Fring
Sedgeford
Heacham
Norfolk Lavender
Peddars Way & Norfolk Coast Path
Summerfield
Ringstead
Hunstanton
Old Hunstanton
Holme Dunes
Holme next the Sea
Thornham
Titchwell
Brancaster Bay
The Wash
Great Ouse
Skegness
59
50
39

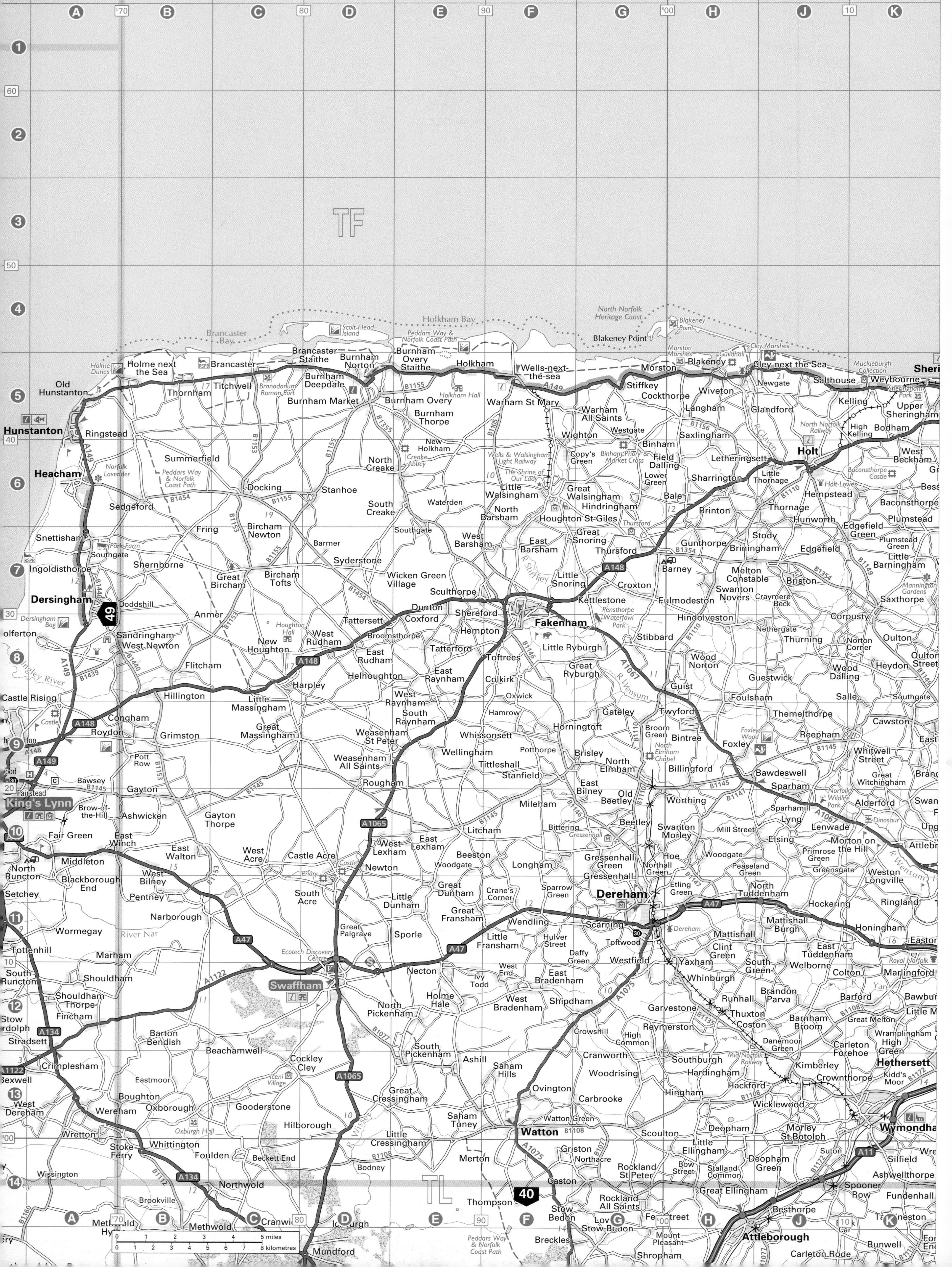

TF
TL
North Norfolk Heritage Coast
Holkham Bay
Brancaster Bay
Scolt Head Island
Peddars Way & Norfolk Coast Path
Blakeney Point
Morston Marshes
Cley Marshes
Muckleburgh Collection
Holme Dunes
Holme next the Sea
Brancaster
Brancaster Staithe
Burnham Deepdale
Burnham Norton
Burnham Overy Staithe
Holkham
Wells-next-the-sea
Morston
Blakeney
Cley next the Sea
Salthouse
Weybourne
Old Hunstanton
Thornham
Titchwell
Branodunum Roman Fort
Burnham Market
Burnham Overy
Holkham Hall
Warham St Mary
Stiffkey
Cockthorpe
Wiveton
Newgate
Kelling
Sheringham Park
Upper Sheringham
Hunstanton
Ringstead
Burnham Thorpe
Warham All Saints
Langham
Glandford
Wighton
Westgate
Binham
Saxlingham
North Norfolk Railway
High Kelling
Bodham
Holt
Heacham
Norfolk Lavender
Summerfield
Peddars Way & Norfolk Coast Path
North Creake
New Holkham
Creake Abbey
Wells & Walsingham Light Railway
Copy's Green
Binham Priory & Market Cross
Field Dalling
Letheringsett
West Beckham
Docking
Stanhoe
The Shrine of Our Lady
Little Walsingham
Great Walsingham
Lower Green
Sharrington
Little Thornage
Baconsthorpe Castle
Holt Lowes
Hempstead
Sedgeford
South Creake
Waterden
North Barsham
Hindringham
Bale
Brinton
Thornage
Baconsthorpe
Fring
Bircham Newton
Houghton St Giles
Thursford
Hunworth
Plumstead
Snettisham
Park Farm
Southgate
Barmer
Southgate
West Barsham
East Barsham
Great Snoring
Gunthorpe
Stody
Briningham
Edgefield Green
Plumstead Green
Edgefield
Ingoldisthorpe
Shernborne
Syderstone
Thursford
Little Barningham
Dersingham
Great Bircham
Bircham Tofts
Wicken Green Village
Little Snoring
Barney
Melton Constable
Briston
Swanton Novers
Craymere Beck
Mannington Gardens
Sculthorpe
Croxton
Kettlestone
Fulmodeston
Saxthorpe
Doddshill
Dersingham Bog
Anmer
Dunton
Coxford
Shereford
Pensthorpe Waterfowl Park
Fakenham
Hindolveston
Corpusty
Wolferton
Sandringham
West Newton
Houghton Hall
West Rudham
Tattersett
Broomsthorpe
Hempton
Nethergate
Thurning
Oulton
New Houghton
East Rudham
Tatterford
Little Ryburgh
Stibbard
Norton Corner
Flitcham
Toftrees
Wood Norton
Heydon
Babingley River
Helhoughton
East Raynham
Colkirk
Great Ryburgh
Wood Dalling
Harpley
West Raynham
Guist
Guestwick
Castle Rising
Hillington
Little Massingham
Oxwick
Salle
Southgate
South Raynham
Twyford
Foulsham
Congham
Hamrow
Gateley
Themelthorpe
Cawston
Great Massingham
Roydon
Grimston
Weasenham St Peter
Whissonsett
Horningtoft
Broom Green
Bintree
Foxley Wood
Reepham
Foxley
Weasenham All Saints
Wellingham
Potthorpe
Brisley
North Elmham Chapel
Whitwell Street
Pott Row
Tittleshall
North Elmham
Billingford
Bawdeswell
Great Witchingham
Bawsey
Stanfield
Sparham
King's Lynn
Gayton
Rougham
East Bilney
Old Beetley
Worthing
Fairstead
Mileham
Norfolk Wildlife Park
Alderford
Brow-of-the-Hill
Ashwicken
Gayton Thorpe
Beetley
Swanton Morley
Sparhamill
Lyng
Lenwade
Dinosaur
Bittering
Gressenhall
Mill Street
Fair Green
East Winch
Litcham
Elsing
Morton on the Hill
Attlebridge
West Lexham
East Lexham
Beeston
Hoe
Woodgate
Primrose Green
North Runcton
Middleton
East Walton
West Acre
Castle Acre
Castle Acre Priory
Newton
Woodgate
Longham
Gressenhall Green
Northall Green
Peaseland Green
Greensgate
Weston Longville
Setchey
Blackborough End
West Bilney
Pentney
South Acre
Little Dunham
Great Dunham
Crane's Corner
Sparrow Green
Etling Green
North Tuddenham
Dereham
Ringland
Hockering
Narborough
Great Fransham
Wendling
Scarning
Mattishall Burgh
Wormegay
River Nar
Great Palgrave
Sporle
Little Fransham
Hulver Street
Toftwood
Mattishall
Honingham
Easton
Tottenhill
Marham
Ecotech Discovery Centre
Daffy Green
Clint Green
East Tuddenham
Royal Norfolk
Shouldham
Swaffham
Necton
Ivy Todd
West End
East Bradenham
Westfield
Yaxham
South Green
Welborne
Colton
Marlingford
South Runcton
Whinburgh
Shouldham Thorpe
Holme Hale
North Pickenham
West Bradenham
Shipdham
Runhall
Brandon Parva
Barford
Fincham
Garvestone
Thuxton
Coston
Barnham Broom
Little Melton
Great Melton
Stow Bardolph
Barton Bendish
Reymerston
Wramplingham
Stradsett
Crowshill
High Common
Danemoor Green
Mid Norfolk Railway
Carleton Forehoe
High Green
Beachamwell
South Pickenham
Cranworth
Southburgh
Crimplesham
Cockley Cley
Iceni Village
Ashill
Saham Hills
Woodrising
Hardingham
Kimberley
Hethersett
Crownthorpe
Kidd's Moor
Bexwell
Eastmoor
Great Cressingham
Ovington
Carbrooke
Hingham
Hackford
West Dereham
Boughton
Wereham
Oxborough
Gooderstone
Hilborough
Saham Toney
Watton Green
Wicklewood
Oxburgh Hall
Watton
Scoulton
Deopham
Morley St Botolph
Wymondham
Wretton
Stoke Ferry
Whittington
Foulden
Beckett End
Little Cressingham
Merton
Griston
Northacre
Little Ellingham
Deopham Green
Sutton
Silfield
Wissington
Bodney
Rockland St Peter
Bow Street
Stalland Common
Ashwellthorpe
Northwold
Caston
Great Ellingham
Spooner Row
Brookville
Thompson
Stow Bedon
Rockland All Saints
Fundenhall
Methwold Hythe
Methwold
Cranwich
Ickburgh
Low Street
Stow Bedon
Fen Street
Besthorpe
Attleborough
Tacolneston
Mount Pleasant
Breckles
Mundford
Shropham
Bunwell
Carleton Rode
Peddars Way & Norfolk Coast Path
R. Stiffkey
R. Glaven
R. Wensum
R. Wissey
R. Yare
A149
A148
A1065
A1067
A47
A1122
A134
A1075
A11
B1155
B1355
B1105
B1153
B1454
B1156
B1110
B1354
B1149
B1146
B1145
B1440
B1439
B1077
B1108
B1135
B1147
B1141
B1112
B1160
B1172
B1113
49
40
0 1 2 3 4 5 miles
0 1 2 3 4 5 6 7 8 kilometres

L 20 M N 30 P Q 40 R S 50 T U 60 V

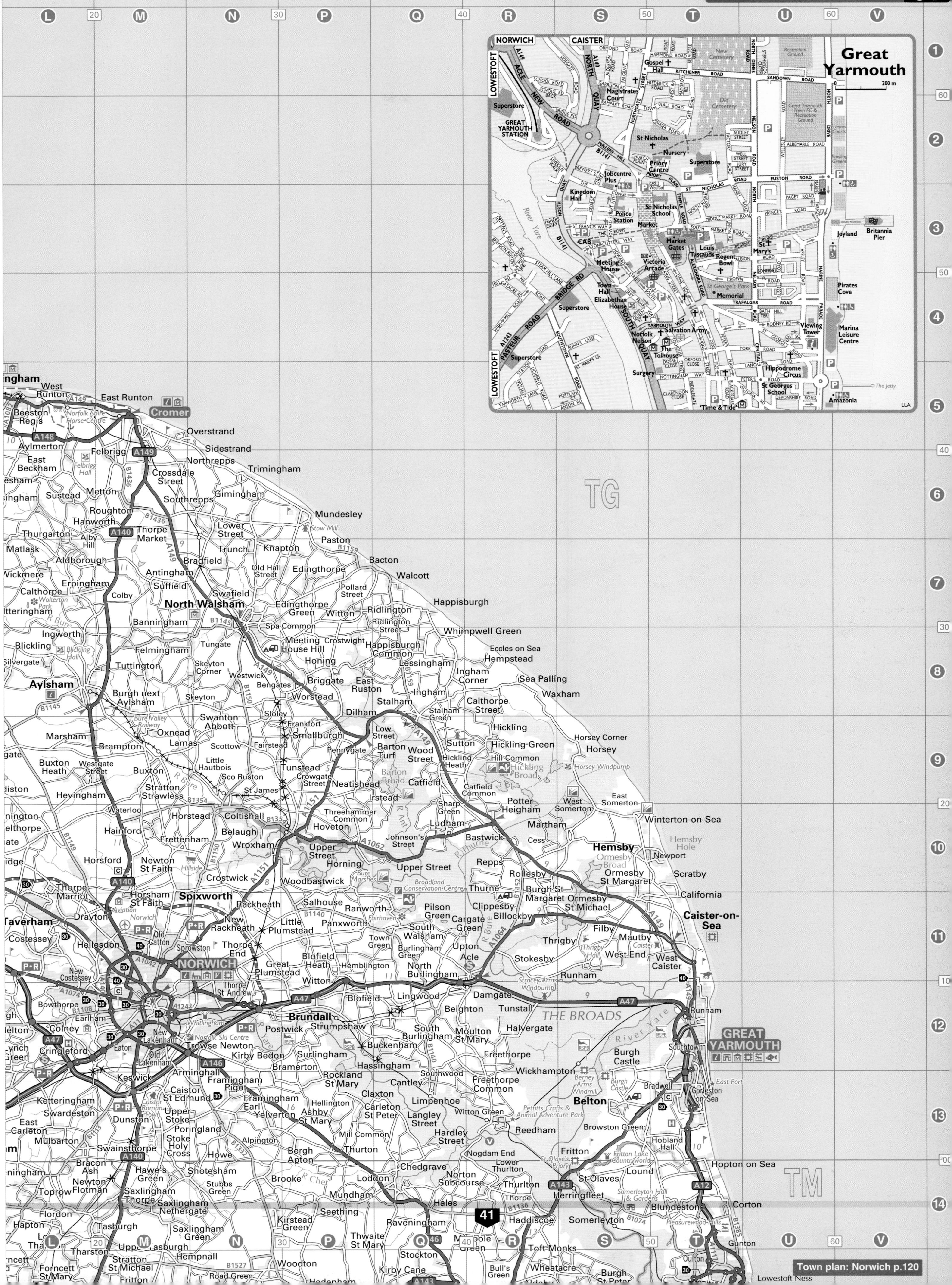

Great Yarmouth (inset town plan)

NORWICH · CAISTER
LOWESTOFT
Great Yarmouth Station
St Nicholas
Market Gates
Joyland
Britannia Pier
Pirates Cove
Marina Leisure Centre
Hippodrome Circus
Time & Tide
Amazonia

TG

Sheringham · West Runton · East Runton · Cromer
Beeston Regis · Overstrand
Aylmerton · Felbrigg · Sidestrand · Northrepps · Trimingham
East Beckham · Metton · Crossdale Street · Mundesley
Sustead · Roughton · Gimingham
Thurgarton · Hanworth · Southrepps
Matlask · Alby Hill · Lower Street · Paston · Bacton
Aldborough · Thorpe Market · Trunch · Knapton · Walcott
Wickmere · Antingham · Bradfield · Old Hall Street · Edingthorpe
Erpingham · Suffield · Swafield · Pollard Street
Calthorpe · Colby · Edingthorpe Green · Witton · Ridlington · Happisburgh
Itteringham · **North Walsham** · Ridlington Street · Whimpwell Green
Ingworth · Banningham · Spa Common · Crostwight · Happisburgh Common · Eccles on Sea · Hempstead
Blickling · Felmingham · Meeting House Hill · Honing · Lessingham · Ingham Corner · Sea Palling
Silvergate · Tungate · Skeyton Corner · Westwick · Briggate · East Ruston · Ingham · Waxham
Aylsham · Skeyton · Bengates · Worstead · Stalham · Stalham Green
Burgh next Aylsham · Little Hautbois · Sloley · Frankfort · Low Street · Sutton · Hickling · Hickling Green · Horsey Corner · Horsey
Marsham · Swanton Abbott · Smallburgh · Barton Turf · Hickling Heath · Horsey Windpump
Brampton · Oxnead · Scottow · Fairstead · Wood Street · Hill Common · Hickling Broad
Buxton Heath · Westgate Street · Buxton · Sco Ruston · Tunstead · Crowgate Street · Neatishead · Catfield · Catfield Common · West Somerton · East Somerton
Hevingham · Stratton Strawless · Lamas · St James · Pennygate · Irstead · Sharp Green · Potter Heigham · Winterton-on-Sea
Waterloo · Horstead · Coltishall · Threehammer Common · Ludham · Cess · Martham · Hemsby Hole
Hainford · Belaugh · Hoveton · Johnson's Street · Bastwick · Newport
Frettenham · Wroxham · Upper Street · Horning · Upper Street · Repps · **Hemsby** · Ormesby Broad · Scratby
Horsford · Newton St Faith · Crostwick · Woodbastwick · Thurne · Rollesby · Ormesby St Margaret · California
Thorpe Marriot · Horsham St Faith · Rackheath · Salhouse · Ranworth · Pilson Green · Clippesby · Burgh St Margaret · Ormesby St Michael · **Caister-on-Sea**
Drayton · Spixworth · New Rackheath · Little Plumstead · Panxworth · South Walsham · Cargate Green · Billockby · Filby · Mautby · West End · West Caister
Taverham · Hellesdon · Sprowston · Thorpe End · Town Green · Burlington Green · Upton · Thrigby · Thrigby Hall
Costessey · Old Catton · Great Plumstead · Blofield Heath · Hemblington · Acle · Stokesby · Runham
New Costessey · Thorpe St Andrew · Witton · North Burlingham · Runham
Bowthorpe · **NORWICH** · Blofield · Lingwood · Beighton · Damgate · Tunstall · Runham
Colney · Earlham · Postwick · **Brundall** · Strumpshaw · Moulton St Mary · Halvergate · THE BROADS · **GREAT YARMOUTH**
Cringleford · New Lakenham · Trowse Newton · Buckenham · South Burlingham · Southtown
Eaton · Old Lakenham · Surlingham · Hassingham · Southwood · Wickhampton · Burgh Castle
Keswick · Kirby Bedon · Bramerton · Rockland St Mary · Freethorpe · Berney Arms Windmill · Bradwell · Gorleston-on-Sea
Armingham · Framingham Pigot · Cantley · Freethorpe Common · **Belton** · Browston Green · East Port
Caistor St Edmund · Framingham Earl · Claxton · Carleton St Peter · Langley Street · Witton Green · Reedham · Pettitts Crafts & Animal Adventure Park · Hobland Hall
Swardeston · Dunston · Yelverton · Hellington · Limpenhoe · Hardley Street · Reedham
East Carleton · Upper Stoke · Alpington · Mill Common · Thurton · Hales · Fritton · Fritton Lake Countryworld · Hopton on Sea
Mulbarton · Poringland · Howe · Bergh Apton · Chedgrave · Lound
Swainsthorpe · Stoke Holy Cross · Shotesham · Brooke · Loddon · Norton Subcourse · Lower Thurlton · St Olaves · St Olave's Priory · Somerleyton Hall & Gardens
Bracon Ash · Hawe's Green · Stubbs Green · Mundham · Thurlton · Thorpe · Herringfleet · Blundeston · Corton
Newton Flotman · Saxlingham · Seething · Ravingham · Haddiscoe · Somerleyton · Pleasurewood Hills
Flordon · Saxlingham Nethergate · Kirstead Green · Hales · Wheatacre · Oulton
Hapton · Tasburgh · Thwaite St Mary · Maypole Green · Toft Monks · Burgh St Peter · Lowestoft Ness
Tharston · Upper Tasburgh · Hempnall · Stockton · Bull's Green
Forncett St Mary · Forncett St Michael · Fritton · Woodton · Kirby Cane · Hedenham

41

TM

Town plan: Norwich p.120

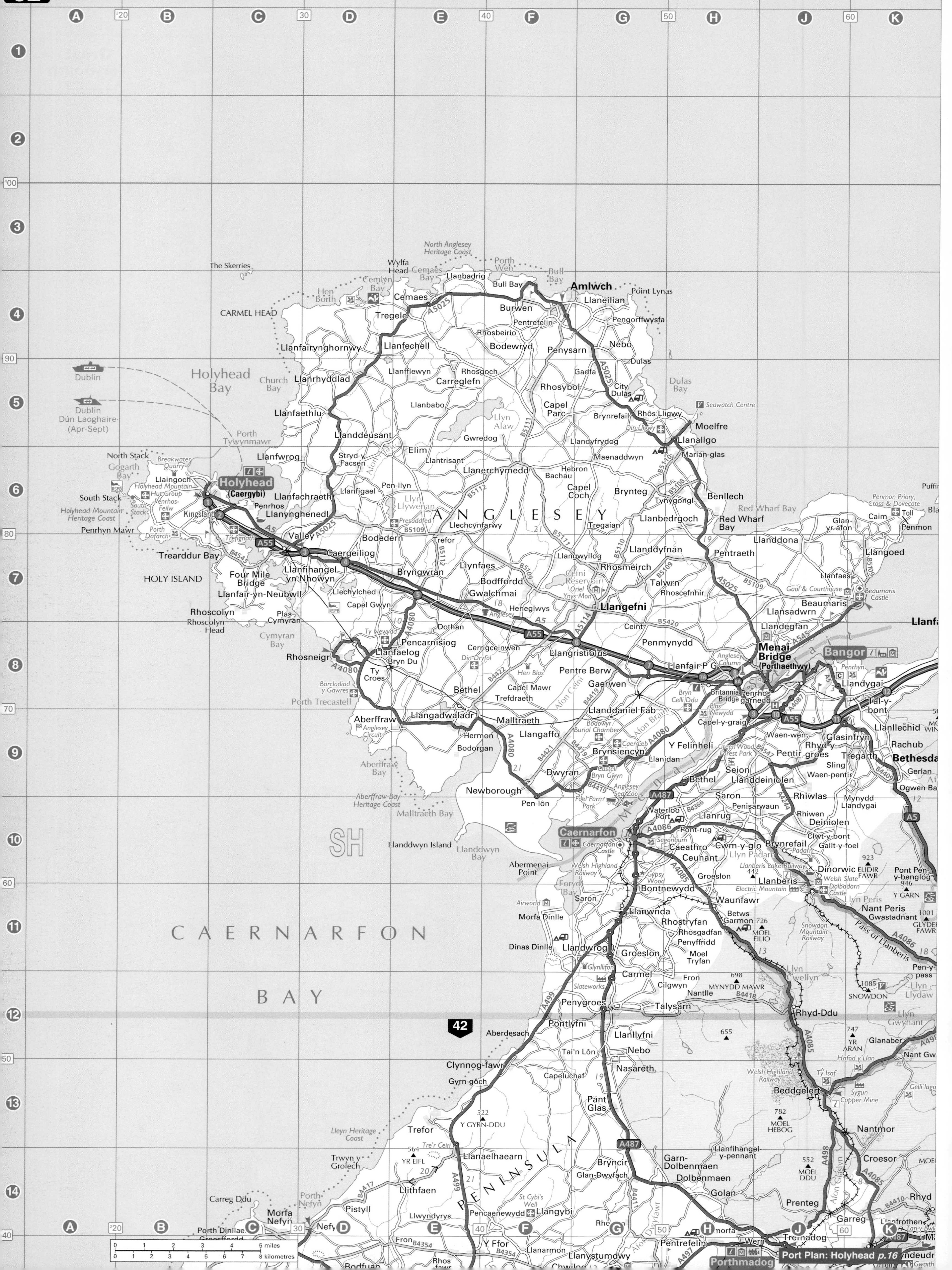

The Skerries
North Anglesey Heritage Coast
Wylfa Head
Cemlyn Bay
Cemaes Bay
Hen Borth
Llanbadrig
Porth Wen
Bull Bay
Amlwch
Point Lynas
Llaneilian
CARMEL HEAD
Cemaes
Tregele
Burwen
Pentrefelin
Pengorffwysfa
Rhosbeirio
Bodewryd
Llanfairynghornwy
Llanfechell
Penysarn
Nebo
Dulas
Dublin
Holyhead Bay
Church Bay
Llanrhyddlad
Llanfflewyn
Rhosgoch
Carreglefn
Gadfa
Rhosybol
City Dulas
Dulas Bay
Dublin Dún Laoghaire (Apr-Sept)
Llanfaethlu
Llanbabo
Llyn Alaw
Capel Parc
Brynrefail
Rhôs Lligwy
Din Lligwy
Seawatch Centre
Moelfre
Porth Tywynmawr
Llanddeusant
Gwredog
Llandyfrydog
Llanallgo
North Stack
Breakwater Quarry
Llanfwrog
Elim
Maenaddwyn
Marian-glas
Gogarth Bay
Stryd-y-Facsen
Llantrisant
Hebron
Bachau
Llaingoch
Holyhead (Caergybi)
Llanerchymedd
Holyhead Mountain Hut Group
Llanfachraeth
Pen-llyn
Capel Coch
Brynteg
Benllech
South Stack
Penrhos-Feilw
Llanfigael
Llyn Llywenan
Tynygongl
Holyhead Mountain Heritage Coast
Kingsland
Penrhos
Llanynghenedl
ANGLESEY
Red Wharf Bay
Penmon Priory, Cross & Dovecote
Caim
Toll
Penmon
Penrhyn Mawr
Porth Dafarch
Trefignath
Presaddfed
Llechcynfarwy
Tregaian
Llanbedrgoch
Red Wharf Bay
Glan-yr-afon
Valley
Bodedern
Trefor
Llanddona
Trearddur Bay
Caergeiliog
Llangwyllog
Llanddyfnan
Pentraeth
Llangoed
HOLY ISLAND
Four Mile Bridge
Llanfihangel yn Nhowyn
Bryngwran
Llynfaes
Cefni Reservoir
Rhosmeirch
Talwrn
Llanfaes
Llanfair-yn-Neubwll
Llechylched
Bodffordd
Oriel Ynys Môn
Rhoscefnhir
Gaol & Courthouse
Beaumaris Castle
Beaumaris
Rhoscolyn
Capel Gwyn
Gwalchmai
Heneglwys
Llangefni
Llansadwrn
Rhoscolyn Head
Plas Cymyran
Anglesey
Cymyran Bay
Ty Newydd
Dothan
Ceint
Llandegfan
Llanfa
Pencarnisiog
Penmynydd
Rhosneigr
Llanfaelog
Bryn Du
Cerrigceinwen
Din Dryfol
Llangristiolus
Anglesey Column
Menai Bridge (Porthaethwy)
Bangor
Penrhyn
Ty Croes
Hen Blas
Pentre Berw
Llanfair P G
Llandygai
Barclodiad y Gawres
Porth Trecastell
Bethel
Capel Mawr
Trefdraeth
Gaerwen
Bryn Celli Ddu
Britannia Bridge
Penrhos garnedd
Tal-y-bont
Aberffraw
Anglesey Circuit
Llangadwaladr
Malltraeth
Llanddaniel Fab
Plas Newydd
Capel-y-graig
Llanllechid
Bodowyr Burial Chamber
Waen-wen
Glasinfryn
Rachub
Hermon
Llangaffo
Caer Leb
Y Felinheli
Rhyd-y-groes
Tregarth
Bethesda
Bodorgan
Brynsiencyn
Pentir
Aberffraw Bay
Castell Bryn Gwyn
Llanidan
Green Wood Forest Park
Seion
Sling
Gerlan
Dwyran
Waen-pentir
Ogwen Ba
Newborough
Anglesey Sea Zoo
Bethel
Llanddeiniolen
Aberffraw Bay Heritage Coast
Pen-lôn
Foel Farm Park
Saron
Rhiwlas
Mynydd Llandygai
Malltraeth Bay
Waterloo Port
Penisarwaun
Rhiwen
Llanrug
Deiniolen
Caernarfon
Pont-rug
Clwt-y-bont
SH
Llanddwyn Island
Llanddwyn Bay
Caernarfon Castle
Segontium
Caeathro
Cwm-y-glo
Brynrefail
Gallt-y-foel
Padarn
Ceunant
Llyn Padarn
Abermenai Point
Welsh Highland Railway
Llanberis Lake Railway
Dinorwic
923 ELIDIR FAWR
Pont Pen-y-benglog
Gypsy Wood
Groeslon
442
Llanberis
Welsh Slate
946
Foryd Bay
Bontnewydd
Electric Mountain
Dolbadarn Castle
Y GARN
Saron
Waunfawr
Llyn Peris
Airworld
Nant Peris
Morfa Dinlle
Llanwnda
Betws Garmon
726 MOEL EILIO
Gwastadnant
1001 GLYDER FAWR
Rhostryfan
Snowdon Mountain Railway
Pass of Llanberis
CAERNARFON
Rhosgadfan
Penyffridd
Dinas Dinlle
Llandwrog
Groeslon
Moel Tryfan
Pen-y-pass
Glynllifon
Llyn Cwellyn
Carmel
Fron
698 MYNYDD MAWR
1085 SNOWDON
Llyn Llydaw
Slateworks
Cilgwyn
Nantlle
BAY
Penygroes
Talysarn
Rhyd-Ddu
Llyn Gwynant
42
Pontlyfni
Aberdesach
655
747 YR ARAN
Glanaber
Llanllyfni
Tai'n Lôn
Nebo
Hafod y Llan
Nant Gw
Clynnog-fawr
Nasareth
Welsh Highland Railway
Ty Isaf
Gyrn-goch
Capeluchaf
Beddgelert
Sygun Copper Mine
Gelli lago
Pant Glas
522 Y GYRN-DDU
782 MOEL HEBOG
Lleyn Heritage Coast
Trefor
Nantmor
Tre'r Ceiri
564 YR EIFL
Llanaelhaearn
PENINSULA
Bryncir
Garn-Dolbenmaen
Llanfihangel-y-pennant
Croesor
Trwyn y Gorlech
Glan-Dwyfach
Dolbenmaen
552 MOEL DDU
Llithfaen
Golan
Afon Glaslyn
Carreg Ddu
Porth Nefyn
Pistyll
St Cybi's Well
Llangybi
Prenteg
Rhyd
Morfa Nefyn
Llwyndyrys
Pencaenewydd
Garreg
Llanfrothen
Porth Dinllae
Nefyn
Rhos
Pentrefelin
Tremadog
Fron
Y Ffor
Llanarmon
Llanystumdwy
Porthmadog
Wern
Port Plan: Holyhead p.16
Rhos fawr
Bodfuan
Chwilog
Gwaith

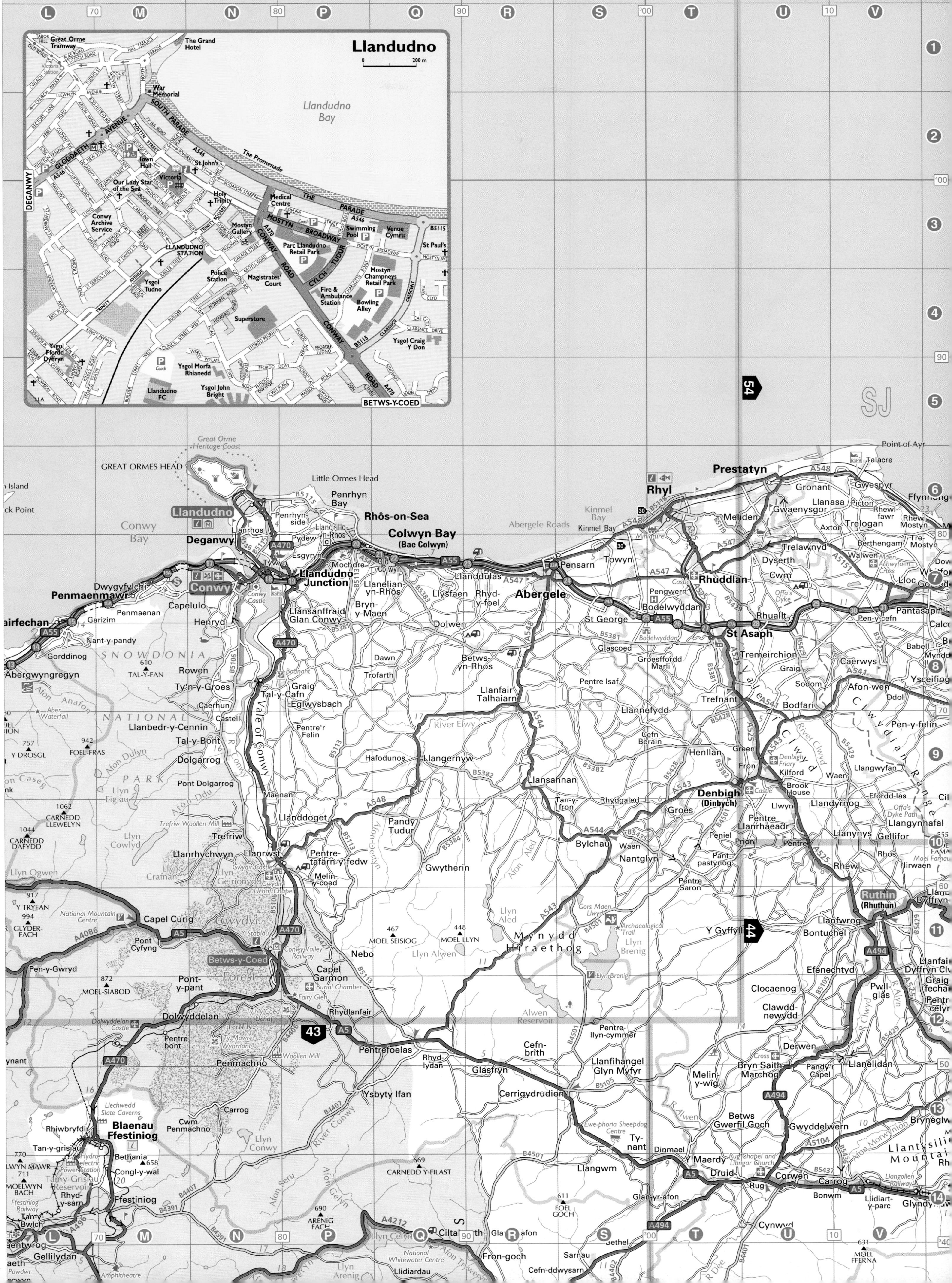
Llandudno
Llandudno Bay
Great Orme Tramway
The Grand Hotel
War Memorial
SOUTH PARADE
The Promenade
THE PARADE
MOSTYN STREET
GLODDAETH AVENUE
St John's
Town Hall
Victoria
Our Lady Star of the Sea
Holy Trinity
Medical Centre
Conwy Archive Service
Mostyn Gallery
Swimming Pool
Venue Cymru
St Paul's
LLANDUDNO STATION
Parc Llandudno Retail Park
Mostyn Champneys Retail Park
Police Station
Magistrates' Court
Fire & Ambulance Station
Bowling Alley
Superstore
Ysgol Tudno
Ysgol Ffordd Dyffryn
Ysgol Morfa Rhianedd
Ysgol John Bright
Ysgol Craig Y Don
Llandudno FC
CONWAY ROAD
CYLCH TUDUR
BETWS-Y-COED
DEGANWY
SJ
Point of Ayr
Talacre
GREAT ORMES HEAD
Great Orme Heritage Coast
Little Ormes Head
Penrhyn Bay
Rhôs-on-Sea
Colwyn Bay (Bae Colwyn)
Llandudno
Deganwy
Conwy Bay
Conwy
Llandudno Junction
Penmaenmawr
Dwygyfylchi
Penmaenan
Capelulo
Llanfairfechan
Abergwyngregyn
Prestatyn
Rhyl
Gronant
Gwespyr
Llanasa
Meliden
Kinmel Bay
Abergele Roads
Towyn
Pensarn
Abergele
Llanddulas
Rhuddlan
Dyserth
Bodelwyddan
St Asaph
St George
Trefnant
Denbigh (Dinbych)
Ruthin (Rhuthun)
Llansannan
Llangernyw
Bylchau
Nantglyn
Gwytherin
Llanrwst
Trefriw
Betws-y-Coed
Capel Curig
Dolwyddelan
Penmachno
Pentrefoelas
Cerrigydrudion
Blaenau Ffestiniog
Ffestiniog
Llangwm
Corwen
Druid
Gwyddelwern
Betws Gwerfil Goch
Llanfihangel Glyn Myfyr
Clocaenog
Efenechtyd
Llanfwrog
Bontuchel
Y Gyffylliog
Mynydd Hiraethog
Llyn Brenig
Llyn Alwen
Alwen Reservoir
Nebo
Capel Garmon
SNOWDONIA NATIONAL PARK
Vale of Conwy
Vale of Clwyd
Clwydian Range
Gwydyr Forest
Tal-y-Bont
Dolgarrog
Rowen
Henryd
Llanbedr-y-Cennin
Eglwysbach
Llanddoget
Maenan
Llansanffraid Glan Conwy
Betws-yn-Rhos
Llanfair Talhaiarn
Llannefydd
Henllan
Bodfari
Caerwys
Tremeirchion
Llandyrnog
Llanynys
Rhewl
Pentre Llanrhaeadr
Melin-y-wig
Clawdd-newydd
Derwen
Bryn Saith Marchog
Llanelidan
Carrog
Glan-yr-afon
Ysbyty Ifan
Glasfryn
Rhydlydan
North Wales 53

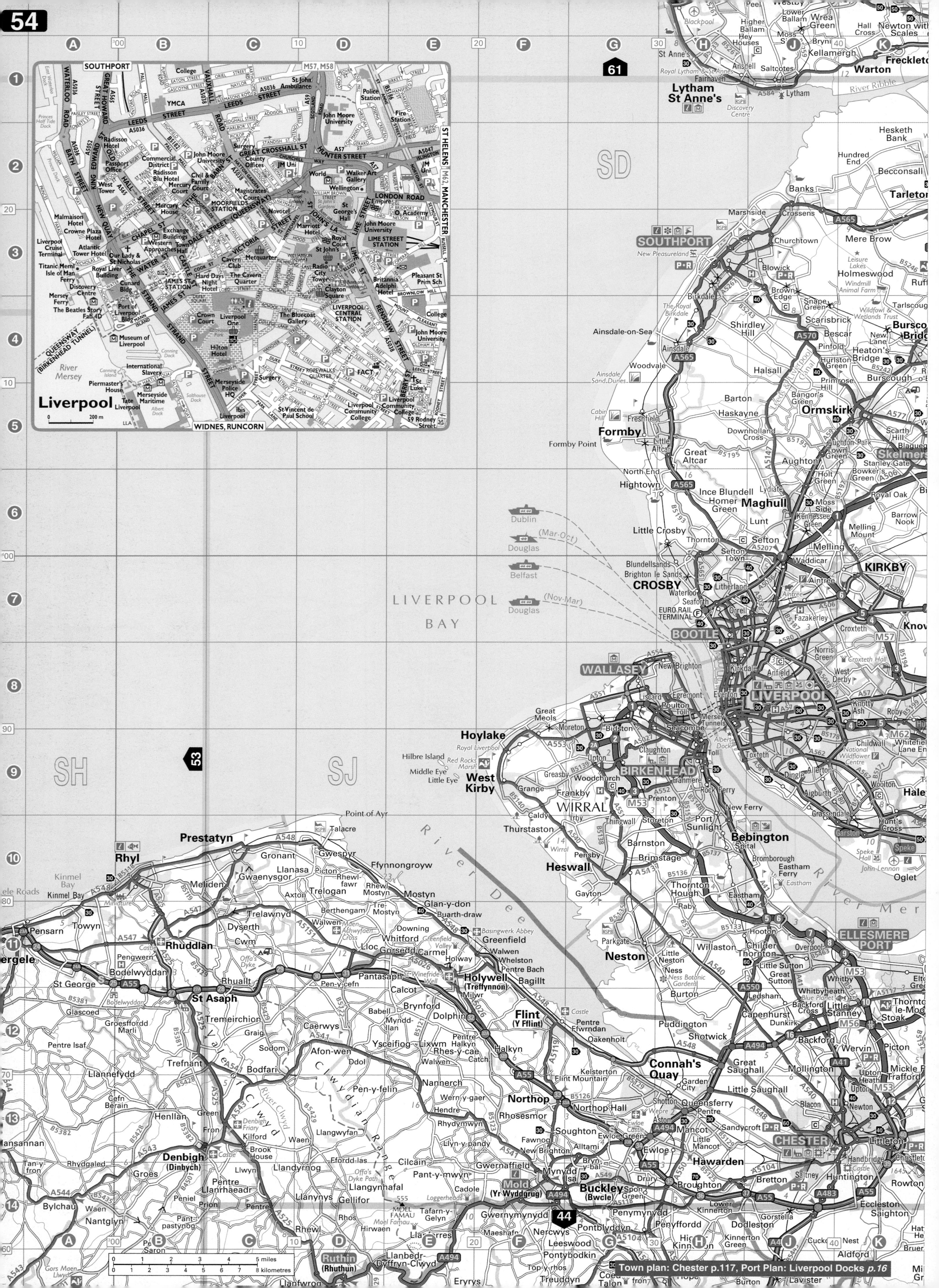

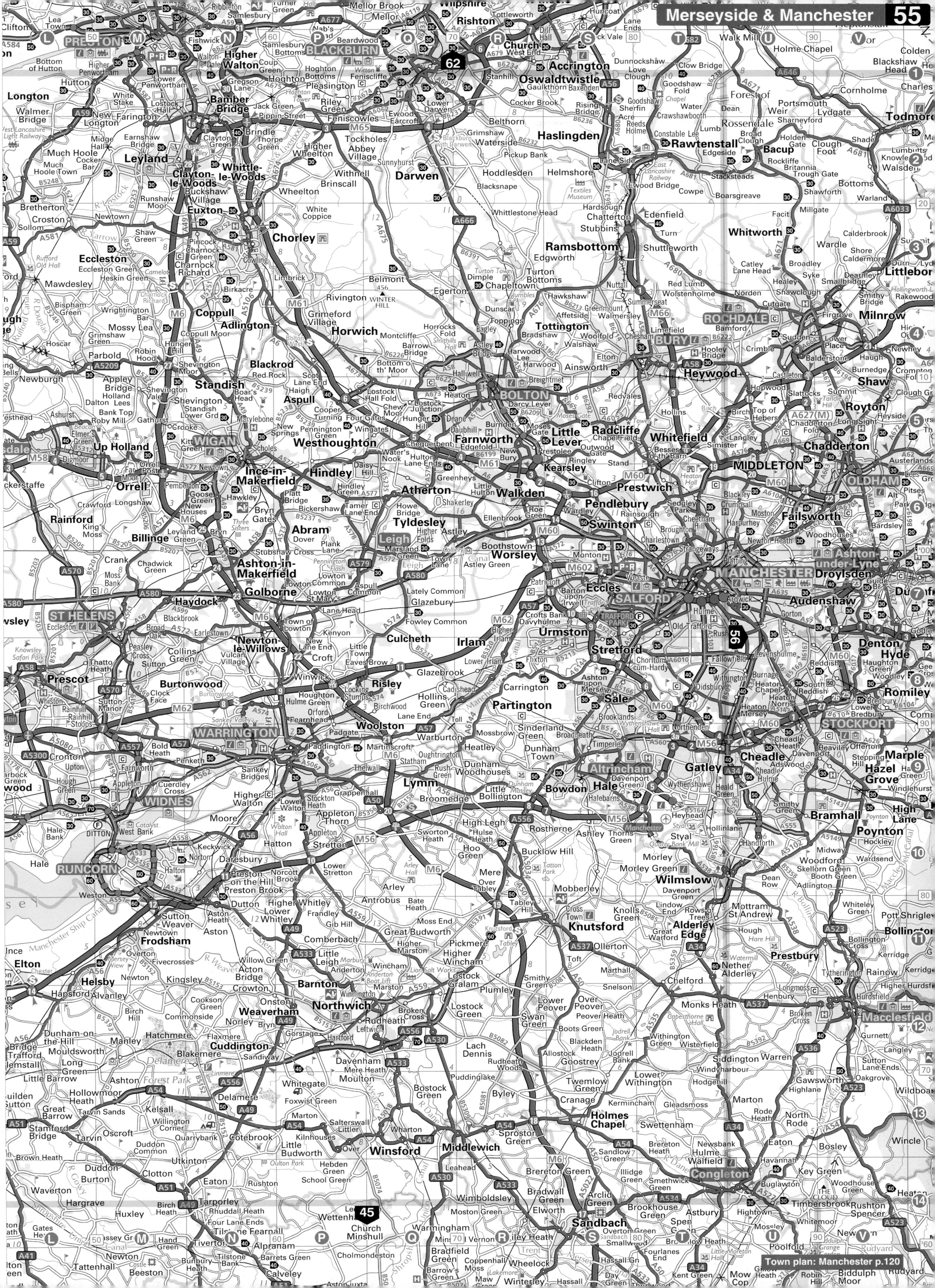
PRESTON
BLACKBURN
Accrington
Oswaldtwistle
Haslingden
Rawtenstall
Bacup
Darwen
Chorley
Leyland
Ramsbottom
ROCHDALE
BURY
Heywood
BOLTON
Horwich
WIGAN
Westhoughton
Farnworth
Radcliffe
Whitefield
MIDDLETON
OLDHAM
Hindley
Atherton
Walkden
Prestwich
Swinton
Leigh
Worsley
Eccles
SALFORD
MANCHESTER
Ashton-under-Lyne
ST HELENS
Haydock
Golborne
Urmston
Stretford
Sale
Irlam
Partington
Altrincham
STOCKPORT
Cheadle
Gatley
WARRINGTON
WIDNES
RUNCORN
Lymm
Knutsford
Wilmslow
Macclesfield
Frodsham
Helsby
Northwich
Winsford
Middlewich
Sandbach
Congleton
Holmes Chapel
Manchester
62
56
45

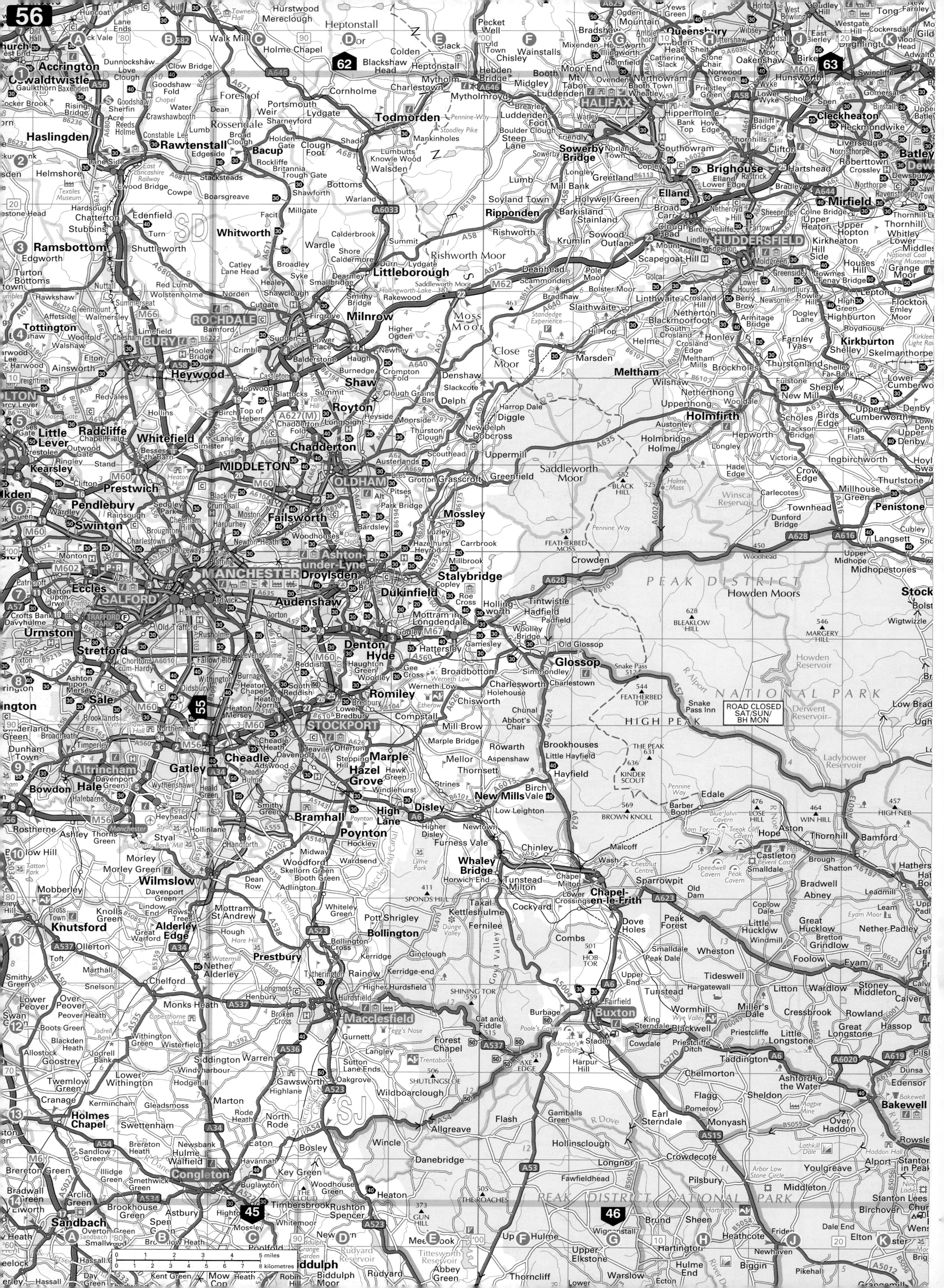
62
63
55
45
46
Accrington
Oswaldtwistle
Haslingden
Rawtenstall
Bacup
Todmorden
Heptonstall
Hebden Bridge
Halifax
Queensbury
Cleckheaton
Heckmondwike
Batley
Brighouse
Elland
Sowerby Bridge
Ripponden
Mirfield
Huddersfield
Whitworth
Littleborough
Milnrow
Rochdale
Bury
Ramsbottom
Tottington
Heywood
Shaw
Royton
Radcliffe
Whitefield
Middleton
Chadderton
Oldham
Little Lever
Kearsley
Prestwich
Pendlebury
Swinton
Failsworth
Eccles
Salford
Manchester
Droylsden
Ashton-under-Lyne
Stalybridge
Dukinfield
Mossley
Audenshaw
Urmston
Stretford
Denton
Hyde
Romiley
Stockport
Sale
Cheadle
Gatley
Altrincham
Hale
Bowdon
Marple
Hazel Grove
Bramhall
Poynton
High Lane
Disley
New Mills
Glossop
Hadfield
Hayfield
Whaley Bridge
Chapel-en-le-Frith
Buxton
Wilmslow
Knutsford
Alderley Edge
Bollington
Prestbury
Macclesfield
Holmes Chapel
Congleton
Sandbach
Biddulph
Bakewell
Holmfirth
Meltham
Marsden
Penistone
Kirkburton
Saddleworth Moor
Howden Moors
Peak District
Peak District National Park
High Peak
Road closed Sat/Sun/BH Mon
0 1 2 3 4 5 miles
0 1 2 3 4 5 6 7 8 kilometres

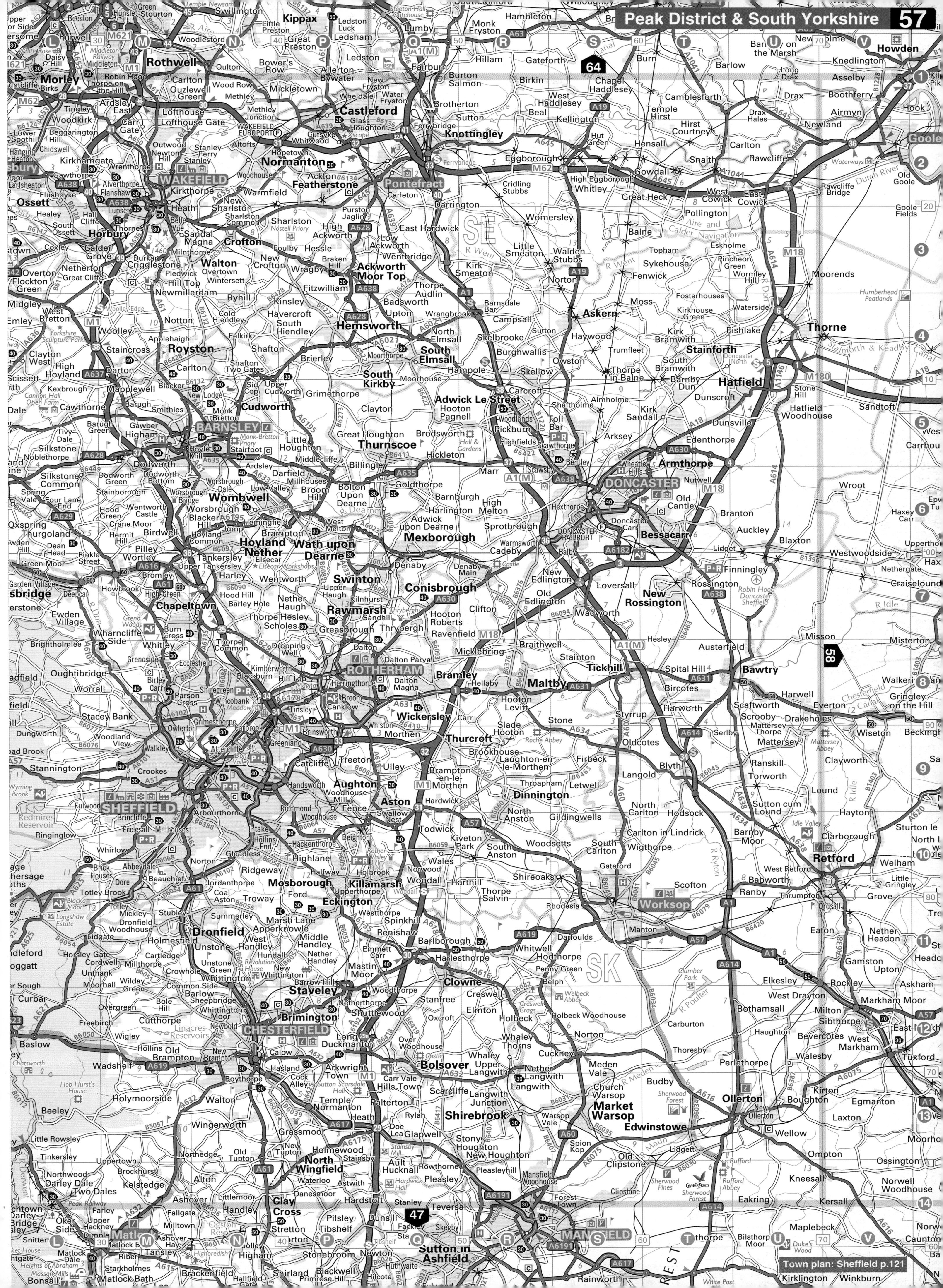
Wakefield
Pontefract
Castleford
Knottingley
Normanton
Featherstone
Rothwell
Morley
Ossett
Horbury
Crofton
Hemsworth
Royston
Cudworth
Barnsley
Wombwell
Hoyland Nether
Wath upon Dearne
Mexborough
Swinton
Conisbrough
Rawmarsh
Rotherham
Chapeltown
Sheffield
Doncaster
Bessacarr
Armthorpe
Askern
Thorne
Stainforth
Hatfield
New Rossington
Tickhill
Maltby
Bawtry
Wickersley
Thurcroft
Dinnington
Aughton
Aston
Worksop
Retford
Mosborough
Killamarsh
Eckington
Dronfield
Staveley
Clowne
Chesterfield
Brimington
Bolsover
Shirebrook
Market Warsop
Edwinstowe
Ollerton
Clay Cross
North Wingfield
Sutton in Ashfield
Mansfield
Matlock
Goole
Howden
Kippax
Thurnscoe
Adwick Le Street
Thorpe Audlin
South Elmsall
South Kirkby
Whitley
Snaith
Tuxford
SE
SK

64
58
47
Town plan: Sheffield p.121

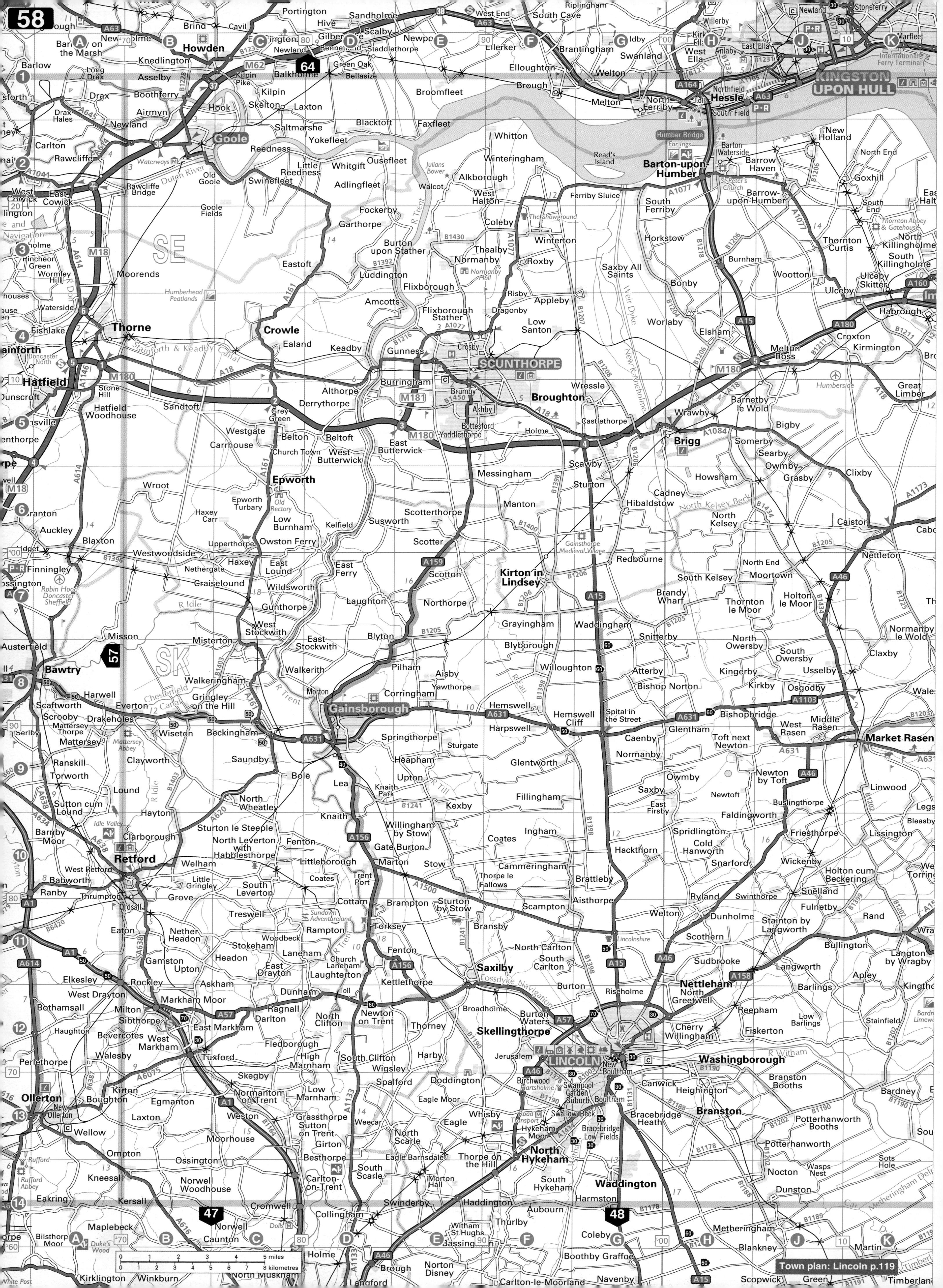

Howden
Goole
Thorne
Hatfield
Crowle
Epworth
Bawtry
Gainsborough
Retford
Ollerton
Tuxford
Saxilby
Skellingthorpe
LINCOLN
North Hykeham
Waddington
Washingborough
Branston
Nettleham
Market Rasen
Caistor
Brigg
Broughton
SCUNTHORPE
Kirton in Lindsey
Barton-upon-Humber
Hessle
KINGSTON UPON HULL
Humber Bridge
Portington
Sandholme
Scalby
Gilberdyke
Newport
South Cave
Brantingham
Ellerker
Elloughton
Welton
Brough
Melton
North Ferriby
Swanland
Kirk Ella
West Ella
Anlaby
Willerby
East Ella
Newland
Marfleet
Stoneferry
Barlow
Long Drax
Drax
Asselby
Knedlington
Boothferry
Airmyn
Hook
Kilpin
Skelton
Laxton
Saltmarshe
Blacktoft
Yokefleet
Faxfleet
Broomfleet
Reedness
Swinefleet
Whitgift
Ousefleet
Adlingfleet
Fockerby
Garthorpe
Old Goole
Goole Fields
Rawcliffe
Rawcliffe Bridge
Carlton
West Cowick
East Cowick
Moorends
Eastoft
Luddington
Whitton
Winteringham
Alkborough
West Halton
Coleby
Thealby
Normanby
Burton upon Stather
Flixborough
Flixborough Stather
Amcotts
Winterton
Roxby
Appleby
Risby
Dragonby
Low Santon
Ferriby Sluice
South Ferriby
Horkstow
Saxby All Saints
Bonby
Worlaby
Elsham
Barrow Haven
Barrow-upon-Humber
New Holland
Goxhill
Thornton Curtis
North Killingholme
South Killingholme
Wootton
Ulceby
Ulceby Skitter
Habrough
Croxton
Kirmington
Melton Ross
Great Limber
Humberside
Barnetby le Wold
Wrawby
Bigby
Somerby
Searby
Owmby
Grasby
Clixby
Howsham
Cadney
Hibaldstow
North Kelsey
Nettleton
Redbourne
South Kelsey
Moortown
North End
Brandy Wharf
Thornton le Moor
Holton le Moor
Normanby le Wold
Claxby
Snitterby
North Owersby
South Owersby
Usselby
Kingerby
Atterby
Bishop Norton
Kirkby
Osgodby
Bishopbridge
West Rasen
Middle Rasen
Glentham
Caenby
Normanby
Owmby
Saxby
Toft next Newton
Newton by Toft
Newtoft
Linwood
Buslingthorpe
Faldingworth
East Firsby
Spridlington
Cold Hanworth
Friesthorpe
Lissington
Hackthorn
Snarford
Wickenby
Holton cum Beckering
Snelland
Ryland
Welton
Dunholme
Fulnetby
Stainton by Langworth
Rand
Scothern
Sudbrooke
Langworth
Bullington
Barlings
Apley
Langton by Wragby
Reepham
Cherry Willingham
Fiskerton
Low Barlings
Stainfield
Heighington
Canwick
Branston Booths
Bracebridge Heath
Potterhanworth
Potterhanworth Booths
Nocton
Dunston
Metheringham
Blankney
Martin
Scopwick
Timberland
Harmston
Coleby
Boothby Graffoe
Navenby
Sots Hole
Wasps Nest
Bardney
Riseholme
Burton
North Carlton
South Carlton
Scampton
Brattleby
Aisthorpe
Cammeringham
Ingham
Fillingham
Glentworth
Harpswell
Hemswell
Hemswell Cliff
Spital in the Street
Willoughton
Blyborough
Grayingham
Waddingham
Northorpe
Scotton
Scotter
Susworth
Scotterthorpe
Messingham
Manton
Scawby
Sturton
Castlethorpe
Holme
Bottesford
Yaddlethorpe
Ashby
Brumby
Burringham
Gunness
Crosby
Keadby
Ealand
Althorpe
Derrythorpe
Sandtoft
Grey Green
Belton
Beltoft
East Butterwick
West Butterwick
Church Town
Westgate
Carrhouse
Wroot
Epworth Turbary
Haxey Carr
Low Burnham
Kelfield
Owston Ferry
Upperthorpe
Haxey
East Lound
Westwoodside
Nethergate
Craiselound
Wildsworth
East Ferry
Laughton
Gunthorpe
West Stockwith
East Stockwith
Blyton
Pilham
Aisby
Yawthorpe
Corringham
Springthorpe
Sturgate
Heapham
Upton
Kexby
Knaith Park
Knaith
Lea
Willingham by Stow
Gate Burton
Marton
Stow
Coates
Thorpe le Fallows
Brampton
Sturton by Stow
Bransby
Torksey
Fenton
Kettlethorpe
Newton on Trent
Thorney
Broadholme
Harby
Doddington
Eagle
Eagle Moor
Eagle Barnsdale
Whisby
Thorpe on the Hill
Morton Hall
South Hykeham
Haddington
Aubourn
Thurlby
Witham St Hughs
Bassingham
Norton Disney
Carlton-le-Moorland
Swinderby
Collingham
South Scarle
North Scarle
Besthorpe
Girton
Carlton-on-Trent
Sutton on Trent
Grassthorpe
Weecar
Low Marnham
High Marnham
South Clifton
North Clifton
Wigsley
Spalford
Dunham
Ragnall
Darlton
Laughterton
Church Laneham
Laneham
East Drayton
Rampton
Stokeham
Woodbeck
Treswell
Cottam
Trent Port
Littleborough
Fenton
Sturton le Steeple
North Leverton with Habblesthorpe
South Leverton
North Wheatley
Saundby
Bole
Beckingham
Walkeringham
Gringley on the Hill
Misterton
Walkerith
Misson
Everton
Harwell
Scaftworth
Scrooby
Drakeholes
Wiseton
Mattersey
Mattersey Thorpe
Clayworth
Ranskill
Torworth
Lound
Hayton
Sutton cum Lound
Barnby Moor
Clarborough
Welham
Little Gringley
Grove
West Retford
Babworth
Ranby
Ordsall
Thrumpton
Eaton
Nether Headon
Headon
Upton
Gamston
Rockley
Askham
Markham Moor
East Markham
West Markham
Milton
Sibthorpe
West Drayton
Elkesley
Bothamsall
Haughton
Bevercotes
Walesby
Perlethorpe
Kirton
Boughton
Egmanton
Laxton
Normanton on Trent
Skegby
Weston
Moorhouse
Ossington
Ompton
Wellow
New Ollerton
Kneesall
Eakring
Kersall
Norwell Woodhouse
Norwell
Cromwell
Caunton
Maplebeck
Bilsthorpe Moor
Holme
Brough
Langford
North Muskham
Kirklington
Winkburn
Austerfield
Finningley
Auckley
Blaxton
Stone Hill
Hatfield Woodhouse
Dunscroft
Fishlake
Waterside
Humberhead Peatlands
Julians Bower
Read's Island
Stainforth & Keadby Canal
Dutch River
Chesterfield Canal
Fossdyke Navigation
R Trent
R Idle
R Witham
R Till
New R Ancholme
Weir Dyke
North Kelsey Beck
Gainsthorpe Medieval Village
Normanby Hall
Thornton Abbey & Gatehouse
St Peter's Church
Sundown Adventureland
Mattersey Abbey
Idle Valley
Robin Hood Doncaster Sheffield
Rufford Abbey
Duke's Wood
Lincolnshire
SE
SK
M18
M62
M180
M181
A63
A1
A15
A18
A46
A57
A156
A159
A161
A614
A631
A638
A1077
A1103
A1500
International Ferry Terminal
0 1 2 3 4 5 miles
0 1 2 3 4 5 6 7 8 kilometres

57
64
47
48
Town plan: Lincoln p.119

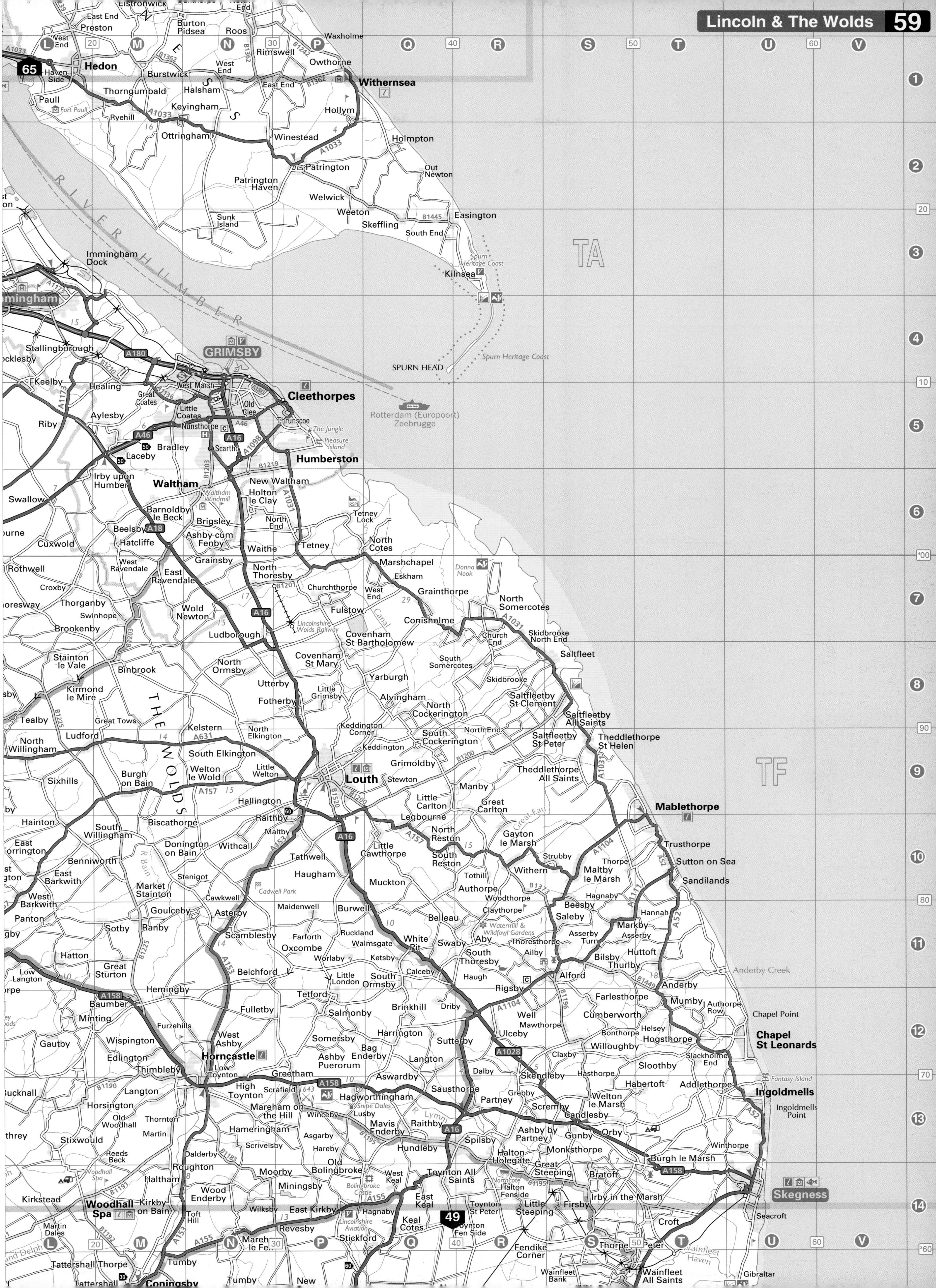
East End
Preston
Burton Pidsea
Roos
Waxholme
West End
Hedon
Haven Side
Burstwick
Rimswell
West End
Owthorne
Withernsea
Thorngumbald
Halsham
East End
Paull
Fort Paull
Keyingham
Hollym
Ryehill
Ottringham
Winestead
Holmpton
Patrington
Out Newton
Patrington Haven
Welwick
Weeton
Easington
Sunk Island
Skeffling
South End
RIVER HUMBER
Immingham Dock
Spurn Heritage Coast
Kilnsea
TA
Immingham
Stallingborough
Keelby
Healing
GRIMSBY
Great Coates
West Marsh
Cleethorpes
Old Clee
Little Coates
Aylesby
Riby
Nunsthorpe
Scartho
Thrunscoe
SPURN HEAD
Rotterdam (Europoort) Zeebrugge
The Jungle
Pleasure Island
Bradley
Laceby
Humberston
Irby upon Humber
Waltham
Waltham Windmill
New Waltham
Holton le Clay
Swallow
Barnoldby le Beck
Brigsley
North End
Tetney Lock
Beelsby
Hatcliffe
Ashby cum Fenby
Cuxwold
Waithe
Tetney
North Cotes
Rothwell
West Ravendale
Grainsby
East Ravendale
North Thoresby
Marshchapel
Eskham
Donna Nook
Croxby
Churchthorpe
West End
Grainthorpe
Thorganby
Swinhope
Wold Newton
Fulstow
North Somercotes
Brookenby
Ludborough
Lincolnshire Wolds Railway
Covenham St Bartholomew
Conisholme
Church End
Skidbrooke North End
Saltfleet
Stainton le Vale
Binbrook
North Ormsby
Covenham St Mary
South Somercotes
Yarburgh
Skidbrooke
Kirmond le Mire
Utterby
Fotherby
Little Grimsby
Alvingham
North Cockerington
Saltfleetby St Clement
Tealby
Great Tows
THE WOLDS
Saltfleetby All Saints
Theddlethorpe St Helen
Ludford
Kelstern
North Elkington
Keddington Corner
South Cockerington
North End
Saltfleetby St Peter
North Willingham
South Elkington
Keddington
Sixhills
Burgh on Bain
Welton le Wold
Little Welton
Louth
Stewton
Grimoldby
Theddlethorpe All Saints
TF
Manby
Hallington
Raithby
Little Carlton
Great Carlton
Legbourne
Mablethorpe
Hainton
South Willingham
Biscathorpe
Maltby
Little Cawthorpe
North Reston
Gayton le Marsh
Trusthorpe
East Torrington
Donington on Bain
Withcall
Tathwell
South Reston
Strubby
Thorpe
Sutton on Sea
Benniworth
Maltby le Marsh
Withern
East Barkwith
Stenigot
Haugham
Muckton
Tothill
Sandilands
West Barkwith
Market Stainton
Cadwell Park
Authorpe
Woodthorpe
Hagnaby
Panton
Cawkwell
Goulceby
Asterby
Maidenwell
Burwell
Claythorpe
Beesby
Saleby
Hannah
Belleau
Markby
Sotby
Ranby
Scamblesby
Farforth
Ruckland
White Pit
Watermill & Wildfowl Gardens
Asserby Turn
Asserby
Walmsgate
Swaby
Aby
Thoresthorpe
Hatton
Oxcombe
Ketsby
South Thoresby
Ailby
Bilsby
Huttoft
Great Sturton
Worlaby
Thurlby
Anderby Creek
Belchford
Little London
Calceby
Haugh
Alford
Low Langton
South Ormsby
Rigsby
Anderby
Hemingby
Tetford
Farlesthorpe
Baumber
Fulletby
Brinkhill
Mumby
Authorpe Row
Salmonby
Driby
Minting
Well
Cumberworth
Chapel Point
Mawthorpe
Furzehills
Helsey
Gautby
Wispington
West Ashby
Harrington
Somersby
Ulceby
Bonthorpe
Chapel St Leonards
Hogsthorpe
Willoughby
Edlington
Horncastle
Bag Enderby
Sutterby
Thimbleby
Ashby Puerorum
Langton
Claxby
Low Toynton
Slackholme End
Sloothby
Greetham
Dalby
Bucknall
High Toynton
Aswardby
Skendleby
Hasthorpe
Fantasy Island
Langton
Scrafield
Sausthorpe
Habertoft
Addlethorpe
Hagworthingham
Grebby
Horsington
Mareham on the Hill
Partney
Welton le Marsh
Ingoldmells
Snipe Dales
Scremby
Ingoldmells Point
Old Woodhall
Thornton
Winceby
Lusby
Candlesby
Martin
Hameringham
Mavis Enderby
Raithby
Orby
Stixwould
Asgarby
Ashby by Partney
Gunby
Scrivelsby
Hareby
Hundleby
Spilsby
Winthorpe
Reeds Beck
Monksthorpe
Dalderby
Halton Holegate
Great Steeping
Burgh le Marsh
Woodhall Spa
Roughton
Old Bolingbroke
Toynton All Saints
Bratoft
Haltham
Moorby
West Keal
Northcote Heavy Horse Centre
Halton Fenside
Kirkstead
Wood Enderby
Miningsby
Bolingbroke Castle
Irby in the Marsh
Skegness
Woodhall Spa
Kirkby on Bain
East Keal
Wilksby
East Kirkby
Toynton St Peter
Little Steeping
Firsby
Toft Hill
Hagnaby
Lincolnshire Aviation
Keal Cotes
Croft
Martin Dales
Revesby
Toynton Fen Side
Seacroft
Mareham le Fen
Stickford
Fendike Corner
Thorpe
Peter
Wainfleet Haven
Tattershall Thorpe
Tumby
Wainfleet Bank
Wainfleet All Saints
Gibraltar
Tattershall
Coningsby
Tumby
New

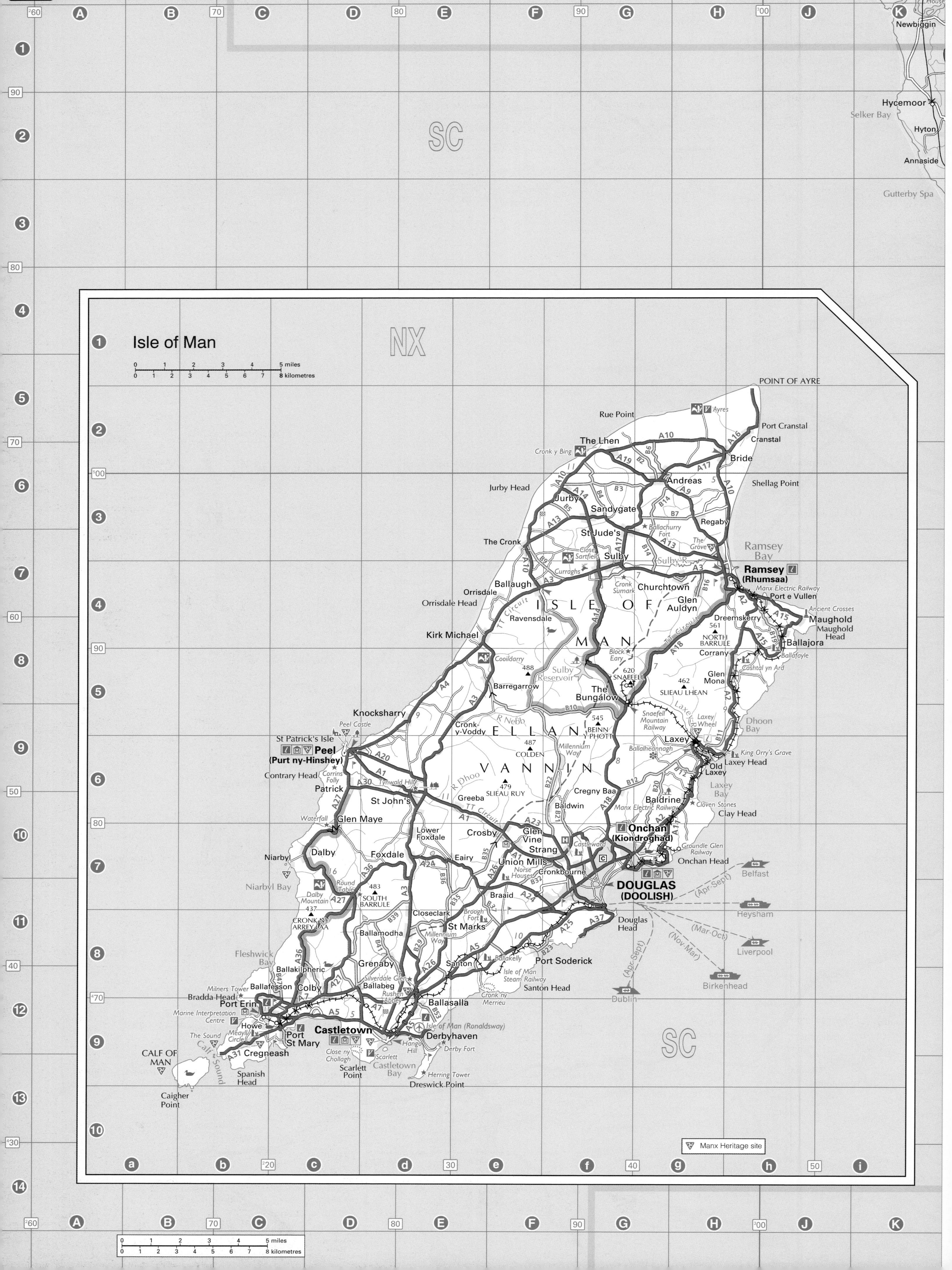

Ravenglass
Newbiggin
Hycemoor
Selker Bay
Hyton
Annaside
Gutterby Spa
Roman Bath House

Isle of Man

0 1 2 3 4 5 miles
0 1 2 3 4 5 6 7 8 kilometres

SC

NX

POINT OF AYRE

Rue Point   Ayres   Port Cranstal
The Lhen   Cranstal
Cronk y Bing   A10   A16   Bride
                    A19   A17
Jurby Head   Andreas   5   Shellag Point
        Jurby   A14   B3   A9   A10
        A13   B5   Sandygate   B14
The Cronk   B9   St Jude's   B7   Regaby
                Close   Sulby-R   A13   The Grove   Ramsey
        A10   Sartfield Sulby   A3   Bay
Ballaugh   Curraghs   Churchtown   Ramsey
Orrisdale   Cronk   Glen   (Rhumsaa)
Orrisdale Head   TT Circuit Sumark   Auldyn   Port e Vullen
                ISLE OF   Maughold
Kirk Michael   Ravensdale   561   Dreemskerry   Maughold
                488   Block NORTH   Head
        Cooildarry   Sulby   Eary BARRULE   A15   Ballajora
        Barregarrow Reservoir 620   Corrany   Ballafayle
                SNAEFELL   462
Knocksharry   The   FELL SLIEAU LHEAN Glen Mona
Peel Castle   Bungalow   Dhoon
St Patrick's Isle   R Nebb   545   Laxey   Bay
Peel   A4   Cronk- ELLAN BEINN   Snaefell Wheel
(Purt ny-Hinshey) y-Voddy   Y PHOTT Mountain
Contrary Head   Corrins A20   Millennium Railway Old
        Folly   VANNIN   487 Way   Laxey   Laxey Head
Patrick   A30   Tynwald Hill   COLDEN   King Orry's Grave
        A1 St John's   Greeba R Dhoo 479   B12   Cregny Baa Cloven
        Waterfall   SLIEAU RUY   Baldrine Stones
Glen Maye   A1   TT Circuit Lower   A18   Manx Electric Clay Head
Niarbyl   Foxdale Crosby Glen A23   Railway   Laxey
        Dalby   Glen Vine   Onchan   Bay
Niarbyl Bay   A36   Foxdale Eairy Strang (Kiondroghad)
        A27   A24   Castleward Groudle Glen
        Round 483   B35 Union Mills   Railway
        Table SOUTH   Norse   C   Onchan Head
        Dalby BARRULE Houses   Belfast
        437 Cronkbourne   DOUGLAS (Apr-Sept)
CRONK-NY-   B39   Braaid A24   (DOOLISH)
ARREY-LAA   Closeclark Brough A37   Heysham
        Ballamodha   Fort A5   (Mar-Oct)
Fleshwick   St Marks   10 A25   Douglas
Bay   Millennium   Head   Liverpool
Ballakilpheric   Way   A5   (Nov-Mar) Birkenhead
        Grenaby   Santon Isle of Man   (Apr-Sept)
Milners Tower   Silverdale Glen   Steam Railway Dublin
Bradda Head Ballafesson Colby Ballabeg Santon Head
Port Erin   A7   Rushen Ballakelly
Marine   Howe   Abbey   Port Soderick
Interpretation   Meayll   Ballasalla
Centre   Circle Port Castletown   Derbyhaven
The Sound   St Mary   Isle of Man (Ronaldsway)
CALF OF Cregneash   Close ny   Hango   Derby Fort
MAN   Chollagh   Hill Scarlett
        Spanish   Scarlett   Castletown
        Head   Point   Bay   Herring Tower
Caigher   Dreswick Point
Point

SC

▽ Manx Heritage site

0 1 2 3 4 5 miles
0 1 2 3 4 5 6 7 8 kilometres

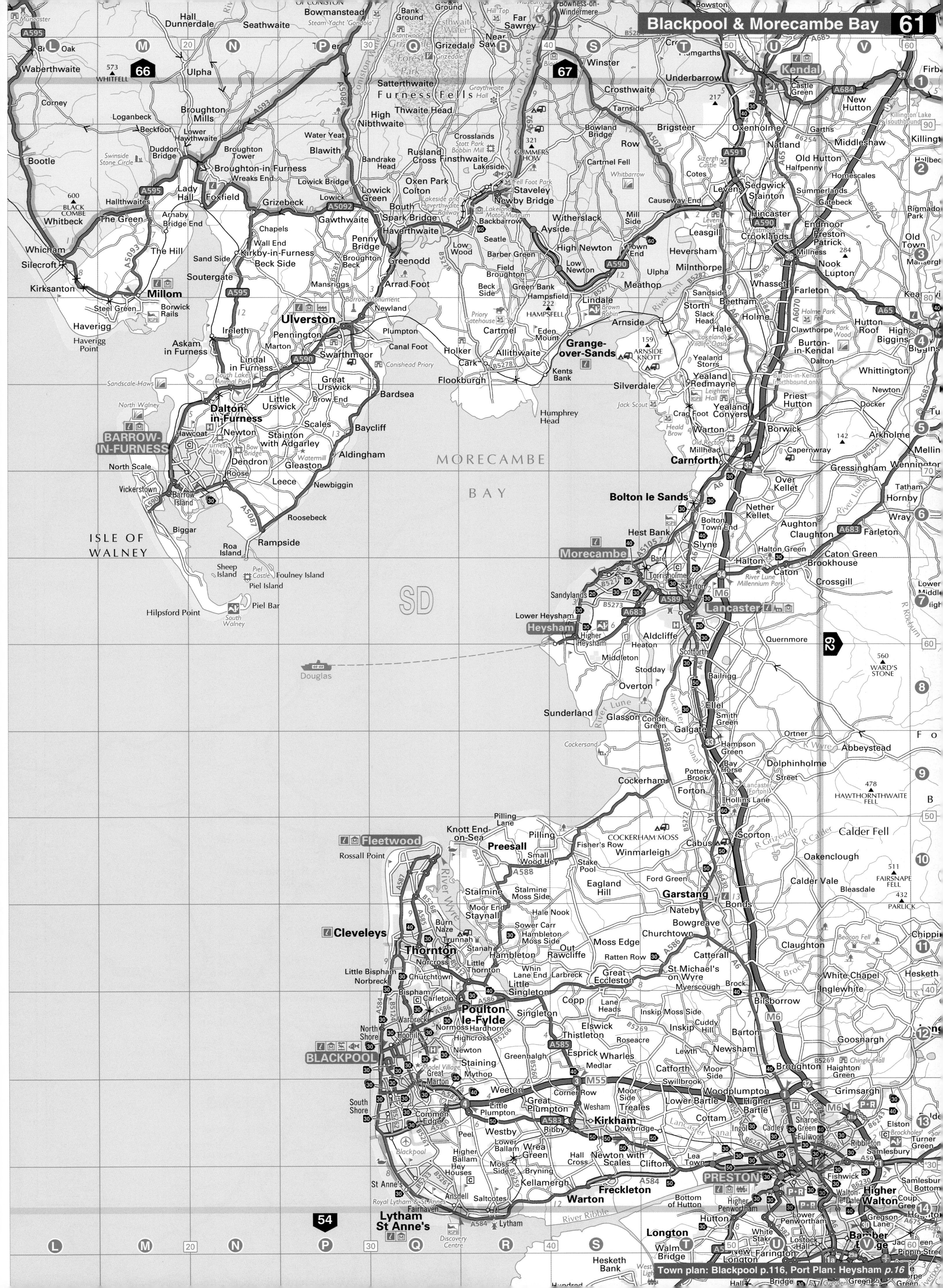
MORECAMBE
BAY
ISLE OF
WALNEY
SD
Blackpool
Lytham St Anne's
Fleetwood
Cleveleys
Thornton
Poulton-le-Fylde
Kirkham
Preston
Lancaster
Morecambe
Heysham
Carnforth
Bolton le Sands
Garstang
Preesall
Knott End-on-Sea
Pilling
Cockerham
Glasson
Sunderland
Overton
Freckleton
Warton
Longton
Barrow-in-Furness
Dalton-in-Furness
Ulverston
Millom
Grange-over-Sands
Kendal
Cartmel
Flookburgh
Arnside
Silverdale
Milnthorpe
Askam in Furness
Broughton-in-Furness
Satterthwaite
Furness Fells
Newby Bridge
Haverthwaite
Bardsea
Aldingham
Roa Island
Piel Island
Foulney Island
Rampside
Biggar
Douglas
Humphrey Head
Hest Bank
Carnforth
Galgate
Scorton
Calder Fell
Bilsborrow
Broughton
Singleton
Hambleton
Stalmine
Weeton
Wrea Green
Warton
Higher Walton
Bamber Bridge
Hesketh Bank
River Ribble
River Wyre
River Lune
Whitbeck
Bootle
Silecroft
Haverigg
Kirksanton
Ulpha
Seathwaite
Waberthwaite
Corney
Crooklands
Burton-in-Kendal
Whittington
Arkholme
Hornby
Caton
Quernmore
Abbeystead
Dolphinholme
Forton
Winmarleigh
Cabus
Inskip
Elswick
Newsham
Goosnargh
Grimsargh
Lea
Hutton
Penwortham
Walton-le-Dale
Samlesbury
Blackpool
M6
M55
A6
A590
A595
A683
A585
A584
A583
A588
A586
A589
54
62
66
67

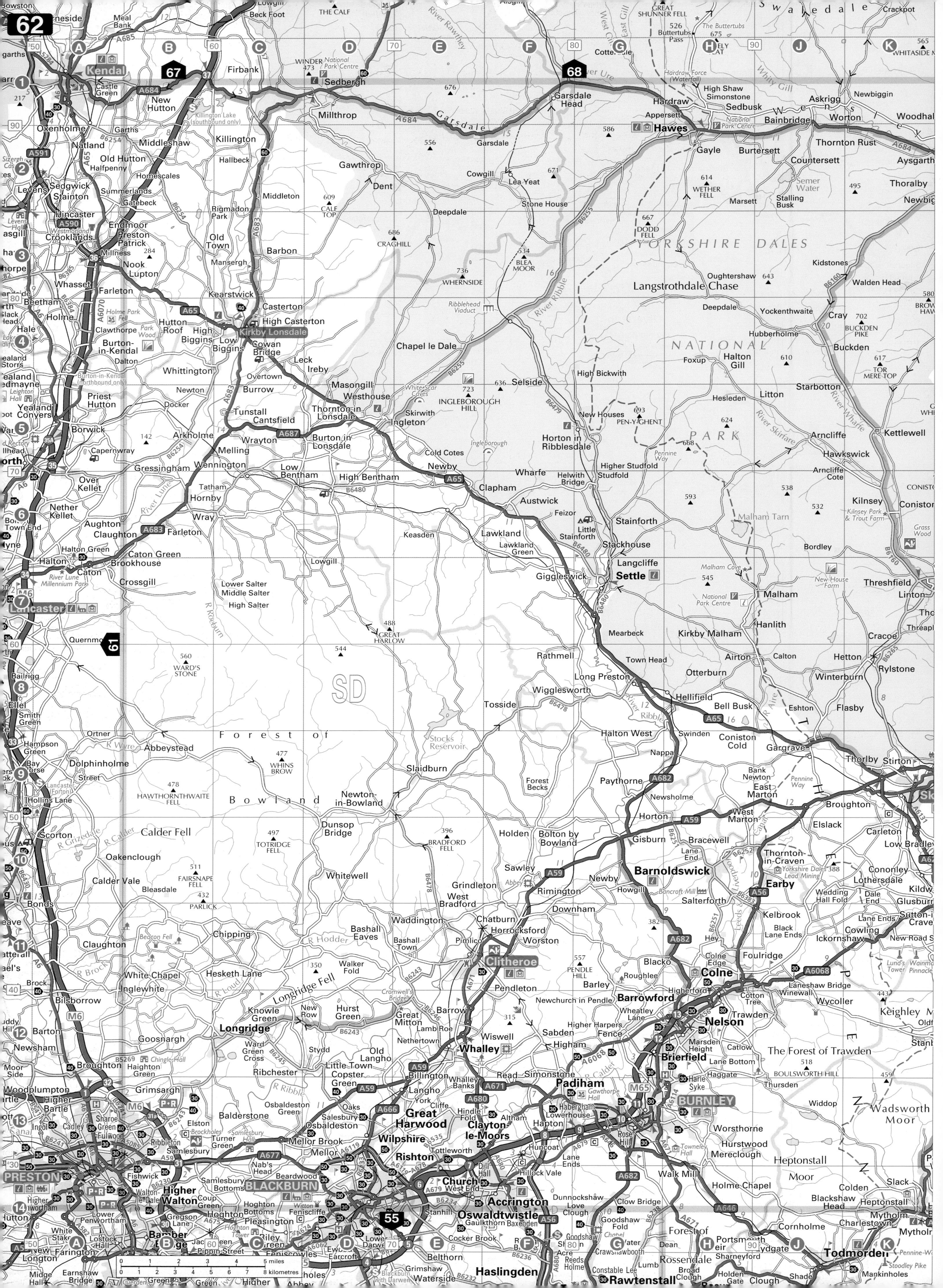
Kendal
Sedbergh
Firbank
Millthrop
Garsdale
Garsdale Head
Hawes
Hardraw
Sedbusk
Askrigg
Bainbridge
Worton
Newbiggin
Thornton Rust
Aysgarth
Gayle
Burtersett
Countersett
Thoralby
Marsett
Stalling Busk
Semer Water
Appersett
High Shaw
Simonstone
Swaledale
Crackpot
Oxenholme
Natland
Old Hutton
Halfpenny
Middleshaw
Killington
Hallbeck
Homescales
Summerlands
Gatebeck
Sedgwick
Stainton
Levens
Hincaster
Crooklands
Endmoor
Preston Patrick
Millness
Nook
Lupton
Whasset
Farleton
Beetham
Holme
Hale
Burton-in-Kendal
Dalton
Clawthorpe
Hutton Roof
High Biggins
Low Biggins
Kirkby Lonsdale
Casterton
High Casterton
Cowan Bridge
Leck
Ireby
Barbon
Mansergh
Old Town
Rigmadon Park
Middleton
Gawthrop
Dent
Deepdale
Cowgill
Lea Yeat
Stone House
Whernside
Blea Moor
Ribblehead Viaduct
Chapel le Dale
Selside
Ingleborough Hill
Ingleton
Thornton in Lonsdale
Masongill
Westhouse
Burton in Lonsdale
Newby
Clapham
Austwick
Feizor
Lawkland
Lawkland Green
Keasden
Wharfe
Helwith Bridge
Studfold
Higher Studfold
Horton in Ribblesdale
New Houses
Pen-y-ghent
High Bickwith
Stainforth
Little Stainforth
Stackhouse
Langcliffe
Settle
Giggleswick
Malham
Malham Tarn
Malham Cove
Kirkby Malham
Hanlith
Airton
Calton
Otterburn
Hetton
Rylstone
Winterburn
Flasby
Eshton
Gargrave
Thorlby
Stirton
Kilnsey
Conistone
Arncliffe
Arncliffe Cote
Hawkswick
Kettlewell
Litton
Starbotton
Halton Gill
Foxup
Hesleden
Buckden
Cray
Hubberholme
Yockenthwaite
Deepdale
Langstrothdale Chase
Oughtershaw
Kidstones
Walden Head
YORKSHIRE DALES
NATIONAL PARK
Threshfield
Linton
Bordley
Mearbeck
Rathmell
Long Preston
Wigglesworth
Hellifield
Bell Busk
Halton West
Swinden
Coniston Cold
Nappa
Tosside
Slaidburn
Newton-in-Bowland
Dunsop Bridge
Forest of Bowland
Stocks Reservoir
Holden
Bolton by Bowland
Paythorne
Newsholme
Horton
Gisburn
West Marton
East Marton
Bank Newton
Broughton
Elslack
Carleton
Thornton-in-Craven
Barnoldswick
Earby
Salterforth
Kelbrook
Foulridge
Colne
Nelson
Barrowford
Brierfield
Burnley
Padiham
Clitheroe
Whalley
Sawley
Rimington
Downham
Chatburn
Grindleton
West Bradford
Waddington
Worston
Pendleton
Sabden
Barley
Roughlee
Newchurch in Pendle
Higham
Simonstone
Read
Wiswell
Barrow
Great Mitton
Whitewell
Chipping
Bashall Eaves
Longridge
Ribchester
Hurst Green
Knowle Green
Goosnargh
Broughton
Grimsargh
Preston
Blackburn
Darwen
Great Harwood
Clayton-le-Moors
Accrington
Oswaldtwistle
Church
Rishton
Wilpshire
Langho
Billington
Haslingden
Rawtenstall
Rossendale
Todmorden
Hebden
Heptonstall
Colden
Slack
Holme Chapel
Walk Mill
Worsthorne
Hurstwood
Mereclough
Wycoller
Trawden
The Forest of Trawden
Boulsworth Hill
Keighley Moor
Wadsworth Moor
Widdop
Lancaster
Caton
Halton
Brookhouse
Crossgill
Wray
Hornby
Tatham
Wennington
Melling
Wrayton
Arkholme
Gressingham
Capernwray
Borwick
Priest Hutton
Yealand Conyers
Over Kellet
Nether Kellet
Aughton
Claughton
Farleton
Caton Green
Low Bentham
High Bentham
Lowgill
Lower Salter
Middle Salter
High Salter
Great Harlow
Ward's Stone
Abbeystead
Dolphinholme
Hawthornthwaite Fell
Whins Brow
Calder Fell
Oakenclough
Calder Vale
Bleasdale
Fairsnape Fell
Parlick
Totridge Fell
Bradford Fell
Claughton
Hesketh Lane
White Chapel
Inglewhite
Bilsborrow
Barton
Longridge Fell
Ellel
Scorton
Garstang
Bay Horse
Hampson Green
Tunstall
Cantsfield
Burrow
Overtown
Whittington
Newton
Docker
Kirkby Lonsdale
Oxenholme
Levens
Preston
Bamber Bridge
Higher Walton
Samlesbury
Hoghton
Mellor
Mellor Brook
Salesbury
Osbaldeston
Balderstone
Copster Green
Old Langho
Stydd
Ward Green Cross
Dinckley
Walker Fold
Cowark
Huncoat
Altham
Hapton
Rose Hill
Habergham
Higherford
Blacko
Roughlee
Laneshaw Bridge
Cowling
Glusburn
Sutton-in-Craven
Cononley
Lothersdale
Ickornshaw
Yorkshire Dales Lead Mining Museum
SD
5 miles
8 kilometres

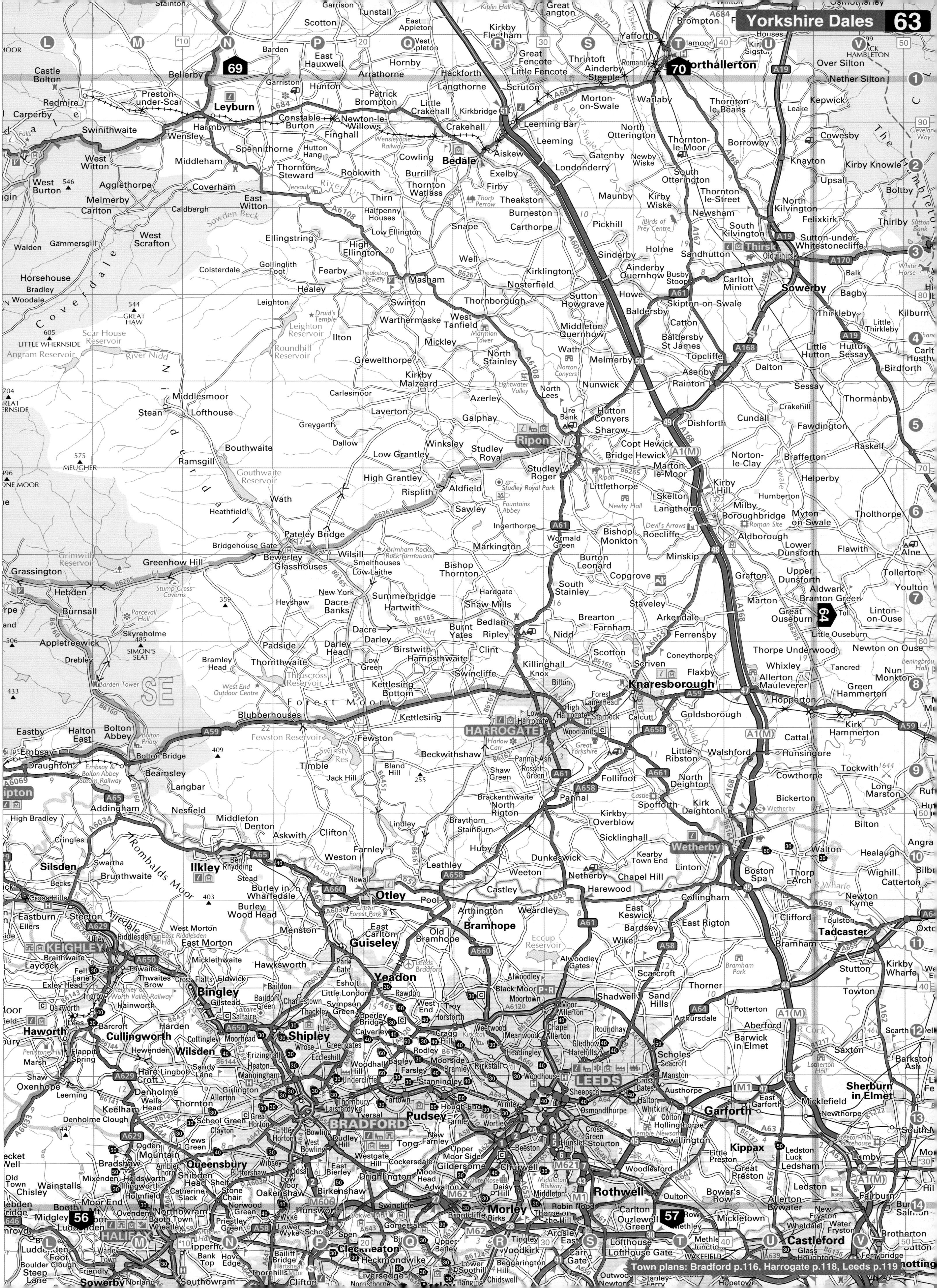

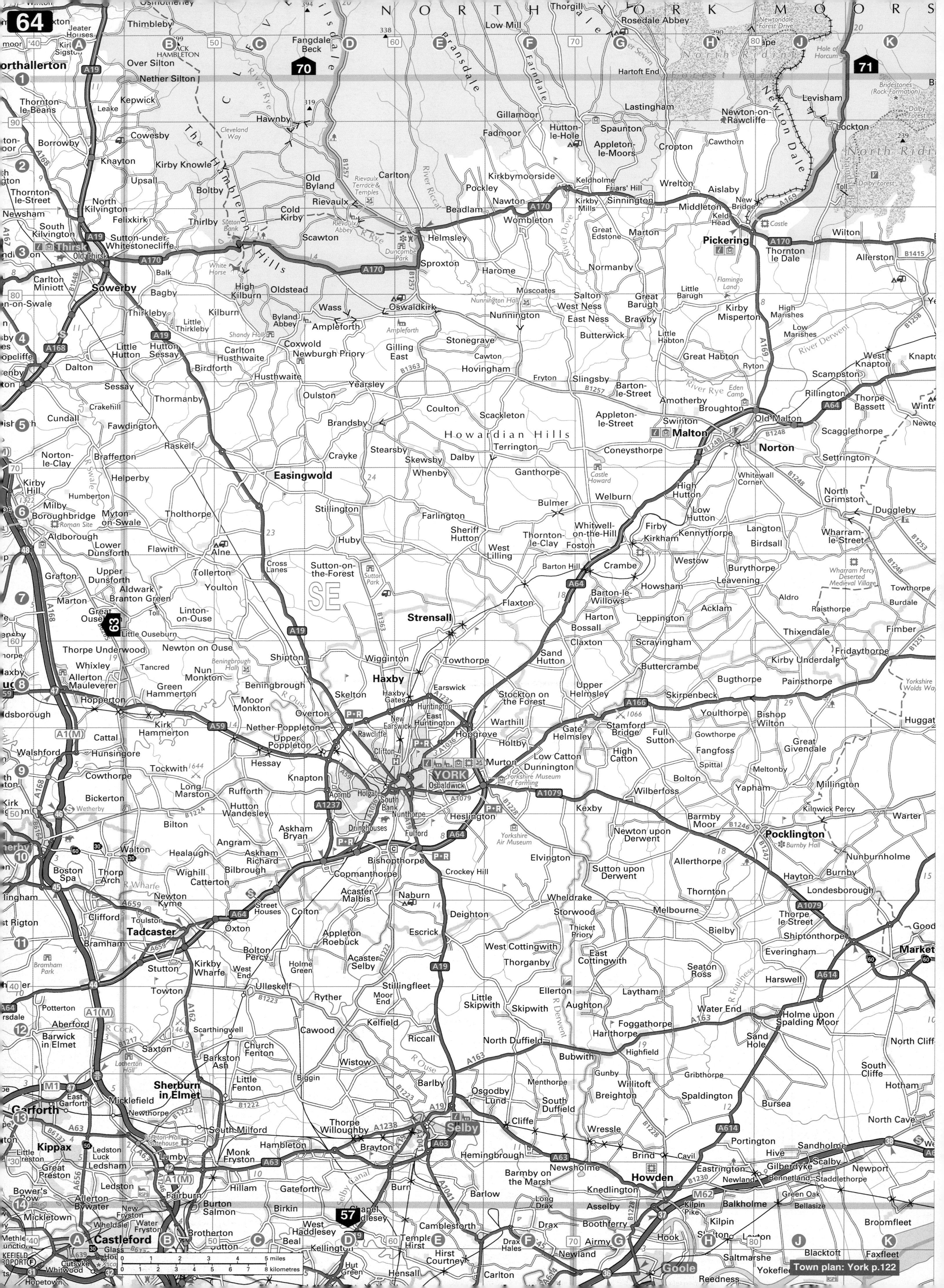
NORTH YORK MOORS
Northallerton
Thimbleby
Over Silton
Nether Silton
Osmotherley
Fangdale Beck
Bilsdale
Bransdale
Farndale
Rosedale Abbey
Thorgill
Low Mill
Hartoft End
North Riding Forest Park
Newton Dale
Levisham
Lockton
Bridestones (Rock Formation)
Dalby Forest Drive
Hole of Horcum
Newtondale Forest Drive
Thornton-le-Beans
Kepwick
Leake
Hawnby
Cleveland Way
The Hambleton Hills
River Rye
Borrowby
Cowesby
Knayton
Kirby Knowle
Upsall
Thornton-le-Street
North Kilvington
South Kilvington
Newsham
Felixkirk
Boltby
Thirlby
Sutton Bank
Sutton-under-Whitestonecliffe
Thirsk
Old Thirsk
Sowerby
Carlton Miniott
Balk
Bagby
Kilburn
White Horse
High Kilburn
Oldstead
Old Byland
Cold Kirby
Rievaulx
Rievaulx Terrace & Temples
Rievaulx Abbey
Scawton
Carlton
River Riccal
Helmsley
Duncombe Park
Sproxton
Wass
Byland Abbey
Ampleforth
Oswaldkirk
Gillamoor
Fadmoor
Hutton-le-Hole
Lastingham
Spaunton
Appleton-le-Moors
Cropton
Cawthorn
Newton-on-Rawcliffe
Kirkbymoorside
Pockley
Beadlam
Nawton
Wombleton
Keldholme
Kirkby Mills
Friars' Hill
Sinnington
Great Edstone
Marton
Wrelton
Aislaby
Middleton
Keld Head
New Bridge
Pickering
Castle
Thornton le Dale
Wilton
Allerston
Dalby Forest
Toll
Harome
Normanby
Muscoates
Nunnington Hall
Nunnington
Salton
West Ness
East Ness
Great Barugh
Little Barugh
Flamingo Land
Kirby Misperton
Brawby
Butterwick
High Marishes
Low Marishes
Little Habton
Great Habton
Ryton
River Derwent
West Knapton
Scampston
Rillington
Thorpe Bassett
Thirkleby
Little Thirkleby
Shandy Hall
Coxwold
Newburgh Priory
Gilling East
Stonegrave
Cawton
Hovingham
Fryton
Slingsby
Barton-le-Street
Eden Camp
Amotherby
Broughton
Swinton
Malton
Old Malton
Norton
Scagglethorpe
Settrington
Little Hutton
Hutton Sessay
Carlton Husthwaite
Birdforth
Husthwaite
Yearsley
Oulston
Sessay
Dalton
Thormanby
Crakehill
Cundall
Fawdington
Brandsby
Coulton
Scackleton
Howardian Hills
Terrington
Appleton-le-Street
Coneysthorpe
Castle Howard
Raskelf
Brafferton
Helperby
Norton-le-Clay
Kirby Hill
Humberton
Milby
Boroughbridge
Roman Site
Aldborough
Myton-on-Swale
Tholthorpe
Easingwold
Crayke
Stearsby
Skewsby
Dalby
Whenby
Ganthorpe
Welburn
Whitewall Corner
High Hutton
Low Hutton
North Grimston
Duggleby
Stillington
Farlington
Bulmer
Sheriff Hutton
West Lilling
Thornton-le-Clay
Foston
Whitwell-on-the-Hill
Firby
Kirkham
Priory
Kennythorpe
Langton
Birdsall
Wharram-le-Street
Wharram Percy Deserted Medieval Village
Huby
Lower Dunsforth
Upper Dunsforth
Flawith
Alne
Tollerton
Youlton
Cross Lanes
Sutton-on-the-Forest
Sutton Park
Grafton
Aldwark
Branton Green
Linton-on-Ouse
Marton
Great Ouseburn
Little Ouseburn
Barton Hill
Crambe
Westow
Burythorpe
Leavening
Howsham
Barton-le-Willows
Towthorpe
Burdale
Aldro
Raisthorpe
Flaxton
Strensall
Harton
Bossall
Leppington
Acklam
Thixendale
Fimber
Claxton
Scrayingham
Fridaythorpe
Kirby Underdale
Thorpe Underwood
Newton on Ouse
Beningbrough Hall
Whixley
Tancred
Nun Monkton
Allerton Mauleverer
Green Hammerton
Beningbrough
Shipton
Wigginton
Haxby
Towthorpe
Sand Hutton
Buttercrambe
Bugthorpe
Painsthorpe
Yorkshire Wolds Way
Hopperton
Moor Monkton
Skelton
Haxby Gates
Earswick
Huntington
Stockton on the Forest
Upper Helmsley
Skirpenbeck
Knaresborough
Overton
Nether Poppleton
Upper Poppleton
Rawcliffe
New Earswick
East Huntington
Hopgrove
Warthill
Gate Helmsley
Stamford Bridge
1066
Youlthorpe
Bishop Wilton
Huggate
Kirk Hammerton
Cattal
Walshford
Hunsingore
Hessay
Clifton
Holtby
Low Catton
High Catton
Full Sutton
Gowthorpe
Fangfoss
Great Givendale
Cowthorpe
Tockwith
1644
Long Marston
Knapton
Murton
Dunnington
Yorkshire Museum of Farming
Spittal
Meltonby
Millington
YORK
Osbaldwick
Acomb
Holgate
South Bank
Bolton
Yapham
Bickerton
Rufforth
Hutton Wandesley
Nunthorpe
Heslington
Kexby
Wilberfoss
Kilnwick Percy
Wetherby
Bilton
Askham Bryan
Dringhouses
Fulford
Yorkshire Air Museum
Barmby Moor
Newton upon Derwent
Pocklington
Burnby Hall
Warter
Angram
Walton
Healaugh
Askham Richard
Bishopthorpe
Crockey Hill
Elvington
Sutton upon Derwent
Allerthorpe
Nunburnholme
Boston Spa
Thorp Arch
Wighill
Bilbrough
Catterton
Copmanthorpe
Hayton
Burnby
Londesborough
Wharfe
Newton Kyme
Acaster Malbis
Naburn
Wheldrake
Thornton
Street Houses
Colton
Deighton
Storwood
Melbourne
Thorpe le Street
Clifford
Toulston
Tadcaster
Oxton
Appleton Roebuck
Escrick
Thicket Priory
Bielby
Shiptonthorpe
Bramham
Bramham Park
Bolton Percy
Acaster Selby
Holme Green
West Cottingwith
East Cottingwith
Thorganby
Everingham
Market Weighton
Stutton
Kirkby Wharfe
West End
Seaton Ross
Harswell
Towton
Ulleskelf
Stillingfleet
Ryther
Moor End
Ellerton
Laytham
Little Skipwith
Skipwith
Aughton
Water End
River Foulness
Potterton
Aberford
Scarthingwell
Cawood
Kelfield
Foggathorpe
Harlthorpe
Holme upon Spalding Moor
Barwick in Elmet
Saxton
Church Fenton
Riccall
North Duffield
Highfield
Bubwith
Sand Hole
North Cliffe
Lotherton Hall
Barkston Ash
Wistow
Biggin
Barlby
Gunby
Willitoft
Gribthorpe
South Cliffe
Hotham
Sherburn in Elmet
Little Fenton
Micklefield
East Garforth
Garforth
Newthorpe
Osgodby
Lund
Menthorpe
South Duffield
Breighton
Spaldington
Bursea
North Cave
Kippax
South Milford
Steeton Hall Gatehouse
Thorpe Willoughby
Selby
Cliffe
Wressle
Little Preston
Ledston Luck
Ledsham
Hambleton
Brayton
Hemingbrough
Portington
Hive
Sandholme
Great Preston
Lumby
Monk Fryston
Newsholme
Brind
Cavil
Howden
Eastrington
Gilberdyke
Scalby
Newland
Bennetland
Staddlethorpe
Newport
Ledston
Hillam
Gateforth
Burn
Barmby on the Marsh
Knedlington
Green Oak
Bellasize
Bowers Row
Allerton Bywater
Fairburn
Burton Salmon
Birkin
Barlow
Long Drax
Asselby
Balkholme
Mickletown
New Fryston
Water Fryston
Wheldale
Brotherton
West Haddlesey
Chapel Haddlesey
Camblesforth
Drax
Boothferry
Kilpin Pike
Kilpin
Broomfleet
Castleford
Sutton
Beal
Kellington
Temple Hirst
Hirst Courtney
Drax Hales
Airmyn
Hook
Skelton
Laxton
Blacktoft
Faxfleet
Glasshoughton
Cutsyke
Whitwood
Hopetown
Hut Green
Hensall
Carlton
Newland
Goole
Saltmarshe
Yokefleet
Reedness
Methley Junction
Wakefield Europort
Selby Canal
River Ouse
River Derwent
SE
0 1 2 3 4 5 miles
0 1 2 3 4 5 6 7 8 kilometres

70
71
63
57

Town plan: York p.122

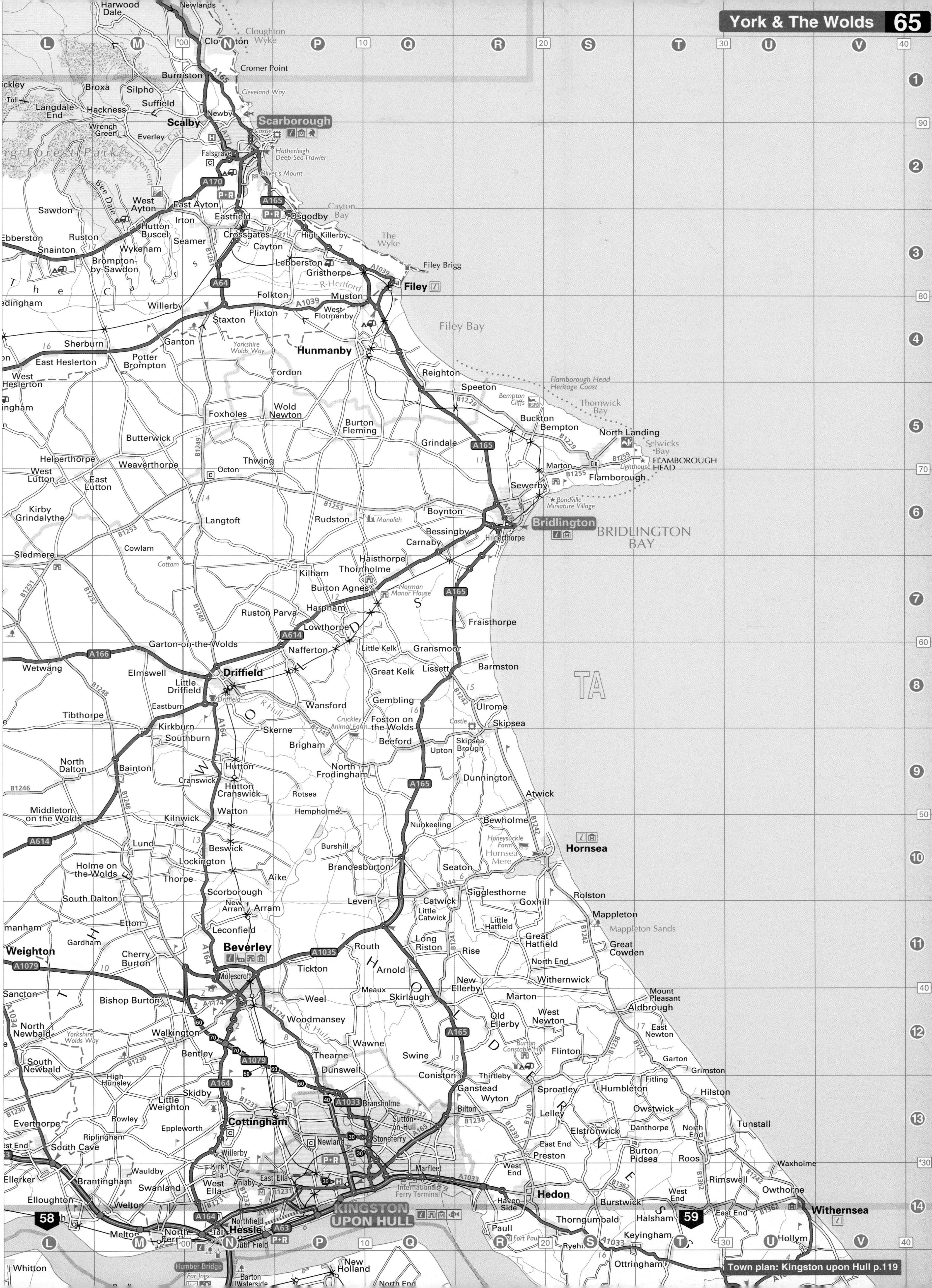
Harwood Dale
Newlands
Cloughton Wyke
Cloughton
Cromer Point
Burniston
Cleveland Way
Broxa
Silpho
Suffield
Langdale End
Hackness
Newby
Scalby
Scarborough
Castle
Wrench Green
Everley
Forest Park
Falsgrave
Hatherleigh Deep Sea Trawler
River Derwent
Sea Cut
Oliver's Mount
Bee Dale
A170
A165
A171
P+R
Cayton Bay
West Ayton
East Ayton
Sawdon
Irton
Eastfield
Osgodby
Hutton Buscel
Ebberston
Ruston
Crossgates
High Killerby
The Wyke
Snainton
Seamer
Cayton
Wykeham
Brompton-by-Sawdon
Lebberston
Filey Brigg
Gristhorpe
R Hertford
A1039
A64
B1261
Filey
Folkton
Muston
Willerby
A1039
West Flotmanby
Staxton
Flixton
Filey Bay
Sherburn
Ganton
Yorkshire Wolds Way
Hunmanby
East Heslerton
Potter Brompton
West Heslerton
Fordon
Reighton
Speeton
Flamborough Head Heritage Coast
B1229
Bempton Cliffs
Thornwick Bay
Foxholes
Wold Newton
Buckton
Bempton
North Landing
Burton Fleming
Butterwick
Grindale
A165
Selwicks Bay
FLAMBOROUGH HEAD
Lighthouse
B1259
Helperthorpe
Thwing
Weaverthorpe
B1249
Octon
Marton
B1255
Flamborough
West Lutton
East Lutton
Sewerby
Bondville Miniature Village
Kirby Grindalythe
Langtoft
B1253
Rudston
Monolith
Boynton
Bridlington
BRIDLINGTON BAY
Bessingby
Hilderthorpe
B1253
Cowlam
Carnaby
Sledmere
Cottam
Haisthorpe
Thornholme
Kilham
Burton Agnes
Norman Manor House
B1251
B1252
A165
B1249
Ruston Parva
Harpham
Fraisthorpe
Lowthorpe
A614
Garton-on-the-Wolds
Nafferton
Little Kelk
Gransmoor
A166
Wetwang
Elmswell
Driffield
Lissett
Barmston
Great Kelk
Little Driffield
TA
B1248
Eastburn
R Hull
Wansford
Gembling
B1242
Ulrome
Tibthorpe
Cruckley Animal Farm
Foston on the Wolds
Castle
Skipsea
Kirkburn
Skerne
B1249
Southburn
A164
Brigham
Beeford
Upton
Skipsea Brough
North Dalton
Bainton
Hutton
North Frodingham
Dunnington
Cranswick
B1246
Hutton Cranswick
Rotsea
A165
Atwick
Middleton on the Wolds
B1248
Watton
Hempholme
Kilnwick
Nunkeeling
Bewholme
A614
Lund
Beswick
Burshill
Honeysuckle Farm
Hornsea Mere
B1242
Hornsea
Holme on the Wolds
Lockington
Aike
Brandesburton
Seaton
Thorpe
Scorborough
B1244
Sigglesthorne
Rolston
South Dalton
Leven
Catwick
Goxhill
New Arram
Arram
Little Catwick
Mappleton
Mappleton Sands
Etton
Little Hatfield
Great Hatfield
Leconfield
Long Riston
B1243
B1242
Great Cowden
Weighton
Gardham
Beverley
Routh
Rise
Cherry Burton
A1035
North End
A1079
Tickton
Arnold
Withernwick
Sancton
Molescroft
Meaux
New Ellerby
Marton
Mount Pleasant
Bishop Burton
A1174
Weel
Skirlaugh
Aldbrough
A1034
North Newbald
Woodmansey
Old Ellerby
West Newton
East Newton
Yorkshire Wolds Way
Walkington
A1174
R Hull
A165
B1238
B1242
Burton Constable Hall
Flinton
Bentley
Wawne
A1079
South Newbald
B1230
Thearne
Swine
Garton
Grimston
High Hunsley
A164
Dunswell
Coniston
Thirtleby
Fitling
Skidby
Ganstead
Sproatley
Humbleton
Hilston
Little Weighton
B1233
A1033
Bransholme
Wyton
B1230
Sutton-on-Hull
B1237
Bilton
B1240
Owstwick
Everthorpe
Rowley
Cottingham
B1238
Lelley
B1239
Elstronwick
Danthorpe
North End
Tunstall
Riplingham
Eppleworth
Newland
Stoneferry
East End
South Cave
A1079
East End
Preston
Burton Pidsea
Roos
Willerby
Waxholme
Kirk Ella
Wauldby
West Ella
East Ella
Marfleet
A1033
West End
B1362
Rimswell
Ellerker
Brantingham
Swanland
Anlaby
International Ferry Terminal
Hedon
West End
Owthorne
Elloughton
B1231
Haven Side
Burstwick
B1362
Withernsea
Welton
KINGSTON UPON HULL
East End
Northfield
A164
A63
Halsham
Paull
Thorngumbald
Melton
North Ferriby
Hessle
Fort Paull
A1033
Keyingham
Hollym
Ryehill
South Field
Whitton
New Holland
Ottringham
Humber Bridge
Far Ings
Barton Waterside
North End
58
59
L
M
N
P
Q
R
S
T
U
V
00
10
20
30
40
90
80
70
60
50
40
30
1
2
3
4
5
6
7
8
9
10
11
12
13
14

Town plan: Kingston upon Hull p.119

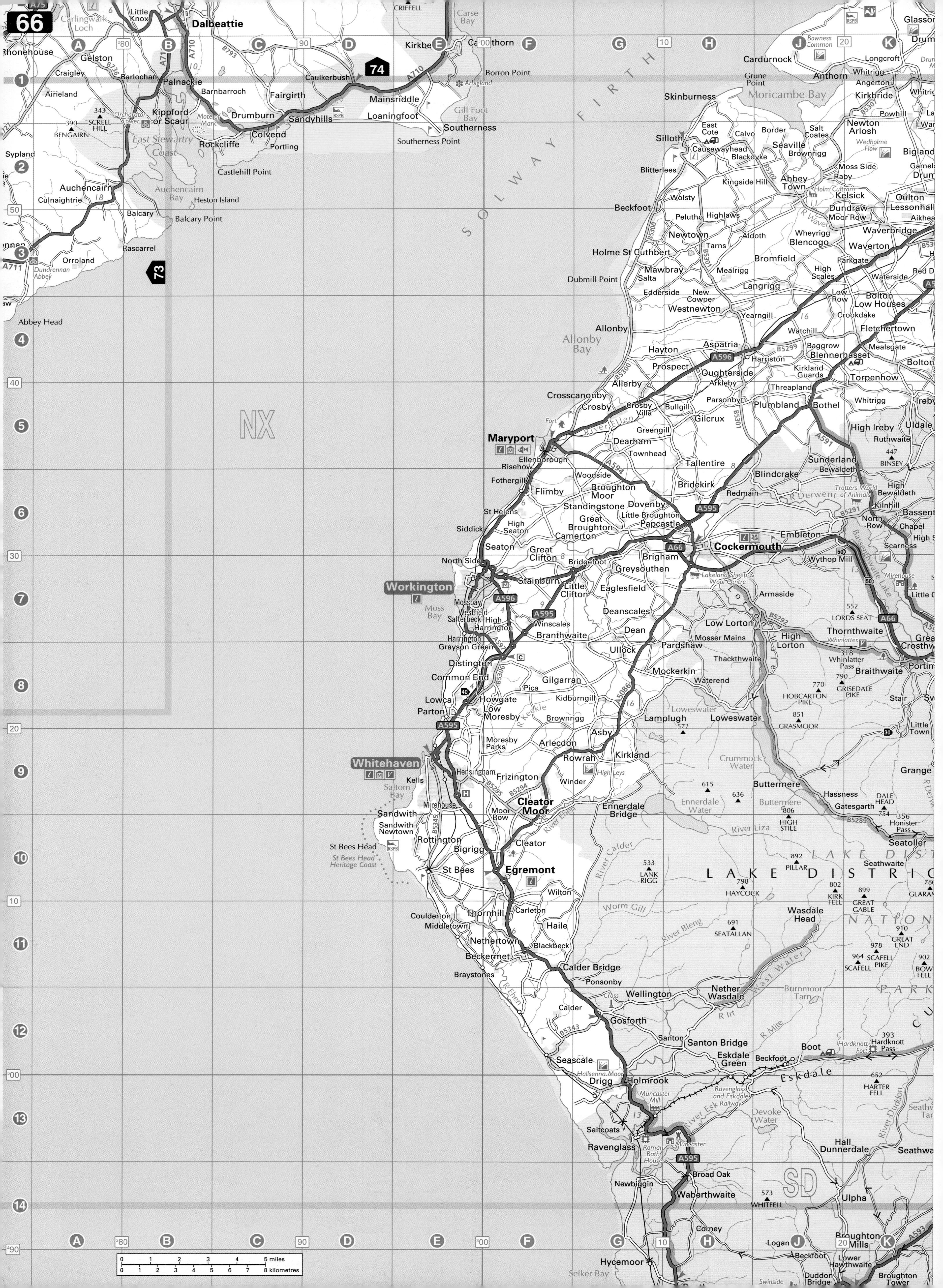

Dalbeattie
Little Knox
Carlingwark Loch
CRIFFELL
Carse Bay
Kirkbean
Carsethorn
Rhonehouse
Gelston
Craigley
Barlochan
Palnackie
Airieland
Barnbarroch
Caulkerbush
Fairgirth
Mainsriddle
Borron Point
Arbigland
Kippford or Scaur
Drumburn
Sandyhills
Loaningfoot
Gill Foot Bay
Southerness
Southerness Point
343 SCREEL HILL
390 BENGAIRN
Orchardton Tower
Mote of Mark
Colvend
Rockcliffe
Portling
East Stewartry Coast
Sypland
Castlehill Point
Auchencairn
Culnaightrie
Auchencairn Bay
Heston Island
Balcary
Balcary Point
Rascarrel
Orroland
Dundrennan Abbey
Abbey Head
74
73
SOLWAY FIRTH
Bowness Common
Glasson
Drum
Cardurnock
Longcroft
Grune Point
Anthorn
Whitrigg
Angerton
Moricambe Bay
Kirkbride
Skinburness
Powhill
East Cote
Calvo
Border
Salt Coates
Newton Arlosh
Silloth
Causewayhead
Seaville
Wedholme Flow
Blackdyke
Brownrigg
Bigland
Blitterlees
Abbey Town
Moss Side
Kingside Hill
Raby
Holm Cultram
Kelsick
Oulton
Lessonhall
Wolsty
Dundraw
Moor Row
Aikhead
Beckfoot
Pelutho
Highlaws
R Waver
Newtown
Aldoth
Wheyrigg
Waverbridge
Blencogo
Waverton
Holme St Cuthbert
Tarns
Bromfield
Mawbray
Salta
Mealrigg
Parkgate
High Scales
Waterside
Dubmill Point
Edderside
New Cowper
Langrigg
Low Row
Bolton Low Houses
Westnewton
Yearngill
Crookdake
Allonby
Allonby Bay
Watchill
Fletchertown
Aspatria
Baggrow
Mealsgate
Hayton
Harriston
Blennerhasset
Prospect
Oughterside
Kirkland Guards
Torpenhow
Allerby
Arkleby
Threapland
Crosscanonby
Parsonby
Plumbland
Bothel
Whitrigg
Crosby
Crosby Villa
Bullgill
Gilcrux
Fort
River Ellen
High Ireby
Uldale
Maryport
Greengill
Dearham
Ruthwaite
447 BINSEY
Ellenborough
Townhead
Risehow
Tallentire
Sunderland
Bewaldeth
Fothergill
Woodside
Broughton Moor
Blindcrake
Flimby
Bridekirk
High Bewaldeth
Redmain
R Derwent
Trotters World of Animals
Kilnhill
St Helens
Standingstone
Dovenby
Bassenthwaite
Little Broughton
Great Broughton
Papcastle
North Row
Chapel
Siddick
High Seaton
Camerton
Seaton
Embleton
Cockermouth
Great Clifton
Brigham
Wythop Mill
Scarness
North Side
Bridgefoot
Greysouthen
Lakeland Sheep & Wool Centre
Bassenthwaite Lake
Mirehouse
Stainburn
Workington
Little Clifton
Eaglesfield
Armaside
Moss Bay
Mossbay
Westfield
Salterbeck
High Harrington
Winscales
Deanscales
552 LORDS SEAT
Little Crosthwaite
Low Lorton
Dean
Harrington
Branthwaite
Mosser Mains
High Lorton
Thornthwaite
Grayson Green
Ullock
Pardshaw
Whinlatter
Crosthwaite
318 Whinlatter Pass
Distington
Thackthwaite
Braithwaite
Mockerkin
Portinscale
Common End
Waterend
Gilgarran
770 HOBCARTON PIKE
790 GRISEDALE PIKE
Lowca
Pica
Howgate
Kidburngill
Stair
Parton
Low Moresby
Brownrigg
Loweswater
Lamplugh
Loweswater
851 GRASMOOR
Little Town
572
Moresby Parks
Asby
Arlecdon
Kirkland
Whitehaven
Rowrah
Crummock Water
Grange
Kells
Hensingham
Frizington
Winder
High Leys
Saltom Bay
615
636
Buttermere
Hassness
DALE HEAD
Cleator Moor
Mirehouse
Moor Row
Ennerdale Bridge
Gatesgarth
Sandwith
Sandwith Newtown
Ennerdale Water
Buttermere
806 HIGH STILE
754
356 Honister Pass
River Ehen
Rottington
River Liza
Seatoller
Cleator
St Bees Head
Bigrigg
St Bees Head Heritage Coast
892 PILLAR
Seathwaite
River Calder
533 LANK RIGG
LAKE DISTRICT
St Bees
Egremont
798 HAYCOCK
802 KIRK FELL
899 GREAT GABLE
Wilton
Worm Gill
Carleton
Wasdale Head
NATIONAL
Coulderton
Thornhill
910 GREAT END
Middletown
Haile
691 SEATALLAN
River Bleng
Nethertown
978 SCAFELL PIKE
964 SCAFELL
902 BOW FELL
Beckermet
Blackbeck
Calder Bridge
Braystones
Wast Water
Ponsonby
Nether Wasdale
Burnmoor Tarn
Cross
Wellington
Calder
PARK
R Irt
Gosforth
R Mite
393 Hardknott Pass
Hardknott Fort
Santon
Santon Bridge
Boot
Seascale
Eskdale Green
Beckfoot
Hallsenna Moor
Drigg
Holmrook
Eskdale
652 HARTER FELL
Muncaster Mill
Ravenglass and Eskdale Railway
River Esk
Devoke Water
Saltcoats
Ravenglass
Roman Bath House
Muncaster
Hall Dunnerdale
River Duddon
Seathwaite
Broad Oak
Newbiggin
Waberthwaite
573 WHITFELL
Ulpha
Corney
Logan
Beckfoot
Broughton Mills
Lower Hawthwaite
Hycemoor
Selker Bay
Duddon Bridge
Broughton Tower
Swinside
NX
SD
A B C D E F G H J K
1 2 3 4 5 6 7 8 9 10 11 12 13 14
A711 A710 A75 B736 B793 A596 A595 A66 A591 A594 A5086 B5300 B5302 B5301 B5299 B5291 B5292 B5289 B5306 B5294 B5295 B5345 B5343 A593
0 1 2 3 4 5 miles
0 1 2 3 4 5 6 7 8 kilometres

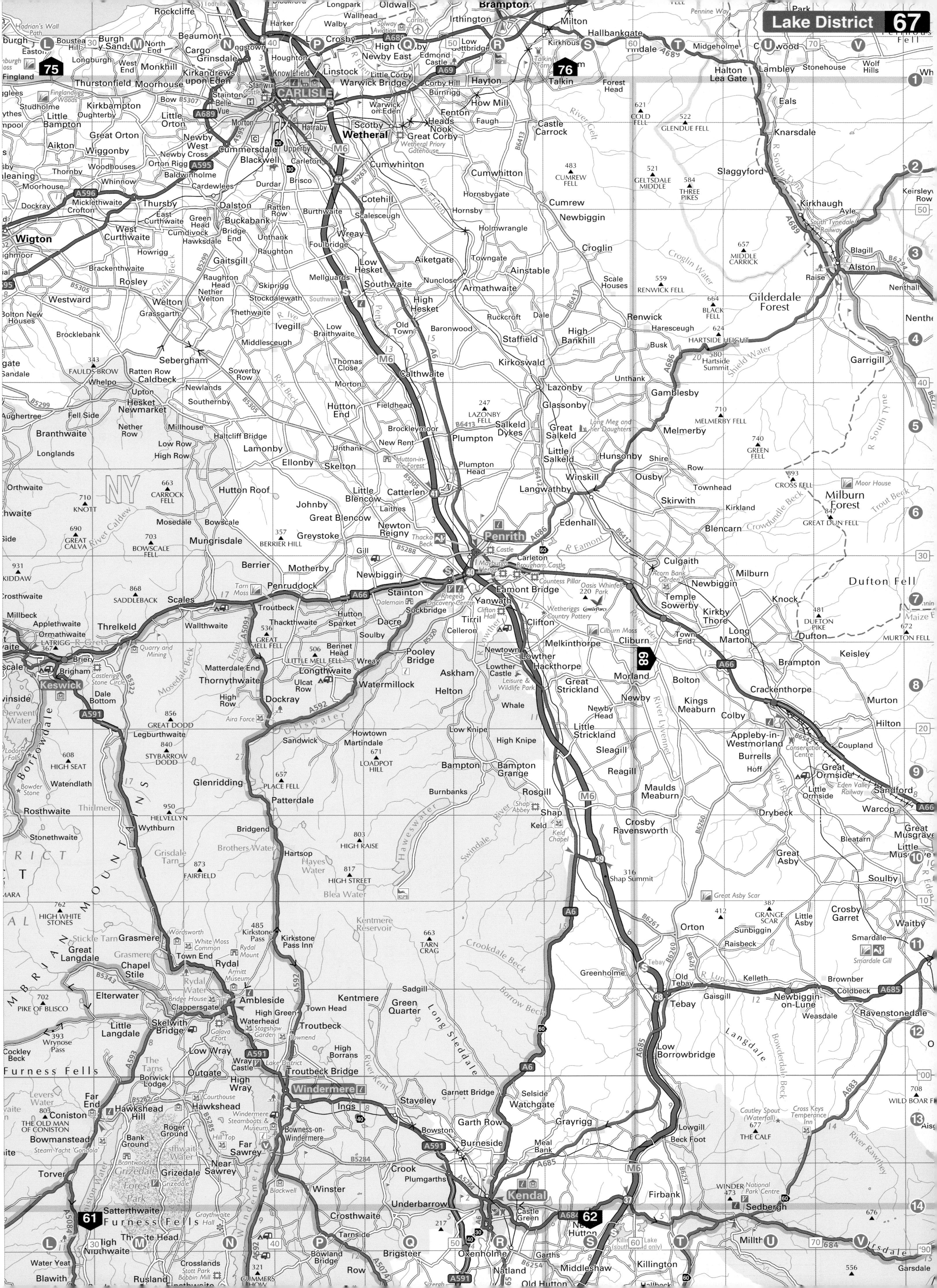
Rockcliffe
Brampton
Milton
Hallbankgate
Carlisle
CARLISLE
Wetheral
Great Corby
Cumwhinton
Cumwhitton
Wigton
Thursby
Dalston
Sebergham
Caldbeck
Hesket Newmarket
Calthwaite
Kirkoswald
Lazonby
Penrith
Temple Sowerby
Appleby-in-Westmorland
Alston
Gilderdale Forest
Milburn Forest
Dufton Fell
Keswick
Threlkeld
Pooley Bridge
Ullswater
Glenridding
Patterdale
Helvellyn
Shap
Orton
Tebay
Grasmere
Ambleside
Windermere
Bowness-on-Windermere
Coniston
Staveley
Kendal
Sedbergh
Ravenstonedale
Low Borrowbridge
Kirkby Thore
Long Marton
Brough
Haweswater
Thirlmere
Skiddaw
Saddleback
Hartside Height
Cross Fell
Great Dun Fell
Furness Fells
Grizedale Forest Park
Long Sleddale
Kentmere
Langdale

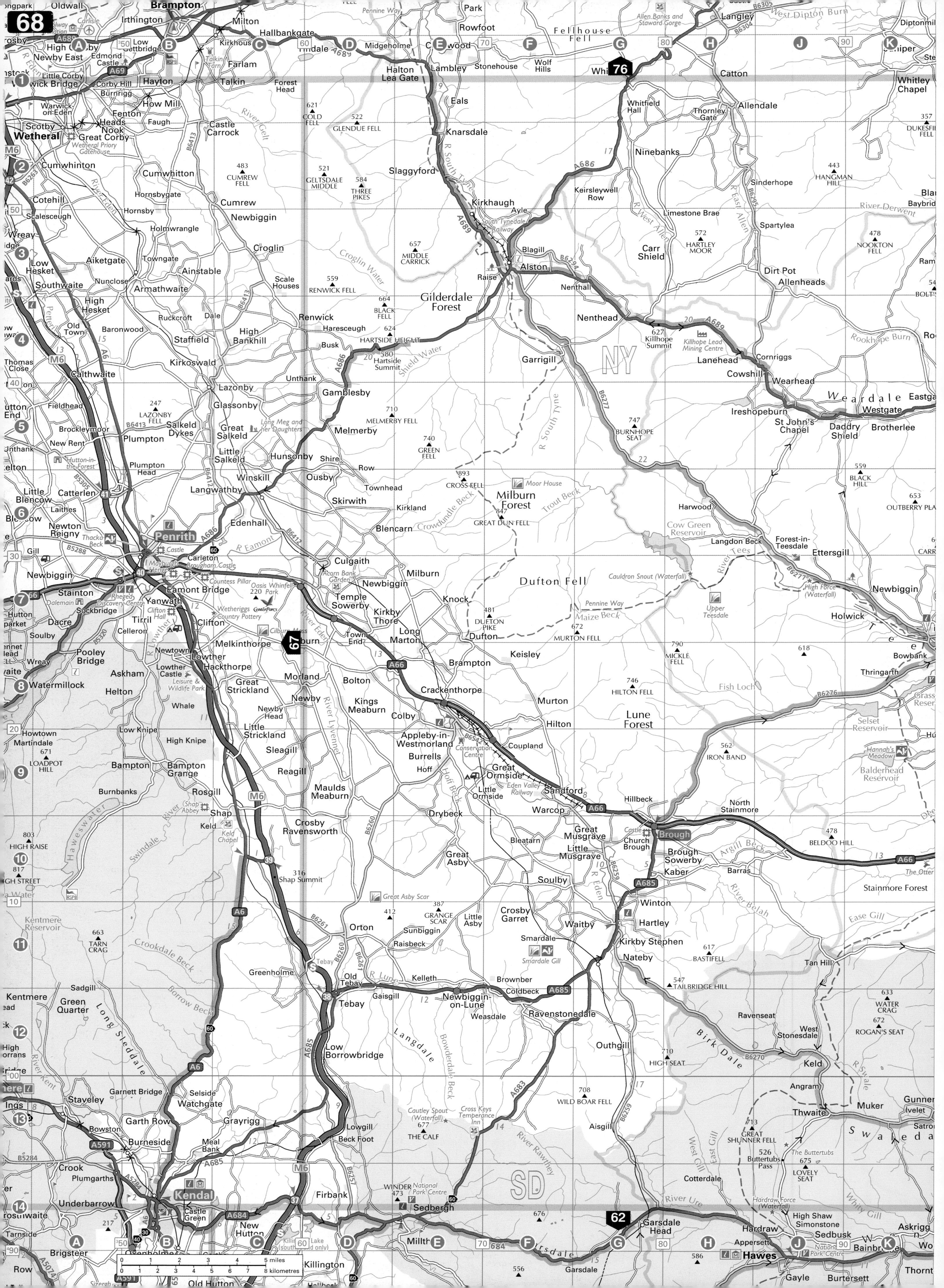
Brampton
Irthington
Oldwall
Milton
Hallbankgate
Midgeholme
Park
Rowfoot
Fellhouse Fell
Allen Banks and Staward Gorge
Langley
West Dipton Burn
Diptonmill
Low Gelt Bridge
Kirkhouse
Tindale
Halton Lea Gate
Lambley
Stonehouse
Wolf Hills
Catton
Newby East
Edmond Castle
Little Corby
Corby Hill
Hayton
Talkin
Farlam
Forest Head
Whitley Chapel
Warwick Bridge
Burnrigg
How Mill
Eals
Whitfield Hall
Thornley Gate
Allendale
Warwick-on-Eden
Fenton
Heads Nook
Faugh
Castle Carrock
621 COLD FELL
522 GLENDUE FELL
Knarsdale
357 DUKESFIELD FELL
Scotby
Wetheral
Great Corby
Wetheral Priory Gatehouse
Ninebanks
Cumwhinton
Cumwhitton
483 CUMREW FELL
521 GELTSDALE MIDDLE
584 THREE PIKES
Slaggyford
443 HANGMAN HILL
Sinderhope
Keirsleywell Row
Hornsbygate
Cotehill
Cumrew
Kirkhaugh
Ayle
South Tynedale Railway
Baybridge
River Derwent
Scalesceugh
Hornsby
Newbiggin
Limestone Brae
Spartylea
Wreay
Holmwrangle
657 MIDDLE CARRICK
572 HARTLEY MOOR
478 NOOKTON FELL
Croglin
Croglin Water
Blagill
Carr Shield
Low Hesket
Aiketgate
Towngate
Ainstable
Alston
Nunclose
Scale Houses
559 RENWICK FELL
Raise
Dirt Pot
Allenheads
Southwaite
Armathwaite
Nenthall
High Hesket
664 BLACK FELL
Gilderdale Forest
Nenthead
Old Town
Ruckcroft
Dale
Renwick
Harescough
624 HARTSIDE HEIGHT
627 Killhope Summit
Killhope Lead Mining Centre
Rookhope Burn
Baronwood
Staffield
High Bankhill
Busk
580 Hartside Summit
Shield Water
Thomas Close
Kirkoswald
Garrigill
Lanehead
Cornriggs
Calthwaite
Unthank
NY
Cowshill
Wearhead
Lazonby
Gamblesby
Weardale
Eastgate
Westgate
Fieldhead
247 LAZONBY FELL
Glassonby
710 MELMERBY FELL
Ireshopeburn
St John's Chapel
Daddry Shield
Brotherlee
Salkeld Dykes
Great Salkeld
Long Meg and her Daughters
Melmerby
747 BURNHOPE SEAT
Brockleymoor
Plumpton
R South Tyne
New Rent
Little Salkeld
740 GREEN FELL
Hutton-in-the-Forest
Hunsonby
Shire
Row
559 BLACK HILL
Plumpton Head
Winskill
Ousby
893 CROSS FELL
Moor House
Little Blencow
Catterlen
Langwathby
Townhead
Milburn Forest
653 OUTBERRY PLAIN
Laithes
Skirwith
Kirkland
847 GREAT DUN FELL
Harwood
Newton Reigny
Edenhall
Blencarn
Crowdundle Beck
Trout Beck
Cow Green Reservoir
Thacka Beck
Penrith
R Eamont
Langdon Beck
Forest-in-Teesdale
Ettersgill
Gill
Castle
Carleton
Culgaith
Brougham Castle
Newbiggin
Mayburgh Henge
Milburn
Dufton Fell
Cauldron Snout (Waterfall)
High Force (Waterfall)
Stainton
Countess Pillar
Eamont Bridge
Oasis Whinfell Park
Acorn Bank Garden
Newbiggin
Knock
Pennine Way
Dalemain
Rheged Discovery Centre
Yanwath
Temple Sowerby
Holwick
Hutton
Dacre
Sockbridge
Tirril
Clifton Hall
Wetheriggs Country Pottery
Kirkby Thore
481 DUFTON PIKE
Maize Beck
Upper Teesdale
Celleron
Clifton
Cliburn Moss
Cliburn
Town End
Long Marton
Dufton
672 MURTON FELL
Soulby
Newtown
Melkinthorpe
618
Bowbank
Pooley Bridge
Lowther
Keisley
790 MICKLE FELL
Wreay
Lowther Castle
Hackthorpe
Brampton
Thringarth
Askham
Leisure & Wildlife Park
Great Strickland
Morland
Bolton
Fish Loch
Watermillock
Helton
Crackenthorpe
746 HILTON FELL
Newby
Murton
Whale
Kings Meaburn
Newby Head
River Lyvennet
Colby
Lune Forest
Selset Reservoir
Low Knipe
Howtown
Martindale
Little Strickland
Appleby-in-Westmorland
Hilton
High Knipe
671 LOADPOT HILL
Sleagill
Conservation Centre
Coupland
562 IRON BAND
Hannah's Meadow
Burrells
Bampton
Bampton Grange
Hoff
Reagill
Great Ormside
Balderhead Reservoir
Hoff Beck
Eden Valley Railway
Burnbanks
Rosgill
Maulds Meaburn
Little Ormside
Sandford
Hillbeck
North Stainmore
Shap Abbey
Shap
Warcop
Drybeck
Keld
Crosby Ravensworth
Great Musgrave
Brough
Keld Chapel
Church Brough
803 HIGH RAISE
Bleatarn
Little Musgrave
478 BELDOO HILL
Great Asby
Brough Sowerby
Argill Beck
Haweswater
Swindale
Kaber
817 HIGH STREET
316 Shap Summit
Soulby
Barras
The Otter
Stainmore Forest
Great Asby Scar
Winton
River Belah
Kentmere Reservoir
387 GRANGE SCAR
Little Asby
Crosby Garret
412
Hartley
Orton
Waitby
Ease Gill
Sunbiggin
663 TARN CRAG
Smardale
Kirkby Stephen
Crookdale Beck
Raisbeck
Smardale Gill
617 BASTIFELL
Nateby
Greenholme
Tebay
Tan Hill
Old Tebay
Kelleth
Brownber
547 TAILBRIDGE HILL
Sadgill
Coldbeck
Kentmere
Gaisgill
Newbiggin-on-Lune
Ravenstonedale
633 WATER CRAG
Green Quarter
Tebay
Weasdale
672 ROGAN'S SEAT
Borrow Beck
Ravenseat
West Stonesdale
Long Sleddale
Langdale
Bowderdale Beck
Birk Dale
Outhgill
High Borrans
Low Borrowbridge
710 HIGH SEAT
Keld
River Kent
Angram
Swaledale
R Swale
Garnett Bridge
Selside
708 WILD BOAR FELL
Muker
Gunnerside
Ivelet
Staveley
Watchgate
Thwaite
Cautley Spout (Waterfall)
Cross Keys Temperance Inn
713 GREAT SHUNNER FELL
Garth Row
Grayrigg
677 THE CALF
Aisgill
Bowston
Lowgill
Beck Foot
River Rawthey
526 Buttertubs Pass
The Buttertubs
675 LOVELY SEAT
Burneside
Meal Bank
West Gill
East Gill
Crook
SD
Plumgarths
Cotterdale
Kendal
Firbank
WINDER 473
National Park Centre
Underbarrow
Castle Green
River Ure
Hardraw Force (Waterfall)
Sedbergh
676
High Shaw
Simonstone
Askrigg
Brigsteer
New Hutton
Garsdale Head
Hardraw
Sedbusk
Appersett
Killington Lake
Millthrop
Garsdale
Hawes
Bainbridge
Oxenholme
586
National Park Centre
556
Gayle
Burtersett
Killington
Old Hutton
Thornton Rust
M6
A6
A66
A686
A689
A685
A683
A684
A591
5 miles
8 kilometres

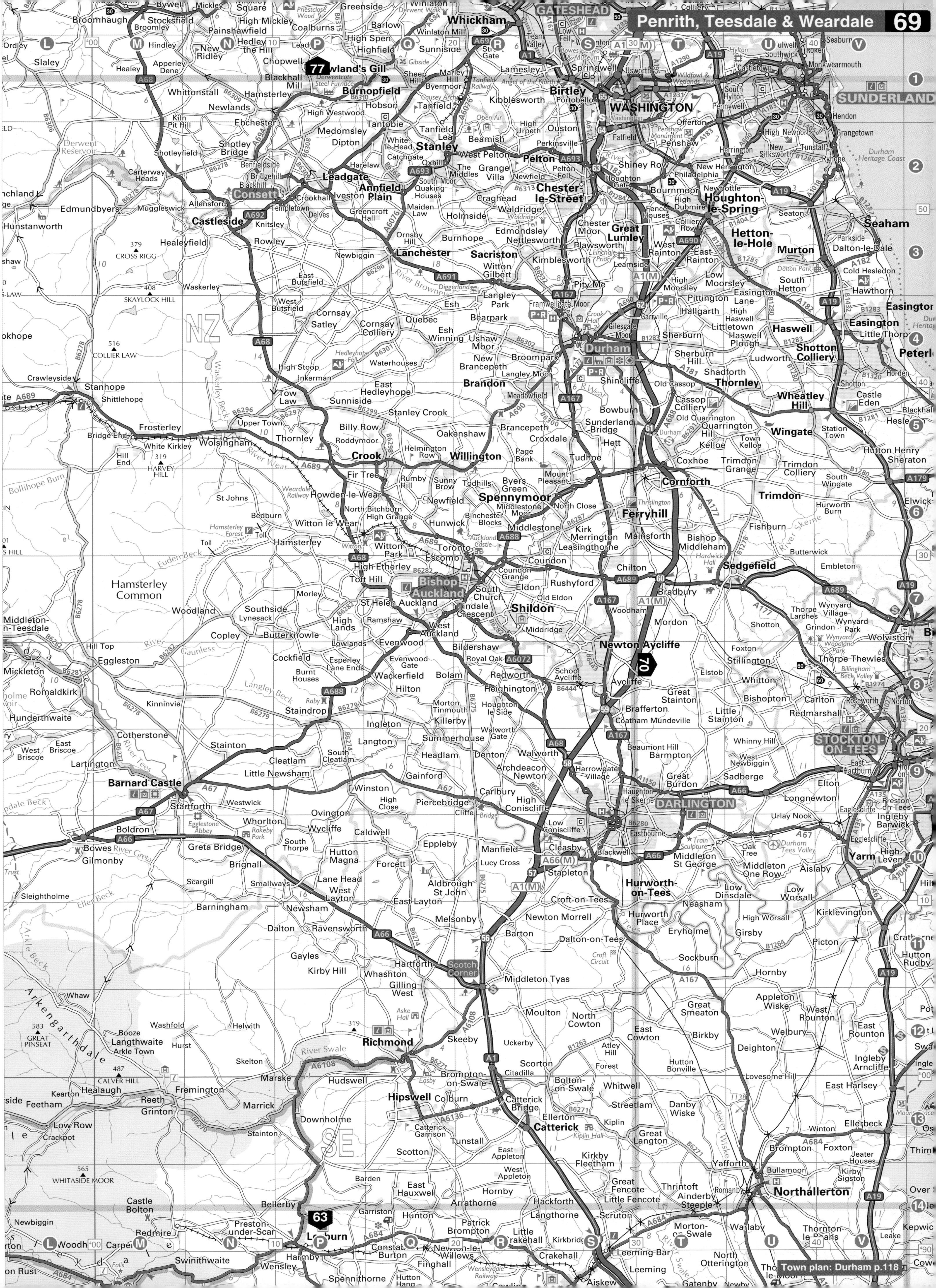
GATESHEAD
Whickham
Birtley
WASHINGTON
SUNDERLAND
Stanley
Consett
Leadgate
Annfield Plain
Pelton
Chester-le-Street
Houghton-le-Spring
Seaham
Hetton-le-Hole
Murton
Lanchester
Sacriston
Great Lumley
Durham
Shotton Colliery
Easington
Haswell
Castleside
Stanhope
Frosterley
Wolsingham
Crook
Willington
Brandon
Spennymoor
Ferryhill
Cornforth
Wingate
Trimdon
Sedgefield
Bishop Auckland
Shildon
Newton Aycliffe
Aycliffe
Hamsterley Common
Middleton-in-Teesdale
Eggleston
Romaldkirk
Staindrop
Barnard Castle
Startforth
Bowes
Greta Bridge
DARLINGTON
STOCKTON-ON-TEES
Yarm
Hurworth-on-Tees
Scotch Corner
Middleton Tyas
Richmond
Hipswell
Catterick
Catterick Garrison
Northallerton
Leyburn
Bedale
Reeth
Marske
Romanby
Brompton
Town plan: Durham p.118

Town plan: Durham p.118

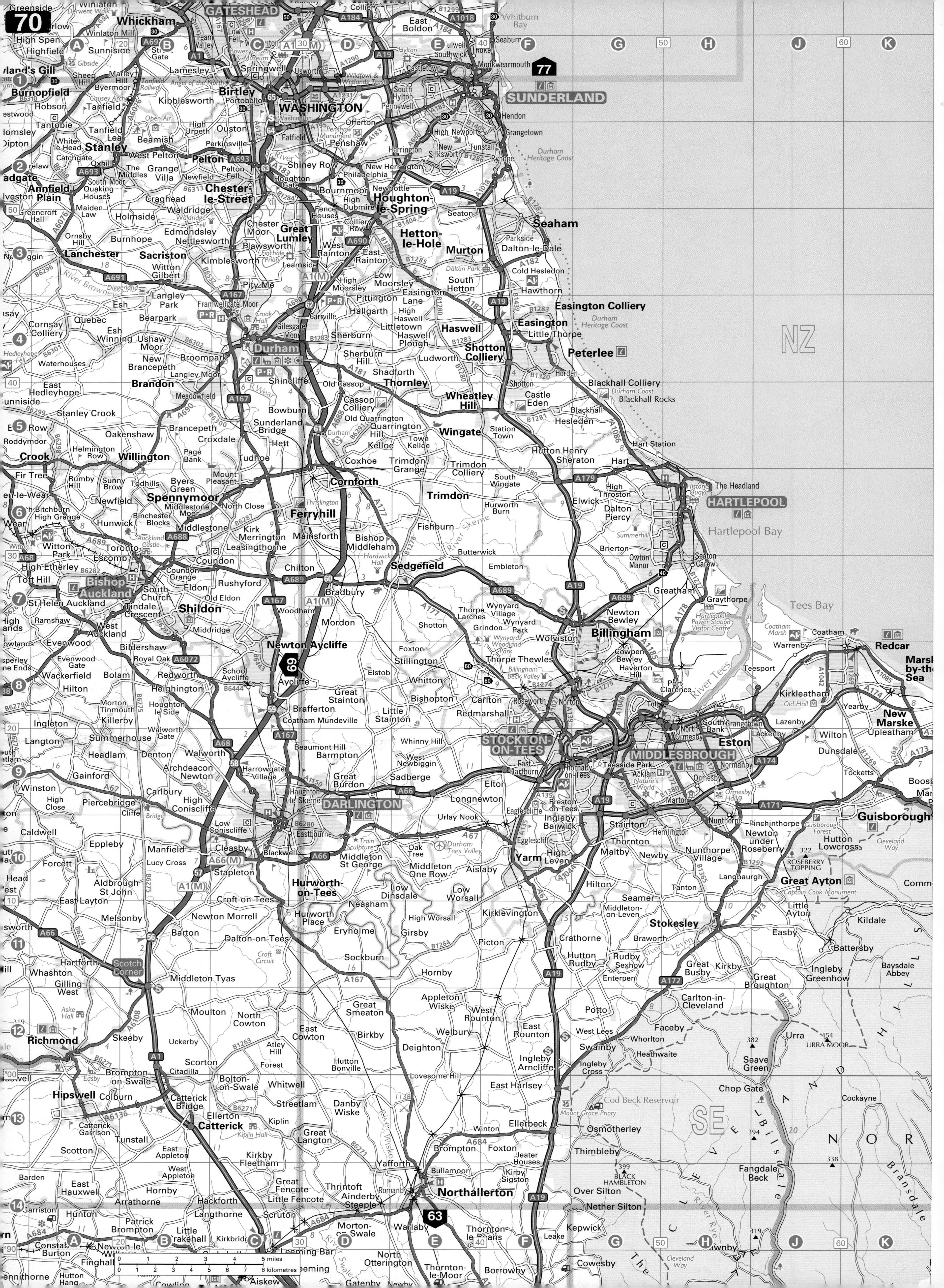

GATESHEAD
Whickham
WASHINGTON
SUNDERLAND
Whitburn Bay
East Boldon
Seaburn
Monkwearmouth
77
Birtley
Burnopfield
Stanley
Pelton
Chester-le-Street
Houghton-le-Spring
Seaham
Annfield Plain
Lanchester
Sacriston
Great Lumley
Hetton-le-Hole
Murton
Dalton-le-Dale
Hawthorn
Easington Colliery
Easington
Peterlee
Haswell
Shotton Colliery
Durham
Brandon
Thornley
Wheatley Hill
Blackhall Colliery
Blackhall Rocks
Durham Heritage Coast
NZ
Crook
Willington
Spennymoor
Ferryhill
Cornforth
Trimdon
Wingate
Hart Station
The Headland
HARTLEPOOL
Hartlepool Bay
Bishop Auckland
Shildon
Sedgefield
Newton Aycliffe
69
Aycliffe
Billingham
Tees Bay
Redcar
Marske-by-the-Sea
STOCKTON-ON-TEES
MIDDLESBROUGH
New Marske
Eston
Guisborough
DARLINGTON
Yarm
Hurworth-on-Tees
Great Ayton
Stokesley
Richmond
Scotch Corner
Hipswell
Catterick
Northallerton
63
Osmotherley
SE
CLEVELAND HILLS
NORTH YORK MOORS
Bilsdale
Bransdale
URRA MOOR
BLACK HAMBLETON
Cod Beck Reservoir
A1(M)
A19
A66
A167
A689
A174
A171
A172
A684
0 1 2 3 4 5 miles
0 1 2 3 4 5 6 7 8 kilometres

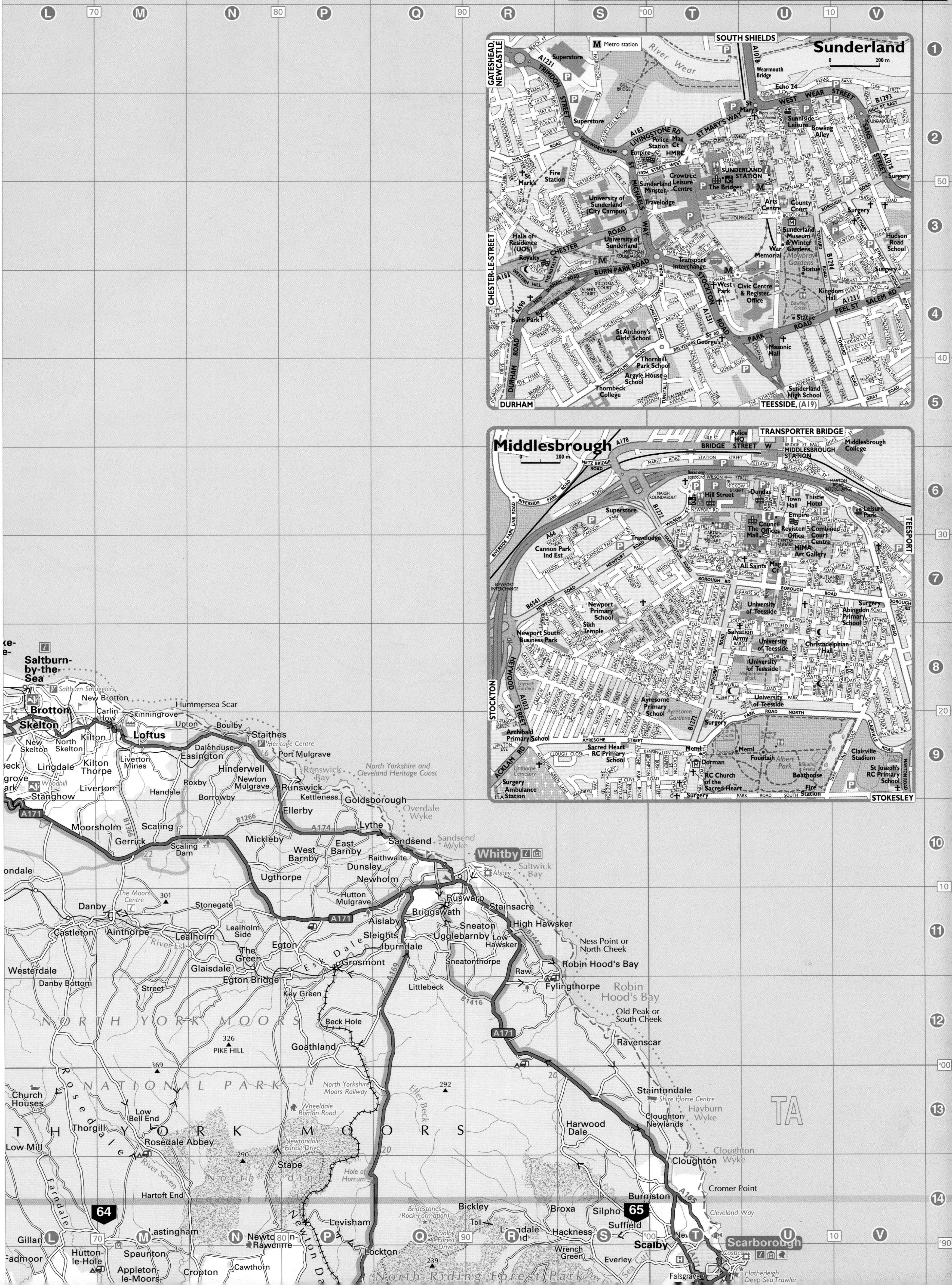

Sunderland

SOUTH SHIELDS

GATESHEAD, NEWCASTLE

River Wear

M Metro station

Superstore
Superstore
Wearmouth Bridge
Echo 24
Sunniside Leisure
Bowling Alley
St Mary's
Empire
Police Station
Mag Ct
HMRC
Fire Station
St Mark's
University of Sunderland (City Campus)
Sunderland Minster
Travelodge
Sunderland Station
The Bridges
Crowtree Leisure Centre
Arts Centre
County Court
Halls of Residence (UOS)
University of Sunderland
Royalty
CHESTER
Sunderland Museum & Winter Gardens
War Memorial
Statue
Hudson Road School
Transport Interchange
Civic Centre & Register Office
West Park
Kingdom Hall
Burn Park
Statue
Masonic Hall
St Anthony's Girls' School
George
Sunderland High School
Thornhill Park School
Argyle House School
Thornbeck College

CHESTER-LE-STREET
DURHAM
TEESSIDE, (A19)

Middlesbrough

TRANSPORTER BRIDGE
Police HQ
MIDDLESBROUGH STATION
Middlesbrough College
Hill Street
Dundas
Town Hall
Thistle Hotel
Leisure Park
Superstore
Council Offices
Empire
The Offices
Register Office
Combined Court Centre
Cannon Park Ind Est
Travelodge
MIMA Art Gallery
Cannon Park
All Saints
Mag Ct
Newport
Newport Primary School
University of Teesside
Surgery
Abingdon Primary School
Sikh Temple
Salvation Army
Newport South Business Park
University of Teesside
Christadelphian Hall
University of Teesside
Ayresome Primary School
Ayresome Gardens
University of Teesside
Archibald Primary School
Surgery
Meml
Meml
Clairville Stadium
Sacred Heart RC Primary School
Dorman
Fountain
Albert Park
St Joseph's RC Primary School
Surgery
KC Church of the Sacred Heart
Beathouse
Fire Station
Surgery

STOCKTON
STOKESLEY

Saltburn-by-the-Sea
Saltburn Smugglers
New Brotton
Brotton
Skelton
New Skelton
North Skelton
Kilton
Loftus
Lingdale
Kilton Thorpe
Liverton Mines
Staithes
Port Mulgrave
Stanghow
Liverton
Handale
Dalehouse
Easington
Hinderwell
Newton Mulgrave
Runswick
Kettleness
Goldsborough
Moorsholm
Scaling
Roxby
Borrowby
Ellerby
Lythe
Overdale Wyke
Gerrick
Scaling Dam
Mickleby
West Barnby
East Barnby
Sandsend
Sandsend Wyke
Ugthorpe
Dunsley
Newholm
Whitby
Saltwick Bay
Hutton Mulgrave
Ruswarp
Stainsacre
Danby
Stonegate
Aislaby
Briggswath
Sneaton
High Hawsker
Castleton
Ainthorpe
Lealholm Side
Sleights
Ugglebarnby
Low Hawsker
Ness Point or North Cheek
The Green
Iburndale
Sneatonthorpe
Lealholm
Egton
Grosmont
Robin Hood's Bay
Glaisdale
Key Green
Raw
Westerdale
Egton Bridge
Littlebeck
Fylingthorpe
Robin Hood's Bay
Danby Bottom
Street
Old Peak or South Cheek
Beck Hole
Ravenscar

NORTH YORK MOORS
326 PIKE HILL
369
Goathland
Staintondale
Shire Horse Centre
Hayburn Wyke
Church Houses
NATIONAL PARK
292
North Yorkshire Moors Railway
Cloughton Newlands
Low Bell End
Thorgill
Wheeldale Roman Road
Harwood Dale
Cloughton
Low Mill
Rosedale Abbey
Newtondale Forest Drive
Cloughton Wyke
290
Cromer Point
Stape
Hole of Horcum
Hartoft End
Burniston
TA
Lastingham
Bridestones (Rock Formation)
Bickley
Broxa
Silpho
Scalby
Gillam
Levisham
Toll
Hackness
Suffield
Scarborough
Fadmoor
Hutton-le-Hole
Spaunton
Appleton-le-Moors
Cropton
Cawthorn
Lockton
Wrench Green
Everley
North Riding Forest Park

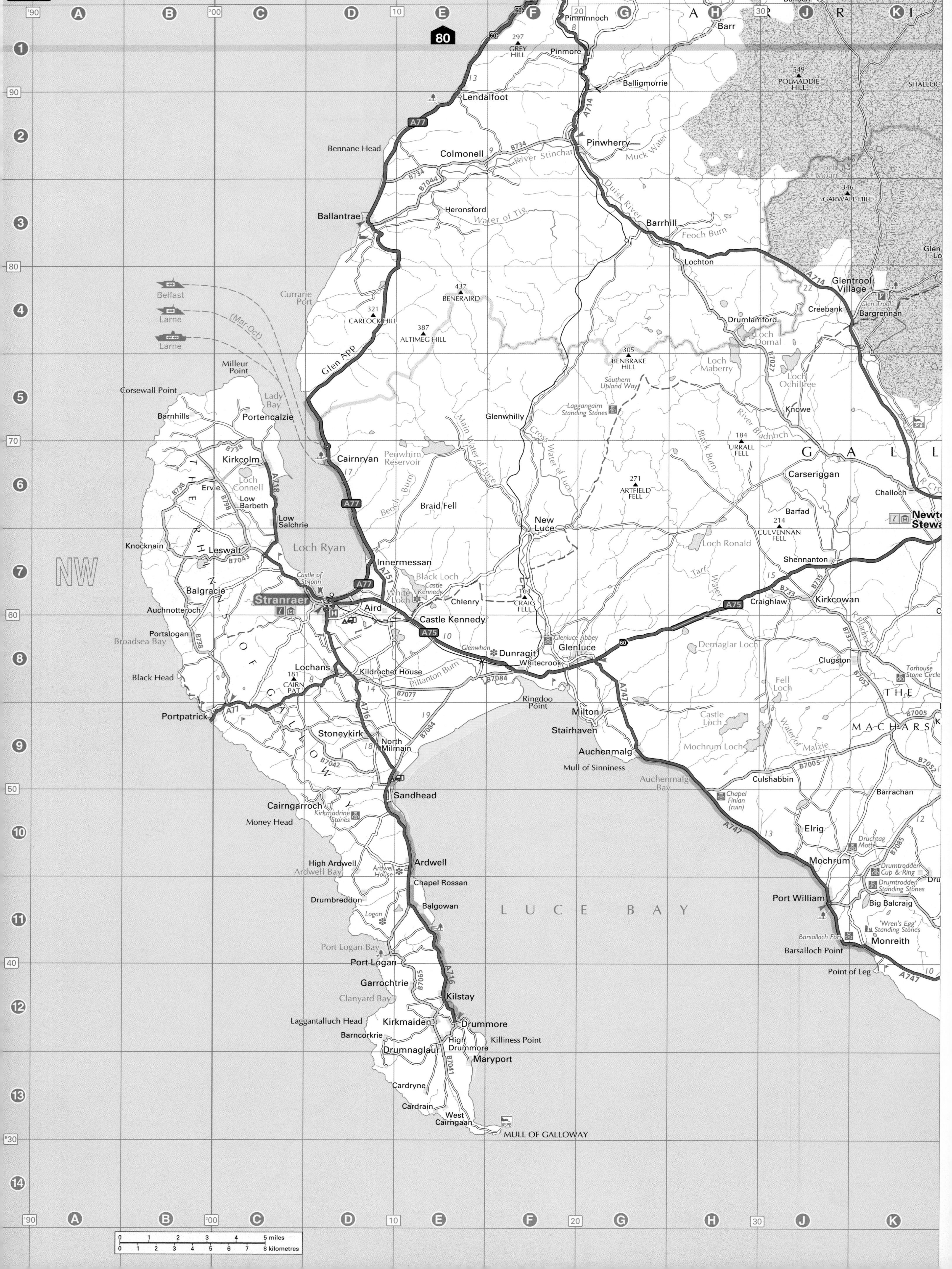
80
Dalquhairn
Knockeen
Balloch
River Stinchar
Woodland
Pinminnoch
Barr
297
GREY HILL
Pinmore
549
POLMADDIE HILL
Balligmorrie
SHALLOCH
Lendalfoot
A77
A714
Pinwherry
Muck Water
Bennane Head
Colmonell
B734
River Stinchar
B7044
Loch Moan
346
GARWALL HILL
Heronsford
Water of Tig
Duisk River
Ballantrae
Barrhill
Feoch Burn
Lochton
Glentrool Village
437
BENERAIRD
Belfast
Currarie Port
Larne
(Mar-Oct)
321
CARLOCK HILL
387
ALTIMEG HILL
Creebank
Bargrennan
Drumlamford
Loch Dornal
Larne
Glen App
305
BENBRAKE HILL
Loch Maberry
Milleur Point
B7027
Loch Ochiltree
Corsewall Point
Lady Bay
Southern Upland Way
Laggangairn Standing Stones
Barnhills
Portencalzie
Glenwhilly
Knowe
River Bladnoch
Main Water of Luce
184
URRALL FELL
B738
Cairnryan
Penwhirn Reservoir
Kirkcolm
Cross Water of Luce
Black Burn
Carseriggan
THE RHINNS OF GALLOWAY
Loch Connell
271
ARTFIELD FELL
Challoch
Ervie
A718
B798
Low Barbeth
A77
Beoch Burn
Braid Fell
Barfad
Newton Stewart
214
CULVENNAN FELL
Low Salchrie
New Luce
Knocknain
Leswalt
Loch Ryan
Loch Ronald
Innermessan
B7043
Shennanton
NW
Castle of St John
Black Loch
A751
A77
Tarf Water
B735
Balgracie
Castle Kennedy
White Loch
104
CRAIG FELL
B733
Kirkcowan
Stranraer
Aird
Chlenry
Craighlaw
A75
Auchnotteroch
Castle Kennedy
Portslogan
Broadsea Bay
A75
Glenluce Abbey
Glenwhan
Dunragit
Glenluce
Dernaglar Loch
Whitecrook
Clugston
Lochans
Kildrochet House
B7084
Pilanton Burn
Torhouse Stone Circle
Black Head
181
CAIRN PAT
B7077
A747
Fell Loch
B7052
THE MACHARS
Ringdoo Point
Milton
A716
B7005
Portpatrick
A77
Castle Loch
Stairhaven
Stoneykirk
North Milmain
B7084
Water of Malzie
Mochrum Loch
Auchenmalg
B7042
Mull of Sinniness
Culshabbin
B7005
Auchenmalg Bay
Sandhead
Chapel Finian (ruin)
Barrachan
Cairngarroch
Kirkmadrine Stones
Money Head
Elrig
A747
Druchtag Motte
High Ardwell
Ardwell Bay
Ardwell
Ardwell House
Mochrum
B7085
Drumtroddan Cup & Ring
Drumtroddan Standing Stones
Chapel Rossan
Drumbreddon
Port William
Big Balcraig
Balgowan
LUCE BAY
Logan
'Wren's Egg' Standing Stones
Barsalloch Fort
Monreith
Port Logan Bay
Barsalloch Point
Port Logan
A716
Point of Leg
A747
Garrochtrie
B7065
Clanyard Bay
Kilstay
Laggantalluch Head
Kirkmaiden
Drummore
Barncorkrie
High Drummore
Killiness Point
Drumnaglaur
B7041
Maryport
Cardryne
Cardrain
West Cairngaan
RSPB
MULL OF GALLOWAY
5 miles
8 kilometres

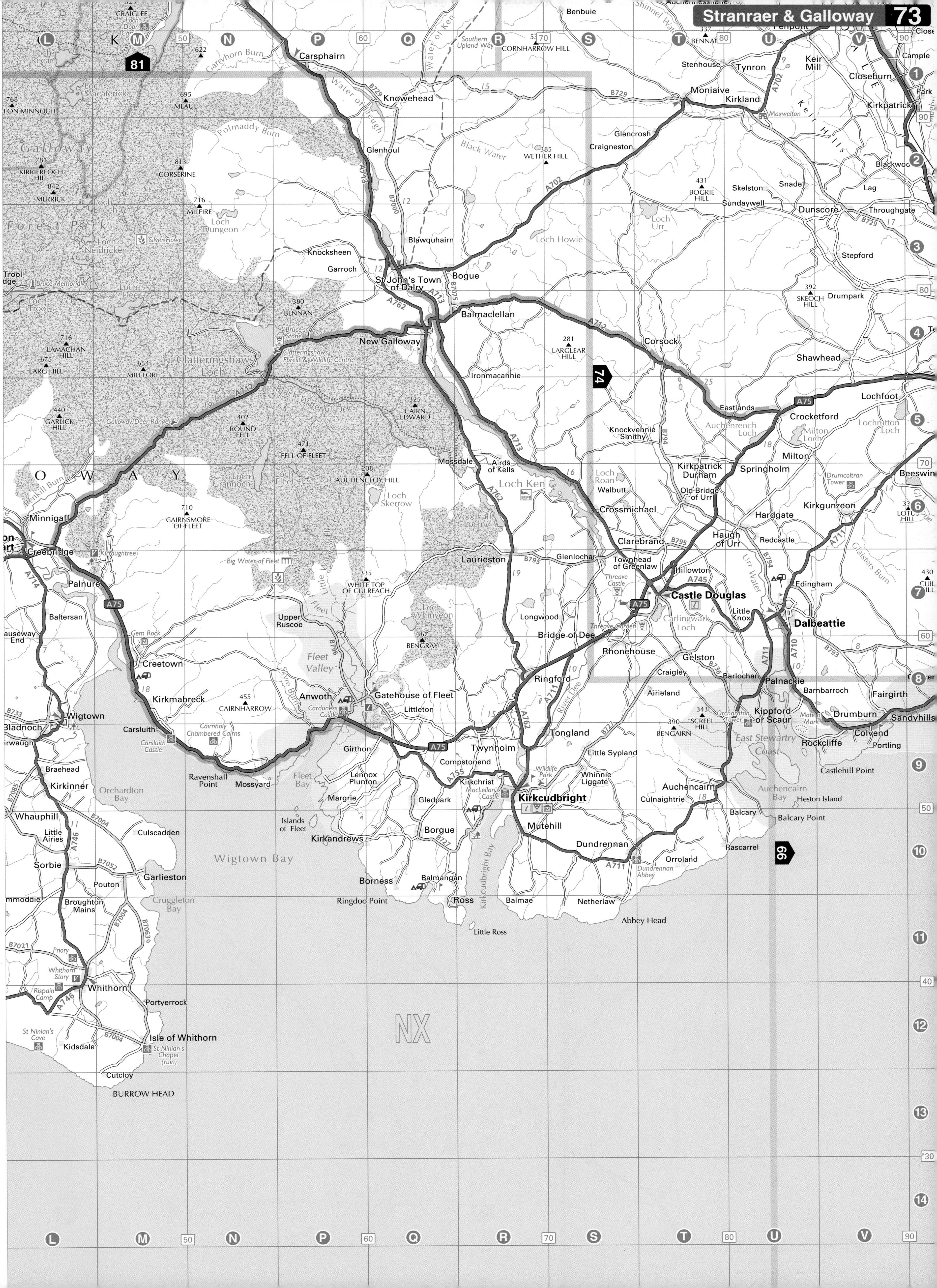
Carsphairn
Knowehead
Glenhoul
Blawquhairn
Knocksheen
Garroch
St John's Town of Dalry
Bogue
Balmaclellan
New Galloway
Ironmacannie
Benbuie
CORNHARROW HILL
Southern Upland Way
Stenhouse
Tynron
Moniaive
Kirkland
Keir Mill
Closeburn
Kirkpatrick
Maxwelton
Keir Hills
Glencrosh
Craigneston
WETHER HILL
BOGRIE HILL
Skelston
Snade
Sundaywell
Dunscore
Lag
Throughgate
Stepford
SKEOCH HILL
Drumpark
Corsock
LARGLEAR HILL
Shawhead
Eastlands
Crocketford
Lochfoot
Auchenreoch Loch
Milton Loch
Milton
Lochrutton Loch
Springholm
Kirkpatrick Durham
Old Bridge of Urr
Walbutt
Crossmichael
Knockvennie Smithy
Hardgate
Kirkgunzeon
Beeswing
Drumcoltran Tower
Clarebrand
Haugh of Urr
Redcastle
Glenlochar
Townhead of Greenlaw
Hillowton
Castle Douglas
Threave Castle
Carlingwark Loch
Threave Garden
Little Knox
Dalbeattie
Edingham
Urr Water
Glaisters Burn
Longwood
Bridge of Dee
Rhonehouse
Gelston
Craigley
Barlochan
Palnackie
Barnbarroch
Fairgirth
Ringford
Airieland
SCREEL HILL
BENGAIRN
Orchardton Tower
Kippford or Scaur
Mote of Mark
Drumburn
Sandyhills
Colvend
Portling
Rockcliffe
East Stewartry Coast
Castlehill Point
Tongland
Little Sypland
Whinnie Liggate
Auchencairn
Culnaightrie
Auchencairn Bay
Heston Island
Balcary
Balcary Point
Rascarrel
Orroland
Dundrennan
Dundrennan Abbey
Netherlaw
Abbey Head
Mutehill
Kirkcudbright
Wildlife Park
Kirkchrist
MacLellan's Castle
Twynholm
Compstonend
Gledpark
Borgue
Balmangan
Ross
Little Ross
Balmae
Kirkcudbright Bay
Borness
Ringdoo Point
Kirkandrews
Islands of Fleet
Margrie
Lennox Plunton
Girthon
Fleet Bay
Gatehouse of Fleet
Littleton
Cardoness Castle
Anwoth
Fleet Valley
BENGRAY
Loch Whinyeon
Laurieston
Loch Ken
Airds of Kells
Mossdale
Woodhall Loch
Loch Skerrow
AUCHENCLOY HILL
FELL OF FLEET
CAIRN EDWARD
ROUND FELL
Black Water of Dee
Clatteringshaws Loch
Clatteringshaws Forest & Wildlife Centre
Bruce's Stone
BENNAN
MILLFORE
LARG HILL
LAMACHAN HILL
GARLICK HILL
Galloway Deer Range
Loch Grannoch
Loch Fleet
CAIRNSMORE OF FLEET
WHITE TOP OF CULREACH
Big Water of Fleet
Upper Ruscoe
Kirroughtree
Minnigaff
Creebridge
Palnure
Baltersan
Causeway End
Gem Rock
Creetown
Kirkmabreck
CAIRNHARROW
Carsluith
Carsluith Castle
Cairnholy Chambered Cairns
Ravenshall Point
Mossyard
Wigtown
Bladnoch
Braehead
Kirkinner
Orchardton Bay
Whauphill
Little Airies
Culscadden
Sorbie
Garlieston
Pouton
Wigtown Bay
Broughton Mains
Cruggleton Bay
Priory
Whithorn Story
Whithorn
Rispain Camp
Portyerrock
St Ninian's Cave
Kidsdale
Isle of Whithorn
St Ninian's Chapel (ruin)
Cutcloy
BURROW HEAD
NX
Loch Dungeon
MILFIRE
Polmaddy Burn
MEAUL
CORSERINE
Loch Enoch
Loch Neldricken
Silver Flowe
Bruce Memorial
Loch Dee
Loch Trool
MERRICK
KIRRIEREOCH HILL
Galloway Forest Park
CRAIGLEE
Loch Doon
Loch Recar
Loch Macaterick
Black Water
Water of Ken
Water of Deugh
Loch Urr
Loch Howie
Loch Roan
Loch Whinyeon
Benkill Burn
Skyre Burn
Little Water of Fleet
River Dee
Shinnel Water
A75
A702
A713
A762
A712
A711
A710
A745
A755
A746
A714
B729
B7000
B7075
B795
B794
B727
B736
B7004
B7052
B7063
B7085
B7021
B733
B793
81
74
69
L M N P Q R S T U V
1 2 3 4 5 6 7 8 9 10 11 12 13 14
50 60 70 80 90
30 40

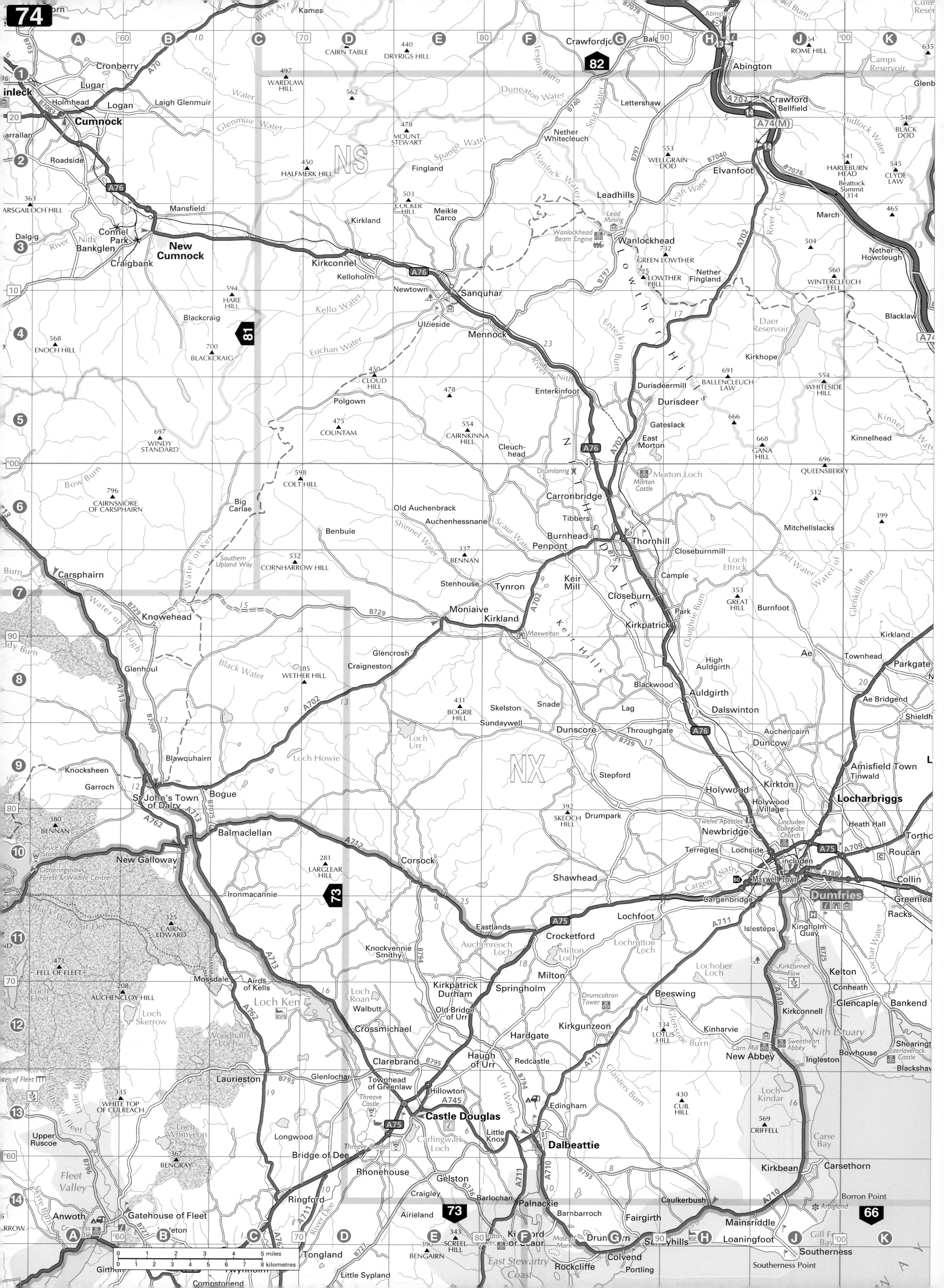
Cronberry
Lugar
Holmhead
Logan
Laigh Glenmuir
Cumnock
Roadside
Mansfield
Connel Park
Bankglen
Craigbank
New Cumnock
Dalgig
Kirkconnel
Kelloholm
Newtown
Sanquhar
Ulzieside
Mennock
Kames
CAIRN TABLE
DRYRIGS HILL
WARDLAW HILL
MOUNT STEWART
HALFMERK HILL
Fingland
COCKER HILL
Meikle Carco
Kirkland
HARE HILL
Blackcraig
ENOCH HILL
BLACKCRAIG
CLOUD HILL
Polgown
COUNTAM
CAIRNKINNA HILL
WINDY STANDARD
COLT HILL
CAIRNSMORE OF CARSPHAIRN
Big Carlae
Old Auchenbrack
Auchenhessnane
Benbuie
BENNAN
CORNHARROW HILL
Southern Upland Way
Carsphairn
Knowehead
Stenhouse
Tynron
Moniaive
Kirkland
Glencrosh
Craigneston
Glenhoul
WETHER HILL
BOGRIE HILL
Skelston
Sundaywell
Snade
Blawquhairn
Knocksheen
Garroch
St John's Town of Dalry
Bogue
Loch Howie
Loch Urr
BENNAN
Balmaclellan
New Galloway
Clatteringshaws Forest & Wildlife Centre
LARGLEAR HILL
Ironmacannie
Corsock
Eastlands
CAIRN EDWARD
FELL OF FLEET
Mossdale
Airds of Kells
AUCHENCLOY HILL
Loch Ken
Loch Skerrow
Woodhall Loch
Knockvennie Smithy
Auchenreoch Loch
Loch Roan
Walbutt
Crossmichael
Kirkpatrick Durham
Old Bridge of Urr
Springholm
Clarebrand
Glenlochar
Laurieston
Townhead of Greenlaw
Threave Castle
Hillowton
Castle Douglas
Carlingwark Loch
Threave Garden
Longwood
Bridge of Dee
Rhonehouse
WHITE TOP OF CULREACH
Loch Whinyeon
BENGRAY
Upper Ruscoe
Fleet Valley
Anwoth
Gatehouse of Fleet
Ringford
Airieland
Gelston
Craigley
Barlochan
Palnackie
SCREEL HILL
BENGAIRN
Tongland
Little Sypland
Compstonend
East Stewartry Coast
Crawfordjohn
Abington
Crawford
Bellfield
Lettershaw
Duneaton Water
Nether Whitecleuch
WELLGRAIN DOD
Elvanfoot
Leadhills
Lead Mining
Wanlockhead
Wanlockhead Beam Engine
GREEN LOWTHER
LOWTHER HILL
Nether Fingland
Lowther Hills
ROME HILL
Camps Reservoir
BLACK DOD
HARLEBURN HEAD
Beattock Summit
CLYDE LAW
March
Nether Howcleugh
WINTERCLEUCH FELL
Daer Reservoir
Blacklaw
Kirkhope
BALLENCLEUCH LAW
WHITESIDE HILL
Durisdeermill
Durisdeer
Enterkinfoot
Gateslack
East Morton
GANA HILL
Kinnelhead
QUEENSBERRY
Cleuch-head
Drumlanrig
Morton Loch
Morton Castle
Carronbridge
Tibbers
Burnhead
Penpont
Thornhill
Closeburnmill
Mitchellslacks
Loch Ettrick
Keir Mill
Cample
Closeburn
GREAT HILL
Burnfoot
Park
Kirkpatrick
Maxwelton
Keir Hills
Nithsdale
Kirkland
Ae
Townhead
Parkgate
High Auldgirth
Blackwood
Auldgirth
Ae Bridgend
Lag
Dalswinton
Dunscore
Throughgate
Auchencairn
Duncow
Stepford
Amisfield Town
Tinwald
Kirkton
Holywood
Holywood Village
Locharbriggs
SKEOCH HILL
Drumpark
Twelve Apostles
Lincluden Collegiate Church
Newbridge
Heath Hall
Terregles
Lochside
Lincluden
Maxwell Town
Dumfries
Roucan
Collin
Shawhead
Cargenbridge
Greenlea
Racks
Lochfoot
Crocketford
Lochrutton Loch
Islesteps
Kingholm Quay
Milton Loch
Milton
Lochober Loch
Kelton
Conheath
Drumcoltran Tower
Beeswing
Glencaple
Bankend
Kirkconnell
Kirkgunzeon
LOTUS HILL
Kinharvie
Nith Estuary
Sweetheart Abbey
Corn Mill
New Abbey
Shearington
Caerlaverock Castle
Bowhouse
Ingleston
Blackshaw
Hardgate
Haugh of Urr
Redcastle
Edingham
CUIL HILL
Loch Kindar
CRIFFELL
Little Knox
Dalbeattie
Carse Bay
Kirkbean
Carsethorn
Caulkerbush
Barnbarroch
Fairgirth
Borron Point
Arbigland
Mainsriddle
Loaningfoot
Colvend
Portling
Rockcliffe
Southerness
Southerness Point
NS
NX
0 1 2 3 4 5 miles
0 1 2 3 4 5 6 7 8 kilometres

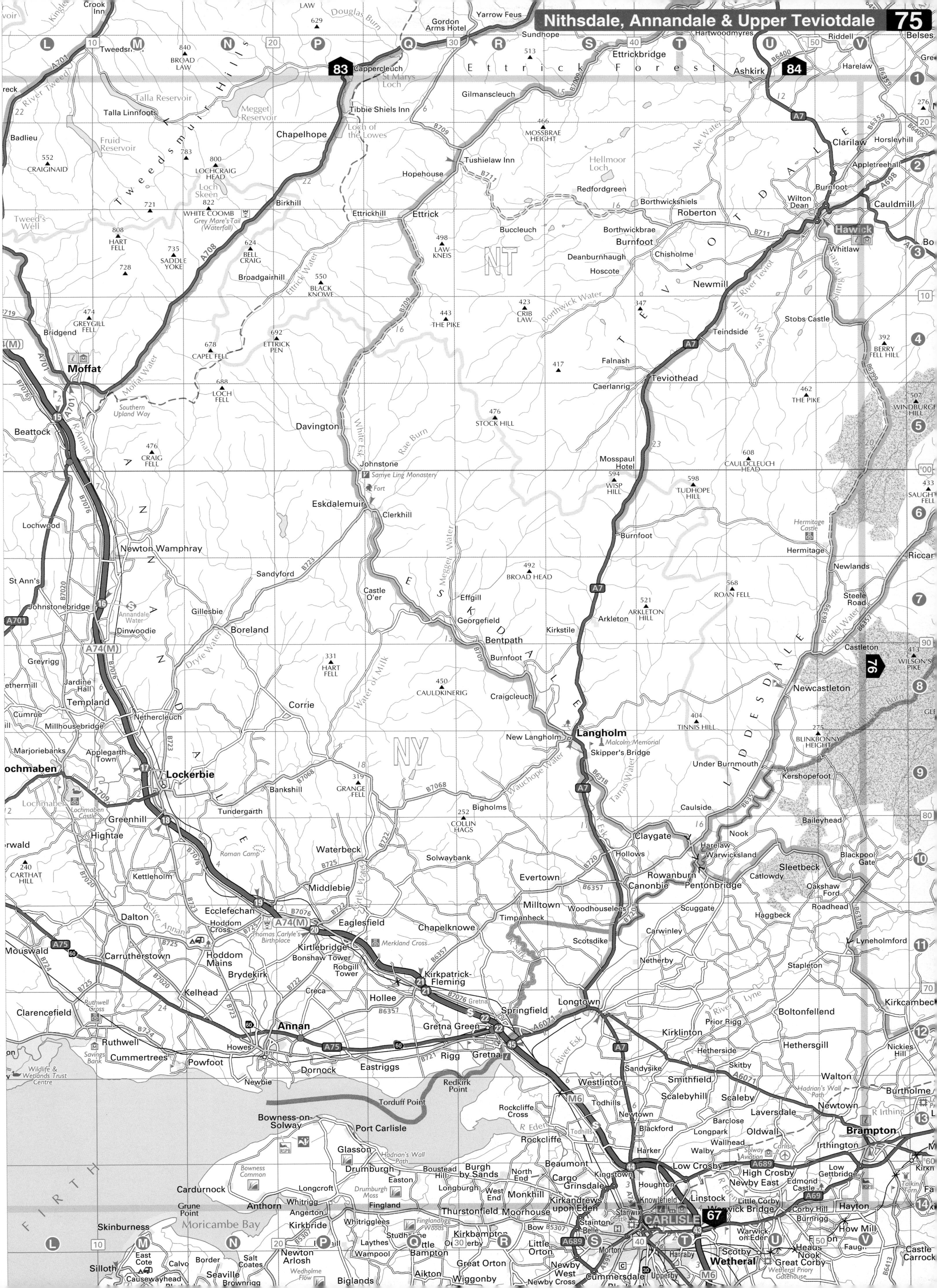
Crook Inn
Tweedsmuir
Broad Law
Douglas Burn
Gordon Arms Hotel
Yarrow Feus
Sundhope
Hartwoodmyres
Riddell
Belses
Cappercleuch
St Marys Loch
Ettrick Forest
Ettrickbridge
Ashkirk
Harelaw
Talla Reservoir
Talla Linnfoots
Megget Reservoir
Tibbie Shiels Inn
Gilmanscleuch
Loch of the Lowes
Chapelhope
Badlieu
Fruid Reservoir
Mossbrae Height
Clarilaw
Horsleyhill
Craiginaid
Tweedsmuir Hills
Lochcraig Head
Tushielaw Inn
Hellmoor Loch
Appletreehall
Hopehouse
Burnfoot
Loch Skeen
Redfordgreen
Wilton Dean
Cauldmill
White Coomb
Grey Mare's Tail (Waterfall)
Birkhill
Ettrickhill
Ettrick
Borthwickshiels
Roberton
Tweed's Well
Hart Fell
Buccleuch
Borthwickbrae
Hawick
Saddle Yoke
Bell Craig
Law Kneis
Burnfoot
Chisholme
Whitlaw
Deanburnhaugh
Hoscote
Broadgairhill
Black Knowe
Newmill
Crib Law
Greygill Fell
The Pike
Stobs Castle
Bridgend
Ettrick Pen
Teindside
Berry Fell Hill
Capel Fell
Falnash
Moffat
Loch Fell
Teviothead
Caerlanrig
Southern Upland Way
Stock Hill
The Pike
Windburgh Hill
Davington
Beattock
Craig Fell
Johnstone
Samye Ling Monastery
Mosspaul Hotel
Cauldcleuch Head
Wisp Hill
Tudhope Hill
Saughtree Fell
Eskdalemuir
Clerkhill
Lochwood
Burnfoot
Hermitage Castle
Newton Wamphray
Hermitage
Sandyford
Broad Head
St Ann's
Newlands
Castle O'er
Roan Fell
Steele Road
Johnstonebridge
Effgill
Arkleton Hill
Annandale Water
Gillesbie
Georgefield
Arkleton
Boreland
Dinwoodie
Bentpath
Kirkstile
Castleton
Wilson's Pike
Greyrigg
Hart Fell
Burnfoot
Jardine Hall
Cauldkinerig
Craigcleuch
Newcastleton
Templand
Corrie
Cumrue
Nethercleuch
Millhousebridge
Tinnis Hill
Langholm
Blinkbonny Height
New Langholm
Malcolm Memorial
Skipper's Bridge
Marjoriebanks
Applegarth Town
Lochmaben
Lockerbie
Under Burnmouth
Kershopefoot
Bankshill
Grange Fell
Lochmaben Castle
Tundergarth
Bigholms
Caulside
Greenhill
Collin Hags
Baileyhead
Hightae
Nook
Claygate
Harelaw
Warwicksland
Hollows
Blackpool Gate
Roman Camp
Waterbeck
Solwaybank
Carthat Hill
Kettleholm
Sleetbeck
Evertown
Rowanburn
Catlowdy
Middlebie
Canonbie
Pentonbridge
Oakshaw Ford
Milltown
Woodhouselees
Roadhead
Ecclefechan
Dalton
Hoddom Cross
Thomas Carlyle's Birthplace
Eaglesfield
Timpanheck
Scuggate
Haggbeck
Chapelknowe
Carwinley
Merkland Cross
Scotsdike
Lyneholmford
Mouswald
Carrutherstown
Hoddom Mains
Kirtlebridge
Bonshaw Tower
Netherby
Robgill Tower
Kirkpatrick-Fleming
Stapleton
Brydekirk
Kelhead
Creca
Hollee
Clarencefield
Ruthwell Cross
Springfield
Longtown
Kirkcambeck
Annan
Gretna Green
Boltonfellend
Prior Rigg
Ruthwell
Kirklinton
Howes
Cummertrees
Rigg
Gretna
Hethersgill
Nickies Hill
Savings Bank
Powfoot
Hetherside
Dornock
Eastriggs
Sandysike
Skitby
Wildlife & Wetlands Trust Centre
Westlinton
Smithfield
Walton
Newbie
Redkirk Point
Hadrian's Wall Path
Burtholme
Tordiff Point
Scalebyhill
Scaleby
Todhills
Rockcliffe Cross
Newtown
Newtown
Irthing
Bowness-on-Solway
Laversdale
Port Carlisle
Blackford
Barclose
Brampton
Longpark
Oldwall
Tordiff Point
Rockcliffe
Harker
Walby
Irthington
Glasson
Wallhead
Solway Aviation
Carlisle
Drumburgh
Hadrian's Wall Path
Beaumont
Bowness Common
Boustead Hill
Burgh by Sands
Low Crosby
North End
Cargo
Kingstown
Grinsdale
Houghton
High Crosby
Low Gettbridge
Easton
Cardurnock
Longcroft
Drumburgh Moss
Longburgh
West End
Monkhill
Newby East
Edmond Castle
Kirkandrews upon Eden
Linstock
Knowlefield
Talkin Tarn
Grune Point
Anthorn
Whitrigg
Fingland
Little Corby
Angerton
Thurstonfield
Moorhouse
Stanwix
Warwick Bridge
Corby Hill
Hayton
Moricambe Bay
Kirkbride
Whitrigglees
Finglandrigg Woods
Stainton
Carlisle
Burnrigg
Skinburness
Studholme
Kirkbampton
Belle Vue
Bow
Warwick-on-Eden
How Mill
Newton Arlosh
Laythes
Little Bampton
Oulton
Little Orton
Morton
Harraby
Scotby
Heads Nook
Fenton
Faugh
East Cote
Calvo
Border
Salt Coates
Wampool
Great Orton
Wetheral
Great Corby
Castle Carrock
Silloth
Seaville
Wedholme Flow
Newby West
Wetheral Priory Gatehouse
Causewayhead
Brownrigg
Biglands
Aikton
Wiggonby
Cummersdale
Upperby
Newby Cross
Firth
River Tweed
River Annan
White Esk
Rae Burn
Ettrick Water
Ale Water
Borthwick Water
River Teviot
Allan Water
Slitrig Water
Moffat Water
Dryfe Water
Water of Milk
Megget Water
Wauchope Water
Tarras Water
River Esk
Liddel Water
River Sark
River Lyne
River Eden
Kershope Burn
Kirtle Water
Teviotdale
Eskdale
Annandale
Liddesdale
NT
NY
A701
A708
A7
A698
A74(M)
A75
A709
A6071
A689
A69
A595
M6
B709
B711
B723
B7076
B7020
B722
B725
B7068
B6357
B6318
B6399
B6359
B6400
B6405
B6320
B724
B721
B6264
B5307
B5302
B6413
B7009
Hadrian's Wall Path
83
84
76
67

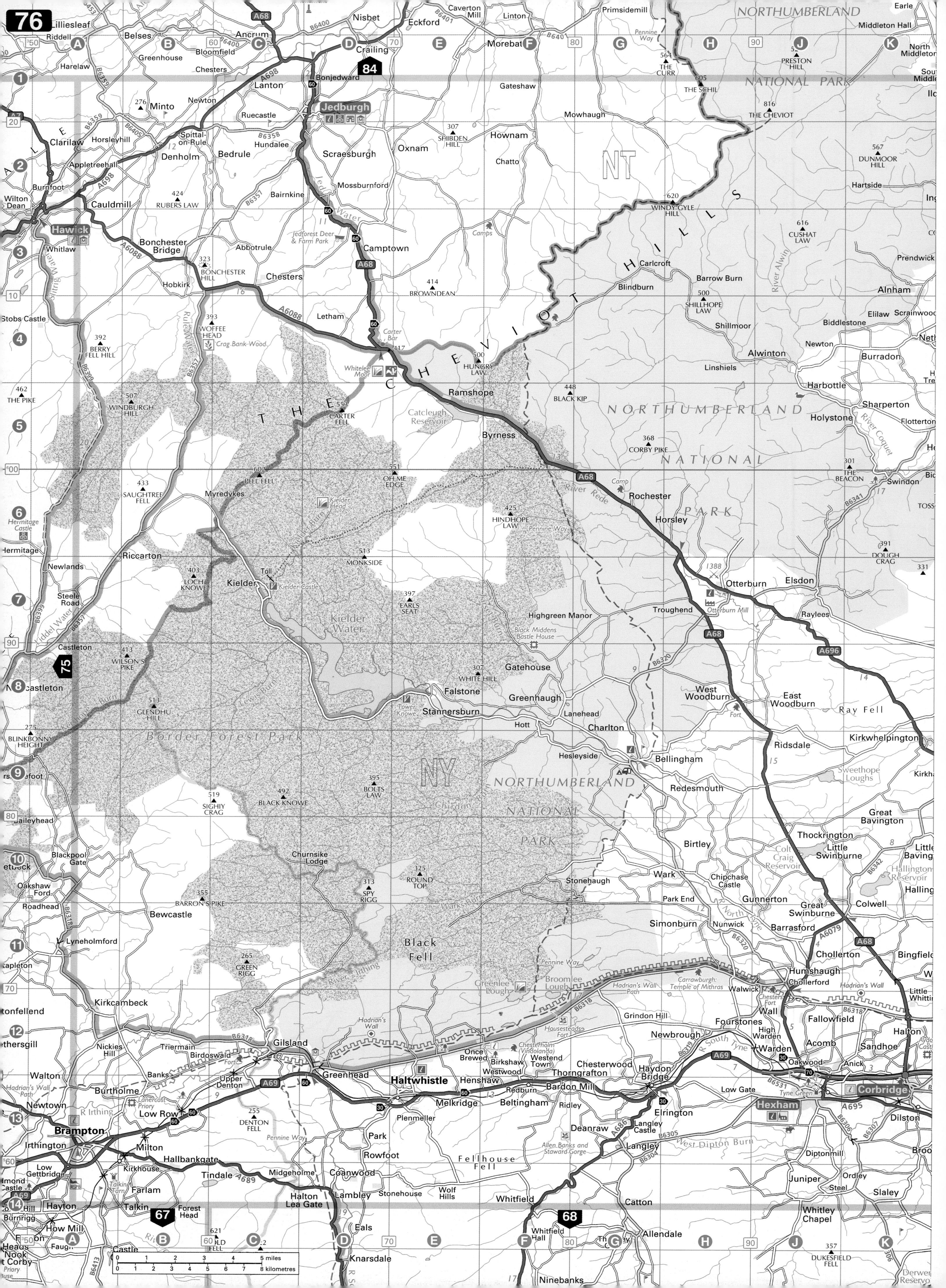
Lilliesleaf
Riddell
Belses
Ancrum
Nisbet
Eckford
Caverton Mill
Linton
Primsidemill
NORTHUMBERLAND
Earle
Middleton Hall
Harelaw
Greenhouse
Bloomfield
Crailing
Morebattle
Pennine Way
564 THE CURR
PRESTON HILL
North Middleton
Chesters
Bonjedward
84
605 THE SCHIL
NATIONAL PARK
Lanton
Gateshaw
276 Minto
Newton
Jedburgh
816 THE CHEVIOT
Ruecastle
Mowhaugh
Clarilaw
Horsleyhill
Spittal-on-Rule
Hundalee
307 SHIBDEN HILL
Hownam
Denholm
Bedrule
Scraesburgh
Oxnam
Chatto
NT
567 DUNMOOR HILL
Appletreehall
Burnfoot
Mossburnford
Hartside
Wilton Dean
424 RUBERS LAW
Bairnkine
620 WINDY GYLE HILL
Cauldmill
Hawick
Jed Water
Jedforest Deer & Farm Park
Camps
616 CUSHAT LAW
Whitlaw
Bonchester Bridge
Abbotrule
Camptown
Prendwick
323 BONCHESTER HILL
Carlcroft
Barrow Burn
Hobkirk
Chesters
414 BROWNDEAN
Blindburn
River Alwin
Alnham
500 SHILLHOPE LAW
Stobs Castle
393 WOFFEE HEAD
Letham
Shillmoor
Elilaw
Scrainwood
Crag Bank Wood
Carter Bar
Biddlestone
392 BERRY FELL HILL
Whitelee Moor
500 HUNGRY LAW
Alwinton
Newton
Burradon
THE CHEVIOT HILLS
Linshiels
462 THE PIKE
507 WINDBURGH HILL
553 CARTER FELL
448 BLACK KIP
Harbottle
Ramshope
Sharperton
Catcleugh Reservoir
NORTHUMBERLAND
Holystone
Byrness
Flotterton
368 CORBY PIKE
NATIONAL
River Coquet
602 PEEL FELL
551 OH ME EDGE
301 THE BEACON
433 SAUGHTREE FELL
Myredykes
Camp
Rochester
River Rede
Swindon
Kielder Head
PARK
Hermitage Castle
425 HINDHOPE LAW
Horsley
Pennine Way
391 DOUGH CRAG
Hermitage
Riccarton
513 MONKSIDE
Newlands
403 LOCH KNOWE
Kielder
Toll
Kielder Castle
Otterburn
Elsdon
Steele Road
397 EARLS SEAT
Troughend
Otterburn Mill
Raylees
Liddel Water
Kielder Water
Highgreen Manor
Black Middens Bastle House
Castleton
413 WILSON'S PIKE
75
307 WHITE HILL
Gatehouse
Newcastleton
Falstone
Greenhaugh
West Woodburn
East Woodburn
Ray Fell
513 GLENDHU HILL
Lewis Burn
Tower Knowe
Stannersburn
Lanehead
Fort
275 BLINKBONNY HEIGHT
Border Forest Park
Hott
Charlton
Kirkwhelpington
Ridsdale
Hesleyside
Bellingham
NY
395 BOLTS LAW
Sweethope Loughs
519 SIGHTY CRAG
492 BLACK KNOWE
NORTHUMBERLAND
Redesmouth
Baileyhead
NATIONAL
Great Bavington
PARK
Chirdon Burn
Blackpool Gate
Churnsike Lodge
Birtley
Thockrington
Little Swinburne
Colt Crag Reservoir
Oakshaw Ford
313 SPY RIGG
325 ROUND TOP
Stonehaugh
Wark
Chipchase Castle
Hallington Reservoir
355 BARRON'S PIKE
Roadhead
Park End
Gunnerton
Colwell
Bewcastle
Warks Burn
Great Swinburne
Simonburn
Nunwick
Barrasford
Lyneholmford
Black Fell
Chollerton
265 GREEN RIGG
Humshaugh
Pennine Way
River Irthing
Greenlee Lough
Broomlee Lough
Carrawburgh: Temple of Mithras
Hadrian's Wall Path
Walwick
Chollerford
Hadrian's Wall
Chesters Fort
Kirkcambeck
Wall
Fallowfield
Hadrian's Wall
Housesteads Fort
Grindon Hill
Fourstones
High Warden
Halton
Gilsland
Newbrough
Acomb
Sandhoe
Nickies Hill
Triermain
Birdoswald Fort
Chesterholm (Vindolanda)
Once Brewed
Birkshaw
Westend Town
R South Tyne
Warden
Walton
Banks
Upper Denton
Greenhead
Westwood
Chesterwood
Haydon Bridge
Oakwood
Anick
Thorngrafton
Haltwhistle
Henshaw
Redburn
Bardon Mill
Low Gate
Corbridge
Burtholme
Lanercost Priory
Melkridge
Beltingham
Ridley
Tyne Green
Hexham
Newtown
R Irthing
Low Row
255 DENTON FELL
Plenmeller
Elrington
Dilston
Brampton
Deanraw
Langley Castle
Park
Pennine Way
Irthington
Milton
Rowfoot
Allen Banks and Staward Gorge
Langley
West Dipton Burn
Low Gettbridge
Kirkhouse
Hallbankgate
Fellhouse Fell
Diptonmill
Tindale
Midgeholme
Coanwood
Talkin Tarn
Farlam
Juniper
Ordley
Steel
Hayton
Talkin
67
Forest Head
Halton Lea Gate
Lambley
Stonehouse
Wolf Hills
Whitfield
Catton
Slaley
68
How Mill
Eals
Whitfield Hall
Allendale
Whitley Chapel
Faugh
Castle Carrock
Knarsdale
Ninebanks
357 DUKESFIELD FELL
0 1 2 3 4 5 miles
0 1 2 3 4 5 6 7 8 kilometres

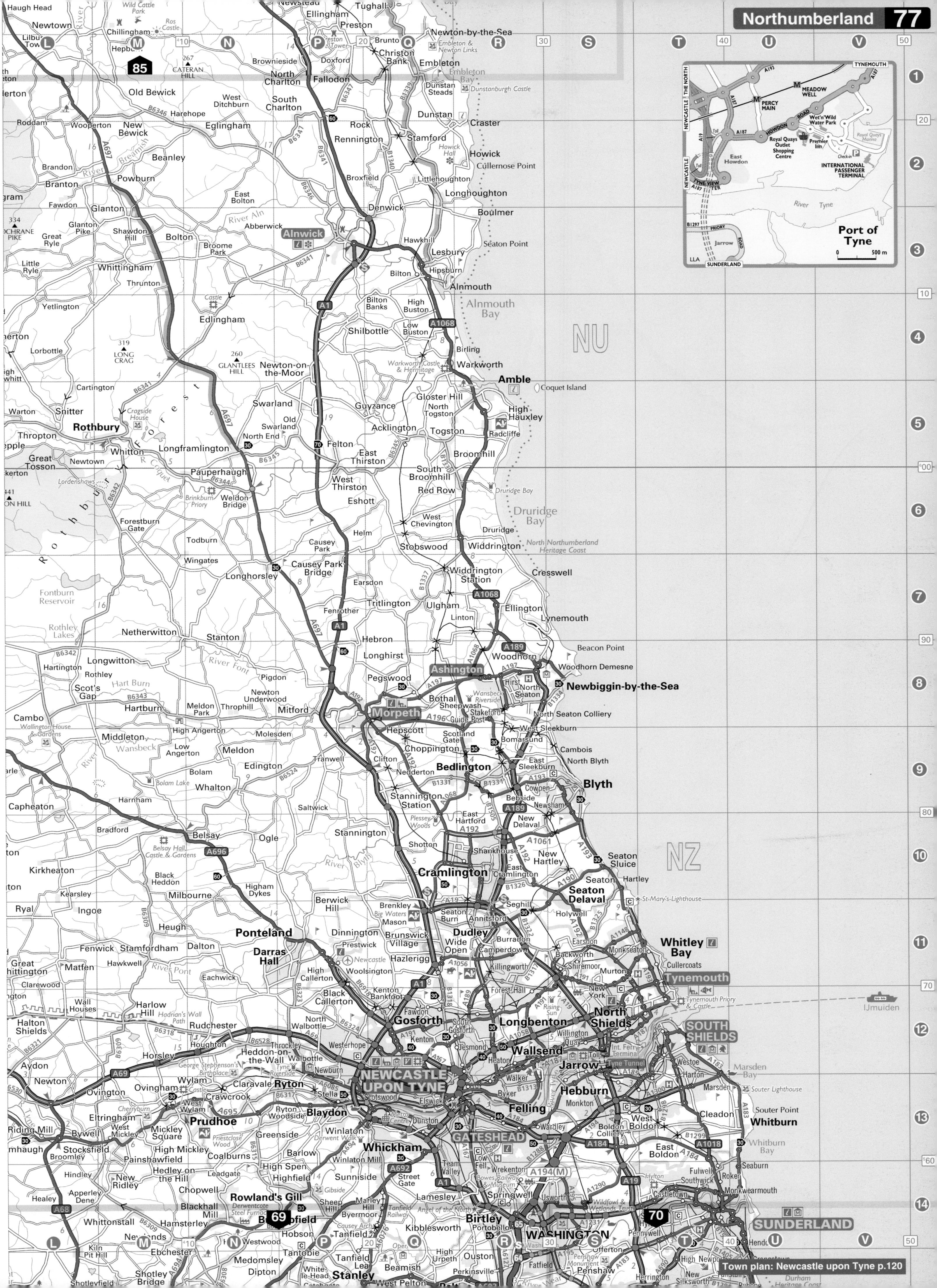
Port of Tyne
TYNEMOUTH
MEADOW WELL
PERCY MAIN
Wet'n'Wild Water Park
Royal Quays Outlet Shopping Centre
East Howdon
INTERNATIONAL PASSENGER TERMINAL
River Tyne
Jarrow
SUNDERLAND
Haugh Head
Newtown
Chillingham
Hepburn
85
Old Bewick
Ellingham
Preston
Tughall
Newton-by-the-Sea
Embleton & Newton Links
Christon Bank
Embleton
Embleton Bay
Brownieside
Doxford
North Charlton
Fallodon
South Charlton
West Ditchburn
Harehope
Dunstan Steads
Dunstanburgh Castle
Dunstan
Craster
Roddam
Wooperton
New Bewick
Eglingham
Rock
Rennington
Stamford
Howick Hall
Howick
Cullernose Point
Beanley
Brandon
Branton
Powburn
Broxfield
Littlehoughton
Longhoughton
Fawdon
Glanton
East Bolton
Denwick
Boulmer
Glanton Pike
Shawdon Hill
River Aln
Abberwick
Great Ryle
Bolton
Broome Park
Alnwick
Hawkhill
Lesbury
Seaton Point
Little Ryle
Whittingham
Bilton
Hipsburn
Thrunton
Alnmouth
Alnmouth Bay
Yetlington
Edlingham
Bilton Banks
High Buston
A1068
Shilbottle
Low Buston
NU
Lorbottle
Long Crag
Birling
Glantlees Hill
Newton-on-the-Moor
Warkworth Castle & Hermitage
Warkworth
Amble
Coquet Island
Cartington
Gloster Hill
Warton
Snitter
Cragside House
Swarland
Guyzance
North Togston
High Hauxley
Rothbury
Old Swarland
Acklington
Togston
Thropton
North End
Radcliffe
Felton
East Thirston
Broomhill
Great Tosson
Newtown
Whitton
Longframlington
Pauperhaugh
South Broomhill
West Thirston
Red Row
Brinkburn Priory
Weldon Bridge
Druridge Bay
Eshott
Forestburn Gate
West Chevington
Druridge
Helm
Todburn
Causey Park
Stobswood
Widdrington
North Northumberland Heritage Coast
Wingates
Causey Park Bridge
Widdrington Station
Cresswell
Longhorsley
Fontburn Reservoir
Earsdon
Tritlington
Ulgham
Ellington
Fenrother
Linton
Lynemouth
Rothley Lakes
Netherwitton
Stanton
Hebron
Beacon Point
Longhirst
Woodhorn
Woodhorn Demesne
Hartington
Longwitton
Rothley
River Font
Ashington
Newbiggin-by-the-Sea
Scot's Gap
Hart Burn
Pigdon
Pegswood
North Seaton
Newton Underwood
Bothal
Wansbeck Riverside
Hartburn
Meldon Park
Throphill
Mitford
Morpeth
Sheepwash
Stakeford
North Seaton Colliery
Cambo
Wallington House & Gardens
High Angerton
Molesden
Hepscott
Guide Post
West Sleekburn
Middleton
Scotland Gate
Bomarsund
Wansbeck
Low Angerton
Meldon
Choppington
Cambois
Edington
Tranwell
Clifton
East Sleekburn
North Blyth
Bolam
Bedlington
Bolam Lake
Whalton
Nedderton
Blyth
Cowpen
Capheaton
Harnham
Saltwick
Stannington Station
Bebside
Newsham
East Hartford
Plessey Woods
New Delaval
Bradford
Belsay
Ogle
Stannington
Belsay Hall, Castle & Gardens
Shotton
Shankhouse
New Hartley
Seaton Sluice
NZ
Kirkheaton
Black Heddon
Cramlington
East Cramlington
Hartley
Higham Dykes
Seaton
Milbourne
Seaton Delaval
St Mary's Lighthouse
Kearsley
Ryal
Ingoe
Berwick Hill
Brenkley
Big Waters
Mason
Seaton Burn
Seghill
Annitsford
Holywell
Heugh
Ponteland
Dinnington
Brunswick Village
Dudley
Earsdon
Whitley Bay
Wide Open
Burradon
Fenwick
Stamfordham
Dalton
Darras Hall
Prestwick
Newcastle Airport
Hazlerigg
Camperdown
Backworth
Monkseaton
Great Whittington
Matfen
Hawkwell
River Pont
Woolsington
Shiremoor
Cullercoats
High Callerton
Killingworth
Murton
Tynemouth
Clarewood
Eachwick
Kenton Bankfoot
Forest Hall
New York
Tynemouth Priory & Castle
IJmuiden
Wall Houses
Harlow Hill
Black Callerton
Fawdon
Halton Shields
Hadrian's Wall Path
Rudchester
North Walbottle
Gosforth
South Gosforth
Longbenton
North Shields
South Shields
Houghton
Westerhope
Kenton
Willington Quay
Horsley
Heddon-on-the-Wall
Walbottle
Throckley
Jesmond
Wallsend
Int. Ferry Terminal
Aydon
George Stephenson's Birthplace
Newburn
Heaton
Jarrow
Tyne Tunnel
Westoe
Marsden Bay
Newton
Wylam
Tyne Riverside
Newcastle upon Tyne
Walker
Harton
Ovingham
Claravale
Ryton
Byker
Hebburn
Marsden
Souter Lighthouse
Ovington
Cherryburn
Crawcrook
Stella
Scotswood
Elswick
Monkton
Cleadon
Eltringham
West Wylam
Ryton Woodside
Blaydon
Felling
Souter Point
Riding Mill
Bywell
West Mickley
Mickley Square
Prudhoe
Metro Centre
Dunston
West Boldon
Whitburn
Greenside
Winlaton
Wardley
Boldon Colliery
Broomhaugh
Stocksfield
High Mickley
Priestclose Wood
Derwent Walk
Whickham
Gateshead
East Boldon
Whitburn Bay
Broomley
Painshawfield
Coalburns
Barlow
Winlaton Mill
High Spen
Low Fell
Team Valley
Seaburn
Hindley
Hedley on the Hill
Leadgate
Highfield
Sunniside
Street Gate
Wrekenton
Bowes Railway & Museum
Fulwell
Southwick
Roker
New Ridley
Chopwell
Gibside
Springwell
Usworth
Wildfowl & Wetlands Trust
Hylton Castle
Monkwearmouth
Healey
Apperley Dene
Rowland's Gill
Marley Hill
Lamesley
Castletown
Blackhall Mill
Derwentcote Steel Furnace
Sheep Hill
Byermoor
Tanfield Railway
Angel of the North
Birtley
Portobello
Sunderland
Whittonstall
Hamsterley
69
70
Causey Arch
Tanfield
Kibblesworth
Washington
Pennywell
Newlands
Westwood
Hobson
Kiln Pit Hill
Ebchester
Tantobie
High Urpeth
Ouston
Offerton
Medomsley
Dipton
Tanfield Lea
Beamish
Perkinsville
Fatfield
Penshaw Monument
Penshaw
Herrington
High Newport
New Silksworth
Durham Heritage Coast
Shotley Bridge
White-le-Head
Stanley
West Pelton

Town plan: Newcastle upon Tyne p.120

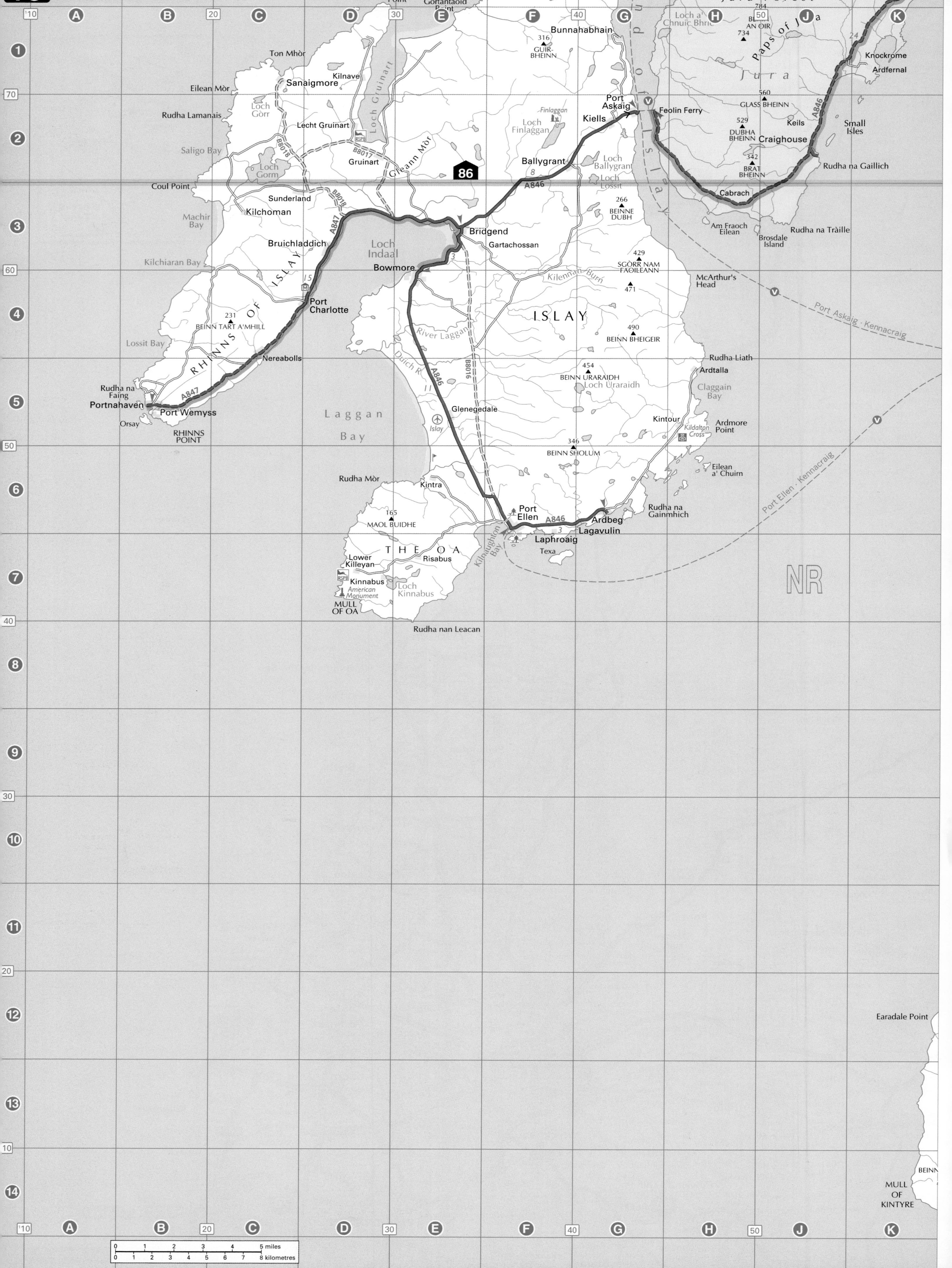

Nave Island
Ardnave Point
Gortantaoid Point
Bunnahabhain
316 GUIR-BHEINN
Jura Forest
398 BEINN TARSUINN
Loch a' Chnuic Bhric
784 BEINN AN OIR
734
Paps of Jura
Jura
Knockrome
Ardfernal
Ton Mhòr
Kilnave
Sanaigmore
Eilean Mòr
Loch Gorm
Loch Gòrr
Rudha Lamanais
Lecht Gruinart
Loch Gruinart
RSPB
Port Askaig
Feolin Ferry
Kiells
Finlaggan
Loch Finlaggan
560 GLASS BHEINN
529 DUBHA BHEINN
Keils
Craighouse
Small Isles
A846
Saligo Bay
B8018
B8017
Gruinart
Gleann Mòr
86
Ballygrant
Loch Ballygrant
Loch Lossit
Sound of Islay
342 BRAT BHEINN
Rudha na Gaillich
Coul Point
Sunderland
Kilchoman
Machir Bay
A847
Bridgend
266 BEINNE DUBH
Cabrach
Am Fraoch Eilean
Brosdale Island
Rudha na Tràille
Bruichladdich
Loch Indaal
Gartachossan
Kilchiaran Bay
Bowmore
429 SGÒRR NAM FAOILEANN
Kilennan Burn
McArthur's Head
ISLAY
Port Charlotte
471
231 BEINN TART A'MHILL
RHINNS OF ISLAY
Lossit Bay
River Laggan
490 BEINN BHEIGEIR
Port Askaig - Kennacraig
Nereabolls
Rudha Liath
Ardtalla
Duich R.
B8016
454 BEINN URARAIDH
Loch Uraraidh
Claggain Bay
Rudha na Faing
Portnahaven
Port Wemyss
Orsay
RHINNS POINT
Laggan Bay
Glenegedale
Islay
Kintour
Ardmore Point
Kildalton Cross
346 BEINN SHOLUM
Eilean a' Chuirn
Rudha Mòr
Kintra
Port Ellen
Ardbeg
Lagavulin
Laphroaig
Rudha na Gainmhich
Port Ellen - Kennacraig
165 MAOL BUIDHE
THE OA
Kilnaughton Bay
Texa
Lower Killeyan
Risabus
Kinnabus
Loch Kinnabus
American Monument
MULL OF OA
NR
Rudha nan Leacan
Earadale Point
MULL OF KINTYRE
0 1 2 3 4 5 miles
0 1 2 3 4 5 6 7 8 kilometres

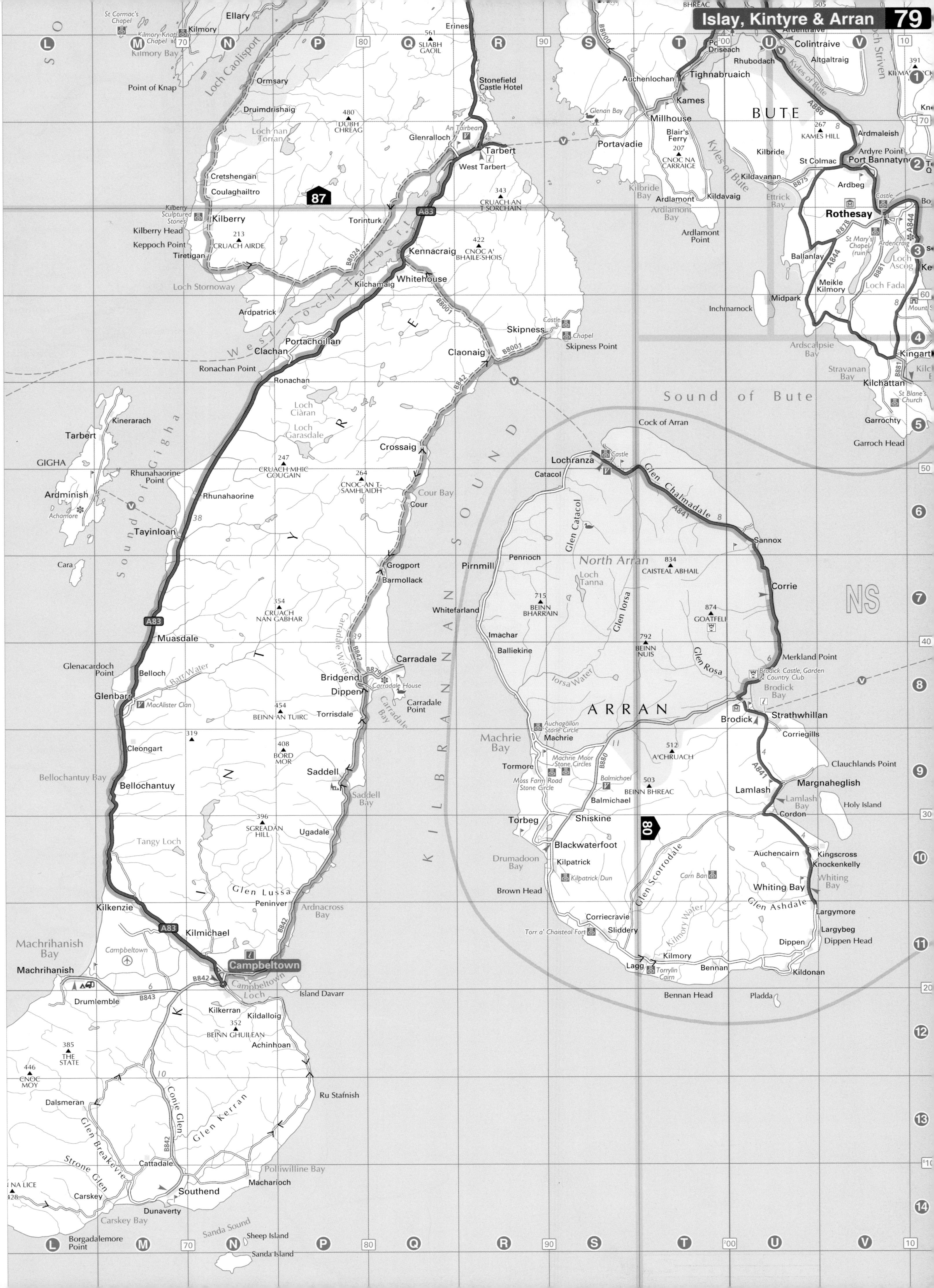
St Cormac's Chapel
Kilmory Knap Chapel
Kilmory
Ellary
Kilmory Bay
Loch Caolisport
Erines
561 SLIABH GAOIL
Point of Knap
Ormsary
Stonefield Castle Hotel
Druimdrishaig
480 DUBH CHREAG
Loch nan Torran
An Tairbeart
Glenralloch
Tarbert
West Tarbert
Cretshengan
Coulaghailtro
87
343 CRUACH AN T SORCHAIN
Kilberry Sculptured Stones
Kilberry
Torinturk
A83
Kilberry Head
213 CRUACH AIRDE
Keppoch Point
Tiretigan
B8024
Kennacraig
422 CNOC A' BHAILE-SHOIS
West Loch Tarbert
Kilchamaig
Whitehouse
Loch Stornoway
B8001
Ardpatrick
Skipness
Castle
Chapel
Skipness Point
Portachoillan
Clachan
Claonaig
B8001
Ronachan Point
Ronachan
B842
Loch Ciàran
Loch Garasdale
Kinerarach
Tarbert
Crossaig
247 CRUACH MHIC GOUGAIN
GIGHA
Rhunahaorine Point
264 CNOC-AN T-SAMHLAIDH
Ardminish
Rhunahaorine
Cour Bay
Cour
Achamore
Sound of Gigha
38
Tayinloan
Cara
Grogport
Barmollack
Pirnmill
354 CRUACH NAN GABHAR
Whitefarland
A83
Muasdale
Carradale Water
39
Glenacardoch Point
Belloch
Barr Water
Carradale
Bridgend
B879
Carradale House
Dippen
Glenbarr
MacAlister Clan
Carradale Point
Carradale Bay
454 BEINN AN TUIRC
Torrisdale
319
Cleongart
408 BORD MOR
Saddell
Bellochantuy Bay
Bellochantuy
Saddell Bay
396 SGREADAN HILL
Ugadale
Tangy Loch
Glen Lussa
Peninver
Kilkenzie
Ardnacross Bay
A83
Kilmichael
B842
Machrihanish Bay
Campbeltown
Machrihanish
Campbeltown Loch
B842
Island Davarr
Drumlemble
B843
6
Kilkerran
Kildalloig
352 BEINN GHUILEAN
Achinhoan
385 THE STATE
446 CNOC MOY
10
Conie Glen
Ru Stafnish
Dalsmeran
Glen Kerran
Glen Breakerie
B842
Strone Glen
Cattadale
Polliwilline Bay
NA LICE 428
Machariocb
Southend
Carskey
Dunaverty
Carskey Bay
Sanda Sound
Borgadalemore Point
Sheep Island
Sanda Island
KILBRANNAN SOUND
KINTYRE
BHREAC
505
B8000
Ardentraive
Colintraive
Portavadie
Driseach
Rhubodach
Altgaltraig
Loch Striven
Auchenlochan
Tighnabruaich
391
Kyles of Bute
Kames
Glenan Bay
Millhouse
BUTE
A886
Blair's Ferry
267 KAMES HILL
8
Ardmaleish
Portavadie
207 CNOC NA CARRAIGE
Kilbride
Ardyre Point
St Colmac
Port Bannatyne
Kyles of Bute
Kildavanan
Kilbride Bay
B875
Ardbeg
Ardlamont
Kildavaig
Ettrick Bay
Castle
Ardlamont Bay
Rothesay
A844
B878
St Mary's Chapel (ruin)
Ardencraig
Ardlamont Point
Ballanlay
A844
Loch Ascog
B881
Meikle Kilmory
Loch Fada
Midpark
Inchmarnock
Mount Stuart
Ardscalpsie Bay
Stravanan Bay
Kingarth
B881
Kilchattan
St Blane's Church
Sound of Bute
Garrochty
Cock of Arran
Garroch Head
Castle
Lochranza
Catacol
Glen Chalmadale
A841
8
Glen Catacol
Sannox
Penrioch
North Arran
834 CAISTEAL ABHAIL
Loch Tanna
Corrie
715 BEINN BHARRAIN
Glen Iorsa
874 GOATFELL
NS
Imachar
792 BEINN NUIS
Balliekine
Glen Rosa
Merkland Point
6
Iorsa Water
Brodick Castle, Garden & Country Club
Brodick Bay
ARRAN
Strathwhillan
Auchagallon Stone Circle
Brodick
Machrie Bay
Machrie
Corriegills
11
512 A'CHRUACH
B880
Tormore
Machrie Moor Stone Circles
Clauchlands Point
Moss Farm Road Stone Circle
Balmichael
503 BEINN BHREAC
A841
Margnaheglish
Balmichael
Lamlash
Lamlash Bay
Holy Island
Torbeg
Shiskine
Cordon
80
Blackwaterfoot
Glen Scorrodale
Auchencairn
Kingscross
Drumadoon Bay
Kilpatrick
Knockenkelly
Carn Ban
Kilpatrick Dun
Whiting Bay
Brown Head
Whiting Bay
Glen Ashdale
Largymore
Kilmory Water
Corriecravie
Largybeg
Torr a' Chaisteal Fort
Sliddery
Dippen
Dippen Head
Kilmory
Lagg
Torrylin Cairn
Bennan
Kildonan
Bennan Head
Pladda

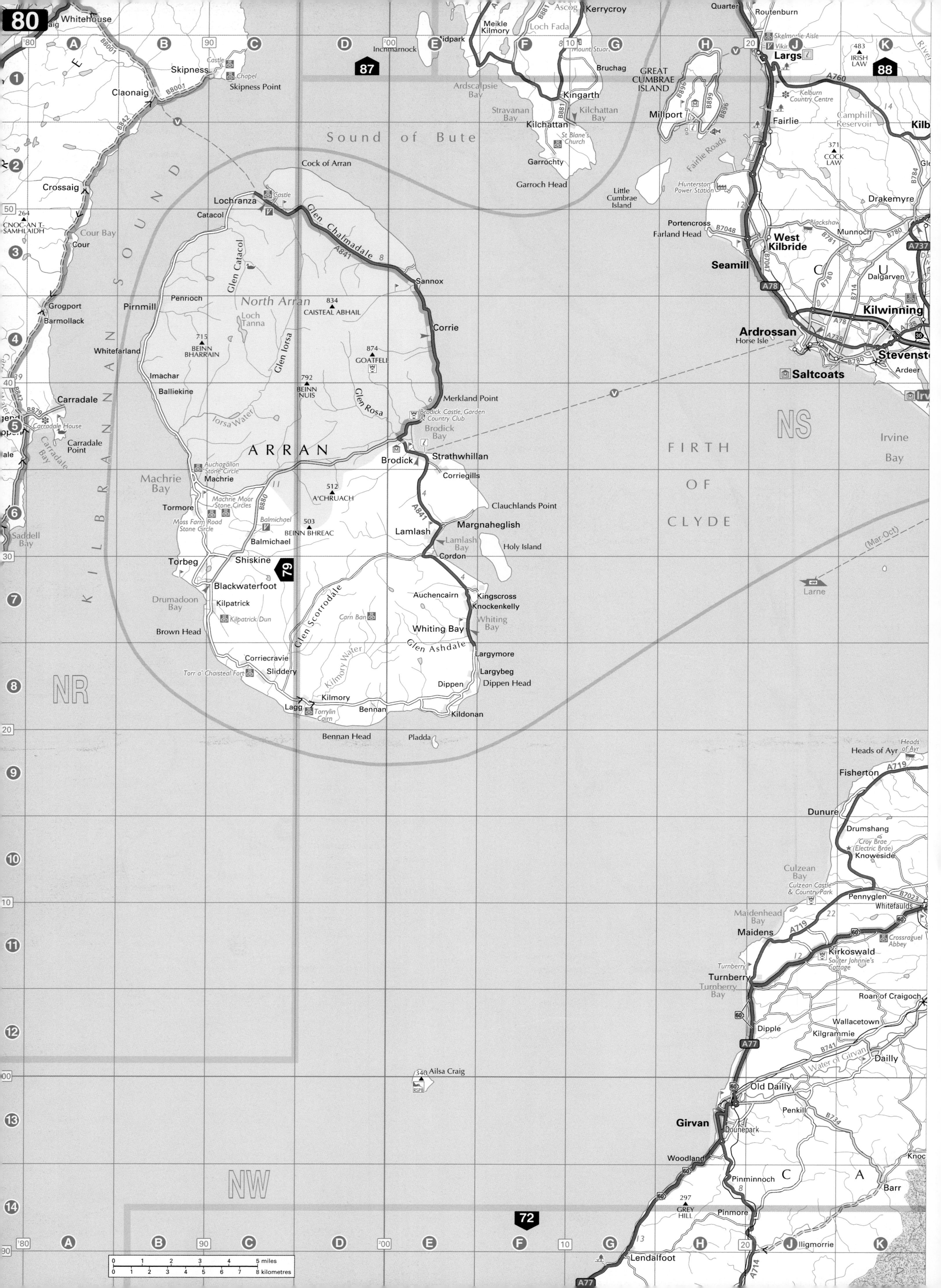
Whitehouse
Skipness
Castle
Chapel
Skipness Point
Claonaig
Crossaig
264
CNOC-AN T-SAMHLAIDH
Cour Bay
Cour
Grogport
Barmollack
Whitefarland
Carradale
Carradale House
Carradale Point
Carradale Bay
Saddell Bay
87
Inchmarnock
Midpark
Meikle Kilmory
Loch Fada
Ascog
Kerrycroy
Mount Stuart
Bruchag
Ardscalpsie Bay
Stravanan Bay
Kingarth
Kilchattan Bay
Kilchattan
St Blane's Church
Garrochty
Garroch Head
Sound of Bute
GREAT CUMBRAE ISLAND
Millport
Fairlie Roads
Little Cumbrae Island
Hunterston Power Station
Portencross
Farland Head
Quarter
Routenburn
Skelmorlie Aisle
Vikingar!
Largs
483
IRISH LAW
88
Kelburn Country Centre
Fairlie
Camphill Reservoir
Kilb
371
COCK LAW
Drakemyre
Blackshaw
Munnoch
West Kilbride
Seamill
Dalgarven
Kilwinning
Ardrossan
Horse Isle
Stevenston
Saltcoats
Ardeer
Irvine Bay
NS
FIRTH OF CLYDE
Cock of Arran
Castle
Lochranza
Catacol
Glen Chalmadale
Glen Catacol
North Arran
834
CAISTEAL ABHAIL
Loch Tanna
Sannox
Penrioch
Pirnmill
715
BEINN BHARRAIN
Glen Iorsa
874
GOATFELL
Corrie
Imachar
Balliekine
792
BEINN NUIS
Glen Rosa
Merkland Point
Brodick Castle, Garden & Country Club
Brodick Bay
Iorsa Water
ARRAN
Brodick
Strathwhillan
Corriegills
Auchagallon Stone Circle
Machrie Bay
Machrie
512
A'CHRUACH
Machrie Moor Stone Circles
Tormore
Moss Farm Road Stone Circle
Balmichael
503
BEINN BHREAC
Clauchlands Point
Margnaheglish
Lamlash
Lamlash Bay
Holy Island
Cordon
Balmichael
Torbeg
Shiskine
79
Blackwaterfoot
KILBRANNAN SOUND
Drumadoon Bay
Kilpatrick
Kilpatrick Dun
Brown Head
Glen Scorrodale
Carn Ban
Auchencairn
Kingscross
Knockenkelly
Whiting Bay
Whiting Bay
Glen Ashdale
Largymore
Kilmory Water
Corriecravie
Sliddery
Torr a' Chaisteal Fort
Largybeg
Dippen Head
Dippen
Kilmory
Lagg
Torrylin Cairn
Bennan
Kildonan
Bennan Head
Pladda
NR
(Mar-Oct)
Larne
Heads of Ayr
Heads of Ayr
Fisherton
Dunure
Drumshang
Croy Brae (Electric Brae)
Knoweside
Culzean Bay
Culzean Castle & Country Park
Pennyglen
Whitefaulds
Maidenhead Bay
Maidens
Crossraguel Abbey
Kirkoswald
Souter Johnnie's Cottage
Turnberry
Turnberry
Turnberry Bay
Roan of Craigoch
Wallacetown
Kilgrammie
Dipple
Water of Girvan
Dailly
340
Ailsa Craig
RSPB
Old Dailly
Penkill
Girvan
Dunepark
Woodland
Pinminnoch
Knoc
Barr
NW
297
GREY HILL
Pinmore
72
Illigmorrie
Lendalfoot
0 1 2 3 4 5 miles
0 1 2 3 4 5 6 7 8 kilometres

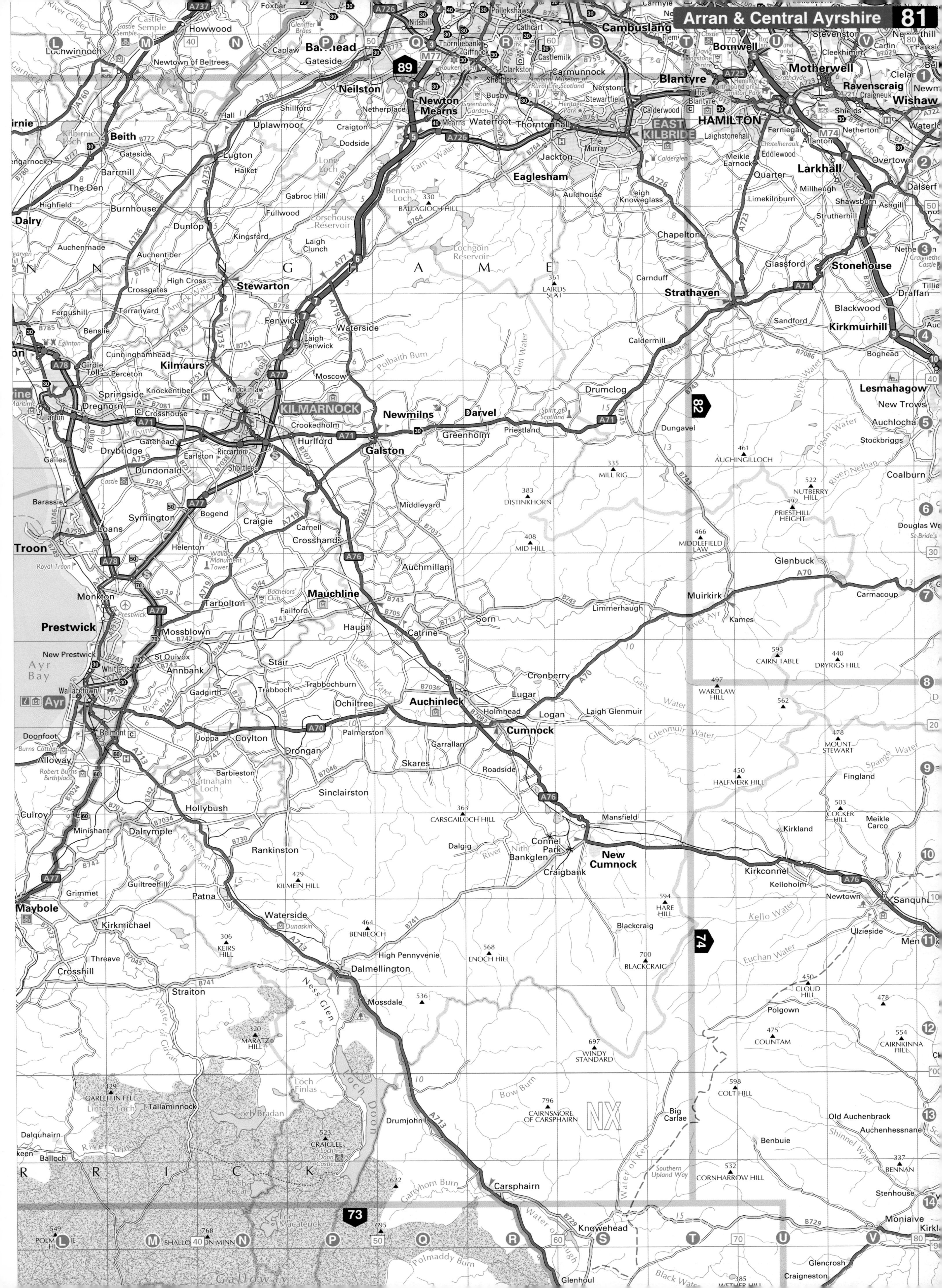

Howwood
Lochwinnoch
Newtown of Beltrees
Foxbar
Barrhead
Gateside
Caplaw
Nitshill
Pollokshaws
Thornliebank
Giffnock
Cathcart
Cambuslang
Castlemilk
Rouken Glen
Clarkston
Carmunnock
Blantyre
Bothwell
Motherwell
Stevenston
Carfin
Cleekhimin
Ravenscraig
Craigneuk
Wishaw
Neilston
Netherplace
Newton Mearns
Busby
Sheddens
Nerston
Stewartfield
Calderwood
HAMILTON
Shillford
Uplawmoor
Craigton
Dodside
Mearns
Waterfoot
Thorntonhall
EAST KILBRIDE
Laighstonehall
Ferniegair
Allanton
Netherton
Kilbirnie
Beith
Gateside
Lugton
Halket
Jackton
The Murray
Meikle Earnock
Eddlewood
Overtown
Barrmill
The Den
Burnhouse
Highfield
Dalry
Eaglesham
Quarter
Larkhall
Millheugh
Dalserf
Gabroc Hill
Bennan Loch
330 BALLAGIOCH HILL
Auldhouse
Leigh Knoweglass
Limekilnburn
Shawsburn
Ashgill
Dunlop
Fullwood
Corsehouse Reservoir
Strutherhill
Kingsford
Laigh Clunch
Lochgoin Reservoir
Chapelton
Auchenmade
Auchentiber
Glassford
Stonehouse
High Cross
Crossgates
Stewarton
361 LAIRDS SEAT
Carnduff
Strathaven
Tillie
Draffan
Fergushill
Torranyard
Blackwood
Fenwick
Waterside
Sandford
Kirkmuirhill
Benslie
Laigh Fenwick
Caldermill
Eglinton
Cunninghamhead
Girdle Toll
Kilmaurs
Perceton
Moscow
Polbaith Burn
Glen Water
Boghead
Springside
Knockentiber
Knockinlaw
Drumclog
Lesmahagow
New Trows
Dreghorn
Crosshouse
KILMARNOCK
Newmilns
Darvel
Priestland
Spirit of Scotland
Fullarton
Crookedholm
Greenholm
Dungavel
Auchlochan
Gatehead
Hurlford
Galston
Drybridge
Riccarton
Earlston
Shortlees
Stockbriggs
Gailes
Dundonald
461 AUCHINGILLOCH
335 MILL RIG
Coalburn
Castle
522 NUTBERRY HILL
383 DISTINKHORN
Barassie
Middleyard
492 PRIESTHILL HEIGHT
Symington
Bogend
Craigie
Loans
Carnell
466 MIDDLEFIELD LAW
Douglas West
St Bride's
Troon
Crosshands
408 MID HILL
Helenton
Royal Troon
Wallace Monument Tower
Auchmillan
Glenbuck
Bachelors' Club
Mauchline
Muirkirk
Carmacoup
Monkton
Tarbolton
Failford
Limmerhaugh
Prestwick
Sorn
Kames
Mossblown
Haugh
Catrine
River Ayr
New Prestwick
St Quivox
593 CAIRN TABLE
440 DRYRIGS HILL
Ayr Bay
Whitletts
Annbank
Stair
Cronberry
Wallacetown
Trabbochburn
Gass Water
497 WARDLAW HILL
562
Ayr
Gadgirth
Trabboch
Lugar
Ochiltree
Auchinleck
Holmhead
Logan
Laigh Glenmuir
Doonfoot
Belmont
Joppa
Coylton
Palmerston
Cumnock
Glenmuir Water
478 MOUNT STEWART
Burns Cottage
Alloway
Drongan
Garrallan
Spango Water
Robert Burns Birthplace
Skares
Roadside
Barbieston
450 HALFMERK HILL
Fingland
Martnaham Loch
Sinclairston
Hollybush
503 COCKER HILL
Meikle Carco
Culroy
363 CARSGAILOCH HILL
Mansfield
Minishant
Dalrymple
Kirkland
Rankinston
Connel Park
Dalgig
Bankglen
New Cumnock
River Doon
Craigbank
Kirkconnel
429 KILMEIN HILL
Kelloholm
Grimmet
Guiltreehill
Newtown
Sanquhar
Maybole
Patna
594 HARE HILL
Kello Water
Kirkmichael
Waterside
Dunaskin
464 BENBEOCH
Blackcraig
Ulzieside
306 KEIRS HILL
Menock
Threave
High Pennyvenie
568 ENOCH HILL
700 BLACKCRAIG
Euchan Water
Crosshill
Dalmellington
Straiton
Ness Glen
Mossdale
536
450 CLOUD HILL
478
Polgown
Water of Girvan
320 MARAZT HILL
697 WINDY STANDARD
475 COUNTAM
554 CAIRNKINNA HILL
Loch Finlas
Loch Doon
Bow Burn
598 COLT HILL
429 GARLEFFIN FELL
Linfern Loch
Tallaminnock
Loch Bradan
796 CAIRNSMORE OF CARSPHAIRN
NX
Big Carlae
Old Auchenbrack
Drumjohn
Auchenhessnane
Dalquhairn
River Stinchar
523 CRAIGLEE
Loch Doon Castle
Benbuie
Shinnel Water
Balloch
Water of Ken
Southern Upland Way
532 CORNHARROW HILL
337 BENNAN
R R I C K
622
Loch Recar
Garryhorn Burn
Carsphairn
Stenhouse
Loch Macaterick
695
Knowehead
Moniaive
549 POLMAIE HILL
768 SHALLOCH ON MINNOCH
Water of Deugh
Polmaddy Burn
Glencrosh
Galloway
Black Water
Craigneston
Glenhoul
385 WETHER HILL
89
82
74
73

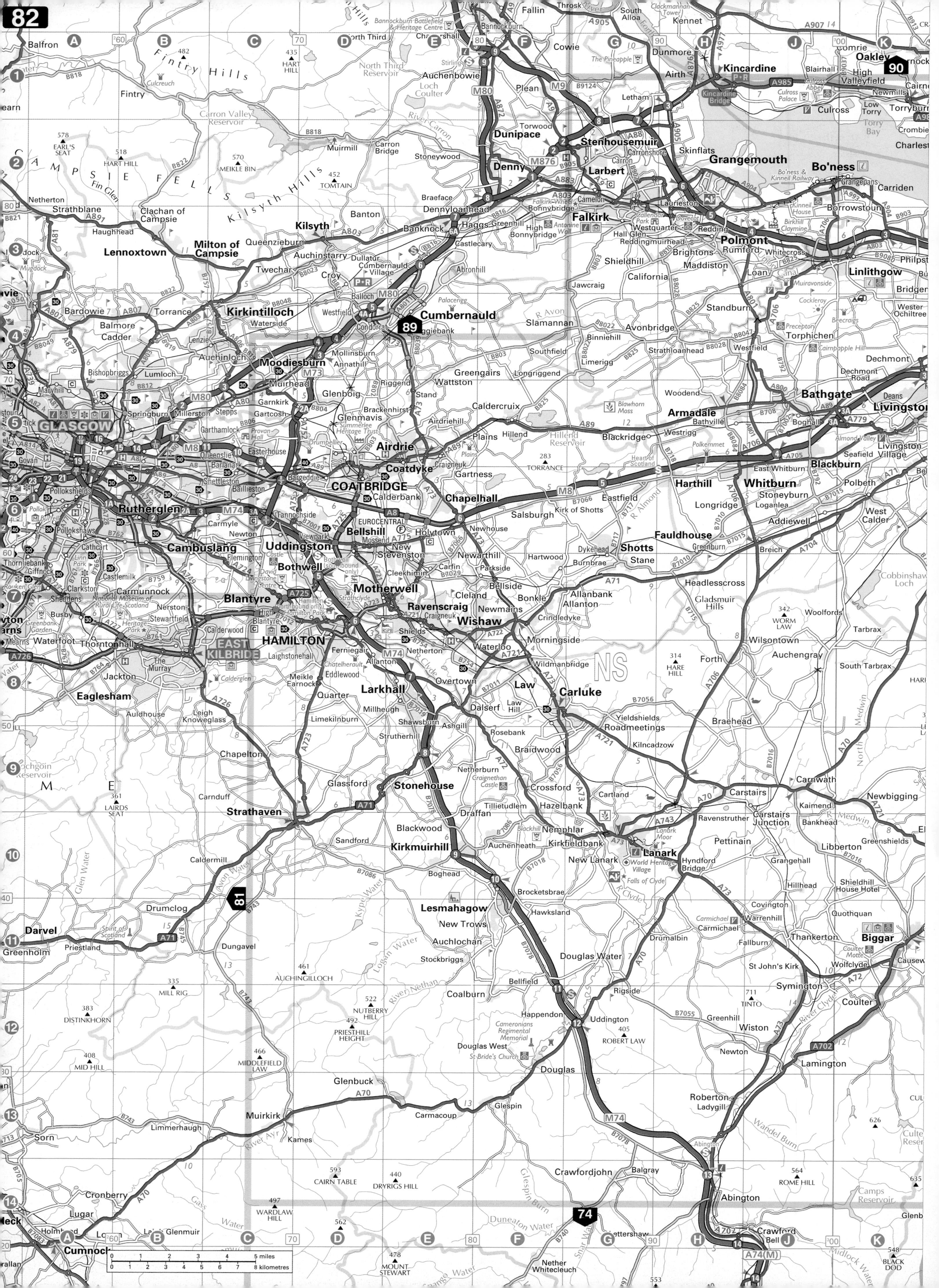
Balfron
Fintry Hills
Fintry
Culcreuch
North Third Reservoir
Bannockburn Battlefield & Heritage Centre
Bannockburn
Fallin
Throsk
South Alloa
Clackmannan Tower
Kennet
Stirling
Cowie
The Pineapple
Dunmore
Kincardine
Airth
Auchenbowie
Loch Coulter
Plean
Letham
Kincardine Bridge
Blairhall
Culross Abbey
Culross Palace
Culross
High Valleyfield
Newmills
Low Torry
Torryburn
Torry Bay
Crombie
Charlestown
Oakley
Comrie
Carron Valley Reservoir
Campsie Fells
Fin Glen
Kilsyth Hills
Earl's Seat
Hart Hill
Meikle Bin
Tomtain
Muirmill
Carron Bridge
Stoneywood
Torwood
Dunipace
Stenhousemuir
Denny
Larbert
Carron
Carronshore
Skinflats
Grangemouth
Bo'ness
Bo'ness & Kinneil Railway
Grangepans
Carriden
Netherton
Strathblane
Clachan of Campsie
Haughhead
Lennoxtown
Milton of Campsie
Kilsyth
Banton
Braefoot
Dennyloanhead
Banknock
Haggs
Greenhill
Bonnybridge
High Bonnybridge
Antonine Wall
Falkirk Wheel
Camelon
Falkirk
Callendar Park
Westquarter
Hall Glen
Reddingmuirhead
Laurieston
Redding
Polmont
Brightons
Rumford
Whitecross
Maddiston
Kinneil House
Birkhill Claymine
Borrowstoun
Linlithgow
Philpstoun
Queenzieburn
Auchinstarry
Dullatur
Cumbernauld Village
Croy
Twechar
Castlecary
Abronhill
Shieldhill
California
Jawcraig
Muiravonside
Cockleroy
Beecraigs
Bridgend
Wester Ochiltree
Mugdock
Bardowie
Torrance
Kirkintilloch
Westfield
Balloch
Condorrat
Cumbernauld
Palacerigg
Slamannan
Avonbridge
Standburn
Torphichen
Preceptory
Cairnpapple Hill
Balmore
Cadder
Waterside
Lenzie
Auchinloch
Moodiesburn
Mollinsburn
Annathill
Binniehill
Southfield
Limerigg
Strathloanhead
Westfield
Dechmont
Dechmont Road
Bishopbriggs
Lumloch
Muirhead
Glenboig
Riggend
Greengairs
Longriggend
Wattston
Stand
Woodend
Bathgate
Deans
Livingston
Maryhill
Springburn
Millerston
Stepps
Garnkirk
Gartcosh
Brackenhirst
Glenmavis
Summerlee Heritage Trust
Caldercruix
Airdriehill
Blawhorn Moss
Armadale
Bathville
Boghall
Glasgow
Garthamlock
Provan Hall
Easterhouse
Drumpellier
Airdrie
Plains
Hillend
Hillend Reservoir
Blackridge
Westrigg
Polkemmet
Almond Valley
Livingston Village
Seafield
Blackburn
Govan
Queenslie
Barlanark
Shettleston
Baillieston
Bargeddie
Coatdyke
Craigneuk
Gartness
Torrance
Heart of Scotland
East Whitburn
Harthill
Whitburn
Polbeth
Pollokshields
Rutherglen
Coatbridge
Calderbank
Chapelhall
Eastfield
Longridge
Stoneyburn
Loganlea
West Calder
Pollok
Burrell
Pollokshaws
Carmyle
Newton
Tannochside
Eurocentral
Holytown
Newhouse
Salsburgh
Kirk of Shotts
Addiewell
Fauldhouse
Cathcart
Cambuslang
Uddingston
Bellshill
Mossend
New Stevenson
Newarthill
Hartwood
Dykehead
Shotts
Greenburn
Breich
Thornliebank
Giffnock
Linn Park
Flemington
Bothwell Castle
Bothwell
Cleekhimin
Carfin
Parkside
Burnbrae
Stane
Castlemilk
Clarkston
Rouken Glen
David Livingstone Centre
Motherwell
Bellside
Headlesscross
Cobbinshaw Loch
Sheddens
Carmunnock
National Museum of Rural Life Scotland
Blantyre
Hamilton
Strathclyde
Ravenscraig
Cleland
Bonkle
Allanbank
Allanton
Gladsmuir Hills
Busby
Nerston
Stewartfield
Newmains
Crindledyke
Worm Law
Woolfords
Greenbank Garden
Calderwood
Calderpark
Hamilton Park
Shields
Wishaw
Tarbrax
Waterfoot
Thorntonhall
East Kilbride
Hamilton
Ferniegair
Netherton
Waterloo
Morningside
Wilsontown
Auchengray
The Murray
Laighstonehall
Chatelherault
Allanton
Wildmanbridge
Hare Hill
Forth
South Tarbrax
Jackton
Calderglen
Meikle Earnock
Eddlewood
Overtown
Law
Carluke
Eaglesham
Quarter
Larkhall
Dalserf
Law Hill
Yieldshields
Braehead
Auldhouse
Leigh Knoweglass
Limekilnburn
Millheugh
Shawsburn
Ashgill
Roadmeetings
Kilncadzow
Strutherhill
Rosebank
Braidwood
Chapelton
Netherburn
Craignethan Castle
Carnwath
Crossford
Cartland
Carstairs
Newbigging
Lochgoin Reservoir
Glassford
Stonehouse
Hazelbank
Kaimend
Carnduff
Tillietudlem
Ravenstruther
Carstairs Junction
Bankhead
Laird's Seat
Strathaven
Draffan
Blackhill
Nemphlar
Lanark Moor
Pettinain
Greenshields
Blackwood
Kirkfieldbank
Libberton
Sandford
Kirkmuirhill
Auchenheath
Lanark
New Lanark
World Heritage Village
Falls of Clyde
Hyndford Bridge
Grangehall
Caldermill
Boghead
Shieldhill House Hotel
Glen Water
Avon Water
Brocketsbrae
Hillhead
Kype Water
Drumclog
Lesmahagow
Hawksland
Covington
Spirit of Scotland
New Trows
Carmichael
Warrenhill
Quothquan
Darvel
Greenholm
Priestland
Dungavel
Auchlochan
Drumalbin
Fallburn
Thankerton
Biggar
Logan Water
Stockbriggs
Douglas Water
Coulter Motte
Wolfclyde
St John's Kirk
Auchingilloch
Bellfield
Symington
Mill Rig
River Nethan
Coalburn
Rigside
Tinto
Coulter
Distinkhorn
Nutberry Hill
Happendon
Uddington
Greenhill
Priesthill Height
Cameronians Regimental Memorial
Robert Law
Wiston
River Clyde
Douglas West
St Bride's Church
Newton
Lamington
Mid Hill
Middlefield Law
Douglas
Glenbuck
Robertson
Ladygill
Muirkirk
Carmacoup
Glespin
Limmerhaugh
Sorn
Kames
River Ayr
Wandel Burn
Culter Reservoir
Crawfordjohn
Balgray
Abington
Cairn Table
Dryrigs Hill
Rome Hill
Camps Reservoir
Cronberry
Wardlaw Hill
Glespin Burn
Duneaton Water
Lugar
Glenmuir
Holmhead
Cumnock
Nether Whitecleuch
Snar Water
Crawford
Bell
Midlock Water
Mount Stewart
Black Dod
5 miles
8 kilometres
NS
89
90
81
74

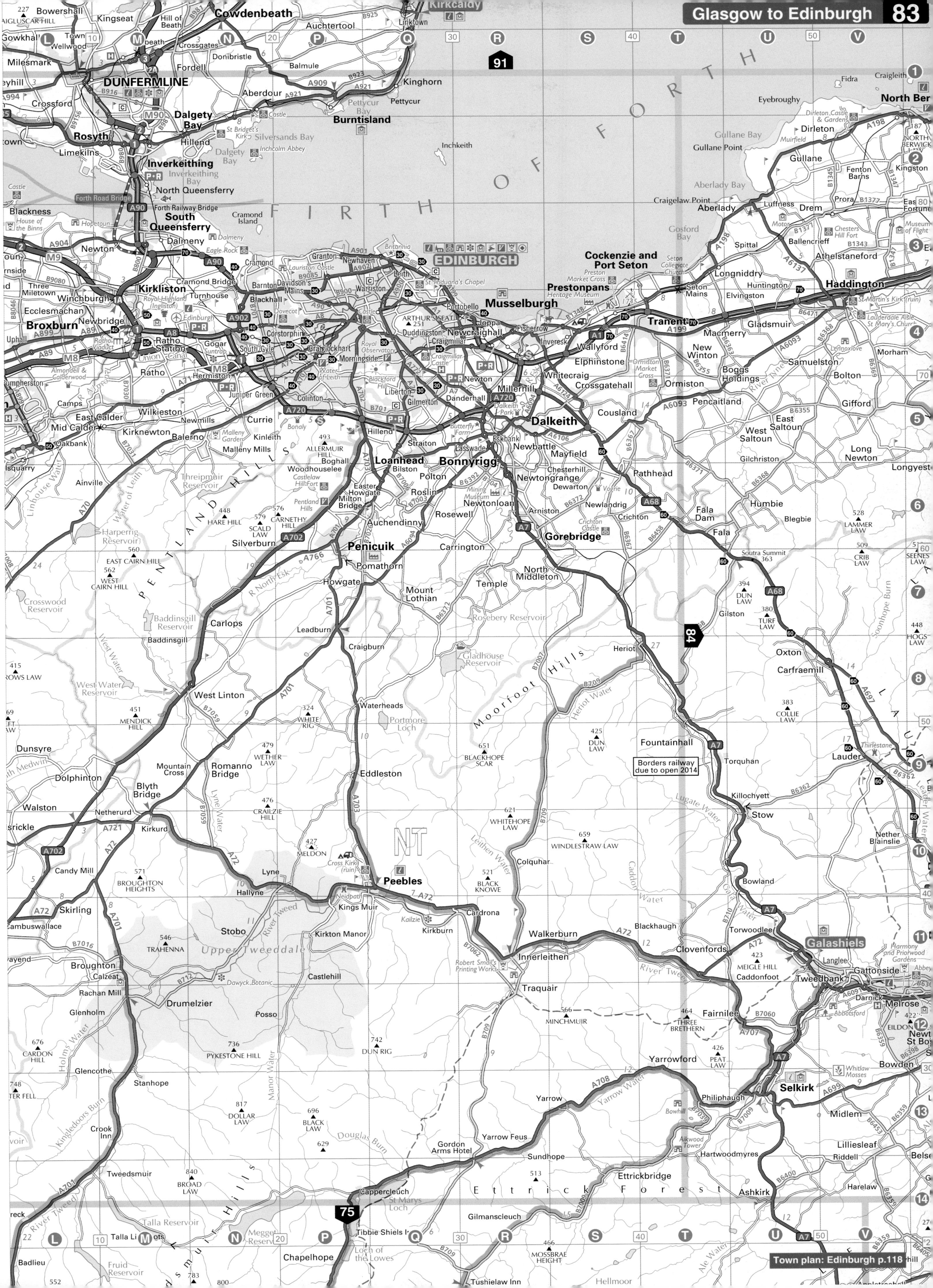
Kirkcaldy
Cowdenbeath
Kingseat
Bowershall
Auchtertool
Linktown
Kinghorn
Pettycur
Burntisland
Aberdour
Dalgety Bay
DUNFERMLINE
Crossford
Rosyth
Limekilns
Inverkeithing
North Queensferry
Forth Road Bridge
Forth Railway Bridge
South Queensferry
Dalmeny
Hopetoun
Blackness
Newton
Kirkliston
Winchburgh
Ecclesmachan
Broxburn
Newbridge
Ratho
Ratho Station
Gogar
Uphall
Inchkeith
FIRTH OF FORTH
Cramond Island
Cramond
Cramond Bridge
Granton
Newhaven
Leith
EDINBURGH
Portobello
Musselburgh
Prestonpans
Cockenzie and Port Seton
Tranent
Longniddry
Aberlady
Aberlady Bay
Gullane
Gullane Bay
Gullane Point
Dirleton
North Berwick
Fidra
Craigleith
Eyebrowby
Craigelaw Point
Gosford Bay
Luffness
Drem
Spittal
Athelstaneford
Haddington
Elvington
Gladsmuir
Macmerry
New Winton
Samuelston
Morham
Bolton
Ormiston
Pencaitland
Gifford
East Saltoun
West Saltoun
Long Newton
Longyester
Humbie
Fala
Fala Dam
Pathhead
Cousland
Dalkeith
Eskbank
Bonnyrigg
Lasswade
Loanhead
Newtongrange
Gorebridge
Penicuik
Rosewell
Roslin
Carrington
Temple
North Middleton
Mount Lothian
Howgate
Leadburn
Carlops
Silverburn
Currie
Balerno
Juniper Green
Colinton
Hermiston
Wilkieston
East Calder
Mid Calder
Kirknewton
Pentland Hills
Heriot
Soutra Summit 363
Oxton
Carfraemill
Lauder
Fountainhall
Borders railway due to open 2014
Stow
Torquhan
Moorfoot Hills
Gladhouse Reservoir
Rosebery Reservoir
West Linton
Eddleston
Peebles
Romanno Bridge
Mountain Cross
Dolphinton
Blyth Bridge
Kirkurd
Candy Mill
Skirling
Lyne
Hallyne
Kings Muir
Cardrona
Walkerburn
Innerleithen
Traquair
Clovenfords
Galashiels
Tweedbank
Melrose
Gattonside
Fairnilee
Selkirk
Philiphaugh
Yarrowford
Yarrow
Yarrow Feus
Ettrick Forest
Ettrickbridge
Ashkirk
Broughton
Drumelzier
Stobo
Upper Tweeddale
Tweedsmuir
Talla Reservoir
Cappercleuch
St Marys Loch
Tibbie Shiels Inn
Chapelhope
Tushielaw Inn
Town plan: Edinburgh p.118

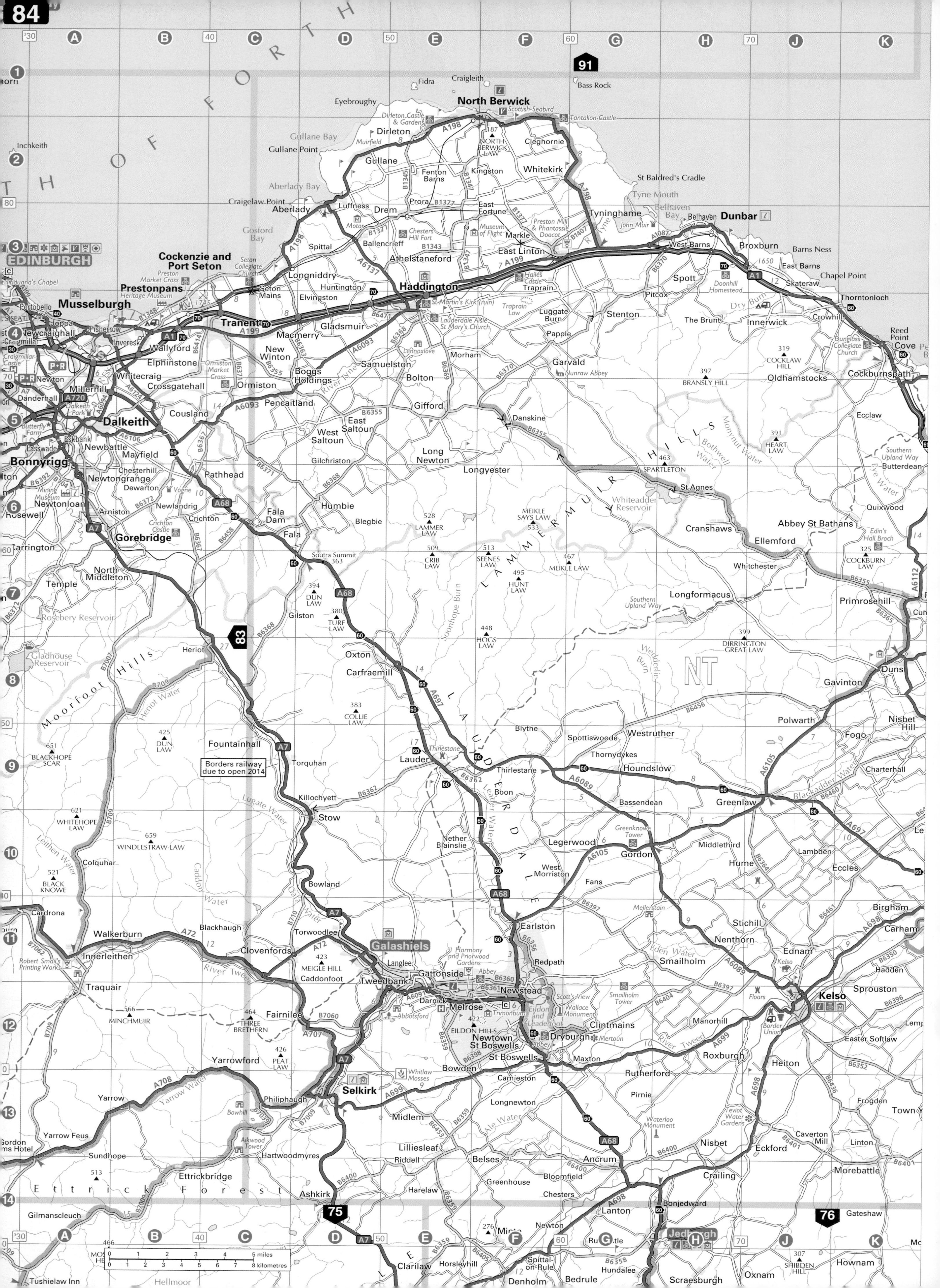
91
Bass Rock
Fidra
Craigleith
Eyebroughy
North Berwick
Scottish Seabird
Dirleton Castle & Gardens
Tantallon Castle
Dirleton
Gullane Bay
Gullane Point
Muirfield
Gullane
187 NORTH BERWICK LAW
Cleghornie
Fenton Barns
Kingston
Whitekirk
St Baldred's Cradle
Tyne Mouth
Aberlady Bay
Craigelaw Point
Aberlady
Luffness
Drem
Prora
East Fortune
Tyninghame
Belhaven Bay
Belhaven
Dunbar
Museum of Flight
Preston Mill & Phantassie Doocot
John Muir
Gosford Bay
Chesters Hill Fort
Markle
Spittal
Ballencrieff
East Linton
West Barns
Broxburn
Barns Ness
East Barns
Chapel Point
Skateraw
Cockenzie and Port Seton
Seton Collegiate Church
Preston Market Cross
Athelstaneford
Hailes Castle
Traprain
EDINBURGH
Prestonpans
Heritage Museum
Seton Mains
Longniddry
Huntington
Haddington
Spott
Doonhill Homestead
Pitcox
Thorntonloch
Portobello
Musselburgh
Elvington
St Martin's Kirk (ruin)
Lauderdale Aisle St Mary's Church
Traprain Law
Luggate Burn
Stenton
Dry Burn
Crowhill
Joppa
Newcraighall
Craigmillar Castle
Fisherrow
Inveresk
Tranent
Gladsmuir
Macmerry
The Brunt
Innerwick
Reed Point
Cove
Wallyford
Elphinstone
New Winton
Samuelston
Lennoxlove
Morham
Pappie
Garvald
Nunraw Abbey
319 COCKLAW HILL
Dunglass Collegiate Church
Newton
Millerhill
Whitecraig
Crossgatehall
Ormiston Market Cross
Ormiston
Boggs Holdings
River Tyne
Bolton
397 BRANSLY HILL
Oldhamstocks
Cockburnspath
Danderhall
Dalkeith Park
Dalkeith
Cousland
Pencaitland
Gifford
Danskine
Ecclaw
Butterfly Farm
Lasswade
Eskbank
Newbattle
Mayfield
West Saltoun
East Saltoun
Long Newton
LAMMERMUIR HILLS
Bothwell Water
Monynut Water
391 HEART LAW
Southern Upland Way
Butterdean
Bonnyrigg
Chesterhill
Pathhead
Gilchriston
Longyester
463 SPARTLETON
St Agnes
Newtongrange
Dewarton
Mining Museum
Vogrie
Newtonloan
Newlandrig
Humbie
Whiteadder Reservoir
Eye Water
Quixwood
Rosewell
Arniston
Crichton Castle
Crichton
Fala Dam
Blegbie
528 LAMMER LAW
MEIKLE SAYS LAW 533
Cranshaws
Abbey St Bathans
Edin's Hall Broch
Gorebridge
Fala
Ellemford
Carrington
Soutra Summit 363
509 CRIB LAW
513 SEENES LAW
467 MEIKLE LAW
325 COCKBURN LAW
Whitchester
North Middleton
Temple
394 DUN LAW
495 HUNT LAW
Longformacus
Primrosehill
Rosebery Reservoir
Gilston
380 TURF LAW
Soonhope Burn
Southern Upland Way
83
448 HOGS LAW
399 DIRRINGTON GREAT LAW
Gladhouse Reservoir
Heriot
Oxton
Carfraemill
Watch Water
NT
Duns
Moorfoot Hills
Heriot Water
Gavinton
383 COLLIE LAW
LAUDERDALE
Blythe
Spottiswoode
Westruther
Polwarth
Nisbet Hill
425 DUN LAW
651 BLACKHOPE SCAR
Fountainhall
Thirlestane
Lauder
Thornydykes
Houndslow
Fogo
Torquhan
Borders railway due to open 2014
Thirlestane
Charterhall
Killochyett
Boon
Leader Water
Bassendean
Greenlaw
Blackadder Water
Lugate Water
Stow
621 WHITEHOPE LAW
659 WINDLESTRAW LAW
Nether Blainslie
Greenknowe Tower
Legerwood
Middlethird
Leithen Water
Colquhar
West Morriston
Gordon
Hume
Lambden
Eccles
521 BLACK KNOWE
Caddon Water
Bowland
Fans
Mellerstain
Birgham
Carham
Cardrona
Gala Water
Stichill
Walkerburn
Blackhaugh
Torwoodlee
Earlston
Nenthorn
Ednam
Innerleithen
Clovenfords
Galashiels
Harmony and Priorwood Gardens
Redpath
Eden Water
Smailholm
Robert Smail's Printing Works
423 MEIGLE HILL
Langlee
Hadden
River Tweed
Caddonfoot
Tweedbank
Gattonside
Abbey
Newstead
Scott's View
Smailholm Tower
Kelso
Sprouston
Traquair
Darnick
Melrose
Trimontium
Wallace Monument
Floors
566 MINCHMUIR
464 THREE BRETHREN
Fairnilee
Abbotsford
422 EILDON HILLS
Eildon and Leaderfoot
Manorhill
Border Union
Lempitlaw
Newtown St Boswells
Dryburgh
Mertoun
Clintmains
Easter Softlaw
426 PEAT LAW
Yarrowford
Bowden
St Boswells
Maxton
Roxburgh
Heiton
Whitlaw Mosses
Camieston
Rutherford
Yarrow
Yarrow Water
Bowhill
Philiphaugh
Selkirk
Longnewton
Pirnie
Frogden
Town Yetholm
Midlem
Ale Water
Waterloo Monument
Teviot Water Gardens
Gordon Arms Hotel
Yarrow Feus
Aikwood Tower
Lilliesleaf
Nisbet
Caverton Mill
Linton
Sundhope
Hartwoodmyres
Riddell
Belses
Ancrum
Eckford
513
Ettrickbridge
Bloomfield
Crailing
Morebattle
Ettrick Forest
Ashkirk
Harelaw
Greenhouse
Chesters
Gilmanscleuch
75
Lanton
Bonjedward
76
Gateshaw
276 Minto
Newton
Jedburgh
Rulecastle
466 MOSSHEAD
307 SHIBDEN HILL
Hownam
Clarilaw
Horsleyhill
Spittal-on-Rule
Hundalee
Oxnam
Tushielaw Inn
Hellmoor
Denholm
Bedrule
Scraesburgh
5 miles
8 kilometres

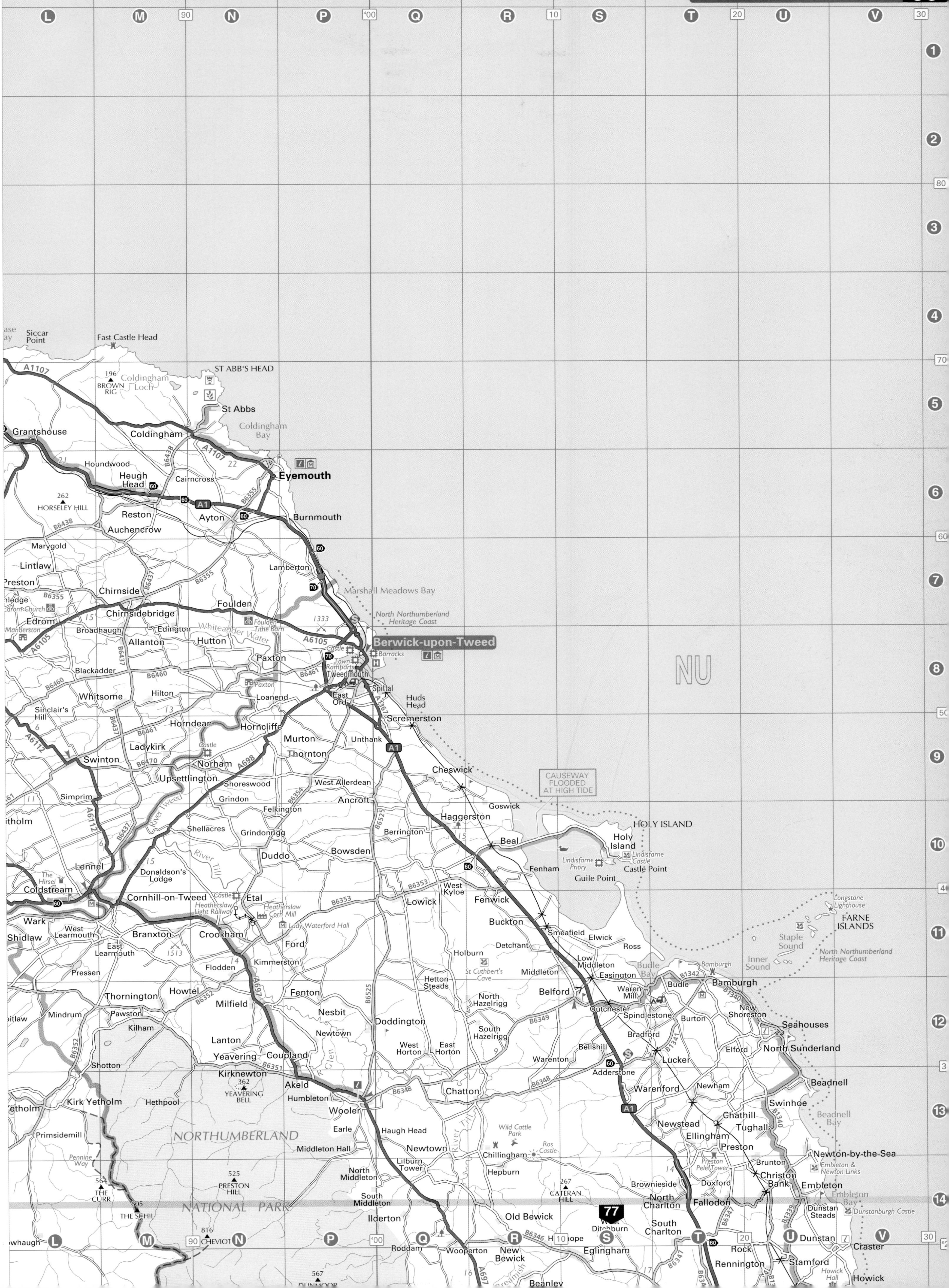

ase Bay
Siccar Point
Fast Castle Head
A1107
196
Coldingham Loch
ST ABB'S HEAD
BROWN RIG
St Abbs
Coldingham Bay
Grantshouse
Coldingham
B6438
A1107   22
Eyemouth
Houndwood
Heugh Head   60
Cairncross
262
HORSELEY HILL
Reston
Ayton   60
A1
B6355
Burnmouth
Marygold
Lintlaw
Lamberton
60
Preston
Marshall Meadows Bay
ledge   B6355
Chirnside
Foulden
70
Edrom   15
Chirnsidebridge
North Northumberland Heritage Coast
Broadhaugh
Edington
Foulden Tithe Barn   1333
Allanton
Hutton
Whitadder Water
A6105
Berwick-upon-Tweed
Blackadder
B6460
Paxton
70
Barracks
Whitsome
Hilton
B6460
Paxton   Castle   Tweedmouth
Loanend
East Ord   Spittal
Sinclair's Hill
Horndean
Huds Head
A6112
Ladykirk
Horncliffe
Scremerston
Swinton
B6470
Norham   A698
Murton
Thornton
Unthank   A1
Upsettlington
Shoreswood
West Allerdean
Cheswick
Simprim
A6112   Grindon
Felkington
Ancroft
Goswick
tholm
Shellacres
Grindonrigg
Berrington
Haggerston
HOLY ISLAND
Lennel
River Till
Duddo
Bowsden
B6353
Beal
Holy Island
Lindisfarne Priory
Coldstream
The Hirsel
80
Donaldson's Lodge
West Kyloe
Fenham
Lindisfarne Castle
Castle Point
Guile Point
Wark
Cornhill-on-Tweed   Etal   Castle
Lowick
Fenwick
West Learmouth
Heatherslaw Light Railway
B6353
Buckton
Shidlaw
Branxton   Crookham
Ford
Holburn
Smeafield   Elwick
Ross
Longstone Lighthouse
FARNE ISLANDS
East Learmouth   1513
Flodden
Kimmerston
Detchant
Low Middleton
Staple Sound
Inner Sound
North Northumberland Heritage Coast
Pressen
Thornington
Howtel
Milfield
Fenton
Hetton Steads
St Cuthbert's Cave
Middleton
Easington   Budle Bay   Bamburgh
Waren Mill   Budle
B1342
New Shoreston
itlaw
Mindrum
Pawston
Nesbit
North Hazelrigg
Belford
Outchester
Spindlestone   Burton
Seahouses
Kilham
Lanton
Newtown
Doddington
South Hazelrigg
B6349
Bradford
Bellshill
Elford
North Sunderland
Shotton
Yeavering
Coupland
West Horton
East Horton
Warenton
Lucker
A1
Kirknewton   362
YEAVERING BELL
Akeld   B6348
Chatton
Adderstone
Warenford
Newham
Beadnell
Kirk Yetholm
Hethpool
Humbleton
Wooler
Chathill   Swinhoe
Beadnell Bay
etholm
Earle
Haugh Head
Wild Cattle Park
Newstead
Tughall
NORTHUMBERLAND
Middleton Hall
Newtown
Ros Castle
Ellingham
Preston
Newton-by-the-Sea
Primsidemill
Pennine Way
Lilburn Tower
Chillingham
CATERAN HILL   267
Brownieside
Doxford
Brunton
Christon Bank
Embleton
Embleton & Newton Links
564
THE CURR
525
PRESTON HILL
North Middleton
Hepburn
North Charlton
Falloden
Dunstan Steads
Embleton Bay
Dunstanburgh Castle
816
CHEVIOT
South Middleton
Old Bewick
77
Ditchburn
South Charlton
Rock
Dunstan
THE SCHIL   605
NATIONAL PARK
Ilderton
hope   10
Eglingham
Stamford
Craster
whaugh
567
Roddam
Wooperton
New Bewick
B6346
Rennington
Howick
Beanley

NU

CAUSEWAY FLOODED AT HIGH TIDE

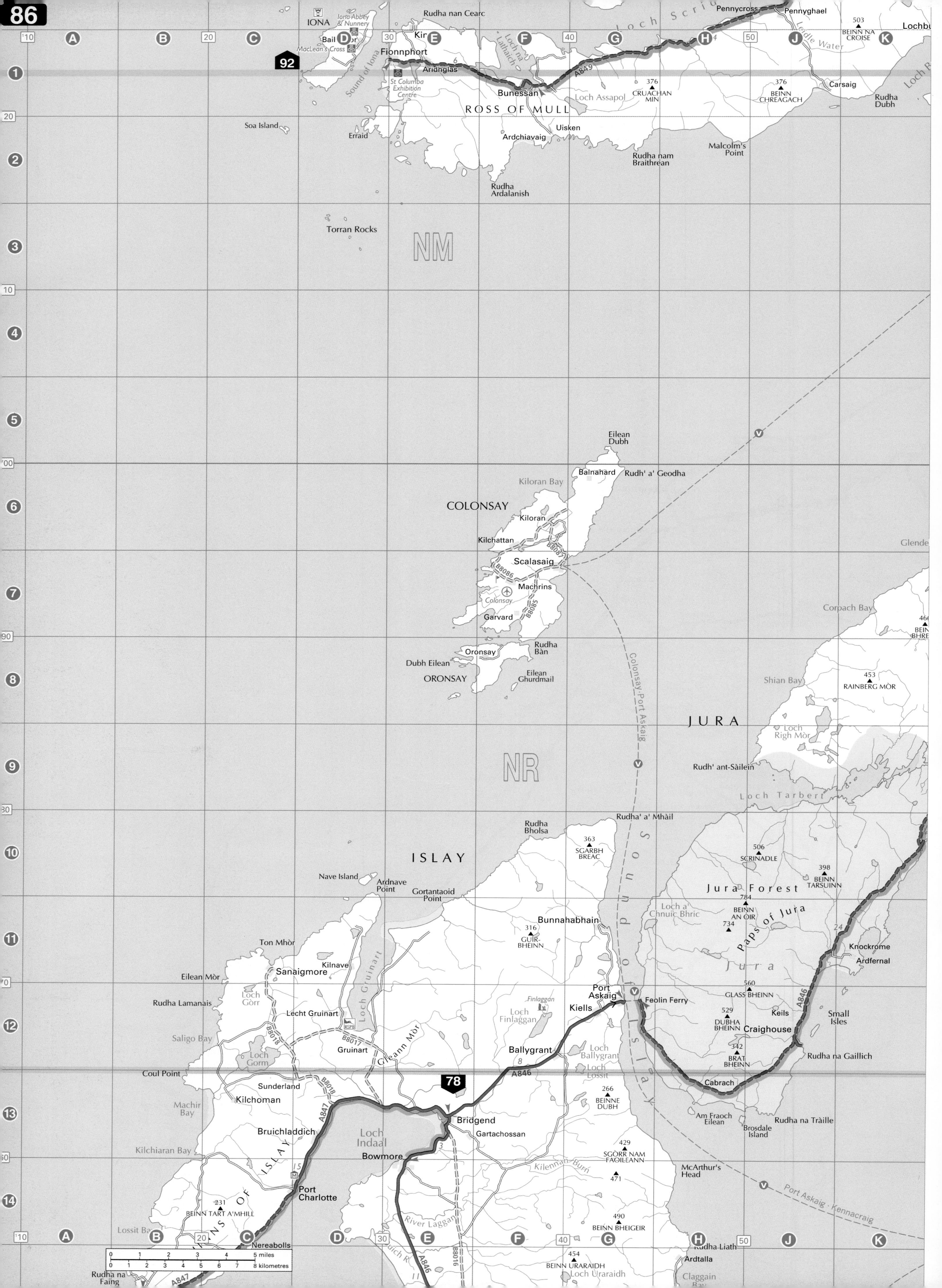
92
78
NM
NR
IONA
Iona Abbey & Nunnery
Baile Mòr
MacLean's Cross
Rudha nan Cearc
Fionnphort
Aridhglas
St Columba Exhibition Centre
Sound of Iona
Loch na Lathaich
Pennycross
Pennyghael
Loch Scridain
Leidle Water
503 BEINN NA CROISE
Lochbuie
A849
Bunessan
Loch Assapol
376 CRUACHAN MIN
376 BEINN CHREAGACH
Carsaig
Rudha Dubh
Loch Buie
ROSS OF MULL
Soa Island
Erraid
Ardchiavaig
Uisken
Rudha nam Braithrean
Malcolm's Point
Rudha Ardalanish
Torran Rocks
Eilean Dubh
Balnahard
Rudh' a' Geodha
Kiloran Bay
COLONSAY
Kiloran
Kilchattan
B8087
Scalasaig
B8086
Machrins
Colonsay
B8085
Garvard
Glendebadel
Corpach Bay
466 BEINN BHREAC
Oronsay
Rudha Bàn
Dubh Eilean
ORONSAY
Eilean Ghurdmail
Colonsay-Port Askaig
453 RAINBERG MÒR
Shian Bay
JURA
Loch Righ Mòr
Rudh' ant-Sàilein
Loch Tarbert
Rudha' a' Mhàil
Rudha Bholsa
363 SGARBH BREAC
ISLAY
506 SCRINADLE
398 BEINN TARSUINN
Nave Island
Ardnave Point
Gortantaoid Point
Jura Forest
784 BEINN AN OIR
Loch a' Chnuic Bhric
734
Paps of Jura
Bunnahabhain
316 GUIR-BHEINN
Sound of Islay
Ton Mhòr
Kilnave
Loch Gruinart
Knockrome
Ardfernal
Jura
Eilean Mòr
Sanaigmore
Loch Gòrr
Rudha Lamanais
Lecht Gruinart
RSPB
Port Askaig
Feolin Ferry
560 GLASS BHEINN
Finlaggan
Loch Finlaggan
Kiells
529 DUBHA BHEINN
Keils
Craighouse
Small Isles
A846
Saligo Bay
B8018
B8017
Gruinart
Gleann Mòr
Ballygrant
Loch Gorm
Loch Ballygrant
342 BRAT BHEINN
Rudha na Gaillich
Coul Point
Loch Lossit
Sunderland
Cabrach
266 BEINNE DUBH
Machir Bay
Kilchoman
A847
Bridgend
Am Fraoch Eilean
Rudha na Tràille
Brosdale Island
Bruichladdich
Gartachossan
Loch Indaal
429 SGÒRR NAM FAOILEANN
Kilchiaran Bay
Bowmore
Kilennan Burn
McArthur's Head
471
RINNS OF ISLAY
Port Charlotte
Port Askaig - Kennacraig
231 BEINN TART A'MHILL
River Laggan
490 BEINN BHEIGEIR
Lossit Bay
Nereabolls
B8016
Rudha Liath
454 BEINN URARAIDH
Loch Uraraidh
Ardtalla
Claggain Bay
Rudha na Faing
0 1 2 3 4 5 miles
0 1 2 3 4 5 6 7 8 kilometres

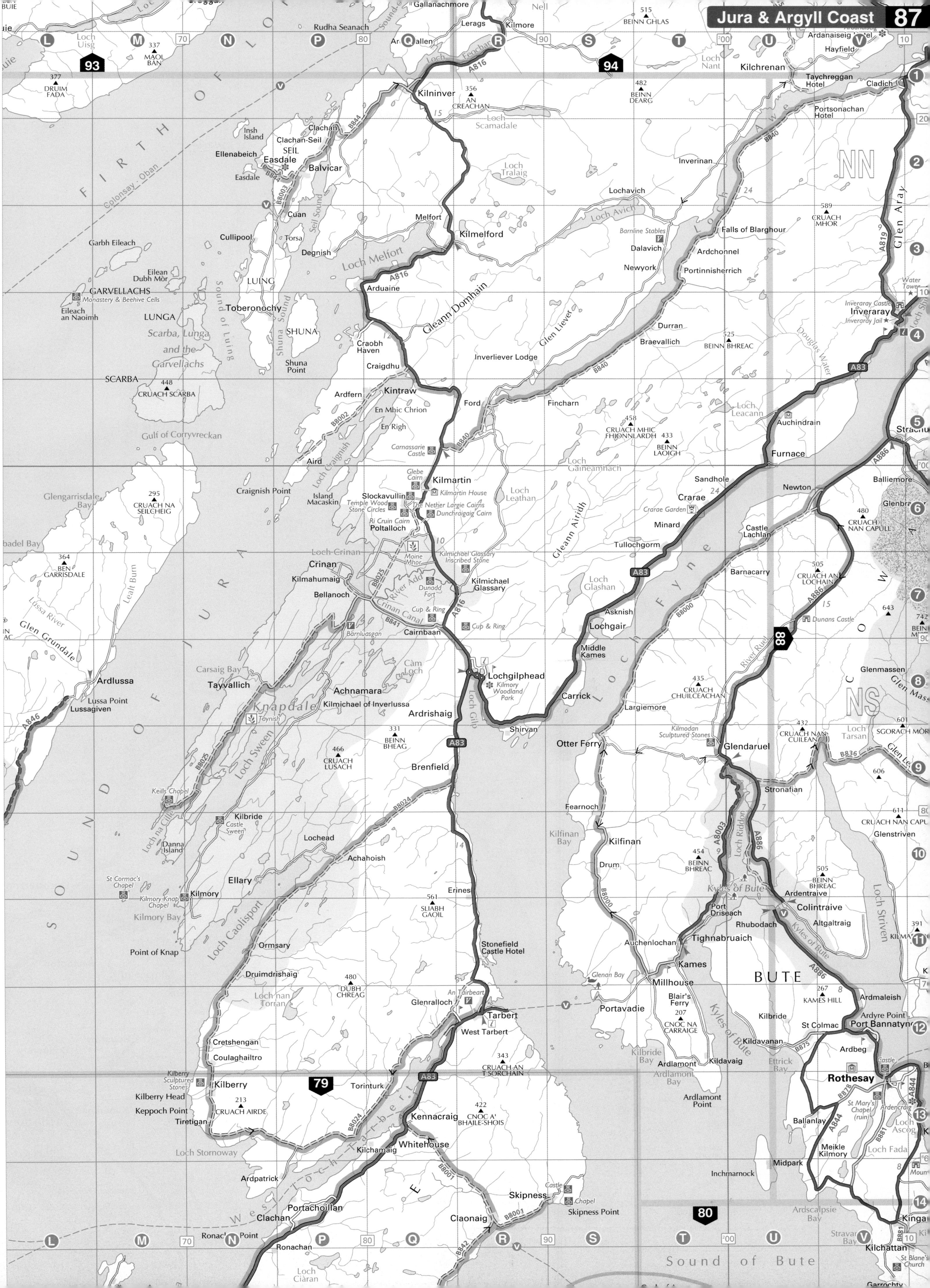

93
94

L M 337 N P Q R S T U V
MAOL
BAN

Gallanachmore
Nell
Lerags Kilmore
Rudha Seanach
515
BEINN GHLAS
Ardanaiseig Hotel
Ardanaiseig Hotel
Hayfield
Ar Allen
Kilchrenan
377 Loch
DRUIM
FADA
70 80 A816
Kilninver
356
AN
CREACHAN
90 A816 Loch
Scamadale
A85
Loch
Nant
Taychreggan
Hotel
Cladich
Portsonachan
Hotel
Kilchrenan

Insh Island
Clachan
B844
15
Inverinan
NN
Clachan-Seil
Ellenabeich
SEIL
Easdale
Balvicar
Loch
Tralaig
Lochavich
589
CRUACH
MHOR

Easdale
B8003
Cuan
Melfort
Kilmelford
Barnline Stables
Dalavich
Falls of Blarghour
Ardchonnel

Cullipool
Torsa
Sell Sound
Degnish
Loch Melfort
Newyork
Portinnisherrich
Water
Tower

Garbh Eileach
LUING
A816
Arduaine
Durran
525
BEINN BHREAC
Inveraray Castle
INVERARAY
Inveraray Jail

GARVELLACHS
Monastery & Beehive Cells
Toberonochy
SHUNA
Gleann Domhain
Glen Lievet
Braevallich

Eileach
an Naoimh
LUNGA
Craobh
Haven
Inverliever Lodge
458
CRUACH MHIC
FHIONNLAIRDH 433
BEINN
LAOIGH
Auchindrain
Strachu

Scarba, Lunga
and the
Garvellachs
Craigdhu
Ford
Fincharn

SCARBA
448
CRUACH SCARBA
Ardfern
Kintraw
En Mhic Chrion
Loch
Gaineamhach
Sandhole
Newton
Balliemore

Gulf of Corryvreckan
Aird
En Righ
Loch
Leacann
480
CRUACH
NAN CAPULL
Glenbra

295
CRUACH NA
SEILCHEIG
Craignish Point
Island
Macaskin
Glebe
Cairn
Kilmartin
Kilmartin House
Loch
Leathan
Crarae
24
Crarae Garden
Minard

364
BEN
GARRISDALE
Slockavullin
Temple Wood
Stone Circles
The Nether Largie Cairns
Dunchraigaig Cairn
Castle
Lachlan
505
CRUACH AN
LOCHAIN

Ri Cruin Cairn
Poltalloch
Kilmichael Glassary
Inscribed Stone
Tullochgorm
Barnacarry

Loch Crinan
Moine
Mhor
643

Crinan
Dunadd
Fort
Kilmichael
Glassary
Loch
Glashan
A83
642

Kilmahumaig
B8025
Cup & Ring
Asknish
Dunans Castle
C
O

Bellanoch
River Add
Cup & Ring
Lochgair
B8000
15
NS

Crinan Canal
B841
Cairnbaan
Middle
Kames
435
CRUACH
CHUILCEACHAN
Glenmassan

Ardlussa
Carsaig Bay
Cam
Loch
Lochgilphead
Kilmory
Woodland
Park
Carrick
Largiemore
432
CRUACH NAN
CUILEAN
606

Lussa Point
Lussagiven
Tayvallich
Achnamara
Kilmory
Sculptured
Stones
Shirvan
Kilmodan
Sculptured Stones
Glendaruel
Stronafian

A846
Knapdale
Kilmichael of Inverlussa
Ardrishaig
331
BEINN
BHEAG
Otter Ferry
611
CRUACH NAN CAPU

Glen Grundale
Taynish
A83
Fearnoch
B836
Glen Le

Keills Chapel
466
CRUACH
LUSACH
Brenfield
Kilfinan
Bay
Kilfinan
A8003
A886
Glenstriven

Kilbride
Castle
Sween
Lochead
454
BEINN
BHREAC
Drum
Loch
Riddon
505
BEINN
BHREAC
Ardentraive
391
KILMA

Danna
Island
Achahoish
Erines
Kyles of Bute
Colintraive
Altgaltraig

St Cormac's
Chapel
Ellary
Port
Driseach
Rhubodach

Kilmory Knap
Chapel
Kilmory
561
SLIABH
GAOIL
Tighnabruaich
Auchenlochan
Kyles of Bute

Kilmory Bay
Ormsary
Stonefield
Castle Hotel
Kames
BUTE
267 8
KAMES HILL
Ardmaleish

Point of Knap
Druimdrishaig
480
DUBH
CHREAG
An Tairbeart
Glenralloch
Millhouse
Glenan Bay
Blair's
Ferry
Portavadie
Kilbride
St Colmac
Ardbeg
Port Bannatyne

Cretshengan
Coulaghailtro
Tarbert
West Tarbert
Kildavanan
B875
Ardyre Point

Kilberry
Sculptured
Stones
Kilberry
79
Torinturk
A83
343
CRUACH AN
SORCHAIN
Kilbride
Bay
Ardlamont
Kildavaig
Ardmaleish
Rothesay

Kilberry Head
Keppoch Point
Tiretigan
213
CRUACH AIRDE
422
CNOC A'
BHAILE-SHOIS
Ardlamont
Bay
Ardlamont
Point
St Mary's
Chapel
Ardencraig
A844

Kennacraig
CNOC A'
BHAILE-SHOIS
Meikle
Kilmory
Loch
Ascog

Ardpatrick
Whitehouse
Ballanlay
B875

Portachoillan
Clachan
Kilchamaig
Midpark
Inchmarnock
Loch Fadai
Kinga

Loch Stornoway
Castle
Skipness
Chapel
Ardscalpsie
Bay

L M 70 N 80 P Q 90 R S 00 T U V
Ronac
Point
Ronachan
Loch
Ciaran
Claonaig
B8001
B842
Skipness Point
80
Sound of Bute
Stravar
Bay
Kilchattan

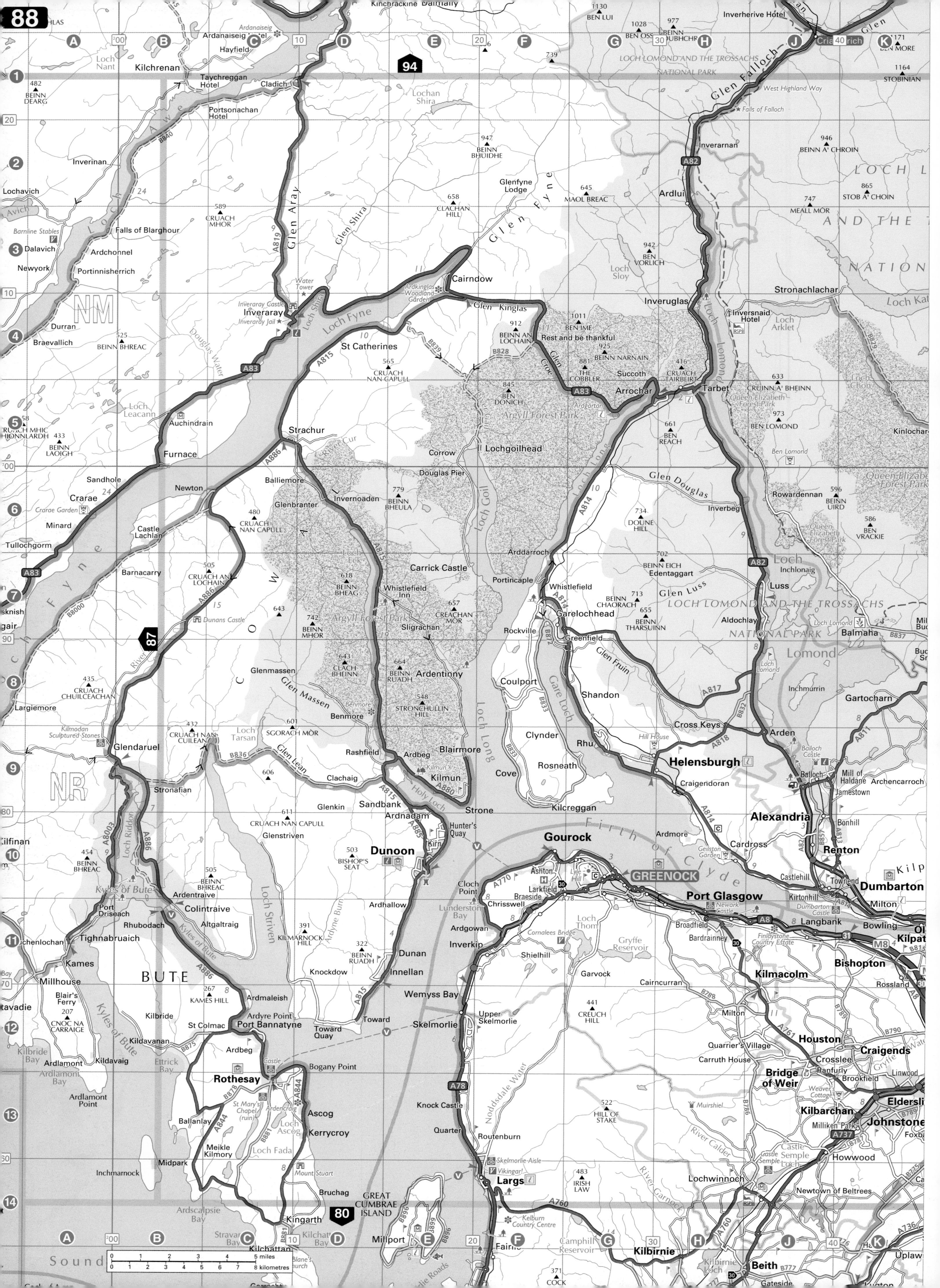

94
87
80
NM
NR
Ardanaiseig Hotel
Hayfield
Kilchrenan
Loch Nant
Taychreggan Hotel
Cladich
Portsonachan Hotel
Loch Awe
Inverinan
Lochavich
Barnline Stables
Falls of Blarghour
Dalavich
Ardchonnel
Portinnisherrich
Newyork
CRUACH MHOR
BEINN DEARG
Durran
Braevallich
BEINN BHREAC
Inveraray Castle
Inveraray
Inveraray Jail
Douglas Water
Loch Leacann
Auchindrain
Furnace
Sandhole
Crarae
Crarae Garden
Minard
Newton
Castle Lachlan
Tullochgorm
Loch Fyne
Barnacarry
Lochan Shira
Glen Aray
Glen Shira
BEINN BHUIDHE
CLACHAN HILL
Glenfyne Lodge
Glen Fyne
Water Tower
Ardkinglas Woodland Garden
Cairndow
Glen Kinglas
St Catherines
CRUACH NAN CAPULL
Strachur
River Cur
Balliemore
Glenbranter
Invernoaden
BEINN BHEULA
Corrow
Douglas Pier
Lochgoilhead
Loch Goil
Argyll Forest Park
Carrick Castle
Whistlefield Inn
CREACHAN MOR
Sligrachan
BEINN MHOR
BEINN BHEAG
Dunans Castle
Glenmassen
Glen Massen
CLACH BHEINN
BEINN RUADH
Ardentinny
Benmore
STRONCHULLIN HILL
SGORACH MOR
Loch Tarsan
CRUACH NAN CUILEAN
Glen Lean
Rashfield
Ardbeg
Kilmun
Blairmore
Clachaig
Holy Loch
Loch Long
Glendaruel
Kilmodan Sculptured Stones
Largiemore
CRUACH CHUILCEACHAN
Stronafian
Loch Riddon
Glenkin
Sandbank
Ardnadam
Strone
Hunter's Quay
Kirn
Dunoon
BISHOP'S SEAT
Glenstriven
Loch Striven
Ardhallow
KILMARNOCK HILL
Ardyne Burn
BEINN RUADH
Dunan
Innellan
Knockdow
Toward
Toward Quay
Kilfinan
BEINN BHREAC
Kyles of Bute
Port Driseach
Tighnabruaich
Rhubodach
Colintraive
Ardentraive
Altgaltraig
Kames
Millhouse
BUTE
Blair's Ferry
CNOC NA CARRAIGE
KAMES HILL
Kilbride
Ardmaleish
Ardyre Point
Port Bannatyne
St Colmac
Kildavanan
Ardbeg
Ettrick Bay
Kilbride Bay
Ardlamont
Kildavaig
Ardlamont Bay
Ardlamont Point
Rothesay
Castle
Bogany Point
St Mary's Chapel (ruin)
Ardencraig
Ascog
Loch Ascog
Kerrycroy
Ballanlay
Meikle Kilmory
Loch Fada
Mount Stuart
Midpark
Inchmarnock
Bruchag
Kingarth
Ardscalpsie Bay
Stravanan Bay
Kilchattan
Kilchattan Bay
GREAT CUMBRAE ISLAND
Millport
Sound of Bute
Blane's Church
BEN LUI
BEN OSS
BEINN DUBHCHRAIG
Inverherive Hotel
BEN MORE
STOBINIAN
LOCH LOMOND AND THE TROSSACHS NATIONAL PARK
Glen Falloch
West Highland Way
Falls of Falloch
Inverarnan
BEINN A' CHROIN
STOB A' CHOIN
MEALL MOR
MAOL BREAC
Ardlui
BEN VORLICH
Loch Sloy
Inveruglas
Stronachlachar
Loch Katrine
Inversnaid Hotel
Loch Arklet
BEN IME
BEINN AN LOCHAIN
Rest and be thankful
BEINN NARNAIN
Glen Croe
THE COBBLER
Succoth
CRUACH TAIRBEIRT
Arrochar
Tarbet
Loch Lomond
CRUINN A' BHEINN
Queen Elizabeth Forest Park
BEN LOMOND
Loch Chon
Kinlochard
BEN DONICH
Ardgartan
BEN REACH
Glen Douglas
Inverbeg
Rowardennan
BEINN UIRD
BEN VRACKIE
DOUNE HILL
Arddarroch
BEINN EICH
Edentaggart
Inchlonaig
Luss
Glen Luss
Portincaple
Whistlefield
Garelochhead
BEINN CHAORACH
BEINN THARSUINN
Aldochlay
Balmaha
Rockville
Greenfield
Glen Fruin
Coulport
Shandon
Gare Loch
Inchmurrin
Gartocharn
Clynder
Rhu
Cross Keys
Hill House
Arden
Helensburgh
Rosneath
Cove
Kilcreggan
Craigendoran
Balloch Castle
Balloch
Mill of Haldane
Jamestown
Archencarroch
Alexandria
Bonhill
Ardmore
Cardross
Renton
Geilston Garden
Firth of Clyde
Gourock
Ashton
Lyle Hill
GREENOCK
Port Glasgow
Newark Castle
Castlehill
Townend
Dumbarton
Kirktonhill
Dumbarton Castle
Milton
Langbank
Bowling
Old Kilpatrick
Cloch Point
Larkfield
Braeside
Chrisswell
Lunderston Bay
Ardgowan
Inverkip
Loch Thom
Cornalees Bridge
Gryffe Reservoir
Shielhill
Broadfield
Bardrainney
Finlaystone Country Estate
Garvock
Kilmacolm
Bishopton
Cairncurran
Rossland
Wemyss Bay
Upper Skelmorlie
Skelmorlie
CREUCH HILL
Milton
Houston
Quarrier's Village
Carruth House
Craigends
Crosslee
Ranfurly
Bridge of Weir
Brookfield
Linwood
Weaver's Cottage
Muirshiel
Kilbarchan
Elderslie
Milliken Park
Johnstone
Knock Castle
Quarter
Noddsdale Water
HILL OF STAKE
River Calder
Castle Semple
Semple Loch
Howwood
Routenburn
Skelmorlie Aisle
Vikingar!
Largs
IRISH LAW
River Garnock
Lochwinnoch
Newtown of Beltrees
Kelburn Country Centre
Fairlie
Camphill Reservoir
Kilbirnie
Kilbirnie Loch
Beith
Gateside
Uplawmoor
COCK

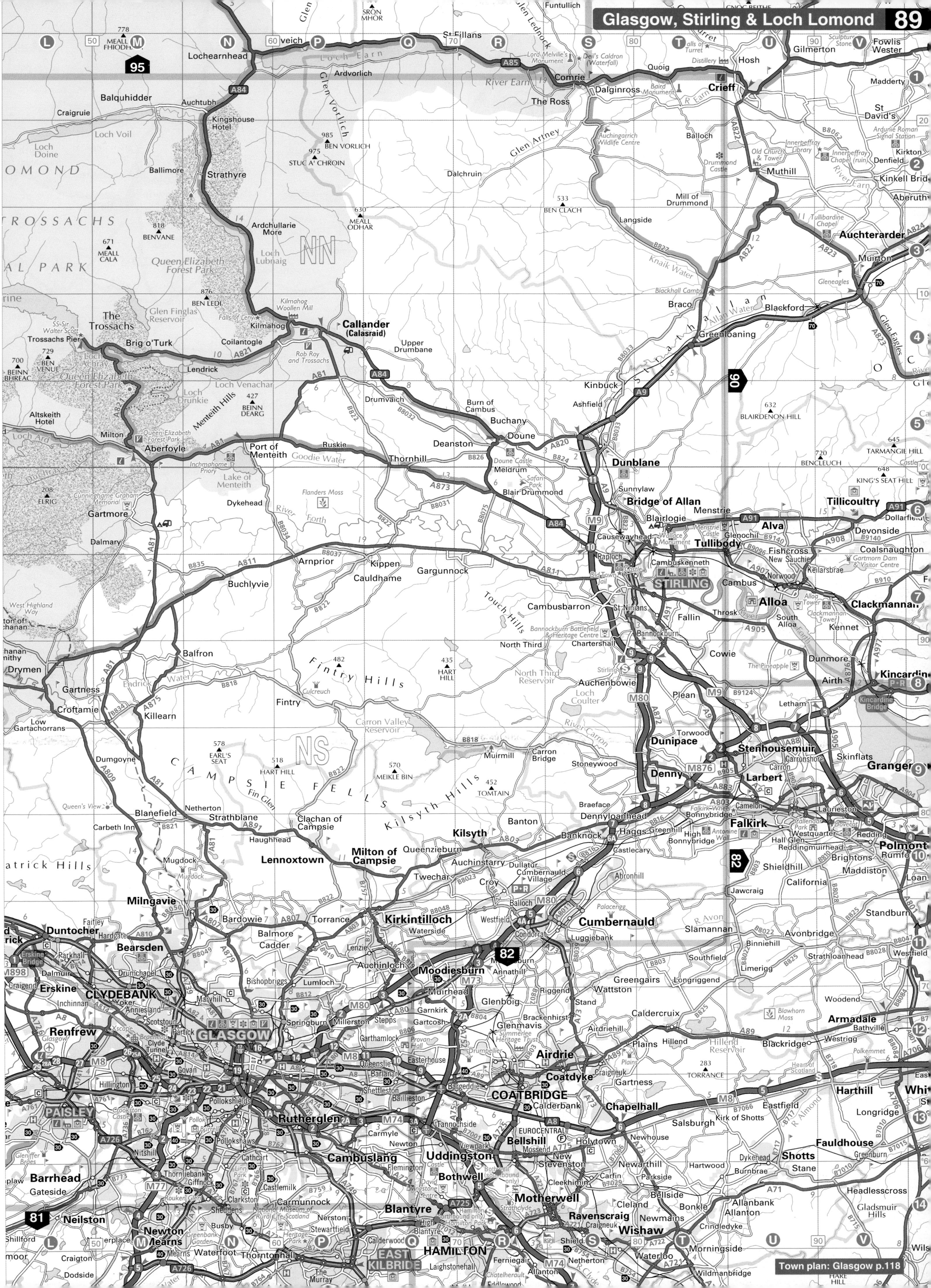
Lochearnhead
Loch Earn
St Fillans
Comrie
Crieff
Gilmerton
Balquhidder
Strathyre
Callander (Calasraid)
Aberfoyle
Port of Menteith
Doune
Dunblane
Bridge of Allan
STIRLING
Alloa
Tullibody
Alva
Tillicoultry
Clackmannan
Auchterarder
Blackford
Braco
Greenloaning
Kinbuck
Deanston
Thornhill
Kippen
Gargunnock
Buchlyvie
Arnprior
Balfron
Drymen
Killearn
Fintry
Fintry Hills
CAMPSIE FELLS
Kilsyth Hills
Kilsyth
Lennoxtown
Milton of Campsie
Strathblane
Milngavie
Bearsden
Kirkintilloch
Cumbernauld
Denny
Dunipace
Larbert
Stenhousemuir
Falkirk
Grangemouth
Polmont
Airdrie
COATBRIDGE
CLYDEBANK
GLASGOW
PAISLEY
Renfrew
Rutherglen
Cambuslang
Uddingston
Bothwell
Motherwell
Wishaw
Blantyre
HAMILTON
EAST KILBRIDE
Barrhead
Newton Mearns
Neilston
Shotts
Harthill
Armadale
Bellshill
Chapelhall
Loch Lomond
The Trossachs
Queen Elizabeth Forest Park
NN
NS

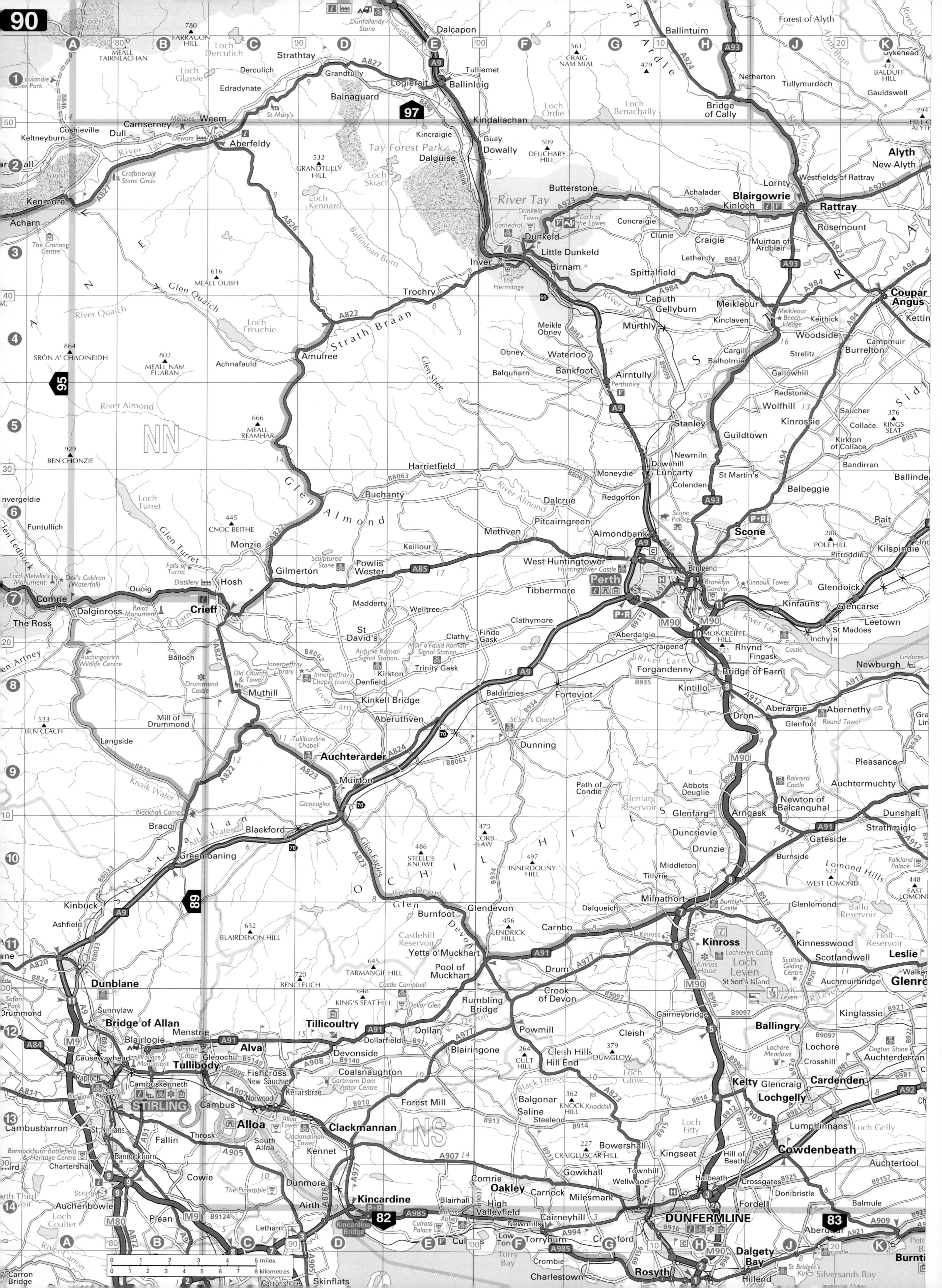
Dalcapon
Ballintuim
Forest of Alyth
Strathtay
Grandtully
Logierait
Ballinluig
Tulliemet
Derculich
Edradynate
Balnaguard
Loch Derculich
Loch Glassie
Weem
Camserney
Dull
Coshieville
Keltneyburn
Aberfeldy
Kenmore
Acharn
Kindallachan
Kincraigie
Guay
Dowally
Dalguise
Tay Forest Park
Loch Ordie
Loch Benachally
Bridge of Cally
Netherton
Tullymurdoch
Gauldswell
Alyth
New Alyth
Lornty
Westfields of Rattray
Butterstone
Achalader
Blairgowrie
Kinloch
Rattray
Rosemount
River Tay
Dunkeld
Little Dunkeld
Birnam
Inver
Concraigie
Clunie
Craigie
Muirton of Ardblair
Lethendy
Spittalfield
Caputh
Gellyburn
Meikleour
Kinclaven
Coupar Angus
Keithick
Woodside
Burrelton
Campmuir
Strelitz
Murthly
Meikle Obney
Obney
Waterloo
Bankfoot
Balquharn
Airntully
Cargill
Balholmie
Gallowhill
Redstone
Wolfhill
Saucher
Collace
Kinrossie
Kirkton of Collace
Bandirran
Stanley
Guildtown
Newmiln
Downhill
Luncarty
Moneydie
St Martin's
Colenden
Balbeggie
Trochry
Amulree
Strath Braan
Glen Quaich
Loch Freuchie
Achnafauld
Glen Shee
River Almond
Harrietfield
Buchanty
Glen Almond
Dalcrue
Redgorton
Pitcairngreen
Methven
Almondbank
Scone
Scone Palace
Rait
Kilspindie
Pitroddie
Keillour
Fowlis Wester
Gilmerton
Monzie
Glen Turret
Loch Turret
Hosh
Crieff
Quoig
Comrie
Dalginross
The Ross
West Huntingtower
Huntingtower Castle
Tibbermore
Perth
Bridgend
Kinnoull Tower
Glendoick
Kinfauns
Glencarse
Leetown
St Madoes
Inchyra
Madderty
Welltree
St David's
Clathy
Findo Gask
Clathymore
Aberdalgie
Craigend
Moncreiffe Hill
Rhynd
Fingask
Elcho Castle
Newburgh
Forgandenny
Bridge of Earn
Kintillo
Balloch
Drummond Castle
Muthill
Innerpeffray Library
Kirkton
Trinity Gask
Denfield
Kinkell Bridge
Aberuthven
Baldinnies
Forteviot
St Serf's Church
Dunning
Aberargie
Abernethy
Dron
Glenfoot
Mill of Drummond
Langside
Auchterarder
Muirton
Gleneagles
Blackford
Braco
Greenloaning
Strathallan
Path of Condie
Glenfarg Reservoir
Abbots Deuglie
Glenfarg
Arngask
Balvaird Castle
Auchtermuchty
Newton of Balcanquhal
Pleasance
Dunshalt
Strathmiglo
Gateside
Burnside
Duncrievie
Drunzie
Middleton
Tillyrie
Milnathort
Ochil Hills
Glen Eagles
Glendevon
Burnfoot
Carnbo
Dalqueich
Kinross
Loch Leven
St Serf's Island
Kinnesswood
Scotlandwell
Leslie
Glenrothes
Auchmuirbridge
Kinbuck
Ashfield
Dunblane
Castlehill Reservoir
Yetts o'Muckhart
Pool of Muckhart
Drum
Crook of Devon
Rumbling Bridge
Gairneybridge
Ballingry
Lochore
Kinglassie
Bridge of Allan
Sunnylaw
Tillicoultry
Dollar
Powmill
Cleish
Menstrie
Blairlogie
Alva
Dollarfield
Blairingone
Cleish Hills
Hill End
Tullibody
Devonside
Coalsnaughton
Fishcross
New Sauchie
Kelty
Glencraig
Lochgelly
Cardenden
Auchterderran
Cambuskenneth
Stirling
Cambus
Norwood
Keilarsbrae
Forest Mill
Balgonar
Saline
Steelend
Alloa
Clackmannan
Lumphinnans
Cambusbarron
St Ninians
Fallin
Throsk
South Alloa
Kennet
Bowershall
Kingseat
Hill of Beath
Cowdenbeath
Auchtertool
Bannockburn
Chartershall
Cowie
Dunmore
Comrie
Oakley
Carnock
Gowkhall
Townhill
Wellwood
Milesmark
Halbeath
Crossgates
Donibristle
Auchenbowie
Plean
Airth
Kincardine
Blairhall
High Valleyfield
Newmills
Cairneyhill
Dunfermline
Fordell
Balmule
Letham
Culross
Torryburn
Crossford
Aberdour
Dalgety Bay
Carron Bridge
Skinflats
Crombie
Charlestown
Rosyth
Hillend
Burntisland
Silversands Bay
NN
NS
97
95
89
82
83
0 1 2 3 4 5 miles
0 1 2 3 4 5 6 7 8 kilometres

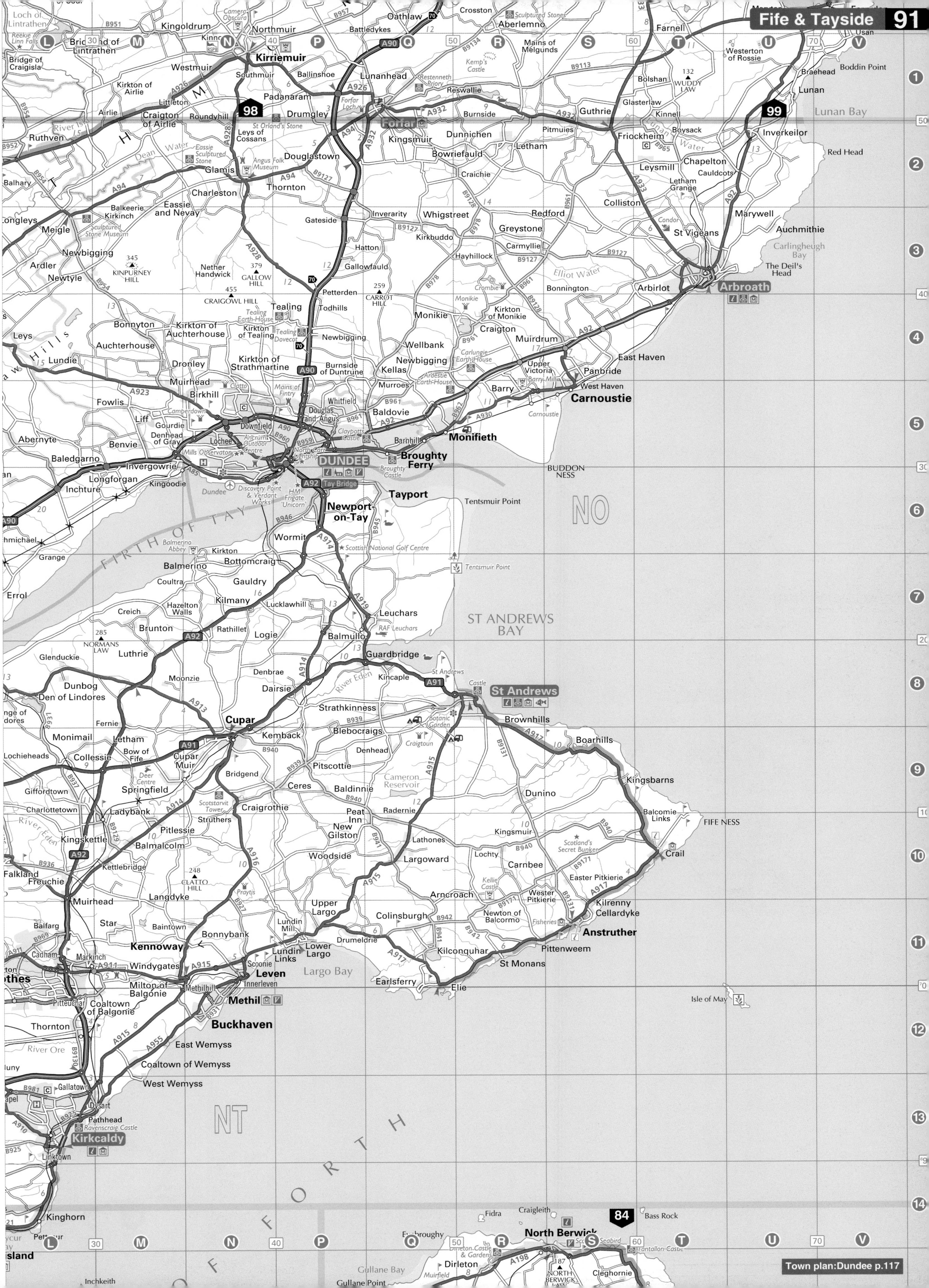
Loch of Lintrathen
Reekie Linn Falls
Bridge of Lintrathen
Bridge of Craigisla
Kingoldrum
Northmuir
Kirriemuir
Westmuir
Southmuir
Kirkton of Airlie
Airlie
Littleton
Craigton of Airlie
Roundyhill
Padanaram
Ballinshoe
Lunanhead
Drumgley
Forfar Loch
Forfar
Oathlaw
Battledykes
Crosston
Sculptured Stones
Aberlemno
Mains of Melgunds
Kemp's Castle
Restenneth Priory
Reswallie
Burnside
Guthrie
Farnell
Westerton of Rossie
Braehead
Boddin Point
Bolshan
132 WUDDY LAW
Lunan
Lunan Bay
Glasterlaw
Kinnell
Friockheim
Boysack
Inverkeilor
Red Head
Chapelton
Cauldcots
Leysmill
Letham Grange
Colliston
Marywell
Auchmithie
Carlingheugh Bay
The Deil's Head
St Vigeans
Condor
Arbroath
Arbirlot
Bonnington
Elliot Water
Ruthven
River Isla
Leys of Cossans
St Orland's Stone
Eassie Sculptured Stone
Glamis
Angus Folk Museum
Douglastown
Kingsmuir
Dunnichen
Bowriefauld
Letham
Pitmuies
Craichie
Balhary
Dean Water
Thornton
Charleston
Eassie and Nevay
Balkeerie
Kirkinch
Sculptured Stone Museum
Meigle
Longleys
Newbigging
Ardler
Newtyle
345 KINPURNEY HILL
Nether Handwick
379 GALLOW HILL
455 CRAIGOWL HILL
Gateside
Inverarity
Whigstreet
Redford
Greystone
Kirkbuddo
Carmyllie
Hatton
Hayhillock
Gallowfauld
Crombie
Petterden
259 CARROT HILL
Monikie
Kirkton of Monikie
Craigton
Muirdrum
Tealing
Tealing Earth-House
Kirkton of Tealing
Tealing Dovecot
Todhills
Bonnyton
Kirkton of Auchterhouse
Auchterhouse
Leys
Lundie
Sidlaw Hills
Newbigging
Wellbank
Newbigging
Kellas
Carlungie Earth-House
Ardestie Earth-House
Dronley
Kirkton of Strathmartine
Burnside of Duntrune
Upper Victoria
Barry Mill
East Haven
Panbride
West Haven
Carnoustie
Barry
Muirhead
Birkhill
Clatto
Mains of Fintry
Murroes
Fowlis
Liff
Camperdown
Whitfield
Douglas and Angus
Baldovie
Gourdie
Denhead of Gray
Downfield
Lochee
Ancrum Outdoor Centre
Claypotts Castle
Barnhill
Monifieth
Abernyte
Benvie
Mills Observatory
North Carr Lightship
DUNDEE
Broughty Ferry
Broughty Castle
BUDDON NESS
Baledgarno
Invergowrie
Longforgan
Kingoodie
Inchture
Dundee
Discovery Point & Verdant Works
HM Frigate 'Unicorn'
Tay Bridge
Tayport
Tentsmuir Point
NO
Newport-on-Tay
Wormit
FIRTH OF TAY
Balmerino Abbey
Kirkton
Scottish National Golf Centre
Tentsmuir Point
Grange
Balmerino
Bottomcraig
Errol
Coultra
Gauldry
Kilmany
Lucklawhill
Leuchars
RAF Leuchars
ST ANDREWS BAY
Creich
Hazelton Walls
Brunton
Rathillet
Logie
Balmullo
285 NORMANS LAW
Luthrie
Glenduckie
Guardbridge
Denbrae
Kincaple
St Andrews
Castle
St Andrews
Dunbog
Den of Lindores
Moonzie
Dairsie
River Eden
Strathkinness
Botanic Garden
Brownhills
Fernie
Cupar
Kemback
Blebocraigs
Craigtoun
Boarhills
Monimail
Letham
Bow of Fife
Cupar Muir
Denhead
Lochieheads
Collessie
Deer Centre
Bridgend
Pitscottie
Cameron Reservoir
Kingsbarns
Giffordtown
Springfield
Ceres
Baldinnie
Dunino
Charlottetown
Ladybank
Scotstarvit Tower
Struthers
Craigrothie
Peat Inn
Radernie
Balcomie Links
FIFE NESS
Kingskettle
Pitlessie
New Gilston
Kingsmuir
Balmalcolm
Lathones
Scotland's Secret Bunker
Falkland
Freuchie
Kettlebridge
Woodside
Largoward
Lochty
Crail
248 CLATTO HILL
Carnbee
Easter Pitkierie
Muirhead
Langdyke
Praytis
Kellie Castle
Arncroach
Wester Pitkierie
Kilrenny
Cellardyke
Balfarg
Star
Upper Largo
Colinsburgh
Newton of Balcormo
Fisheries Museum
Anstruther
Baintown
Lundin Mill
Cadham
Kennoway
Bonnybank
Drumeldrie
Pittenweem
Markinch
Lundin Links
Lower Largo
Kilconquhar
St Monans
Glenrothes
Windygates
Scoonie
Leven
Largo Bay
Milton of Balgonie
Methilhill
Innerleven
Earlsferry
Elie
Isle of May
Pitteuchar
Coaltown of Balgonie
Methil
Thornton
Buckhaven
River Ore
East Wemyss
Coaltown of Wemyss
West Wemyss
Gallatown
Dysart
Pathhead
Ravenscraig Castle
NT
Kirkcaldy
Linktown
FIRTH OF FORTH
Kinghorn
Fidra
Craigleith
Bass Rock
North Berwick
Seabird Centre
Tantallon Castle
Dirleton Castle & Gardens
Dirleton
187 NORTH BERWICK LAW
Gullane Bay
Gullane Point
Muirfield
Cleghornie
Inchkeith
98
99
84
A90 A926 A928 A94 A932 A933 A92 A923 A930 A914 A919 A91 A913 A915 A916 A917 A911 A955 A921 A198 A985
B951 B957 B9134 B9113 B965 B954 B9127 B9128 B961 B978 B962 B959 B960 B946 B945 B939 B940 B9131 B9171 B942 B941 B937 B936 B9129 B927 B969 B931 B930 B981 B925

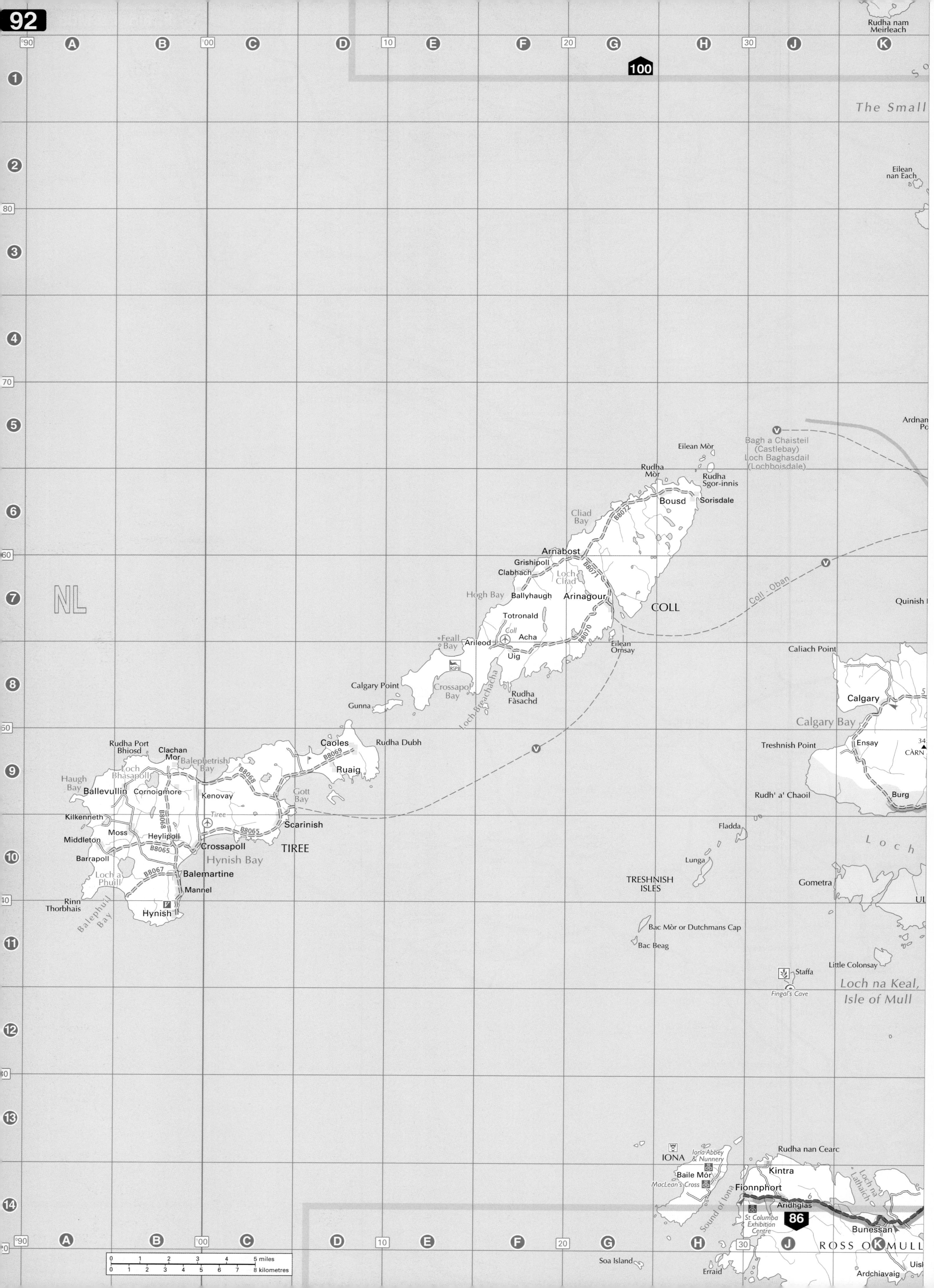

NL

COLL

Rudha nam
Meirleach

The Small

Eilean
nan Each

Ardnan
Po

Bagh a Chaisteil
(Castlebay)
Loch Baghasdail
(Lochboisdale)

Eilean Mòr

Rudha
Mòr

Rudha
Sgor-innis

Sorisdale

Bousd

B8072

Cliad
Bay

Coll – Oban

Arnabost

Grishipoll
Clabhach

Loch
Cliad

B8071

Quinish P

Hogh Bay

Ballyhaugh

Arinagour

Totronald

Coll

Acha

Caliach Point

Feall
Bay

Arileod

Uig

B8070

Eilean
Ornsay

RSPB

Crossapol
Bay

Rudha
Fàsachd

Calgary

Calgary Bay

Calgary Point

Gunna

Loch Breachaidh

Treshnish Point

Ensay

CÀRN

34

5

Rudha Port
Bhiosd

Clachan
Mor

Balephetrish
Bay

Caoles

Rudha Dubh

Rudh' a' Chaoil

Burg

B8069

Haugh
Bay

Loch
Bhasapoll

Ruaig

B8068

Ballevullin

Cornoigmore

Kenovay

Gott
Bay

Fladda

Kilkenneth

Tiree

Lunga

Gometra

Moss

Heylipoll

B8068

Scarinish

Middleton

B8065

Crossapoll

TIREE

TRESHNISH
ISLES

Loch

Barrapoll

B8065

Hynish Bay

Loch a
Phuill

B8067

Balemartine

Mannel

Rinn
Thorbhais

Bac Mòr or Dutchmans Cap

Little Colonsay

Hynish

Balephuil
Bay

Bac Beag

Staffa

Fingal's Cave

Loch na Keal,
Isle of Mull

Rudha nan Cearc

Iona Abbey
& Nunnery

IONA

Baile Mòr

Kintra

MacLean's Cross

Fionnphort

Aridhglas

St Columba
Exhibition
Centre

86

Bunessan

ROSS O**K**MULL

Soa Island

Erraid

Ardchiavaig

Uisl

UL

100

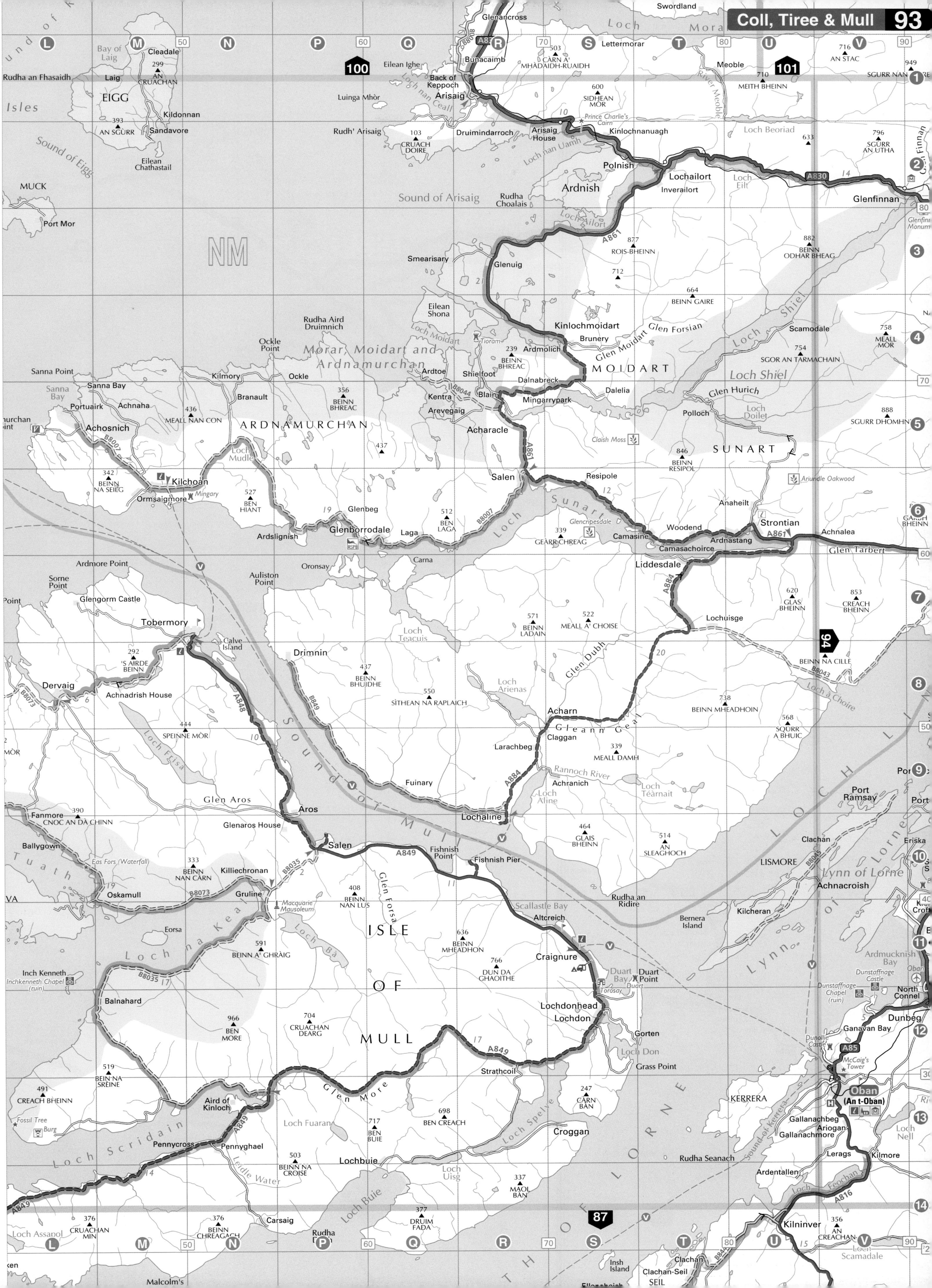
Swordland
Glenancross
Loch Morar
L
M
N
P
Q
R
S
T
U
V
50
60
70
80
90
100
101
Bay of Laig
Cleadale
299 AN CRUACHAN
Rudha an Fhasaidh
Laig
EIGG
Isles
Kildonnan
393 AN SGURR
Sandavore
Sound of Eigg
Eilean Chathastail
MUCK
Port Mor
NM
Eilean Ighe
Bunacaimb
503 CARN A' MHADAIDH-RUAIDH
Lettermorar
Meoble
716 AN STAC
949 SGURR NAN
Back of Keppoch
Arisaig
Loch nan Ceall
Luinga Mhòr
600 SIDHEAN MÒR
River Meoble
710 MEITH BHEINN
Prince Charlie's Cairn
Rudh' Arisaig
103 CRUACH DOIRE
Druimindarroch
Arisaig House
Kinlochnanuagh
Loch Beoriad
633
796 SGURR AN UTHA
Loch nan Uamh
Polnish
Lochailort
A830
Loch Eilt
Ardnish
Inverailort
Glenfinnan
Sound of Arisaig
Rudha Choalais
Loch Ailort
A861
877 ROIS-BHEINN
882 BEINN ODHAR BHEAG
Smearisary
Glenuig
712
664 BEINN GAIRE
Eilean Shona
Rudha Aird Druimnich
Kinlochmoidart
Glen Forsian
Scamodale
758 MEALL MÒR
Loch Moidart
Tioram
Ockle Point
Morar, Moidart and Ardnamurchan
239 BEINN BHREAC
Ardmolich
Brunery
Glen Moidart
Loch Shiel
754 SGOR AN TARMACHAIN
MOIDART
Sanna Point
Kilmory
Ockle
Ardtoe
Shielfoot
Dalnabreck
Loch Shiel
Sanna Bay
Sanna Bay
Branault
356 BEINN BHREAC
Kentra
Blain
B8044
Dalelia
Glen Hurich
Portuairk
Achnaha
Arevegaig
Mingarrypark
Loch Doilet
Polloch
888 SGURR DHOMHNUILL
436 MEALL NAN CON
ARDNAMURCHAN
Acharacle
Achosnich
B8007
437
Claish Moss
846 BEINN RESIPOL
SUNART
Loch Mudle
Ariundle Oakwood
342 BEINN NA SEILG
Kilchoan
Mingary
Ormsaigmore
527 BEN HIANT
Salen
Resipole
Loch Sunart
19
Glenbeg
512 BEN LAGA
B8007
Anaheilt
Strontian
Ardslignish
Glenborrodale
RSPB
Laga
Loch
339 GEARR CHREAG
Glencripesdale
Camasine
Woodend
Ardnastang
A861
Achnalea
Camasachoirce
Glen Tarbert
Ardmore Point
Carna
Oronsay
Auliston Point
Liddesdale
A884
Sorne Point
Glengorm Castle
620 GLAS BHEINN
853 CREACH BHEINN
Tobermory
571 BEINN LADAIN
522 MEALL A' CHOISE
Lochuisge
Calve Island
Loch Teacuis
94
Drimnin
292 'S AIRDE BEINN
Glen Dubh
20
BEINN NA CILLE
B8043
Dervaig
Achnadrish House
437 BEINN BHUIDHE
Loch Arienas
Loch a' Choire
B8073
A848
B849
550 SÌTHEAN NA RAPLAICH
Acharn
738 BEINN MHEADHOIN
Gleann Geal
Claggan
444 SPEINNE MÒR
Loch Frisa
Larachbeg
339 MEALL DAMH
568 SGURR A' BHUIC
Sound of Mull
Rannoch River
Achranich
Fuinary
A884
Loch Aline
Loch Tèarnait
Port Ramsay
Glen Aros
Fanmore
390 CNOC AN DÀ CHINN
Aros
Lochaline
Glenaros House
464 GLAIS BHEINN
514 AN SLEAGHOCH
Clachan
Ballygown
Salen
Fishnish Point
Fishnish Pier
A849
LISMORE
Eas Fors (Waterfall)
333 BEINN NAN CARN
Killiechronan
B8035
Lynn of Lorne
Achnacroish
Oskamull
B8073
Gruline
408 BEINN NAN LUS
Glen Forsa
Rudha an Ridire
Scallastle Bay
Macquarie Mausoleum
Altcreich
Kilcheran
Bernera Island
Eorsa
ISLE
636 BEINN MHEADHON
Loch na Keal
Loch Bà
591 BEINN A' GHRÀIG
Craignure
Ardmucknish Bay
766 DÙN DA GHAOITHE
Inch Kenneth
Inchkenneth Chapel (ruin)
OF
Duart Bay
Duart Point
Dunstaffnage Castle
B8035
Balnahard
Torosay
Duart
Dunstaffnage Chapel (ruin)
North Connel
Lynn of Lorne
Lochdonhead
Lochdon
966 BEN MORE
704 CRUACHAN DEARG
MULL
Dunbeg
Ganavan Bay
Gorten
Loch Don
A849
Dunollie Castle
A85
519 BEINN NA SREINE
Grass Point
Strathcoil
McCaig's Tower
Oban (An t-Oban)
Glen More
491 CREACH BHEINN
247 CARN BAN
KERRERA
Aird of Kinloch
Fossil Tree
Burg
698 BEN CREACH
Gallanachbeg
Ariogan
Gallanachmore
Loch Nell
Loch Fuaran
717 BEN BUIE
Loch Spelve
Croggan
Sound of Kerrera
Loch Scridain
A849
Pennycross
Pennyghael
Leidle Water
503 BEINN NA CROISE
Lochbuie
Loch Uisg
Rudha Seanach
Lerags
Kilmore
Ardentallen
Loch Feochan
337 MAOL BAN
A816
376 CRUACHAN MIN
376 BEINN CHREAGACH
Carsaig
Loch Buie
377 DRUIM FADA
87
Kilninver
356 AN CREACHAN
Loch Assapol
Rudha
Loch Scamadale
THE FIRTH OF LORNE
Insh Island
Clachan
Clachan-Seil
SEIL
B844
Malcolm's
1
2
3
4
5
6
7
8
9
10
11
12
13
14

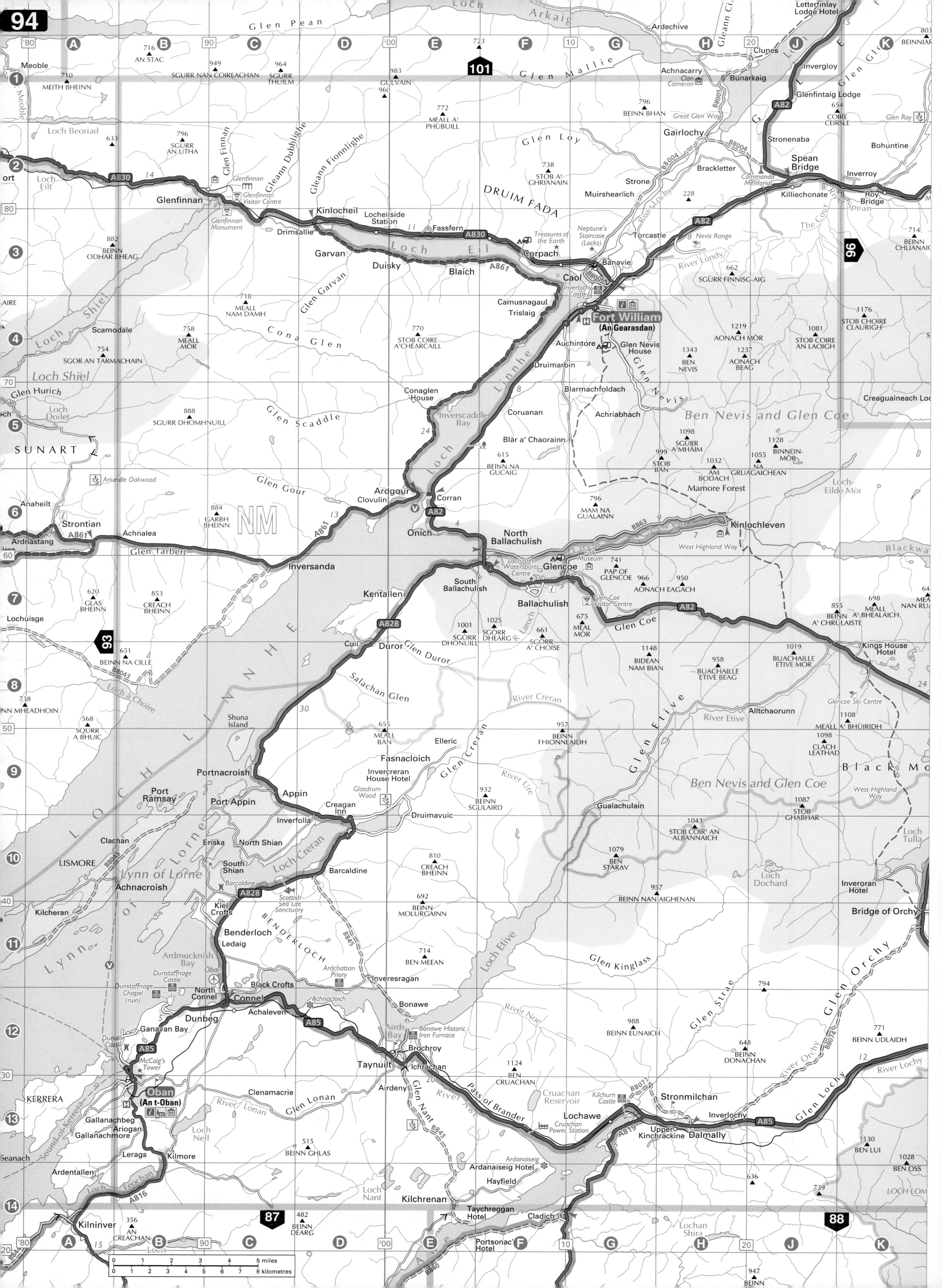
Glen Pean
Loch Arkaig
Letterfinlay Lodge Hotel
Ardechive
Meoble
AN STAC
SGURR NAN COIREACHAN
SGURR THUILM
GULVAIN
101
Glen Mallie
Achnacarry
Clan Cameron
Clunes
Bunarkaig
Invergloy
Glenfintaig Lodge
COIRE CEIRSLE
Glen Roy
MEITH BHEINN
Loch Beoriad
SGURR AN UTHA
MEALL A' PHUBUILL
BEINN BHAN
Great Glen Way
Gairlochy
Stronenaba
Bohuntine
Glen Finnan
Gleann Dubhlighe
Gleann Fionnlighe
Glen Loy
STOB A' GHRIANAIN
Brackletter
Spean Bridge
Inverroy
Loch Eilt
A830
Glenfinnan
Glenfinnan Visitor Centre
Glenfinnan Monument
DRUIM FADA
Strone
Muirshearlich
Commando Memorial
Killiechonate
Roy Bridge
River Spean
Kinlocheil
Locheilside Station
Fassfern
Drimsallie
BEINN ODHAR BHEAG
Treasures of the Earth
Neptune's Staircase (Locks)
Torcastle
Nevis Range
The Cour
BEINN CHLIANAIG
96
Garvan
Duisky
Blaich
Loch Eil
A861
Corpach
Banavie
Caol
River Lundy
SGÙRR FINNISG-AIG
Inverlochy Castle
Loch Shiel
Scamodale
MEALL NAM DAMH
Glen Garvan
Camusnagaul
Trislaig
Fort William
(An Gearasdan)
STOB CHOIRE CLAURIGH
SGOR AN TARMACHAIN
MEALL MÒR
Cona Glen
STOB COIRE A'CHEARCAILL
Auchintore
Glen Nevis House
AONACH MÒR
STOB COIRE AN LAOIGH
BEN NEVIS
AONACH BEAG
Druimarbin
Glen Hurich
Loch Doilet
SGURR DHOMHNUILL
Glen Scaddle
Conaglen House
Inverscaddle Bay
Loch Linnhe
Blarmachfoldach
Glen Nevis
Creaguaineach Lodge
Coruanan
Achriabhach
Ben Nevis and Glen Coe
SUNART
Blàr a' Chaorainn
SGURR A' MHAIM
BINNEIN MÒR
STOB BAN
AM BODACH
GRUAGAICHEAN
BEINN NA GUCAIG
Mamore Forest
Loch Eilde Mòr
Ariundle Oakwood
Glen Gour
Ardgour
Clovulin
Corran
A82
Anaheilt
Strontian
GARBH BHEINN
NM
Onich
MAM NA GUALAINN
Kinlochleven
North Ballachulish
Ardnastang
Achnalea
Glen Tarbert
Inversanda
Lochaber Watersports Centre
Glencoe
Glencoe Folk Museum
PAP OF GLENCOE
AONACH EAGACH
West Highland Way
Blackwater
GLAS BHEINN
CREACH BHEINN
Kentallen
South Ballachulish
Ballachulish
Glen Coe Visitor Centre
MEALL A' BHEALAICH
BEINN A' CHRULAISTE
Lochuisge
93
A828
SGORR DHONUILL
SGORR DHEARG
SGORR A' CHOISE
MEAL MÒR
Glen Coe
Kings House Hotel
BEINN NA CILLE
Cuil
Duror
Glen Duror
BIDEAN NAM BIAN
BUACHAILLE ETIVE BEAG
BUACHAILLE ETIVE MOR
Loch a' Choire
SGURR MHEADHOIN
Salachan Glen
River Creran
Glencoe Ski Centre
SGURR A BHUIC
Shuna Island
MEALL BAN
Elleric
BEINN FHIONNLAIDH
Glen Etive
River Etive
Alltchaorunn
MEALL A' BHÙIRIDH
CLACH LEATHAD
Fasnacloich
Glen Creran
Portnacroish
LOCH LINNHE
Invercreran House Hotel
Glasdrum Wood
River Ure
Black Mount
Port Ramsay
Port Appin
Appin
Creagan Inn
BEINN SGULAIRD
Druimavuic
Gualachulain
West Highland Way
STOB GHABHAR
Inverfolla
Clachan
Eriska
North Shian
STOB COIR' AN ALBANNAICH
Loch Tulla
Lynn of Lorne
LISMORE
South Shian
Loch Creran
Barcaldine
CREACH BHEINN
BEN STARAV
Loch Dochard
Achnacroish
Barcaldine Castle
Scottish Sea Life Sanctuary
BEINN NAN AIGHENAN
Inveroran Hotel
Kilcheran
Kiel Crofts
BEINN MOLURGAINN
BENDERLOCH
Bridge of Orchy
Benderloch
Ledaig
B845
Loch Etive
Glen Kinglass
Glen Orchy
Ardmucknish Bay
Dunstaffnage Castle
Oban
Ardchattan Priory
BEN MEEAN
Dunstaffnage Chapel (ruin)
Black Crofts
Inveresragan
Glen Strae
North Connel
Connel
Achnacloich
Bonawe
Dunbeg
Achaleven
A85
River Noe
BEINN EUNAICH
BEINN UDLAIDH
Ganavan Bay
Dunollie Castle
Airds Bay
Bonawe Historic Iron Furnace
Brochroy
BEINN DONACHAN
McCaig's Tower
Taynuilt
Ichrachan
BEN CRUACHAN
River Orchy
River Lochy
Pass of Brander
Cruachan Reservoir
Kilchurn Castle
B8077
B8074
Oban
(An t-Oban)
KERRERA
Clenamacrie
Airdeny
River Awe
River Lonan
Glen Lonan
Glen Nant
Stronmilchan
Lochawe
Inverlochy
Glen Lochy
Gallanachbeg
Ariogan
Gallanachmore
Loch Nell
Cruachan Power Station
A819
Upper Kinchrackine
Dalmally
Sound of Kerrera
BEN LUI
BEINN GHLAS
Lerags
Kilmore
Ardanaiseig
Ardanaiseig Hotel
BEN OSS
Seanach
Ardentallen
Loch Feochan
Hayfield
LOCH LOMOND
A816
Loch Nant
Kilchrenan
Taychreggan Hotel
Kilninver
AN CREACHAN
87
BEINN DEARG
Cladich
Lochan Shira
88
Portsonachan Hotel
Loch Awe
B840
BEINN
0 1 2 3 4 5 miles
0 1 2 3 4 5 6 7 8 kilometres

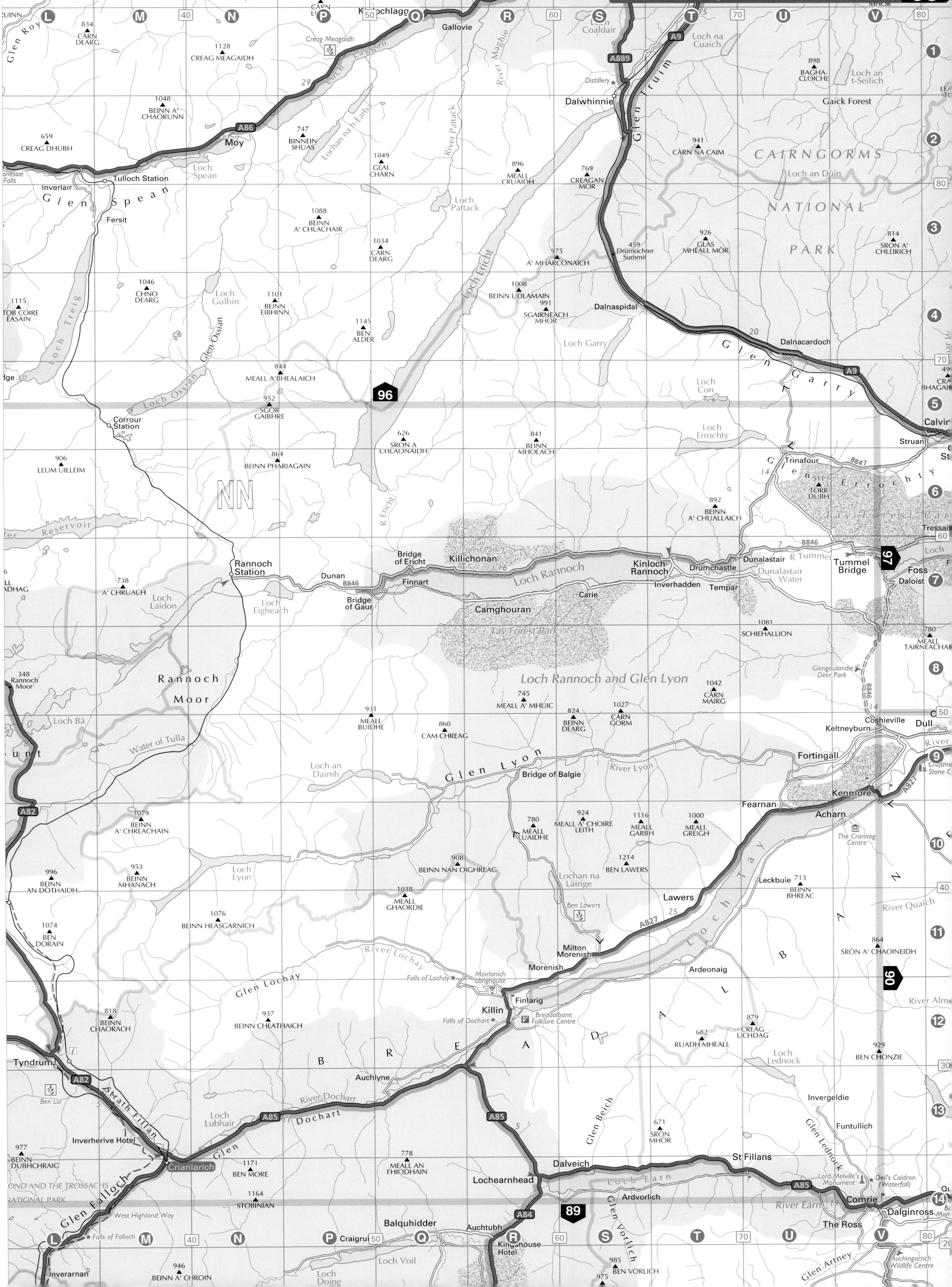
Brae Roy Lodge
Glen Roy
834 CARN DEARG
1128 CREAG MEAGAIDH
1005 CARN LIATH
Kinlochlaggan
Creag Meagaidh
Loch Laggan
Gallovie
River Mashie
Strathmashie House
BLACK CRAIG
Loch Coaldair
Loch na Cuaich
A9
A889
Distillery
Dalwhinnie
Glen Truim
898 BAGHA-CLOICHE
Loch an t-Seilich
Gaick Forest
1048 BEINN A' CHAORUNN
A86
747 BINNEIN SHUAS
Lochan na h-Earba
River Pattack
659 CREAG DHUBH
Moy
1049 GEAL CHARN
Loch Spean
Tulloch Station
Inverlair
Glen Spean
Fersit
896 MEALL CRUAIDH
769 CREAGAN MOR
941 CÀRN NA CAIM
CAIRNGORMS NATIONAL PARK
Loch an Dùin
Loch Pattack
1088 BEINN A' CHLACHAIR
1034 CARN DEARG
975 A' MHARCONAICH
459 Drumochter Summit
926 GLAS MHEALL MÒR
814 SRON A' CHLEIRICH
Loch Ericht
1046 CHNO DEARG
Loch Gulbin
1101 BEINN EIBHINN
1008 BEINN UDLAMAIN
991 SGAIRNEACH MHOR
Dalnaspidal
1115 STOB COIRE EASAIN
Loch Treig
Glen Ossian
1145 BEN ALDER
Loch Garry
Dalnacardoch
Glen Garry
844 MEALL A'BHEALAICH
Loch Ossian
96
Loch Con
952 SGOR GAIBHRE
Corrour Station
626 SRON A CHLAONAIDH
841 BEINN MHOLACH
Loch Errochty
Calvine
Struan
906 LEUM UILLEIM
864 BEINN PHARIAGAIN
Trinafour
B847
Glen Errochty
511 TORR DUBH
NN
R Ericht
892 BEINN A' CHUALLAICH
Tay Forest Park
Tressait
Reservoir
Rannoch Station
Bridge of Ericht
Killichonan
Loch Rannoch
Kinloch Rannoch
Drumchastle
Dunalastair
B846
R Tummel
Tummel Bridge
97
Foss
Dunan
Finnart
Carie
Inverhadden
Tempar
Dunalastair Water
Daloist
738 A' CHRUACH
Loch Laidon
Loch Eigheach
Bridge of Gaur
Camghouran
1081 SCHIEHALLION
780 MEALL TAIRNEACHAN
348 Rannoch Moor
Rannoch Moor
Loch Rannoch and Glen Lyon
Glengoulandie Deer Park
745 MEALL A' MHUIC
1042 CARN MAIRG
931 MEALL BUIDHE
860 CAM CHREAG
824 BEINN DEARG
1027 CARN GORM
Coshieville
Keltneyburn
Dull
Loch Bà
Water of Tulla
Glen Lyon
River Lyon
Bridge of Balgie
Fortingall
Loch an Daimh
Fearnan
Kenmore
A827
Croftmoraig Stone Circle
A82
1079 BEINN A' CHREACHAIN
780 MEALL LUAIDHE
924 MEALL A' CHOIRE LEITH
1116 MEALL GARBH
1000 MEALL GREIGH
Acharn
The Crannog Centre
996 BEINN AN DOTHAIDH
953 BEINN MHANACH
Loch Lyon
908 BEINN NAN OIGHREAG
1214 BEN LAWERS
Lochan na Làirige
Leckbuie
713 BEINN BHREAC
1038 MEALL GHAORDIE
Lawers
Loch Tay
River Quaich
1074 BEN DORAIN
1076 BEINN HEASGARNICH
Ben Lawers
864 SRÒN A' CHAOINEIDH
River Lochay
Milton Morenish
Morenish
Glen Lochay
Falls of Lochay
Moirlanich Longhouse
Ardeonaig
90
BREADALBANE
River Almond
818 BEINN CHAORACH
937 BEINN CHEATHAICH
Killin
Finlarig
Breadalbane Folklore Centre
Falls of Dochart
879 CREAG UCHDAG
682 RUADH MHEALL
929 BEN CHONZIE
Loch Lednock
Tyndrum
Auchlyne
River Dochart
Ben Lui
Strath Fillan
Loch Lubhair
A85
Glen Dochart
Glen Beich
671 SRÒN MHOR
Invergeldie
Funtullich
Inverherive Hotel
Glen Lednock
977 BEINN DUBHCHRAIG
Crianlarich
1171 BEN MORE
778 MEALL AN FHIODHAIN
Dalveich
St Fillans
Lochearnhead
Loch Earn
Lord Melville's Monument
Deil's Caldron (Waterfall)
LOMOND AND THE TROSSACHS NATIONAL PARK
1164 STOBINIAN
Ardvorlich
Glen Vorlich
River Earn
Comrie
Dalginross
89
Glen Falloch
West Highland Way
Balquhidder
Auchtubh
A84
The Ross
Falls of Falloch
Craigruie
Kingshouse Hotel
Loch Voil
Loch Doine
985 BEN VORLICH
975
Glen Artney
Auchingarrich Wildlife Centre
Inverarnan
946 BEINN A' CHROIN
L M N P Q R S T U V
40 50 60 70 80
1 2 3 4 5 6 7 8 9 10 11 12 13 14

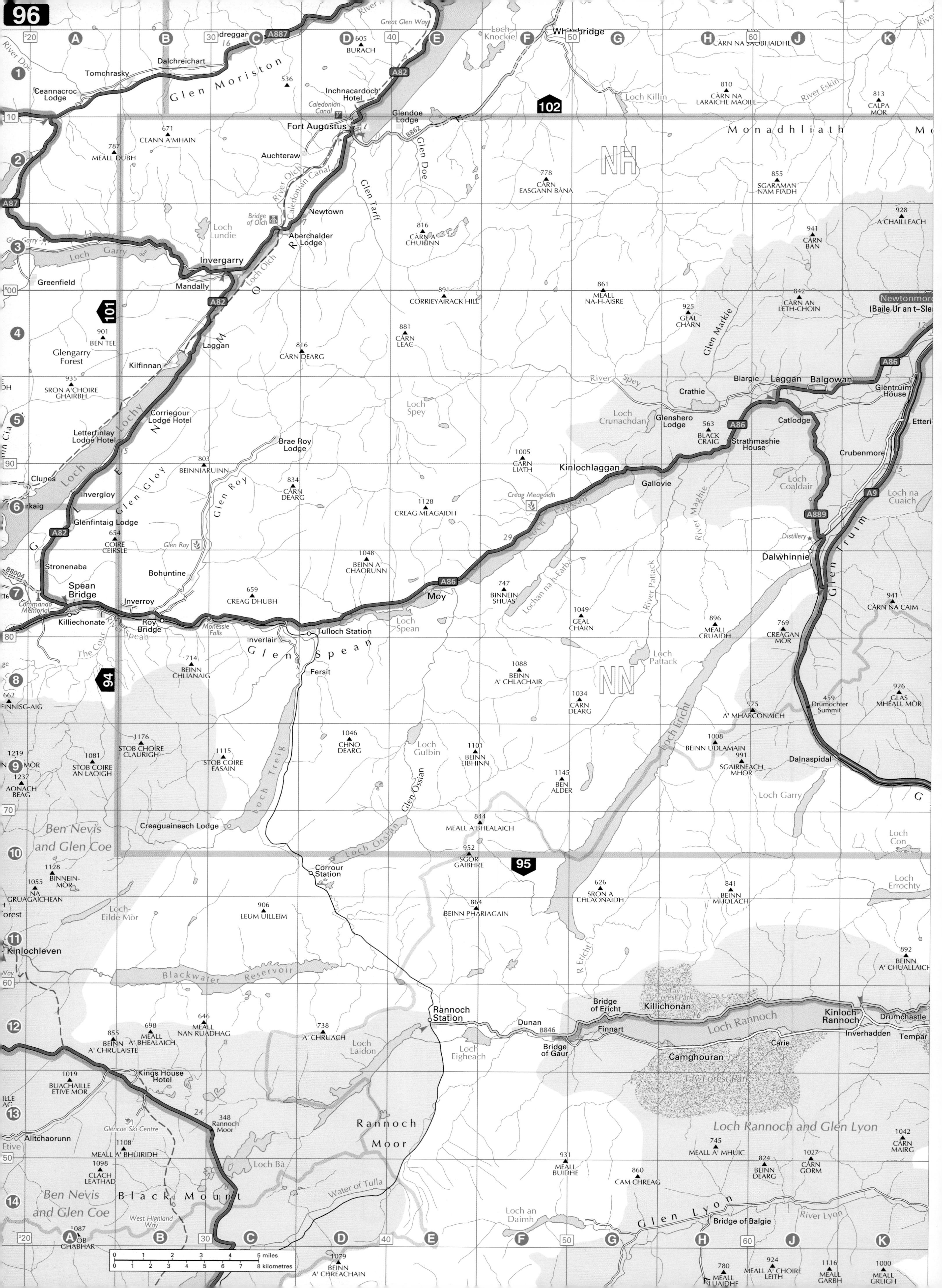
Whitebridge
Loch Knockie
Great Glen Way
605 BURACH
Dalchreichart
Tomchrasky
Ceannacroc Lodge
Glen Moriston
536
Inchnacardoch Hotel
Caledonian Canal
Fort Augustus
Glendoe Lodge
Loch Killin
River Eskin
810 CÀRN NA LARAICHE MAOILE
813 CALPA MÒR
102
Monadhliath
671 CEANN A' MHAIN
787 MEALL DUBH
Auchteraw
Glen Doe
Glen Tarff
River Oich
778 CARN EASGANN BÀNA
855 SGARAMAN NAM FIADH
NH
Newtown
Bridge of Oich
Loch Lundie
Aberchalder Lodge
816 CÀRN A' CHUILINN
928 A' CHAILLEACH
941 CÀRN BÀN
Loch Garry
Invergarry
Loch Oich
Greenfield
Mandally
891 CORRIEYAIRACK HILL
861 MEALL NA-H-AISRE
842 CÀRN AN LETH-CHOIN
925 GEAL CHÀRN
Newtonmore (Baile Ùr an t-Slèibh)
101
901 BEN TEE
Glengarry Forest
Laggan
Kilfinnan
881 CÀRN LEAC
816 CÀRN DEARG
Glen Markie
River Spey
Blargie
Laggan
Balgowan
Crathie
Glentruim House
935 SRON A' CHOIRE GHAIRBH
Loch Spey
Loch Crunachdan
Glenshero Lodge
563 BLACK CRAIG
Strathmashie House
Catlodge
Corriegour Lodge Hotel
Letterfinlay Lodge Hotel
Brae Roy Lodge
803 BEINNIARUINN
834 CÀRN DEARG
1005 CÀRN LIATH
Kinlochlaggan
Gallovie
Crubenmore
Loch Coaldair
Loch na Cuaich
Clunes
Loch Lochy
Invergloy
Glen Gloy
Glen Roy
1128 CREAG MEAGAIDH
Creag Meagaidh
Loch Laggan
River Maghie
A889
Distillery
Glenfintaig Lodge
654 COIRE CEIRSLE
Glen Roy
1048 BEINN A' CHAORUNN
Dalwhinnie
Glen Truim
Stronenaba
Spean Bridge
Commando Memorial
Bohuntine
659 CREAG DHUBH
Moy
747 BINNEIN SHUAS
Lochan na h-Earba
River Pattack
1049 GEAL CHÀRN
896 MEALL CRUAIDH
769 CREAGAN MÒR
941 CÀRN NA CAIM
Inverroy
Killiechonate
Roy Bridge
Monessie Falls
River Spean
Inverlair
Tulloch Station
Loch Spean
Glen Spean
The Cour
94
714 BEINN CHLIANAIG
Fersit
1088 BEINN A' CHLACHAIR
Loch Pattack
NN
1034 CÀRN DEARG
975 A' MHARCONAICH
459 Drumochter Summit
926 GLAS MHEALL MÒR
662 FINNISG-AIG
1176 STOB CHOIRE CLAURIGH
1081 STOB COIRE AN LAOIGH
1115 STOB COIRE EASAIN
1046 CHNO DEARG
Loch Gulbin
1101 BEINN EIBHINN
Loch Ericht
1008 BEINN UDLAMAIN
991 SGAIRNEACH MHOR
Dalnaspidal
1219
1237 AONACH BEAG
Loch Treig
Glen Ossian
1145 BEN ALDER
Loch Garry
Creaguaineach Lodge
844 MEALL A' BHEALAICH
Ben Nevis and Glen Coe
Loch Ossian
952 SGOR GAIBHRE
95
Corrour Station
Loch Con
1128 BINNEIN MÒR
1055 NA GRUAGAICHEAN
626 SRON A' CHLAONAIDH
841 BEINN MHOLACH
Loch Errochty
Loch Eilde Mòr
906 LEUM UILLEIM
864 BEINN PHARIAGAIN
Kinlochleven
R Ericht
892 BEINN A' CHUALLAICH
Blackwater Reservoir
Tay Forest Park
Rannoch Station
Bridge of Ericht
Killichonan
Kinloch Rannoch
Drumchastle
855 BEINN A' CHRULAISTE
698 MEALL A' BHEALAICH
646 MEALL NAN RUADHAG
738 A' CHRUACH
Loch Laidon
Dunan
B846
Finnart
Loch Rannoch
Inverhadden
Tempar
Loch Eigheach
Bridge of Gaur
Carie
Camghouran
Tay Forest Park
1019 BUACHAILLE ETIVE MÒR
Kings House Hotel
Glencoe Ski Centre
348 Rannoch Moor
Rannoch Moor
Loch Rannoch and Glen Lyon
Alltchaorunn
1108 MEALL A' BHÙIRIDH
745 MEALL A' MHUIC
1042 CÀRN MAIRG
931 MEALL BUIDHE
824 BEINN DEARG
1027 CÀRN GORM
1098 CLACH LEATHAD
Loch Bà
860 CAM CHREAG
Ben Nevis and Glen Coe
Black Mount
Water of Tulla
West Highland Way
Loch an Daimh
Glen Lyon
Bridge of Balgie
River Lyon
1087 STOB GHABHAR
1079 BEINN A' CHREACHAIN
780 MEALL LUAIDHE
924 MEALL A' CHOIRE LEITH
1116 MEALL GARBH
1000 MEALL GREIGH
0 1 2 3 4 5 miles
0 1 2 3 4 5 6 7 8 kilometres
A87
A887
A82
B862
A86
A9
A889
B8004
B846

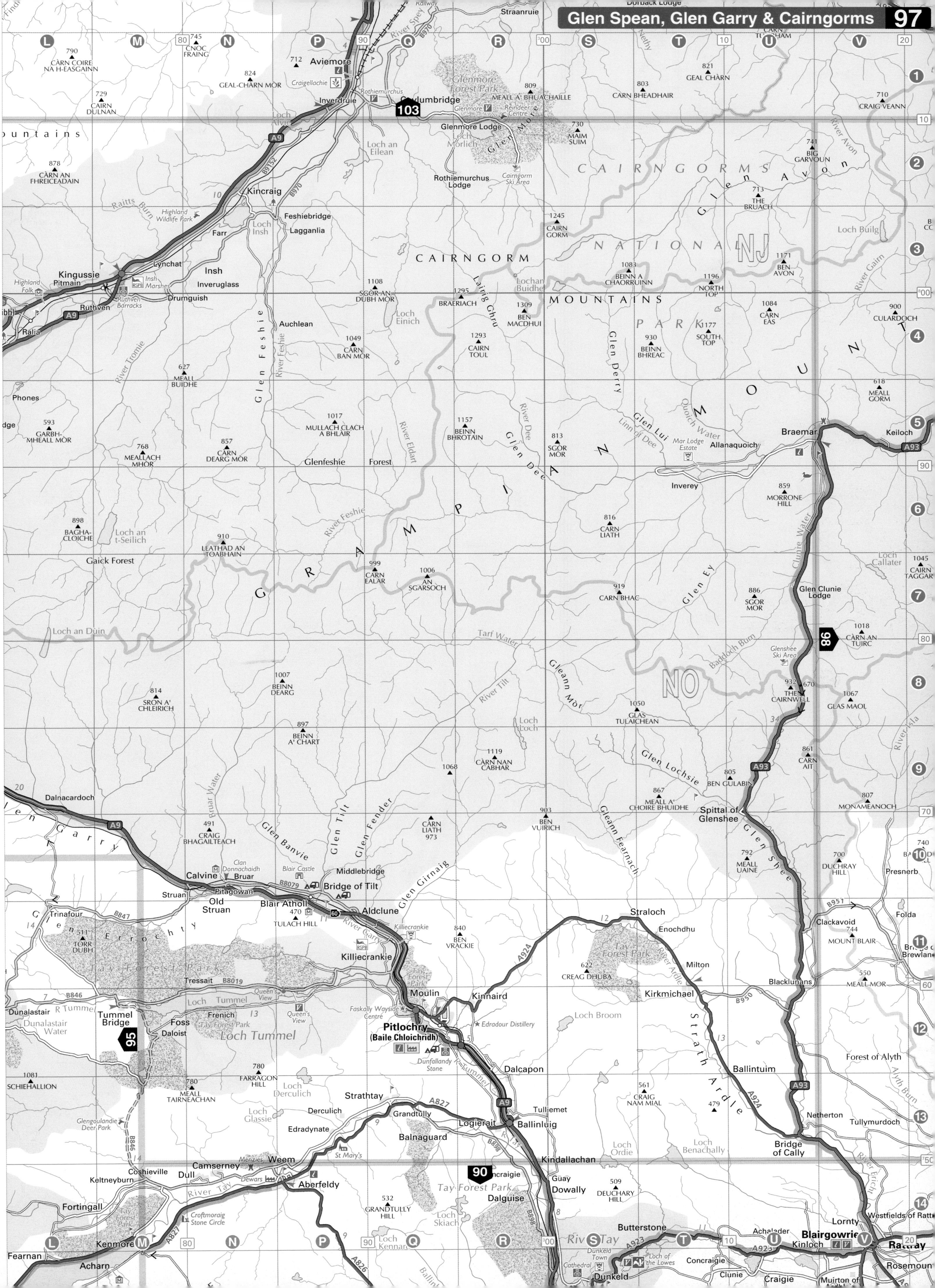
Aviemore
Craigellachie
Rothiemurchus
Coylumbridge
Inverdruie
Loch Alvie
Glenmore Forest Park
Glenmore
Reindeer Centre
Glenmore Lodge
Loch Morlich
Glen More
Loch an Eilean
Rothiemurchus Lodge
Cairngorm Ski Area
103
Straanruie
River Spey
River Nethy
Dorback Lodge
712
824
GEAL-CHARN MOR
790
CARN COIRE NA H-EASGAINN
745
CNOC FRAING
729
CAIRN DULNAN
809
MEALL A' BHUACHAILLE
730
MAIM SUIM
803
CARN BHEADHAIR
821
GEAL CHARN
710
CRAIG VEANN
CARN TUTHAM
741
BIG GARVOUN
713
THE BRUACH
River Avon
Glen Avon
Loch Builg
878
CARN AN FHREICEADAIN
Kincraig
Highland Wildlife Park
Raitts Burn
Feshiebridge
Loch Insh
Lagganlia
Farr
Lynchat
Insh
Inveruglass
Kingussie
Pitmain
Highland Folk
Insh Marshes
Ruthven Barracks
Ruthven
Drumguish
Ralia
A9
B9152
B970
CAIRNGORMS
CAIRNGORM MOUNTAINS
NATIONAL PARK
NJ
1245
CAIRN GORM
1083
BEINN A CHAORRUINN
1171
BEN AVON
1196
NORTH TOP
1177
SOUTH TOP
1084
CARN EAS
900
CULARDOCH
River Gairn
1108
SGOR AN DUBH MOR
Loch Einich
1295
BRAERIACH
Lairig Ghru
Lochan Buidhe
1309
BEN MACDHUI
1293
CAIRN TOUL
930
BEINN BHREAC
Glen Derry
Auchlean
Glen Feshie
River Feshie
1049
CARN BAN MOR
627
MEALL BUIDHE
River Tromie
Phones
593
GARBH-MHEALL MOR
768
MEALLACH MHOR
857
CARN DEARG MOR
1017
MULLACH CLACH A BHLAIR
Glenfeshie Forest
River Eidart
1157
BEINN BHROTAIN
River Dee
Glen Dee
813
SGOR MOR
Glen Lui
Linn of Dee
Quoich Water
Mar Lodge Estate
Allanaquoich
Braemar
Keiloch
A93
Inverey
859
MORRONE HILL
618
MEALL GORM
GRAMPIAN MOUNTAINS
898
BAGHA-CLOICHE
Loch an t-Seilich
910
LEATHAD AN TOABHAIN
Gaick Forest
816
CARN LIATH
999
CARN EALAR
1006
AN SGARSOCH
919
CARN BHAC
Glen Ey
886
SGOR MOR
Clunie Water
Glen Clunie Lodge
Loch Callater
1045
CAIRN TAGGAR
Loch an Duin
Tarf Water
Baddoch Burn
Glenshee Ski Area
1018
CARN AN TUIRC
98
NO
814
SRON A' CHLEIRICH
1007
BEINN DEARG
River Tilt
Gleann Mor
932
THE CAIRNWELL
670
1067
GLAS MAOL
1050
GLAS TULAICHEAN
Loch Loch
897
BEINN A' CHART
1119
CARN NAN CABHAR
Glen Lochsie
805
BEN GULABIN
861
CARN AIT
River Isla
1068
Dalnacardoch
Bruar Water
Glen Tilt
Glen Fender
867
MEALL A' CHOIRE BHUIDHE
903
BEN VUIRICH
Gleann Fearnach
Spittal of Glenshee
807
MONAMEANOCH
Glen Garry
491
CRAIG BHAGAILTEACH
Glen Banvie
973
CARN LIATH
Glen Shee
792
MEALL UAINE
700
DUCHRAY HILL
740
Presnerb
Clan Donnachaidh
Blair Castle
Calvine
Bruar
Middlebridge
Bridge of Tilt
Glen Girnaig
Struan
Pitagowan
Old Struan
B8079
Blair Atholl
470
TULACH HILL
Aldclune
River Garry
Trinafour
B847
Glen Errochty
511
TORR DUBH
Killiecrankie
840
BEN VRACKIE
Straloch
Enochdhu
Clackavoid
744
MOUNT BLAIR
B951
Folda
Bridge of Brewlands
Tay Forest Park
A924
622
CREAG DHUBA
River Ardle
Milton
Blacklunans
550
MEALL MOR
Tressait
B8019
Loch Tummel
Queen's View
Moulin
Kinnaird
Kirkmichael
B950
B846
Dunalastair
Dunalastair Water
River Tummel
Tummel Bridge
Foss
Daloist
Frenich
95
Faskally Wayside Centre
Pitlochry
(Baile Chloichridh)
Edradour Distillery
Loch Broom
Strath Ardle
Forest of Alyth
Dunfallandy Stone
Dalcapon
Ballintuim
Alyth Burn
1081
SCHIEHALLION
780
FARRAGON HILL
Loch Derculich
780
MEALL TAIRNEACHAN
Strathtay
561
CRAIG NAM MIAL
479
A93
Glengoulandie Deer Park
Loch Glassie
Derculich
Edradynate
Grandtully
A827
Logierait
Tulliemet
Ballinluig
Netherton
Tullymurdoch
Balnaguard
B898
Loch Ordie
Loch Benachally
Bridge of Cally
River Ericht
St Mary's
Menzies
Weem
Camserney
Coshieville
Dull
Keltneyburn
Kindallachan
90
Craigie
Guay
Dowally
509
DEUCHARY HILL
Dewars
River Tay
Aberfeldy
532
GRANDTULLY HILL
Loch Skiach
Dalguise
Fortingall
Croftmoraig Stone Circle
Loch Kennard
Kenmore
A827
A826
Fearnan
Acharn
Butterstone
Achalader
Lornty
Westfields of Rattray
Blairgowrie
Rattray
Kinloch
A923
Dunkeld Town
Loch of the Lowes
Cathedral
Dunkeld
Concraigie
Clunie
Craigie
Muirton of Ardblair
Rosemount

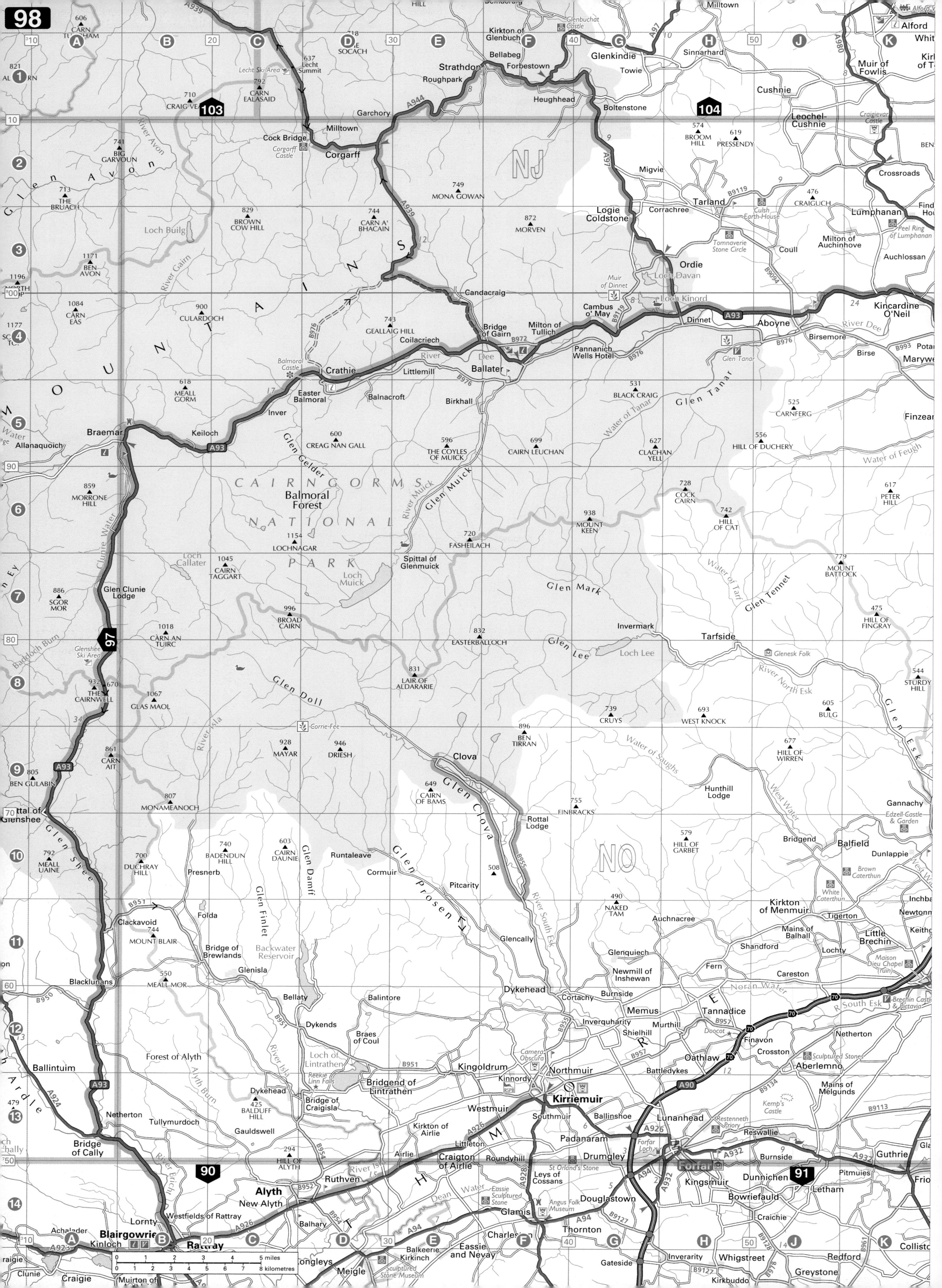
A939
606 CARN TULACHAM
718 DE SOCACH
637 Lecht Summit
Lecht Ski Area
792 CARN EALASAID
710 CRAIG VEAN
103
Kirkton of Glenbuchat
Glenbuchat Castle
Milltown
Alford
Glenkindie
Sinnarhard
Muir of Fowlis
Strathdon
Bellabeg
Forbestown
Towie
Roughpark
Cushnie
Heughhead
Boltenstone
104
Leochel-Cushnie
Craigievar Castle
Garchory
A944
Milltown
Cock Bridge
Corgarff Castle
Corgarff
741 BIG GARVOUN
574 BROOM HILL
619 PRESSENDY
NJ
Migvie
Crossroads
Glen Avon
River Avon
713 THE BRUACH
749 MONA GOWAN
829 BROWN COW HILL
744 CARN A' BHACAIN
872 MORVEN
Logie Coldstone
Corrachree
Tarland
B9119
Culsh Earth-House
476 CRAIGUCH
Lumphanan
Peel Ring of Lumphanan
Loch Builg
Tomnaverie Stone Circle
Milton of Auchinhove
Coull
1171 BEN AVON
River Gairn
Ordie
Loch Davan
Auchlossan
Muir of Dinnet
1196 NORTH TOP
Candacraig
Loch Kinord
Kincardine O'Neil
1084 CARN EAS
900 CULARDOCH
Cambus o' May
Dinnet
A93
1177
B976
743 GEALLAIG HILL
Coilacriech
Bridge of Gairn
Milton of Tullich
Aboyne
River Dee
Birsemore
B972
Pannanich Wells Hotel
Birse
Balmoral Castle
Crathie
Littlemill
Ballater
Glen Tanar
Marywell
M O U N T A I N S
618 MEALL GORM
Easter Balmoral
Balnacroft
531 BLACK CRAIG
525 CARNFERG
Inver
Birkhall
Glen Tanar
Water of Tanar
Braemar
Keiloch
Finzean
Allanaquoich
Glen Gelder
600 CREAG NAN GALL
596 THE COYLES OF MUICK
699 CAIRN LEUCHAN
627 CLACHAN YELL
556 HILL OF DUCHERY
Water of Feugh
CAIRNGORMS NATIONAL PARK
859 MORRONE HILL
Balmoral Forest
River Muick
Glen Muick
728 COCK CAIRN
617 PETER HILL
742 HILL OF CAT
938 MOUNT KEEN
Clunie Water
1154 LOCHNAGAR
720 FASHEILACH
Loch Callater
1045 CAIRN TAGGART
Spittal of Glenmuick
Loch Muick
779 MOUNT BATTOCK
Water of Tarf
Glen Tennet
886 SGOR MOR
Glen Clunie Lodge
Glen Mark
996 BROAD CAIRN
475 HILL OF FINGRAY
Invermark
Tarfside
1018 CARN AN TUIRC
832 EASTERBALLOCH
Glen Lee
Loch Lee
97
Baddoch Burn
Glenshee Ski Area
Glenesk Folk Museum
River North Esk
831 LAIR OF ALDARARIE
544 STURDY HILL
932 THE CAIRNWELL
670
1067 GLAS MAOL
Glen Doll
739 CRUYS
693 WEST KNOCK
605 BULG
Glen Esk
Corrie-Fee
896 BEN TIRRAN
861 CARN AIT
River Isla
928 MAYAR
946 DRIESH
Clova
Water of Saughs
677 HILL OF WIRREN
805 BEN GULABIN
A93
649 CAIRN OF BAMS
Glen Clova
Hunthill Lodge
West Water
807 MONAMEANOCH
755 FINBRACKS
Gannachy
Spittal of Glenshee
Rottal Lodge
Edzell Castle & Garden
Glen Shee
740 BADENDUN HILL
603 CAIRN DAUNIE
579 HILL OF GARBET
Bridgend
Balfield
792 MEALL UAINE
700 DUCHRAY HILL
Presnerb
Glen Damff
Runtaleave
Cormuir
Glen Prosen
508
B955
NO
Dunlappie
Brown Caterthun
White Caterthun
Pitcarity
B951
Glen Finlet
Folda
River South Esk
490 NAKED TAM
Kirkton of Menmuir
Auchnacree
Tigerton
Clackavoid
744 MOUNT BLAIR
Bridge of Brewlands
Backwater Reservoir
Glencally
Mains of Balhall
Little Brechin
Shandford
Glenquiech
Glenisla
Lochty
550 MEALL MOR
Fern
Newmill of Inshewan
Maison Dieu Chapel (ruin)
Careston
Blacklunans
B950
Bellaty
Balintore
Dykehead
Cortachy
Burnside
Noran Water
A90
Brechin Castle & Pictavia
Memus
Tannadice
R. South Esk
B951
Dykends
Braes of Coul
Inverquharity
Shielhill
Murthill
B957
Doocot
Netherton
Finavon
Forest of Alyth
Loch of Lintrathen
Camera Obscura
Crosston
Sculptured Stones
Ballintuim
B951
Kingoldrum
Northmuir
Oathlaw
Aberlemno
River Isla
Reekie Linn Falls
Bridgend of Lintrathen
Kinnordy
Battledykes
A93
Alyth Burn
Mains of Melgunds
Dykehead
425 BALDUFF HILL
Bridge of Craigisla
Kirriemuir
B9134
A924
Westmuir
Southmuir
Ballinshoe
Lunanhead
Kemp's Castle
Restenneth Priory
B9113
479
Netherton
Tullymurdoch
Gauldswell
Kirkton of Airlie
A926
Reswallie
Bridge of Cally
Littleton
Padanaram
Forfar Loch
294 HILL OF ALYTH
B954
Airlie
Craigton of Airlie
Roundyhill
Drumgley
A932
Burnside
Guthrie
River Ericht
90
St Orland's Stone
Forfar
91
Pitmuies
Ruthven
Leys of Cossans
A94
Dunnichen
Kingsmuir
Alyth
New Alyth
B952
Eassie Sculptured Stone
Letham
Bowriefauld
Lornty
Westfields of Rattray
Glamis
Angus Folk Museum
Douglastown
A926
Balhary
Dean Water
A928
B9127
Craichie
Achalader
Blairgowrie
Kinloch
Rattray
A94
Balkeerie
Kirkinch
Charleston
Thornton
Eassie and Nevay
Inverarity
Whigstreet
Redford
Colliston
Craigie
Clunie
Muirton of
Longleys
Meigle
Meigle Sculptured Stone Museum
Gateside
Kirkbuddo
Greystone
B9127
B9128
B978
0 1 2 3 4 5 miles
0 1 2 3 4 5 6 7 8 kilometres

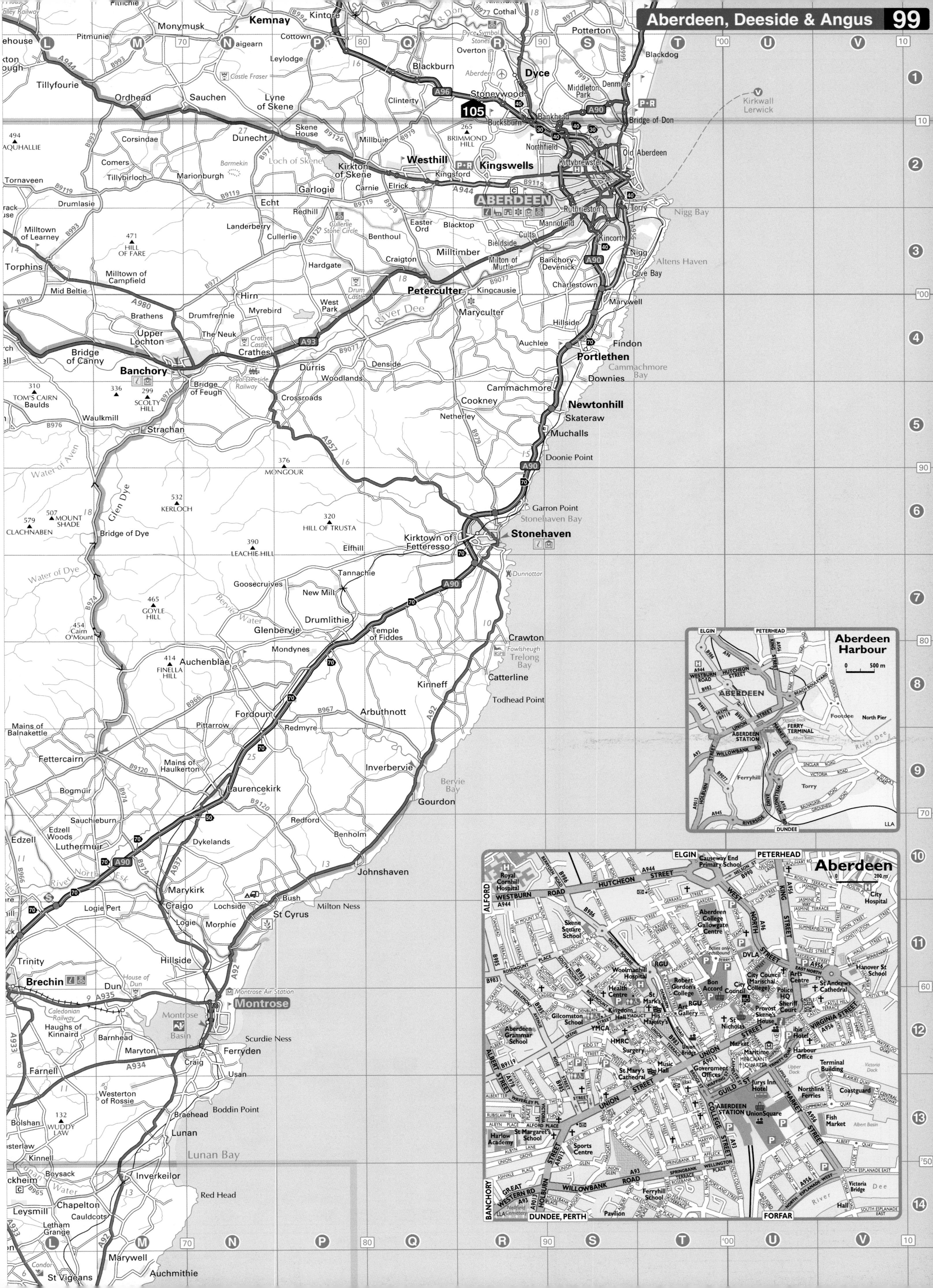
Kemnay
Kintore
Monymusk
Pitmunie
Naigearn
Cottown
Cothal
Potterton
Blackdog
Leylodge
Blackburn
Overton
Dyce
Tillyfourie
Ordhead
Sauchen
Lyne of Skene
Clinterty
Stoneywood
Middleton Park
Denmore
Castle Fraser
Kirkwall
Lerwick
Bucksburn
Bankhead
Bridge of Don
Corsindae
Dunecht
Skene House
Millbuie
BRIMMOND HILL
Northfield
Old Aberdeen
Comers
Tillybirloch
Marionburgh
Barmekin
Loch of Skene
Kirkton of Skene
Westhill
Kingswells
Kingsford
Kittybrewster
Tornaveen
Drumlasie
Garlogie
Carnie
Elrick
ABERDEEN
Echt
Redhill
Ruthrieston
Torry
Nigg Bay
Milltown of Learney
Landerberry
Cullerlie
Cullerlie Stone Circle
Benthoul
Easter Ord
Blacktop
Bieldside
Cults
Mannofield
Kincorth
HILL OF FARE
Milltimber
Nigg
Torphins
Hardgate
Craigton
Milton of Murtle
Banchory-Devenick
Altens Haven
Cove Bay
Milltown of Campfield
Drum Castle
Peterculter
Kingcausie
Charlestown
Mid Beltie
Hirn
West Park
Marywell
Brathens
Drumfrennie
Myrebird
River Dee
Maryculter
Hillside
Upper Lochton
The Neuk
Crathes Castle
Crathes
Auchlee
Findon
Bridge of Canny
Banchory
Durris
Denside
Portlethen
Cammachmore Bay
Woodlands
Downies
TOM'S CAIRN
Baulds
SCOLTY HILL
Bridge of Feugh
Royal Deeside Railway
Crossroads
Cammachmore
Cookney
Newtonhill
Waulkmill
Netherley
Skateraw
Strachan
Muchalls
Water of Aven
MONGOUR
Doonie Point
KERLOCH
Glen Dye
Garron Point
Stonehaven Bay
MOUNT SHADE
CLACHNABEN
HILL OF TRUSTA
Bridge of Dye
Kirktown of Fetteresso
Stonehaven
LEACHIE HILL
Elfhill
Water of Dye
Dunnottar
Tannachie
Goosecruives
New Mill
GOYLE HILL
Bervie Water
Drumlithie
Cairn O'Mount
Glenbervie
Temple of Fiddes
Crawton
Mondynes
Fowlsheugh
Trelong Bay
FINELLA HILL
Auchenblae
Catterline
Kinneff
Todhead Point
Mains of Balnakettle
Fordoun
Arbuthnott
Pittarrow
Redmyre
Fettercairn
Mains of Haulkerton
Inverbervie
Bervie Bay
Bogmuir
Laurencekirk
Gourdon
Sauchieburn
Redford
Edzell Woods
Edzell
Luthermuir
Dykelands
Benholm
River North Esk
Johnshaven
Marykirk
Craigo
Bush
Milton Ness
Logie Pert
Lochside
St Cyrus
Logie
Morphie
Trinity
Hillside
Brechin
Dun
House of Dun
Montrose Air Station
Montrose
Caledonian Railway
Montrose Basin
Haughs of Kinnaird
Barnhead
Scurdie Ness
Maryton
Ferryden
Craig
Farnell
Usan
Westerton of Rossie
Braehead
Boddin Point
Bolshan
WUDDY LAW
Lunan
Lunan Bay
Kinnell
Boysack
Inverkeilor
Red Head
Leysmill
Chapelton
Cauldcots
Letham Grange
Marywell
St Vigeans
Auchmithie
Aberdeen Harbour
ELGIN
PETERHEAD
HUTCHEON STREET
WESTBURN ROAD
ABERDEEN
SKENE STREET
UNION STREET
ABERDEEN STATION
FERRY TERMINAL
Footdee
North Pier
WILLOWBANK RD
Ferryhill
Torry
River Dee
RIVERSIDE
DUNDEE
Aberdeen
Causeway End Primary School
Royal Cornhill Hospital
City Hospital
Aberdeen College Gallowgate Centre
Skene Square School
Woolmanhill Hospital
Robert Gordon's College
Bon Accord Centre
Marischal College
City Council
Police HQ
Sheriff Court
Arts Centre
St Andrews Cathedral
Hanover St School
Health Centre
Art Gallery
Provost Skene's House
St Nicholas
Gilcomston School
Aberdeen Grammar School
YMCA
HMRC
His Majesty's
Union Bridge
Market
Maritime Museum
Merchant Quarter
Harbour Office
ibis Hotel
Music Hall
St Mary's Cathedral
Government Offices
Jurys Inn Hotel
Terminal Building
Northlink Ferries
Coastguard
ABERDEEN STATION
Union Square
Fish Market
Harlow Academy
St Margaret's School
Sports Centre
Ferryhill School
Pavilion
Victoria Bridge
Hall
DUNDEE, PERTH
FORFAR
BANCHORY
ALFORD

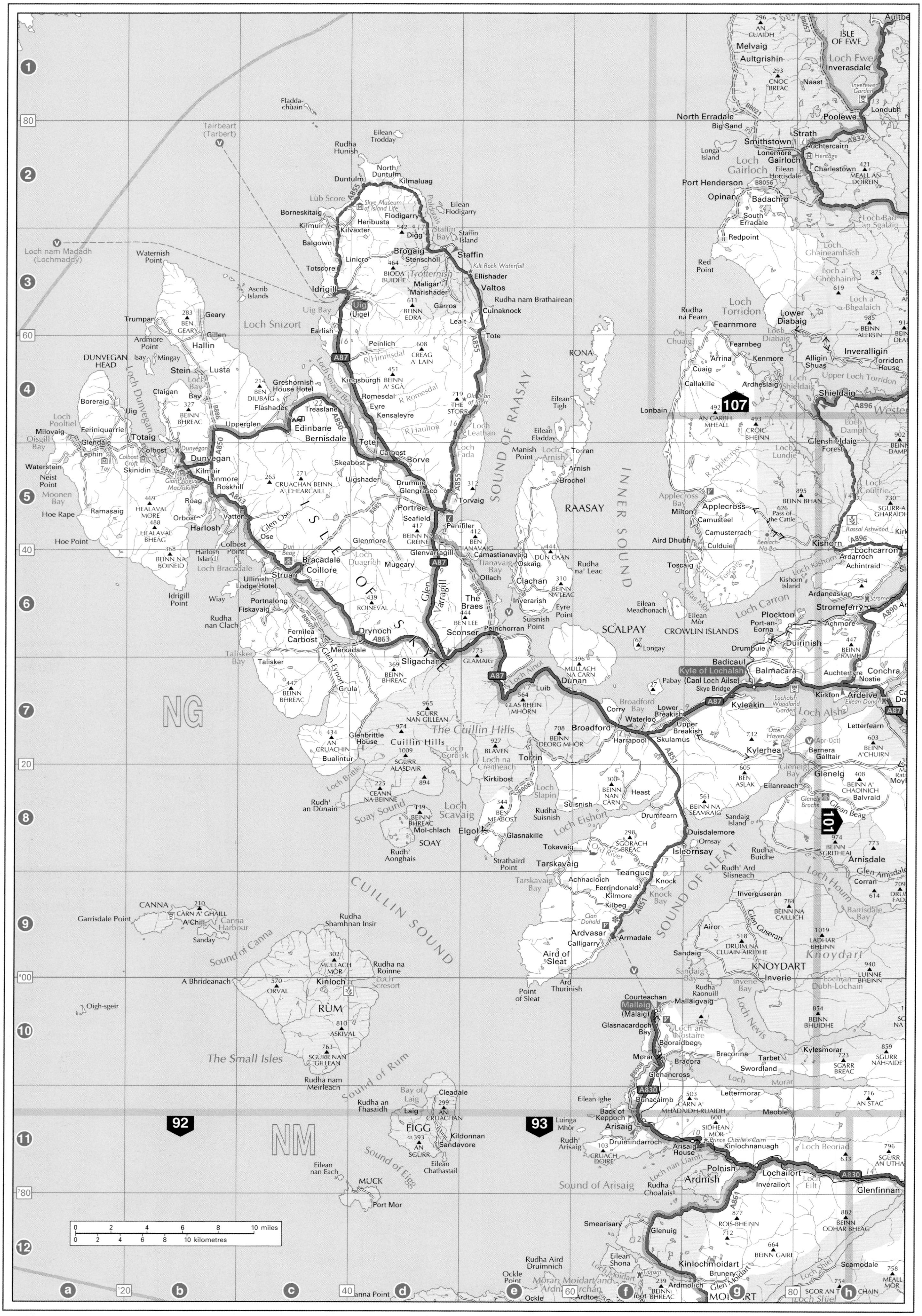

Fladda-chùain
Tairbeart (Tarbert)
Loch nam Madadh (Lochmaddy)
Eilean Trodday
Rudha Hunish
North Duntulm
Duntulm
Kilmaluag
Lùb Score
Skye Museum of Island Life
Eilean Flodigarry
Borneskitaig
Kilmuir
Flodigarry
Heribusta
Kilvaxter
Digg
Staffin Bay
Staffin Island
Balgown
Brogaig
Staffin
Stenscholl
Kilt Rock Waterfall
Linicro
BIODA BUIDHE
Trotternish
Ellishader
Maligar
Marishader
Valtos
Rudha nam Brathairean
Totscore
Idrigill
Uig (Uige)
Uig Bay
Garros
Culnaknock
Waternish Point
Ascrib Islands
Loch Snizort
Earlish
BEINN EDRA
Lealt
Tote
Trumpan
Geary
BEN GEARY
Gillen
Hallin
Ardmore Point
Isay
Mingay
DUNVEGAN HEAD
Stein
Lusta
Loch Bay
Peinlich
CREAG A' LAIN
R. Hinnisdal
Kingsburgh
BEINN A' SGA
Romesdal
R. Romesdal
Eyre
Kensaleyre
Greshornish House Hotel
BEN DIUBAIG
Flashader
Claigan
Borereraig
Loch Dunvegan
Uig
BEINN BHREAC
Upperglen
Treaslane
Edinbane
Bernisdale
THE STORR
Old Man of Storr
Loch Leathan
R. Haultin
Loch Pooltiel
Milovaig
Feriniquarrie
Totaig
Glendale
Lephin
Loch Osgaill Bay
Toy
Colbost Croft
Colbost
Dunvegan
Skinidin
Waterstein
Kilmuir
Lonmore
Roskhill
Neist Point
Moonen Bay
Giant Angus MacAskill
Tote
Carbost
Borve
Skeabost
CRUACHAN BEINN A' CHEARCAILL
Uigshader
Drumuie
Glengrasco
Loch Fada
Torvaig
SOUND OF RAASAY
Roag
Orbost
Ramasaig
Hoe Rape
HEALAVAL MORE
HEALAVAL BHEAG
Harlosh
Vatten
Glen Ose
Ose
ISLE OF SKYE
Portree
Seafield
BEINN NA GREINE
Penifiler
TIANAVAIG
Hoe Point
Colbost Point
Harlosh Island
BEINN NA BOINEID
Loch Bracadale
Dun Beag
Bracadale
Coillore
Glenmore
Loch Duagrich
Glenvarragill
Mugeary
Camastianavaig
Tianavaig Bay
Ollach
Struan
Ullinish Lodge Hotel
Wiay
Idrigill Point
Portnalong
Fiskavaig
Rudha nan Clach
Loch Harport
ROINEVAL
Glen Varragill
The Braes
BEN LEE
Fernilea
Carbost
Drynoch
Merkadale
Sconser
Peinchorran
Talisker Bay
Talisker
Glen Eynort
Sligachan
GLAMAIG
BEINN BHREAC
Grula
NG
SGURR NAN GILLEAN
The Cuillin Hills
Cuillin Hills
Loch Coruisk
AN CRUACHAN
Glenbrittle House
Bualintur
SGURR ALASDAIR
Loch Brittle
CEANN NA BEINNE
Rudh' an Dùnain
Soay Sound
BEINN BHREAC
Mol-chlach
SOAY
Rudh' Aonghais
Loch Scavaig
Elgol
BLAVEN
Loch na Creitheach
Torrin
Kirkibost
BEN MEABOST
Glasnakille
Strathaird Point
Loch Ainort
Luib
GLAS BHEIN MHÒR
Loch Slapin
CUILLIN SOUND
RONA
Eilean Tigh
Eilean Fladday
Manish Point
Loch Arnish
Torran
Arnish
Brochel
RAASAY
INNER SOUND
DÙN CAAN
Oskaig
Rudha na' Leac
Clachan
BEINN NA LEAC
Inverarish
Eyre Point
Suisnish Point
SCALPAY
Longay
MULLACH NA CARN
Dunan
Pabay
Broadford Bay
Corry
Waterloo
Broadford
BEINN DEARG MHÒR
Harrapool
Lower Breakish
Upper Breakish
Skulamus
Suisnish
BEINN NAN CARN
Heast
Rudha Suisnish
Loch Eishort
Drumfearn
BEINN NA SEAMRAIG
SGORACH BREAC
Tokavaig
Ord River
Tarskavaig
Tarskavaig Bay
Teangue
Achnacloich
Ferrindonald
Kilmore
Kilbeg
Knock
Knock Bay
Clan Donald
Ardvasar
Calligarry
Armadale
Aird of Sleat
Point of Sleat
Ard Thurinish
SOUND OF SLEAT
Duisdalemore
Ornsay
Isleornsay
Sandaig Island
Rudha Buidhe
Rudh' Ard Slisneach
CANNA
CARN A' GHAILL
A'Chill
Canna Harbour
Sanday
Garrisdale Point
Sound of Canna
Rudha Shamhnan Insir
MULLACH MÒR
Kinloch
Rudha na Roinne
Loch Scresort
A Bhrideanach
ORVAL
RÙM
ASKIVAL
SGÙRR NAN GILLEAN
Oigh-sgeir
The Small Isles
Rudha nam Meirleach
Sound of Rum
Rudha an Fhasaidh
Bay of Laig
Laig
Cleadale
AN CRUACHAN
EIGG
AN SGÙRR
Kildonnan
Sandavore
Eilean Chathastail
Eilean nan Each
Sound of Eigg
MUCK
Port Mor
NM
92
93
Luinga Mhòr
Rudh' Arisaig
Eilean Ighe
Back of Keppoch
Arisaig
Druimindarroch
CRUACH DOIRE
Arisaig House
Sound of Arisaig
Loch nan Uamh
Rudha Chaolais
Ardnish
Polnish
Smearisary
Rudha Aird Druimnich
Eilean Shona
Ockle Point
Ockle
Moidart
Ardnamurchan
Ardtoe
Courteachan
Mallaig (Malaig)
Mallaigvaig
Glasnacardoch Bay
Loch an Nostaire
Beoraidbeg
Morar
Bracora
Bracorina
Glenancross
Loch Morar
Bunacaimb
CARN A' MHADAIDH-RUAIDH
Lettermorar
SIDHEAN MÒR
Prince Charlie's Cairn
Kinlochnanuagh
Meoble
Lochailort
Inverailort
Loch Eilt
Loch Beoraid
Glenfinnan
ROIS-BHEINN
Glenuig
BEINN GAIRE
Kinlochmoidart
Brunery
Glen Moidart
Ardmolich
BEINN BHREAC
Tioram
MOIDART
Loch Shiel
SGÙRR AN UTHA
BEINN ODHAR BHEAG
Scamodale
SGOR AN
MEALL MÒR
Sandaig
Sandaig Bay
Airor
Inverguseran
Glen Guseran
DRUIM NA CLUAIN-AIRIDHE
KNOYDART
Knoydart
Inverie
Inverie Bay
Rudha Raonuill
Loch Nevis
Loch Hourn
BEINN NA CAILLICH
LADHAR BHEINN
Barrisdale Bay
LUINNE BHEINN
Loch an Dubh-Lochain
BEINN BHUIDHE
Kylesmorar
Tarbet
Swordland
SGÙRR NA h-AIDE
SGURR BREAC
AN STAC
Corran
Arnisdale
Glen Arnisdale
BEINN SGRITHEAL
101
Glenelg
Glenelg Bay
Glenelg Brochs
Glen Beag
BEINN A' CHAOINICH
Balvraid
Eilanreach
BEN ASLAK
Kylerhea
Kyle Rhea
Otter Haven
Bernera
Galltair
BEINN A'CHUIRN
Letterfearn
Kyleakin
Lochalsh Woodland Garden
Loch Alsh
Kyle of Lochalsh (Caol Loch Ailse)
Skye Bridge
Badicaul
Balmacara
Kirkton
Ardelve
Eilean Donan
Auchtertyre
Conchra
Nostie
Drumbuie
Duirinish
Achmore
BEINN RAIMH
Plockton
Port-an-Eorna
Stromeferry
Loch Carron
Eilean Mòr
CROWLIN ISLANDS
Eilean Meadhonach
Caolas Mòr
Kishorn Island
Ardaneaskan
Toscaig
Culduie
Camusterrach
Aird Dhubh
Camusteel
Milton
Applecross Bay
Applecross
R. Applecross
Pass of the Cattle
Bealach-Na-Bà
Kishorn
Loch Kishorn
Lochcarron
Ardarroch
Achintraid
Rassal Ashwood
BEINN BHAN
Glenshieldaig Forest
Loch Lundie
Loch Coultrie
Loch Damph
SGURR A' GHARAIDH
Lonbain
AN GARBH-MHEALL
CROIC-BHEINN
107
Callakille
Cuaig
Arrina
Fearnbeg
Kenmore
Ardheslaig
Loch Shieldaig
Shieldaig
Upper Loch Torridon
Torridon House
Inverallgin
Alligin Shuas
Loch Diabaig
Lower Diabaig
Fearnmore
Rudha na Fearn
Ob Chuaig
Loch Torridon
Red Point
Redpoint
South Erradale
Badachro
Opinan
Port Henderson
Loch Gairloch
Gairloch
Eilean Horrisdale
Longa Island
Lonemore
Smithstown
Big Sand
North Erradale
Strath
Auchtercairn
Heritage
Charlestown
MEALL AN DOIRIEN
Loch Bad an Sgalaig
Loch Ghaineamhach
Loch a' Ghobhainn
Loch a' Bhealaich
BEINN ALLIGIN
Melvaig
Aultgrishin
AN CUAIDH
CNOC BREAC
ISLE OF EWE
Loch Ewe
Inverasdale
Naast
Inverewe Garden
Poolewe
Londubh
Aultbea

0 2 4 6 8 10 miles
0 2 4 6 8 10 kilometres

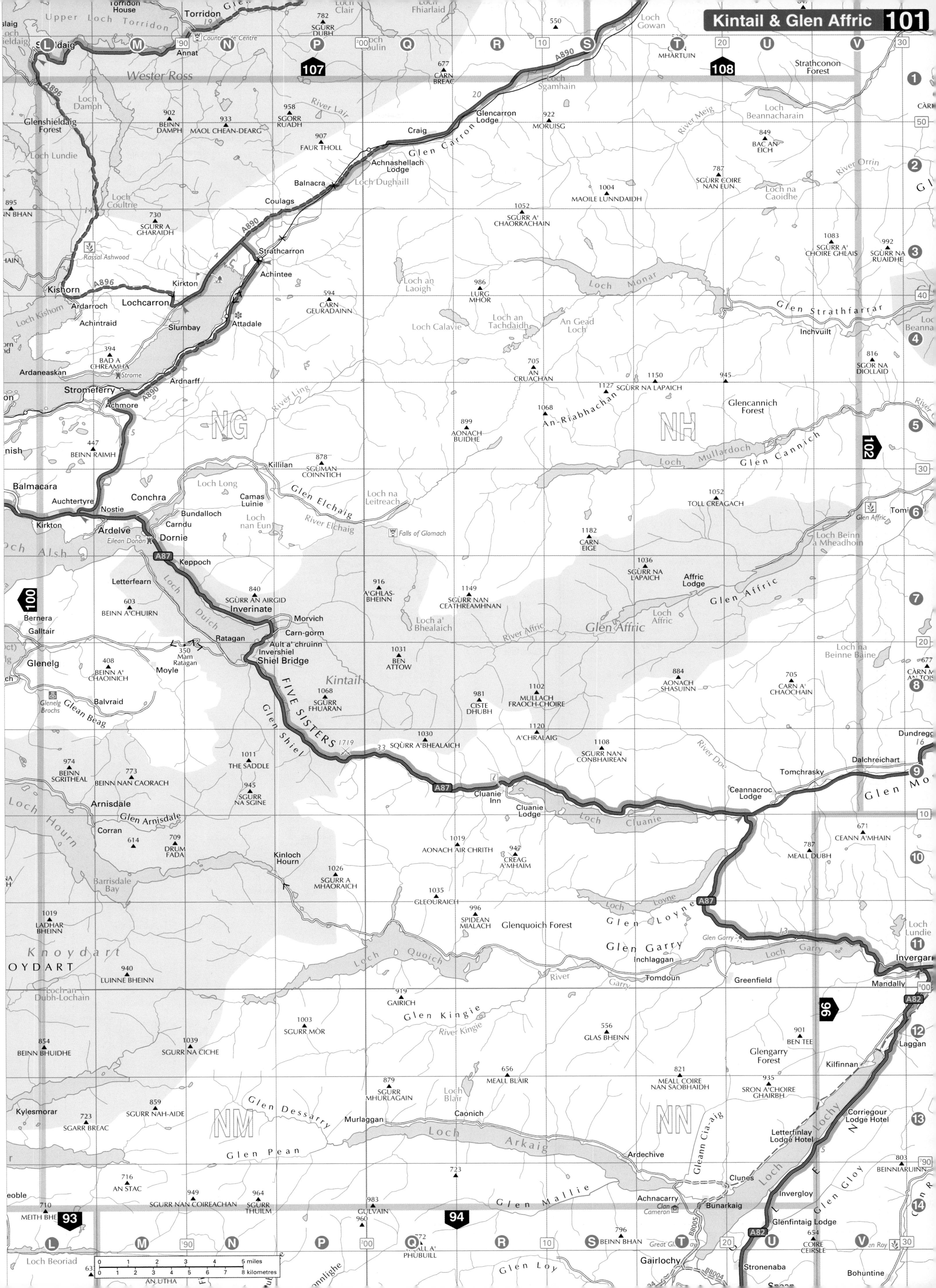

Upper Loch Torridon
Torridon House
Torridon
Glen Clair
Loch Fhiarlaid
Loch Gowan
A890
Strathconon Forest

Wester Ross
Annat
Countryside Centre
782 SGURR DUBH
107
Loch Coulin
Loch Sgamhain
108

550
CARN

Loch Damph
902 BEINN DAMPH
933 MAOL CHEAN-DEARG
958 SGURR RUADH
River Lair
Craig
Glencarron Lodge
922 MORUISG

Glenshieldaig Forest
907 FUAR THOLL
Achnashellach Lodge
Glen Carron
677 CARN BREAC

Loch Coultrie
730 SGURR A GHARAIDH
Balnacra
Loch Dughaill
Coulags

1052 SGURR A' CHAORRACHAIN
1004
MAOILE LUNNDAIDH
1083 SGURR A' CHOIRE GHLAIS
992 SGURR NA RUAIDHE

Loch Lundie
Rassal Ashwood
Strathcarron
Achintee
1086 LURG MHOR
Loch Monar
Glen Strathfarrar

Kishorn
A896
Kirkton
Attadale
594 CARN GEURADAINN
Loch an Laoigh
986
Loch Calavie
An Gead Loch
Inchvuilt
Loch Beanna

Ardarroch
Lochcarron
Slumbay
705 AN CRUACHAN
1150
816 SGOR NA DIOLLAID

Ardaneaskan
394 BAD A CHREAMHA
Strome
Ardnarff
1127 SGURR NA LAPAICH
945

Stromeferry
Achmore
River Ling
1068
An-Riabhachan
NH
Glencannich Forest

447 BEINN RAIMH
NG
899 AONACH BUIDHE
Loch Mullardoch
Glen Cannich
102

Balmacara
Auchtertyre
Nostie
Killilan
878 SGUMAN COINNTICH
1052 TOLL CREAGACH
Glen Affric

Kirkton
Ardelve
Conchra
Loch Long
Camas Luinie
Glen Elchaig
Loch na Leitreach
Tomi
Glen Affric

Bernera
Galltair
Eilean Donan
Dornie
A87
Keppoch
Bundalloch
Carndu
Loch nan Eun
River Elchaig
Falls of Glomach
1182 CARN EIGE
1036 SGURR NA LAPAICH
Affric Lodge
Loch Beinn a Mheadhoin

100
Letterfearn
603 BEINN A'CHUIRN
840 SGURR AN AIRGID
Inverinate
916 A'GHLAS-BHEINN
1149 SGURR NAN CEATHREAMHNAN
Glen Affric

Glenelg
408 BEINN A' CHAOINICH
350 Ratagan
Mam Ratagan
Morvich
Carn-gorm
Ault a' chruinn
Invershiel
Shiel Bridge
Loch a' Bhealaich
River Affric
Loch Affric
1102 MULLACH FRAOCH-CHOIRE
884 AONACH SHASUINN
705 CARN A' CHAOCHAIN
CARN AN TOIS

Glenelg Brochs
Balvraid
Glean Beag
Moyle
Kintail
1031 BEN ATTOW
981 CISTE DHUBH
Loch na Beinne Baine

974 BEINN SGRITHEAL
773 BEINN NAN CAORACH
1068 SGURR FHUARAN
FIVE SISTERS
1719
1030 SGURR A'BHEALAICH
1120 A'CHRALAIG
1108 SGURR NAN CONBHAIREAN
River Doe
Dundreggan

Arnisdale
Corran
1011 THE SADDLE
Glen Shiel
33
A87
Tomchrasky
Dalchreichart
Glen Mo

Loch Hourn
614
709 DRUM FADA
945 SGURR NA SGINE
Kinloch Hourn
i
Cluanie Inn
Cluanie Lodge
Ceannacroc Lodge
671 CEANN A'MHAIN

1019 AONACH AIR CHRITH
947 CREAG A'MHAIM
Loch Cluanie
787 MEALL DUBH

1026 SGURR A MHAORAICH
1035 GLEOURAICH
996 SPIDEAN MIALACH
Glenquoich Forest
A87
Glen Loyne
Loch Lundie

1019 LADHAR BHEINN
Knoydart
Glen Garry
Inchlaggan
Loch Garry
Invergarr

854 BEINN BHUIDHE
940 LUINNE BHEINN
Loch Quoich
919 GAIRICH
Tomdoun
Greenfield
Mandally
A82

Eochan Dubh-Lochain
1003 SGURR MOR
Glen Kingie
River Kingie
556 GLAS BHEINN
96
901 BEN TEE
Laggan

Kylesmorar
723 SGARR BREAC
859 SGURR NA-H-AIDE
1039 SGURR NA CICHE
NM
Murlaggan
Caonich
879 SGURR MHURLAGAIN
Loch Blair
821 MEALL COIRE NAN SAOBHAIDH
935 SRON A'CHOIRE GHAIRBH
Glengarry Forest
Kilfinnan

723 MEITH BHE
93
716 AN STAC
949 SGURR NAN COIREACHAN
964 SGURR THUILM
983 GULVAIN
656 MEALL BLAIR
Loch Arkaig
Ardechive
Letterfinlay Lodge Hotel
Corriegour Lodge Hotel

eoble
710
Glen Pean
960
572 CARN MHIC AN UTHA
Glen Mallie
723
Clunes
Achnacarry
Clan Cameron
Bunarkaig
Invergloy
Glen Gloy
803 BEINNIARUINN

Loch Beoriad
AN UTHA
94
Glen Loy
796
SGALL A' PHUBUILL
BEINN BHAN
NN
Glenfintaig Lodge
654 COIRE CEIRSLE

L
M
N
P
Q
R
S
T
U
V

Gairlochy
Stronenaba
Bohuntine

0 1 2 3 4 5 miles
0 1 2 3 4 5 6 7 8 kilometres

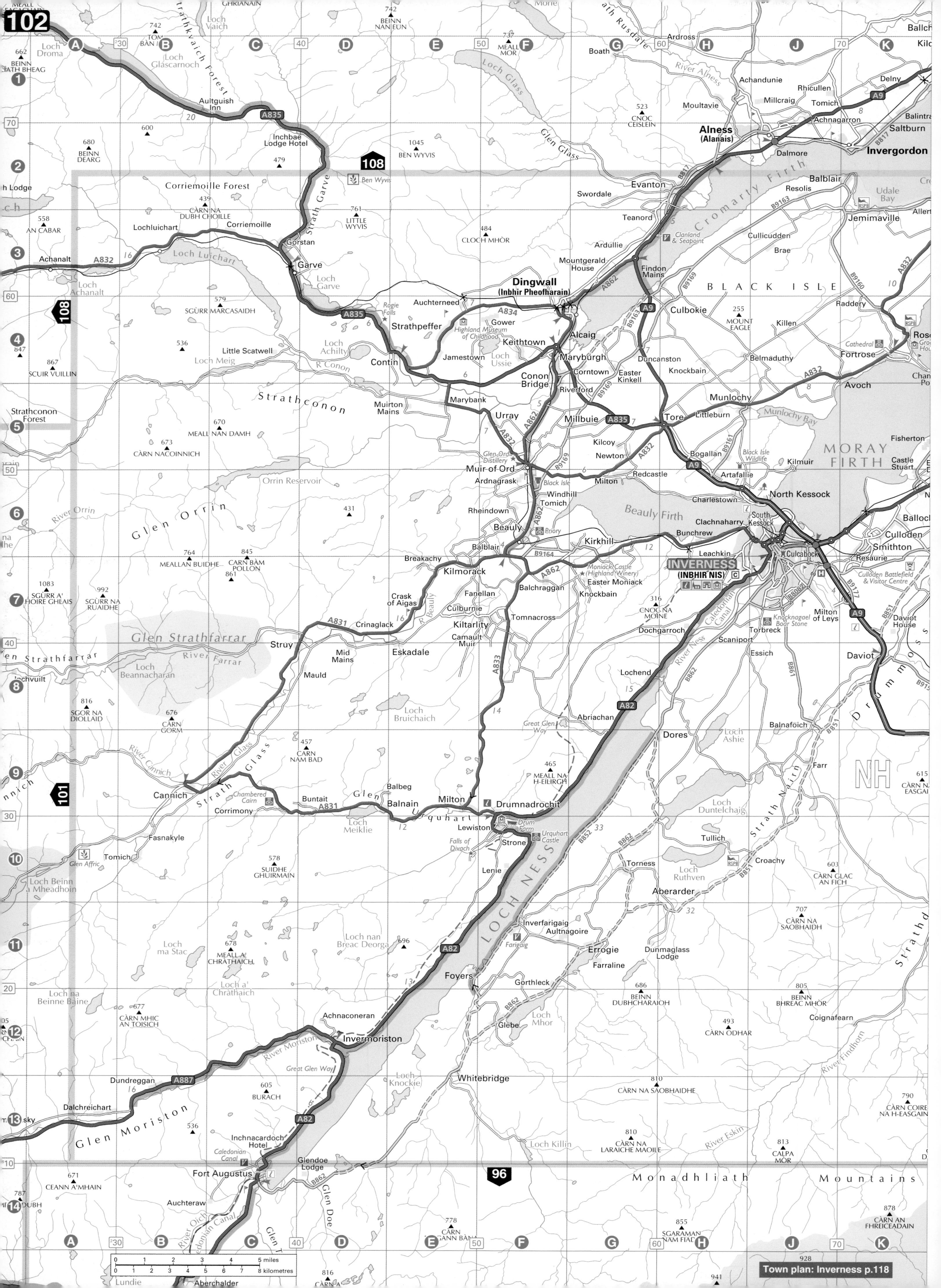

Loch Droma
662 BEINN LIATH BHEAG
742 TOM BÀN
Loch Glascarnoch
Strathvaich Forest
Loch Vaich
742 BEINN NAN EUN
737 MEALL MÒR
Loch Glass
Boath
Strath Rusdale
Ardross
River Alness
Achandunie
Rhicullen
Delny
Millcraig
Tomich
Moultavie
Achnagarron
Balintraid
Saltburn
523 CNOC CEISLEIN
Alness (Alanais)
Invergordon
Dalmore
Aultguish Inn
A835
Inchbae Lodge Hotel
600
680 BEINN DEARG
479
1045 BEN WYVIS
108
Ben Wyvis
Glen Glass
Evanton
Swordale
Balblair
Resolis
Udale Bay
Cromarty Firth
Corriemoille Forest
439 CÀRN NA DUBH CHOILLE
Corriemoille
Lochluichart
558 AN CABAR
Strath Garve
761 LITTLE WYVIS
484 CLOCH MHÒR
Teanord
Clanland & Seaport
Jemimaville
Cullicudden
Brae
Ardullie
Gorstan
Loch Luichart
Achanalt
A832
Garve
Loch Garve
Loch Achanalt
Mountgerald House
Findon Mains
Dingwall (Inbhir Pheofharain)
BLACK ISLE
579 SGÙRR MARCASAIDH
Rogie Falls
Auchterneed
A834
A835
Gower
Highland Museum of Childhood
Strathpeffer
Culbokie
255 MOUNT EAGLE
Killen
Raddery
Rosemarkie
Alcaig
847
536
Little Scatwell
Loch Achilty
Keithtown
Jamestown
Loch Ussie
Maryburgh
Duncanston
Cathedral
Fortrose
Belmaduthy
867 SCUIR VUILLIN
Loch Meig
R Conon
Contin
Conon Bridge
Corntown
Easter Kinkell
Knockbain
Chanonry Point
Avoch
Strathconon Forest
Strathconon
Muirton Mains
Marybank
Riverford
A832
Munlochy
Littleburn
Munlochy Bay
670 MEALL NAN DAMH
Urray
Millbuie
A835
Tore
673 CÀRN NACOINNICH
Kilcoy
Newton
Glen Ord Distillery
Black Isle Wildlife
Bogallan
MORAY FIRTH
Kilmuir
Fisherton
Castle Stuart
Muir of Ord
Ardnagrask
Black Isle
Milton
Redcastle
A9
Artafallie
Orrin Reservoir
Windhill
Tomich
North Kessock
River Orrin
431
Rheindown
Charlestown
Beauly Firth
South Kessock
Clachnaharry
Glen Orrin
Beauly
Priory
Bunchrew
Balloch
Culloden
Kirkhill
Smithton
Balblair
B9164
Leachkin
Culcabock
764 MEALLAN BUIDHE
845 CÀRN BÀN POLLON
861
Breakachy
Kilmorack
A862
Moniack Castle (Highland Winery)
Easter Moniack
INVERNESS (INBHIR NIS)
Resaurie
Culloden Battlefield & Visitor Centre
1083 SGÙRR A' CHOIRE GHLAIS
992 SGÙRR NA RUAIDHE
Crask of Aigas
Fanellan
Balchraggan
Knockbain
316 CNOC NA MOINE
Caledonian Canal
Milton of Leys
Daviot House
R Beauly
Culburnie
Tomnacross
A831
Crinaglack
Kiltarlity
Knocknagael Boar Stone
Dochgarroch
Torbreck
Glen Strathfarrar
Struy
Camault Muir
Scaniport
River Farrar
Strathfarrar
Mid Mains
Eskadale
River Ness
Essich
Daviot
Loch Beannacharan
Inchvuilt
Mauld
A833
Lochend
B862
B861
Drummossie
816 SGOR NA DIOLLAID
676 CÀRN GORM
Loch Bruiachaich
Great Glen Way
Abriachan
A82
Dores
Balnafoich
457 CARN NAM BAD
Loch Ashie
River Cannich
River Glass
Strath Glass
465 MEALL NA H-EILRIGH
Farr
NH
615 CÀRN NA EASGAIN
101
Cannich
Chambered Cairn
Glen
Balbeg
Buntait
Balnain
Milton
Drumnadrochit
Corrimony
A831
Urquhart
Loch Meiklie
Lewiston
Drum Farm
Urquhart Castle
Loch Duntelchaig
Strath Nairn
Fasnakyle
Falls of Divach
Strone
B852
B862
Tullich
Tomich
Glen Affric
578 SUIDHE GHUIRMAIN
Torness
Croachy
603 CÀRN GLAC AN FICH
Loch Beinn a Mheadhoin
Lenie
Loch Ruthven
Aberarder
LOCH NESS
B851
707 CÀRN NA SAOBHAIDH
Inverfarigaig
Aultnagoire
Loch ma Stac
678 MEALL A' CHRATHAICH
Loch nan Breac Deorga
696
Farigaig
Errogie
Dunmaglass Lodge
Farraline
Strathdearn
Loch a' Chràthaich
Foyers
Gorthleck
Loch na Beinne Bàine
677 CÀRN MHIC AN TOISICH
686 BEINN DUBHCHARAIDH
805 BEINN BHREAC MHÒR
Coignafearn
Achnaconeran
Loch Mhor
Glebe
493 CÀRN ODHAR
Invermoriston
River Moriston
Great Glen Way
Loch Knockie
Whitebridge
River Findhorn
Dundreggan
A887
605 BURACH
810 CÀRN NA SAOBHAIDHE
790 CÀRN COIRE NA H-EASGAIN
Dalchreichart
Glen Moriston
536
A82
Inchnacardoch Hotel
810 CÀRN NA LARAICHE MAOILE
River Eskin
Loch Killin
813 CALPA MÒR
Caledonian Canal
Glendoe Lodge
Fort Augustus
96
Monadhliath Mountains
671 CEANN A' MHAIM
B862
Glen Doe
787
Auchteraw
River Oich
Caledonian Canal
Glen Tarff
778 CÀRN GANN BÀN
855 SGARAMAN NAM FIADH
878 CÀRN AN FHREICEADAIN
0 1 2 3 4 5 miles
0 1 2 3 4 5 6 7 8 kilometres
Lundie
Aberchalder
816 CÀRN A'
928
941

Town plan: Inverness p.118

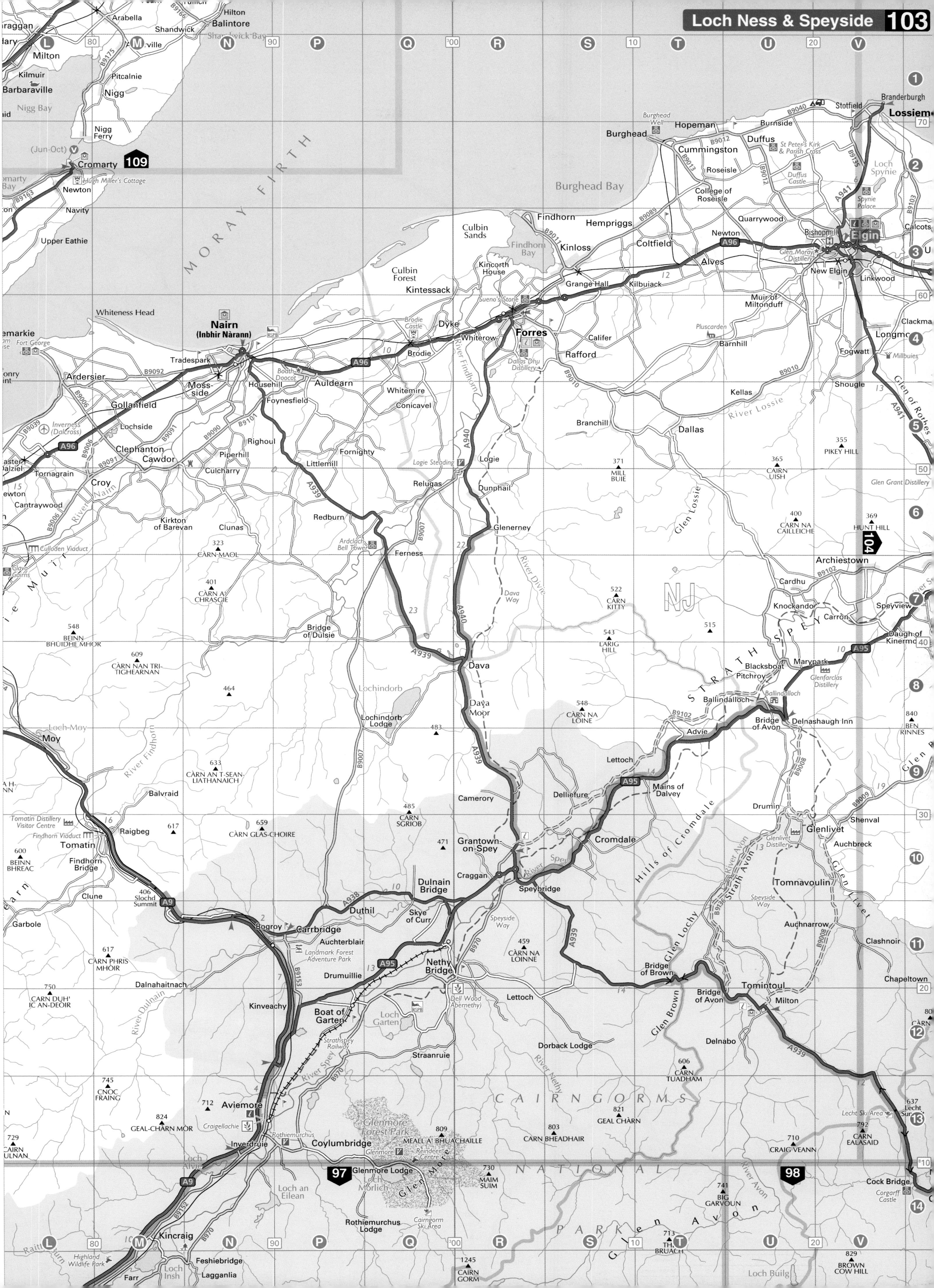

MORAY FIRTH
Burghead Bay
Nigg Bay
Findhorn Bay
Culbin Sands
Culbin Forest
Whiteness Head
Cromarty
Hugh Miller's Cottage
Nigg
Nigg Ferry
Pitcalnie
Barbaraville
Kilmuir
Milton
Arabella
Shandwick
Balintore
Hilton
Newton
Navity
Upper Eathie
Fort George
Nairn
(Inbhir Nàrann)
Tradespark
Ardersier
Gollanfield
Inverness (Dalcross)
Lochside
Clephanton
Cawdor
Croy
Tornagrain
Cantraywood
Culcharry
Piperhill
Righoul
Moss-side
Househill
Foynesfield
Auldearn
Boath Doocot
Kirkton of Barevan
Clunas
Culloden Viaduct
Clava Cairns
Kintessack
Brodie
Brodie Castle
Dyke
Whiterow
Forres
Kincorth House
Sueno's Stone
Dallas Dhu Distillery
Findhorn
Kinloss
Hempriggs
Coltfield
Grange Hall
Kilbuiack
Alves
Rafford
Califer
Pluscarden
Barnhill
Burghead
Burghead Well
Hopeman
Cummingston
Roseisle
College of Roseisle
Duffus
Duffus Castle
St Peter's Kirk & Parish Cross
Burnside
Stotfield
Branderburgh
Lossiemouth
Loch Spynie
Spynie Palace
Quarrywood
Newton
Bishopmill
Elgin
Glen Moray Distillery
New Elgin
Linkwood
Calcots
Muir of Miltonduff
Clackmarras
Longmorn
Fogwatt
Millbuies
Shougle
Kellas
Glen of Rothes
River Lossie
Dallas
Branchill
Whitemire
Conicavel
Logie Steading
Logie
Littlemill
Fornighty
Relugas
Dunphail
Redburn
Ardclach Bell Tower
Ferness
Glenerney
River Findhorn
River Divie
Dava Way
323 CÀRN MAOL
401 CÀRN A' CHRASGIE
548 BEINN BHUIDHE MHOR
609 CÀRN NAN TRI-TIGHEARNAN
464
Bridge of Dulsie
Dava
Dava Moor
Lochindorb
Lochindorb Lodge
483
371 MILL BUIE
365 CAIRN UISH
355 PIKEY HILL
400 CARN NA CAILLEICHE
369 HUNT HILL
104
Glen Grant Distillery
Glen Lossie
522 CARN KITTY
543 LARIG HILL
515
548 CÀRN NA LOINE
NJ
Archiestown
Cardhu
Knockando
Carron
Speyview
Daugh of Kinermony
STRATH SPEY
Blacksboat
Pitchroy
Marypark
Glenfarclas Distillery
Ballindalloch
Bridge of Avon
Delnashaugh Inn
840 BEN RINNES
Advie
Lettoch
Mains of Dalvey
Dellifure
Cromdale
Hills of Cromdale
Cameron
Grantown-on-Spey
Craggan
Speybridge
471
485 CARN SGRIOB
659 CÀRN GLAS-CHOIRE
633 CÀRN AN T-SEAN-LIATHANAICH
617
Loch Moy
Moy
Balvraid
Raigbeg
Tomatin Distillery Visitor Centre
Findhorn Viaduct
Tomatin
600 BEINN BHREAC
Findhorn Bridge
Clune
406 Slochd Summit
Garbole
Dulnain Bridge
Duthil
Skye of Curr
Carrbridge
Bogroy
Auchterblair
Landmark Forest Adventure Park
617 CARN PHRIS MHÒIR
750 CARN DUH' IC AN-DEOIR
Dalnahaitnach
River Dulnain
Drumuillie
Kinveachy
Boat of Garten
Loch Garten
Nethy Bridge
Dell Wood (Abernethy)
Lettoch
459 CÀRN NA LOINNE
Speyside Way
Strathspey Railway
River Spey
Straanruie
Dorback Lodge
River Nethy
Bridge of Brown
Glen Brown
Glen Lochy
Drumin
Glenlivet
Glenlivet Distillery
Shenval
Auchbreck
Strath Avon
River Avon
Tomnavoulin
Glen Livet
Auchnarrow
Clashnoir
Tomintoul
Bridge of Avon
Milton
Chapeltown
Delnabo
606 CARN TUADHAM
CAIRNGORMS NATIONAL PARK
821 GEAL CHÀRN
803 CARN BHEADHAIR
809 MEALL A' BHUACHAILLE
710 CRAIG VEANN
792 CARN EALASAID
637 Lecht Summit
Lecht Ski Area
Cock Bridge
Corgarff Castle
745 CNOC FRAING
712
Aviemore
824 GEAL-CHARN MOR
Craigellachie
729 CAIRN ULNAN
Inverdruie
Rothiemurchus
Coylumbridge
Glenmore Forest Park
Glenmore
Reindeer Centre
Glenmore Lodge
97
98
109
730 MAIM SUIM
Loch Morlich
Glen More
Loch Alvie
Loch an Eilean
Rothiemurchus Lodge
Cairngorm Ski Area
741 BIG GARVOUN
Glen Avon
713 THE BRUACH
829 BROWN COW HILL
1245 CAIRN GORM
Loch Builg
Kincraig
Highland Wildlife Park
Loch Insh
Feshiebridge
Lagganlia
Farr
A9
A95
A96
A938
A939
A940
A941
B9007
B9006
B9010
B9089
B9091
B9092
B9101
B9102
B9008
B9009
B9013
B9012
B9040
B9135
B9136
B9153
B9152
B970

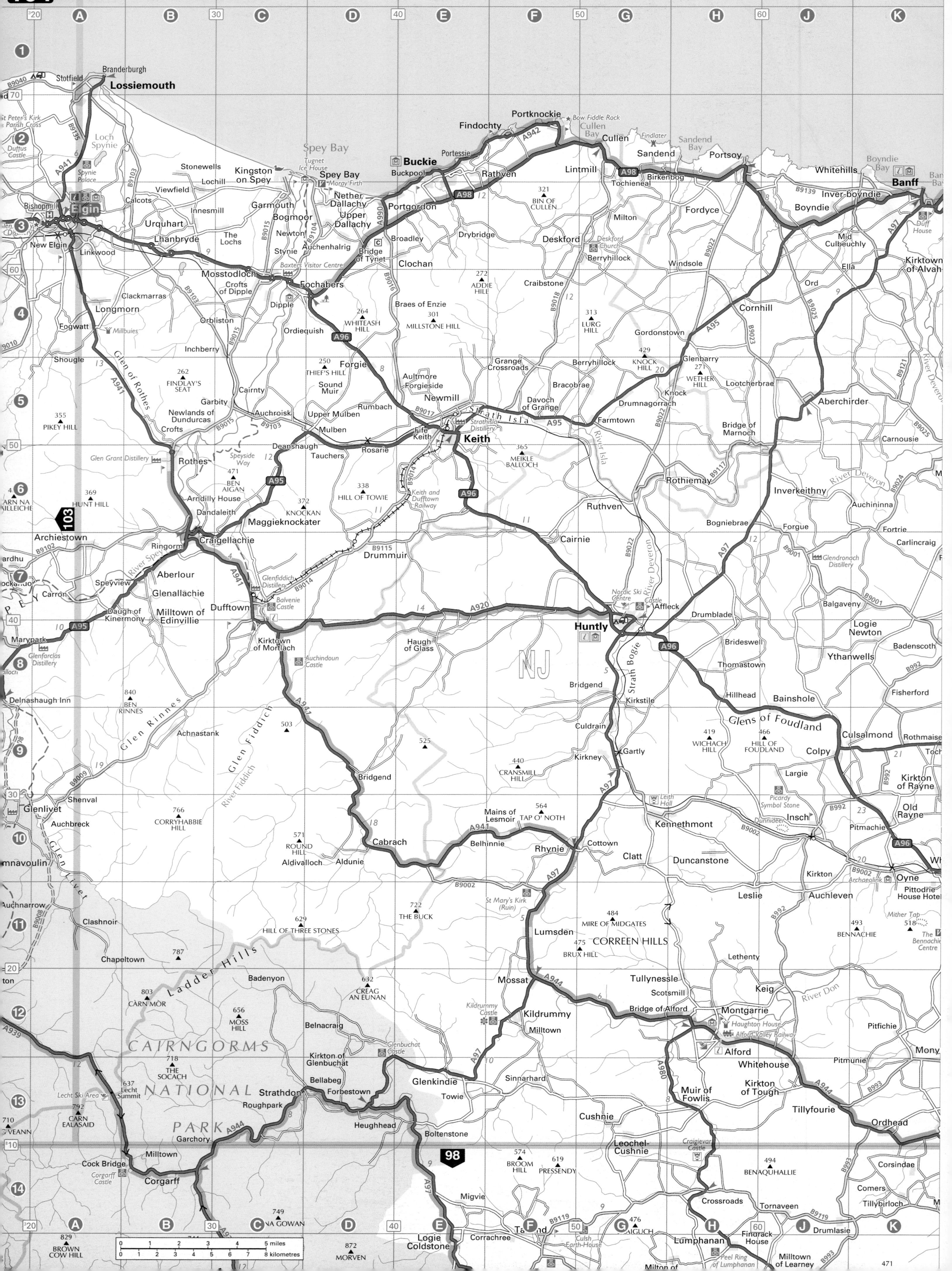
Lossiemouth
Branderburgh
Stotfield
Loch Spynie
Spynie Palace
Elgin
Bishopmill
New Elgin
Linkwood
Calcots
Urquhart
Lhanbryde
Innesmill
Stonewells
Lochill
Viewfield
Kingston on Spey
Spey Bay
Tugnet Ice House
Garmouth
Bogmoor
Newton
Stynie
The Lochs
Nether Dallachy
Upper Dallachy
Auchenhalrig
Mosstodloch
Crofts of Dipple
Dipple
Fochabers
Baxters Visitor Centre
Bridge of Tynet
Buckie
Buckpool
Portessie
Portgordon
Findochty
Portknockie
Bow Fiddle Rock
Cullen Bay
Cullen
Findlater
Sandend
Sandend Bay
Portsoy
Rathven
Lintmill
Tochieneal
Birkenbog
Whitehills
Boyndie Bay
Banff
Inver-boyndie
Boyndie
Fordyce
Milton
Deskford
Berryhillock
Drybridge
Broadley
Clochan
Windsole
Craibstone
Clackmarras
Longmorn
Fogwatt
Orbliston
Ordiequish
Braes of Enzie
Millstone Hill
Whiteash Hill
Addie Hill
Bin of Cullen
Lurg Hill
Gordonstown
Cornhill
Ord
Ella
Mid Culbeuchly
Duff House
Kirktown of Alvah
Shougle
Inchberry
Findlay's Seat
Glen of Rothes
Cairnty
Garbity
Newlands of Dundurcas
Crofts
Pikey Hill
Auchroisk
Upper Mulben
Mulben
Thief's Hill
Sound Muir
Forgie
Rumbach
Aultmore
Forgieside
Newmill
Grange Crossroads
Berryhillock
Knock Hill
Glenbarry
Wether Hill
Lootcherbrae
Bracobrae
Davoch of Grange
Knock
Drumnagorrach
Farmtown
Aberchirder
Bridge of Marnoch
Carnousie
Strath Isla
Strathisla Distillery
Fife Keith
Keith
Rosarie
Deanshaugh
Tauchers
Meikle Balloch
River Isla
Glen Grant Distillery
Rothes
Speyside Way
Ben Aigan
Arndilly House
Dandaleith
Hill of Towie
Knockan
Keith and Dufftown Railway
Rothiemay
Inverkeithny
River Deveron
Auchininna
Hunt Hill
Maggieknockater
Ruthven
Bogniebrae
Forgue
Fortrie
Archiestown
Craigellachie
Ringorm
Drummuir
Cairnie
Carlincraig
Glendronach Distillery
Aberlour
Speyview
Carron
Glenallachie
River Spey
Glenfiddich Distillery
Balvenie Castle
Dufftown
Milltown of Edinvillie
Daugh of Kinermony
Marypark
Glenfarclas Distillery
Nordic Ski Centre
Castle
Affleck
Huntly
Drumblade
Balgaveny
Logie Newton
Kirktown of Mortlach
Auchindoun Castle
Haugh of Glass
NJ
Brideswell
Badenscoth
Thomastown
Ythanwells
Delnashaugh Inn
Ben Rinnes
Glen Rinnes
Glen Fiddich
River Fiddich
Bridgend
Strath Bogie
Kirkstile
Hillhead
Bainshole
Fisherford
Glens of Foudland
Culdrain
Achnastank
Wichach Hill
Hill of Foudland
Culsalmond
Rothmaise
Colpy
Gartly
Kirkney
Cransmill Hill
Largie
Kirkton of Rayne
Old Rayne
Glenlivet
Shenval
Auchbreck
Corryhabbie Hill
Leith Hall
Picardy Symbol Stone
Insch
Dunnideer
Pitmachie
Mains of Lesmoir
Tap o' Noth
Kennethmont
Round Hill
Cabrach
Belhinnie
Rhynie
Cottown
Clatt
Duncanstone
Aldivalloch
Aldunie
Glen Livet
St Mary's Kirk (Ruin)
Leslie
Kirkton
Archaeolink
Oyne
Pittodrie House Hotel
Auchleven
Auchnarrow
Clashnoir
The Buck
Hill of Three Stones
Mire of Midgates
Correen Hills
Lumsden
Brux Hill
Bennachie
Mither Tap
The Bennachie Centre
Chapeltown
Lethenty
Ladder Hills
Badenyon
Creag an Eunan
Carn Mor
Moss Hill
Mossat
Tullynessle
Scotsmill
Keig
River Don
Bridge of Alford
Montgarrie
Haughton House
Alford Valley Railway
Pitfichie
Kildrummy Castle
Kildrummy
Milltown
Belnacraig
Glenbuchat Castle
Kirkton of Glenbuchat
Alford
Whitehouse
Pitmunie
Cairngorms National Park
The Socach
Lecht Ski Area
Lecht Summit
Carn Ealasaid
Bellabeg
Strathdon
Forbestown
Glenkindie
Towie
Sinnarhard
Muir of Fowlis
Kirkton of Tough
Tillyfourie
Roughpark
Heughhead
Cushnie
Ordhead
Garchory
Boltenstone
Leochel-Cushnie
Craigievar Castle
Cock Bridge
Corgarff Castle
Corgarff
Broom Hill
Pressendy
Benaquhallie
Corsindae
Migvie
Crossroads
Tornaveen
Comers
Tillybirloch
Na Gowan
Tarland
Cairnmore
Brown Cow Hill
Morven
Logie Coldstone
Corrachree
Culsh Earth-House
Lumphanan
Findrack House
Peel Ring of Lumphanan
Milltown of Learney
Drumlasie
A941
A96
A95
A98
A942
A990
A97
A920
A944
A939
A980
B9015
B9103
B9104
B9016
B9018
B9022
B9023
B9025
B9139
B9017
B9014
B9115
B9117
B9024
B9121
B9001
B9002
B992
B9009
B9008
B9102
B9119
B993
103
98
0 1 2 3 4 5 miles
0 1 2 3 4 5 6 7 8 kilometres

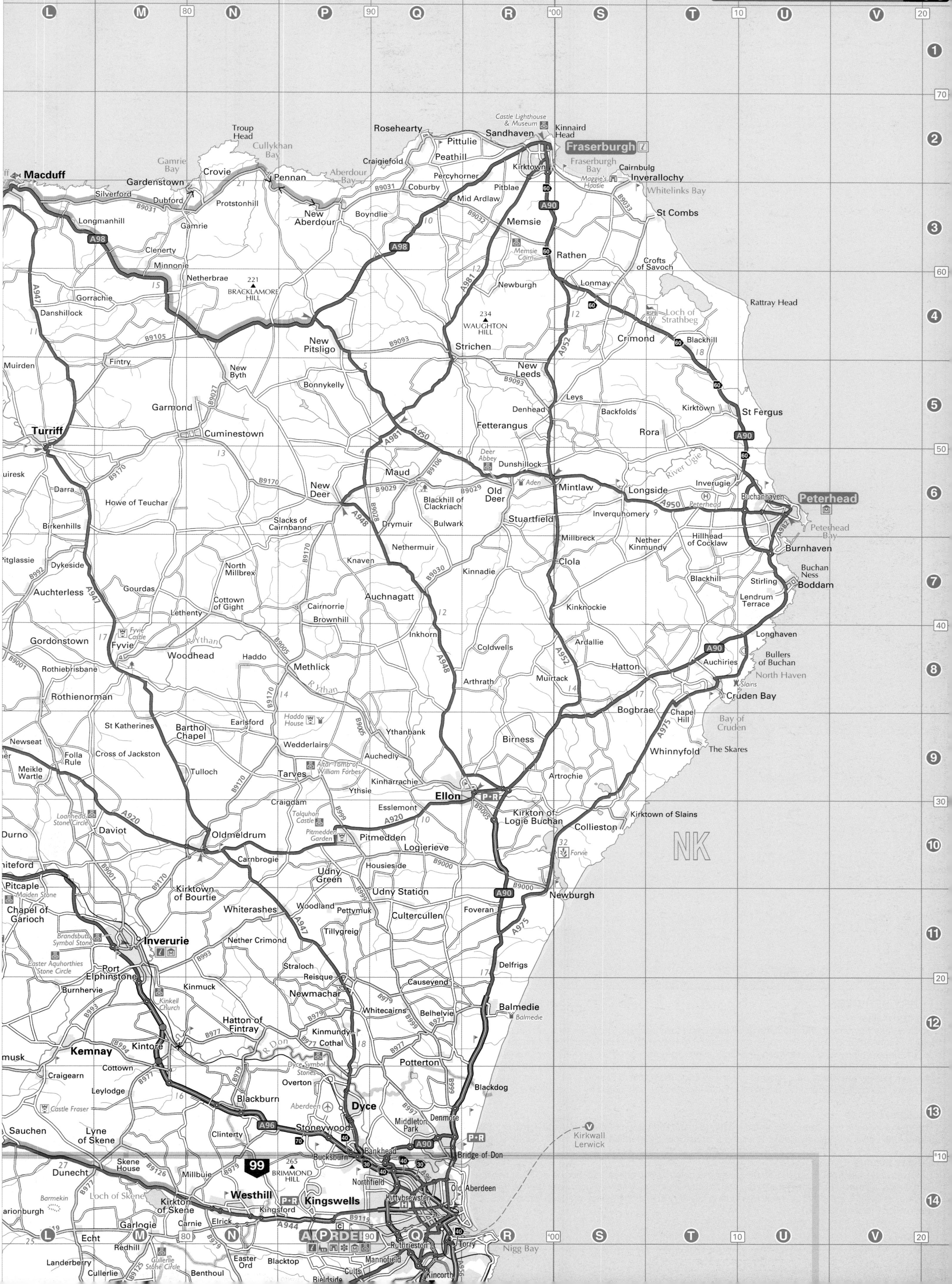

Troup Head
Rosehearty
Castle Lighthouse & Museum
Sandhaven
Kinnaird Head
Fraserburgh
Cullykhan Bay
Gamrie Bay
Pittulie
Peathill
Craigiefold
Fraserburgh Bay
Cairnbulg
Inverallochy
Macduff
Gardenstown
Crovie
Pennan
Aberdour Bay
Percyhorner
Kirktown
Maggie's Hoosie
Whitelinks Bay
Silverford
Dubford
Coburby
Mid Ardlaw
Pitblae
Protstonhill
New Aberdour
Boyndlie
Memsie
St Combs
Longmanhill
Gamrie
Clenerty
Minnonie
Memsie Cairn
Rathen
Crofts of Savoch
Netherbrae
221 BRACKLAMORE HILL
Newburgh
Lonmay
Gorrachie
Danshillock
234 WAUGHTON HILL
Loch of Strathbeg
Rattray Head
Crimond
Blackhill
New Pitsligo
Strichen
Muirden
Fintry
New Byth
New Leeds
Bonnykelly
Leys
Garmond
Denhead
Backfolds
Kirktown
St Fergus
Turriff
Cuminestown
Fetterangus
Rora
Deer Abbey
Dunshillock
Maud
Aden
Mintlaw
Longside
Inverugie
River Ugie
Peterhead
uiresk
Darra
New Deer
Blackhill of Clackriach
Old Deer
Buchanhaven
Howe of Teuchar
Inverquhomery
Stuartfield
Peterhead Bay
Slacks of Cairnbanno
Drymuir
Bulwark
Millbreck
Nether Kinmundy
Hillhead of Cocklaw
Birkenhills
Nethermuir
Burnhaven
Itglassie
Dykeside
Knaven
North Millbrex
Kinnadie
Clola
Buchan Ness
Boddam
Auchterless
Gourdas
Cottown of Gight
Auchnagatt
Blackhill
Stirling
Lendrum Terrace
Lethenty
Cairnorrie
Brownhill
Kinknockie
Fyvie Castle
Gordonstown
Fyvie
Inkhorn
Longhaven
Woodhead
R. Ythan
Haddo
Coldwells
Ardallie
Rothiebrisbane
Methlick
Hatton
Auchiries
Buller of Buchan
Arthrath
Muirtack
North Haven
Slains
Rothienorman
Cruden Bay
Bogbrae
Chapel Hill
Haddo House
Bay of Cruden
St Katherines
Barthol Chapel
Earlsford
Ythanbank
Birness
Newseat
Folla Rule
Cross of Jackston
Wedderlairs
Auchedly
Whinnyfold
The Skares
Meikle Wartle
Tulloch
Altar Tomb of William Forbes
Tarves
Kinharrachie
Artrochie
Ythsie
Ellon
Craigdam
Esslemont
Kirkton of Logie Buchan
Kirktown of Slains
Loanhead Stone Circle
Tolquhon Castle
Daviot
Collieston
Durno
Oldmeldrum
Pitmedden Garden
Pitmedden
Logierieve
NK
Forvie
iteford
Carnbrogie
Housieside
Udny Green
Pitcaple
Maiden Stone
Udny Station
Newburgh
Chapel of Garioch
Kirktown of Bourtie
Whiterashes
Woodland
Pettymuk
Cultercullen
Foveran
Brandsbutt Symbol Stone
Tillygreig
Inverurie
Nether Crimond
Easter Aquhorthies Stone Circle
Straloch
Delfrigs
Port Elphinstone
Reisque
Causeyend
Burnhervie
Kinmuck
Newmachar
Kinkell Church
Whitecairns
Belhelvie
Balmedie
Hatton of Fintray
Kinmundy
Kemnay
Kintore
R. Don
Cothal
musk
Cottown
Dyce Symbol Stones
Potterton
Craigearn
Leylodge
Overton
Blackdog
Blackburn
Castle Fraser
Aberdeen
Dyce
Middleton Park
Denmore
Sauchen
Lyne of Skene
Clinterty
Stoneywood
Kirkwall
Lerwick
Bankhead
Skene House
Bucksburn
Bridge of Don
Dunecht
Millbuie
265 BRIMMOND HILL
Northfield
Old Aberdeen
Barmekin
Loch of Skene
Westhill
Kingswells
Kittybrewster
arionburgh
Kirkton of Skene
Kingsford
Garlogie
Carnie
Elrick
ABERDEEN
Echt
Ruthrieston
Torry
Nigg Bay
Redhill
Gullerie Stone Circle
Easter Ord
Blacktop
Mannofield
Landerberry
Cullerlie
Benthoul
Cults
Bieldside
Kincorth
A98
A90
A981
A950
A952
A948
A947
A920
A975
A96
A944
A982
99

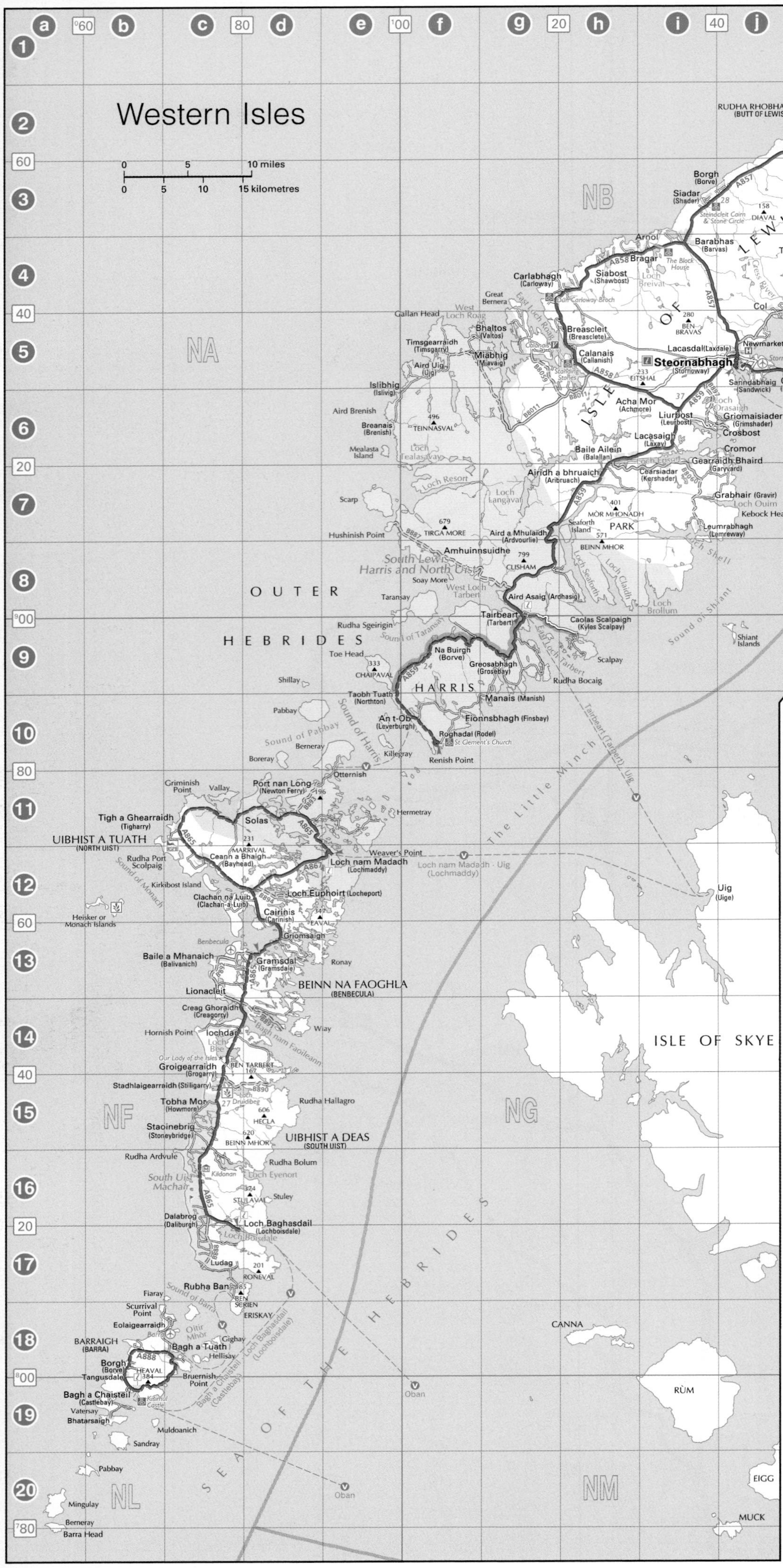

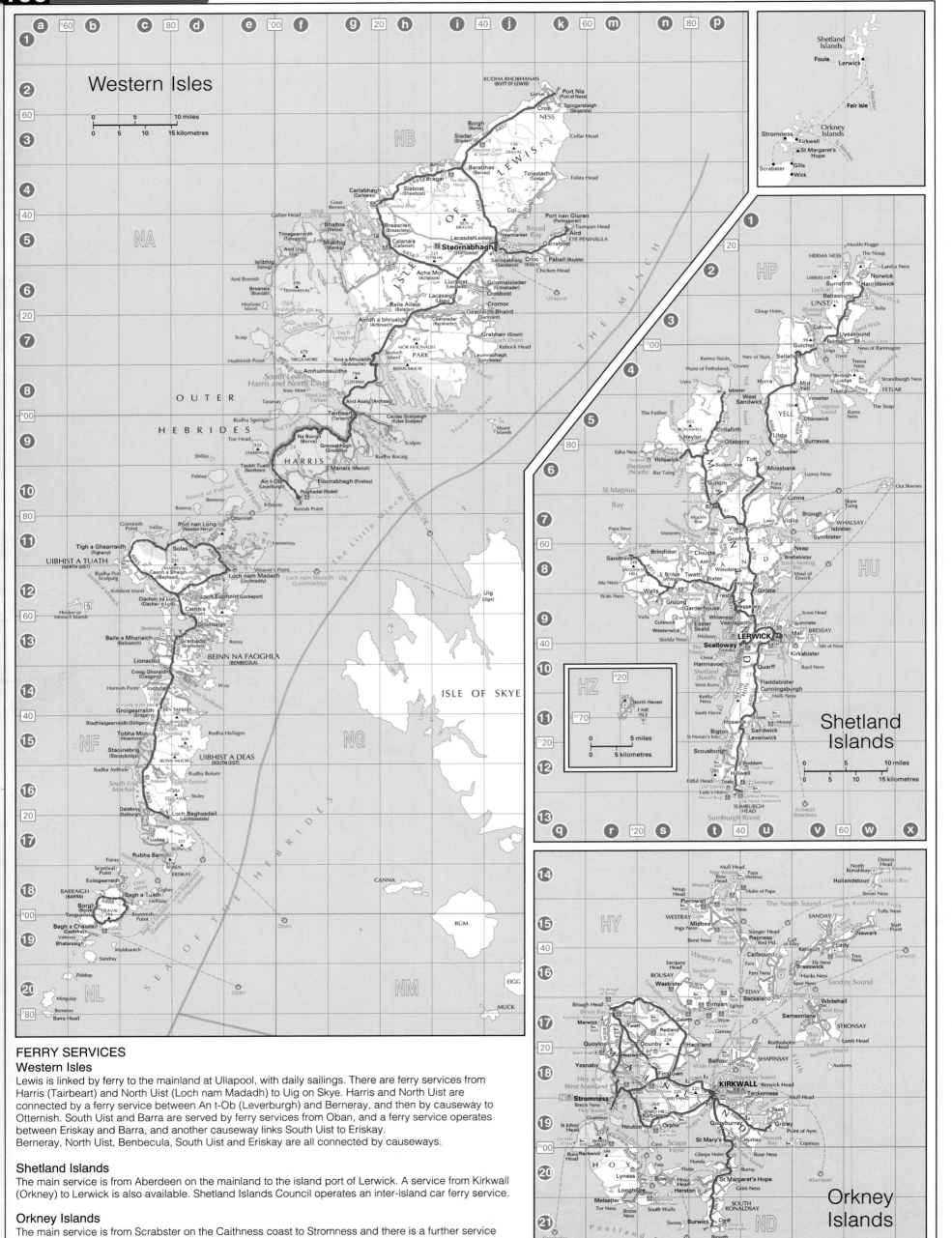

FERRY SERVICES

Western Isles

Lewis is linked by ferry to the mainland at Ullapool, with daily sailings. There are ferry services from Harris (Tairbeart) and North Uist (Loch nam Madadh) to Uig on Skye. Harris and North Uist are connected by a ferry service between An t-Ob (Leverburgh) and Berneray, and then by causeway to Otternish. South Uist and Barra are served by ferry services from Oban, and a ferry service operates between Eriskay and Barra, and another causeway links South Uist to Eriskay.
Berneray, North Uist, Benbecula, South Uist and Eriskay are all connected by causeways.

Shetland Islands

The main service is from Aberdeen on the mainland to the island port of Lerwick. A service from Kirkwall (Orkney) to Lerwick is also available. Shetland Islands Council operates an inter-island car ferry service.

Orkney Islands

The main service is from Scrabster on the Caithness coast to Stromness and there is a further service from Gills (Caithness) to St Margaret's Hope on South Ronaldsay. A service from Aberdeen to Kirkwall provides a link to Shetland at Lerwick. Inter-island car ferry services are also operated (advance reservations recommended).

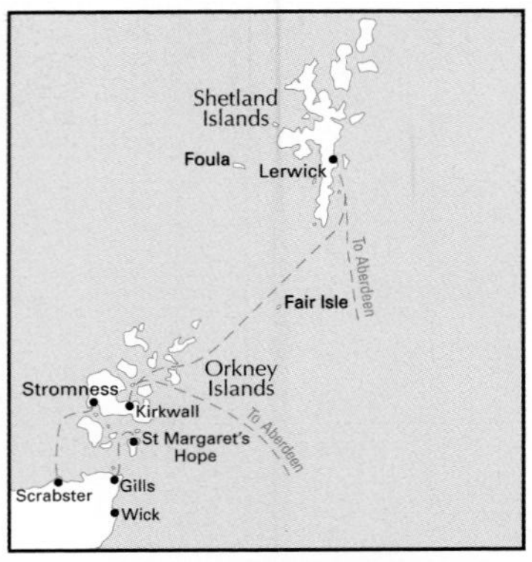

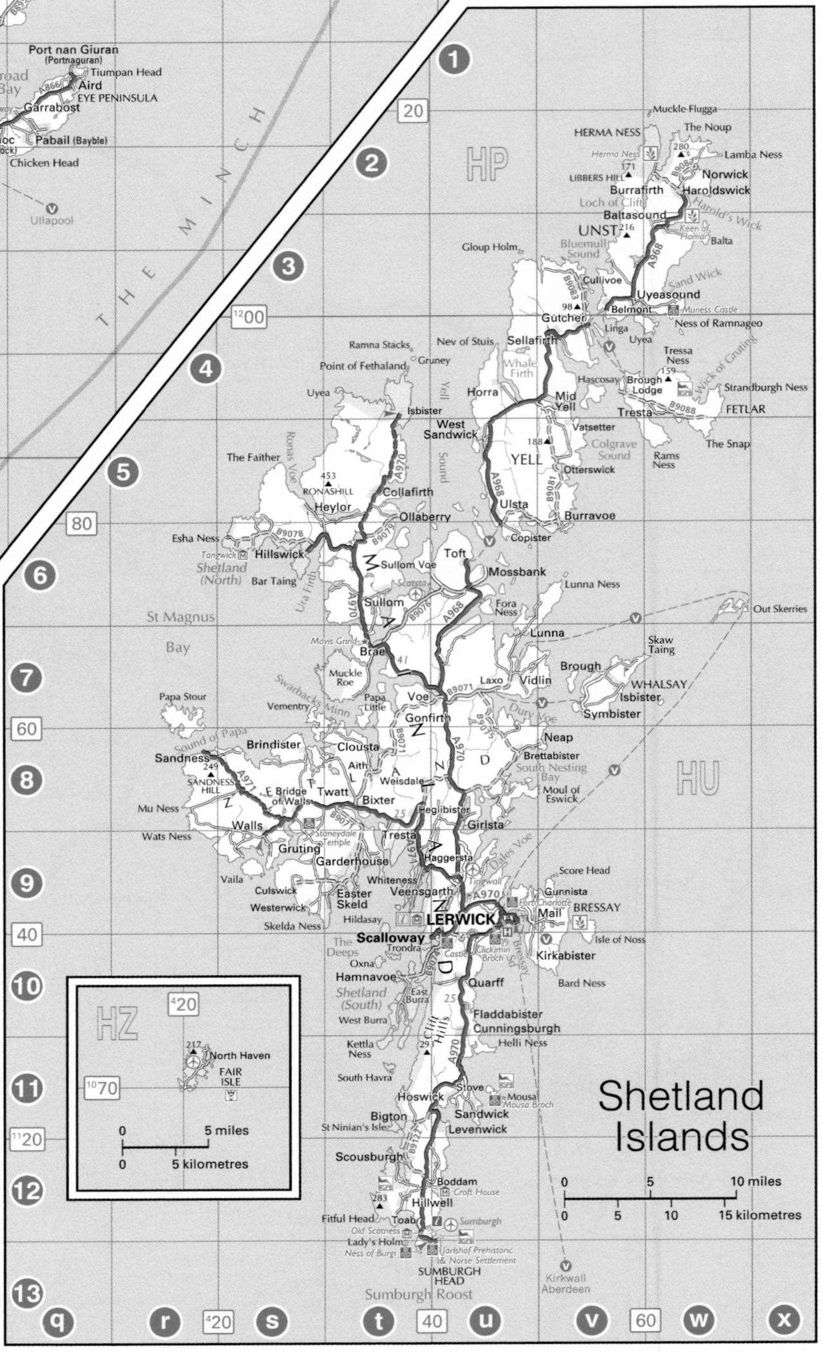

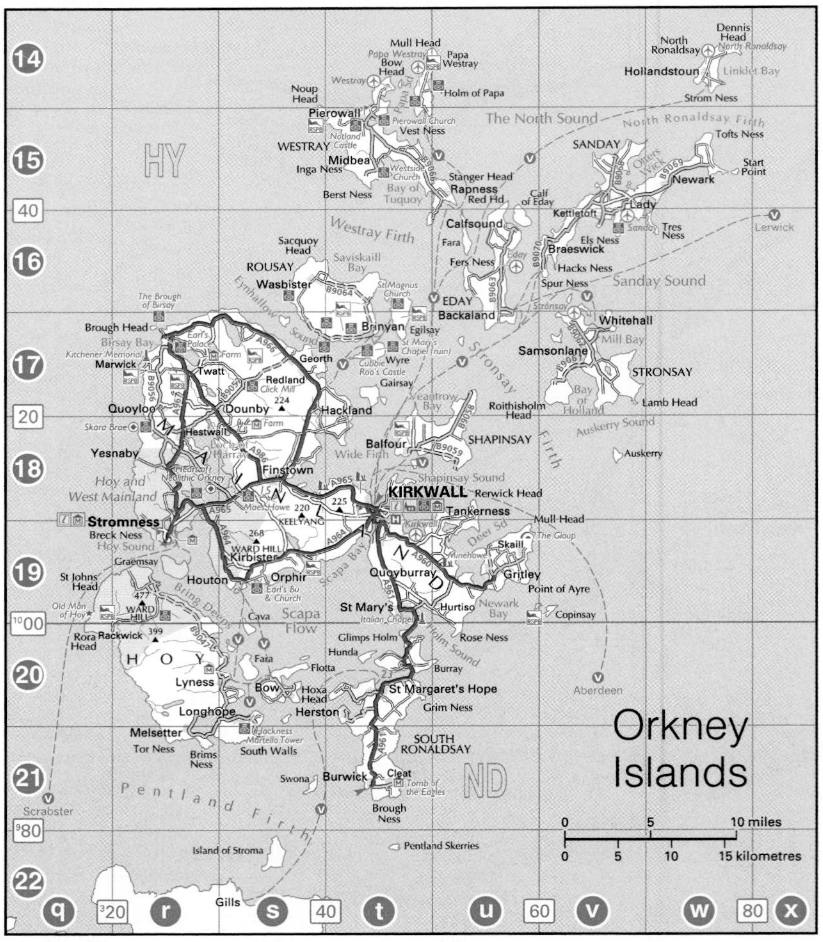

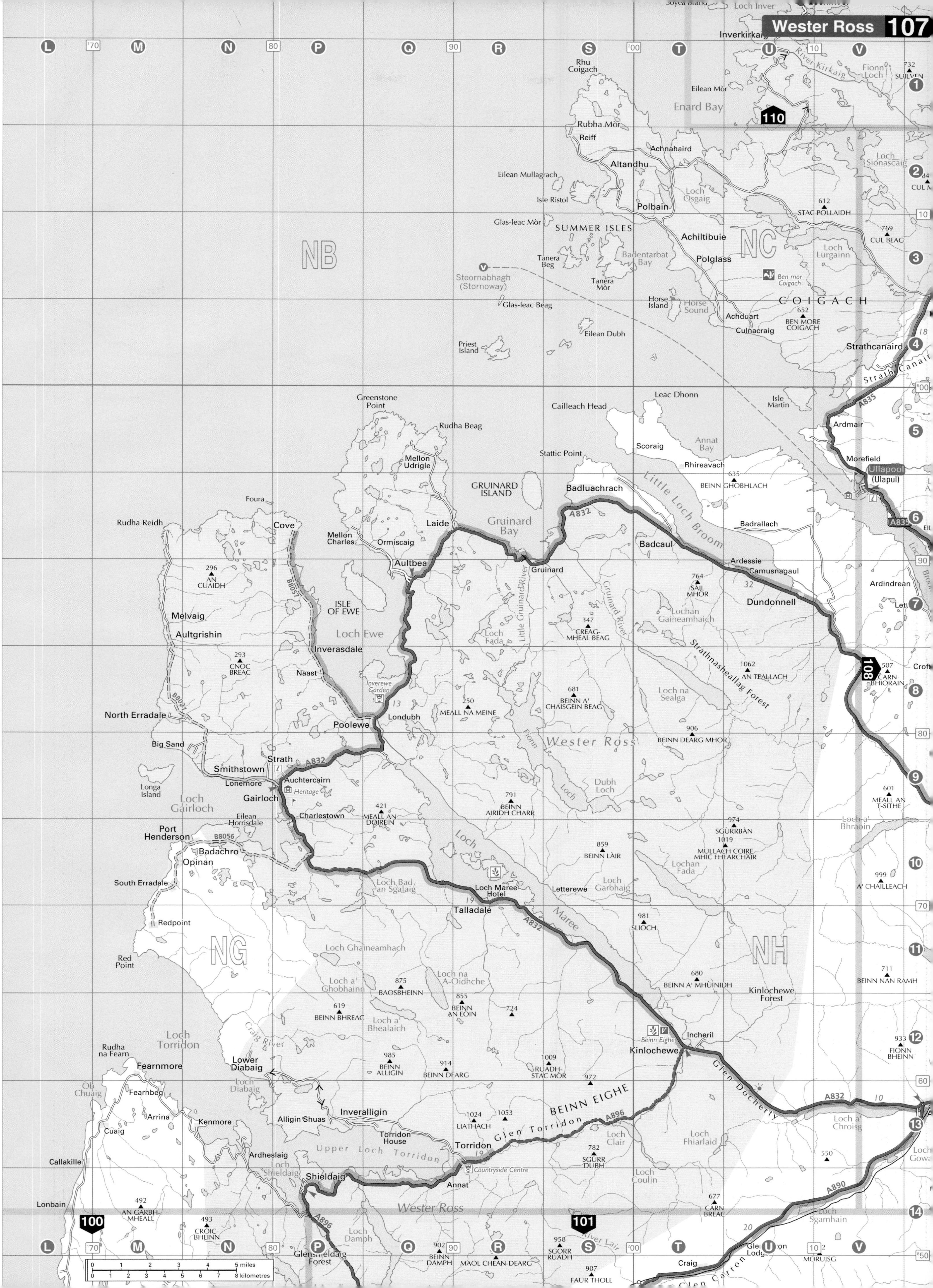

Inverkirkaig

River Kirkaig

Fionn
Loch

732
SUILVEN

1

110

Joyea Island

Loch Inver

Eilean Mòr

Enard Bay

Loch
Sionascaig

2

CUL M

Rhu
Coigach

Achnahaird

Rubha Mòr

Reiff

Altandhu

Eilean Mullagrach

Isle Ristol

Polbain

SUMMER ISLES

Badentarbat
Bay

Tanera
Beg

Steòrnabhagh
(Stornoway)

Tanera
Mòr

Glas-leac Mòr

Glas-leac Beag

Priest
Island

Eilean Dubh

Achiltibuie

Polglass

Horse
Island

Horse
Sound

Achduart

Culnacraig

612
STAC POLLAIDH

769
CUL BEAG

3

Loch
Osgaig

Loch
Lurgainn

Ben mòr
Coigach

NC

COIGACH

652
BEN MORE
COIGACH

18

4

Strathcanaird

Strath Canaird

A835

00

Greenstone
Point

Leac Dhonn

Cailleach Head

Isle
Martin

Ardmair

5

Rudha Beag

Scoraig

Annat
Bay

Rhireavach

Morefield

Ullapool
(Ulapul)

6

Mellon
Udrigle

Stattic Point

635

BEINN GHOBHLACH

Badluachrach

A832

Little Loch Broom

A835

GRUINARD
ISLAND

Gruinard
Bay

Gruinard

Badcaul

Badrallach

Ardessie
Camusnagaul

764
SAIL
MHOR

32

Dundonnell

Ardindrean

Lett

7

Rudha Reidh

Cove

Foura

Laide

Mellon
Charles

Ormiscaig

Aultbea

296
AN
CUAIDH

B8057

Little Gruinard River

Gruinard River

347
CREAG-
MHEAL BEAG

Lochan
Gaineamhaich

1062
AN TEALLACH

Strathnasheallag Forest

507
CARN
BHIORAIN

Croft

8

108

Melvaig

Aultgrishin

Inverasdale

ISLE
OF EWE

Loch Ewe

293
CNOC
BREAC

Naast

Inverewe
Garden

13

Loch
Fada

681
BEINN A'
CHAISGEIN BEAG

Loch na
Sealga

906
BEINN DEARG MHOR

Wester Ross

B8021

North Erradale

Poolewe

Londubh

250
MEALL NA MEINE

Fionn
Loch

601
MEALL AN
T-SITHE

9

80

Big Sand

Smithstown

Longa
Island

Strath

A832

Auchtercairn

Heritage

Gairloch

Lonemore

Eilean
Horrisdale

Charlestown

421
MEALL AN
DOIREIN

791
BEINN
AIRIDH CHARR

Dubh
Loch

Loch
Maree

974
SGÙRR BÀN

1019
MULLACH COIRE
MHIC FHEARCHAIR

Loch-a'
Bhraoin

Loch
Gairloch

Port
Henderson

B8056

Badachro

Opinan

South Erradale

Loch Bad
an Sgalaig

19

Loch Maree
Hotel

Talladale

A832

Maree

859
BEINN LAIR

Letterewe

Loch
Garbhaig

Lochan
Fada

999
A' CHAILLEACH

10

70

Redpoint

NG

Craig River

Loch Ghaineamhach

981
SLIOCH

A832

680
BEINN A' MHÙINIDH

Kinlochewe
Forest

711
BEINN NAN RAMH

NH

11

Red
Point

Loch
Torridon

Loch a'
Ghobhainn

875
BAOSBHEINN

Loch na
A-Oidhche

855
BEINN
AN EOIN

724

933
FIONN
BHEINN

12

60

Rudha
na Fearn

Fearnmore

Lower
Diabaig

619
BEINN BHREAC

Loch a'
Bhealaich

Beinn Eighe

Incheril

Kinlochewe

Glen Docherty

A832

10

13

Fearnberg

Arrina

Kenmore

Loch
Diabaig

Inveralligin

985
BEINN
ALLIGIN

914
BEINN DEARG

1009
RUADH-
STAC MOR

972

BEINN EIGHE

A896

Loch a'
Chroisg

Cuaig

All[?]

Callakille

Alligin Shuas

1024
LIATHACH

1053

Glen Torridon

Loch
Clair

Loch
Fhiarlaid

550

Loch
Gowa[?]

Lonbain

An Garbh-
Mheall

Torridon
House

Torridon

782
SGÙRR
DUBH

677
CARN
BREAC

14

492
AN GARBH-
MHEALL

Upper Loch Torridon

Ardheslaig

Loch
Shieldaig

Countryside Centre

Annat

Loch
Coulin

A890

100

493
CROIC-
BHEINN

Shieldaig

A896

Wester Ross

Loch
Sgamhain

20

101

Glensheildaig
Forest

Loch
Damph

902
BEINN
DAMPH

958
SGORR
RUADH

907
FUAR THOLL

River Lair

00

Glen Carron

Craig

Glen
Lodge

MORUISG

Glen Garron

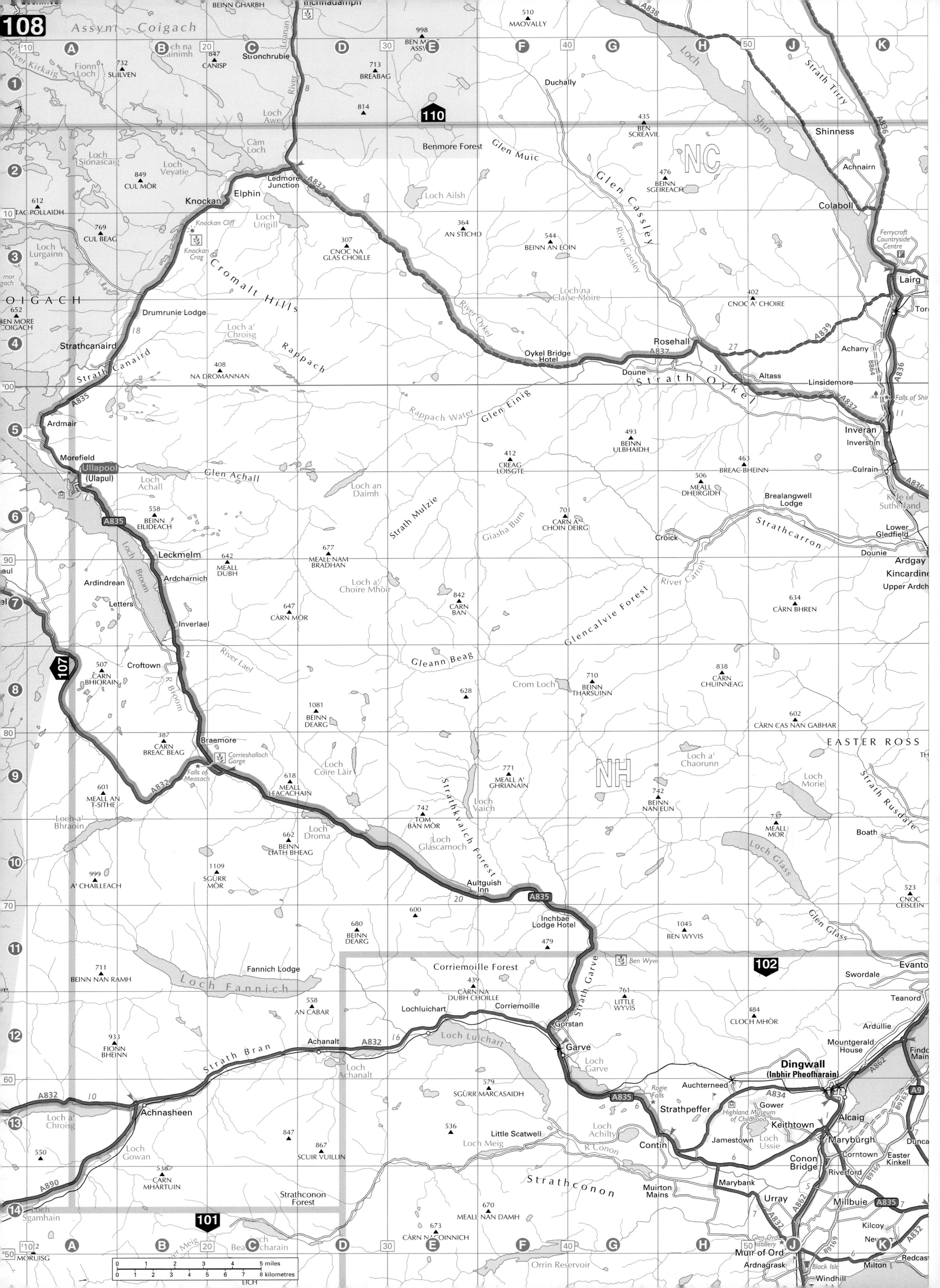
Assynt - Coigach
BEINN GHARBH
Inchnadamph
510
MAOVALLY
A838
A B C D E F G H J K
Fionn Loch
732
SUILVEN
Loch na Gainimh
847
CANISP
Stronchrubie
998
BEN MORE ASSYNT
713
BREABAG
Loch Shin
Strath Tirry
Duchally
814
110
Loch Awe
Càm Loch
Benmore Forest
Glen Muic
435
BEN SCREAVIL
NC
Shinness
A836
Loch Sionascaig
Loch Veyatie
849
CUL MÒR
Ledmore Junction
A837
Elphin
Knockan
476
BEINN SGEIREACH
Achnairn
612
TAC POLLAIDH
Knockan Cliff
Loch Urigill
Loch Ailsh
Glen Cassley
Colaboll
769
CUL BEAG
364
AN STICHD
Loch Lurgainn
Knockan Crag
307
CNOC NA GLAS CHOILLE
544
BEINN AN EOIN
River Cassley
Ferrycroft Countryside Centre
Lairg
Cromalt Hills
COIGACH
652
BEN MORE COIGACH
Drumrunie Lodge
Loch na Claise Mòire
402
CNOC A' CHOIRE
Tor
Loch a' Chroisg
River Oykel
A839
Strathcanaird
Rappach
Rosehall
Achany
Oykel Bridge Hotel
408
NA DROMANNAN
Doune
Strath Oykel
Altass
Linsidemore
B864
Strath Canaird
A835
Falls of Shin
Rappach Water
Glen Einig
Ardmair
Inveran
Invershin
493
BEINN ULBHAIDH
Morefield
412
CREAG LOISGTE
463
BREAC BHEINN
Culrain
Ullapool
(Ulapul)
Glen Achall
Loch Achall
Loch an Daimh
506
MEALL DHEIRGIDH
Kyle of Sutherland
558
BEINN EILIDEACH
Strath Mulzie
Brealangwell Lodge
701
CARN A' CHOIN DEIRG
Giasha Burn
Strathcarron
Croick
Lower Gledfield
Loch Broom
Leckmelm
642
MEALL DUBH
677
MEALL NAM BRADHAN
Dounie
Ardgay
Kincardine
Upper Ardch
Ardindrean
Ardcharnich
River Carron
Loch a' Choire Mhòir
842
CARN BAN
634
CÀRN BHREN
Letters
Glencalvie Forest
647
CÀRN MÒR
Inverlael
River Lael
Gleann Beag
107
507
CARN BHIORAIN
Croftown
R Broom
838
CARN CHUINNEAG
Crom Loch
710
BEINN THARSUINN
628
1081
BEINN DEARG
602
CÀRN CAS NAN GABHAR
Braemore
387
CARN BREAC BEAG
Corrieshalloch Gorge
EASTER ROSS
NH
Loch a' Chaorunn
Loch Coire Làir
Falls of Measach
771
MEALL A' GHRIANAIN
Loch Morie
A832
618
MEALL LEACACHAIN
Strathkvaich Forest
742
BEINN NAN EUN
Strath Rusdale
601
MEALL AN T-SITHE
Loch Vaich
742
TOM BÀN MÒR
737
MEALL MÒR
Loch a' Bhraoin
Loch Droma
Boath
662
BEINN LIATH BHEAG
Loch Glascarnoch
Loch Glass
1109
SGÙRR MÒR
999
A' CHAILLEACH
Aultguish Inn
523
CNOC CEISLEIN
600
Inchbae Lodge Hotel
680
BEINN DEARG
1045
BEN WYVIS
Glen Glass
479
Ben Wyvis
102
Evanto
Strath Garve
711
BEINN NAN RAMH
Fannich Lodge
Corriemoille Forest
Swordale
Loch Fannich
439
CÀRN NA DUBH CHOILLE
761
LITTLE WYVIS
558
AN CABAR
Teanord
Lochluichart
Corriemoille
484
CLOCH MHÒR
933
FIONN BHEINN
Gorstan
Ardullie
Loch Luichart
Mountgerald House
Strath Bran
Achanalt
Garve
Loch Achanalt
Loch Garve
Dingwall
(Inbhir Pheofharain)
A832
579
SGÙRR MARCASAIDH
Auchterneed
Rogie Falls
A834
A9
Loch a' Chroisg
Achnasheen
Strathpeffer
Gower
Highland Museum of Childhood
Alcaig
Keithtown
536
Little Scatwell
Loch Achilty
Jamestown
Loch Ussie
Maryburgh
Loch Gowan
Loch Meig
Contin
R Conon
Duncan
847
867
SCUIR VUILLIN
Conon Bridge
Corntown
Easter Kinkell
550
538
CARN MHARTUIN
Riverford
B9169
A890
Strathconon
Muirton Mains
Marybank
Strathconon Forest
Urray
Millbuie
A862
Loch Sgamhain
670
MEALL NAN DAMH
Kilcoy
101
673
CÀRN NA COINNICH
Glen Ord Distillery
MORUISG
Muir of Ord
Redcast
Ardnagrask
Black Isle
Milton
Orrin Reservoir
Windhill
0 1 2 3 4 5 miles
0 1 2 3 4 5 6 7 8 kilometres

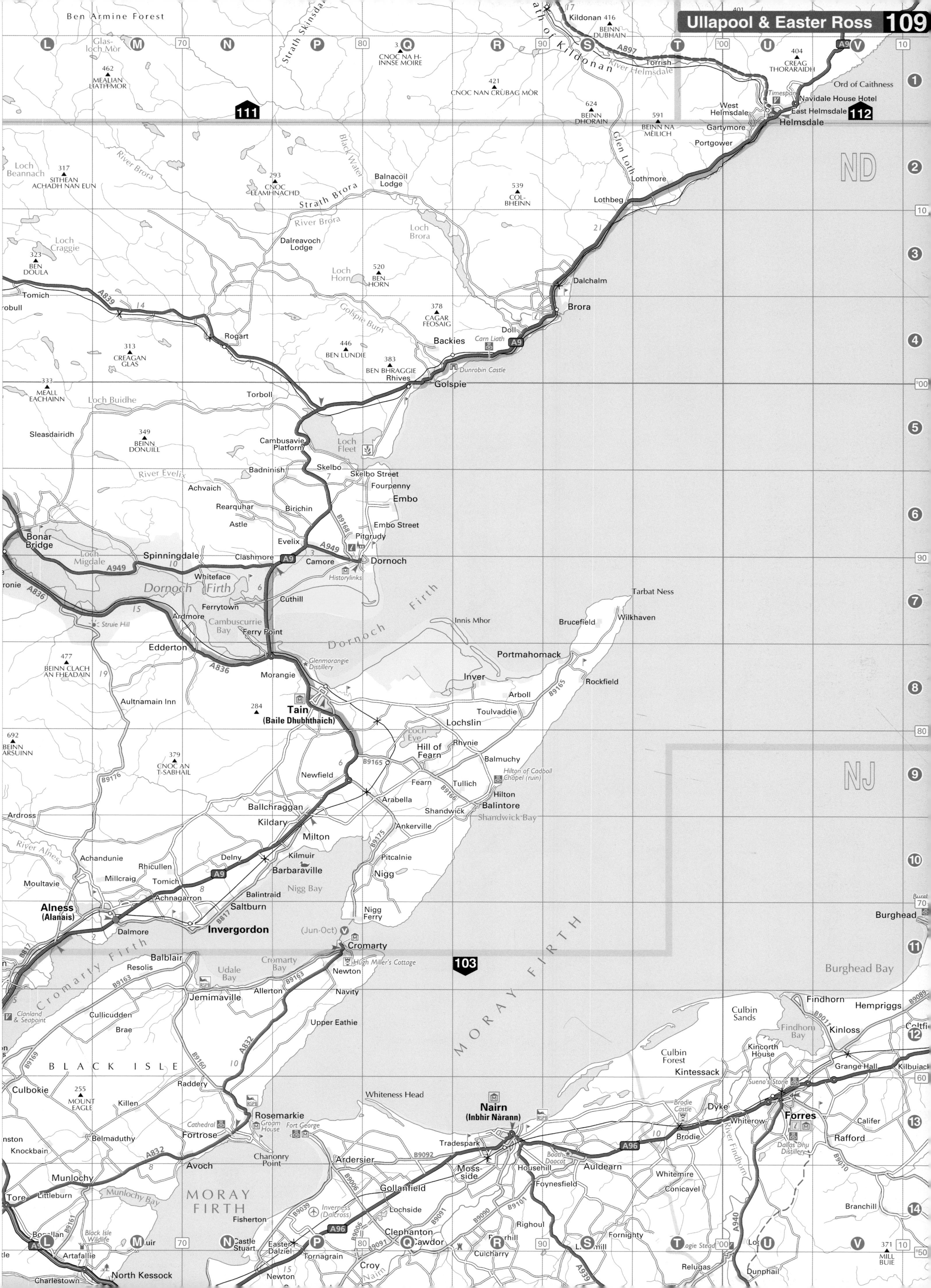
Ben Armine Forest
Glas-loch Mòr
462 MEALLAN LIATH MÒR
Strath Skinsdale
CNOC NA H-INNSE MOIRE
421 CNOC NAN CRÙBAG MÒR
Kildonan 416
BEINN DUBHAIN
Strath of Kildonan
River Helmsdale
A897
Torrish
404 CREAG THORARAIDH
Ord of Caithness
Timespan
Navidale House Hotel
West Helmsdale
East Helmsdale
Helmsdale
111
112
624 BEINN DHORAIN
591 BEINN NA MEILICH
Gartymore
Portgower
ND
Loch Beannach
317 SITHEAN ACHADH NAN EUN
River Brora
Black Water
293 CNOC LEAMHNACHD
Strath Brora
Balnacoil Lodge
539 COL-BHEINN
Glen Loth
Lothmore
Lothbeg
River Brora
Loch Brora
Loch Craggie
323 BEN DOULA
Dalreavoch Lodge
Loch Horn
520 BEN HORN
Dalchalm
Brora
Tomich
A839
Golspie Burn
378 CAGAR FEOSAIG
Rogart
313 CREAGAN GLAS
446 BEN LUNDIE
Backies
Carn Liath
Doll
A9
383 BEN BHRAGGIE
Rhives
Dunrobin Castle
Golspie
333 MEALL EACHAINN
Loch Buidhe
Torboll
Sleasdairidh
349 BEINN DONUILL
Cambusavie Platform
Loch Fleet
River Evelix
Badninish
Skelbo
Skelbo Street
Fourpenny
Embo
Achvaich
Rearquhar
Birichin
B9168
Embo Street
Astle
Pitgrudy
Bonar Bridge
Evelix
A949
Loch Migdale
Spinningdale
Clashmore
Camore
Dornoch
A949
Whiteface
Historylinks
Dornoch Firth
Cuthill
A836
Ferrytown
Tarbat Ness
Ardmore
Wilkhaven
Struie Hill
Cambuscurrie Bay
Ferry Point
Innis Mhor
Brucefield
Dornoch
Edderton
477 BEINN CLACH AN FHEADAIN
A836
Glenmorangie Distillery
Portmahomack
Morangie
Inver
Rockfield
Aultnamain Inn
284
Tain (Baile Dhubhthaich)
Arboll
B9165
Toulvaddie
Lochslin
692 BEINN ARSUINN
379 CNOC AN T-SABHAIL
Loch Eye
Hill of Fearn
Rhynie
B9165
Balmuchy
NJ
B9176
Newfield
Fearn
Tullich
Hilton of Cadboll Chapel (ruin)
Hilton
B9166
Arabella
Ardross
Ballchraggan
Shandwick
Balintore
Kildary
Shandwick Bay
Ankerville
Milton
River Alness
B9175
Achandunie
Kilmuir
Pitcalnie
Rhicullen
Delny
Barbaraville
Millcraig
Tomich
Nigg
Moultavie
Nigg Bay
Balintraid
Achnagarron
Saltburn
Alness (Alanais)
Nigg Ferry
Burghead
B817
Dalmore
Invergordon
(Jun-Oct)
Cromarty
MORAY FIRTH
Balblair
Cromarty Firth
Resolis
Cromarty Bay
Hugh Miller's Cottage
103
Udale Bay
Newton
Burghead Bay
B9163
Allerton
Jemimaville
Navity
Clanland & Seaport
Findhorn
Hempriggs
Culbin Sands
Cullicudden
Findhorn Bay
Kinloss
Brae
Upper Eathie
Kincorth House
A832
Culbin Forest
B9169
B9160
Grange Hall
BLACK ISLE
Kintessack
Kilbuiack
Culbokie
255 MOUNT EAGLE
Raddery
Sueno's Stone
Killen
Whiteness Head
Nairn (Inbhir Nàrann)
Dyke
Rosemarkie
Brodie Castle
Forres
Groam House
Whiterow
Califer
Cathedral
Fort George
Belmaduthy
Fortrose
Brodie
Rafford
Knockbain
A832
Tradespark
A96
River Findhorn
Dallas Dhu Distillery
Chanonry Point
Avoch
Ardersier
B9092
Boath Doocot
Auldearn
Munlochy
Moss-side
Househill
Whitemire
B9010
B9006
Foynesfield
Tore
Littleburn
Gollanfield
Conicavel
MORAY FIRTH
Munlochy Bay
B9039
Inverness (Dalcross)
Lochside
B9091
B9090
B9101
Branchill
A940
B9161
Black Isle Wildlife
Fisherton
Righoul
Clephanton
Castle Stuart
Cawdor
Fornighty
Bogallan
Muir
Easter Dalziel
A96
B9091
Culcharry
Logie Steading
371 MILL BUIE
Artafallie
Tornagrain
Croy
Relugas
Dunphail
North Kessock
Charlestown
Newton
A939

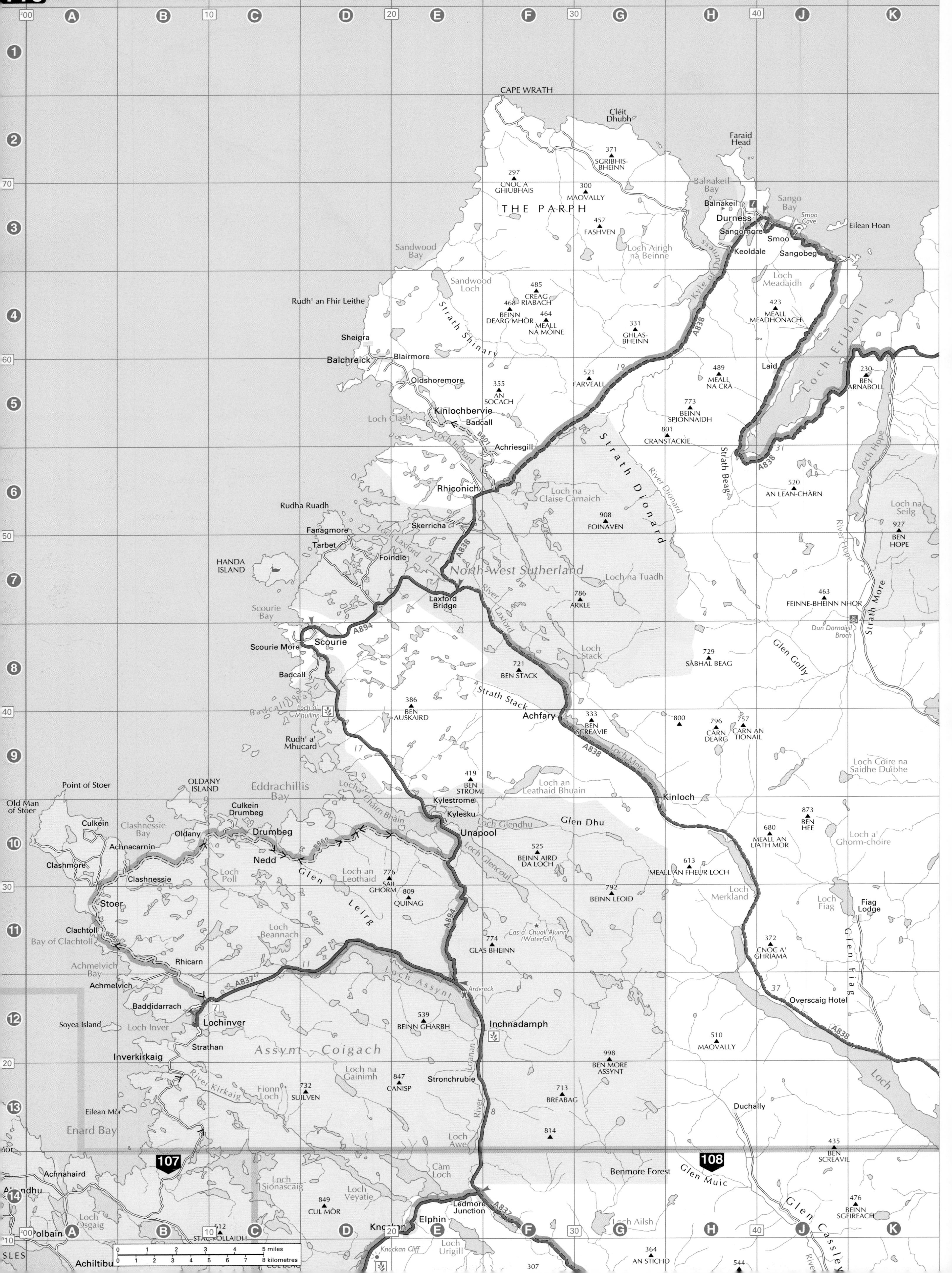
A
B
C
D
E
F
G
H
J
K
CAPE WRATH
Cléit Dhubh
Faraid Head
371 SGRIBHIS-BHEINN
297 CNOC A' GHIUBHAIS
300 MAOVALLY
THE PARPH
Balnakeil Bay
Balnakeil
Durness
Sango Bay
Smoo Cave
Eilean Hoan
457 FASHVEN
Sangomore
Smoo
Keoldale
Sangobeg
Loch Airigh na Beinne
Kyle of Durness
Sandwood Bay
Sandwood Loch
485 CREAG RIABACH
468 BEINN DEARG MHÒR
464 MEALL NA MOINE
Loch Meadaidh
423 MEALL MEADHONACH
Rudh' an Fhir Leithe
Strath Shinary
331 GHLAS-BHEINN
A838
Loch Eriboll
Sheigra
Balchreick
Blairmore
Oldshoremore
355 AN SOCACH
521 FARVEALL
489 MEALL NA CRA
Laid
230 BEN ARNABOLL
773 BEINN SPIONNAIDH
Kinlochbervie
Loch Clash
Badcall
B801
Loch Inchard
Achriesgill
801 CRANSTACKIE
Strath Dionard
River Dionard
Strath Beag
Loch Hope
520 AN LEAN-CHÀRN
Rhiconich
Loch na Claise Carnaich
Rudha Ruadh
908 FOINAVEN
Loch na Seilg
927 BEN HOPE
River Hope
Fanagmore
Skerricha
Tarbet
Loch Laxford
Foindle
HANDA ISLAND
North-west Sutherland
Loch na Tuadh
786 ARKLE
463 FEINNE-BHEINN NHOR
Strath More
Scourie Bay
Laxford Bridge
River Laxford
Dun Dornaigil Broch
A894
Scourie
Scourie More
Loch Stack
729 SÀBHAL BEAG
Glen Golly
Badcall
721 BEN STACK
Strath Stack
Badcall Bay
Loch a' Mhuilinn
386 BEN AUSKAIRD
Achfary
333 BEN SCREAVIE
800
796 CARN DEARG
757 CARN AN TIONAIL
Rudh' a' Mhucard
Loch More
Loch Coire na Saidhe Duibhe
Point of Stoer
OLDANY ISLAND
Eddrachillis Bay
419 BEN STROME
Loch an Leathaid Bhuain
Old Man of Stoer
Culkein Drumbeg
Loch a' Chàirn Bhàin
Kylestrome
Kinloch
Culkein
Clashnessie Bay
Kylesku
Loch Glendhu
Glen Dhu
873 BEN HEE
Oldany
Drumbeg
Unapool
680 MEALL AN LIATH MOR
Loch a' Ghorm-choire
Achnacarnin
B869
525 BEINN AIRD DA LOCH
Clashmore
Nedd
Loch Glencoul
613 MEALL AN FHEUR LOCH
Clashnessie
Loch Poll
Loch an Leothaid
776 SAIL GHORM
Glen Leirg
792 BEINN LEOID
Loch Merkland
Loch Fiag
Fiag Lodge
809 QUINAG
Stoer
Clachtoll
Loch Beannach
Eas a' Chuall Aluinn (Waterfall)
372 CNOC A' GHRIAMA
Glen Fiag
Bay of Clachtoll
774 GLAS BHEINN
Achmelvich Bay
Rhicarn
A837
Loch Assynt
Ardvreck
Achmelvich
Overscaig Hotel
Baddidarrach
539 BEINN GHARBH
Lochinver
Inchnadamph
Soyea Island
Loch Inver
Strathan
Assynt - Coigach
510 MAOVALLY
Inverkirkaig
998 BEN MORE ASSYNT
Loch na Gainimh
847 CANISP
Stronchrubie
River Loanan
Loch
River Kirkaig
Fionn Loch
732 SUILVEN
713 BREABAG
Eilean Mòr
Duchally
Enard Bay
814
Loch Awe
435 BEN SCREAVIL
107
108
Achnahaird
Càm Loch
Benmore Forest
Glen Muic
Loch Sionascaig
Loch Veyatie
849 CUL MÒR
476 BEINN SGEIREACH
Loch Osgaig
Ledmore Junction
Glen Cassley
Polbain
612 STAC POLLAIDH
Knockan
Elphin
A837
Loch Ailsh
Loch Urigill
Knockan Cliff
Achiltibuie
364 AN STICHD
544
307
0 1 2 3 4 5 miles
0 1 2 3 4 5 6 7 8 kilometres

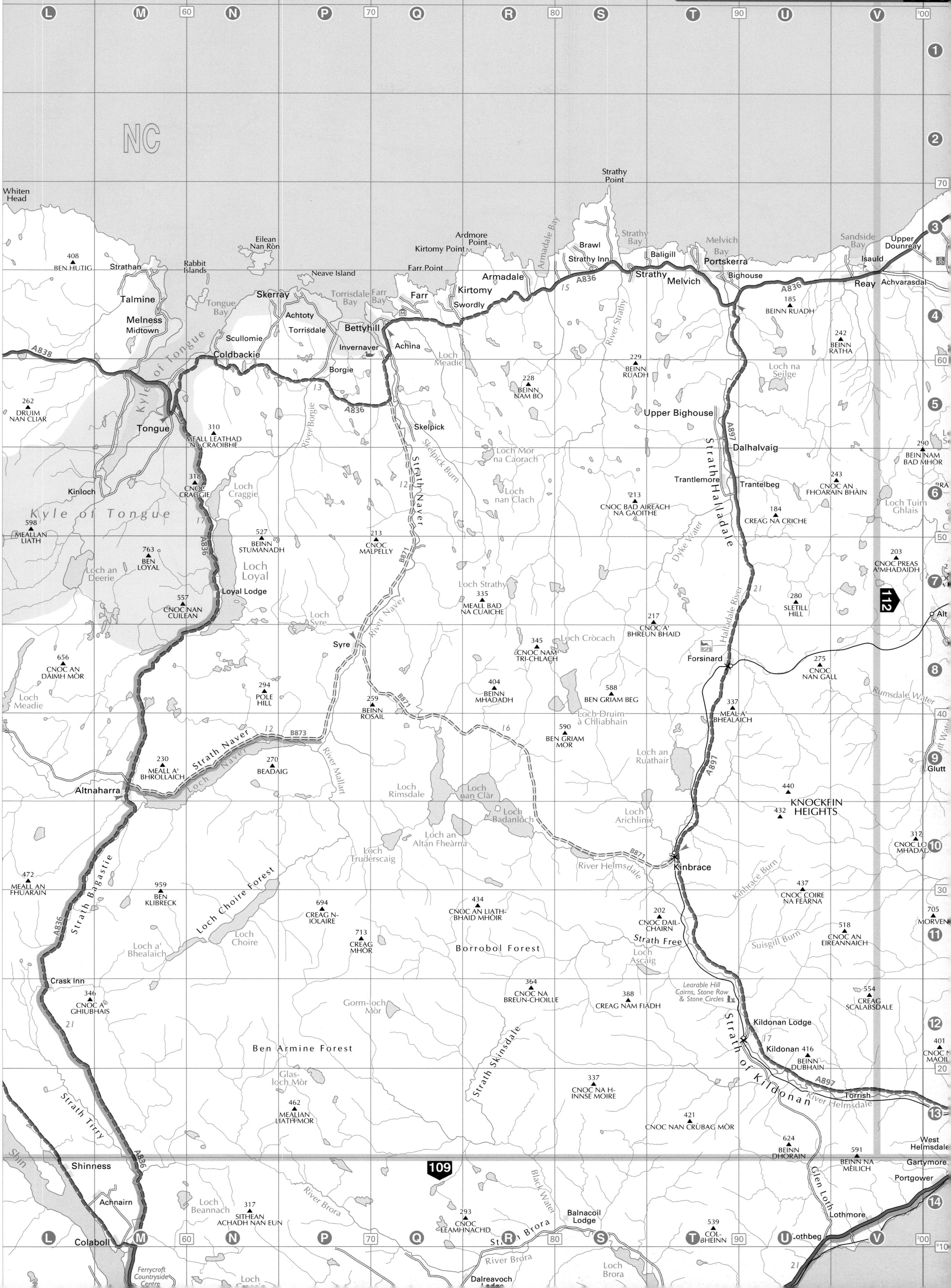

NC

L M 60 N O P 70 Q R 80 S T 90 U V '00

Whiten
Head

408
BEN HUTIG

Strathan
Talmine
Melness
Midtown

Rabbit
Islands

Eilean
Nan Ròn

Skerray
Achtoty
Torrisdale
Scullomie

Neave Island

Torrisdale
Bay

Farr Point
Kirtomy Point

Ardmore
Point

Strathy
Point

Strathy
Bay

Brawl
Strathy Inn

Baligill

Melvich
Bay

Sandside
Bay

Upper
Dounreay

Isauld

Farr
Kirtomy
Swordly

Armadale

Armadale Bay

Strathy

Portskerra

Melvich

Bighouse

A836

Reay

Achvarasdal

185
BEINN RUADH

242
BEINN
RATHA

262
DRUIM
NAN CLIAR

A838

Tongue

Coldbackie

Kyle of Tongue

Borgie

Bettyhill
Invernaver

Achina

River Borgie

13

A836

Skelpick

Loch
Meadie

Loch na
Seilge

A836

229
BEINN
RUADH

228
BEINN
NAM BO

15

Upper Bighouse

290
BEIN NAM
BAD MHOR

310
MEALL LEATHAD
NA CRAOIBHE

Loch
Craggie

Skelpick Burn

Strath Naver

12

Loch Mòr
na Caorach

Loch
nan Clach

213
CNOC BAD AIREACH
NA GAOITHE

Trantlemore

Dalhalvaig

Trantelbeg

Strath Halladale

A897

243
CNOC AN
FHOARAIN BHÀIN

184
CREAG NA CRICHE

203
CNOC PREAS
A'MHADAIDH

Kinloch

318
CNOC
CRAGGIE

A836

17

Kyle of Tongue

598
MEALLAN
LIATH

527
BEINN
STUMANADH

763
BEN
LOYAL

Loch an
Deerie

Loyal Lodge

Loch
Loyal

213
CNOC
MALPELLY

B871

River Naver

Loch
a Syre

Meall Bad
na Cuaiche

335
MEALL BAD
NA CUAICHE

Loch Strathy

Loch Cròcach

217
CNOC A'
BHREUN BHAID

Dyke Water

Halladale River

21

RSPB

Forsinard

280
SLETILL
HILL

112

Alt

557
CNOC NAN
CUILEAN

Syre

345
CNOC NAM
TRI-CHLACH

275
CNOC
NAN GALL

656
CNOC AN
DÀIMH MOR

294
POLE
HILL

259
BEINN
ROSAIL

B871

404
BEINN
MHADADH

588
BEN GRIAM BEG

Loch Druim
à Chliabhain

Rumsdale Water

337
MEALL A'
BHEALAICH

40

Loch
Meadie

Strath Naver

12

B873

590
BEN GRIAM
MOR

16

Glutt

230
MEALL A'
BHROLLAICH

270
BEADAIG

River Mallart

Loch
Rimsdale

Loch
nan Clàr

Loch an
Ruathair

440

KNOCKFIN
HEIGHTS

317
CNOC LO
MHADAI

Altnaharra

Strath Bagastie

Loch Naver

Loch
Badanloch

Loch
Arichlinie

432

River Helmsdale

B871

Kinbrace

Loch an
Altàn Fheàrna

472
MEALL AN
FHUARAIN

959
BEN
KLIBRECK

Loch Choire Forest

694
CREAG N-
IOLAIRE

434
CNOC AN LIATH-
BHAID MHOIR

Kinbrace Burn

437
CNOC COIRE
NA FEARNA

30

705
MORVEN

713
CREAG
MHOR

Borrobol Forest

202
CNOC DAIL-
CHAIRN

518
CNOC AN
EIREANNAICH

Crask Inn

Loch a'
Bhealaich

Loch
Choire

Strath Free

Loch
Ascaig

Suisgill Burn

346
CNOC A'
GHIUBHAIS

21

Gorm-loch
Mòr

364
CNOC NA
BREUN-CHOILLE

388
CREAG NAM FIADH

Learable Hill
Cairns, Stone Row
& Stone Circles

554
CREAG
SCALABSDALE

Ben Armine Forest

Kildonan Lodge

Strath of Kildonan

12

401
CNOC
MAOIL

Kildonan

416
BEINN
DUBHAIN

A897

Glas-
loch Mòr

462
MEALAN
LIATH-MOR

Strath Skinsdale

337
CNOC NA H-
INNSE MOIRE

17

Torrish

River Helmsdale

13

421
CNOC NAN CRUBAG MÒR

624
BEINN
DHORAIN

West
Helmsdale

Shin

Shinness

Achnairn

Strath Tirry

A836

Loch
Beannach

317
SITHEAN
ACHADH NAN EUN

River Brora

109

293
CNOC
LEAMHNACHD

Str R Brora

Black Water

Balnacoil
Lodge

Str R Brora

539
COL-
BHEINN

591
BEINN NA
MEILICH

Gartymore

Portgower

Lothmore

Coldboll

L M 60 N O P 70 Q R 80 S T 90 U V '00

Ferrycroft
Countryside
Centre

Loch

Dalreavoch
Lodge

River Brora

Loch Brora

Glen Loth

21

Lothbeg

14

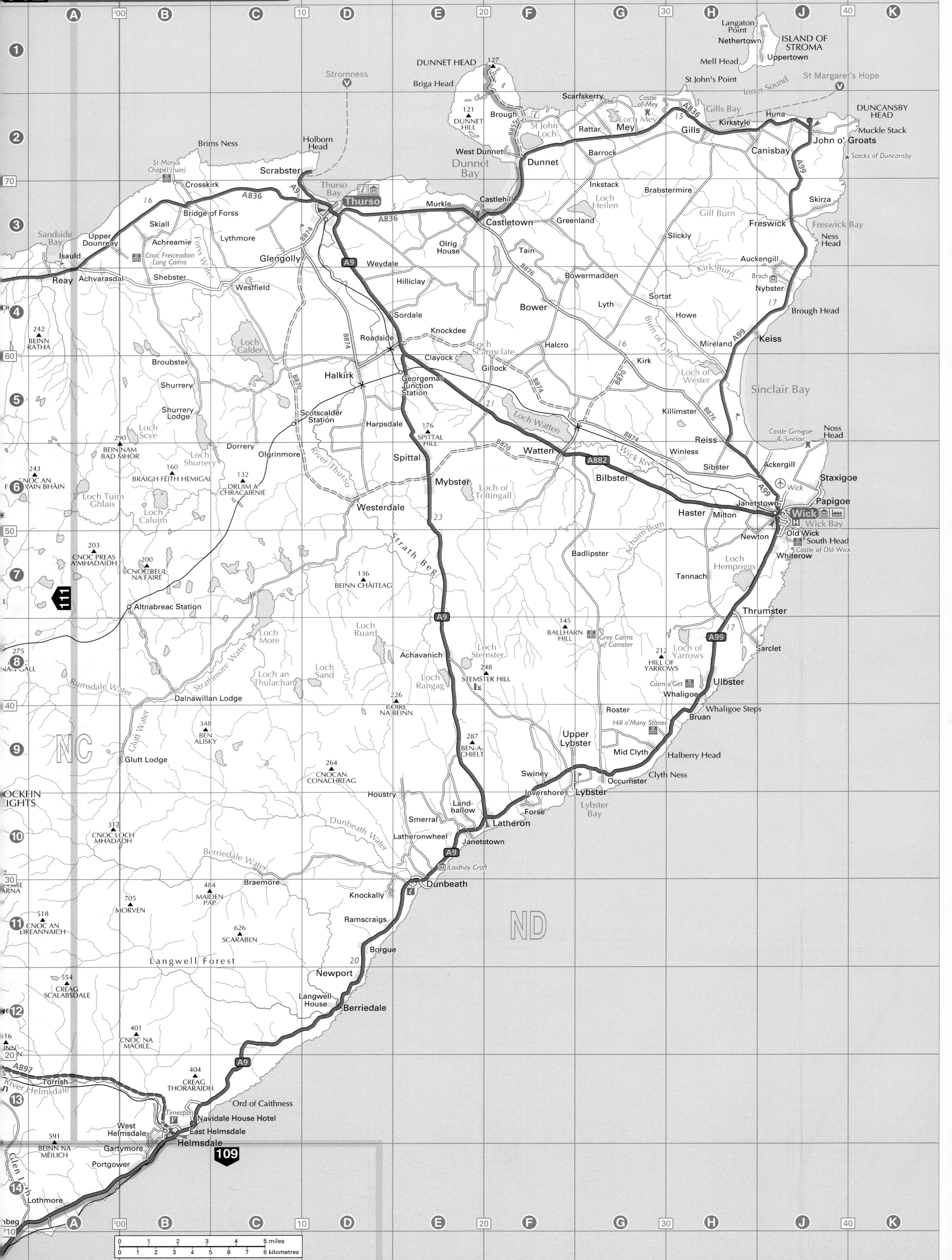
PENTLAND FIRTH
Langaton Point
Nethertown
ISLAND OF STROMA
Uppertown
Mell Head
St John's Point
Inner Sound
St Margaret's Hope
DUNCANSBY HEAD
Muckle Stack
John o' Groats
Stacks of Duncansby
DUNNET HEAD
127
Briga Head
Stromness
121
DUNNET HILL
Brough
St John's Loch
B855
West Dunnet
Dunnet Bay
Dunnet
Scarfskerry
Castle of Mey
Loch Mey
Mey
Rattar
Gills
Gills Bay
Kirkstyle
Huna
Canisbay
Barrock
A836
A99
Brims Ness
Holborn Head
St Mary's Chapel (ruin)
Scrabster
Thurso Bay
Thurso
Crosskirk
A836
Bridge of Forss
Murkle
Castlehill
Castletown
Inkstack
Loch Heilen
Brabstermire
Skirza
Gill Burn
Freswick
Freswick Bay
Ness Head
Greenland
Slickly
Sandside Bay
Upper Dounreay
Isauld
Reay
Achvarasdal
Skiall
Achreamie
Cnoc Freiceadain Long Cairns
Forss Water
Lythmore
Glengolly
B874
A9
Weydale
Olrig House
Tain
Hilliclay
B876
Bowermadden
Auckengill
Kirk Burn
Broch
Nybster
Shebster
Westfield
Sordale
Bower
Lyth
Sortat
Howe
Brough Head
Burn of Lyth
242
BEINN RATHA
Loch Calder
Roadside
Knockdee
Loch Scarmclate
Halcro
Mireland
Keiss
Broubster
Clayock
Gillock
Kirk
Halkirk
Georgemas Junction Station
B870
B874
Loch of Wester
Shurrery
Shurrery Lodge
Scotscalder Station
Loch Watten
Sinclair Bay
Killimster
Loch Scye
Harpsdale
176
SPITTAL HILL
Reiss
Castle Girnigoe & Sinclair
Noss Head
290
BEIN NAM BAD MHOR
Dorrery
Loch Shurrery
Olgrinmore
River Thurso
Spittal
Watten
B874
Winless
Sibster
Ackergill
Staxigoe
243
CNOC AN FRAIN BHÀIN
160
BRAIGH FEITH HEMIGAL
132
DRUIM A' CHRACAIRNIE
Mybster
Loch of Toftingall
A882
Bilbster
Wick River
Wick
Papigoe
Loch Tuim Ghlais
Loch Caluim
Westerdale
Haster
Milton
Janetstown
Wick Bay
Old Wick
South Head
Castle of Old Wick
Newton
Whiterow
Strath Beg
Achairn Burn
Badlipster
203
CNOC PREAS A' MHADAIDH
200
CNOC BEUL NA FAIRE
136
BEINN CHAITEAG
Loch Hempriggs
Tannach
111
Altnabreac Station
Thrumster
Loch More
Loch Ruard
145
BALLHARN HILL
Grey Cairns of Camster
Loch Stemster
212
HILL OF YARROWS
Loch of Yarrows
Sarclet
275
Achavanich
248
STEMSTER HILL
Cairn o' Get
Whaligoe
Ulbster
Rumsdale Water
Strathmore Water
Loch an Thulachan
Loch Sand
Loch Rangag
Dalnawillan Lodge
226
COIRE NA BEINN
Roster
Whaligoe Steps
Bruan
Hill o' Many Stanes
Glutt Water
348
BEN ALISKY
287
BEN-A-CHIELT
Upper Lybster
Mid Clyth
Halberry Head
NC
Glutt Lodge
264
CNOCAN CONACHREAG
Swiney
Occumster
Clyth Ness
Inversnore
Lybster
Lybster Bay
Houstry
Landhallow
Forse
Smerral
Latheron
Dunbeath Water
317
CNOC LOCH MHADADH
Latheronwheel
Janetstown
Berriedale Water
Laidhay Croft
484
MAIDEN PAP
Braemore
Dunbeath
705
MORVEN
Knockally
518
CNOC AN EIREANNAICH
626
SCARABEN
Ramscraigs
ND
Borgue
Langwell Forest
554
CREAG SCALABSDALE
Newport
Langwell House
Berriedale
401
CNOC NA MAOILE
A897
Torrish
River Helmsdale
404
CREAG THORARAIDH
Ord of Caithness
Timespan
Navidale House Hotel
West Helmsdale
East Helmsdale
Helmsdale
109
591
BEINN NA MEILICH
Gartymore
Portgower
Glen Loth
Lothmore
0 1 2 3 4 5 miles
0 1 2 3 4 5 6 7 8 kilometres

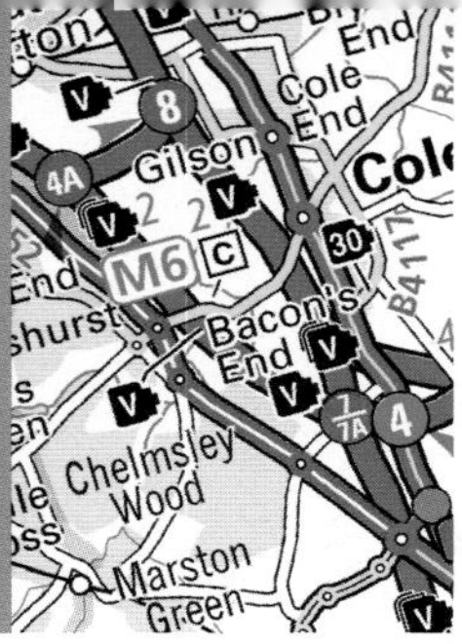

Restricted junctions

Motorway and Primary Route junctions which have access or exit restrictions are shown on the map pages thus:

M1 London - Leeds

Junction	Northbound	Southbound
2	Access only from A1 (northbound)	Exit only to A1 (southbound)
4	Access only from A41 (northbound)	Exit only to A41 (southbound)
6A	Access only from M25 (no link from A405)	Exit only to M25 (no link from A405)
7	Access only from A414	Exit only to A414
17	Exit only to M45	Access only from M45
19	Exit only to M6 (northbound)	Access only from M6
21A	Exit only, no access	Access only, no exit
23A	Access only from A42	No restriction
24A	Access only, no exit	Exit only, no access
35A	Exit only, no access	Access only, no exit
43	Exit only to M621	Access only from M621
48	Exit only to A1(M) (northbound)	Access only from A1(M) (southbound)

M2 Rochester - Faversham

Junction	Westbound	Eastbound
1	No exit to A2 (eastbound)	No access from A2 (westbound)

M3 Sunbury - Southampton

Junction	Northeastbound	Southwestbound
8	Access only from A303, no exit	Exit only to A303, no access
10	Exit only, no access	Access only, no exit
14	Access from M27 only, no exit	No access to M27 (westbound)

M4 London - South Wales

Junction	Westbound	Eastbound
1	Access only from A4 (westbound)	Exit only to A4 (eastbound)
4A	No exit to A4 (westbound)	No restriction
21	Exit only to M48	Access only from M48
23	Access only from M48	Exit only to M48
25	Exit only, no access	Access only, no exit
25A	Exit only, no access	Access only, no exit
29	Exit only to A48(M)	Access only from A48(M)
38	Exit only, no access	No restriction
39	Access only, no exit	No access or exit

M5 Birmingham - Exeter

Junction	Northeastbound	Southwestbound
10	Access only, no exit	Exit only, no access
11A	Access only from A417 (westbound)	Exit only to A417 (eastbound)
18	Exit only, no access	Access only, no exit
18A	Exit only to M49	Access only from M49
29	No restriction	Access only from A30 (westbound)

M6 Toll Motorway

Junction	Northwestbound	Southeastbound
T1	Access only, no exit	No access or exit
T2	No access or exit	Exit only, no access
T3	Staggered junction, follow signs - access only from A38 (northbound)	Staggered junction, follow signs - access only from A38 (southbound)
T5	Access only, no exit	Exit only to A5148 (northbound), no access
T7	Exit only, no access	Access only, no exit
T8	Exit only, no access	Access only, no exit

M6 Rugby - Carlisle

Junction	Northbound	Southbound
3A	Exit only to M6 Toll	Access only from M6 Toll
4A	Access only from M42 (southbound)	Exit only to M42
5	Exit only, no access	Access only, no exit
10A	Exit only to M54	Access only from M54
11A	Access only from M6 Toll	Exit only to M6 Toll
with M56 (jct 20A)	No restriction	Access only from M56 (eastbound)
20	Access only, no exit	No restriction
24	Access only, no exit	Exit only, no access
25	Exit only, no access	Access only, no exit
29	No direct access, use adjacent slip road to jct 29A	No direct exit, use adjacent slip road from jct 29A
29A	Access only, no exit	Exit only, no access
30	Access only from M61	Exit only to M61
31A	Exit only, no access	Access only, no exit
45	Exit only, no access	Access only, no exit

M8 Edinburgh - Bishopton

Junction	Westbound	Eastbound
8	No access from M73 (southbound) or from A8 (eastbound) & A89	No exit to M73 (northbound) or to A8 (westbound) & A89
9	Access only, no exit	Exit only, no access
13	Access only from M80 (southbound)	Exit only to M80 (northbound)
14	Access only, no exit	Exit only, no access
16	Exit only to A804	Access only from A879
17	Exit only to A82	No restriction
18	Access only from A82 (eastbound)	Exit only to A814
19	No access from A814 (westbound)	Exit only to A814 (westbound)
20	Exit only, no access	Access only, no exit
21	Access only, no exit	Exit only to A8
22	Exit only to M77 (southbound)	Access only from M77 (northbound)
23	Exit only to B768	Access only from B768
25	No access or exit from or to A8	No access or exit from or to A8
25A	Exit only, no access	Access only, no exit
28	Exit only, no access	Access only, no exit
28A	Exit only to A737	Access only from A737

M9 Edinburgh - Dunblane

Junction	Northwestbound	Southeastbound
1A	Exit only to M9 spur	Access only from M9 spur
2	Access only, no exit	Exit only, no access
3	Exit only, no access	Access only, no exit
6	Access only, no exit	Exit only to A905
8	Exit only to M876 (southwestbound)	Access only from M876 (northeastbound)

M11 London - Cambridge

Junction	Northbound	Southbound
4	Access only from A406 (eastbound)	Exit only to A406
5	Exit only, no access	Access only, no exit
9	Exit only to A11	Access only from A11
13	Exit only, no access	Access only, no exit
14	Exit only, no access	Access only, no exit

M20 Swanley - Folkestone

Junction	Northwestbound	Southeastbound
2	Staggered junction; follow signs - access only	Staggered junction; follow signs - exit only
3	Exit only to M26 (westbound)	Access only from M26 (eastbound)
5	Access only from A20	For access follow signs - exit only to A20
6	No restriction	For exit follow signs
11A	Access only, no exit	Exit only, no access

M23 Hooley - Crawley

Junction	Northbound	Southbound
7	Exit only to A23 (northbound)	Access only from A23 (southbound)
10A	Access only, no exit	Exit only, no access

M25 London Orbital Motorway

Junction	Clockwise	Anticlockwise
1B	No direct access, use slip road to Jct 2. Exit only	Access only, no exit
5	No exit to M26 (eastbound)	No access from M26
19	Exit only, no access	Access only, no exit
21	Access only from M1 (southbound). Exit only to M1 (northbound)	Access only from M1 (southbound). Exit only to M1 (northbound)
31	No exit (use slip road via jct 30), access only	No access (use slip road via jct 30), exit only

M26 Sevenoaks - Wrotham

Junction	Westbound	Eastbound
with M25 (jct 5)	Exit only to clockwise M25 (westbound)	Access only from anticlockwise M25 (eastbound)
with M20 (jct 3)	Access only from M20 (northwestbound)	Exit only to M20 (southeastbound)

M27 Cadnam - Portsmouth

Junction	Westbound	Eastbound
4	Staggered junction; follow signs - access only from M3 (southbound). Exit only to M3 (northbound)	Staggered junction; follow signs - access only from M3 (southbound). Exit only to M3 (northbound)
10	Exit only, no access	Access only, no exit
12	Staggered junction; follow signs - exit only to M275 (southbound)	Staggered junction; follow signs - access only from M275 (northbound)

M40 London - Birmingham

Junction	Northwestbound	Southeastbound
3	Exit only, no access	Access only, no exit
7	Exit only, no access	Access only, no exit
8	Exit only to M40/A40	Access only from M40/A40
13	Exit only, no access	Access only, no exit
14	Access only, no exit	Exit only, no access
16	Access only, no exit	Exit only, no access

M42 Bromsgrove - Measham

Junction	Northeastbound	Southwestbound
1	Access only, no exit	Exit only, no access
7	Exit only to M6 (northwestbound)	Access only from M6 (northwestbound)
7A	Exit only to M6 (southeastbound)	No access or exit
8	Access only from M6 (southeastbound)	Exit only to M6 (northwestbound)

M45 Coventry - M1

Junction	Westbound	Eastbound
Dunchurch (unnumbered)	Access only from A45	Exit only, no access
with M1 (jct 17)	Access only from M1 (northbound)	Exit only to M1 (southbound)

M53 Mersey Tunnel - Chester

Junction	Northbound	Southbound
11	Access only from M56 (westbound). Exit only to M56 (eastbound)	Access only from M56 (westbound). Exit only to M56 (eastbound)

M54 Telford

Junction	Westbound	Eastbound
with M6 (jct 10A)	Access only from M6 (northbound)	Exit only to M6 (southbound)

M56 North Cheshire

Junction	Westbound	Eastbound
1	Access only from M60 (westbound)	Exit only to M60 (eastbound) & A34 (northbound)
2	Exit only, no access	Access only, no exit
3	Access only, no exit	Exit only, no access
4	Exit only, no access	Access only, no exit
7	Exit only, no access	No restriction
8	Access only, no exit	No access or exit
15	Exit only to M53	Access only from M53

M57 Liverpool Outer Ring Road

Junction	Northwestbound	Southeastbound
3	Access only, no exit	Exit only, no access
5	Access only from A580 (westbound)	Exit only, no access

M58 Liverpool - Wigan

Junction	Westbound	Eastbound
1	Exit only, no access	Access only, no exit

M60 Manchester Orbital

Junction	Clockwise	Anticlockwise
2	Access only, no exit	Exit only, no access
3	No access from M56	Access only from A34 (northbound)
4	Access only from A34 (northbound). Exit only to M56	Access only from M56 (eastbound). Exit only to A34 (southbound)
5	Access and exit only from and to A5103 (northbound)	Access and exit only from and to A5103 (southbound)
7	No direct access, use slip road to jct 8. Exit only to A56	Access only from A56. No exit - use jct 8
14	Access from A580 (eastbound)	Exit only to A580 (westbound)
16	Access only, no exit	Exit only, no access
20	Exit only, no access	Access only, no exit
22	No restriction	Exit only, no access
25	Exit only, no access	No restriction
26	No restriction	Exit only, no access
27	Access only, no exit	Exit only, no access

M61 Manchester - Preston

Junction	Northwestbound	Southeastbound
3	No access or exit	Exit only, no access
with M6 (jct 30)	Exit only to M6 (northbound)	Access only from M6 (southbound)

M62 Liverpool - Kingston upon Hull

Junction	Westbound	Eastbound
23	Access only, no exit	Exit only, no access
32A	No access to A1(M) (southbound)	No restriction

M65 Preston - Colne

Junction	Northeastbound	Southwestbound
9	Exit only, no access	Access only, no exit
11	Access only, no exit	Exit only, no access

M66 Bury

Junction	Northbound	Southbound
with A56	Exit only to A56 (northbound)	Access only from A56 (southbound)
1	Exit only, no access	Access only, no exit

M67 Hyde Bypass

Junction	Westbound	Eastbound
1	Access only, no exit	Exit only, no access
2	Exit only, no access	Access only, no exit
3	Exit only, no access	No restriction

M69 Coventry - Leicester

Junction	Northbound	Southbound
2	Access only, no exit	Exit only, no access

M73 East of Glasgow

Junction	Northbound	Southbound
2	No access from or exit to A89. No access from M8 (eastbound).	No access from or exit to A89. No exit to M8 (westbound)

M74 and A74(M) Glasgow - Gretna

Junction	Northbound	Southbound
3	Exit only, no access	Access only, no exit
3A	Access only, no exit	Exit only, no access
7	Access only, no exit	Exit only, no access
9	No access or exit	Exit only, no access
10	No restrictions	Access only, no exit
11	Access only, no exit	Exit only, no access
12	Exit only, no access	Access only, no exit
18	Exit only, no access	Access only, no exit

M77 South of Glasgow

Junction	Northbound	Southbound
with M8 (jct 22)	No exit to M8 (westbound)	No access from M8 (eastbound)
4	Access only, no exit	Exit only, no access
6	Access only, no exit	Exit only, no access
7	Access only, no exit	No restriction

M80 Glasgow - Stirling

Junction	Northbound	Southbound
4A	Exit only, no access	Access only, no exit
6A	Access only, no exit	Exit only, no access
8	Exit only to M876 (northeastbound)	Access only from M876 (southwestbound)

M90 Forth Road Bridge - Perth

Junction	Northbound	Southbound
2A	Exit only to A92 (eastbound)	Access only from A92 (westbound)
7	Access only, no exit	Exit only, no access
8	Exit only, no access	Access only, no exit
10	No access from A912. No exit to A912 (southbound)	No access from A912 (northbound). No exit to A912

M180 Doncaster - Grimsby

Junction	Westbound	Eastbound
1	Access only, no exit	Exit only, no access

M606 Bradford Spur

Junction	Northbound	Southbound
2	Exit only, no access	No restriction

M621 Leeds - M1

Junction	Clockwise	Anticlockwise
2A	Access only, no exit	Exit only, no access
4	No exit or access	No restriction
5	Access only, no exit	Exit only, no access
6	Exit only, no access	Access only, no exit
with M1 (jct 43)	Exit only to M1 (southbound)	Access only from M1 (northbound)

M876 Bonnybridge - Kincardine Bridge

Junction	Northeastbound	Southwestbound
with M80 (jct 5)	Access only from M80 (northbound)	Exit only to M80 (southbound)
with M9 (jct 8)	Exit only to M9 (eastbound)	Access only from M9 (westbound)

A1(M) South Mimms - Baldock

Junction	Northbound	Southbound
2	Exit only, no access	Access only, no exit
3	No restriction	Exit only, no access
5	Access only, no exit	No access or exit

A1(M) East of Leeds

Junction	Northbound	Southbound
41	No access to M62 (eastbound)	No restriction
43	Access only from M1 (northbound)	Exit only to M1 (southbound)

A1(M) Scotch Corner - Newcastle upon Tyne

Junction	Northbound	Southbound
57	Exit only to A66(M) (eastbound)	Access only from A66(M) (westbound)
65	No access. Exit only to A194(M) & A1 (northbound)	No exit. Access only from A194(M) & A1 (southbound)

A3(M) Horndean - Havant

Junction	Northbound	Southbound
1	Access only from A3	Exit only to A3
4	Exit only, no access	Access only, no exit

A48(M) Cardiff Spur

Junction	Westbound	Eastbound
29	Access only from M4 (westbound)	Exit only to M4 (eastbound)
29A	Exit only to A48 (westbound)	Access only from A48 (eastbound)

A66(M) Darlington Spur

Junction	Westbound	Eastbound
with A1(M) (jct 57)	Exit only to A1(M) (southbound)	Access only from A1(M) (northbound)

A194(M) Newcastle upon Tyne

Junction	Northbound	Southbound
with A1(M) (jct 65)	Access only from A1(M) (northbound)	Exit only to A1(M) (southbound)

A12 M25 - Ipswich

Junction	Northeastbound	Southwestbound
13	Access only, no exit	No restriction
14	Exit only, no access	Access only, no exit
20A	Exit only, no access	Access only, no exit
20B	Access only, no exit	Exit only, no access
21	No restriction	Access only, no exit
23	Exit only, no access	Access only, no exit
24	Access only, no exit	Exit only, no access
27	Exit only, no access	Access only, no exit
with A120 (unnumbered)	Exit only, no access	Access only, no exit
29	Access only, no exit	Exit only, no access
Dedham & Stratford St Mary (unnumbered)	Exit only	Access only

A14 M1 - Felixstowe

Junction	Westbound	Eastbound
With M1/M6 (jct19)	Exit only to M6 and M1 (northbound)	Access only from M6 and M1 (southbound)
4	Exit only, no access	Access only, no exit
31	Access only from A1307	Exit only, to A1307
34	Access only, no exit	Exit only, no access
36	Exit only to A11	Access only from A11
38	Access only from A11	Exit only to A11
39	Exit only, no access	Access only, no exit
61	Access only, no exit	Exit only, no access

A55 Holyhead - Chester

Junction	Westbound	Eastbound
8A	Exit only, no access	Access only, no exit
23A	Access only, no exit	Exit only, no access
24A	Exit only, no access	No access or exit
33A	Exit only, no access	No access or exit
33B	Exit only, no access	Access only, no exit
36A	Exit only to A5104	Access only from A5104

C12 Abbeydorney
D12 Abbeyfeale
G11 Abbeyleix
H12 Adamstown
D12 Adare
C14 Adrigole
H4 Aghadowey
E9 Ahascragh
J4 Ahoghill
B15 Allihies
B13 Anascaul
E4 An Bun Beag
E5 An Charraig
E4 An Clochán Liath
B14 An Coireán
B13 An Daingean
C9 An Fhairche
J7 Annalong
G13 Annestown
G13 An Rinn
D9 An Spidéal
J5 Antrim
D12 Ardagh
E5 Ardara
H8 Ardee
C12 Ardfert
F12 Ardfinnan
K6 Ardglass
B14 Ardgroom
F14 Ardmore
J11 Arklow
H11 Arless
H6 Armagh
J3 Armoy
H13 Arthurstown
G7 Arvagh
J9 Ashbourne
J10 Ashford
D12 Askeaton
H8 Athboy
D12 Athea
E9 Athenry
E8 Athleague
F9 Athlone
H10 Athy
G6 Augher
H6 Aughnacloy
J11 Aughrim
J11 Avoca

H11 Bagenalstown
D14 Baile Mhic Íre
H7 Bailieborough
J8 Balbriggan
D8 Balla
E7 Ballaghaderreen
D7 Ballina
E11 Ballina
E7 Ballinafad
G7 Ballinagh
G11 Ballinakill
F8 Ballinalee
G6 Ballinamallard
F7 Ballinamore
D14 Ballinascarty
E9 Ballinasloe
D8 Ballindine
D14 Ballineen
D12 Ballingarry
G12 Ballingarry
D14 Ballingeary
E14 Ballinhassig
E8 Ballinlough
D8 Ballinrobe
E15 Ballinspittle
E8 Ballintober
F5 Ballintra
H9 Ballivor
H11 Ballon
E9 Ballybaun
H7 Ballybay
F5 Ballybofey
C12 Ballybunion
J11 Ballycanew
K5 Ballycarry
J3 Ballycastle
C6 Ballycastle
J5 Ballyclare
G11 Ballycolla
B9 Ballyconneely
G7 Ballyconnell
F14 Ballycotton
F9 Ballycumber
C15 Ballydehob
D13 Ballydesmond
C12 Ballyduff
F13 Ballyduff
E7 Ballyfarnan
J4 Ballygalley
E9 Ballygar
E6 Ballygawley
H6 Ballygawley
K5 Ballygowan
H13 Ballyhack
G7 Ballyhaise
G12 Ballyhale
E8 Ballyhaunis
D8 Ballyhean
C12 Ballyheige
G8 Ballyjamesduff
F9 Ballykeeran
E12 Ballylanders
C14 Ballylickey
G3 Ballyliffin
C12 Ballylongford
F12 Ballylooby
H10 Ballylynan
F13 Ballymacarbry
F8 Ballymahon
D14 Ballymakeery
J4 Ballymena
E8 Ballymoe
H4 Ballymoney
F9 Ballymore
H10 Ballymore Eustace
E7 Ballymote
J6 Ballynahinch
J5 Ballynure
F13 Ballyporeen
G11 Ballyragget
G10 Ballyroan
H5 Ballyronan
E6 Ballysadare
F5 Ballyshannon
D10 Ballyvaughan
K5 Ballywalter
J8 Balrothery
C15 Baltimore
H10 Baltinglass
F10 Banagher
J6 Banbridge
E14 Bandon
K5 Bangor
C7 Bangor Erris
F12 Bansha
D13 Banteer
C14 Bantry
D9 Barna
B6 Béal an Mhuirthead
D14 Béal Átha an Ghaorthaidh
D9 Bearna
C13 Beaufort
F6 Belcoo
J5 Belfast
E14 Belgooly
H4 Bellaghy
F6 Belleek
B6 Belmullet
G7 Belturbet
H6 Benburb
G12 Bennettsbridge
G5 Beragh
J8 Bettystown
F10 Birr
F6 Blacklion
J9 Blackrock
J12 Blackwater
E14 Blarney
H10 Blessington
D13 Boherbue
H12 Borris
F10 Borris in Ossory
F10 Borrisokane
F11 Borrisoleigh
E7 Boyle
G10 Bracknagh
J10 Bray
H13 Bridgetown
J9 Brittas
E11 Broadford
D12 Broadford
J4 Broughshane
E12 Bruff
E12 Bruree
E4 Bunbeg
H11 Bunclody
G3 Buncrana
E6 Bundoran
G13 Bunmahon
C6 Bun na hAbhna
C6 Bunnahowen
D7 Bunnyconnellan
D11 Bunratty
E13 Burnfort
H3 Bushmills
E13 Buttevant

F10 Cadamstown
E12 Caherconlish
B14 Caherdaniel
B14 Cahersiveen
F12 Cahir
H6 Caledon
G12 Callan
E9 Caltra
B13 Camp
H13 Campile
F12 Cappagh White
E11 Cappamore
F13 Cappoquin
H8 Carlanstown
J7 Carlingford
H11 Carlow
C9 Carna
G3 Carndonagh
J11 Carnew
J4 Carnlough
E7 Carracastle
F3 Carraig Airt
E5 Carrick
F3 Carrickart
K5 Carrickfergus
H7 Carrickmacross
G5 Carrickmore or Termon Rock
F7 Carrick-on-Shannon
G12 Carrick-on-Suir
F10 Carrigahorig
E14 Carrigaline
F7 Carrigallen
D14 Carriganimmy
G4 Carrigans
E14 Carrigtohill
J5 Carryduff
C9 Cashel
F12 Cashel
D8 Castlebar
J7 Castlebellingham
H7 Castleblayney
J12 Castlebridge
G11 Castlecomer
E11 Castleconnell
G5 Castlederg
H11 Castledermot
B13 Castlegregory
C13 Castleisland
C13 Castlemaine
F14 Castlemartyr
E8 Castleplunket
G8 Castlepollard
E8 Castlerea
H3 Castlerock
H6 Castleshane
G10 Castletown
B15 Castletownbere
E13 Castletownroche
D15 Castletownshend
J6 Castlewellan
B14 Cathair Dónall
C12 Causeway
G7 Cavan
H9 Celbridge
D7 Charlestown
E12 Charleville
H13 Cheekpoint
E5 Cill Charthaigh
C9 Cill Chiaráin
G5 Clady
H9 Clane
G9 Clara
D11 Clarecastle
D8 Claremorris
D10 Clarinbridge
F13 Clashmore
G4 Claudy
B9 Clifden
E6 Cliffony
G11 Clogh
F10 Cloghan
F13 Clogheen
G6 Clogher
H11 Clohamon
D15 Clonakilty
H9 Clonard
G10 Clonaslee
G9 Clonbulloge
C9 Clonbur
J9 Clondalkin
G7 Clones
E11 Clonlara
G3 Clonmany
F12 Clonmel
H8 Clonmellon
F11 Clonmore
F10 Clonony
F12 Clonoulty
H12 Clonroche
H6 Clontibret
F8 Cloondara
K6 Clough
F10 Cloughjordan
F14 Cloyne
H5 Coagh
H5 Coalisland
E14 Cobh
H3 Coleraine
G8 Collinstown
H8 Collon
E6 Collooney
K5 Comber
D9 Cong
F13 Conna
H5 Cookstown
G8 Coole
C11 Cooraclare
G7 Cootehill
E14 Cork
C9 Cornamona
C9 Corr na Móna
D10 Corrofin
E15 Courtmacsherry
J11 Courtown
J6 Craigavon
E10 Craughwell
K5 Crawfordsburn
E8 Creegs
F4 Creeslough
D12 Croagh
E4 Croithlí
E4 Crolly
G8 Crookedwood
C15 Crookhaven
D14 Crookstown
E12 Croom
H8 Crossakeel
E14 Cross Barry
E14 Crosshaven
H7 Crossmaglen
D7 Crossmolina
J5 Crumlin
D10 Crusheen
G3 Culdaff
J4 Cullybackey
J12 Curracloe
F9 Curraghboy
E7 Curry
J4 Cushendall
J3 Cushendun

G9 Daingean
J10 Delgany
G8 Delvin
G4 Derry
F6 Derrygonnelly
G6 Derrylin
H3 Dervock
B13 Dingle
J5 Doagh
K5 Donaghadee
G11 Donaghmore
H10 Donard
F5 Donegal
E13 Doneraile
C10 Doolin
E12 Doon
C11 Doonbeg
F9 Doon Cross Roads
E14 Douglas
K6 Downpatrick
F6 Dowra
H5 Draperstown
D15 Drimoleague
E14 Dripsey
J8 Drogheda
E6 Dromahair
D12 Dromcolliher
J6 Dromore
G5 Dromore
D6 Dromore West
E6 Drumcliff
H8 Drumcondra
F7 Drumkeeran
F8 Drumlish
F8 Drumod
G5 Drumquin
F7 Drumshanbo
F7 Drumsna
C12 Duagh
J9 Dublin
J8 Duleek
J9 Dunboyne
H13 Duncormick
J7 Dundalk
E14 Dunderrow
K5 Dundonald
K6 Dundrum
F12 Dundrum
F3 Dunfanaghy
H5 Dungannon
G12 Dungarvan
G13 Dungarvan
H4 Dungiven
E4 Dunglow
F14 Dungourney
E5 Dunkineely
J9 Dún Laoghaire
H10 Dunlavin
J8 Dunleer
J4 Dunloy
D14 Dunmanway
E8 Dunmore
H13 Dunmore East
J5 Dunmurry
H9 Dunshaughlin
G11 Durrow
C15 Durrus
E9 Dysart

D6 Easky
H9 Edenderry
G8 Edgeworthstown
G4 Eglinton
F8 Elphin
H6 Emyvale
H9 Enfield
D11 Ennis
H12 Enniscorthy
D14 Enniskean
F6 Enniskillen
D10 Ennistymon
F10 Eyrecourt

G4 Fahan
C13 Farranfore
E10 Feakle
F7 Fenagh
F9 Ferbane
E13 Fermoy
J12 Ferns
F12 Fethard
H13 Fethard
G8 Finnea
G6 Fintona
G6 Fivemiletown
H10 Fontstown
H12 Foulkesmill
D7 Foxford
D11 Foynes
D13 Freemount
E8 Frenchpark
G11 Freshford
E8 Fuerty

E12 Galbally
D9 Galway
F6 Garrison
J8 Garristown
F14 Garryvoe
H4 Garvagh
G10 Geashill
J6 Gilford
D15 Glandore
E14 Glanmire
E13 Glanworth
H6 Glaslough
F9 Glassan
E5 Gleann Cholm Cille
J4 Glenarm
J5 Glenavy
B13 Glenbeigh
E5 Glencolumbkille
J10 Glenealy
C14 Glengarriff
H12 Glenmore
E8 Glennamaddy
E5 Glenties
D12 Glin
C9 Glinsce
C9 Glinsk
F12 Golden
C15 Goleen
H11 Goresbridge
J11 Gorey
D10 Gort
G5 Gortin
H11 Gowran
H12 Graiguenamanagh
G8 Granard
E6 Grange
J7 Greenore
K5 Greyabbey
J10 Greystones
H4 Gulladuff

H11 Hacketstown
D9 Headford
E12 Herbertstown
J6 Hillsborough
J6 Hilltown
F11 Holycross
K5 Holywood
G9 Horseleap
E12 Hospital
J9 Howth

B13 Inch
D14 Inchigeelagh
E14 Inishannon
D6 Inishcrone
H12 Inistioge
F6 Irvinestown

G11 Johnstown

D13 Kanturk
F7 Keadew
H6 Keady
B7 Keel
F8 Keenagh
J4 Kells
H8 Kells
C14 Kenmare
F5 Kesh
G9 Kilbeggan
H8 Kilberry
E14 Kilbrittain
E5 Kilcar
H9 Kilcock
D10 Kilcolgan
E9 Kilconnell
J10 Kilcoole
F10 Kilcormac
H10 Kilcullen
J7 Kilcurry
H10 Kildare
H11 Kildavin
E13 Kildorrery
D10 Kilfenora
C14 Kilgarvan
C11 Kilkee
J7 Kilkeel
D7 Kilkelly
G11 Kilkenny
C9 Kilkieran
C12 Kilkinlea Lower
H9 Kill
G13 Kill
D11 Killadysert
D6 Killala
E11 Killaloe
C13 Killarney
G7 Killashandra
F14 Killeagh
G10 Killeigh
F12 Killenaule
C11 Killimer
E10 Killimor
J9 Killiney
J13 Killinick
C13 Killorglin
K6 Killough
G9 Killucan
E5 Killybegs
K6 Killyleagh
J10 Kilmacanoge
F4 Kilmacrenan
G13 Kilmacthomas
G12 Kilmaganny
D8 Kilmaine
E12 Kilmallock
G11 Kilmanagh
G13 Kilmeadan
H9 Kilmeage
D12 Kilmeedy
D14 Kilmichael
H13 Kilmore Quay
J12 Kilmuckridge
G8 Kilnaleck
H4 Kilrea
C11 Kilrush
G12 Kilsheelan
D8 Kiltamagh
H12 Kiltealy
H11 Kiltegan
F9 Kiltoom
H7 Kingscourt
E6 Kinlough
G9 Kinnegad
F10 Kinnitty
E14 Kinsale
D10 Kinvarra
K5 Kircubbin
D8 Knock
F8 Knockcroghery
F12 Knocklofty
G12 Knocktopher

C10 Lahinch
F8 Lanesborough
J10 Laragh
K4 Larne
C14 Lauragh
F10 Laurencetown
D15 Leap
C8 Leenane
H11 Leighlinbridge
F7 Leitrim
H9 Leixlip
G13 Lemybrien
B8 Letterfrack
F4 Letterkenny
G4 Lifford
H4 Limavady
E11 Limerick
G6 Lisbellaw
J5 Lisburn
C10 Liscannor
D13 Liscarroll
D10 Lisdoonvarna
F13 Lismore
G6 Lisnaskea
G8 Lisryan
C12 Listowel
D12 Loghill
G4 Londonderry
F8 Longford
J6 Loughbrickland
H6 Loughgall
E8 Loughglinn
E10 Loughrea
C8 Louisburgh
J9 Lucan
J6 Lurgan
J9 Lusk

F3 Machair Loiscthe
D14 Macroom
J6 Maghera
H4 Maghera
H5 Magherafelt
G6 Maguiresbridge
J9 Malahide
E5 Málainn Mhóir
G3 Malin
E5 Malin More
E13 Mallow
F6 Manorhamilton
H6 Markethill
J4 Martinstown
H9 Maynooth
J5 Mazetown
H6 Middletown
F14 Midleton
F4 Millford
D13 Millstreet
C13 Milltown
C11 Milltown Malbay
E13 Mitchelstown
F9 Moate
F7 Mohill
H6 Monaghan
G10 Monasterevin
F11 Moneygall
H5 Moneymore
E9 Monivea
G13 Mooncoin
J4 Moorfields
E9 Mountbellew Bridge
F5 Mountcharles
G10 Mountmellick
G10 Mountrath
E10 Mountshannon
G3 Moville
H6 Moy
H8 Moynalty
F9 Moyvore
C13 Muckross
G4 Muff
E6 Mullaghmore
G12 Mullinavat
G9 Mullingar
C7 Mulrany
H11 Myshall

H10 Naas
J8 Naul
H8 Navan
D8 Neale
E11 Nenagh
G7 Newbliss
H10 Newbridge
J6 Newcastle
D12 Newcastle West
F12 Newinn
D13 Newmarket
D11 Newmarket-on-Fergus
C7 Newport
E11 Newport
H12 New Ross
J6 Newry
G11 Newtown
J5 Newtownabbey
K5 Newtownards
G7 Newtownbutler
F8 Newtown Forbes
H6 Newtownhamilton
J10 Newtown Mount Kennedy
G5 Newtownstewart
H8 Nobber

E11 Ogonnelloe
H12 Oilgate
G8 Oldcastle
G5 Omagh
J7 Omeath
E12 Oola
D9 Oranmore
D9 Oughterard
E14 Ovens

E12 Pallas Grean New
B14 Parknasilla
D8 Partry
H13 Passage East
E14 Passage West
E12 Patrickswell
H11 Paulstown
F5 Pettigo
G5 Plumbridge
H5 Pomeroy
H6 Portadown
K6 Portaferry
G10 Portarlington
K6 Portavogie
H3 Portballintrae
H4 Portglenone
G10 Portlaoise
J9 Portmarnock
E4 Portnoo
J9 Portraine
E11 Portroe
H3 Portrush
H3 Portstewart
E10 Portumna
C13 Poulgorm Bridge
J6 Poyntz Pass

G9 Raharney
J5 Randalstown
H4 Rasharkin
H10 Rathangan
J9 Rathcoole
E13 Rathcormack
G11 Rathdowney
J10 Rathdrum
J6 Rathfriland
D12 Rathkeale
F4 Rathmelton
D13 Rathmore
H9 Rathmoylon
G4 Rathmullan
J10 Rathnew
G8 Rathowen
H11 Rathvilly
J9 Ratoath
G4 Ray
C9 Recess
B8 Renvyle
E14 Ringaskiddy
G13 Ringville
H7 Rockcorry
F8 Roosky
H12 Rosbercon
F8 Roscommon
F10 Roscrea
F3 Rosepenna
D15 Ross Carbery
E6 Rosses Point
J13 Rosslare
J13 Rosslare Harbour
G6 Rosslea
F5 Rossnowlagh
J7 Rostrevor
B9 Roundstone
J10 Roundwood
J9 Rush

K6 Saintfield
G4 St Johnston
H9 Sallins
D9 Salthill
E11 Scarriff
C13 Scartaglin
J6 Scarva
C15 Schull
F8 Scramoge
G5 Seskinore
F14 Shanagarry
D12 Shanagolden
J9 Shankill
D11 Shannon
F9 Shannonbridge
H7 Shercock
H11 Shillelagh
F10 Shinrone
D9 Shrule
E11 Silvermines
G5 Sion Mills
D11 Sixmilebridge
J8 Skerries
D15 Skibbereen
H8 Slane
E6 Sligo
G6 Smithborough
B14 Sneem
C11 Spanish Point
D9 Spiddal
C9 Sraith Salach
H5 Stewartstown
J9 Stillorgan
G12 Stonyford
G4 Strabane
G10 Stradbally
G7 Stradone
H9 Straffan
E6 Strandhill
K6 Strangford
F5 Stranorlar
F8 Strokestown
H9 Summerhill
F6 Swanlinbar
H4 Swatragh
D7 Swinford
J9 Swords

H12 Taghmon
J13 Tagoat
C14 Tahilla
J9 Tallaght
F13 Tallow
F13 Tallowbridge
J6 Tandragee
F9 Tang
C12 Tarbert
F11 Templemore
F11 Templetouhy
J8 Termonfeckin
G12 Thomastown
F11 Thurles
G10 Timahoe
D15 Timoleague
J11 Tinahely
F12 Tipperary
E7 Tobercurry
H4 Tobermore
F11 Toomyvara
C15 Toormore
C13 Tralee
G13 Tramore
H8 Trim
D9 Tuam
E11 Tuamgraney
D11 Tulla
G9 Tullamore
H11 Tullow
E8 Tulsk
D7 Turlough
G9 Tyrrellspass

G11 Urlingford

G8 Virginia

J7 Warrenpoint
G13 Waterford
E13 Watergrasshill
B14 Waterville
C8 Westport
J12 Wexford
E14 Whitegate
K5 Whitehead
J10 Wicklow
J11 Woodenbridge
E10 Woodford

F14 Youghal

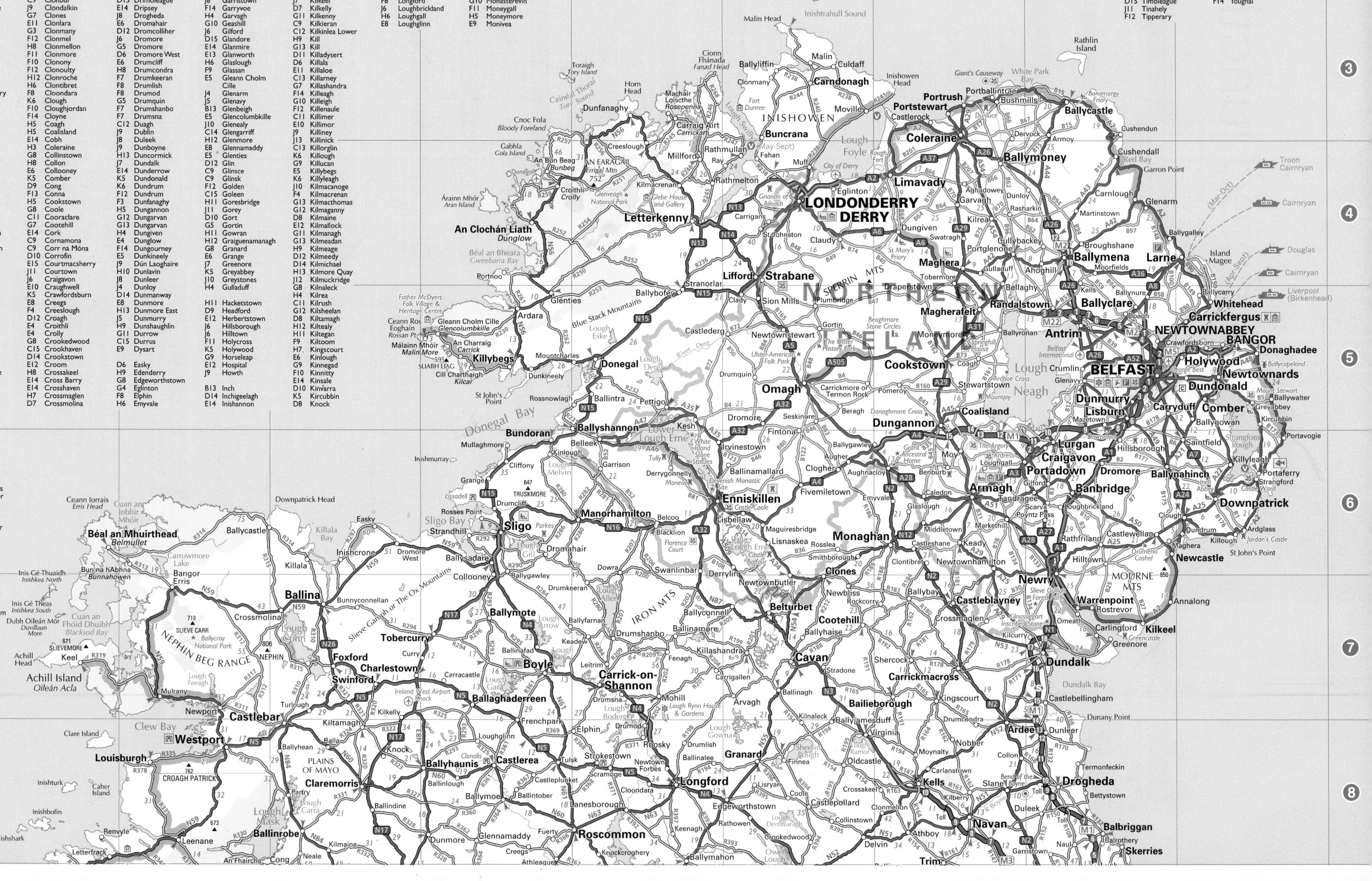

Malin Head
Inishtrahull Sound
Rathlin Island
Giant's Causeway
White Park Bay
Toraigh
Tory Island
Cnoc Fola
Bloody Foreland
Gabhla
Gola Island
Árainn Mhór
Aran Island
An Clochán Liath
Dunglow
Letterkenny
LONDONDERRY
DERRY
Coleraine
Ballymoney
Ballycastle
Portrush
Portstewart
Limavady
Ballymena
Larne
Antrim
Ballyclare
Carrickfergus
Whitehead
NEWTOWNABBEY
BANGOR
Donaghadee
Holywood
BELFAST
Newtownards
Dundonald
Dunmurry
Lisburn
Lurgan
Craigavon
Portadown
Banbridge
Armagh
Downpatrick
Newcastle
Newry
Warrenpoint
Kilkeel
Dundalk
Drogheda
Balbriggan
Skerries
Navan
Kells
Trim
Ardee
Cookstown
Dungannon
Magherafelt
Omagh
Strabane
Lifford
Enniskillen
Donegal
Killybegs
Ardara
Glenties
Ballyshannon
Bundoran
Sligo
Ballina
Castlebar
Westport
Louisburgh
Béal an Mhuirthead
Belmullet
Achill Island
Oileán Acla
Claremorris
Ballyhaunis
Castlerea
Boyle
Carrick-on-Shannon
Longford
Roscommon
Monaghan
Cavan
Castleblayney
Carrickmacross
Clones
Belturbet
Cootehill
Granard
Ballinrobe
Charlestown
Swinford
Foxford
Tobercurry
Ballymote
Manorhamilton
Donegal Bay
Clew Bay
Dundalk Bay
Lough Neagh
Lough Foyle
NEPHIN BEG RANGE
CROAGH PATRICK
MOURNE MTS
SPERRIN MTS
IRON MTS
PLAINS OF MAYO
INISHOWEN
NORTHERN IRELAND
Blue Stack Mountains
Troon
Cairnryan
Douglas
Liverpool (Birkenhead)

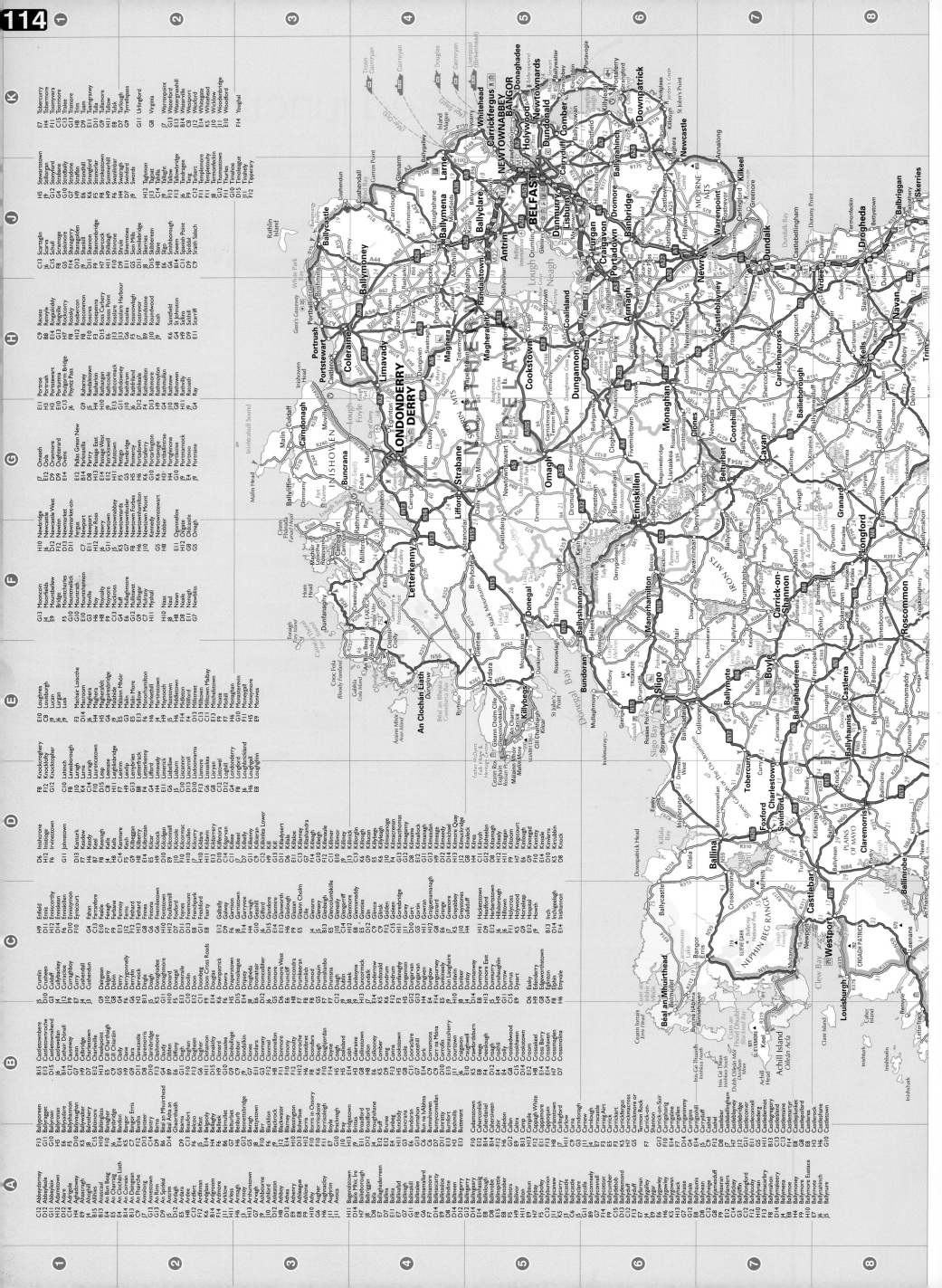

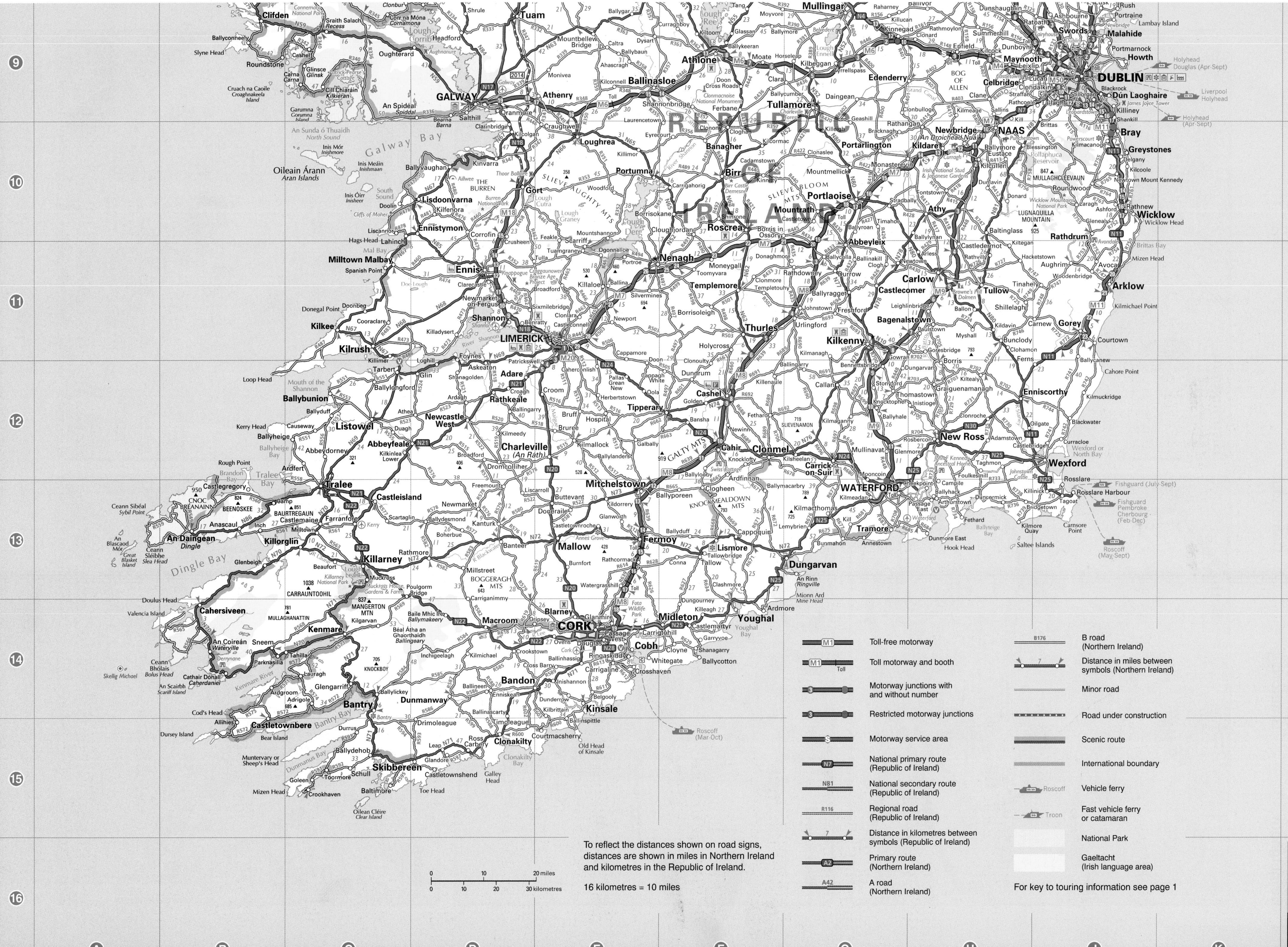
REPUBLIC OF IRELAND
DUBLIN
Dún Laoghaire
Howth
Malahide
Swords
Maynooth
Celbridge
NAAS
Bray
Greystones
Wicklow
Arklow
Gorey
Wexford
Rosslare Harbour
Enniscorthy
New Ross
WATERFORD
Tramore
Dungarvan
Youghal
Midleton
Cobh
CORK
Kinsale
Bandon
Clonakilty
Skibbereen
Bantry
Castletownbere
Kenmare
Cahersiveen
An Daingean
Dingle
Tralee
Killarney
Killorglin
Castleisland
Listowel
Abbeyfeale
Newcastle West
Charleville
Mallow
Fermoy
Mitchelstown
Macroom
LIMERICK
Shannon
Ennis
Kilrush
Kilkee
Milltown Malbay
Ennistymon
Lisdoonvarna
GALWAY
Clifden
Tuam
Athenry
Loughrea
Gort
Ballinasloe
Athlone
Mullingar
Tullamore
Portlaoise
Kilkenny
Carlow
Thurles
Nenagh
Roscrea
Birr
Tipperary
Cashel
Cahir
Clonmel
Carrick-on-Suir
Lismore
Galway Bay
Dingle Bay
Aran Islands
THE BURREN
SLIEVE AUGHTY MTS
SLIEVE BLOOM MTS
GALTY MTS
KNOCKMEALDOWN MTS
BOGGERAGH MTS
Toll-free motorway
Toll motorway and booth
Motorway junctions with and without number
Restricted motorway junctions
Motorway service area
National primary route (Republic of Ireland)
National secondary route (Republic of Ireland)
Regional road (Republic of Ireland)
Distance in kilometres between symbols (Republic of Ireland)
Primary route (Northern Ireland)
A road (Northern Ireland)
B road (Northern Ireland)
Distance in miles between symbols (Northern Ireland)
Minor road
Road under construction
Scenic route
International boundary
Vehicle ferry
Fast vehicle ferry or catamaran
National Park
Gaeltacht (Irish language area)
For key to touring information see page 1
To reflect the distances shown on road signs, distances are shown in miles in Northern Ireland and kilometres in the Republic of Ireland.
16 kilometres = 10 miles
0 10 20 miles
0 10 20 30 kilometres

116
Bath
Birmingham
Blackpool
Bradford
Bristol
Cambridge

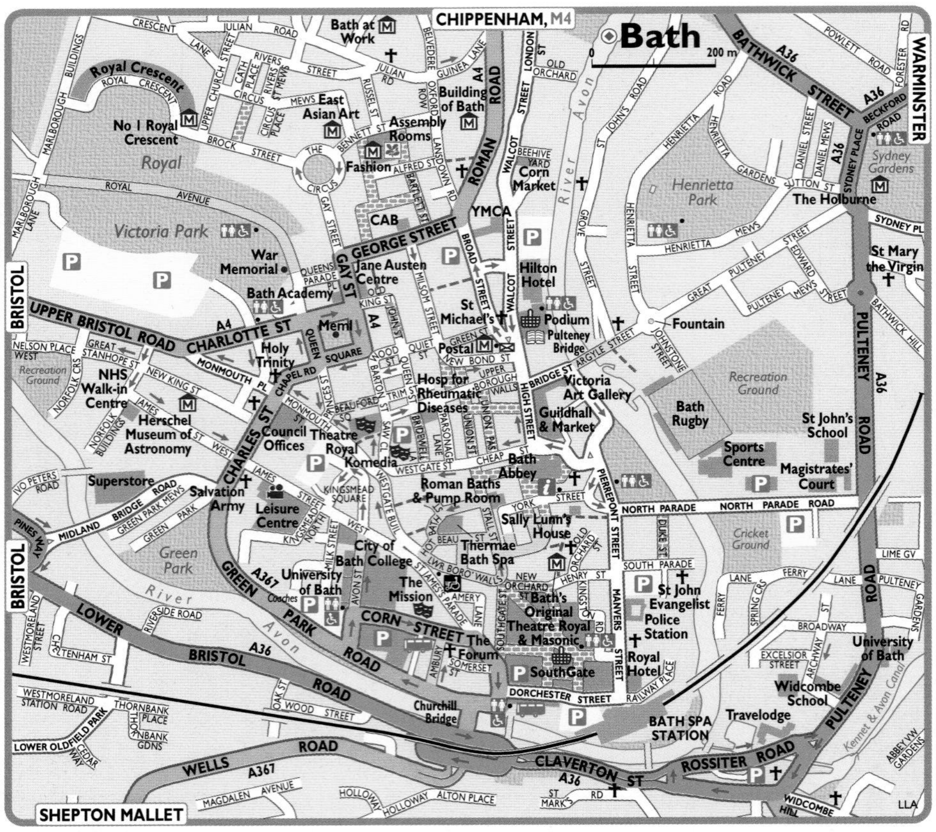

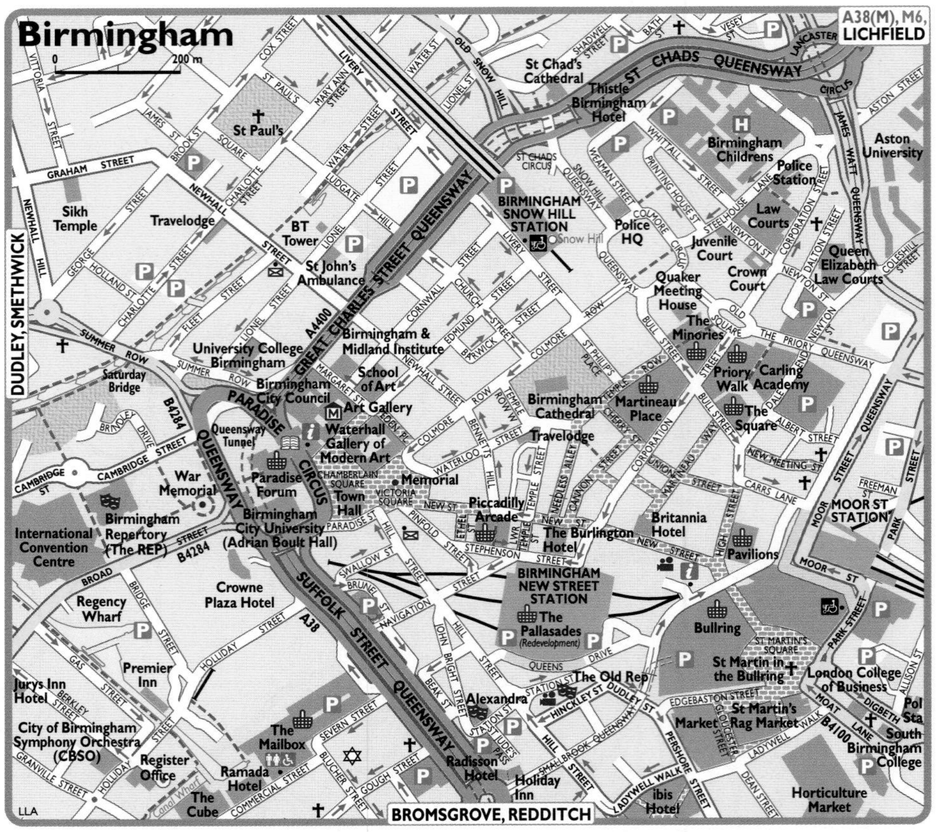

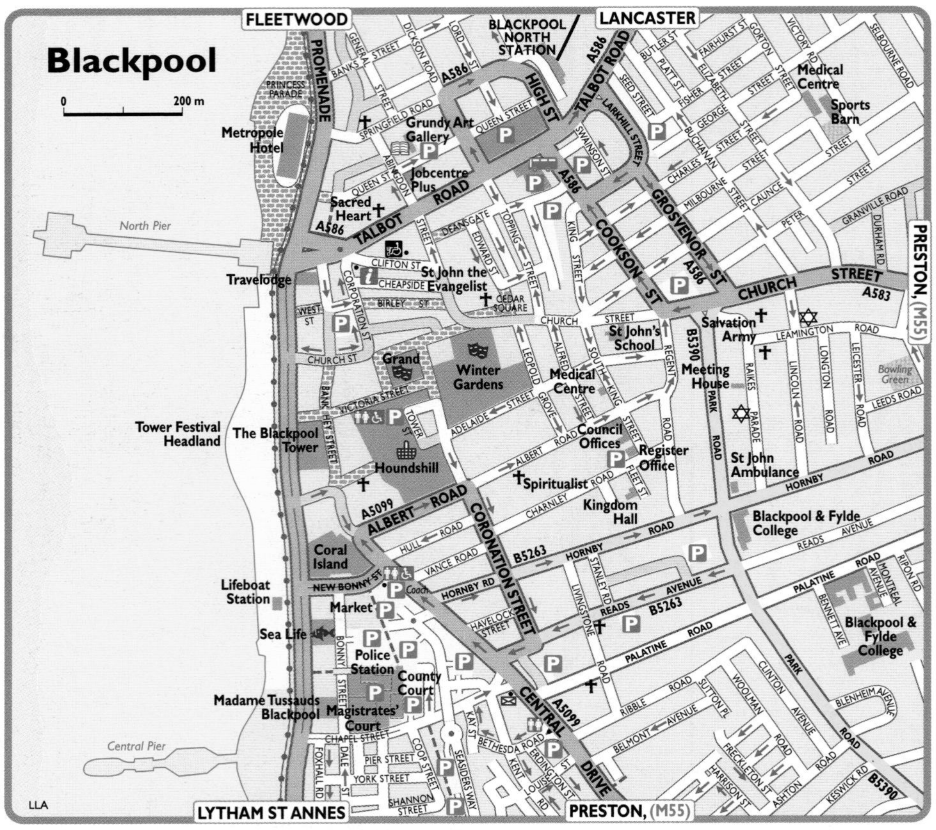

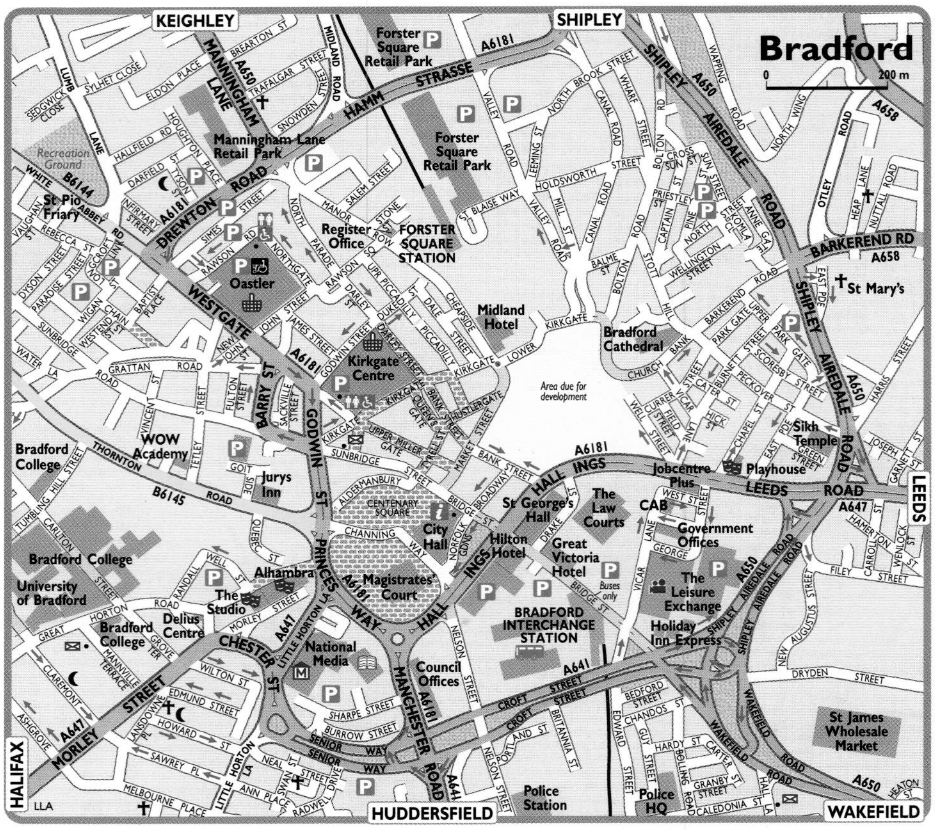

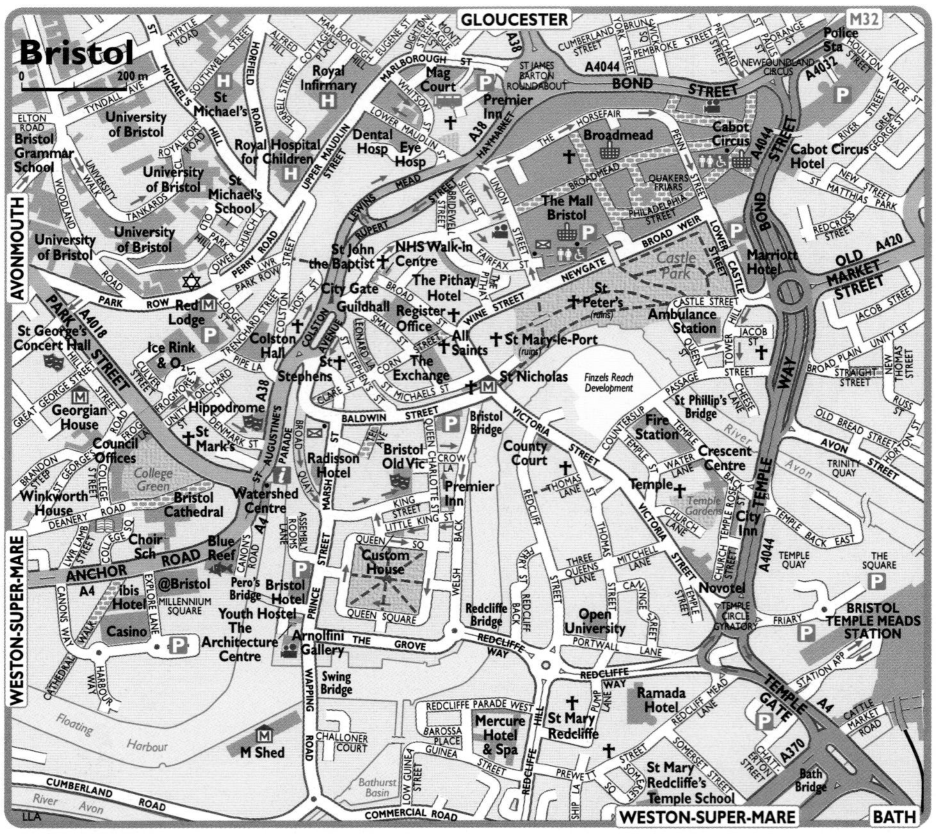

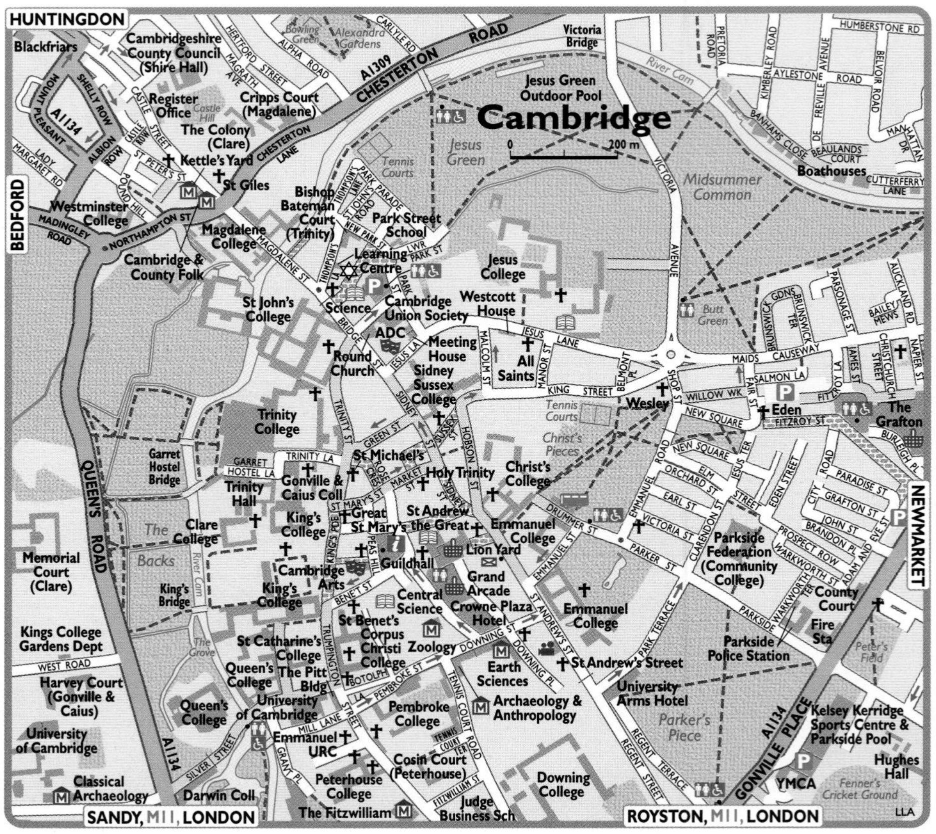

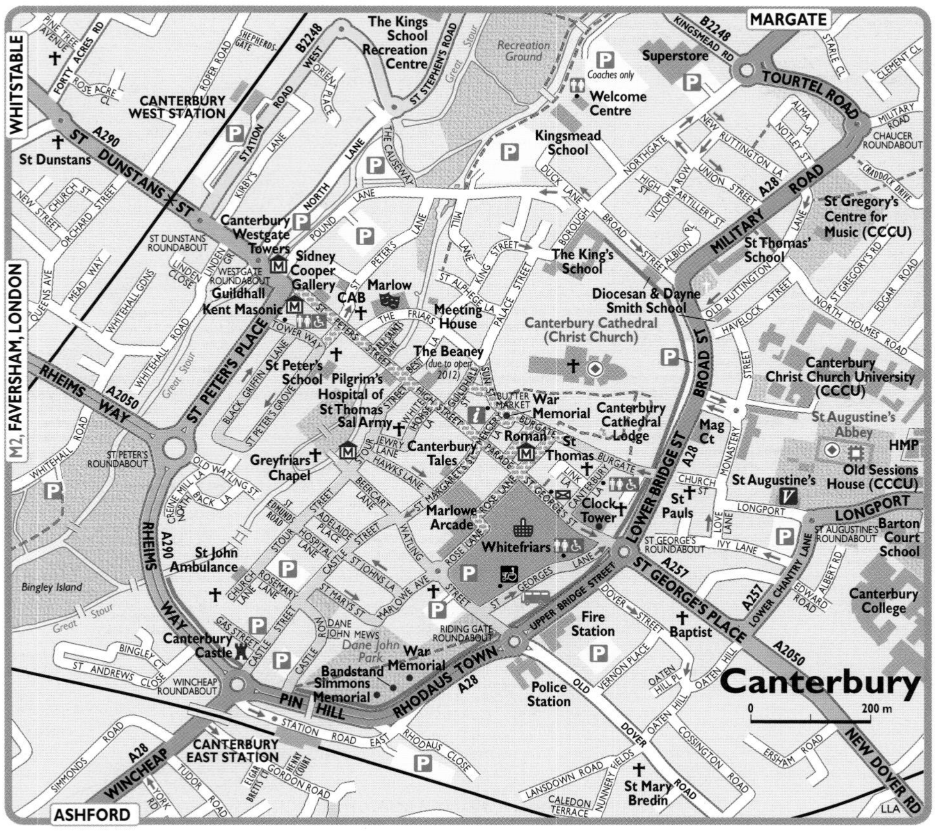

Canterbury

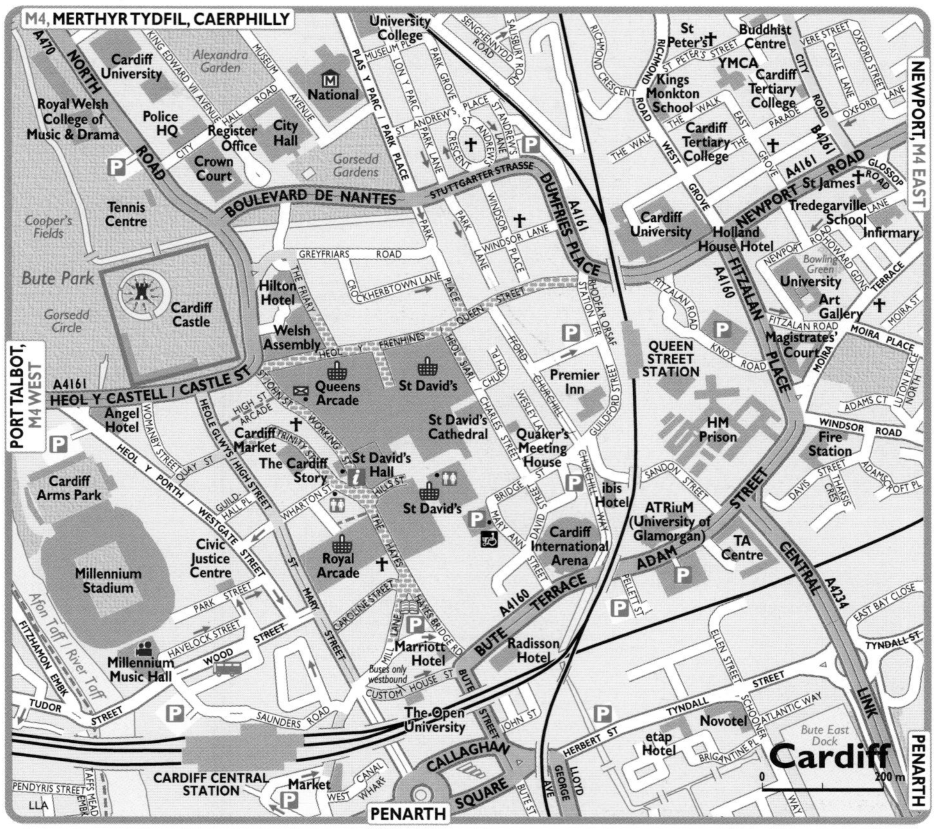

Cardiff

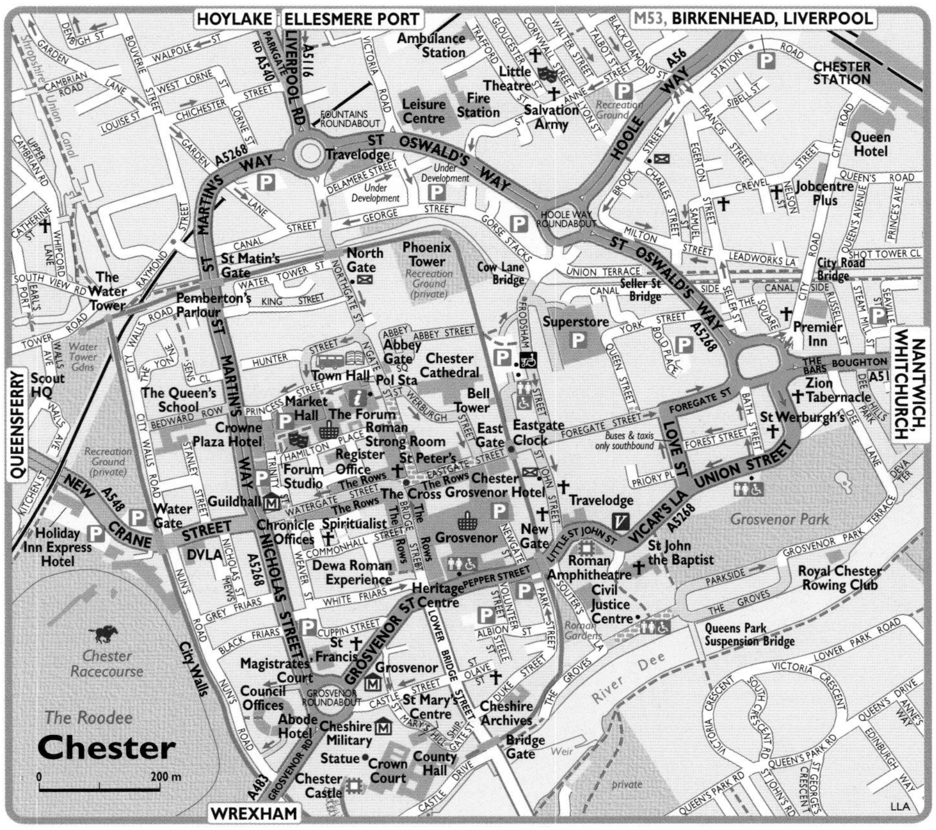

Chester

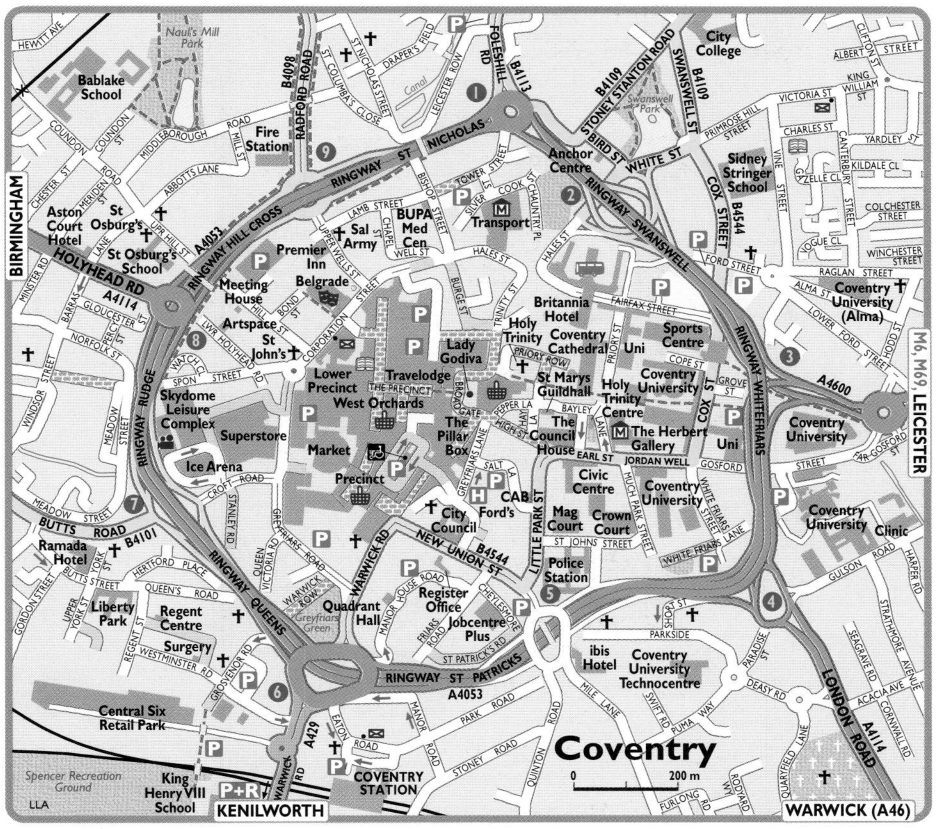

Coventry

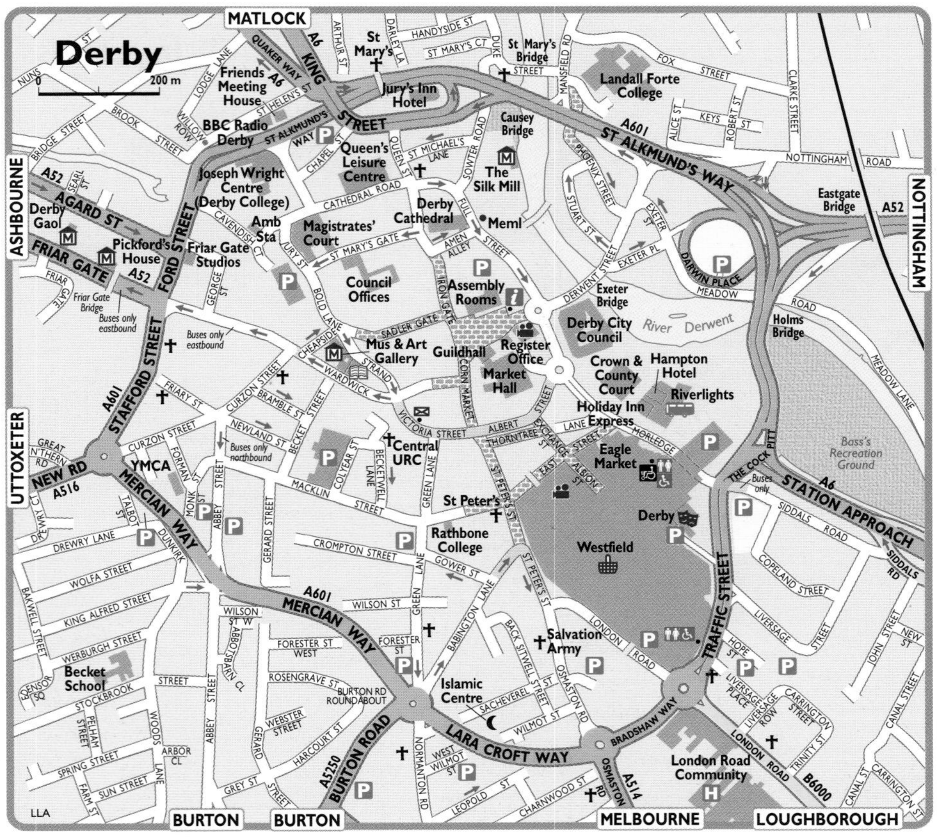

Derby

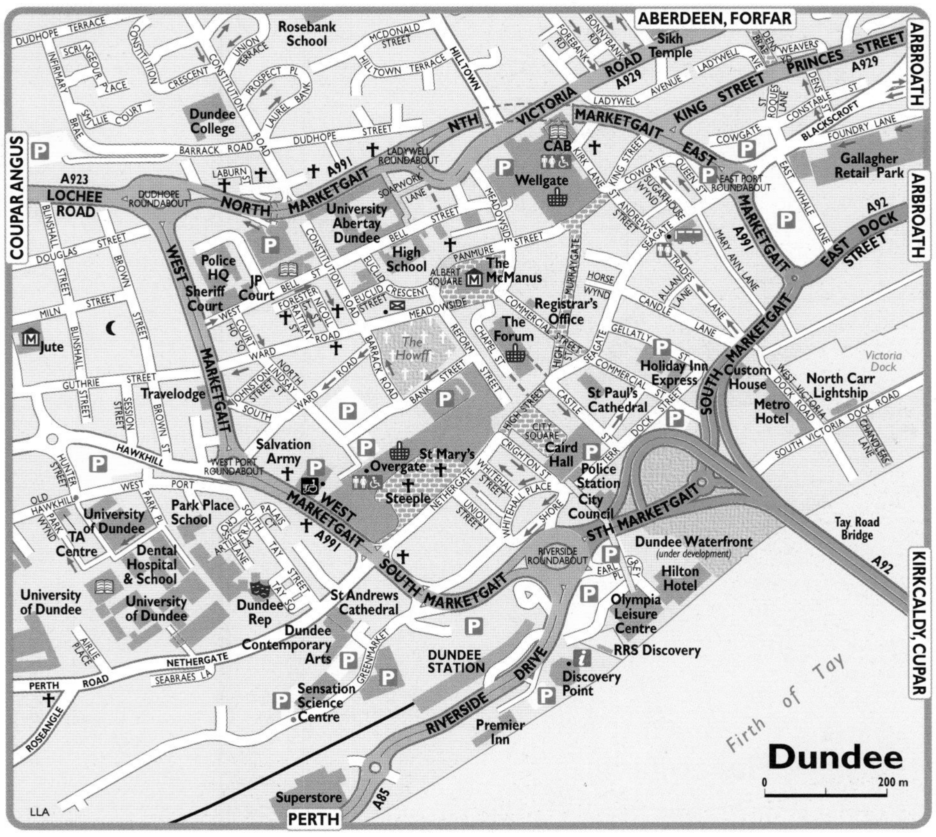

Dundee

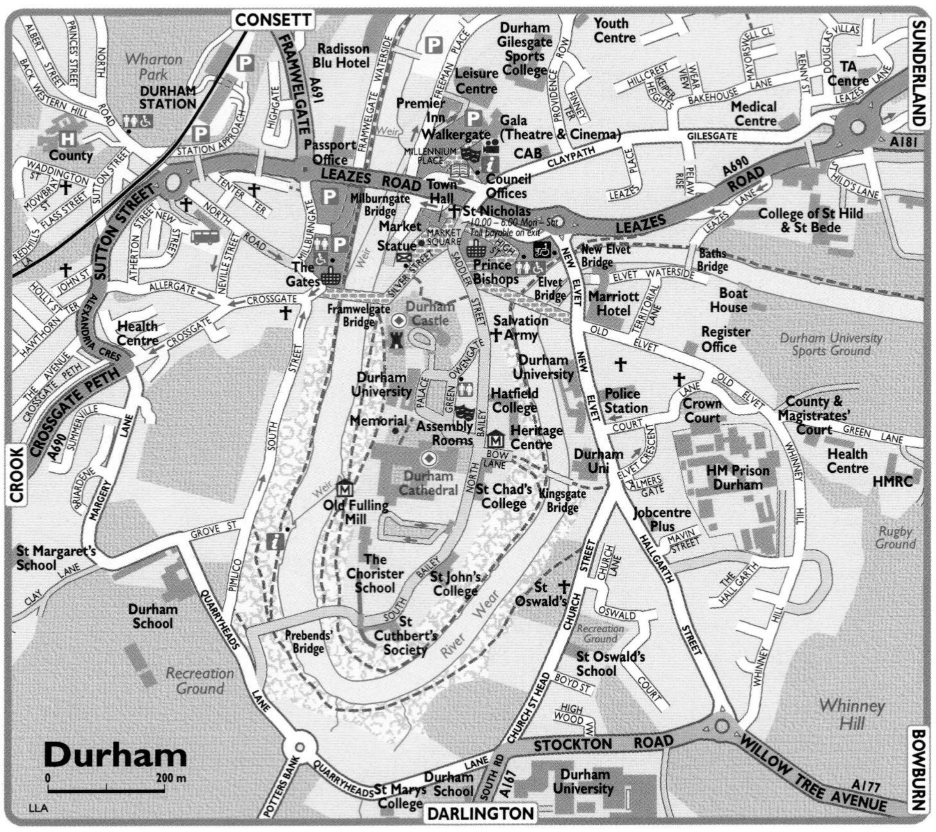

Durham

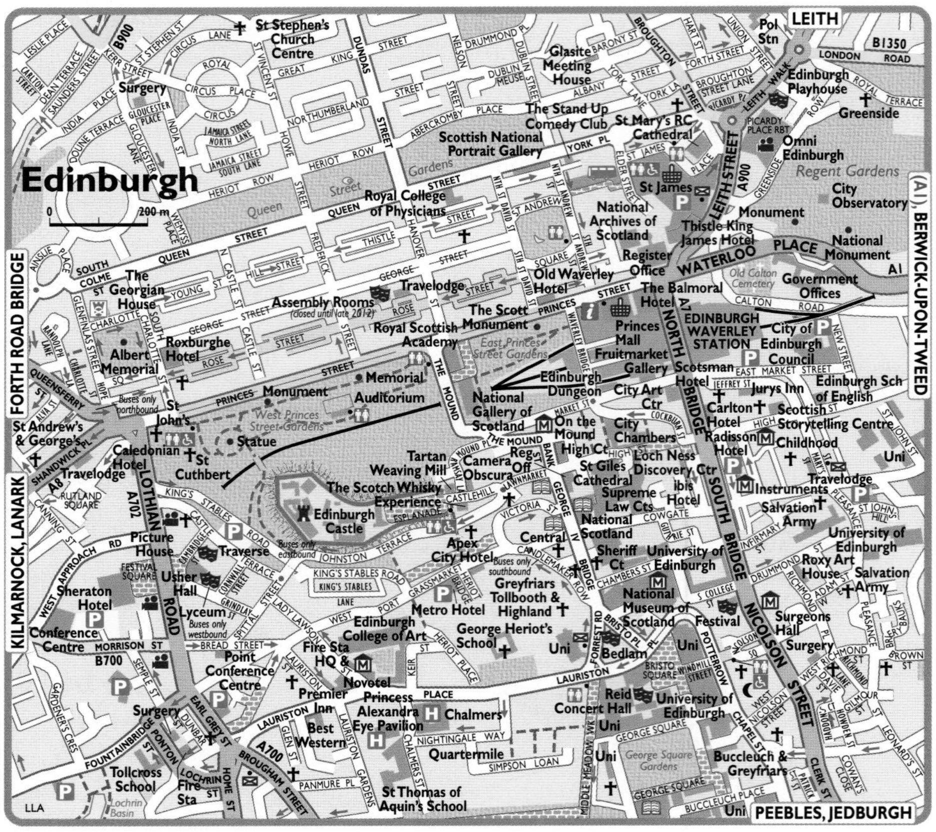

Edinburgh

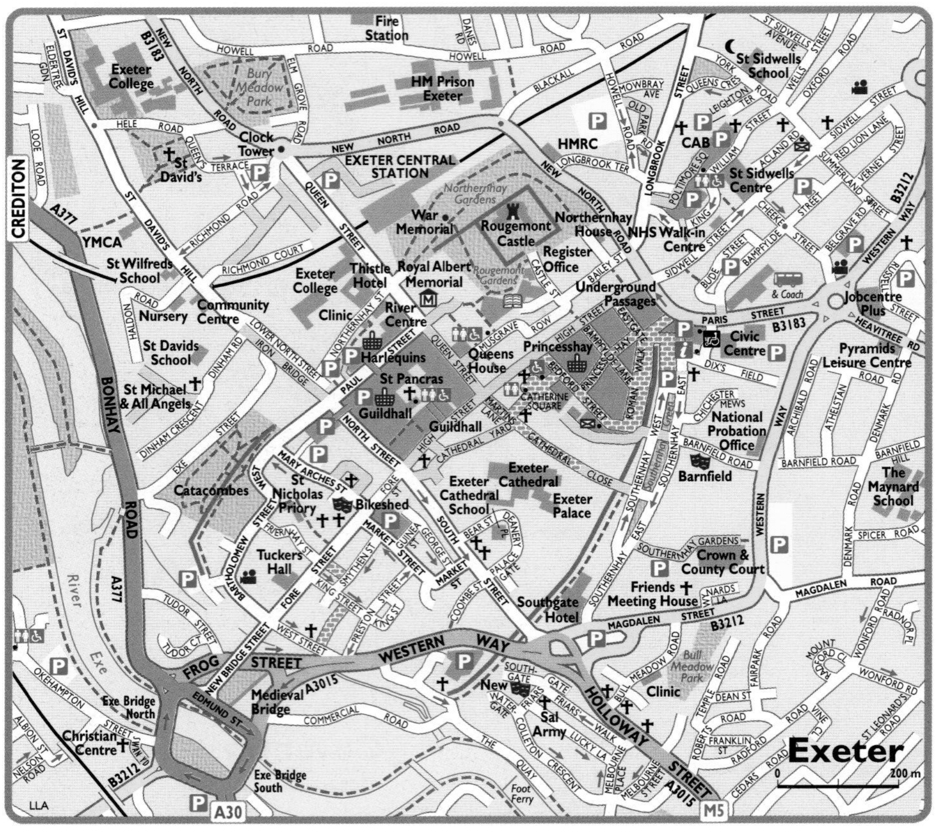

Exeter

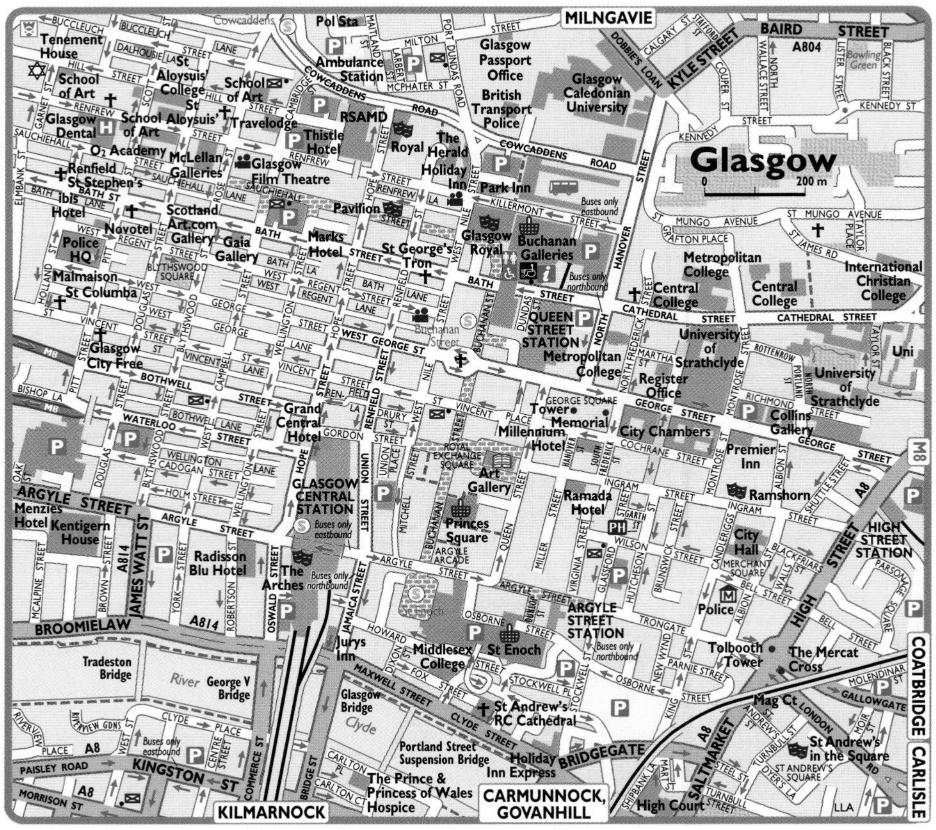

Glasgow

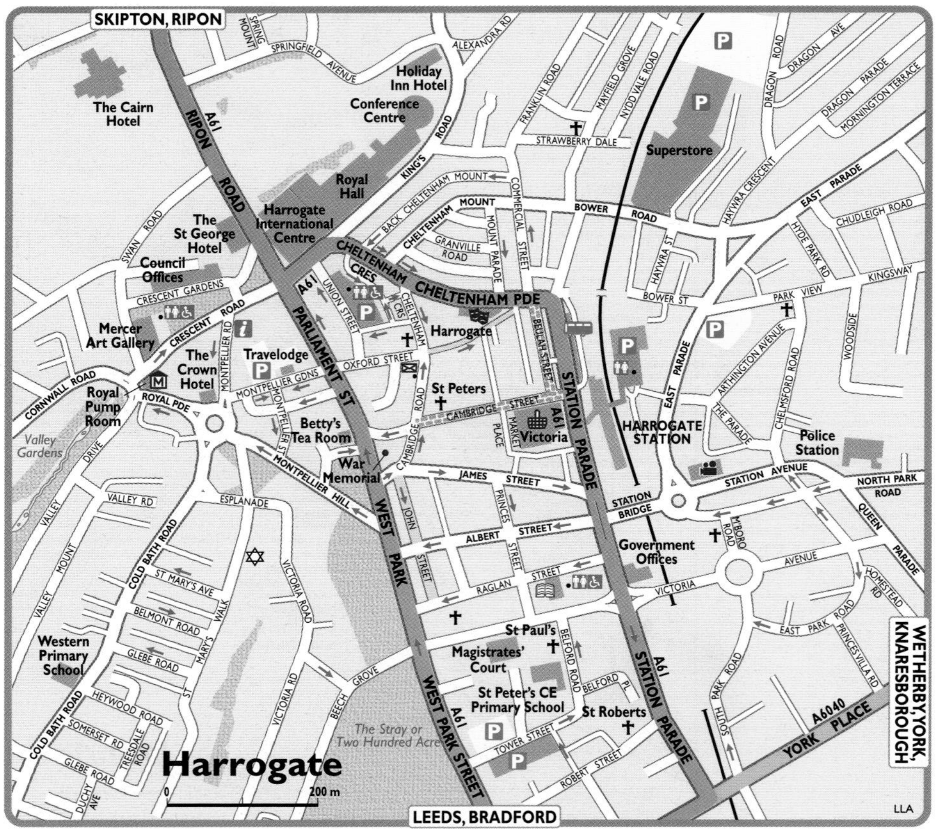

Harrogate

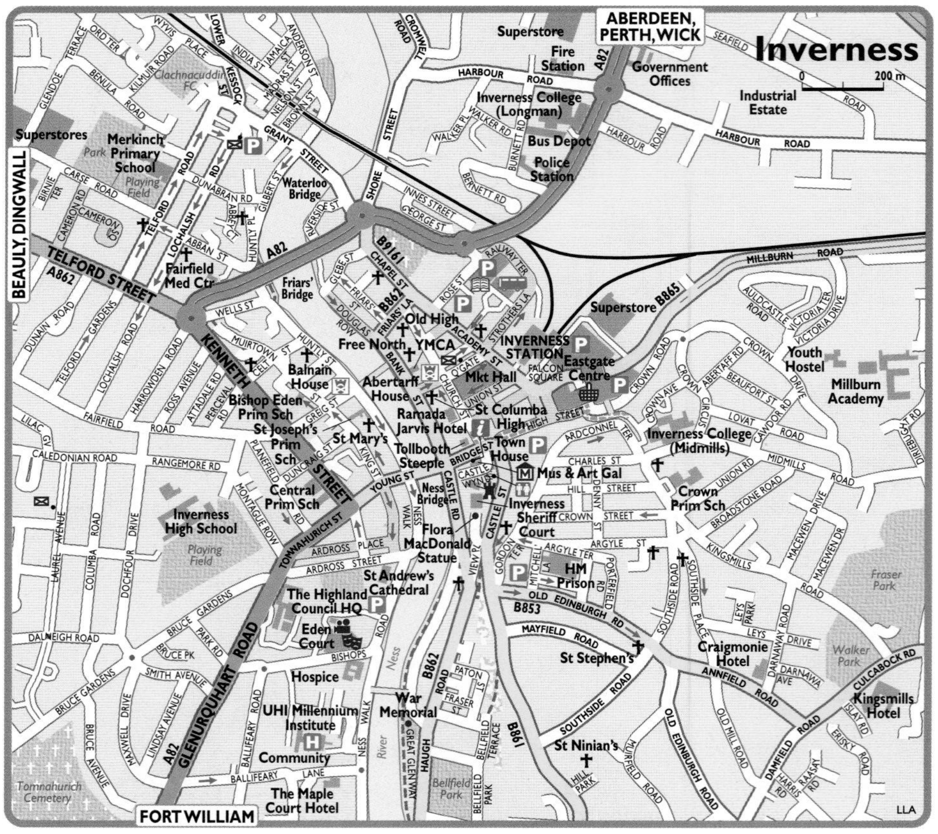

Inverness

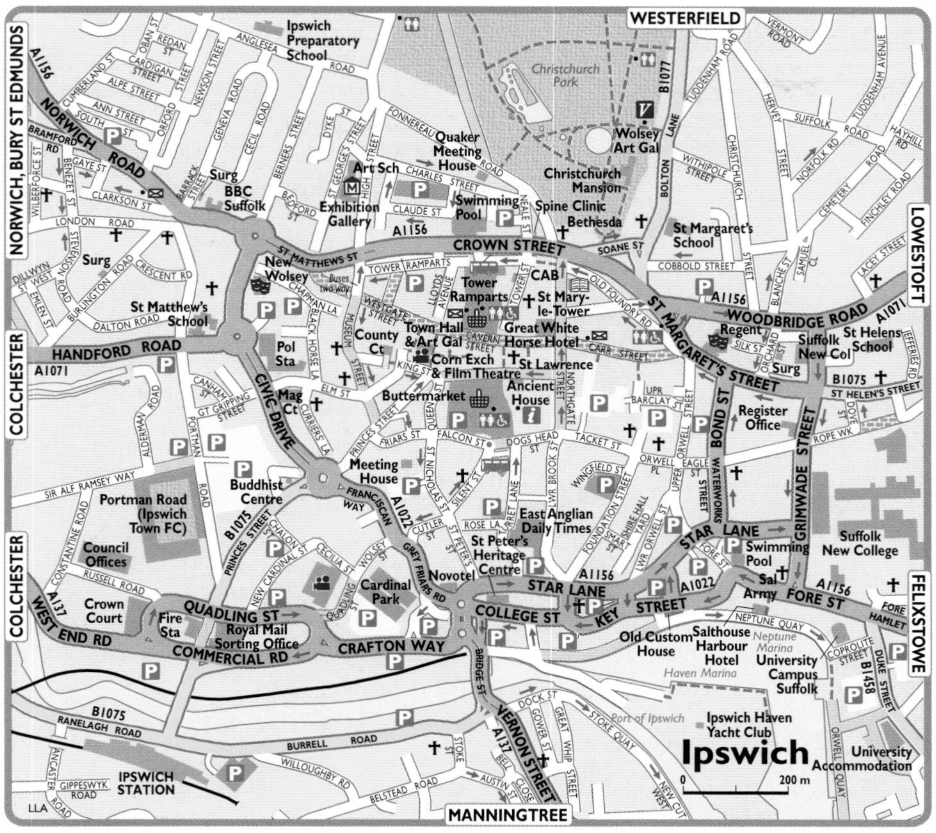

Ipswich

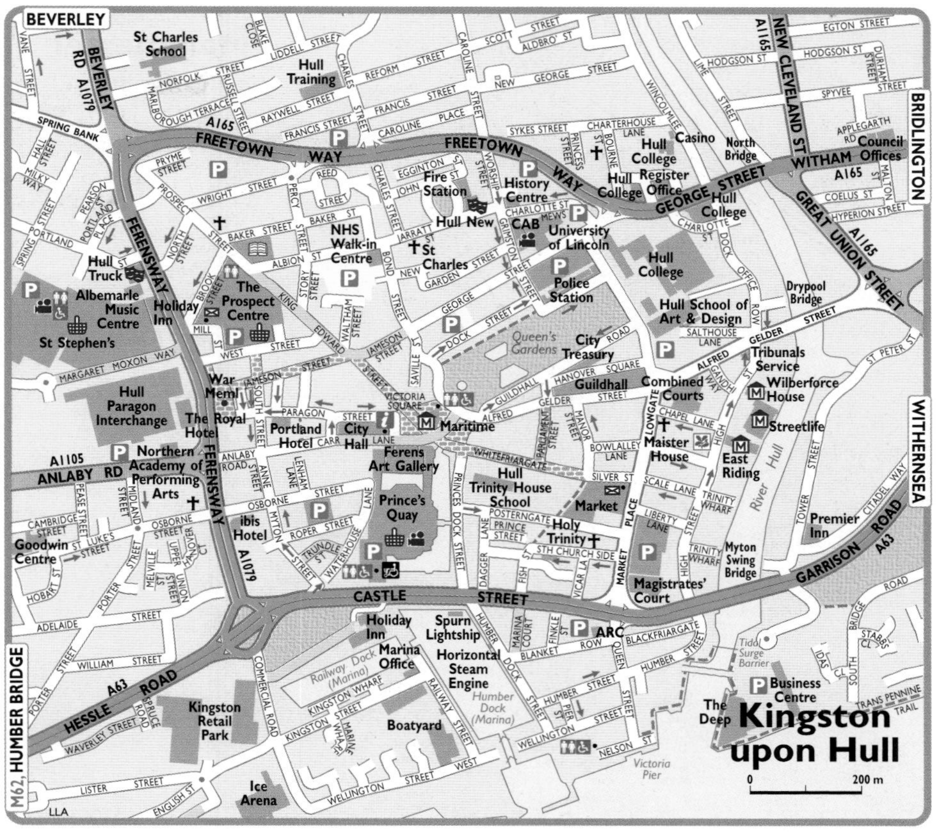

Kingston upon Hull

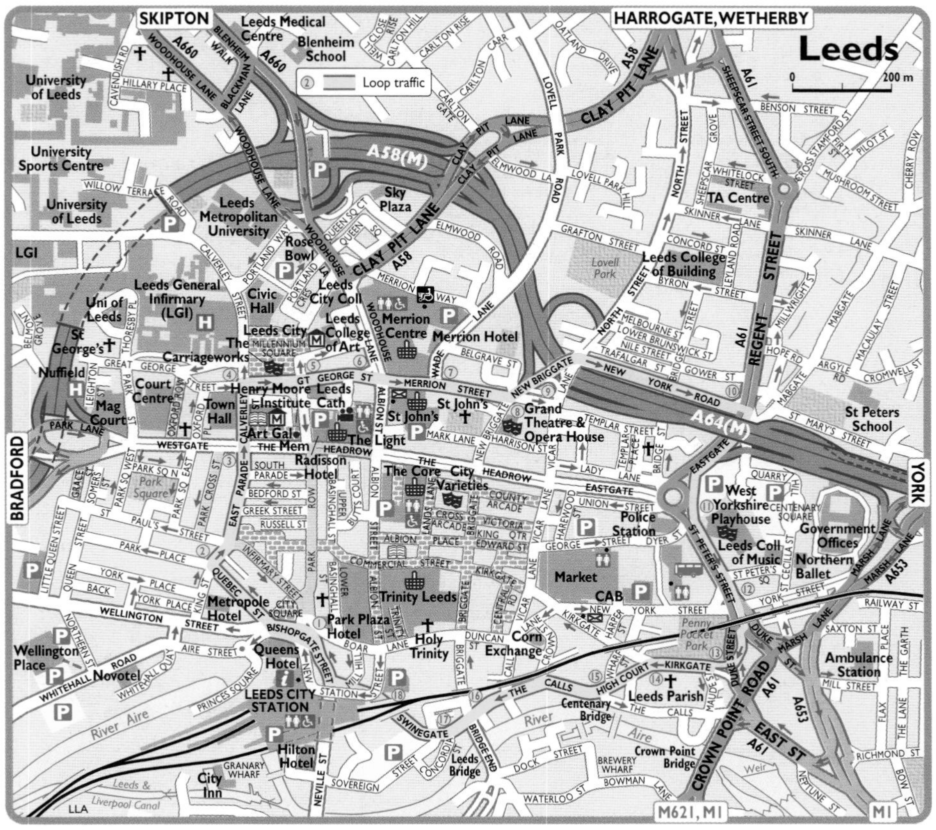

Leeds

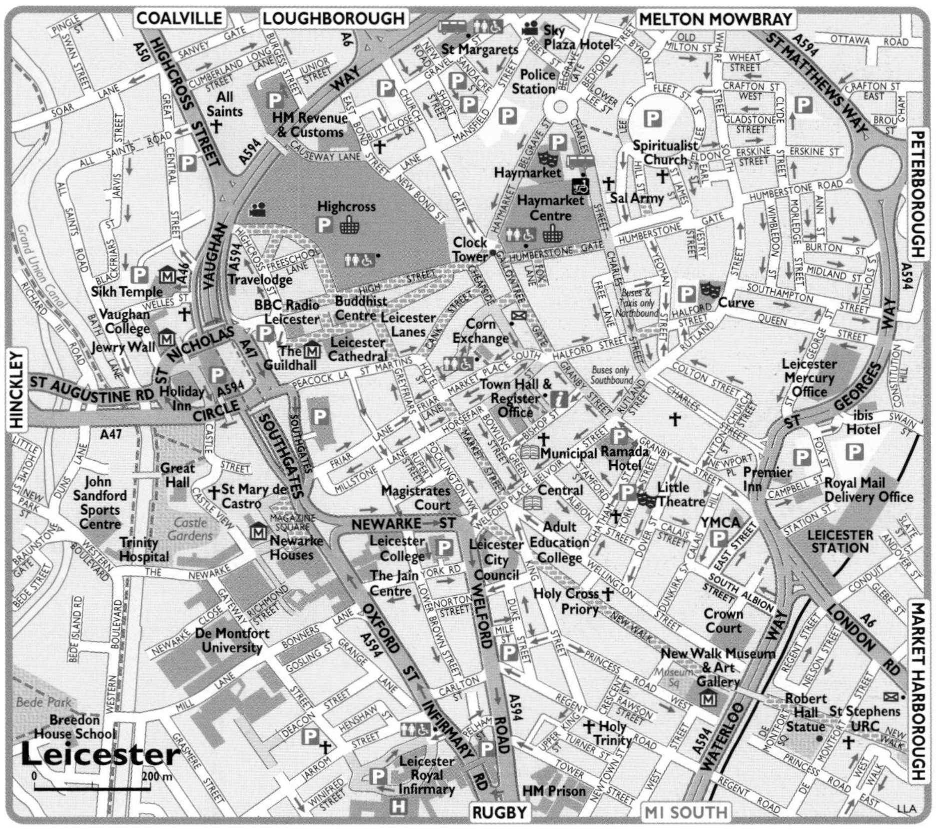

Leicester

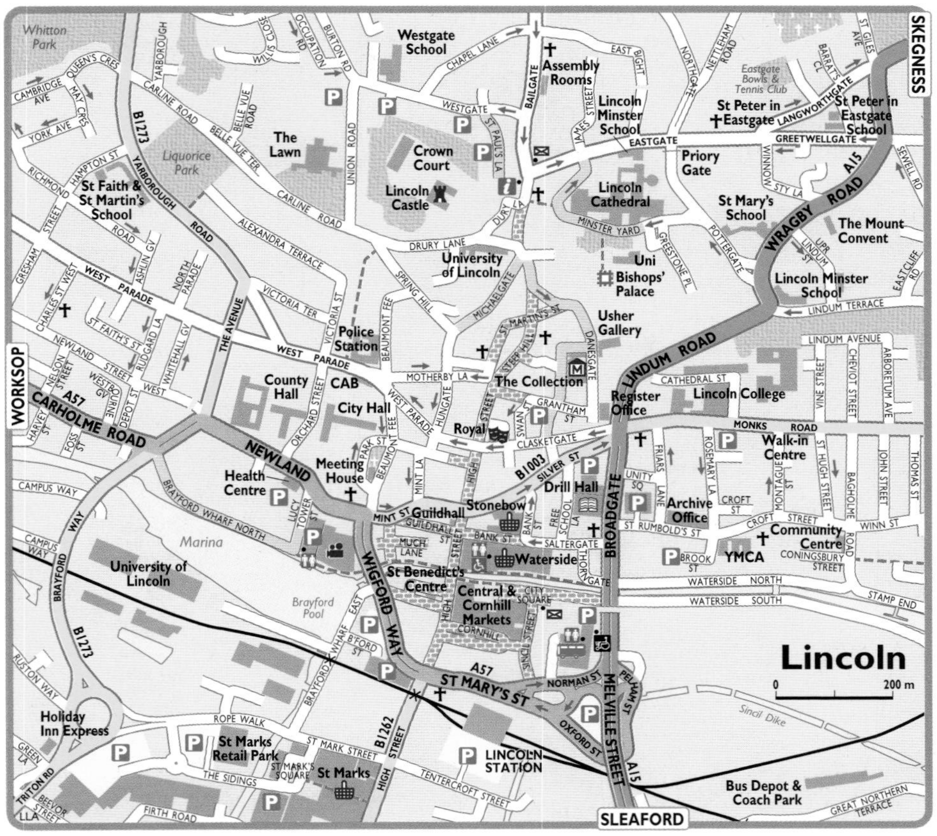

Lincoln

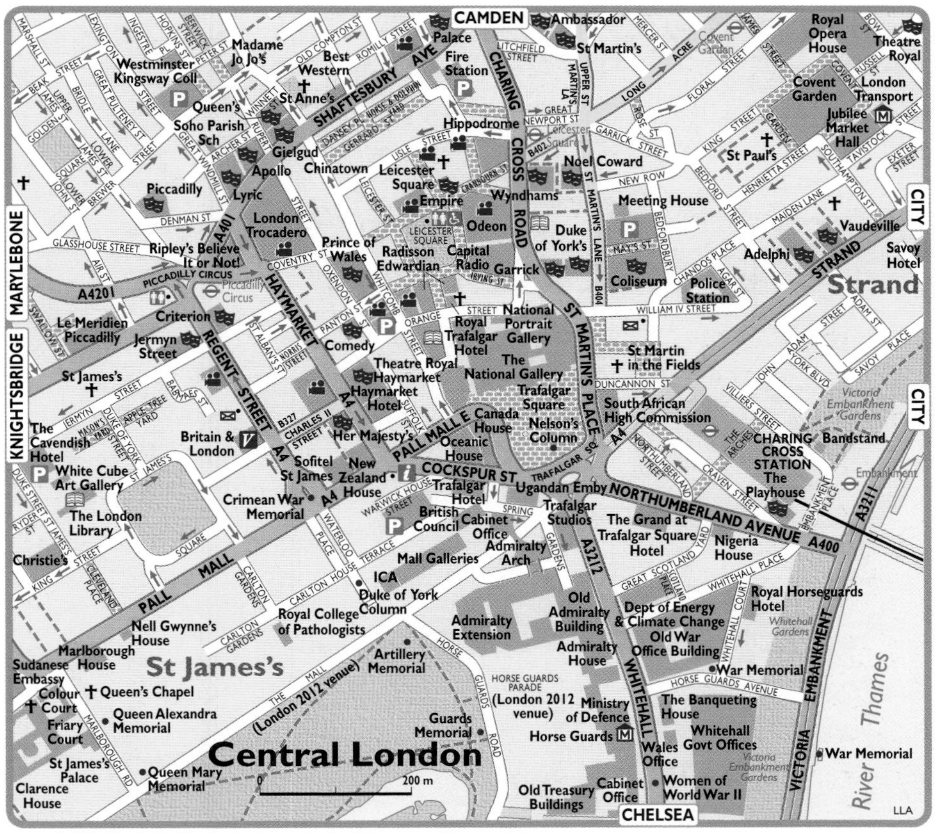

Central London

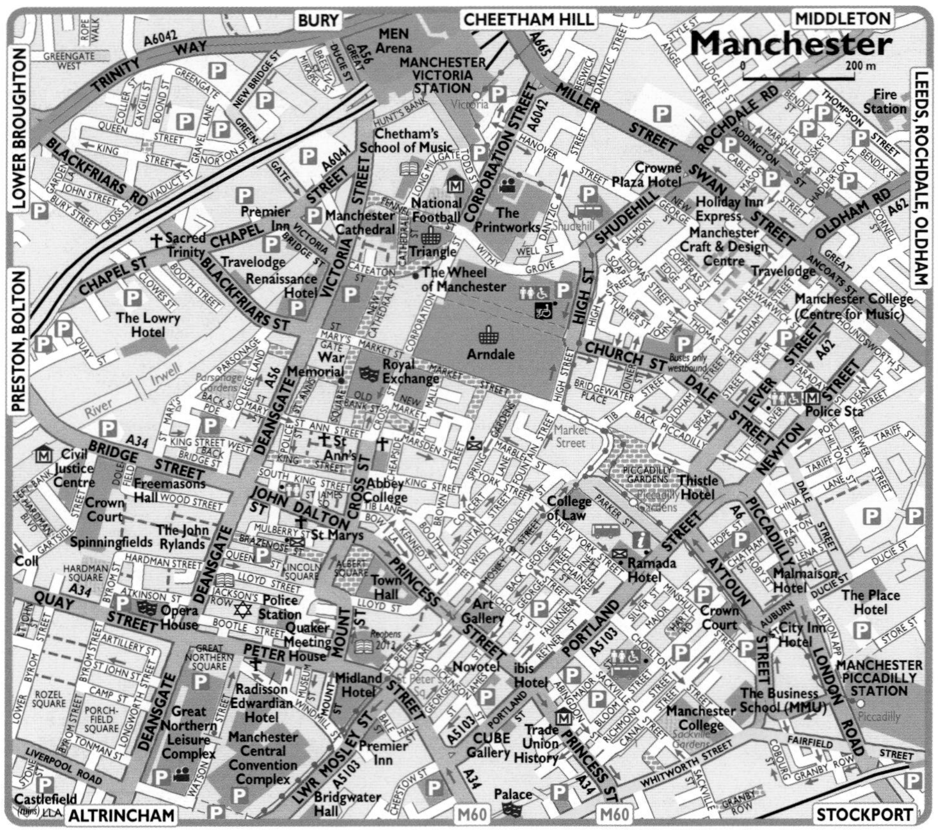
Manchester
0 200 m
BURY
CHEETHAM HILL
MIDDLETON
LEEDS, ROCHDALE, OLDHAM
LOWER BROUGHTON
PRESTON, BOLTON
ALTRINCHAM
M60
STOCKPORT
MANCHESTER VICTORIA STATION
MANCHESTER PICCADILLY STATION
Arndale
Chetham's School of Music
Manchester Cathedral
National Football Museum
The Printworks
Royal Exchange
Town Hall
Opera House
Great Northern Leisure Complex
Manchester Central Convention Complex
Bridgewater Hall
Palace
Piccadilly Gardens
The Lowry Hotel
LLA

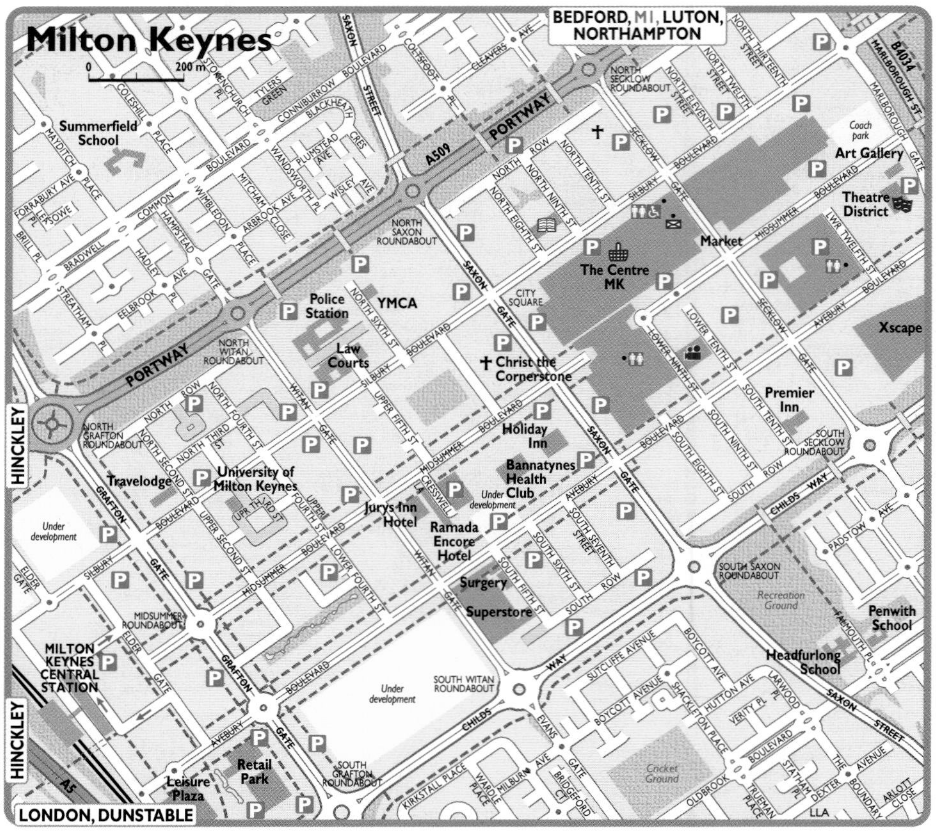
Milton Keynes
0 200 m
BEDFORD, M1, LUTON, NORTHAMPTON
HINCKLEY
LONDON, DUNSTABLE
MILTON KEYNES CENTRAL STATION
The Centre MK
Market
Theatre District
Art Gallery
Xscape
Police Station
YMCA
Law Courts
Christ the Cornerstone
University of Milton Keynes
Holiday Inn
Bannatynes Health Club
Jurys Inn Hotel
Ramada Encore Hotel
Superstore
Retail Park
Leisure Plaza
Summerfield School
Penwith School
Headfurlong School
Premier Inn
Travelodge
LLA

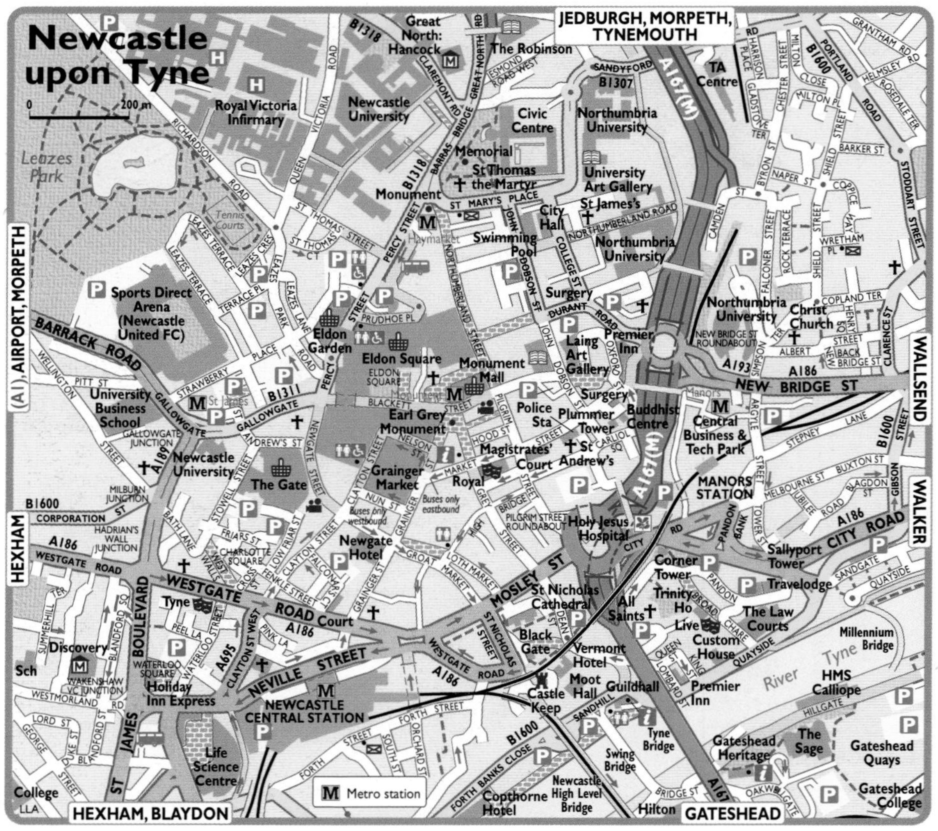
Newcastle upon Tyne
0 200 m
JEDBURGH, MORPETH, TYNEMOUTH
(A1), AIRPORT, MORPETH
WALLSEND
WALKER
HEXHAM
HEXHAM, BLAYDON
GATESHEAD
Royal Victoria Infirmary
Newcastle University
Northumbria University
Civic Centre
Sports Direct Arena (Newcastle United FC)
Eldon Square
Monument
Grey's Monument
Grainger Market
St Nicholas Cathedral
Castle Keep
NEWCASTLE CENTRAL STATION
MANORS STATION
Millennium Bridge
Tyne Bridge
Swing Bridge
High Level Bridge
The Sage Gateshead
Gateshead Quays
Life Science Centre
Discovery
M Metro station
LLA

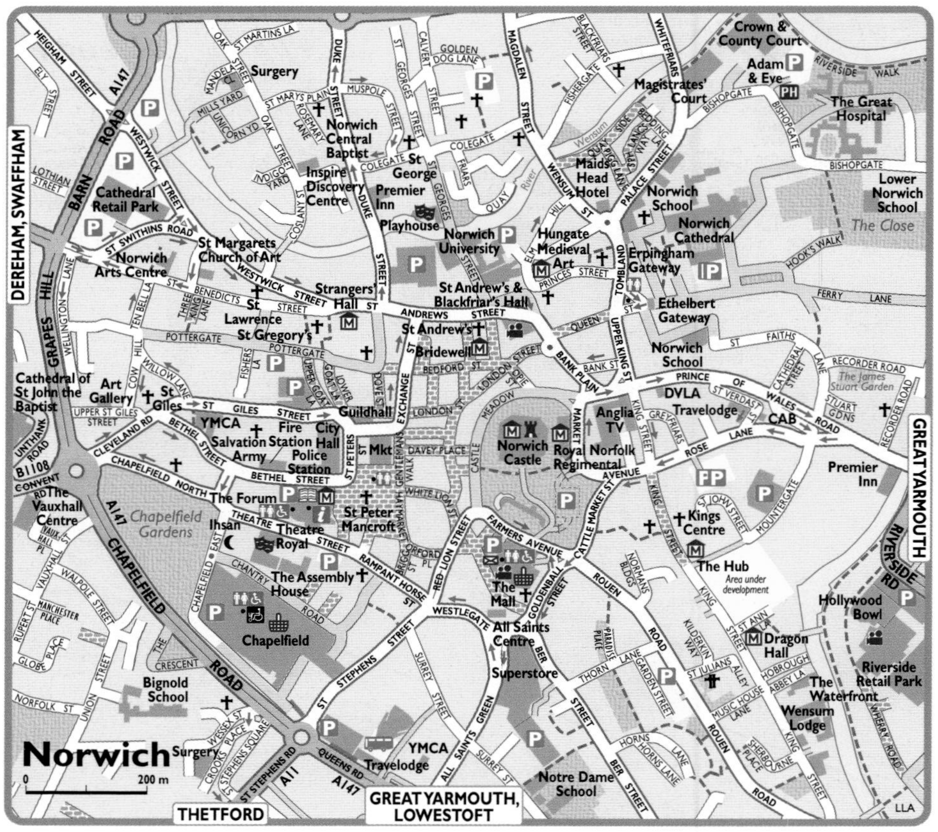
Norwich
0 200 m
DEREHAM, SWAFFHAM
GREAT YARMOUTH
THETFORD
GREAT YARMOUTH, LOWESTOFT
Norwich Cathedral
Norwich Castle
Cathedral of St John the Baptist
Chapelfield Gardens
Chapelfield
The Forum
City Hall
Guildhall
Theatre Royal
The Assembly House
St Andrew's & Blackfriar's Hall
Bridewell
Anglia TV
Dragon Hall
Riverside Retail Park
Hollywood Bowl
The Great Hospital
Norwich School
Norwich University
Superstore
LLA

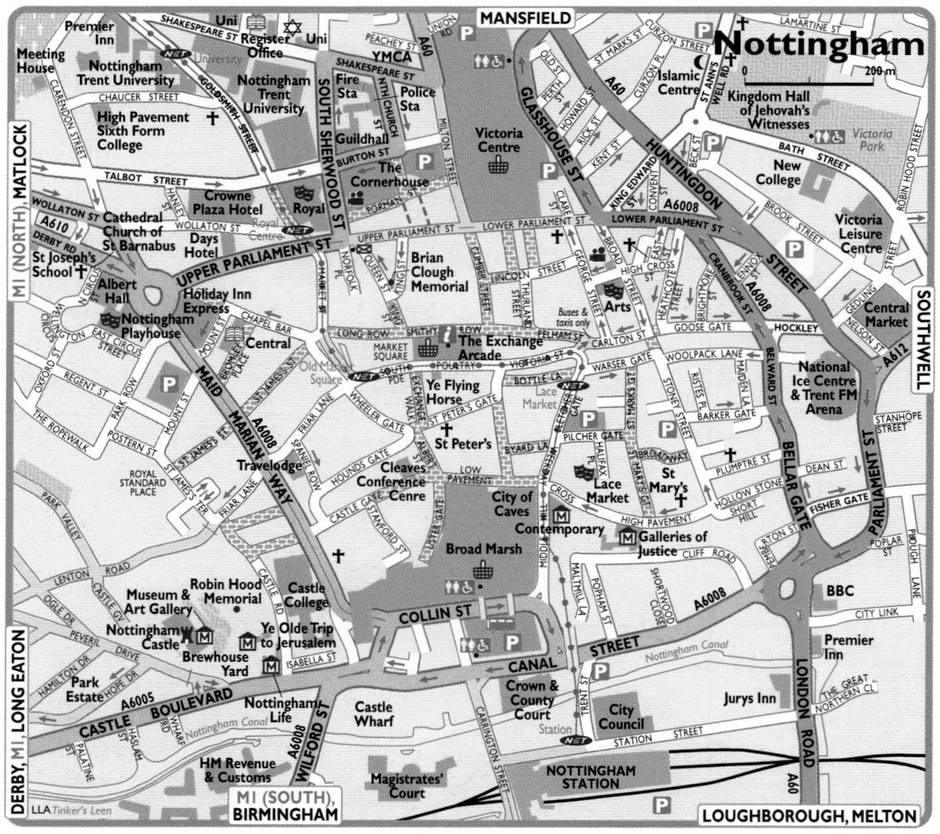
Nottingham
0 200 m
MANSFIELD
M1 (NORTH), MATLOCK
SOUTHWELL
DERBY, M1, LONG EATON
M1 (SOUTH), BIRMINGHAM
LOUGHBOROUGH, MELTON
NOTTINGHAM STATION
Nottingham Trent University
Victoria Centre
Theatre Royal
Royal Concert Hall
Nottingham Playhouse
The Exchange Arcade
Broad Marsh
National Ice Centre & Trent FM Arena
Galleries of Justice
Lace Market
Nottingham Castle
Ye Olde Trip to Jerusalem
Brewhouse Yard
Castle Wharf
Nottingham Canal
City Council
LLA Tinker's Leen

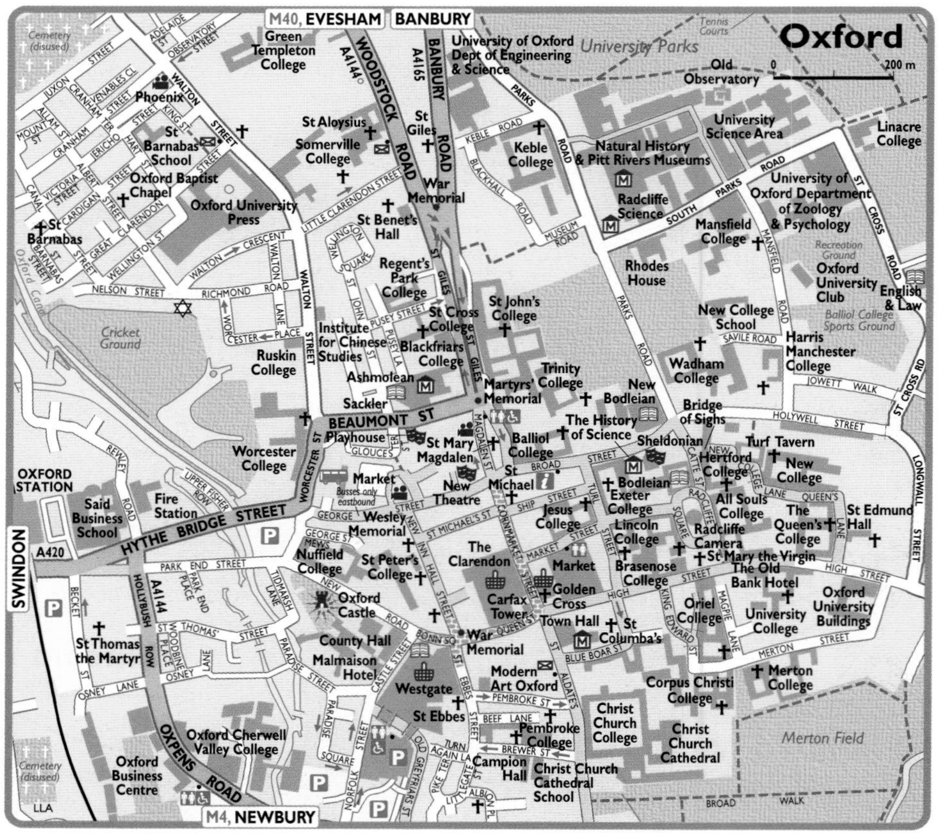
Oxford
0 200 m
M40, EVESHAM
BANBURY
CROSS RD
SWINDON
M4, NEWBURY
OXFORD STATION
University Parks
Natural History & Pitt Rivers Museums
Keble College
Radcliffe Science
Somerville College
St John's College
Balliol College
Trinity College
Ashmolean
Martyrs' Memorial
New Bodleian
Sheldonian
Bodleian
Radcliffe Camera
Oxford Castle
Westgate
Carfax Tower
Christ Church Cathedral
Merton College
Merton Field
Magdalen
Worcester College
Cricket Ground
LLA

**Peterborough
Plymouth**

**Portsmouth
Salisbury**

**Sheffield
Southampton**

121

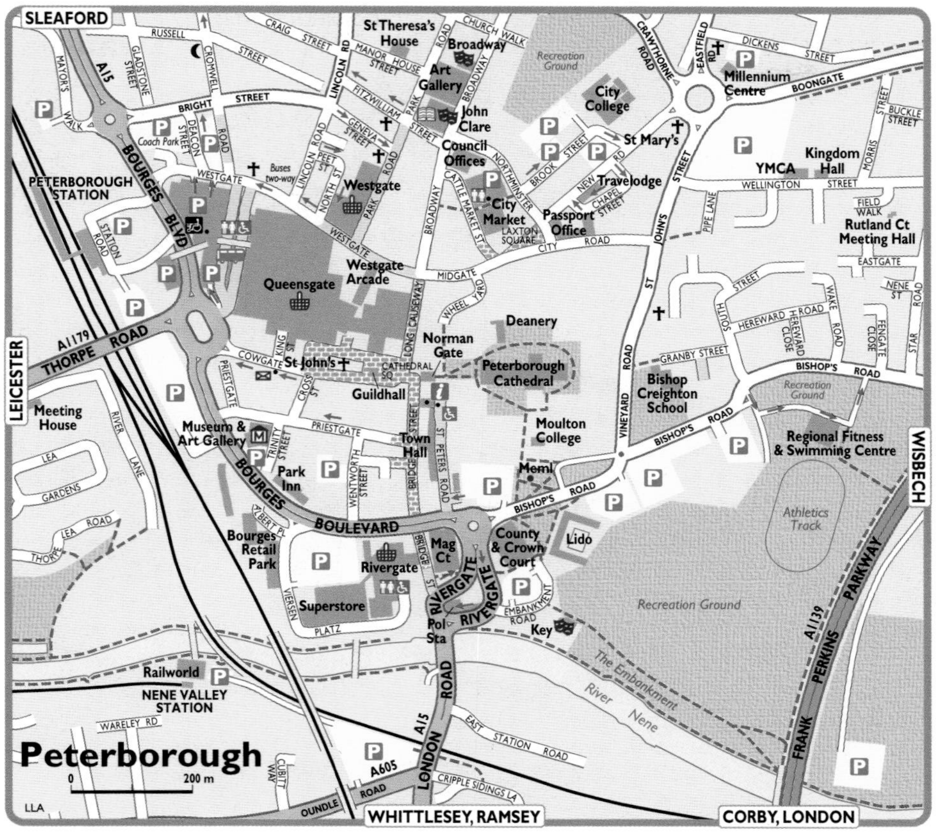

Peterborough

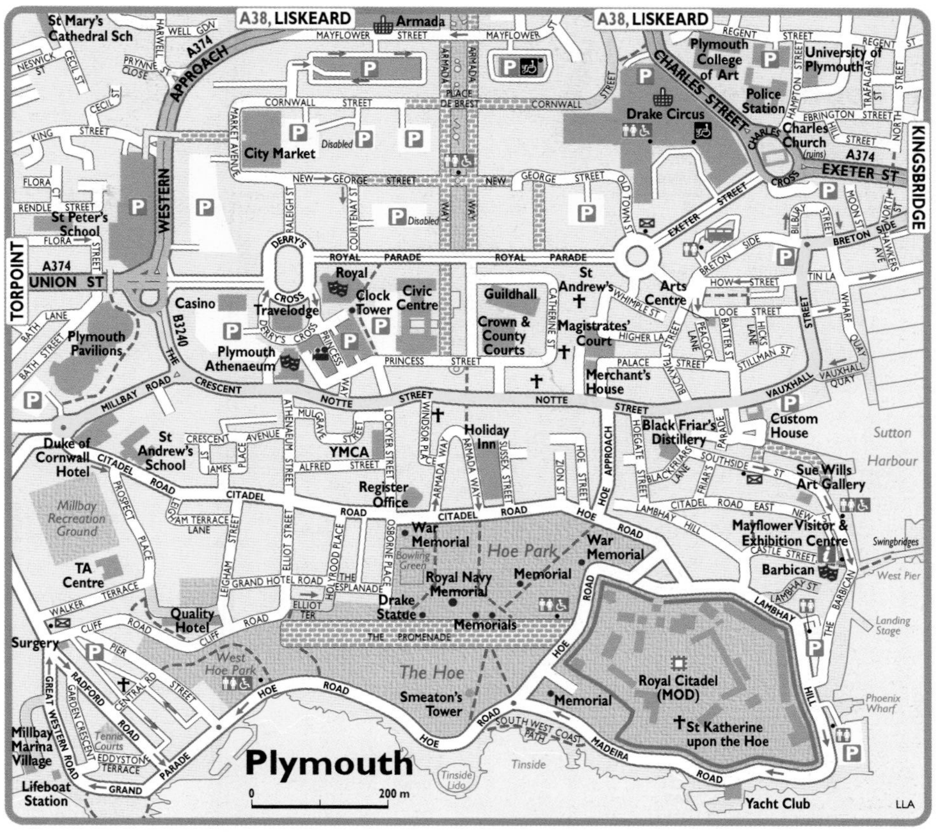

Plymouth

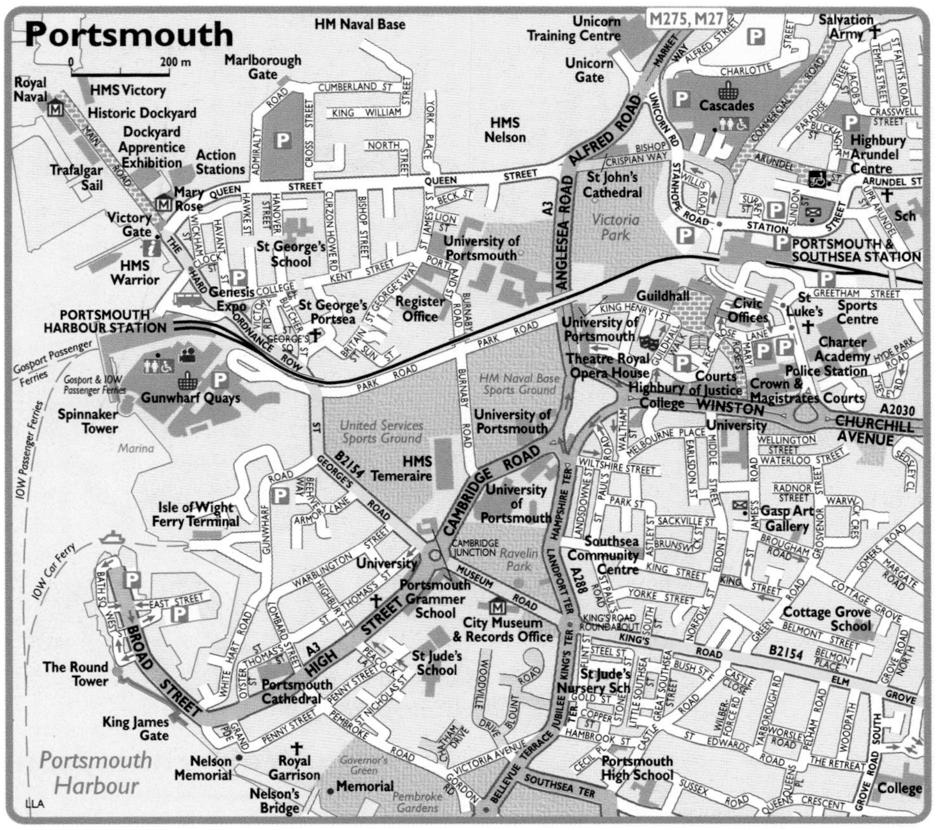

Portsmouth

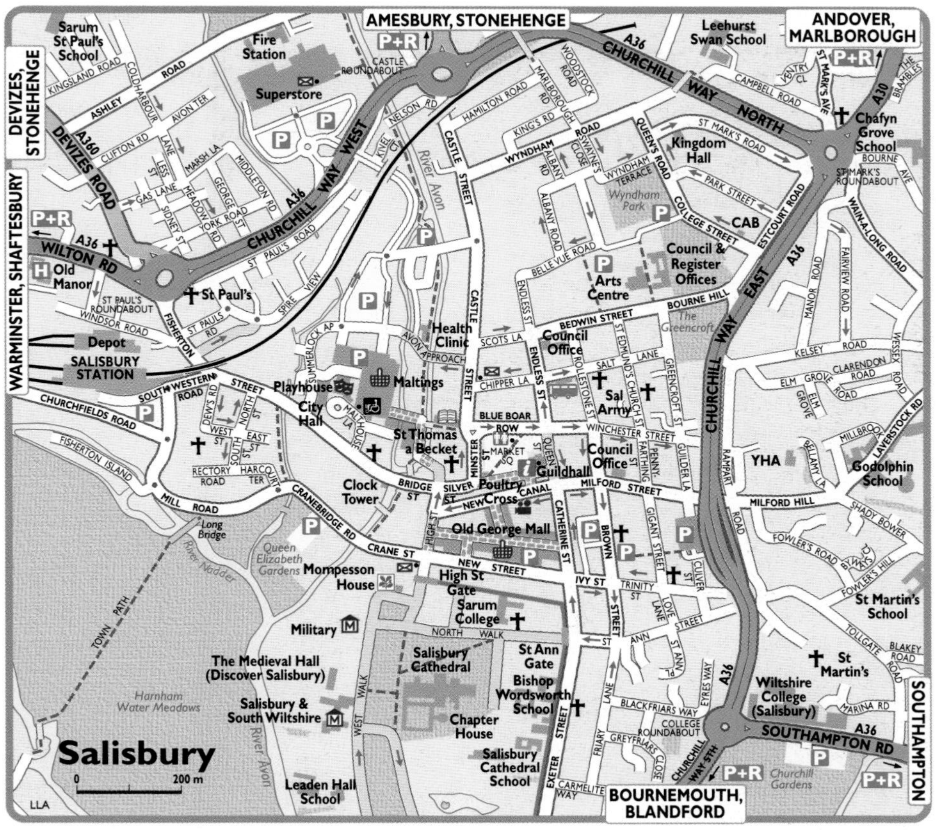

Salisbury

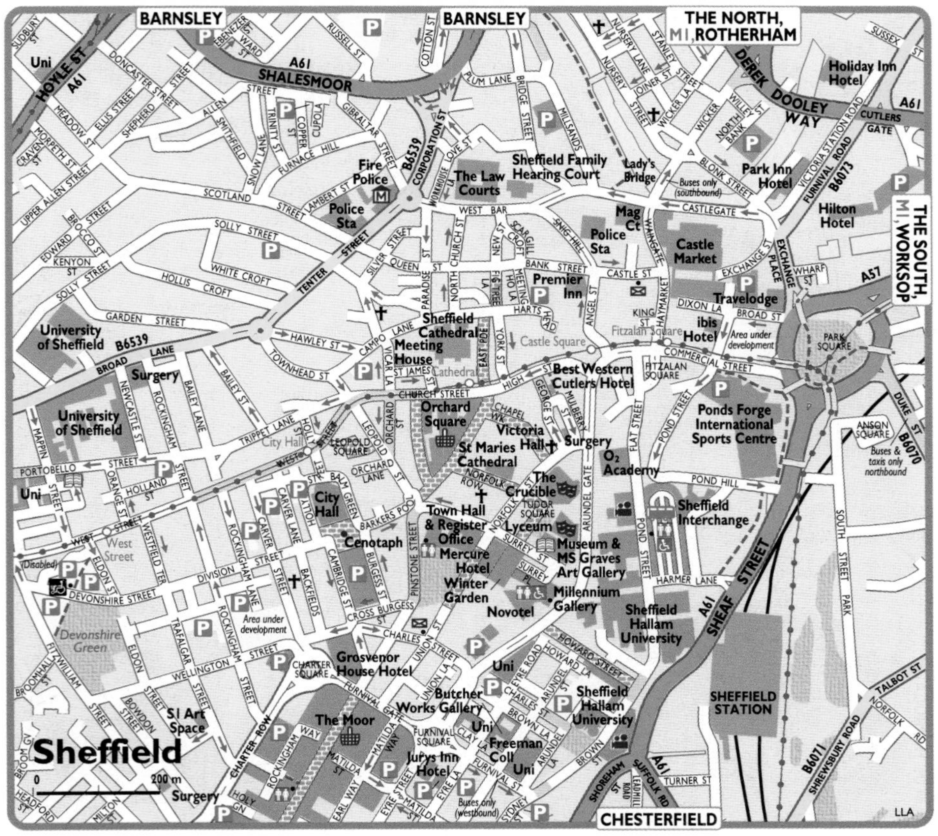

Sheffield

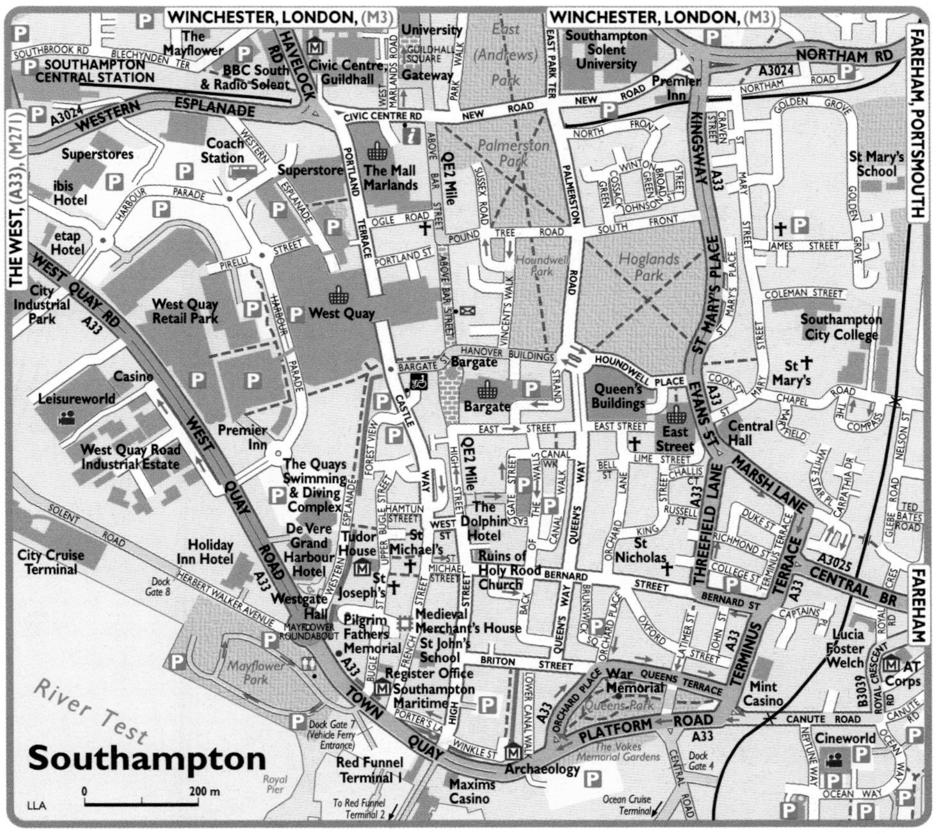

Southampton

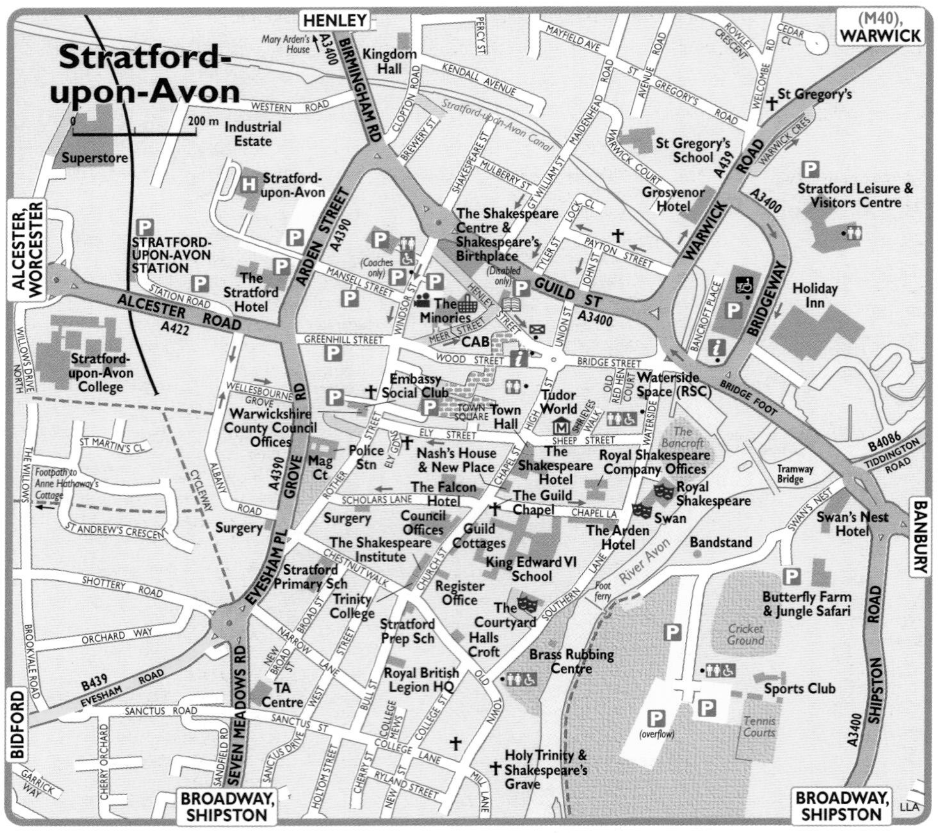
Stratford-upon-Avon
200 m
HENLEY
(M40), WARWICK
ALCESTER, WORCESTER
BANBURY
BIDFORD
BROADWAY, SHIPSTON
BROADWAY, SHIPSTON
Kingdom Hall
Superstore
Industrial Estate
Stratford-upon-Avon Hotel
STRATFORD-UPON-AVON STATION
The Stratford Hotel
The Shakespeare Centre & Shakespeare's Birthplace
St Gregory's
St Gregory's School
Grosvenor Hotel
Stratford Leisure & Visitors Centre
Holiday Inn
The Minories
CAB
Stratford-upon-Avon College
Embassy Social Club
Warwickshire County Council Offices
Town Hall
Tudor World
Waterside Space (RSC)
Police Stn
Nash's House & New Place
The Shakespeare Hotel
Royal Shakespeare Company Offices
The Falcon Hotel
The Guild Chapel
Royal Shakespeare
Swan
Swan's Nest Hotel
Surgery
Council Offices
Guild Cottages
The Arden Hotel
Bandstand
The Shakespeare Institute
King Edward VI School
Stratford Primary Sch
Trinity College
Register Office
The Courtyard
Butterfly Farm & Jungle Safari
Stratford Prep Sch
Halls Croft
Brass Rubbing Centre
Royal British Legion HQ
Sports Club
TA Centre
Holy Trinity & Shakespeare's Grave
River Avon
ALCESTER ROAD
BIRMINGHAM RD
ARDEN STREET
GUILD ST
WARWICK ROAD
BRIDGEWAY
GROVE
EVESHAM PL
SEVEN MEADOWS RD
SHIPSTON ROAD
TIDDINGTON ROAD
A422
A3400
A439
A4390
B439
B4086

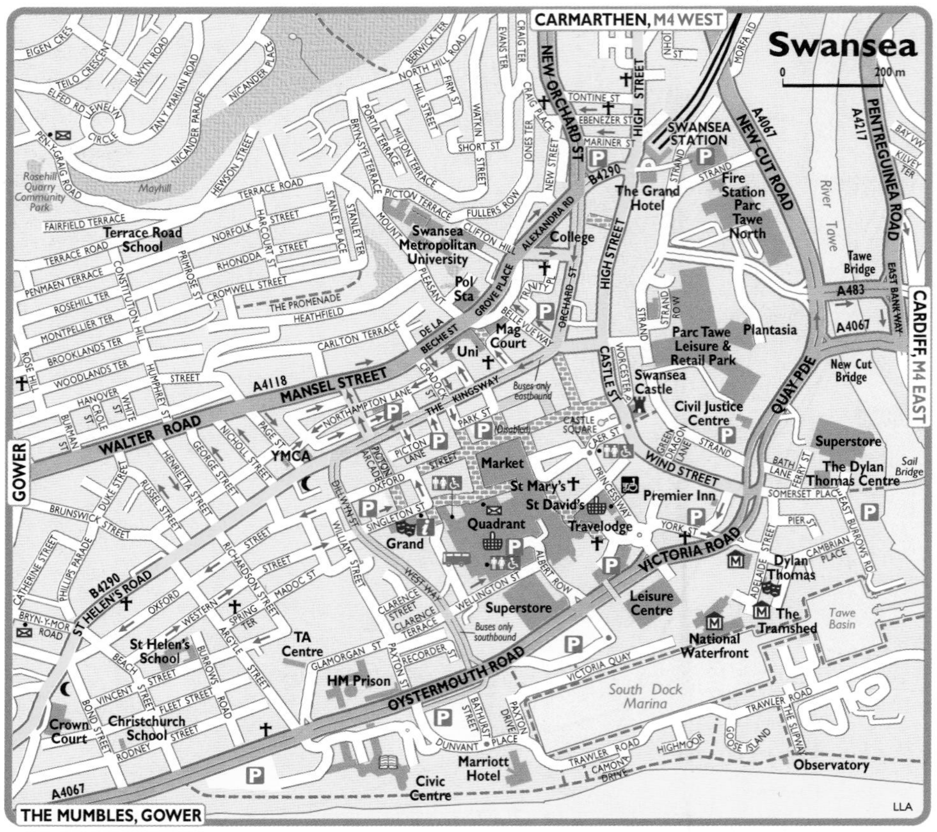
Swansea
200 m
CARMARTHEN, M4 WEST
CARDIFF, M4 EAST
GOWER
THE MUMBLES, GOWER
SWANSEA STATION
Fire Station
Parc Tawe North
The Grand Hotel
Tawe Bridge
Terrace Road School
Swansea Metropolitan University
College
Pol Sta
Mag Court
Uni
Parc Tawe Leisure & Retail Park
Plantasia
New Cut Bridge
Swansea Castle
Civil Justice Centre
YMCA
Market
St Mary's
St David's
Premier Inn
Superstore
The Dylan Thomas Centre
Grand
Quadrant
Travelodge
Dylan Thomas
Superstore
Leisure Centre
National Waterfront
The Tramshed
St Helen's School
TA Centre
HM Prison
Crown Court
Christchurch School
Marriott Hotel
Civic Centre
Observatory
South Dock Marina
WALTER ROAD
MANSEL STREET
OYSTERMOUTH ROAD
VICTORIA ROAD
NEW ORCHARD ST
HIGH STREET
NEW CUT ROAD
QUAY PDE
WIND STREET
A4118
A4067
A483
A4217
B4290

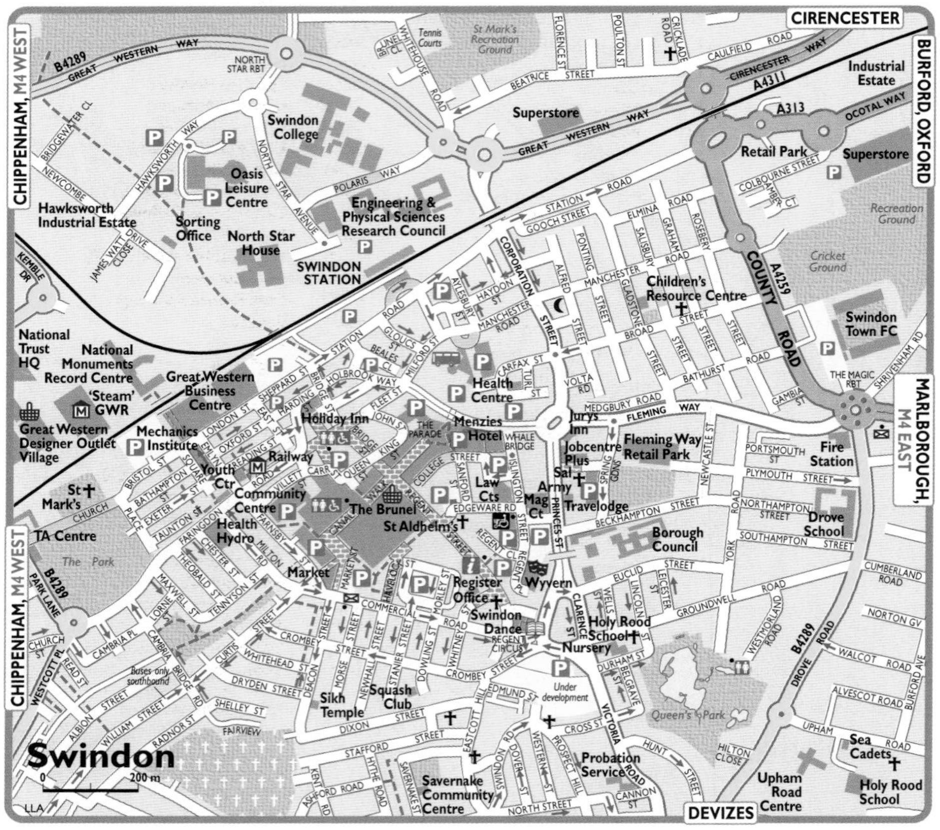
Swindon
200 m
CIRENCESTER
BURFORD, OXFORD
CHIPPENHAM, M4 WEST
MARLBOROUGH, M4 EAST
DEVIZES
Industrial Estate
Superstore
Swindon College
Retail Park
Superstore
Oasis Leisure Centre
Hawksworth Industrial Estate
Sorting Office
North Star House
Engineering & Physical Sciences Research Council
SWINDON STATION
Children's Resource Centre
Swindon Town FC
National Trust HQ
National Monuments Record Centre
Great Western Business Centre
'Steam' GWR
Great Western Designer Outlet Village
Mechanics Institute
Holiday Inn
Health Centre
Menzies Hotel
Jurys Inn
Jobcentre Plus
Fleming Way Retail Park
Fire Station
Youth Ctr
Community Centre
Law Cts
Mag Ct
Sal Army
Travelodge
Drove School
The Brunel
St Aldhelm's
Borough Council
Health Hydro
TA Centre
Market
Register Office
Swindon Dance
Holy Rood School
Nursery
Squash Club
Sikh Temple
Savernake Community Centre
Probation Service
Upham Road Centre
Sea Cadets
Holy Rood School
GREAT WESTERN WAY
COUNTY ROAD
A4311
A4259
A313
B4289

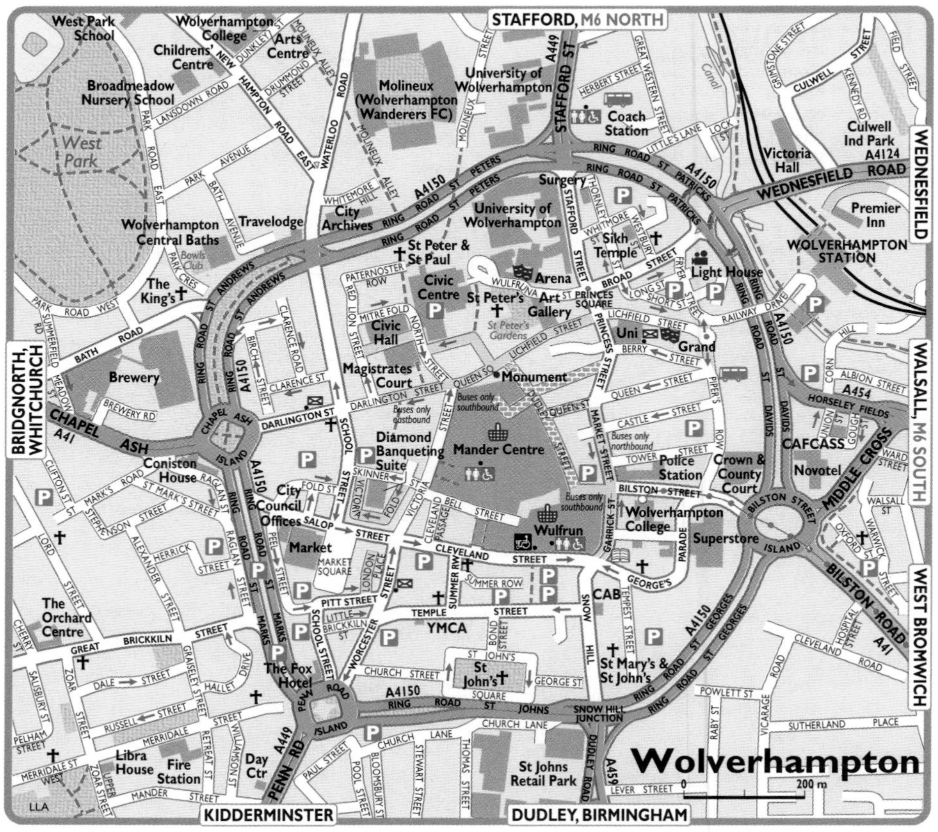
Wolverhampton
200 m
STAFFORD, M6 NORTH
WEDNESFIELD
WALSALL, M6 SOUTH
WEST BROMWICH
BRIDGNORTH, WHITCHURCH
KIDDERMINSTER
DUDLEY, BIRMINGHAM
West Park School
Wolverhampton College
Arts Centre
Children's Centre
Broadmeadow Nursery School
Molineux (Wolverhampton Wanderers FC)
University of Wolverhampton
Coach Station
Culwell Ind Park
Victoria Hall
Premier Inn
WOLVERHAMPTON STATION
Wolverhampton Central Baths
Travelodge
City Archives
Surgery
University of Wolverhampton
St Peter & St Paul
Sikh Temple
Light House
Civic Centre
St Peter's
Arena
Art Gallery
Uni
Grand
Civic Hall
Brewery
Magistrates Court
Monument
Diamond Banqueting Suite
Mander Centre
CAFCASS
Novotel
Police Station
Crown & County Court
Coniston House
City Council Offices
Wolverhampton College
Superstore
Market
Wulfrun
CAB
The Orchard Centre
YMCA
St Mary's & St John's
The Fox Hotel
St John's
Libra House
Fire Station
Day Ctr
St Johns Retail Park
RING ROAD
CHAPEL ASH
WEDNESFIELD ROAD
PENN RD
BILSTON ROAD
MIDDLE CROSS
A4150
A449
A41
A459
A454
A4124

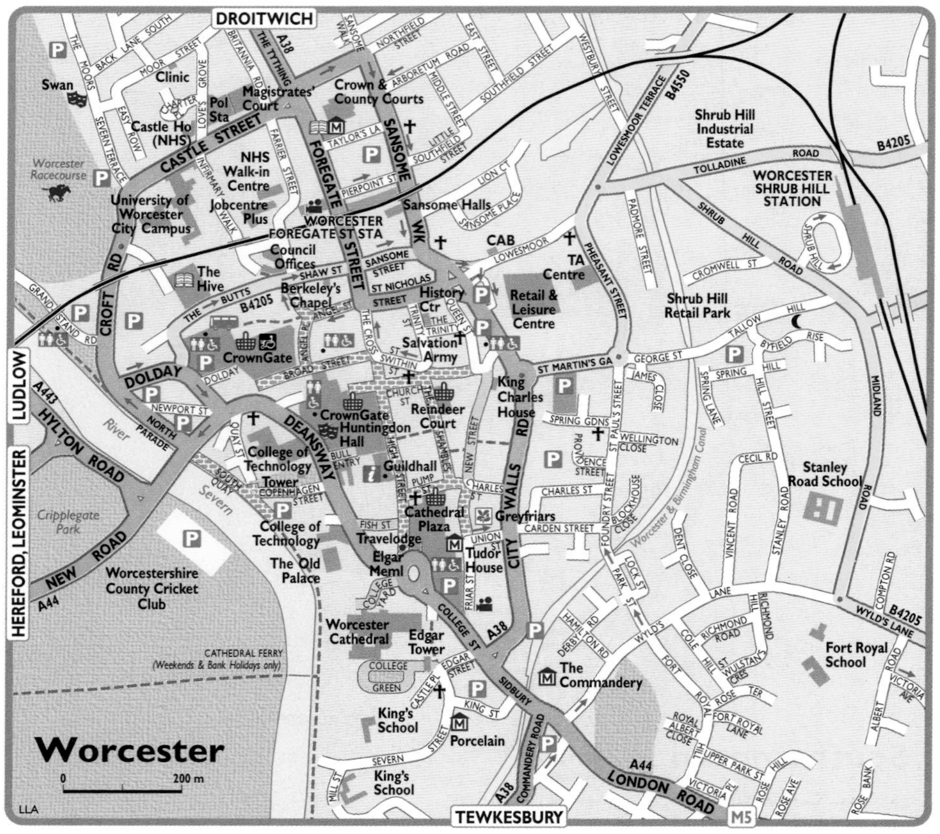
Worcester
200 m
DROITWICH
LUDLOW
HEREFORD, LEOMINSTER
TEWKESBURY
M5
Swan
Clinic
Magistrates' Court
Crown & County Courts
Castle Ho (NHS)
Pol Sta
NHS Walk-in Centre
Shrub Hill Industrial Estate
WORCESTER SHRUB HILL STATION
University of Worcester City Campus
Jobcentre Plus
WORCESTER FOREGATE ST STA
Sansome Halls
CAB
TA Centre
Council Offices
The Hive
Berkeley's Chapel
History Ctr
Retail & Leisure Centre
Shrub Hill Retail Park
CrownGate
Salvation Army
King Charles House
CrownGate Huntingdon Hall
Reindeer Court
College of Technology Tower
Guildhall
Stanley Road School
Cathedral Plaza
College of Technology
Greyfriars
Travelodge
The Old Palace
Elgar Meml
Tudor House
Worcestershire County Cricket Club
Worcester Cathedral
Edgar Tower
The Commandery
Fort Royal School
King's School
Porcelain
King's School
CATHEDRAL FERRY (Weekends & Bank Holidays only)
CASTLE STREET
FOREGATE STREET
SANSOME WALK
CROFT RD
DOLDAY
DEANSWAY
CITY WALLS RD
LONDON ROAD
HYLTON ROAD
NEW ROAD
A38
A44
A449
B4205
B4550

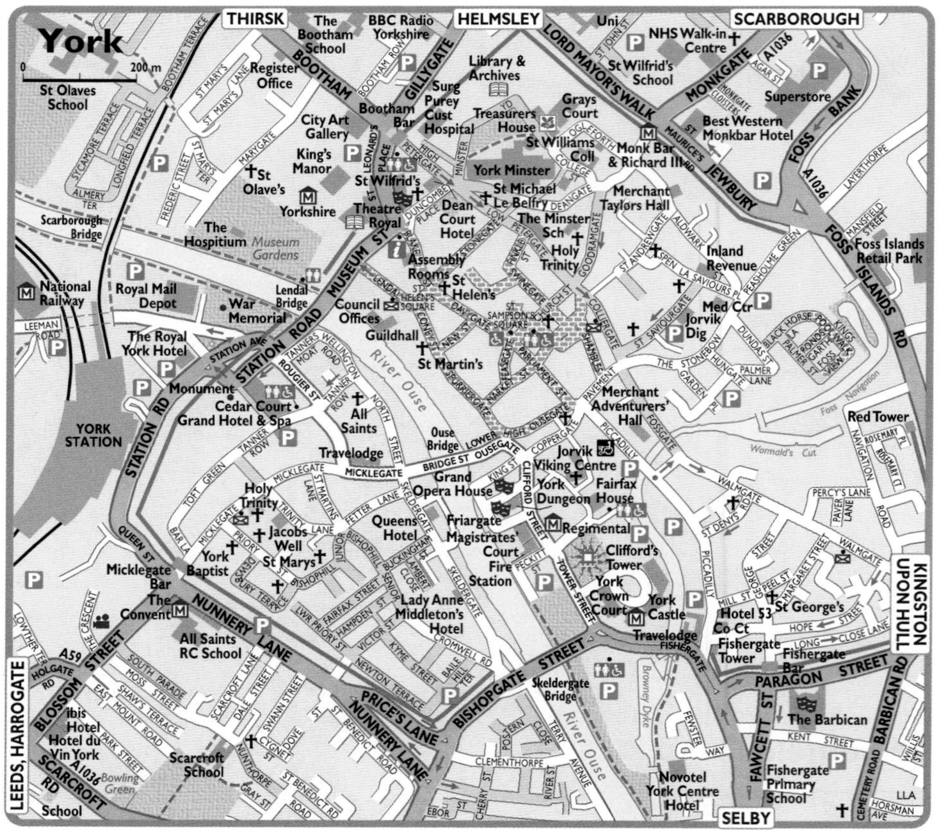
York
200 m
THIRSK
HELMSLEY
SCARBOROUGH
KINGSTON UPON HULL
LEEDS, HARROGATE
SELBY
The Bootham School
BBC Radio Yorkshire
Uni
NHS Walk-in Centre
St Wilfrid's School
St Olaves School
Register Office
Library & Archives
Superstore
Best Western Monkbar Hotel
City Art Gallery
Bootham Bar
Surg Purey Cust Hospital
Treasurers House
Grays Court
St Williams Coll
Monk Bar & Richard III
King's Manor
St Olave's
York Minster
St Michael Le Belfry
Merchant Taylors Hall
Yorkshire
Theatre Royal
Dean Court Hotel
The Minster Sch
Holy Trinity
Foss Islands Retail Park
The Hospitium
Museum Gardens
Inland Revenue
National Railway
Royal Mail Depot
Assembly Rooms
St Helen's
War Memorial
Council Offices
Guildhall
Med Ctr
Jorvik Dig
The Royal York Hotel
St Martin's
YORK STATION
Monument
Cedar Court Grand Hotel & Spa
All Saints
Merchant Adventurers' Hall
Red Tower
Travelodge
Grand Opera House
Jorvik Viking Centre
York Dungeon
Fairfax House
Holy Trinity
Jacobs Well
St Marys
Queens Hotel
Friargate
Magistrates Court
Fire Station
Regimental
Clifford's Tower
York Baptist
Lady Anne Middleton's Hotel
York Crown Court
York Castle
Hotel 53
St George's
Micklegate Bar
The Convent
Travelodge
Fishergate Tower
Fishergate Bar
All Saints RC School
Skeldergate Bridge
The Barbican
Ibis Hotel
Hotel du Vin York
Scarcroft School
Novotel York Centre Hotel
Fishergate Primary School
BOOTHAM
GILLYGATE
LORD MAYOR'S WALK
MONKGATE
JEWBURY
FOSS ISLANDS RD
STATION RD
STATION ROAD
MUSEUM STREET
NUNNERY LANE
PRICE'S LANE
BISHOPGATE STREET
PARAGON STREET
BARBICAN RD
BLOSSOM STREET
FAWCETT ST
A59
A1036
River Ouse

Index to place names

This index lists places appearing in the main-map section of the atlas in alphabetical order. The reference before each name gives the atlas page number and grid reference of the square in which the place appears. The map shows counties, unitary authorities and administrative areas, together with a list of the abbreviated name forms used in the index. The top 100 places of tourist interest are indexed in **red** (or **green** if a World Heritage site), motorway service areas in **blue** and airports in blue *italic*.

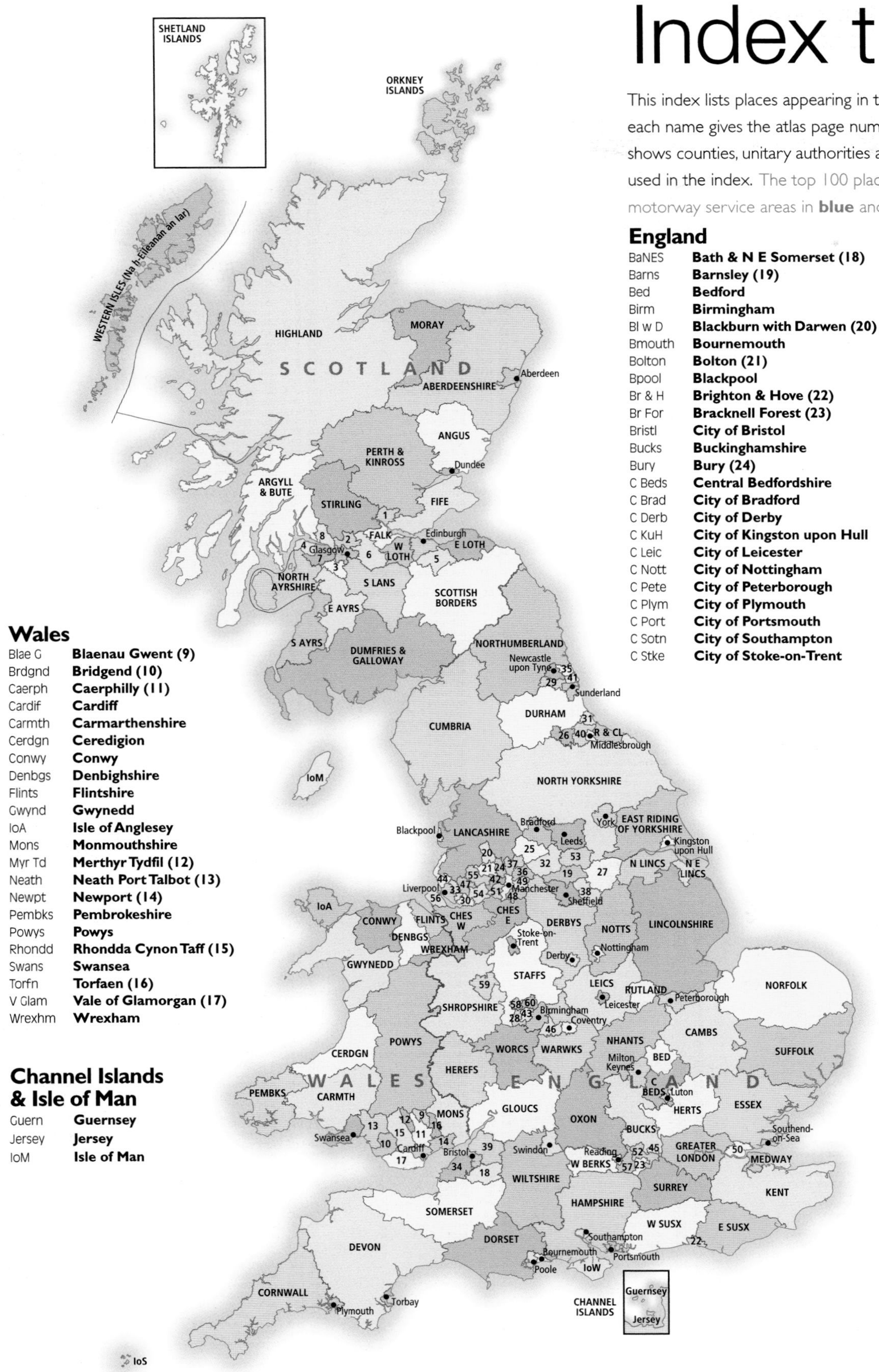

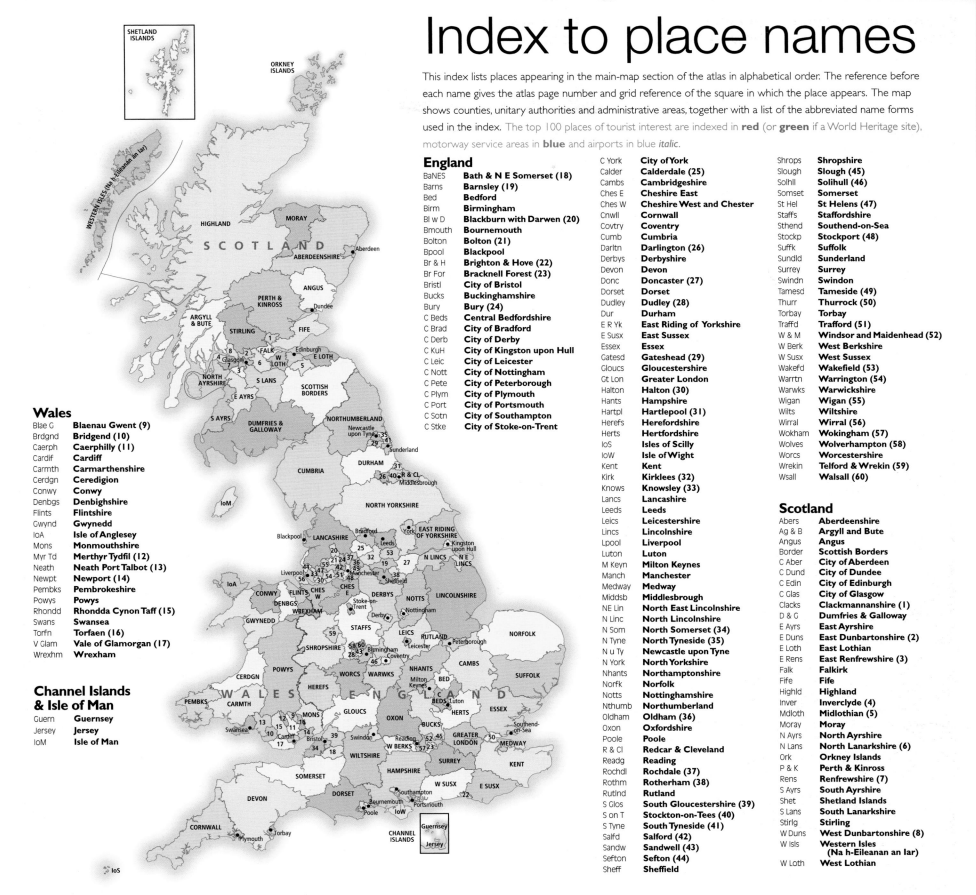

Wales

Blae G	**Blaenau Gwent (9)**
Brdgnd	**Bridgend (10)**
Caerph	**Caerphilly (11)**
Cardif	**Cardiff**
Carmth	**Carmarthenshire**
Cerdgn	**Ceredigion**
Conwy	**Conwy**
Denbgs	**Denbighshire**
Flints	**Flintshire**
Gwynd	**Gwynedd**
IoA	**Isle of Anglesey**
Mons	**Monmouthshire**
Myr Td	**Merthyr Tydfil (12)**
Neath	**Neath Port Talbot (13)**
Newpt	**Newport (14)**
Pembks	**Pembrokeshire**
Powys	**Powys**
Rhondd	**Rhondda Cynon Taff (15)**
Swans	**Swansea**
Torfn	**Torfaen (16)**
V Glam	**Vale of Glamorgan (17)**
Wrexhm	**Wrexham**

Channel Islands & Isle of Man

Guern	**Guernsey**
Jersey	**Jersey**
IoM	**Isle of Man**

England

BaNES	**Bath & N E Somerset (18)**
Barns	**Barnsley (19)**
Bed	**Bedford**
Birm	**Birmingham**
Bl w D	**Blackburn with Darwen (20)**
Bmouth	**Bournemouth**
Bolton	**Bolton (21)**
Bpool	**Blackpool**
Br & H	**Brighton & Hove (22)**
Br For	**Bracknell Forest (23)**
Bristl	**City of Bristol**
Bucks	**Buckinghamshire**
Bury	**Bury (24)**
C Beds	**Central Bedfordshire**
C Brad	**City of Bradford**
C Derb	**City of Derby**
C KuH	**City of Kingston upon Hull**
C Leic	**City of Leicester**
C Nott	**City of Nottingham**
C Pete	**City of Peterborough**
C Plym	**City of Plymouth**
C Port	**City of Portsmouth**
C Sotn	**City of Southampton**
C Stke	**City of Stoke-on-Trent**
C York	**City of York**
Calder	**Calderdale (25)**
Cambs	**Cambridgeshire**
Ches E	**Cheshire East**
Ches W	**Cheshire West and Chester**
Cnwll	**Cornwall**
Covtry	**Coventry**
Cumb	**Cumbria**
Darltn	**Darlington (26)**
Derbys	**Derbyshire**
Devon	**Devon**
Donc	**Doncaster (27)**
Dorset	**Dorset**
Dudley	**Dudley (28)**
Dur	**Durham**
E R Yk	**East Riding of Yorkshire**
E Susx	**East Sussex**
Essex	**Essex**
Gatesd	**Gateshead (29)**
Gloucs	**Gloucestershire**
Gt Lon	**Greater London**
Halton	**Halton (30)**
Hants	**Hampshire**
Hartpl	**Hartlepool (31)**
Herefs	**Herefordshire**
Herts	**Hertfordshire**
IoS	**Isles of Scilly**
IoW	**Isle of Wight**
Kent	**Kent**
Kirk	**Kirklees (32)**
Knows	**Knowsley (33)**
Lancs	**Lancashire**
Leeds	**Leeds**
Leics	**Leicestershire**
Lincs	**Lincolnshire**
Lpool	**Liverpool**
Luton	**Luton**
M Keyn	**Milton Keynes**
Manch	**Manchester**
Medway	**Medway**
Middsb	**Middlesbrough**
NE Lin	**North East Lincolnshire**
N Linc	**North Lincolnshire**
N Som	**North Somerset (34)**
N Tyne	**North Tyneside (35)**
N u Ty	**Newcastle upon Tyne**
N York	**North Yorkshire**
Nhants	**Northamptonshire**
Norfk	**Norfolk**
Notts	**Nottinghamshire**
Nthumb	**Northumberland**
Oldham	**Oldham (36)**
Oxon	**Oxfordshire**
Poole	**Poole**
R & Cl	**Redcar & Cleveland**
Readg	**Reading**
Rochdl	**Rochdale (37)**
Rothm	**Rotherham (38)**
Rutlnd	**Rutland**
S Glos	**South Gloucestershire (39)**
S on T	**Stockton-on-Tees (40)**
S Tyne	**South Tyneside (41)**
Salfd	**Salford (42)**
Sandw	**Sandwell (43)**
Sefton	**Sefton (44)**
Sheff	**Sheffield**
Shrops	**Shropshire**
Slough	**Slough (45)**
Solhll	**Solihull (46)**
Somset	**Somerset**
St Hel	**St Helens (47)**
Staffs	**Staffordshire**
Sthend	**Southend-on-Sea**
Stockp	**Stockport (48)**
Suffk	**Suffolk**
Sundld	**Sunderland**
Surrey	**Surrey**
Swindn	**Swindon**
Tamesd	**Tameside (49)**
Thurr	**Thurrock (50)**
Torbay	**Torbay**
Traffd	**Trafford (51)**
W & M	**Windsor and Maidenhead (52)**
W Berk	**West Berkshire**
W Susx	**West Sussex**
Wakefd	**Wakefield (53)**
Warrtn	**Warrington (54)**
Warwks	**Warwickshire**
Wigan	**Wigan (55)**
Wilts	**Wiltshire**
Wirral	**Wirral (56)**
Wokham	**Wokingham (57)**
Wolves	**Wolverhampton (58)**
Worcs	**Worcestershire**
Wrekin	**Telford & Wrekin (59)**
Wsall	**Walsall (60)**

Scotland

Abers	**Aberdeenshire**
Ag & B	**Argyll and Bute**
Angus	**Angus**
Border	**Scottish Borders**
C Aber	**City of Aberdeen**
C Dund	**City of Dundee**
C Edin	**City of Edinburgh**
C Glas	**City of Glasgow**
Clacks	**Clackmannanshire (1)**
D & G	**Dumfries & Galloway**
E Ayrs	**East Ayrshire**
E Duns	**East Dunbartonshire (2)**
E Loth	**East Lothian**
E Rens	**East Renfrewshire (3)**
Falk	**Falkirk**
Fife	**Fife**
Highld	**Highland**
Inver	**Inverclyde (4)**
Mdloth	**Midlothian (5)**
Moray	**Moray**
N Ayrs	**North Ayrshire**
N Lans	**North Lanarkshire (6)**
Ork	**Orkney Islands**
P & K	**Perth & Kinross**
Rens	**Renfrewshire (7)**
S Ayrs	**South Ayrshire**
Shet	**Shetland Islands**
S Lans	**South Lanarkshire**
Stirlg	**Stirling**
W Duns	**West Dunbartonshire (8)**
W Isls	**Western Isles (Na h-Eileanan an Iar)**
W Loth	**West Lothian**

Using the National Grid

With an Ordnance Survey National Grid reference you can pinpoint anywhere in the country in this atlas. The blue grid lines which divide the main-map pages into 5km squares for ease of indexing also match the National Grid. A National Grid reference gives two letters and some figures. An example is how to find the summit of mount Snowdon using its 4-figure grid reference of **SH6154**.

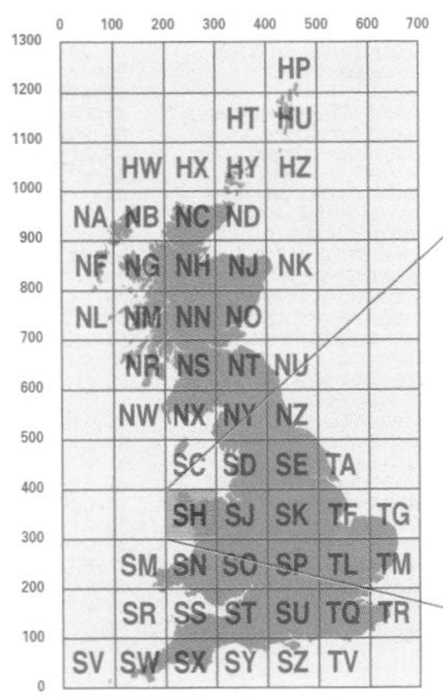

The letters **SH** indicate the 100km square of the National Grid in which Snowdon is located.

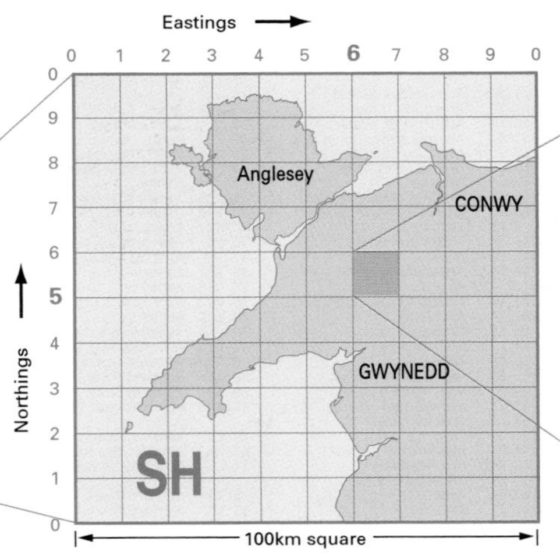

In a 4-figure grid reference the first two figures (eastings) are read along the map from left to right, the second two (northings) up the map. The figures **6** and **5**, the first and third figures of the Snowdon reference, indicate the 10km square within the **SH** square, lying above (north) and right (east) of the intersection of the vertical (easting) line **6** and horizontal (northing) line **5**.

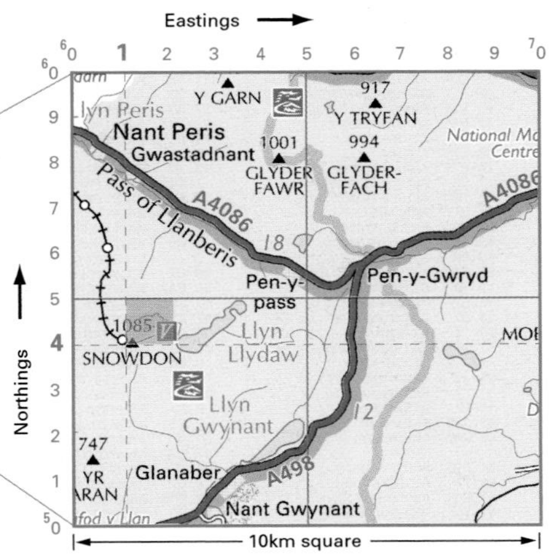

The summit is finally pinpointed by figures **1** and **4** which locate a 1km square within the 10km square. At road atlas scales these grid lines are normally estimated by eye.

124 Abbas Combe - Bampton

A

17 T12 Abbas Combe Somset
35 S7 Abberley Worcs
35 R7 Abberley Common Worcs
23 P4 Abberton Essex
36 C10 Abberton Worcs
77 N3 Abberwick Nthumb
22 E5 Abbess Roding Essex
6 F2 Abbey Devon
34 C6 Abbey-Cwm-Hir Powys
57 M10 Abbeydale Sheff
27 R1 Abbey Dore Herefs
46 C2 Abbey Green Staffs
16 J13 Abbey Hill Somset
84 K6 Abbey St Bathans Border
62 B9 Abbeystead Lancs
66 J2 Abbey Town Cumb
55 P2 Abbey Village Lancs
21 S7 Abbey Wood Gt Lon
76 C3 Abbotrule Border
14 J10 Abbots Bickington Devon
46 E9 Abbots Bromley Staffs
7 Q7 Abbotsbury Dorset
56 F8 Abbot's Chair Derbys
90 H9 Abbots Deuglie P & K
14 K7 Abbotsham Devon
5 V7 Abbotskerswell Devon
31 N12 Abbots Langley Herts
5 U11 Abbotsleigh Devon
27 U13 Abbots Leigh N Som
38 K9 Abbotsley Cambs
36 D9 Abbots Morton Worcs
38 K5 Abbots Ripton Cambs
36 E10 Abbot's Salford Warwks
9 R2 Abbotstone Hants
9 M4 Abbotswood Hants
9 P2 Abbots Worthy Hants
19 M12 Abbotts Ann Hants
8 D8 Abbott Street Dorset
34 J5 Abcott Shrops
35 N3 Abdon Shrops
28 C4 Abenhall Gloucs
32 J8 Aberaeron Cerdgn
26 J7 Aberaman Rhondd
43 R11 Aberangell Gwynd
32 F12 Aber-arad Carmth
102 H10 Aberarder Highld
90 J8 Aberargie P & K
32 J8 Aberarth Cerdgn
26 C10 Aberavon Neath
32 G12 Aber-banc Cerdgn
27 M7 Aberbargoed Caerph
27 N7 Aberbeeg Blae G
26 K7 Abercanaid Myr Td
27 N9 Abercarn Caerph
24 E4 Abercastle Pembks
43 R13 Abercegir Powys
96 C3 Aberchalder Lodge Highld
104 J5 Aberchirder Abers
27 L3 Aber Clydach Powys
26 E5 Abercraf Powys
26 E8 Abercregan Neath
26 J8 Abercwmboi Rhondd
32 D12 Abercych Pembks
26 K9 Abercynon Rhondd
90 G7 Aberdalgie P & K
26 J7 Aberdare Rhondd
42 C8 Aberdaron Gwynd
99 S2 Aberdeen C Aber
105 P13 Aberdeen Airport C Aber
99 R2 Aberdeen Crematorium C Aber
42 H3 Aberdesach Gwynd
83 N1 Aberdour Fife
26 D8 Aberdulais Neath
33 M1 Aberdyfi Gwynd
34 C11 Aberedw Powys
24 C4 Abereiddy Pembks
42 G6 Abererch Gwynd
26 K7 Aberfan Myr Td
90 C2 Aberfeldy P & K
52 E9 Aberffraw IoA
33 N5 Aberffrwd Cerdgn
63 U12 Aberford Leeds
89 M5 Aberfoyle Stirlg
26 G11 Abergarw Brdgnd
26 E7 Abergarwed Neath
27 P5 Abergavenny Mons
53 R7 Abergele Conwy
32 K12 Aber-giar Carmth
25 U4 Abergorlech Carmth
33 S10 Abergwesyn Powys
25 R6 Abergwili Carmth
43 Q13 Abergwydol Powys
26 F8 Abergwynfi Neath
53 L8 Abergwyngregyn Gwynd
43 N12 Abergynolwyn Gwynd
34 C2 Aberhafesp Powys
33 R1 Aberhosan Powys
26 F11 Aberkenfig Brdgnd
84 D3 Aberlady E Loth
98 J12 Aberlemno Angus
43 Q12 Aberllefenni Gwynd
34 E13 Aberllynfi Powys
104 B7 Aberlour Moray
33 N6 Aber-Magwr Cerdgn
33 L9 Aber-meurig Cerdgn
44 H2 Abermorddu Flints
34 E2 Abermule Powys
25 P6 Abernant Carmth
26 J7 Aber-nant Rhondd
90 J8 Abernethy P & K
91 L5 Abernyte P & K
32 E10 Aberporth Cerdgn
42 F8 Abersoch Gwynd
27 P7 Abersychan Torfn
26 J13 Aberthin V Glam
27 N7 Abertillery Blae G
27 L10 Abertridwr Caerph
44 B10 Abertridwr Powys
27 L6 Abertysswg Caerph
90 E8 Aberuthven P & K
26 H2 Aberyscir Powys
33 L4 Aberystwyth Cerdgn
33 M4 Aberystwyth Crematorium Cerdgn
29 U8 Abingdon-on-Thames Oxon
20 K13 Abinger Common Surrey
20 J13 Abinger Hammer Surrey
37 U8 Abington Nhants
82 H14 Abington S Lans
31 T4 Abington Pigotts Cambs
82 H14 Abington Services S Lans
10 J7 Abingworth W Susx
47 T9 Ab Kettleby Leics
36 D10 Ab Lench Worcs
29 M6 Ablington Gloucs
18 J11 Ablington Wilts
56 J10 Abney Derbys
46 D3 Above Church Staffs
98 J4 Aboyne Abers
55 P6 Abram Wigan
102 G8 Abriachan Highld
21 S3 Abridge Essex
89 S10 Abronhill N Lans
28 D13 Abson S Glos
37 R11 Abthorpe Nhants
59 R11 Aby Lincs
64 D10 Acaster Malbis C York
64 D11 Acaster Selby N York
62 F14 Accrington Lancs
62 F14 Accrington Crematorium Lancs
92 F8 Acha Ag & B
87 P10 Achahoish Ag & B
90 H2 Achalader P & K
94 C12 Achaleven Ag & B
106 i6 Acha Mor W Isls
108 D12 Achanalt Highld
109 L10 Achandunie Highld
108 K4 Achany Highld
93 R5 Acharacle Highld
93 S8 Acharn Highld
95 V10 Acharn P & K
112 E8 Achavanich Highld
107 T4 Achduart Highld
110 F9 Achfary Highld
100 b9 A'Chill Highld
107 T3 Achiltibuie Highld
111 Q4 Achina Highld
79 P12 Achinhoan Ag & B
101 N3 Achintee Highld
101 L4 Achintraid Highld
110 B12 Achmelvich Highld
101 M5 Achmore Highld
106 i6 Achmore W Isls
110 A10 Achnacarnin Highld
101 T14 Achnacarry Highld
100 e9 Achnacloich Highld
102 D12 Achnaconeran Highld
94 B10 Achnacroish Ag & B
93 M8 Achnadrish House Ag & B
90 C4 Achnafauld P & K
109 M10 Achnagarron Highld
93 M5 Achnaha Highld
107 T2 Achnahaird Highld
108 K2 Achnairn Highld
94 B6 Achnalea Highld
87 P8 Achnamara Ag & B
108 B13 Achnasheen Highld
101 Q2 Achnashellach Lodge Highld
104 B9 Achnastank Moray
93 L5 Achosnich Highld
93 S9 Achranich Highld
112 B3 Achreamie Highld
94 G5 Achriabhach Highld
110 F6 Achriesgill Highld
111 P4 Achtoty Highld
38 F4 Achurch Nhants
109 N6 Achvaich Highld
112 A4 Achvarasdal Highld
112 J6 Ackergill Highld
70 G9 Acklam Middsb
64 H7 Acklam N York
45 S14 Ackleton Shrops
77 Q5 Acklington Nthumb
57 P2 Ackton Wakefd
57 P3 Ackworth Moor Top Wakefd
51 R11 Acle Norfk
36 F4 Acock's Green Birm
13 R2 Acol Kent
64 D9 Acomb C York
76 J12 Acomb Nthumb
6 G2 Acombe Somset
35 M14 Aconbury Herefs
55 S2 Acre Lancs
44 G5 Acrefair Wrexhm
45 P3 Acton Ches E
8 D13 Acton Dorset
21 M6 Acton Gt Lon
34 H4 Acton Shrops
45 T5 Acton Staffs
40 E11 Acton Suffk
35 T7 Acton Worcs
35 Q10 Acton Beauchamp Herefs
55 N11 Acton Bridge Ches W
45 M13 Acton Burnell Shrops
35 Q10 Acton Green Herefs
44 H3 Acton Park Wrexhm
45 M13 Acton Pigott Shrops
35 P1 Acton Round Shrops
35 L3 Acton Scott Shrops
46 B10 Acton Trussell Staffs
18 B4 Acton Turville S Glos
45 S8 Adbaston Staffs
17 Q12 Adber Dorset
47 Q6 Adbolton Notts
37 N13 Adderbury Oxon
45 Q6 Adderley Shrops
85 S12 Adderstone Nthumb
82 J6 Addiewell W Loth
63 M10 Addingham C Brad
30 F7 Addington Bucks
21 Q10 Addington Gt Lon
12 C4 Addington Kent
21 P9 Addiscombe Gt Lon
20 J10 Addlestone Surrey
20 J9 Addlestonemoor Surrey
59 T13 Addlethorpe Lincs
45 Q10 Adeney Wrekin
31 N11 Adeyfield Herts
44 C13 Adfa Powys
34 K6 Adforton Herefs
13 P5 Adisham Kent
29 P2 Adlestrop Gloucs
58 D2 Adlingfleet E R Yk
56 D10 Adlington Ches E
55 P4 Adlington Lancs
46 D9 Admaston Staffs
45 P11 Admaston Wrekin
36 H11 Admington Warwks
32 F12 Adpar Cerdgn
16 J11 Adsborough Somset
16 G9 Adscombe Somset
30 F7 Adstock Bucks
37 Q10 Adstone Nhants
56 C9 Adswood Stockp
10 H6 Adversane W Susx
103 T9 Advie Highld
63 Q14 Adwalton Leeds
30 E13 Adwell Oxon
57 R5 Adwick Le Street Donc
57 Q6 Adwick upon Dearne Donc
74 J8 Ae D & G
74 K8 Ae Bridgend D & G
26 F8 Afan Forest Park Neath
55 S4 Affetside Bury
104 H7 Affleck Abers
7 V6 Affpuddle Dorset
101 T7 Affric Lodge Highld
54 D12 Afon-wen Flints
5 U8 Afton Devon
9 L11 Afton IoW
55 T6 Agecroft Crematorium Salfd
63 M2 Agglethorpe N York
54 J9 Aigburth Lpool
65 N10 Aike E R Yk
67 Q3 Aiketgate Cumb
66 K3 Aikhead Cumb
67 L2 Aikton Cumb
59 R11 Ailby Lincs
34 H11 Ailey Herefs
48 H14 Ailsworth C Pete
63 S3 Ainderby Quernhow N York
63 S1 Ainderby Steeple N York
23 R3 Aingers Green Essex
54 H4 Ainsdale Sefton
54 G4 Ainsdale-on-Sea Sefton
67 R3 Ainstable Cumb
55 S4 Ainsworth Bury
71 M11 Ainthorpe N York
54 J7 Aintree Sefton
83 M6 Ainville W Loth
87 P5 Aird Ag & B
72 D7 Aird D & G
106 k5 Aird W Isls
106 g7 Aird a Mhulaidh W Isls
106 g8 Aird Asaig W Isls
100 g5 Aird Dhubh Highld
94 D13 Airdeny Ag & B
93 N13 Aird of Kinloch Ag & B
100 e9 Aird of Sleat Highld
82 E5 Airdrie N Lans
82 E5 Airdriehill N Lans
73 R5 Airds of Kells D & G
106 f5 Aird Uig W Isls
106 h7 Airidh a bhruaich W Isls
73 T8 Airieland D & G
98 E13 Airlie Angus
58 B2 Airmyn E R Yk
90 G4 Airntully P & K
100 g9 Airor Highld
82 H1 Airth Falk
62 J8 Airton N York
48 F6 Aisby Lincs
58 E8 Aisby Lincs
68 G13 Aisgill Cumb
5 R8 Aish Devon
5 U9 Aish Devon
16 G9 Aisholt Somset
63 R2 Aiskew N York
64 H2 Aislaby N York
71 Q11 Aislaby N York
70 F10 Aislaby S on T
58 F10 Aisthorpe Lincs
106 t8 Aith Shet
85 P13 Akeld Nthumb
30 F5 Akeley Bucks
40 K11 Akenham Suffk
5 L6 Albaston Cnwll
44 J11 Alberbury Shrops
11 M7 Albourne W Susx
11 M7 Albourne Green W Susx
45 L10 Albrighton Shrops
45 T13 Albrighton Shrops
41 N3 Alburgh Norfk
22 B3 Albury Herts
30 E11 Albury Oxon
20 H13 Albury Surrey
22 B3 Albury End Herts
20 J13 Albury Heath Surrey
51 L7 Alby Hill Norfk
102 G4 Alcaig Highld
35 L3 Alcaston Shrops
36 E9 Alcester Warwks
36 E4 Alcester Lane End Birm
11 S9 Alciston E Susx
16 C7 Alcombe Somset
18 B7 Alcombe Wilts
38 J5 Alconbury Cambs
38 J5 Alconbury Weston Cambs
63 U6 Aldborough N York
51 L7 Aldborough Norfk
19 L5 Aldbourne Wilts
65 S12 Aldbrough E R Yk
69 R10 Aldbrough St John N York
31 L10 Aldbury Herts
61 T7 Aldcliffe Lancs
97 P11 Aldclune P & K
41 S9 Aldeburgh Suffk
41 R2 Aldeby Norfk
20 K3 Aldenham Herts
8 H3 Alderbury Wilts
47 M4 Aldercar Derbys
50 K10 Alderford Norfk
8 G6 Alderholt Dorset
28 E9 Alderley Gloucs
55 T11 Alderley Edge Ches E
37 L4 Aldermans Green Covtry
19 S7 Aldermaston W Berk
36 H11 Alderminster Warwks
46 H8 Alder Moor Staffs
45 L2 Aldersey Green Ches W
20 E12 Aldershot Hants
36 D14 Alderton Gloucs
37 T11 Alderton Nhants
45 L9 Alderton Shrops
41 P12 Alderton Suffk
28 F11 Alderton Wilts
46 K3 Alderwasley Derbys
63 R6 Aldfield N York
44 K2 Aldford Ches W
48 E13 Aldgate Rutlnd
23 M2 Aldham Essex
40 J11 Aldham Suffk
10 E9 Aldingbourne W Susx
61 P5 Aldingham Cumb
13 L8 Aldington Kent
36 E12 Aldington Worcs
13 L8 Aldington Corner Kent
104 D10 Aldivalloch Moray
88 J7 Aldochlay Ag & B
34 K5 Aldon Shrops
66 H3 Aldoth Cumb
39 P6 Aldreth Cambs
46 E13 Aldridge Wsall
41 R8 Aldringham Suffk
64 J7 Aldro N York
29 N6 Aldsworth Gloucs
10 B9 Aldsworth W Susx
104 D10 Aldunie Moray
46 H2 Aldwark Derbys
64 B7 Aldwark N York
10 E11 Aldwick W Susx
38 F4 Aldwincle Nhants
19 S5 Aldworth W Berk
88 J10 Alexandria W Duns
16 G9 Aley Somset
14 G10 Alfardisworthy Devon
6 F5 Alfington Devon
10 G4 Alfold Surrey
10 G4 Alfold Bars W Susx
10 G3 Alfold Crossways Surrey
104 H12 Alford Abers
59 S11 Alford Lincs
17 R10 Alford Somset
59 R11 Alford Crematorium Lincs
47 M2 Alfreton Derbys
35 R10 Alfrick Worcs
35 R10 Alfrick Pound Worcs
11 S10 Alfriston E Susx
49 L6 Algarkirk Lincs
17 R10 Alhampton Somset
58 E2 Alkborough N Linc
28 E6 Alkerton Gloucs
37 L12 Alkerton Oxon
13 Q7 Alkham Kent
45 M6 Alkington Shrops
46 G6 Alkmonton Derbys
5 U10 Allaleigh Devon
97 U5 Allanaquoich Abers
82 F7 Allanbank N Lans
85 M8 Allanton Border
82 F7 Allanton N Lans
82 D8 Allanton S Lans
28 B7 Allaston Gloucs
9 P4 Allbrook Hants
18 G8 All Cannings Wilts
68 H1 Allendale Nthumb
36 G1 Allen End Warwks
68 J3 Allenheads Nthumb
69 N2 Allensford Dur
22 C4 Allen's Green Herts
35 L13 Allensmore Herefs
47 L7 Allenton C Derb
15 S7 Aller Devon
17 M11 Aller Somset
66 G5 Allerby Cumb
6 D6 Allercombe Devon
16 B7 Allerford Somset
64 K3 Allerston N York
64 H10 Allerthorpe E R Yk
63 N13 Allerton C Brad
103 L2 Allerton Highld
54 J9 Allerton Lpool
63 U14 Allerton Bywater Leeds
63 U8 Allerton Mauleverer N York
36 K4 Allesley Covtry
46 K6 Allestree C Derb
2 K7 Allet Common Cnwll
48 B13 Allexton Leics
56 E13 Allgreave Ches E
22 K12 Allhallows Medway
22 K12 Allhallows-on-Sea Medway
107 P13 Alligin Shuas Highld
45 U10 Allimore Green Staffs
7 N6 Allington Dorset
12 E4 Allington Kent
48 C5 Allington Lincs
18 C5 Allington Wilts
18 G8 Allington Wilts
18 K13 Allington Wilts
61 R4 Allithwaite Cumb
90 C13 Alloa Clacks
66 G4 Allonby Cumb
55 R12 Allostock Ches W
81 L9 Alloway S Ayrs
7 L2 Allowenshay Somset
41 P4 All Saints South Elmham Suffk
35 R1 Allscott Shrops
45 P11 Allscott Wrekin
35 L1 All Stretton Shrops
54 G13 Alltami Flints
94 H8 Alltchaorunn Highld
34 C11 Alltmawr Powys
25 R4 Alltwalis Carmth
26 C7 Alltwen Neath
32 K11 Alltyblaca Cerdgn
7 S2 Allweston Dorset
40 H6 Allwood Green Suffk
34 H10 Almeley Herefs
34 H10 Almeley Wooton Herefs
8 C9 Almer Dorset
57 S5 Almholme Donc
45 R7 Almington Staffs
10 C11 Almodington W Susx
90 G6 Almondbank P & K
56 J4 Almondbury Kirk
28 B11 Almondsbury S Glos
64 B6 Alne N York
109 M11 Alness Highld
76 K3 Alnham Nthumb
77 Q3 Alnmouth Nthumb
77 P3 Alnwick Nthumb
21 L6 Alperton Gt Lon
40 E13 Alphamstone Essex
40 E10 Alpheton Suffk
6 B6 Alphington Devon
51 N13 Alpington Norfk
56 K14 Alport Derbys
45 N2 Alpraham Ches E
23 Q3 Alresford Essex
46 G11 Alrewas Staffs
45 S2 Alsager Ches E
45 S4 Alsagers Bank Staffs
46 G3 Alsop en le Dale Derbys
68 F3 Alston Cumb
6 K4 Alston Devon
36 C14 Alstone Gloucs
16 K7 Alstone Somset
46 F2 Alstonefield Staffs
17 M6 Alston Sutton Somset
15 R8 Alswear Devon
56 D6 Alt Oldham
107 S2 Altandhu Highld
4 G4 Altarnun Cnwll
108 J4 Altass Highld
93 R11 Altcreich Ag & B
88 B11 Altgaltraig Ag & B
62 F13 Altham Lancs
23 M8 Althorne Essex
58 D5 Althorpe N Linc
112 B7 Altnabreac Station Highld
111 M9 Altnaharra Highld
57 N2 Altofts Wakefd
57 N14 Alton Derbys
19 V13 Alton Hants
46 E5 Alton Staffs
18 J11 Alton Wilts
18 H8 Alton Barnes Wilts
7 T4 Alton Pancras Dorset
18 H8 Alton Priors Wilts
46 E5 Alton Towers Staffs
55 S9 Altrincham Traffd
55 R9 Altrincham Crematorium Traffd
89 L5 Altskeith Hotel Stirlg
90 C12 Alva Clacks
55 L12 Alvanley Ches W
47 L7 Alvaston C Derb
36 D6 Alvechurch Worcs
46 H13 Alvecote Warwks
8 D4 Alvediston Wilts
35 S4 Alveley Shrops
15 M7 Alverdiscott Devon
9 S9 Alverstoke Hants
9 R11 Alverstone IoW
57 M2 Alverthorpe Wakefd
47 U5 Alverton Notts
103 T3 Alves Moray
29 Q7 Alvescot Oxon
28 B10 Alveston S Glos
36 H9 Alveston Warwks
59 Q8 Alvingham Lincs
28 B7 Alvington Gloucs
38 H1 Alwalton C Pete
76 J4 Alwinton Nthumb
63 R11 Alwoodley Leeds
63 S11 Alwoodley Gates Leeds
90 K2 Alyth P & K
46 K3 Ambergate Derbys
48 K4 Amber Hill Lincs
28 G7 Amberley Gloucs
10 G8 Amberley W Susx
47 L2 Amber Row Derbys
11 T8 Amberstone E Susx
77 R5 Amble Nthumb
35 U3 Amblecote Dudley
63 M14 Ambler Thorn C Brad
67 N12 Ambleside Cumb
24 H5 Ambleston Pembks
30 D9 Ambrosden Oxon
58 E4 Amcotts N Linc
39 P5 America Cambs
20 G3 Amersham Bucks
20 G3 Amersham Common Bucks
20 G3 Amersham Old Town Bucks
20 G3 Amersham on the Hill Bucks
46 C8 Amerton Staffs
18 J12 Amesbury Wilts
106 f8 Amhuinnsuidhe W Isls
46 H13 Amington Staffs
74 K9 Amisfield Town D & G
52 F4 Amlwch IoA
26 A5 Ammanford Carmth
64 G5 Amotherby N York
9 N4 Ampfield Hants
64 D4 Ampleforth N York
29 L7 Ampney Crucis Gloucs
29 L7 Ampney St Mary Gloucs
29 L7 Ampney St Peter Gloucs
19 M12 Amport Hants
31 M5 Ampthill C Beds
40 E6 Ampton Suffk
25 L9 Amroth Pembks
90 C4 Amulree P & K
31 Q10 Amwell Herts
93 U6 Anaheilt Highld
48 E5 Ancaster Lincs
34 E3 Anchor Shrops
85 P9 Ancroft Nthumb
84 G14 Ancrum Border
10 F10 Ancton W Susx
59 T11 Anderby Lincs
16 K10 Andersea Somset
16 H10 Andersfield Somset
8 B9 Anderson Dorset
55 P11 Anderton Ches W
5 L10 Anderton Cnwll
19 N11 Andover Hants
28 K4 Andoversford Gloucs
60 g3 Andreas IoM
42 C8 Anelog Gwynd
21 P9 Anerley Gt Lon
54 J8 Anfield Lpool
54 J8 Anfield Crematorium Lpool
2 F9 Angarrack Cnwll
2 K9 Angarrick Cnwll
35 N5 Angelbank Shrops
16 G13 Angersleigh Somset
66 K1 Angerton Cumb
24 E10 Angle Pembks
52 F6 Anglesey IoA
10 H10 Angmering W Susx
64 C10 Angram N York
68 J13 Angram N York
2 H13 Angrouse Cnwll
76 J12 Anick Nthumb
109 Q10 Ankerville Highld
47 U10 Ankle Hill Leics
65 N14 Anlaby E R Yk
50 B8 Anmer Norfk
9 T6 Anmore Hants
75 N12 Annan D & G
75 M7 Annandale Water Services D & G
60 K2 Annaside Cumb
107 Q14 Annat Highld
82 D4 Annathill N Lans
19 N12 Anna Valley Hants
81 N8 Annbank S Ayrs
36 G10 Anne Hathaway's Cottage Warwks
47 P3 Annesley Notts
47 N3 Annesley Woodhouse Notts
69 Q2 Annfield Plain Dur
89 M12 Anniesland C Glas
77 R11 Annitsford N Tyne
45 L12 Annscroft Shrops
61 Q14 Ansdell Lancs
17 R10 Ansford Somset
36 K2 Ansley Warwks
46 H8 Anslow Staffs
46 G9 Anslow Gate Staffs
46 H9 Anslow Lees Staffs
10 E4 Ansteadbrook Surrey
10 A2 Anstey Hants
39 P14 Anstey Herts
47 Q12 Anstey Leics
91 S11 Anstruther Fife
11 M6 Ansty W Susx
37 M4 Ansty Warwks
8 D3 Ansty Wilts
7 U4 Ansty Cross Dorset
9 S6 Anthill Common Hants
20 H10 Anthonys Surrey
75 N14 Anthorn Cumb
51 N7 Antingham Norfk
106 f10 An t-Ob W Isls
49 M4 Anton's Gowt Lincs
5 L10 Antony Cnwll
55 P11 Antrobus Ches W
14 J12 Anvil Corner Devon
13 M6 Anvil Green Kent
48 H3 Anwick Lincs
73 P8 Anwoth D & G
21 R11 Aperfield Gt Lon
36 C6 Apes Dale Worcs
38 F1 Apethorpe Nhants
45 U10 Apeton Staffs
58 K11 Apley Lincs
57 N11 Apperknowle Derbys
28 G2 Apperley Gloucs
63 P12 Apperley Bridge C Brad
77 M14 Apperley Dene Nthumb
62 H1 Appersett N York
94 C9 Appin Ag & B
58 G4 Appleby N Linc
68 E8 Appleby-in-Westmorland Cumb
46 K12 Appleby Magna Leics
46 K12 Appleby Parva Leics
31 T12 Appleby Street Herts
100 g5 Applecross Highld
6 E2 Appledore Devon
15 L6 Appledore Devon
12 J10 Appledore Kent
12 J9 Appledore Heath Kent
19 R2 Appleford Oxon
75 M9 Applegarth Town D & G
57 N4 Applehaigh Wakefd
19 M11 Appleshaw Hants
67 L7 Applethwaite Cumb
55 M9 Appleton Halton
29 T7 Appleton Oxon
55 P10 Appleton Warrtn
64 G2 Appleton-le-Moors N York
64 G5 Appleton-le-Street N York
64 D11 Appleton Roebuck N York
55 P10 Appleton Thorn Warrtn
70 E12 Appleton Wiske N York
75 V2 Appletreehall Border
63 M7 Appletreewick N York
16 E12 Appley Somset
55 M5 Appley Bridge Lancs
9 R12 Apse Heath IoW
31 P6 Apsley End C Beds
10 C10 Apuldram W Susx
109 Q9 Arabella Highld
91 T3 Arbirlot Angus
109 R8 Arboll Highld
20 C9 Arborfield Wokham
20 C9 Arborfield Cross Wokham
57 N9 Arbourthorne Sheff
91 T3 Arbroath Angus
99 P8 Arbuthnott Abers
12 G8 Arcadia Kent
25 R10 Archddu Carmth
69 S9 Archdeacon Newton Darltn
88 K9 Archencarroch W Duns
104 A7 Archiestown Moray
7 f2 Archirondel Jersey
45 S1 Arclid Green Ches E
105 S8 Ardallie Abers
94 F14 Ardanaiseig Hotel Ag & B
101 L4 Ardaneaskan Highld
101 L4 Ardarroch Highld
78 G6 Ardbeg Ag & B
88 C12 Ardbeg Ag & B
88 E9 Ardbeg Ag & B
108 B7 Ardcharnich Highld
86 F2 Ardchiavaig Ag & B
87 T3 Ardchonnel Ag & B
89 N3 Ardchullarie More Stirlg
88 F7 Arddarroch Ag & B
44 G10 Arddleen Powys
101 S13 Ardechive Highld
80 K4 Ardeer N Ayrs
31 T7 Ardeley Herts
101 M6 Ardelve Highld
88 J9 Arden Ag & B
36 F10 Ardens Grafton Warwks
93 U14 Ardentallen Ag & B
88 E8 Ardentinny Ag & B
88 B11 Ardentraive Ag & B
95 T11 Ardeonaig Stirlg
103 L5 Ardersier Highld
107 U7 Ardessie Highld
87 Q5 Ardfern Ag & B
86 K11 Ardfernal Ag & B
108 K6 Ardgay Highld
94 E6 Ardgour Highld
88 F11 Ardgowan Inver
88 E11 Ardhallow Ag & B
106 g8 Ardhasig W Isls
107 N13 Ardheslaig Highld
108 B7 Ardindrean Highld
11 N5 Ardingly W Susx
29 T10 Ardington Oxon
29 T10 Ardington Wick Oxon
87 T12 Ardlamont Ag & B
23 Q2 Ardleigh Essex
23 P1 Ardleigh Heath Essex
91 L3 Ardler P & K
30 B7 Ardley Oxon
22 D5 Ardley End Essex
88 H2 Ardlui Ag & B
87 L8 Ardlussa Ag & B
107 V5 Ardmair Highld
88 C12 Ardmaleish Ag & B
79 L6 Ardminish Ag & B
93 S4 Ardmolich Highld
88 H10 Ardmore Ag & B
109 N7 Ardmore Highld
88 E9 Ardnadam Ag & B
102 F6 Ardnagrask Highld
101 M4 Ardnarff Highld
93 U6 Ardnastang Highld
79 P4 Ardpatrick Ag & B
87 R8 Ardrishaig Ag & B
109 L10 Ardross Highld
80 J4 Ardrossan N Ayrs
57 N5 Ardsley Barns
57 M1 Ardsley East Leeds
93 P6 Ardslignish Highld
78 H5 Ardtalla Ag & B
93 Q4 Ardtoe Highld
87 P3 Arduaine Ag & B
102 G3 Ardullie Highld
100 f9 Ardvasar Highld
95 S14 Ardvorlich P & K
106 g7 Ardvourlie W Isls
72 E10 Ardwell D & G
56 C7 Ardwick Manch
35 S6 Areley Kings Worcs
93 R5 Arevegaig Highld
10 C3 Arford Hants
27 M8 Argoed Caerph
44 H9 Argoed Shrops
33 U8 Argoed Mill Powys
11 T5 Argos Hill E Susx
88 F5 Argyll Forest Park Ag & B
106 h7 Aribruach W Isls
92 J14 Aridhglas Ag & B
92 F8 Arileod Ag & B
92 G7 Arinagour Ag & B
94 B13 Ariogan Ag & B
93 R1 Arisaig Highld
93 R2 Arisaig House Highld
63 T7 Arkendale N York
39 Q14 Arkesden Essex
62 B5 Arkholme Lancs
66 H5 Arkleby Cumb
75 S7 Arkleton D & G
69 M12 Arkle Town N York
21 M3 Arkley Gt Lon
57 S5 Arksey Donc
57 P12 Arkwright Town Derbys
28 H3 Arle Gloucs
66 F9 Arlecdon Cumb
37 L11 Arlescote Warwks
31 Q5 Arlesey C Beds
45 Q11 Arleston Wrekin
55 Q10 Arley Ches E
36 J2 Arley Warwks
28 D5 Arlingham Gloucs
15 P4 Arlington Devon
11 S9 Arlington E Susx
29 M6 Arlington Gloucs
15 P4 Arlington Beccott Devon
100 f9 Armadale Highld
111 R4 Armadale Highld
82 H5 Armadale W Loth
66 J7 Armaside Cumb
67 R3 Armathwaite Cumb
51 N13 Arminghall Norfk
46 E10 Armitage Staffs
56 H4 Armitage Bridge Kirk
63 R13 Armley Leeds
36 H12 Armscote Warwks
46 B4 Armshead Staffs
38 G3 Armston Nhants
57 T6 Armthorpe Donc
92 G6 Arnabost Ag & B
61 M3 Arnaby Cumb
62 J5 Arncliffe N York
62 J5 Arncliffe Cote N York
91 R10 Arncroach Fife
104 B6 Arndilly House Moray
8 D11 Arne Dorset
37 R2 Arnesby Leics
90 H9 Arngask P & K
101 L9 Arnisdale Highld
100 e5 Arnish Highld
83 R6 Arniston Mdloth
106 i4 Arnol W Isls
65 Q11 Arnold E R Yk
47 Q4 Arnold Notts
89 P7 Arnprior Stirlg
61 T4 Arnside Cumb
93 P9 Aros Ag & B
45 L6 Arowry Wrexhm
61 Q3 Arrad Foot Cumb
65 N11 Arram E R Yk
79 S8 Arran N Ayrs
69 R14 Arrathorne N York
9 Q11 Arreton IoW
107 M13 Arrina Highld
39 M10 Arrington Cambs
88 G5 Arrochar Ag & B
36 E9 Arrow Warwks
36 D6 Arrowfield Top Worcs
44 K12 Arscott Shrops
102 H6 Artafallie Highld
63 R11 Arthington Leeds
37 U4 Arthingworth Nhants
43 M11 Arthog Gwynd
105 R8 Arthrath Abers
63 T12 Arthursdale Leeds
105 S9 Artrochie Abers
10 G9 Arundel W Susx
66 G8 Asby Cumb
88 D13 Ascog Ag & B
20 F9 Ascot W & M
36 K14 Ascott Warwks
29 R4 Ascott Earl Oxon
29 R4 Ascott-under-Wychwood Oxon
63 T4 Asenby N York
47 T10 Asfordby Leics
47 T10 Asfordby Hill Leics
48 H4 Asgarby Lincs
59 P13 Asgarby Lincs
5 U11 Ash Devon
15 M11 Ash Devon
8 B6 Ash Dorset
12 B3 Ash Kent
13 Q4 Ash Kent
16 J12 Ash Somset
17 N12 Ash Somset
20 F12 Ash Surrey
19 S5 Ashampstead W Berk
19 S5 Ashampstead Green W Berk
41 L10 Ashbocking Suffk
46 G4 Ashbourne Derbys
16 E12 Ashbrittle Somset
12 C13 Ashburnham Place E Susx
5 T6 Ashburton Devon
15 M13 Ashbury Devon
29 Q10 Ashbury Oxon
58 E5 Ashby N Linc
59 R13 Ashby by Partney Lincs
59 N6 Ashby cum Fenby NE Lin
48 G2 Ashby de la Launde Lincs
47 L10 Ashby-de-la-Zouch Leics
47 T11 Ashby Folville Leics
37 Q2 Ashby Magna Leics
37 P3 Ashby Parva Leics
59 P12 Ashby Puerorum Lincs
37 Q7 Ashby St Ledgers Nhants
51 P13 Ashby St Mary Norfk
36 B14 Ashchurch Gloucs
6 B9 Ashcombe Devon
16 K4 Ashcombe N Som
17 M9 Ashcott Somset
39 S12 Ashdon Essex
19 R10 Ashe Hants
23 N7 Asheldham Essex
40 B12 Ashen Essex
30 F10 Ashendon Bucks
30 K12 Asheridge Bucks
9 M5 Ashfield Hants
28 A3 Ashfield Herefs
89 S5 Ashfield Stirlg
41 M8 Ashfield cum Thorpe Suffk
40 C9 Ashfield Green Suffk
41 N6 Ashfield Green Suffk
11 L5 Ashfold Crossways W Susx
5 R11 Ashford Devon
15 M5 Ashford Devon
12 K7 Ashford Kent
20 J8 Ashford Surrey
35 M6 Ashford Bowdler Shrops
35 M6 Ashford Carbonell Shrops
19 S8 Ashford Hill Hants
56 J13 Ashford in the Water Derbys
82 E8 Ashgill S Lans
20 F13 Ash Green Surrey
36 K4 Ash Green Warwks
6 E2 Ashill Devon
50 E13 Ashill Norfk
16 K13 Ashill Somset
23 L9 Ashingdon Essex
77 R8 Ashington Nthumb
8 E9 Ashington Poole
17 Q12 Ashington Somset
10 J7 Ashington W Susx
75 U1 Ashkirk Border
9 P8 Ashlett Hants
28 F2 Ashleworth Gloucs
28 F2 Ashleworth Quay Gloucs
39 U8 Ashley Cambs
55 S10 Ashley Ches E
15 Q10 Ashley Devon
8 G8 Ashley Dorset
28 H9 Ashley Gloucs
8 K9 Ashley Hants
9 M2 Ashley Hants
13 R6 Ashley Kent
37 U2 Ashley Nhants
45 S6 Ashley Staffs
18 B7 Ashley Wilts
31 L11 Ashley Green Bucks
46 J3 Ashleyhay Derbys
8 G8 Ashley Heath Dorset
35 L7 Ashley Moor Herefs
45 N6 Ash Magna Shrops
19 P9 Ashmansworth Hants
14 H9 Ashmansworthy Devon
28 E8 Ashmead Green Gloucs
14 J13 Ashmill Devon
15 S8 Ash Mill Devon
8 C5 Ashmore Dorset
19 R7 Ashmore Green W Berk
36 K9 Ashorne Warwks
57 M14 Ashover Derbys
46 K1 Ashover Hay Derbys
36 K6 Ashow Warwks
45 N6 Ash Parva Shrops
35 P12 Ashperton Herefs
5 U9 Ashprington Devon
16 G11 Ash Priors Somset
15 P10 Ashreigney Devon
40 H11 Ash Street Suffk
21 L11 Ashtead Surrey
6 D2 Ash Thomas Devon
48 H12 Ashton C Pete
55 M13 Ashton Ches W
2 G11 Ashton Cnwll
5 V4 Ashton Devon
9 Q5 Ashton Hants
35 M8 Ashton Herefs
88 F10 Ashton Inver
37 U11 Ashton Nhants
38 G3 Ashton Nhants
17 M7 Ashton Somset
18 C9 Ashton Common Wilts
18 D9 Ashton Hill Wilts
55 N7 Ashton-in-Makerfield Wigan
28 K9 Ashton Keynes Wilts
36 C13 Ashton under Hill Worcs
56 D7 Ashton-under-Lyne Tamesd
55 S8 Ashton upon Mersey Traffd
9 L6 Ashurst Hants
11 S3 Ashurst Kent
55 L5 Ashurst Lancs
10 K7 Ashurst W Susx
11 Q3 Ashurstwood W Susx
20 E12 Ash Vale Surrey
14 J13 Ashwater Devon
31 S5 Ashwell Herts
48 C11 Ashwell Rutlnd
17 L13 Ashwell Somset
31 S4 Ashwell End Herts
50 K14 Ashwellthorpe Norfk
17 R7 Ashwick Somset
50 B10 Ashwicken Norfk
35 U3 Ashwood Staffs
61 N4 Askam in Furness Cumb
57 S4 Askern Donc
7 P6 Askerswell Dorset
30 H11 Askett Bucks
67 R8 Askham Cumb
58 B12 Askham Notts
64 D10 Askham Bryan C York
64 C10 Askham Richard C York
87 S7 Asknish Ag & B
62 J1 Askrigg N York
63 P10 Askwith N York
48 G7 Aslackby Lincs
41 L2 Aslacton Norfk
47 T6 Aslockton Notts
17 N9 Asney Somset
41 L8 Aspall Suffk
66 H4 Aspatria Cumb
31 U7 Aspenden Herts
56 F9 Aspenshaw Derbys
49 L6 Asperton Lincs
45 T7 Aspley Staffs
30 K5 Aspley Guise C Beds
30 K6 Aspley Heath C Beds
36 E6 Aspley Heath Warwks
55 P5 Aspull Wigan
55 P7 Aspull Common Wigan
64 G14 Asselby E R Yk
59 S11 Asserby Lincs
59 S11 Asserby Turn Lincs
40 F13 Assington Suffk
40 C10 Assington Green Suffk
45 T1 Astbury Ches E
37 S10 Astcote Nhants
59 N11 Asterby Lincs
44 J12 Asterley Shrops
34 J2 Asterton Shrops
29 Q5 Asthall Oxon
29 R5 Asthall Leigh Oxon
109 N6 Astle Highld
45 M10 Astley Shrops
36 K3 Astley Warwks
55 R6 Astley Wigan
35 S7 Astley Worcs
35 R1 Astley Abbots Shrops
55 R4 Astley Bridge Bolton
35 T7 Astley Cross Worcs
55 R7 Astley Green Wigan
36 E3 Aston Birm
45 P4 Aston Ches E
55 N11 Aston Ches W
56 J10 Aston Derbys
54 H13 Aston Flints
35 L8 Aston Herefs
31 S8 Aston Herts
29 R7 Aston Oxon
57 Q9 Aston Rothm
35 T2 Aston Shrops
45 M8 Aston Shrops
45 S5 Aston Staffs
45 U9 Aston Staffs
20 C6 Aston Wokham
45 P12 Aston Wrekin
30 H8 Aston Abbotts Bucks
35 P4 Aston Botterell Shrops
46 B7 Aston-by-Stone Staffs
36 F8 Aston Cantlow Warwks
30 J10 Aston Clinton Bucks
28 C3 Aston Crews Herefs
36 B14 Aston Cross Gloucs
31 S8 Aston End Herts
35 Q2 Aston-Eyre Shrops
36 C7 Aston Fields Worcs
37 N2 Aston Flamville Leics
55 N11 Aston Heath Ches W
28 C3 Aston Ingham Herefs
45 P2 Aston juxta Mondrum Ches E
37 N10 Aston le Walls Nhants
36 G13 Aston Magna Gloucs
35 M3 Aston Munslow Shrops
34 J4 Aston on Clun Shrops
44 H12 Aston Pigott Shrops
44 H12 Aston Rogers Shrops
20 B3 Aston Rowant Oxon
30 G11 Aston Sandford Bucks
36 D13 Aston Somerville Worcs
36 F12 Aston-sub-Edge Gloucs
19 S3 Aston Tirrold Oxon
47 M8 Aston-upon-Trent Derbys
19 S3 Aston Upthorpe Oxon
30 B5 Astrop Nhants
30 J10 Astrope Herts
31 R5 Astwick C Beds
57 P14 Astwith Derbys
38 E11 Astwood M Keyn
36 B7 Astwood Worcs
36 D8 Astwood Bank Worcs
35 U9 Astwood Crematorium Worcs
48 G6 Aswarby Lincs
59 Q12 Aswardby Lincs
45 M12 Atcham Shrops
36 D10 Atch Lench Worcs
7 U6 Athelhampton Dorset
41 M6 Athelington Suffk
16 K11 Athelney Somset
84 E3 Athelstaneford E Loth
9 P13 Atherfield Green IoW
15 N8 Atherington Devon
10 G10 Atherington W Susx
17 L13 Atherstone Somset
46 K14 Atherstone Warwks
36 H10 Atherstone on Stour Warwks
55 Q6 Atherton Wigan
69 S12 Atley Hill N York
46 H4 Atlow Derbys
101 N4 Attadale Highld
47 P7 Attenborough Notts
58 G8 Atterby Lincs
57 N9 Attercliffe Sheff
45 P14 Atterley Shrops
47 L14 Atterton Leics
40 H1 Attleborough Norfk
37 L2 Attleborough Warwks
50 K10 Attlebridge Norfk
40 B10 Attleton Green Suffk
65 R9 Atwick E R Yk
18 C7 Atworth Wilts
35 L11 Auberrow Herefs
58 F14 Aubourn Lincs
103 V10 Auchbreck Moray
105 P9 Auchedly Abers
99 N8 Auchenblae Abers
89 S8 Auchenbowie Stirlg
73 T9 Auchencairn D & G
74 J9 Auchencairn D & G
80 E7 Auchencairn N Ayrs
85 M6 Auchencrow Border
83 Q6 Auchendinny Mdloth
82 J8 Auchengray S Lans
104 D3 Auchenhalrig Moray
82 F10 Auchenheath S Lans
74 F6 Auchenhessnane D & G
87 T11 Auchenlochan Ag & B
81 M3 Auchenmade N Ayrs
72 G9 Auchenmalg D & G
81 M3 Auchentiber N Ayrs
88 B5 Auchindrain Ag & B
108 B8 Auchindrean Highld
104 K6 Auchininna Abers
81 R8 Auchinleck E Ayrs
89 Q11 Auchinloch N Lans
89 R10 Auchinstarry N Lans
94 F4 Auchintore Highld
105 T8 Auchiries Abers
97 P4 Auchlean Highld
99 R4 Auchlee Abers
104 J11 Auchleven Abers
82 F11 Auchlochan S Lans
98 K3 Auchlossan Abers
95 Q13 Auchlyne Stirlg
81 Q7 Auchmillan E Ayrs
91 U3 Auchmithie Angus
90 K11 Auchmuirbridge Fife
98 H11 Auchnacree Angus
105 Q7 Auchnagatt Abers
103 V11 Auchnarrow Moray
72 B7 Auchnotteroch D & G
104 C5 Auchroisk Moray
90 D9 Auchterarder P & K
96 D2 Auchteraw Highld
103 P11 Auchterblair Highld
107 P9 Auchtercairn Highld
90 K12 Auchterderran Fife
91 M4 Auchterhouse Angus
105 L7 Auchterless Abers
90 K9 Auchtermuchty Fife
102 E4 Auchterneed Highld
90 K13 Auchtertool Fife
101 L6 Auchtertyre Highld
89 N1 Auchtubh Stirlg
112 J3 Auckengill Highld
57 T6 Auckley Donc
56 D7 Audenshaw Tamesd
45 Q5 Audlem Ches E
45 S3 Audley Staffs
39 R13 Audley End Essex
40 D13 Audley End Essex
40 E10 Audley End Suffk
39 R13 Audley End House Essex
45 T9 Audmore Staffs
35 U3 Audnam Dudley
67 L5 Aughertree Cumb
64 G12 Aughton E R Yk
54 J5 Aughton Lancs
62 B6 Aughton Lancs
57 Q9 Aughton Rothm
18 K9 Aughton Wilts
54 K5 Aughton Park Lancs
103 P4 Auldearn Highld
35 L10 Aulden Herefs
74 H8 Auldgirth D & G
81 S2 Auldhouse S Lans
101 N7 Ault a' chruinn Highld
107 Q7 Aultbea Highld
107 M7 Aultgrishin Highld
108 F10 Aultguish Inn Highld
57 Q13 Ault Hucknall Derbys
104 E5 Aultmore Moray
102 F11 Aultnagoire Highld
109 M8 Aultnamain Inn Highld
48 F11 Aunby Lincs
6 D4 Aunk Devon
48 F6 Aunsby Lincs
28 A10 Aust S Glos
49 L9 Austendike Lincs
57 U8 Austerfield Donc
56 E5 Austerlands Oldham
63 T13 Austhorpe Leeds
56 H5 Austonley Kirk
46 J12 Austrey Warwks
62 F6 Austwick N York
59 Q10 Authorpe Lincs
59 T12 Authorpe Row Lincs
18 H7 Avebury Wilts
18 G7 Avebury Trusloe Wilts
22 E11 Aveley Thurr
28 G8 Avening Gloucs
47 U3 Averham Notts
5 R11 Aveton Gifford Devon
103 N13 Aviemore Highld
19 N7 Avington W Berk
102 K4 Avoch Highld
8 G9 Avon Hants
82 H4 Avonbridge Falk
37 M10 Avon Dassett Warwks
27 U12 Avonmouth Bristl
5 S9 Avonwick Devon
9 L4 Awbridge Hants
28 A10 Awkley S Glos
6 F4 Awliscombe Devon
28 D6 Awre Gloucs
47 N5 Awsworth Notts
35 U5 Axborough Worcs
17 M6 Axbridge Somset
19 T12 Axford Hants
18 K6 Axford Wilts
6 J5 Axminster Devon
6 J6 Axmouth Devon
54 D10 Axton Flints
69 S8 Aycliffe Dur
77 L12 Aydon Nthumb
28 B7 Aylburton Gloucs
68 F3 Ayle Nthumb
6 D6 Aylesbeare Devon
30 H10 Aylesbury Bucks
59 M5 Aylesby NE Lin
12 D4 Aylesford Kent
13 P5 Aylesham Kent
47 Q13 Aylestone C Leic
47 Q13 Aylestone Park C Leic
51 L6 Aylmerton Norfk
51 L8 Aylsham Norfk
35 Q13 Aylton Herefs
29 M3 Aylworth Gloucs
34 K7 Aymestrey Herefs
30 B6 Aynho Nhants
31 R10 Ayot Green Herts
31 Q9 Ayot St Lawrence Herts
31 R9 Ayot St Peter Herts
81 L8 Ayr S Ayrs
63 L2 Aysgarth N York
16 D13 Ayshford Devon
61 R3 Ayside Cumb
48 C13 Ayston Rutlnd
22 E4 Aythorpe Roding Essex
85 N6 Ayton Border
63 R5 Azerley N York

B

6 B11 Babbacombe Torbay
47 N5 Babbington Notts
44 H8 Babbinswood Shrops
31 U9 Babbs Green Herts
17 Q11 Babcary Somset
33 R13 Babel Carmth
40 B11 Babel Green Suffk
54 E12 Babell Flints
5 R5 Babeny Devon
29 T7 Bablock Hythe Oxon
39 R10 Babraham Cambs
57 U10 Babworth Notts
52 F6 Bachau IoA
35 L4 Bache Shrops
34 F2 Bacheldre Powys
12 F13 Bachelor's Bump E Susx
106 u16 Backaland Ork
61 R3 Backbarrow Cumb
25 N7 Backe Carmth
105 S5 Backfolds Abers
54 J12 Backford Ches W
54 J12 Backford Cross Ches W
109 Q4 Backies Highld
100 f11 Back of Keppoch Highld
46 E3 Back o' th' Brook Staffs
40 B9 Back Street Suffk
17 N3 Backwell N Som
77 S11 Backworth N Tyne
36 G3 Bacon's End Solhll
50 K6 Baconsthorpe Norfk
27 R1 Bacton Herefs
51 P7 Bacton Norfk
40 J7 Bacton Suffk
40 H7 Bacton Green Suffk
56 C2 Bacup Lancs
107 N10 Badachro Highld
18 J4 Badbury Swindn
37 Q9 Badby Nhants
110 D8 Badcall Highld
110 E5 Badcall Highld
107 T6 Badcaul Highld
46 B3 Baddeley Edge C Stke
46 B3 Baddeley Green C Stke
36 H6 Baddesley Clinton Warwks
46 J14 Baddesley Ensor Warwks
110 B12 Baddidarrach Highld
83 M8 Baddinsgill Border
104 K8 Badenscoth Abers
104 C12 Badenyon Abers
4 G3 Badgall Cnwll
39 P1 Badgeney Cambs
45 S14 Badger Shrops
2 D10 Badger's Cross Cnwll
21 S10 Badgers Mount Kent
28 H4 Badgeworth Gloucs
17 L6 Badgworth Somset
4 H3 Badharlick Cnwll
100 g7 Badicaul Highld
41 P7 Badingham Suffk
12 K5 Badlesmere Kent
75 L2 Badlieu Border
112 F7 Badlipster Highld
107 S6 Badluachrach Highld
109 P6 Badninish Highld
107 U6 Badrallach Highld
36 E12 Badsey Worcs
20 E13 Badshot Lea Surrey
57 Q4 Badsworth Wakefd
40 G7 Badwell Ash Suffk
40 H7 Badwell Green Suffk
7 U2 Bagber Dorset
64 B3 Bagby N York
59 Q12 Bag Enderby Lincs
28 K6 Bagendon Gloucs
35 Q4 Bagginswood Shrops
66 J4 Baggrow Cumb
106 b19 Bagh a Chaisteil W Isls
13 L5 Bagham Kent
106 c18 Bagh a Tuath W Isls
54 F11 Bagillt Flints
36 K6 Baginton Warwks
26 C9 Baglan Neath
63 Q12 Bagley Leeds
44 K8 Bagley Shrops
17 N7 Bagley Somset
19 U12 Bagmore Hants
46 B3 Bagnall Staffs
19 Q7 Bagnor W Berk
35 N6 Bagot Shrops
20 F10 Bagshot Surrey
19 M7 Bagshot Wilts
28 C10 Bagstone S Glos
47 N3 Bagthorpe Notts
47 M12 Bagworth Leics
27 S2 Bagwy Llydiart Herefs
63 P12 Baildon C Brad
63 N12 Baildon Green C Brad
106 h6 Baile Ailein W Isls
106 c13 Baile a Mhanaich W Isls
92 H14 Baile Mor Ag & B
9 T3 Bailey Green Hants
75 V10 Baileyhead Cumb
56 H1 Bailiff Bridge Calder
82 C6 Baillieston C Glas
61 T8 Bailrigg Lancs
62 J1 Bainbridge N York
104 J8 Bainshole Abers
48 G12 Bainton C Pete
65 M9 Bainton E R Yk
30 C7 Bainton Oxon
91 N11 Baintown Fife
76 D2 Bairnkine Border
31 U9 Baker's End Herts
22 F11 Baker Street Thurr
56 K13 Bakewell Derbys
43 T6 Bala Gwynd
106 h6 Balallan W Isls
102 D9 Balbeg Highld
90 J6 Balbeggie P & K
102 F6 Balblair Highld
102 K2 Balblair Highld
57 S6 Balby Donc
73 U10 Balcary D & G
102 F7 Balchraggan Highld
110 D4 Balchreick Highld
11 N4 Balcombe W Susx
11 N4 Balcombe Lane W Susx
91 T10 Balcomie Links Fife
63 T4 Baldersby N York
63 T4 Baldersby St James N York
62 C13 Balderstone Lancs
56 D4 Balderstone Rochdl
48 B3 Balderton Notts
2 K8 Baldhu Cnwll
91 P9 Baldinnie Fife
90 F8 Baldinnies P & K
31 R6 Baldock Herts
31 R5 Baldock Services Herts
91 Q5 Baldovie C Dund
60 g6 Baldrine IoM
12 F13 Baldslow E Susx
60 f6 Baldwin IoM
67 M2 Baldwinholme Cumb
45 S6 Baldwin's Gate Staffs
11 P3 Baldwin's Hill W Susx
50 H6 Bale Norfk
91 L5 Baledgarno P & K
92 B10 Balemartine Ag & B
83 N5 Balerno C Edin
91 L11 Balfarg Fife
98 J10 Balfield Angus
106 t18 Balfour Ork
89 M8 Balfron Stirlg
104 K7 Balgaveny Abers
90 F13 Balgonar Fife
72 E11 Balgowan D & G
96 J5 Balgowan Highld
100 c3 Balgown Highld
72 B7 Balgracie D & G
82 G14 Balgray S Lans
21 N8 Balham Gt Lon
91 L2 Balhary P & K
90 H4 Balholmie P & K
111 T3 Baligill Highld
98 D12 Balintore Angus
109 R9 Balintore Highld
109 N10 Balintraid Highld
106 c13 Balivanich W Isls
64 B3 Balk N York
91 M3 Balkeerie Angus
64 H14 Balkholme E R Yk
60 d8 Ballabeg IoM
94 F7 Ballachulish Highld
60 c8 Ballafesson IoM
60 h4 Ballajora IoM
60 c8 Ballakilpheric IoM
60 d8 Ballamodha IoM
88 B13 Ballanlay Ag & B
72 D3 Ballantrae S Ayrs
23 M9 Ballards Gore Essex
36 J2 Ballards Green Warwks
60 d8 Ballasalla IoM
98 F4 Ballater Abers
60 e4 Ballaugh IoM
109 P9 Ballchraggan Highld
84 D3 Ballencrieff E Loth
92 B9 Ballevullin Ag & B
45 U3 Ball Green C Stke
46 C2 Ball Haye Green Staffs
19 P8 Ball Hill Hants
46 H3 Ballidon Derbys
79 R8 Balliekine N Ayrs
88 D6 Balliemore Ag & B
72 G1 Balligmorrie S Ayrs
89 M2 Ballimore Stirlg
103 U8 Ballindalloch Moray
91 L6 Ballindean P & K
40 E12 Ballingdon Suffk
30 K12 Ballinger Common Bucks
28 A1 Ballingham Herefs
90 J12 Ballingry Fife
97 R13 Ballinluig P & K
98 G13 Ballinshoe Angus
97 U12 Ballintuim P & K
102 K6 Balloch Highld
89 R11 Balloch N Lans
89 T2 Balloch P & K
81 L13 Balloch S Ayrs
88 J9 Balloch W Duns
10 F5 Balls Cross W Susx
11 R3 Balls Green E Susx
28 G8 Ball's Green Gloucs
93 L10 Ballygown Ag & B
86 F12 Ballygrant Ag & B
92 F7 Ballyhaugh Ag & B
100 h7 Balmacara Highld
73 R4 Balmaclellan D & G
73 R11 Balmae D & G
88 K7 Balmaha Stirlg
91 M10 Balmalcolm Fife
73 Q10 Balmangan D & G
105 R12 Balmedie Abers
44 K7 Balmer Heath Shrops
91 N7 Balmerino Fife
9 L8 Balmerlawn Hants
79 S9 Balmichael N Ayrs
98 D5 Balmoral Castle Grounds Abers
89 N11 Balmore E Duns
109 R9 Balmuchy Highld
90 K14 Balmule Fife
91 P7 Balmullo Fife
109 Q2 Balnacoil Lodge Highld
101 P2 Balnacra Highld
98 D5 Balnacroft Abers
102 J8 Balnafoich Highld
97 Q13 Balnaguard P & K
86 G6 Balnahard Ag & B
93 M12 Balnahard Ag & B
102 D9 Balnain Highld
110 H3 Balnakeil Highld
57 S3 Balne N York
90 F4 Balquharn P & K
89 M1 Balquhidder Stirlg
36 H5 Balsall Common Solhll
36 E4 Balsall Heath Birm
36 H5 Balsall Street Solhll
37 L12 Balscote Oxon
39 S10 Balsham Cambs
106 w3 Baltasound Shet
45 S3 Balterley Staffs
45 S3 Balterley Green Staffs
45 R3 Balterley Heath Staffs
73 L7 Baltersan D & G
17 P10 Baltonsborough Somset
87 P2 Balvicar Ag & B
101 L8 Balvraid Highld
103 M9 Balvraid Highld
2 F10 Balwest Cnwll
55 N1 Bamber Bridge Lancs
22 E3 Bamber's Green Essex
85 T12 Bamburgh Nthumb
85 T11 Bamburgh Castle Nthumb
56 K10 Bamford Derbys
56 C4 Bamford Rochdl
67 R9 Bampton Cumb
16 C12 Bampton Devon
29 R7 Bampton Oxon

67 M13 Borwick Lodge Cumb
61 M4 Borwick Rails Cumb
2 B10 Bosavern Cnwll
35 Q12 Bosbury Herefs
3 Q3 Boscarne Cnwll
4 D2 Boscastle Cnwll
8 G10 Boscombe Bmouth
18 K13 Boscombe Wilts
3 Q6 Boscoppa Cnwll
10 C10 Bosham W Susx
10 C10 Bosham Hoe W Susx
24 G12 Bosherston Pembks
2 C10 Boskednan Cnwll
2 C12 Boskenna Cnwll
56 D13 Bosley Ches E
3 M4 Bosoughan Cnwll
64 G7 Bossall N York
4 D3 Bossiney Cnwll
13 N6 Bossingham Kent
15 U3 Bossington Somset
55 Q13 Bostock Green Ches W
49 M5 Boston Lincs
49 M4 Boston Crematorium Lincs
63 U10 Boston Spa Leeds
2 C10 Boswarthan Cnwll
3 P8 Boswinger Cnwll
2 B10 Botallack Cnwll
21 N3 Botany Bay Gt Lon
47 N13 Botcheston Leics
40 H5 Botesdale Suffk
77 Q8 Bothal Nthumb
19 R5 Bothampstead W Berk
57 U12 Bothamsall Notts
66 J5 Bothel Cumb
7 N6 Bothenhampton Dorset
82 D7 Bothwell S Lans
82 D7 Bothwell Services S Lans
31 L12 Botley Bucks
9 Q6 Botley Hants
29 U6 Botley Oxon
30 F8 Botolph Claydon Bucks
10 K9 Botolphs W Susx
13 M9 Botolph's Bridge Kent
48 B6 Bottesford Leics
58 E5 Bottesford N Linc
39 R8 Bottisham Cambs
91 N7 Bottomcraig Fife
55 L1 Bottom of Hutton Lancs
55 Q4 Bottom o' th' Moor Bolton
56 D2 Bottoms Calder
2 B12 Bottoms Cnwll
36 H2 Botts Green Warwks
5 L8 Botusfleming Cnwll
42 E7 Botwnnog Gwynd
21 S13 Bough Beech Kent
34 D13 Boughrood Powys
27 V8 Boughspring Gloucs
37 U7 Boughton Nhants
50 B13 Boughton Norfk
57 U13 Boughton Notts
12 K6 Boughton Aluph Kent
31 L5 Boughton End C Beds
12 E5 Boughton Green Kent
12 G6 Boughton Malherbe Kent
12 E5 Boughton Monchelsea Kent
13 L4 Boughton Street Kent
71 N9 Boulby R & Cl
56 F2 Boulder Clough Calder
9 M11 Bouldnor IoW
35 M3 Bouldon Shrops
77 R3 Boulmer Nthumb
24 G8 Boulston Pembks
58 G13 Boultham Lincs
39 M9 Bourn Cambs
48 G9 Bourne Lincs
22 D9 Bournebridge Essex
36 D4 Bournebrook Birm
38 F8 Bourne End Bed
20 E5 Bourne End Bucks
31 L4 Bourne End C Beds
31 M11 Bourne End Herts
8 F10 Bournemouth Bmouth
8 G9 Bournemouth Airport Dorset
8 G10 Bournemouth Crematorium Bmouth
28 H7 Bournes Green Gloucs
23 M10 Bournes Green Sthend
36 C6 Bournheath Worcs
70 D2 Bournmoor Dur
28 D9 Bournstream Gloucs
36 D4 Bournville Birm
17 U10 Bourton Dorset
17 L4 Bourton N Som
29 P10 Bourton Oxon
35 N1 Bourton Shrops
18 F8 Bourton Wilts
37 M6 Bourton on Dunsmore Warwks
29 N1 Bourton-on-the-Hill Gloucs
29 N3 Bourton-on-the-Water Gloucs
92 H6 Bousd Ag & B
75 Q14 Boustead Hill Cumb
61 Q2 Bouth Cumb
63 N5 Bouthwaite N York
36 D9 Bouts Worcs
20 F7 Boveney Bucks
8 F6 Boveridge Dorset
5 U5 Bovey Tracey Devon
31 M12 Bovingdon Herts
20 D5 Bovingdon Green Bucks
22 D6 Bovinger Essex
8 A11 Bovington Dorset
8 A11 Bovington Camp Dorset
8 A11 Bovington Tank Museum Dorset
67 M1 Bow Cumb
5 U9 Bow Devon
15 R12 Bow Devon
21 Q6 Bow Gt Lon
106 s20 Bow Ork
68 K8 Bowbank Dur
30 K6 Bow Brickhill M Keyn
28 G6 Bowbridge Gloucs
70 D5 Bowburn Dur
9 P11 Bowcombe IoW
6 F6 Bowd Devon
84 F12 Bowden Border
5 U11 Bowden Devon
18 D7 Bowden Hill Wilts
55 S9 Bowdon Traffd
112 F4 Bower Highld
17 Q2 Bower Ashton Bristl
8 E4 Bowerchalke Wilts
18 D8 Bowerhill Wilts
17 N13 Bower Hinton Somset
40 G12 Bower House Tye Suffk
112 F4 Bowermadden Highld
45 T6 Bowers Staffs
22 J10 Bowers Gifford Essex
90 G13 Bowershall Fife
63 U14 Bower's Row Leeds
69 L10 Bowes Dur
61 T11 Bowgreave Lancs
74 K12 Bowhouse D & G
4 F4 Bowithick Cnwll
54 K6 Bowker's Green Lancs
84 D10 Bowland Border
61 S2 Bowland Bridge Cumb
35 M10 Bowley Herefs
35 M10 Bowley Town Herefs
10 E3 Bowlhead Green Surrey
63 P13 Bowling C Brad
88 K11 Bowling W Duns
44 J4 Bowling Bank Wrexhm
35 T10 Bowling Green Worcs
67 M13 Bowmanstead Cumb
78 E4 Bowmore Ag & B
75 P13 Bowness-on-Solway Cumb
67 P13 Bowness-on-Windermere Cumb
91 M9 Bow of Fife Fife
91 R2 Bowriefauld Angus
67 N6 Bowscale Cumb
85 P10 Bowsden Nthumb
67 Q13 Bowston Cumb
33 M3 Bow Street Cerdgn
50 H14 Bow Street Norfk
51 L12 Bowthorpe Norfk
28 G7 Box Gloucs
18 B7 Box Wilts
28 C3 Boxbush Gloucs
28 D5 Boxbush Gloucs
38 F11 Box End Bed
40 G12 Boxford Suffk
19 P6 Boxford W Berk
10 E9 Boxgrove W Susx
21 L12 Box Hill Surrey
12 E4 Boxley Kent
31 M11 Boxmoor Herts
14 F12 Box's Shop Cnwll
23 P1 Boxted Essex
40 G14 Boxted Essex
40 D10 Boxted Suffk
23 P1 Boxted Cross Essex
28 F9 Boxwell Gloucs
39 M8 Boxworth Cambs
39 N7 Boxworth End Cambs
40 B9 Boyden End Suffk
13 P2 Boyden Gate Kent
46 G6 Boylestone Derbys
104 J3 Boyndie Abers
105 Q3 Boyndlie Abers
65 Q6 Boynton E R Yk
91 T2 Boysack Angus
7 S2 Boys Hill Dorset
57 N13 Boythorpe Derbys
4 J2 Boyton Cnwll
41 Q11 Boyton Suffk
18 E13 Boyton Wilts
22 F6 Boyton Cross Essex
40 B12 Boyton End Suffk
38 D9 Bozeat Nhants
60 e7 Braaid IoM
41 N8 Brabling Green Suffk
13 M7 Brabourne Kent
13 L7 Brabourne Lees Kent
112 H3 Brabstermire Highld
100 c6 Bracadale Highld
48 G11 Braceborough Lincs
58 G13 Bracebridge Heath Lincs
58 G13 Bracebridge Low Fields Lincs
48 F6 Braceby Lincs
62 H10 Bracewell Lancs
47 L2 Brackenfield Derbys
82 D5 Brackenhirst N Lans
67 L3 Brackenthwaite Cumb
63 R9 Brackenthwaite N York
10 C11 Bracklesham W Susx
94 H2 Brackletter Highld
30 C5 Brackley Nhants
30 D4 Brackley Hatch Nhants
20 E9 Bracknell Br For
89 T4 Braco P & K
104 G5 Bracobrae Moray
51 L14 Bracon Ash Norfk
100 g10 Bracora Highld
100 g10 Bracorina Highld
4 K2 Bradaford Devon
46 H3 Bradbourne Derbys
70 D7 Bradbury Dur
37 R11 Bradden Nhants
4 F8 Braddock Cnwll
45 U3 Bradeley C Stke
20 D3 Bradenham Bucks
18 F5 Bradenstoke Wilts
6 E3 Bradfield Devon
23 R1 Bradfield Essex
51 N7 Bradfield Norfk
57 L8 Bradfield Sheff
19 T6 Bradfield W Berk
40 E9 Bradfield Combust Suffk
45 Q2 Bradfield Green Ches E
23 R1 Bradfield Heath Essex
40 F9 Bradfield St Clare Suffk
40 F9 Bradfield St George Suffk
63 P13 Bradford C Brad
4 E5 Bradford Cnwll
14 K11 Bradford Devon
77 M10 Bradford Nthumb
85 T12 Bradford Nthumb
7 Q2 Bradford Abbas Dorset
18 B8 Bradford Leigh Wilts
18 B8 Bradford-on-Avon Wilts
16 G12 Bradford-on-Tone Somset
7 S6 Bradford Peverell Dorset
15 N6 Bradiford Devon
9 S11 Brading IoW
46 H4 Bradley Derbys
19 T12 Bradley Hants
56 J2 Bradley Kirk
63 L3 Bradley N York
59 M5 Bradley NE Lin
45 U10 Bradley Staffs
36 C1 Bradley Wolves
36 C8 Bradley Worcs
44 H3 Bradley Wrexhm
45 M4 Bradley Common Ches W
16 J9 Bradley Green Somset
46 J13 Bradley Green Warwks
36 C8 Bradley Green Worcs
46 E5 Bradley in the Moors Staffs
28 B11 Bradley Stoke S Glos
47 Q7 Bradmore Notts
16 K9 Bradney Somset
6 C4 Bradninch Devon
15 P6 Bradninch Devon
46 D2 Bradnop Staffs
34 G9 Bradnor Green Herefs
7 N6 Bradpole Dorset
55 R4 Bradshaw Bolton
63 M14 Bradshaw Calder
56 G4 Bradshaw Kirk
4 K4 Bradstone Devon
55 S14 Bradwall Green Ches E
56 J10 Bradwell Derbys
15 M4 Bradwell Devon
22 K3 Bradwell Essex
30 H4 Bradwell M Keyn
51 T13 Bradwell Norfk
45 U4 Bradwell Crematorium Staffs
23 P6 Bradwell-on-Sea Essex
23 N6 Bradwell Waterside Essex
14 H10 Bradworthy Devon
102 J3 Brae Highld
106 t7 Brae Shet
89 S9 Braeface Falk
99 M13 Braehead Angus
73 L9 Braehead D & G
82 J8 Braehead S Lans
98 B5 Braemar Abers
108 B9 Braemore Highld
112 C11 Braemore Highld
96 C5 Brae Roy Lodge Highld
88 F11 Braeside Inver
98 D12 Braes of Coul Angus
104 D4 Braes of Enzie Moray
106 v16 Braeswick Ork
87 T4 Braevallich Ag & B
69 S8 Brafferton Darltn
63 U5 Brafferton N York
38 B9 Brafield-on-the-Green Nhants
106 h4 Bragar W Isls
31 S8 Bragbury End Herts
82 F9 Braidwood S Lans
46 J5 Brailsford Derbys
46 J5 Brailsford Green Derbys
28 C6 Brain's Green Gloucs
22 J3 Braintree Essex
40 K6 Braiseworth Suffk
9 M3 Braishfield Hants
63 L11 Braithwaite C Brad
66 K8 Braithwaite Cumb
57 R8 Braithwell Donc
57 P3 Braken Hill Wakefd
10 K8 Bramber W Susx
9 P4 Brambridge Hants
47 P6 Bramcote Notts
37 M3 Bramcote Warwks
47 P6 Bramcote Crematorium Notts
9 S3 Bramdean Hants
51 N13 Bramerton Norfk
31 S9 Bramfield Herts
41 Q6 Bramfield Suffk
40 K11 Bramford Suffk
56 C10 Bramhall Stockp
63 U11 Bramham Leeds
63 R11 Bramhope Leeds
19 U9 Bramley Hants
63 Q12 Bramley Leeds
57 Q8 Bramley Rothm
10 G2 Bramley Surrey
19 T9 Bramley Corner Hants
19 U9 Bramley Green Hants
63 N8 Bramley Head N York
13 P4 Bramling Kent
6 B5 Brampford Speke Devon
38 K6 Brampton Cambs
68 E8 Brampton Cumb
76 A13 Brampton Cumb
58 D11 Brampton Lincs
51 M9 Brampton Norfk
57 P6 Brampton Rothm
41 R4 Brampton Suffk
28 B2 Brampton Abbotts Herefs
37 U3 Brampton Ash Nhants
34 J6 Brampton Bryan Herefs
57 Q9 Brampton-en-le-Morthen Rothm
46 E7 Bramshall Staffs
8 K5 Bramshaw Hants
20 B10 Bramshill Hants
10 C4 Bramshott Hants
17 M11 Bramwell Somset
93 N5 Branault Highld
50 C5 Brancaster Norfk
50 C5 Brancaster Staithe Norfk
69 R5 Brancepeth Dur
103 S5 Branchill Moray
49 N4 Brand End Lincs
104 A1 Branderburgh Moray
65 Q10 Brandesburton E R Yk
41 M8 Brandeston Suffk
28 D2 Brand Green Gloucs
14 K12 Brandis Corner Devon
50 K9 Brandiston Norfk
69 R4 Brandon Dur
48 D4 Brandon Lincs
77 L2 Brandon Nthumb
40 C3 Brandon Suffk
37 M5 Brandon Warwks
39 T3 Brandon Bank Norfk
39 T2 Brandon Creek Norfk
50 J12 Brandon Parva Norfk
64 D5 Brandsby N York
58 H7 Brandy Wharf Lincs
2 C11 Brane Cnwll
22 G2 Bran End Essex
8 E10 Branksome Poole
8 F10 Branksome Park Poole
19 P12 Bransbury Hants
58 E11 Bransby Lincs
6 G7 Branscombe Devon
35 S10 Bransford Worcs
8 H9 Bransgore Hants
65 Q13 Bransholme C KuH
35 Q5 Bransley Shrops
36 E6 Branson's Cross Worcs
48 B8 Branston Leics
58 H13 Branston Lincs
46 H9 Branston Staffs
58 J13 Branston Booths Lincs
9 R12 Branstone IoW
48 D3 Brant Broughton Lincs
40 K14 Brantham Suffk
66 G8 Branthwaite Cumb
67 L5 Branthwaite Cumb
65 L14 Brantingham E R Yk
57 T6 Branton Donc
77 L2 Branton Nthumb
63 U7 Branton Green N York
85 M11 Branxton Nthumb
45 M1 Brassey Green Ches W
46 H3 Brassington Derbys
21 S11 Brasted Kent
21 S12 Brasted Chart Kent
99 M4 Brathens Abers
59 S14 Bratoft Lincs
58 F10 Brattleby Lincs
16 B7 Bratton Somset
18 D10 Bratton Wilts
45 P11 Bratton Wrekin
5 M2 Bratton Clovelly Devon
15 P5 Bratton Fleming Devon
17 S11 Bratton Seymour Somset
31 U7 Braughing Herts
22 B3 Braughing Friars Herts
37 P7 Braunston Nhants
48 B12 Braunston Rutlnd
47 Q13 Braunstone Leics
15 L5 Braunton Devon
64 G4 Brawby N York
111 S3 Brawl Highld
70 H11 Braworth N York
20 F7 Bray W & M
37 U4 Braybrooke Nhants
28 K10 Braydon Wilts
28 J9 Braydon Brook Wilts
28 K10 Braydon Side Wilts
15 Q6 Brayford Devon
12 C13 Bray's Hill E Susx
4 J6 Bray Shop Cnwll
66 F11 Braystones Cumb
63 Q10 Braythorn N York
64 E13 Brayton N York
20 E7 Braywick W & M
20 E7 Braywoodside W & M
4 H2 Brazacott Cnwll
12 F2 Breach Kent
13 N6 Breach Kent
31 Q8 Breachwood Green Herts
44 K6 Breaden Heath Shrops
47 L6 Breadsall Derbys
28 D7 Breadstone Gloucs
34 G10 Breadward Herefs
2 G11 Breage Cnwll
102 E7 Breakachy Highld
20 J5 Breakspear Crematorium Gt Lon
108 J6 Brealangwell Lodge Highld
28 B6 Bream Gloucs
8 H5 Breamore Hants
16 J5 Brean Somset
106 e6 Breanais W Isls
56 F1 Brearley Calder
63 S7 Brearton N York
106 h5 Breascleit W Isls
106 h5 Breasclete W Isls
47 N7 Breaston Derbys
25 T4 Brechfa Carmth
99 L11 Brechin Angus
40 G2 Breckles Norfk
26 J2 Brecon Powys
26 J3 Brecon Beacons National Park
56 D8 Bredbury Stockp
12 F12 Brede E Susx
35 P9 Bredenbury Herefs
41 N10 Bredfield Suffk
12 G3 Bredgar Kent
12 E3 Bredhurst Kent
36 B13 Bredon Worcs
36 B13 Bredon's Hardwick Worcs
36 B13 Bredon's Norton Worcs
34 H12 Bredwardine Herefs
47 M9 Breedon on the Hill Leics
82 J6 Breich W Loth
55 R5 Breightmet Bolton
64 G13 Breighton E R Yk
35 L13 Breinton Herefs
18 E6 Bremhill Wilts
15 Q7 Bremridge Devon
12 C7 Brenchley Kent
14 J11 Brendon Devon
15 S3 Brendon Devon
16 D10 Brendon Hill Somset
87 Q9 Brenfield Ag & B
106 e6 Brenish W Isls
77 Q10 Brenkley N u Ty
40 F11 Brent Eleigh Suffk
21 L7 Brentford Gt Lon
47 U10 Brentingby Leics
16 K6 Brent Knoll Somset
5 R9 Brent Mill Devon
22 B1 Brent Pelham Herts
22 E9 Brentwood Essex
12 K10 Brenzett Kent
12 K10 Brenzett Green Kent
46 E10 Brereton Staffs
55 S14 Brereton Green Ches E
55 T13 Brereton Heath Ches E
46 E10 Brereton Hill Staffs
106 v9 Bressay Shet
40 J4 Bressingham Norfk
40 J4 Bressingham Common Norfk
46 J9 Bretby Derbys
46 J9 Bretby Crematorium Derbys
37 M5 Bretford Warwks
36 E12 Bretforton Worcs
55 L2 Bretherton Lancs
106 u8 Brettabister Shet
40 F4 Brettenham Norfk
40 G10 Brettenham Suffk
56 K11 Bretton Derbys
54 J14 Bretton Flints
22 E3 Brewers End Essex
21 P12 Brewer Street Surrey
45 U12 Brewood Staffs
7 V6 Briantspuddle Dorset
22 E2 Brick End Essex
31 T11 Brickendon Herts
31 P12 Bricket Wood Herts
57 M10 Brick Houses Sheff
22 H1 Brickkiln Green Essex
36 C12 Bricklehampton Worcs
60 g2 Bride IoM
66 H6 Bridekirk Cumb
32 C12 Bridell Pembks
5 N3 Bridestowe Devon
104 H8 Brideswell Abers
5 U3 Bridford Devon
13 N5 Bridge Kent
61 M3 Bridge End Cumb
67 N3 Bridge End Cumb
5 R11 Bridge End Devon
69 M5 Bridge End Dur
22 G1 Bridge End Essex
48 H6 Bridge End Lincs
66 G7 Bridgefoot Cumb
39 Q13 Bridge Green Essex
17 Q12 Bridgehampton Somset
63 S5 Bridge Hewick N York
69 N2 Bridgehill Dur
63 P6 Bridgehouse Gate N York
9 R8 Bridgemary Hants
45 R4 Bridgemere Ches E
104 G8 Bridgend Abers
78 E3 Bridgend Ag & B
79 P8 Bridgend Ag & B
98 J10 Bridgend Angus
26 G12 Bridgend Brdgnd
32 C11 Bridgend Cerdgn
67 P10 Bridgend Cumb
75 L4 Bridgend D & G
5 P11 Bridgend Devon
91 N9 Bridgend Fife
104 D9 Bridgend Moray
90 H7 Bridgend P & K
82 K3 Bridgend W Loth
98 D13 Bridgend of Lintrathen Angus
104 H12 Bridge of Alford Abers
89 S6 Bridge of Allan Stirlg
103 U11 Bridge of Avon Moray
103 U8 Bridge of Avon Moray
95 R9 Bridge of Balgie P & K
98 B11 Bridge of Brewlands Angus
103 T11 Bridge of Brown Highld
97 U13 Bridge of Cally P & K
99 M4 Bridge of Canny Abers
98 D13 Bridge of Craigisla Angus
74 D14 Bridge of Dee D & G
99 S2 Bridge of Don C Aber
103 P7 Bridge of Dulsie Highld
99 M6 Bridge of Dye Abers
90 H8 Bridge of Earn P & K
95 Q7 Bridge of Ericht P & K
99 N5 Bridge of Feugh Abers
112 B3 Bridge of Forss Highld
98 F4 Bridge of Gairn Abers
95 Q7 Bridge of Gaur P & K
104 H5 Bridge of Marnoch Abers
94 K11 Bridge of Orchy Ag & B
97 P10 Bridge of Tilt P & K
104 D3 Bridge of Tynet Moray
106 s8 Bridge of Walls Shet
88 J12 Bridge of Weir Rens
15 Q10 Bridge Reeve Devon
14 G12 Bridgerule Devon
34 J1 Bridges Shrops
34 K12 Bridge Sollers Herefs
40 E11 Bridge Street Suffk
4 J3 Bridgetown Cnwll
16 B10 Bridgetown Somset
55 L12 Bridge Trafford Ches W
28 C13 Bridge Yate S Glos
40 G3 Bridgham Norfk
35 R2 Bridgnorth Shrops
16 J9 Bridgwater Somset
16 K10 Bridgwater Services Somset
65 R6 Bridlington E R Yk
7 N6 Bridport Dorset
28 A3 Bridstow Herefs
62 G12 Brierfield Lancs
57 P4 Brierley Barns
28 B4 Brierley Gloucs
35 L9 Brierley Herefs
36 B3 Brierley Hill Dudley
70 G6 Brierton Hartpl
67 L8 Briery Cumb
58 H5 Brigg N Linc
51 P8 Briggate Norfk
71 Q11 Briggswath N York
66 G6 Brigham Cumb
67 L8 Brigham Cumb
65 P9 Brigham E R Yk
56 H2 Brighouse Calder
9 N12 Brighstone IoW
46 J2 Brightgate Derbys
29 S7 Brighthampton Oxon
57 L7 Brightholmlee Sheff
15 P13 Brightley Devon
12 C11 Brightling E Susx
23 Q4 Brightlingsea Essex
11 N10 Brighton Br & H
3 N6 Brighton Cnwll
54 H7 Brighton le Sands Sefton
82 H3 Brightons Falk
19 P5 Brightwalton W Berk
19 P5 Brightwalton Green W Berk
19 P5 Brightwalton Holt W Berk
41 N12 Brightwell Suffk
30 E13 Brightwell Baldwin Oxon
19 S2 Brightwell-cum-Sotwell Oxon
19 U2 Brightwell Upperton Oxon
69 N10 Brignall Dur
89 M4 Brig o'Turk Stirlg
59 N6 Brigsley NE Lin
61 T2 Brigsteer Cumb
38 D3 Brigstock Nhants
30 E10 Brill Bucks
2 J11 Brill Cnwll
34 G11 Brilley Herefs
35 M7 Brimfield Herefs
35 M7 Brimfield Cross Herefs
57 P12 Brimington Derbys
5 U5 Brimley Devon
28 H5 Brimpsfield Gloucs
19 S8 Brimpton W Berk
19 S8 Brimpton Common W Berk
28 G7 Brimscombe Gloucs
54 H10 Brimstage Wirral
57 M10 Brincliffe Sheff
64 G13 Brind E R Yk
17 P9 Brindham Somset
106 s8 Brindister Shet
55 N2 Brindle Lancs
45 T11 Brineton Staffs
38 B2 Bringhurst Leics
35 R9 Bringsty Common Herefs
38 G5 Brington Cambs
50 H7 Briningham Norfk
47 T3 Brinkely Notts
59 Q12 Brinkhill Lincs
39 T10 Brinkley Cambs
37 M5 Brinklow Warwks
28 K11 Brinkworth Wilts
55 P2 Brinscall Lancs
17 M6 Brinscombe Somset
17 M4 Brinsea N Som
47 N4 Brinsley Notts
34 K12 Brinsop Herefs
57 P9 Brinsworth Rothm
50 H6 Brinton Norfk
106 t17 Brinyan Ork
67 P2 Brisco Cumb
50 F9 Brisley Norfk
17 R2 Brislington Bristl
12 H8 Brissenden Green Kent
28 A13 Bristol Bristl
17 P3 Bristol Airport N Som
27 V13 Bristol Zoo Bristl
50 J7 Briston Norfk
5 P7 Brisworthy Devon
56 C2 Britannia Lancs
8 H3 Britford Wilts
27 L7 Brithdir Caerph
43 Q10 Brithdir Gwynd
12 D4 British Legion Village Kent
26 C9 Briton Ferry Neath
19 U2 Britwell Salome Oxon
6 B13 Brixham Torbay
5 P10 Brixton Devon
21 P7 Brixton Gt Lon
18 C13 Brixton Deverill Wilts
37 T6 Brixworth Nhants
29 Q6 Brize Norton Oxon
29 Q6 Brize Norton Airport Oxon
35 U7 Broad Alley Worcs
29 M9 Broad Blunsdon Swindn
56 E8 Broadbottom Tamesd
10 C9 Broadbridge W Susx
10 J4 Broadbridge Heath W Susx
36 G13 Broad Campden Gloucs
56 G3 Broad Carr Calder
8 E3 Broad Chalke Wilts
56 C2 Broad Clough Lancs
6 C5 Broadclyst Devon
88 H11 Broadfield Inver
24 K10 Broadfield Pembks
100 f7 Broadford Highld
12 D8 Broad Ford Kent
10 H6 Broadford Bridge W Susx
75 P3 Broadgairhill Border
40 G8 Broadgrass Green Suffk
39 U8 Broad Green Cambs
23 L3 Broad Green Essex
35 S9 Broad Green Worcs
36 C6 Broad Green Worcs
85 M7 Broadhaugh Border
24 E8 Broad Haven Pembks
55 S9 Broadheath Traffd
35 Q7 Broadheath Worcs
6 F4 Broadhembury Devon
5 U7 Broadhempston Devon
39 S5 Broad Hill Cambs
18 H5 Broad Hinton Wilts
58 E12 Broadholme Lincs
12 F12 Broadland Row E Susx
25 Q9 Broadlay Carmth
19 P8 Broad Layings Hants
22 B6 Broadley Essex
56 C3 Broadley Lancs
104 D3 Broadley Moray
22 B6 Broadley Common Essex
36 F11 Broad Marston Worcs
7 T7 Broadmayne Dorset
45 T4 Broad Meadow Staffs
19 T11 Broadmere Hants
28 B4 Broadmoor Gloucs
24 J9 Broadmoor Pembks
15 R12 Broadnymett Devon
66 H14 Broad Oak Cumb
7 M5 Broadoak Dorset
11 U6 Broad Oak E Susx
12 F12 Broad Oak E Susx
28 C5 Broadoak Gloucs
20 C12 Broad Oak Hants
27 T3 Broad Oak Herefs
13 N3 Broad Oak Kent
55 M7 Broad Oak St Hel
44 J2 Broadoak Wrexhm
41 N5 Broad Road Suffk
22 G5 Broad's Green Essex
13 S2 Broadstairs Kent
27 U7 Broadstone Mons
8 E9 Broadstone Poole
35 M3 Broadstone Shrops
12 G12 Broad Street E Susx
22 E4 Broad Street Essex
12 F4 Broad Street Kent
13 M7 Broad Street Kent
22 J13 Broad Street Medway
18 H9 Broad Street Wilts
23 L6 Broad Street Green Essex
18 G5 Broad Town Wilts
35 S9 Broadwas Worcs
31 R8 Broadwater Herts
10 J10 Broadwater W Susx
35 T5 Broadwaters Worcs
25 N8 Broadway Carmth
25 Q9 Broadway Carmth
24 E8 Broadway Pembks
16 K13 Broadway Somset
41 Q5 Broadway Suffk
36 E13 Broadway Worcs
28 A5 Broadwell Gloucs
29 P2 Broadwell Gloucs
29 Q7 Broadwell Oxon
37 N7 Broadwell Warwks
7 S8 Broadwey Dorset
7 M4 Broadwindsor Dorset
15 P11 Broadwood Kelly Devon
5 L3 Broadwoodwidger Devon
34 H12 Brobury Herefs
100 e5 Brochel Highld
94 E12 Brochroy Ag & B
61 U11 Brock Lancs
35 S10 Brockamin Worcs
9 S5 Brockbridge Hants
41 M5 Brockdish Norfk
35 U6 Brockencote Worcs
9 L8 Brockenhurst Hants
82 F11 Brocketsbrae S Lans
40 K7 Brockford Green Suffk
40 K7 Brockford Street Suffk
37 R8 Brockhall Nhants
21 L13 Brockham Surrey
28 H2 Brockhampton Gloucs
28 K3 Brockhampton Gloucs
9 U7 Brockhampton Hants
28 A1 Brockhampton Herefs
35 Q9 Brockhampton Estate Herefs
7 T3 Brockhampton Green Dorset
56 J4 Brockholes Kirk
57 M14 Brockhurst Derbys
37 N4 Brockhurst Warwks
67 M4 Brocklebank Cumb
58 K4 Brocklesby Lincs
17 N3 Brockley N Som
40 D6 Brockley Suffk
40 B11 Brockley Green Suffk
40 D10 Brockley Green Suffk
67 Q5 Brockleymoor Cumb
36 B3 Brockmoor Dudley
15 L13 Brockscombe Devon
19 R8 Brock's Green Hants
34 H3 Brockton Shrops
35 N2 Brockton Shrops
44 H13 Brockton Shrops
45 R13 Brockton Shrops
45 T7 Brockton Staffs
27 U7 Brockweir Gloucs
9 S3 Brockwood Park Hants
28 G4 Brockworth Gloucs
3 Q3 Brocton Cnwll
46 C10 Brocton Staffs
80 E5 Brodick N Ayrs
103 Q4 Brodie Moray
57 R5 Brodsworth Donc
100 d3 Brogaig Highld
31 L5 Brogborough C Beds
28 H10 Brokenborough Wilts
56 C12 Broken Cross Ches E
55 Q12 Broken Cross Ches W
18 B10 Brokerswood Wilts
54 J10 Bromborough Wirral
40 K5 Brome Suffk
41 L5 Brome Street Suffk
41 P10 Bromeswell Suffk
66 J3 Bromfield Cumb
35 L5 Bromfield Shrops
38 F10 Bromham Bed
18 E7 Bromham Wilts
57 M7 Bromley Barns
36 B3 Bromley Dudley
21 R9 Bromley Gt Lon
35 R1 Bromley Shrops
21 R9 Bromley Common Gt Lon
23 Q2 Bromley Cross Essex
12 J8 Bromley Green Kent
44 H13 Bromlow Shrops
12 E2 Brompton Medway
70 E13 Brompton N York
65 L3 Brompton-by-Sawdon N York
69 R13 Brompton-on-Swale N York
16 E10 Brompton Ralph Somset
16 C10 Brompton Regis Somset
28 C3 Bromsash Herefs
35 R14 Bromsberrow Gloucs
35 R14 Bromsberrow Heath Gloucs
36 C6 Bromsgrove Worcs
45 S10 Bromstead Heath Staffs
35 Q10 Bromyard Herefs
35 Q9 Bromyard Downs Herefs
43 P7 Bronaber Gwynd
33 M7 Bronant Cerdgn
35 M3 Broncroft Shrops
32 F11 Brongest Cerdgn
45 L6 Bronington Wrexhm
34 D14 Bronllys Powys
25 R6 Bronwydd Carmth
34 F11 Bronydd Powys
44 G6 Bronygarth Shrops
53 P7 Bron-y-Nant Crematorium Conwy
25 N9 Brook Carmth
8 K6 Brook Hants
9 L3 Brook Hants
9 M12 Brook IoW
13 L7 Brook Kent
10 E3 Brook Surrey
20 J13 Brook Surrey
51 N14 Brooke Norfk
48 B12 Brooke Rutlnd
59 M7 Brookenby Lincs
38 G8 Brook End Bed
38 J11 Brook End C Beds
38 G6 Brook End Cambs
30 K4 Brook End M Keyn
88 K13 Brookfield Rens
30 D13 Brookhampton Oxon
17 R11 Brookhampton Somset
8 K6 Brook Hill Hants
54 C13 Brook House Denbgs
61 U7 Brookhouse Lancs
57 R9 Brookhouse Rothm
45 T1 Brookhouse Green Ches E
56 F9 Brookhouses Derbys
12 J10 Brookland Kent
55 S8 Brooklands Traffd
31 R12 Brookmans Park Herts
44 D14 Brooks Powys
47 S10 Brooksby Leics
13 Q2 Brooks End Kent
10 J6 Brooks Green W Susx
22 E9 Brook Street Essex
12 H9 Brook Street Kent
40 D11 Brook Street Suffk
11 N5 Brook Street W Susx
28 F5 Brookthorpe Gloucs
40 B1 Brookville Norfk
20 G11 Brookwood Surrey
31 Q4 Broom C Beds
57 P8 Broom Rothm
36 E10 Broom Warwks
41 Q2 Broome Norfk
34 K4 Broome Shrops
36 B5 Broome Worcs
55 R9 Broomedge Warrtn
77 N3 Broome Park Nthumb
10 J6 Broomer's Corner W Susx
10 H7 Broomershill W Susx
22 H5 Broomfield Essex
12 F5 Broomfield Kent
13 N2 Broomfield Kent
16 H10 Broomfield Somset
44 K10 Broomfields Shrops
58 E1 Broomfleet E R Yk
50 G9 Broom Green Norfk
20 G9 Broomhall W & M
77 L13 Broomhaugh Nthumb
57 P6 Broom Hill Barns
8 E8 Broom Hill Dorset
47 P4 Broom Hill Notts
77 Q5 Broomhill Nthumb
36 B5 Broom Hill Worcs
45 P4 Broomhill Green Ches E
77 L13 Broomley Nthumb
69 R4 Broompark Dur
35 R14 Broom's Green Gloucs
50 D8 Broomsthorpe Norfk
12 K3 Broom Street Kent
109 S4 Brora Highld
45 Q13 Broseley Shrops
49 L11 Brotherhouse Bar Lincs
68 K5 Brotherlee Dur
49 L4 Brothertoft Lincs
57 Q1 Brotherton N York
71 L9 Brotton R & Cl
112 B5 Broubster Highld
68 G10 Brough Cumb
56 J10 Brough Derbys
58 F1 Brough E R Yk
112 F2 Brough Highld
48 B2 Brough Notts
106 v7 Brough Shet
45 N5 Broughall Shrops
106 v4 Brough Lodge Shet
68 G10 Brough Sowerby Cumb
83 M11 Broughton Border
30 H10 Broughton Bucks
39 L5 Broughton Cambs
54 H14 Broughton Flints
9 L2 Broughton Hants
61 U13 Broughton Lancs
30 J5 Broughton M Keyn
58 G5 Broughton N Linc
62 J9 Broughton N York
64 H5 Broughton N York
38 B5 Broughton Nhants
37 M13 Broughton Oxon
55 T6 Broughton Salfd
45 S7 Broughton Staffs
16 B2 Broughton V Glam
37 P2 Broughton Astley Leics
61 P3 Broughton Beck Cumb
18 C8 Broughton Gifford Wilts
36 C8 Broughton Green Worcs
36 B10 Broughton Hackett Worcs
61 N2 Broughton-in-Furness Cumb
73 M10 Broughton Mains D & G
61 N1 Broughton Mills Cumb
66 G6 Broughton Moor Cumb
29 P7 Broughton Poggs Oxon
61 N2 Broughton Tower Cumb
91 Q5 Broughty Ferry C Dund
61 P5 Brow End Cumb
68 F11 Brownber Cumb
19 S13 Brown Candover Hants
54 J4 Brown Edge Lancs
46 B3 Brown Edge Staffs
55 L14 Brown Heath Ches W
45 L8 Brownheath Shrops
105 P7 Brownhill Abers
91 R8 Brownhills Fife
46 D12 Brownhills Wsall
85 T14 Brownieside Nthumb
19 S9 Browninghill Green Hants
45 U2 Brown Lees Staffs
45 T1 Brownlow Heath Ches E
66 F8 Brownrigg Cumb
66 J2 Brownrigg Cumb
8 E11 Brownsea Island Dorset
36 E2 Brown's Green Birm
14 G7 Brownsham Devon
28 G7 Browns Hill Gloucs
37 P5 Brownsover Warwks
5 R10 Brownston Devon
40 J8 Brown Street Suffk
49 U10 Brow-of-the-Hill Norfk
51 S13 Browston Green Norfk
65 L1 Broxa N York
31 U11 Broxbourne Herts
84 H3 Broxburn E Loth
83 L4 Broxburn W Loth
77 Q2 Broxfield Nthumb
22 E2 Broxted Essex
45 L3 Broxton Ches W
11 R8 Broyle Side E Susx
112 H9 Bruan Highld
97 N10 Bruar P & K
109 S7 Brucefield Highld
88 D14 Bruchag Ag & B
44 K1 Bruera Ches W
29 Q3 Bruern Abbey Oxon
78 D3 Bruichladdich Ag & B
41 P7 Bruisyard Suffk
41 P7 Bruisyard Street Suffk
58 E5 Brumby N Linc
46 F1 Brund Staffs
51 P12 Brundall Norfk
41 N7 Brundish Suffk
41 N6 Brundish Street Suffk
93 S4 Brunery Highld
2 E9 Brunnion Cnwll
34 J4 Brunslow Shrops
77 Q11 Brunswick Village N u Ty
57 L1 Bruntcliffe Leeds
63 M10 Brunthwaite C Brad
37 R3 Bruntingthorpe Leics
91 M7 Brunton Fife
85 U14 Brunton Nthumb
18 K9 Brunton Wilts
15 Q11 Brushford Devon
16 B11 Brushford Somset
17 S9 Bruton Somset
35 U7 Bryan's Green Worcs
8 B7 Bryanston Dorset
20 E3 Bryant's Bottom Bucks
75 N11 Brydekirk D & G
2 b2 Bryher IoS
44 G3 Brymbo Wrexhm
17 P13 Brympton Somset
25 T10 Bryn Carmth
55 P12 Bryn Ches W
26 E9 Bryn Neath
34 G3 Bryn Shrops
55 N6 Bryn Wigan
26 C5 Brynamman Carmth
24 K3 Brynberian Pembks
26 D9 Brynbryddan Neath
43 M6 Bryn-bwbach Gwynd
26 H11 Bryncae Rhondd
26 G11 Bryncethin Brdgnd
42 J5 Bryncir Gwynd
26 C8 Bryn-coch Neath
42 D7 Bryncroes Gwynd
43 M13 Bryncrug Gwynd
52 D8 Bryn Du IoA
43 P8 Bryn-Eden Gwynd
44 D4 Bryneglwys Denbgs
44 H5 Brynfields Wrexhm
54 E12 Brynford Flints
55 N6 Bryn Gates Wigan
26 J10 Bryn Golau Rhondd
52 E7 Bryngwran IoA
27 R6 Bryngwyn Mons
34 E11 Bryngwyn Powys
24 H3 Bryn-Henllan Pembks
32 F10 Brynhoffnant Cerdgn
61 S14 Bryning Lancs
27 N7 Brynithel Blae G
27 M5 Brynmawr Blae G
42 D7 Bryn-mawr Gwynd
26 G11 Brynmenyn Brdgnd
26 A9 Brynmill Swans
26 H11 Brynna Rhondd
44 D13 Bryn-penarth Powys
52 J10 Brynrefail Gwynd
52 G5 Brynrefail IoA
26 J11 Brynsadler Rhondd
44 C3 Bryn Saith Marchog Denbgs
52 G9 Brynsiencyn IoA
52 G6 Brynteg IoA
54 G14 Bryn-y-bal Flints
53 P7 Bryn-y-Maen Conwy
44 G5 Bryn-yr-Eos Wrexhm
100 d7 Bualintur Highld
54 E11 Buarth-draw Flints
37 L6 Bubbenhall Warwks
64 G12 Bubwith E R Yk
75 R3 Buccleuch Border
89 L8 Buchanan Smithy Stirlg
105 U6 Buchanhaven Abers
90 D6 Buchanty P & K
89 R5 Buchany Stirlg
89 N7 Buchlyvie Stirlg
67 N3 Buckabank Cumb
38 J7 Buckden Cambs
62 J4 Buckden N York
51 Q12 Buckenham Norfk
6 F4 Buckerell Devon
5 S7 Buckfast Devon
5 S7 Buckfastleigh Devon
91 N12 Buckhaven Fife
27 U4 Buckholt Mons
14 J13 Buckhorn Devon
17 U12 Buckhorn Weston Dorset
21 R4 Buckhurst Hill Essex
104 E2 Buckie Moray
30 E6 Buckingham Bucks
30 J10 Buckland Bucks
5 R12 Buckland Devon
36 E13 Buckland Gloucs
9 L9 Buckland Hants
31 U6 Buckland Herts
13 R7 Buckland Kent
29 R8 Buckland Oxon
21 M12 Buckland Surrey
14 K8 Buckland Brewer Devon
30 K11 Buckland Common Bucks
17 U6 Buckland Dinham Somset
15 L11 Buckland Filleigh Devon
5 S6 Buckland in the Moor Devon
5 M7 Buckland Monachorum Devon
7 S3 Buckland Newton Dorset
7 S8 Buckland Ripers Dorset
6 J2 Buckland St Mary Somset
5 T11 Buckland-Tout-Saints Devon
19 S6 Bucklebury W Berk
9 N8 Bucklers Hard Hants
41 M12 Bucklesham Suffk
54 G14 Buckley Flints
36 G7 Buckley Green Warwks
55 R10 Bucklow Hill Ches E
48 C9 Buckminster Leics
46 B4 Bucknall C Stke
59 L13 Bucknall Lincs
30 C7 Bucknell Oxon
34 J6 Bucknell Shrops
104 E2 Buckpool Moray
99 R2 Bucksburn C Aber
14 J8 Buck's Cross Devon
10 H4 Bucks Green W Susx
55 N2 Buckshaw Village Lancs
31 N12 Bucks Hill Herts
10 C2 Bucks Horn Oak Hants
14 J8 Buck's Mills Devon
65 R5 Buckton E R Yk
34 J6 Buckton Herefs
85 R11 Buckton Nthumb
38 H5 Buckworth Cambs
57 T13 Budby Notts
45 R4 Buddileigh Staffs
14 F11 Bude Cnwll
4 J9 Budge's Shop Cnwll
6 C4 Budlake Devon
85 T11 Budle Nthumb
6 E8 Budleigh Salterton Devon
11 R6 Budlett's Common E Susx
2 K10 Budock Water Cnwll
45 Q5 Buerton Ches E
37 S9 Bugbrooke Nhants
5 U10 Bugford Devon
56 C14 Buglawton Ches E
3 Q5 Bugle Cnwll
17 U12 Bugley Dorset
64 H8 Bugthorpe E R Yk
45 P13 Buildwas Shrops
34 B10 Builth Road Powys
34 B10 Builth Wells Powys
30 K10 Bulbourne Herts
8 F2 Bulbridge Wilts
48 G8 Bulby Lincs
18 J12 Bulford Wilts
18 J12 Bulford Camp Wilts
45 M3 Bulkeley Ches E
37 L3 Bulkington Warwks
18 D9 Bulkington Wilts
14 J10 Bulkworthy Devon
70 E14 Bullamoor N York
52 F4 Bull Bay IoA
47 L3 Bullbridge Derbys
20 E9 Bullbrook Br For
31 R11 Bullen's Green Herts
28 E4 Bulley Gloucs
66 G5 Bullgill Cumb
35 M13 Bullinghope Herefs
19 Q12 Bullington Hants
58 J11 Bullington Lincs
13 N2 Bullockstone Kent
31 S9 Bull's Green Herts
41 R2 Bull's Green Norfk
40 D12 Bulmer Essex
64 F6 Bulmer N York
40 D13 Bulmer Tye Essex
22 F10 Bulphan Thurr
6 G7 Bulstone Devon
31 M12 Bulstrode Herts
12 E14 Bulverhythe E Susx
105 Q6 Bulwark Abers
47 P5 Bulwell C Nott
38 E2 Bulwick Nhants
22 B6 Bumble's Green Essex
100 f11 Bunacaimb Highld
101 T14 Bunarkaig Highld
45 N2 Bunbury Ches E
45 N2 Bunbury Heath Ches E
102 H6 Bunchrew Highld
10 J8 Buncton W Susx
101 M6 Bundalloch Highld
86 F1 Bunessan Ag & B
41 P3 Bungay Suffk
49 L3 Bunker's Hill Lincs
86 G11 Bunnahabhain Ag & B
47 Q8 Bunny Notts
102 D9 Buntait Highld
31 U7 Buntingford Herts
40 K2 Bunwell Norfk
40 K2 Bunwell Hill Norfk
46 H6 Bupton Derbys
56 F12 Burbage Derbys
37 M2 Burbage Leics
18 K8 Burbage Wilts
34 H8 Burcher Herefs
12 C9 Burchett's Green E Susx
20 D6 Burchett's Green W & M
8 F2 Burcombe Wilts
30 C13 Burcot Oxon
36 C6 Burcot Worcs
35 R1 Burcote Shrops
30 H9 Burcott Bucks
30 J8 Burcott Bucks
64 K7 Burdale N York
40 F14 Bures Essex
29 Q5 Burford Oxon
35 N7 Burford Shrops
92 K9 Burg Ag & B
40 J5 Burgate Suffk
10 B5 Burgates Hants
31 P6 Burge End Herts
11 N7 Burgess Hill W Susx
41 M10 Burgh Suffk
75 R14 Burgh by Sands Cumb
51 S12 Burgh Castle Norfk
19 Q8 Burghclere Hants
103 T2 Burghead Moray
19 U7 Burghfield W Berk
19 U7 Burghfield Common W Berk
21 M11 Burgh Heath Surrey
12 D10 Burgh Hill E Susx
35 L12 Burghill Herefs
5 Q12 Burgh Island Devon
59 T13 Burgh le Marsh Lincs
51 M8 Burgh next Aylsham Norfk
59 M9 Burgh on Bain Lincs
51 R11 Burgh St Margaret Norfk
41 S2 Burgh St Peter Norfk
57 R4 Burghwallis Donc
12 D3 Burham Kent
9 U5 Buriton Hants
45 P3 Burland Ches E
3 P2 Burlawn Cnwll
28 G7 Burleigh Gloucs
16 E13 Burlescombe Devon
7 U6 Burleston Dorset
5 U11 Burlestone Devon
8 J8 Burley Hants
48 C11 Burley Rutlnd
35 L4 Burley Shrops
45 P5 Burleydam Ches E
35 N11 Burley Gate Herefs
63 P10 Burley in Wharfedale C Brad
8 J8 Burley Lawn Hants
8 J8 Burley Street Hants
63 P11 Burley Wood Head C Brad
51 Q11 Burlingham Green Norfk
34 G9 Burlingjobb Powys
45 S11 Burlington Shrops
45 L8 Burlton Shrops
13 M9 Burmarsh Kent
36 J13 Burmington Warwks
64 D14 Burn N York
56 C8 Burnage Manch
46 J7 Burnaston Derbys
67 R9 Burnbanks Cumb
82 G7 Burnbrae N Lans
64 J10 Burnby E R Yk
57 M7 Burn Cross Sheff
10 F10 Burndell W Susx
55 R5 Burnden Bolton
56 D4 Burnedge Rochdl
67 R13 Burneside Cumb
63 S3 Burneston N York
17 S3 Burnett BaNES
75 T3 Burnfoot Border
75 V2 Burnfoot Border
74 J7 Burnfoot D & G
75 R8 Burnfoot D & G
75 S6 Burnfoot D & G
90 E11 Burnfoot P & K
20 F6 Burnham Bucks
58 J3 Burnham N Linc
50 D5 Burnham Deepdale Norfk
31 S9 Burnham Green Herts
50 D5 Burnham Market Norfk
50 D5 Burnham Norton Norfk
23 M8 Burnham-on-Crouch Essex
16 K7 Burnham-on-Sea Somset
50 D5 Burnham Overy Norfk
50 D5 Burnham Overy Staithe Norfk
50 E5 Burnham Thorpe Norfk
105 U7 Burnhaven Abers
74 G6 Burnhead D & G
105 L12 Burnhervie Abers
45 S13 Burnhill Green Staffs
69 Q3 Burnhope Dur
81 M2 Burnhouse N Ayrs
71 T14 Burniston N York
62 G13 Burnley Lancs
62 G13 Burnley Crematorium Lancs
85 P6 Burnmouth Border
61 Q11 Burn Naze Lancs
89 R5 Burn of Cambus Stirlg
69 Q1 Burnopfield Dur
67 Q1 Burnrigg Cumb
63 L7 Burnsall N York
98 G12 Burnside Angus
98 J13 Burnside Angus
90 J10 Burnside Fife
103 U2 Burnside Moray
83 L3 Burnside W Loth
91 P5 Burnside of Duntrune Angus
20 H12 Burntcommon Surrey
46 H7 Burntheath Derbys
23 Q2 Burnt Heath Essex
19 S6 Burnt Hill W Berk
2 K9 Burnthouse Cnwll
69 P8 Burnt Houses Dur
83 P1 Burntisland Fife
11 S5 Burnt Oak E Susx
46 E12 Burntwood Staffs
46 E12 Burntwood Green Staffs
63 R7 Burnt Yates N York
16 G13 Burnworthy Somset
20 H12 Burpham Surrey
10 G9 Burpham W Susx
77 R11 Burradon N Tyne
76 K4 Burradon Nthumb
106 w2 Burrafirth Shet
2 H10 Burras Cnwll
5 L7 Burraton Cnwll
106 v5 Burravoe Shet
68 E9 Burrells Cumb
90 K4 Burrelton P & K
6 K3 Burridge Devon
15 N5 Burridge Devon
9 Q6 Burridge Hants
63 Q2 Burrill N York
58 D5 Burringham N Linc
15 P9 Burrington Devon
34 K6 Burrington Herefs
17 N5 Burrington N Som
39 T9 Burrough End Cambs
39 T9 Burrough Green Cambs
47 U11 Burrough on the Hill Leics
62 C5 Burrow Lancs
16 B8 Burrow Somset
17 L10 Burrow Bridge Somset
20 G10 Burrowhill Surrey
20 J13 Burrows Cross Surrey
25 S12 Burry Swans
25 S12 Burry Green Swans
25 R10 Burry Port Carmth
54 K4 Burscough Lancs
54 K4 Burscough Bridge Lancs
64 J13 Bursea E R Yk
65 P10 Burshill E R Yk
9 P7 Bursledon Hants
45 U4 Burslem C Stke
40 J12 Burstall Suffk
7 M4 Burstock Dorset
40 K4 Burston Norfk
46 B7 Burston Staffs
11 N2 Burstow Surrey
65 S14 Burstwick E R Yk
62 H2 Burtersett N York
76 A13 Burtholme Cumb
40 C8 Burthorpe Green Suffk
67 P3 Burthwaite Cumb
3 N5 Burthy Cnwll
17 L8 Burtle Hill Somset
49 L6 Burtoft Lincs
54 H12 Burton Ches W
55 M14 Burton Ches W
7 S6 Burton Dorset
8 H10 Burton Dorset
58 G12 Burton Lincs
85 T12 Burton Nthumb
24 G9 Burton Pembks
7 P2 Burton Somset
16 G8 Burton Somset
17 V10 Burton Wilts
18 B5 Burton Wilts
65 Q7 Burton Agnes E R Yk
7 N7 Burton Bradstock Dorset
48 E8 Burton Coggles Lincs
65 R12 Burton Constable Hall E R Yk
37 L10 Burton Dassett Warwks
22 D3 Burton End Essex
39 U11 Burton End Suffk
65 P5 Burton Fleming E R Yk
36 J5 Burton Green Warwks
44 H2 Burton Green Wrexhm
37 M3 Burton Hastings Warwks
61 U4 Burton-in-Kendal Cumb
61 U4 Burton-in-Kendal Services Cumb
62 D5 Burton in Lonsdale N York
47 R5 Burton Joyce Notts
38 D6 Burton Latimer Nhants
47 U10 Burton Lazars Leics
63 S7 Burton Leonard N York
47 Q9 Burton on the Wolds Leics
47 S14 Burton Overy Leics
48 H5 Burton Pedwardine Lincs
65 S13 Burton Pidsea E R Yk
57 Q1 Burton Salmon N York
22 K2 Burton's Green Essex
58 E3 Burton upon Stather N Linc
46 H9 Burton upon Trent Staffs
58 F12 Burton Waters Lincs
55 N8 Burtonwood Warrtn
55 N8 Burtonwood Services Warrtn
45 M2 Burwardsley Ches W
35 P3 Burwarton Shrops
12 C11 Burwash E Susx
11 U6 Burwash Common E Susx
11 V6 Burwash Weald E Susx
39 S7 Burwell Cambs
59 Q11 Burwell Lincs
52 F4 Burwen IoA
106 t21 Burwick Ork
55 T4 Bury Bury
39 L4 Bury Cambs
16 B11 Bury Somset
10 G8 Bury W Susx
31 P5 Bury End C Beds
22 C3 Bury Green Herts
40 E8 Bury St Edmunds Suffk
64 H7 Burythorpe N York
81 R1 Busby E Rens
63 T3 Busby Stoop N York
29 P8 Buscot Oxon
99 P10 Bush Abers
14 F11 Bush Cnwll
35 L10 Bush Bank Herefs
46 B13 Bushbury Wolves
46 B13 Bushbury Crematorium Wolves
47 S13 Bushby Leics
20 K3 Bushey Herts
20 K4 Bushey Heath Herts
41 M3 Bush Green Norfk
40 F9 Bush Green Suffk
21 P3 Bush Hill Park Gt Lon
35 U14 Bushley Worcs
35 U14 Bushley Green Worcs
38 H8 Bushmead Bed
34 K3 Bushmoor Shrops
18 G5 Bushton Wilts
68 D4 Busk Cumb
58 J9 Buslingthorpe Lincs
28 G7 Bussage Gloucs
17 L9 Bussex Somset
11 T5 Butcher's Cross E Susx
17 P4 Butcombe N Som
88 B12 Bute Ag & B
17 P10 Butleigh Somset
17 P9 Butleigh Wootton Somset
30 H11 Butler's Cross Bucks
47 P4 Butler's Hill Notts
36 K10 Butlers Marston Warwks
41 Q10 Butley Suffk
41 Q11 Butley High Corner Suffk
64 G8 Buttercrambe N York
84 K6 Butterdean Border
69 P7 Butterknowle Dur
6 C3 Butterleigh Devon
47 M3 Butterley Derbys
66 J9 Buttermere Cumb
19 M8 Buttermere Wilts
45 T3 Butters Green Staffs
63 N14 Buttershaw C Brad
90 G2 Butterstone P & K
45 T5 Butterton Staffs
46 E2 Butterton Staffs
70 E6 Butterwick Dur
49 N4 Butterwick Lincs
64 G4 Butterwick N York
65 M5 Butterwick N York
45 Q3 Butt Green Ches E
44 F12 Buttington Powys
35 R5 Buttonbridge Shrops
35 S5 Buttonoak Shrops
9 N7 Buttsash Hants
14 G12 Buttsbear Cross Cnwll
22 J7 Butt's Green Essex
40 H9 Buxhall Suffk
40 H9 Buxhall Fen Street Suffk
11 R6 Buxted E Susx
56 G12 Buxton Derbys
51 M9 Buxton Norfk
51 L9 Buxton Heath Norfk
27 M3 Bwlch Powys
44 G3 Bwlchgwyn Wrexhm
33 L9 Bwlchllan Cerdgn
25 Q6 Bwlchnewydd Carmth
42 F8 Bwlchtocyn Gwynd
44 E10 Bwlch-y-cibau Powys
44 E9 Bwlch-y-Ddar Powys
32 H11 Bwlchyfadfa Cerdgn
34 C1 Bwlch-y-ffridd Powys
25 M3 Bwlch-y-groes Pembks
25 U11 Bwlchymyrdd Swans
34 B6 Bwlch-y-sarnau Powys
69 Q1 Byermoor Gatesd
69 R6 Byers Green Dur
37 P10 Byfield Nhants
20 J10 Byfleet Surrey
34 J12 Byford Herefs
31 S5 Bygrave Herts
77 R13 Byker N u Ty
64 C4 Byland Abbey N York
53 S10 Bylchau Conwy
55 R13 Byley Ches W
25 T11 Bynea Carmth
76 F5 Byrness Nthumb
6 D8 Bystock Devon
38 G5 Bythorn Cambs
34 J8 Byton Herefs
77 L13 Bywell Nthumb
10 F6 Byworth W Susx

Cabbacott - Clifton 127

C

14 K8 Cabbacott Devon
58 K6 Cabourne Lincs
78 H3 Cabrach Ag & B
104 D10 Cabrach Moray
61 T10 Cabus Lancs
11 R5 Cackle Street E Susx
12 C12 Cackle Street E Susx
12 F12 Cackle Street E Susx
6 B3 Cadbury Devon
15 Q9 Cadbury Barton Devon
89 P11 Cadder E Duns
31 N9 Caddington C Beds
84 D11 Caddonfoot Border
57 R6 Cadeby Donc
47 M13 Cadeby Leics
6 B3 Cadeleigh Devon
11 U6 Cade Street E Susx
2 J14 Cadgwith Cnwll
91 L11 Cadham Fife
55 R8 Cadishead Salfd
25 V11 Cadle Swans
61 U13 Cadley Lancs
18 K10 Cadley Wilts
18 K7 Cadley Wilts
20 C4 Cadmore End Bucks
9 L6 Cadnam Hants
58 H6 Cadney N Linc
54 F14 Cadole Flints
16 F3 Cadoxton V Glam
26 D8 Cadoxton Juxta-Neath Neath
44 B6 Cadwst Denbgs
52 H10 Caeathro Gwynd
26 E5 Caehopkin Powys
58 G9 Caenby Lincs
33 N12 Caeo Carmth
26 F9 Caerau Brdgnd
27 L12 Caerau Cardif
26 E5 Cae'r-bont Powys
25 U8 Cae'r bryn Carmth
43 N10 Caerdeon Gwynd
24 C5 Caer Farchell Pembks
52 D7 Caergeiliog IoA
44 H2 Caergwrle Flints
53 N8 Caerhun Conwy
75 S5 Caerlanrig Border
27 Q9 Caerleon Newpt
27 Q9 Caerleon Roman Amphitheatre Newpt
52 G10 Caernarfon Gwynd
52 G10 Caernarfon Castle Gwynd
27 M10 Caerphilly Caerph
34 B2 Caersws Powys
32 G9 Caerwedros Cerdgn
27 T9 Caerwent Mons
54 D12 Caerwys Flints
43 Q10 Caerynwch Gwynd
27 R4 Caggle Street Mons
52 K6 Caim IoA
106 d12 Cairinis W Isls
87 Q7 Cairnbaan Ag & B
105 S2 Cairnbulg Abers
85 M6 Cairncross Border
88 H11 Cairncurran Inver
88 E3 Cairndow Ag & B
82 K1 Cairneyhill Fife
72 D10 Cairngarroch D & G
97 T3 Cairngorms National Park
104 F7 Cairnie Abers
105 P7 Cairnorrie Abers
72 D6 Cairnryan D & G
104 C5 Cairnty Moray
51 T11 Caister-on-Sea Norfk
58 K6 Caistor Lincs
51 M13 Caistor St Edmund Norfk
35 U6 Cakebole Worcs
40 J2 Cake Street Norfk
40 G13 Calais Street Suffk
106 h5 Calanais W Isls
9 N11 Calbourne IoW
59 Q11 Calceby Lincs
54 E12 Calcot Flints
29 L5 Calcot Gloucs
19 U6 Calcot W Berk
19 U6 Calcot Row W Berk
104 B3 Calcots Moray
13 N3 Calcott Kent
44 K11 Calcott Shrops
63 S8 Calcutt N York
29 M9 Calcutt Wilts
67 M4 Caldbeck Cumb
63 M2 Caldbergh N York
38 H3 Caldecote Cambs
39 M9 Caldecote Cambs
31 R5 Caldecote Herts
37 S10 Caldecote Nhants
39 N9 Caldecote Highfields Cambs
38 E7 Caldecott Nhants
29 U8 Caldecott Oxon
38 C2 Caldecott RutInd
30 J5 Caldecotte M Keyn
66 F12 Calder Cumb
82 E6 Calderbank N Lans
66 F11 Calder Bridge Cumb
56 D3 Calderbrook Rochdl
82 F5 Caldercruix N Lans
57 M3 Calder Grove Wakefd
81 T4 Caldermill S Lans
56 D3 Caldermore Rochdl
61 U10 Calder Vale Lancs
81 T1 Calderwood S Lans
24 K11 Caldey Island Pembks
27 T10 Caldicot Mons
46 D14 Caldmore Wsall
69 Q10 Caldwell N York
54 F9 Caldy Wirral
26 B2 Caledfwlch Carmth
3 L8 Calenick Cnwll
60 b9 Calf of Man IoM
40 B11 Calford Green Suffk
106 u16 Calfsound Ork
92 K8 Calgary Ag & B
103 S4 Califer Moray
82 H3 California Falk
51 T10 California Norfk
5 S10 California Cross Devon
47 L9 Calke Derbys
107 L13 Callakille Highld
89 P4 Callander Stirlg
106 h5 Callanish W Isls
45 P14 Callaughton Shrops
2 K6 Callestick Cnwll
100 f9 Calligarry Highld
4 K7 Callington Cnwll
46 G9 Callingwood Staffs
35 L14 Callow Herefs
35 T10 Callow End Worcs
28 K11 Callow Hill Wilts
35 R6 Callow Hill Worcs
36 D8 Callow Hill Worcs
35 N7 Callows Grave Worcs
9 L6 Calmore Hants
28 K6 Calmsden Gloucs
18 E6 Calne Wilts
57 P12 Calow Derbys
9 P8 Calshot Hants
5 L7 Calstock Cnwll
18 F7 Calstone Wellington Wilts
51 L7 Calthorpe Norfk
51 R8 Calthorpe Street Norfk
67 Q4 Calthwaite Cumb
62 J8 Calton N York
46 F4 Calton Staffs
45 N2 Calveley Ches E
56 K12 Calver Derbys
45 P6 Calverhall Shrops
34 J11 Calver Hill Herefs
6 B2 Calverleigh Devon
63 Q12 Calverley Leeds
56 K12 Calver Sough Derbys
30 E8 Calvert Bucks
30 G5 Calverton M Keyn
47 R4 Calverton Notts
97 N10 Calvine P & K
66 H2 Calvo Cumb
83 M11 Calzeat Border
28 E8 Cam Gloucs
93 T6 Camasachoirce Highld
93 T6 Camasine Highld
101 N6 Camas Luinie Highld
100 e6 Camastianavaig Highld
102 F7 Camault Muir Highld
12 J12 Camber E Susx
20 E10 Camberley Surrey
21 P7 Camberwell Gt Lon
57 T1 Camblesforth N York
77 L8 Cambo Nthumb
77 S9 Cambois Nthumb
2 G8 Camborne Cnwll
39 M9 Cambourne Cambs
39 Q9 Cambridge Cambs
28 D7 Cambridge Gloucs
39 Q9 Cambridge Airport Cambs
39 N8 Cambridge City Crematorium Cambs
2 H7 Cambrose Cnwll
90 C13 Cambus Clacks
109 P5 Cambusavie Platform Highld
89 S7 Cambusbarron Stirlg
89 T7 Cambuskenneth Stirlg
89 P13 Cambuslang S Lans
98 G4 Cambus o' May Abers
82 K11 Cambuswallace S Lans
21 N6 Camden Town Gt Lon
17 R5 Cameley BaNES
4 E4 Camelford Cnwll
82 G2 Camelon Falk
103 R9 Camerory Highld
35 S13 Camer's Green Worcs
17 S5 Camerton BaNES
66 F6 Camerton Cumb
95 R7 Camghouran P & K
84 F12 Camieston Border
99 S4 Cammachmore Abers
58 F10 Cammeringham Lincs
109 P7 Camore Highld
79 N11 Campbeltown Ag & B
79 M11 Campbeltown Airport Ag & B
77 R11 Camperdown N Tyne
74 G7 Cample D & G
90 K4 Campmuir P & K
83 L5 Camps W Loth
57 R4 Campsall Donc
41 P9 Campsea Ash Suffk
39 T12 Camps End Cambs
31 P5 Campton C Beds
76 D3 Camptown Border
24 F6 Camrose Pembks
90 B2 Camserney P & K
94 F4 Camusnagaul Highld
107 U7 Camusnagaul Highld
100 g5 Camusteel Highld
100 g5 Camusterrach Highld
8 K5 Canada Hants
61 Q4 Canal Foot Cumb
24 J7 Canaston Bridge Pembks
98 E4 Candacraig Abers
59 S13 Candlesby Lincs
40 H6 Candle Street Suffk
45 M12 Candover Green Shrops
83 L10 Candy Mill Border
19 U5 Cane End Oxon
23 M9 Canewdon Essex
8 E8 Canford Bottom Dorset
8 F11 Canford Cliffs Poole
27 V12 Canford Crematorium Bristl
8 E10 Canford Heath Poole
8 E9 Canford Magna Poole
40 J7 Canhams Green Suffk
112 H2 Canisbay Highld
57 P8 Canklow Rothm
36 K5 Canley Covtry
36 K5 Canley Crematorium Covtry
8 B4 Cann Dorset
100 b9 Canna Highld
102 B9 Cannich Highld
16 J9 Cannington Somset
21 R6 Canning Town Gt Lon
46 C11 Cannock Staffs
46 C10 Cannock Chase Staffs
46 D11 Cannock Wood Staffs
34 K12 Cannon Bridge Herefs
75 S10 Canonbie D & G
35 P12 Canon Frome Herefs
35 L11 Canon Pyon Herefs
37 Q10 Canons Ashby Nhants
2 E9 Canonstown Cnwll
13 M4 Canterbury Kent
13 N4 Canterbury Cathedral Kent
51 Q13 Cantley Norfk
45 M12 Cantlop Shrops
27 M12 Canton Cardif
103 L6 Cantraywood Highld
62 C5 Cantsfield Lancs
22 J11 Canvey Island Essex
58 G13 Canwick Lincs
4 G2 Canworthy Water Cnwll
94 G3 Caol Highld
106 h9 Caolas Scalpaigh W Isls
92 D9 Caoles Ag & B
101 R13 Caonich Highld
12 B7 Capel Kent
10 K2 Capel Surrey
33 N4 Capel Bangor Cerdgn
33 M9 Capel Betws Lleucu Cerdgn
52 G6 Capel Coch IoA
53 M11 Capel Curig Conwy
32 G11 Capel Cynon Cerdgn
25 S6 Capel Dewi Carmth
32 J12 Capel Dewi Cerdgn
33 M4 Capel-Dewi Cerdgn
53 P11 Capel Garmon Conwy
41 Q11 Capel Green Suffk
25 S6 Capel Gwyn Carmth
52 D7 Capel Gwyn IoA
26 C3 Capel Gwynfe Carmth
25 U8 Capel Hendre Carmth
25 U5 Capel Isaac Carmth
25 N3 Capel Iwan Carmth
13 Q8 Capel le Ferne Kent
6 d2 Capelles Guern
26 K12 Capel Llanilltern Cardif
52 F8 Capel Mawr IoA
52 F5 Capel Parc IoA
41 Q11 Capel St Andrew Suffk
40 J13 Capel St Mary Suffk
33 M5 Capel Seion Cerdgn
33 P5 Capel Trisant Cerdgn
42 H4 Capeluchaf Gwynd
53 M7 Capelulo Conwy
27 P1 Capel-y-ffin Powys
52 H9 Capel-y-graig Gwynd
54 J12 Capenhurst Ches W
61 U5 Capernwray Lancs
77 L9 Capheaton Nthumb
88 K14 Caplaw E Rens
41 N7 Capon's Green Suffk
83 P14 Cappercleuch Border
12 E2 Capstone Medway
5 U10 Capton Devon
16 E9 Capton Somset
90 G3 Caputh P & K
4 H6 Caradon Town Cnwll
89 M10 Carbeth Inn Stirlg
3 Q5 Carbis Cnwll
2 E9 Carbis Bay Cnwll
100 c6 Carbost Highld
100 d5 Carbost Highld
57 N9 Carbrook Sheff
50 F13 Carbrooke Norfk
57 T12 Carburton Notts
3 Q6 Carclaze Cnwll
47 T5 Car Colston Notts
57 R5 Carcroft Donc
90 K12 Cardenden Fife
44 J11 Cardeston Shrops
67 N2 Cardewlees Cumb
103 U7 Cardhu Moray
27 M12 Cardiff Cardif
16 E3 Cardiff Airport V Glam
27 N11 Cardiff Gate Services Cardif
26 K12 Cardiff West Services Cardif
32 C11 Cardigan Cerdgn
39 T11 Cardinal's Green Cambs
38 G11 Cardington Bed
35 M1 Cardington Shrops
4 E7 Cardinham Cnwll
72 E13 Cardrain D & G
83 R11 Cardrona Border
88 H10 Cardross Ag & B
88 H10 Cardross Crematorium Ag & B
72 E13 Cardryne D & G
75 N14 Cardurnock Cumb
48 F10 Careby Lincs
98 J11 Careston Angus
24 H10 Carew Pembks
24 H10 Carew Cheriton Pembks
24 H10 Carew Newton Pembks
27 V1 Carey Herefs
82 E7 Carfin N Lans
84 E8 Carfraemill Border
51 Q11 Cargate Green Norfk
74 J10 Cargenbridge D & G
90 J4 Cargill P & K
75 S14 Cargo Cumb
5 L8 Cargreen Cnwll
3 M9 Cargurrel Cnwll
84 K11 Carham Nthumb
16 D8 Carhampton Somset
2 J8 Carharrack Cnwll
95 S7 Carie P & K
106 d12 Carinish W Isls
9 P11 Carisbrooke IoW
61 R4 Cark Cumb
5 L8 Carkeel Cnwll
106 h4 Carlabhagh W Isls
3 M6 Carland Cross Cnwll
69 R9 Carlbury Darltn
48 F11 Carlby Lincs
76 G3 Carlcroft Nthumb
56 J6 Carlecotes Barns
2 G10 Carleen Cnwll
63 Q5 Carlesmoor N York
66 F11 Carleton Cumb
67 P2 Carleton Cumb
67 R7 Carleton Cumb
61 Q12 Carleton Lancs
62 K10 Carleton N York
57 Q2 Carleton Wakefd
61 Q12 Carleton Crematorium Bpool
50 J12 Carleton Forehoe Norfk
40 K2 Carleton Rode Norfk
51 P13 Carleton St Peter Norfk
2 K11 Carlidnack Cnwll
104 K7 Carlincraig Abers
17 S5 Carlingcott BaNES
71 M9 Carlin How R & Cl
67 N1 Carlisle Cumb
75 U13 Carlisle Airport Cumb
67 N2 Carlisle Crematorium Cumb
3 M3 Carloggas Cnwll
83 N7 Carlops Border
106 h4 Carloway W Isls
57 N4 Carlton Barns
38 E9 Carlton Bed
39 T10 Carlton Cambs
57 M1 Carlton Leeds
47 L13 Carlton Leics
57 T2 Carlton N York
63 M3 Carlton N York
64 E2 Carlton N York
47 R5 Carlton Notts
70 E8 Carlton S on T
41 Q8 Carlton Suffk
41 T3 Carlton Colville Suffk
37 S1 Carlton Curlieu Leics
39 T10 Carlton Green Cambs
64 B4 Carlton Husthwaite N York
70 H12 Carlton-in-Cleveland N York
57 S10 Carlton in Lindrick Notts
48 D2 Carlton-le-Moorland Lincs
63 T3 Carlton Miniott N York
58 C14 Carlton-on-Trent Notts
48 D4 Carlton Scroop Lincs
82 F8 Carluke S Lans
3 R6 Carlyon Bay Cnwll
82 E13 Carmacoup S Lans
25 R6 Carmarthen Carmth
25 U7 Carmel Carmth
54 E11 Carmel Flints
52 G12 Carmel Gwynd
82 H11 Carmichael S Lans
46 B4 Carmountside Crematorium C Stke
89 N14 Carmunnock C Glas
89 P13 Carmyle C Glas
91 R3 Carmyllie Angus
65 Q6 Carnaby E R Yk
91 R10 Carnbee Fife
90 G11 Carnbo P & K
2 H8 Carn Brea Cnwll
105 P10 Carnbrogie Abers
101 M6 Carndu Highld
81 T3 Carnduff S Lans
2 K12 Carne Cnwll
3 N9 Carne Cnwll
3 P5 Carne Cnwll
81 P6 Carnell E Ayrs
3 M3 Carnewas Cnwll
61 T5 Carnforth Lancs
101 P7 Carn-gorm Highld
24 D5 Carnhedryn Pembks
2 G9 Carnhell Green Cnwll
99 Q2 Carnie Abers
2 H8 Carnkie Cnwll
2 J10 Carnkie Cnwll
2 K6 Carnkiet Cnwll
33 U1 Carno Powys
90 F14 Carnock Fife
2 K8 Carnon Downs Cnwll
104 K5 Carnousie Abers
91 S5 Carnoustie Angus
3 Q5 Carnsmerry Cnwll
82 J9 Carnwath S Lans
2 B10 Carnyorth Cnwll
36 J5 Carol Green Solhll
3 P6 Carpalla Cnwll
63 L2 Carperby N York
57 R8 Carr Rothm
79 Q8 Carradale Ag & B
103 P11 Carrbridge Highld
56 E6 Carrbrook Tamesd
7 c2 Carrefour Jersey
52 E5 Carreglefn IoA
57 M2 Carr Gate Wakefd
58 C5 Carrhouse N Linc
87 S8 Carrick Ag & B
88 E7 Carrick Castle Ag & B
82 K2 Carriden Falk
49 M2 Carrington Lincs
83 R6 Carrington Mdloth
55 R8 Carrington Traffd
43 Q4 Carrog Conwy
44 D5 Carrog Denbgs
82 G2 Carron Falk
103 V7 Carron Moray
74 G6 Carronbridge D & G
89 R9 Carron Bridge Stirlg
82 G2 Carronshore Falk
27 S9 Carrow Hill Mons
68 H3 Carr Shield Nthumb
75 M11 Carrutherstown D & G
88 J12 Carruth House Inver
57 Q13 Carr Vale Derbys
70 D4 Carrville Dur
86 J1 Carsaig Ag & B
72 J6 Carseriggan D & G
74 J14 Carsethorn D & G
21 N10 Carshalton Gt Lon
46 J3 Carsington Derbys
79 M14 Carskey Ag & B
73 M9 Carsluith D & G
81 R14 Carsphairn D & G
82 H9 Carstairs S Lans
82 J9 Carstairs Junction S Lans
29 R8 Carswell Marsh Oxon
9 L4 Carter's Clay Hants
22 D5 Carters Green Essex
29 Q6 Carterton Oxon
69 M2 Carterway Heads Nthumb
3 Q5 Carthew Cnwll
63 S3 Carthorpe N York
77 L5 Cartington Nthumb
82 G9 Cartland S Lans
57 M11 Cartledge Derbys
61 R4 Cartmel Cumb
61 S2 Cartmel Fell Cumb
25 S9 Carway Carmth
75 T11 Carwinley Cumb
28 F6 Cashe's Green Gloucs
8 D6 Cashmoor Dorset
29 U5 Cassington Oxon
70 D5 Cassop Colliery Dur
2 D11 Castallack Cnwll
6 d3 Castel Guern
53 N9 Castell Conwy
27 P9 Castell-y-bwch Torfn
62 C4 Casterton Cumb
3 R5 Castle Cnwll
50 D10 Castle Acre Norfk
38 C9 Castle Ashby Nhants
106 b19 Castlebay W Isls
63 L1 Castle Bolton N York
36 F3 Castle Bromwich Solhll
48 E10 Castle Bytham Lincs
24 H5 Castlebythe Pembks
44 E12 Castle Caereinion Powys
39 T12 Castle Camps Cambs
67 R1 Castle Carrock Cumb
89 S10 Castlecary Falk
17 R10 Castle Cary Somset
18 B5 Castle Combe Wilts
47 M8 Castle Donington Leics
74 E13 Castle Douglas D & G
29 M8 Castle Eaton Swindn
70 F5 Castle Eden Dur
48 H12 Castle End C Pete
57 P1 Castleford Wakefd
35 Q11 Castle Frome Herefs
2 D10 Castle Gate Cnwll
61 U1 Castle Green Cumb
20 G10 Castle Green Surrey
46 J10 Castle Gresley Derbys
40 C13 Castle Hedingham Essex
83 P11 Castlehill Border
112 E3 Castlehill Highld
12 C7 Castle Hill Kent
40 K11 Castle Hill Suffk
88 J10 Castlehill W Duns
72 E8 Castle Kennedy D & G
87 U6 Castle Lachlan Ag & B
24 F11 Castlemartin Pembks
89 N14 Castlemilk C Glas
24 F4 Castle Morris Pembks
35 S13 Castlemorton Worcs
35 S13 Castlemorton Common Worcs
75 P7 Castle O'er D & G
44 K13 Castle Pulverbatch Shrops
67 L8 Castlerigg Stone Circle Cumb
49 U9 Castle Rising Norfk
69 N3 Castleside Dur
102 K6 Castle Stuart Highld
30 H4 Castlethorpe M Keyn
58 G5 Castlethorpe N Linc
75 V8 Castleton Border
56 J10 Castleton Derbys
71 L11 Castleton N York
27 P11 Castleton Newpt
56 C4 Castleton Rochdl
7 S10 Castletown Dorset
112 E3 Castletown Highld
60 d9 Castletown IoM
77 T14 Castletown Sundld
63 R10 Castley N York
50 G14 Caston Norfk
48 H14 Castor C Pete
25 U13 Caswell Bay Swans
79 S6 Catacol N Ayrs
56 F12 Cat and Fiddle Derbys
27 V11 Catbrain S Glos
27 U7 Catbrook Mons
54 F12 Catch Flints
2 C11 Catchall Cnwll
36 J5 Catchem's Corner Solhll
69 Q2 Catchgate Dur
57 P9 Catcliffe Rothm
18 F5 Catcomb Wilts
17 L9 Catcott Somset
17 M8 Catcott Burtle Somset
21 P11 Caterham Surrey
51 Q9 Catfield Norfk
51 R9 Catfield Common Norfk
21 Q8 Catford Gt Lon
61 T12 Catforth Lancs
89 N13 Cathcart C Glas
27 L2 Cathedine Powys
36 G4 Catherine-de-Barnes Solhll
63 M14 Catherine Slack C Brad
9 T6 Catherington Hants
7 L6 Catherston Leweston Dorset
35 Q5 Catherton Shrops
9 R7 Catisfield Hants
35 Q12 Catley Herefs
56 C3 Catley Lane Head Rochdl
96 J5 Catlodge Highld
62 H12 Catlow Lancs
75 U10 Catlowdy Cumb
39 Q13 Catmere End Essex
19 Q4 Catmore W Berk
5 T6 Caton Devon
61 U7 Caton Lancs
62 B6 Caton Green Lancs
5 R5 Cator Court Devon
81 Q7 Catrine E Ayrs
27 R9 Cat's Ash Newpt
12 D13 Catsfield E Susx
12 D13 Catsfield Stream E Susx
17 P11 Catsgore Somset
17 Q10 Catsham Somset
36 C6 Catshill Worcs
35 R1 Catstree Shrops
79 M13 Cattadale Ag & B
63 U9 Cattal N York
40 K14 Cattawade Suffk
61 T11 Catterall Lancs
45 N5 Catteralslane Shrops
69 R13 Catterick N York
69 R13 Catterick Bridge N York
69 Q13 Catterick Garrison N York
67 Q6 Catterlen Cumb
99 R8 Catterline Abers
64 C10 Catterton N York
10 F2 Catteshall Surrey
37 Q5 Catthorpe Leics
40 E7 Cattishall Suffk
7 Q5 Cattistock Dorset
63 T4 Catton N York
76 G14 Catton Nthumb
65 Q10 Catwick E R Yk
38 G6 Catworth Cambs
28 H5 Caudle Green Gloucs
31 M4 Caulcott C Beds
30 B8 Caulcott Oxon
91 U2 Cauldcots Angus
89 P7 Cauldhame Stirlg
76 A2 Cauldmill Border
46 E4 Cauldon Staffs
46 E4 Cauldon Lowe Staffs
46 J10 Cauldwell Derbys
66 D1 Caulkerbush D & G
75 T9 Caulside D & G
7 S2 Caundle Marsh Dorset
35 U4 Caunsall Worcs
47 T1 Caunton Notts
9 U4 Causeway Hants
61 T2 Causeway End Cumb
73 L8 Causeway End D & G
22 G4 Causeway End Essex
82 K11 Causewayend S Lans
66 H2 Causewayhead Cumb
89 T6 Causewayhead Stirlg
105 Q12 Causeyend Abers
77 P7 Causey Park Nthumb
77 P7 Causey Park Bridge Nthumb
40 D11 Cavendish Suffk
40 C6 Cavenham Suffk
30 C7 Caversfield Oxon
20 B8 Caversham Readg
46 C5 Caverswall Staffs
84 J13 Caverton Mill Border
64 H13 Cavil E R Yk
103 M5 Cawdor Highld
59 N11 Cawkwell Lincs
64 D12 Cawood N York
5 L10 Cawsand Cnwll
50 K9 Cawston Norfk
37 N6 Cawston Warwks
64 H2 Cawthorn N York
57 L5 Cawthorne Barns
64 E4 Cawton N York
39 M9 Caxton Cambs
39 M9 Caxton End Cambs
39 L8 Caxton Gibbet Cambs
35 N6 Caynham Shrops
48 D4 Caythorpe Lincs
47 S4 Caythorpe Notts
65 P3 Cayton N York
106 c12 Ceann a Bhaigh W Isls
101 U9 Ceannacroc Lodge Highld
106 i6 Cearsiadar W Isls
27 U7 Ceciliford Mons
27 P10 Cefn Newpt
53 S9 Cefn Berain Conwy
43 T3 Cefn-brith Conwy
26 C5 Cefn-bryn-brain Carmth
26 E5 Cefn Byrle Powys
44 F7 Cefn Canel Powys
44 D8 Cefn Coch Powys
26 J6 Cefn-coed-y-cymmer Myr Td
26 F11 Cefn Cribwr Brdgnd
26 F11 Cefn Cross Brdgnd
43 U6 Cefn-ddwysarn Gwynd
34 G3 Cefn-Einion Shrops
25 U8 Cefneithin Carmth
33 T11 Cefngorwydd Powys
44 G5 Cefn-mawr Wrexhm
26 J7 Cefnpennar Rhondd
44 H2 Cefn-y-bedd Flints
25 L5 Cefn-y-pant Carmth
52 G7 Ceint IoA
33 M11 Cellan Cerdgn
91 S11 Cellardyke Fife
46 C4 Cellarhead Staffs
67 Q7 Celleron Cumb
27 N8 Celynen Caerph
52 E4 Cemaes IoA
43 R12 Cemmaes Powys
43 R13 Cemmaes Road Powys
32 E12 Cenarth Cerdgn
24 D5 Cerbyd Pembks
91 P9 Ceres Fife
7 S4 Cerne Abbas Dorset
29 L8 Cerney Wick Gloucs
52 F8 Cerrigceinwen IoA
43 U4 Cerrigydrudion Conwy
51 R10 Cess Norfk
52 H10 Ceunant Gwynd
28 G1 Chaceley Gloucs
2 K8 Chacewater Cnwll
30 E5 Chackmore Bucks
37 N12 Chacombe Nhants
36 D11 Chadbury Worcs
56 D5 Chadderton Oldham
56 D5 Chadderton Fold Oldham
47 L6 Chaddesden C Derb
35 U6 Chaddesley Corbett Worcs
5 M5 Chaddlehanger Devon
19 P5 Chaddleworth W Berk
29 R3 Chadlington Oxon
36 K10 Chadshunt Warwks
47 U9 Chadwell Leics
45 S11 Chadwell Shrops
38 G7 Chadwell End Bed
21 S5 Chadwell Heath Gt Lon
22 F12 Chadwell St Mary Thurr
35 T7 Chadwick Worcs
36 H6 Chadwick End Solhll
55 M7 Chadwick Green St Hel
7 L2 Chaffcombe Somset
22 F12 Chafford Hundred Thurr
5 S3 Chagford Devon
11 P7 Chailey E Susx
49 P13 Chainbridge Cambs
12 D6 Chainhurst Kent
8 E7 Chalbury Dorset
8 E7 Chalbury Common Dorset
21 P11 Chaldon Surrey
9 P13 Chale IoW
9 P13 Chale Green IoW
20 H4 Chalfont Common Bucks
20 G4 Chalfont St Giles Bucks
20 H4 Chalfont St Peter Bucks
28 G7 Chalford Gloucs
30 F12 Chalford Oxon
18 C10 Chalford Wilts
31 M7 Chalgrave C Beds
30 D13 Chalgrove Oxon
22 G13 Chalk Kent
22 F5 Chalk End Essex
20 B7 Chalkhouse Green Oxon
7 L3 Chalkway Somset
12 G3 Chalkwell Kent
5 R12 Challaborough Devon
15 Q4 Challacombe Devon
72 K6 Challoch D & G
12 K5 Challock Kent
7 Q4 Chalmington Dorset
31 M7 Chalton C Beds
38 H10 Chalton C Beds
9 U5 Chalton Hants
20 G7 Chalvey Slough
11 S9 Chalvington E Susx
12 H7 Chambers Green Kent
20 J3 Chandler's Cross Herts
35 S13 Chandlers Cross Worcs
9 N5 Chandler's Ford Hants
38 H9 Channel's End Bed
65 P13 Chanterlands Crematorium C KuH
17 T7 Chantry Somset
40 K12 Chantry Suffk
66 K6 Chapel Cumb
91 L13 Chapel Fife
63 S12 Chapel Allerton Leeds
17 M6 Chapel Allerton Somset
3 P1 Chapel Amble Cnwll
37 T7 Chapel Brampton Nhants
39 L2 Chapelbridge Cambs
45 T6 Chapel Chorlton Staffs
11 U6 Chapel Cross E Susx
38 H9 Chapel End Bed
31 N4 Chapel End C Beds
38 H4 Chapel End Cambs
36 K2 Chapel End Warwks
40 B13 Chapelend Way Essex
56 G10 Chapel-en-le-Frith Derbys
55 S5 Chapel Field Bury
49 P9 Chapelgate Lincs
36 J3 Chapel Green Warwks
37 N8 Chapel Green Warwks
57 S1 Chapel Haddlesey N York
82 E6 Chapelhall N Lans
105 T8 Chapel Hill Abers
48 K3 Chapel Hill Lincs
27 U8 Chapel Hill Mons
63 S10 Chapel Hill N York
75 P2 Chapelhope Border
75 R11 Chapelknowe D & G
34 H5 Chapel Lawn Shrops
62 E4 Chapel le Dale N York
16 F11 Chapel Leigh Somset
56 G10 Chapel Milton Derbys
105 L11 Chapel of Garioch Abers
72 E11 Chapel Rossan D & G
11 U8 Chapel Row E Susx
22 J7 Chapel Row Essex
19 S7 Chapel Row W Berk
61 N3 Chapels Cumb
59 U12 Chapel St Leonards Lincs
67 M11 Chapel Stile Cumb
91 T2 Chapelton Angus
15 N7 Chapelton Devon
82 C9 Chapelton S Lans
55 R3 Chapeltown Bl w D
3 M5 Chapel Town Cnwll
104 A11 Chapeltown Moray
57 N7 Chapeltown Sheff
18 B11 Chapmanslade Wilts
4 K2 Chapmans Well Devon
31 T9 Chapmore End Herts
23 L2 Chappel Essex
4 J7 Charaton Cnwll
6 K3 Chard Somset
6 K4 Chard Junction Somset
6 K2 Chardleigh Green Somset
6 K4 Chardstock Devon
28 D9 Charfield S Glos
28 H4 Chargrove Gloucs
12 J6 Charing Kent
12 J6 Charing Crematorium Kent
12 H6 Charing Heath Kent
12 J5 Charing Hill Kent
36 G13 Charingworth Gloucs
29 S4 Charlbury Oxon
17 T3 Charlcombe BaNES
18 E5 Charlcutt Wilts
36 J9 Charlecote Warwks
36 D2 Charlemont Sandw
15 Q6 Charles Devon
10 D2 Charleshill Surrey
91 N2 Charleston Angus
99 S3 Charlestown C Aber
63 P12 Charlestown C Brad
56 E1 Charlestown Calder
3 Q6 Charlestown Cnwll
56 F8 Charlestown Derbys
7 S9 Charlestown Dorset
83 L2 Charlestown Fife
102 H6 Charlestown Highld
107 P10 Charlestown Highld
55 T6 Charlestown Salfd
40 H10 Charles Tye Suffk
56 F8 Charlesworth Derbys
16 H9 Charlinch Somset
91 L9 Charlottetown Fife
21 R7 Charlton Gt Lon
19 N11 Charlton Hants
31 Q7 Charlton Herts
30 B5 Charlton Nhants
76 G9 Charlton Nthumb
29 T10 Charlton Oxon
16 J11 Charlton Somset
17 R8 Charlton Somset
17 S6 Charlton Somset
20 J9 Charlton Surrey
10 D8 Charlton W Susx
8 C4 Charlton Wilts
28 J10 Charlton Wilts
35 T6 Charlton Worcs
36 D11 Charlton Worcs
45 N11 Charlton Wrekin
28 K3 Charlton Abbots Gloucs
17 P11 Charlton Adam Somset
8 H4 Charlton-All-Saints Wilts
7 S5 Charlton Down Dorset
45 N12 Charlton Hill Shrops
17 S12 Charlton Horethorne Somset
28 J3 Charlton Kings Gloucs
17 P11 Charlton Mackrell Somset
8 C8 Charlton Marshall Dorset
17 T11 Charlton Musgrove Somset
30 C9 Charlton-on-Otmoor Oxon
8 B8 Charlton on the Hill Dorset
18 H9 Charlton St Peter Wilts
9 T2 Charlwood Hants
11 L2 Charlwood Surrey
7 S6 Charminster Dorset
7 L6 Charmouth Dorset
30 E8 Charndon Bucks
29 S9 Charney Bassett Oxon
55 N3 Charnock Green Lancs
55 N3 Charnock Richard Lancs
55 N3 Charnock Richard Crematorium Lancs
55 M3 Charnock Richard Services Lancs
41 N9 Charsfield Suffk
12 E5 Chart Corner Kent
19 S9 Charter Alley Hants
84 K9 Charterhall Border
17 N5 Charterhouse Somset
89 S7 Chartershall Stirlg
29 R5 Charterville Allotments Oxon
13 M5 Chartham Kent
13 M4 Chartham Hatch Kent
12 E6 Chart Hill Kent
30 K12 Chartridge Bucks
12 F6 Chart Sutton Kent
12 F5 Chartway Street Kent
20 C7 Charvil Wokham
37 P9 Charwelton Nhants
46 D12 Chase Terrace Staffs
46 D12 Chasetown Staffs
29 P2 Chastleton Oxon
14 H12 Chasty Devon
62 F11 Chatburn Lancs
45 S7 Chatcull Staffs
27 N10 Chatham Caerph
12 E2 Chatham Medway
22 H4 Chatham Green Essex
85 T13 Chathill Nthumb
35 U8 Chatley Worcs
57 L12 Chatsworth House Derbys
22 J13 Chattenden Medway
22 C2 Chatter End Essex
39 N3 Chatteris Cambs
55 S3 Chatterton Lancs
40 J12 Chattisham Suffk
76 F2 Chatto Border
85 R13 Chatton Nthumb
31 N8 Chaul End C Beds
15 R10 Chawleigh Devon
29 U7 Chawley Oxon
38 J9 Chawston Bed
19 V13 Chawton Hants
28 D5 Chaxhill Gloucs
19 U5 Chazey Heath Oxon
46 D5 Cheadle Staffs
56 C9 Cheadle Stockp
56 C9 Cheadle Heath Stockp
56 C9 Cheadle Hulme Stockp
21 M10 Cheam Gt Lon
20 F9 Cheapside W & M
30 F10 Chearsley Bucks
45 U8 Chebsey Staffs
19 U4 Checkendon Oxon
45 R4 Checkley Ches E
35 N13 Checkley Herefs
46 D6 Checkley Staffs
45 R4 Checkley Green Ches E
40 C9 Chedburgh Suffk
17 N6 Cheddar Somset
30 K9 Cheddington Bucks
46 C3 Cheddleton Staffs
46 C3 Cheddleton Heath Staffs
16 H11 Cheddon Fitzpaine Somset
28 H9 Chedglow Wilts
51 Q14 Chedgrave Norfk
7 N3 Chedington Dorset
41 Q5 Chediston Suffk
41 Q5 Chediston Green Suffk
29 L5 Chedworth Gloucs
16 K9 Chedzoy Somset
12 K8 Cheeseman's Green Kent
55 T6 Cheetham Hill Manch
15 R10 Cheldon Devon
55 T12 Chelford Ches E
47 L7 Chellaston C Derb
38 E9 Chellington Bed
35 R3 Chelmarsh Shrops
35 L2 Chelmick Shrops
41 M13 Chelmondiston Suffk
56 H13 Chelmorton Derbys
22 H6 Chelmsford Essex
22 G6 Chelmsford Crematorium Essex
36 G3 Chelmsley Wood Solhll
21 N7 Chelsea Gt Lon
21 S10 Chelsfield Gt Lon
21 Q11 Chelsham Surrey
16 G12 Chelston Somset
40 G11 Chelsworth Suffk
28 H3 Cheltenham Gloucs
28 J3 Cheltenham Crematorium Gloucs
38 E7 Chelveston Nhants
17 N3 Chelvey N Som
17 R4 Chelwood BaNES
11 Q5 Chelwood Common E Susx
11 Q4 Chelwood Gate E Susx
28 J9 Chelworth Wilts
29 L9 Chelworth Lower Green Wilts
29 L9 Chelworth Upper Green Wilts
34 K4 Cheney Longville Shrops
20 H3 Chenies Bucks
27 U9 Chepstow Mons
55 Q5 Chequerbent Bolton
49 Q12 Chequers Corner Norfk
18 F6 Cherhill Wilts
28 H8 Cherington Gloucs
36 J13 Cherington Warwks
15 R3 Cheriton Devon
9 R3 Cheriton Hants
13 P8 Cheriton Kent
25 S12 Cheriton Swans
5 T2 Cheriton Bishop Devon
15 U11 Cheriton Fitzpaine Devon
24 G11 Cheriton or Stackpole Elidor Pembks
45 Q10 Cherrington Wrekin
65 M11 Cherry Burton E R Yk
39 Q9 Cherry Hinton Cambs
35 U10 Cherry Orchard Worcs
58 H12 Cherry Willingham Lincs
20 H9 Chertsey Surrey
30 B7 Cherwell Valley Services Oxon
7 U5 Cheselbourne Dorset
31 L12 Chesham Bucks
55 T4 Chesham Bury
20 G3 Chesham Bois Bucks
31 U12 Cheshunt Herts
7 R9 Chesil Beach Dorset
12 G3 Chesley Kent
46 C12 Cheslyn Hay Staffs
36 G6 Chessetts Wood Warwks
21 L10 Chessington Gt Lon
21 L10 Chessington World of Adventures Gt Lon
54 K13 Chester Ches W
17 S8 Chesterblade Somset
54 K13 Chester Cathedral Ches W
54 J13 Chester Crematorium Ches W
57 N12 Chesterfield Derbys
46 E12 Chesterfield Staffs
57 N12 Chesterfield Crematorium Derbys
47 M1 Chesterfield Services Derbys
83 S6 Chesterhill Mdloth
69 S2 Chester-le-Street Dur
69 S3 Chester Moor Dur
76 C3 Chesters Border
84 G14 Chesters Border
55 L12 Chester Services Ches W
38 H1 Chesterton Cambs
39 Q8 Chesterton Cambs
28 K7 Chesterton Gloucs
30 C8 Chesterton Oxon
35 S1 Chesterton Shrops
45 T4 Chesterton Staffs
37 L9 Chesterton Green Warwks
76 G12 Chesterwood Nthumb
54 K12 Chester Zoo Ches W
13 M2 Chestfield Kent
12 G3 Chestnut Street Kent
5 R9 Cheston Devon
45 R7 Cheswardine Shrops
85 Q9 Cheswick Nthumb
36 F5 Cheswick Green Solhll
7 R3 Chetnole Dorset
6 C2 Chettiscombe Devon
39 R4 Chettisham Cambs
8 D6 Chettle Dorset
35 Q2 Chetton Shrops
30 D7 Chetwode Bucks
45 R9 Chetwynd Wrekin
45 S10 Chetwynd Aston Wrekin
39 U8 Cheveley Cambs
21 S11 Chevening Kent
9 P12 Cheverton IoW
40 C9 Chevington Suffk
76 F4 Cheviot Hills
16 C13 Chevithorne Devon
17 Q4 Chew Magna BaNES
55 Q5 Chew Moor Bolton
17 Q4 Chew Stoke BaNES
17 S3 Chewton Keynsham BaNES
17 Q6 Chewton Mendip Somset
15 P13 Chichacott Devon
38 D11 Chicheley M Keyn
10 D10 Chichester W Susx
10 D9 Chichester Crematorium W Susx
7 R8 Chickerell Dorset
41 M5 Chickering Suffk
8 C2 Chicklade Wilts
34 G10 Chickward Herefs
9 T5 Chidden Hants
10 F3 Chiddingfold Surrey
11 S8 Chiddingly E Susx
21 T14 Chiddingstone Kent
21 T13 Chiddingstone Causeway Kent
7 M6 Chideock Dorset
10 B10 Chidham W Susx
57 L2 Chidswell Kirk
19 Q6 Chieveley W Berk
22 G5 Chignall St James Essex
22 G5 Chignall Smealy Essex
21 R4 Chigwell Essex
21 S4 Chigwell Row Essex
19 N12 Chilbolton Hants
9 Q3 Chilcomb Hants
7 P6 Chilcombe Dorset
17 R6 Chilcompton Somset
46 J11 Chilcote Leics
54 J11 Childer Thornton Ches W
8 A6 Child Okeford Dorset
29 S10 Childrey Oxon
45 Q8 Child's Ercall Shrops
36 E13 Childswickham Worcs
54 K9 Childwall Lpool
31 P10 Childwick Bury Herts
31 P10 Childwick Green Herts
7 Q5 Chilfrome Dorset
10 C8 Chilgrove W Susx
13 L5 Chilham Kent
14 K12 Chilla Devon
5 L4 Chillaton Devon
13 Q5 Chillenden Kent
9 P12 Chillerton IoW
41 Q10 Chillesford Suffk
85 R13 Chillingham Nthumb
5 T12 Chillington Devon
7 L2 Chillington Somset
8 D2 Chilmark Wilts
12 J7 Chilmington Green Kent
29 R4 Chilson Oxon
5 L6 Chilsworthy Cnwll
14 H11 Chilsworthy Devon
31 P9 Chiltern Green C Beds
20 C3 Chiltern Hills
20 F3 Chilterns Crematorium Bucks
17 P13 Chilthorne Domer Somset
30 E10 Chilton Bucks
15 U12 Chilton Devon
69 S7 Chilton Dur
13 Q7 Chilton Kent
29 U10 Chilton Oxon
40 E12 Chilton Suffk
19 S12 Chilton Candover Hants
17 Q12 Chilton Cantelo Somset
19 M6 Chilton Foliat Wilts
17 L8 Chilton Polden Somset
40 C11 Chilton Street Suffk
16 J9 Chilton Trinity Somset
47 P6 Chilwell Notts
9 N5 Chilworth Hants
20 H13 Chilworth Surrey
29 S7 Chimney Oxon
19 U9 Chineham Hants
21 Q4 Chingford Gt Lon
56 F10 Chinley Derbys
30 G12 Chinnor Oxon
76 H10 Chipchase Castle Nthumb
45 R7 Chipnall Shrops
39 U7 Chippenham Cambs
18 D6 Chippenham Wilts
31 M12 Chipperfield Herts
31 U6 Chipping Herts
62 C11 Chipping Lancs
36 G13 Chipping Campden Gloucs
22 K4 Chipping Hill Essex
29 R2 Chipping Norton Oxon
22 E7 Chipping Ongar Essex
28 D11 Chipping Sodbury S Glos
37 N11 Chipping Warden Nhants
16 D11 Chipstable Somset
21 T11 Chipstead Kent
21 N11 Chipstead Surrey
44 G14 Chirbury Shrops
44 G6 Chirk Wrexhm
85 M7 Chirnside Border
85 M7 Chirnsidebridge Border
18 G9 Chirton Wilts
19 L7 Chisbury Wilts
7 N2 Chiselborough Somset
18 J4 Chiseldon Swindn
30 C13 Chiselhampton Oxon
75 T3 Chisholme Border
21 R8 Chislehurst Gt Lon
13 P3 Chislet Kent
63 L14 Chisley Calder
31 P12 Chiswell Green Herts
21 M7 Chiswick Gt Lon
39 N11 Chiswick End Cambs
56 E8 Chisworth Derbys
12 F11 Chitcombe E Susx
10 C6 Chithurst W Susx
39 Q7 Chittering Cambs
18 E12 Chitterne Wilts
15 Q8 Chittlehamholt Devon
15 P7 Chittlehampton Devon
18 E7 Chittoe Wilts
5 T13 Chivelstone Devon
15 M6 Chivenor Devon
72 E7 Chlenry D & G
20 G10 Chobham Surrey
18 K12 Cholderton Wilts
30 K11 Cholesbury Bucks
76 J11 Chollerford Nthumb
76 J11 Chollerton Nthumb
45 P2 Cholmondeston Ches E
19 S3 Cholsey Oxon
35 L9 Cholstrey Herefs
70 J13 Chop Gate N York
77 R9 Choppington Nthumb
77 N14 Chopwell Gatesd
45 N3 Chorley Ches E
55 N3 Chorley Lancs
35 Q4 Chorley Shrops
46 E11 Chorley Staffs
20 H3 Chorleywood Herts
20 H3 Chorleywood West Herts
45 R3 Chorlton Ches E
55 T8 Chorlton-cum-Hardy Manch
45 L4 Chorlton Lane Ches W
34 J3 Choulton Shrops
45 L2 Chowley Ches W
39 P13 Chrishall Essex
88 F11 Chrisswell Inver
39 Q1 Christchurch Cambs
8 H10 Christchurch Dorset
27 V5 Christchurch Gloucs
27 Q10 Christchurch Newpt
18 E5 Christian Malford Wilts
54 K13 Christleton Ches W
20 B4 Christmas Common Oxon
17 L5 Christon N Som
85 U14 Christon Bank Nthumb
5 U3 Christow Devon
10 J5 Christ's Hospital W Susx
11 R4 Chuck Hatch E Susx
5 V5 Chudleigh Devon
5 U5 Chudleigh Knighton Devon
15 Q10 Chulmleigh Devon
56 F8 Chunal Derbys
62 E14 Church Lancs
28 E4 Churcham Gloucs
45 R10 Church Aston Wrekin
37 T7 Church Brampton Nhants
68 G10 Church Brough Cumb
46 H7 Church Broughton Derbys
2 J14 Church Cove Cnwll
20 D12 Church Crookham Hants
28 G4 Churchdown Gloucs
45 T10 Church Eaton Staffs
38 G9 Church End Bed
38 H9 Church End Bed
30 F11 Church End Bucks
31 L6 Church End C Beds
31 L8 Church End C Beds
31 M6 Church End C Beds
31 M9 Church End C Beds
31 Q5 Church End C Beds
38 J10 Church End C Beds
38 G6 Church End Cambs
38 K4 Church End Cambs
39 M5 Church End Cambs
39 Q9 Church End Cambs
22 F3 Church End Essex
22 H2 Church End Essex
22 H4 Church End Essex
23 P9 Churchend Essex
35 U13 Church End Gloucs
21 M4 Church End Gt Lon
19 U9 Church End Hants
22 B3 Church End Herts
31 P10 Church End Herts
31 S6 Church End Herts
48 K7 Church End Lincs
59 R7 Church End Lincs
36 H2 Church End Warwks
36 J2 Church End Warwks
29 S2 Church Enstone Oxon
64 C12 Church Fenton N York
36 D2 Churchfield Sandw
31 T12 Churchgate Herts
22 C5 Churchgate Street Essex
6 G5 Church Green Devon
46 J10 Church Gresley Derbys
29 T5 Church Hanborough Oxon
46 D11 Church Hill Staffs
71 L13 Church Houses N York
6 J4 Churchill Devon
15 N4 Churchill Devon
17 M5 Churchill N Som
29 Q3 Churchill Oxon
35 U5 Churchill Worcs
36 B10 Churchill Worcs
6 H2 Churchinford Somset
8 C12 Church Knowle Dorset
58 D11 Church Laneham Notts
37 T2 Church Langton Leics
37 N5 Church Lawford Warwks
45 T2 Church Lawton Ches E
46 D6 Church Leigh Staffs
36 D10 Church Lench Worcs
46 G5 Church Mayfield Staffs
45 Q1 Church Minshull Ches E
10 D11 Church Norton W Susx
37 P4 Churchover Warwks
45 M14 Church Preen Shrops
44 K13 Church Pulverbatch Shrops
6 G2 Churchstanton Somset
34 G2 Churchstoke Powys
5 S11 Churchstow Devon
37 R9 Church Stowe Nhants
40 C12 Church Street Essex
22 H13 Church Street Kent
41 S4 Church Street Suffk
35 L2 Church Stretton Shrops
59 P7 Churchthorpe Lincs
61 Q11 Churchtown Bpool
4 D5 Churchtown Cnwll
57 L14 Churchtown Derbys
15 Q4 Churchtown Devon
60 g4 Churchtown IoM
61 T11 Churchtown Lancs
58 C5 Church Town N Linc
54 J3 Churchtown Sefton
26 K10 Church Village Rhondd
57 S13 Church Warsop Notts
47 M7 Church Wilne Derbys
76 D10 Churnsike Lodge Nthumb
6 B13 Churston Ferrers Torbay
10 D3 Churt Surrey
44 K2 Churton Ches W
63 R14 Churwell Leeds
42 H6 Chwilog Gwynd
2 D10 Chyandour Cnwll
2 H12 Chyanvounder Cnwll
2 K8 Chyeowling Cnwll
2 D10 Chysauster Cnwll
2 H12 Chyvarloe Cnwll
44 E13 Cil Powys
54 E13 Cilcain Flints
32 K8 Cilcennin Cerdgn
44 F13 Cilcewydd Powys
26 D7 Cilfrew Neath
26 K9 Cilfynydd Rhondd
32 C12 Cilgerran Pembks
26 C2 Cilgwyn Carmth
52 G12 Cilgwyn Gwynd
32 K9 Ciliau-Aeron Cerdgn
26 C6 Cilmaengwyn Neath
34 B10 Cilmery Powys
25 N4 Cilrhedyn Pembks
25 U6 Cilsan Carmth
43 S5 Ciltalgarth Gwynd
33 Q13 Cilycwm Carmth
26 D8 Cimla Neath
28 C5 Cinderford Gloucs
36 B2 Cinder Hill Wolves
20 G6 Cippenham Slough
28 K7 Cirencester Gloucs
69 R13 Citadilla N York
21 P6 City Gt Lon
26 H12 City V Glam
21 R6 City Airport Gt Lon
52 G5 City Dulas IoA
21 R5 City of London Crematorium Gt Lon
92 F7 Clabhach Ag & B
88 D9 Clachaig Ag & B
79 P4 Clachan Ag & B
87 P2 Clachan Ag & B
94 B10 Clachan Ag & B
100 e6 Clachan Highld
106 d12 Clachan-a-Luib W Isls
92 B9 Clachan Mor Ag & B
106 d12 Clachan na Luib W Isls
89 P10 Clachan of Campsie E Duns
87 P2 Clachan-Seil Ag & B
102 H6 Clachnaharry Highld
110 A11 Clachtoll Highld
97 U11 Clackavoid P & K
21 R12 Clacket Lane Services Surrey
90 D13 Clackmannan Clacks
104 A4 Clackmarras Moray
23 S4 Clacton-on-Sea Essex
88 C1 Cladich Ag & B
36 E9 Cladswell Worcs
93 S9 Claggan Highld
100 b4 Claigan Highld
17 S5 Clandown BaNES
9 T5 Clanfield Hants
29 Q7 Clanfield Oxon
15 R12 Clannaborough Devon
19 M11 Clanville Hants
17 R10 Clanville Somset
79 R4 Claonaig Ag & B
8 E8 Clapgate Dorset
22 B3 Clapgate Herts
38 F10 Clapham Bed
6 A7 Clapham Devon
21 N7 Clapham Gt Lon
62 E6 Clapham N York
10 H9 Clapham W Susx
38 F10 Clapham Green Bed
13 L8 Clap Hill Kent
67 N12 Clappersgate Cumb
7 M3 Clapton Somset
17 R6 Clapton Somset
27 T13 Clapton-in-Gordano N Som
29 N4 Clapton-on-the-Hill Gloucs
15 Q8 Clapworthy Devon
33 M4 Clarach Cerdgn
77 N13 Claravale Gatesd
24 J6 Clarbeston Pembks
24 H6 Clarbeston Road Pembks
58 B10 Clarborough Notts
40 C11 Clare Suffk
74 E12 Clarebrand D & G
75 L12 Clarencefield D & G
77 L12 Clarewood Nthumb
76 A2 Clarilaw Border
19 S10 Clarken Green Hants
10 K3 Clark's Green Surrey
89 N14 Clarkston E Rens
109 N7 Clashmore Highld
110 A10 Clashmore Highld
110 B10 Clashnessie Highld
104 A11 Clashnoir Moray
90 E7 Clathy P & K
90 F7 Clathymore P & K
104 G10 Clatt Abers
33 U2 Clatter Powys
22 F5 Clatterford End Essex
16 E10 Clatworthy Somset
61 U11 Claughton Lancs
62 B6 Claughton Lancs
54 H9 Claughton Wirral
16 J10 Clavelshay Somset
36 G7 Claverdon Warwks
17 N3 Claverham N Som
22 C1 Clavering Essex
35 S2 Claverley Shrops
17 U4 Claverton BaNES
17 U4 Claverton Down BaNES
26 K12 Clawdd-coch V Glam
44 C3 Clawdd-newydd Denbgs
61 U4 Clawthorpe Cumb
14 J13 Clawton Devon
58 K8 Claxby Lincs
59 S12 Claxby Lincs
64 F8 Claxton N York
51 P13 Claxton Norfk
37 N3 Claybrooke Magna Leics
41 S4 Clay Common Suffk
37 Q5 Clay Coton Nhants
57 N14 Clay Cross Derbys
37 N11 Claydon Oxon
40 K11 Claydon Suffk
31 T8 Clay End Herts
75 S10 Claygate D & G
12 D7 Claygate Kent
21 L10 Claygate Surrey
12 B4 Claygate Cross Kent
21 R4 Clayhall Gt Lon
16 D12 Clayhanger Devon
46 D13 Clayhanger Wsall
16 G13 Clayhidon Devon
12 F11 Clayhill E Susx
9 L7 Clayhill Hants
39 R8 Clayhithe Cambs
112 E5 Clayock Highld
39 N10 Claypit Hill Cambs
28 E6 Claypits Gloucs
48 B4 Claypole Lincs
59 R11 Claythorpe Lincs
63 N13 Clayton C Brad
57 Q5 Clayton Donc
11 M8 Clayton W Susx
55 N2 Clayton Green Lancs
62 F13 Clayton-le-Moors Lancs
55 N2 Clayton-le-Woods Lancs
57 L4 Clayton West Kirk
58 B9 Clayworth Notts
100 d11 Cleadale Highld
77 T13 Cleadon S Tyne
5 N7 Clearbrook Devon
27 V6 Clearwell Gloucs
28 A6 Clearwell Meend Gloucs
69 S10 Cleasby N York
106 t21 Cleat Ork
69 P9 Cleatlam Dur
66 F10 Cleator Cumb
66 F9 Cleator Moor Cumb
56 J1 Cleckheaton Kirk
35 N4 Cleedownton Shrops
35 N5 Cleehill Shrops
82 E7 Cleekhimin N Lans
35 N4 Clee St Margaret Shrops
35 N5 Cleestanton Shrops
59 P5 Cleethorpes NE Lin
35 P5 Cleeton St Mary Shrops
17 N3 Cleeve N Som
19 T4 Cleeve Oxon
28 J2 Cleeve Hill Gloucs
36 E11 Cleeve Prior Worcs
84 F2 Cleghornie E Loth
34 K13 Clehonger Herefs
90 G12 Cleish P & K
82 E7 Cleland N Lans
31 M10 Clement's End C Beds
22 D13 Clement Street Kent
94 C13 Clenamacrie Ag & B
18 J7 Clench Common Wilts
49 S9 Clenchwarton Norfk
105 M3 Clenerty Abers
36 B5 Clent Worcs
35 Q5 Cleobury Mortimer Shrops
35 P3 Cleobury North Shrops
79 M9 Cleongart Ag & B
103 M5 Clephanton Highld
75 Q6 Clerkhill D & G
74 F5 Cleuch-head D & G
18 G5 Clevancy Wilts
17 M2 Clevedon N Som
29 S3 Cleveley Oxon
61 Q11 Cleveleys Lancs
28 J10 Cleverton Wilts
17 M6 Clewer Somset
50 H5 Cley next the Sea Norfk
67 S8 Cliburn Cumb
19 T11 Cliddesden Hants
46 H14 Cliff Warwks
62 E13 Cliffe Lancs
22 H12 Cliffe Medway
64 F13 Cliffe N York
69 R9 Cliffe N York
12 G13 Cliff End E Susx
22 H13 Cliffe Woods Medway
34 F11 Clifford Herefs
63 U11 Clifford Leeds
36 G10 Clifford Chambers Warwks
28 D3 Clifford's Mesne Gloucs
13 R3 Cliffsend Kent
27 V13 Clifton Bristl
31 Q5 Clifton C Beds
47 P7 Clifton C Nott
64 D9 Clifton C York

57 T13 Edwinstowe Notts
31 R4 Edworth C Beds
35 P9 Edwyn Ralph Herefs
99 L10 Edzell Angus
99 L10 Edzell Woods Abers
26 D8 Efail-fach Neath
26 K11 Efail Isaf Rhondd
42 G6 Efailnewydd Gwynd
44 E8 Efail-Rhyd Powys
24 K5 Efailwen Carmth
44 D2 Efenechtyd Denbgs
75 R7 Effgill D & G
20 K12 Effingham Surrey
46 G10 Efflinch Staffs
15 U12 Efford Devon
5 N9 Efford Crematorium C Plym
19 P10 Egbury Hants
10 F6 Egdean W Susx
55 R4 Egerton Bolton
12 H6 Egerton Kent
12 G6 Egerton Forstal Kent
57 S2 Eggborough N York
5 N9 Eggbuckland C Plym
15 Q10 Eggesford Devon
31 L7 Eggington C Beds
46 J8 Egginton Derbys
70 F10 Egglescliffe S on T
69 L8 Eggleston Dur
20 H8 Egham Surrey
20 G8 Egham Wick Surrey
48 C12 Egleton Rutlnd
77 N2 Eglingham Nthumb
3 Q2 Egloshayle Cnwll
4 H3 Egloskerry Cnwll
53 P8 Eglwysbach Conwy
16 D3 Eglwys-Brewis V Glam
45 L5 Eglwys Cross Wrexhm
33 N1 Eglwys Fach Cerdgn
24 K3 Eglwyswrw Pembks
58 B13 Egmanton Notts
66 F10 Egremont Cumb
54 H8 Egremont Wirral
71 P11 Egton N York
71 P12 Egton Bridge N York
20 G5 Egypt Bucks
19 Q12 Egypt Hants
93 M1 Eigg Highld
23 M2 Eight Ash Green Essex
100 h8 Eilanreach Highld
33 Q4 Eisteddfa Gurig Cerdgn
33 S8 Elan Valley Powys
33 T8 Elan Village Powys
28 B10 Elberton S Glos
10 E10 Elbridge W Susx
5 N10 Elburton C Plym
18 H4 Elcombe Swindn
19 N7 Elcot W Berk
49 M14 Eldernell Cambs
28 E1 Eldersfield Worcs
88 K13 Elderslie Rens
39 S14 Elder Street Essex
69 R7 Eldon Dur
63 N11 Eldwick C Brad
99 Q6 Elfhill Abers
85 T12 Elford Nthumb
46 G11 Elford Staffs
103 V3 Elgin Moray
100 e8 Elgol Highld
13 N7 Elham Kent
91 Q11 Elie Fife
76 K4 Elilaw Nthumb
52 E6 Elim IoA
9 M6 Eling Hants
57 U11 Elkesley Notts
28 J5 Elkstone Gloucs
104 J4 Ella Abers
6 B12 Ellacombe Torbay
56 H2 Elland Calder
56 H2 Elland Lower Edge Calder
87 N10 Ellary Ag & B
46 F5 Ellastone Staffs
61 T8 Ellel Lancs
84 J6 Ellemford Border
87 N2 Ellenabeich Ag & B
66 F5 Ellenborough Cumb
55 R6 Ellenbrook Salfd
45 T8 Ellenhall Staffs
10 H3 Ellen's Green Surrey
70 F13 Ellerbeck N York
71 N10 Ellerby N York
45 P9 Ellerdine Heath Wrekin
6 C4 Ellerhayes Devon
94 E9 Elleric Ag & B
65 L14 Ellerker E R Yk
63 L11 Ellers N York
64 G12 Ellerton E R Yk
69 S13 Ellerton N York
45 R8 Ellerton Shrops
30 H11 Ellesborough Bucks
44 J7 Ellesmere Shrops
54 K11 Ellesmere Port Ches W
8 G7 Ellingham Hants
41 Q2 Ellingham Norfk
85 T13 Ellingham Nthumb
63 P3 Ellingstring N York
38 J6 Ellington Cambs
77 R7 Ellington Nthumb
38 J6 Ellington Thorpe Cambs
17 U7 Elliots Green Somset
19 T11 Ellisfield Hants
100 e3 Ellishader Highld
47 M11 Ellistown Leics
105 R9 Ellon Abers
67 P5 Ellonby Cumb
41 R3 Ellough Suffk
65 L14 Elloughton E R Yk
28 A6 Ellwood Gloucs
49 Q12 Elm Cambs
36 B7 Elmbridge Worcs
39 Q13 Elmdon Essex
36 G4 Elmdon Solhll
36 G4 Elmdon Heath Solhll
10 F10 Elmer W Susx
21 Q9 Elmers End Gt Lon
55 M5 Elmer's Green Lancs
37 N1 Elmesthorpe Leics
22 J6 Elm Green Essex
46 F11 Elmhurst Staffs
36 C12 Elmley Castle Worcs
35 U7 Elmley Lovett Worcs
28 E4 Elmore Gloucs
28 E4 Elmore Back Gloucs
22 D10 Elm Park Gt Lon
14 F8 Elmscott Devon
40 J11 Elmsett Suffk
35 R7 Elms Green Worcs
23 Q3 Elmstead Heath Essex
23 Q3 Elmstead Market Essex
23 Q3 Elmstead Row Essex
13 M7 Elmsted Kent
13 Q3 Elmstone Kent
28 H2 Elmstone Hardwicke Gloucs
65 M8 Elmswell E R Yk
40 G8 Elmswell Suffk
57 R12 Elmton Derbys
108 C2 Elphin Highld
83 S4 Elphinstone E Loth
99 Q2 Elrick Abers
72 J10 Elrig D & G
76 H13 Elrington Nthumb
76 J7 Elsdon Nthumb
57 N7 Elsecar Barns
22 D2 Elsenham Essex
30 B10 Elsfield Oxon
58 H4 Elsham N Linc
50 J10 Elsing Norfk
62 J10 Elslack N York
9 S8 Elson Hants
44 J6 Elson Shrops
83 L10 Elsrickle S Lans
10 E2 Elstead Surrey
10 C7 Elsted W Susx
48 G9 Elsthorpe Lincs
70 D8 Elstob Dur
62 B13 Elston Lancs
47 U4 Elston Notts
18 G12 Elston Wilts
15 Q9 Elstone Devon
38 G11 Elstow Bed
21 L3 Elstree Herts
65 S13 Elstronwick E R Yk
61 S12 Elswick Lancs
77 Q13 Elswick N u Ty
39 M8 Elsworth Cambs
67 M12 Elterwater Cumb
21 R8 Eltham Gt Lon
21 R8 Eltham Crematorium Gt Lon
39 L9 Eltisley Cambs
55 S4 Elton Bury
38 G2 Elton Cambs
55 L11 Elton Ches W
46 H1 Elton Derbys
28 D5 Elton Gloucs
35 L6 Elton Herefs
47 U6 Elton Notts
70 F9 Elton S on T
55 L12 Elton Green Ches W
77 M13 Eltringham Nthumb
74 J2 Elvanfoot S Lans
47 M7 Elvaston Derbys
40 D4 Elveden Suffk
20 D11 Elvetham Heath Hants
84 D4 Elvingston E Loth
64 G10 Elvington C York
13 Q5 Elvington Kent
15 Q6 Elwell Devon
70 G6 Elwick Hartpl
85 S11 Elwick Nthumb
45 R1 Elworth Ches E
16 E10 Elworthy Somset
39 R4 Ely Cambs
27 L12 Ely Cardif
38 C11 Emberton M Keyn
66 J6 Embleton Cumb
70 F7 Embleton Dur
85 U14 Embleton Nthumb
109 Q6 Embo Highld
17 R6 Emborough Somset
109 Q6 Embo Street Highld
63 L9 Embsay N York
8 K7 Emery Down Hants
56 K4 Emley Kirk
56 K4 Emley Moor Kirk
20 D9 Emmbrook Wokham
20 B7 Emmer Green Readg
57 Q11 Emmett Carr Derbys
30 F12 Emmington Oxon
49 Q12 Emneth Norfk
49 R12 Emneth Hungate Norfk
48 D12 Empingham Rutlnd
10 B4 Empshott Hants
9 U2 Empshott Green Hants
45 M11 Emstrey Crematorium Shrops
9 U7 Emsworth Hants
19 P7 Enborne W Berk
19 P8 Enborne Row W Berk
35 M1 Enchmarsh Shrops
47 P14 Enderby Leics
61 U3 Endmoor Cumb
46 B3 Endon Staffs
46 B3 Endon Bank Staffs
21 Q3 Enfield Gt Lon
21 P3 Enfield Crematorium Gt Lon
21 Q3 Enfield Lock Gt Lon
21 Q3 Enfield Wash Gt Lon
18 H10 Enford Wilts
28 C11 Engine Common S Glos
35 M10 England's Gate Herefs
19 T6 Englefield W Berk
20 G8 Englefield Green Surrey
45 S3 Engleseabrook Ches E
28 A4 English Bicknor Gloucs
17 T4 Englishcombe BaNES
45 L8 English Frankton Shrops
3 M2 Engollan Cnwll
19 N11 Enham-Alamein Hants
16 H9 Enmore Somset
8 B4 Enmore Green Dorset
66 G9 Ennerdale Bridge Cumb
3 P5 Enniscaven Cnwll
97 T11 Enochdhu P & K
92 K9 Ensay Ag & B
8 F9 Ensbury Bmouth
44 K10 Ensdon Shrops
15 N7 Ensis Devon
46 B8 Enson Staffs
29 S3 Enstone Oxon
74 G5 Enterkinfoot D & G
70 G11 Enterpen N York
35 T3 Enville Staffs
106 c18 Eolaigearraidh W Isls
28 E5 Epney Gloucs
47 S4 Epperstone Notts
22 C7 Epping Essex
22 B6 Epping Green Essex
31 S11 Epping Green Herts
22 B7 Epping Upland Essex
69 Q10 Eppleby N York
65 N13 Eppleworth E R Yk
21 M10 Epsom Surrey
37 L12 Epwell Oxon
58 C6 Epworth N Linc
58 C6 Epworth Turbary N Linc
44 J5 Erbistock Wrexhm
36 F2 Erdington Birm
11 T3 Eridge Green E Susx
11 S4 Eridge Station E Susx
87 R10 Erines Ag & B
94 C10 Eriska Ag & B
106 c18 Eriskay W Isls
40 B5 Eriswell Suffk
22 D12 Erith Gt Lon
18 E10 Erlestoke Wilts
5 Q10 Ermington Devon
51 L7 Erpingham Norfk
12 H4 Erriottwood Kent
102 G11 Errogie Highld
90 K7 Errol P & K
89 L11 Erskine Rens
72 C6 Ervie D & G
41 M14 Erwarton Suffk
34 C12 Erwood Powys
70 D11 Eryholme N York
44 F2 Eryrys Denbgs
2 B11 Escalls Cnwll
69 Q6 Escomb Dur
16 E9 Escott Somset
64 E11 Escrick N York
25 Q5 Esgair Carmth
33 L7 Esgair Cerdgn
43 Q12 Esgairgeiliog Powys
33 M12 Esgerdawe Carmth
53 P7 Esgyryn Conwy
69 Q4 Esh Dur
20 K10 Esher Surrey
63 P11 Esholt C Brad
77 Q6 Eshott Nthumb
62 J8 Eshton N York
69 Q4 Esh Winning Dur
102 E7 Eskadale Highld
83 R5 Eskbank Mdloth
66 H12 Eskdale Green Cumb
75 Q6 Eskdalemuir D & G
59 Q7 Eskham Lincs
57 T3 Eskholme Donc
69 P8 Esperley Lane Ends Dur
61 S12 Esprick Lancs
48 F11 Essendine Rutlnd
31 S11 Essendon Herts
102 H8 Essich Highld
46 C13 Essington Staffs
105 Q10 Esslemont Abers
70 H9 Eston R & Cl
85 N11 Etal Nthumb
18 F8 Etchilhampton Wilts
12 D10 Etchingham E Susx
13 N8 Etchinghill Kent
46 D10 Etchinghill Staffs
11 S6 Etchingwood E Susx
50 H11 Etling Green Norfk
28 C6 Etloe Gloucs
20 G7 Eton W & M
20 F7 Eton Wick W & M
45 U4 Etruria C Stke
96 K5 Etteridge Highld
68 J7 Ettersgill Dur
45 R1 Ettiley Heath Ches E
36 B1 Ettingshall Wolves
36 J11 Ettington Warwks
48 H12 Etton C Pete
65 M11 Etton E R Yk
75 Q3 Ettrick Border
83 S14 Ettrickbridge Border
75 Q3 Ettrickhill Border
46 J7 Etwall Derbys
35 Q3 Eudon George Shrops
40 E5 Euston Suffk
49 Q14 Euximoor Drove Cambs
55 N3 Euxton Lancs
34 G8 Evancoyd Powys
102 H2 Evanton Highld
48 G4 Evedon Lincs
45 R12 Evelith Shrops
109 P6 Evelix Highld
34 G8 Evenjobb Powys
30 C6 Evenley Nhants
29 P2 Evenlode Gloucs
69 Q8 Evenwood Dur
69 Q8 Evenwood Gate Dur
17 R9 Evercreech Somset
64 J11 Everingham E R Yk
18 K10 Everleigh Wilts
65 M2 Everley N York
31 L6 Eversholt C Beds
7 Q4 Evershot Dorset
20 C10 Eversley Hants
20 C10 Eversley Cross Hants
65 L13 Everthorpe E R Yk
38 K10 Everton C Beds
8 K10 Everton Hants
54 H8 Everton Lpool
57 U8 Everton Notts
75 S10 Evertown D & G
35 Q11 Evesbatch Herefs
36 D12 Evesham Worcs
47 R13 Evington C Leic
57 L7 Ewden Village Sheff
21 M10 Ewell Surrey
13 Q7 Ewell Minnis Kent
19 T2 Ewelme Oxon
28 K8 Ewen Gloucs
26 G12 Ewenny V Glam
48 H4 Ewerby Lincs
48 H4 Ewerby Thorpe Lincs
10 H2 Ewhurst Surrey
12 E11 Ewhurst Green E Susx
10 H3 Ewhurst Green Surrey
54 H13 Ewloe Flints
54 G13 Ewloe Green Flints
55 Q1 Ewood Bl w D
55 S2 Ewood Bridge Lancs
14 K13 Eworthy Devon
20 D13 Ewshot Hants
27 R2 Ewyas Harold Herefs
15 P12 Exbourne Devon
16 B12 Exbridge Somset
9 N8 Exbury Hants
11 S11 Exceat E Susx
63 R2 Exelby N York
6 B6 Exeter Devon
6 C6 Exeter Airport Devon
6 B6 Exeter & Devon Crematorium Devon
6 C6 Exeter Services Devon
15 U5 Exford Somset
45 L12 Exfordsgreen Shrops
36 F9 Exhall Warwks
37 L3 Exhall Warwks
19 U4 Exlade Street Oxon
63 L11 Exley Head C Brad
6 B7 Exminster Devon
15 U5 Exmoor National Park
6 D8 Exmouth Devon
39 T7 Exning Suffk
13 N7 Exted Kent
6 C7 Exton Devon
9 S4 Exton Hants
48 D11 Exton Rutlnd
16 B10 Exton Somset
6 B6 Exwick Devon
56 K11 Eyam Derbys
37 P11 Eydon Nhants
48 K13 Eye C Pete
35 L8 Eye Herefs
40 K6 Eye Suffk
48 K13 Eye Green C Pete
47 T10 Eye Kettleby Leics
85 N6 Eyemouth Border
39 L11 Eyeworth C Beds
12 F5 Eyhorne Street Kent
41 P10 Eyke Suffk
38 J9 Eynesbury Cambs
21 T9 Eynsford Kent
29 T6 Eynsham Oxon
7 M6 Eype Dorset
100 d4 Eyre Highld
13 Q6 Eythorne Kent
35 L8 Eyton Herefs
34 J3 Eyton Shrops
44 J11 Eyton Shrops
44 K9 Eyton Shrops
44 J5 Eyton Wrexhm
45 N12 Eyton on Severn Shrops
45 Q11 Eyton upon the Weald Moors Wrekin

F

19 N9 Faccombe Hants
70 G12 Faceby N York
44 B10 Fachwen Powys
56 C3 Facit Lancs
47 N1 Fackley Notts
45 N3 Faddiley Ches E
64 F2 Fadmoor N York
26 B7 Faerdre Swans
26 B7 Fagwyr Swans
89 L11 Faifley W Duns
17 P2 Failand N Som
81 P7 Failford S Ayrs
56 C6 Failsworth Oldham
43 M11 Fairbourne Gwynd
64 B14 Fairburn N York
56 G12 Fairfield Derbys
12 J10 Fairfield Kent
36 B5 Fairfield Worcs
29 N7 Fairford Gloucs
29 N7 Fairford Park Gloucs
66 C1 Fairgirth D & G
49 U10 Fair Green Norfk
61 Q14 Fairhaven Lancs
106 r11 Fair Isle Shet
20 G12 Fairlands Surrey
80 J2 Fairlie N Ayrs
12 G13 Fairlight E Susx
6 E5 Fairmile Devon
20 K10 Fairmile Surrey
84 D12 Fairnilee Border
9 P5 Fair Oak Hants
45 S7 Fairoak Staffs
19 U8 Fair Oak Green Hants
12 B3 Fairseat Kent
22 J4 Fairstead Essex
49 T9 Fairstead Norfk
51 N9 Fairstead Norfk
11 R5 Fairwarp E Susx
27 L12 Fairwater Cardif
14 K8 Fairy Cross Devon
50 F8 Fakenham Norfk
40 F5 Fakenham Magna Suffk
84 C6 Fala Mdloth
84 C6 Fala Dam Mdloth
30 C4 Falcut Nhants
58 J10 Faldingworth Lincs
7 f2 Faldouet Jersey
28 C9 Falfield S Glos
41 N13 Falkenham Suffk
82 G2 Falkirk Falk
82 G2 Falkirk Crematorium Falk
91 L10 Falkland Fife
82 J11 Fallburn S Lans
47 L1 Fallgate Derbys
89 T7 Fallin Stirlg
85 T14 Fallodon Nthumb
56 C8 Fallowfield Manch
76 J12 Fallowfield Nthumb
87 T3 Falls of Blarghour Ag & B
11 P9 Falmer E Susx
3 L10 Falmouth Cnwll
75 S4 Falnash Border
65 N2 Falsgrave N York
76 E8 Falstone Nthumb
110 D7 Fanagmore Highld
31 M7 Fancott C Beds
102 E7 Fanellan Highld
70 J14 Fangdale Beck N York
64 H9 Fangfoss E R Yk
93 L10 Fanmore Ag & B
108 C11 Fannich Lodge Highld
84 G10 Fans Border
30 J6 Far Bletchley M Keyn
38 K2 Farcet Cambs
37 U9 Far Cotton Nhants
35 N5 Farden Shrops
9 R7 Fareham Hants
67 M13 Far End Cumb
46 E11 Farewell Staffs
35 R5 Far Forest Worcs
59 P11 Farforth Lincs
28 E7 Far Green Gloucs
29 Q8 Faringdon Oxon
55 M1 Farington Lancs
76 B14 Farlam Cumb
17 P3 Farleigh N Som
21 Q10 Farleigh Surrey
18 B9 Farleigh Hungerford Somset
19 T11 Farleigh Wallop Hants
59 S12 Farlesthorpe Lincs
61 U3 Farleton Cumb
62 B6 Farleton Lancs
46 J1 Farley Derbys
46 E5 Farley Staffs
8 J3 Farley Wilts
40 B10 Farley Green Suffk
20 J13 Farley Green Surrey
20 B10 Farley Hill Wokham
28 E5 Farleys End Gloucs
9 T7 Farlington C Port
64 E6 Farlington N York
35 P4 Farlow Shrops
17 S4 Farmborough BaNES
22 F5 Farmbridge End Essex
29 L2 Farmcote Gloucs
35 S2 Farmcote Shrops
33 M12 Farmers Carmth
29 M4 Farmington Gloucs
29 U6 Farmoor Oxon
55 M6 Far Moor Wigan
2 H10 Farms Common Cnwll
47 L10 Farm Town Leics
104 G5 Farmtown Moray
46 K4 Farnah Green Derbys
21 R10 Farnborough Gt Lon
20 E12 Farnborough Hants
19 P4 Farnborough W Berk
37 M11 Farnborough Warwks
20 E11 Farnborough Park Hants
20 E11 Farnborough Street Hants
10 F2 Farncombe Surrey
38 D8 Farndish Bed
44 K3 Farndon Ches W
47 U3 Farndon Notts
85 V11 Farne Islands Nthumb
99 L12 Farnell Angus
8 D5 Farnham Dorset
22 C3 Farnham Essex
63 S7 Farnham N York
41 Q8 Farnham Suffk
20 D13 Farnham Surrey
20 G5 Farnham Common Bucks
22 C2 Farnham Green Essex
20 G6 Farnham Royal Bucks
21 T9 Farningham Kent
63 R13 Farnley Leeds
63 Q10 Farnley N York
56 J4 Farnley Tyas Kirk
47 R2 Farnsfield Notts
55 R5 Farnworth Bolton
55 M9 Farnworth Halton
28 H7 Far Oakridge Gloucs
97 N3 Farr Highld
102 J9 Farr Highld
111 Q4 Farr Highld
102 G11 Farraline Highld
6 D6 Farringdon Devon
17 R5 Farrington Gurney BaNES
67 N13 Far Sawrey Cumb
63 Q12 Farsley Leeds
22 K7 Farther Howegreen Essex
12 F6 Farthing Green Kent
30 B5 Farthinghoe Nhants
13 Q7 Farthingloe Kent
37 R10 Farthingstone Nhants
21 R10 Farthing Street Gt Lon
56 J3 Fartown Kirk
63 Q13 Fartown Leeds
6 G5 Farway Devon
94 E9 Fasnacloich Ag & B
102 B10 Fasnakyle Highld
94 E3 Fassfern Highld
69 S2 Fatfield Sundld
67 R2 Faugh Cumb
46 G8 Fauld Staffs
82 H6 Fauldhouse W Loth
22 J4 Faulkbourne Essex
17 T6 Faulkland Somset
45 N7 Fauls Shrops
12 K3 Faversham Kent
63 U5 Fawdington N York
77 Q12 Fawdon N u Ty
77 L2 Fawdon Nthumb
56 G14 Fawfieldhead Staffs
21 U9 Fawkham Green Kent
29 S4 Fawler Oxon
20 C5 Fawley Bucks
9 P8 Fawley Hants
19 N4 Fawley W Berk
28 A2 Fawley Chapel Herefs
54 F13 Fawnog Flints
37 Q9 Fawsley Nhants
58 E2 Faxfleet E R Yk
11 L4 Faygate W Susx
54 J7 Fazakerley Lpool
46 H13 Fazeley Staffs
63 P3 Fearby N York
109 Q9 Fearn Highld
95 U10 Fearnan P & K
107 M13 Fearnbeg Highld
55 P8 Fearnhead Warrtn
107 M12 Fearnmore Highld
87 S10 Fearnoch Ag & B
46 B12 Featherstone Staffs
57 P2 Featherstone Wakefd
36 D8 Feckenham Worcs
23 L3 Feering Essex
69 L13 Feetham N York
62 F6 Feizor N York
11 P3 Felbridge Surrey
51 M6 Felbrigg Norfk
11 P2 Felcourt Surrey
31 M12 Felden Herts
25 Q3 Felindre Carmth
25 U6 Felindre Carmth
26 C2 Felindre Carmth
33 L9 Felindre Cerdgn
27 M3 Felindre Powys
34 E4 Felindre Powys
26 A7 Felindre Swans
24 K3 Felindre Farchog Pembks
32 K9 Felin Fach Cerdgn
34 C14 Felinfach Powys
25 T10 Felinfoel Carmth
25 T6 Felingwm Isaf Carmth
25 T6 Felingwm Uchaf Carmth
34 D13 Felin-newydd Powys
64 B3 Felixkirk N York
41 P14 Felixstowe Suffk
41 P13 Felixstowe Ferry Suffk
85 N10 Felkington Nthumb
57 N4 Felkirk Wakefd
77 R13 Felling Gatesd
63 L11 Fell Lane C Brad
67 M5 Fell Side Cumb
38 E9 Felmersham Bed
51 N8 Felmingham Norfk
10 E11 Felpham W Susx
40 F9 Felsham Suffk
22 G3 Felsted Essex
20 K8 Feltham Gt Lon
20 J8 Felthamhill Surrey
51 L10 Felthorpe Norfk
35 N11 Felton Herefs
17 P3 Felton N Som
77 P5 Felton Nthumb
44 J10 Felton Butler Shrops
40 B2 Feltwell Norfk
56 J3 Fenay Bridge Kirk
62 G12 Fence Lancs
57 P9 Fence Rothm
70 D3 Fence Houses Sundld
30 C9 Fencott Oxon
49 Q1 Fendike Corner Lincs
39 Q8 Fen Ditton Cambs
39 M7 Fen Drayton Cambs
48 K9 Fen End Lincs
36 H6 Fen End Solhll
85 R10 Fenham Nthumb
55 Q1 Feniscliffe Bl w D
55 P1 Feniscowles Bl w D
6 F5 Feniton Devon
39 P2 Fenland Crematorium Cambs
35 S4 Fenn Green Shrops
22 J12 Fenn Street Medway
46 G4 Fenny Bentley Derbys
6 F5 Fenny Bridges Devon
37 M10 Fenny Compton Warwks
37 L1 Fenny Drayton Leics
30 J6 Fenny Stratford M Keyn
77 P7 Fenrother Nthumb
39 M7 Fenstanton Cambs
40 D10 Fenstead End Suffk
40 G1 Fen Street Norfk
41 L8 Fen Street Suffk
45 U5 Fenton C Stke
39 M5 Fenton Cambs
67 R1 Fenton Cumb
48 C3 Fenton Lincs
58 D11 Fenton Lincs
58 C10 Fenton Notts
85 P12 Fenton Nthumb
84 E2 Fenton Barns E Loth
57 S3 Fenwick Donc
81 P4 Fenwick E Ayrs
77 M11 Fenwick Nthumb
85 R10 Fenwick Nthumb
3 L9 Feock Cnwll
86 G12 Feolin Ferry Ag & B
81 L4 Fergushill N Ayrs
100 a4 Feriniquarrie Highld
6 e3 Fermain Bay Guern
98 H11 Fern Angus
26 H8 Ferndale Rhondd
8 F8 Ferndown Dorset
103 Q6 Ferness Highld
29 Q9 Fernham Oxon
35 U9 Fernhill Heath Worcs
10 D5 Fernhurst W Susx
91 M8 Fernie Fife
82 D8 Ferniegair S Lans
100 c6 Fernilea Highld
56 F11 Fernilee Derbys
48 B3 Fernwood Notts
63 T7 Ferrensby N York
58 G2 Ferriby Sluice N Linc
100 f9 Ferrindonald Highld
10 H10 Ferring W Susx
57 Q2 Ferrybridge Wakefd
57 Q2 Ferrybridge Services Wakefd
99 N12 Ferryden Angus
69 S6 Ferryhill Dur
109 N7 Ferry Point Highld
25 Q8 Ferryside Carmth
109 N7 Ferrytown Highld
40 J4 Fersfield Norfk
96 D8 Fersit Highld
97 P3 Feshiebridge Highld
20 K11 Fetcham Surrey
106 w4 Fetlar Shet
105 R5 Fetterangus Abers
99 M9 Fettercairn Abers
30 B7 Fewcott Oxon
63 P9 Fewston N York
26 A3 Ffairfach Carmth
33 P7 Ffair Rhos Cerdgn
33 M12 Ffald-y-Brenin Carmth
27 N4 Ffawyddog Powys
43 P5 Ffestiniog Gwynd
43 N5 Ffestiniog Railway Gwynd
54 D14 Ffordd-las Denbgs
25 U10 Fforest Carmth
27 P3 Fforest Mons
26 A8 Fforest Fach Swans
26 C7 Fforest Goch Neath
32 G11 Ffostrasol Cerdgn
44 G2 Ffrith Flints
32 G10 Ffynnonddewi Cerdgn
54 D10 Ffynnongroyw Flints
32 K10 Ffynnon-Oer Cerdgn
110 K11 Fiag Lodge Highld
21 Q10 Fickleshole Surrey
28 H1 Fiddington Gloucs
16 H8 Fiddington Somset
7 V2 Fiddleford Dorset
3 L5 Fiddlers Green Cnwll
22 C7 Fiddlers Hamlet Essex
46 D7 Field Staffs
61 R3 Field Broughton Cumb
50 H6 Field Dalling Norfk
67 Q5 Fieldhead Cumb
47 N12 Field Head Leics
17 U12 Fifehead Magdalen Dorset
7 U2 Fifehead Neville Dorset
7 U2 Fifehead St Quintin Dorset
104 E5 Fife Keith Moray
29 P4 Fifield Oxon
20 F7 Fifield W & M
18 H10 Fifield Wilts
18 J11 Figheldean Wilts
28 H10 Filands Wilts
51 S11 Filby Norfk
65 Q3 Filey N York
38 C11 Filgrave M Keyn
29 P7 Filkins Oxon
15 Q7 Filleigh Devon
15 R10 Filleigh Devon
58 F9 Fillingham Lincs
36 J3 Fillongley Warwks
9 T3 Filmore Hill Hants
28 B12 Filton S Glos
64 K7 Fimber E R Yk
98 H12 Finavon Angus
49 U12 Fincham Norfk
20 C10 Finchampstead Wokham
87 S5 Fincharn Ag & B
9 U6 Finchdean Hants
39 U14 Finchingfield Essex
21 N4 Finchley Gt Lon
46 K7 Findern Derbys
103 R3 Findhorn Moray
103 M10 Findhorn Bridge Highld
104 F2 Findochty Moray
90 F8 Findo Gask P & K
99 S4 Findon Abers
10 J9 Findon W Susx
102 H3 Findon Mains Highld
99 L3 Findrack House Abers
38 D6 Finedon Nhants
48 E14 Fineshade Nhants
41 M7 Fingal Street Suffk
90 J8 Fingask P & K
20 C4 Fingest Bucks
63 P2 Finghall N York
67 L1 Fingland Cumb
74 E2 Fingland D & G
13 R5 Finglesham Kent
23 P3 Fingringhoe Essex
40 B12 Finkle Green Essex
57 M7 Finkle Street Barns
95 R12 Finlarig Stirlg
30 D6 Finmere Oxon
95 Q7 Finnart P & K
40 J7 Finningham Suffk
57 U7 Finningley Donc
106 f10 Finsbay W Isls
36 C6 Finstall Worcs
61 R2 Finsthwaite Cumb
29 S4 Finstock Oxon
106 s18 Finstown Ork
105 M5 Fintry Abers
89 P8 Fintry Stirlg
99 L5 Finzean Abers
92 J14 Fionnphort Ag & B
106 f10 Fionnsbhagh W Isls
68 D14 Firbank Cumb
57 S9 Firbeck Rothm
63 R2 Firby N York
64 G6 Firby N York
56 D4 Firgrove Rochdl
11 R9 Firle E Susx
59 S14 Firsby Lincs
8 J2 Firsdown Wilts
69 P6 Fir Tree Dur
9 R10 Fishbourne IoW
10 C10 Fishbourne W Susx
10 C9 Fishbourne Roman Palace W Susx
70 E6 Fishburn Dur
90 C12 Fishcross Clacks
10 D10 Fisher W Susx
104 K8 Fisherford Abers
83 R4 Fisherrow E Loth
9 P4 Fisher's Pond Hants
61 S10 Fisher's Row Lancs
10 E4 Fisherstreet W Susx
102 K5 Fisherton Highld
80 K9 Fisherton S Ayrs
18 F13 Fisherton de la Mere Wilts
46 G12 Fisherwick Staffs
20 E6 Fishery Estate W & M
24 G3 Fishguard Pembks
57 U4 Fishlake Donc
15 M11 Fishleigh Devon
49 L6 Fishmere End Lincs
93 R10 Fishnish Pier Ag & B
7 L5 Fishpond Bottom Dorset
28 B12 Fishponds Bristl
49 N5 Fishtoft Lincs
49 M4 Fishtoft Drove Lincs
62 B14 Fishwick Lancs
100 c6 Fiskavaig Highld
58 H12 Fiskerton Lincs
47 T3 Fiskerton Notts
65 T13 Fitling E R Yk
18 H11 Fittleton Wilts
10 G7 Fittleworth W Susx
49 P11 Fitton End Cambs
44 K10 Fitz Shrops
16 F11 Fitzhead Somset
16 G11 Fitzroy Somset
57 P3 Fitzwilliam Wakefd
11 R6 Five Ash Down E Susx
11 T5 Five Ashes E Susx
16 E8 Five Bells Somset
35 P11 Five Bridges Herefs
55 M11 Fivecrosses Ches W
17 L12 Fivehead Somset
4 G4 Fivelanes Cnwll
27 S9 Five Lanes Mons
12 B6 Five Oak Green Kent
7 e3 Five Oaks Jersey
10 H5 Five Oaks W Susx
25 S9 Five Roads Carmth
12 F5 Five Wents Kent
22 J5 Flack's Green Essex
20 E5 Flackwell Heath Bucks
36 C11 Fladbury Worcs
106 u10 Fladdabister Shet
56 H13 Flagg Derbys
65 S5 Flamborough E R Yk
65 T5 Flamborough Head E R Yk
64 H4 Flamingo Land Theme Park N York
31 N10 Flamstead Herts
10 F10 Flansham W Susx
57 M2 Flanshaw Wakefd
63 M12 Flappit Spring C Brad
62 J8 Flasby N York
56 F13 Flash Staffs
100 c4 Flashader Highld
31 M12 Flaunden Herts
47 U5 Flawborough Notts
64 B6 Flawith N York
17 P3 Flax Bourton N Som
63 T8 Flaxby N York
28 C4 Flaxley Gloucs
55 N12 Flaxmere Ches W
16 F9 Flaxpool Somset
64 F7 Flaxton N York
37 R2 Fleckney Leics
37 P8 Flecknoe Warwks
58 D12 Fledborough Notts
7 R8 Fleet Dorset
9 U8 Fleet Hants
20 D12 Fleet Hants
49 N9 Fleet Lincs
9 Q7 Fleetend Hants
49 N9 Fleet Hargate Lincs
20 C11 Fleet Services Hants
61 Q10 Fleetwood Lancs
16 D3 Flemingston V Glam
89 Q14 Flemington S Lans
40 D7 Flempton Suffk
21 T13 Fletcher Green Kent
4 E7 Fletchersbridge Cnwll
66 K4 Fletchertown Cumb
11 Q6 Fletching E Susx
27 M8 Fleur-de-lis Caerph
14 F11 Flexbury Cnwll
20 F12 Flexford Surrey
66 F6 Flimby Cumb
12 D9 Flimwell E Susx
54 F12 Flint Flints
47 T4 Flintham Notts
54 F12 Flint Mountain Flints
65 S12 Flinton E R Yk
36 J4 Flint's Green Solhll
12 E8 Flishinghurst Kent
50 B8 Flitcham Norfk
31 N5 Flitton C Beds
31 M6 Flitwick C Beds
58 E4 Flixborough N Linc
58 E4 Flixborough Stather N Linc
65 N4 Flixton N York
41 P3 Flixton Suffk
55 R8 Flixton Traffd
56 K4 Flockton Kirk
57 L3 Flockton Green Kirk
85 N11 Flodden Nthumb
100 d2 Flodigarry Highld
61 R4 Flookburgh Cumb
41 L1 Flordon Norfk
37 R8 Flore Nhants
76 K5 Flotterton Nthumb
11 U8 Flowers Green E Susx
40 J11 Flowton Suffk
57 L2 Flushdyke Wakefd
3 L10 Flushing Cnwll
6 E6 Fluxton Devon
36 C9 Flyford Flavell Worcs
22 H11 Fobbing Thurr
104 C4 Fochabers Moray
27 L6 Fochriw Caerph
58 E3 Fockerby N Linc
17 Q11 Foddington Somset
43 U11 Foel Powys
25 T8 Foelgastell Carmth
26 F9 Foel y Dyffryn Brdgnd
64 H12 Foggathorpe E R Yk
84 K9 Fogo Border
104 A4 Fogwatt Moray
110 D7 Foindle Highld
98 B11 Folda Angus
46 D6 Fole Staffs
37 L4 Foleshill Covtry
7 S2 Folke Dorset
13 P8 Folkestone Kent
48 G7 Folkingham Lincs
11 T10 Folkington E Susx
38 H3 Folksworth Cambs
65 P4 Folkton N York
105 L9 Folla Rule Abers
63 S9 Follifoot N York
15 N13 Folly Gate Devon
20 D13 Folly Hill Surrey
16 D3 Fonmon V Glam
8 C2 Fonthill Bishop Wilts
8 C2 Fonthill Gifford Wilts
8 B5 Fontmell Magna Dorset
8 A6 Fontmell Parva Dorset
10 E9 Fontwell W Susx
16 E3 Font-y-gary V Glam
56 J11 Foolow Derbys
21 S8 Foots Cray Gt Lon
104 D13 Forbestown Abers
69 Q10 Forcett N York
87 R5 Ford Ag & B
30 G11 Ford Bucks
57 P10 Ford Derbys
5 Q10 Ford Devon
5 T12 Ford Devon
14 K8 Ford Devon
29 L2 Ford Gloucs
85 N11 Ford Nthumb
44 K11 Ford Shrops
16 E11 Ford Somset
17 Q6 Ford Somset
46 E3 Ford Staffs
10 F10 Ford W Susx
8 H2 Ford Wilts
18 B5 Ford Wilts
5 N2 Forda Devon
11 S2 Fordcombe Kent
90 J14 Fordell Fife
44 F13 Forden Powys
22 G4 Ford End Essex
5 T7 Forder Green Devon
61 T10 Ford Green Lancs
39 T6 Fordham Cambs
23 M2 Fordham Essex
49 T14 Fordham Norfk
23 M2 Fordham Heath Essex
44 K11 Ford Heath Shrops
8 G6 Fordingbridge Hants
65 N4 Fordon E R Yk
99 N8 Fordoun Abers
40 J7 Ford's Green Suffk
23 M2 Fordstreet Essex
16 G13 Ford Street Somset
15 T13 Fordton Devon
29 R5 Fordwells Oxon
13 N4 Fordwich Kent
104 H3 Fordyce Abers
46 B9 Forebridge Staffs
46 K8 Foremark Derbys
6 d4 Forest Guern
69 S12 Forest N York
62 F9 Forest Becks Lancs
77 M6 Forestburn Gate Nthumb
56 E12 Forest Chapel Ches E
21 R5 Forest Gate Gt Lon
10 J2 Forest Green Surrey
77 R12 Forest Hall N Tyne
76 B14 Forest Head Cumb
21 Q8 Forest Hill Gt Lon
30 C11 Forest Hill Oxon
68 J6 Forest-in-Teesdale Dur
63 S8 Forest Lane Head N York
90 E13 Forest Mill Clacks
28 B5 Forest of Dean Gloucs
21 S4 Forest Park Crematorium Gt Lon
11 Q4 Forest Row E Susx
9 P11 Forest Side IoW
10 B8 Forestside W Susx
47 Q1 Forest Town Notts
98 H13 Forfar Angus
90 G8 Forgandenny P & K
43 Q14 Forge Powys
27 P8 Forge Hammer Torfn
27 N6 Forge Side Torfn
104 D5 Forgie Moray
104 E5 Forgieside Moray
104 J6 Forgue Abers
36 E5 Forhill Worcs
54 H5 Formby Sefton
40 K2 Forncett End Norfk
41 L2 Forncett St Mary Norfk
41 L2 Forncett St Peter Norfk
40 D7 Fornham All Saints Suffk
40 E7 Fornham St Martin Suffk
103 P5 Fornighty Highld
103 R4 Forres Moray
46 C5 Forsbrook Staffs
112 F10 Forse Highld
36 E6 Forshaw Heath Warwks
111 T8 Forsinard Highld
7 S5 Forston Dorset
96 D2 Fort Augustus Highld
90 G8 Forteviot P & K
82 H8 Forth S Lans
28 G1 Forthampton Gloucs
6 c2 Fort Hommet Guern
95 U9 Fortingall P & K
6 e1 Fort le Marchant Guern
19 P12 Forton Hants
61 T9 Forton Lancs
44 K10 Forton Shrops
6 K3 Forton Somset
45 S9 Forton Staffs
104 K6 Fortrie Abers
102 K4 Fortrose Highld
7 S10 Fortuneswell Dorset
94 G4 Fort William Highld
20 F4 Forty Green Bucks
21 P3 Forty Hill Gt Lon
40 K9 Forward Green Suffk
19 M9 Fosbury Wilts
29 P3 Foscot Oxon
37 S11 Foscote Nhants
49 M7 Fosdyke Lincs
49 M7 Fosdyke Bridge Lincs
97 M12 Foss P & K
29 L5 Fossebridge Gloucs
32 H8 Foss-y-ffin Cerdgn
57 U4 Fosterhouses Donc
22 C6 Foster Street Essex
46 G7 Foston Derbys
37 R2 Foston Leics
48 C5 Foston Lincs
64 F6 Foston N York
65 Q8 Foston on the Wolds E R Yk
59 P8 Fotherby Lincs
66 F6 Fothergill Cumb
38 G2 Fotheringhay Nhants
67 P3 Foulbridge Cumb
57 N3 Foulby Wakefd
85 N7 Foulden Border
50 C14 Foulden Norfk
36 H2 Foul End Warwks
11 U7 Foul Mile E Susx
23 N9 Foulness Island Essex
6 d3 Foulon Vale Crematorium Guern
62 H11 Foulridge Lancs
50 H9 Foulsham Norfk
84 C9 Fountainhall Border
36 G5 Four Ashes Solhll
35 T3 Four Ashes Staffs
46 B12 Four Ashes Staffs
40 H6 Four Ashes Suffk
6 d3 Four Cabots Guern
44 G10 Four Crosses Powys
46 C12 Four Crosses Staffs
21 S13 Four Elms Kent
17 Q10 Four Foot Somset
16 H9 Four Forks Somset
55 P5 Four Gates Bolton
49 Q10 Four Gotes Cambs
57 L6 Four Lane End Barns
45 N1 Four Lane Ends Ches W
2 H9 Four Lanes Cnwll
45 T2 Fourlanes End Ches E
19 U13 Four Marks Hants
52 C7 Four Mile Bridge IoA
46 F14 Four Oaks Birm
12 G11 Four Oaks E Susx
28 C2 Four Oaks Gloucs
36 H4 Four Oaks Solhll
109 Q6 Fourpenny Highld
19 S5 Four Points W Berk
25 R9 Four Roads Carmth
29 P1 Four Shire Stone Warwks
76 H12 Fourstones Nthumb
12 E10 Four Throws Kent
12 B5 Four Wents Kent
8 E3 Fovant Wilts
105 R11 Foveran Abers
4 E10 Fowey Cnwll
55 Q7 Fowley Common Warrtn
12 C6 Fowlhall Kent
91 M5 Fowlis Angus
90 D7 Fowlis Wester P & K
39 P11 Fowlmere Cambs
35 N14 Fownhope Herefs
89 L13 Foxbar Rens
5 M3 Foxcombe Devon
20 G12 Fox Corner Surrey
28 K4 Foxcote Gloucs
17 T5 Foxcote Somset
60 d7 Foxdale IoM
40 D12 Foxearth Essex
12 B2 Foxendown Kent
61 N2 Foxfield Cumb
18 E5 Foxham Wilts
22 E8 Fox Hatch Essex
9 L6 Foxhills Hants
3 P6 Foxhole Cnwll
65 N5 Foxholes N York
11 S7 Foxhunt Green E Susx
37 R10 Foxley Nhants
50 H9 Foxley Norfk
28 G10 Foxley Wilts
36 D7 Foxlydiate Worcs
23 P2 Fox Street Essex
46 D4 Foxt Staffs
39 P11 Foxton Cambs
70 E8 Foxton Dur
37 T3 Foxton Leics
70 F13 Foxton N York
62 H4 Foxup N York
55 P13 Foxwist Green Ches W
35 P5 Foxwood Shrops
28 A2 Foy Herefs
102 E11 Foyers Highld
103 N5 Foynesfield Highld
2 F10 Fraddam Cnwll
3 N5 Fraddon Cnwll
46 G11 Fradley Staffs
46 C7 Fradswell Staffs
65 R7 Fraisthorpe E R Yk
11 R6 Framfield E Susx
51 N13 Framingham Earl Norfk
51 N13 Framingham Pigot Norfk
41 N8 Framlingham Suffk
7 R5 Frampton Dorset
49 M6 Frampton Lincs
28 C11 Frampton Cotterell S Glos
28 H7 Frampton Mansell Gloucs
28 D6 Frampton on Severn Gloucs
49 M5 Frampton West End Lincs
41 L9 Framsden Suffk
69 S4 Framwellgate Moor Dur
35 T5 Franche Worcs
55 P11 Frandley Ches W
4 K2 Frankaborough Devon
54 F9 Frankby Wirral
51 P9 Frankfort Norfk
35 M11 Franklands Gate Herefs
36 C4 Frankley Worcs
36 C4 Frankley Services Worcs
34 D9 Franksbridge Powys
37 M6 Frankton Warwks
11 T3 Frant E Susx
105 R2 Fraserburgh Abers
23 Q3 Frating Essex
23 Q3 Frating Green Essex
9 T8 Fratton C Port
4 K10 Freathy Cnwll
39 U6 Freckenham Suffk
61 S14 Freckleton Lancs
57 M12 Freebirch Derbys
48 B9 Freeby Leics
19 Q11 Freefolk Hants
46 D5 Freehay Staffs
29 T5 Freeland Oxon
51 R12 Freethorpe Norfk
51 R13 Freethorpe Common Norfk
49 N5 Freiston Lincs
15 M6 Fremington Devon
69 M13 Fremington N York
28 B12 Frenchay S Glos
5 R3 Frenchbeer Devon
21 S12 French Street Kent
97 N12 Frenich P & K
10 C2 Frensham Surrey
54 G5 Freshfield Sefton
17 U4 Freshford Wilts
9 L11 Freshwater IoW
9 L11 Freshwater Bay IoW
24 H11 Freshwater East Pembks
41 N5 Fressingfield Suffk
41 L13 Freston Suffk
112 J3 Freswick Highld
28 D5 Fretherne Gloucs
51 M10 Frettenham Norfk
91 L10 Freuchie Fife
24 G8 Freystrop Pembks
36 D2 Friar Park Sandw
11 R4 Friar's Gate E Susx
64 G2 Friars' Hill N York
7 R7 Friar Waddon Dorset
49 Q13 Friday Bridge Cambs
41 M9 Friday Street Suffk
41 P10 Friday Street Suffk
41 Q8 Friday Street Suffk
20 K13 Friday Street Surrey
64 K8 Fridaythorpe E R Yk
46 G1 Friden Derbys
56 G2 Friendly Calder
21 N4 Friern Barnet Gt Lon
58 J10 Friesthorpe Lincs
48 D4 Frieston Lincs
20 C4 Frieth Bucks
47 N3 Friezeland Notts
29 T8 Frilford Oxon
19 R6 Frilsham W Berk
20 E11 Frimley Surrey
20 E11 Frimley Green Surrey
12 D2 Frindsbury Medway
50 B7 Fring Norfk
30 D7 Fringford Oxon
12 G4 Frinsted Kent
23 T3 Frinton-on-Sea Essex
91 S2 Friockheim Angus
43 M11 Friog Gwynd
47 S10 Frisby on the Wreake Leics
49 Q2 Friskney Lincs
49 Q2 Friskney Eaudike Lincs
11 T11 Friston E Susx
41 R8 Friston Suffk
47 L3 Fritchley Derbys
8 J6 Fritham Hants
49 M4 Frith Bank Lincs
35 Q7 Frith Common Worcs
15 L9 Frithelstock Devon
15 L9 Frithelstock Stone Devon
10 C3 Frithend Hants
31 M11 Frithsden Herts
49 M3 Frithville Lincs
12 F7 Frittenden Kent
5 U12 Frittiscombe Devon
41 M2 Fritton Norfk
51 S13 Fritton Norfk
30 B7 Fritwell Oxon
63 N12 Frizinghall C Brad
66 F9 Frizington Cumb
28 E7 Frocester Gloucs
45 M13 Frodesley Shrops
55 M11 Frodsham Ches W
84 K13 Frogden Border
39 N11 Frog End Cambs
39 R9 Frog End Cambs
56 K11 Froggatt Derbys
46 D4 Froghall Staffs
8 H6 Frogham Hants
13 Q5 Frogham Kent
5 T12 Frogmore Devon
48 J11 Frognall Lincs
2 K8 Frogpool Cnwll
35 T7 Frog Pool Worcs
4 J7 Frogwell Cnwll
37 P2 Frolesworth Leics
17 U7 Frome Somset
7 Q4 Frome St Quintin Dorset
35 Q11 Fromes Hill Herefs
54 C13 Fron Denbgs
42 G6 Fron Gwynd
52 H12 Fron Gwynd
44 E14 Fron Powys
44 F13 Fron Powys
44 G5 Froncysyllte Denbgs
43 T6 Fron-goch Gwynd
44 G5 Fron Isaf Wrexhm
41 S4 Frostenden Suffk
69 M5 Frosterley Dur
31 L6 Froxfield C Beds
19 L7 Froxfield Wilts
9 U3 Froxfield Green Hants
9 N4 Fryern Hill Hants
22 F7 Fryerning Essex
64 F5 Fryton N York
93 Q9 Fuinary Highld
48 D3 Fulbeck Lincs
39 R9 Fulbourn Cambs
29 Q5 Fulbrook Oxon
9 P2 Fulflood Hants
64 E10 Fulford C York
16 H11 Fulford Somset
46 C6 Fulford Staffs
21 N7 Fulham Gt Lon
11 L8 Fulking W Susx
15 Q5 Fullaford Devon
81 L5 Fullarton N Ayrs
22 D2 Fuller's End Essex
45 L3 Fuller's Moor Ches W
22 H4 Fuller Street Essex
21 U11 Fuller Street Kent
19 N13 Fullerton Hants
59 N12 Fulletby Lincs
36 J11 Fullready Warwks
64 G8 Full Sutton E R Yk
81 N2 Fullwood E Ayrs
20 G5 Fulmer Bucks
50 G7 Fulmodeston Norfk
58 J11 Fulnetby Lincs
49 L9 Fulney Lincs
56 J5 Fulstone Kirk
59 P7 Fulstow Lincs
29 S3 Fulwell Oxon
77 T14 Fulwell Sundld
61 U13 Fulwood Lancs
47 N2 Fulwood Notts
57 M9 Fulwood Sheff
16 H12 Fulwood Somset
41 L1 Fundenhall Norfk
10 C9 Funtington W Susx
9 R7 Funtley Hants
95 V13 Funtullich P & K
6 J4 Furley Devon
87 U5 Furnace Ag & B
25 T10 Furnace Carmth
33 N1 Furnace Cerdgn
36 H2 Furnace End Warwks
11 Q5 Furner's Green E Susx
56 F10 Furness Vale Derbys
22 B2 Furneux Pelham Herts
12 G8 Further Quarter Kent
30 G4 Furtho Nhants
15 R3 Furzehill Devon
8 E8 Furzehill Dorset
59 N12 Furzehills Lincs
9 T6 Furzeley Corner Hants
20 E6 Furze Platt W & M
8 K5 Furzley Hants
6 H2 Fyfett Somset
22 E6 Fyfield Essex
19 L11 Fyfield Hants
29 T8 Fyfield Oxon
18 H7 Fyfield Wilts
18 J8 Fyfield Wilts
8 E3 Fyfield Bavant Wilts
71 R12 Fylingthorpe N York
10 C6 Fyning W Susx
105 M8 Fyvie Abers

G

81 P2 Gabroc Hill E Ayrs
47 S11 Gaddesby Leics
31 N10 Gaddesden Row Herts
52 G5 Gadfa IoA
81 N8 Gadgirth S Ayrs
44 J6 Gadlas Shrops
27 M3 Gaer Powys
27 S8 Gaer-llwyd Mons
52 G8 Gaerwen IoA
29 T2 Gagingwell Oxon
81 L5 Gailes N Ayrs
46 B11 Gailey Staffs
69 Q9 Gainford Dur
58 D9 Gainsborough Lincs
40 B13 Gainsford End Essex
107 P9 Gairloch Highld
94 H2 Gairlochy Highld
90 H12 Gairneybridge P & K
68 D11 Gaisgill Cumb
67 N3 Gaitsgill Cumb
84 D11 Galashiels Border
61 T8 Galgate Lancs
17 R11 Galhampton Somset
93 U13 Gallanachbeg Ag & B
93 U13 Gallanachmore Ag & B
45 M3 Gallantry Bank Ches E
91 L13 Gallatown Fife
36 K2 Galley Common Warwks
22 H7 Galleywood Essex
96 H6 Gallovie Highld
73 L2 Galloway Forest Park
91 P3 Gallowfauld Angus
90 J4 Gallowhill P & K
23 M2 Gallows Green Essex
36 B8 Gallows Green Worcs
19 U4 Gallowstree Common Oxon
100 h7 Galltair Highld
52 J10 Gallt-y-foel Gwynd
20 D12 Gally Hill Hants
11 R3 Gallypot Street E Susx
5 R12 Galmpton Devon
6 A13 Galmpton Torbay
63 R5 Galphay N York
81 Q5 Galston E Ayrs
56 F13 Gamballs Green Staffs
68 D5 Gamblesby Cumb
22 J5 Gambles Green Essex
67 L2 Gamelsby Cumb
56 F8 Gamesley Derbys
38 K10 Gamlingay Cambs
38 K10 Gamlingay Cinques Cambs
38 K10 Gamlingay Great Heath Cambs
63 M3 Gammersgill N York
105 M3 Gamrie Abers
47 Q6 Gamston Notts
58 B11 Gamston Notts
27 U4 Ganarew Herefs
94 B12 Ganavan Bay Ag & B
4 J7 Gang Cnwll
43 P9 Ganllwyd Gwynd
98 K9 Gannachy Angus
65 Q13 Ganstead E R Yk
64 F5 Ganthorpe N York
65 M4 Ganton N York
21 N3 Ganwick Corner Herts
5 V5 Gappah Devon
104 C5 Garbity Moray
40 H4 Garboldisham Norfk
103 L11 Garbole Highld
104 C13 Garchory Abers
54 H13 Garden City Flints
20 D9 Gardeners Green Wokham
105 N3 Gardenstown Abers
57 L7 Garden Village Sheff
106 t9 Garderhouse Shet
65 M11 Gardham E R Yk
17 U8 Gare Hill Somset
88 F7 Garelochhead Ag & B
29 T8 Garford Oxon
63 U13 Garforth Leeds
62 J9 Gargrave N York
89 R7 Gargunnock Stirlg
53 L7 Garizim Conwy
41 M4 Garlic Street Norfk
73 M10 Garlieston D & G
13 R2 Garlinge Kent
13 M5 Garlinge Green Kent
99 P2 Garlogie Abers
105 N5 Garmond Abers
104 C3 Garmouth Moray
45 P12 Garmston Shrops
26 B5 Garnant Carmth
42 J5 Garn-Dolbenmaen Gwynd
67 R13 Garnett Bridge Cumb
42 E7 Garnfadryn Gwynd
82 C5 Garnkirk N Lans
26 A6 Garnswllt Swans
27 N6 Garn-yr-erw Torfn
106 k5 Garrabost W Isls
81 Q9 Garrallan E Ayrs
2 J12 Garras Cnwll
43 M5 Garreg Gwynd
68 F4 Garrigill Cumb
69 Q14 Garriston N York
73 P3 Garroch D & G
72 E12 Garrochtrie D & G
80 F2 Garrochty Ag & B
100 d3 Garros Highld
62 E2 Garsdale Cumb
62 F1 Garsdale Head Cumb
28 J10 Garsdon Wilts
46 C7 Garshall Green Staffs
30 C12 Garsington Oxon
61 T10 Garstang Lancs
31 P12 Garston Herts
54 K10 Garston Lpool
78 E3 Gartachossan Ag & B
82 C5 Gartcosh N Lans
26 F9 Garth Brdgnd
27 Q9 Garth Mons
33 U11 Garth Powys
34 G6 Garth Powys
44 G5 Garth Wrexhm
89 Q12 Garthamlock C Glas
34 B14 Garthbrengy Powys
33 L9 Gartheli Cerdgn
44 E14 Garthmyl Powys
48 B9 Garthorpe Leics
58 D3 Garthorpe N Linc
33 M4 Garth Penrhyncoch Cerdgn
67 R13 Garth Row Cumb
61 U2 Garths Cumb
104 G9 Gartly Abers
89 M6 Gartmore Stirlg
82 E6 Gartness N Lans
89 M8 Gartness Stirlg
88 K8 Gartocharn W Duns
65 T12 Garton E R Yk
65 M8 Garton-on-the-Wolds E R Yk
109 U2 Gartymore Highld
84 F4 Garvald E Loth
94 D3 Garvan Highld
86 F7 Garvard Ag & B
102 C3 Garve Highld
87 M3 Garvellachs Ag & B
50 H12 Garvestone Norfk
88 G11 Garvock Inver
27 T3 Garway Herefs
27 T3 Garway Common Herefs
27 S2 Garway Hill Herefs
106 i7 Garyvard W Isls
17 U10 Gasper Wilts
18 C7 Gastard Wilts
40 G4 Gasthorpe Norfk
22 C4 Gaston Green Essex
9 P11 Gatcombe IoW
61 U2 Gatebeck Cumb
58 D10 Gate Burton Lincs
57 S10 Gateford Notts
64 D14 Gateforth N York
81 M5 Gatehead E Ayrs
64 F8 Gate Helmsley N York
76 F8 Gatehouse Nthumb
73 P8 Gatehouse of Fleet D & G
50 G9 Gateley Norfk
63 S2 Gatenby N York
66 J9 Gatesgarth Cumb
76 F1 Gateshaw Border
77 R13 Gateshead Gatesd
45 L1 Gates Heath Ches W
91 P3 Gateside Angus
89 L14 Gateside E Rens
90 J10 Gateside Fife
81 M2 Gateside N Ayrs
74 G5 Gateslack D & G
55 M5 Gathurst Wigan
55 T9 Gatley Stockp
21 N12 Gatton Surrey
84 E11 Gattonside Border
11 M2 Gatwick Airport W Susx
33 U7 Gaufron Powys
47 S13 Gaulby Leics
91 N7 Gauldry Fife
98 C13 Gauldswell P & K

9 P5 Horton Heath Hants
62 G5 Horton in Ribblesdale N York
21 U9 Horton Kirby Kent
55 P4 Horwich Bolton
56 F10 Horwich End Derbys
15 M7 Horwood Devon
55 L4 Hoscar Lancs
75 S3 Hoscote Border
47 T8 Hose Leics
21 S12 Hosey Hill Kent
90 C7 Hosh P & K
106 u11 Hoswick Shet
64 K13 Hotham E R Yk
12 J7 Hothfield Kent
47 Q9 Hoton Leics
76 F8 Hott Nthumb
45 R3 Hough Ches E
56 C11 Hough Ches E
48 C5 Hougham Lincs
63 Q13 Hough End Leeds
55 L9 Hough Green Halton
48 D4 Hough-on-the-Hill Lincs
39 L6 Houghton Cambs
75 T14 Houghton Cumb
9 L2 Houghton Hants
77 N12 Houghton Nthumb
24 G9 Houghton Pembks
10 G8 Houghton W Susx
31 M4 Houghton Conquest C Beds
70 D2 Houghton Gate Dur
12 H11 Houghton Green E Susx
55 P8 Houghton Green Warrtn
69 R8 Houghton le Side Darltn
70 D3 Houghton-le-Spring Sundld
47 S13 Houghton on the Hill Leics
31 M8 Houghton Regis C Beds
50 F6 Houghton St Giles Norfk
20 B11 Hound Green Hants
84 G9 Houndslow Border
16 F11 Houndsmoor Somset
85 L6 Houndwood Border
20 K7 Hounslow Gt Lon
103 N4 Househill Highld
56 J3 Houses Hill Kirk
105 P10 Housieside Abers
88 K12 Houston Rens
112 E10 Houstry Highld
106 s19 Houton Ork
11 M10 Hove Br & H
56 H2 Hove Edge Calder
47 S4 Hoveringham Notts
51 P10 Hoveton Norfk
64 F4 Hovingham N York
57 M7 Howbrook Barns
28 B1 How Caple Herefs
64 G14 Howden E R Yk
69 Q6 Howden-le-Wear Dur
112 H4 Howe Highld
60 b9 Howe IoM
63 T3 Howe N York
51 N14 Howe Norfk
55 Q6 Howe Bridge Wigan
55 Q6 Howe Bridge Crematorium Wigan
22 H7 Howe Green Essex
22 K7 Howegreen Essex
48 H4 Howell Lincs
31 M4 How End C Beds
105 M6 Howe of Teuchar Abers
75 N12 Howes D & G
22 G5 Howe Street Essex
39 U14 Howe Street Essex
34 C9 Howey Powys
66 E8 Howgate Cumb
83 P7 Howgate Mdloth
62 G10 Howgill Lancs
77 R2 Howick Nthumb
45 Q9 Howle Wrekin
28 B3 Howle Hill Herefs
39 S14 Howlett End Essex
6 J3 Howley Somset
67 R1 How Mill Cumb
106 c15 Howmore W Isls
76 F2 Hownam Border
67 M3 Howrigg Cumb
58 H6 Howsham N Linc
64 G7 Howsham N York
85 M12 Howtel Nthumb
12 G2 Howt Green Kent
27 S2 Howton Herefs
67 P9 Howtown Cumb
88 J13 Howwood Rens
41 L5 Hoxne Suffk
106 r20 Hoy Ork
54 F9 Hoylake Wirral
57 N6 Hoyland Common Barns
57 N6 Hoyland Nether Barns
57 L6 Hoyland Swaine Barns
10 E7 Hoyle W Susx
57 N5 Hoyle Mill Barns
62 J4 Hubberholme N York
24 E9 Hubberston Pembks
49 L5 Hubbert's Bridge Lincs
63 R10 Huby N York
64 D6 Huby N York
5 R6 Huccaby Devon
28 G4 Hucclecote Gloucs
12 F4 Hucking Kent
47 P4 Hucknall Notts
56 H3 Huddersfield Kirk
56 H2 Huddersfield Crematorium Kirk
36 B9 Huddington Worcs
31 M10 Hudnall Herts
69 P12 Hudswell N York
64 K8 Huggate E R Yk
47 M11 Hugglescote Leics
20 E3 Hughenden Valley Bucks
45 N14 Hughley Shrops
2 c2 Hugh Town IoS
15 M10 Huish Devon
18 H8 Huish Wilts
16 E11 Huish Champflower Somset
17 M11 Huish Episcopi Somset
30 K5 Hulcote C Beds
30 J9 Hulcott Bucks
6 D8 Hulham Devon
46 H4 Hulland Derbys
46 J4 Hulland Ward Derbys
18 C4 Hullavington Wilts
22 K8 Hullbridge Essex
65 P14 Hull, Kingston upon C KuH
55 T7 Hulme Manch
46 B4 Hulme Staffs
55 P8 Hulme Warrtn
46 F2 Hulme End Staffs
55 T13 Hulme Walfield Ches E
55 R10 Hulse Heath Ches E
55 Q5 Hulton Lane Ends Bolton
9 M12 Hulverstone IoW
50 F11 Hulver Street Norfk
41 S3 Hulver Street Suffk
6 A9 Humber Devon
35 M9 Humber Herefs
58 J4 Humberside Airport N Linc
59 P5 Humberston NE Lin
47 R12 Humberstone C Leic
63 U6 Humberton N York
84 D6 Humbie E Loth
65 S13 Humbleton E R Yk
85 P13 Humbleton Nthumb
48 F7 Humby Lincs
84 J10 Hume Border
76 J11 Humshaugh Nthumb
112 J2 Huna Highld
62 F13 Huncoat Lancs
47 P14 Huncote Leics
76 C2 Hundalee Border
57 N11 Hundall Derbys
69 L8 Hunderthwaite Dur
59 Q13 Hundleby Lincs
48 K3 Hundle Houses Lincs
24 G10 Hundleton Pembks
40 B11 Hundon Suffk
54 K2 Hundred End Lancs
34 D10 Hundred House Powys
47 S12 Hungarton Leics
8 H6 Hungerford Hants
16 D8 Hungerford Somset
19 M7 Hungerford W Berk
19 N6 Hungerford Newtown W Berk
55 Q5 Hunger Hill Bolton
55 M4 Hunger Hill Lancs
34 K13 Hungerstone Herefs
48 C8 Hungerton Lincs
45 Q8 Hungryhatton Shrops
65 P4 Hunmanby N York
37 L7 Hunningham Warwks
36 C4 Hunnington Worcs
37 T9 Hunsbury Hill Nhants
22 B5 Hunsdon Herts
63 U9 Hunsingore N York
63 S13 Hunslet Leeds
67 S5 Hunsonby Cumb
49 U5 Hunstanton Norfk
68 K3 Hunstanworth Dur
45 Q4 Hunsterson Ches E
40 G7 Hunston Suffk
10 D10 Hunston W Susx
40 G7 Hunston Green Suffk
17 R4 Hunstrete BaNES
56 J1 Hunsworth Kirk
36 D8 Hunt End Worcs
15 Q3 Hunter's Inn Devon
88 E10 Hunter's Quay Ag & B
16 K11 Huntham Somset
98 H9 Hunthill Lodge Angus
38 K6 Huntingdon Cambs
41 P6 Huntingfield Suffk
17 V11 Huntingford Dorset
64 E8 Huntington C York
54 K14 Huntington Ches W
84 D4 Huntington E Loth
34 G10 Huntington Herefs
35 L12 Huntington Herefs
46 C11 Huntington Staffs
28 D4 Huntley Gloucs
104 G8 Huntly Abers
19 Q12 Hunton Hants
12 D6 Hunton Kent
63 P1 Hunton N York
31 N12 Hunton Bridge Herts
40 J3 Hunt's Corner Norfk
16 B8 Huntscott Somset
54 K9 Hunt's Cross Lpool
30 J12 Hunts Green Bucks
36 G1 Hunts Green Warwks
16 D12 Huntsham Devon
15 M8 Huntshaw Devon
15 M8 Huntshaw Cross Devon
16 K7 Huntspill Somset
16 J10 Huntstile Somset
16 K10 Huntworth Somset
69 Q6 Hunwick Dur
50 J6 Hunworth Norfk
17 L13 Hurcott Somset
8 H2 Hurdcott Wilts
56 D12 Hurdsfield Ches E
20 D6 Hurley W & M
36 H1 Hurley Warwks
20 D6 Hurley Bottom W & M
36 H1 Hurley Common Warwks
81 P5 Hurlford E Ayrs
54 J4 Hurlston Green Lancs
8 G9 Hurn Dorset
49 P4 Hurn's End Lincs
9 N3 Hursley Hants
7 U6 Hurst Dorset
69 M12 Hurst N York
17 N13 Hurst Somset
20 C8 Hurst Wokham
19 P11 Hurstbourne Priors Hants
19 N10 Hurstbourne Tarrant Hants
12 D10 Hurst Green E Susx
23 Q4 Hurst Green Essex
62 D12 Hurst Green Lancs
21 Q12 Hurst Green Surrey
36 B2 Hurst Hill Dudley
34 J11 Hurstley Herefs
11 M7 Hurstpierpoint W Susx
11 M7 Hurst Wickham W Susx
62 H13 Hurstwood Lancs
106 u19 Hurtiso Ork
20 F13 Hurtmore Surrey
70 F6 Hurworth Burn Dur
70 D11 Hurworth-on-Tees Darltn
69 S11 Hurworth Place Darltn
69 L9 Hury Dur
37 R4 Husbands Bosworth Leics
31 L5 Husborne Crawley C Beds
64 C5 Husthwaite N York
5 T10 Hutcherleigh Devon
57 M10 Hutcliffe Wood Crematorium Sheff
57 S2 Hut Green N York
47 N2 Huthwaite Notts
59 T11 Huttoft Lincs
85 N8 Hutton Border
67 P7 Hutton Cumb
65 N9 Hutton E R Yk
22 F8 Hutton Essex
55 L1 Hutton Lancs
17 L5 Hutton N Som
70 D12 Hutton Bonville N York
65 M3 Hutton Buscel N York
63 S5 Hutton Conyers N York
65 N9 Hutton Cranswick E R Yk
67 Q5 Hutton End Cumb
63 P2 Hutton Hang N York
70 F5 Hutton Henry Dur
64 G1 Hutton-le-Hole N York
70 J10 Hutton Lowcross R & Cl
69 P10 Hutton Magna Dur
71 P11 Hutton Mulgrave N York
62 B4 Hutton Roof Cumb
67 N6 Hutton Roof Cumb
70 G11 Hutton Rudby N York
64 B4 Hutton Sessay N York
64 C9 Hutton Wandesley N York
6 B5 Huxham Devon
17 Q9 Huxham Green Somset
45 M1 Huxley Ches W
54 K8 Huyton Knows
60 K2 Hycemoor Cumb
28 G7 Hyde Gloucs
8 H6 Hyde Hants
56 D8 Hyde Tamesd
20 B9 Hyde End Wokham
30 K12 Hyde Heath Bucks
46 B10 Hyde Lea Staffs
10 F2 Hydestile Surrey
58 F13 Hykeham Moor Lincs
82 H10 Hyndford Bridge S Lans
92 B11 Hynish Ag & B
34 H2 Hyssington Powys
28 C8 Hystfield Gloucs
9 N7 Hythe Hants
13 N9 Hythe Kent
17 M6 Hythe Somset
20 H8 Hythe End W & M
60 K2 Hyton Cumb

I

7 U3 Ibberton Dorset
46 H2 Ible Derbys
8 H7 Ibsley Hants
47 M12 Ibstock Leics
20 C4 Ibstone Bucks
19 N10 Ibthorpe Hants
71 Q11 Iburndale N York
19 S10 Ibworth Hants
17 L3 Icelton N Som
94 E12 Ichrachan Ag & B
40 D1 Ickburgh Norfk
20 J5 Ickenham Gt Lon
30 D11 Ickford Bucks
13 P4 Ickham Kent
31 Q6 Ickleford Herts
12 G12 Icklesham E Susx
39 Q12 Ickleton Cambs
40 C6 Icklingham Suffk
62 K11 Ickornshaw N York
38 J11 Ickwell Green C Beds
40 D8 Ickworth Suffk
29 P3 Icomb Gloucs
29 P4 Idbury Oxon
15 N11 Iddesleigh Devon
6 A6 Ide Devon
6 A9 Ideford Devon
21 S12 Ide Hill Kent
12 H11 Iden E Susx
12 D8 Iden Green Kent
12 F9 Iden Green Kent
63 P12 Idle C Brad
3 L7 Idless Cnwll
36 J12 Idlicote Warwks
18 J13 Idmiston Wilts
25 R7 Idole Carmth
46 J4 Idridgehay Derbys
100 c3 Idrigill Highld
29 Q11 Idstone Oxon
30 B12 Iffley Oxon
11 M3 Ifield W Susx
10 G4 Ifold W Susx
8 G10 Iford Bmouth
11 Q9 Iford E Susx
27 T10 Ifton Mons
44 H6 Ifton Heath Shrops
45 N6 Ightfield Shrops
21 U11 Ightham Kent
41 R9 Iken Suffk
46 F3 Ilam Staffs
17 P12 Ilchester Somset
77 L1 Ilderton Nthumb
21 R5 Ilford Gt Lon
17 L13 Ilford Somset
15 M3 Ilfracombe Devon
47 N5 Ilkeston Derbys
41 Q3 Ilketshall St Andrew Suffk
41 Q3 Ilketshall St John Suffk
41 Q4 Ilketshall St Lawrence Suffk
41 P3 Ilketshall St Margaret Suffk
63 N10 Ilkley C Brad
4 H5 Illand Cnwll
36 C4 Illey Dudley
55 S14 Illidge Green Ches E
63 M14 Illingworth Calder
2 H8 Illogan Cnwll
47 T14 Illston on the Hill Leics
30 G11 Ilmer Bucks
36 H12 Ilmington Warwks
7 L2 Ilminster Somset
5 T5 Ilsington Devon
7 U6 Ilsington Dorset
25 U12 Ilston Swans
63 P4 Ilton N York
17 L13 Ilton Somset
79 R7 Imachar N Ayrs
59 L4 Immingham NE Lin
59 L3 Immingham Dock NE Lin
39 P8 Impington Cambs
55 L11 Ince Ches W
54 H6 Ince Blundell Sefton
55 N6 Ince-in-Makerfield Wigan
108 G11 Inchbae Lodge Hotel Highld
99 L10 Inchbare Angus
104 C4 Inchberry Moray
107 T12 Incheril Highld
89 L12 Inchinnan Rens
101 T11 Inchlaggan Highld
90 K6 Inchmichael P & K
102 C13 Inchnacardoch Hotel Highld
110 F12 Inchnadamph Highld
91 L6 Inchture P & K
101 U4 Inchvuilt Highld
90 J7 Inchyra P & K
3 N5 Indian Queens Cnwll
41 R3 Ingate Place Suffk
22 F8 Ingatestone Essex
56 K5 Ingbirchworth Barns
63 R6 Ingerthorpe N York
46 C9 Ingestre Staffs
58 F10 Ingham Lincs
51 Q8 Ingham Norfk
40 E6 Ingham Suffk
51 Q8 Ingham Corner Norfk
49 Q10 Ingleborough Norfk
46 K8 Ingleby Derbys
70 F12 Ingleby Arncliffe N York
70 F10 Ingleby Barwick S on T
70 G12 Ingleby Cross N York
70 J11 Ingleby Greenhow N York
15 P11 Ingleigh Green Devon
17 T4 Inglesbatch BaNES
29 P8 Inglesham Swindn
74 J12 Ingleston D & G
69 Q8 Ingleton Dur
62 D5 Ingleton N York
61 U12 Inglewhite Lancs
77 L11 Ingoe Nthumb
61 U13 Ingol Lancs
49 U7 Ingoldisthorpe Norfk
59 U13 Ingoldmells Lincs
48 F8 Ingoldsby Lincs
77 L2 Ingram Nthumb
22 F9 Ingrave Essex
63 M12 Ingrow C Brad
67 P13 Ings Cumb
28 A10 Ingst S Glos
48 E12 Ingthorpe Rutlnd
51 L8 Ingworth Norfk
36 D9 Inkberrow Worcs
69 P5 Inkerman Dur
105 Q8 Inkhorn Abers
19 N8 Inkpen W Berk
112 G2 Inkstack Highld
18 D8 Inmarsh Wilts
88 E11 Innellan Ag & B
83 R11 Innerleithen Border
91 N11 Innerleven Fife
72 D7 Innermessan D & G
84 J4 Innerwick E Loth
104 B3 Innesmill Moray
104 J10 Insch Abers
97 N3 Insh Highld
61 T12 Inskip Lancs
61 T12 Inskip Moss Side Lancs
15 L6 Instow Devon
5 L10 Insworke Cnwll
57 N10 Intake Sheff
98 C5 Inver Abers
109 R8 Inver Highld
90 F3 Inver P & K
93 T2 Inverailort Highld
107 P13 Inveralligin Highld
105 S2 Inverallochy Abers
108 K5 Inveran Highld
88 C4 Inveraray Ag & B
100 e6 Inverarish Highld
91 Q3 Inverarity Angus
88 H2 Inverarnan Stirlg
107 P8 Inverasdale Highld
88 H6 Inverbeg Ag & B
99 Q9 Inverbervie Abers
104 K3 Inver-boyndie Abers
94 E9 Invercreran House Hotel Ag & B
103 N13 Inverdruie Highld
83 R4 Inveresk E Loth
94 D11 Inveresragan Ag & B
107 Q8 Inverewe Garden Highld
97 T6 Inverey Abers
102 F11 Inverfarigaig Highld
94 D10 Inverfolla Ag & B
96 C3 Invergarry Highld
95 U13 Invergeldie P & K
101 U14 Invergloy Highld
109 N11 Invergordon Highld
91 M5 Invergowrie P & K
100 g9 Inverguseran Highld
95 T7 Inverhadden P & K
95 M13 Inverherive Hotel Stirlg
100 g9 Inverie Highld
87 T2 Inverinan Ag & B
101 N7 Inverinate Highld
91 U2 Inverkeilor Angus
83 M2 Inverkeithing Fife
104 J6 Inverkeithny Abers
88 F11 Inverkip Inver
110 B13 Inverkirkaig Highld
108 B7 Inverlael Highld
96 C8 Inverlair Highld
87 R4 Inverliever Lodge Ag & B
94 H13 Inverlochy Ag & B
98 G7 Invermark Angus
102 D12 Invermoriston Highld
111 Q4 Invernaver Highld
102 J6 Inverness Highld
102 H7 Inverness Crematorium Highld
103 L5 Inverness Dalcross Airport Highld
88 D6 Invernoaden Ag & B
94 K10 Inveroran Hotel Ag & B
98 G12 Inverquharity Angus
105 S6 Inverquhomery Abers
96 B7 Inverroy Highld
94 C7 Inversanda Highld
101 N8 Invershiel Highld
108 K5 Invershin Highld
112 F9 Invershore Highld
88 H4 Inversnaid Hotel Stirlg
105 T6 Inverugie Abers
88 H4 Inveruglas Ag & B
97 N3 Inveruglass Highld
105 M11 Inverurie Abers
15 N13 Inwardleigh Devon
23 L4 Inworth Essex
106 c14 Iochdar W Isls
92 H13 Iona Ag & B
10 D6 Iping W Susx
5 U7 Ipplepen Devon
19 T3 Ipsden Oxon
46 D4 Ipstones Staffs
41 L12 Ipswich Suffk
41 L11 Ipswich Crematorium Suffk
54 G10 Irby Wirral
59 S14 Irby in the Marsh Lincs
59 L6 Irby upon Humber NE Lin
38 D7 Irchester Nhants
66 K5 Ireby Cumb
62 D4 Ireby Lancs
31 P4 Ireland C Beds
61 N4 Ireleth Cumb
68 J5 Ireshopeburn Dur
46 J4 Ireton Wood Derbys
55 R8 Irlam Salfd
48 F8 Irnham Lincs
28 C11 Iron Acton S Glos
49 Q14 Iron Bridge Cambs
45 Q13 Ironbridge Wrekin
45 Q13 Ironbridge Gorge Shrops
36 E10 Iron Cross Warwks
73 R4 Ironmacannie D & G
21 M13 Irons Bottom Surrey
47 M3 Ironville Derbys
51 Q9 Irstead Norfk
75 U13 Irthington Cumb
38 D6 Irthlingborough Nhants
65 N3 Irton N York
81 L5 Irvine N Ayrs
81 L5 Irvine Maritime Centre N Ayrs
112 A3 Isauld Highld
106 t4 Isbister Shet
106 v7 Isbister Shet
11 Q7 Isfield E Susx
38 C6 Isham Nhants
10 B2 Isington Hants
35 U4 Islandpool Worcs
86 F10 Islay Ag & B
78 E5 Islay Airport Ag & B
17 L12 Isle Abbotts Somset
17 L12 Isle Brewers Somset
39 T6 Isleham Cambs
21 Q7 Isle of Dogs Gt Lon
23 L12 Isle of Grain Medway
106 i5 Isle of Lewis W Isls
60 f5 Isle of Man IoM
60 d9 Isle of Man Ronaldsway Airport IoM
93 Q11 Isle of Mull Ag & B
8 E12 Isle of Purbeck Dorset
12 J2 Isle of Sheppey Kent
100 d6 Isle of Skye Highld
13 R2 Isle of Thanet Kent
61 M6 Isle of Walney Cumb
73 M12 Isle of Whithorn D & G
9 Q11 Isle of Wight IoW
9 Q10 Isle of Wight Crematorium IoW
100 g8 Isleornsay Highld
2 c2 Isles of Scilly St Mary's Airport IoS
74 J11 Islesteps D & G
6 e2 Islet Village Guern
21 L7 Isleworth Gt Lon
47 M9 Isley Walton Leics
106 f6 Islibhig W Isls
21 P6 Islington Gt Lon
21 N4 Islington Crematorium Gt Lon
38 E5 Islip Nhants
30 B10 Islip Oxon
106 f6 Islivig W Isls
45 P11 Isombridge Wrekin
22 F13 Istead Rise Kent
9 Q2 Itchen Abbas Hants
9 R2 Itchen Stoke Hants
10 J5 Itchingfield W Susx
28 C10 Itchington S Glos
50 K7 Itteringham Norfk
15 Q13 Itton Devon
27 T8 Itton Mons
27 T8 Itton Common Mons
67 P4 Ivegill Cumb
68 K13 Ivelet N York
20 H6 Iver Bucks
20 H6 Iver Heath Bucks
69 P2 Iveston Dur
30 K9 Ivinghoe Bucks
31 L9 Ivinghoe Aston Bucks
35 L9 Ivington Herefs
35 L9 Ivington Green Herefs
5 Q9 Ivybridge Devon
12 K10 Ivychurch Kent
8 B4 Ivy Cross Dorset
21 U12 Ivy Hatch Kent
50 E12 Ivy Todd Norfk
12 H2 Iwade Kent
8 B6 Iwerne Courtney or Shroton Dorset
8 B6 Iwerne Minster Dorset
40 F6 Ixworth Suffk
40 F6 Ixworth Thorpe Suffk

J

55 N1 Jack Green Lancs
63 P9 Jack Hill N York
6 D5 Jack-in-the-Green Devon
19 L13 Jack's Bush Hants
47 M3 Jacksdale Notts
56 J5 Jackson Bridge Kirk
81 R2 Jackton S Lans
14 E13 Jacobstow Cnwll
15 N12 Jacobstowe Devon
20 H12 Jacobs Well Surrey
24 J11 Jameston Pembks
102 E4 Jamestown Highld
88 J9 Jamestown W Duns
112 E10 Janetstown Highld
112 J6 Janets-town Highld
75 M8 Jardine Hall D & G
77 S13 Jarrow S Tyne
11 S5 Jarvis Brook E Susx
22 H2 Jasper's Green Essex
89 T10 Jawcraig Falk
23 S5 Jaywick Essex
20 E8 Jealott's Hill Br For
70 F14 Jeater Houses N York
76 C1 Jedburgh Border
24 J9 Jeffreyston Pembks
102 K2 Jemimaville Highld
6 e4 Jerbourg Guern
7 b2 Jersey Airport Jersey
7 d3 Jersey Crematorium Jersey
26 C9 Jersey Marine Neath
58 F12 Jerusalem Lincs
77 R12 Jesmond N u Ty
11 T10 Jevington E Susx
27 T5 Jingle Street Mons
31 M10 Jockey End Herts
55 S12 Jodrell Bank Ches E
67 P6 Johnby Cumb
54 K10 John Lennon Airport Lpool
112 J2 John o' Groats Highld
12 D11 John's Cross E Susx
99 P10 Johnshaven Abers
51 Q10 Johnson's Street Norfk
24 F8 Johnston Pembks
75 P5 Johnstone D & G
88 K13 Johnstone Rens
75 M7 Johnstonebridge D & G
25 Q7 Johnstown Carmth
44 H4 Johnstown Wrexhm
83 R4 Joppa C Edin
33 L7 Joppa Cerdgn
81 N9 Joppa S Ayrs
20 G4 Jordans Bucks
24 F4 Jordanston Pembks
57 N10 Jordanthorpe Sheff
22 D13 Joyden's Wood Kent
12 F6 Jubilee Corner Kent
57 N6 Jump Barns
11 R4 Jumper's Town E Susx
76 J14 Juniper Nthumb
83 N5 Juniper Green C Edin
86 J9 Jura Ag & B
60 f3 Jurby IoM
5 R4 Jurston Devon

K

68 G10 Kaber Cumb
82 J9 Kaimend S Lans
87 T11 Kames Ag & B
82 C13 Kames E Ayrs
3 L8 Kea Cnwll
58 D4 Keadby N Linc
49 N1 Keal Cotes Lincs
63 S10 Kearby Town End N York
55 S6 Kearsley Bolton
77 L10 Kearsley Nthumb
13 Q7 Kearsney Kent
62 C4 Kearstwick Cumb
69 L13 Kearton N York
62 E6 Keasden N York
5 Q10 Keaton Devon
55 N10 Keckwick Halton
59 P9 Keddington Lincs
59 Q9 Keddington Corner Lincs
40 B11 Kedington Suffk
46 K5 Kedleston Derbys
59 L4 Keelby Lincs
45 T4 Keele Staffs
45 T5 Keele Services Staffs
45 T4 Keele University Staffs
38 F11 Keeley Green Bed
63 M13 Keelham C Brad
24 F7 Keeston Pembks
18 D9 Keevil Wilts
47 N8 Kegworth Leics
2 G8 Kehelland Cnwll
104 J12 Keig Abers
63 M11 Keighley C Brad
63 L12 Keighley Crematorium C Brad
90 C13 Keilarsbrae Clacks
90 E6 Keillour P & K
98 B5 Keiloch Abers
86 J12 Keils Ag & B
17 P10 Keinton Mandeville Somset
74 G7 Keir Mill D & G
68 G2 Keirsleywell Row Nthumb
48 F8 Keisby Lincs
68 F8 Keisley Cumb
112 H4 Keiss Highld
104 E5 Keith Moray
90 K4 Keithick P & K
99 L11 Keithock Angus
102 F4 Keithtown Highld
62 J11 Kelbrook Lancs
48 F5 Kelby Lincs
67 S10 Keld Cumb
68 J12 Keld N York
64 H3 Keld Head N York
64 G2 Keldholme N York
58 D6 Kelfield N Linc
64 D12 Kelfield N York
47 U2 Kelham Notts
75 M12 Kelhead D & G
5 L3 Kellacott Devon
61 S14 Kellamergh Lancs
91 Q4 Kellas Angus
103 U5 Kellas Moray
5 U13 Kellaton Devon
68 E11 Kelleth Cumb
50 J5 Kelling Norfk
57 S2 Kellington N York
70 D5 Kelloe Dur
74 D3 Kelloholm D & G
66 E9 Kells Cumb
4 K4 Kelly Devon
4 K6 Kelly Bray Cnwll
37 T5 Kelmarsh Nhants
29 P8 Kelmscott Oxon
41 Q7 Kelsale Suffk
55 M13 Kelsall Ches W
31 T5 Kelshall Herts
66 J2 Kelsick Cumb
84 J12 Kelso Border
57 M14 Kelstedge Derbys
59 M9 Kelstern Lincs
54 G12 Kelsterton Flints
17 T3 Kelston BaNES
95 V9 Keltneyburn P & K
74 J11 Kelton D & G
90 H13 Kelty Fife
23 L4 Kelvedon Essex
22 E8 Kelvedon Hatch Essex
2 B11 Kelynack Cnwll
15 Q3 Kemacott Devon
91 P9 Kemback Fife
45 R13 Kemberton Shrops
28 J8 Kemble Gloucs
28 J8 Kemble Wick Gloucs
36 C13 Kemerton Worcs
27 Q7 Kemeys Commander Mons
105 L12 Kemnay Abers
12 K6 Kempe's Corner Kent
28 C2 Kempley Gloucs
28 C2 Kempley Green Gloucs
35 U11 Kempsey Worcs
29 N8 Kempsford Gloucs
36 F6 Kemps Green Warwks
19 T10 Kempshott Hants
38 F11 Kempston Bed
31 M4 Kempston Hardwick Bed
34 J4 Kempton Shrops
11 N10 Kemp Town Br & H
21 U11 Kemsing Kent
12 H2 Kemsley Kent
12 F3 Kemsley Street Kent
12 J9 Kenardington Kent
34 K12 Kenchester Herefs
29 Q7 Kencot Oxon
67 R14 Kendal Cumb
27 S2 Kenderchurch Herefs
28 C12 Kendleshire S Glos
26 E11 Kenfig Brdgnd
26 E11 Kenfig Hill Brdgnd
36 J6 Kenilworth Warwks
21 P10 Kenley Gt Lon
45 N13 Kenley Shrops
107 N13 Kenmore Highld
95 V9 Kenmore P & K
6 B7 Kenn Devon
17 M3 Kenn N Som
79 Q3 Kennacraig Ag & B
4 H4 Kennards House Cnwll
2 F11 Kenneggy Cnwll
15 T11 Kennerleigh Devon
54 J6 Kennessee Green Sefton
90 D13 Kennet Clacks
104 G10 Kennethmont Abers
39 U7 Kennett Cambs
6 B7 Kennford Devon
40 H3 Kenninghall Norfk
12 K6 Kennington Kent
30 B12 Kennington Oxon
91 N11 Kennoway Fife
16 K13 Kenny Somset
39 U5 Kennyhill Suffk
64 H6 Kennythorpe N York
92 B9 Kenovay Ag & B
100 d4 Kensaleyre Highld
21 N7 Kensington Gt Lon
31 M9 Kensworth Common C Beds
94 E7 Kentallen Highld
11 T3 Kent and Sussex Crematorium Kent
27 S2 Kentchurch Herefs
40 B7 Kentford Suffk
45 T2 Kent Green Ches E
13 R2 Kent International Airport Kent
6 E3 Kentisbeare Devon
15 P4 Kentisbury Devon
15 P4 Kentisbury Ford Devon
21 N6 Kentish Town Gt Lon
67 Q12 Kentmere Cumb
6 C8 Kenton Devon
21 L5 Kenton Gt Lon
77 Q12 Kenton N u Ty
41 L7 Kenton Suffk
77 Q12 Kenton Bankfoot N u Ty
93 R5 Kentra Highld
61 R4 Kents Bank Cumb
28 D3 Kent's Green Gloucs
9 L4 Kent's Oak Hants
12 E12 Kent Street E Susx
12 C5 Kent Street Kent
44 K7 Kenwick Shrops
3 L7 Kenwyn Cnwll
55 P7 Kenyon Warrtn
110 H3 Keoldale Highld
101 M7 Keppoch Highld
64 B1 Kepwick N York
36 K4 Keresley Covtry
55 T13 Kermincham Ches E
5 T12 Kernborough Devon
28 A4 Kerne Bridge Herefs
93 U13 Kerrera Ag & B
56 D11 Kerridge Ches E
56 D11 Kerridge-end Ches E
2 C11 Kerris Cnwll
34 D2 Kerry Powys
88 D13 Kerrycroy Ag & B
47 T1 Kersall Notts
6 E8 Kersbrook Devon
15 P7 Kerscott Devon
40 H12 Kersey Suffk
40 G12 Kersey Tye Suffk
40 G12 Kersey Upland Suffk
106 i6 Kershader W Isls
75 U9 Kershopefoot Cumb
36 C12 Kersoe Worcs
6 E3 Kerswell Devon
35 U11 Kerswell Green Worcs
2 F10 Kerthen Wood Cnwll
41 M11 Kesgrave Suffk
41 T3 Kessingland Suffk
41 T3 Kessingland Beach Suffk
3 P7 Kestle Cnwll
3 L5 Kestle Mill Cnwll
21 R10 Keston Gt Lon
67 L8 Keswick Cumb
51 M13 Keswick Norfk
59 Q11 Ketsby Lincs
38 C5 Kettering Nhants
38 C5 Kettering Crematorium Nhants
51 L13 Ketteringham Norfk
90 K4 Kettins P & K
40 G10 Kettlebaston Suffk
91 M10 Kettlebridge Fife
46 H13 Kettlebrook Staffs
41 N8 Kettleburgh Suffk
22 B4 Kettle Green Herts
75 M10 Kettleholm D & G
71 P9 Kettleness N York
56 E11 Kettleshulme Ches E
63 Q8 Kettlesing N York
63 Q8 Kettlesing Bottom N York
50 G7 Kettlestone Norfk
58 D11 Kettlethorpe Lincs
106 v16 Kettletoft Ork
62 K5 Kettlewell N York
48 E13 Ketton Rutlnd
21 L7 Kew Gt Lon
16 K4 Kewstoke N Som
57 M5 Kexbrough Barns
64 G9 Kexby C York
58 E9 Kexby Lincs
56 C14 Key Green Ches E
71 P12 Key Green N York
47 S12 Keyham Leics
9 L10 Keyhaven Hants
59 M1 Keyingham E R Yk
11 N7 Keymer W Susx
17 S3 Keynsham BaNES
38 G8 Keysoe Bed
38 G8 Keysoe Row Bed
38 F5 Keyston Cambs
12 G3 Key Street Kent
47 R7 Keyworth Notts
16 H12 Kibbear Somset
69 R1 Kibblesworth Gatesd
37 S2 Kibworth Beauchamp Leics
37 S2 Kibworth Harcourt Leics
21 R7 Kidbrooke Gt Lon
66 G8 Kidburngill Cumb
45 U12 Kiddemore Green Staffs
35 T5 Kidderminster Worcs
29 T3 Kiddington Oxon
50 K13 Kidd's Moor Norfk
29 U5 Kidlington Oxon
19 U5 Kidmore End Oxon
73 L12 Kidsdale D & G
45 T3 Kidsgrove Staffs
62 K3 Kidstones N York
25 R9 Kidwelly Carmth
94 C11 Kiel Crofts Ag & B
76 C7 Kielder Nthumb
86 G12 Kiells Ag & B
88 K13 Kilbarchan Rens
100 f9 Kilbeg Highld
79 N3 Kilberry Ag & B
81 L2 Kilbirnie N Ayrs
87 N10 Kilbride Ag & B
88 B12 Kilbride Ag & B
103 S3 Kilbuiack Moray
47 L4 Kilburn Derbys
21 M6 Kilburn Gt Lon
64 C4 Kilburn N York
37 R1 Kilby Leics
79 Q3 Kilchamaig Ag & B
80 G2 Kilchattan Ag & B
86 F6 Kilchattan Ag & B
93 U11 Kilcheran Ag & B
93 M6 Kilchoan Highld
78 C3 Kilchoman Ag & B
94 E14 Kilchrenan Ag & B
91 Q11 Kilconquhar Fife
28 C2 Kilcot Gloucs
102 G5 Kilcoy Highld
88 F9 Kilcreggan Ag & B
70 K11 Kildale N York
79 P12 Kildalloig Ag & B
109 P10 Kildary Highld
87 T12 Kildavaig Ag & B
88 B12 Kildavanan Ag & B
111 U12 Kildonan Highld
80 E8 Kildonan N Ayrs
111 U12 Kildonan Lodge Highld
93 M1 Kildonnan Highld
72 D8 Kildrochet House D & G
104 F12 Kildrummy Abers
63 L10 Kildwick N York
87 S10 Kilfinan Ag & B
96 B4 Kilfinnan Highld
54 C13 Kilford Denbgs
24 K9 Kilgetty Pembks
80 K12 Kilgrammie S Ayrs
27 T8 Kilgwrrwg Common Mons
65 P7 Kilham E R Yk
85 M12 Kilham Nthumb
92 A10 Kilkenneth Ag & B
79 M11 Kilkenzie Ag & B
79 N12 Kilkerran Ag & B
14 G10 Kilkhampton Cnwll
57 Q10 Killamarsh Derbys
25 V12 Killay Swans
89 M8 Killearn Stirlg
102 J4 Killen Highld
69 Q9 Killerby Darltn
6 C4 Killerton Devon
95 Q7 Killichonan P & K
94 J2 Killiechonate Highld
93 N10 Killiechronan Ag & B
97 Q11 Killiecrankie P & K
101 N5 Killilan Highld
112 H5 Killimster Highld
95 R12 Killin Stirlg
63 R8 Killinghall N York
62 C2 Killington Cumb
15 Q3 Killington Devon
62 B1 Killington Lake Services Cumb
77 R11 Killingworth N Tyne
3 L8 Killiow Cnwll
84 D9 Killochyett Border
88 J11 Kilmacolm Inver
89 P4 Kilmahog Stirlg
87 P7 Kilmahumaig Ag & B
100 d2 Kilmaluag Highld
91 N7 Kilmany Fife
81 N5 Kilmarnock E Ayrs
87 Q6 Kilmartin Ag & B
81 N4 Kilmaurs E Ayrs
87 R3 Kilmelford Ag & B
17 S6 Kilmersdon Somset
9 R3 Kilmeston Hants
79 M11 Kilmichael Ag & B
87 R7 Kilmichael Glassary Ag & B
87 P8 Kilmichael of Inverlussa Ag & B
6 J5 Kilmington Devon
17 U9 Kilmington Wilts
17 U9 Kilmington Common Wilts
17 U9 Kilmington Street Wilts
102 E7 Kilmorack Highld
94 B13 Kilmore Ag & B
100 f9 Kilmore Highld
87 N11 Kilmory Ag & B
93 N4 Kilmory Highld
80 D8 Kilmory N Ayrs
100 b5 Kilmuir Highld
100 c2 Kilmuir Highld
102 J6 Kilmuir Highld
109 P10 Kilmuir Highld
88 E9 Kilmun Ag & B
86 D11 Kilnave Ag & B
82 G9 Kilncadzow S Lans
12 D8 Kilndown Kent
20 D7 Kiln Green Wokham
66 K6 Kilnhill Cumb
55 P13 Kilnhouses Ches W
57 Q7 Kilnhurst Rothm
87 Q1 Kilninver Ag & B
69 M1 Kiln Pit Hill Nthumb
59 R3 Kilnsea E R Yk
62 K6 Kilnsey N York
65 M10 Kilnwick E R Yk
64 J10 Kilnwick Percy E R Yk
86 F6 Kiloran Ag & B
79 S10 Kilpatrick N Ayrs
27 S1 Kilpeck Herefs
58 C1 Kilpin E R Yk
58 C1 Kilpin Pike E R Yk
91 S11 Kilrenny Fife
37 Q6 Kilsby Nhants
90 K6 Kilspindie P & K
72 E12 Kilstay D & G
89 R10 Kilsyth N Lans
102 F7 Kiltarlity Highld
71 M9 Kilton R & Cl
71 L9 Kilton Thorpe R & Cl
100 c3 Kilvaxter Highld
16 F8 Kilve Somset
48 B5 Kilvington Notts
81 L4 Kilwinning N Ayrs
50 J13 Kimberley Norfk
47 N5 Kimberley Notts
57 P8 Kimberworth Rothm
69 S3 Kimblesworth Dur
30 H11 Kimble Wick Bucks
38 H7 Kimbolton Cambs
35 M8 Kimbolton Herefs
37 Q3 Kimcote Leics
8 C13 Kimmeridge Dorset
85 P11 Kimmerston Nthumb
19 L11 Kimpton Hants
31 Q9 Kimpton Herts
14 H10 Kimworthy Devon
111 T10 Kinbrace Highld
89 S4 Kinbuck Stirlg
91 Q8 Kincaple Fife
90 D14 Kincardine Fife
109 L7 Kincardine Highld
98 K4 Kincardine O'Neil Abers
90 J4 Kinclaven P & K
99 S3 Kincorth C Aber
103 R3 Kincorth House Moray
97 N2 Kincraig Highld
90 E2 Kincraigie P & K
90 E2 Kindallachan P & K
79 M5 Kinerarach Ag & B
29 L2 Kineton Gloucs
36 K10 Kineton Warwks
90 J7 Kinfauns P & K
80 F1 Kingarth Ag & B
43 Q12 King Arthur's Labyrinth Gwynd
99 R4 Kingcausie Abers
27 S6 Kingcoed Mons
58 J8 Kingerby Lincs
14 G11 Kingford Devon
29 Q3 Kingham Oxon
74 J11 Kingholm Quay D & G
83 Q1 Kinghorn Fife
90 K12 Kinglassie Fife
98 E12 Kingoldrum Angus
91 M6 Kingoodie P & K
35 L12 King's Acre Herefs
5 L10 Kingsand Cnwll
30 J11 Kingsash Bucks
91 S9 Kingsbarns Fife
5 S12 Kingsbridge Devon
16 C9 Kingsbridge Somset
25 U11 Kings Bridge Swans
46 F10 King's Bromley Staffs
100 c4 Kingsburgh Highld
21 L5 Kingsbury Gt Lon
36 H1 Kingsbury Warwks
17 M12 Kingsbury Episcopi Somset
27 V2 King's Caple Herefs
19 R9 Kingsclere Hants
38 F1 King's Cliffe Nhants
28 F8 Kingscote Gloucs
15 M9 Kingscott Devon
36 E9 King's Coughton Warwks
80 E7 Kingscross N Ayrs
17 P11 Kingsdon Somset
13 S6 Kingsdown Kent
29 N10 Kingsdown Swindn
18 B7 Kingsdown Wilts
29 N10 Kingsdown Crematorium Swindn
90 H13 Kingseat Fife
30 F11 Kingsey Bucks
10 K3 Kingsfold W Susx
99 R2 Kingsford C Aber
81 N3 Kingsford E Ayrs
35 T4 Kingsford Worcs
13 S1 Kingsgate Kent
35 S14 Kings Green Gloucs
40 F8 Kingshall Street Suffk
15 N5 Kingsheanton Devon
36 E4 King's Heath Birm
12 C4 Kings Hill Kent
36 C1 King's Hill Wsall
94 K8 Kings House Hotel Highld
89 N1 Kingshouse Hotel Stirlg
36 G3 Kingshurst Solhll
66 J2 Kingside Hill Cumb
6 A11 Kingskerswell Devon
91 M10 Kingskettle Fife
7 N5 Kingsland Dorset
34 K8 Kingsland Herefs
52 C6 Kingsland IoA
31 N12 Kings Langley Herts
55 N12 Kingsley Ches W
10 B3 Kingsley Hants
46 D4 Kingsley Staffs
10 D4 Kingsley Green W Susx
37 U8 Kingsley Park Nhants
45 S14 Kingslow Shrops
49 T9 King's Lynn Norfk
68 D8 Kings Meaburn Cumb
9 R6 Kingsmead Hants
6 c3 King's Mills Guern
55 M6 King's Moss St Hel
91 Q2 Kingsmuir Angus
83 Q11 Kings Muir Border
91 R10 Kingsmuir Fife
37 N5 Kings Newnham Warwks
47 L8 King's Newton Derbys
12 K8 Kingsnorth Kent
36 E5 King's Norton Birm
47 S13 King's Norton Leics
15 Q9 Kings Nympton Devon
34 K10 King's Pyon Herefs
39 L5 Kings Ripton Cambs
9 M2 King's Somborne Hants
7 T2 King's Stag Dorset
28 F7 King's Stanley Gloucs
37 N13 King's Sutton Nhants
36 E2 Kingstanding Birm
5 V6 Kingsteignton Devon
56 G12 King Sterndale Derbys
27 T1 Kingsthorne Herefs
37 U8 Kingsthorpe Nhants
39 M9 Kingston Cambs
4 K5 Kingston Cnwll
5 Q11 Kingston Devon
6 E7 Kingston Devon
7 U3 Kingston Dorset
8 D13 Kingston Dorset
84 E2 Kingston E Loth
8 G8 Kingston Hants
9 P12 Kingston IoW
13 N5 Kingston Kent
10 H10 Kingston W Susx
29 T8 Kingston Bagpuize Oxon
20 B3 Kingston Blount Oxon
18 B13 Kingston Deverill Wilts
34 K13 Kingstone Herefs
7 L2 Kingstone Somset
46 E8 Kingstone Staffs
29 Q10 Kingstone Winslow Oxon
29 R10 Kingston Lisle Oxon
11 P9 Kingston near Lewes E Susx
47 P8 Kingston on Soar Notts
104 C2 Kingston on Spey Moray
7 Q6 Kingston Russell Dorset
16 H11 Kingston St Mary Somset
17 M3 Kingston Seymour N Som
30 F12 Kingston Stert Oxon
65 P14 Kingston upon Hull C KuH
21 L9 Kingston upon Thames Gt Lon
21 L9 Kingston upon Thames Crematorium Gt Lon
75 S14 Kingstown Cumb
31 Q8 King's Walden Herts
5 V10 Kingswear Devon
99 R2 Kingswells C Aber
27 U12 Kings Weston Bristl
35 U3 Kingswinford Dudley
30 E9 Kingswood Bucks
28 D9 Kingswood Gloucs
12 F5 Kingswood Kent
44 F13 Kingswood Powys
28 B13 Kingswood S Glos
16 F9 Kingswood Somset
21 M11 Kingswood Surrey
36 G6 Kingswood Warwks
36 G6 Kingswood Brook Warwks
34 G10 Kingswood Common Herefs
45 T13 Kingswood Common Staffs
9 P2 Kings Worthy Hants
58 K11 Kingthorpe Lincs
34 G9 Kington Herefs
28 B9 Kington S Glos
36 C9 Kington Worcs
18 D5 Kington Langley Wilts
17 U12 Kington Magna Dorset
18 D5 Kington St Michael Wilts
97 M3 Kingussie Highld
17 P10 Kingweston Somset
105 Q9 Kinharrachie Abers
74 H12 Kinharvie D & G
90 D8 Kinkell Bridge P & K
105 S7 Kinknockie Abers
83 N5 Kinleith C Edin
35 R4 Kinlet Shrops
100 d10 Kinloch Highld
110 G10 Kinloch Highld
111 M6 Kinloch Highld
90 H3 Kinloch P & K
89 L5 Kinlochard Stirlg
110 E5 Kinlochbervie Highld
94 D3 Kinlocheil Highld
107 T12 Kinlochewe Highld
101 P10 Kinloch Hourn Highld
96 G6 Kinlochlaggan Highld
94 H6 Kinlochleven Highld
93 S4 Kinlochmoidart Highld
93 S2 Kinlochnanuagh Highld
95 T7 Kinloch Rannoch P & K
103 S3 Kinloss Moray
53 S6 Kinmel Bay Conwy
105 N12 Kinmuck Abers
105 P12 Kinmundy Abers
78 D7 Kinnabus Ag & B
105 R7 Kinnadie Abers
97 R12 Kinnaird P & K
99 Q8 Kinneff Abers
74 K5 Kinnelhead D & G
99 L13 Kinnell Angus
44 H9 Kinnerley Shrops
34 H11 Kinnersley Herefs
35 U12 Kinnersley Worcs
34 F8 Kinnerton Powys
34 J1 Kinnerton Shrops
44 H1 Kinnerton Green Flints
90 J11 Kinnesswood P & K
69 N8 Kinninvie Dur
98 F12 Kinnordy Angus
47 S7 Kinoulton Notts
90 H11 Kinross P & K
90 J5 Kinrossie P & K
90 H11 Kinross Services P & K
31 P9 Kinsbourne Green Herts
45 Q5 Kinsey Heath Ches E
34 J7 Kinsham Herefs
36 B13 Kinsham Worcs
57 P4 Kinsley Wakefd
8 F9 Kinson Bmouth
101 P8 Kintail Highld
19 N7 Kintbury W Berk
103 R3 Kintessack Moray
90 H8 Kintillo P & K
34 K6 Kinton Herefs
44 J10 Kinton Shrops
105 M12 Kintore Abers
78 H5 Kintour Ag & B
78 E6 Kintra Ag & B
92 J13 Kintra Ag & B
87 Q5 Kintraw Ag & B
79 N8 Kintyre Ag & B
103 P12 Kinveachy Highld
35 T4 Kinver Staffs
69 S13 Kiplin N York
63 U13 Kippax Leeds
89 P7 Kippen Stirlg
66 B2 Kippford or Scaur D & G
12 B7 Kipping's Cross Kent
106 s19 Kirbister Ork
51 N12 Kirby Bedon Norfk
47 T10 Kirby Bellars Leics
41 Q2 Kirby Cane Norfk
36 J5 Kirby Corner Covtry
23 T3 Kirby Cross Essex
47 P13 Kirby Fields Leics
65 L6 Kirby Grindalythe N York
63 T6 Kirby Hill N York
69 P11 Kirby Hill N York
64 B2 Kirby Knowle N York
23 T3 Kirby le Soken Essex
64 H4 Kirby Misperton N York
47 P13 Kirby Muxloe Leics
70 F14 Kirby Sigston N York
64 J8 Kirby Underdale E R Yk
63 T3 Kirby Wiske N York
10 G5 Kirdford W Susx
112 G5 Kirk Highld
106 u10 Kirkabister Shet
73 Q10 Kirkandrews D & G
75 S14 Kirkandrews upon Eden Cumb
67 M1 Kirkbampton Cumb
74 J14 Kirkbean D & G
57 T4 Kirk Bramwith Donc
66 K1 Kirkbride Cumb
63 R1 Kirkbridge N York
91 R3 Kirkbuddo Angus
83 Q11 Kirkburn Border
65 M8 Kirkburn E R Yk
56 J4 Kirkburton Kirk
54 K7 Kirkby Knows
58 J8 Kirkby Lincs
70 H11 Kirkby N York
69 S14 Kirkby Fleetham N York
48 G2 Kirkby Green Lincs
47 N2 Kirkby in Ashfield Notts
61 N3 Kirkby-in-Furness Cumb
48 G4 Kirkby la Thorpe Lincs
62 C4 Kirkby Lonsdale Cumb
62 H7 Kirkby Malham N York
47 N13 Kirkby Mallory Leics
63 Q5 Kirkby Malzeard N York
64 G2 Kirkby Mills N York
64 F2 Kirkbymoorside N York
48 K1 Kirkby on Bain Lincs
63 S10 Kirkby Overblow N York
68 G11 Kirkby Stephen Cumb
68 D7 Kirkby Thore Cumb
48 G8 Kirkby Underwood Lincs
64 C11 Kirkby Wharf N York
47 N3 Kirkby Woodhouse Notts
91 L13 Kirkcaldy Fife
91 L13 Kirkcaldy Crematorium Fife
76 A12 Kirkcambeck Cumb
73 R9 Kirkchrist D & G
72 C6 Kirkcolm D & G
74 D3 Kirkconnel D & G
74 J12 Kirkconnell D & G
72 J7 Kirkcowan D & G
73 R9 Kirkcudbright D & G
54 H8 Kirkdale Lpool
63 T9 Kirk Deighton N York
65 N14 Kirk Ella E R Yk
82 G10 Kirkfieldbank S Lans
74 G12 Kirkgunzeon D & G
47 N5 Kirk Hallam Derbys
61 S13 Kirkham Lancs
64 G6 Kirkham N York
57 L2 Kirkhamgate Wakefd
64 B8 Kirk Hammerton N York
77 L9 Kirkharle Nthumb
68 E3 Kirkhaugh Nthumb
56 J3 Kirkheaton Kirk
77 L10 Kirkheaton Nthumb
102 G6 Kirkhill Highld
74 J4 Kirkhope S Lans
76 B14 Kirkhouse Cumb
57 T4 Kirkhouse Green Donc
100 e8 Kirkibost Highld
91 M3 Kirkinch P & K
73 L9 Kirkinner D & G
89 Q11 Kirkintilloch E Duns
46 J3 Kirk Ireton Derbys
66 G9 Kirkland Cumb
68 D6 Kirkland Cumb
74 D3 Kirkland D & G
74 F7 Kirkland D & G
74 K8 Kirkland D & G
66 J4 Kirkland Guards Cumb
46 J6 Kirk Langley Derbys
70 J8 Kirkleatham R & Cl
70 F11 Kirklevington S on T
41 T2 Kirkley Suffk
63 S3 Kirklington N York
47 S2 Kirklington Notts
75 T12 Kirklinton Cumb
83 M4 Kirkliston C Edin
73 M8 Kirkmabreck D & G
72 E12 Kirkmaiden D & G
69 S6 Kirk Merrington Dur
60 e4 Kirk Michael IoM
97 T12 Kirkmichael P & K
81 L11 Kirkmichael S Ayrs
82 E10 Kirkmuirhill S Lans
85 N12 Kirknewton Nthumb
83 M5 Kirknewton W Loth
104 G9 Kirkney Abers
82 F6 Kirk of Shotts N Lans
67 S4 Kirkoswald Cumb
80 J11 Kirkoswald S Ayrs
74 H7 Kirkpatrick D & G
74 E11 Kirkpatrick Durham D & G
75 Q11 Kirkpatrick-Fleming D & G
57 T5 Kirk Sandall Donc
61 L3 Kirksanton Cumb
57 R3 Kirk Smeaton N York
63 R12 Kirkstall Leeds
48 J1 Kirkstead Lincs
104 G8 Kirkstile Abers
75 S7 Kirkstile D & G
67 P11 Kirkstone Pass Inn Cumb
112 H2 Kirkstyle Highld
57 N2 Kirkthorpe Wakefd
104 J10 Kirkton Abers
74 J9 Kirkton D & G
91 N6 Kirkton Fife
101 L6 Kirkton Highld
101 N3 Kirkton Highld
90 E8 Kirkton P & K
83 P11 Kirkton Manor Border
98 E13 Kirkton of Airlie Angus
91 M4 Kirkton of Auchterhouse Angus
103 M6 Kirkton of Barevan Highld
90 J5 Kirkton of Collace P & K
104 D12 Kirkton of Glenbuchat Abers
105 R10 Kirkton of Logie Buchan Abers
98 J11 Kirkton of Menmuir Angus
91 R4 Kirkton of Monikie Angus
104 K9 Kirkton of Rayne Abers
99 Q2 Kirkton of Skene Abers
91 N4 Kirkton of Strathmartine Angus
91 P4 Kirkton of Tealing Angus
104 J13 Kirkton of Tough Abers
105 R2 Kirktown Abers
105 T5 Kirktown Abers
104 K3 Kirktown of Alvah Abers
105 N10 Kirktown of Bourtie Abers
99 R6 Kirktown of Fetteresso Abers
104 C8 Kirktown of Mortlach Moray
105 S10 Kirktown of Slains Abers
83 M10 Kirkurd Border
106 t18 Kirkwall Ork
106 t19 Kirkwall Airport Ork
76 K9 Kirkwhelpington Nthumb
85 L13 Kirk Yetholm Border
58 K4 Kirmington N Linc
59 L8 Kirmond le Mire Lincs
88 E10 Kirn Ag & B
98 F13 Kirriemuir Angus
41 N1 Kirstead Green Norfk
75 P11 Kirtlebridge D & G
39 U9 Kirtling Cambs
39 U9 Kirtling Green Cambs
29 U4 Kirtlington Oxon
111 Q4 Kirtomy Highld
49 M6 Kirton Lincs
57 U13 Kirton Notts
41 N12 Kirton Suffk
49 L5 Kirton End Lincs
88 J10 Kirtonhill W Duns
49 L5 Kirton Holme Lincs
58 F7 Kirton in Lindsey N Linc
73 L9 Kirwaugh D & G
101 L4 Kishorn Highld
37 S9 Kislingbury Nhants
29 P1 Kitebrook Warwks
36 G7 Kite Green Warwks
37 N7 Kites Hardwick Warwks
14 F13 Kitleigh Cnwll
55 M5 Kitt Green Wigan
16 E12 Kittisford Somset
25 U13 Kittle Swans
36 G3 Kitt's Green Birm
99 S2 Kittybrewster C Aber
9 T2 Kitwood Hants
27 T1 Kivernoll Herefs
57 Q10 Kiveton Park Rothm
58 D10 Knaith Lincs
58 D9 Knaith Park Lincs
17 V12 Knap Corner Dorset
20 G11 Knaphill Surrey
16 K11 Knapp Somset
9 N4 Knapp Hill Hants
47 T2 Knapthorpe Notts
64 D9 Knapton C York
64 K4 Knapton N York
51 P7 Knapton Norfk
34 K10 Knapton Green Herefs
39 M8 Knapwell Cambs
63 T8 Knaresborough N York
68 E2 Knarsdale Nthumb
105 P7 Knaven Abers
63 U2 Knayton N York
31 S8 Knebworth Herts
64 G14 Knedlington E R Yk
58 B14 Kneesall Notts
31 T4 Kneesworth Cambs
47 T4 Kneeton Notts
25 S13 Knelston Swans
46 B6 Knenhall Staffs
40 G4 Knettishall Suffk
15 Q5 Knightacott Devon
37 M10 Knightcote Warwks
45 T8 Knightley Staffs
45 T9 Knightley Dale Staffs
47 R13 Knighton C Leic
5 N11 Knighton Devon
7 R2 Knighton Dorset
8 E9 Knighton Poole
34 G6 Knighton Powys
16 G8 Knighton Somset
45 R5 Knighton Staffs
45 S8 Knighton Staffs
19 L6 Knighton Wilts
35 P7 Knighton on Teme Worcs
28 G2 Knightsbridge Gloucs
4 D4 Knightsmill Cnwll
35 R9 Knightwick Worcs
34 G8 Knill Herefs
48 B7 Knipton Leics
69 P3 Knitsley Dur
46 H3 Kniveton Derbys

136 Merry Lees - Newton of Balcanquhal

47 N12 **Merry Lees** Leics
4 H7 **Merrymeet** Cnwll
23 P4 **Mersea Island** Essex
13 L7 **Mersham** Kent
21 N12 **Merstham** Surrey
10 D10 **Merston** W Susx
9 Q11 **Merstone** IoW
3 M8 **Merther** Cnwll
25 Q6 **Merthyr** Carmth
33 U13 **Merthyr Cynog** Powys
16 F3 **Merthyr Dyfan** V Glam
26 F12 **Merthyr Mawr** Brdgnd
26 J6 **Merthyr Tydfil** Myr Td
26 K8 **Merthyr Vale** Myr Td
15 M10 **Merton** Devon
21 N8 **Merton** Gt Lon
50 F14 **Merton** Norfk
30 C9 **Merton** Oxon
15 S9 **Meshaw** Devon
23 L4 **Messing** Essex
58 E6 **Messingham** N Linc
41 N4 **Metfield** Suffk
5 L7 **Metherell** Cnwll
48 G1 **Metheringham** Lincs
91 N12 **Methil** Fife
91 N11 **Methilhill** Fife
57 N1 **Methley** Leeds
57 N1 **Methley Junction** Leeds
105 P8 **Methlick** Abers
90 F6 **Methven** P & K
40 B2 **Methwold** Norfk
40 B2 **Methwold Hythe** Norfk
41 Q3 **Mettingham** Suffk
51 M6 **Metton** Norfk
3 Q8 **Mevagissey** Cnwll
57 Q6 **Mexborough** Donc
112 G2 **Mey** Highld
42 D7 **Meyllteyrn** Gwynd
29 M7 **Meysey Hampton** Gloucs
106 f5 **Miabhig** W Isls
106 f5 **Miavaig** W Isls
27 U2 **Michaelchurch** Herefs
34 H14 **Michaelchurch Escley** Herefs
34 F10 **Michaelchurch-on-Arrow** Powys
27 N11 **Michaelstone-y-Fedw** Newpt
27 M13 **Michaelston-le-Pit** V Glam
4 D5 **Michaelstow** Cnwll
28 D8 **Michaelwood Services** Gloucs
5 R7 **Michelcombe** Devon
19 R13 **Micheldever** Hants
19 R12 **Micheldever Station** Hants
9 L3 **Michelmersh** Hants
40 K8 **Mickfield** Suffk
57 R8 **Micklebring** Donc
71 P10 **Mickleby** N York
63 U13 **Micklefield** Leeds
20 H3 **Micklefield Green** Herts
21 L12 **Mickleham** Surrey
46 K7 **Mickleover** C Derb
63 N11 **Micklethwaite** C Brad
67 L2 **Micklethwaite** Cumb
69 L8 **Mickleton** Dur
36 G12 **Mickleton** Gloucs
57 P1 **Mickletown** Leeds
54 K13 **Mickle Trafford** Ches W
57 M11 **Mickley** Derbys
63 R4 **Mickley** N York
40 D9 **Mickley Green** Suffk
77 M13 **Mickley Square** Nthumb
105 Q3 **Mid Ardlaw** Abers
106 t15 **Midbea** Ork
99 L3 **Mid Beltie** Abers
8 H9 **Mid Bockhampton** Dorset
83 L5 **Mid Calder** W Loth
112 G9 **Mid Clyth** Highld
104 K3 **Mid Culbeuchly** Abers
20 B5 **Middle Assendon** Oxon
29 U2 **Middle Aston** Oxon
29 T2 **Middle Barton** Oxon
75 P10 **Middlebie** D & G
97 P10 **Middlebridge** P & K
7 N2 **Middle Chinnock** Somset
30 F7 **Middle Claydon** Bucks
57 P5 **Middlecliffe** Barns
5 S3 **Middlecott** Devon
28 J6 **Middle Duntisbourne** Gloucs
63 N2 **Middleham** N York
57 P11 **Middle Handley** Derbys
40 G3 **Middle Harling** Norfk
4 H7 **Middlehill** Cnwll
18 B7 **Middlehill** Wilts
35 L3 **Middlehope** Shrops
87 S8 **Middle Kames** Ag & B
36 E11 **Middle Littleton** Worcs
45 S4 **Middle Madeley** Staffs
34 H14 **Middle Maes-coed** Herefs
7 S3 **Middlemarsh** Dorset
46 F5 **Middle Mayfield** Staffs
24 D5 **Middle Mill** Pembks
5 M6 **Middlemore** Devon
12 G8 **Middle Quarter** Kent
58 J9 **Middle Rasen** Lincs
6 B11 **Middle Rocombe** Devon
62 C7 **Middle Salter** Lancs
70 G9 **Middlesbrough** Middsb
67 P4 **Middlesceugh** Cumb
62 B2 **Middleshaw** Cumb
63 M5 **Middlesmoor** N York
16 G12 **Middle Stoford** Somset
22 K12 **Middle Stoke** Medway
69 S6 **Middlestone** Dur
69 R6 **Middlestone Moor** Dur
17 M7 **Middle Stoughton** Somset
57 L3 **Middlestown** Wakefd
28 E7 **Middle Street** Gloucs
4 F8 **Middle Taphouse** Cnwll
84 H10 **Middlethird** Border
92 A10 **Middleton** Ag & B
62 C2 **Middleton** Cumb
46 J2 **Middleton** Derbys
56 J14 **Middleton** Derbys
40 E13 **Middleton** Essex
19 P12 **Middleton** Hants
35 M7 **Middleton** Herefs
61 S8 **Middleton** Lancs
63 S14 **Middleton** Leeds
63 N10 **Middleton** N York
64 H2 **Middleton** N York
38 B3 **Middleton** Nhants
49 U10 **Middleton** Norfk
77 M9 **Middleton** Nthumb
85 S11 **Middleton** Nthumb
90 H10 **Middleton** P & K
56 C5 **Middleton** Rochdl
35 M5 **Middleton** Shrops
44 H8 **Middleton** Shrops
41 R7 **Middleton** Suffk
25 R13 **Middleton** Swans
46 G14 **Middleton** Warwks
37 N12 **Middleton Cheney** Nhants
56 C5 **Middleton Crematorium** Rochdl
46 C6 **Middleton Green** Staffs
85 P13 **Middleton Hall** Nthumb
68 K7 **Middleton-in-Teesdale** Dur
41 R7 **Middleton Moor** Suffk
70 E10 **Middleton One Row** Darltn
70 G11 **Middleton-on-Leven** N York
10 F10 **Middleton-on-Sea** W Susx
35 M8 **Middleton on the Hill** Herefs
65 L10 **Middleton on the Wolds** E R Yk
105 Q13 **Middleton Park** C Aber
35 P2 **Middleton Priors** Shrops
63 S4 **Middleton Quernhow** N York
70 D10 **Middleton St George** Darltn
35 Q3 **Middleton Scriven** Shrops
30 B8 **Middleton Stoney** Oxon
69 R11 **Middleton Tyas** N York
66 E11 **Middletown** Cumb
2 b3 **Middle Town** IoS
17 N2 **Middletown** N Som
44 H11 **Middletown** Powys
36 K12 **Middle Tysoe** Warwks
19 L13 **Middle Wallop** Hants
55 R13 **Middlewich** Ches E
8 J2 **Middle Winterslow** Wilts
4 H5 **Middlewood** Cnwll
34 G12 **Middlewood** Herefs
18 H13 **Middle Woodford** Wilts
40 J8 **Middlewood Green** Suffk
81 Q6 **Middleyard** E Ayrs
28 F7 **Middle Yard** Gloucs
17 L10 **Middlezoy** Somset
69 R7 **Middridge** Dur
17 U4 **Midford** BaNES
55 M2 **Midge Hall** Lancs
76 C14 **Midgeholme** Cumb
19 S7 **Midgham** W Berk
56 F1 **Midgley** Calder
57 L4 **Midgley** Wakefd
21 L13 **Mid Holmwood** Surrey
56 K7 **Midhopestones** Sheff
10 D6 **Midhurst** W Susx
10 D9 **Mid Lavant** W Susx
84 E13 **Midlem** Border
102 D8 **Mid Mains** Highld
17 N11 **Midney** Somset
87 U14 **Midpark** Ag & B
17 S6 **Midsomer Norton** BaNES
111 M4 **Midtown** Highld
49 N2 **Midville** Lincs
36 K9 **Mid Warwickshire Crematorium** Warwks
56 D10 **Midway** Ches E
106 v4 **Mid Yell** Shet
98 G2 **Migvie** Abers
17 S13 **Milborne Port** Somset
7 V5 **Milborne St Andrew** Dorset
17 S12 **Milborne Wick** Somset
77 N10 **Milbourne** Nthumb
28 J10 **Milbourne** Wilts
68 E7 **Milburn** Cumb
28 C9 **Milbury Heath** S Glos
63 U6 **Milby** N York
37 M14 **Milcombe** Oxon
40 G11 **Milden** Suffk
40 B6 **Mildenhall** Suffk
18 K7 **Mildenhall** Wilts
34 H6 **Milebrook** Powys
12 E6 **Milebush** Kent
18 E7 **Mile Elm** Wilts
23 N2 **Mile End** Essex
28 A5 **Mile End** Gloucs
41 P3 **Mile End** Suffk
50 F10 **Mileham** Norfk
11 L9 **Mile Oak** Br & H
12 C7 **Mile Oak** Kent
46 G13 **Mile Oak** Staffs
35 N8 **Miles Hope** Herefs
90 G14 **Milesmark** Fife
56 C7 **Miles Platting** Manch
23 M13 **Mile Town** Kent
85 N12 **Milfield** Nthumb
47 L4 **Milford** Derbys
14 F8 **Milford** Devon
34 C2 **Milford** Powys
46 C9 **Milford** Staffs
10 E2 **Milford** Surrey
24 F9 **Milford Haven** Pembks
8 K10 **Milford on Sea** Hants
28 A6 **Milkwall** Gloucs
7 a1 **Millais** Jersey
10 C5 **Milland** W Susx
10 C5 **Milland Marsh** W Susx
56 F2 **Mill Bank** Calder
67 L7 **Millbeck** Cumb
105 S7 **Millbreck** Abers
10 C2 **Millbridge** Surrey
31 M5 **Millbrook** C Beds
9 M6 **Millbrook** C Sotn
5 L10 **Millbrook** Cnwll
7 c3 **Millbrook** Jersey
56 E7 **Millbrook** Tamesd
56 E9 **Mill Brow** Stockp
99 P2 **Millbuie** Abers
102 G5 **Millbuie** Highld
5 U11 **Millcombe** Devon
51 P13 **Mill Common** Norfk
41 R4 **Mill Common** Suffk
12 F11 **Millcorner** E Susx
109 M10 **Millcraig** Highld
5 S8 **Mill Cross** Devon
46 F3 **Milldale** Staffs
20 C5 **Mill End** Bucks
39 M4 **Mill End** Cambs
28 D8 **Millend** Gloucs
31 T6 **Mill End** Herts
83 R5 **Millerhill** Mdloth
56 H12 **Miller's Dale** Derbys
46 J3 **Millers Green** Derbys
22 E6 **Miller's Green** Essex
89 P12 **Millerston** C Glas
56 C3 **Millgate** Lancs
39 T11 **Mill Green** Cambs
22 F7 **Mill Green** Essex
31 R10 **Mill Green** Herts
48 K9 **Mill Green** Lincs
40 K4 **Mill Green** Norfk
45 Q8 **Millgreen** Shrops
46 E13 **Mill Green** Staffs
46 E9 **Mill Green** Staffs
40 G12 **Mill Green** Suffk
40 G9 **Mill Green** Suffk
40 K8 **Mill Green** Suffk
41 P8 **Mill Green** Suffk
34 G11 **Millhalf** Herefs
6 H4 **Millhayes** Devon
61 T5 **Millhead** Lancs
82 D8 **Millheugh** S Lans
11 U9 **Mill Hill** E Susx
21 M4 **Mill Hill** Gt Lon
87 T11 **Millhouse** Ag & B
67 N5 **Millhouse** Cumb
75 M8 **Millhousebridge** D & G
56 K6 **Millhouse Green** Barns
57 P6 **Millhouses** Barns
57 M10 **Millhouses** Sheff
88 K13 **Milliken Park** Rens
24 G8 **Millin Cross** Pembks
64 J9 **Millington** E R Yk
45 T7 **Millmeece** Staffs
61 U3 **Millness** Cumb
89 T2 **Mill of Drummond** P & K
88 J9 **Mill of Haldane** W Duns
61 M3 **Millom** Cumb
14 E13 **Millook** Cnwll
2 F10 **Millpool** Cnwll
4 E6 **Millpool** Cnwll
80 H2 **Millport** N Ayrs
61 S3 **Mill Side** Cumb
12 C4 **Mill Street** Kent
50 J10 **Mill Street** Norfk
40 J6 **Mill Street** Suffk
57 M11 **Millthorpe** Derbys
62 D1 **Millthrop** Cumb
99 R3 **Milltimber** C Aber
98 D2 **Milltown** Abers
104 F12 **Milltown** Abers
4 E9 **Milltown** Cnwll
75 R10 **Milltown** D & G
47 L1 **Milltown** Derbys
15 N5 **Milltown** Devon
99 M3 **Milltown of Campfield** Abers
104 B7 **Milltown of Edinvillie** Moray
99 L3 **Milltown of Learney** Abers
90 H11 **Milnathort** P & K
89 N11 **Milngavie** E Duns
56 D4 **Milnrow** Rochdl
61 T3 **Milnthorpe** Cumb
57 M3 **Milnthorpe** Wakefd
100 a5 **Milovaig** Highld
35 P6 **Milson** Shrops
12 H4 **Milstead** Kent
18 J11 **Milston** Wilts
48 H7 **Milthorpe** Lincs
37 Q11 **Milthorpe** Nhants
46 B3 **Milton** C Stke
39 Q8 **Milton** Cambs
76 B13 **Milton** Cumb
72 G9 **Milton** D & G
74 F11 **Milton** D & G
46 K8 **Milton** Derbys
100 g5 **Milton** Highld
102 E9 **Milton** Highld
102 G6 **Milton** Highld
109 P10 **Milton** Highld
112 H6 **Milton** Highld
88 J12 **Milton** Inver
22 G13 **Milton** Kent
103 U12 **Milton** Moray
104 G3 **Milton** Moray
16 K4 **Milton** N Som
27 R10 **Milton** Newpt
58 B12 **Milton** Notts
29 U9 **Milton** Oxon
37 N13 **Milton** Oxon
97 T11 **Milton** P & K
24 H10 **Milton** Pembks
17 N12 **Milton** Somset
89 M5 **Milton** Stirlg
88 K11 **Milton** W Duns
7 V4 **Milton Abbas** Dorset
5 L5 **Milton Abbot** Devon
83 Q6 **Milton Bridge** Mdloth
31 L6 **Milton Bryan** C Beds
17 S9 **Milton Clevedon** Somset
5 M7 **Milton Combe** Devon
30 E12 **Milton Common** Oxon
14 J10 **Milton Damerel** Devon
28 D5 **Milton End** Gloucs
29 M7 **Milton End** Gloucs
38 F9 **Milton Ernest** Bed
45 L2 **Milton Green** Ches W
29 U9 **Milton Hill** Oxon
30 J5 **Milton Keynes** M Keyn
18 J8 **Milton Lilbourne** Wilts
37 T9 **Milton Malsor** Nhants
95 S11 **Milton Morenish** P & K
98 K3 **Milton of Auchinhove** Abers
91 M11 **Milton of Balgonie** Fife
88 K7 **Milton of Buchanan** Stirlg
89 Q10 **Milton of Campsie** E Duns
102 J7 **Milton of Leys** Highld
99 R3 **Milton of Murtle** C Aber
98 F4 **Milton of Tullich** Abers
17 U11 **Milton on Stour** Dorset
12 H3 **Milton Regis** Kent
11 S10 **Milton Street** E Susx
29 Q4 **Milton-under-Wychwood** Oxon
16 F11 **Milverton** Somset
36 K7 **Milverton** Warwks
46 C7 **Milwich** Staffs
54 E12 **Milwr** Flints
87 T6 **Minard** Ag & B
8 D6 **Minchington** Dorset
28 G7 **Minchinhampton** Gloucs
85 L12 **Mindrum** Nthumb
16 C7 **Minehead** Somset
44 G3 **Minera** Wrexhm
28 K9 **Minety** Wilts
43 L6 **Minffordd** Gwynd
93 R5 **Mingarrypark** Highld
59 P14 **Miningsby** Lincs
4 H6 **Minions** Cnwll
81 L10 **Minishant** S Ayrs
43 S11 **Minllyn** Gwynd
73 L6 **Minnigaff** D & G
13 Q2 **Minnis Bay** Kent
105 M3 **Minnonie** Abers
45 Q1 **Minshull Vernon** Ches E
63 T7 **Minskip** N York
8 K6 **Minstead** Hants
10 D6 **Minsted** W Susx
13 R3 **Minster** Kent
23 N13 **Minster** Kent
44 J12 **Minsterley** Shrops
29 R5 **Minster Lovell** Oxon
28 E4 **Minsterworth** Gloucs
7 S4 **Minterne Magna** Dorset
7 S4 **Minterne Parva** Dorset
59 L12 **Minting** Lincs
105 R6 **Mintlaw** Abers
49 U10 **Mintlyn Crematorium** Norfk
76 B1 **Minto** Border
34 K2 **Minton** Shrops
24 H8 **Minwear** Pembks
36 G2 **Minworth** Birm
66 E9 **Mirehouse** Cumb
112 H4 **Mireland** Highld
56 K3 **Mirfield** Kirk
28 H6 **Miserden** Gloucs
26 J11 **Miskin** Rhondd
26 J8 **Miskin** Rhondd
57 U8 **Misson** Notts
37 Q4 **Misterton** Leics
58 C8 **Misterton** Notts
7 N3 **Misterton** Somset
23 R1 **Mistley** Essex
23 R1 **Mistley Heath** Essex
21 N9 **Mitcham** Gt Lon
28 C4 **Mitcheldean** Gloucs
3 M6 **Mitchell** Cnwll
74 J6 **Mitchellslacks** D & G
27 T5 **Mitchel Troy** Mons
77 P8 **Mitford** Nthumb
2 J6 **Mithian** Cnwll
45 U10 **Mitton** Staffs
30 D6 **Mixbury** Oxon
63 M14 **Mixenden** Calder
40 H9 **Moats Tye** Suffk
55 S11 **Mobberley** Ches E
46 D5 **Mobberley** Staffs
34 J12 **Moccas** Herefs
53 P7 **Mochdre** Conwy
34 C3 **Mochdre** Powys
72 J10 **Mochrum** D & G
8 H7 **Mockbeggar** Hants
12 D6 **Mockbeggar** Kent
66 G8 **Mockerkin** Cumb
5 R10 **Modbury** Devon
46 B6 **Moddershall** Staffs
52 H5 **Moelfre** IoA
44 E8 **Moelfre** Powys
52 H11 **Moel Tryfan** Gwynd
75 L4 **Moffat** D & G
38 H11 **Moggerhanger** C Beds
46 K10 **Moira** Leics
12 K5 **Molash** Kent
100 d8 **Mol-chlach** Highld
54 F14 **Mold** Flints
56 J3 **Moldgreen** Kirk
22 E3 **Molehill Green** Essex
22 H3 **Molehill Green** Essex
65 N11 **Molescroft** E R Yk
77 N9 **Molesden** Nthumb
38 G5 **Molesworth** Cambs
15 T7 **Molland** Devon
54 J12 **Mollington** Ches W
37 M11 **Mollington** Oxon
82 D4 **Mollinsburn** N Lans
32 K8 **Monachty** Cerdgn
99 P8 **Mondynes** Abers
41 M9 **Monewden** Suffk
90 G6 **Moneydie** P & K
20 E7 **Moneyrow Green** W & M
74 E7 **Moniaive** D & G
91 Q5 **Monifieth** Angus
91 Q4 **Monikie** Angus
91 L9 **Monimail** Fife
32 B12 **Monington** Pembks
57 N5 **Monk Bretton** Barns
21 M3 **Monken Hadley** Gt Lon
64 C14 **Monk Fryston** N York
35 P12 **Monkhide** Herefs
75 R14 **Monkhill** Cumb
35 P2 **Monkhopton** Shrops
35 L9 **Monkland** Herefs
15 L8 **Monkleigh** Devon
16 B2 **Monknash** V Glam
15 N11 **Monkokehampton** Devon
77 S11 **Monkseaton** N Tyne
40 G11 **Monks Eleigh** Suffk
11 L5 **Monk's Gate** W Susx
55 T12 **Monks Heath** Ches E
19 T9 **Monk Sherborne** Hants
13 M7 **Monks Horton** Kent
16 E9 **Monksilver** Somset
37 N4 **Monks Kirby** Warwks
41 M7 **Monk Soham** Suffk
36 F5 **Monkspath** Solhll
30 H12 **Monks Risborough** Bucks
59 R13 **Monksthorpe** Lincs
22 F2 **Monk Street** Essex
27 Q7 **Monkswood** Mons
6 G4 **Monkton** Devon
13 Q3 **Monkton** Kent
81 M7 **Monkton** S Ayrs
77 S13 **Monkton** S Tyne
16 B2 **Monkton** V Glam
17 U4 **Monkton Combe** BaNES
18 C13 **Monkton Deverill** Wilts
18 B7 **Monkton Farleigh** Wilts
16 J11 **Monkton Heathfield** Somset
8 E6 **Monkton Up Wimborne** Dorset
6 K5 **Monkton Wyld** Dorset
77 T14 **Monkwearmouth** Sundld
9 T2 **Monkwood** Hants
46 B14 **Monmore Green** Wolves
27 U5 **Monmouth** Mons
34 J12 **Monnington on Wye** Herefs
72 K11 **Monreith** D & G
17 N13 **Montacute** Somset
55 Q4 **Montcliffe** Bolton
44 K11 **Montford** Shrops
44 K10 **Montford Bridge** Shrops
104 H12 **Montgarrie** Abers
34 F1 **Montgomery** Powys
55 S7 **Monton** Salfd
99 N12 **Montrose** Angus
6 c3 **Mont Saint** Guern
19 M12 **Monxton** Hants
56 J13 **Monyash** Derbys
104 K12 **Monymusk** Abers
90 C6 **Monzie** P & K
82 C4 **Moodiesburn** N Lans
91 M8 **Moonzie** Fife
63 S12 **Moor Allerton** Leeds
7 M5 **Moorbath** Dorset
59 N14 **Moorby** Lincs
34 J9 **Moorcot** Herefs
8 D7 **Moor Crichel** Dorset
8 F10 **Moordown** Bmouth
55 N10 **Moore** Halton
31 L8 **Moor End** C Beds
63 M14 **Moor End** Calder
15 Q11 **Moor End** Devon
28 D7 **Moorend** Gloucs
61 R11 **Moor End** Lancs
64 E12 **Moor End** N York
57 U3 **Moorends** Donc
9 P5 **Moorgreen** Hants
31 T7 **Moor Green** Herts
47 N4 **Moorgreen** Notts
57 M12 **Moorhall** Derbys
34 J11 **Moorhampton** Herefs
63 N12 **Moorhead** C Brad
63 Q14 **Moor Head** Leeds
67 L2 **Moorhouse** Cumb
67 M1 **Moorhouse** Cumb
57 Q4 **Moorhouse** Donc
58 C13 **Moorhouse** Notts
21 R12 **Moorhouse Bank** Surrey
16 K10 **Moorland** Somset
17 L9 **Moorlinch** Somset
64 C8 **Moor Monkton** N York
66 F10 **Moor Row** Cumb
66 K3 **Moor Row** Cumb
71 L10 **Moorsholm** R & Cl
17 U13 **Moorside** Dorset
61 S13 **Moor Side** Lancs
61 T12 **Moor Side** Lancs
63 Q12 **Moorside** Leeds
49 L2 **Moor Side** Lincs
56 D5 **Moorside** Oldham
13 M8 **Moorstock** Kent
36 C4 **Moor Street** Birm
12 F2 **Moor Street** Medway
4 G8 **Moorswater** Cnwll
57 Q4 **Moorthorpe** Wakefd
5 N6 **Moortown** Devon
8 H8 **Moortown** Hants
9 N12 **Moortown** IoW
63 R12 **Moortown** Leeds
58 J7 **Moortown** Lincs
45 P10 **Moortown** Wrekin
109 P8 **Morangie** Highld
100 f10 **Morar** Highld
104 D3 **Moray Crematorium** Moray
38 H2 **Morborne** Cambs
15 S11 **Morchard Bishop** Devon
7 M6 **Morcombelake** Dorset
48 D13 **Morcott** Rutlnd
44 G8 **Morda** Shrops
8 C9 **Morden** Dorset
21 N9 **Morden** Gt Lon
35 N13 **Mordiford** Herefs
70 D7 **Mordon** Dur
34 H2 **More** Shrops
16 C11 **Morebath** Devon
84 K14 **Morebattle** Border
61 S7 **Morecambe** Lancs
29 M10 **Moredon** Swindn
107 V5 **Morefield** Highld
13 P8 **Morehall** Kent
5 T10 **Moreleigh** Devon
95 S11 **Morenish** P & K
66 E9 **Moresby Parks** Cumb
9 Q3 **Morestead** Hants
7 V7 **Moreton** Dorset
22 D6 **Moreton** Essex
35 M8 **Moreton** Herefs
30 E12 **Moreton** Oxon
45 S10 **Moreton** Staffs
46 F8 **Moreton** Staffs
54 G9 **Moreton** Wirral
45 N9 **Moreton Corbet** Shrops
5 T3 **Moretonhampstead** Devon
29 P1 **Moreton-in-Marsh** Gloucs
35 P11 **Moreton Jeffries** Herefs
45 N9 **Moretonmill** Shrops
36 K9 **Moreton Morrell** Warwks
35 M11 **Moreton on Lugg** Herefs
36 K10 **Moreton Paddox** Warwks
37 Q11 **Moreton Pinkney** Nhants
45 P7 **Moreton Say** Shrops
28 E6 **Moreton Valence** Gloucs
32 F10 **Morfa** Cerdgn
42 K6 **Morfa Bychan** Gwynd
52 F11 **Morfa Dinlle** Gwynd
26 F6 **Morfa Glas** Neath
42 E5 **Morfa Nefyn** Gwynd
27 L11 **Morganstown** Cardif
8 H4 **Morgan's Vale** Wilts
84 F4 **Morham** E Loth
33 M5 **Moriah** Cerdgn
68 D8 **Morland** Cumb
55 T10 **Morley** Ches E
47 L5 **Morley** Derbys
69 P7 **Morley** Dur
57 L1 **Morley** Leeds
55 T10 **Morley Green** Ches E
50 J14 **Morley St Botolph** Norfk
4 J6 **Mornick** Cnwll
83 P4 **Morningside** C Edin
82 F7 **Morningside** N Lans
41 M2 **Morningthorpe** Norfk
77 P8 **Morpeth** Nthumb
99 N11 **Morphie** Abers
46 F10 **Morrey** Staffs
46 D3 **Morridge Side** Staffs
26 B8 **Morriston** Swans
50 H5 **Morston** Norfk
15 L3 **Mortehoe** Devon
57 Q9 **Morthen** Rothm
19 U8 **Mortimer** W Berk
19 U7 **Mortimer Common** W Berk
34 K8 **Mortimer's Cross** Herefs
19 T8 **Mortimer West End** Hants
21 M7 **Mortlake** Gt Lon
21 L7 **Mortlake Crematorium** Gt Lon
67 N2 **Morton** Cumb
67 Q5 **Morton** Cumb
47 M1 **Morton** Derbys
9 S11 **Morton** IoW
48 G9 **Morton** Lincs
58 D8 **Morton** Lincs
47 T3 **Morton** Notts
44 G9 **Morton** Shrops
58 E14 **Morton Hall** Lincs
83 Q5 **Mortonhall Crematorium** C Edin
63 S1 **Morton-on-Swale** N York
50 K10 **Morton on the Hill** Norfk
69 Q8 **Morton Tinmouth** Dur
2 C9 **Morvah** Cnwll
4 H9 **Morval** Cnwll
101 P7 **Morvich** Highld
35 Q2 **Morville** Shrops
35 Q2 **Morville Heath** Shrops
5 L7 **Morwellham Quay** Devon
14 F9 **Morwenstow** Cnwll
57 P10 **Mosborough** Sheff
81 P4 **Moscow** E Ayrs
35 S2 **Mose** Shrops
67 N6 **Mosedale** Cumb
36 E4 **Moseley** Birm
46 B14 **Moseley** Wolves
35 T9 **Moseley** Worcs
55 R5 **Moses Gate** Bolton
92 B10 **Moss** Ag & B
57 S4 **Moss** Donc
44 H3 **Moss** Wrexhm
104 F12 **Mossat** Abers
106 u6 **Mossbank** Shet
55 M7 **Moss Bank** St Hel
66 E7 **Mossbay** Cumb
81 N8 **Mossblown** S Ayrs
55 R9 **Mossbrow** Traffd
76 D2 **Mossburnford** Border
73 R5 **Mossdale** D & G
81 P12 **Mossdale** E Ayrs
61 S11 **Moss Edge** Lancs
55 Q11 **Moss End** Ches E
82 D6 **Mossend** N Lans
66 H7 **Mosser Mains** Cumb
45 U1 **Mossley** Ches E
56 E6 **Mossley** Tamesd
75 S6 **Mosspaul Hotel** Border
66 J2 **Moss Side** Cumb
103 N4 **Moss-side** Highld
61 R13 **Moss Side** Lancs
54 J6 **Moss Side** Sefton
104 C4 **Mosstodloch** Moray
73 N9 **Mossyard** D & G
55 M4 **Mossy Lea** Lancs
7 N3 **Mosterton** Dorset
56 C6 **Moston** Manch
45 N8 **Moston** Shrops
45 R1 **Moston Green** Ches E
54 E10 **Mostyn** Flints
8 B3 **Motcombe** Dorset
5 Q11 **Mothecombe** Devon
67 P7 **Motherby** Cumb
82 D7 **Motherwell** N Lans
21 M9 **Motspur Park** Gt Lon
21 R8 **Mottingham** Gt Lon
9 L3 **Mottisfont** Hants
9 N12 **Mottistone** IoW
56 E7 **Mottram in Longdendale** Tamesd
56 C11 **Mottram St Andrew** Ches E
6 d3 **Mouilpied** Guern
55 M12 **Mouldsworth** Ches W
97 Q12 **Moulin** P & K
11 N9 **Moulsecoomb** Br & H
19 S4 **Moulsford** Oxon
30 K4 **Moulsoe** M Keyn
109 L10 **Moultavie** Highld
55 Q13 **Moulton** Ches W
49 M9 **Moulton** Lincs
69 R12 **Moulton** N York
37 U7 **Moulton** Nhants
39 U8 **Moulton** Suffk
16 E3 **Moulton** V Glam
49 L10 **Moulton Chapel** Lincs
51 Q12 **Moulton St Mary** Norfk
49 M8 **Moulton Seas End** Lincs
2 K5 **Mount** Cnwll
4 E7 **Mount** Cnwll
56 G3 **Mount** Kirk
63 M13 **Mountain** C Brad
26 J8 **Mountain Ash** Rhondd
83 N9 **Mountain Cross** Border
13 L5 **Mountain Street** Kent
2 J8 **Mount Ambrose** Cnwll
40 F14 **Mount Bures** Essex
12 D11 **Mountfield** E Susx
102 G3 **Mountgerald House** Highld
2 J7 **Mount Hawke** Cnwll
2 H13 **Mount Hermon** Cnwll
3 M4 **Mountjoy** Cnwll
83 Q7 **Mount Lothian** Mdloth
22 F8 **Mountnessing** Essex
27 U9 **Mounton** Mons
45 T2 **Mount Pleasant** Ches E
46 J10 **Mount Pleasant** Derbys
46 K4 **Mount Pleasant** Derbys
69 S6 **Mount Pleasant** Dur
65 T12 **Mount Pleasant** E R Yk
11 Q7 **Mount Pleasant** E Susx
40 G2 **Mount Pleasant** Norfk
40 B11 **Mount Pleasant** Suffk
36 D8 **Mount Pleasant** Worcs
69 Q2 **Mountsett Crematorium** Dur
47 Q11 **Mountsorrel** Leics
8 E4 **Mount Sorrel** Wilts
56 G1 **Mount Tabor** Calder
10 E2 **Mousehill** Surrey
2 D11 **Mousehole** Cnwll
75 L11 **Mouswald** D & G
45 U2 **Mow Cop** Ches E
76 G1 **Mowhaugh** Border
47 Q12 **Mowmacre Hill** C Leic
37 R3 **Mowsley** Leics
96 E7 **Moy** Highld
103 L9 **Moy** Highld
101 M8 **Moyle** Highld
32 B12 **Moylegrove** Pembks
79 M7 **Muasdale** Ag & B
99 S5 **Muchalls** Abers
27 U1 **Much Birch** Herefs
35 P11 **Much Cowarne** Herefs
27 T1 **Much Dewchurch** Herefs
17 M12 **Muchelney** Somset
17 M12 **Muchelney Ham** Somset
22 B4 **Much Hadham** Herts
55 L2 **Much Hoole** Lancs
55 L2 **Much Hoole Town** Lancs
4 G9 **Muchlarnick** Cnwll
35 Q14 **Much Marcle** Herefs
45 P14 **Much Wenlock** Shrops
93 L3 **Muck** Highld
22 G11 **Mucking** Thurr
22 G12 **Muckingford** Thurr
50 K5 **Muckleburgh Collection** Norfk
7 R6 **Muckleford** Dorset
45 R6 **Mucklestone** Staffs
35 P1 **Muckley** Shrops
59 Q10 **Muckton** Lincs
15 N5 **Muddiford** Devon
11 S8 **Muddles Green** E Susx
8 H10 **Mudeford** Dorset
17 Q13 **Mudford** Somset
17 Q13 **Mudford Sock** Somset
17 N7 **Mudgley** Somset
23 P13 **Mud Row** Kent
89 N10 **Mugdock** Stirlg
100 d6 **Mugeary** Highld
46 J5 **Mugginton** Derbys
46 J5 **Muggintonlane End** Derbys
69 M3 **Muggleswick** Dur
105 L5 **Muirden** Abers
91 S4 **Muirdrum** Angus
104 K6 **Muiresk** Abers
91 M5 **Muirhead** Angus
91 L10 **Muirhead** Fife
82 C5 **Muirhead** N Lans
82 C13 **Muirkirk** E Ayrs
89 R9 **Muirmill** Stirlg
104 H13 **Muir of Fowlis** Abers
103 U4 **Muir of Miltonduff** Moray
102 F5 **Muir of Ord** Highld
94 G2 **Muirshearlich** Highld
105 R8 **Muirtack** Abers
90 D9 **Muirton** P & K
102 E5 **Muirton Mains** Highld
90 J3 **Muirton of Ardblair** P & K
68 K13 **Muker** N York
51 L13 **Mulbarton** Norfk
104 D5 **Mulben** Moray
2 D10 **Mulfra** Cnwll
93 Q12 **Mull** Ag & B
15 M4 **Mullacott Cross** Devon
2 H13 **Mullion** Cnwll
2 H13 **Mullion Cove** Cnwll
59 T12 **Mumby** Lincs
35 P10 **Munderfield Row** Herefs
35 Q10 **Munderfield Stocks** Herefs
51 P6 **Mundesley** Norfk
40 D2 **Mundford** Norfk
51 P14 **Mundham** Norfk
23 L7 **Mundon Hill** Essex
12 H6 **Mundy Bois** Kent
67 N6 **Mungrisdale** Cumb
102 H5 **Munlochy** Highld
80 K3 **Munnoch** N Ayrs
35 Q12 **Munsley** Herefs
35 M3 **Munslow** Shrops
5 R3 **Murchington** Devon
36 E12 **Murcot** Worcs
30 C9 **Murcott** Oxon
28 J9 **Murcott** Wilts
112 E3 **Murkle** Highld
101 Q13 **Murlaggan** Highld
20 B11 **Murrell Green** Hants
91 Q4 **Murroes** Angus
49 N12 **Murrow** Cambs
30 H7 **Mursley** Bucks
12 H3 **Murston** Kent
98 H12 **Murthill** Angus
90 H4 **Murthly** P & K
64 E9 **Murton** C York
68 F8 **Murton** Cumb
70 E3 **Murton** Dur
77 S11 **Murton** N Tyne
85 P9 **Murton** Nthumb
6 J6 **Musbury** Devon
64 F4 **Muscoates** N York
83 R4 **Musselburgh** E Loth
48 B6 **Muston** Leics
65 P4 **Muston** N York
35 U6 **Mustow Green** Worcs
21 N5 **Muswell Hill** Gt Lon
73 R10 **Mutehill** D & G
41 S3 **Mutford** Suffk
90 C8 **Muthill** P & K
6 D3 **Mutterton** Devon
45 R11 **Muxton** Wrekin
112 E6 **Mybster** Highld
26 D1 **Myddfai** Carmth
45 L9 **Myddle** Shrops
32 J9 **Mydroilyn** Cerdgn
61 T12 **Myerscough** Lancs
3 L9 **Mylor** Cnwll
3 L9 **Mylor Bridge** Cnwll
24 K4 **Mynachlog ddu** Pembks
54 E12 **Myndd-llan** Flints
34 J3 **Myndtown** Shrops
27 T9 **Mynydd-bach** Mons
26 B8 **Mynydd-Bach** Swans
33 P5 **Mynydd Buch** Cerdgn
25 R9 **Mynyddgarreg** Carmth
54 G14 **Mynydd Isa** Flints
52 K9 **Mynydd Llandygai** Gwynd
42 F7 **Mynytho** Gwynd
99 N4 **Myrebird** Abers
76 B6 **Myredykes** Border
20 E11 **Mytchett** Surrey
56 E1 **Mytholm** Calder
56 F1 **Mytholmroyd** Calder
61 R13 **Mythop** Lancs
63 U6 **Myton-on-Swale** N York

N

107 P8 **Naast** Highld
62 C14 **Nab's Head** Lancs
106 f9 **Na Buirgh** W Isls
64 D10 **Naburn** C York
63 N12 **Nab Wood Crematorium** C Brad
13 L7 **Naccolt** Kent
13 N5 **Nackington** Kent
41 M12 **Nacton** Suffk
65 P8 **Nafferton** E R Yk
28 G8 **Nag's Head** Gloucs
28 B4 **Nailbridge** Gloucs
16 H11 **Nailsbourne** Somset
17 N2 **Nailsea** N Som
47 M12 **Nailstone** Leics
28 F8 **Nailsworth** Gloucs
103 N4 **Nairn** Highld
21 M13 **Nalderswood** Surrey
2 G10 **Nancegollan** Cnwll
2 D9 **Nancledra** Cnwll
42 E7 **Nanhoron** Gwynd
54 E13 **Nannerch** Flints
47 P10 **Nanpantan** Leics
3 P5 **Nanpean** Cnwll
2 B11 **Nanquidno** Cnwll
3 Q3 **Nanstallon** Cnwll
26 J5 **Nant-ddu** Powys
32 G9 **Nanternis** Cerdgn
25 S6 **Nantgaredig** Carmth
27 L10 **Nantgarw** Rhondd
33 U7 **Nant-glas** Powys
53 T10 **Nantglyn** Denbgs
33 U5 **Nantgwyn** Powys
43 M3 **Nant Gwynant** Gwynd
52 H12 **Nantlle** Gwynd
44 G9 **Nantmawr** Shrops
34 B7 **Nantmel** Powys
43 M4 **Nantmor** Gwynd
52 K11 **Nant Peris** Gwynd
45 Q3 **Nantwich** Ches E
27 L5 **Nant-y-Bwch** Blae G
25 S7 **Nant-y-caws** Carmth
27 Q6 **Nant-y-derry** Mons
26 E9 **Nantyffyllon** Brdgnd
27 M5 **Nantyglo** Blae G
44 F8 **Nant-y-gollen** Shrops
26 G9 **Nant-y-moel** Brdgnd
53 L8 **Nant-y-pandy** Conwy
20 D3 **Naphill** Bucks
35 U11 **Napleton** Worcs
62 H9 **Nappa** N York
37 N8 **Napton on the Hill** Warwks
24 K8 **Narberth** Pembks
37 P1 **Narborough** Leics
50 B11 **Narborough** Norfk
4 J9 **Narkurs** Cnwll
42 J4 **Nasareth** Gwynd
37 S5 **Naseby** Nhants
30 G6 **Nash** Bucks
21 R10 **Nash** Gt Lon
34 H8 **Nash** Herefs
27 Q11 **Nash** Newpt
35 P6 **Nash** Shrops
35 S4 **Nash End** Worcs
30 H11 **Nash Lee** Bucks
19 U11 **Nash's Green** Hants
12 B2 **Nash Street** Kent
38 G1 **Nassington** Nhants
28 E6 **Nastend** Gloucs
31 U8 **Nasty** Herts
68 G11 **Nateby** Cumb
61 T11 **Nateby** Lancs
46 G11 **National Memorial Arboretum** Staffs
47 Q12 **National Space Science Centre** C Leic
61 U2 **Natland** Cumb
40 H11 **Naughton** Suffk
29 M3 **Naunton** Gloucs
35 U13 **Naunton** Worcs
36 C10 **Naunton Beauchamp** Worcs
48 E2 **Navenby** Lincs
22 D8 **Navestock** Essex
22 E8 **Navestock Side** Essex
112 B13 **Navidale House Hotel** Highld
103 L3 **Navity** Highld
64 F3 **Nawton** N York
40 G14 **Nayland** Suffk
22 B6 **Nazeing** Essex
22 B6 **Nazeing Gate** Essex
8 H9 **Neacroft** Hants
36 K4 **Neal's Green** Warwks
106 v8 **Neap** Shet
46 E4 **Near Cotton** Staffs
67 N13 **Near Sawrey** Cumb
21 M5 **Neasden** Gt Lon
70 D10 **Neasham** Darltn
26 D8 **Neath** Neath
10 A2 **Neatham** Hants
51 P9 **Neatishead** Norfk
32 K7 **Nebo** Cerdgn
53 P11 **Nebo** Conwy
42 J3 **Nebo** Gwynd
52 G4 **Nebo** IoA
50 E12 **Necton** Norfk
110 C10 **Nedd** Highld
77 Q9 **Nedderton** Nthumb
40 G11 **Nedging** Suffk
40 H11 **Nedging Tye** Suffk
41 M4 **Needham** Norfk
40 J9 **Needham Market** Suffk
40 B7 **Needham Street** Suffk
39 M6 **Needingworth** Cambs
35 Q5 **Neen Savage** Shrops
35 Q6 **Neen Sollars** Shrops
35 P3 **Neenton** Shrops
42 F5 **Nefyn** Gwynd
81 P1 **Neilston** E Rens
27 L8 **Nelson** Caerph
62 H12 **Nelson** Lancs
82 G10 **Nemphlar** S Lans
17 P4 **Nempnett Thrubwell** BaNES
68 G3 **Nenthall** Cumb
68 G4 **Nenthead** Cumb
84 H11 **Nenthorn** Border
15 S13 **Neopardy** Devon
11 L7 **Nep Town** W Susx
44 F1 **Nercwys** Flints
78 C4 **Nereabolls** Ag & B
81 S1 **Nerston** S Lans
85 P12 **Nesbit** Nthumb
63 M10 **Nesfield** N York
54 H11 **Ness** Ches W
54 H11 **Ness Botanic Gardens** Ches W
44 J10 **Nesscliffe** Shrops
54 G11 **Neston** Ches W
18 C7 **Neston** Wilts
35 P2 **Netchwood** Shrops
55 T11 **Nether Alderley** Ches E
18 H11 **Netheravon** Wilts
84 E10 **Nether Blainslie** Border
105 M4 **Netherbrae** Abers
47 S8 **Nether Broughton** Leics
82 E9 **Netherburn** S Lans
7 N5 **Netherbury** Dorset
75 S11 **Netherby** Cumb
63 S10 **Netherby** N York
7 S5 **Nether Cerne** Dorset
75 M8 **Nethercleuch** D & G
17 Q13 **Nether Compton** Dorset
37 P8 **Nethercote** Warwks
14 J13 **Nethercott** Devon
15 L5 **Nethercott** Devon
105 N11 **Nether Crimond** Abers
104 D3 **Nether Dallachy** Moray
28 A7 **Netherend** Gloucs
6 B4 **Nether Exe** Devon
12 D12 **Netherfield** E Susx
47 Q10 **Netherfield** Leics
47 R5 **Netherfield** Notts
74 H3 **Nether Fingland** S Lans
58 C7 **Nethergate** N Linc
50 J8 **Nethergate** Norfk
8 G3 **Netherhampton** Wilts
57 P11 **Nether Handley** Derbys
91 N3 **Nether Handwick** Angus
57 P7 **Nether Haugh** Rothm
7 M3 **Netherhay** Dorset
58 B11 **Nether Headon** Notts
47 L3 **Nether Heage** Derbys
37 S9 **Nether Heyford** Nhants
74 K3 **Nether Howcleugh** S Lans
61 U6 **Nether Kellet** Lancs
105 T7 **Nether Kinmundy** Abers
46 F7 **Netherland Green** Staffs
57 R12 **Nether Langwith** Notts
73 S11 **Netherlaw** D & G
99 R5 **Netherley** Abers
74 K8 **Nethermill** D & G
105 Q7 **Nethermuir** Abers
21 N11 **Netherne-on-the-Hill** Surrey
56 H3 **Netheroyd Hill** Kirk
56 K11 **Nether Padley** Derbys
81 Q1 **Netherplace** E Rens
64 D9 **Nether Poppleton** C York
67 M5 **Nether Row** Cumb
46 J11 **Netherseal** Derbys
64 B1 **Nether Silton** N York
34 G6 **Nether Skyborry** Shrops
16 G9 **Nether Stowey** Somset
22 E5 **Nether Street** Essex
18 E8 **Netherstreet** Wilts
56 H5 **Netherthong** Kirk
57 P12 **Netherthorpe** Derbys
98 J12 **Netherton** Angus
6 A10 **Netherton** Devon
36 B3 **Netherton** Dudley
19 N9 **Netherton** Hants
27 U2 **Netherton** Herefs
56 H4 **Netherton** Kirk
82 E8 **Netherton** N Lans
76 K4 **Netherton** Nthumb
29 T8 **Netherton** Oxon
97 U13 **Netherton** P & K
35 R4 **Netherton** Shrops
89 N10 **Netherton** Stirlg
57 L3 **Netherton** Wakefd
36 C12 **Netherton** Worcs
66 E11 **Nethertown** Cumb
112 J1 **Nethertown** Highld
62 E12 **Nethertown** Lancs
46 F10 **Nethertown** Staffs
83 M10 **Netherurd** Border
19 M13 **Nether Wallop** Hants
66 H12 **Nether Wasdale** Cumb
67 N3 **Nether Welton** Cumb
29 P3 **Nether Westcote** Gloucs
36 H2 **Nether Whitacre** Warwks
74 F2 **Nether Whitecleuch** S Lans
30 F10 **Nether Winchendon** Bucks
77 M7 **Netherwitton** Nthumb
103 R11 **Nethy Bridge** Highld
9 P7 **Netley** Hants
9 L6 **Netley Marsh** Hants
19 U3 **Nettlebed** Oxon
17 R7 **Nettlebridge** Somset
7 P5 **Nettlecombe** Dorset
9 Q13 **Nettlecombe** IoW
31 M10 **Nettleden** Herts
58 H11 **Nettleham** Lincs
12 C5 **Nettlestead** Kent
12 C5 **Nettlestead Green** Kent
9 S10 **Nettlestone** IoW
69 S3 **Nettlesworth** Dur
58 K6 **Nettleton** Lincs
18 B5 **Nettleton** Wilts
18 B5 **Nettleton Shrub** Wilts
5 P11 **Netton** Devon
18 H13 **Netton** Wilts
26 C3 **Neuadd** Carmth
33 T5 **Neuadd-ddu** Powys
22 J9 **Nevendon** Essex
32 A12 **Nevern** Pembks
38 B2 **Nevill Holt** Leics
74 J12 **New Abbey** D & G
105 P3 **New Aberdour** Abers
21 Q10 **New Addington** Gt Lon
63 P10 **Newall** Leeds
9 R2 **New Alresford** Hants
90 K2 **New Alyth** P & K
48 K13 **Newark** C Pete
106 w15 **Newark** Ork
47 U3 **Newark-on-Trent** Notts
65 N11 **New Arram** E R Yk
82 E7 **Newarthill** N Lans
12 B2 **New Ash Green** Kent
48 B3 **New Balderton** Notts
12 B2 **New Barn** Kent
13 N7 **Newbarn** Kent
21 N3 **New Barnet** Gt Lon
38 C8 **New Barton** Nhants
83 R5 **Newbattle** Mdloth
77 M1 **New Bewick** Nthumb
75 N12 **Newbie** D & G
61 P6 **Newbiggin** Cumb
66 G14 **Newbiggin** Cumb
67 Q7 **Newbiggin** Cumb
67 S3 **Newbiggin** Cumb
68 D7 **Newbiggin** Cumb
68 K7 **Newbiggin** Dur
69 P3 **Newbiggin** Dur
62 K1 **Newbiggin** N York
63 L2 **Newbiggin** N York
77 S8 **Newbiggin-by-the-Sea** Nthumb
91 L3 **Newbigging** Angus
91 P4 **Newbigging** Angus
91 Q4 **Newbigging** Angus
82 K9 **Newbigging** S Lans
68 F12 **Newbiggin-on-Lune** Cumb
37 N5 **New Bilton** Warwks
57 N12 **Newbold** Derbys
47 M10 **Newbold** Leics
37 N5 **Newbold on Avon** Warwks
36 H11 **Newbold on Stour** Warwks
36 J9 **Newbold Pacey** Warwks
37 N4 **Newbold Revel** Warwks
47 M13 **Newbold Verdon** Leics
49 M2 **New Bolingbroke** Lincs
48 K12 **Newborough** C Pete
52 F9 **Newborough** IoA
46 F8 **Newborough** Staffs
30 B5 **Newbottle** Nhants
70 D2 **Newbottle** Sundld
58 G12 **New Boultham** Lincs
41 N12 **Newbourne** Suffk
30 H4 **New Bradwell** M Keyn
57 N12 **New Brampton** Derbys
69 R4 **New Brancepeth** Dur
83 M4 **Newbridge** C Edin
27 N8 **Newbridge** Caerph
32 K9 **Newbridge** Cerdgn
2 C10 **Newbridge** Cnwll
2 K8 **Newbridge** Cnwll
74 H10 **Newbridge** D & G
8 K5 **Newbridge** Hants
9 N11 **Newbridge** IoW
64 J2 **New Bridge** N York
29 T7 **Newbridge** Oxon
44 G5 **Newbridge** Wrexhm
35 T13 **Newbridge Green** Worcs
27 R9 **Newbridge-on-Usk** Mons
34 B9 **Newbridge on Wye** Powys
54 G13 **New Brighton** Flints
54 H8 **New Brighton** Wirral
47 N3 **New Brinsley** Notts
71 L8 **New Brotton** R & Cl
76 H12 **Newbrough** Nthumb
44 H3 **New Broughton** Wrexhm
40 J2 **New Buckenham** Norfk
15 S12 **Newbuildings** Devon
105 R10 **Newburgh** Abers
105 R4 **Newburgh** Abers
90 K8 **Newburgh** Fife
55 L4 **Newburgh** Lancs
64 C4 **Newburgh Priory** N York
77 P12 **Newburn** N u Ty
55 R6 **New Bury** Bolton
17 S7 **Newbury** Somset
19 Q7 **Newbury** W Berk
18 B12 **Newbury** Wilts
21 R5 **Newbury Park** Gt Lon
67 S8 **Newby** Cumb
62 G10 **Newby** Lancs
62 E6 **Newby** N York
65 N1 **Newby** N York
70 H10 **Newby** N York
61 R2 **Newby Bridge** Cumb
67 N2 **Newby Cross** Cumb
75 U14 **Newby East** Cumb
67 S8 **Newby Head** Cumb
105 N5 **New Byth** Abers
67 N2 **Newby West** Cumb
63 T2 **Newby Wiske** N York
27 S4 **Newcastle** Mons
34 G4 **Newcastle** Shrops
77 P11 *Newcastle Airport* Nthumb
32 F12 **Newcastle Emlyn** Carmth
75 U8 **Newcastleton** Border
45 T4 **Newcastle-under-Lyme** Staffs
77 Q13 **Newcastle upon Tyne** N u Ty
25 M3 **Newchapel** Pembks
45 U3 **Newchapel** Staffs
11 P2 **Newchapel** Surrey
27 M5 **Newchurch** Blae G
34 J10 **Newchurch** Herefs
9 R11 **Newchurch** IoW
13 L9 **Newchurch** Kent
27 T8 **Newchurch** Mons
34 F10 **Newchurch** Powys
46 F9 **Newchurch** Staffs
62 G12 **Newchurch in Pendle** Lancs
51 L11 **New Costessey** Norfk
66 H3 **New Cowper** Cumb
83 R4 **Newcraighall** C Edin
57 N3 **New Crofton** Wakefd
33 M5 **New Cross** Cerdgn
21 Q7 **New Cross** Gt Lon
17 M13 **New Cross** Somset
81 S10 **New Cumnock** E Ayrs
12 F12 **New Cut** E Susx
105 P6 **New Deer** Abers
77 R10 **New Delaval** Nthumb
56 E5 **New Delph** Oldham
20 H6 **New Denham** Bucks
10 K2 **Newdigate** Surrey
37 T8 **New Duston** Nhants
64 E8 **New Earswick** C York
47 N4 **New Eastwood** Notts
57 R7 **New Edlington** Donc
103 V3 **New Elgin** Moray
65 R12 **New Ellerby** E R Yk
20 E8 **Newell Green** Br For
21 R8 **New Eltham** Gt Lon
36 E8 **New End** Worcs
12 F10 **Newenden** Kent
48 J13 **New England** C Pete
40 B12 **New England** Essex
28 D2 **Newent** Gloucs
63 R13 **New Farnley** Leeds
54 H9 **New Ferry** Wirral
69 R2 **Newfield** Dur
69 R6 **Newfield** Dur
109 P9 **Newfield** Highld
48 J14 **New Fletton** C Pete
8 K7 **New Forest National Park**
19 S10 **Newfound** Hants
57 Q1 **New Fryston** Wakefd
24 E6 **Newgale** Pembks
73 Q4 **New Galloway** D & G
50 H5 **Newgate** Norfk
31 T11 **Newgate Street** Herts
91 P10 **New Gilston** Fife
2 b1 **New Grimsby** IoS
45 P4 **Newhall** Ches E
46 J9 **Newhall** Derbys
85 T13 **Newham** Nthumb
77 S10 **New Hartley** Nthumb
83 Q3 **Newhaven** C Edin
46 G1 **Newhaven** Derbys
11 Q10 **Newhaven** E Susx
20 J10 **New Haw** Surrey
24 K10 **New Hedges** Pembks
70 D2 **New Herrington** Sundld
56 D4 **Newhey** Rochdl
50 E6 **New Holkham** Norfk
58 J2 **New Holland** N Linc
71 Q10 **Newholm** N York
57 Q13 **New Houghton** Derbys
50 C8 **New Houghton** Norfk
82 E6 **Newhouse** N Lans
62 G5 **New Houses** N York
55 N6 **New Houses** Wigan
62 B1 **New Hutton** Cumb
12 D4 **New Hythe** Kent
11 Q6 **Newick** E Susx
13 M8 **Newingreen** Kent
12 G3 **Newington** Kent
13 N8 **Newington** Kent
30 D13 **Newington** Oxon
34 K4 **Newington** Shrops
28 F9 **Newington Bagpath** Gloucs
25 S3 **New Inn** Carmth
27 Q8 **New Inn** Torfn
34 G5 **New Invention** Shrops
51 M12 **New Lakenham** Norfk
82 G10 **New Lanark** S Lans
65 P13 **Newland** C KuH
61 Q4 **Newland** Cumb
64 J14 **Newland** E R Yk
27 V6 **Newland** Gloucs
57 U2 **Newland** N York
29 S6 **Newland** Oxon
15 T5 **Newland** Somset
35 S11 **Newland** Worcs
83 S6 **Newlandrig** Mdloth
75 V7 **Newlands** Border
67 M5 **Newlands** Cumb
69 N1 **Newlands** Nthumb
104 B5 **Newlands of Dundurcas** Moray
54 K4 **New Lane** Lancs
55 P8 **New Lane End** Warrtn
75 S9 **New Langholm** D & G
49 P2 **New Leake** Lincs
105 R5 **New Leeds** Abers
57 N5 **New Lodge** Barns
55 M1 **New Longton** Lancs
72 F7 **New Luce** D & G
2 D11 **Newlyn** Cnwll
3 L5 **Newlyn East** Cnwll
105 P12 **Newmachar** Abers
82 F7 **Newmains** N Lans
21 M9 **New Malden** Gt Lon
22 D5 **Newman's End** Essex
40 E12 **Newman's Green** Suffk
39 T8 **Newmarket** Suffk
106 j5 **Newmarket** W Isls
70 K8 **New Marske** R & Cl
30 B11 **New Marston** Oxon
44 H7 **New Marton** Shrops
99 P7 **New Mill** Abers
75 U3 **Newmill** Border
2 D10 **New Mill** Cnwll
30 K10 **New Mill** Herts
56 J5 **New Mill** Kirk
104 E5 **Newmill** Moray
57 M3 **Newmillerdam** Wakefd
98 G11 **Newmill of Inshewan** Angus
83 N5 **Newmills** C Edin
3 M6 **New Mills** Cnwll
56 F9 **New Mills** Derbys
82 K1 **Newmills** Fife
27 U6 **Newmills** Mons
44 C13 **New Mills** Powys
90 H5 **Newmiln** P & K
81 Q5 **Newmilns** E Ayrs
8 J9 **New Milton** Hants
23 R1 **New Mistley** Essex
24 J5 **New Moat** Pembks
44 J7 **Newnes** Shrops
22 G6 **Newney Green** Essex
28 C5 **Newnham** Gloucs
20 B12 **Newnham** Hants
31 R5 **Newnham** Herts
12 J4 **Newnham** Kent
37 Q9 **Newnham** Nhants
35 P7 **Newnham** Worcs
57 U13 **New Ollerton** Notts
36 E2 **New Oscott** Birm
105 P4 **New Pitsligo** Abers
4 A5 **New Polzeath** Cnwll
4 J3 **Newport** Cnwll
8 B9 **Newport** Dorset
64 K13 **Newport** E R Yk
39 R14 **Newport** Essex
28 D8 **Newport** Gloucs
112 D12 **Newport** Highld
9 Q11 **Newport** IoW
27 Q10 **Newport** Newpt
51 T10 **Newport** Norfk
24 J3 **Newport** Pembks
45 R10 **Newport** Wrekin
91 P6 **Newport-on-Tay** Fife
30 J4 **Newport Pagnell** M Keyn
30 J4 **Newport Pagnell Services** M Keyn
10 H5 **Newpound Common** W Susx
81 L8 **New Prestwick** S Ayrs
32 G9 **New Quay** Cerdgn
3 L4 **Newquay** Cnwll
23 P3 **New Quay** Essex
3 M4 *Newquay Airport* Cnwll
51 N11 **New Rackheath** Norfk
34 F8 **New Radnor** Powys
67 Q5 **New Rent** Cumb
77 M14 **New Ridley** Nthumb
62 K11 **New Road Side** N York
13 L11 **New Romney** Kent
57 T7 **New Rossington** Donc
33 P6 **New Row** Cerdgn
62 C12 **New Row** Lancs
90 C13 **New Sauchie** Clacks
55 T13 **Newsbank** Ches E
105 L9 **Newseat** Abers
61 U12 **Newsham** Lancs
63 T3 **Newsham** N York
69 P10 **Newsham** N York
77 S10 **Newsham** Nthumb
57 N3 **New Sharlston** Wakefd
64 G14 **Newsholme** E R Yk
62 G9 **Newsholme** Lancs
85 T12 **New Shoreston** Nthumb
70 E2 **New Silksworth** Sundld
71 L9 **New Skelton** R & Cl
56 J4 **Newsome** Kirk
48 D6 **New Somerby** Lincs
21 N4 **New Southgate Crematorium** Gt Lon
55 N5 **New Springs** Wigan
84 F12 **Newstead** Border
47 P3 **Newstead** Notts
85 T13 **Newstead** Nthumb
82 E7 **New Stevenston** N Lans
34 H9 **New Street** Herefs
47 M10 **New Swannington** Leics
64 B13 **Newthorpe** N York
47 N4 **Newthorpe** Notts
22 J10 **New Thundersley** Essex
11 M8 **Newtimber** W Susx
58 H9 **Newtoft** Lincs
88 B6 **Newton** Ag & B
76 C1 **Newton** Border
26 E12 **Newton** Brdgnd
31 R4 **Newton** C Beds
39 P11 **Newton** Cambs
49 P11 **Newton** Cambs
27 N12 **Newton** Cardif
45 M2 **Newton** Ches W
54 K13 **Newton** Ches W
55 M11 **Newton** Ches W
61 N5 **Newton** Cumb
47 M2 **Newton** Derbys
34 H14 **Newton** Herefs
34 J7 **Newton** Herefs
35 M10 **Newton** Herefs
102 G5 **Newton** Highld
102 K6 **Newton** Highld
103 L2 **Newton** Highld
112 H7 **Newton** Highld
61 Q12 **Newton** Lancs
62 B5 **Newton** Lancs
48 F6 **Newton** Lincs
83 R5 **Newton** Mdloth
103 U3 **Newton** Moray
104 C3 **Newton** Moray
64 K5 **Newton** N York
38 C4 **Newton** Nhants
50 D10 **Newton** Norfk
47 S5 **Newton** Notts
76 J4 **Newton** Nthumb
77 L13 **Newton** Nthumb
82 H12 **Newton** S Lans
89 Q13 **Newton** S Lans
36 D2 **Newton** Sandw
44 K7 **Newton** Shrops
16 F9 **Newton** Somset
46 D8 **Newton** Staffs
40 F12 **Newton** Suffk
83 L3 **Newton** W Loth
37 P5 **Newton** Warwks
8 J4 **Newton** Wilts
5 V6 **Newton Abbot** Devon
66 K1 **Newton Arlosh** Cumb
69 S8 **Newton Aycliffe** Dur
70 G7 **Newton Bewley** Hartpl
38 D10 **Newton Blossomville** M Keyn
38 E7 **Newton Bromswold** Nhants
47 L12 **Newton Burgoland** Leics
85 U13 **Newton-by-the-Sea** Nthumb
58 H9 **Newton by Toft** Lincs
4 J7 **Newton Ferrers** Cnwll
5 P11 **Newton Ferrers** Devon
106 d11 **Newton Ferry** W Isls
51 M14 **Newton Flotman** Norfk
83 R6 **Newtongrange** Mdloth
27 U9 **Newton Green** Mons
37 R1 **Newton Harcourt** Leics
56 C6 **Newton Heath** Manch
99 S5 **Newtonhill** Abers
57 M2 **Newton Hill** Wakefd
62 D9 **Newton-in-Bowland** Lancs
64 B11 **Newton Kyme** N York
63 Q2 **Newton-le-Willows** N York
55 N7 **Newton-le-Willows** St Hel
83 R6 **Newtonloan** Mdloth
30 H6 **Newton Longville** Bucks
81 Q1 **Newton Mearns** E Rens
99 L11 **Newtonmill** Angus
97 L4 **Newtonmore** Highld
69 R11 **Newton Morrell** N York
24 G9 **Newton Mountain** Pembks
71 N9 **Newton Mulgrave** N York
90 J9 **Newton of Balcanquhal** P & K

91 R11 **Newton of Balcormo** Fife
64 C8 **Newton on Ouse** N York
64 J1 **Newton-on-Rawcliffe** N York
45 L9 **Newton on the Hill** Shrops
77 P4 **Newton-on-the-Moor** Nthumb
58 D12 **Newton on Trent** Lincs
6 E7 **Newton Poppleford** Devon
30 D6 **Newton Purcell** Oxon
46 J12 **Newton Regis** Warwks
67 Q6 **Newton Reigny** Cumb
15 U13 **Newton St Cyres** Devon
51 M10 **Newton St Faith** Norfk
17 T4 **Newton St Loe** BaNES
14 K10 **Newton St Petrock** Devon
46 J8 **Newton Solney** Derbys
19 P12 **Newton Stacey** Hants
73 L6 **Newton Stewart** D & G
18 K12 **Newton Tony** Wilts
15 M7 **Newton Tracey** Devon
70 J10 **Newton under Roseberry** R & Cl
77 N8 **Newton Underwood** Nthumb
64 G10 **Newton upon Derwent** E R Yk
9 U2 **Newton Valence** Hants
75 M7 **Newton Wamphray** D & G
61 T13 **Newton with Scales** Lancs
27 M6 **Newtown** Blae G
55 M11 **Newtown** Ches W
2 F11 **Newtown** Cnwll
4 H5 **Newtown** Cnwll
66 H3 **Newtown** Cumb
67 R8 **Newtown** Cumb
75 S13 **Newtown** Cumb
75 V13 **Newtown** Cumb
74 E3 **Newtown** D & G
56 E10 **Newtown** Derbys
6 E5 **Newtown** Devon
15 S7 **Newtown** Devon
7 N4 **Newtown** Dorset
8 D5 **New Town** Dorset
8 D5 **New Town** Dorset
8 D7 **New Town** Dorset
11 R6 **New Town** E Susx
28 C7 **Newtown** Gloucs
8 K6 **Newtown** Hants
9 S6 **Newtown** Hants
19 Q8 **Newtown** Hants
35 L9 **Newtown** Herefs
35 M14 **Newtown** Herefs
35 P11 **Newtown** Herefs
35 R13 **Newtown** Herefs
96 D3 **Newtown** Highld
9 N10 **Newtown** IoW
55 M3 **Newtown** Lancs
38 E5 **New Town** Nhants
77 L5 **Newtown** Nthumb
85 P12 **Newtown** Nthumb
85 Q13 **Newtown** Nthumb
8 E10 **Newtown** Poole
34 D2 **Newtown** Powys
26 K8 **Newtown** Rhondd
44 K9 **Newtown** Shrops
45 L7 **Newtown** Shrops
6 J2 **Newtown** Somset
46 B1 **Newtown** Staffs
46 C13 **Newtown** Staffs
55 N6 **Newtown** Wigan
8 C3 **Newtown** Wilts
19 L6 **New Town** Wilts
19 L8 **Newtown** Wilts
35 U9 **Newtown** Worcs
36 B5 **Newtown** Worcs
2 J12 **Newtown-in-St Martin** Cnwll
47 P12 **Newtown Linford** Leics
88 J14 **Newtown of Beltrees** Rens
84 F12 **Newtown St Boswells** Border
47 N13 **Newtown Unthank** Leics
27 L7 **New Tredegar** Caerph
82 F11 **New Trows** S Lans
57 N13 **New Tupton** Derbys
91 L3 **Newtyle** Angus
49 Q12 **New Walsoken** Cambs
59 N6 **New Waltham** NE Lin
57 N11 **New Whittington** Derbys
84 C4 **New Winton** E Loth
29 S5 **New Yatt** Oxon
20 J5 **Newyears Green** Gt Lon
87 T3 **Newyork** Ag & B
48 K2 **New York** Lincs
77 S11 **New York** N Tyne
63 P7 **New York** N York
34 H9 **Nextend** Herefs
24 G9 **Neyland** Pembks
60 c7 **Niarbyl** IoM
28 C6 **Nibley** Gloucs
28 C11 **Nibley** S Glos
28 D8 **Nibley Green** Gloucs
16 F13 **Nicholashayne** Devon
25 T13 **Nicholaston** Swans
76 A12 **Nickies Hill** Cumb
63 S7 **Nidd** N York
99 S3 **Nigg** C Aber
109 Q10 **Nigg** Highld
109 P11 **Nigg Ferry** Highld
17 T2 **Nimlet** BaNES
68 G2 **Ninebanks** Nthumb
29 M10 **Nine Elms** Swindn
24 C6 **Nine Wells** Pembks
12 D13 **Ninfield** E Susx
9 M11 **Ningwood** IoW
84 H13 **Nisbet** Border
84 K8 **Nisbet Hill** Border
9 Q13 **Niton** IoW
89 M13 **Nitshill** C Glas
21 U11 **Noah's Ark** Kent
22 G9 **Noak Bridge** Essex
22 D9 **Noak Hill** Gt Lon
57 L5 **Noblethorpe** Barns
45 L11 **Nobold** Shrops
37 S8 **Nobottle** Nhants
58 J14 **Nocton** Lincs
51 Q13 **Nogdam End** Norfk
30 B10 **Noke** Oxon
24 E7 **Nolton** Pembks
24 E7 **Nolton Haven** Pembks
45 M4 **No Man's Heath** Ches W
46 J12 **No Man's Heath** Warwks
4 H9 **No Man's Land** Cnwll
15 T10 **Nomansland** Devon
8 K5 **Nomansland** Wilts
45 L8 **Noneley** Shrops
13 Q5 **Nonington** Kent
61 U3 **Nook** Cumb
75 U10 **Nook** Cumb
21 L9 **Norbiton** Gt Lon
61 Q11 **Norbreck** Bpool
35 R12 **Norbridge** Herefs
45 N4 **Norbury** Ches E
46 F5 **Norbury** Derbys
21 P9 **Norbury** Gt Lon
34 J2 **Norbury** Shrops
45 S9 **Norbury** Staffs
45 N4 **Norbury Common** Ches E
45 S9 **Norbury Junction** Staffs
35 T7 **Norchard** Worcs
55 P10 **Norcott Brook** Ches W
61 Q11 **Norcross** Lancs
49 S13 **Nordelph** Norfk
56 C4 **Norden** Rochdl
35 Q1 **Nordley** Shrops
51 S12 **Norfolk Broads** Norfk
85 N9 **Norham** Nthumb
56 G2 **Norland Town** Calder
55 N12 **Norley** Ches W
9 M9 **Norleywood** Hants
11 Q8 **Norlington** E Susx
58 G9 **Normanby** Lincs
58 E3 **Normanby** N Linc
64 G3 **Normanby** N York
70 H9 **Normanby** R & Cl
58 K7 **Normanby le Wold** Lincs
38 J2 **Norman Cross** Cambs
20 F12 **Normandy** Surrey
12 C14 **Norman's Bay** E Susx
6 E4 **Norman's Green** Devon
46 K7 **Normanton** C Derb
48 B5 **Normanton** Leics
48 D4 **Normanton** Lincs
47 T3 **Normanton** Notts
48 D12 **Normanton** Rutlnd
57 N2 **Normanton** Wakefd
18 H12 **Normanton** Wilts
47 L11 **Normanton le Heath** Leics
47 P9 **Normanton on Soar** Notts
47 R7 **Normanton on the Wolds** Notts
58 C13 **Normanton on Trent** Notts
61 Q12 **Normoss** Lancs
10 E2 **Norney** Surrey
18 C8 **Norrington Common** Wilts
5 L7 **Norris Green** Cnwll
54 J8 **Norris Green** Lpool
46 K10 **Norris Hill** Leics
56 K2 **Norristhorpe** Kirk
50 G14 **Northacre** Norfk
31 L8 **Northall** Bucks
70 E14 **Northallerton** N York
50 G11 **Northall Green** Norfk
9 N6 **Northam** C Sotn
15 L7 **Northam** Devon
37 U8 **Northampton** Nhants
35 T7 **Northampton** Worcs
57 R10 **North Anston** Rothm
20 F9 **North Ascot** Br For
29 U2 **North Aston** Oxon
31 S12 **Northaw** Herts
6 J2 **Northay** Somset
9 M4 **North Baddesley** Hants
94 F6 **North Ballachulish** Highld
17 R11 **North Barrow** Somset
50 F6 **North Barsham** Norfk
22 J10 **North Benfleet** Essex
10 E10 **North Bersted** W Susx
84 E1 **North Berwick** E Loth
69 Q6 **North Bitchburn** Dur
77 S9 **North Blyth** Nthumb
9 S6 **North Boarhunt** Hants
8 H9 **North Bockhampton** Dorset
48 J12 **Northborough** C Pete
13 R5 **Northbourne** Kent
5 S4 **North Bovey** Devon
18 C9 **North Bradley** Wilts
5 M4 **North Brentor** Devon
17 T9 **North Brewham** Somset
10 F3 **North Bridge** Surrey
12 D11 **Northbridge Street** E Susx
19 R13 **Northbrook** Hants
29 U3 **Northbrook** Oxon
31 S4 **North Brook End** Cambs
15 L4 **North Buckland** Devon
51 Q12 **North Burlingham** Norfk
17 R11 **North Cadbury** Somset
58 F11 **North Carlton** Lincs
57 S10 **North Carlton** Notts
64 K13 **North Cave** E R Yk
28 K6 **North Cerney** Gloucs
11 P6 **North Chailey** E Susx
10 F5 **Northchapel** W Susx
8 H5 **North Charford** Hants
85 T14 **North Charlton** Nthumb
21 M9 **North Cheam** Gt Lon
17 S11 **North Cheriton** Somset
7 M6 **North Chideock** Dorset
31 L11 **Northchurch** Herts
64 K12 **North Cliffe** E R Yk
58 D12 **North Clifton** Notts
69 S6 **North Close** Dur
59 Q8 **North Cockerington** Lincs
94 C12 **North Connel** Ag & B
26 E11 **North Cornelly** Brdgnd
2 K13 **North Corner** Cnwll
59 P6 **North Cotes** Lincs
4 J2 **Northcott** Devon
6 E2 **Northcott** Devon
6 F3 **Northcott** Devon
2 H8 **North Country** Cnwll
29 U8 **Northcourt** Oxon
41 S3 **North Cove** Suffk
69 S12 **North Cowton** N York
30 K4 **North Crawley** M Keyn
21 S8 **North Cray** Gt Lon
50 E6 **North Creake** Norfk
16 K11 **North Curry** Somset
65 L9 **North Dalton** E R Yk
63 T9 **North Deighton** N York
15 M6 **North Devon Crematorium** Devon
13 S1 **Northdown** Kent
12 H4 **North Downs**
64 F12 **North Duffield** N York
100 d2 **North Duntulm** Highld
21 M9 **North East Surrey Crematorium** Gt Lon
57 N13 **Northedge** Derbys
13 N7 **North Elham** Kent
59 N8 **North Elkington** Lincs
50 G9 **North Elmham** Norfk
57 Q4 **North Elmsall** Wakefd
20 B4 **Northend** Bucks
9 T8 **North End** C Port
75 R14 **North End** Cumb
8 A3 **North End** Dorset
65 R11 **North End** E R Yk
65 T13 **North End** E R Yk
22 G4 **North End** Essex
8 G5 **North End** Hants
9 R3 **North End** Hants
47 Q10 **North End** Leics
48 K5 **North End** Lincs
58 H7 **North End** Lincs
59 P6 **North End** Lincs
59 R9 **North End** Lincs
58 K2 **North End** N Linc
17 M3 **North End** N Som
38 E7 **North End** Nhants
40 G2 **North End** Norfk
77 N5 **North End** Nthumb
54 H6 **North End** Sefton
10 F10 **North End** W Susx
10 J9 **North End** W Susx
37 L10 **Northend** Warwks
55 T9 **Northenden** Manch
20 F5 **Northend Woods** Bucks
107 M8 **North Erradale** Highld
47 R13 **North Evington** C Leic
23 L8 **North Fambridge** Essex
58 G1 **North Ferriby** E R Yk
36 D5 **Northfield** Birm
99 S2 **Northfield** C Aber
58 H1 **Northfield** E R Yk
48 F12 **Northfields** Lincs
22 F13 **Northfleet** Kent
65 Q9 **North Frodingham** E R Yk
8 H6 **North Gorley** Hants
41 M3 **North Green** Norfk
41 P8 **North Green** Suffk
41 Q7 **North Green** Suffk
58 H12 **North Greetwell** Lincs
64 J6 **North Grimston** N York
12 D2 **North Halling** Medway
9 U8 **North Hayling** Hants
85 R12 **North Hazelrigg** Nthumb
15 R6 **North Heasley** Devon
10 H6 **North Heath** W Susx
16 D12 **North Hele** Devon
4 H5 **North Hill** Cnwll
20 J6 **North Hillingdon** Gt Lon
29 U6 **North Hinksey Village** Oxon
21 L13 **North Holmwood** Surrey
5 S9 **North Huish** Devon
58 F13 **North Hykeham** Lincs
12 F11 **Northiam** E Susx
38 H11 **Northill** C Beds
28 D6 **Northington** Gloucs
19 S13 **Northington** Hants
58 H6 **North Kelsey** Lincs
102 J6 **North Kessock** Highld
58 K3 **North Killingholme** N Linc
63 U2 **North Kilvington** N York
37 R4 **North Kilworth** Leics
8 H8 **North Kingston** Hants
48 J3 **North Kyme** Lincs
65 S5 **North Landing** E R Yk
49 M3 **Northlands** Lincs
29 M5 **Northleach** Gloucs
30 H11 **North Lee** Bucks
63 R5 **North Lees** N York
6 G5 **Northleigh** Devon
15 P6 **Northleigh** Devon
13 M6 **North Leigh** Kent
29 S5 **North Leigh** Oxon
58 C10 **North Leverton with Habblesthorpe** Notts
15 M13 **Northlew** Devon
36 E11 **North Littleton** Worcs
17 N9 **Northload Bridge** Somset
40 H4 **North Lopham** Norfk
48 D13 **North Luffenham** Rutlnd
10 C7 **North Marden** W Susx
30 G8 **North Marston** Bucks
83 S7 **North Middleton** Mdloth
85 P14 **North Middleton** Nthumb
105 N7 **North Millbrex** Abers
72 D9 **North Milmain** D & G
15 R7 **North Molton** Devon
29 T7 **Northmoor** Oxon
19 S3 **North Moreton** Oxon
98 F13 **Northmuir** Angus
10 D10 **North Mundham** W Susx
47 U2 **North Muskham** Notts
65 L12 **North Newbald** E R Yk
37 M12 **North Newington** Oxon
18 H9 **North Newnton** Wilts
16 K10 **North Newton** Somset
9 U8 **Northney** Hants
28 D8 **North Nibley** Gloucs
19 R10 **North Oakley** Hants
22 E10 **North Ockendon** Gt Lon
20 K6 **Northolt** Gt Lon
54 F13 **Northop** Flints
54 G13 **Northop Hall** Flints
70 H9 **North Ormesby** Middsb
59 N8 **North Ormsby** Lincs
56 K2 **Northorpe** Kirk
48 G10 **Northorpe** Lincs
48 K6 **Northorpe** Lincs
58 E7 **Northorpe** Lincs
63 T2 **North Otterington** N York
17 N9 **Northover** Somset
17 P12 **Northover** Somset
58 J8 **North Owersby** Lincs
56 H1 **Northowram** Calder
7 N3 **North Perrott** Somset
16 J10 **North Petherton** Somset
4 H3 **North Petherwin** Cnwll
50 E12 **North Pickenham** Norfk
36 C10 **North Piddle** Worcs
7 P5 **North Poorton** Dorset
8 C11 **Northport** Dorset
8 H7 **North Poulner** Hants
83 M2 **North Queensferry** Fife
15 S6 **North Radworthy** Devon
48 F4 **North Rauceby** Lincs
51 M6 **Northrepps** Norfk
59 Q10 **North Reston** Lincs
63 R10 **North Rigton** N York
8 H9 **North Ripley** Hants
56 C13 **North Rode** Ches E
106 w14 **North Ronaldsay** Ork
106 w14 *North Ronaldsay Airport* Ork
66 K6 **North Row** Cumb
49 T10 **North Runcton** Norfk
61 M6 **North Scale** Cumb
58 D13 **North Scarle** Lincs
77 R8 **North Seaton** Nthumb
77 R8 **North Seaton Colliery** Nthumb
94 C10 **North Shian** Ag & B
77 T12 **North Shields** N Tyne
23 M10 **North Shoebury** Sthend
61 Q12 **North Shore** Bpool
49 L14 **North Side** C Pete
66 E7 **North Side** Cumb
71 L9 **North Skelton** R & Cl
59 R7 **North Somercotes** Lincs
63 R4 **North Stainley** N York
68 H10 **North Stainmore** Cumb
22 F11 **North Stifford** Thurr
17 T3 **North Stoke** BaNES
19 T3 **North Stoke** Oxon
10 G8 **North Stoke** W Susx
39 S7 **North Street** Cambs
8 H5 **North Street** Hants
9 S2 **North Street** Hants
12 K4 **North Street** Kent
22 K13 **North Street** Medway
19 T6 **North Street** W Berk
85 U12 **North Sunderland** Nthumb
14 H13 **North Tamerton** Cnwll
15 Q12 **North Tawton** Devon
89 S8 **North Third** Stirlg
59 N7 **North Thoresby** Lincs
77 Q5 **North Togston** Nthumb
106 e10 **Northton** W Isls
15 M11 **North Town** Devon
17 Q8 **North Town** Somset
20 E6 **North Town** W & M
50 H11 **North Tuddenham** Norfk
106 c11 **North Uist** W Isls
76 H5 **Northumberland National Park** Nthumb
77 P12 **North Walbottle** N u Ty
51 N7 **North Walsham** Norfk
19 S11 **North Waltham** Hants
20 B12 **North Warnborough** Hants
16 F11 **Northway** Somset
25 U13 **Northway** Swans
22 C7 **North Weald Bassett** Essex
58 C9 **North Wheatley** Notts
5 V7 **North Whilborough** Devon
55 Q12 **Northwich** Ches W
17 Q3 **North Wick** BaNES
27 V10 **Northwick** S Glos
17 L7 **Northwick** Somset
35 T9 **Northwick** Worcs
17 Q5 **North Widcombe** BaNES
59 L9 **North Willingham** Lincs
57 P13 **North Wingfield** Derbys
48 D9 **North Witham** Lincs
40 C1 **Northwold** Norfk
45 U4 **Northwood** C Stke
57 L14 **Northwood** Derbys
20 J4 **Northwood** Gt Lon
9 P10 **Northwood** IoW
45 L7 **Northwood** Shrops
28 D4 **Northwood Green** Gloucs
7 S2 **North Wootton** Dorset
49 T9 **North Wootton** Norfk
17 Q8 **North Wootton** Somset
18 B5 **North Wraxall** Wilts
18 H4 **North Wroughton** Swindn
71 M12 **North York Moors National Park**
57 R3 **Norton** Donc
11 R10 **Norton** E Susx
28 G3 **Norton** Gloucs
55 N10 **Norton** Halton
31 R6 **Norton** Herts
9 L11 **Norton** IoW
27 S3 **Norton** Mons
16 K4 **Norton** N Som
64 H5 **Norton** N York
37 Q8 **Norton** Nhants
57 S12 **Norton** Notts
34 H7 **Norton** Powys
70 F8 **Norton** S on T
57 N10 **Norton** Sheff
35 L4 **Norton** Shrops
35 P4 **Norton** Shrops
45 N12 **Norton** Shrops
45 R13 **Norton** Shrops
40 G7 **Norton** Suffk
25 V13 **Norton** Swans
10 E9 **Norton** W Susx
28 G11 **Norton** Wilts
35 U10 **Norton** Worcs
36 D11 **Norton** Worcs
18 D12 **Norton Bavant** Wilts
45 U7 **Norton Bridge** Staffs
46 D12 **Norton Canes** Staffs
46 D12 **Norton Canes Services** Staffs
34 J11 **Norton Canon** Herefs
50 J8 **Norton Corner** Norfk
48 C2 **Norton Disney** Lincs
17 U9 **Norton Ferris** Wilts
16 G11 **Norton Fitzwarren** Somset
9 L11 **Norton Green** IoW
17 Q4 **Norton Hawkfield** BaNES
22 F7 **Norton Heath** Essex
45 R6 **Norton in Hales** Shrops
45 U3 **Norton in the Moors** C Stke
46 K12 **Norton-Juxta-Twycross** Leics
63 U5 **Norton-le-Clay** N York
36 H8 **Norton Lindsey** Warwks
40 G7 **Norton Little Green** Suffk
17 R4 **Norton Malreward** BaNES
22 E7 **Norton Mandeville** Essex
17 U5 **Norton St Philip** Somset
51 R14 **Norton Subcourse** Norfk
17 N13 **Norton sub Hamdon** Somset
34 J11 **Norton Wood** Herefs
47 U1 **Norwell** Notts
58 B14 **Norwell Woodhouse** Notts
51 M12 **Norwich** Norfk
51 M11 *Norwich Airport* Norfk
51 M12 **Norwich Cathedral** Norfk
51 M10 **Norwich (St Faith) Crematorium** Norfk
106 w2 **Norwick** Shet
90 C13 **Norwood** Clacks
57 Q10 **Norwood** Derbys
13 L9 **Norwood** Kent
22 E6 **Norwood End** Essex
56 H1 **Norwood Green** Calder
20 K7 **Norwood Green** Gt Lon
11 L2 **Norwood Hill** Surrey
49 P14 **Norwoodside** Cambs
47 T14 **Noseley** Leics
5 P11 **Noss Mayo** Devon
63 R3 **Nosterfield** N York
39 T12 **Nosterfield End** Cambs
101 M6 **Nostie** Highld
29 M3 **Notgrove** Gloucs
26 E12 **Nottage** Brdgnd
4 K8 **Notter** Cnwll
47 Q6 **Nottingham** C Nott
7 S8 **Nottington** Dorset
57 M4 **Notton** Wakefd
18 D7 **Notton** Wilts
22 J5 **Nounsley** Essex
35 T7 **Noutard's Green** Worcs
40 E8 **Nowton** Suffk
44 K11 **Nox** Shrops
19 U3 **Nuffield** Oxon
64 J10 **Nunburnholme** E R Yk
47 P3 **Nuncargate** Notts
67 Q3 **Nunclose** Cumb
37 L2 **Nuneaton** Warwks
30 C13 **Nuneham Courtenay** Oxon
21 P7 **Nunhead** Gt Lon
65 Q10 **Nunkeeling** E R Yk
64 C8 **Nun Monkton** N York
17 T7 **Nunney** Somset
17 T8 **Nunney Catch** Somset
35 N12 **Nunnington** Herefs
64 F4 **Nunnington** N York
59 N5 **Nunsthorpe** NE Lin
64 E9 **Nunthorpe** C York
70 H10 **Nunthorpe** Middsb
70 H10 **Nunthorpe Village** Middsb
8 H3 **Nunton** Wilts
63 S5 **Nunwick** N York
76 H11 **Nunwick** Nthumb
28 B8 **Nupdown** S Glos
30 J9 **Nup End** Bucks
28 E6 **Nupend** Gloucs
20 E8 **Nuptown** Br For
9 M5 **Nursling** Hants
10 B6 **Nursted** Hants
18 F8 **Nursteed** Wilts
45 T14 **Nurton** Staffs
10 B9 **Nutbourne** W Susx
10 H7 **Nutbourne** W Susx
21 P12 **Nutfield** Surrey
47 P5 **Nuthall** Notts
39 P14 **Nuthampstead** Herts
10 K5 **Nuthurst** W Susx
11 Q5 **Nutley** E Susx
19 T12 **Nutley** Hants
55 S3 **Nuttall** Bury
57 T6 **Nutwell** Donc
112 J4 **Nybster** Highld
10 D11 **Nyetimber** W Susx
10 C6 **Nyewood** W Susx
15 R11 **Nymet Rowland** Devon
15 R12 **Nymet Tracey** Devon
28 F7 **Nympsfield** Gloucs
16 F12 **Nynehead** Somset
17 M10 **Nythe** Somset
10 E9 **Nyton** W Susx

O

47 R13 **Oadby** Leics
12 G3 **Oad Street** Kent
35 T8 **Oakall Green** Worcs
46 D5 **Oakamoor** Staffs
83 L5 **Oakbank** W Loth
15 M13 **Oak Cross** Devon
27 M8 **Oakdale** Caerph
16 G11 **Oake** Somset
45 U13 **Oaken** Staffs
61 U10 **Oakenclough** Lancs
45 R11 **Oakengates** Wrekin
54 G12 **Oakenholt** Flints
69 Q5 **Oakenshaw** Dur
63 P14 **Oakenshaw** Kirk
47 L3 **Oakerthorpe** Derbys
32 J9 **Oakford** Cerdgn
16 B12 **Oakford** Devon
16 B12 **Oakfordbridge** Devon
56 D13 **Oakgrove** Ches E
48 C12 **Oakham** Rutlnd
45 S3 **Oakhanger** Ches E
10 B3 **Oakhanger** Hants
17 R7 **Oakhill** Somset
21 U12 **Oakhurst** Kent
39 P8 **Oakington** Cambs
34 B10 **Oaklands** Powys
28 E4 **Oakle Street** Gloucs
38 F10 **Oakley** Bed
30 D10 **Oakley** Bucks
90 F14 **Oakley** Fife
19 S10 **Oakley** Hants
30 G12 **Oakley** Oxon
8 E9 **Oakley** Poole
41 L5 **Oakley** Suffk
20 F7 **Oakley Green** W & M
33 U3 **Oakley Park** Powys
28 H7 **Oakridge** Gloucs
62 D13 **Oaks** Lancs
44 K13 **Oaks** Shrops
28 J9 **Oaksey** Wilts
46 G7 **Oaks Green** Derbys
75 V10 **Oakshaw Ford** Cumb
9 U3 **Oakshott** Hants
46 K11 **Oakthorpe** Leics
70 E10 **Oak Tree** Darltn
47 L6 **Oakwood** C Derb
76 J12 **Oakwood** Nthumb
63 L12 **Oakworth** C Brad
12 K3 **Oare** Kent
15 S3 **Oare** Somset
18 J8 **Oare** Wilts
48 F6 **Oasby** Lincs
17 L11 **Oath** Somset
98 H12 **Oathlaw** Angus
20 J9 **Oatlands Park** Surrey
94 B13 **Oban** Ag & B
94 C11 *Oban Airport* Ag & B
34 H5 **Obley** Shrops
90 F4 **Obney** P & K
17 S13 **Oborne** Dorset
48 G11 **Obthorpe** Lincs
41 L6 **Occold** Suffk
112 G9 **Occumster** Highld
81 Q8 **Ochiltree** E Ayrs
47 M6 **Ockbrook** Derbys
36 C2 **Ocker Hill** Sandw
35 S8 **Ockeridge** Worcs
20 J11 **Ockham** Surrey
93 P4 **Ockle** Highld
10 J2 **Ockley** Surrey
35 N11 **Ocle Pychard** Herefs
65 N6 **Octon** E R Yk
17 P13 **Odcombe** Somset
17 T4 **Odd Down** BaNES
36 B9 **Oddingley** Worcs
29 P2 **Oddington** Gloucs
30 C9 **Oddington** Oxon
38 E9 **Odell** Bed
15 L12 **Odham** Devon
20 B12 **Odiham** Hants
63 P14 **Odsal** C Brad
31 S5 **Odsey** Cambs
8 G3 **Odstock** Wilts
47 L12 **Odstone** Leics
37 L7 **Offchurch** Warwks
36 E11 **Offenham** Worcs
56 D9 **Offerton** Stockp
70 D1 **Offerton** Sundld
11 Q8 **Offham** E Susx
12 C4 **Offham** Kent
10 G9 **Offham** W Susx
45 S8 **Offleymarsh** Staffs
38 K7 **Offord Cluny** Cambs
38 K7 **Offord D'Arcy** Cambs
40 J11 **Offton** Suffk
6 G5 **Offwell** Devon
18 J6 **Ogbourne Maizey** Wilts
18 J6 **Ogbourne St Andrew** Wilts
18 K6 **Ogbourne St George** Wilts
63 M13 **Ogden** Calder
77 N10 **Ogle** Nthumb
54 K10 **Oglet** Lpool
26 F12 **Ogmore** V Glam
26 F12 **Ogmore-by-Sea** V Glam
26 G9 **Ogmore Vale** Brdgnd
52 K9 **Ogwen Bank** Gwynd
7 V2 **Okeford Fitzpaine** Dorset
15 N13 **Okehampton** Devon
46 J1 **Oker Side** Derbys
10 J3 **Okewood Hill** Surrey
6 A9 **Olchard** Devon
37 U6 **Old** Nhants
99 S2 **Old Aberdeen** C Aber
9 R2 **Old Alresford** Hants
110 B10 **Oldany** Highld
74 E6 **Old Auchenbrack** D & G
47 Q5 **Old Basford** C Nott
19 U10 **Old Basing** Hants
50 G10 **Old Beetley** Norfk
36 F7 **Oldberrow** Warwks
77 M1 **Old Bewick** Nthumb
59 Q13 **Old Bolingbroke** Lincs
63 Q11 **Old Bramhope** Leeds
57 M12 **Old Brampton** Derbys
74 E12 **Old Bridge of Urr** D & G
40 J2 **Old Buckenham** Norfk
19 Q9 **Old Burghclere** Hants
21 U11 **Oldbury** Kent
36 C3 **Oldbury** Sandw
35 R2 **Oldbury** Shrops
36 K2 **Oldbury** Warwks
28 B9 **Oldbury Naite** S Glos
28 B9 **Oldbury-on-Severn** S Glos
28 F10 **Oldbury on the Hill** Gloucs
64 D2 **Old Byland** N York
57 T6 **Old Cantley** Donc
70 D5 **Old Cassop** Dur
26 G12 **Old Castle** Brdgnd
27 Q3 **Oldcastle** Mons
45 L4 **Oldcastle Heath** Ches W
51 M11 **Old Catton** Norfk
34 G2 **Old Churchstoke** Powys
59 N5 **Old Clee** NE Lin
16 D8 **Old Cleeve** Somset
57 T14 **Old Clipstone** Notts
53 Q7 **Old Colwyn** Conwy
57 S9 **Oldcotes** Notts
80 J13 **Old Dailly** S Ayrs
47 S9 **Old Dalby** Leics
56 H11 **Old Dam** Derbys
105 R6 **Old Deer** Abers
17 P7 **Old Ditch** Somset
57 R7 **Old Edlington** Donc
69 R7 **Old Eldon** Dur
65 R12 **Old Ellerby** E R Yk
41 P13 **Old Felixstowe** Suffk
63 L12 **Oldfield** C Brad
35 T8 **Oldfield** Worcs
38 J1 **Old Fletton** C Pete
17 U6 **Oldford** Somset
27 V4 **Old Forge** Herefs
27 T3 **Old Furnace** Herefs
56 F8 **Old Glossop** Derbys
58 B2 **Old Goole** E R Yk
2 b1 **Old Grimsby** IoS
31 U8 **Old Hall Green** Herts
40 E9 **Oldhall Green** Suffk
51 P7 **Old Hall Street** Norfk
56 D6 **Oldham** Oldham
84 J4 **Oldhamstocks** E Loth
22 C5 **Old Harlow** Essex
23 P3 **Old Heath** Essex
49 U5 **Old Hunstanton** Norfk
39 M5 **Old Hurst** Cambs
62 B2 **Old Hutton** Cumb
3 L8 **Old Kea** Cnwll
89 L11 **Old Kilpatrick** W Duns
31 R8 **Old Knebworth** Herts
51 M12 **Old Lakenham** Norfk
17 S2 **Oldland** S Glos
62 E12 **Old Langho** Lancs
60 g6 **Old Laxey** IoM
49 P3 **Old Leake** Lincs
64 H5 **Old Malton** N York
105 N10 **Oldmeldrum** Abers
4 K6 **Oldmill** Cnwll
36 J7 **Old Milverton** Warwks
16 K5 **Oldmixon** N Som
40 J8 **Old Newton** Suffk
70 D5 **Old Quarrington** Dur
47 Q5 **Old Radford** C Nott
34 G9 **Old Radnor** Powys
104 K10 **Old Rayne** Abers
12 K11 **Old Romney** Kent
11 L9 **Old Shoreham** W Susx
110 E5 **Oldshoremore** Highld
12 B5 **Old Soar** Kent
28 E11 **Old Sodbury** S Glos
48 E7 **Old Somerby** Lincs
64 C4 **Oldstead** N York
30 G4 **Old Stratford** Nhants
97 N10 **Old Struan** P & K
77 P5 **Old Swarland** Nthumb
36 B4 **Old Swinford** Dudley
68 D11 **Old Tebay** Cumb
63 U3 **Old Thirsk** N York
63 L14 **Old Town** Calder
62 B3 **Old Town** Cumb
67 Q4 **Old Town** Cumb
11 T11 **Old Town** E Susx
2 c2 **Old Town** IoS
55 T7 **Old Trafford** Traffd
57 N13 **Old Tupton** Derbys
75 U13 **Oldwall** Cumb
25 S12 **Oldwalls** Swans
31 P4 **Old Warden** C Beds
15 U8 **Oldways End** Somset
38 G5 **Old Weston** Cambs
112 J7 **Old Wick** Highld
20 G8 **Old Windsor** W & M
13 L5 **Old Wives Lees** Kent
20 H11 **Old Woking** Surrey
30 H4 **Old Wolverton** M Keyn
59 M13 **Old Woodhall** Lincs
45 L9 **Old Woods** Shrops
112 C6 **Olgrinmore** Highld
46 F10 **Olive Green** Staffs
9 P3 **Oliver's Battery** Hants
106 t5 **Ollaberry** Shet
100 e6 **Ollach** Highld
55 S11 **Ollerton** Ches E
57 U13 **Ollerton** Notts
45 P8 **Ollerton** Shrops
33 M9 **Olmarch** Cerdgn
39 T12 **Olmstead Green** Cambs
38 C10 **Olney** M Keyn
112 E3 **Olrig House** Highld
36 F4 **Olton** Solhll
28 B10 **Olveston** S Glos
35 T8 **Ombersley** Worcs
57 U13 **Ompton** Notts
76 E12 **Once Brewed** Nthumb
60 f7 **Onchan** IoM
46 D2 **Onecote** Staffs
40 H9 **Onehouse** Suffk
27 S5 **Onen** Mons
34 J7 **Ongar Street** Herefs
35 L5 **Onibury** Shrops
94 E6 **Onich** Highld
26 E5 **Onllwyn** Neath
45 S5 **Onneley** Staffs
22 G4 **Onslow Green** Essex
20 G13 **Onslow Village** Surrey
55 N12 **Onston** Ches W
47 L4 **Openwoodgate** Derbys
107 M10 **Opinan** Highld
104 C4 **Orbliston** Moray
100 b5 **Orbost** Highld
59 S13 **Orby** Lincs
16 H12 **Orchard Portman** Somset
18 G11 **Orcheston** Wilts
27 T2 **Orcop** Herefs
27 T2 **Orcop Hill** Herefs
104 J4 **Ord** Abers
104 K13 **Ordhead** Abers
98 H3 **Ordie** Abers
104 C4 **Ordiequish** Moray
76 J14 **Ordley** Nthumb
58 B11 **Ordsall** Notts
12 F13 **Ore** E Susx
35 L7 **Oreleton Common** Herefs
35 Q4 **Oreton** Shrops
41 R10 **Orford** Suffk
55 P8 **Orford** Warrtn
8 C10 **Organford** Dorset
46 F10 **Orgreave** Staffs
12 K9 **Orlestone** Kent
35 L7 **Orleton** Herefs
35 R7 **Orleton** Worcs
38 C6 **Orlingbury** Nhants
67 L7 **Ormathwaite** Cumb
70 H9 **Ormesby** R & Cl
51 S11 **Ormesby St Margaret** Norfk
51 S11 **Ormesby St Michael** Norfk
107 Q6 **Ormiscaig** Highld
83 T5 **Ormiston** E Loth
93 M6 **Ormsaigmore** Highld
87 N11 **Ormsary** Ag & B
54 K5 **Ormskirk** Lancs
69 Q3 **Ornsby Hill** Dur
86 F8 **Oronsay** Ag & B
106 s19 **Orphir** Ork
21 S9 **Orpington** Gt Lon
54 H7 **Orrell** Sefton
55 M6 **Orrell** Wigan
55 M5 **Orrell Post** Wigan
60 e4 **Orrisdale** IoM
73 T10 **Orroland** D & G
22 F11 **Orsett** Thurr
45 T10 **Orslow** Staffs
47 U5 **Orston** Notts
67 L6 **Orthwaite** Cumb
61 U9 **Ortner** Lancs
68 D11 **Orton** Cumb
38 B5 **Orton** Nhants
35 U1 **Orton** Staffs
38 J1 **Orton Longueville** C Pete
46 K13 **Orton-on-the-Hill** Leics
67 M2 **Orton Rigg** Cumb
38 J1 **Orton Waterville** C Pete
39 N10 **Orwell** Cambs
62 C13 **Osbaldeston** Lancs
62 C13 **Osbaldeston Green** Lancs
64 E9 **Osbaldwick** C York
47 M13 **Osbaston** Leics
44 H9 **Osbaston** Shrops
9 Q10 **Osborne** IoW
9 Q10 **Osborne House** IoW
48 G6 **Osbournby** Lincs
55 M13 **Oscroft** Ches W
100 c5 **Ose** Highld
47 M10 **Osgathorpe** Leics
58 J8 **Osgodby** Lincs
64 E13 **Osgodby** N York
65 P3 **Osgodby** N York
100 e6 **Oskaig** Highld
93 M10 **Oskamull** Ag & B
46 G5 **Osmaston** Derbys
7 T8 **Osmington** Dorset
7 T8 **Osmington Mills** Dorset
63 S13 **Osmondthorpe** Leeds
70 G13 **Osmotherley** N York
29 U6 **Osney** Oxon
12 K3 **Ospringe** Kent
57 L2 **Ossett** Wakefd
58 C14 **Ossington** Notts
23 M8 **Ostend** Essex
21 L7 **Osterley** Gt Lon
64 E4 **Oswaldkirk** N York
55 R1 **Oswaldtwistle** Lancs
44 G8 **Oswestry** Shrops
21 T11 **Otford** Kent
12 E5 **Otham** Kent
12 F5 **Otham Hole** Kent
17 L10 **Othery** Somset
63 Q10 **Otley** Leeds
41 M9 **Otley** Suffk
41 M9 **Otley Green** Suffk
9 P4 **Otterbourne** Hants
62 H8 **Otterburn** N York
76 H7 **Otterburn** Nthumb
87 S9 **Otter Ferry** Ag & B
4 F2 **Otterham** Cnwll
16 H8 **Otterhampton** Somset
12 F2 **Otterham Quay** Kent
4 F3 **Otterham Station** Cnwll
106 e11 **Otternish** W Isls
20 H10 **Ottershaw** Surrey
106 v5 **Otterswick** Shet
6 E7 **Otterton** Devon
9 N8 **Otterwood** Hants
6 F5 **Ottery St Mary** Devon
13 N7 **Ottinge** Kent
59 N2 **Ottringham** E R Yk
67 L1 **Oughterby** Cumb
62 H3 **Oughtershaw** N York
66 H4 **Oughterside** Cumb
57 M8 **Oughtibridge** Sheff
55 Q9 **Oughtrington** Warrtn
64 C5 **Oulston** N York
66 K2 **Oulton** Cumb
63 T14 **Oulton** Leeds
50 K8 **Oulton** Norfk
45 S9 **Oulton** Staffs
46 B6 **Oulton** Staffs
41 T2 **Oulton** Suffk
41 T2 **Oulton Broad** Suffk
51 L8 **Oulton Street** Norfk
38 F3 **Oundle** Nhants
35 U2 **Ounsdale** Staffs
68 D6 **Ousby** Cumb
40 B9 **Ousden** Suffk
58 D2 **Ousefleet** E R Yk
69 S2 **Ouston** Dur
85 S12 **Outchester** Nthumb
13 P5 **Out Elmstead** Kent
67 N13 **Outgate** Cumb
68 G12 **Outhgill** Cumb
36 F7 **Outhill** Warwks
45 S7 **Outlands** Staffs
56 G3 **Outlane** Kirk
59 Q2 **Out Newton** E R Yk
61 S11 **Out Rawcliffe** Lancs
49 R13 **Outwell** Norfk
8 G5 **Outwick** Hants
21 P13 **Outwood** Surrey
57 M2 **Outwood** Wakefd
55 S5 **Outwood Gate** Bury
47 M10 **Outwoods** Leics
45 S10 **Outwoods** Staffs
57 M1 **Ouzlewell Green** Leeds
56 G1 **Ovenden** Calder
39 N6 **Over** Cambs
55 P13 **Over** Ches W
28 F4 **Over** Gloucs
28 A11 **Over** S Glos
46 J6 **Over Burrows** Derbys
36 C13 **Overbury** Worcs
7 S8 **Overcombe** Dorset
17 Q13 **Over Compton** Dorset
55 Q5 **Overdale Crematorium** Bolton
38 G2 **Over End** Cambs
57 M12 **Overgreen** Derbys
36 G2 **Over Green** Warwks
56 K13 **Over Haddon** Derbys
61 U6 **Over Kellet** Lancs
29 T3 **Over Kiddington** Oxon
17 N9 **Overleigh** Somset
46 G10 **Overley** Staffs
27 U5 **Over Monnow** Mons
29 R2 **Over Norton** Oxon
55 S12 **Over Peover** Ches E
54 J11 **Overpool** Ches W
110 J12 **Overscaig Hotel** Highld
46 J10 **Overseal** Derbys
70 F14 **Over Silton** N York
13 L4 **Oversland** Kent
36 E9 **Oversley Green** Warwks
37 U7 **Overstone** Nhants
16 G9 **Over Stowey** Somset
51 M5 **Overstrand** Norfk
17 M13 **Over Stratton** Somset
18 G13 **Overstreet** Wilts
55 R11 **Over Tabley** Ches E
37 N12 **Overthorpe** Nhants
105 P13 **Overton** C Aber
55 M11 **Overton** Ches W
19 R11 **Overton** Hants
61 S8 **Overton** Lancs
64 D8 **Overton** N York
35 M6 **Overton** Shrops
25 S13 **Overton** Swans
57 L3 **Overton** Wakefd
44 J5 **Overton** Wrexhm
44 J5 **Overton Bridge** Wrexhm
45 T1 **Overton Green** Ches E
62 C4 **Overtown** Lancs
82 F8 **Overtown** N Lans
18 J5 **Overtown** Swindn
57 N3 **Overtown** Wakefd
19 L13 **Over Wallop** Hants
36 J2 **Over Whitacre** Warwks
57 Q12 **Over Woodhouse** Derbys
29 T2 **Over Worton** Oxon
19 S2 **Overy** Oxon
30 G8 **Oving** Bucks
10 E10 **Oving** W Susx
11 P10 **Ovingdean** Br & H
77 M13 **Ovingham** Nthumb
69 P10 **Ovington** Dur
40 C12 **Ovington** Essex
9 R2 **Ovington** Hants
50 F13 **Ovington** Norfk
77 M13 **Ovington** Nthumb
9 L5 **Ower** Hants
9 P8 **Ower** Hants
7 U7 **Owermoigne** Dorset
34 H2 **Owlbury** Shrops
57 M9 **Owlerton** Sheff
28 E8 **Owlpen** Gloucs
41 N7 **Owl's Green** Suffk
20 D10 **Owlsmoor** Br For
30 G11 **Owlswick** Bucks
58 H9 **Owmby** Lincs
58 J6 **Owmby** Lincs
9 Q4 **Owslebury** Hants
57 S4 **Owston** Donc
47 U12 **Owston** Leics
58 D6 **Owston Ferry** N Linc
65 T13 **Owstwick** E R Yk
65 U14 **Owthorne** E R Yk
47 S7 **Owthorpe** Notts
70 G7 **Owton Manor** Hartpl
50 B13 **Oxborough** Norfk
7 N5 **Oxbridge** Dorset
59 P11 **Oxcombe** Lincs
57 Q12 **Oxcroft** Derbys
22 G2 **Oxen End** Essex
61 U2 **Oxenholme** Cumb
63 L13 **Oxenhope** C Brad
61 Q2 **Oxen Park** Cumb
17 M8 **Oxenpill** Somset
28 J1 **Oxenton** Gloucs
19 M9 **Oxenwood** Wilts
30 B11 **Oxford** Oxon
29 U4 *Oxford Airport* Oxon
30 C11 **Oxford Crematorium** Oxon
30 D12 **Oxford Services** Oxon
20 K3 **Oxhey** Herts
69 Q2 **Oxhill** Dur
36 K11 **Oxhill** Warwks
46 B13 **Oxley** Wolves
23 M5 **Oxley Green** Essex
12 C11 **Oxley's Green** E Susx
39 Q3 **Oxlode** Cambs
76 D2 **Oxnam** Border
51 M9 **Oxnead** Norfk
20 K10 **Oxshott** Surrey
20 K10 **Oxshott Heath** Surrey
57 L6 **Oxspring** Barns
21 Q12 **Oxted** Surrey
84 D8 **Oxton** Border
64 C11 **Oxton** N York
47 R3 **Oxton** Notts
25 S13 **Oxwich** Swans
25 S13 **Oxwich Green** Swans
50 F8 **Oxwick** Norfk
108 F4 **Oykel Bridge Hotel** Highld
104 K10 **Oyne** Abers
25 V13 **Oystermouth** Swans
28 E9 **Ozleworth** Gloucs

P

106 k5 **Pabail** W Isls
7 T2 **Packers Hill** Dorset
47 L11 **Packington** Leics
45 U3 **Packmoor** C Stke
36 J7 **Packmores** Warwks
98 G13 **Padanaram** Angus
30 F6 **Padbury** Bucks
21 N6 **Paddington** Gt Lon
55 P9 **Paddington** Warrtn
12 C3 **Paddlesworth** Kent
13 N8 **Paddlesworth** Kent
12 C7 **Paddock Wood** Kent
45 M7 **Paddolgreen** Shrops
56 F7 **Padfield** Derbys
55 P9 **Padgate** Warrtn
22 F8 **Padhams Green** Essex
62 F13 **Padiham** Lancs
63 P8 **Padside** N York
3 N1 **Padstow** Cnwll
19 T7 **Padworth** W Berk
69 R5 **Page Bank** Dur
10 D11 **Pagham** W Susx
23 M9 **Paglesham** Essex
6 A12 **Paignton** Torbay
37 N4 **Pailton** Warwks
11 U6 **Paine's Cross** E Susx
46 D7 **Painleyhill** Staffs
34 E11 **Painscastle** Powys
77 M13 **Painshawfield** Nthumb
64 J8 **Painsthorpe** E R Yk
28 G6 **Painswick** Gloucs
12 J4 **Painter's Forstal** Kent
89 L13 **Paisley** Rens
89 L13 **Paisley Woodside Crematorium** Rens
41 T2 **Pakefield** Suffk
40 F7 **Pakenham** Suffk
43 U6 **Pale** Gwynd
39 U12 **Pale Green** Essex
19 L12 **Palestine** Hants
20 E7 **Paley Street** W & M
36 D1 **Palfrey** Wsall
40 K5 **Palgrave** Suffk
7 U6 **Pallington** Dorset
4 F5 **Palmersbridge** Cnwll
21 P4 **Palmers Green** Gt Lon
81 Q9 **Palmerston** E Ayrs
16 F3 **Palmerstown** V Glam
73 U8 **Palnackie** D & G
73 M7 **Palnure** D & G
57 Q13 **Palterton** Derbys
19 T9 **Pamber End** Hants
19 T9 **Pamber Green** Hants
19 T8 **Pamber Heath** Hants
36 B14 **Pamington** Gloucs
8 D8 **Pamphill** Dorset
39 Q11 **Pampisford** Cambs
17 N7 **Panborough** Somset
91 S4 **Panbride** Angus
14 G11 **Pancrasweek** Devon
16 D3 **Pancross** V Glam
27 M10 **Pandy** Caerph
43 M13 **Pandy** Gwynd
43 S8 **Pandy** Gwynd
27 Q3 **Pandy** Mons
43 T13 **Pandy** Powys
44 E6 **Pandy** Wrexhm
44 C3 **Pandy'r Capel** Denbgs
53 Q10 **Pandy Tudur** Conwy
22 H2 **Panfield** Essex
19 T5 **Pangbourne** W Berk
11 M8 **Pangdean** W Susx
35 P11 **Panks Bridge** Herefs
63 S9 **Pannal** N York
63 R9 **Pannal Ash** N York
98 G4 **Pannanich Wells Hotel** Abers
44 G9 **Pant** Shrops
54 E11 **Pantasaph** Flints
24 F4 **Panteg** Pembks
4 F7 **Pantersbridge** Cnwll
26 G11 **Pant-ffrwyth** Brdgnd
42 J4 **Pant Glas** Gwynd
43 Q14 **Pantglas** Powys
25 U5 **Pant-Gwyn** Carmth
26 B7 **Pant-lasau** Swans
33 R4 **Pant Mawr** Powys
59 L11 **Panton** Lincs
53 T10 **Pant-pastynog** Denbgs
43 P13 **Pantperthog** Gwynd
33 U6 **Pant-y-dwr** Powys
44 E13 **Pant-y-ffridd** Powys
25 V8 **Pantyffynnon** Carmth
27 P8 **Pantygaseg** Torfn
26 G9 **Pant-y-gog** Brdgnd
24 K5 **Pantymenyn** Carmth
54 E14 **Pant-y-mwyn** Flints
51 Q11 **Panxworth** Norfk
106 t14 *Papa Westray Airport* Ork
66 H6 **Papcastle** Cumb
112 J6 **Papigoe** Highld
84 F4 **Papple** E Loth
47 P3 **Papplewick** Notts
39 L8 **Papworth Everard** Cambs
39 L8 **Papworth St Agnes** Cambs
3 R6 **Par** Cnwll
13 Q3 **Paramour Street** Kent
55 L4 **Parbold** Lancs
17 Q9 **Parbrook** Somset
10 H5 **Parbrook** W Susx
43 S7 **Parc** Gwynd
24 K8 **Parc Gwyn Crematorium** Pembks
32 D10 **Parcllyn** Cerdgn
27 S9 **Parc Seymour** Newpt
66 G8 **Pardshaw** Cumb
41 P8 **Parham** Suffk
74 H7 **Park** D & G
76 D13 **Park** Nthumb
2 H8 **Park Bottom** Cnwll
56 D6 **Park Bridge** Tamesd
11 S3 **Park Corner** E Susx
19 U3 **Park Corner** Oxon
20 E6 **Park Corner** W & M
61 R14 **Park Crematorium** Lancs
38 E10 **Park End** Bed
28 B6 **Parkend** Gloucs
76 H10 **Park End** Nthumb
12 B6 **Parkers Green** Kent
23 T1 **Parkeston** Essex
41 M14 **Parkeston Quay** Essex
12 K8 **Park Farm** Kent
54 G11 **Parkgate** Ches W
66 K3 **Parkgate** Cumb
74 K8 **Parkgate** D & G
12 D13 **Parkgate** E Susx
22 G2 **Parkgate** Essex
9 Q7 **Park Gate** Hants
12 G9 **Parkgate** Kent
21 T10 **Parkgate** Kent
63 P11 **Park Gate** Leeds
11 L2 **Parkgate** Surrey
36 B6 **Park Gate** Worcs
22 C2 **Park Green** Essex
40 K8 **Park Green** Suffk
91 T2 **Parkgrove Crematorium** Angus
89 L11 **Parkhall** W Duns
14 J8 **Parkham** Devon
14 J8 **Parkham Ash** Devon
47 L3 **Park Head** Derbys
27 V8 **Park Hill** Gloucs
27 U7 **Parkhouse** Mons
25 T13 **Parkmill** Swans
21 L6 **Park Royal** Gt Lon
70 F3 **Parkside** Dur
82 F7 **Parkside** N Lans
44 J2 **Parkside** Wrexhm
8 E10 **Parkstone** Poole
31 P12 **Park Street** Herts
10 J4 **Park Street** W Susx
56 H2 **Park Wood Crematorium** Calder
8 G9 **Parley Green** Dorset
20 C5 **Parmoor** Bucks
22 B6 **Parndon** Essex
22 B6 **Parndon Wood Crematorium** Essex
15 Q3 **Parracombe** Devon
24 J3 **Parrog** Pembks
66 H5 **Parsonby** Cumb
57 M8 **Parson Cross** Sheff
49 N12 **Parson Drove** Cambs
23 P2 **Parson's Heath** Essex
46 J8 **Parson's Hill** Derbys
89 M12 **Partick** C Glas
55 R8 **Partington** Traffd
59 R13 **Partney** Lincs
66 E8 **Parton** Cumb
10 K7 **Partridge Green** W Susx
27 P3 **Partrishow** Powys
46 G3 **Parwich** Derbys
22 E7 **Paslow Wood Common** Essex
30 G5 **Passenham** Nhants
10 C4 **Passfield** Hants
22 D8 **Passingford Bridge** Essex
48 J13 **Paston** C Pete
51 P7 **Paston** Norfk
46 C9 **Pasturefields** Staffs
15 L13 **Patchacott** Devon
11 N9 **Patcham** Br & H
20 K3 **Patchetts Green** Herts
10 H9 **Patching** W Susx
15 P4 **Patchole** Devon
28 B11 **Patchway** S Glos
63 P6 **Pateley Bridge** N York
23 M4 **Paternoster Heath** Essex
17 L10 **Pathe** Somset
91 L13 **Pathhead** Fife
83 S6 **Pathhead** Mdloth
36 G9 **Pathlow** Warwks
90 G9 **Path of Condie** P & K
22 B2 **Patmore Heath** Herts
81 N10 **Patna** E Ayrs
18 G9 **Patney** Wilts
60 c6 **Patrick** IoM
63 Q1 **Patrick Brompton** N York
55 S7 **Patricroft** Salfd
59 P2 **Patrington** E R Yk
59 P2 **Patrington Haven** E R Yk
13 N4 **Patrixbourne** Kent
67 N9 **Patterdale** Cumb
45 T14 **Pattingham** Staffs
37 S10 **Pattishall** Nhants
22 K3 **Pattiswick Green** Essex
35 N1 **Patton** Shrops
2 D11 **Paul** Cnwll
37 T11 **Paulerspury** Nhants
59 L1 **Paull** E R Yk
8 G2 **Paul's Dene** Wilts
17 S5 **Paulton** BaNES
35 Q10 **Paunton** Herefs
77 N6 **Pauperhaugh** Nthumb
45 S10 **Pave Lane** Wrekin
38 E9 **Pavenham** Bed
16 J8 **Pawlett** Somset
85 M12 **Pawston** Nthumb
36 G13 **Paxford** Gloucs
85 N8 **Paxton** Border
12 H5 **Payden Street** Kent
6 E4 **Payhembury** Devon
2 H8 **Paynter's Lane End** Cnwll
62 G9 **Paythorne** Lancs
34 K6 **Paytoe** Herefs
11 Q10 **Peacehaven** E Susx
56 G11 **Peak Dale** Derbys
56 J8 **Peak District National Park**
56 H11 **Peak Forest** Derbys
49 L10 **Peak Hill** Lincs
48 J12 **Peakirk** C Pete
12 C7 **Pearson's Green** Kent
35 N14 **Peartree Green** Herefs
17 T5 **Peasedown St John** BaNES
47 M4 **Peasehill** Derbys
50 J10 **Peaseland Green** Norfk
19 Q5 **Peasemore** W Berk
41 Q7 **Peasenhall** Suffk
11 M4 **Pease Pottage** W Susx
10 H2 **Peaslake** Surrey
55 M8 **Peasley Cross** St Hel
12 G11 **Peasmarsh** E Susx
6 K2 **Peasmarsh** Somset
20 G13 **Peasmarsh** Surrey
105 Q2 **Peathill** Abers
91 Q10 **Peat Inn** Fife
37 Q2 **Peatling Magna** Leics
37 Q3 **Peatling Parva** Leics
35 M3 **Peaton** Shrops
40 E14 **Pebmarsh** Essex
36 F11 **Pebworth** Worcs
62 K14 **Pecket Well** Calder
45 M2 **Peckforton** Ches E
21 P7 **Peckham** Gt Lon
47 N13 **Peckleton** Leics
44 D9 **Pedairffordd** Powys
13 M8 **Pedlinge** Kent
36 B4 **Pedmore** Dudley
17 M9 **Pedwell** Somset
83 Q10 **Peebles** Border
60 c6 **Peel** IoM
61 R13 **Peel** Lancs
9 R8 **Peel Common** Hants
13 N8 **Peene** Kent
12 G10 **Peening Quarter** Kent
47 M10 **Peggs Green** Leics
31 P6 **Pegsdon** C Beds
77 Q8 **Pegswood** Nthumb
13 S3 **Pegwell** Kent
100 e6 **Peinchorran** Highld
100 d4 **Peinlich** Highld
24 F7 **Pelcomb** Pembks
24 F7 **Pelcomb Bridge** Pembks
24 F7 **Pelcomb Cross** Pembks
23 N4 **Peldon** Essex
12 B9 **Pell Green** E Susx
46 D13 **Pelsall** Wsall
46 D13 **Pelsall Wood** Wsall
69 S2 **Pelton** Dur
69 S2 **Pelton Fell** Dur
66 H3 **Pelutho** Cumb
4 G9 **Pelynt** Cnwll
25 T10 **Pemberton** Carmth
55 N6 **Pemberton** Wigan
12 G6 **Pembles Cross** Kent
25 R10 **Pembrey** Carmth
34 J9 **Pembridge** Herefs
24 G10 **Pembroke** Pembks
24 G10 **Pembroke Dock** Pembks
24 D6 **Pembrokeshire Coast National Park** Pembks
12 B7 **Pembury** Kent
27 V2 **Pen-allt** Herefs
27 U5 **Penallt** Mons
24 K11 **Penally** Pembks
3 P8 **Penare** Cnwll
16 G2 **Penarth** V Glam
24 K7 **Penblewin** Pembks
33 N4 **Pen-bont Rhydybeddau** Cerdgn
32 E10 **Penbryn** Cerdgn
25 R3 **Pencader** Carmth
42 H5 **Pencaenewydd** Gwynd
84 C5 **Pencaitland** E Loth
52 E8 **Pencarnisiog** IoA
32 K11 **Pencarreg** Carmth
4 E4 **Pencarrow** Cnwll
26 K2 **Pencelli** Powys
25 T11 **Penclawdd** Swans
26 H11 **Pencoed** Brdgnd
35 N10 **Pencombe** Herefs
27 U2 **Pencoyd** Herefs
27 V3 **Pencraig** Herefs
44 B8 **Pencraig** Powys
2 B10 **Pendeen** Cnwll
26 G6 **Penderyn** Rhondd
25 M9 **Pendine** Carmth
55 S6 **Pendlebury** Salfd
62 F12 **Pendleton** Lancs
35 S14 **Pendock** Worcs
4 C5 **Pendoggett** Cnwll
7 P2 **Pendomer** Somset
26 K12 **Pendoylan** V Glam
26 G11 **Pendre** Brdgnd
43 Q13 **Penegoes** Powys
3 L8 **Penelewey** Cnwll
24 J6 **Pen-ffordd** Pembks
27 M8 **Pengam** Caerph
27 N12 **Pengam** Cardif
21 Q8 **Penge** Gt Lon
4 D4 **Pengelly** Cnwll
52 G4 **Pengorffwysfa** IoA
4 H7 **Pengover Green** Cnwll
27 Q6 **Pen-groes-oped** Mons
53 T7 **Pengwern** Denbgs
2 H13 **Penhale** Cnwll
3 N5 **Penhale** Cnwll
3 R4 **Penhale** Cnwll
5 L10 **Penhale** Cnwll
2 K6 **Penhallow** Cnwll
2 J9 **Penhalurick** Cnwll
2 J9 **Penhalvean** Cnwll
29 N10 **Penhill** Swindn
27 S9 **Penhow** Newpt
12 C12 **Penhurst** E Susx
43 M12 **Peniarth** Gwynd
83 P7 **Penicuik** Mdloth
25 R6 **Peniel** Carmth
53 T10 **Peniel** Denbgs
100 d5 **Penifiler** Highld
79 P11 **Peninver** Ag & B
52 J10 **Penisarwaun** Gwynd
56 K6 **Penistone** Barns
2 K10 **Penjerrick** Cnwll
55 N9 **Penketh** Warrtn
80 J13 **Penkill** S Ayrs
46 B11 **Penkridge** Staffs
14 F13 **Penlean** Cnwll
18 C10 **Penleigh** Wilts
44 K5 **Penley** Wrexhm
25 V11 **Penllergaer** Swans
52 E6 **Pen-llyn** IoA
26 H12 **Penllyn** V Glam
52 F9 **Pen-lon** IoA
43 Q3 **Penmachno** Conwy
27 M8 **Penmaen** Caerph
25 T13 **Penmaen** Swans
53 M7 **Penmaenan** Conwy
53 M7 **Penmaenmawr** Conwy
43 N10 **Penmaenpool** Gwynd
16 E3 **Penmark** V Glam
52 K6 **Penmon** IoA
42 K5 **Penmorfa** Gwynd
3 L7 **Penmount Crematorium** Cnwll
52 H8 **Penmynydd** IoA
20 F4 **Penn** Bucks
35 U1 **Penn** Wolves
43 N13 **Pennal** Gwynd
105 N2 **Pennan** Abers
32 K8 **Pennant** Cerdgn
44 B7 **Pennant** Denbgs
43 S14 **Pennant** Powys
44 B8 **Pennant-Melangell** Powys
25 U13 **Pennard** Swans
44 J14 **Pennerley** Shrops
15 U12 **Pennicott** Devon
62 K12 **Pennines**
61 P4 **Pennington** Cumb
9 L9 **Pennington** Hants
55 P5 **Pennington Green** Wigan
27 L2 **Pennorth** Powys
20 F3 **Penn Street** Bucks
28 D13 **Pennsylvania** S Glos
61 Q3 **Penny Bridge** Cumb
93 N13 **Pennycross** Ag & B
51 P9 **Pennygate** Norfk
93 N13 **Pennyghael** Ag & B
80 K10 **Pennyglen** S Ayrs
57 R11 **Penny Green** Derbys
49 N8 **Penny Hill** Lincs
15 U10 **Pennymoor** Devon
70 E1 **Pennywell** Sundld
32 D11 **Penparc** Cerdgn
33 L4 **Penparcau** Cerdgn
27 L8 **Penpedairheol** Caerph
27 Q7 **Penpedairheol** Mons
27 Q7 **Penperlleni** Mons
4 D3 **Penpethy** Cnwll
3 R5 **Penpillick** Cnwll
3 L9 **Penpol** Cnwll
4 E10 **Penpoll** Cnwll
2 G9 **Penponds** Cnwll
3 R2 **Penpont** Cnwll
74 F7 **Penpont** D & G
26 H2 **Penpont** Powys
5 Q10 **Penquit** Devon
4 J5 **Penrest** Cnwll
25 N3 **Penrherber** Carmth
32 D12 **Pen-rhiw** Pembks
26 K8 **Penrhiwceiber** Rhondd
26 C5 **Pen Rhiwfawr** Neath
32 G12 **Penrhiw-llan** Cerdgn
32 F11 **Penrhiw-pal** Cerdgn
42 F7 **Penrhos** Gwynd
52 C6 **Penrhos** IoA
27 S5 **Penrhos** Mons
26 E5 **Penrhos** Powys
52 J8 **Penrhos garnedd** Gwynd
53 P6 **Penrhyn Bay** Conwy
52 K8 **Penrhyn Castle** Gwynd
33 M4 **Penrhyncoch** Cerdgn
43 M6 **Penrhyndeudraeth** Gwynd
53 P6 **Penrhyn-side** Conwy

138 Penrice - Ring's End

25 S13 Penrice Swans
79 R7 Penrioch N Ayrs
67 R6 Penrith Cumb
3 M2 Penrose Cnwll
67 P7 Penruddock Cumb
2 K10 Penryn Cnwll
53 S7 Pensarn Conwy
35 R7 Pensax Worcs
54 G10 Pensby Wirral
17 U10 Penselwood Somset
17 R4 Pensford BaNES
36 B12 Pensham Worcs
70 D2 Penshaw Sundld
11 S2 Penshurst Kent
21 T13 Penshurst Station Kent
4 H6 Pensilva Cnwll
36 B3 Pensnett Dudley
15 S12 Penstone Devon
34 C2 Penstrowed Powys
3 Q7 Pentewan Cnwll
52 J9 Pentir Gwynd
2 K4 Pentire Cnwll
24 K9 Pentlepoir Pembks
40 D11 Pentlow Essex
40 D11 Pentlow Street Essex
50 B11 Pentney Norfk
75 T10 Pentonbridge Cumb
19 M11 Penton Grafton Hants
19 M11 Penton Mewsey Hants
52 H7 Pentraeth IoA
54 C14 Pentre Denbgs
54 H13 Pentre Flints
27 Q6 Pentre Mons
27 S7 Pentre Mons
34 C3 Pentre Powys
34 E3 Pentre Powys
34 G2 Pentre Powys
26 H8 Pentre Rhondd
44 J10 Pentre Shrops
44 G5 Pentre Wrexhm
33 L11 Pentre bach Cerdgn
54 F11 Pentre Bach Flints
26 K7 Pentrebach Myr Td
33 T14 Pentre-bach Powys
44 E11 Pentrebeirdd Powys
52 G8 Pentre Berw IoA
43 P3 Pentre-bont Conwy
44 H4 Pentrebychan Crematorium Wrexhm
32 F12 Pentre-cagel Carmth
44 D3 Pentre-celyn Denbgs
43 S12 Pentre-celyn Powys
26 B9 Pentre-chwyth Swans
44 G7 Pentre-clawdd Shrops
25 Q3 Pentre-cwrt Carmth
44 E4 Pentredwr Denbgs
42 K6 Pentrefelin Gwynd
52 F4 Pentrefelin IoA
54 G12 Pentre Ffwrndan Flints
43 S3 Pentrefoelas Conwy
25 L4 Pentregalar Pembks
32 G10 Pentregat Cerdgn
25 V7 Pentre-Gwenlais Carmth
43 L8 Pentre Gwynfryn Gwynd
54 F12 Pentre Halkyn Flints
34 H5 Pentre Hodrey Shrops
53 S8 Pentre Isaf Conwy
54 C14 Pentre Llanrhaeadr Denbgs
44 E14 Pentre Llifior Powys
33 U10 Pentre-llwyn-llwyd Powys
33 M5 Pentre-llyn Cerdgn
43 U3 Pentre-llyn-cymmer Conwy
43 S13 Pentre-Maw Powys
26 H12 Pentre Meyrick V Glam
27 P7 Pentre-piod Torfn
27 P10 Pentre-poeth Newpt
32 G10 Pentre'rbryn Cerdgn
33 M11 Pentre'r-felin Cerdgn
53 P9 Pentre'r Felin Conwy
26 G1 Pentre'r-felin Powys
53 T10 Pentre Saron Denbgs
53 P10 Pentre-tafarn-y-fedw Conwy
33 R13 Pentre ty gwyn Carmth
47 L3 Pentrich Derbys
8 E5 Pentridge Dorset
27 N7 Pen-twyn Caerph
27 U6 Pen-twyn Mons
27 P7 Pen-twyn Torfn
27 M8 Pentwynmaur Caerph
27 L11 Pentyrch Cardif
3 Q5 Penwithick Cnwll
19 P8 Penwood Hants
26 F4 Penwyllt Powys
25 V6 Penybanc Carmth
34 D8 Penybont Powys
44 F9 Pen-y-bont Powys
44 C9 Pen-y-bont-fawr Powys
32 C12 Pen-y-bryn Pembks
26 E5 Pen-y-cae Powys
44 G4 Penycae Wrexhm
27 S8 Pen-y-cae-mawr Mons
42 C8 Penycaerau Gwynd
54 D11 Pen-y-cefn Flints
27 T6 Pen-y-clawdd Mons
26 K10 Pen-y-coedcae Rhondd
24 E6 Pen-y-cwn Pembks
26 F11 Pen-y-fai Brdgnd
54 E13 Pen-y-felin Flints
44 H1 Penyffordd Flints
52 H11 Penyffridd Gwynd
33 M3 Pen-y-garn Cerdgn
44 D9 Pen-y-Garnedd Powys
27 M2 Pen-y-genffordd Powys
42 D7 Pen-y-graig Gwynd
26 J9 Penygraig Rhondd
25 U8 Penygroes Carmth
52 G12 Penygroes Gwynd
53 L11 Pen-y-Gwryd Gwynd
26 H12 Pen-y-lan V Glam
25 S10 Pen-y-Mynydd Carmth
44 H1 Penymynydd Flints
52 K11 Pen-y-pass Gwynd
27 S5 Pen-yr-Heol Mons
26 J6 Pen-yr-Heolgerrig Myr Td
52 G4 Penysarn IoA
44 F3 Pen-y-stryt Denbgs
26 H7 Penywaun Rhondd
2 D10 Penzance Cnwll
2 D10 Penzance Heliport Cnwll
36 B10 Peopleton Worcs
55 S12 Peover Heath Ches E
10 E2 Peper Harow Surrey
45 P9 Peplow Shrops
22 F5 Pepper's Green Essex
31 N9 Pepperstock C Beds
81 M4 Perceton N Ayrs
105 R2 Percyhorner Abers
6 c3 Perelle Guern
19 L11 Perham Down Wilts
16 C7 Periton Somset
21 L6 Perivale Gt Lon
6 D6 Perkins Village Devon
69 S2 Perkinsville Dur
57 T12 Perlethorpe Notts
2 K9 Perranarworthal Cnwll
2 K6 Perranporth Cnwll
2 E11 Perranuthnoe Cnwll
2 K6 Perranwell Cnwll
2 K9 Perranwell Cnwll
2 K9 Perran Wharf Cnwll
2 K6 Perranzabuloe Cnwll
28 K6 Perrott's Brook Gloucs
36 E2 Perry Birm
36 E2 Perry Barr Birm
36 E2 Perry Barr Crematorium Birm
22 K3 Perry Green Essex
22 B4 Perry Green Herts
28 J10 Perry Green Wilts
28 B2 Perrystone Hill Herefs
6 K3 Perry Street Somset
45 T8 Pershall Staffs
36 B11 Pershore Worcs
38 G7 Pertenhall Bed
90 H7 Perth P & K
90 G6 Perth Crematorium P & K
44 J7 Perthy Shrops
35 N12 Perton Herefs
45 U14 Perton Staffs
18 C13 Pertwood Wilts
48 J14 Peterborough C Pete
48 J13 Peterborough Crematorium C Pete
38 H2 Peterborough Services Cambs
34 H13 Peterchurch Herefs
99 Q3 Peterculter C Aber
105 U6 Peterhead Abers
70 F4 Peterlee Dur
9 U4 Petersfield Hants
31 P9 Peter's Green Herts
21 L8 Petersham Gt Lon
15 L10 Peters Marland Devon
27 P12 Peterstone Wentlooge Newpt
26 K12 Peterston-super-Ely V Glam
27 V3 Peterstow Herefs
5 N5 Peter Tavy Devon
13 M5 Petham Kent
4 H3 Petherwin Gate Cnwll
15 M11 Petrockstow Devon
38 C11 Petsoe End M Keyn
13 L6 Pet Street Kent
12 G13 Pett E Susx
41 L9 Pettaugh Suffk
13 N5 Pett Bottom Kent
91 P3 Petterden Angus
82 J10 Pettinain S Lans
41 P9 Pettistree Suffk
16 D12 Petton Devon
44 K8 Petton Shrops
21 S9 Petts Wood Gt Lon
83 Q1 Pettycur Fife
28 E10 Petty France S Glos
105 Q11 Pettymuk Abers
10 F6 Petworth W Susx
11 U9 Pevensey E Susx
11 V10 Pevensey Bay E Susx
18 J8 Pewsey Wilts
20 C5 Pheasant's Hill Bucks
36 B9 Phepson Worcs
70 D2 Philadelphia Sundld
14 G8 Philham Devon
84 C13 Philiphaugh Border
2 F9 Phillack Cnwll
3 M9 Philleigh Cnwll
22 F4 Philpot End Essex
83 L3 Philpstoun W Loth
28 B2 Phocle Green Herefs
20 C11 Phoenix Green Hants
97 L5 Phones Highld
17 M11 Pibsbury Somset
66 F8 Pica Cumb
46 H14 Piccadilly Warwks
31 M11 Piccotts End Herts
57 R5 Pickburn Donc
64 H3 Pickering N York
19 N11 Picket Piece Hants
8 H7 Picket Post Hants
36 J4 Pickford Covtry
36 J4 Pickford Green Covtry
63 S3 Pickhill N York
44 K14 Picklescott Shrops
55 Q11 Pickmere Ches E
16 G11 Pickney Somset
45 R9 Pickstock Wrekin
55 R2 Pickup Bank Bl w D
15 L4 Pickwell Devon
47 U11 Pickwell Leics
18 C6 Pickwick Wilts
48 F7 Pickworth Lincs
48 E11 Pickworth Rutlnd
54 K12 Picton Ches W
54 D10 Picton Flints
70 F11 Picton N York
11 Q10 Piddinghoe E Susx
20 D4 Piddington Bucks
38 B10 Piddington Nhants
30 D9 Piddington Oxon
7 T5 Piddlehinton Dorset
7 T5 Piddletrenthide Dorset
39 M5 Pidley Cambs
69 R9 Piercebridge Darltn
106 t15 Pierowall Ork
28 H2 Piff's Elm Gloucs
77 P8 Pigdon Nthumb
36 H8 Pigeon Green Warwks
8 E8 Pig Oak Dorset
34 J11 Pig Street Herefs
46 G2 Pikehall Derbys
8 E8 Pilford Dorset
22 E8 Pilgrims Hatch Essex
58 E8 Pilham Lincs
27 U12 Pill N Som
4 K8 Pillaton Cnwll
4 K8 Pillatonmill Cnwll
36 J11 Pillerton Hersey Warwks
36 J11 Pillerton Priors Warwks
34 G7 Pilleth Powys
57 M6 Pilley Barns
9 L9 Pilley Hants
9 L9 Pilley Bailey Hants
27 Q10 Pillgwenlly Newpt
15 L7 Pillhead Devon
61 S10 Pilling Lancs
61 R10 Pilling Lane Lancs
27 V10 Pilning S Glos
13 L12 Pilot Inn Kent
56 H14 Pilsbury Derbys
7 M5 Pilsdon Dorset
48 G12 Pilsgate C Pete
47 M1 Pilsley Derbys
56 K12 Pilsley Derbys
51 Q11 Pilson Green Norfk
11 Q6 Piltdown E Susx
15 N6 Pilton Devon
38 F4 Pilton Nhants
48 D13 Pilton Rutlnd
17 Q8 Pilton Somset
25 R13 Pilton Green Swans
62 E11 Pimlico Lancs
30 D4 Pimlico Nhants
8 C7 Pimperne Dorset
48 K8 Pinchbeck Lincs
48 J8 Pinchbeck Bars Lincs
48 K9 Pinchbeck West Lincs
57 U3 Pincheon Green Donc
70 J10 Pinchinthorpe R & Cl
55 M3 Pincock Lancs
54 J4 Pinfold Lancs
40 D9 Pinford End Suffk
25 R10 Pinged Carmth
19 U7 Pingewood W Berk
31 S7 Pin Green Herts
6 C6 Pinhoe Devon
36 J4 Pinkett's Booth Covtry
28 G10 Pinkney Wilts
37 L5 Pinley Covtry
36 H7 Pinley Green Warwks
41 M13 Pin Mill Suffk
80 H14 Pinminnoch S Ayrs
72 G1 Pinmore S Ayrs
6 F7 Pinn Devon
20 K5 Pinner Gt Lon
20 K5 Pinner Green Gt Lon
45 N4 Pinsley Green Ches E
36 C11 Pinvin Worcs
72 G2 Pinwherry S Ayrs
47 N3 Pinxton Derbys
35 M12 Pipe and Lyde Herefs
35 L6 Pipe Aston Herefs
45 R5 Pipe Gate Shrops
46 E12 Pipehill Staffs
103 N5 Piperhill Highld
4 H4 Pipers Pool Cnwll
38 B3 Pipewell Nhants
15 M5 Pippacott Devon
55 N2 Pippin Street Lancs
34 E13 Pipton Powys
20 F11 Pirbright Surrey
20 F11 Pirbright Camp Surrey
84 H13 Pirnie Border
79 R7 Pirnmill N Ayrs
31 P6 Pirton Herts
35 U11 Pirton Worcs
33 N5 Pisgah Cerdgn
20 B5 Pishill Oxon
42 F5 Pistyll Gwynd
97 N10 Pitagowan P & K
105 R3 Pitblae Abers
90 G6 Pitcairngreen P & K
109 Q10 Pitcalnie Highld
105 L10 Pitcaple Abers
98 E10 Pitcarity Angus
28 G6 Pitchcombe Gloucs
30 G8 Pitchcott Bucks
49 L7 Pitcher Row Lincs
45 M13 Pitchford Shrops
30 G12 Pitch Green Bucks
10 D3 Pitch Place Surrey
20 G12 Pitch Place Surrey
103 U8 Pitchroy Moray
17 S10 Pitcombe Somset
26 F13 Pitcot V Glam
84 G3 Pitcox E Loth
104 K12 Pitfichie Abers
104 K7 Pitglassie Abers
109 P6 Pitgrudy Highld
91 M10 Pitlessie Fife
97 Q12 Pitlochry P & K
104 K10 Pitmachie Abers
97 L3 Pitmain Highld
105 P10 Pitmedden Abers
105 P10 Pitmedden Garden Abers
16 H13 Pitminster Somset
91 S2 Pitmuies Angus
104 K13 Pitmunie Abers
17 N11 Pitney Somset
90 K6 Pitroddie P & K
91 P9 Pitscottie Fife
22 H10 Pitsea Essex
56 D6 Pitses Oldham
37 U7 Pitsford Nhants
30 K9 Pitstone Bucks
16 D13 Pitt Devon
9 P3 Pitt Hants
99 N9 Pittarrow Abers
28 D8 Pitt Court Gloucs
91 S11 Pittenweem Fife
91 L12 Pitteuchar Fife
70 D4 Pittington Dur
104 K11 Pittodrie House Hotel Abers
8 J2 Pitton Wilts
12 B6 Pitt's Wood Kent
105 R2 Pittulie Abers
3 P1 Pityme Cnwll
69 S3 Pity Me Dur
12 H6 Pivington Kent
41 M5 Pixey Green Suffk
21 L12 Pixham Surrey
82 E5 Plains N Lans
4 B5 Plain Street Cnwll
35 M1 Plaish Shrops
21 R6 Plaistow Gt Lon
10 G4 Plaistow W Susx
8 K5 Plaitford Hants
55 P7 Plank Lane Wigan
52 C7 Plas Cymyran IoA
19 R8 Plastow Green Hants
12 B4 Platt Kent
55 P6 Platt Bridge Wigan
45 M6 Platt Lane Shrops
12 G5 Platts Heath Kent
69 S3 Plawsworth Dur
12 B5 Plaxtol Kent
12 H11 Playden E Susx
41 M11 Playford Suffk
20 B7 Play Hatch Oxon
3 L8 Playing Place Cnwll
28 E1 Playley Green Gloucs
44 K12 Plealey Shrops
89 T8 Plean Stirlg
90 K9 Pleasance Fife
55 P1 Pleasington Bl w D
55 P1 Pleasington Crematorium Bl w D
57 R14 Pleasley Derbys
57 R14 Pleasleyhill Notts
7 T2 Pleck Dorset
22 E2 Pledgdon Green Essex
57 M3 Pledwick Wakefd
6 d2 Pleinheaume Guern
7 a1 Plemont Jersey
55 L12 Plemstall Ches W
76 E13 Plenmeller Nthumb
22 G5 Pleshey Essex
100 h6 Plockton Highld
34 J3 Plowden Shrops
44 J13 Plox Green Shrops
12 H6 Pluckley Kent
12 H7 Pluckley Station Kent
12 H7 Pluckley Thorne Kent
13 Q3 Plucks Gutter Kent
66 J5 Plumbland Cumb
67 Q14 Plumgarths Cumb
55 R12 Plumley Ches E
61 Q4 Plumpton Cumb
67 Q5 Plumpton Cumb
11 P8 Plumpton E Susx
37 Q11 Plumpton Nhants
30 F4 Plumpton End Nhants
11 P7 Plumpton Green E Susx
67 R5 Plumpton Head Cumb
21 R7 Plumstead Gt Lon
50 K7 Plumstead Norfk
50 K6 Plumstead Green Norfk
47 R7 Plumtree Notts
12 F6 Plumtree Green Kent
47 U7 Plungar Leics
12 H8 Plurenden Kent
7 T4 Plush Dorset
4 H4 Plusha Cnwll
4 J6 Plushabridge Cnwll
32 G10 Plwmp Cerdgn
5 M10 Plymouth C Plym
5 N8 Plymouth Airport C Plym
5 N9 Plympton C Plym
5 N10 Plymstock C Plym
6 E4 Plymtree Devon
64 E2 Pockley N York
64 J10 Pocklington E R Yk
48 K9 Pode Hole Lincs
17 P12 Podimore Somset
38 D8 Podington Bed
45 S6 Podmore Staffs
23 R5 Point Clear Essex
48 H7 Pointon Lincs
8 G10 Pokesdown Bmouth
107 S2 Polbain Highld
4 J9 Polbathic Cnwll
82 K6 Polbeth W Loth
3 Q3 Polbrock Cnwll
2 H10 Poldark Mine Cnwll
38 G3 Polebrook Nhants
35 T10 Pole Elm Worcs
11 T10 Polegate E Susx
56 G3 Pole Moor Kirk
46 J13 Polesworth Warwks
2 B12 Polgigga Cnwll
107 T3 Polglass Highld
3 P6 Polgooth Cnwll
74 D5 Polgown D & G
10 G10 Poling W Susx
10 G9 Poling Corner W Susx
3 R6 Polkerris Cnwll
51 P7 Pollard Street Norfk
57 T3 Pollington E R Yk
93 T5 Polloch Highld
89 N13 Pollokshaws C Glas
89 N13 Pollokshields C Glas
3 P7 Polmassick Cnwll
3 R6 Polmear Cnwll
82 H3 Polmont Falk
93 T2 Polnish Highld
4 G10 Polperro Cnwll
4 E10 Polruan Cnwll
17 P8 Polsham Somset
40 G13 Polstead Suffk
40 G12 Polstead Heath Suffk
87 Q6 Poltalloch Ag & B
2 J13 Poltescoe Cnwll
6 C5 Poltimore Devon
83 Q6 Polton Mdloth
84 J8 Polwarth Border
4 H4 Polyphant Cnwll
4 A5 Polzeath Cnwll
83 P7 Pomathorn Mdloth
56 H13 Pomeroy Derbys
34 D13 Ponde Powys
39 L2 Pondersbridge Cambs
21 Q3 Ponders End Gt Lon
2 K9 Ponsanooth Cnwll
66 G11 Ponsonby Cumb
2 K13 Ponsongath Cnwll
5 S6 Ponsworthy Devon
25 U9 Pont Abraham Services Carmth
7 e4 Pontac Jersey
26 A5 Pontamman Carmth
25 R8 Pontantwn Carmth
26 C7 Pontardawe Neath
25 U10 Pontarddulais Swans
25 T6 Pont-ar-gothi Carmth
26 F2 Pont-ar-Hydfer Powys
26 C3 Pont-ar-llechau Carmth
25 R5 Pontarsais Carmth
44 G1 Pontblyddyn Flints
53 M11 Pont Cyfyng Conwy
53 N9 Pont Dolgarrog Conwy
34 B2 Pontdolgoch Powys
27 P10 Pont-Ebbw Newpt
57 Q2 Pontefract Wakefd
57 P2 Pontefract Crematorium Wakefd
77 P11 Ponteland Nthumb
33 P4 Ponterwyd Cerdgn
44 J12 Pontesbury Shrops
44 J12 Pontesbury Hill Shrops
44 K12 Pontesford Shrops
44 F6 Pontfadog Wrexhm
24 H4 Pontfaen Pembks
33 U14 Pont-faen Powys
32 F10 Pontgarreg Cerdgn
32 B12 Pontgarreg Pembks
25 S9 Ponthenry Carmth
27 Q9 Ponthir Torfn
32 E11 Ponthirwaun Cerdgn
27 M8 Pontllanfraith Caerph
25 V11 Pontlliw Swans
27 L6 Pontlottyn Caerph
42 H3 Pontlyfni Gwynd
25 T9 Pont Morlais Carmth
26 G6 Pontneddfechan Neath
27 P8 Pontnewydd Torfn
27 P7 Pontnewynydd Torfn
53 L10 Pont Pen-y-benglog Gwynd
33 P7 Pontrhydfendigaid Cerdgn
43 S8 Pont Rhyd-sarn Gwynd
26 F10 Pont Rhyd-y-cyff Brdgnd
26 D9 Pont-rhyd-y-fen Neath
33 P6 Pontrhydygroes Cerdgn
27 P8 Pontrhydyrun Torfn
27 R2 Pontrilas Herefs
44 D11 Pont Robert Powys
52 H10 Pont-rug Gwynd
12 C12 Ponts Green E Susx
32 H11 Pontshaen Cerdgn
28 B3 Pontshill Herefs
26 K5 Pontsticill Myr Td
26 F6 Pont Walby Neath
32 H12 Pontwelly Carmth
25 S9 Pontyates Carmth
25 T8 Pontyberem Carmth
44 H6 Pont-y-blew Wrexhm
44 G2 Pontybodkin Flints
26 J11 Pontyclun Rhondd
26 G9 Pontycymer Brdgnd
24 K3 Pontyglasier Pembks
26 J9 Pontygwaith Rhondd
24 K3 Pontygynon Pembks
53 N12 Pont-y-pant Conwy
27 P7 Pontypool Torfn
27 Q8 Pontypool Road Torfn
26 K10 Pontypridd Rhondd
24 F5 Pont-yr-hafod Pembks
26 G10 Pont-yr-Rhyl Brdgnd
27 N9 Pontywaun Caerph
2 H8 Pool Cnwll
2 b2 Pool IoS
63 Q10 Pool Leeds
8 E10 Poole Poole
8 E9 Poole Crematorium Poole
28 J8 Poole Keynes Gloucs
107 Q8 Poolewe Highld
67 Q8 Pooley Bridge Cumb
40 J4 Pooley Street Norfk
45 U2 Poolfold Staffs
35 N10 Pool Head Herefs
28 D2 Poolhill Gloucs
90 F11 Pool of Muckhart Clacks
44 G11 Pool Quay Powys
40 C13 Pool Street Essex
21 S13 Pooting's Kent
19 S12 Popham Hants
21 Q6 Poplar Gt Lon
41 R7 Poplar Street Suffk
9 N10 Porchfield IoW
51 N13 Poringland Norfk
2 H10 Porkellis Cnwll
15 U3 Porlock Somset
15 U3 Porlock Weir Somset
79 P4 Portachoillan Ag & B
100 g6 Port-an-Eorna Highld
94 C9 Port Appin Ag & B
86 G12 Port Askaig Ag & B
87 S12 Portavadie Ag & B
88 C12 Port Bannatyne Ag & B
27 U12 Portbury N Som
75 P13 Port Carlisle Cumb
78 D4 Port Charlotte Ag & B
9 S7 Portchester Hants
9 S7 Portchester Crematorium Hants
70 G8 Port Clarence S on T
87 T11 Port Driseach Ag & B
78 F6 Port Ellen Ag & B
105 M11 Port Elphinstone Abers
72 C5 Portencalzie D & G
80 H3 Portencross N Ayrs
60 b9 Port Erin IoM
7 R7 Portesham Dorset
104 E2 Portessie Moray
60 h4 Port e Vullen IoM
25 S13 Port Eynon Swans
24 F7 Portfield Gate Pembks
5 L3 Portgate Devon
4 C4 Port Gaverne Cnwll
88 H11 Port Glasgow Inver
104 D3 Portgordon Moray
109 U2 Portgower Highld
3 L4 Porth Cnwll
26 J9 Porth Rhondd
2 K12 Porthallow Cnwll
4 G10 Porthallow Cnwll
26 E12 Porthcawl Brdgnd
3 M2 Porthcothan Cnwll
2 B12 Porthcurno Cnwll
42 E5 Porth Dinllaen Gwynd
107 N10 Port Henderson Highld
24 D4 Porthgain Pembks
2 B12 Porthgwarra Cnwll
45 T4 Porthill Staffs
3 L8 Porthkea Cnwll
16 E3 Porthkerry V Glam
2 G11 Porthleven Cnwll
43 L6 Porthmadog Gwynd
2 C9 Porthmeor Cnwll
2 K11 Porth Navas Cnwll
3 P8 Portholland Cnwll
3 L12 Porthoustock Cnwll
3 Q6 Porthpean Cnwll
2 H7 Porthtowan Cnwll
44 J4 Porthwgan Wrexhm
25 T7 Porthyrhyd Carmth
44 G9 Porth-y-Waen Shrops
88 F7 Portincaple Ag & B
7 a1 Portinfer Jersey
64 H13 Portington E R Yk
87 T3 Portinnisherrich Ag & B
67 L8 Portinscale Cumb
4 B4 Port Isaac Cnwll
27 T12 Portishead N Som
104 F2 Portknockie Moray
7 S10 Portland Dorset
99 S4 Portlethen Abers
66 C2 Portling D & G
3 N9 Portloe Cnwll
72 D11 Port Logan D & G
4 G10 Portlooe Cnwll
109 S8 Portmahomack Highld
43 L6 Portmeirion Gwynd
3 Q8 Portmellon Cnwll
93 L3 Port Mor Highld
9 L9 Portmore Hants
71 N9 Port Mulgrave N York
94 C9 Portnacroish Ag & B
106 k5 Portnaguran W Isls
78 B5 Portnahaven Ag & B
100 c6 Portnalong Highld
106 k5 Port nan Giuran W Isls
106 d11 Port nan Long W Isls
106 k2 Port Nis W Isls
83 R4 Portobello C Edin
69 S1 Portobello Gatesd
46 C14 Portobello Wolves
89 N5 Port of Menteith Stirlg
106 k2 Port of Ness W Isls
18 J13 Porton Wilts
5 L5 Portontown Devon
72 B9 Portpatrick D & G
4 B4 Port Quin Cnwll
94 B9 Port Ramsay Ag & B
2 H7 Portreath Cnwll
100 d5 Portree Highld
60 c9 Port St Mary IoM
3 M9 Portscatho Cnwll
9 S8 Portsea C Port
111 T3 Portskerra Highld
27 T10 Portskewett Mons
11 M9 Portslade Br & H
11 M9 Portslade-by-Sea Br & H
72 B8 Portslogan D & G
9 S9 Portsmouth C Port
56 D1 Portsmouth Calder
60 e8 Port Soderick IoM
9 S7 Port Solent C Port
88 B1 Portsonachan Hotel Ag & B
104 H2 Portsoy Abers
54 H10 Port Sunlight Wirral
9 N6 Portswood C Sotn
26 D10 Port Talbot Neath
26 B9 Port Tennant Swans
93 L5 Portuairk Highld
35 L12 Portway Herefs
35 L13 Portway Herefs
36 C3 Portway Sandw
36 E6 Portway Worcs
78 B5 Port Wemyss Ag & B
72 J11 Port William D & G
4 K10 Portwrinkle Cnwll
73 M12 Portyerrock D & G
15 T13 Posbury Devon
45 Q13 Posenhall Shrops
40 C11 Poslingford Suffk
83 P12 Posso Border
5 R5 Postbridge Devon
30 F12 Postcombe Oxon
8 D10 Post Green Dorset
13 M8 Postling Kent
51 N12 Postwick Norfk
99 L4 Potarch Abers
31 L6 Potsgrove C Beds
31 M11 Potten End Herts
13 Q2 Potten Street Kent
65 M4 Potter Brompton N York
41 L2 Pottergate Street Norfk
58 J13 Potterhanworth Lincs
58 J13 Potterhanworth Booths Lincs
51 R10 Potter Heigham Norfk
18 E9 Potterne Wilts
18 E9 Potterne Wick Wilts
30 K12 Potter Row Bucks
31 R12 Potters Bar Herts
61 T9 Potters Brook Lancs
35 T4 Potter's Cross Staffs
31 P11 Potters Crouch Herts
12 G6 Potter's Forstal Kent
37 L4 Potters Green Covtry
11 S6 Potter's Green E Susx
31 U8 Potter's Green Herts
31 R9 Pottersheath Herts
37 N1 Potters Marston Leics
46 F6 Potter Somersal Derbys
30 G4 Potterspury Nhants
105 Q12 Potterton Abers
63 U12 Potterton Leeds
50 F9 Potthorpe Norfk
18 B12 Pottle Street Wilts
70 G12 Potto N York
38 K11 Potton C Beds
50 B9 Pott Row Norfk
23 M3 Pott's Green Essex
56 D11 Pott Shrigley Ches E
14 F11 Poughill Cnwll
15 U11 Poughill Devon
8 H7 Poulner Hants
18 E9 Poulshot Wilts
29 L7 Poulton Gloucs
54 H8 Poulton Wirral
61 Q12 Poulton-le-Fylde Lancs
29 L8 Poulton Priory Gloucs
35 R6 Pound Bank Worcs
7 S6 Poundbury Dorset
25 U12 Poundffald Swans
11 R5 Poundgate E Susx
11 S6 Pound Green E Susx
40 B10 Pound Green Suffk
35 S5 Pound Green Worcs
11 M3 Pound Hill W Susx
30 D7 Poundon Bucks
11 S2 Poundsbridge Kent
5 S6 Poundsgate Devon
14 F13 Poundstock Cnwll
19 Q8 Pound Street Hants
11 S6 Pounsley E Susx
73 M10 Pouton D & G
41 Q6 Pouy Street Suffk
11 M2 Povey Cross Surrey
77 M2 Powburn Nthumb
6 C8 Powderham Devon
7 P5 Powerstock Dorset
75 M12 Powfoot D & G
35 R12 Pow Green Herefs
66 K1 Powhill Cumb
35 T10 Powick Worcs
90 F12 Powmill P & K
7 T8 Poxwell Dorset
20 H7 Poyle Slough
11 M8 Poynings W Susx
17 S12 Poyntington Dorset
56 D10 Poynton Ches E
45 N10 Poynton Wrekin
45 N10 Poynton Green Wrekin
24 G7 Poyston Cross Pembks
40 G9 Poystreet Green Suffk
2 F11 Praa Sands Cnwll
21 S10 Pratt's Bottom Gt Lon
2 G9 Praze-an-Beeble Cnwll
2 H13 Predannack Wollas Cnwll
45 N7 Prees Shrops
61 R10 Preesall Lancs
45 N7 Prees Green Shrops
44 G6 Preesgweene Shrops
45 N6 Prees Heath Shrops
45 N6 Prees Higher Heath Shrops
45 N7 Prees Lower Heath Shrops
77 L3 Prendwick Nthumb
32 H12 Pren-gwyn Cerdgn
43 L5 Prenteg Gwynd
54 H9 Prenton Wirral
55 L8 Prescot Knows
6 E2 Prescott Devon
35 Q4 Prescott Shrops
44 K9 Prescott Shrops
98 B10 Presnerb Angus
85 L11 Pressen Nthumb
54 C10 Prestatyn Denbgs
56 C11 Prestbury Ches E
28 J3 Prestbury Gloucs
34 H8 Presteigne Powys
17 R8 Prestleigh Somset
55 S5 Prestolee Bolton
84 K7 Preston Border
11 N9 Preston Br & H
5 V6 Preston Devon
7 T8 Preston Dorset
65 R13 Preston E R Yk
28 K7 Preston Gloucs
31 Q8 Preston Herts
12 K3 Preston Kent
13 P3 Preston Kent
61 U14 Preston Lancs
85 T13 Preston Nthumb
48 C13 Preston Rutlnd
45 M11 Preston Shrops
16 E9 Preston Somset
40 F10 Preston Suffk
6 A12 Preston Torbay
18 F5 Preston Wilts
19 L6 Preston Wilts
36 G7 Preston Bagot Warwks
30 E7 Preston Bissett Bucks
16 F11 Preston Bowyer Somset
45 M9 Preston Brockhurst Shrops
55 N10 Preston Brook Halton
19 T12 Preston Candover Hants
37 Q10 Preston Capes Nhants
62 B13 Preston Crematorium Lancs
19 T2 Preston Crowmarsh Oxon
37 U9 Preston Deanery Nhants
36 G7 Preston Green Warwks
45 L10 Preston Gubbals Shrops
44 K11 Preston Montford Shrops
36 H11 Preston on Stour Warwks
70 F9 Preston on Tees S on T
55 N10 Preston on the Hill Halton
34 J12 Preston on Wye Herefs
83 S4 Prestonpans E Loth
61 U3 Preston Patrick Cumb
17 P13 Preston Plucknett Somset
13 Q3 Preston Street Kent
63 M1 Preston-under-Scar N York
45 Q10 Preston upon the Weald Moors Wrekin
35 N11 Preston Wynne Herefs
55 T6 Prestwich Bury
77 P11 Prestwick Nthumb
81 M7 Prestwick S Ayrs
81 M7 Prestwick Airport S Ayrs
30 J12 Prestwood Bucks
35 U3 Prestwood Staffs
26 G9 Price Town Brdgnd
39 S4 Prickwillow Cambs
17 P6 Priddy Somset
14 K11 Priestacott Devon
56 H12 Priestcliffe Derbys
56 H12 Priestcliffe Ditch Derbys
61 U5 Priest Hutton Lancs
81 R5 Priestland E Ayrs
56 H1 Priestley Green Calder
34 G1 Priest Weston Shrops
12 C3 Priestwood Green Kent
37 P2 Primethorpe Leics
50 J10 Primrose Green Norfk
84 K7 Primrosehill Border
39 N3 Primrose Hill Cambs
47 M2 Primrose Hill Derbys
36 B3 Primrose Hill Dudley
54 J5 Primrose Hill Lancs
85 L13 Primsidemill Border
24 K8 Princes Gate Pembks
30 H12 Princes Risborough Bucks
37 M6 Princethorpe Warwks
5 P6 Princetown Devon
10 B9 Prinsted W Susx
44 C1 Prion Denbgs
75 U12 Prior Rigg Cumb
35 L5 Priors Halton Shrops
37 N9 Priors Hardwick Warwks
45 R11 Priorslee Wrekin
37 N9 Priors Marston Warwks
28 G3 Priors Norton Gloucs
29 M10 Priory Vale Swindn
34 G11 Priory Wood Herefs
26 J12 Prisk V Glam
17 S4 Priston BaNES
40 K3 Pristow Green Norfk
23 L10 Prittlewell Sthend
9 T3 Privett Hants
15 N5 Prixford Devon
3 M7 Probus Cnwll
84 E3 Prora E Loth
66 H4 Prospect Cumb
2 G10 Prospidnick Cnwll
105 N3 Protstonhill Abers
77 M13 Prudhoe Nthumb
2 F11 Prussia Cove Cnwll
17 R4 Publow BaNES
31 U8 Puckeridge Herts
17 L13 Puckington Somset
28 C12 Pucklechurch S Glos
35 U13 Puckrup Gloucs
55 R13 Puddinglake Ches W
54 H12 Puddington Ches W
15 T10 Puddington Devon
40 J2 Puddledock Norfk
7 U6 Puddletown Dorset
35 N9 Pudleston Herefs
63 Q13 Pudsey Leeds
10 G7 Pulborough W Susx
45 R9 Puleston Wrekin
44 J2 Pulford Ches W
7 T3 Pulham Dorset
41 L3 Pulham Market Norfk
41 M3 Pulham St Mary Norfk
28 B9 Pullens Green S Glos
31 N6 Pulloxhill C Beds
83 L5 Pumpherston W Loth
33 N12 Pumsaint Carmth
24 H5 Puncheston Pembks
7 P7 Puncknowle Dorset
11 U6 Punnett's Town E Susx
9 T7 Purbrook Hants
22 E12 Purfleet Thurr
16 K8 Puriton Somset
22 K7 Purleigh Essex
21 P10 Purley Gt Lon
19 U5 Purley W Berk
34 G5 Purlogue Shrops
18 C7 Purlpit Wilts
39 Q3 Purls Bridge Cambs
17 S13 Purse Caundle Dorset
35 U6 Purshull Green Worcs
34 J4 Purslow Shrops
57 P3 Purston Jaglin Wakefd
7 L3 Purtington Somset
28 C6 Purton Gloucs
28 C7 Purton Gloucs
29 L10 Purton Wilts
29 L9 Purton Stoke Wilts
37 T11 Pury End Nhants
29 S8 Pusey Oxon
35 P13 Putley Herefs
35 P13 Putley Green Herefs
28 E6 Putloe Gloucs
21 M8 Putney Gt Lon
21 M8 Putney Vale Crematorium Gt Lon
14 K4 Putsborough Devon
30 J10 Puttenham Herts
20 F13 Puttenham Surrey
40 D12 Puttock End Essex
7 R8 Putton Dorset
30 G4 Puxley Nhants
17 M4 Puxton N Som
25 S10 Pwll Carmth
24 F10 Pwllcrochan Pembks
27 N5 Pwll-du Mons
44 D3 Pwll-glas Denbgs
34 B14 Pwllgloyw Powys
42 G6 Pwllheli Gwynd
27 U9 Pwllmeyric Mons
25 N7 Pwll Trap Carmth
26 D9 Pwll-y-glaw Neath
53 P7 Pydew Conwy
47 M3 Pye Bridge Derbys
11 M8 Pyecombe W Susx
27 Q10 Pye Corner Newpt
46 C11 Pye Green Staffs
26 E11 Pyle Brdgnd
16 F10 Pyleigh Somset
17 R9 Pylle Somset
39 Q3 Pymoor Cambs
7 N6 Pymore Dorset
20 H11 Pyrford Surrey
30 E13 Pyrton Oxon
38 C6 Pytchley Nhants
14 H12 Pyworthy Devon

Q

34 F4 Quabbs Shrops
48 K7 Quadring Lincs
48 K7 Quadring Eaudike Lincs
30 F8 Quainton Bucks
26 K8 Quaker's Yard Myr Td
69 Q2 Quaking Houses Dur
16 G9 Quantock Hills Somset
106 u10 Quarff Shet
19 L12 Quarley Hants
46 K5 Quarndon Derbys
9 R10 Quarr Hill IoW
88 J12 Quarrier's Village Inver
48 G5 Quarrington Lincs
70 D5 Quarrington Hill Dur
55 N13 Quarrybank Ches W
36 B3 Quarry Bank Dudley
103 U3 Quarrywood Moray
88 E13 Quarter N Ayrs
82 D8 Quarter S Lans
35 R2 Quatford Shrops
35 S3 Quatt Shrops
69 Q4 Quebec Dur
28 F5 Quedgeley Gloucs
39 S4 Queen Adelaide Cambs
23 M13 Queenborough Kent
17 Q12 Queen Camel Somset
17 R3 Queen Charlton BaNES
15 T9 Queen Dart Devon
89 M5 Queen Elizabeth Forest Park Stirlg
35 U13 Queenhill Worcs
17 U10 Queen Oak Dorset
9 R12 Queen's Bower IoW
63 N13 Queensbury C Brad
54 H13 Queensferry Flints
44 H8 Queen's Head Shrops
89 Q12 Queenslie C Glas
38 F11 Queen's Park Bed
37 U8 Queen's Park Nhants
12 C6 Queen Street Kent
28 K10 Queen Street Wilts
89 Q10 Queenzieburn N Lans
22 D1 Quendon Essex
47 R11 Queniborough Leics
29 M7 Quenington Gloucs
61 U7 Quernmore Lancs
36 E2 Queslett Birm
4 J8 Quethiock Cnwll
19 S5 Quick's Green W Berk
40 H3 Quidenham Norfk
19 R10 Quidhampton Hants
8 G2 Quidhampton Wilts
45 M7 Quina Brook Shrops
37 R10 Quinbury End Nhants
36 C4 Quinton Dudley
37 U10 Quinton Nhants
37 U10 Quinton Green Nhants
3 L4 Quintrell Downs Cnwll
46 F5 Quixhall Staffs
84 K6 Quixwood Border
14 K13 Quoditch Devon
90 B7 Quoig P & K
47 Q10 Quorn Leics
82 J11 Quothquan S Lans
106 u19 Quoyburray Ork
106 r17 Quoyloo Ork

R

100 e5 Raasay Highld
12 E6 Rabbit's Cross Kent
31 R9 Rableyheath Herts
66 J2 Raby Cumb
54 H11 Raby Wirral
83 M12 Rachan Mill Border
52 K9 Rachub Gwynd
15 U9 Rackenford Devon
10 G8 Rackham W Susx
51 N11 Rackheath Norfk
74 K11 Racks D & G
106 r20 Rackwick Ork
46 J6 Radbourne Derbys
55 S5 Radcliffe Bury
77 R5 Radcliffe Nthumb
47 R6 Radcliffe on Trent Notts
30 E6 Radclive Bucks
29 Q8 Radcot Oxon
102 K4 Raddery Highld
16 D11 Raddington Somset
91 Q10 Radernie Fife
36 K4 Radford Covtry
36 K8 Radford Semele Warwks
16 H9 Radlet Somset
31 Q12 Radlett Herts
15 R8 Radley Devon
30 B13 Radley Oxon
22 F6 Radley Green Essex
45 N2 Radmore Green Ches E
20 C3 Radnage Bucks
17 S6 Radstock BaNES
30 C4 Radstone Nhants
37 L11 Radway Warwks
38 F9 Radwell Bed
31 R5 Radwell Herts
39 T13 Radwinter Essex
39 T13 Radwinter End Essex
27 L11 Radyr Cardif
48 F4 RAF College (Cranwell) Lincs
103 S4 Rafford Moray
47 S10 Ragdale Leics
35 L2 Ragdon Shrops
2 D11 Raginnis Cnwll
27 S6 Raglan Mons
58 D12 Ragnall Notts
103 M10 Raigbeg Highld
35 U9 Rainbow Hill Worcs
55 L6 Rainford St Hel
22 D11 Rainham Gt Lon
12 F2 Rainham Medway
55 L8 Rainhill St Hel
55 M8 Rainhill Stoops St Hel
56 D11 Rainow Ches E
55 T6 Rainsough Bury
63 T4 Rainton N York
47 Q2 Rainworth Notts
68 D11 Raisbeck Cumb
68 F3 Raise Cumb
64 K7 Raisthorpe N York
90 K6 Rait P & K
59 P10 Raithby Lincs
59 Q13 Raithby Lincs
71 Q10 Raithwaite N York
10 C5 Rake Hants
56 D4 Rakewood Rochdl
97 L4 Ralia Highld
33 L11 Ram Carmth
100 a5 Ramasaig Highld
2 J10 Rame Cnwll
5 L11 Rame Cnwll
28 C12 Ram Hill S Glos
12 J6 Ram Lane Kent
7 Q4 Rampisham Dorset
61 N6 Rampside Cumb
39 P7 Rampton Cambs
58 D11 Rampton Notts
55 S3 Ramsbottom Bury
19 L6 Ramsbury Wilts
112 D11 Ramscraigs Highld
9 U4 Ramsdean Hants
19 S9 Ramsdell Hants
29 S4 Ramsden Oxon
36 B11 Ramsden Worcs
22 H9 Ramsden Bellhouse Essex
22 H8 Ramsden Heath Essex
39 L3 Ramsey Cambs
23 T1 Ramsey Essex
60 h4 Ramsey IoM
39 M3 Ramsey Forty Foot Cambs
38 K4 Ramsey Heights Cambs
23 M6 Ramsey Island Essex
24 B6 Ramsey Island Pembks
39 L3 Ramsey Mereside Cambs
39 L3 Ramsey St Mary's Cambs
13 S2 Ramsgate Kent
63 N5 Ramsgill N York
69 L3 Ramshaw Dur
69 P7 Ramshaw Dur
41 P12 Ramsholt Suffk
76 E5 Ramshope Nthumb
46 E4 Ramshorn Staffs
5 R2 Ramsley Devon
10 E4 Ramsnest Common Surrey
59 M11 Ranby Lincs
57 U10 Ranby Notts
58 K11 Rand Lincs
21 L11 Randalls Park Crematorium Surrey
28 F6 Randwick Gloucs
88 J12 Ranfurly Rens
46 G9 Rangemore Staffs
28 C10 Rangeworthy S Glos
81 P10 Rankinston E Ayrs
48 B11 Ranksborough Rutlnd
22 H4 Rank's Green Essex
95 N7 Rannoch Station P & K
16 B8 Ranscombe Somset
57 U9 Ranskill Notts
45 U9 Ranton Staffs
45 T9 Ranton Green Staffs
51 Q11 Ranworth Norfk
89 S7 Raploch Stirlg
106 u15 Rapness Ork
16 K13 Rapps Somset
73 T10 Rascarrel D & G
88 D9 Rashfield Ag & B
36 B7 Rashwood Worcs
64 B5 Raskelf N York
27 M5 Rassau Blae G
56 H2 Rastrick Calder
101 N8 Ratagan Highld
47 P12 Ratby Leics
46 K14 Ratcliffe Culey Leics
47 N8 Ratcliffe on Soar Notts
47 R11 Ratcliffe on the Wreake Leics
18 J12 Ratfyn Wilts
105 R3 Rathen Abers
91 N7 Rathillet Fife
62 G8 Rathmell N York
83 M4 Ratho C Edin
83 M4 Ratho Station C Edin
104 E2 Rathven Moray
9 N4 Ratlake Hants
37 L11 Ratley Warwks
13 P5 Ratling Kent
34 K1 Ratlinghope Shrops
49 R11 Rattan Row Norfk
112 G2 Rattar Highld
67 M4 Ratten Row Cumb
67 N3 Ratten Row Cumb
61 S11 Ratten Row Lancs
5 S8 Rattery Devon
40 G9 Rattlesden Suffk
11 T10 Ratton Village E Susx
90 J2 Rattray P & K
67 N3 Raughton Cumb
67 N3 Raughton Head Cumb
38 E6 Raunds Nhants
57 Q7 Ravenfield Rothm
66 G13 Ravenglass Cumb
35 R10 Ravenhills Green Worcs
41 Q1 Raveningham Norfk
71 S12 Ravenscar N York
82 E7 Ravenscraig N Lans
60 f4 Ravensdale IoM
38 G10 Ravensden Bed
68 J12 Ravenseat N York
47 Q3 Ravenshead Notts
45 P3 Ravensmoor Ches E
56 K2 Ravensthorpe Kirk
37 S6 Ravensthorpe Nhants
47 M11 Ravenstone Leics
38 B10 Ravenstone M Keyn
68 F12 Ravenstonedale Cumb
82 H9 Ravenstruther S Lans
69 P11 Ravensworth N York
71 R11 Raw N York
64 D9 Rawcliffe C York
57 U2 Rawcliffe E R Yk
57 U2 Rawcliffe Bridge E R Yk
63 Q12 Rawdon Leeds
63 Q12 Rawdon Crematorium Leeds
12 H4 Rawling Street Kent
57 P7 Rawmarsh Rothm
46 D11 Rawnsley Staffs
22 J9 Rawreth Essex
6 H3 Rawridge Devon
55 T2 Rawtenstall Lancs
40 H13 Raydon Suffk
76 J7 Raylees Nthumb
22 K9 Rayleigh Essex
6 K5 Raymond's Hill Devon
22 H3 Rayne Essex
21 M9 Raynes Park Gt Lon
39 S7 Reach Cambs
62 F13 Read Lancs
20 B8 Reading Readg
20 B7 Reading Crematorium Readg
19 U7 Reading Services W Berk
12 H9 Reading Street Kent
13 S2 Reading Street Kent
68 D9 Reagill Cumb
2 G9 Realwa Cnwll
109 N6 Rearquhar Highld
47 S11 Rearsby Leics
45 P3 Rease Heath Ches E
111 V4 Reay Highld
13 P2 Reculver Kent
16 E13 Red Ball Devon
24 J10 Redberth Pembks
31 P10 Redbourn Herts
58 G7 Redbourne N Linc
27 U6 Redbrook Gloucs
45 M5 Redbrook Wrexhm
12 H8 Redbrook Street Kent
103 P6 Redburn Highld
76 F13 Redburn Nthumb
70 K8 Redcar R & Cl
74 F12 Redcastle D & G
102 G6 Redcastle Highld
67 L3 Red Dial Cumb
82 H3 Redding Falk
82 H3 Reddingmuirhead Falk
56 C8 Reddish Stockp
36 D7 Redditch Worcs
36 D7 Redditch Crematorium Worcs
40 D9 Rede Suffk
41 N4 Redenhall Norfk
19 M11 Redenham Hants
76 H9 Redesmouth Nthumb
99 P9 Redford Abers
91 S3 Redford Angus
10 D5 Redford W Susx
75 S2 Redfordgreen Border
26 J10 Redgate Rhondd
90 G6 Redgorton P & K
40 H5 Redgrave Suffk
99 P3 Redhill Abers
8 F9 Red Hill Bmouth
31 T6 Redhill Herts
17 N4 Redhill N Som
21 N12 Redhill Surrey
36 F9 Red Hill Warwks
41 R4 Redisham Suffk
28 A12 Redland Bristl
106 s17 Redland Ork
41 L6 Redlingfield Suffk
41 L6 Redlingfield Green Suffk
39 U6 Red Lodge Suffk
55 T3 Red Lumb Rochdl
17 T10 Redlynch Somset
8 J4 Redlynch Wilts
66 H6 Redmain Cumb
35 S7 Redmarley Worcs
28 E1 Redmarley D'Abitot Gloucs
70 E8 Redmarshall S on T
47 U6 Redmile Leics
63 L1 Redmire N York
99 P8 Redmyre Abers
36 D5 Rednal Birm
44 J8 Rednal Shrops
84 F11 Redpath Border
107 M11 Redpoint Highld
14 G11 Red Post Cnwll
55 N5 Red Rock Wigan
25 M8 Red Roses Carmth
77 R6 Red Row Nthumb
2 H8 Redruth Cnwll
18 D8 Redstocks Wilts
90 J5 Redstone P & K
24 K7 Redstone Cross Pembks
45 T3 Red Street Staffs
55 T5 Redvales Bury
52 H6 Red Wharf Bay IoA
27 S11 Redwick Newpt
27 U10 Redwick S Glos
69 R8 Redworth Darltn
31 U5 Reed Herts
51 R13 Reedham Norfk
58 C2 Reedness E R Yk
59 M13 Reeds Beck Lincs
55 T2 Reeds Holme Lancs
58 H12 Reepham Lincs
50 K9 Reepham Norfk
69 M13 Reeth N York
36 J5 Reeves Green Solhll
60 g3 Regaby IoM
17 P4 Regil N Som
107 S2 Reiff Highld
21 N12 Reigate Surrey
65 Q4 Reighton N York
105 P12 Reisque Abers
112 H6 Reiss Highld
2 K5 Rejerrah Cnwll
2 H10 Releath Cnwll
2 F10 Relubbus Cnwll
103 Q6 Relugas Moray
20 C6 Remenham Wokham
20 C6 Remenham Hill Wokham
47 Q9 Rempstone Notts
28 K6 Rendcomb Gloucs
41 P8 Rendham Suffk
41 P10 Rendlesham Suffk
89 M12 Renfrew Rens
38 G10 Renhold Bed
57 Q11 Renishaw Derbys
77 Q2 Rennington Nthumb
88 J10 Renton W Duns
67 S4 Renwick Cumb
51 R10 Repps Norfk
46 K8 Repton Derbys
102 K6 Resaurie Highld
3 P8 Rescassa Cnwll
3 P7 Rescorla Cnwll
93 S6 Resipole Highld
2 G8 Reskadinnick Cnwll
102 J2 Resolis Highld
26 E7 Resolven Neath
88 F4 Rest and be thankful Ag & B
85 M6 Reston Border
3 L9 Restronguet Cnwll
98 J13 Reswallie Angus
3 N4 Reterth Cnwll
58 B10 Retford Notts
3 Q4 Retire Cnwll
22 J8 Rettendon Essex
3 M5 Retyn Cnwll
49 L1 Revesby Lincs
5 S13 Rew Devon
5 T6 Rew Devon
6 B5 Rewe Devon
9 P10 Rew Street IoW
5 L3 Rexon Devon
41 S5 Reydon Suffk
50 H12 Reymerston Norfk
24 J9 Reynalton Pembks
25 S13 Reynoldston Swans
4 K5 Rezare Cnwll
27 R7 Rhadyr Mons
33 Q12 Rhandirmwyn Carmth
33 U7 Rhayader Powys
102 F6 Rheindown Highld
54 E12 Rhes-y-cae Flints
44 D1 Rhewl Denbgs
44 E5 Rhewl Denbgs
54 D10 Rhewl-fawr Flints
54 E10 Rhewl Mostyn Flints
110 B11 Rhicarn Highld
110 F6 Rhiconich Highld
109 M10 Rhicullen Highld
26 G6 Rhigos Rhondd
107 T5 Rhireavach Highld
109 Q4 Rhives Highld
27 M11 Rhiwbina Cardif
43 N4 Rhiwbryfdir Gwynd
27 P10 Rhiwderyn Newpt
52 J10 Rhiwen Gwynd
26 J10 Rhiwinder Rhondd
43 T6 Rhiwlas Gwynd
52 J9 Rhiwlas Gwynd
44 E7 Rhiwlas Powys
26 K11 Rhiwsaeson Rhondd
16 J10 Rhode Somset
12 C6 Rhoden Green Kent
57 S11 Rhodesia Notts
13 N7 Rhodes Minnis Kent
24 C5 Rhodiad-y-brenin Pembks
74 D14 Rhonehouse D & G
16 E3 Rhoose V Glam
25 Q3 Rhos Carmth
44 D1 Rhos Denbgs
26 C7 Rhos Neath
52 E4 Rhosbeirio IoA
52 H7 Rhoscefnhir IoA
52 C7 Rhoscolyn IoA
24 F10 Rhoscrowther Pembks
54 F13 Rhosesmor Flints
42 G6 Rhos-fawr Gwynd
52 H11 Rhosgadfan Gwynd
52 F5 Rhosgoch IoA
34 E11 Rhosgoch Powys
32 K8 Rhos Haminiog Cerdgn
32 C12 Rhoshill Pembks
42 D8 Rhoshirwaun Gwynd
42 J5 Rhoslan Gwynd
43 L12 Rhoslefain Gwynd
44 G4 Rhosllanerchrugog Wrexhm
52 G5 Rhôs Lligwy IoA
26 A3 Rhosmaen Carmth
52 G7 Rhosmeirch IoA
52 D8 Rhosneigr IoA
44 J3 Rhosnesni Wrexhm
53 P6 Rhôs-on-Sea Conwy
44 H3 Rhosrobin Wrexhm
25 R13 Rhossili Swans
52 G11 Rhostryfan Gwynd
44 H4 Rhostyllen Wrexhm
52 F5 Rhosybol IoA
44 D9 Rhos y-brithdir Powys
44 H7 Rhosygadfa Shrops
33 M6 Rhos-y-garth Cerdgn
43 T7 Rhos-y-gwaliau Gwynd
42 D6 Rhos-y-llan Gwynd
44 G5 Rhosymedre Wrexhm
34 G7 Rhos-y-meirch Powys
88 G9 Rhu Ag & B
54 C11 Rhualit Denbgs
88 B11 Rhubodach Ag & B
45 N1 Rhuddall Heath Ches W
32 J12 Rhuddlan Cerdgn
53 T7 Rhuddlan Denbgs
34 D11 Rhulen Powys
79 N6 Rhunahaorine Ag & B
43 M5 Rhyd Gwynd
25 R5 Rhydargaeau Carmth
25 U3 Rhydcymerau Carmth
35 T11 Rhydd Worcs
52 J12 Rhyd-Ddu Gwynd
26 C8 Rhydding Neath
53 S10 Rhydgaled Conwy
53 P12 Rhydlanfair Conwy
32 F11 Rhydlewis Cerdgn
42 C8 Rhydlios Gwynd
43 S3 Rhyd-lydan Conwy
32 H11 Rhydowen Cerdgn
33 L7 Rhydrosser Cerdgn
34 F11 Rhydspence Herefs
44 F3 Rhydtalog Flints
43 T6 Rhyd-uchaf Gwynd
42 F7 Rhyd-y-clafdy Gwynd
44 F7 Rhydycroesau Shrops
33 L5 Rhydyfelin Cerdgn
26 K10 Rhydyfelin Rhondd
53 R7 Rhyd-y-foel Conwy
26 C6 Rhydyfro Neath
52 J9 Rhyd-y-groes Gwynd
43 R9 Rhydymain Gwynd
27 Q6 Rhyd-y-meirch Mons
54 F13 Rhydymwyn Flints
33 M3 Rhyd-y pennau Cerdgn
43 M13 Rhyd-yr-onnen Gwynd
43 N5 Rhyd-y-sarn Gwynd
53 T6 Rhyl Denbgs
27 L6 Rhymney Caerph
90 J7 Rhynd P & K
104 F10 Rhynie Abers
109 Q9 Rhynie Highld
35 S6 Ribbesford Worcs
62 B13 Ribbleton Lancs
61 S13 Ribby Lancs
62 D12 Ribchester Lancs
46 K2 Riber Derbys
59 L5 Riby Lincs
64 E12 Riccall N York
76 A7 Riccarton Border
81 N5 Riccarton E Ayrs
35 L7 Richards Castle Herefs
20 H7 Richings Park Bucks
21 L8 Richmond Gt Lon
69 Q12 Richmond N York
57 P9 Richmond Sheff
6 c2 Richmond Fort Guern
16 F10 Rich's Holford Somset
46 B9 Rickerscote Staffs
17 N5 Rickford N Som
5 T13 Rickham Devon
40 H5 Rickinghall Suffk
22 C1 Rickling Essex
22 D2 Rickling Green Essex
20 J4 Rickmansworth Herts
84 E14 Riddell Border
47 M3 Riddings Derbys
15 P10 Riddlecombe Devon
63 M11 Riddlesden C Brad
17 Q5 Ridge BaNES
8 C11 Ridge Dorset
31 R12 Ridge Herts
8 D2 Ridge Wilts
34 C8 Ridgebourne Powys
21 P13 Ridge Green Surrey
36 J2 Ridge Lane Warwks
13 P7 Ridge Row Kent
57 P10 Ridgeway Derbys
36 D8 Ridgeway Worcs
35 R11 Ridgeway Cross Herefs
40 B12 Ridgewell Essex
11 R7 Ridgewood E Susx
31 L5 Ridgmont C Beds
77 L13 Riding Mill Nthumb
12 B3 Ridley Kent
76 F13 Ridley Nthumb
45 N3 Ridley Green Ches E
51 P7 Ridlington Norfk
48 B13 Ridlington Rutlnd
51 P7 Ridlington Street Norfk
76 J9 Ridsdale Nthumb
64 D2 Rievaulx N York
64 D3 Rievaulx Abbey N York
75 Q12 Rigg D & G
82 E4 Riggend N Lans
103 N5 Righoul Highld
62 C3 Rigmadon Park Cumb
59 R11 Rigsby Lincs
82 G11 Rigside S Lans
55 P1 Riley Green Lancs
46 F11 Rileyhill Staffs
4 H6 Rilla Mill Cnwll
4 H6 Rillaton Cnwll
64 K5 Rillington N York
62 G10 Rimington Lancs
17 R12 Rimpton Somset
65 U14 Rimswell E R Yk
24 G5 Rinaston Pembks
35 R1 Rindleford Shrops
73 R8 Ringford D & G
57 L10 Ringinglow Sheff
50 K11 Ringland Norfk
11 R6 Ringles Cross E Susx
12 G4 Ringlestone Kent
55 S5 Ringley Bolton
11 Q8 Ringmer E Susx
5 R11 Ringmore Devon
6 B10 Ringmore Devon
55 L4 Ring o'Bells Lancs
104 B7 Ringorm Moray
49 N13 Ring's End Cambs

Ringsfield - Shiplake 139

41 R3 Ringsfield Suffk
41 R3 Ringsfield Corner Suffk
31 L10 Ringshall Herts
40 H10 Ringshall Suffk
40 J10 Ringshall Stocks Suffk
38 E5 Ringstead Nhants
50 B5 Ringstead Norfk
8 H7 Ringwood Hants
13 S6 Ringwould Kent
2 F11 Rinsey Cnwll
2 G11 Rinsey Croft Cnwll
11 S8 Ripe E Susx
47 L3 Ripley Derbys
8 H9 Ripley Hants
63 R7 Ripley N York
20 J11 Ripley Surrey
65 M13 Riplingham E R Yk
9 T4 Riplington Hants
63 S5 Ripon N York
48 G8 Rippingale Lincs
13 S5 Ripple Kent
35 U13 Ripple Worcs
56 F3 Ripponden Calder
78 E7 Risabus Ag & B
35 M10 Risbury Herefs
58 F4 Risby N Linc
40 D7 Risby Suffk
27 N9 Risca Caerph
65 R11 Rise E R Yk
11 U4 Riseden E Susx
12 D8 Riseden Kent
48 K8 Risegate Lincs
58 G11 Riseholme Lincs
66 F6 Risehow Cumb
38 F8 Riseley Bed
20 B10 Riseley Wokham
41 L7 Rishangles Suffk
62 E13 Rishton Lancs
56 F3 Rishworth Calder
55 S1 Rising Bridge Lancs
47 N6 Risley Derbys
55 Q8 Risley Warrtn
63 Q6 Risplith N York
19 M8 Rivar Wilts
22 K4 Rivenhall End Essex
13 Q7 River Kent
10 E6 River W Susx
39 R7 River Bank Cambs
102 F5 Riverford Highld
21 T11 Riverhead Kent
7 U2 Rivers Corner Dorset
55 P4 Rivington Lancs
15 U8 Roachill Devon
37 U10 Roade Nhants
41 N2 Road Green Norfk
75 V11 Roadhead Cumb
82 G9 Roadmeetings S Lans
81 R9 Roadside E Ayrs
112 E4 Roadside Highld
16 D9 Roadwater Somset
100 b5 Roag Highld
61 N6 Roa Island Cumb
80 K12 Roan of Craigoch S Ayrs
39 Q14 Roast Green Essex
27 M12 Roath Cardif
75 T3 Roberton Border
82 H13 Roberton S Lans
12 D11 Robertsbridge E Susx
56 J2 Roberttown Kirk
24 J7 Robeston Wathen Pembks
75 P11 Robgill Tower D & G
46 B2 Robin Hill Staffs
55 M4 Robin Hood Lancs
57 M1 Robin Hood Leeds
36 F4 Robin Hood Crematorium Solhll
57 U7 *Robin Hood Doncaster Sheffield Airport* Donc
40 B13 Robinhood End Essex
71 S11 Robin Hood's Bay N York
5 N8 Roborough Devon
15 N9 Roborough Devon
54 K8 Roby Knows
55 M5 Roby Mill Lancs
46 F6 Rocester Staffs
24 E6 Roch Pembks
56 C4 Rochdale Rochdl
56 C4 Rochdale Crematorium Rochdl
3 P4 Roche Cnwll
12 D2 Rochester Medway
76 G6 Rochester Nthumb
23 L9 Rochford Essex
35 P7 Rochford Worcs
24 E6 Roch Gate Pembks
3 N1 Rock Cnwll
26 D9 Rock Neath
77 Q1 Rock Nthumb
10 J8 Rock W Susx
35 R6 Rock Worcs
6 D6 Rockbeare Devon
8 G5 Rockbourne Hants
75 S13 Rockcliffe Cumb
66 B2 Rockcliffe D & G
75 R13 Rockcliffe Cross Cumb
45 U2 Rock End Staffs
6 B12 Rockend Torbay
54 H9 Rock Ferry Wirral
109 S8 Rockfield Highld
27 T5 Rockfield Mons
15 S3 Rockford Devon
8 H7 Rockford Hants
35 M5 Rockgreen Shrops
28 C9 Rockhampton S Glos
4 D4 Rockhead Cnwll
34 G5 Rockhill Shrops
36 C7 Rock Hill Worcs
38 C2 Rockingham Nhants
40 G1 Rockland All Saints Norfk
51 P13 Rockland St Mary Norfk
40 G1 Rockland St Peter Norfk
58 B12 Rockley Notts
18 J6 Rockley Wilts
56 C2 Rockliffe Lancs
88 F7 Rockville Ag & B
20 C5 Rockwell End Bucks
16 F12 Rockwell Green Somset
28 F7 Rodborough Gloucs
29 M10 Rodbourne Swindn
28 H11 Rodbourne Wilts
34 H8 Rodd Herefs
77 L1 Roddam Nthumb
7 R8 Rodden Dorset
69 Q5 Roddymoor Dur
18 B10 Rode Somset
45 T2 Rode Heath Ches E
56 C13 Rode Heath Ches E
106 f10 Rodel W Isls
45 N10 Roden Wrekin
16 D9 Rodhuish Somset
45 N11 Rodington Wrekin
45 N11 Rodington Heath Wrekin
28 D5 Rodley Gloucs
63 Q12 Rodley Leeds
28 H8 Rodmarton Gloucs
11 Q9 Rodmell E Susx
12 H3 Rodmersham Kent
12 H3 Rodmersham Green Kent
17 N7 Rodney Stoke Somset
46 H5 Rodsley Derbys
16 J8 Rodway Somset
63 T6 Roecliffe N York
56 E7 Roe Cross Tamesd
31 R11 Roe Green Herts
31 T6 Roe Green Herts
55 S6 Roe Green Salfd
21 M8 Roehampton Gt Lon
10 K4 Roffey W Susx
109 N4 Rogart Highld
10 C6 Rogate W Susx
67 N13 Roger Ground Cumb
27 P10 Rogerstone Newpt
106 f10 Roghadal W Isls
27 T10 Rogiet Mons
19 T2 Roke Oxon
77 U14 Roker Sundld
51 R10 Rollesby Norfk
47 T13 Rolleston Leics
47 T3 Rolleston Notts
46 H8 Rolleston on Dove Staffs
65 S11 Rolston E R Yk
17 L4 Rolstone N Som
12 F9 Rolvenden Kent
12 G9 Rolvenden Layne Kent
69 L8 Romaldkirk Dur
17 U4 Roman Baths & Pump Room BaNES
70 E14 Romanby N York
83 N9 Romanno Bridge Border
15 R8 Romansleigh Devon
12 G7 Romden Castle Kent
100 d4 Romesdal Highld
8 F7 Romford Dorset
22 D10 Romford Gt Lon
56 D8 Romiley Stockp
21 U10 Romney Street Kent
9 M4 Romsey Hants
35 S4 Romsley Shrops
36 C4 Romsley Worcs
100 f4 Rona Highld
79 N5 Ronachan Ag & B
18 C9 Rood Ashton Wilts
68 K4 Rookhope Dur
9 Q12 Rookley IoW
9 Q12 Rookley Green IoW
17 L6 Rooks Bridge Somset
16 E10 Rooks Nest Somset
63 Q2 Rookwith N York
65 T13 Roos E R Yk
61 N6 Roose Cumb
61 P6 Roosebeck Cumb
38 G9 Roothams Green Bed
9 S2 Ropley Hants
9 S2 Ropley Dean Hants
9 T2 Ropley Soke Hants
48 E7 Ropsley Lincs
105 T5 Rora Abers
44 H13 Rorrington Shrops
104 D5 Rosarie Moray
2 K6 Rose Cnwll
61 S12 Roseacre Lancs
15 S8 Rose Ash Devon
82 F9 Rosebank S Lans
24 J5 Rosebush Pembks
14 E13 Rosecare Cnwll
3 L5 Rosecliston Cnwll
71 M13 Rosedale Abbey N York
23 M2 Rose Green Essex
40 F13 Rose Green Suffk
40 G12 Rose Green Suffk
10 E11 Rose Green W Susx
108 H4 Rosehall Highld
105 Q2 Rosehearty Abers
11 R7 Rose Hill E Susx
62 G13 Rose Hill Lancs
45 L10 Rosehill Shrops
103 T2 Roseisle Moray
11 U10 Roselands E Susx
24 G9 Rosemarket Pembks
102 K4 Rosemarkie Highld
6 G2 Rosemary Lane Devon
90 J3 Rosemount P & K
3 P3 Rosenannon Cnwll
3 L12 Rosenithon Cnwll
11 S6 Roser's Cross E Susx
3 Q5 Rosevean Cnwll
3 M9 Rosevine Cnwll
2 G9 Rosewarne Cnwll
83 Q6 Rosewell Mdloth
70 F8 Roseworth S on T
2 G9 Roseworthy Cnwll
67 R9 Rosgill Cumb
2 B12 Roskestal Cnwll
100 b5 Roskhill Highld
2 K12 Roskorwell Cnwll
67 M3 Rosley Cumb
83 Q6 Roslin Mdloth
46 H10 Rosliston Derbys
88 G9 Rosneath Ag & B
73 Q11 Ross D & G
85 S11 Ross Nthumb
44 J2 Rossett Wrexhm
63 R9 Rossett Green N York
57 T7 Rossington Donc
88 K11 Rossland Rens
28 A3 Ross-on-Wye Herefs
112 G9 Roster Highld
55 R10 Rostherne Ches E
67 L10 Rosthwaite Cumb
46 F5 Roston Derbys
2 F11 Rosudgeon Cnwll
83 M2 Rosyth Fife
77 M5 Rothbury Nthumb
47 S10 Rotherby Leics
11 T5 Rotherfield E Susx
20 B6 Rotherfield Greys Oxon
20 B6 Rotherfield Peppard Oxon
57 P8 Rotherham Rothm
57 Q8 Rotherham Crematorium Rothm
37 T9 Rothersthorpe Nhants
37 T9 Rothersthorpe Services Nhants
20 B11 Rotherwick Hants
104 B6 Rothes Moray
88 C13 Rothesay Ag & B
105 L8 Rothiebrisbane Abers
104 H6 Rothiemay Moray
97 R2 Rothiemurchus Lodge Highld
105 L8 Rothienorman Abers
47 Q11 Rothley Leics
77 L8 Rothley Nthumb
104 K9 Rothmaise Abers
63 S14 Rothwell Leeds
58 K7 Rothwell Lincs
38 B4 Rothwell Nhants
65 P9 Rotsea E R Yk
98 F10 Rottal Lodge Angus
11 P10 Rottingdean Br & H
66 E10 Rottington Cumb
74 K10 Roucan D & G
74 K10 Roucan Loch Crematorium D & G
9 Q12 Roud IoW
50 D9 Rougham Norfk
40 F8 Rougham Green Suffk
46 B6 Rough Close Staffs
13 M4 Rough Common Kent
62 G11 Roughlee Lancs
104 C13 Roughpark Abers
59 M14 Roughton Lincs
51 M6 Roughton Norfk
35 S2 Roughton Shrops
12 B5 Roughway Kent
23 L7 Roundbush Essex
20 K3 Round Bush Herts
22 E5 Roundbush Green Essex
31 P8 Round Green Luton
7 M3 Roundham Somset
63 S12 Roundhay Leeds
36 C3 Rounds Green Sandw
12 C2 Round Street Kent
10 H5 Roundstreet Common W Susx
18 F8 Roundway Wilts
98 F13 Roundyhill Angus
106 s16 Rousay Ork
6 J6 Rousdon Devon
29 U3 Rousham Oxon
36 D10 Rous Lench Worcs
88 E13 Routenburn N Ayrs
65 P11 Routh E R Yk
20 C3 Rout's Green Bucks
3 R1 Row Cnwll
61 T2 Row Cumb
68 D6 Row Cumb
75 T10 Rowanburn D & G
88 J6 Rowardennan Stirlg
56 F9 Rowarth Derbys
9 Q6 Row Ash Hants
17 N5 Rowberrow Somset
9 P12 Rowborough IoW
18 E8 Rowde Wilts
15 P13 Rowden Devon
53 N8 Rowen Conwy
46 G4 Rowfield Derbys
76 D13 Rowfoot Nthumb
16 H11 Rowford Somset
22 H3 Row Green Essex
23 P3 Rowhedge Essex
10 J4 Rowhook W Susx
36 H7 Rowington Warwks
56 K12 Rowland Derbys
9 U6 Rowland's Castle Hants
77 P14 Rowland's Gill Gatesd
10 C2 Rowledge Surrey
69 N3 Rowley Dur
65 M13 Rowley E R Yk
44 H12 Rowley Shrops
56 J4 Rowley Hill Kirk
36 C3 Rowley Regis Sandw
36 C3 Rowley Regis Crematorium Sandw
27 R2 Rowlstone Herefs
10 G2 Rowly Surrey
9 R8 Rowner Hants
36 D6 Rowney Green Worcs
9 M5 Rownhams Hants
9 M5 Rownhams Services Hants
66 G9 Rowrah Cumb
30 H9 Rowsham Bucks
57 L13 Rowsley Derbys
55 T11 Rows of Trees Ches E
29 U10 Rowstock Oxon
48 G2 Rowston Lincs
57 Q14 Rowthorne Derbys
54 K14 Rowton Ches W
34 K4 Rowton Shrops
44 J11 Rowton Shrops
45 P10 Rowton Wrekin
20 H10 Row Town Surrey
84 H12 Roxburgh Border
58 F3 Roxby N Linc
71 N9 Roxby N York
38 J10 Roxton Bed
22 F6 Roxwell Essex
21 L7 Royal Botanic Gardens Gt Lon
69 R8 Royal Oak Darltn
54 K6 Royal Oak Lancs
45 P5 Royal's Green Ches E
96 B7 Roy Bridge Highld
56 K4 Roydhouse Kirk
22 B5 Roydon Essex
40 K4 Roydon Norfk
50 B9 Roydon Norfk
22 B6 Roydon Hamlet Essex
57 N4 Royston Barns
31 U4 Royston Herts
56 D5 Royton Oldham
7 e2 Rozel Jersey
44 H5 Ruabon Wrexhm
92 D9 Ruaig Ag & B
3 N9 Ruan High Lanes Cnwll
3 M8 Ruan Lanihorne Cnwll
2 J13 Ruan Major Cnwll
2 J13 Ruan Minor Cnwll
28 B4 Ruardean Gloucs
28 B4 Ruardean Hill Gloucs
28 B4 Ruardean Woodside Gloucs
36 C5 Rubery Birm
106 c17 Rubha Ban W Isls
67 R4 Ruckcroft Cumb
35 L13 Ruckhall Herefs
12 K9 Ruckinge Kent
59 P11 Ruckland Lincs
45 M13 Ruckley Shrops
70 G11 Rudby N York
77 N12 Rudchester Nthumb
47 Q7 Ruddington Notts
28 C5 Ruddle Gloucs
3 Q6 Ruddlemoor Cnwll
28 E3 Rudford Gloucs
18 B10 Rudge Somset
28 B10 Rudgeway S Glos
10 H4 Rudgwick W Susx
28 B2 Rudhall Herefs
55 Q12 Rudheath Ches W
55 R12 Rudheath Woods Ches E
22 K7 Rudley Green Essex
18 B6 Rudloe Wilts
27 N10 Rudry Caerph
65 P6 Rudston E R Yk
46 C2 Rudyard Staffs
76 C1 Ruecastle Border
55 L3 Rufford Lancs
64 C9 Rufforth C York
44 C5 Rug Denbgs
37 P5 Rugby Warwks
46 D10 Rugeley Staffs
16 J11 Ruishton Somset
20 J5 Ruislip Gt Lon
100 c10 Rùm Highld
104 D5 Rumbach Moray
90 F12 Rumbling Bridge P & K
41 P4 Rumburgh Suffk
69 Q6 Rumby Hill Dur
3 M2 Rumford Cnwll
82 H3 Rumford Falk
27 N12 Rumney Cardif
16 G12 Rumwell Somset
55 M10 Runcorn Halton
10 D10 Runcton W Susx
49 T12 Runcton Holme Norfk
20 E13 Runfold Surrey
50 J12 Runhall Norfk
51 S11 Runham Norfk
51 T12 Runham Norfk
16 F12 Runnington Somset
22 J6 Runsell Green Essex
55 M3 Runshaw Moor Lancs
71 P9 Runswick N York
98 D10 Runtaleave Angus
22 J9 Runwell Essex
20 C7 Ruscombe Wokham
35 P13 Rushall Herefs
41 L4 Rushall Norfk
18 H9 Rushall Wilts
46 D13 Rushall Wsall
40 E8 Rushbrooke Suffk
35 M2 Rushbury Shrops
31 T6 Rushden Herts
38 E7 Rushden Nhants
23 M13 Rushenden Kent
11 U5 Rusher's Cross E Susx
5 M5 Rushford Devon
40 F4 Rushford Norfk
23 S4 Rush Green Essex
22 D10 Rush Green Gt Lon
31 R8 Rush Green Herts
55 Q9 Rush Green Warrtn
11 U7 Rushlake Green E Susx
41 S3 Rushmere Suffk
41 L11 Rushmere St Andrew Suffk
10 D2 Rushmoor Surrey
34 H9 Rushock Herefs
35 U6 Rushock Worcs
56 C8 Rusholme Manch
55 N14 Rushton Ches W
38 B4 Rushton Nhants
45 P12 Rushton Shrops
46 B1 Rushton Spencer Staffs
35 T10 Rushwick Worcs
69 S7 Rushyford Dur
89 P5 Ruskie Stirlg
48 G3 Ruskington Lincs
61 Q2 Rusland Cross Cumb
11 L3 Rusper W Susx
28 C5 Ruspidge Gloucs
22 H5 Russell Green Essex
20 B5 Russell's Water Oxon
41 N6 Russel's Green Suffk
11 L2 Russ Hill Surrey
11 T3 Rusthall Kent
10 G10 Rustington W Susx
65 M3 Ruston N York
65 P7 Ruston Parva E R Yk
71 Q11 Ruswarp N York
35 N2 Ruthall Shrops
84 G12 Rutherford Border
89 P13 Rutherglen S Lans
3 Q3 Ruthernbridge Cnwll
44 D2 Ruthin Denbgs
99 S3 Ruthrieston C Aber
104 G6 Ruthven Abers
91 L2 Ruthven Angus
97 M4 Ruthven Highld
3 N4 Ruthvoes Cnwll
66 K5 Ruthwaite Cumb
75 L12 Ruthwell D & G
21 S8 Ruxley Corner Gt Lon
27 U4 Ruxton Green Herefs
44 J9 Ruyton-XI-Towns Shrops
77 L11 Ryal Nthumb
7 M5 Ryall Dorset
35 U12 Ryall Worcs
12 C3 Ryarsh Kent
30 E11 Rycote Oxon
67 N11 Rydal Cumb
9 R10 Ryde IoW
12 H11 Rye E Susx
45 M7 Ryebank Shrops
28 B3 Ryeford Herefs
12 G11 Rye Foreign E Susx
12 H12 Rye Harbour E Susx
59 M1 Ryehill E R Yk
20 B9 Ryeish Green Wokham
35 S13 Rye Street Worcs
48 F11 Ryhall Rutlnd
57 N4 Ryhill Wakefd
70 F2 Ryhope Sundld
57 Q13 Rylah Derbys
58 H11 Ryland Lincs
47 P6 Rylands Notts
62 K8 Rylstone N York
7 Q2 Ryme Intrinseca Dorset
64 D12 Ryther N York
77 P13 Ryton Gatesd
64 H4 Ryton N York
45 S13 Ryton Shrops
37 M3 Ryton Warwks
37 L6 Ryton-on-Dunsmore Warwks
77 N13 Ryton Woodside Gatesd

S

62 F12 Sabden Lancs
22 D8 Sabine's Green Essex
31 T9 Sacombe Herts
31 T9 Sacombe Green Herts
69 R3 Sacriston Dur
70 D9 Sadberge Darltn
79 P9 Saddell Ag & B
37 S2 Saddington Leics
49 T10 Saddle Bow Norfk
11 M8 Saddlescombe W Susx
67 Q11 Sadgill Cumb
39 R13 Saffron Walden Essex
24 J10 Sageston Pembks
50 F13 Saham Hills Norfk
50 E13 Saham Toney Norfk
44 K1 Saighton Ches W
85 N5 St Abbs Border
84 H6 St Agnes Border
2 J6 St Agnes Cnwll
2 b3 St Agnes IoS
31 P11 St Albans Herts
3 L6 St Allen Cnwll
6 d3 St Andrew Guern
91 R8 St Andrews Fife
91 R8 St Andrews Botanic Garden Fife
16 F2 St Andrew's Major V Glam
7 N6 St Andrews Well Dorset
61 Q14 St Anne's Lancs
75 L7 St Ann's D & G
5 L6 St Ann's Chapel Cnwll
5 R11 St Ann's Chapel Devon
2 K11 St Anthony Cnwll
11 U10 St Anthony's Hill E Susx
27 U8 St Arvans Mons
53 T8 St Asaph Denbgs
16 D3 St Athan V Glam
7 c3 St Aubin Jersey
3 Q6 St Austell Cnwll
66 E10 St Bees Cumb
3 R6 St Blazey Cnwll
3 R6 St Blazey Gate Cnwll
84 F12 St Boswells Border
7 b3 St Brelade Jersey
7 b3 St Brelade's Bay Jersey
3 P2 St Breock Cnwll
3 R1 St Breward Cnwll
27 V7 St Briavels Gloucs
24 D8 St Brides Pembks
26 F13 St Bride's Major V Glam
27 S10 St Brides Netherwent Mons
26 K12 St Brides super-Ely V Glam
27 P11 St Brides Wentlooge Newpt
5 M9 St Budeaux C Plym
36 F13 Saintbury Gloucs
2 C11 St Buryan Cnwll
17 U3 St Catherine BaNES
88 D4 St Catherines Ag & B
28 F7 St Chloe Gloucs
25 N7 St Clears Carmth
4 G7 St Cleer Cnwll
3 M8 St Clement Cnwll
7 e4 St Clement Jersey
4 G4 St Clether Cnwll
88 B12 St Colmac Ag & B
3 N4 St Columb Major Cnwll
3 L4 St Columb Minor Cnwll
3 N5 St Columb Road Cnwll
105 T3 St Combs Abers
41 N4 St Cross South Elmham Suffk
99 N11 St Cyrus Abers
90 D7 St David's P & K
24 C5 St David's Pembks
2 J8 St Day Cnwll
16 E8 St Decumans Somset
3 P5 St Dennis Cnwll
27 S1 St Devereux Herefs
32 C11 St Dogmaels Pembks
24 G5 St Dogwells Pembks
5 L7 St Dominick Cnwll
16 B3 St Donats V Glam
18 E8 St Edith's Marsh Wilts
4 B5 St Endellion Cnwll
3 M5 St Enoder Cnwll
3 L7 St Erme Cnwll
4 K9 St Erney Cnwll
2 F9 St Erth Cnwll
2 F9 St Erth Praze Cnwll
3 M2 St Ervan Cnwll
3 M3 St Eval Cnwll
3 P7 St Ewe Cnwll
27 L12 St Fagans Cardif
27 L12 St Fagans Welsh Life Museum Cardif
105 T5 St Fergus Abers
95 T14 St Fillans P & K
24 J10 St Florence Pembks
14 D13 St Gennys Cnwll
53 S7 St George Conwy
17 L4 St Georges N Som
27 L12 St George's V Glam
20 J10 St George's Hill Surrey
4 K9 St Germans Cnwll
15 M9 St Giles in the Wood Devon
4 K2 St Giles-on-the-Heath Devon
2 K10 St Gluvia's Cnwll
33 U6 St Harmon Powys
69 Q7 St Helen Auckland Dur
66 F6 St Helens Cumb
12 F13 St Helens E Susx
9 S11 St Helens IoW
55 M7 St Helens St Hel
55 L7 St Helens Crematorium St Hel
21 N9 St Helier Gt Lon
7 d3 St Helier Jersey
2 E10 St Hilary Cnwll
26 J13 St Hilary V Glam
6 E3 Saint Hill Devon
11 P3 Saint Hill W Susx
27 N7 St Illtyd Blae G
31 Q7 St Ippollitts Herts
24 D9 St Ishmael's Pembks
3 N2 St Issey Cnwll
4 J7 St Ive Cnwll
4 J7 St Ive Cross Cnwll
39 M6 St Ives Cambs
2 E8 St Ives Cnwll
8 G8 St Ives Dorset
51 N9 St James Norfk
37 T8 St James's End Nhants
41 P4 St James South Elmham Suffk
3 N3 St Jidgey Cnwll
5 L10 St John Cnwll
7 c1 St John Jersey
69 N6 St Johns Dur
60 d6 St John's IoM
21 T11 St Johns Kent
20 G11 St Johns Surrey
35 T10 St Johns Worcs
15 M7 St John's Chapel Devon
68 J5 St John's Chapel Dur
49 R11 St John's Fen End Norfk
49 R11 St John's Highway Norfk
82 J11 St John's Kirk S Lans
73 Q3 St John's Town of Dalry D & G
21 N6 St John's Wood Gt Lon
60 f3 St Jude's IoM
2 B10 St Just Cnwll
3 L9 St Just-in-Roseland Cnwll
105 M9 St Katherines Abers
2 K12 St Keverne Cnwll
3 Q1 St Kew Cnwll
3 Q1 St Kew Highway Cnwll
4 G8 St Keyne Cnwll
3 Q3 St Lawrence Cnwll
23 N7 St Lawrence Essex
9 Q13 St Lawrence IoW
7 c2 St Lawrence Jersey
13 S2 St Lawrence Kent
30 K11 St Leonards Bucks
8 G8 St Leonards Dorset
12 F14 St Leonards E Susx
12 C4 St Leonard's Street Kent
2 B12 St Levan Cnwll
27 L13 St Lythans V Glam
3 Q2 St Mabyn Cnwll
90 J7 St Madoes P & K
34 J14 St Margarets Herefs
31 U10 St Margarets Herts
13 S7 St Margaret's at Cliffe Kent
106 t20 St Margaret's Hope Ork
41 P4 St Margaret South Elmham Suffk
60 d8 St Marks IoM
2 J12 St Martin Cnwll
4 H9 St Martin Cnwll
6 d3 St Martin Guern
7 e2 St Martin Jersey
2 c1 St Martin's IoS
90 J5 St Martin's P & K
44 H6 St Martins Shrops
44 H6 St Martin's Moor Shrops
7 c2 St Mary Jersey
19 P10 St Mary Bourne Hants
6 B11 St Marychurch Torbay
16 D2 St Mary Church V Glam
21 S9 St Mary Cray Gt Lon
26 H12 St Mary Hill V Glam
13 L10 St Mary in the Marsh Kent
21 N5 St Marylebone Crematorium Gt Lon
2 c2 St Mary's IoS
106 t19 St Mary's Ork
13 L10 St Mary's Bay Kent
17 N3 St Mary's Grove N Som
22 K12 St Mary's Hoo Medway
27 T4 St Maughans Mons
27 T4 St Maughans Green Mons
3 L10 St Mawes Cnwll
3 M3 St Mawgan Cnwll
4 K7 St Mellion Cnwll
27 N11 St Mellons Cardif
3 M2 St Merryn Cnwll
3 P6 St Mewan Cnwll
3 P8 St Michael Caerhays Cnwll
16 K10 St Michael Church Somset
3 M8 St Michael Penkevil Cnwll
12 G8 St Michaels Kent
35 N7 St Michaels Worcs
61 T11 St Michael's on Wyre Lancs
41 P4 St Michael South Elmham Suffk
4 B5 St Minver Cnwll
91 R11 St Monans Fife
4 F7 St Neot Cnwll
38 J8 St Neots Cambs
24 F3 St Nicholas Pembks
26 K13 St Nicholas V Glam
13 Q2 St Nicholas at Wade Kent
89 S7 St Ninians Stirlg
51 S14 St Olaves Norfk
23 R4 St Osyth Essex
7 b2 St Ouen Jersey
27 U3 St Owens Cross Herefs
21 S9 St Pauls Cray Gt Lon
31 Q8 St Paul's Walden Herts
7 b2 St Peter Jersey
6 e3 St Peter Port Guern
6 c3 St Peter's Guern
13 S2 St Peter's Kent
38 K6 St Peter's Hill Cambs
24 G11 St Petrox Pembks
4 G8 St Pinnock Cnwll
81 M8 St Quivox S Ayrs
2 J13 St Ruan Cnwll
6 e2 St Sampson Guern
6 c3 St Saviour Guern
7 d3 St Saviour Jersey
3 N6 St Stephen Cnwll
4 J3 St Stephens Cnwll
5 L9 St Stephens Cnwll
4 D4 St Teath Cnwll
3 R1 St Tudy Cnwll
24 G11 St Twynnells Pembks
4 E9 St Veep Cnwll
91 T3 St Vigeans Angus
3 P4 St Wenn Cnwll
27 T3 St Weonards Herefs
26 K12 St y-Nyll V Glam
5 S13 Salcombe Devon
6 G7 Salcombe Regis Devon
23 M5 Salcott-cum-Virley Essex
55 S8 Sale Traffd
59 S11 Saleby Lincs
36 B9 Sale Green Worcs
12 E11 Salehurst E Susx
25 V5 Salem Carmth
33 N4 Salem Cerdgn
93 P10 Salen Ag & B
93 R6 Salen Highld
62 D13 Salesbury Lancs
30 K5 Salford C Beds
29 Q2 Salford Oxon
55 T7 Salford Salfd
36 E10 Salford Priors Warwks
21 N13 Salfords Surrey
51 P11 Salhouse Norfk
90 F13 Saline Fife
8 G3 Salisbury Wilts
8 G3 Salisbury Cathedral Wilts
8 H2 Salisbury Crematorium Wilts
18 G12 Salisbury Plain Wilts
67 R5 Salkeld Dykes Cumb
50 K9 Salle Norfk
59 P12 Salmonby Lincs
29 L3 Salperton Gloucs
38 G10 Salph End Bed
82 F6 Salsburgh N Lans
46 C8 Salt Staffs
66 G3 Salta Cumb
63 N12 Saltaire C Brad
5 L9 Saltash Cnwll
109 N10 Saltburn Highld
71 L8 Saltburn-by-the-Sea R & Cl
48 C8 Saltby Leics
66 J2 Salt Coates Cumb
66 G13 Saltcoats Cumb
80 J4 Saltcoats N Ayrs
61 R14 Saltcotes Lancs
11 P10 Saltdean Br & H
66 E7 Salterbeck Cumb
62 H10 Salterforth Lancs
55 P13 Salterswall Ches W
18 H13 Salterton Wilts
59 S8 Saltfleet Lincs
59 S8 Saltfleetby All Saints Lincs
59 S8 Saltfleetby St Clement Lincs
59 R9 Saltfleetby St Peter Lincs
17 S3 Saltford BaNES
50 J5 Salthouse Norfk
36 F3 Saltley Birm
27 Q11 Saltmarsh Newpt
58 C2 Saltmarshe E R Yk
54 J14 Saltney Flints
64 G4 Salton N York
15 L8 Saltrens Devon
77 R13 Saltwell Crematorium Gatesd
77 P9 Saltwick Nthumb
13 N8 Saltwood Kent
10 J9 Salvington W Susx
35 U8 Salwarpe Worcs
7 N5 Salway Ash Dorset
36 E8 Sambourne Warwks
45 R9 Sambrook Wrekin
62 B13 Samlesbury Lancs
62 C14 Samlesbury Bottoms Lancs
16 F13 Sampford Arundel Somset
16 E8 Sampford Brett Somset
15 P12 Sampford Courtenay Devon
16 F13 Sampford Moor Somset
6 D2 Sampford Peverell Devon
5 N6 Sampford Spiney Devon
106 v17 Samsonlane Ork
23 Q4 Samson's Corner Essex
84 D4 Samuelston E Loth
86 C11 Sanaigmore Ag & B
2 C11 Sancreed Cnwll
64 K12 Sancton E R Yk
17 M7 Sand Somset
100 g9 Sandaig Highld
66 K4 Sandale Cumb
57 M3 Sandal Magna Wakefd
93 M2 Sandavore Highld
106 v15 Sanday Ork
106 v15 *Sanday Airport* Ork
45 S1 Sandbach Ches E
45 S1 Sandbach Services Ches E
88 E9 Sandbank Ag & B
8 E11 Sandbanks Poole
104 H2 Sandend Abers
21 P10 Sanderstead Gt Lon
68 F9 Sandford Cumb
15 T12 Sandford Devon
8 C11 Sandford Dorset
8 H8 Sandford Hants
9 Q12 Sandford IoW
17 M5 Sandford N Som
82 D10 Sandford S Lans
44 H9 Sandford Shrops
45 N7 Sandford Shrops
30 B12 Sandford-on-Thames Oxon
17 R12 Sandford Orcas Dorset
29 T2 Sandford St Martin Oxon
13 P8 Sandgate Kent
105 R2 Sandhaven Abers
72 D10 Sandhead D & G
57 P7 Sandhill Rothm
7 Q4 Sandhills Dorset
7 S2 Sandhills Dorset
63 T12 Sand Hills Leeds
30 C11 Sandhills Oxon
10 E3 Sandhills Surrey
76 K12 Sandhoe Nthumb
87 U6 Sandhole Ag & B
64 J12 Sand Hole E R Yk
64 J13 Sandholme E R Yk
49 M6 Sandholme Lincs
20 D10 Sandhurst Br For
28 F3 Sandhurst Gloucs
12 F10 Sandhurst Kent
12 E10 Sandhurst Cross Kent
63 T3 Sandhutton N York
64 F8 Sand Hutton N York
47 N6 Sandiacre Derbys
59 T10 Sandilands Lincs
55 P12 Sandiway Ches W
8 G5 Sandleheath Hants
29 U7 Sandleigh Oxon
17 U12 Sandley Dorset
12 E4 Sandling Kent
55 S13 Sandlow Green Ches E
106 r8 Sandness Shet
22 H7 Sandon Essex
31 T6 Sandon Herts
46 B8 Sandon Staffs
46 B8 Sandon Bank Staffs
9 R12 Sandown IoW
4 H9 Sandplace Cnwll
31 Q10 Sandridge Herts
18 D7 Sandridge Wilts
49 U8 Sandringham Norfk
20 D4 Sands Bucks
71 Q10 Sandsend N York
61 N3 Sand Side Cumb
61 T3 Sandside Cumb
58 B5 Sandtoft N Linc
12 G5 Sandway Kent
13 R4 Sandwich Kent
67 P9 Sandwick Cumb
106 u11 Sandwick Shet
106 j5 Sandwick W Isls
66 E10 Sandwith Cumb
66 E10 Sandwith Newtown Cumb
38 J11 Sandy C Beds
49 L2 Sandy Bank Lincs
54 H13 Sandycroft Flints
11 T6 Sandy Cross E Susx
35 Q9 Sandy Cross Herefs
75 P7 Sandyford D & G
5 V6 Sandygate Devon
60 f3 Sandygate IoM
24 E9 Sandy Haven Pembks
66 C1 Sandyhills D & G
61 S7 Sandylands Lancs
63 N12 Sandy Lane C Brad
45 R6 Sandylane Staffs
25 U13 Sandylane Swans
18 E7 Sandy Lane Wilts
44 K5 Sandy Lane Wrexhm
5 S3 Sandy Park Devon
75 S12 Sandysike Cumb
27 T2 Sandyway Herefs
110 J3 Sangobeg Highld
110 J3 Sangomore Highld
55 N9 Sankey Bridges Warrtn
35 S7 Sankyn's Green Worcs
93 L5 Sanna Bay Highld
106 j5 Sanndabhaig W Isls
80 E3 Sannox N Ayrs
74 E4 Sanquhar D & G
66 H12 Santon Cumb
60 e8 Santon IoM
66 H12 Santon Bridge Cumb
40 D3 Santon Downham Suffk
37 N2 Sapcote Leics
35 R8 Sapey Common Herefs
40 F5 Sapiston Suffk
38 K6 Sapley Cambs
46 G7 Sapperton Derbys
28 H7 Sapperton Gloucs
48 F7 Sapperton Lincs
49 M8 Saracen's Head Lincs
112 H8 Sarclet Highld
9 Q7 Sarisbury Hants
26 G11 Sarn Brdgnd
42 D7 Sarn Gwynd
34 F2 Sarn Powys
43 U14 Sarn Powys
25 P7 Sarnau Carmth
32 F10 Sarnau Cerdgn
43 U6 Sarnau Gwynd
34 B14 Sarnau Powys
44 F10 Sarnau Powys
42 F8 Sarn Bach Gwynd
34 J10 Sarnesfield Herefs
26 G11 Sarn Park Services Brdgnd
44 G10 Sarn-wen Powys
25 Q3 Saron Carmth
25 V8 Saron Carmth
52 G11 Saron Gwynd
52 H9 Saron Gwynd
20 H3 Sarratt Herts
13 Q2 Sarre Kent
29 Q3 Sarsden Oxon
19 M12 Sarson Hants
69 P4 Satley Dur
13 Q8 Satmar Kent
68 K13 Satron N York
15 Q8 Satterleigh Devon
61 Q1 Satterthwaite Cumb
20 B6 Satwell Oxon
105 L13 Sauchen Abers
90 J5 Saucher P & K
99 M10 Sauchieburn Abers
28 D6 Saul Gloucs
58 C9 Saundby Notts
24 K10 Saundersfoot Pembks
30 G12 Saunderton Bucks
15 L5 Saunton Devon
59 Q13 Sausthorpe Lincs
2 K7 Saveock Cnwll
46 C6 Saverley Green Staffs
56 K2 Savile Town Kirk
37 P7 Sawbridge Warwks
22 C5 Sawbridgeworth Herts
65 L3 Sawdon N York
47 N7 Sawley Derbys
62 F10 Sawley Lancs
63 Q6 Sawley N York
39 Q11 Sawston Cambs
38 J4 Sawtry Cambs
48 B10 Saxby Leics
58 H9 Saxby Lincs
58 G3 Saxby All Saints N Linc
47 S9 Saxelbye Leics
40 J8 Saxham Street Suffk
58 E11 Saxilby Lincs
50 H6 Saxlingham Norfk
41 M1 Saxlingham Green Norfk
41 M1 Saxlingham Nethergate Norfk
41 M1 Saxlingham Thorpe Norfk
41 Q8 Saxmundham Suffk
47 S6 Saxondale Notts
39 U9 Saxon Street Cambs
41 N7 Saxtead Suffk
41 N8 Saxtead Green Suffk
41 M7 Saxtead Little Green Suffk
50 K7 Saxthorpe Norfk
64 B12 Saxton N York
11 M7 Sayers Common W Susx
64 E5 Scackleton N York
66 K11 Scafell Pike Cumb
57 U8 Scaftworth Notts
64 J5 Scagglethorpe N York
86 F7 Scalasaig Ag & B
64 J14 Scalby E R Yk
65 N1 Scalby N York
38 F9 Scald End Bed
37 U6 Scaldwell Nhants
75 T13 Scaleby Cumb
75 T13 Scalebyhill Cumb
67 S3 Scale Houses Cumb
61 P5 Scales Cumb
67 M7 Scales Cumb
67 P3 Scalesceugh Cumb
47 U9 Scalford Leics
71 M10 Scaling N York
71 M10 Scaling Dam R & Cl
106 u10 Scalloway Shet
100 f6 Scalpay Highld
59 N11 Scamblesby Lincs
56 G3 Scammonden Kirk
93 U4 Scamodale Highld
64 K4 Scampston N York
58 G11 Scampton Lincs
102 H8 Scaniport Highld
56 G3 Scapegoat Hill Kirk
87 M5 Scarba Ag & B
65 N2 Scarborough N York
3 N6 Scarcewater Cnwll
57 Q13 Scarcliffe Derbys
63 T11 Scarcroft Leeds
112 G2 Scarfskerry Highld
69 N10 Scargill Dur
92 C10 Scarinish Ag & B
54 J4 Scarisbrick Lancs
66 K6 Scarness Cumb
50 G11 Scarning Norfk
47 T5 Scarrington Notts
54 K5 Scarth Hill Lancs
64 B12 Scarthingwell N York
59 N5 Scartho NE Lin
106 t6 *Scatsta Airport* Shet
58 G5 Scawby N Linc
57 R6 Scawsby Donc
57 S5 Scawthorpe Donc
64 C3 Scawton N York
11 P6 Scayne's Hill W Susx
27 L2 Scethrog Powys
45 T2 Scholar Green Ches E
63 N13 Scholemoor Crematorium C Brad
56 J1 Scholes Kirk
56 J5 Scholes Kirk
63 T12 Scholes Leeds
57 N7 Scholes Rothm
55 N5 Scholes Wigan
69 S8 School Aycliffe Dur
63 N13 School Green C Brad
55 P14 School Green Ches W
20 B9 Schoolgreen Wokham
7 L4 School House Dorset
56 K4 Scissett Kirk
24 F4 Scleddau Pembks
57 T10 Scofton Notts
41 L5 Scole Norfk
90 H6 Scone P & K
100 e6 Sconser Highld
91 N11 Scoonie Fife
48 G2 Scopwick Lincs
107 T5 Scoraig Highld
65 N10 Scorborough E R Yk
2 J8 Scorrier Cnwll
5 S7 Scorriton Devon
61 U10 Scorton Lancs
69 S12 Scorton N York
51 N9 Sco Ruston Norfk
67 P1 Scotby Cumb
69 R11 Scotch Corner N York
61 T8 Scotforth Lancs
45 S4 Scot Hay Staffs
58 H11 Scothern Lincs
48 F7 Scotland Lincs
77 R9 Scotland Gate Nthumb
90 J11 Scotlandwell P & K
55 P5 Scot Lane End Bolton
112 C5 Scotscalder Station Highld
75 S11 Scotsdike Cumb
77 L8 Scot's Gap Nthumb
104 H12 Scotsmill Abers
89 M12 Scotstoun C Glas
77 Q13 Scotswood N u Ty
58 E6 Scotter Lincs
58 E6 Scotterthorpe Lincs
48 G9 Scottlethorpe Lincs
58 E7 Scotton Lincs
63 S8 Scotton N York
69 Q13 Scotton N York
51 N9 Scottow Norfk
48 G6 Scott Willoughby Lincs
50 G13 Scoulton Norfk
46 E8 Scounslow Green Staffs
110 D8 Scourie Highld
110 C8 Scourie More Highld
106 t12 Scousburgh Shet
56 E5 Scouthead Oldham
112 D2 Scrabster Highld
76 D2 Scraesburgh Border
59 P13 Scrafield Lincs
76 K4 Scrainwood Nthumb
49 N5 Scrane End Lincs
47 R12 Scraptoft Leics
51 T10 Scratby Norfk
64 G8 Scrayingham N York
12 E12 Scrays E Susx
48 G5 Scredington Lincs
59 R13 Scremby Lincs
85 Q9 Scremerston Nthumb
47 T5 Screveton Notts
59 N13 Scrivelsby Lincs
63 S8 Scriven N York
57 U8 Scrooby Notts
46 G7 Scropton Derbys
48 K2 Scrub Hill Lincs
63 R1 Scruton N York
75 T11 Scuggate Cumb
111 N4 Scullomie Highld
50 E7 Sculthorpe Norfk
58 E4 Scunthorpe N Linc
25 S13 Scurlage Swans
6 K2 Sea Somset
7 M3 Seaborough Dorset
45 T5 Seabridge Staffs
13 N8 Seabrook Kent
77 U14 Seaburn Sundld
54 H8 Seacombe Wirral
63 T12 Seacroft Leeds
49 S1 Seacroft Lincs
49 M6 Seadyke Lincs
100 d5 Seafield Highld
82 K5 Seafield W Loth
83 Q3 Seafield Crematorium C Edin
11 R11 Seaford E Susx
54 H7 Seaforth Sefton
47 R10 Seagrave Leics
18 E4 Seagry Heath Wilts
70 F3 Seaham Dur
85 U12 Seahouses Nthumb
21 U11 Seal Kent
20 E13 Seale Surrey
65 N3 Seamer N York
70 G10 Seamer N York
80 J3 Seamill N Ayrs
51 R8 Sea Palling Norfk
58 J5 Searby Lincs
13 L3 Seasalter Kent
66 F12 Seascale Cumb
66 K10 Seathwaite Cumb
66 K13 Seathwaite Cumb
61 R3 Seatle Cumb
66 K10 Seatoller Cumb
4 J10 Seaton Cnwll
66 F6 Seaton Cumb
6 H6 Seaton Devon
70 E3 Seaton Dur
65 R10 Seaton E R Yk
13 P4 Seaton Kent
77 S10 Seaton Nthumb
48 D14 Seaton Rutlnd
77 Q11 Seaton Burn N Tyne
70 H7 Seaton Carew Hartpl
77 S10 Seaton Delaval Nthumb
64 H11 Seaton Ross E R Yk
77 S10 Seaton Sluice Nthumb
7 M6 Seatown Dorset
70 J12 Seave Green N York
9 S10 Seaview IoW
66 J2 Seaville Cumb
7 M2 Seavington St Mary Somset
17 M13 Seavington St Michael Somset
27 P8 Sebastopol Torfn
67 N4 Sebergham Cumb
46 J12 Seckington Warwks
62 D1 Sedbergh Cumb
27 U9 Sedbury Gloucs
62 H1 Sedbusk N York
36 D13 Sedgeberrow Worcs
48 C6 Sedgebrook Lincs
39 U4 Sedge Fen Suffk
70 E7 Sedgefield Dur
50 B6 Sedgeford Norfk
8 B3 Sedgehill Wilts
17 L6 Sedgemoor Services Somset
36 B2 Sedgley Dudley
55 T6 Sedgley Park Bury
61 U2 Sedgwick Cumb
12 E12 Sedlescombe E Susx
30 H10 Sedrup Bucks
12 H4 Seed Kent
18 D8 Seend Wilts
18 D8 Seend Cleeve Wilts
20 G4 Seer Green Bucks
41 P1 Seething Norfk
54 J6 Sefton Sefton
54 H6 Sefton Town Sefton
77 R11 Seghill Nthumb
45 U8 Seighford Staffs
52 H9 Seion Gwynd
35 T1 Seisdon Staffs
44 G7 Selattyn Shrops
9 U2 Selborne Hants
64 E13 Selby N York
10 E6 Selham W Susx
21 P9 Selhurst Gt Lon
84 D13 Selkirk Border
27 V2 Sellack Herefs
106 v4 Sellafirth Shet
2 C10 Sellan Cnwll
16 H13 Sellick's Green Somset
13 L8 Sellindge Kent
12 K4 Selling Kent
18 D8 Sells Green Wilts
36 D4 Selly Oak Birm
11 S9 Selmeston E Susx
21 Q10 Selsdon Gt Lon
28 F7 Selsey Gloucs
10 D12 Selsey W Susx
11 N4 Selsfield Common W Susx
67 R13 Selside Cumb
62 F4 Selside N York
13 P7 Selsted Kent
47 N3 Selston Notts
16 B7 Selworthy Somset
40 G11 Semer Suffk
18 C8 Semington Wilts
8 B3 Semley Wilts
48 H7 Sempringham Lincs
20 H11 Send Surrey
20 H11 Send Marsh Surrey
27 L9 Senghenydd Caerph
2 B11 Sennen Cnwll
2 B11 Sennen Cove Cnwll
26 G2 Sennybridge Powys
57 T9 Serlby Notts
64 B4 Sessay N York
49 T11 Setchey Norfk
9 L8 Setley Hants
84 C3 Seton Mains E Loth
62 G7 Settle N York
64 J5 Settrington N York
16 G10 Seven Ash Somset
28 K3 Sevenhampton Gloucs
29 P9 Sevenhampton Swindn
41 M12 Seven Hills Crematorium Suffk
21 S5 Seven Kings Gt Lon
21 T11 Sevenoaks Kent
21 T12 Sevenoaks Weald Kent
26 E6 Seven Sisters Neath
28 J4 Seven Springs Gloucs
23 M2 Seven Star Green Essex
27 U11 Severn Beach S Glos
35 U12 Severn Stoke Worcs
27 V10 Severn View Services S Glos
38 G10 Sevick End Bed
12 K7 Sevington Kent
39 S13 Sewards End Essex
21 Q3 Sewardstonebury Essex
31 L8 Sewell C Beds
65 R6 Sewerby E R Yk
2 J10 Seworgan Cnwll
48 C9 Sewstern Leics
70 G11 Sexhow N York
29 N1 Sezincote Gloucs
106 k2 Sgiogarstaigh W Isls
30 E11 Shabbington Bucks
45 T12 Shackerley Shrops
47 L12 Shackerstone Leics
47 M7 Shacklecross Derbys
20 F13 Shackleford Surrey
56 D2 Shade Calder
106 i3 Shader W Isls
70 D4 Shadforth Dur
41 R4 Shadingfield Suffk
12 J8 Shadoxhurst Kent
63 S12 Shadwell Leeds
40 F4 Shadwell Norfk
39 P13 Shaftenhoe End Herts
8 B4 Shaftesbury Dorset
57 S5 Shaftholme Donc
57 N4 Shafton Barns
57 N4 Shafton Two Gates Barns
55 Q6 Shakerley Wigan
19 M8 Shalbourne Wilts
9 M11 Shalcombe IoW
19 U12 Shalden Hants
19 V12 Shalden Green Hants
6 B10 Shaldon Devon
9 N11 Shalfleet IoW
22 H2 Shalford Essex
20 H13 Shalford Surrey
22 H2 Shalford Green Essex
45 U8 Shallowford Staffs
13 L5 Shalmsford Street Kent
30 D5 Shalstone Bucks
10 G2 Shamley Green Surrey
98 H11 Shandford Angus
88 G8 Shandon Ag & B
109 R9 Shandwick Highld
37 T1 Shangton Leics
77 R10 Shankhouse Nthumb
9 R12 Shanklin IoW
67 S9 Shap Cumb
106 u18 Shapinsay Ork
8 C8 Shapwick Dorset
17 M9 Shapwick Somset
36 G3 Shard End Birm
47 M7 Shardlow Derbys
46 B12 Shareshill Staffs
57 N3 Sharlston Wakefd
57 N3 Sharlston Common Wakefd
36 F5 Sharman's Cross Solhll
22 J13 Sharnal Street Medway
38 E9 Sharnbrook Bed
56 C2 Sharneyford Lancs
37 N2 Sharnford Leics
7 T3 Sharnhill Green Dorset
61 U13 Sharoe Green Lancs
63 S5 Sharow N York
31 N6 Sharpenhoe C Beds
76 K5 Sharperton Nthumb
51 Q9 Sharp Green Norfk
28 C7 Sharpness Gloucs
11 P4 Sharpthorne W Susx
4 H6 Sharptor Cnwll
36 C7 Sharpway Gate Worcs
50 H6 Sharrington Norfk
35 S4 Shatterford Worcs
13 Q4 Shatterling Kent
56 K10 Shatton Derbys
5 N8 Shaugh Prior Devon
7 M5 Shave Cross Dorset
45 Q3 Shavington Ches E
63 L12 Shaw C Brad
56 D5 Shaw Oldham
29 M10 Shaw Swindn
19 Q7 Shaw W Berk
18 C7 Shaw Wilts
45 P11 Shawbirch Wrekin
106 h4 Shawbost W Isls
45 N9 Shawbury Shrops
56 C4 Shawclough Rochdl
28 C2 Shaw Common Gloucs
77 M3 Shawdon Hill Nthumb
37 P4 Shawell Leics
9 P3 Shawford Hants
56 C2 Shawforth Lancs
31 T6 Shaw Green Herts
55 M3 Shaw Green Lancs
63 R9 Shaw Green N York
74 G10 Shawhead D & G
63 R7 Shaw Mills N York
82 E8 Shawsburn S Lans
18 C12 Shear Cross Wilts
74 K12 Shearington D & G
37 R2 Shearsby Leics
16 J10 Shearston Somset
14 K11 Shebbear Devon
45 S8 Shebdon Staffs
112 B4 Shebster Highld
81 R1 Sheddens E Rens
9 R6 Shedfield Hants
46 F1 Sheen Staffs
57 N12 Sheepbridge Derbys
69 Q1 Sheep Hill Dur
56 J3 Sheepridge Kirk
63 S13 Sheepscar Leeds
28 G5 Sheepscombe Gloucs
5 P7 Sheepstor Devon
15 L11 Sheepwash Devon
77 R8 Sheepwash Nthumb
27 T12 Sheepway N Som
46 K13 Sheepy Magna Leics
46 K13 Sheepy Parva Leics
22 D5 Sheering Essex
23 M13 Sheerness Kent
20 H10 Sheerwater Surrey
10 B6 Sheet Hants
2 D11 Sheffield Cnwll
57 N9 Sheffield Sheff
19 T7 Sheffield Bottom W Berk
57 N9 Sheffield City Road Crematorium Sheff
11 Q5 Sheffield Green E Susx
31 P5 Shefford C Beds
110 D4 Sheigra Highld
45 P13 Sheinton Shrops
34 K5 Shelderton Shrops
36 G4 Sheldon Birm
56 J13 Sheldon Derbys
6 F3 Sheldon Devon
12 K4 Sheldwich Kent
12 K4 Sheldwich Lees Kent
63 N14 Shelf Calder
40 K4 Shelfanger Norfk
36 F8 Shelfield Warwks
46 D13 Shelfield Wsall
36 F8 Shelfield Green Warwks
47 S5 Shelford Notts
37 M3 Shelford Warwks
85 M10 Shellacres Nthumb
22 E6 Shelley Essex
56 K4 Shelley Kirk
40 H13 Shelley Suffk
56 K4 Shelley Far Bank Kirk
29 R9 Shellingford Oxon
22 F6 Shellow Bowells Essex
35 R8 Shelsley Beauchamp Worcs
35 R8 Shelsley Walsh Worcs
38 F7 Shelton Bed
41 M2 Shelton Norfk
47 U5 Shelton Notts
45 L11 Shelton Shrops
41 M2 Shelton Green Norfk
47 L7 Shelton Lock C Derb
45 T6 Shelton Under Harley Staffs
44 H14 Shelve Shrops
35 M12 Shelwick Herefs
22 F8 Shenfield Essex
37 L12 Shenington Oxon
31 Q12 Shenley Herts
30 H5 Shenley Brook End M Keyn
31 Q12 Shenleybury Herts
30 H5 Shenley Church End M Keyn
34 J13 Shenmore Herefs
72 J7 Shennanton D & G
46 F13 Shenstone Staffs
35 U6 Shenstone Worcs
46 F13 Shenstone Woodend Staffs
47 L14 Shenton Leics
103 V10 Shenval Moray
49 M11 Shepeau Stow Lincs
31 S8 Shephall Herts
21 M6 Shepherd's Bush Gt Lon
20 B6 Shepherd's Green Oxon
28 D7 Shepherds Patch Gloucs
13 Q6 Shepherdswell Kent
56 J5 Shepley Kirk
28 B8 Shepperdine S Glos
20 J9 Shepperton Surrey
20 J9 Shepperton Green Surrey
39 N11 Shepreth Cambs
47 N10 Shepshed Leics
17 M13 Shepton Beauchamp Somset
17 R8 Shepton Mallet Somset
17 S10 Shepton Montague Somset
12 E5 Shepway Kent
70 F5 Sheraton Dur
17 R13 Sherborne Dorset
29 N5 Sherborne Gloucs
17 Q5 Sherborne Somset
19 T9 Sherborne St John Hants
36 J8 Sherbourne Warwks
70 D4 Sherburn Dur
65 M4 Sherburn N York
70 D4 Sherburn Hill Dur
64 B13 Sherburn in Elmet N York
20 J13 Shere Surrey
50 E8 Shereford Norfk
8 K4 Sherfield English Hants
19 U9 Sherfield on Loddon Hants
55 S1 Sherfin Lancs
5 T12 Sherford Devon
8 C10 Sherford Dorset
45 S11 Sheriffhales Shrops
64 F6 Sheriff Hutton N York
51 L5 Sheringham Norfk
38 C11 Sherington M Keyn
11 L7 Shermanbury W Susx
50 B7 Shernborne Norfk
18 E13 Sherrington Wilts
28 G10 Sherston Wilts
47 Q5 Sherwood C Nott
47 R2 Sherwood Forest Notts
57 U13 Sherwood Forest Crematorium Notts
89 P13 Shettleston C Glas
55 M5 Shevington Wigan
55 M4 Shevington Moor Wigan
55 M5 Shevington Vale Wigan
4 K9 Sheviock Cnwll
63 M14 Shibden Head C Brad
9 Q11 Shide IoW
85 L11 Shidlaw Nthumb
101 N8 Shiel Bridge Highld
107 P14 Shieldaig Highld
74 K8 Shieldhill D & G
82 G3 Shieldhill Falk
82 K10 Shieldhill House Hotel S Lans
82 E7 Shields N Lans
93 R4 Shielfoot Highld
98 G12 Shielhill Angus
88 F11 Shielhill Inver
29 S7 Shifford Oxon
45 R12 Shifnal Shrops
77 P4 Shilbottle Nthumb
69 R7 Shildon Dur
81 P1 Shillford E Rens
16 C12 Shillingford Devon
19 S2 Shillingford Oxon
6 B7 Shillingford Abbot Devon
6 B7 Shillingford St George Devon
8 A6 Shillingstone Dorset
31 P6 Shillington C Beds
76 H4 Shillmoor Nthumb
29 Q6 Shilton Oxon
37 M4 Shilton Warwks
41 L4 Shimpling Norfk
40 E10 Shimpling Suffk
40 E10 Shimpling Street Suffk
69 S4 Shincliffe Dur
70 D2 Shiney Row Sundld
20 B9 Shinfield Wokham
39 M11 Shingay Cambs
41 Q12 Shingle Street Suffk
5 T8 Shinnersbridge Devon
108 J2 Shinness Highld
21 U12 Shipbourne Kent
50 G12 Shipdham Norfk
17 M5 Shipham Somset
6 A11 Shiphay Torbay
20 C7 Shiplake Oxon

140 Shiplake Row - Storridge

20 B7 Shiplake Row Oxon
17 L5 Shiplate N Som
63 P12 Shipley C Brad
47 M5 Shipley Derbys
35 T1 Shipley Shrops
10 J6 Shipley W Susx
11 N2 Shipley Bridge Surrey
12 K8 Shipley Hatch Kent
41 Q2 Shipmeadow Suffk
39 T4 Shippea Hill Station Cambs
29 U8 Shippon Oxon
36 J12 Shipston on Stour Warwks
30 G7 Shipton Bucks
28 K4 Shipton Gloucs
64 D8 Shipton N York
35 N2 Shipton Shrops
18 K11 Shipton Bellinger Hants
7 N6 Shipton Gorge Dorset
10 C11 Shipton Green W Susx
28 G10 Shipton Moyne Gloucs
29 U4 Shipton-on-Cherwell Oxon
64 K11 Shiptonthorpe E R Yk
29 Q4 Shipton-under-Wychwood Oxon
30 E13 Shirburn Oxon
54 J4 Shirdley Hill Lancs
68 D5 Shire Cumb
57 R13 Shirebrook Derbys
57 N8 Shiregreen Sheff
27 U12 Shirehampton Bristl
77 S11 Shiremoor N Tyne
27 T9 Shirenewton Mons
46 E13 Shire Oak Wsall
57 S10 Shireoaks Notts
12 H8 Shirkoak Kent
47 M2 Shirland Derbys
45 P14 Shirlett Shrops
9 N6 Shirley C Sotn
46 H5 Shirley Derbys
21 Q9 Shirley Gt Lon
36 F5 Shirley Solhll
34 K9 Shirl Heath Herefs
9 R6 Shirrell Heath Hants
87 R9 Shirvan Ag & B
15 P5 Shirwell Devon
79 S10 Shiskine N Ayrs
69 M5 Shittlehope Dur
34 K8 Shobdon Herefs
8 H7 Shobley Hants
15 U12 Shobrooke Devon
47 S9 Shoby Leics
44 K4 Shocklach Ches W
44 K4 Shocklach Green Ches W
23 M10 Shoeburyness Sthend
13 S5 Sholden Kent
9 P6 Sholing C Sotn
44 K11 Shoot Hill Shrops
3 M2 Shop Cnwll
14 F10 Shop Cnwll
10 D9 Shopwyke W Susx
56 D3 Shore Rochdl
21 P6 Shoreditch Gt Lon
16 H12 Shoreditch Somset
21 T10 Shoreham Kent
11 L9 Shoreham Airport W Susx
11 L9 Shoreham-by-Sea W Susx
85 N9 Shoreswood Nthumb
9 R3 Shorley Hants
28 K8 Shorncote Gloucs
22 G13 Shorne Kent
4 H9 Shorta Cross Cnwll
11 R6 Shortbridge E Susx
10 C2 Shortfield Common Surrey
11 R7 Shortgate E Susx
36 E2 Short Heath Birm
10 B3 Shortheath Hants
46 C13 Short Heath Wsall
3 L7 Shortlanesend Cnwll
81 N5 Shortlees E Ayrs
38 G11 Shortstown Bed
9 P12 Shorwell IoW
17 T5 Shoscombe BaNES
51 M14 Shotesham Norfk
22 J9 Shotgate Essex
41 M13 Shotley Suffk
69 N2 Shotley Bridge Dur
69 N2 Shotleyfield Nthumb
41 M14 Shotley Gate Suffk
41 M13 Shotley Street Suffk
12 K5 Shottenden Kent
10 D4 Shottermill Surrey
36 G10 Shottery Warwks
37 M11 Shotteswell Warwks
41 P12 Shottisham Suffk
46 K4 Shottle Derbys
46 K4 Shottlegate Derbys
70 E7 Shotton Dur
70 F5 Shotton Dur
54 H13 Shotton Flints
77 Q10 Shotton Nthumb
85 L12 Shotton Nthumb
70 E4 Shotton Colliery Dur
82 G7 Shotts N Lans
54 H12 Shotwick Ches W
103 V4 Shougle Moray
49 U12 Shouldham Norfk
49 U12 Shouldham Thorpe Norfk
35 T9 Shoulton Worcs
12 C9 Shover's Green E Susx
45 S4 Shraleybrook Staffs
44 J10 Shrawardine Shrops
35 T7 Shrawley Worcs
20 H6 Shreding Green Bucks
36 H7 Shrewley Warwks
45 L11 Shrewsbury Shrops
18 G12 Shrewton Wilts
10 E10 Shripney W Susx
29 P10 Shrivenham Oxon
40 G2 Shropham Norfk
23 N3 Shrub End Essex
35 N12 Shucknall Herefs
39 T12 Shudy Camps Cambs
87 P4 Shuna Ag & B
28 H4 Shurdington Gloucs
20 D8 Shurlock Row W & M
36 D8 Shurnock Worcs
112 B5 Shurrery Highld
112 B5 Shurrery Lodge Highld
16 H8 Shurton Somset
36 H2 Shustoke Warwks
6 J5 Shute Devon
15 U12 Shute Devon
37 L12 Shutford Oxon
45 U9 Shut Heath Staffs
35 U13 Shuthonger Gloucs
37 T11 Shutlanger Nhants
6 C9 Shutterton Devon
45 U12 Shutt Green Staffs
46 J12 Shuttington Warwks
57 Q12 Shuttlewood Derbys
55 T3 Shuttleworth Bury
106 h4 Siabost W Isls
106 i3 Siadar W Isls
37 S4 Sibbertoft Nhants
34 K4 Sibdon Carwood Shrops
37 L13 Sibford Ferris Oxon
37 L13 Sibford Gower Oxon
40 C14 Sible Hedingham Essex
22 F2 Sibley's Green Essex
4 G6 Siblyback Cnwll
49 N3 Sibsey Lincs
49 M3 Sibsey Fenside Lincs
38 G1 Sibson Cambs
47 L13 Sibson Leics
112 H6 Sibster Highld
47 U4 Sibthorpe Notts
58 B12 Sibthorpe Notts
41 Q7 Sibton Suffk
40 E8 Sicklesmere Suffk
63 T10 Sicklinghall N York
16 J11 Sidbrook Somset
6 F6 Sidbury Devon
35 Q3 Sidbury Shrops
57 N5 Sid Cop Barns
17 M5 Sidcot N Som
21 S8 Sidcup Gt Lon
66 F6 Siddick Cumb
55 T12 Siddington Ches E
28 K8 Siddington Gloucs
36 C6 Sidemoor Worcs
51 N6 Sidestrand Norfk
6 F6 Sidford Devon
10 D11 Sidlesham W Susx
10 D11 Sidlesham Common W Susx
12 D14 Sidley E Susx
6 F7 Sidmouth Devon
35 L4 Siefton Shrops
5 T6 Sigford Devon
65 R10 Sigglesthorne E R Yk
16 C2 Sigingstone V Glam
29 P5 Signet Oxon
19 T8 Silchester Hants
47 R10 Sileby Leics
61 L3 Silecroft Cumb
50 K14 Silfield Norfk
33 L10 Silian Cerdgn
9 N4 Silkstead Hants
57 L5 Silkstone Barns
57 L6 Silkstone Common Barns
48 G5 Silk Willoughby Lincs
66 H2 Silloth Cumb
65 M1 Silpho N York
63 L10 Silsden C Brad
31 N5 Silsoe C Beds
17 U11 Silton Dorset
83 P6 Silverburn Mdloth
61 T5 Silverdale Lancs
45 T4 Silverdale Staffs
22 K4 Silver End Essex
105 M3 Silverford Abers
51 L8 Silvergate Norfk
41 P8 Silverlace Green Suffk
41 N5 Silverley's Green Suffk
30 E4 Silverstone Nhants
12 G3 Silver Street Kent
17 P10 Silver Street Somset
6 C4 Silverton Devon
2 J7 Silverwell Cnwll
35 P5 Silvington Shrops
55 T5 Simister Bury
56 F8 Simmondley Derbys
76 H11 Simonburn Nthumb
15 S5 Simonsbath Somset
16 F13 Simonsburrow Devon
62 F13 Simonstone Lancs
62 H1 Simonstone N York
85 L9 Simprim Border
30 J5 Simpson M Keyn
24 E7 Simpson Cross Pembks
85 L8 Sinclair's Hill Border
81 P9 Sinclairston E Ayrs
63 S3 Sinderby N York
68 H2 Sinderhope Nthumb
55 R9 Sinderland Green Traffd
20 C9 Sindlesham Wokham
46 K7 Sinfin C Derb
30 G6 Singleborough Bucks
21 R11 Single Street Gt Lon
12 K7 Singleton Kent
61 R12 Singleton Lancs
10 D8 Singleton W Susx
22 G13 Singlewell Kent
12 F7 Sinkhurst Green Kent
104 F13 Sinnarhard Abers
64 G2 Sinnington N York
35 T8 Sinton Worcs
35 T8 Sinton Worcs
35 T8 Sinton Green Worcs
20 J7 Sipson Gt Lon
27 L5 Sirhowy Blae G
12 E8 Sissinghurst Kent
28 C12 Siston S Glos
4 K2 Sitcott Devon
2 G11 Sithney Cnwll
2 G11 Sithney Common Cnwll
2 G11 Sithney Green Cnwll
12 H3 Sittingbourne Kent
35 S3 Six Ashes Shrops
27 N7 Six Bells Blae G
59 L9 Sixhills Lincs
39 S9 Six Mile Bottom Cambs
13 M7 Sixmile Cottages Kent
8 D5 Sixpenny Handley Dorset
7 c2 Six Rues Jersey
61 T2 Sizergh Castle Cumb
41 S8 Sizewell Suffk
106 u19 Skaill Ork
81 Q9 Skares E Ayrs
99 S5 Skateraw Abers
84 J3 Skateraw E Loth
100 d5 Skeabost Highld
69 Q12 Skeeby N York
47 T13 Skeffington Leics
59 Q3 Skeffling E R Yk
47 N1 Skegby Notts
58 C13 Skegby Notts
59 U14 Skegness Lincs
109 P5 Skelbo Highld
109 P6 Skelbo Street Highld
57 R4 Skelbrooke Donc
49 M6 Skeldyke Lincs
58 F12 Skellingthorpe Lincs
56 D10 Skellorn Green Ches E
57 R4 Skellow Donc
56 K4 Skelmanthorpe Kirk
55 L5 Skelmersdale Lancs
88 E12 Skelmorlie N Ayrs
111 Q5 Skelpick Highld
74 F8 Skelston D & G
64 D8 Skelton C York
67 P5 Skelton Cumb
58 C1 Skelton E R Yk
63 T6 Skelton N York
69 N12 Skelton N York
71 L9 Skelton R & Cl
67 M12 Skelwith Bridge Cumb
59 R13 Skendleby Lincs
105 M13 Skene House Abers
27 T3 Skenfrith Mons
65 N8 Skerne E R Yk
111 P4 Skerray Highld
110 E6 Skerricha Highld
61 T7 Skerton Lancs
37 M2 Sketchley Leics
25 V12 Sketty Swans
26 C8 Skewen Neath
64 E5 Skewsby N York
51 M8 Skeyton Norfk
51 N8 Skeyton Corner Norfk
112 B3 Skiall Highld
59 R8 Skidbrooke Lincs
59 R7 Skidbrooke North End Lincs
65 N13 Skidby E R Yk
106 k2 Skigersta W Isls
16 C11 Skilgate Somset
48 C8 Skillington Lincs
66 H1 Skinburness Cumb
82 H2 Skinflats Falk
100 b5 Skinidin Highld
19 P7 Skinners Green W Berk
71 M9 Skinningrove R & Cl
79 S4 Skipness Ag & B
75 S9 Skipper's Bridge D & G
67 N3 Skiprigg Cumb
65 R9 Skipsea E R Yk
65 R9 Skipsea Brough E R Yk
62 K9 Skipton N York
63 T4 Skipton-on-Swale N York
64 F12 Skipwith N York
65 Q12 Skirlaugh E R Yk
83 L11 Skirling Border
20 C4 Skirmett Bucks
64 G8 Skirpenbeck E R Yk
68 D6 Skirwith Cumb
62 E5 Skirwith N York
112 J3 Skirza Highld
75 T12 Skitby Cumb
30 G12 Skittle Green Bucks
24 B10 Skokholm Island Pembks
24 B9 Skomer Island Pembks
100 f7 Skulamus Highld
34 G6 Skyborry Green Shrops
23 L3 Skye Green Essex
103 Q11 Skye of Curr Highld
63 M7 Skyreholme N York
62 K14 Slack Calder
56 E5 Slackcote Oldham
61 T4 Slack Head Cumb
59 T12 Slackholme End Lincs
105 N6 Slacks of Cairnbanno Abers
28 G6 Slad Gloucs
6 F3 Slade Devon
15 M3 Slade Devon
15 T7 Slade Devon
19 S2 Slade End Oxon
22 D12 Slade Green Gt Lon
46 B12 Slade Heath Staffs
57 R9 Slade Hooton Rothm
3 Q2 Sladesbridge Cnwll
35 T14 Slades Green Worcs
68 E2 Slaggyford Nthumb
62 E9 Slaidburn Lancs
56 G4 Slaithwaite Kirk
46 J2 Slaley Derbys
76 K14 Slaley Nthumb
82 G4 Slamannan Falk
30 K8 Slapton Bucks
5 U11 Slapton Devon
37 R11 Slapton Nhants
56 C5 Slattocks Rochdl
11 M5 Slaugham W Susx
18 B6 Slaughterford Wilts
37 U2 Slawston Leics
10 C3 Sleaford Hants
48 G4 Sleaford Lincs
67 S9 Sleagill Cumb
45 L8 Sleap Shrops
45 P10 Sleapford Wrekin
31 Q11 Sleapshyde Herts
109 L5 Sleasdairidh Highld
24 H7 Slebech Pembks
35 T14 Sledge Green Worcs
65 L7 Sledmere E R Yk
75 V10 Sleetbeck Cumb
8 D9 Sleight Dorset
69 L10 Sleightholme Dur
71 Q11 Sleights N York
8 C10 Slepe Dorset
112 G3 Slickly Highld
79 S11 Sliddery N Ayrs
100 d7 Sligachan Highld
88 E7 Sligrachan Ag & B
28 D7 Slimbridge Gloucs
45 T7 Slindon Staffs
10 F9 Slindon W Susx
10 J4 Slinfold W Susx
52 K9 Sling Gwynd
64 F5 Slingsby N York
31 N9 Slip End C Beds
31 S5 Slip End Herts
38 E5 Slipton Nhants
46 D10 Slitting Mill Staffs
87 Q6 Slockavullin Ag & B
51 N9 Sloley Norfk
5 S3 Sloncombe Devon
59 S12 Sloothby Lincs
20 G7 Slough Slough
20 G6 Slough Crematorium Bucks
16 J13 Slough Green Somset
11 M5 Slough Green W Susx
101 M4 Slumbay Highld
20 G12 Slyfield Green Surrey
61 T6 Slyne Lancs
84 G11 Smailholm Border
56 D3 Smallbridge Rochdl
15 U13 Smallbrook Devon
28 A7 Smallbrook Gloucs
51 P9 Smallburgh Norfk
56 G11 Smalldale Derbys
56 J10 Smalldale Derbys
11 L8 Small Dole W Susx
47 M5 Smalley Derbys
47 M5 Smalley Common Derbys
47 M5 Smalley Green Derbys
11 N2 Smallfield Surrey
36 F3 Small Heath Birm
12 G9 Small Hythe Kent
6 K4 Smallridge Devon
45 U3 Smallthorne C Stke
69 P10 Smallways N York
45 T1 Smallwood Ches E
61 R10 Small Wood Hey Lancs
40 H4 Smallworth Norfk
19 N11 Smannell Hants
68 F11 Smardale Cumb
12 G7 Smarden Kent
12 G7 Smarden Bell Kent
11 S2 Smart's Hill Kent
85 R11 Smeafield Nthumb
93 Q3 Smearisary Highld
6 G2 Smeatharpe Devon
13 L8 Smeeth Kent
37 S2 Smeeton Westerby Leics
63 P7 Smelthouses N York
112 E10 Smerral Highld
35 U2 Smestow Staffs
36 D3 Smethwick Sandw
55 T14 Smethwick Green Ches E
46 K10 Smisby Derbys
9 Q10 Smitheclose IoW
35 S10 Smith End Green Worcs
75 T12 Smithfield Cumb
61 T8 Smith Green Lancs
57 N5 Smithies Barns
6 E2 Smithincott Devon
39 P13 Smith's End Herts
22 E3 Smith's Green Essex
39 U12 Smith's Green Essex
107 N9 Smithstown Highld
102 K6 Smithton Highld
56 D3 Smithy Bridge Rochdl
55 R12 Smithy Green Ches E
56 C9 Smithy Green Stockp
47 L4 Smithy Houses Derbys
37 N3 Smockington Leics
110 J3 Smoo Highld
23 M4 Smythe's Green Essex
74 F8 Snade D & G
44 J13 Snailbeach Shrops
39 T7 Snailwell Cambs
65 L3 Snainton N York
57 T2 Snaith E R Yk
56 H8 Snake Pass Inn Derbys
63 R3 Snape N York
41 Q9 Snape Suffk
54 J4 Snape Green Lancs
41 Q9 Snape Street Suffk
21 R5 Snaresbrook Gt Lon
46 K12 Snarestone Leics
58 H10 Snarford Lincs
12 J10 Snargate Kent
12 K10 Snave Kent
36 B10 Sneachill Worcs
34 H2 Snead Powys
41 L3 Sneath Common Norfk
71 Q11 Sneaton N York
71 R11 Sneatonthorpe N York
58 J10 Snelland Lincs
55 T12 Snelson Ches E
46 G5 Snelston Derbys
40 G2 Snetterton Norfk
49 U7 Snettisham Norfk
47 M11 Snibston Leics
28 E2 Snig's End Gloucs
77 L5 Snitter Nthumb
58 G8 Snitterby Lincs
36 H9 Snitterfield Warwks
46 J1 Snitterton Derbys
35 N5 Snitton Shrops
12 H7 Snoadhill Kent
34 H12 Snodhill Herefs
12 D3 Snodland Kent
12 C6 Snoll Hatch Kent
57 L6 Snowden Hill Barns
52 K12 Snowdon Gwynd
43 R8 Snowdonia National Park
22 B1 Snow End Herts
36 E14 Snowshill Gloucs
40 J4 Snow Street Norfk
9 T6 Soake Hants
26 K11 Soar Cardif
5 S13 Soar Devon
26 H1 Soar Powys
100 d8 Soay Highld
9 S5 Soberton Hants
9 S6 Soberton Heath Hants
67 Q7 Sockbridge Cumb
70 D11 Sockburn Darltn
54 C12 Sodom Denbgs
44 H6 Sodylt Bank Shrops
39 S6 Soham Cambs
39 S5 Soham Cotes Cambs
106 d11 Solas W Isls
24 E8 Solbury Pembks
14 H10 Soldon Devon
14 H10 Soldon Cross Devon
19 U13 Soldridge Hants
12 C2 Sole Street Kent
13 L6 Sole Street Kent
36 G5 Solihull Solhll
34 K9 Sollers Dilwyn Herefs
35 P14 Sollers Hope Herefs
55 L3 Sollom Lancs
24 D6 Solva Pembks
75 R10 Solwaybank D & G
47 U11 Somerby Leics
58 J5 Somerby Lincs
47 M3 Somercotes Derbys
8 H10 Somerford Dorset
28 K8 Somerford Keynes Gloucs
10 C11 Somerley W Susx
41 S1 Somerleyton Suffk
46 F6 Somersal Herbert Derbys
59 P12 Somersby Lincs
39 N5 Somersham Cambs
40 J11 Somersham Suffk
29 U2 Somerton Oxon
17 N11 Somerton Somset
40 D10 Somerton Suffk
45 N11 Somerwood Shrops
10 K9 Sompting W Susx
20 C7 Sonning Wokham
20 B6 Sonning Common Oxon
20 B7 Sonning Eye Oxon
44 H4 Sontley Wrexhm
8 H9 Sopley Hants
28 F10 Sopworth Wilts
73 L10 Sorbie D & G
112 D4 Sordale Highld
92 H6 Sorisdale Ag & B
81 R7 Sorn E Ayrs
112 G4 Sortat Highld
59 M11 Sotby Lincs
58 K14 Sots Hole Lincs
41 R4 Sotterley Suffk
54 F13 Soughton Flints
30 J7 Soulbury Bucks
67 Q7 Soulby Cumb
68 F10 Soulby Cumb
30 B6 Souldern Oxon
38 E8 Souldrop Bed
45 P4 Sound Ches E
104 D5 Sound Muir Moray
28 C12 Soundwell S Glos
5 N2 Sourton Devon
61 N3 Soutergate Cumb
50 D11 South Acre Norfk
13 P7 South Alkham Kent
20 K7 Southall Gt Lon
5 T13 South Allington Devon
90 C13 South Alloa Falk
28 J2 Southam Gloucs
37 M8 Southam Warwks
10 E6 South Ambersham W Susx
9 N6 Southampton C Sotn
9 P5 Southampton Airport Hants
9 N5 Southampton Crematorium Hants
57 R10 South Anston Rothm
20 F9 South Ascot W & M
12 K7 South Ashford Kent
9 M9 South Baddesley Hants
94 F7 South Ballachulish Highld
64 D9 South Bank C York
70 H8 South Bank R & Cl
17 R11 South Barrow Somset
21 N10 South Beddington Gt Lon
4 J2 South Beer Cnwll
22 J10 South Benfleet Essex
10 E10 South Bersted W Susx
8 H9 South Bockhampton Dorset
21 R9 Southborough Gt Lon
11 T2 Southborough Kent
8 G10 Southbourne Bmouth
10 B9 Southbourne W Susx
7 M5 South Bowood Dorset
57 T4 South Bramwith Donc
5 R8 South Brent Devon
17 T9 South Brewham Somset
17 Q3 South Bristol Crematorium Bristl
77 Q6 South Broomhill Nthumb
50 H12 Southburgh Norfk
51 Q12 South Burlingham Norfk
65 M9 Southburn E R Yk
17 R11 South Cadbury Somset
58 F11 South Carlton Lincs
57 S10 South Carlton Notts
65 L13 South Cave E R Yk
28 K8 South Cerney Gloucs
11 P7 South Chailey E Susx
6 K3 South Chard Somset
77 P1 South Charlton Nthumb
17 S12 South Cheriton Somset
69 R7 South Church Dur
23 M10 Southchurch Sthend
69 P9 South Cleatlam Dur
64 K12 South Cliffe E R Yk
58 D12 South Clifton Notts
59 Q9 South Cockerington Lincs
26 E11 South Cornelly Brdgnd
14 E13 Southcott Cnwll
5 T4 Southcott Devon
14 K9 Southcott Devon
15 M13 Southcott Devon
18 J9 Southcott Wilts
30 H10 Southcourt Bucks
41 S4 South Cove Suffk
50 E6 South Creake Norfk
56 H4 South Crosland Kirk
47 S11 South Croxton Leics
65 M10 South Dalton E R Yk
21 U9 South Darenth Kent
11 P9 South Downs National Park
64 F13 South Duffield N York
11 Q9 Southease E Susx
59 N9 South Elkington Lincs
57 Q4 South Elmsall Wakefd
79 M14 Southend Ag & B
59 Q3 South End E R Yk
8 G5 South End Hants
35 R12 South End Herefs
58 K2 South End N Linc
40 G2 South End Norfk
18 J6 Southend Wilts
23 L10 Southend Airport Essex
23 L10 Southend Crematorium Sthend
23 L10 Southend-on-Sea Sthend
67 N5 Southernby Cumb
12 G6 Southernden Kent
26 F13 Southerndown V Glam
66 E2 Southerness D & G
107 M10 South Erradale Highld
6 E6 Southerton Devon
39 T2 Southery Norfk
22 E10 South Essex Crematorium Gt Lon
23 L9 South Fambridge Essex
19 N4 South Fawley W Berk
58 G2 South Ferriby N Linc
58 H1 South Field E R Yk
82 F4 Southfield Falk
22 F13 Southfleet Kent
9 Q13 Southford IoW
21 N4 Southgate Gt Lon
49 U7 Southgate Norfk
50 E6 Southgate Norfk
50 K9 Southgate Norfk
25 U13 Southgate Swans
21 Q13 South Godstone Surrey
8 H6 South Gorley Hants
77 Q12 South Gosforth N u Ty
22 G9 South Green Essex
23 P4 South Green Essex
12 G3 South Green Kent
50 J11 South Green Norfk
41 L5 South Green Suffk
83 N4 South Gyle C Edin
22 H8 South Hanningfield Essex
10 B7 South Harting W Susx
9 U9 South Hayling Hants
85 R12 South Hazelrigg Nthumb
30 K12 South Heath Bucks
11 Q10 South Heighton E Susx
70 E3 South Hetton Dur
57 N4 South Hiendley Wakefd
4 J6 South Hill Cnwll
17 N11 South Hill Somset
30 B12 South Hinksey Oxon
14 F8 South Hole Devon
10 K2 South Holmwood Surrey
22 D11 South Hornchurch Gt Lon
17 Q7 South Horrington Somset
5 R12 South Huish Devon
58 F14 South Hykeham Lincs
70 E1 South Hylton Sundld
31 Q4 Southill C Beds
19 R11 Southington Hants
58 H7 South Kelsey Lincs
102 J6 South Kessock Highld
58 K3 South Killingholme N Linc
63 U3 South Kilvington N York
37 R4 South Kilworth Leics
57 P4 South Kirkby Wakefd
5 U6 South Knighton Devon
48 J4 South Kyme Lincs
82 C7 South Lanarkshire Crematorium S Lans
6 H6 Southleigh Devon
29 S6 South Leigh Oxon
58 C10 South Leverton Notts
36 E11 South Littleton Worcs
21 N9 South London Crematorium Gt Lon
40 H4 South Lopham Norfk
48 D13 South Luffenham Rutlnd
11 Q8 South Malling E Susx
29 N10 South Marston Swindn
21 N12 South Merstham Surrey
85 P14 South Middleton Nthumb
64 B13 South Milford N York
5 S12 South Milton Devon
31 R12 South Mimms Herts
31 R12 South Mimms Services Herts
23 N8 Southminster Essex
15 R7 South Molton Devon
69 Q2 South Moor Dur
29 S8 Southmoor Oxon
19 S3 South Moreton Oxon
98 F13 Southmuir Angus
10 D10 South Mundham W Susx
47 U2 South Muskham Notts
65 L12 South Newbald E R Yk
37 M14 South Newington Oxon
8 F2 South Newton Wilts
47 M2 South Normanton Derbys
21 P9 South Norwood Gt Lon
21 P13 South Nutfield Surrey
22 E11 South Ockendon Thurr
38 J8 Southoe Cambs
41 L7 Southolt Suffk
59 Q11 South Ormsby Lincs
48 G13 Southorpe C Pete
57 L3 South Ossett Wakefd
63 T2 South Otterington N York
7 R6 Southover Dorset
12 C10 Southover E Susx
58 J8 South Owersby Lincs
56 H2 Southowram Calder
21 M13 South Park Surrey
7 N3 South Perrott Dorset
17 M13 South Petherton Somset
4 J4 South Petherwin Cnwll
50 E13 South Pickenham Norfk
5 L9 South Pill Cnwll
5 T12 South Pool Devon
7 P5 South Poorton Dorset
54 H3 Southport Sefton
54 J4 Southport Crematorium Lancs
83 M3 South Queensferry C Edin
15 R6 South Radworthy Devon
48 F4 South Rauceby Lincs
50 E9 South Raynham Norfk
56 C8 South Reddish Stockp
51 N6 Southrepps Norfk
59 R10 South Reston Lincs
58 K13 Southrey Lincs
106 t21 South Ronaldsay Ork
29 N7 Southrop Gloucs
19 U12 Southrope Hants
49 T12 South Runcton Norfk
58 D14 South Scarle Notts
9 T9 Southsea C Port
44 H3 Southsea Wrexhm
94 C10 South Shian Ag & B
77 T12 South Shields S Tyne
77 S13 South Shields Crematorium S Tyne
61 Q13 South Shore Bpool
69 P7 Southside Dur
59 R8 South Somercotes Lincs
63 S7 South Stainley N York
22 E12 South Stifford Thurr
17 T4 South Stoke BaNES
19 S4 South Stoke Oxon
10 G9 South Stoke W Susx
12 K8 South Stour Kent
12 B3 South Street Kent
13 L4 South Street Kent
13 M2 South Street Kent
82 K8 South Tarbrax S Lans
5 R2 South Tawton Devon
2 H8 South Tehidy Cnwll
59 R11 South Thoresby Lincs
69 P10 South Thorpe Dur
19 U13 South Town Hants
51 T12 Southtown Norfk
16 K13 Southtown Somset
106 d15 South Uist W Isls
67 P3 Southwaite Cumb
67 P3 Southwaite Services Cumb
51 Q11 South Walsham Norfk
21 P7 Southwark Gt Lon
20 B13 South Warnborough Hants
10 K5 Southwater W Susx
10 J5 Southwater Street W Susx
17 P8 Southway Somset
22 E9 South Weald Essex
7 S10 Southwell Dorset
47 S3 Southwell Notts
20 K8 South West Middlesex Crematorium Gt Lon
20 B3 South Weston Oxon
4 G2 South Wheatley Cnwll
9 S7 Southwick Hants
38 F2 Southwick Nhants
17 L7 Southwick Somset
77 T14 Southwick Sundld
11 L9 Southwick W Susx
18 B9 Southwick Wilts
17 Q5 South Widcombe BaNES
47 Q14 South Wigston Leics
12 K7 South Willesborough Kent
59 L10 South Willingham Lincs
70 F6 South Wingate Dur
47 L2 South Wingfield Derbys
48 D10 South Witham Lincs
41 T5 Southwold Suffk
19 Q13 South Wonston Hants
51 Q12 Southwood Norfk
17 Q10 Southwood Somset
22 K8 South Woodham Ferrers Essex
49 T9 South Wootton Norfk
18 B8 South Wraxall Wilts
5 R2 South Zeal Devon
56 F2 Sowerby Calder
63 U3 Sowerby N York
56 G2 Sowerby Bridge Calder
67 N4 Sowerby Row Cumb
61 R11 Sower Carr Lancs
15 U8 Sowerhill Somset
27 P7 Sowhill Torfn
40 B10 Sowley Green Suffk
56 G3 Sowood Calder
5 N7 Sowton Devon
6 C6 Sowton Devon
56 F2 Soyland Town Calder
51 N7 Spa Common Norfk
39 U13 Spain's End Essex
48 K9 Spalding Lincs
64 H13 Spaldington E R Yk
38 H6 Spaldwick Cambs
58 D13 Spalford Notts
48 G6 Spanby Lincs
19 U9 Spanish Green Hants
50 J10 Sparham Norfk
50 J10 Sparhamill Norfk
61 Q3 Spark Bridge Cumb
67 P7 Sparket Cumb
17 R11 Sparkford Somset
36 F4 Sparkhill Birm
5 P9 Sparkwell Devon
50 F11 Sparrow Green Norfk
56 G10 Sparrowpit Derbys
12 B9 Sparrows Green E Susx
9 N2 Sparsholt Hants
29 R10 Sparsholt Oxon
68 J3 Spartylea Nthumb
46 E6 Spath Staffs
64 G2 Spaunton N York
16 H9 Spaxton Somset
94 J2 Spean Bridge Highld
10 J7 Spear Hill W Susx
9 L3 Spearywell Hants
20 D3 Speen Bucks
19 Q7 Speen W Berk
65 R5 Speeton N York
54 K10 Speke Lpool
11 T2 Speldhurst Kent
22 C4 Spellbrook Herts
12 D8 Spelmonden Kent
29 R3 Spelsbury Oxon
56 J1 Spen Kirk
20 B9 Spencers Wood Wokham
45 T1 Spen Green Ches E
63 N2 Spennithorne N York
69 S6 Spennymoor Dur
36 E8 Spernall Warwks
35 U10 Spetchley Worcs
8 C8 Spetisbury Dorset
41 Q4 Spexhall Suffk
104 D2 Spey Bay Moray
103 R10 Speybridge Highld
104 B7 Speyview Moray
59 R13 Spilsby Lincs
85 T12 Spindlestone Nthumb
57 Q11 Spinkhill Derbys
109 M7 Spinningdale Highld
57 S13 Spion Kop Notts
18 E5 Spirthill Wilts
54 H10 Spital Wirral
57 T8 Spital Hill Donc
58 G8 Spital in the Street Lincs
11 Q7 Spithurst E Susx
84 D3 Spittal E Loth
64 H9 Spittal E R Yk
112 E6 Spittal Highld
85 Q8 Spittal Nthumb
24 G6 Spittal Pembks
90 H3 Spittalfield P & K
98 E6 Spittal of Glenmuick Abers
97 U10 Spittal of Glenshee P & K
76 B2 Spittal-on-Rule Border
51 M10 Spixworth Norfk
3 N1 Splatt Cnwll
4 G3 Splatt Cnwll
15 P11 Splatt Devon
11 Q6 Splayne's Green E Susx
27 N12 Splottlands Cardif
63 T9 Spofforth N York
47 M6 Spondon C Derb
54 G14 Spon Green Flints
40 J1 Spooner Row Norfk
50 D11 Sporle Norfk
84 H3 Spott E Loth
84 G9 Spottiswoode Border
37 T7 Spratton Nhants
10 C2 Spreakley Surrey
15 Q13 Spreyton Devon
5 N10 Spriddlestone Devon
58 H10 Spridlington Lincs
89 P12 Springburn C Glas
75 R12 Springfield D & G
22 H6 Springfield Essex
91 M9 Springfield Fife
46 C13 Springhill Staffs
46 E12 Springhill Staffs
74 F11 Springholm D & G
81 M5 Springside N Ayrs
58 E9 Springthorpe Lincs
57 L6 Spring Vale Barns
77 R14 Springwell Sundld
54 K9 Springwood Crematorium Lpool
65 R13 Sproatley E R Yk
55 R13 Sproston Green Ches W
57 R6 Sprotbrough Donc
40 K12 Sproughton Suffk
84 K11 Sprouston Border
51 N11 Sprowston Norfk
48 C9 Sproxton Leics
64 E3 Sproxton N York
44 K7 Spunhill Shrops
45 N2 Spurstow Ches E
7 P6 Spyway Dorset
24 D4 Square & Compass Pembks
45 S14 Stableford Shrops
45 T6 Stableford Staffs
57 L8 Stacey Bank Sheff
62 G6 Stackhouse N York
24 G11 Stackpole Pembks
40 J2 Stacksford Norfk
56 C2 Stacksteads Lancs
5 N10 Staddiscombe C Plym
64 J14 Staddlethorpe E R Yk
56 G12 Staden Derbys
30 D13 Stadhampton Oxon
106 c15 Stadhlaigearraidh W Isls
67 R4 Staffield Cumb
100 d3 Staffin Highld
46 B9 Stafford Staffs
46 C9 Stafford Crematorium Staffs
45 U7 Stafford Services (northbound) Staffs
45 U7 Stafford Services (southbound) Staffs
38 E11 Stagsden Bed
57 M6 Stainborough Barns
66 F7 Stainburn Cumb
63 R10 Stainburn N York
48 D9 Stainby Lincs
57 M4 Staincross Barns
69 P8 Staindrop Dur
20 H8 Staines-upon-Thames Surrey
48 G9 Stainfield Lincs
58 K12 Stainfield Lincs
57 T4 Stainforth Donc
62 G6 Stainforth N York
61 Q12 Staining Lancs
56 G3 Stainland Calder
71 R11 Stainsacre N York
57 Q13 Stainsby Derbys
61 U2 Stainton Cumb
67 N1 Stainton Cumb
67 Q7 Stainton Cumb
57 S8 Stainton Donc
69 N9 Stainton Dur
70 G10 Stainton Middsb
69 P13 Stainton N York
58 J11 Stainton by Langworth Lincs
71 S13 Staintondale N York
59 L8 Stainton le Vale Lincs
61 N5 Stainton with Adgarley Cumb
66 K8 Stair Cumb
81 N8 Stair E Ayrs
57 N5 Stairfoot Barns
72 G9 Stairhaven D & G
71 N9 Staithes N York
77 R8 Stakeford Nthumb
61 S10 Stake Pool Lancs
9 T7 Stakes Hants
17 T13 Stalbridge Dorset
17 T13 Stalbridge Weston Dorset
51 Q8 Stalham Norfk
51 Q9 Stalham Green Norfk
12 J5 Stalisfield Green Kent
50 H14 Stalland Common Norfk
17 R13 Stallen Dorset
59 L4 Stallingborough NE Lin
62 J2 Stalling Busk N York
46 B6 Stallington Staffs
61 R10 Stalmine Lancs
61 R10 Stalmine Moss Side Lancs
56 E7 Stalybridge Tamesd
40 B13 Stambourne Essex
39 U13 Stambourne Green Essex
48 F12 Stamford Lincs
77 Q2 Stamford Nthumb
55 L13 Stamford Bridge Ches W
64 G8 Stamford Bridge E R Yk
77 M11 Stamfordham Nthumb
21 P5 Stamford Hill Gt Lon
61 R11 Stanah Lancs
31 R10 Stanborough Herts
31 L8 Stanbridge C Beds
8 E8 Stanbridge Dorset
63 L12 Stanbury C Brad
55 S5 Stand Bury
82 E5 Stand N Lans
82 H4 Standburn Falk
46 B12 Standeford Staffs
12 G7 Standen Kent
12 F9 Standen Street Kent
18 B10 Standerwick Somset
10 C4 Standford Hants
66 G6 Standingstone Cumb
28 E6 Standish Gloucs
55 N4 Standish Wigan
55 N5 Standish Lower Ground Wigan
29 S7 Standlake Oxon
9 N3 Standon Hants
31 U8 Standon Herts
45 T6 Standon Staffs
31 U9 Standon Green End Herts
40 K7 Standwell Green Suffk
82 G7 Stane N Lans
50 F9 Stanfield Norfk
31 Q4 Stanford C Beds
13 M8 Stanford Kent
44 H11 Stanford Shrops
35 Q10 Stanford Bishop Herefs
35 R7 Stanford Bridge Worcs
45 R9 Stanford Bridge Wrekin
19 S6 Stanford Dingley W Berk
29 R9 Stanford in the Vale Oxon
22 G11 Stanford le Hope Thurr
37 Q5 Stanford on Avon Nhants
47 P9 Stanford on Soar Notts
35 R7 Stanford on Teme Worcs
22 D7 Stanford Rivers Essex
57 Q12 Stanfree Derbys
71 L9 Stanghow R & Cl
38 K1 Stanground C Pete
62 E14 Stanhill Lancs
50 D6 Stanhoe Norfk
83 M13 Stanhope Border
69 L5 Stanhope Dur
12 K7 Stanhope Kent
46 J9 Stanhope Bretby Derbys
38 D3 Stanion Nhants
35 U6 Stanklin Worcs
47 M5 Stanley Derbys
69 Q2 Stanley Dur
47 N1 Stanley Notts
90 H5 Stanley P & K
35 R4 Stanley Shrops
46 B3 Stanley Staffs
57 M2 Stanley Wakefd
47 M5 Stanley Common Derbys
69 Q5 Stanley Crook Dur
57 N2 Stanley Ferry Wakefd
54 K5 Stanley Gate Lancs
46 B3 Stanley Moor Staffs
28 K1 Stanley Pontlarge Gloucs
11 N9 Stanmer Br & H
21 L4 Stanmore Gt Lon
9 P3 Stanmore Hants
19 Q5 Stanmore W Berk
76 E8 Stannersburn Nthumb
40 E9 Stanningfield Suffk
63 Q13 Stanningley Leeds
77 Q10 Stannington Nthumb
57 L9 Stannington Sheff
77 Q9 Stannington Station Nthumb
34 H8 Stansbatch Herefs
40 C10 Stansfield Suffk
46 F3 Stanshope Staffs
40 D11 Stanstead Suffk
31 U10 Stanstead Abbotts Herts
12 B3 Stansted Kent
22 D3 Stansted Airport Essex
22 D2 Stansted Mountfitchet Essex
46 J10 Stanton Derbys
36 E14 Stanton Gloucs
27 Q3 Stanton Mons
77 N7 Stanton Nthumb
46 F4 Stanton Staffs
40 G6 Stanton Suffk
47 L8 Stanton by Bridge Derbys
47 N6 Stanton by Dale Derbys
17 Q4 Stanton Drew BaNES
29 N9 Stanton Fitzwarren Swindn
29 T6 Stanton Harcourt Oxon
47 N1 Stanton Hill Notts
56 K14 Stanton in Peak Derbys
35 L5 Stanton Lacy Shrops
57 L14 Stanton Lees Derbys
35 N2 Stanton Long Shrops
47 R7 Stanton on the Wolds Notts
17 S4 Stanton Prior BaNES
18 G8 Stanton St Bernard Wilts
30 C11 Stanton St John Oxon
18 D5 Stanton St Quintin Wilts
40 G7 Stanton Street Suffk
47 N11 Stanton under Bardon Leics
45 N9 Stanton upon Hine Heath Shrops
17 R4 Stanton Wick BaNES
28 D5 Stantway Gloucs
44 K9 Stanwardine in the Field Shrops
44 K8 Stanwardine in the Wood Shrops
23 M3 Stanway Essex
29 L1 Stanway Gloucs
23 N3 Stanway Green Essex
41 M6 Stanway Green Suffk
20 J8 Stanwell Surrey
20 H8 Stanwell Moor Surrey
38 E6 Stanwick Nhants
67 P1 Stanwix Cumb
106 c15 Staoinebrig W Isls
71 N14 Stape N York
8 F8 Stapehill Dorset
45 Q4 Stapeley Ches E
46 J9 Stapenhill Staffs
13 Q4 Staple Kent
16 D12 Staple Cross Devon
12 E11 Staple Cross E Susx
11 M5 Staplefield W Susx
16 J13 Staple Fitzpaine Somset
39 Q10 Stapleford Cambs
31 T9 Stapleford Herts
48 B10 Stapleford Leics
48 C2 Stapleford Lincs
47 N6 Stapleford Notts
18 G13 Stapleford Wilts
22 D9 Stapleford Abbotts Essex
22 D8 Stapleford Tawney Essex
16 H11 Staplegrove Somset
16 H12 Staplehay Somset
36 C6 Staple Hill Worcs
12 E7 Staplehurst Kent
9 Q11 Staplers IoW
13 L3 Staplestreet Kent
75 V11 Stapleton Cumb
34 H7 Stapleton Herefs
47 M14 Stapleton Leics
69 S10 Stapleton N York
45 L13 Stapleton Shrops
17 N12 Stapleton Somset
6 G2 Stapley Somset
38 J8 Staploe Bed
35 Q12 Staplow Herefs
91 M11 Star Fife
25 M4 Star Pembks
17 M5 Star Somset
63 S8 Starbeck N York
62 K5 Starbotton N York
6 C8 Starcross Devon
36 K6 Stareton Warwks
46 K2 Starkholmes Derbys
22 C1 Starlings Green Essex
12 E12 Starr's Green E Susx
41 M4 Starston Norfk
5 U12 Start Devon
69 M9 Startforth Dur
18 D4 Startley Wilts
13 R4 Statenborough Kent
55 Q9 Statham Warrtn
17 L11 Stathe Somset
47 U7 Stathern Leics
70 F5 Station Town Dur
38 H7 Staughton Green Cambs
38 H8 Staughton Highway Cambs
27 V5 Staunton Gloucs
28 E2 Staunton Gloucs
48 B5 Staunton in the Vale Notts
34 J8 Staunton on Arrow Herefs
34 J12 Staunton on Wye Herefs
61 R2 Staveley Cumb
67 Q13 Staveley Cumb
57 P12 Staveley Derbys
63 T7 Staveley N York
5 T8 Staverton Devon
28 G3 Staverton Gloucs
37 P8 Staverton Nhants
18 C8 Staverton Wilts
28 G3 Staverton Bridge Gloucs
17 L9 Stawell Somset
16 E12 Stawley Somset
112 J6 Staxigoe Highld
65 N4 Staxton N York
33 M3 Staylittle Cerdgn
33 S2 Staylittle Powys
61 R11 Staynall Lancs
47 U3 Staythorpe Notts
63 N10 Stead C Brad
63 M5 Stean N York
64 E5 Stearsby N York
16 J7 Steart Somset
22 G3 Stebbing Essex
22 G3 Stebbing Green Essex
36 F3 Stechford Birm
12 G8 Stede Quarter Kent
10 D6 Stedham W Susx
76 J14 Steel Nthumb
11 S4 Steel Cross E Susx
90 F13 Steelend Fife
76 A7 Steele Road Border
61 M4 Steel Green Cumb
45 M6 Steel Heath Shrops
35 M9 Steen's Bridge Herefs
9 U3 Steep Hants
9 Q13 Steephill IoW
56 F2 Steep Lane Calder
8 C12 Steeple Dorset
23 M7 Steeple Essex
18 D9 Steeple Ashton Wilts
29 U2 Steeple Aston Oxon
29 T3 Steeple Barton Oxon
39 U12 Steeple Bumpstead Essex
30 F7 Steeple Claydon Bucks
38 H4 Steeple Gidding Cambs
18 F13 Steeple Langford Wilts
31 S4 Steeple Morden Cambs
63 L11 Steeton C Brad
100 b4 Stein Highld
77 P13 Stella Gatesd
13 M6 Stelling Minnis Kent
17 M12 Stembridge Somset
3 Q5 Stenalees Cnwll
74 F7 Stenhouse D & G
82 G2 Stenhousemuir Falk
59 M10 Stenigot Lincs
100 d3 Stenscholl Highld
46 K7 Stenson Fields Derbys
84 G4 Stenton E Loth
106 j5 Steornabhagh W Isls
24 K9 Stepaside Pembks
74 G9 Stepford D & G
21 Q6 Stepney Gt Lon
56 D9 Stepping Hill Stockp
31 M5 Steppingley C Beds
89 Q12 Stepps N Lans
41 Q8 Sternfield Suffk
18 F9 Stert Wilts
39 T9 Stetchworth Cambs
31 R7 Stevenage Herts
12 D12 Steven's Crouch E Susx
80 K4 Stevenston N Ayrs
19 R11 Steventon Hants
29 U9 Steventon Oxon
39 S12 Steventon End Essex
38 E10 Stevington Bed
31 M4 Stewartby Bed
81 S1 Stewartfield S Lans
81 N3 Stewarton E Ayrs
30 J7 Stewkley Bucks
16 K13 Stewley Somset
59 Q9 Stewton Lincs
9 S11 Steyne Cross IoW
10 K8 Steyning W Susx
24 F9 Steynton Pembks
14 F10 Stibb Cnwll
50 G8 Stibbard Norfk
14 K10 Stibb Cross Devon
18 K8 Stibb Green Wilts
48 G14 Stibbington Cambs
84 J11 Stichill Border
3 P6 Sticker Cnwll
49 N1 Stickford Lincs
5 Q2 Sticklepath Devon
16 D9 Sticklepath Somset
39 Q14 Stickling Green Essex
49 M2 Stickney Lincs
50 G5 Stiffkey Norfk
35 R11 Stifford's Bridge Herefs
12 G3 Stiff Street Kent
12 E6 Stile Bridge Kent
17 N8 Stileway Somset
106 c15 Stilligarry W Isls
64 D11 Stillingfleet N York
64 D6 Stillington N York
70 E8 Stillington S on T
38 J3 Stilton Cambs
28 D8 Stinchcombe Gloucs
7 T6 Stinsford Dorset
44 J13 Stiperstones Shrops
36 E4 Stirchley Birm
45 Q12 Stirchley Wrekin
105 U7 Stirling Abers
89 S7 Stirling Stirlg
89 T8 Stirling Services Stirlg
38 J7 Stirtloe Cambs
62 K9 Stirton N York
22 K3 Stisted Essex
18 K7 Stitchcombe Wilts
2 J9 Stithians Cnwll
36 K5 Stivichall Covtry
59 L13 Stixwould Lincs
13 S7 St Margaret's Bay Kent
54 K12 Stoak Ches W
83 N11 Stobo Border
8 C11 Stoborough Dorset
8 C11 Stoborough Green Dorset
75 V4 Stobs Castle Border
77 Q6 Stobswood Nthumb
22 G8 Stock Essex
17 N4 Stock N Som
19 N13 Stockbridge Hants
82 E11 Stockbriggs S Lans
12 F3 Stockbury Kent
19 P7 Stockcross W Berk
67 N3 Stockdalewath Cumb
12 J5 Stocker's Hill Kent
48 B14 Stockerston Leics
36 C9 Stock Green Worcs
28 B1 Stocking Herefs
36 K2 Stockingford Warwks
22 C2 Stocking Pelham Herts
6 H4 Stockland Devon
16 H8 Stockland Bristol Somset
11 T2 Stockland Green Kent
15 U11 Stockleigh English Devon
15 U12 Stockleigh Pomeroy Devon
18 E7 Stockley Wilts
34 J13 Stockley Hill Herefs
17 L13 Stocklinch Somset
34 J10 Stockmoor Herefs
56 C8 Stockport Stockp
56 D9 Stockport Crematorium Stockp
57 L7 Stocksbridge Sheff
77 M13 Stocksfield Nthumb
35 M8 Stockton Herefs
41 Q2 Stockton Norfk
44 G13 Stockton Shrops
45 R14 Stockton Shrops
37 M8 Stockton Warwks
18 E13 Stockton Wilts
45 S10 Stockton Wrekin
46 B3 Stockton Brook Staffs
55 P9 Stockton Heath Warrtn
70 F9 Stockton-on-Tees S on T
35 R7 Stockton on Teme Worcs
64 F8 Stockton on the Forest C York
28 H5 Stockwell Gloucs
45 U13 Stockwell End Wolves
46 E9 Stockwell Heath Staffs
17 R3 Stockwood Bristl
7 Q3 Stockwood Dorset
36 D9 Stock Wood Worcs
61 T8 Stodday Lancs
13 P3 Stodmarsh Kent
50 J6 Stody Norfk
110 A11 Stoer Highld
7 Q2 Stoford Somset
18 G13 Stoford Wilts
16 E9 Stogumber Somset
16 H8 Stogursey Somset
37 L5 Stoke Covtry
14 F8 Stoke Devon
9 U8 Stoke Hants
19 P10 Stoke Hants
22 K13 Stoke Medway
7 N4 Stoke Abbott Dorset
38 B3 Stoke Albany Nhants
40 K6 Stoke Ash Suffk
47 R5 Stoke Bardolph Notts
35 Q8 Stoke Bliss Worcs
37 T11 Stoke Bruerne Nhants
40 B12 Stoke by Clare Suffk
40 G13 Stoke-by-Nayland Suffk
6 B5 Stoke Canon Devon
19 Q13 Stoke Charity Hants
4 K6 Stoke Climsland Cnwll
35 P10 Stoke Cross Herefs
20 K11 Stoke D'Abernon Surrey
38 F3 Stoke Doyle Nhants
38 C1 Stoke Dry Rutlnd
35 P12 Stoke Edith Herefs
36 G1 Stoke End Warwks
8 F3 Stoke Farthing Wilts
50 B13 Stoke Ferry Norfk
5 V11 Stoke Fleming Devon
8 B11 Stokeford Dorset
5 V9 Stoke Gabriel Devon
28 B12 Stoke Gifford S Glos
37 L1 Stoke Golding Leics
38 B11 Stoke Goldington M Keyn
20 G6 Stoke Green Bucks
58 C11 Stokeham Notts
30 J7 Stoke Hammond Bucks
45 Q8 Stoke Heath Shrops
36 B7 Stoke Heath Worcs
51 M13 Stoke Holy Cross Norfk
6 B10 Stokeinteignhead Devon
35 P11 Stoke Lacy Herefs
30 C7 Stoke Lyne Oxon
30 H10 Stoke Mandeville Bucks
20 C3 Stokenchurch Bucks
21 P5 Stoke Newington Gt Lon
5 U12 Stokenham Devon
45 U4 Stoke-on-Trent C Stke
28 H2 Stoke Orchard Gloucs
20 G6 Stoke Poges Bucks
36 C7 Stoke Pound Worcs
35 M9 Stoke Prior Herefs
36 B7 Stoke Prior Worcs
15 P5 Stoke Rivers Devon
48 D8 Stoke Rochford Lincs
19 U4 Stoke Row Oxon
16 K11 Stoke St Gregory Somset
16 J12 Stoke St Mary Somset
17 S7 Stoke St Michael Somset
35 N4 Stoke St Milborough Shrops
34 K4 Stokesay Shrops
34 K4 Stokesay Castle Shrops
51 R11 Stokesby Norfk
70 H11 Stokesley N York
17 N13 Stoke sub Hamdon Somset
30 E13 Stoke Talmage Oxon
17 T11 Stoke Trister Somset
45 P8 Stoke upon Tern Shrops
45 U4 Stoke-upon-Trent C Stke
7 U3 Stoke Wake Dorset
36 C7 Stoke Wharf Worcs
16 H7 Stolford Somset
22 E7 Stondon Massey Essex
30 G10 Stone Bucks
28 C8 Stone Gloucs
22 E13 Stone Kent
57 S9 Stone Rothm
17 Q10 Stone Somset
46 B7 Stone Staffs
35 U5 Stone Worcs
39 Q2 Stonea Cambs
17 L6 Stone Allerton Somset
17 R6 Ston Easton Somset
17 L5 Stonebridge N Som
40 F2 Stonebridge Norfk
36 H4 Stonebridge Warwks
49 L13 Stone Bridge Corner C Pete
47 M2 Stonebroom Derbys
63 N14 Stone Chair Calder
11 S5 Stone Cross E Susx
11 U10 Stone Cross E Susx
12 B9 Stone Cross E Susx
11 S3 Stone Cross Kent
12 K8 Stone Cross Kent
13 R4 Stone Cross Kent
40 D9 Stonecross Green Suffk
12 D9 Stonecrouch Kent
17 N2 Stone-edge-Batch N Som
65 Q13 Stoneferry C KuH
87 R11 Stonefield Castle Hotel Ag & B
12 C10 Stonegate E Susx
71 N11 Stonegate N York
64 F4 Stonegrave N York
35 U11 Stonehall Worcs
76 F10 Stonehaugh Nthumb
99 R6 Stonehaven Abers
18 H12 Stonehenge Wilts
57 U5 Stone Hill Donc
5 M10 Stonehouse C Plym
62 F2 Stone House Cumb
28 F6 Stonehouse Gloucs
76 D14 Stonehouse Nthumb
82 E9 Stonehouse S Lans
12 H10 Stone in Oxney Kent
36 K6 Stoneleigh Warwks
45 P3 Stoneley Green Ches E
38 H7 Stonely Cambs
9 U3 Stoner Hill Hants
48 B9 Stonesby Leics
29 S4 Stonesfield Oxon
23 S2 Stones Green Essex
21 U12 Stone Street Kent
40 G13 Stone Street Suffk
40 H12 Stone Street Suffk
41 Q4 Stone Street Suffk
13 L8 Stonestreet Green Kent
67 L10 Stonethwaite Cumb
104 B2 Stonewells Moray
22 E13 Stonewood Kent
106 c15 Stoneybridge W Isls
36 B5 Stoneybridge Worcs
82 J6 Stoneyburn W Loth
8 K6 Stoney Cross Hants
47 R13 Stoneygate C Leic
23 N8 Stoneyhills Essex
72 D9 Stoneykirk D & G
56 K11 Stoney Middleton Derbys
37 N2 Stoney Stanton Leics
17 T10 Stoney Stoke Somset
17 S9 Stoney Stratton Somset
44 J12 Stoney Stretton Shrops
105 P13 Stoneywood C Aber
89 S9 Stoneywood Falk
40 K9 Stonham Aspal Suffk
46 E13 Stonnall Staffs
20 B5 Stonor Oxon
37 T1 Stonton Wyville Leics
35 M7 Stony Cross Herefs
35 R11 Stony Cross Herefs
9 L5 Stonyford Hants
57 Q13 Stony Houghton Derbys
30 G4 Stony Stratford M Keyn
46 E11 Stonywell Staffs
15 Q6 Stoodleigh Devon
16 B13 Stoodleigh Devon
13 M8 Stop 24 Services Kent
10 G7 Stopham W Susx
31 P8 Stopsley Luton
3 N1 Stoptide Cnwll
54 H10 Storeton Wirral
35 R12 Storeyard Green Herefs
106 j5 Stornoway W Isls
106 j5 Stornoway Airport W Isls
35 S11 Storridge Herefs

9 L11 Totland IoW
57 M11 Totley Sheff
57 M10 Totley Brook Sheff
5 U8 Totnes Devon
47 P7 Toton Notts
92 F7 Totronald Ag & B
100 c3 Totscore Highld
21 P4 Tottenham Gt Lon
49 T11 Tottenhill Norfk
21 M4 Totteridge Gt Lon
31 L8 Totternhoe C Beds
55 S4 Tottington Bury
62 E13 Tottleworth Lancs
9 M6 Totton Hants
20 E7 Touchen End W & M
64 B11 Toulston N York
16 G10 Toulton Somset
109 R8 Toulvaddie Highld
12 E5 Tovil Kent
3 M2 Towan Cnwll
3 Q7 Towan Cnwll
88 D12 Toward Ag & B
88 D12 Toward Quay Ag & B
37 S11 Towcester Nhants
2 D9 Towednack Cnwll
30 F11 Towersey Oxon
104 E13 Towie Abers
69 P5 Tow Law Dur
39 P1 Town End Cambs
61 S3 Town End Cumb
67 M11 Town End Cumb
68 D7 Town End Cumb
88 J10 Townend W Duns
67 R3 Towngate Cumb
48 H11 Towngate Lincs
54 K5 Town Green Lancs
51 Q11 Town Green Norfk
56 J6 Townhead Barns
66 G5 Townhead Cumb
67 P12 Town Head Cumb
68 D6 Townhead Cumb
74 K8 Townhead D & G
62 G8 Town Head N York
74 D13 Townhead of Greenlaw D & G
90 H14 Townhill Fife
70 E5 Town Kelloe Dur
5 L6 Townlake Devon
55 Q7 Town Lane Wigan
11 Q7 Town Littleworth E Susx
55 P7 Town of Lowton Wigan
11 T4 Town Row E Susx
19 S9 Towns End Hants
7 L2 Townsend Somset
2 F10 Townshend Cnwll
40 C3 Town Street Suffk
28 D9 Townwell S Glos
85 L13 Town Yetholm Border
64 E8 Towthorpe C York
64 K7 Towthorpe E R Yk
64 B12 Towton N York
53 S7 Towyn Conwy
54 J9 Toxteth Lpool
59 Q14 Toynton All Saints Lincs
49 N1 Toynton Fen Side Lincs
59 R14 Toynton St Peter Lincs
21 S12 Toy's Hill Kent
81 N8 Trabboch E Ayrs
81 P8 Trabbochburn E Ayrs
2 J12 Traboe Cnwll
16 E12 Tracebridge Somset
103 N4 Tradespark Highld
26 H2 Trallong Powys
46 K2 Tramway Museum Derbys
83 T4 Tranent E Loth
54 H9 Tranmere Wirral
111 T6 Trantelbeg Highld
111 T6 Trantlemore Highld
77 P9 Tranwell Nthumb
26 B4 Trapp Carmth
84 F3 Traprain E Loth
36 F7 Trap's Green Warwks
19 N8 Trapshill W Berk
83 R12 Traquair Border
19 U7 Trash Green W Berk
62 J12 Trawden Lancs
33 N6 Trawscoed Cerdgn
43 P6 Trawsfynydd Gwynd
26 J9 Trealaw Rhondd
61 S13 Treales Lancs
52 C7 Trearddur Bay IoA
100 c4 Treaslane Highld
3 N1 Treator Cnwll
16 D2 Tre Aubrey V Glam
26 J9 Trebanog Rhondd
26 C7 Trebanos Neath
4 H5 Trebartha Cnwll
4 D3 Trebarwith Cnwll
4 H3 Trebeath Cnwll
4 A5 Trebetherick Cnwll
16 D9 Treborough Somset
3 M4 Trebudannon Cnwll
4 J5 Trebullett Cnwll
4 D5 Treburgett Cnwll
4 K5 Treburley Cnwll
3 M2 Treburrick Cnwll
3 R4 Trebyan Cnwll
26 F2 Trecastle Powys
4 J4 Trecogo Cnwll
15 P12 Trecott Devon
24 G4 Trecwn Pembks
26 H7 Trecynon Rhondd
4 G4 Tredaule Cnwll
2 D11 Tredavoe Cnwll
27 L6 Tredegar Blae G
3 R2 Tredethy Cnwll
28 H2 Tredington Gloucs
36 J12 Tredington Warwks
3 N2 Tredinnick Cnwll
3 Q5 Tredinnick Cnwll
4 F7 Tredinnick Cnwll
4 G9 Tredinnick Cnwll
4 H9 Tredinnick Cnwll
27 L1 Tredomen Powys
24 J2 Tredrissi Pembks
4 B5 Tredrizzick Cnwll
27 R9 Tredunnock Mons
27 L1 Tredustan Powys
2 B12 Treen Cnwll
2 C9 Treen Cnwll
3 R5 Treesmill Cnwll
57 P9 Treeton Rothm
24 E3 Trefasser Pembks
52 F8 Trefdraeth IoA
27 L1 Trefecca Powys
33 U2 Trefeglwys Powys
33 M7 Trefenter Cerdgn
24 G6 Treffgarne Pembks
24 E5 Treffgarne Owen Pembks
26 K10 Trefforest Rhondd
24 E5 Treffynnon Pembks
27 L5 Trefil Blae G
32 K9 Trefilan Cerdgn
24 D4 Trefin Pembks
44 G8 Treflach Wood Shrops
44 F10 Trefnannau Powys
54 C12 Trefnant Denbgs
44 G8 Trefonen Shrops
42 G4 Trefor Gwynd
52 E6 Trefor IoA
4 E4 Trefrew Cnwll
53 N10 Trefriw Conwy
4 H4 Tregadillett Cnwll
27 U6 Tre-gagle Mons
52 G6 Tregaian IoA
27 S5 Tregare Mons
2 K12 Tregarne Cnwll
33 N9 Tregaron Cerdgn
52 K9 Tregarth Gwynd
3 M4 Tregaswith Cnwll
4 D3 Tregatta Cnwll
3 Q3 Tregawne Cnwll
4 G3 Tregeare Cnwll
44 E7 Tregeiriog Wrexhm
52 E4 Tregele IoA
4 C5 Tregellist Cnwll
3 M8 Tregenna Cnwll
2 B10 Tregeseal Cnwll
3 L10 Tregew Cnwll
26 H6 Tre-Gibbon Rhondd
2 K12 Tregidden Cnwll
3 Q7 Tregiskey Cnwll
24 D5 Treglemais Pembks
14 E13 Tregole Cnwll
2 J9 Tregolls Cnwll
3 N2 Tregonce Cnwll
3 P4 Tregonetha Cnwll
3 N8 Tregony Cnwll
4 E4 Tregoodwell Cnwll
3 Q6 Tregorrick Cnwll
3 P4 Tregoss Cnwll
34 E13 Tregoyd Powys
3 Q6 Tregrehan Mills Cnwll
32 H12 Tre-groes Cerdgn
3 R4 Tregullon Cnwll
3 P2 Tregunna Cnwll
4 G4 Tregunnon Cnwll
3 M3 Tregurrian Cnwll
44 C14 Tregynon Powys
25 R7 Tre-gynwr Carmth
26 J9 Trehafod Rhondd
5 L9 Trehan Cnwll
26 K8 Treharris Myr Td
4 C5 Treharrock Cnwll
3 M2 Trehemborne Cnwll
33 L11 Treherbert Carmth
26 G8 Treherbert Rhondd
4 J8 Trehunist Cnwll
4 J5 Trekenner Cnwll
4 D3 Treknow Cnwll
2 J13 Trelan Cnwll
4 F2 Trelash Cnwll
3 M6 Trelassick Cnwll
4 G10 Trelawne Cnwll
54 C11 Trelawnyd Flints
2 K12 Treleague Cnwll
2 K13 Treleaver Cnwll
25 N4 Trelech Carmth
25 P5 Trelech a'r Betws Carmth
24 C5 Treleddyd-fawr Pembks
3 L9 Trelew Cnwll
27 L8 Trelewis Myr Td
4 C4 Treligga Cnwll
4 B5 Trelights Cnwll
4 C5 Trelill Cnwll
4 J4 Trelinnoe Cnwll
3 N6 Trelion Cnwll
3 L9 Trelissick Cnwll
3 L9 Trelissick Garden Cnwll
27 U6 Trellech Mons
27 T7 Trelleck Grange Mons
54 D10 Trelogan Flints
3 N3 Trelow Cnwll
2 J12 Trelowarren Cnwll
4 H9 Trelowia Cnwll
3 M9 Treluggan Cnwll
44 G13 Trelystan Powys
43 L6 Tremadog Gwynd
4 F3 Tremail Cnwll
32 D11 Tremain Cerdgn
4 G3 Tremaine Cnwll
4 H7 Tremar Cnwll
4 K9 Trematon Cnwll
4 H7 Trembraze Cnwll
54 C12 Tremeirchion Denbgs
2 C10 Tremethick Cross Cnwll
3 Q4 Tremore Cnwll
54 D11 Tre-Mostyn Flints
3 L12 Trenance Cnwll
3 M3 Trenance Cnwll
3 N2 Trenance Cnwll
3 Q7 Trenarren Cnwll
45 Q11 Trench Wrekin
19 U5 Trench Green Oxon
3 M6 Trendeal Cnwll
2 D9 Trendrine Cnwll
3 P2 Treneague Cnwll
2 H10 Trenear Cnwll
4 G3 Treneglos Cnwll
2 G9 Trenerth Cnwll
4 F10 Trenewan Cnwll
4 D5 Trenewth Cnwll
4 F2 Trengune Cnwll
3 L4 Treninnick Cnwll
2 K5 Trenowah Cnwll
2 K10 Trenoweth Cnwll
17 Q13 Trent Dorset
45 U5 Trentham C Stke
15 P3 Trentishoe Devon
47 N7 Trentlock Derbys
58 D10 Trent Port Lincs
45 U5 Trent Vale C Stke
2 G10 Trenwheal Cnwll
26 G12 Treoes V Glam
26 H8 Treorchy Rhondd
4 C5 Trequite Cnwll
33 N2 Tre'r-ddol Cerdgn
26 J12 Trerhyngyll V Glam
4 J9 Trerulefoot Cnwll
32 E10 Tresaith Cerdgn
3 M7 Tresawle Cnwll
2 b2 Tresco IoS
2 b2 Tresco Heliport IoS
35 U1 Trescott Staffs
2 F10 Trescowe Cnwll
2 K5 Tresean Cnwll
28 E9 Tresham Gloucs
92 G10 Treshnish Isles Ag & B
3 M7 Tresillian Cnwll
4 E4 Tresinney Cnwll
14 F13 Treskinnick Cross Cnwll
4 G3 Tresmeer Cnwll
4 E2 Tresparrett Cnwll
97 N11 Tressait P & K
106 t8 Tresta Shet
106 w4 Tresta Shet
58 C11 Treswell Notts
2 G8 Treswithian Cnwll
2 G8 Treswithian Downs Crematorium Cnwll
33 N2 Tre Taliesin Cerdgn
4 D3 Trethevey Cnwll
2 B12 Trethewey Cnwll
27 M10 Trethomas Caerph
3 N6 Trethosa Cnwll
3 Q5 Trethurgy Cnwll
24 C5 Tretio Pembks
27 U3 Tretire Herefs
27 M3 Tretower Powys
44 G2 Treuddyn Flints
4 H5 Trevadlock Cnwll
4 D2 Trevalga Cnwll
44 J2 Trevalyn Wrexhm
4 B5 Trevanger Cnwll
3 P2 Trevanson Cnwll
2 D10 Trevarrack Cnwll
3 N4 Trevarren Cnwll
3 M3 Trevarrian Cnwll
3 P8 Trevarrick Cnwll
2 J8 Trevarth Cnwll
25 M7 Trevaughan Carmth
25 Q6 Tre-Vaughan Carmth
2 D8 Treveal Cnwll
2 K5 Treveal Cnwll
4 D5 Treveighan Cnwll
2 J6 Trevellas Downs Cnwll
4 G8 Trevelmond Cnwll
3 L5 Trevemper Cnwll
3 P8 Treveor Cnwll
3 M7 Treverbyn Cnwll
3 Q5 Treverbyn Cnwll
2 K10 Treverva Cnwll
2 B12 Trevescan Cnwll
27 P7 Trevethin Torfn
4 D4 Trevia Cnwll
4 J7 Trevigro Cnwll
3 L9 Trevilla Cnwll
3 L5 Trevilson Cnwll
3 N5 Treviscoe Cnwll
3 N8 Treviskey Cnwll
3 M4 Trevithick Cnwll
3 P7 Trevithick Cnwll
3 L5 Trevoll Cnwll
3 M1 Trevone Cnwll
44 G5 Trevor Wrexhm
2 C11 Trevorgans Cnwll
3 N2 Trevorrick Cnwll
3 M1 Trevose Cnwll
2 G11 Trew Cnwll
4 D4 Trewalder Cnwll
27 M1 Trewalkin Powys
4 D3 Trewarmett Cnwll
4 E3 Trewassa Cnwll
2 F11 Trewavas Cnwll
4 G4 Treween Cnwll
2 B10 Trewellard Cnwll
4 H4 Trewen Cnwll
2 H11 Trewennack Cnwll
24 H11 Trewent Pembks
44 G11 Trewern Powys
4 C4 Trewetha Cnwll
3 Q1 Trewethern Cnwll
4 H9 Trewidland Cnwll
2 K13 Trewillis Cnwll
4 G4 Trewint Cnwll
4 H8 Trewint Cnwll
3 M9 Trewithian Cnwll
4 J6 Trewoodloe Cnwll
2 H13 Trewoon Cnwll
3 P6 Trewoon Cnwll
3 M8 Treworga Cnwll
3 L7 Treworgan Cnwll
3 M9 Treworlas Cnwll
4 E2 Treworld Cnwll
3 M9 Treworthal Cnwll
27 Q3 Tre-wyn Mons
3 M2 Treyarnon Cnwll
10 C7 Treyford W Susx
8 F8 Trickett's Cross Dorset
76 B12 Triermain Cumb
24 G6 Triffleton Pembks
4 H3 Trillacott Cnwll
70 E6 Trimdon Dur
70 E5 Trimdon Colliery Dur
70 E5 Trimdon Grange Dur
51 N6 Trimingham Norfk
41 N13 Trimley Lower Street Suffk
41 N13 Trimley St Martin Suffk
41 N13 Trimley St Mary Suffk
35 S5 Trimpley Worcs
25 S10 Trimsaran Carmth
22 C4 Trims Green Herts
15 M4 Trimstone Devon
95 U6 Trinafour P & K
27 N8 Trinant Caerph
30 K10 Tring Herts
30 K10 Tringford Herts
30 K10 Tring Wharf Herts
99 L11 Trinity Angus
7 d2 Trinity Jersey
90 E8 Trinity Gask P & K
16 G9 Triscombe Somset
94 F4 Trislaig Highld
3 L6 Trispen Cnwll
77 Q7 Tritlington Nthumb
3 M5 Troan Cnwll
90 E3 Trochry P & K
27 L7 Troedrhiwfuwch Caerph
32 F11 Troedyraur Cerdgn
26 K7 Troedyrhiw Myr Td
53 Q8 Trofarth Conwy
7 c2 Trois Bois Jersey
2 H9 Troon Cnwll
81 L6 Troon S Ayrs
63 S12 Tropical World Roundhay Park Leeds
89 M4 Trossachs Stirlg
89 L4 Trossachs Pier Stirlg
40 E6 Troston Suffk
4 H2 Troswell Cnwll
35 U9 Trotshill Worcs
12 B3 Trottiscliffe Kent
10 C6 Trotton W Susx
76 H7 Troughend Nthumb
56 C2 Trough Gate Lancs
67 N7 Troutbeck Cumb
67 P12 Troutbeck Cumb
67 P12 Troutbeck Bridge Cumb
57 N11 Troway Derbys
18 C9 Trowbridge Wilts
47 N6 Trowell Notts
47 N5 Trowell Services Notts
18 B9 Trowle Common Wilts
31 N10 Trowley Bottom Herts
51 M12 Trowse Newton Norfk
63 Q12 Troy Leeds
17 T8 Trudoxhill Somset
16 H12 Trull Somset
57 T4 Trumfleet Donc
100 b3 Trumpan Highld
35 Q13 Trumpet Herefs
39 P10 Trumpington Cambs
20 G9 Trumpsgreen Surrey
51 N7 Trunch Norfk
61 Q11 Trunnah Lancs
3 L8 Truro Cnwll
3 L8 Truro Cathedral Cnwll
4 H3 Truscott Cnwll
5 V4 Trusham Devon
46 J6 Trusley Derbys
59 T10 Trusthorpe Lincs
35 U2 Trysull Staffs
29 T8 Tubney Oxon
5 U9 Tuckenhay Devon
35 S3 Tuckhill Shrops
2 H8 Tuckingmill Cnwll
8 C3 Tuckingmill Wilts
8 G10 Tuckton Bmouth
3 P7 Tucoyse Cnwll
40 B6 Tuddenham Suffk
41 L11 Tuddenham Suffk
12 B6 Tudeley Kent
69 S5 Tudhoe Dur
28 A3 Tudorville Herefs
42 D6 Tudweiliog Gwynd
10 F2 Tuesley Surrey
28 F5 Tuffley Gloucs
19 Q11 Tufton Hants
24 H5 Tufton Pembks
47 U13 Tugby Leics
35 N3 Tugford Shrops
85 U13 Tughall Nthumb
90 C12 Tullibody Clacks
102 H10 Tullich Highld
109 R9 Tullich Highld
97 S13 Tulliemet P & K
105 N9 Tulloch Abers
87 T6 Tullochgorm Ag & B
96 D7 Tulloch Station Highld
98 B13 Tullymurdoch P & K
104 H12 Tullynessle Abers
21 P8 Tulse Hill Gt Lon
25 T8 Tumble Carmth
22 K2 Tumbler's Green Essex
48 K2 Tumby Lincs
49 L2 Tumby Woodside Lincs
95 V7 Tummel Bridge P & K
11 T3 Tunbridge Wells Kent
75 N9 Tundergarth D & G
51 N8 Tungate Norfk
17 S5 Tunley BaNES
45 U3 Tunstall C Stke
65 U13 Tunstall E R Yk
12 G3 Tunstall Kent
62 C5 Tunstall Lancs
69 R13 Tunstall N York
51 R12 Tunstall Norfk
45 S8 Tunstall Staffs
41 Q9 Tunstall Suffk
70 E2 Tunstall Sundld
56 H12 Tunstead Derbys
51 N9 Tunstead Norfk
56 F10 Tunstead Milton Derbys
19 U11 Tunworth Hants
35 M12 Tupsley Herefs
19 U9 Turgis Green Hants
29 M4 Turkdean Gloucs
37 T2 Tur Langton Leics
18 B8 Turleigh Wilts
35 S3 Turleygreen Shrops
55 T3 Turn Lancs
34 J13 Turnastone Herefs
80 J11 Turnberry S Ayrs
5 M10 Turnchapel C Plym
46 J4 Turnditch Derbys
62 C13 Turner Green Lancs
11 U7 Turner's Green E Susx
36 G7 Turner's Green Warwks
11 N3 Turner's Hill W Susx
8 A10 Turners Puddle Dorset
31 U12 Turnford Herts
83 N4 Turnhouse C Edin
7 V3 Turnworth Dorset
105 L5 Turriff Abers
55 R3 Turton Bottoms Bl w D
39 M1 Turves Cambs
38 D10 Turvey Bed
20 C4 Turville Bucks
20 B4 Turville Heath Bucks
30 D5 Turweston Bucks
75 R2 Tushielaw Inn Border
46 H8 Tutbury Staffs
36 C6 Tutnall Worcs
27 U9 Tutshill Gloucs
51 M8 Tuttington Norfk
4 K5 Tutwell Cnwll
58 B12 Tuxford Notts
106 r17 Twatt Ork
106 t8 Twatt Shet
89 Q10 Twechar E Duns
84 E12 Tweedbank Border
85 P8 Tweedmouth Nthumb
83 M14 Tweedsmuir Border
2 K8 Twelveheads Cnwll
12 C11 Twelve Oaks E Susx
55 S13 Twemlow Green Ches E
48 J9 Twenty Lincs
17 T4 Twerton BaNES
21 L8 Twickenham Gt Lon
28 F3 Twigworth Gloucs
11 M7 Twineham W Susx
11 M6 Twineham Green W Susx
17 U5 Twinhoe BaNES
40 E13 Twinstead Essex
15 S6 Twitchen Devon
34 J5 Twitchen Shrops
13 Q4 Twitham Kent
5 Q6 Two Bridges Devon
57 L14 Two Dales Derbys
46 H13 Two Gates Staffs
5 U7 Two Mile Oak Cross Devon
15 M4 Two Pots Devon
31 N11 Two Waters Herts
46 K13 Twycross Leics
46 K12 Twycross Zoo Leics
30 E7 Twyford Bucks
9 P4 Twyford Hants
47 T11 Twyford Leics
48 D9 Twyford Lincs
50 H9 Twyford Norfk
20 C7 Twyford Wokham
35 M13 Twyford Common Herefs
27 L6 Twyn-carno Caerph
73 R9 Twynholm D & G
36 B13 Twyning Green Gloucs
26 D3 Twynllanan Carmth
27 L13 Twyn-yr-Odyn V Glam
27 S6 Twyn-y-Sheriff Mons
38 E5 Twywell Nhants
34 J13 Tyberton Herefs
36 F2 Tyburn Birm
25 V8 Tycroes Carmth
52 D8 Ty Croes IoA
44 D10 Tycrwyn Powys
49 Q10 Tydd Gote Lincs
49 P10 Tydd St Giles Cambs
49 P10 Tydd St Mary Lincs
9 U8 Tye Hants
22 D3 Tye Green Essex
22 J3 Tye Green Essex
39 S13 Tye Green Essex
63 P13 Tyersal C Brad
55 Q6 Tyldesley Wigan
13 M3 Tyler Hill Kent
20 F4 Tylers Green Bucks
22 D6 Tyler's Green Essex
21 Q12 Tylers Green Surrey
26 J8 Tylorstown Rhondd
33 U4 Tylwch Powys
43 U5 Ty-nant Conwy
43 T8 Ty-nant Gwynd
95 L12 Tyndrum Stirlg
44 F5 Ty'n-dwr Denbgs
77 T12 Tynemouth N Tyne
77 S12 Tynemouth Crematorium N Tyne
26 G8 Tynewydd Rhondd
84 G3 Tyninghame E Loth
74 F7 Tynron D & G
17 P2 Tyntesfield N Som
26 J10 Ty'n-y-bryn Rhondd
27 M10 Ty'n-y-coedcae Caerph
52 H6 Tynygongl IoA
33 N7 Tynygraig Cerdgn
53 N8 Ty'n-y-Groes Conwy
26 K10 Tyn-y-nant Rhondd
38 C11 Tyringham M Keyn
36 F4 Tyseley Birm
26 F12 Tythegston Brdgnd
56 D11 Tytherington Ches E
28 C10 Tytherington S Glos
17 U8 Tytherington Somset
18 D12 Tytherington Wilts
6 K4 Tytherleigh Devon
18 D6 Tytherton Lucas Wilts
31 Q11 Tyttenhanger Herts
3 R6 Tywardreath Cnwll
3 R5 Tywardreath Highway Cnwll
53 N7 Tywyn Conwy
43 L13 Tywyn Gwynd

U

41 P6 Ubbeston Green Suffk
17 P5 Ubley BaNES
69 R12 Uckerby N York
11 R6 Uckfield E Susx
35 U13 Uckinghall Worcs
28 H3 Uckington Gloucs
45 N11 Uckington Shrops
82 C6 Uddingston S Lans
82 G12 Uddington S Lans
12 G12 Udimore E Susx
105 P10 Udny Green Abers
105 Q11 Udny Station Abers
18 H5 Uffcott Wilts
6 E2 Uffculme Devon
48 G12 Uffington Lincs
29 R10 Uffington Oxon
45 M11 Uffington Shrops
48 G13 Ufford C Pete
41 N10 Ufford Suffk
37 L8 Ufton Warwks
19 T7 Ufton Nervet W Berk
79 P10 Ugadale Ag & B
5 R9 Ugborough Devon
41 R4 Uggeshall Suffk
71 Q11 Ugglebarnby N York
57 L8 Ughill Sheff
22 D2 Ugley Essex
22 D2 Ugley Green Essex
71 N10 Ugthorpe N York
106 d15 Uibhist A Deas W Isls
106 c11 Uibhist A Tuath W Isls
92 F8 Uig Ag & B
100 a4 Uig Highld
100 c3 Uig Highld
106 f5 Uig W Isls
100 d5 Uigshader Highld
86 F2 Uisken Ag & B
112 H8 Ulbster Highld
67 P8 Ulcat Row Cumb
59 R12 Ulceby Lincs
58 K4 Ulceby N Linc
58 K3 Ulceby Skitter N Linc
12 F6 Ulcombe Kent
66 K5 Uldale Cumb
28 E8 Uley Gloucs
77 Q7 Ulgham Nthumb
108 A6 Ullapool Highld
36 F7 Ullenhall Warwks
28 H4 Ullenwood Gloucs
64 C12 Ulleskelf N York
37 P3 Ullesthorpe Leics
57 Q9 Ulley Rothm
35 N11 Ullingswick Herefs
100 c6 Ullinish Lodge Hotel Highld
66 G8 Ullock Cumb
67 P8 Ullswater Cumb
61 T3 Ulpha Cumb
66 J14 Ulpha Cumb
65 R8 Ulrome E R Yk
106 u5 Ulsta Shet
22 K6 Ulting Wick Essex
92 K10 Ulva Ag & B
36 F4 Ulverley Green Solhll
61 P4 Ulverston Cumb
8 E12 Ulwell Dorset
74 E4 Ulzieside D & G
15 P8 Umberleigh Devon
110 E10 Unapool Highld
61 T1 Underbarrow Cumb
75 U9 Under Burnmouth Border
63 P13 Undercliffe C Brad
45 M11 Underdale Shrops
12 E6 Underling Green Kent
21 U12 Under River Kent
47 N3 Underwood Notts
39 U4 Undley Suffk
27 S10 Undy Mons
60 f7 Union Mills IoM
12 D9 Union Street E Susx
106 v3 Unst Shet
57 N11 Unstone Derbys
57 N11 Unstone Green Derbys
67 N3 Unthank Cumb
67 Q5 Unthank Cumb
68 D4 Unthank Cumb
57 M11 Unthank Derbys
85 P9 Unthank Nthumb
18 H10 Upavon Wilts
7 S4 Up Cerne Dorset
12 F2 Upchurch Kent
15 S7 Upcott Devon
34 H10 Upcott Herefs
40 B9 Upend Cambs
6 B4 Up Exe Devon
50 K10 Upgate Norfk
40 J2 Upgate Street Norfk
41 N2 Upgate Street Norfk
7 Q4 Uphall Dorset
83 L4 Uphall W Loth
15 U11 Upham Devon
9 Q4 Upham Hants
34 J8 Uphampton Herefs
35 T8 Uphampton Worcs
16 K5 Uphill N Som
55 M5 Up Holland Lancs
81 N1 Uplawmoor E Rens
28 E2 Upleadon Gloucs
70 K9 Upleatham R & Cl
12 K3 Uplees Kent
7 P6 Uploders Dorset
16 D13 Uplowman Devon
6 K6 Uplyme Devon
10 B8 Up Marden W Susx
22 E10 Upminster Gt Lon
17 Q13 Up Mudford Somset
19 U10 Up Nately Hants
6 H3 Upottery Devon
34 K3 Upper Affcot Shrops
109 L7 Upper Ardchronie Highld
35 S4 Upper Arley Worcs
30 D9 Upper Arncott Oxon
30 B5 Upper Astrop Nhants
19 S5 Upper Basildon W Berk
56 K1 Upper Batley Kirk
10 K8 Upper Beeding W Susx
38 E3 Upper Benefield Nhants
36 C7 Upper Bentley Worcs
111 T5 Upper Bighouse Highld
47 M2 Upper Birchwood Derbys
27 L10 Upper Boat Rhondd
37 N10 Upper Boddington Nhants
33 M3 Upper Borth Cerdgn
36 K13 Upper Brailes Warwks
100 f7 Upper Breakish Highld
35 L12 Upper Breinton Herefs
35 T9 Upper Broadheath Worcs
47 S8 Upper Broughton Notts
19 R7 Upper Bucklebury W Berk
8 H5 Upper Burgate Hants
12 C2 Upper Bush Medway
67 P2 Upperby Cumb
38 J11 Upper Caldecote C Beds
17 L5 Upper Canada N Som
8 K6 Upper Canterton Hants
37 P9 Upper Catesby Nhants
36 C6 Upper Catshill Worcs
34 B12 Upper Chapel Powys
16 H11 Upper Cheddon Somset
8 D3 Upper Chicksgrove Wilts
19 L10 Upper Chute Wilts
21 P5 Upper Clapton Gt Lon
19 N12 Upper Clatford Hants
28 J4 Upper Coberley Gloucs
10 K9 Upper Cokeham W Susx
46 E4 Upper Cotton Staffs
45 N12 Upper Cound Shrops
57 N5 Upper Cudworth Barns
56 K5 Upper Cumberworth Kirk
104 D3 Upper Dallachy Moray
13 S5 Upper Deal Kent
38 F7 Upper Dean Bed
56 K5 Upper Denby Kirk
76 C12 Upper Denton Cumb
11 T9 Upper Dicker E Susx
35 L4 Upper Dinchope Shrops
112 B3 Upper Dounreay Highld
23 T1 Upper Dovercourt Essex
89 Q4 Upper Drumbane Stirlg
63 U7 Upper Dunsforth N York
10 F2 Upper Eashing Surrey
103 L3 Upper Eathie Highld
35 P12 Upper Egleton Herefs
46 E2 Upper Elkstone Staffs
46 F5 Upper Ellastone Staffs
56 G11 Upper End Derbys
19 N10 Upper Enham Hants
35 S2 Upper Farmcote Shrops
19 V13 Upper Farringdon Hants
28 E5 Upper Framilode Gloucs
10 B2 Upper Froyle Hants
100 c4 Upperglen Highld
17 N8 Upper Godney Somset
31 P5 Upper Gravenhurst C Beds
27 R4 Upper Green Mons
40 B8 Upper Green Suffk
19 N8 Upper Green W Berk
27 V2 Upper Grove Common Herefs
46 J1 Upper Hackney Derbys
20 D13 Upper Hale Surrey
20 J9 Upper Halliford Surrey
12 C3 Upper Halling Medway
48 D12 Upper Hambleton Rutlnd
13 M4 Upper Harbledown Kent
13 N5 Upper Hardres Court Kent
34 K9 Upper Hardwick Herefs
11 R4 Upper Hartfield E Susx
47 L3 Upper Hartshay Derbys
28 H3 Upper Hatherley Gloucs
45 T6 Upper Hatton Staffs
57 P7 Upper Haugh Rothm
35 M4 Upper Hayton Shrops
56 J3 Upper Heaton Kirk
64 F8 Upper Helmsley N York
34 G10 Upper Hergest Herefs
37 S9 Upper Heyford Nhants
29 U2 Upper Heyford Oxon
35 L10 Upper Hill Herefs
21 T9 Upper Hockenden Kent
56 J3 Upper Hopton Kirk
35 S11 Upper Howsell Worcs
46 D1 Upper Hulme Staffs
10 G4 Upper Ifold Surrey
29 P8 Upper Inglesham Swindn
28 E10 Upper Kilcott Gloucs
25 U12 Upper Killay Swans
94 H13 Upper Kinchrackine Ag & B
19 M4 Upper Lambourn W Berk
46 C12 Upper Landywood Staffs
17 N5 Upper Langford N Som
57 R13 Upper Langwith Derbys
91 P11 Upper Largo Fife
46 D6 Upper Leigh Staffs
17 Q4 Upper Littleton N Som
99 M4 Upper Lochton Abers
46 E11 Upper Longdon Staffs
31 Q6 Upper & Lower Stondon C Beds
35 T1 Upper Ludstone Shrops
112 G9 Upper Lybster Highld
28 B4 Upper Lydbrook Gloucs
35 L12 Upper Lyde Herefs
34 J7 Upper Lye Herefs
34 H14 Upper Maes-coed Herefs
56 K7 Upper Midhope Sheff
56 E5 Uppermill Oldham
35 T6 Upper Milton Worcs
28 K9 Upper Minety Wilts
36 C11 Upper Moor Worcs
63 Q13 Upper Moor Side Leeds
104 D5 Upper Mulben Moray
35 P2 Upper Netchwood Shrops
46 D6 Upper Nobut Staffs
10 E7 Upper Norwood W Susx
56 K11 Upper Padley Derbys
9 L9 Upper Pennington Hants
30 F10 Upper Pollicott Bucks
64 D9 Upper Poppleton C York
36 G11 Upper Quinton Warwks
9 L4 Upper Ratley Hants
29 P4 Upper Rissington Gloucs
35 P7 Upper Rochford Worcs
73 P7 Upper Ruscoe D & G
35 Q8 Upper Sapey Herefs
18 D4 Upper Seagry Wilts
31 L4 Upper Shelton C Beds
50 K5 Upper Sheringham Norfk
88 F12 Upper Skelmorlie N Ayrs
29 N3 Upper Slaughter Gloucs
28 C5 Upper Soudley Gloucs
34 H10 Upper Spond Herefs
13 P7 Upper Standen Kent
38 H9 Upper Staploe Bed
51 N13 Upper Stoke Norfk
37 R9 Upper Stowe Nhants
8 H5 Upper Street Hants
41 L5 Upper Street Norfk
51 P10 Upper Street Norfk
51 Q10 Upper Street Norfk
40 C10 Upper Street Suffk
40 K10 Upper Street Suffk
40 K14 Upper Street Suffk
35 U13 Upper Strensham Worcs
31 M7 Upper Sundon C Beds
29 N2 Upper Swell Gloucs
57 M7 Upper Tankersley Barns
41 M1 Upper Tasburgh Norfk
46 D6 Upper Tean Staffs
56 H5 Upperthong Kirk
57 Q10 Upperthorpe Derbys
58 C6 Upperthorpe N Linc
44 K4 Upper Threapwood Ches W
10 F6 Upperton W Susx
46 H3 Upper Town Derbys
57 M14 Uppertown Derbys
69 N5 Upper Town Dur
35 N11 Upper Town Herefs
112 J1 Uppertown Highld
17 P3 Upper Town N Som
40 F7 Upper Town Suffk
25 T8 Upper Tumble Carmth
36 K12 Upper Tysoe Warwks
41 N10 Upper Ufford Suffk
28 K8 Upperup Gloucs
18 K5 Upper Upham Wilts
22 J13 Upper Upnor Medway
91 R4 Upper Victoria Angus
17 T7 Upper Vobster Somset
37 N11 Upper Wardington Oxon
30 H5 Upper Weald M Keyn
37 R9 Upper Weedon Nhants
35 S12 Upper Welland Worcs
11 Q8 Upper Wellingham E Susx
17 T3 Upper Weston BaNES
41 M5 Upper Weybread Suffk
35 T10 Upper Wick Worcs
19 T13 Upper Wield Hants
30 F10 Upper Winchendon Bucks
46 J2 Upperwood Derbys
18 H13 Upper Woodford Wilts
19 S10 Upper Wootton Hants
18 B6 Upper Wraxall Wilts
35 S12 Upper Wyche Worcs
6 B3 Uppincott Devon
48 C14 Uppingham Rutlnd
8 E7 Uppington Dorset
45 N12 Uppington Shrops
64 B2 Upsall N York
85 M9 Upsettlington Border
22 B7 Upshire Essex
9 M2 Up Somborne Hants
13 P3 Upstreet Kent
7 R4 Up Sydling Dorset
40 G6 Upthorpe Suffk
30 G10 Upton Bucks
48 H13 Upton C Pete
38 J5 Upton Cambs
54 K13 Upton Ches W
4 H6 Upton Cnwll
14 F12 Upton Cnwll
67 M5 Upton Cumb
5 S12 Upton Devon
6 E4 Upton Devon
7 T8 Upton Dorset
8 D10 Upton Dorset
65 Q9 Upton E R Yk
55 L9 Upton Halton
9 M5 Upton Hants
19 N9 Upton Hants
47 L14 Upton Leics
58 E9 Upton Lincs
37 T9 Upton Nhants
51 Q11 Upton Norfk
47 T3 Upton Notts
58 B11 Upton Notts
19 R3 Upton Oxon
29 P5 Upton Oxon
24 H10 Upton Pembks
71 M9 Upton R & Cl
20 G7 Upton Slough
16 C11 Upton Somset
17 N11 Upton Somset
57 Q4 Upton Wakefd
36 F9 Upton Warwks
8 B2 Upton Wilts
54 G9 Upton Wirral
28 C2 Upton Bishop Herefs
17 S2 Upton Cheyney S Glos
35 Q2 Upton Cressett Shrops
28 B2 Upton Crews Herefs
4 H6 Upton Cross Cnwll
31 P6 Upton End C Beds
19 U11 Upton Grey Hants
54 K13 Upton Heath Ches W
15 T12 Upton Hellions Devon
18 D12 Upton Lovell Wilts
45 N11 Upton Magna Shrops
17 T9 Upton Noble Somset
6 B5 Upton Pyne Devon
28 G4 Upton St Leonards Gloucs
18 C11 Upton Scudamore Wilts
36 B10 Upton Snodsbury Worcs
2 F8 Upton Towans Cnwll
35 U12 Upton upon Severn Worcs
36 B7 Upton Warren Worcs
10 E8 Upwaltham W Susx
39 R6 Upware Cambs
49 Q13 Upwell Norfk
7 S7 Upwey Dorset
22 C3 Upwick Green Herts
39 L4 Upwood Cambs
18 F9 Urchfont Wilts
35 M11 Urdimarsh Herefs
63 S5 Ure Bank N York
70 F10 Urlay Nook S on T
55 S8 Urmston Traffd
104 B3 Urquhart Moray
70 J12 Urra N York
102 F5 Urray Highld
99 N13 Usan Angus
69 R4 Ushaw Moor Dur
27 R7 Usk Mons
58 J8 Usselby Lincs
77 S14 Usworth Sundld
55 M13 Utkinton Ches W
63 M11 Utley C Brad
15 T13 Uton Devon
59 P8 Utterby Lincs
46 E7 Uttoxeter Staffs
42 C8 Uwchmynydd Gwynd
20 J6 Uxbridge Gt Lon
106 v3 Uyeasound Shet
24 G8 Uzmaston Pembks

V

6 e2 Vale Guern
16 F2 Vale of Glamorgan Crematorium V Glam
33 P5 Vale of Rheidol Railway Cerdgn
52 C7 Valley IoA
20 G10 Valley End Surrey
4 D4 Valley Truckle Cnwll
100 e3 Valtos Highld
106 f5 Valtos W Isls
22 H10 Vange Essex
27 P6 Varteg Torfn
106 v5 Vatsetter Shet
100 b5 Vatten Highld
26 J5 Vaynor Myr Td
6 c2 Vazon Bay Guern
106 u9 Veensgarth Shet
34 E13 Velindre Powys
16 E9 Vellow Somset
14 G8 Velly Devon
14 J10 Venngreen Devon
44 H12 Vennington Shrops
6 E6 Venn Ottery Devon
15 T13 Venny Tedburn Devon
4 K6 Venterdon Cnwll
9 R13 Ventnor IoW
5 P9 Venton Devon
19 M9 Vernham Dean Hants
19 M9 Vernham Street Hants
35 L4 Vernolds Common Shrops
8 F7 Verwood Dorset
3 N9 Veryan Cnwll
3 N8 Veryan Green Cnwll
6 H7 Vicarage Devon
61 M6 Vickerstown Cumb
56 J5 Victoria Barns
27 M6 Victoria Blae G
3 P4 Victoria Cnwll
106 u7 Vidlin Shet
104 B3 Viewfield Moray
82 D6 Viewpark N Lans
12 B3 Vigo Kent
6 e3 Village de Putron Guern
7 a1 Ville la Bas Jersey
6 c3 Villiaze Guern
12 E11 Vinehall Street E Susx
11 T7 Vines Cross E Susx
12 E4 Vinters Park Crematorium Kent
20 H9 Virginia Water Surrey
4 K2 Virginstow Devon
17 T7 Vobster Somset
106 u7 Voe Shet
34 J13 Vowchurch Herefs
55 N8 Vulcan Village St Hel

W

66 H14 Waberthwaite Cumb
69 Q8 Wackerfield Dur
41 L2 Wacton Norfk
36 B11 Wadborough Worcs
30 F9 Waddesdon Bucks
6 A13 Waddeton Devon
54 J7 Waddicar Sefton
58 G7 Waddingham Lincs
62 E11 Waddington Lancs
58 G14 Waddington Lincs
6 A9 Waddon Devon
7 R7 Waddon Dorset
3 P2 Wadebridge Cnwll
6 K2 Wadeford Somset
38 F4 Wadenhoe Nhants
31 U9 Wadesmill Herts
12 B9 Wadhurst E Susx
57 M12 Wadshelf Derbys
18 B7 Wadswick Wilts
57 S7 Wadworth Donc
53 S10 Waen Denbgs
54 D13 Waen Denbgs
44 F10 Waen Powys
44 F10 Waen Fach Powys
52 J9 Waen-pentir Gwynd
52 J9 Waen-wen Gwynd
44 J13 Wagbeach Shrops
27 P7 Wainfelin Torfn
49 Q2 Wainfleet All Saints Lincs
49 Q2 Wainfleet Bank Lincs
49 Q2 Wainfleet St Mary Lincs
41 P2 Wainford Norfk
14 E13 Wainhouse Corner Cnwll
22 H13 Wainscott Medway
17 L2 Wain's Hill N Som
63 L14 Wainstalls Calder
68 G11 Waitby Cumb
59 N6 Waithe Lincs
57 M2 Wakefield Wakefd
57 M3 Wakefield Crematorium Wakefd
36 E4 Wake Green Birm
48 E14 Wakerley Nhants
23 L2 Wakes Colne Essex
41 S6 Walberswick Suffk
10 F9 Walberton W Susx
77 P12 Walbottle N u Ty
74 D12 Walbutt D & G
75 T13 Walby Cumb
17 Q7 Walcombe Somset
48 G6 Walcot Lincs
58 E2 Walcot N Linc
34 H3 Walcot Shrops
45 N11 Walcot Shrops
29 N11 Walcot Swindn
36 F9 Walcot Warwks
37 Q4 Walcote Leics
40 K4 Walcot Green Norfk
48 H2 Walcott Lincs
51 Q7 Walcott Norfk
63 L3 Walden N York
62 K3 Walden Head N York
57 S3 Walden Stubbs N York
12 E3 Walderslade Medway
10 B8 Walderton W Susx
7 N6 Walditch Dorset
46 F6 Waldley Derbys
69 S3 Waldridge Dur
41 N11 Waldringfield Suffk
11 S7 Waldron E Susx
57 Q10 Wales Rothm
17 Q12 Wales Somset
58 K8 Walesby Lincs
57 U12 Walesby Notts
28 A3 Walford Herefs
34 J6 Walford Herefs
44 K9 Walford Shrops
45 T7 Walford Staffs
44 K10 Walford Heath Shrops
45 Q4 Walgherton Ches E
38 B6 Walgrave Nhants
9 L9 Walhampton Hants
55 R6 Walkden Salfd
77 R13 Walker N u Ty
83 S11 Walkerburn Border
62 D11 Walker Fold Lancs
58 C8 Walkeringham Notts
58 C8 Walkerith Lincs
31 S7 Walkern Herts
35 M11 Walker's Green Herefs
36 E5 Walker's Heath Birm
90 K11 Walkerton Fife
8 J10 Walkford Dorset
5 N7 Walkhampton Devon
65 M12 Walkington E R Yk
57 M9 Walkley Sheff
62 H14 Walk Mill Lancs
36 D8 Walkwood Worcs
76 J12 Wall Nthumb
46 F12 Wall Staffs
80 K12 Wallacetown S Ayrs
81 L8 Wallacetown S Ayrs
11 Q8 Wallands Park E Susx
54 G8 Wallasey Wirral
61 N3 Wall End Cumb
34 K9 Wall End Herefs
23 L12 Wallend Medway
35 Q13 Waller's Green Herefs
75 U13 Wallhead Cumb
35 U3 Wall Heath Dudley
77 L12 Wall Houses Nthumb
19 T3 Wallingford Oxon
21 N10 Wallington Gt Lon
9 R7 Wallington Hants
31 S6 Wallington Herts
46 C13 Wallington Heath Wsall
24 H5 Wallis Pembks
8 F10 Wallisdown Poole
10 J3 Walliswood Surrey
106 s9 Walls Shet
77 R12 Wallsend N Tyne
67 N7 Wallthwaite Cumb
35 M2 Wall under Haywood Shrops
83 S4 Wallyford E Loth
13 S5 Walmer Kent
55 L2 Walmer Bridge Lancs
55 T4 Walmersley Bury
13 Q4 Walmestone Kent
36 F2 Walmley Birm
36 F2 Walmley Ash Birm
59 Q11 Walmsgate Lincs
16 K8 Walpole Somset
41 Q6 Walpole Suffk
49 R10 Walpole Cross Keys Norfk
49 R11 Walpole Highway Norfk
49 R10 Walpole St Andrew Norfk
49 R10 Walpole St Peter Norfk
16 K7 Walrow Somset
46 D14 Walsall Wsall
46 D13 Walsall Wood Wsall
56 D2 Walsden Calder
37 L4 Walsgrave on Sowe Covtry
40 H6 Walsham le Willows Suffk
55 S4 Walshaw Bury
63 U9 Walshford N York
49 Q11 Walsoken Norfk
83 L9 Walston S Lans
31 Q6 Walsworth Herts
20 D3 Walter's Ash Bucks
11 S2 Walters Green Kent
16 E2 Walterston V Glam
27 Q2 Walterstone Herefs
13 M6 Waltham Kent
59 N6 Waltham NE Lin
31 U12 Waltham Abbey Essex
9 R6 Waltham Chase Hants
31 U12 Waltham Cross Herts
48 B9 Waltham on the Wolds Leics
20 D7 Waltham St Lawrence W & M
22 G1 Waltham's Cross Essex
21 Q5 Walthamstow Gt Lon
48 J13 Walton C Pete
75 V13 Walton Cumb
57 N13 Walton Derbys
63 U10 Walton Leeds
37 Q3 Walton Leics
30 J5 Walton M Keyn
34 G9 Walton Powys
35 L5 Walton Shrops
17 N9 Walton Somset
45 U7 Walton Staffs
45 U8 Walton Staffs
41 N13 Walton Suffk
10 C10 Walton W Susx
57 N3 Walton Wakefd
36 J10 Walton Warwks
45 N10 Walton Wrekin
28 H1 Walton Cardiff Gloucs
24 H6 Walton East Pembks
17 U13 Walton Elm Dorset
30 B6 Walton Grounds Nhants
27 S13 Walton-in-Gordano N Som
55 P9 Walton Lea Crematorium Warrtn
62 B14 Walton-le-Dale Lancs
20 K9 Walton-on-Thames Surrey
46 C9 Walton-on-the-Hill Staffs
21 M11 Walton on the Hill Surrey
23 U3 Walton on the Naze Essex
47 Q10 Walton on the Wolds Leics
46 H10 Walton-on-Trent Derbys
17 M2 Walton Park N Som
24 E8 Walton West Pembks
62 K9 Waltonwrays Crematorium N York
54 D11 Walwen Flints
54 E12 Walwen Flints
54 F11 Walwen Flints
76 J11 Walwick Nthumb
69 R9 Walworth Darltn
21 P7 Walworth Gt Lon
69 R8 Walworth Gate Darltn
24 E8 Walwyn's Castle Pembks
6 J3 Wambrook Somset
66 K2 Wampool Cumb
20 F13 Wanborough Surrey
29 P11 Wanborough Swindn
31 P8 Wandon End Herts
21 N8 Wandsworth Gt Lon
41 S5 Wangford Suffk
47 Q11 Wanlip Leics
74 G3 Wanlockhead D & G
11 T10 Wannock E Susx
48 G14 Wansford C Pete
65 P8 Wansford E R Yk
12 E6 Wanshurst Green Kent
21 R5 Wanstead Gt Lon
17 T8 Wanstrow Somset
28 C7 Wanswell Gloucs
29 S10 Wantage Oxon
35 S9 Wants Green Worcs
28 D12 Wapley S Glos
37 L7 Wappenbury Warwks
37 R11 Wappenham Nhants
11 U7 Warbleton E Susx
19 S2 Warborough Oxon
39 M4 Warboys Cambs
61 Q12 Warbreck Bpool
4 G2 Warbstow Cnwll
55 R9 Warburton Traffd
68 F9 Warcop Cumb
23 P13 Warden Kent
76 J12 Warden Nthumb
36 F3 Ward End Birm
31 P4 Warden Street C Beds
40 H8 Ward Green Suffk
62 C12 Ward Green Cross Lancs
31 N5 Wardhedges C Beds
37 N11 Wardington Oxon
45 P2 Wardle Ches E
56 D3 Wardle Rochdl
77 S13 Wardley Gatesd
48 B13 Wardley Rutlnd
55 S6 Wardley Salfd
56 J12 Wardlow Derbys
56 D10 Wardsend Ches E
39 Q4 Wardy Hill Cambs
31 U10 Ware Herts
8 C11 Wareham Dorset
12 J9 Warehorne Kent
85 S13 Warenford Nthumb
85 S12 Waren Mill Nthumb
85 S12 Warenton Nthumb
31 U9 Wareside Herts
39 L10 Waresley Cambs
35 T6 Waresley Worcs
12 E4 Ware Street Kent
20 E8 Warfield Br For
5 V10 Warfleet Devon
48 K7 Wargate Lincs
20 C7 Wargrave Wokham
35 L13 Warham Herefs
50 G5 Warham All Saints Norfk
50 F5 Warham St Mary Norfk
76 H10 Wark Nthumb
85 L11 Wark Nthumb
15 P8 Warkleigh Devon
38 C5 Warkton Nhants
37 N12 Warkworth Nhants
77 Q4 Warkworth Nthumb
63 S1 Warlaby N York
56 D2 Warland Calder
4 F7 Warleggan Cnwll
17 U4 Warleigh BaNES
56 G2 Warley Town Calder
21 Q11 Warlingham Surrey
46 J3 Warmbrook Derbys
57 N2 Warmfield Wakefd
45 R1 Warmingham Ches E
38 G2 Warmington Nhants
37 M11 Warmington Warwks
18 C11 Warminster Wilts
28 C13 Warmley S Glos
57 R6 Warmsworth Donc
7 U7 Warmwell Dorset
35 U9 Warndon Worcs
9 S4 Warnford Hants
10 K4 Warnham W Susx
10 K4 Warnham Court W Susx
10 G9 Warningcamp W Susx
11 L5 Warninglid W Susx
56 C12 Warren Ches E
24 F11 Warren Pembks
70 J7 Warrenby R & Cl
82 H11 Warrenhill S Lans
20 D6 Warren Row W & M
31 S7 Warren's Green Herts
12 H5 Warren Street Kent
38 C10 Warrington M Keyn
55 P9 Warrington Warrtn
83 Q3 Warriston C Edin
83 Q3 Warriston Crematorium C Edin
9 P7 Warsash Hants
46 E2 Warslow Staffs
57 R13 Warsop Vale Notts
64 K9 Warter E R Yk
63 Q4 Warthermaske N York
64 F8 Warthill N York
11 V9 Wartling E Susx
47 T9 Wartnaby Leics
61 S14 Warton Lancs
61 T5 Warton Lancs
77 L5 Warton Nthumb
46 J13 Warton Warwks
36 J7 Warwick Warwks
67 Q1 Warwick Bridge Cumb
36 J8 Warwick Castle Warwks
67 Q1 Warwick-on-Eden Cumb
36 K9 Warwick Services Warwks
75 U10 Warwicksland Cumb
106 s16 Wasbister Ork
66 J11 Wasdale Head Cumb
56 G10 Wash Derbys
22 B1 Washall Green Herts
3 Q3 Washaway Cnwll
5 T10 Washbourne Devon
17 M6 Washbrook Somset
40 K12 Washbrook Suffk
16 B13 Washfield Devon
69 N12 Washfold N York
16 E8 Washford Somset
15 T10 Washford Pyne Devon
58 H12 Washingborough Lincs
70 D1 Washington Sundld
10 J8 Washington W Susx
69 S1 Washington Services Gatesd
36 F3 Washwood Heath Birm
19 S8 Wasing W Berk
69 M3 Waskerley Dur
36 J9 Wasperton Warwks
58 J14 Wasps Nest Lincs
64 D4 Wass N York
16 E8 Watchet Somset
29 P9 Watchfield Oxon
16 K7 Watchfield Somset
67 R13 Watchgate Cumb
66 J4 Watchill Cumb
6 B11 Watcombe Torbay
67 L9 Watendlath Cumb
5 T4 Water Devon
55 T1 Water Lancs
39 Q7 Waterbeach Cambs
10 D9 Waterbeach W Susx
75 P10 Waterbeck D & G
50 E6 Waterden Norfk
30 B10 Water Eaton Oxon
46 B11 Water Eaton Staffs
38 H10 Water End Bed
38 H11 Water End Bed
31 N5 Water End C Beds
66 H8 Waterend Cumb
64 H12 Water End E R Yk
39 S12 Water End Essex
31 M10 Water End Herts
31 R12 Water End Herts
46 E3 Waterfall Staffs
81 R1 Waterfoot E Rens
31 T10 Waterford Herts
57 Q1 Water Fryston Wakefd
4 E4 Watergate Cnwll
67 N12 Waterhead Cumb
83 P8 Waterheads Border
69 Q4 Waterhouses Dur
46 E3 Waterhouses Staffs
12 C5 Wateringbury Kent
28 H7 Waterlane Gloucs
4 E6 Waterloo Cnwll
57 P14 Waterloo Derbys
34 H11 Waterloo Herefs
100 f7 Waterloo Highld
82 F8 Waterloo N Lans
51 M10 Waterloo Norfk
90 G4 Waterloo P & K
24 G10 Waterloo Pembks
8 E10 Waterloo Poole
54 H7 Waterloo Sefton
6 E2 Waterloo Cross Devon
52 G10 Waterloo Port Gwynd
9 T7 Waterlooville Hants
67 P8 Watermillock Cumb
38 H1 Water Newton Cambs
36 G2 Water Orton Warwks
30 D11 Waterperry Oxon
16 E11 Waterrow Somset
10 G7 Watersfield W Susx
55 R2 Waterside Bl w D
31 L12 Waterside Bucks
66 K3 Waterside Cumb
57 U4 Waterside Donc
81 N11 Waterside E Ayrs
81 P4 Waterside E Ayrs
89 Q11 Waterside E Duns
55 Q5 Water's Nook Bolton
100 a5 Waterstein Highld
30 D11 Waterstock Oxon
24 F9 Waterston Pembks
30 E6 Water Stratford Bucks
26 E11 Water Street Neath
45 P10 Waters Upton Wrekin
61 P2 Water Yeat Cumb
20 K3 Watford Herts
37 R7 Watford Nhants
37 R7 Watford Gap Services Nhants
63 N6 Wath N York
63 S4 Wath N York
57 P6 Wath upon Dearne Rothm
49 T11 Watlington Norfk
19 U2 Watlington Oxon
47 P4 Watnall Notts
112 F6 Watten Highld
40 H6 Wattisfield Suffk
40 H10 Wattisham Suffk
7 N6 Watton Dorset
65 N9 Watton E R Yk
50 F13 Watton Norfk
31 T9 Watton-at-Stone Herts
50 F13 Watton Green Norfk
22 D8 Wattons Green Essex
82 E4 Wattston N Lans
26 J9 Wattstown Rhondd
27 N9 Wattsville Caerph
65 M14 Wauldby E R Yk
99 L5 Waulkmill Abers
25 V11 Waunarlwydd Swans
33 M4 Waunfawr Cerdgn
52 H11 Waunfawr Gwynd
25 U10 Waungron Swans
27 M6 Waunlwyd Blae G
30 K5 Wavendon M Keyn
66 K3 Waverbridge Cumb
55 L14 Waverton Ches W
66 K3 Waverton Cumb
65 P12 Wawne E R Yk
51 R8 Waxham Norfk
65 U14 Waxholme E R Yk
13 R2 Way Kent
5 T6 Waye Devon
7 M3 Wayford Somset
7 N5 Waytown Dorset
15 U10 Way Village Devon
17 L4 Way Wick N Som
16 F8 Weacombe Somset
29 R7 Weald Oxon
21 L5 Wealdstone Gt Lon
63 R11 Weardley Leeds
17 M6 Weare Somset
15 L8 Weare Giffard Devon
68 J5 Wearhead Dur
17 M11 Wearne Somset
69 S6 Wear Valley Crematorium Dur
68 E12 Weasdale Cumb
50 D9 Weasenham All Saints Norfk
50 E9 Weasenham St Peter Norfk
55 T7 Weaste Salfd
36 E6 Weatheroak Hill Worcs
55 P12 Weaverham Ches W
46 F10 Weaverslake Staffs
65 M5 Weaverthorpe N York
17 L5 Webbington Somset
28 C13 Webb's Heath S Glos
36 D7 Webheath Worcs
34 K13 Webton Herefs
105 P9 Wedderlairs Abers
62 J10 Wedding Hall Fold N York
13 Q4 Weddington Kent
37 L2 Weddington Warwks
18 G9 Wedhampton Wilts
17 M7 Wedmore Somset
36 C1 Wednesbury Sandw
46 B13 Wednesfield Wolves
58 D13 Weecar Notts
30 H9 Weedon Bucks
37 R9 Weedon Nhants
37 R11 Weedon Lois Nhants
46 F13 Weeford Staffs
5 T8 Week Devon
15 N7 Week Devon
15 R9 Week Devon
15 S11 Weeke Devon
9 P2 Weeke Hants
38 C4 Weekley Nhants
14 F13 Week St Mary Cnwll
65 P12 Weel E R Yk
23 R3 Weeley Essex
23 R3 Weeley Crematorium Essex
23 S3 Weeley Heath Essex
90 B2 Weem P & K
46 B9 Weeping Cross Staffs
36 E9 Weethley Warwks
40 C3 Weeting Norfk

Column 1

59 Q2 Weeton E R Yk
61 R13 Weeton Lancs
63 R10 Weeton N York
46 R12 Weetwood Leeds
5 Q6 Weir Lancs
44 H9 Weirbrook Shrops
5 L7 Weir Quay Devon
106 t8 Weisdale Shet
50 J11 Welborne Norfk
48 E13 Welborn Lincs
64 G6 Welburn N York
70 E12 Welburn N York
48 E6 Welby Lincs
39 Q3 Welches Dam Cambs
16 M6 Welcombe Devon
7 N6 Weldon Bridge Nthumb
37 R4 Weldon Nhants
19 P6 Welford W Berk
36 F10 Welford-on-Avon Warwks
37 U2 Welham Leics
58 B10 Welham Notts
31 R11 Welham Green Herts
20 C12 Well Hants
59 R12 Well Lincs
63 R3 Well N York
35 S12 Welland Worcs
91 Q4 Wellbank Angus
20 E5 Well End Bucks
21 M3 Well End Herts
36 J9 Wellesbourne Warwks
36 J9 Wellesbourne Mountford Warwks
11 Q7 Well Hill Kent
19 R6 Wellhouse W Berk
21 S7 Welling Gt Lon
38 C7 Wellingborough Nhants
50 E9 Wellingham Norfk
48 E12 Wellingore Lincs
66 G12 Wellington Cumb
35 L11 Wellington Herefs
16 F12 Wellington Somset
44 K10 Wellington Wrekin
35 R12 Wellington Heath Herefs
35 L11 Wellington Marsh Herefs
17 T5 Wellow BaNES
9 M11 Wellow IoW
57 N3 Wellow Notts
22 B3 Wellpond Green Herts
17 P7 Wells Somset
47 L13 Wellsborough Leics
45 Q5 Wells Green Ches E
63 M13 Wells Head C Brad
50 F5 Wells-next-the-sea Norfk
22 F4 Wellstye Green Essex
6 B4 Well Town Devon
5 T4 Weltree [P & K]
65 V14 Wellwood Fife
39 R2 Welney Norfk
44 A6 Welshampton Shrops
44 B8 Welsh Bicknor Herefs
45 M6 Welsh End Shrops
44 A7 Welsh Frankton Shrops
24 F5 Welsh Hook Pembks
27 U4 Welsh Newton Herefs
44 F12 Welshpool Powys
26 J12 Welsh St Donats V Glam
67 N4 Welton Cumb
58 G1 Welton E R Yk
59 T7 Welton Lincs
37 S7 Welton Nhants
59 S13 Welton le Marsh Lincs
59 N10 Welton le Wold Lincs
59 R9 Welwick E R Yk
31 R10 Welwyn Herts
31 R10 Welwyn Garden City Herts
45 M8 Wem Shrops
16 J9 Wembdon Somset
21 L5 Wembley Gt Lon
5 N11 Wembury Devon
15 Q11 Wembworthy Devon
88 E12 Wemyss Bay Inver
44 H4 Wenallt Cerdgn
30 C9 Wendens Ambo Essex
30 C9 Wendlebury Oxon
2 J10 Wendron Cnwll
31 P11 Wendy Cambs
41 R5 Wenfordbridge Cnwll
38 K5 Wennington Cambs
21 Q6 Wennington Gt Lon
62 C6 Wennington Lancs
63 M4 Wensley Derbys
63 M2 Wensley N York
57 Q3 Wentbridge Wakefd
34 J2 Wentnor Shrops
39 Q5 Wentworth Cambs
57 N6 Wentworth Rothm
57 M6 Wentworth Castle Barns
16 F2 Wenvoe V Glam
34 K10 Weobley Herefs
34 K10 Weobley Marsh Herefs
10 G9 Wepham W Susx
45 U13 Wergs Wolves
42 K6 Wern Gwynd
43 M11 Wern Powys
44 G11 Wern Powys
56 E8 Werneth Low Tamesd
62 C1 Wernffrwd Swans
7 L15 Wern-y-gaer Flints
48 J13 Werrington C Pete
4 J3 Werrington Cnwll
45 U10 Werrington Staffs
54 K12 Wervin Ches W
9 P5 Wesham Lancs
57 M6 Wessex Vale Crematorium Hants
47 L2 Wessington Derbys
16 D3 West Aberthaw V Glam
57 M8 West Acre Norfk
85 P9 West Allerdean Nthumb
5 S12 West Alvington Devon
18 H12 West Amesbury Wilts
15 U12 West Anstey Devon
69 R4 West Appleton N York
45 U13 West Ashby Lincs
10 C9 West Ashling W Susx
18 B8 West Ashton Wilts
68 D6 West Auckland Dur
65 M3 West Ayton N York
16 J11 West Bagborough Somset
27 N6 West Bank Blae G
59 L10 West Barkwith Lincs
71 P10 West Barnby N York
50 F7 West Barns E Loth
7 N6 West Bay Dorset
50 J8 West Beckham Norfk
21 N9 West Bedfont Surrey
23 N2 West Bergholt Essex
7 P7 West Bexington Dorset
50 B10 West Bilney Norfk
11 M8 West Blatchington Br & H
77 T13 West Boldon S Tyne
48 C5 Westborough Lincs
9 Q10 Westbourne Bmouth
10 B9 Westbourne W Susx
5 U13 West Bourton Dorset
57 S7 West Bradenham Norfk
62 E11 West Bradford Lancs
17 Q8 West Bradley Somset
63 M13 West Bretton Kirk
17 R11 West Bridgford Notts
36 D2 West Bromwich Sandw
36 D2 West Bromwich Crematorium Sandw
11 P6 Westbrook Kent
19 R6 Westbrook W Berk
18 E11 West Buckland Devon
16 G12 West Buckland Somset
63 L12 West Burton N York
10 G12 West Burton W Susx
30 D5 Westbury Bucks
34 J9 Westbury Shrops
18 C11 Westbury Wilts
18 C11 Westbury Leigh Wilts
27 V12 Westbury-on-Trym Brist
17 P7 Westbury-sub-Mendip Somset
59 P4 West Butsfield Dur
58 D5 West Butterwick N Linc
52 B2 Westby Lancs
61 R13 West Byfleet Surrey
72 E13 West Cairngaan D & G
51 T11 West Caister Norfk
17 Q12 West Camel Somset
7 U8 West Chaldon Dorset
29 U10 West Challow Oxon
5 T12 West Charleton Devon
7 P3 West Chelborough Dorset
77 Q6 West Chevington Nthumb

Column 2

10 H7 West Chiltington W Susx
7 N2 West Chinnock Somset
13 R7 West Chisenbury Wilts
20 H12 West Clandon Surrey
13 R7 West Cliffe Kent
23 L10 Westcliff-on-Sea Sthend
7 P2 West Coker Somset
5 T8 West Combe Devon
16 J8 Westcombe Somset
17 Q8 West Compton Somset
7 Q6 West Compton Abbas Dorset
29 P3 Westcote Gloucs
29 T2 Westcote Barton Oxon
30 F9 Westcott Bucks
6 D3 Westcott Devon
20 K13 Westcott Surrey
64 F11 West Cottingwith N York
8 V8 West Dean W Susx
65 L6 West Dean Wilts
17 V13 West Cross Swans
4 H2 West Curry Cnwll
67 M3 West Curthwaite Cumb
11 S11 Westdean E Susx
10 D8 West Dean W Susx
38 K3 West Deeping Lincs
48 H12 West Derby Lpool
55 L13 West Derby Lpool
50 C13 West Dereham Norfk
77 N1 West Ditchburn Nthumb
15 M4 West Down Devon
18 F11 Westdown Camp Wilts
4 D4 Westdowns Cnwll
21 Q8 West Drayton Gt Lon
58 B12 West Drayton Notts
112 F2 West Dunnet Highld
65 N14 West Ella E R Yk
38 E10 West End Bed
20 E8 West End Br For
75 R14 West End Cumb
65 R13 West End E R Yk
65 T14 West End E R Yk
28 E6 West End Gloucs
19 T13 West End Hants
9 P6 West End Hants
19 S11 West End Hants
11 S11 West End Herts
52 E11 West End Lancs
63 Q12 West End Leeds
17 N3 West End N Som
64 C4 West End N York
50 J8 West End Norfk
51 S11 West End Norfk
59 N9 West End Norfk
62 H9 West Marton N York
7 P6 West Melbury Dorset
50 F12 West End Norfk
51 T11 West End Norfk
19 S3 West End Oxon
21 M6 West End S Glos
20 K10 West End Surrey
20 D7 West End W & M
11 L7 West End W Susx
8 D4 West End Wilts
18 E8 West End Wilts
19 U8 West End Green Hants
76 F12 Westend Town Nthumb

Column 3

85 L11 West Learmouth Nthumb
70 G12 West Lees N York
15 L7 West Leigh Devon
5 Q11 West Leigh Devon
16 E13 Westleigh Devon
16 F10 West Leigh Somset
41 R7 Westleton Suffk
50 D10 West Lexham Norfk
44 J12 Westley Shrops
40 D8 Westley Suffk
39 T9 Westley Waterless Cambs
64 E7 West Lilling N York
5 G10 Westlington Bucks
83 N8 West Linton Border
75 S13 Westlinton Cumb
28 E12 West Littleton S Glos
29 T10 West Lockinge Oxon
21 M6 West London Crematorium Gt Lon
67 L4 Westward Cumb
14 K7 Westward Ho! Devon
29 P6 Westwell Oxon
12 J6 Westwell Kent
12 J6 Westwell Leacon Kent
8 K5 West Wellow Hants
5 N11 West Wembury Devon
91 M13 West Wemyss Fife
39 P7 Westwick Cambs
10 T4 West Wick N Som
51 N8 Westwick Norfk
39 T11 West Wickham Cambs
21 Q9 West Wickham Gt Lon
24 H9 West Williamston Pembks
18 D9 West Wiltshire Crematorium Wilts
49 T10 West Winch Norfk
55 P3 West Winterslow Wilts
83 R4 West Wittering W Susx
8 B11 West Wittering W Susx
63 M2 West Witton N York
22 F8 Westwood D & G
6 D5 Westwood Devon
15 S2 Westwood Kent
22 F13 Westwood Kent
47 N3 Westwood Notts
76 F12 Westwood Nthumb
18 B9 Westwood Wilts
76 H8 West Woodburn Nthumb
19 N8 West Woodhay W Berk
36 J5 Westwood Heath Covtry
17 U8 West Woodlands Somset
58 B6 Westwoodside N Linc
10 A3 West Worldham Hants
10 H10 West Worthing W Susx
39 T10 West Wratting Cambs
20 A4 West Wycombe Bucks
67 M13 West Wylam Nthumb
18 C5 West Yatton Wilts
21 V9 West Yoke Kent
14 G9 West Youlstone Cnwll
67 Q2 Wetheral Cumb
63 U10 Wetherby Leeds
63 U9 Wetherby Services N York
40 H8 Wetherden Suffk
40 K7 Wetheringsett Suffk
22 H1 Wethersfield Essex
41 N5 Wetherup Street Suffk
46 C4 Wetley Rocks Staffs
55 P2 Wettenhall Ches E
46 F4 Wetton Staffs
65 L8 Wetwang E R Yk
45 S7 Wetwood Staffs
45 T7 Wexcombe Wilts
20 G6 Wexham Slough
20 G6 Wexham Street Bucks
50 K5 Weybourne Norfk
41 M4 Weybread Suffk
41 M5 Weybread Street Suffk
20 J10 Weybridge Surrey
6 J5 Weycroft Devon
112 E4 Weydale Highld
19 M11 Weyhill Hants
7 S9 Weymouth Dorset
7 S9 Weymouth Crematorium Dorset
35 H6 Whaddon Bucks
39 N11 Whaddon Cambs
28 F5 Whaddon Gloucs
8 H3 Whaddon Wilts
18 C8 Whaddon Wilts
67 R8 Whale Cumb
57 M2 Whaley Derbys
56 F10 Whaley Bridge Derbys
57 M2 Whaley Thorns Derbys
112 H8 Whaligoe Highld
62 E12 Whalley Lancs
62 E12 Whalley Banks Lancs
106 v7 Whalsay Shet
67 N1 Whalton Nthumb
49 M9 Whaplode Lincs
49 M10 Whaplode Drove Lincs
37 M10 Wharf Warwks
62 F6 Wharfe N York
61 S13 Wharles Lancs
50 K4 Wharley End C Beds
57 L8 Wharncliffe Side Sheff
64 K6 Wharram-le-Street N York

Column 4

77 P6 West Thirston Nthumb
10 D10 West Thorney W Susx
57 Q11 Westthorpe Derbys
22 E12 West Thurrock Thurr
22 G12 West Tilbury Thurr
9 T5 West Tisted Hants
58 K10 West Torrington Lincs
17 P4 West Town BaNES
5 U9 West Town Hants
34 K8 West Town N Som
17 N3 West Town N Som
17 P9 West Town Somset
7 T9 West Town Somset
8 K3 West Tytherley Hants
49 Q11 West Walton Norfk
49 Q11 West Walton Highway Norfk
19 T7 Westweed Dorset
29 N5 West Wick N Som
34 G4 Westwell Keysett Shrops
9 R9 Wecham Hants
19 N6 Weston Hants
22 K5 Weston Herts
84 J7 Whitchurch BaNES
30 M8 Whitchurch Bucks
47 M12 Whitchurch Cardif
5 Q11 Whitchurch Devon
19 Q11 Whitchurch Hants
27 V4 Whitchurch Herefs
24 J7 Whitchurch Pembks
45 M5 Whitchurch Shrops
4 L5 Whitchurch Canonicorum Dorset
19 T5 Whitchurch Hill Oxon
57 Q8 Whitchurch-on-Thames Oxon
9 R13 Whitcombe Dorset
34 G4 Whitcot Shrops
34 G4 Whitcott Keysett Shrops
9 H6 Whiteacre Kent
36 H2 Whiteacre Heath Warwks
22 J1 Whiteash Green Essex
102 E12 Whitebridge Highld
27 U6 Whitebrook Mons
45 T9 White Chapel Lancs
25 L3 Whitchurch Pembks
23 M3 Whitcox Hill Warwks
28 D10 White Coppice Lancs
89 R4 White Lackington Lancs
50 J7 Whitecrook Ches W
10 J7 Whitecairns Abers
46 D13 Whitchurch St Paul Essex
46 E13 Whitchurch Maelor Wrexhm [?]
3 L3 Whitchurch Pembks
5 S14 Whitecross Cnwll
2 K4 Whitecross Falk
82 J3 Whitecross Falk
85 S14 Whitefarland N Ayrs
109 N7 Whiteface Highld
76 H8 White Hill Nthumb
80 K11 Whitefaulds S Ayrs
57 N12 Whitefield Bury
16 E11 Whitefield Somset
15 N5 Whitefield Devon
5 G8 Wideombe in the Moor Devon
27 U4 Whitegate Ches W
22 G7 Whitehall Devon
77 Q11 Wide Open N Tyne
106 u17 Widewall Ork
20 J4 Widewall Ork
66 E9 Widdington Essex
49 S11 Widdington Nthumb
77 Q7 Widdrington Station Nthumb
6 J4 Widecombe in the Moor Devon
57 R8 Widmerpool Notts
55 M10 Widnes Halton
56 E11 Widnes Crematorium Halton
5 V2 Widworthy Devon
79 Q5 Wigan Wigan
55 N6 Wigan Crematorium Wigan
17 M3 Wigborough Somset
7 F6 Wiggaton Devon
9 S11 Wiggenhall St Germans Norfk
49 S11 Wiggenhall St Mary Magdalen Norfk
49 S11 Wiggenhall St Mary the Virgin Norfk
39 U12 Wiggens Green Essex
30 H12 Wigginton Herts
44 H5 Wigginton Oxon
29 T1 Wigginton Shrops
36 F10 Wigginton Staffs
45 S7 Wigginton York
45 S7 Wigginton Bottom Herts
62 H9 Wigglesworth N York
67 L2 Wiggonby Cumb
10 H7 Wiggonholt W Susx

Column 5

35 R9 Whitbourne Herefs
77 U13 Whitburn S Tyne
83 Q11 Whitburn W Loth
112 J6 Whitby Ches W
71 R11 Whitby N York
84 J7 Whitchester Border
37 R3 Whitchurch BaNES
30 M8 Whitchurch Bucks
47 M12 Whitchurch Cardif
5 Q11 Whitchurch Devon
19 Q11 Whitchurch Hants
27 V4 Whitchurch Herefs
24 J7 Whitchurch Pembks
45 M5 Whitchurch Shrops
54 J12 Whitchurch Maelor Wrexhm
84 G3 Whiteadder Water Border
78 K13 Whitebeck Cumb
29 M10 Whitecross Gloucs
9 N13 White Cross Wilts
81 M7 Whitecross Falk
34 G4 Whitcott Keysett Shrops
10 C7 White Chapel Lancs
26 J6 White Mill Carmth
25 S6 White Mill Carmth
47 R7 Whitemoor C Nott
41 P5 Whitemoor Devon
47 L4 Whitemoor Staffs
106 t15 Whiteness Shet
22 J4 White Notley Essex
82 G4 Whiteoak Green Oxon
10 C7 White Pit Lincs
59 Q11 White Pit Lincs
12 K3 Whiteparish Wilts
67 N9 Whiterow Highld
57 R10 Whiteshill Gloucs
11 M8 Whitesmith E Susx
8 C8 White Stake Lancs [?]
13 U1 Whitestaunton Somset
5 V2 Whitestone Cross Devon
40 G13 Whitestreet Green Suffk
20 D7 White Waltham W & M
12 H5 Whiteway BaNES
62 H2 Whiteway Gloucs
61 L4 Whitewell Lancs
9 Q5 Whiteworks Devon
91 P5 Whitfield C Dund
13 R8 Whitfield Kent
37 U7 Whitfield Nhants
76 F14 Whitfield Nthumb
9 S12 Whitfield S Glos
68 J9 Whitford Devon
54 C5 Whitford Flints
48 B8 Whitgift E R Yk
46 B8 Whitgreave Staffs
73 L10 Whithorn D & G
75 Q7 Whiting Bay N Ayrs
65 T13 Whitkirk Leeds
14 G7 Whitland Carmth
75 U10 Whitlaw Border
57 M8 Whitletts S Ayrs
77 T11 Whitley N York
63 V14 Whitley Readg
20 H7 Whitley Sheff
77 P11 Whitley Wilts
13 Q3 Whitley Bay N Tyne
77 L9 Whitley Chapel Nthumb
58 E6 Whitley Heath Staffs
15 N10 Whitley Lower Kirk
37 N4 Whitley Row Kent
45 T8 Whitley Staffs
10 D5 Whitlock's End Solhll
37 M3 Whitminster Gloucs
29 M7 Whitmore Dorset
46 D5 Whitmore Staffs
8 H7 Whitnage Devon
36 G11 Whitnash Warwks
27 R11 Whitney-on-Wye Herefs
66 K5 Whitrigg Cumb
67 L2 Whitrigg Cumb
8 C5 Whitsbury Hants
85 M8 Whitsome Border
27 R11 Whitson Newpt
23 L10 Whitstable Kent
4 H4 Whitstone Cnwll
77 N11 Whittingham Nthumb
34 H2 Whittingslow Shrops
57 N12 Whittington Derbys
29 M6 Whittington Gloucs
36 H7 Whittington Lancs
50 C14 Whittington Norfk
44 H6 Whittington Shrops
46 E5 Whittington Staffs
45 U14 Whittington Staffs
35 U13 Whittington Warwks
35 T11 Whittington Worcs
55 M13 Whittington Corner Ches W
62 A11 Whittlebury Nhants
62 F7 Whittle-le-Woods Lancs
39 M1 Whittlesey Cambs
39 P11 Whittlesford Cambs
55 R3 Whittlestone Head Bl w D
58 K2 Whitton N Linc
77 L9 Whitton Nthumb
34 J7 Whitton Powys
45 M7 Whitton S on T
57 M11 Whitton Shrops
40 K11 Whitton Suffk
34 J2 Whittonditch Wilts
76 K13 Whittonstall Nthumb
9 R4 Whitway Hants
57 N13 Whitwell Derbys
31 Q8 Whitwell Herts
9 S13 Whitwell IoW
69 S12 Whitwell N York
50 H10 Whitwell Rutlnd
64 E6 Whitwell-on-the-Hill N York
37 M3 Whitwell Street Norfk
38 F11 Whitwick Leics
62 D13 Whitwood Wakefd
56 H4 Whitworth Lancs
45 M7 Whixall Shrops
64 B7 Whixley N York
69 Q9 Whorlton Dur
70 H12 Whorlton N York
35 N7 Whyle Herefs
21 P11 Whyteleafe Surrey
63 P13 Wibsey C Brad
37 L3 Wibtoft Warwks
35 R9 Wichenford Worcs
12 H4 Wichling Kent

Column 6

8 H10 Wick Bmouth
6 G4 Wick Highld
112 J6 Wick V Glam
5 Q5 Wick V Glam
17 M11 Wick Somset
17 R4 Wick Somset
10 C10 Wick W Susx
8 H4 Wick Wilts
36 C11 Wick Worcs
10 H8 Wick W Susx
36 C11 Wick Worcs
112 J6 Wick Airport Highld
39 S6 Wicken Cambs
37 U6 Wicken Nhants
39 S6 Wicken Bonhunt Essex
58 J10 Wickenby Lincs
45 P8 Wicken Green Village Norfk
57 Q8 Wickersley Rothm
40 Q12 Wicker Street Green Suffk
9 R9 Wickford Hants
19 N6 Wickham Hants
22 K5 Wickham Bishops Essex
40 D13 Wickhambreaux Kent
40 C8 Wickhambrook Suffk
36 C11 Wickhamford Worcs
19 P7 Wickham Green W Berk
41 P9 Wickham Green Suffk
41 R12 Wickham Market Suffk
50 E13 Wickhampton Norfk
40 D13 Wickham St Paul Essex
41 M6 Wickham Skeith Suffk
40 C10 Wickham Street Suffk
40 J7 Wickham Street Suffk
50 J7 Wickmere Norfk
17 L3 Wick St Lawrence N Som
11 S9 Wickstreet E Susx
28 D10 Wickwar S Glos
22 D1 Widdington Essex
22 D13 Widdington Nthumb [Widmerpool]
11 U8 Widdington Surrey
31 M2 Widford Essex
16 K13 Widford Herts
29 L3 Widham Wilts
20 J2 Widmer End Bucks
47 R8 Widmerpool Notts
55 M10 Widnes Halton
56 E11 Widnes Crematorium Halton
6 F1 Widworthy Devon
79 Q5 Widnes Ag & B [Widrow?]
55 N6 Wigan Wigan
17 M3 Wigborough Somset
7 F6 Wiggaton Devon
49 S11 Wiggenhall St Germans Norfk
49 S11 Wiggenhall St Mary Magdalen Norfk
49 S11 Wiggenhall St Mary the Virgin Norfk
39 U12 Wiggens Green Essex
30 H12 Wigginton Herts
44 H5 Wigginton Oxon
29 T1 Wigginton Shrops
36 F10 Wigginton Staffs
64 D10 Wigginton York
64 D9 Wigginton Bottom Herts
62 H9 Wigglesworth N York
67 L2 Wiggonby Cumb
10 H7 Wiggonholt W Susx
63 S11 Wighill N York
50 F6 Wighton Norfk
45 U14 Wightwick Wolves
35 T5 Wigley Hants
34 K7 Wigmore Herefs
12 E4 Wigmore Medway
58 E12 Wigsley Notts
38 G4 Wigsthorpe Nhants
37 Q1 Wigston Leics
37 R13 Wigston Fields Leics
47 M5 Wigston Parva Leics
57 S10 Wigthorpe Notts
49 L6 Wigtoft Lincs
66 K3 Wigton Cumb
73 L8 Wigtown D & G
63 S11 Wigtwizzle Sheff
63 S11 Wike Leeds
38 B1 Wilbarston Nhants
65 L10 Wilberfoss E R Yk
39 P5 Wilburton Cambs
38 C6 Wilby Nhants
50 H14 Wilby Norfk
41 M6 Wilby Suffk
18 H8 Wilcot Wilts
44 J9 Wilcott Shrops
57 M12 Wilday Green Derbys
56 F11 Wildboarclough Ches E
38 G9 Wilden Bed
35 T6 Wilden Worcs
36 G5 Wildmanbridge S Lans
35 T7 Wildmoor Worcs
58 C5 Wildsworth Lincs
37 Q6 Wilford Hill Crematorium Notts
45 L6 Wilkesley Ches E
111 L3 Wilkhaven Highld
83 M5 Wilkieston W Loth
37 N14 Wilkin's Green Herts
75 S14 Willand Somset [?]
8 H2 Willand Devon
45 M3 Willaston Ches E
54 J12 Willaston Ches W
38 C7 Willen M Keyn
37 N5 Willenhall Covtry
46 C1 Willenhall Wsall
65 N13 Willerby E R Yk
65 M3 Willerby N York
36 F13 Willersey Gloucs
34 H12 Willersley Herefs
12 J7 Willesborough Kent
12 J7 Willesborough Lees Kent
21 M6 Willesden Gt Lon
17 T5 Willesleigh Devon
28 G13 Willesley Wilts
16 F11 Willett Somset
45 R13 Willey Shrops
37 N4 Willey Warwks
20 F12 Willey Green Surrey
37 N11 Williamscot Oxon
26 K7 Williamstown Rhondd
31 Q8 Willian Herts
22 E7 Willingale Essex
11 S9 Willingdon E Susx
39 P6 Willingham Cambs
58 E11 Willingham by Stow Lincs
39 S10 Willingham Green Cambs
38 H10 Willington Bed
45 S4 Willington Derbys
57 L1 Willington Dur
46 H8 Willington Kent
36 K4 Willington Warwks
77 S12 Willington Quay N Tyne
45 M2 Willitoft E R Yk [?]
64 G13 Willitoft E R Yk
16 F9 Williton Somset
59 S12 Willoughby Lincs
37 P7 Willoughby Warwks
48 E5 Willoughby-on-the-Wolds Notts
47 S9 Willoughby Waterleys Leics
58 C9 Willoughton Lincs
22 H4 Willows Green Essex
7 M2 Willtown Somset
36 H11 Wilmcote Warwks
6 E5 Wilmington BaNES
17 R4 Wilmington BaNES
11 S10 Wilmington E Susx
22 E13 Wilmington Kent
56 C10 Wilmslow Ches E
62 E12 Wilpshire Lancs
63 M11 Wilsden C Brad
48 E7 Wilsford Lincs
18 H13 Wilsford Wilts
18 J9 Wilsford Wilts
62 K8 Wilshaw Kirk [?]

Column 7

30 K10 Wilstone Green Herts
66 F10 Wilton Cumb
35 A3 Wilton Herefs
63 J9 Wilton N York
70 J9 Wilton R & Cl
18 G13 Wilton Wilts
18 K8 Wilton Wilts
85 U5 Wilton Dean Border
39 S13 Wimbish Essex
39 T13 Wimbish Green Essex
21 M8 Wimbledon Gt Lon
39 P2 Wimblington Cambs
55 N2 Wimboldsley Ches W
8 E9 Wimborne Minster Dorset
8 E6 Wimborne St Giles Dorset
49 T12 Wimbotsham Norfk
39 N11 Wimpole Cambs
36 H11 Wimpstone Warwks
18 E13 Wincanton Somset
99 S11 Wincham Ches W
55 P13 Wincham Ches W
29 M3 Wincle Ches E
28 J2 Winchcombe Gloucs
12 H12 Winchelsea E Susx
12 H12 Winchelsea Beach E Susx
9 P3 Winchester Hants
19 R13 Winchester Services Hants
21 R12 Winchet Hill Kent
20 C12 Winchfield Hants
20 C12 Winchmore Hill Bucks
41 R9 Winchmore Hill Gt Lon
56 F11 Wincle Ches E
57 L8 Wincobank Sheff
67 P3 Windermere Cumb
56 K12 Winderton Warwks
102 F6 Windhill Highld
10 F5 Windlehurst Stockp
20 F10 Windlesham Surrey
3 M2 Windmill Cnwll
2 J13 Windmill Derbys
5 S14 Windmill Hill E Susx
16 K13 Windmill Hill Somset
29 N5 Windrush Gloucs
20 G7 Windsor W & M
20 G7 Windsor Castle W & M
20 G7 Windsoredge Gloucs
40 D13 Winder Green Suffk
77 S11 Windygates Fife
55 T12 Windyharbour Ches E
11 L6 Wineham W Susx
59 R9 Winestead E R Yk
62 J11 Winewall Lancs
40 K3 Winfarthing Norfk
9 V11 Winford IoW
17 P4 Winford N Som
34 G11 Winforton Herefs
7 V8 Winfrith Newburgh Dorset
30 J8 Wing Bucks
48 C13 Wing Rutlnd
70 F8 Wingate Dur
55 Q5 Wingates Bolton
77 M7 Wingates Nthumb
57 N13 Wingerworth Derbys
38 G7 Wingfield C Beds
41 M4 Wingfield Suffk
18 B9 Wingfield Wilts
13 N4 Wingham Kent
13 N4 Wingmore Kent
30 J9 Wingrave Bucks
57 T2 Winkburn Notts
20 D9 Winkfield Br For
20 D10 Winkfield Row Br For
46 D4 Winkhill Staffs
15 P11 Winkleigh Devon
63 R4 Winksley N York
77 Q10 Winlaton Gatesd
77 P13 Winlaton Mill Gatesd
112 G8 Winless Highld
44 H5 Winllan Powys [?]
45 P7 Winmarleigh Lancs
66 F7 Winnard's Perch Cnwll [?]
54 T4 Winnersh Woknm
55 T4 Winscales Cumb
17 N7 Winscombe N Som
55 P13 Winsford Ches W
16 B10 Winsford Somset
46 B14 Winsham Devon
7 L2 Winsham Somset
46 K9 Winshill Staffs
67 S4 Winskill Cumb
19 S9 Winslade Hants
18 B9 Winsley Wilts
30 F7 Winslow Bucks
29 N5 Winson Gloucs
8 K8 Winsor Hants
67 N3 Winster Cumb
46 H1 Winster Derbys
69 P9 Winston Dur
41 L8 Winston Suffk
28 G6 Winstone Gloucs
14 K8 Winswell Devon
7 T7 Winterborne Came Dorset
7 U4 Winterborne Clenston Dorset
7 U4 Winterborne Herringston Dorset
8 B9 Winterborne Houghton Dorset
8 B9 Winterborne Kingston Dorset
7 T6 Winterborne Monkton Dorset
8 B9 Winterborne Stickland Dorset
8 B9 Winterborne Tomson Dorset
8 B9 Winterborne Whitechurch Dorset
7 V5 Winterborne Zelston Dorset
28 B11 Winterbourne S Glos
19 S6 Winterbourne W Berk
8 E7 Winterbourne Abbas Dorset
18 H13 Winterbourne Bassett Wilts
8 G9 Winterbourne Dauntsey Wilts
8 G9 Winterbourne Earls Wilts
8 G9 Winterbourne Gunner Wilts
18 G12 Winterbourne Monkton Wilts
7 N4 Winterbourne Steepleton Dorset
18 G12 Winterbourne Stoke Wilts
60 F7 Winterbrook Oxon
62 F2 Winterburn N York
58 F2 Winteringham N Linc
55 Q1 Winterley Ches E
57 N4 Wintersett Wakefd
8 J3 Winterslow Wilts
58 G2 Winterton N Linc
51 T10 Winterton-on-Sea Norfk
48 K3 Winthorpe Lincs
48 B2 Winthorpe Notts
9 U13 Winton Bmouth
68 G10 Winton Cumb
11 S8 Winton E Susx
64 K3 Wintringham N York
38 H5 Winwick Cambs
37 S6 Winwick Nhants
55 P8 Winwick Warrtn
46 J3 Wirksworth Derbys
44 J2 Wirswall Ches E
49 Q11 Wisbech Cambs
49 R12 Wisbech St Mary Cambs
10 J7 Wisborough Green W Susx
73 Q5 Wiseman's Bridge Pembks
58 C8 Wiseton Notts
82 H7 Wishaw N Lans
36 G2 Wishaw Warwks
20 J11 Wisley Surrey
59 N11 Wispington Lincs
40 J5 Wissett Suffk
34 K12 Wistanstow Shrops
45 R10 Wistanswick Shrops
45 R3 Wistaston Ches E
24 H7 Wiston Pembks
10 J8 Wiston W Susx
38 H5 Wistow Cambs
47 R13 Wistow Leics
63 T13 Wistow N York
62 D11 Wiswell Lancs
39 R4 Witcham Cambs
8 D8 Witchampton Dorset
39 Q3 Witchford Cambs
7 P3 Witcombe Somset
22 K5 Witham Essex
48 C1 Witham St Hughs Lincs
11 N9 Witherenden Hill E Susx
12 B10 Witherenden Hill E Susx
15 T10 Witheridge Devon
47 M14 Witherley Leics
59 R11 Withern Lincs
59 R10 Withernsea E R Yk
41 N4 Withernwick E R Yk
39 U11 Withersdale Street Suffk
39 U11 Withersfield Suffk
61 S3 Witherslack Cumb
16 C12 Withiel Cnwll [?]
3 Q3 Withiel Florey Somset
28 K4 Withington Gloucs
55 T8 Withington Herefs
46 G10 Withington Manch
55 T12 Withington Shrops
11 N8 Withleigh Devon
55 S5 Withnell Lancs
35 U2 Withybrook Warwks
11 R4 Withybush Pembks
17 R5 Withycombe Somset
17 Q3 Withypool Somset
41 M10 Withersfield Suffk
35 N4 Withywood Brist [?]
29 S5 Witney Oxon
48 C13 Wittering C Pete [?]
36 E2 Wittering Pete
12 B10 Wittersham Kent
51 P12 Witton Norfk [?]
57 R7 Witton Gilbert Dur
63 R13 Witton Green Norfk
69 R6 Witton le Wear Dur
69 R6 Witton Park Dur
16 E11 Wiveliscombe Somset
11 N6 Wivelrod Hants
11 N6 Wivelsfield E Susx
11 N6 Wivelsfield Green E Susx
23 P3 Wivenhoe Essex
23 N5 Wivenhoe Cross Essex
50 H6 Wiveton Norfk
23 N3 Wix Essex
23 N3 Wixford Warwks
40 D12 Wixoe Suffk
31 L6 Woburn C Beds
31 L6 Woburn Sands M Keyn
20 H11 Woking Surrey
20 G11 Woking Crematorium Surrey
20 D9 Wokingham Wokhm
20 C9 Woldingham Surrey
65 N5 Wold Newton E R Yk
59 N8 Wold Newton NE Lin
37 U3 Wolfclyde S Lans
35 U8 Wolferlow Herefs
50 B8 Wolferton Norfk
37 R5 Wolfhampcote Warwks
30 J6 Wolfhill P & K
75 J5 Wolf Hills Nthumb
24 K6 Wolf's Castle Pembks
24 F6 Wolfsdale Pembks
36 A1 Wollaston Dudley
38 C8 Wollaston Nhants
44 H11 Wollaston Shrops
47 P6 Wollaton C Nott
44 H7 Wollerton Shrops
36 C4 Wollescote Dudley
84 U4 Wolsingham Dur [?]
88 D9 Wolseley Bridge Staffs
69 N6 Wolsingham Dur
20 H12 Wolston Warwks
46 B14 Wolstanton Staffs
37 L4 Wolston Warwks
29 U4 Wolvercote Oxon
36 C1 Wolverhampton Wolves
36 C1 Wolverhampton Business Airport Staffs
35 L7 Wolverley Shrops
35 T6 Wolverley Worcs
19 R9 Wolverton Hants
38 B9 Wolverton M Keyn
36 J8 Wolverton Warwks
12 K7 Wolverton Kent [?]
18 B11 Wolverton Wilts
17 U9 Wolverton Common Hants
19 S9 Wolvesnewton Mons
27 T8 Wolvey Warwks
37 L3 Wolvey Heath Warwks
70 G6 Wolviston S on T
64 H4 Wombleton N York
35 T2 Wombourne Staffs
57 P5 Wombwell Barns
13 N5 Womenswold Kent
57 R3 Womersley N York
20 B12 Wonersh Surrey
6 B5 Wonford Devon
6 E4 Wonson Devon
9 N3 Wonston Hants
20 G6 Wooburn Bucks
20 G6 Wooburn Green Bucks
20 F5 Wooburn Moor Bucks
14 K12 Woodacott Devon
14 J8 Woodale N York
63 R10 Woodall Rothm
57 Q10 Woodall Services Rothm
51 P10 Woodbastwick Norfk
47 V8 Woodbeck Notts
6 E10 Woodborough Notts [?]
18 H9 Woodborough Wilts
6 E7 Woodbridge Devon
8 C5 Woodbridge Dorset
41 N11 Woodbridge Suffk
6 D8 Woodbury Devon
6 D8 Woodbury Salterton Devon

Column 8

30 K10 Wilstone Green Herts
48 C1 Witham on the Hill Lincs
48 C1 Witham St Hughs Lincs
11 N9 Witherenden Hill E Susx
12 B10 Witherenden Hill E Susx
15 T10 Witheridge Devon
47 M14 Witherley Leics
59 R11 Withern Lincs
59 R10 Withernsea E R Yk
41 N4 Withernwick E R Yk
39 U11 Withersdale Street Suffk
39 U11 Withersfield Suffk
16 C2 Witherslack Cumb
61 S3 Withiel Cnwll
3 Q3 Withiel Florey Somset
28 K4 Withington Gloucs
45 T6 Withington Herefs
46 G10 Withington Manch
34 L9 Withington Shrops
55 T12 Withington Staffs
55 T12 Withington Green Ches E
11 N8 Withleigh Devon
6 B2 Withnell Lancs
35 U2 Withybrook Warwks
13 M4 Withybush Pembks
17 S11 Withycombe Somset
5 V7 Withycombe Raleigh Devon
11 N5 Withyham E Susx
23 V3 Withypool Somset
8 E11 Withywood Brist
35 N13 Witney Oxon
25 T2 Wittering C Pete
12 H10 Wittersham Kent
35 T5 Witton Birm
51 P10 Witton Norfk
51 Q11 Witton Norfk
69 R6 Witton Gilbert Dur
16 E10 Witton Green Norfk
16 E11 Witton le Wear Dur
69 R6 Witton Park Dur
16 E11 Wiveliscombe Somset
11 N6 Wivelrod Hants
11 N6 Wivelsfield E Susx
11 N6 Wivelsfield Green E Susx
23 P3 Wivenhoe Essex
50 H6 Wiveton Norfk
23 S2 Wix Essex
36 E10 Wixford Warwks
40 B12 Wixoe Suffk
31 L5 Woburn C Beds
31 L5 Woburn Sands M Keyn
20 H11 Woking Surrey
20 G11 Woking Crematorium Surrey
20 D9 Wokingham Wokhm
21 P12 Woldingham Surrey
65 N4 Wold Newton E R Yk
59 N7 Wold Newton NE Lin
82 K11 Wolfclyde S Lans
35 S8 Wolferlow Herefs
49 U9 Wolferton Norfk
90 J6 Wolfhill P & K
76 B12 Wolf Hills Nthumb
24 J5 Wolf's Castle Pembks
24 F6 Wolfsdale Pembks
36 B4 Wollaston Dudley
38 C8 Wollaston Nhants
44 H11 Wollaston Shrops
47 P6 Wollaton C Nott
45 P8 Wollerton Shrops
36 C4 Wollescote Dudley
57 N8 Womenswold Kent
88 D9 Wolseley Bridge Staffs
69 N6 Wolsingham Dur
20 H12 Wolston Warwks
46 B14 Wolstanton Staffs
37 L4 Wolston Warwks
29 U4 Wolvercote Oxon
36 C1 Wolverhampton Wolves
36 C1 Wolverhampton Business Airport Staffs
35 L7 Wolverley Shrops
35 T6 Wolverley Worcs
19 R9 Wolverton Hants
38 B9 Wolverton M Keyn
36 J8 Wolverton Warwks
12 K7 Wolverton Kent
18 B11 Wolverton Wilts
17 U9 Wolverton Common Hants
27 S8 Wolvesnewton Mons
37 L3 Wolvey Warwks
37 L3 Wolvey Heath Warwks
70 G6 Wolviston S on T
64 H4 Wombleton N York
35 T2 Wombourne Staffs
57 P5 Wombwell Barns
13 N5 Womenswold Kent
57 R3 Womersley N York
20 B12 Wonersh Surrey
6 B5 Wonford Devon
6 E4 Wonson Devon
9 N3 Wonston Hants
20 F6 Wooburn Bucks
20 F6 Wooburn Green Bucks
20 F5 Wooburn Moor Bucks
14 K12 Woodacott Devon
64 H4 Woodale N York
57 Q10 Woodall Rothm
57 Q10 Woodall Services Rothm
51 P10 Woodbastwick Norfk
47 V8 Woodbeck Notts
47 Q5 Woodborough Notts
18 H9 Woodborough Wilts
6 E7 Woodbridge Devon
8 B9 Woodbridge Dorset
41 N11 Woodbridge Suffk
6 D8 Woodbury Devon
6 D8 Woodbury Salterton Devon
28 E6 Woodchester Gloucs
12 H9 Woodchurch Kent
54 G10 Woodchurch Wirral
54 F9 Woodcombe Somset
20 D11 Woodcote Oxon
45 S10 Woodcote Wrekin
28 D9 Woodcroft Gloucs
49 S14 Wood Dalling Norfk
39 S9 Woodditton Cambs
30 B10 Woodeaton Oxon
40 E5 Wood Eaton Staffs
63 R4 Wood End Bed
22 B2 Wood End Gt Lon
30 J4 Wood End Herts
37 L5 Wood End Warwks
36 G3 Wood End Warwks
36 E3 Wood End Warwks
45 U14 Wood End Wolves
36 E1 Wood Enderby Lincs
22 E2 Woodend Essex
50 K5 Woodend Highld
37 S11 Woodend Nhants
80 C8 Woodend W Loth
10 C9 Woodend W Susx
22 C2 Wood End Green Gt Lon
9 N8 Wood Enderby Lincs
50 E7 Woodfalls Wilts
5 L3 Woodford Cnwll
28 C9 Woodford Gloucs
21 R4 Woodford Gt Lon
56 C10 Woodford Stockp
38 F6 Woodford Nhants
21 R4 Woodford Bridge Gt Lon
36 E2 Woodford Halse Nhants
21 R4 Woodford Wells Gt Lon
37 Q9 Woodgate Birm
16 F12 Woodgate Devon
50 G9 Woodgate Norfk
36 B5 Woodgate Worcs
10 E10 Woodgate W Susx
20 K11 Wood Green Gt Lon
22 J8 Woodham Dur
22 K7 Woodham Ferrers Essex
22 J8 Woodham Mortimer Essex

Be prepared on your journey... just in case

AA Road Safety Kit
Exclusively available at:
theAA.com/shop/safety

Only £25*
NORMALLY £50 AT theAA.com/shop
Includes free P&P**

How to buy:
To buy this kit for only £25*, simply visit **theAA.com/shop/safety** add to your basket, then enter promotion code SAFETY

Half price offer, only with AA Atlases

Durable Zipped Bag Neatly keeps the safety equipment altogether and ready for any breakdown or emergency.

Hazard Warning Triangle Alert oncoming traffic in hazardous situations. RRP £9.99.

Reflective Emergency Jacket For maximum visibility in emergencies. RRP £7.99.

First Aid Kit Contains: plasters, dressings, foil blanket, microporous adhesive tape, wipes, gloves and scissors. RRP £7.99

Fire Extinguisher (950g) Lightweight and easy to operate. RRP £14.99.

3-in-One Emergency Beacon 360 degree flashing beacon, seat belt cutter and an emergency glass hammer all in one. RRP £11.99.

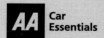
AA Car Essentials

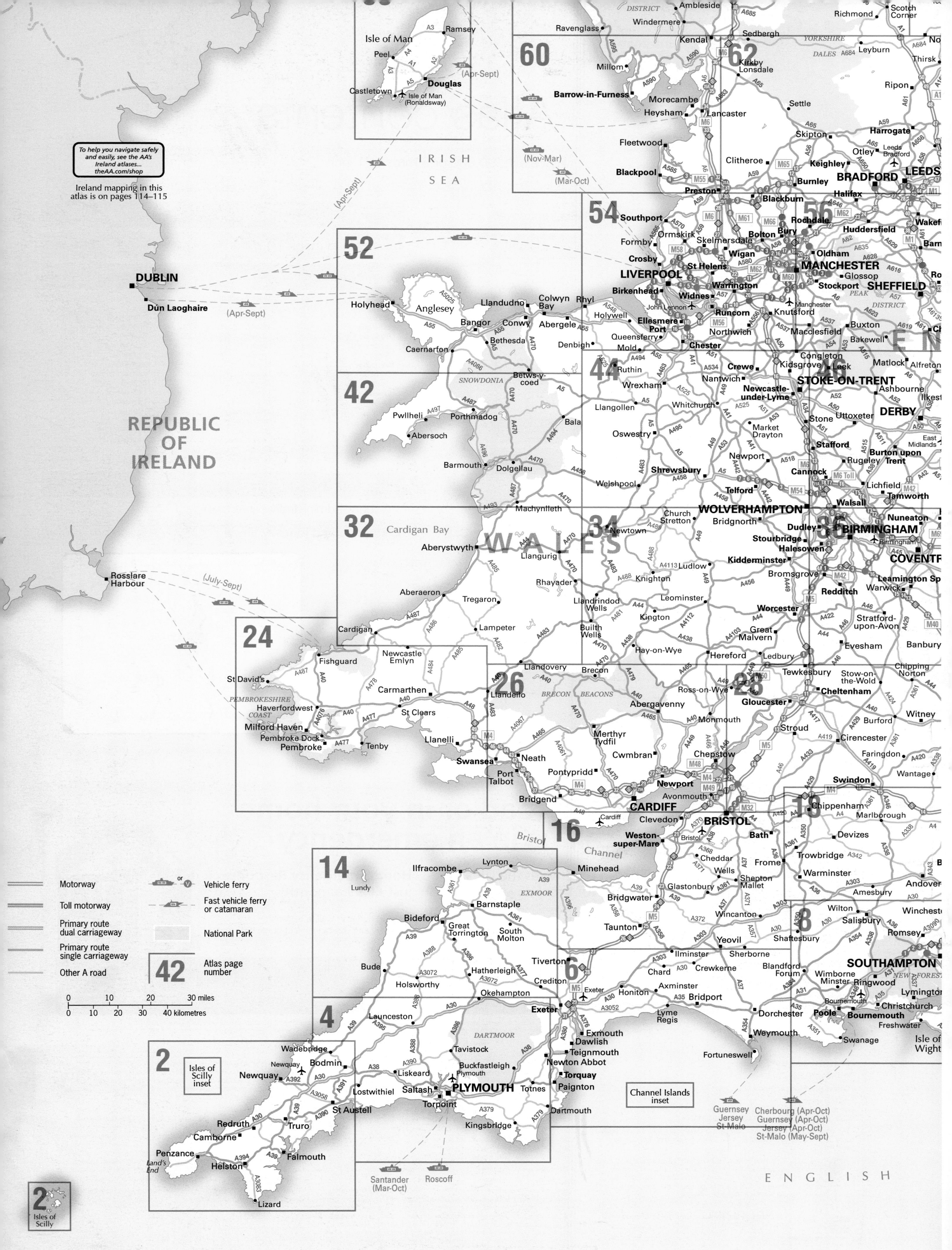
Isle of Man
Ramsey
Peel
Douglas
Castletown
Isle of Man (Ronaldsway)
(Apr-Sept)
To help you navigate safely and easily, see the AA's Ireland atlases... theAA.com/shop
Ireland mapping in this atlas is on pages 114–115
IRISH SEA
REPUBLIC OF IRELAND
DUBLIN
Dún Laoghaire
(Apr-Sept)
Rosslare Harbour
(July-Sept)
60
62
54
56
52
42
44
46
32
34
36
24
26
28
16
18
14
8
6
4
2
Ambleside
Windermere
Ravenglass
Kendal
Sedbergh
Kirkby Lonsdale
Millom
Barrow-in-Furness
Morecambe
Heysham
Lancaster
Fleetwood
Blackpool
Preston
(Nov-Mar)
(Mar-Oct)
Richmond
Scotch Corner
Leyburn
Thirsk
Ripon
Settle
Harrogate
Skipton
Otley
Clitheroe
Keighley
BRADFORD
LEEDS
Burnley
Halifax
Blackburn
Southport
Ormskirk
Formby
Skelmersdale
Bolton
Bury
Rochdale
Huddersfield
Oldham
Wigan
Crosby
LIVERPOOL
St Helens
MANCHESTER
Glossop
Birkenhead
Warrington
Stockport
SHEFFIELD
Widnes
Runcorn
Knutsford
Ellesmere Port
Northwich
Macclesfield
Buxton
Chester
Holyhead
Anglesey
Llandudno
Colwyn Bay
Rhyl
Holywell
Bangor
Conwy
Abergele
Bethesda
Denbigh
Mold
Caernarfon
Ruthin
Wrexham
SNOWDONIA
Betws-y-coed
Crewe
Nantwich
Kidsgrove
Leek
Congleton
Newcastle-under-Lyme
STOKE-ON-TRENT
Ashbourne
Matlock
Pwllheli
Porthmadog
Abersoch
Llangollen
Whitchurch
Bala
Oswestry
Market Drayton
Stone
Uttoxeter
DERBY
Stafford
Burton upon Trent
Barmouth
Dolgellau
Shrewsbury
Newport
Rugeley
Cannock
Lichfield
Tamworth
Welshpool
Telford
Machynlleth
WOLVERHAMPTON
Walsall
Nuneaton
Cardigan Bay
Aberystwyth
WALES
Llangurig
Newtown
Church Stretton
Bridgnorth
Dudley
Stourbridge
Halesowen
BIRMINGHAM
COVENTRY
Kidderminster
Bromsgrove
Redditch
Warwick
Leamington Spa
Rhayader
Knighton
Ludlow
Aberaeron
Tregaron
Llandrindod Wells
Leominster
Worcester
Stratford-upon-Avon
Kington
Great Malvern
Evesham
Lampeter
Builth Wells
Hay-on-Wye
Hereford
Ledbury
Cardigan
Fishguard
Newcastle Emlyn
Llandovery
Brecon
Tewkesbury
Cheltenham
St David's
PEMBROKESHIRE COAST
Carmarthen
Llandeilo
BRECON BEACONS
Abergavenny
Ross-on-Wye
Gloucester
Haverfordwest
St Clears
Monmouth
Stroud
Cirencester
Burford
Witney
Milford Haven
Pembroke Dock
Pembroke
Tenby
Llanelli
Merthyr Tydfil
Cwmbran
Chepstow
Swansea
Neath
Port Talbot
Pontypridd
Newport
Bridgend
CARDIFF
Swindon
Avonmouth
BRISTOL
Chippenham
Marlborough
Clevedon
Weston-super-Mare
Bath
Devizes
Bristol Channel
Lundy
Ilfracombe
Lynton
Minehead
EXMOOR
Cheddar
Wells
Frome
Trowbridge
Warminster
Barnstaple
Glastonbury
Shepton Mallet
Bridgwater
Bideford
Great Torrington
South Molton
Taunton
Wincanton
Salisbury
Yeovil
Shaftesbury
Romsey
SOUTHAMPTON
Bude
Holsworthy
Hatherleigh
Tiverton
Crediton
Ilminster
Crewkerne
Sherborne
Chard
Blandford Forum
Wimborne Minster
Ringwood
Okehampton
Exeter
Honiton
Axminster
Bridport
Lyme Regis
Dorchester
Poole
Bournemouth
Christchurch
Lymington
Launceston
DARTMOOR
Exmouth
Dawlish
Weymouth
Swanage
Isle of Wight
Wadebridge
Bodmin
Newquay
Tavistock
Teignmouth
Newton Abbot
Fortuneswell
Isles of Scilly inset
Liskeard
Buckfastleigh
Torquay
Paignton
Lostwithiel
Saltash
PLYMOUTH
Totnes
Torpoint
St Austell
Dartmouth
Channel Islands inset
Redruth
Truro
Kingsbridge
Guernsey Jersey St-Malo
Cherbourg (Apr-Oct) Guernsey (Apr-Oct) Jersey (Apr-Oct) St-Malo (May-Sept)
Camborne
Penzance
Land's End
Falmouth
Helston
Lizard
Santander (Mar-Oct)
Roscoff
ENGLISH
Isles of Scilly
Motorway
Toll motorway
Primary route dual carriageway
Primary route single carriageway
Other A road
Vehicle ferry
Fast vehicle ferry or catamaran
National Park
Atlas page number
0 10 20 30 miles
0 10 20 30 40 kilometres

Atlas contents

Scale 1:190,000 or 3 miles to 1 inch

22nd edition July 2012
© AA Media Limited 2012
Original edition printed 1991.

Cartography:
All cartography in this atlas edited, designed and produced by the Mapping Services Department of AA Publishing (A04860).

This atlas contains Ordnance Survey data © Crown copyright and database right 2012 and Royal Mail data © Royal Mail copyright and database right 2012.

 Land & Property Services. This atlas is based upon Crown Copyright and is reproduced with the permission of Land and Property Services under delegated authority from the Controller of Her Majesty's Stationery Office, © Crown copyright and database rights 2012, Licence number 100,363. Permit No. 110089.

 Ordnance Survey Ireland. Ireland's National Mapping Agency. © Ordnance Survey Ireland/Government of Ireland. Permit No. MP000611.

Publisher's Notes:
Published by AA Publishing (a trading name of AA Media Limited, whose registered office is Fanum House, Basing View, Basingstoke, Hampshire RG21 4EA, UK. Registered number 06112600).

All rights reserved. No part of this publication may be reproduced, stored in a retrieval system, or transmitted in any form or by any means – electronic, mechanical, photocopying, recording or otherwise – unless the permission of the publisher has been given beforehand.

ISBN: 978 0 7495 7347 8 (spiral bound)
ISBN: 978 0 7495 7369 0 (spiral bound)
ISBN: 978 0 7495 7346 1 (paperback)

A CIP catalogue record for this book is available from The British Library.

Disclaimer:
The contents of this atlas are believed to be correct at the time of the latest revision, it will not contain any subsequent amended, new or temporary information including diversions and traffic control or enforcement systems. The publishers cannot be held responsible or liable for any loss or damage occasioned to any person acting or refraining from action as a result of any use or reliance on material in this atlas, nor for any errors, omissions or changes in such material. This does not affect your statutory rights.

The publishers would welcome information to correct any errors or omissions and to keep this atlas up to date. Please write to the Atlas Editor, AA Publishing, The Automobile Association, Fanum House, Basing View, Basingstoke, Hampshire RG21 4EA, UK.
E-mail: roadatlasfeedback@theaa.com

Acknowledgements:
AA Publishing would like to thank the following for their assistance in producing this atlas:
RoadPilot® Information on fixed speed camera locations provided by and © 2012 RoadPilot® Driving Technology. Crematoria data provided by the Cremation Society of Great Britain. Cadw, English Heritage, Forestry Commission, Historic Scotland, Johnsons, National Trust and National Trust for Scotland, RSPB, The Wildlife Trust, Scottish Natural Heritage, Natural England, The Countryside Council for Wales (road maps).

Road signs are © Crown Copyright 2012. Reproduced under the terms of the Open Government Licence.

Printer:
Printed in Italy by G. Canale & C.
Paper: 80gsm Fenice Matt FSC.